Cyclopedia
of
LITERARY
CHARACTERS

Cyclopedia
of
LITERARY
CHARACTERS

Revised Edition

Volume Four
Pedro Páramo–A Tomb for Boris Davidovich

edited by
A. J. Sobczak

original editions edited by
Frank N. Magill

associate editor
Janet Alice Long

SALEM PRESS, INC.
Pasadena, California   Englewood Cliffs, New Jersey

Editor in Chief: Dawn P. Dawson
Managing Editor: Chris Moose
Project Editor: A. J. Sobczak
Acquisitions Editor: Mark Rehn
Research Supervisor: Jeffry Jensen
Research: Jun Ohnuki
Production Editor: Janet Alice Long
Layout: William Zimmerman

The Revised Edition includes *Cyclopedia of Literary Characters*, 1963 (first edition); *Cyclopedia of Literary Characters II*, 1990; and material new to this edition.

∞ The paper used in these volumes conforms to the American National Standard for Permanence of Paper for Printed Library Materials, Z39.48-1984.

Library of Congress Cataloging-in-Publication Data
Cyclopedia of literary characters / edited by A. J. Sobczak ; associate editor, Janet Alice Long. — Rev. ed.
   p. cm.
"This comprehensive revised edition of Cyclopedia of literary characters combines all the titles from the original Cyclopedia of literary characters and from Cyclopedia of literary characters II . . . adds character descriptions from titles included in Masterplots (revised second edition, 1996) and the Masterplots II sets covering African American literature (1994), women's literature (1995), and American fiction (supplement, 1994) . . . 3,300 titles [in all]."—Publisher's note.
   Includes index
1. Literature—Stories, plots, etc. 2. Literature—Dictionaries. 3. Characters and characteristics in literature. I. Sobczak, A. J. II. Long, Janet Alice.
PN44.M3 1998
809'.927—dc21
ISBN 0-89356-438-9 (set)   97-45813
ISBN 0-89356-442-7 (vol. 4)   CIP

SECOND PRINTING
PRINTED IN THE UNITED STATES OF AMERICA

CONTENTS

CONTENTS

CONTENTS

CONTENTS

KEY TO PRONUNCIATION

As an aid to users of the *Cyclopedia of Literary Characters, Revised Edition*, guides to pronunciation have been provided for particularly difficult character names. These guides are rendered in an easy-to-use phonetic manner. Stressed syllables are indicated by small capital letters. Letters of the English language, particularly vowels, are pronounced in different ways depending on the context. Below are letters and combinations of letters used in the phonetic guides to represent various sounds, along with examples of words in which those sounds appear.

Symbols	Pronounced As In
a	answer, laugh, sample, that
ah	father, hospital
aw	awful, caught
ay	blaze, fade, waiter, weigh
ch	beach, chimp
ee	believe, cedar, leader, liter
eh	bed, head, said
ew	boot, lose
g	beg, disguise, get
i	buy, height, lie, surprise
ih	bitter, pill
j	digit, edge, jet
k	cat, kitten, hex
[n]	bon (French "silent" n)
o	cotton, hot
oh	below, coat, note, wholesome
oo	good, look
ow	couch, how
oy	boy, coin
rr (rolled r)	guerrilla (Spanish pronunciation)
s	cellar, save, scent
sh	champagne, issue, shop
uh	about, butter, enough, other
ur	birth, disturb, earth, letter
y	useful, young
z	business, zest
zh	seizure, vision

Cyclopedia
of
LITERARY
CHARACTERS

PEDRO PÁRAMO

Author: Juan Rulfo (1918-1986)
First published: 1955
Genre: Novel

Locale: Comala, Jalisco, Mexico
Time: Late nineteenth and early twentieth centuries
Plot: Magical Realism

Juan Preciado (hwahn preh-see-AH-doh), the protagonist and point-of-view character of the novel. A young, curious man, Juan decides to research and discover his past after the death of his mother. Juan returns to the dusty provincial town of Comala in search of the man he knows to be his father, Pedro Páramo. Although he finds the town virtually deserted and Páramo dead, he continues to investigate the events that have brought the town to its current state. He talks with the local inhabitants who remain. Literally suffocated by the paralysis and despair of Comala, Juan dies in the middle of the novel. Even after his death, his consciousness remains alive and gives reports on the life and fate of his cruel father.

Pedro Páramo (PEH-droh PAHR-ah-moh), the local chieftain of the village of Comala, dead by the time the novel begins. Pedro Páramo is a loveless man, without soul or pity, who lives to control and dominate others. Although he lacks a distinguished family background, Pedro rises to the top of the village hierarchy by a ruthless process of exploitation. Pedro bullies more timid men and through force and deceit neutralizes other potential power centers in the village, such as Father Rentería and Bartolomé San Juan. Pedro gathers all power to himself and uses it neither to benefit others nor to improve the quality of life in the desperately poor village. Pedro's rampaging, promiscuous sexuality leads him to affairs with many women and the fathering of several children. Unscrupulous, insensitive, and dedicated to graft and tyranny, Pedro has one emotional soft spot: his love for Susana San Juan. When she dies, Pedro, through his semimagical powers, leaves the town dead in revenge. Pedro is finally killed in resentment by one of his many sons, Abundio. Pedro's death marks the end of any sign of life in Comala.

Miguel Páramo (mee-GEHL), Pedro's impetuous son. Miguel has all of his father's machismo and boorishness without his calculating cruelty. He is symbolic of human appetite incarnate, complementing his father's embodiment of cruelty. The only one of Pedro's many sons to be fully acknowledged by him, Miguel is employed as a tool in his father's schemes. Filled with lust and rage, he rapes the young Damiana Cis-

neros and kills the brother of Father Rentería. An avid horseman, he is killed while riding. Although he is hated by Comala, his death further saps the waning life force of the town.

Susana San Juan (sew-SAH-nah sahn hwahn), Pedro's idealized lost love. She is the daughter of Bartolomé San Juan, a dead miner. Susana represents the lost innocence of childhood and youth to Pedro. He cherishes her memory even though he stands for the corruption of all the qualities she represents. Susana is the only figure in the novel exempt from Comala's snares of despair and death.

Abundio Martínez (ah-BEWN-dee-oh mahr-TEE-nehs), one of Pedro's illegitimate sons. He kills his father out of resentment and frustration.

Father Rentería (rrehn-teh-RREE-ah), the local priest, whose potential to present opposition to Pedro's domination of Comala is short-circuited by his own unwillingness to challenge authority. He is the uncle of Damiana Cisneros, who is raped by Miguel, who also murders the brother of the priest, Damiana's father. Through his charitable act of convincing Pedro to accept responsibility for his illegitimate son Miguel, Father Rentería ironically seals the doom of Comala. Father Rentería is a symbol of the subordination of church to state in anticlerical, twentieth century Mexico.

Damiana Cisneros (dah-mee-AH-nah sees-NEH-rohs), Father Rentería's niece. She is raped by Miguel Páramo as a young girl. She becomes a domestic servant of Pedro and takes care of Juan Preciado as a boy, surviving to encounter him years later and provide him with ambiguous information regarding his father.

Dolores Preciado, the mother of Juan. Dolores is seduced and abused by Pedro, as one of his many female conquests. She lives in devastated sorrow the remainder of her life. Her death initiates her son's quest to find his father.

Dorotea (doh-roh-TEH-ah), called "La Curraca," (lah kew-RRAH-kah), a local woman who offers a kind of passive resistance to Pedro Páramo and after his death is the vehicle that the novel uses to portray the collective meditation of the town's inhabitants.

PEDRO SÁNCHEZ

Author: José María de Pereda (1833-1906)
First published: 1883
Genre: Novel

Locale: Santander and Madrid, Spain
Time: 1852-1879
Plot: Picaresque

Pedro Sánchez (PEH-droh SAHN-chehs), a provincial. Ignorant of the world outside his native region, he sets out for Madrid. He finds a job on the antigovernment newspaper *El Clarín*, where he wins a certain notoriety for criticism of a literary work by a member of the opposition; eventually, he catches the revolutionary fever of his fellow employees. When the government is overthrown, Pedro is rewarded with a provincial governorship, and he marries Clara. From this time on,

his fortunes decline. Finally, he returns to his native mountains, where he writes the story of his disillusionment.

Augusto Valenzuela (ow-GEWS-toh vahl-ehn-SWEH-lah), a shady politician who promises Pedro Sánchez that he will see to his future when the boy comes to Madrid. He gives Pedro a cold reception when he presents himself in the city.

Clara (KLAHR-ah), Augusto Valenzuela's daughter, who is later Pedro Sánchez' extravagant and faithless first wife.

Serafín Balduque (sehr-ah-FEEN bahl-DEW-keh), Pedro Sánchez' friend, a former state employee who is killed in street fighting against government forces.

Carmen, Serafín Balduque's daughter and Pedro Sánchez' second wife, who, with their small son, dies during an epidemic.

Mata (MAH-tah), also called **Matica** (mah-TEE-kah), a student who befriends Pedro Sánchez when he arrives in Madrid and finds him a job on *El Clarín*.

Redondo (rreh-DOHN-doh), the editor of *El Clarín*.

Pilita (pee-LEE-tah), the wife of Augusto Valenzuela.

Barrientos (bah-rree-EHN-tohs), Governor Pedro Sánchez' secretary, who is a collector of bribes and the lover of Pedro's wife Clara.

PEER GYNT

Author: Henrik Ibsen (1828-1906)
First published: 1867
Genre: Drama

Locale: Norway
Time: Mid-nineteenth century
Plot: Satire

Peer Gynt, a poetic, contradictious, and intriguing character made of the stuff of legendary heroes and sometimes confused with them in his own mind. He is one of the playwright's greatest character creations and the least Victorian. As Peer himself would have wished to be, he is a citizen of the world. A youthful braggart, idler, brawler, and dreamer, he is a ragged, lying outcast from village life, the joy and despair of Aase, his mother. After stealing a bride from her unwelcome groom, he flees from his village, but he quickly abandons the stolen bride because he has fallen in love with Solveig, an innocent young girl whom he met at the wedding festivities. Later, bewitched by the Troll King's daughter, he promises to marry her and inherit the Troll Kingdom. He puts on Troll clothing and the Troll King's Sunday tail, eats the repulsive Troll food, and drinks the Troll mead, but he demurs when the Troll King wants to scratch one of his eyeballs so that he will see ugly as beautiful and beautiful as ugly. Escaping, he encounters the Great Boyg but is saved from that monster by the ringing of church bells. After his mother's death, he becomes wealthy by slave trading in America and by shipping to China idols and missionaries that counteract one another. When his ship is commandeered off the coast of Morocco, he asks God to "Make something go wrong with the works! Do listen! Leave other folk's matters alone! The world will look after itself while you do." His prayer is answered and the vessel sinks, leaving Peer safe ashore. He poses as an Arab chief; is fleeced by Anitra, a dancing girl; becomes emperor of the insane asylum in Cairo; survives a shipwreck off the coast of Norway; encounters the Button Moulder; meets the Troll King again; tricks the Devil; and at last finds Solveig, who tells him that his real self exists in her faith, hope, and love. Peer's reverence for Solveig and his whimsical devotion to his mother, whom he alternately teases and cherishes, are evidence of gentleness and tenderness underlying his selfish behavior. Inferior as a stage play because of the diffused action, Peer's story is an imaginative dramatic poem that in power of language, humorous insight into human foibles, liveliness of dialogue, and creation of character reaches heights that many of Henrik Ibsen's later plays never attempt.

Aase, Peer's devoted, exasperated mother. A lively and pathetic character, she symbolizes maternal love. Her love permits her to scold Peer but will not allow anyone else to criticize him. As a youth, he sets her on a mill rooftop while he runs off to a wedding. After his escapade of bride stealing, Aase and Solveig cause the church bells to ring, saving him

from the Boyg. When Aase is old and dying, Peer returns, and they play a game in which he pretends that he is driving her on a sleigh to a great party at a castle. God the Father is waiting and overrides St. Peter's refusal to let her enter. With Peer's arms around her, Aase rides happily into eternity.

Solveig, Peer's ideal love, always beautiful and always patient. Although she grows old and almost blind while waiting for Peer's return, she has power to defy the Button Moulder by her belief that her faith and love reveal the real Peer. She seems to represent love, holy and remote but ever-lasting.

Ingrid, the daughter of the owner of Haegstad Farm, the bride whom Peer steals on her wedding day.

Mads Moën, Ingrid's bumbling, cuckolded groom.

Aslak, a young blacksmith who voices the ridicule and dislike that most of the villagers show toward Peer.

Three Cowherd Girls, who take Peer Gynt into their beds after he has abandoned Ingrid.

The Woman in Green, the daughter of the Troll King and the mother of Peer's lame, ugly child.

Brosë, the Troll King of Dovre. He tells Peer that the Troll motto is "To thyself be—enough." Although Peer later believes that he has left Trolldom behind him, this motto is his philosophy in his subsequent adventures in many parts of the world. After the Button Moulder gives Peer leave to find witnesses to prove that he has always been himself, he and the Troll King meet again. The Troll King refuses to testify to a lie; he says that Peer has been a Troll in secret ever since he ate and drank with the Trolls and took away their motto graven on his heart.

The Great Boyg, a grim, impassable monster, identified only by a voice in the darkness, who says that he conquers though he does not fight. His advice is, "Go round about, Peer." He typifies the riddle of existence.

The Button Moulder, an agent of God who is waiting for Peer when he returns, as an old man, to Norway. He intends to take Peer's soul and melt it down with other worthless ones, neither good enough to merit Heaven nor bad enough to deserve Hell, and he carries a huge casting ladle with him for this purpose. To Peer's surprise and indignation, the Button Moulder tells him that he should not mind dissolution because he has never been himself. The Button Moulder grants Peer leave to find witnesses that he has always been himself, to find a witness who will testify that his sins are great enough to merit Hell, and to set his house in order. At the end of the play, though the Button Moulder waits at the next crossroads, Solveig ignores his call while she holds Peer's head in her lap and sings him a lullaby.

Kari, a cotter's wife and Aase's friend.

Mr. Cotton,

Monsieur Ballon,

Herr von Eberkopf, and

Herr Trumpeterstraale, the men who commandeer Peer Gynt's ship in the hope of obtaining his gold. They are destroyed when the vessel blows up after Peer's prayer to God.

A Moroccan Thief and

a Receiver of Stolen Goods, who flee at Peer Gynt's approach, leaving behind them an emperor's stolen robe and charger. With these, Peer impersonates an Arab chieftain.

Anitra, an Arab dancing girl. While Peer Gynt is singing and dancing to show her how young and vigorous he is, she rides away with his horse and moneybag.

Professor Begriffenfeldt, the keeper of a lunatic asylum at Cairo. He introduces Peer to the mad inmates as their emperor.

Huhu, a language reformer from the Malabar coast.

Hussein, a minister of state.

A Fellah, carrying a mummy, who imagines that he is King Apis. He, Huhu, and Hussein are inmates of the asylum.

A Stranger, who encounters Peer Gynt on a ship off the Norwegian coast. He asks Peer for his corpse.

The Ship's Cook, whom Peer, to save his own life, pushes off the keel after the ship capsizes during a storm.

A Thin Person, the Devil dressed in a priest's cassock, whom Peer meets while trying to find someone who will testify to his fitness to enter Hell. Unimpressed by this stranger's recital of his sins, the Devil says that he is searching for Peer Gynt. Peer sends him off to the Cape of Good Hope on a useless search. Fooling the Devil gives Peer a momentary pleasure.

PEG WOFFINGTON

Author: Charles Reade (1814-1884)
First published: 1853
Genre: Novel

Locale: England
Time: The eighteenth century
Plot: Sentimental

Peg Woffington, a celebrated actress of the eighteenth century. She admires Harry Vane as an ideal of goodness and has an affair with him. She comes to see the wrong she has done Mrs. Vane, however, and renounces her lover and becomes Mrs. Vane's friend. Peg is a generous person who helps all who are friendly to her.

Harry Vane, an English gentleman who falls in love with Peg Woffington, sending her notes and flowers anonymously to awaken her interest in him. He truly loves his wife and returns to her after his affair with the actress.

Sir Charles Pomander, a gentleman with great curiosity who watches Harry's pursuit of Peg. He, too, is an admirer of the actress. When he is rebuffed by her, he sets out to stop the affair between her and Harry. He is a crude man.

Mabel Vane, Harry's wife, a beautiful woman with the simplicity of the country. She discovers her husband's affair with Peg through Sir Charles, who tries to make love to her. She is such a sweet and generous woman that she forgives her

husband for his straying and becomes a close friend of Peg.

Colley Cibber, a great actor and playwright of an earlier day. He claims that Peg Woffington is not as great as Mrs. Bracegirdle, an earlier star. Peg disguises herself as Mrs. Bracegirdle at a party backstage and completely fools Cibber, who then acknowledges her brilliance as an actress.

James Triplet, a struggling playwright, scene painter, and poet who is befriended by Peg because he befriended her when she was a girl. To further his career as an artist, she sits for a portrait. When critics arrive to ridicule his work, she cuts a hole in the canvas, inserts her own head, and thus confounds the critics. Disguised in the same way, she hears Mabel's plea for the return of her husband and promptly renounces Harry.

Snarl and

Soaper, arrogant critics made to look foolish by Peg's trick with the portrait.

Mr. Rich, a theater manager who is uninterested in Triplet's plays.

THE PELICAN
(Pelikanen)

Author: August Strindberg (1849-1912)
First published: 1907
Genre: Drama

Locale: Indeterminate, but probably Sweden
Time: Early 1900's
Plot: Mythic

The Mother, Elise, a newly widowed matriarch of a lower-class Swedish household. The Mother considers herself a model of motherhood because of the self-sacrifices she has endured on behalf of her husband and children. Actually, however, her life is a fabric of lies intended to conceal her own extravagance and indulgence. She has eaten well and kept warm while her children have virtually starved and frozen. She does not deny this history to herself, yet she shows no remorse and continues to insist on a frugality that perpetuates hunger and ill health. She is suspicious and defensive, quick to judge

or blame others. She demands obedience and attention and is ready to fight for them. The Mother claims to love her children, yet she manipulates them and treats them with contempt. The only person she trusts is her Son-in-Law, but that trust is based on a mercenary complicity, and she even takes pride in having stolen his attentions from her daughter. Supposedly in mourning for her husband—whom she knows she drove to his death—she cannot stand the smell of the funeral flowers and imagines his ghost to be present as the wind rocks his chair.

The Son, Fredrik, a law student. The Son is a hungry and delicate young man because of the deprivations of his childhood. He is unhappy and racked with coughing and stammering. Basically practical-minded, he hopes to finish his education and become a lawyer, but his ambition is hollow because he has lost all faith in the legal system, and now that his father's estate proves to be worthless, he despairs of ever earning his degree. The Son has no illusions about the Mother, his parents' marriage, and his own upbringing, and he is overwhelmingly cynical about human relationships. Just as a hellish marriage led his father to the taverns and eventually to his death, so do the Son's contempt for life, humanity, community, and himself lead him to drinking as his only escape.

The Daughter, **Gerda**, a frail young newlywed. Because of disease and poor nutrition in childhood, she is underdeveloped and, she reveals to her mother, barren. She has just married the Son-in-Law and is devoted to him to the point of excessive jealousy, for deep down she knows that his passion for her is completely a sham. This, like many truths of her life, she chooses to deny. The Daughter is, by her own confession, a sleepwalker through life. She wants to stay ignorant, so she continues to believe in the sacredness of motherhood and to defend the Mother against the Son's accusations. When forced to face the truth, she allies with her brother and becomes much more powerful and articulate, even pointedly sardonic.

The Son-in-Law, **Axel**, a lieutenant who has just married the Daughter. The Son-in-Law is a scoundrel, an intelligent man with a consuming greed and a basic disregard for others. He does not indulge in pretenses but shrewdly calculates his way through situations. He courted and married the Daughter for her inheritance; at best, he is indifferent to her. Once he discovered the mother to be infinitely stronger and more interesting, he befriended her, and they quickly became intimates, causing the final deterioration of her marriage. Now that the father's estate offers no financial reward, however, the Son-in-Law assumes a position of authority and becomes cruel and contemptuous toward the Mother.

Margaret, the cook, who has been with the family for years. She sees the truth and is willing to accuse and provoke the Mother with it, though she stops short of full-scale confrontation. She has heard too many lies, has felt like a prisoner with this family too long, and is ready to leave.

— *B. P. Mann*

PELLE THE CONQUEROR
(Pelle erobreren)

Author: Martin Andersen Nexø (Martin Andersen, 1869-1954)
First published: 1906-1910
Genre: Novel

Locale: Denmark
Time: Late nineteenth century
Plot: Social realism

Pelle Karlsson, a poor lad who becomes a shoemaker. He becomes interested in the labor movement and the shoemakers' union, rising to become president of the shoemakers. He and his fellow workers live in difficult times. Pelle finds his livelihood cut off; his wife alienates him by becoming a prostitute in order to feed their two children; and he is unjustly convicted of being a counterfeiter. Pelle studies the labor movement and decides that factories will do away with the shoemaker who works by hand. He and Mr. Brun, a librarian, start a cooperative shoe factory, and Pelle devotes the latter part of his life to urging his fellow workers to seek constitutional means of improving their lot, rather than strikes and violence.

Lasse Karlsson, Pelle's father, a farmhand. Attracted by higher wages, he migrates to the island of Bornholm. Because he is weak and worn-out, he is the butt of his fellow worker's jokes.

Rud Pihl, Pelle's playmate in childhood. The illegitimate son of the farm owner, he lives with his mother in a hut.

Master Andres, a master shoemaker under whom Pelle has his apprenticeship. He is not a difficult master, but he dies before Pelle's apprenticeship is finished.

Ellen Stolpe, loved by Pelle. She is the daughter of a leader in the stonemasons' union. She becomes a prostitute during hard times in order to earn a little money to support her family. For this reason, her husband leaves her, but they are reconciled after Pelle completes his six-year prison term.

Mr. Brun, a librarian in whose library Pelle reads up on the labor movement. Brun and Pelle start a cooperative shoe factory that proves quite successful.

Marie Nielsen, a dancer who befriends Pelle.

Sort, a traveling shoemaker with whom Pelle works for a time.

PELLÉAS AND MÉLISANDE
(Pelléas et Mélisande)

Author: Maurice Maeterlinck (1862-1949)
First published: 1892
Genre: Drama

Locale: Allemonde, a mythical kingdom
Time: Unspecified, but distant past
Plot: Symbolism

Pelléas (pay-lay-AHS), the grandson of King Arkël and much younger half brother of Golaud. Although his father lies gravely ill in the castle, Pelléas wishes to journey far away to a dying friend. He stays to welcome Golaud and his childlike bride, Mélisande. He shows Mélisande around the castle's environs. One night, as she is leaning out of a tower, he tangles her long hair in a tree so she cannot escape him; Golaud finds them this way. Golaud tells him that Mélisande is pregnant, so Pelléas resolves again to go away, but only after he tells her of his love. They meet at the Fountain of the Blind and declare their love. They suddenly notice Golaud watching from the shadows. In despair, they kiss passionately as Golaud rushes forward with his sword and strikes down Pelléas.

Mélisande (may-lee-ZAHND), a mysterious, childlike maiden whom Golaud discovers lost and weeping in a dark forest; she has dropped a golden crown in the water. Though frightened, she follows Golaud. Some time later, she and Golaud have married and arrive at his grandfather Arkël's castle. While accompanied by Pelléas, Mélisande loses her wedding ring in the bottomless Fountain of the Blind. She pretends to look for it in a dangerous cave by the sea. Golaud becomes increasingly jealous and suspicious after he finds Pelléas entwined in her hair by the tower. In front of Arkël, Golaud berates her and drags her around the floor by her long hair. She concludes that he no longer loves her. She and Pelléas declare their love shortly before Golaud kills Pelléas. She flees. Slightly wounded by Golaud, she forgives him, denies that she had a guilty love for Pelléas, and dies, after giving birth to a baby girl.

Golaud (goh-LOH), the elder grandson of Arkël, half brother of Pelléas, and widowed father of Yniold. He is a powerfully built man, with gray hair and beard, who loves hunting. While lost in a forest, he discovers Mélisande and later marries her. He initially encourages Pelléas and Mélisande to spend time together but grows jealous after Mélisande loses her wedding ring and he finds Pelléas wrapped in Mélisande's hair. He threatens Pelléas in the dank vaults beneath the castle, warning him to avoid Mélisande. He enlists his young son to spy on them, but the child becomes terrified, deepening Golaud's suspicions. Finally, he brutally drags Mélisande around the floor by her hair, calling her Absalom.

That night, from the shadows, he observes Pelléas and Mélisande embracing. He rushes at them with his sword, killing Pelléas and wounding his wife. As Mélisande is dying following childbirth, Golaud repeatedly asks her if she loved Pelléas with a guilty love; she denies it, but he can never know the truth of her feelings.

Arkël (ahr-KEHL), the king of Allemonde (perhaps, in its hints at German and French, suggesting "all the world") and grandfather of Pelléas and Golaud. He is very old and nearly blind. Sickness, poverty, and hunger pervade his realm. He persuades Pelléas to stay at the castle and verbally defends Mélisande against Golaud's accusations, saying that he sees in her eyes nothing but a great innocence. He repeatedly voices pity for humankind, for every human being is a mystery.

Yniold (een-YOHL), Golaud's young son (sometimes played by a woman). He takes to Mélisande quickly but weeps because he says she will soon go away. He seems to sense things about the relationship between Pelléas and Mélisande, but, when questioned by Golaud, he gives ambiguous answers. Outside Mélisande's window, Golaud makes the child spy on them, but Yniold becomes terrified; it is unclear whether it is because of what he sees or how his father is acting. Shortly before Pelléas and Mélisande meet for the last time, Yniold is seen trying to move a huge stone. He sees a flock of sheep being led away from the fold (perhaps to slaughter, an image that recurs throughout the play).

Geneviève (zhehn-VYEHV), Arkël's daughter, the mother of Golaud and Pelléas.

— *Susan Wladaver-Morgan*

PEÑAS ARRIBA

Author: José María de Pereda (1833-1906)
First published: 1895
Genre: Novel

Locale: Santander, Spain
Time: Late nineteenth century
Plot: Regional

Marcelo (mahr-SEH-loh), a young man from Madrid. Bidden by his lonely, eighty-year-old uncle, Celso Ruiz de Bejos, to come and live with him, the sophisticated Marcelo sets out for the heart of the Pyrenees on a visit to his patriarchal relative. At first, the simple pleasures of the village have little appeal for the urbane young man, but as time passes, the kindness and courage of the mountaineers and the grandeur of the surrounding peaks expand and lift his heart and mind. He finally marries Lita and becomes so much a part of the village life that he dreads leaving home even for short trips.

Celso Ruiz de Bejos (SEHL-soh rrew-EES deh BEH-hohs), Marcelo's eighty-year-old uncle, who is the patriarch of his region in the Pyrenees. He urges his nephew to leave Madrid and join him in his mountain home, where he makes him his heir.

Doctor Neluco (neh-LEW-koh), the friend and confidant of Marcelo in the mountain village. He advises the young man to marry Lita.

Sabas Peñas (SAH-bahs PEHN-yahs), the village priest.

Pedro Nolasco (PEH-droh noh-LAHS-koh) and

Pito Salces (PEE-toh SAHL-sehs), mountaineers whose courage and kindness inspire Marcelo with a love for the mountain village.

Margarita (mahr-gahr-EE-tah), called **Lita** (LEE-tah), Pedro Nolasco's granddaughter, who marries Marcelo.

Mari Pepa (MAH-ree PEH-pah), Pedro Nolasco's daughter.

Chisco (CHEES-koh), Celso Ruiz de Bejos' faithful servant.

Facia (FAH-see-ah), a mountain woman who seeks Marcelo's advice concerning her criminal husband, who is blackmailing her.

Tona (TOH-nah), Facia's daughter.

PENGUIN ISLAND
(L'Île des pingouins)

Author: Anatole France (Jacques-Anatole-François Thibault, 1844-1924)
First published: 1908
Genre: Novel

Locale: Mythical Alca
Time: Ancient to modern times
Plot: Satire

Maël (mah-EHL), a Breton missionary monk who, in ancient times, preached to a group of penguins living on an island at the North Pole. The penguins were baptized and turned into men, and the island was towed to a point off the Breton coast. Thus began a society that is the author's satire of French history.

Kraken (krah-KAH[N]), a clever penguin who lives by his wits and turns to his advantage the ignorance and superstitions of the peasant penguins. By constructing an imitation dragon and "killing" it at an appropriate time, he wins the gratitude of the populace and thereafter accepts annual tribute from them.

Oberosia (oh-beh-ROH-zyah), Kraken's mistress and the most beautiful of the penguin women. She appears as a virgin who conquers a dragon in order that Maël's prophecy might be fulfilled. The "dragon" is one she and Kraken have fashioned. Oberosia is the island's first and most important saint.

Eveline Clarence (ehv-LEEN klah-REHNS), a beautiful, talented charmer who becomes a favorite at political social gatherings. She marries a rising politician and becomes the mistress of the prime minister. She lives a long, happy life and, when she dies, leaves her property to the Charity of Saint Oberosia.

M. Hippolyte Cérès (ee-poh-LEET say-REHS), Eveline's husband, who tries to ruin the prime minister's career when it becomes apparent that Eveline is his mistress. His action has some effect, for the prime minister is finally put out of office.

Father Agaric (ah-gah-REEK) and

Prince des Boscenos (day boh-sah-NOHS), conspirators who attempt to destroy the republic and restore the monarchy. The revolution they launch is short-lived, failing almost as soon as it begins.

Greatank (gray-ah-TAH[N]K), the most powerful of all the penguins, who establishes Penguinia's first government on the island of Alca, its system that of a clan or tribe ruled by a strong warrior.

Draco (drah-KOH), Kraken's son, who founds the first royal family of Penguinia.

Draco the Great, a descendant of Draco who establishes a monastery in honor of Oberosia; thus the Middle Ages come to the island of Alca.

Trinco (tra[n]-KOH), the great soldier who takes command of the army of the republic after the monarchy has been abolished. He quickly conquers and loses most of the known world.

Johannes Talpa (zhoh-AHN tahl-PAH), a learned monk who chronicles the early history of the penguins.

Marbodius (mahr-boh-DYEWS), a literary monk who leaves a record of his descent into Hell.

Viscountess Olive (oh-LEEV), a clever aristocrat who seduces Chatillon in order to gain his support for the royalists' cause.

Viscount Clena (klay-NAH), a suitor whom Eveline rejects when she learns that he is of modest means.

God, a deity who finds it necessary to call the saints together in order to decide what to do about the penguins Maël has baptized.

Chatillon (shah-tee-YOH[N]), an admiral used by Father Agaric and the prince to head the military forces in the unsuccessful revolution.

M. Paul Visire (vee-SEER), prime minister of Penguinia, Eveline's lover.

Madame Clarence, Eveline's mother.

Pyrot (pee-ROH), a scapegoat.

A PENNY FOR A SONG

Author: John Whiting (1917-1963)
First published: 1957
Genre: Drama

Locale: England
Time: 1804
Plot: Comedy

Sir Timothy Bellboys, the eccentric bachelor landowner of a large estate on the Dorset coast in southern England. As Napoleon's power grows in Europe, rumors of invasion circle England, and Timothy is obsessed by them. In fact, he is convinced that the French will land their forces on his property. He has therefore devised a plan to outwit the French, by disguising himself as Napoleon and then ordering the French troops to lay down their arms. He also believes that the local volunteer soldiers' exercise is the real invasion, and he proceeds to put his plan into operation. In the process, he descends a well (twice), rides a balloon, is involved in an explosion, and actually convinces the volunteers that he is Napoleon. For all his bizarre behavior, he shows himself to be a courageous and resourceful gentleman.

Lamprett Bellboys, Timothy's brother, who lives with him and is equally eccentric. Unlike Timothy, Lamprett is married, although the marriage was more or less forced on him to save his wife's honor during his university days; he had been helping her make a protofeminist gesture to prove women intellectually capable of being Oxford students. Lamprett is in charge of the house's fire engine and believes that his is the most important function of the whole community. He is as single-minded as his brother, so they conflict, especially over the function of William Humpage. Later, Lamprett puts out all the warning fires lit in the mistaken belief that Napoleon has landed.

Hester Bellboys, Lamprett's wife. Although Hester may seem far more capable and organized than her husband, it is soon revealed that she has her own obsessions. She is part of an early feminist movement and has been invited to form part of a women's army corps. She is prepared to leave her family, even in the middle of a supposed invasion, to take up her post. Her energies are largely consumed in getting herself ready, especially her dress and equipment. Like the other eccentrics, she believes that the endeavors of the others are largely a waste of time.

Dorcas Bellboys, the seventeen-year-old only child of Lamprett and Hester. Unlike them, she appears quite natural and delightfully innocent. Her mother believes that it is time for Dorcas to behave more maturely. Dorcas falls in love with

Edward Sterne, a veteran who comes to the house. He appears to be one of the first normal men she has met, and she responds to both his personal suffering and his honesty and radical convictions. He does not return her affection, and she intuitively realizes this. She bravely accepts that love can be an unhappy experience.

Hallam Matthews, a middle-aged dandy who arrives at the house from London with his servant, Samuel Breeze. He has been asked by Timothy to bring a number of items to further his Napoleonic disguise scheme. Hallam is as concerned with his own affairs as the other older people; in his case, it is his personal comfort. He does, however, discuss with Edward and Dorcas a number of contemporary issues, such as Romanticism and revolutionary theories. As might be expected, he represents a worldly wisdom that, although somewhat cynical and reactionary, is more than mere prejudice.

Edward Sterne, a mercenary and a radical, about twenty-eight years old. He appears first asking for food, in the company of a small boy whom he has rescued from some European battlefield. (In the first version of the play, Edward was blind, but his sight was reinstated in the final version.) He talks to Dorcas and Hallam Matthews about his experiences of actual fighting and the devastation it brings to civilians as well as soldiers, jarring the pastoral eccentricity of the scene and making many of the older people's obsessions seem absurd and selfish. Hallam's refutation of much of Edward's revolutionary philosophy and Edward's inability to return Dorcas' love temper the audience's natural sympathies for him.

George Selincourt, a man who has taken over as captain of the local volunteers, reared initially by Timothy. There is considerable antagonism between them: Selincourt's plans for military exercises are never communicated to Timothy, giving rise to the plot confusions. He is finally redeemed in Timothy's eyes when it is discovered that he is a first-class cricketer.

William Humpage, the old family servant, who divides his loyalties between Timothy, who wants him as a lookout for the Napoleonic invasion, and Lamprett, who needs him as a lookout for fires. His ensuing behavior is more than slightly bizarre.

— *David Barratt*

THE PEOPLE OF JUVIK
(Juvikfolke)

Author: Olav Duun (1876-1939)
First published: 1918-1923
Genre: Novel

Locale: Namdal district, Norway
Time: 1800-1918
Plot: Family

Per,
Bear Anders,
Big Per, and
Greedy Per, heroic ancestors of Per Anders Juvika.

Per Anders Juvika, a prosperous eighteenth century Norwegian farmer who rules his family as a patriarch.

Ane, Per Anders Juvika's wife.

Jens, Per Anders' son, who is wild and reckless like the old Juvikings.

Per, Per Anders' other son, a gentle and hardworking young man. Like his brother Jens, he is ruled by his father.

Valborg, Per's wife, picked out for him by his father.

Ane,
Aasel, and
Beret, daughters of Per Anders.

Mikkal, Aasel's husband, a hard worker and a good provider.

Anders Haaberg, Per and Valborg's son. He takes over the family farm.

Petter Haaberg, Anders' worthless brother. He is a sly and reckless man.

Solvi, a Laplander, Anders' first wife. Suspected of being a witch, she is sent back to her father, but she and her child are killed on the way home by a rock slide. Having yielded to the pressure of his superstitious neighbors, Anders broods much over her death.

Massi Liness, Anders' second wife.

Ola Engdal, a rival of Anders for the hand of Massi. She accepts Ola, but he is killed in an accident while still young.

Kjersti, Massi's foster daughter, who bears a child by Peter.

Per,
Gjartru,
Aasel,
Jens,
Beret, and
Ola, children of Anders and Massi.

Marja Leinland, Per's wife.

Hall Gronset, who is loved by Gjartru. He is lost at sea.

Petter Liness, Per's friend who, before he is drowned, gives Per some money to pass on secretly to Kjersti.

Johan Arnesen, Gjartru's husband. He is a storekeeper who prospers for a time, but his business finally fails. He and Gjartru go to America with Jens.

Kristen Folden, Aasel's husband, who takes over the Haaberg farm.

Peder,
Elen, and
Marjane, children of Kristen and Aasel.

Kjerstina, Peder's distant cousin. She is pregnant by him.

Andrea Ween, who marries Peder. After his death, she marries Otte Setran.

Arthur Ween, Andrea's brother. He marries Mina Arnesen, a cousin of Peder.

Mina Arnesen, the daughter of Johan and Gjartru, and Arthur's wife. She and her husband inherit Segelsund when Johan and Gjartru go to America.

Otte Setran, Elen's lover and the father of Odin Setran. He eventually marries Andrea, after Peder's death.

Odin Setran, Elen's illegitimate son. He shows promise of being a heroic man, like the first Juvikings. When Elen marries, he is sent to live with foster parents.

Iver Vennestad, who marries Elen. He is disliked by Odin, whom he bullies.

Bendek and

Gurianna Kjelvik, Odin's foster parents.

Lauris Kjelvik, Odin's playmate. Great friends in their youth, they become enemies in later life when Lauris proves to be unscrupulous and overly ambitious. Eventually, Odin sacrifices his life to save Lauris from drowning.

Astri, Odin's cousin, the daughter of Peder and Andrea. They fall in love but cannot marry because Astri's mother decides to marry Odin's natural father. Astri marries Arne Finne.

Ingri Arnesen, who marries Odin. They first meet as youngsters, when they almost drown while crossing the fjord in a storm.

Arne Finne, a childhood sweetheart whom Astri marries, even though he is dying of tuberculosis.

Engelbert Olsen, a leader of the workmen in the community. With Lauris, he plots to discredit Odin, but Odin hunts him down and drives him from the area.

Anders and

Per, sons of Odin and Ingri. Like true Juvikings, they seem to possess their father's great generosity and courage.

PEOPLE OF THE CITY

Author: Cyprian Ekwensi (1921-   )
First published: 1954; revised, 1963
Genre: Novel

Locale: Lagos and eastern Nigeria
Time: Early 1950's
Plot: Social morality

Amusa Sango (ah-MEW-sah SAHN-goh), the protagonist, who lives in Lagos, the capital of Nigeria, where he is employed as a crime reporter on a tabloid newspaper. He exemplifies a new class that has developed in contemporary Africa, that of educated urban workers who relish the opportunities for money and pleasure that social change has brought and who are indifferent, even antagonistic, to the restrictive cultural traditions of their parents. Sango is young, lively, and opportunistic, intelligent but not intellectual. He enjoys his role as a man-about-town; he is handsome, easygoing, and self-confident. He finds enjoyment in the high life of the city. During the evenings, he is the leader of a dance band, which plays in the local nightclubs. This moonlighting gives him access to the many good-time girls who, like him, see Lagos as a city of exotic opportunity. He is not merely a superficial playboy. Although he enjoys passionate sex with several women, in each case he defends himself from the guilt of promiscuity by believing himself to be ardently in love. He takes his work as a journalist seriously as well. His news reports show a serious social awareness of the exploitation suffered by the underprivileged in this rapidly evolving economy that provides benefits not for workers but rather for shrewd, even crooked, manipulators. His convictions are strong enough to require that he challenge the system. He is finally fired because his trenchant columns criticizing corruption offend the elite friends of the newspaper proprietor. Forced into exile in Ghana, he swears that he will return to Nigeria to work toward reform. For all of his private sexual activities, he remains a social idealist. He lives by his own code of honor, one that, if flexible in ultimate moral terms, retains a redeeming measure of dedication and decency.

Aina (AY-nah), a pretty country girl. There is nothing remarkable about her. Like hundreds of others, she has been lured to the city by the exaggerated promises of thrills and profit and is eager to experience the fast, glamorous life no matter the consequences, which she is too innocent to imagine anyway. Her only prospects derive from her sex. She is naïve enough to think that the men who seduce her will marry her but soon realizes the disappointing truth. She finds no work and survives by petty theft until she is caught and sentenced to prison. Humiliated and embittered, she turns viciously on so-

ciety. She creates public scenes and attempts blackmail. At the nadir of her fortunes, she suffers a painful miscarriage. She is a young woman destroyed by the cruelties and indifference of the city. At this point, however, she undergoes a complete (if somewhat improbable) character transformation. She repents of her behavior and displays the heart of gold that exists beneath the angry resentment that has motivated her.

Aina's mother, a strange and ominous person who is powerfully protective of Aina and threatens anyone who might seem to do her harm. Her comings and goings are made so mysterious that it seems as if she may be more than a brooding, attentive mother, a witch who, in the African context, would have great powers for evil. Believing that she is a witch, Sango fears her greatly. When she unexpectedly appears at his mother's deathbed, however, she offers Sango her blessing rather than her curse, so she may be simply an ordinary old woman, devoted and anxious about the uncaring folly of her daughter and the tempting vices among which she lives.

Lajide (lah-JEE-dah), Sango's fat, lustful, greedy, exploitative Syrian landlord, a thoroughly despicable tyrant. He dresses in the Arab style and wears a gilt-edged fez with golden tassels. He has eight wives, but that does not stop him from making lecherous advances to any women who seek to do business with him and becoming incensed if any dares deny him. He has made his fortune with a series of barely legal deals. He is a part-time moneylender at usurious rates, harsh in all of his dealings. With his compatriot Zamil, he exemplifies the rapacious foreign trader, a familiar real-life feature of West African commerce. He drives a large American car to display his wealth ostentatiously and, while living in exceptional luxury, constantly and deliberately grinds and exploits his poor tenants. His greed is his undoing. To acquire still more money, he takes the step into actual criminal activity. His further crooked tradings are uncovered, and his whole empire collapses. The wife he most deeply adores dies. His anguish reveals that even Lajide has some virtues. He dies in a peaceful, drunken, perhaps suicidal, coma that allows him to avoid the jail sentence his activities have earned for him.

Bayo (BAH-yoh), a friend of Sango and, like him, somewhat of a playboy, reveling in the opportunities that Lagos provides for drinking, dancing, and enjoying the transient attentions of innumerable women, preferably very young ones. His cheerfully extravagant way of life makes no provision for the future. Although his behavior is frivolous, he is warmhearted and a good friend capable of real affection, so that it is not implausible that he finally truly falls in love. It is unfortunate that he chooses the daughter of Zamil, however, because Zamil despises the Africans that he swindles. His death by shooting at the hands of Zamil is pointless, but it may suggest the wider pointlessness of Bayo's existence.

Beatrice, an extremely beautiful mature woman. Without moral embarrassment, she acknowledges that she covets the luxuries she can obtain only by being the mistress of a rich man. This life of virtual prostitution brings her neither money nor happiness, only the feeling of being degraded and exploited. After living for years as the mistress of a British engineer, by whom she has three children, she determines to reform her life. With considerable courage and much optimism, she leaves him, trusting that independence will provide the basis for renewed honor. She is still attractive to men, and, when she takes a job in a department store, Lajide pursues her with gifts. In spite of increasingly ill health, she joins up with yet another man. Soon afterward, she dies and is buried in a pauper's grave, proving the sad futility of her mode of life.

Beatrice Two, a morally perfect, idealized presentation of beauteous womanhood. In complete contrast to all the other good-time girls, who are immoral and appeal to men's sexual urges, she has all the virtues a man appreciates and seeks in a wife, including virginity. She is dainty, modest, and well brought up; she dresses well and converses intelligently. She is educated and appropriately destined for the status and comfort of marrying an elite Nigerian at present studying in England. She is so sensitive that an inner conflict about her choice of husbands brings her to a nervous breakdown. She forgives Sango his past affairs because of her infatuation for him.

— *John F. Povey*

PEPITA JIMÉNEZ
(Pepita Ximenez)

Author: Juan Valera (Juan Valera y Alcalá Galiano, 1824-1905)
First published: 1874
Genre: Novel

Locale: Andalusia, Spain
Time: c. 1870
Plot: Psychological realism

Luis de Vargas (lew-EES deh VAHR-gahs), a seminary student, preparing for the priesthood, who is home for a vacation. He corresponds with his uncle, the dean of the seminary, about his own changing attitude toward Pepita, his father's prospective young bride.

Don Pedro de Vargas (PEH-droh), his understanding father, who is well satisfied to have his son give up the priesthood in order to stay home and marry Pepita.

Pepita Jiménez (peh-PEE-tah hee-MEHN-ehs), a charming young widow.

Gumersindo (gew-mehr-SEEN-doh), an elderly moneylender, briefly married to Pepita.

Antoñona (ahn-tohn-YOHN-ah), Pepita's duenna, who does more than her share to further the romance of Luis and Pepita.

The Vicar, who wants Pepita to marry Don Pedro.

Currito (kew-RREE-toh), Luis' cousin, who takes him to the casino. There, he gambles with the count and eventually fights a duel with him.

Count de Genazahar (deh gehn-ah-sah-AHR), who borrowed money from Gumersindo that he will not repay to the widow. When he makes slighting remarks about Pepita, he and Luis wound each other with sabers.

PÈRE GORIOT
(Le Père Goriot)

Author: Honoré de Balzac (1799-1850)
First published: 1834-1835
Genre: Novel

Locale: Paris, France
Time: 1819
Plot: Naturalism

Father Goriot (goh-RYOH), a lonely old lodger at the pension of Madame Vauquer in Paris. Known to the other boarders as Old Goriot, he is a retired manufacturer of vermicelli who sold his prosperous business in order to provide handsome dowries for his two daughters. During his first year at the Maison Vauquer, he occupied the best rooms in the house; in the second year, he asked for less expensive quarters on the floor above; and at the end of the third year he moved into a cheap, dingy room on the third story. Because two fashionably dressed young women have visited him from time to time in the past, the old man has become an object of curiosity and suspicion; the belief is that he has ruined himself by keeping two mistresses. Actually, Old Goriot is a man in whom parental love has become an obsession, a love unappreciated and misused by his two selfish, heartless daughters, who make constant demands on his meager resources. After a life of hard work, careful saving, and fond indulgence of his children, he has outlived his usefulness and is now in his dotage. Happy in the friendship of Eugène de Rastignac, the law student who becomes the lover of one of the daughters, he uses the last of his money to provide an apartment for the young man, a place where Old Goriot will also have his own room. Before the change can be made, however, the daughters drive their father to desperation by fresh demands for money to pay their bills. He dies attended only by Eugène and Bianchon, a poor medical student; in his last moments he speaks lovingly of the daughters who have ruined him and made him the victim of their ingratitude. The daughters send their empty carriages to follow his coffin to the grave.

Countess Anastasie de Restaud (ah-nah-stah-ZEE deh rehs-TOH), the more fashionable of Old Goriot's daughters, constantly in need of money to indulge her extravagant tastes and to provide for her lover. Meeting her at a ball given by his distant relative, Madame de Beauséant, Eugène de Rastignac immediately falls in love with Anastasie. When he calls on her, he finds Old Goriot just leaving. His mention of his fellow lodger causes Anastasie and her husband to treat the young law student with great coldness, and he realizes that he is no longer welcome in their house. Later, Madame de Beauséant explains the mystery, saying that Anastasie is ashamed of her humble origins and her tradesman father.

Baroness Delphine de Nucingen (dehl-FEEN deh new-sahn-ZHAHN), Old Goriot's second daughter, the wife of a German banker. Like her sister Anastasie, she married for position and money, but her place in society is not as exalted as that of the Countess de Restaud, who has been received at court. As a result, the sisters are not on speaking terms. Madame de Beauséant, amused by Eugène de Rastignac's youthful ardor, suggests that he introduce her to the Baroness de Nucingen in order to win Delphine's gratitude and a place for himself in Parisian society. Delphine accepts the young man as her lover. Though self-centered and snobbish, she is less demanding than her sister; she has asked for less, given more of herself, and brought more happiness to her father. When Old Goriot is dying, she goes to the Maison Vauquer at Eugène's insistence, but she arrives too late to receive her father's blessing.

Eugène de Rastignac (yew-ZHEHN deh rahs-tee-NYAHK), an impoverished law student, the son of a landed provincial family. As ambitious as he is handsome, he is determined to conquer Paris. At first, his lack of sophistication makes him almost irresistible to his relative, Madame de Beauséant, and Delphine de Nucingen, whose lover he becomes. He learns cynicism without losing his warm feelings; he never wavers in his regard for Old Goriot, and while he does not attend seriously to the law studies for which his family is making a great sacrifice, he manages to get on in fashionable society, where friendships and influence are important. The revelation of the ways of the world that he gains through the patronage of Madame de Beauséant, his love affair with Delphine, and his regard for Old Goriot, as well as the shabby activities in which he engages in order to maintain himself in the world of fashion, make him all the more ambitious and eager to succeed.

Madame Vauquer (voh-KAY), the sly, shabby, penurious owner of the Maison Vauquer. When Old Goriot first moves into her establishment, she sees him as a possible suitor; after he fails to respond to her coy attentions, she makes him an object of gossip and ridicule.

Monsieur Vautrin (voh-TRAHN), a man living at the Maison Vauquer who claims to be a former tradesman. Reserved, sharp-tongued, secretive, he observes everything that goes on about him and is aware of Old Goriot's efforts to provide money for his daughters. Knowing that Eugène de Rastignac desperately needs money in order to maintain himself in society, he suggests that the young man court Victorine Taillefer, another lodger, an appealing young girl whose father has disinherited her in favor of her brother. Vautrin says that he will arrange to have the brother killed in a duel, a death that will make Victorine an heiress. He gives Eugène two weeks to consider his proposition. Eugène considers Vautrin a devil, but in the end, driven to desperation by his mistress, he begins to court Victorine. True to Vautrin's word, Victorine's brother is fatally wounded in a duel. Vautrin's scheme fails when he is arrested and revealed as a notorious criminal, **Jacques Collin**, nicknamed **Trompe-la-Mort**. Although his identity has been betrayed within the pension, he swears that he will return and continue his climb to good fortune by the same unscrupulous means used by those who call themselves respectable.

Victorine Taillefer (veek-toh-REEN tah-yeh-FEHR), a young girl cast off by her harsh father, who has decided to make his son his only heir. She lives with Madame Couture at the Maison Vauquer.

Madame Couture (kew-TEWR), the widow of a public official and a lodger at the Maison Vauquer. A kind-hearted woman, she fills the place of a mother in the lonely life of Victorine Taillefer.

Monsieur Poiret (pwah-RAY), a lodger at the Maison Vauquer. To him Gondureau, a detective, confides his suspicion that Monsieur Vautrin is in reality the famous criminal, Trompe-la-Mort.

Mademoiselle Michonneau (mee-shoh-NOH), an elderly woman living at the Maison Vauquer. Disliking Monsieur Vautrin, her fellow boarder, she agrees to put a drug in his coffee. While Vautrin is asleep, she discovers the brand of a criminal on his shoulder. Acting on this information, the police appear and arrest Vautrin.

Gondureau (gohn-dew-ROH), the detective who is trying to track down Jacques Collin, called Trompe-la-Mort, a criminal who lives at the Maison Vauquer under the name of Vautrin. Gondureau arranges with Monsieur Poiret and Mademoiselle Michonneau to have Vautrin drugged in order to learn whether he bears a criminal brand on his shoulder.

Count Maxime de Trailles (mahk-SEEM deh TRAH-yeh), an arrogant but impecunious young nobleman, the lover of Anastasie de Restaud. For his sake, she helps to impoverish her father.

Madame de Beauséant (deh boy-say-YAHN), a relative of Eugène de Rastignac. Aristocratic and high-minded, she is the ideal of inherited culture and good manners—kind, reserved, warm-hearted, beautiful. Though saddened by the loss of her lover, she treats Eugène with great kindness, receives Delphine de Nucingen for his sake, and introduces the young man into fashionable Parisian society.

Bianchon (byahn-SHOHN), a poor medical student living at the Maison Vauquer. Like Eugène de Rastignac, he befriends Old Goriot and attends him when the old man is dying. Bianchon extends friendship easily and allows warm human feelings to influence his relations with other people.

Sylvie (seel-VEE), the plump cook at the Maison Vauquer.

Christophe (krees-TOHF), Madame Vauquer's man of all work.

PEREGRINE PICKLE

Author: Tobias Smollett (1721-1771)
First published: 1751
Genre: Novel

Locale: England and the Continent
Time: Early eighteenth century
Plot: Picaresque

Peregrine Pickle, called **Perry** in his younger days, a headstrong, rebellious young man. Bitterly disliked by his mother in his childhood, Peregrine is adopted by his godfather, a retired naval officer who lavishes money on his young ward, educates him, saves him from a love affair regarded as imprudent, and sends him traveling on the Continent. Although wealthy after his benefactor's death, Peregrine suffers reverses caused by his extravagance, his delight in practical jokes, and his foolhardiness in writing satires on public officials after he has stood unsuccessfully for Parliament and has been reduced to near penury. Thrown into prison and without influential friends, he nevertheless refuses the hand and fortune of Emilia Gauntlet, with whom he is in love. He is saved by an inheritance from his father, marries Emilia, and settles down to the life of a country squire. Peregrine Pickle is developed beyond Smollett's other title characters. On his travels, he is thrown with intellectuals, the associations leading to lengthy discussions on political, cultural, and philosophical matters. He is also given to foolhardy and sometimes licentious behavior.

Commodore Hawser Trunnion, Peregrine's godfather and benefactor. An old sea dog, Trunnion keeps his house—called "the garrison"—like a ship; his speech is sharp and salty with naval jargon. His maintenance of a ship's atmosphere makes for much of the comedy in the novel.

Thomas Pipes, Trunnion's companion and servant, retired from the sea. He becomes a companion to Peregrine when he is sent to school and on his travels. Loyal to the young man, Pipes rescues his wayward master from many scrapes.

Lieutenant Jack Hatchway, the commodore's one-legged companion. Like Pipes, he often shows up when Peregrine needs help. Hatchway's most opportune appearance comes when Peregrine is in Fleet Prison after his arrest for writing the political satires.

Emilia Gauntlet, called **Emy** by her family, Peregrine's sweetheart, whom he meets while he is attending Winchester School. The recurrent meetings of these two, tempered by quarrels and avowals of devotion, are for much of the story secondary in importance to Peregrine's pursuit of other women. Eventually, Peregrine offers her his hand, and Emilia accepts.

Godfrey Gauntlet, her brother. After a brief period of animosity, during which he worsts Peregrine in a duel, he becomes a devoted friend on learning that Peregrine is his secret benefactor. Peregrine, in his prosperous days, had anonymously provided funds for Godfrey and had used his influence to secure Godfrey's captaincy in the navy.

Gamaliel Pickle, Peregrine's father, the soul of humbleness and the butt of his wife's ill temper. He is happy to see his son taken by Trunnion, away from the meanness of his wife. Whether unwittingly or not, Gamaliel wins the final victory over his wife; he dies intestate, and his money goes to Peregrine, his first-born son.

Sally Appleby, Gamaliel's termagant wife. Left unprovided for at the death of her husband, she is forced to live on an allowance from Peregrine.

Grizzle Pickle, Gamaliel's sister and his housekeeper until he marries Sally. Refusing to be subjugated by her sister-in-law, Grizzle finds escape when she becomes Mrs. Trunnion. Her death brings sadness to Peregrine, who has considered her more a mother than an aunt.

Gam Pickle, Peregrine's young brother. His mother's favorite child, Gam conspires with his mother in her scheming. Their hatred for Peregrine is shown in their plot to have him murdered. Godfrey Gauntlet, mistaken for Peregrine, suffers from their machinations. Gam faces a dismal future when he is ordered away from the property with his mother, after Peregrine inherits his father's estate.

Julia Pickle, Peregrine's sister and the youngest of the children, who also suffers her mother's ill will. Sympathetic to Peregrine, she is taken in and cared for by Grizzle Trunnion.

Layman Pallet, an English traveler whom Peregrine meets at the Palais Royal in Paris. In addition to his discussion on art and the other aspects of sophistication that he lends to the story, he is pictured, almost in burlesque and in raucous circumstances, trying to seduce a woman in a party traveling to Ghent.

The Doctor, Pallet's traveling companion. His knowledge as a connoisseur of foods and wines adds to the tone of the story, stressing Peregrine's sophistication.

Cadwallader Crabtree, an eccentric old man whom Peregrine meets when he returns to London. Posing as a fortune teller, he allows Peregrine to learn many women's secrets.

Deborah Hornbeck, the attractive wife of an English traveler in Paris. Her elopement with Peregrine threatens to become an international incident. The British ambassador sends Deborah back to her husband. After a second affair with her, Peregrine is put into prison. Freed, he is given three days to leave Paris.

Lady Vane, a notorious lady of quality. Her memoirs, which make up a sizable section of the novel, tell of her many lovers.

Amanda, a young woman traveling to Ghent. Peregrine's efforts to seduce her are exceeded in comedy only by Pallet's simultaneous activities with her traveling companion.

Jolter, a teacher at Winchester School, hired by Trunnion to act as Peregrine's traveling companion on the Continent.

Miss Sophy, Emilia Gauntlet's cousin, who helps Peregrine in his affair with Emilia.

A Young Female Beggar, whom Peregrine encounters on the road to London. In Pygmalion-like manner, he buys her fashionable gowns and teaches her polite phrases in order to pass her off as a lady; however, her gaucherie causes him to lose friends.

Sir Steady Steerwell, the minister of public affairs and the subject of the satire that sends Peregrine to the Fleet Prison.

Charles Clover, Julia Pickle's husband, who informs Peregrine of his father's death. A young justice of the peace, he aborts any plan Gam and his mother may have to forge a will after Gamaliel Pickle dies intestate.

Cecilia Gauntlet, Emilia's mother. She reprimands Peregrine for his conduct toward her daughter. Later, she is much in favor of her son-in-law.

Mr. Sackbut, the curate, who plots with Gam and Sally to murder Peregrine.

Morgan, a Welsh surgeon identified as Dr. Morgan, a character in Smollett's earlier novel *Roderick Random*.

Benjamin Chintz, a merchant who repays with interest a loan of seven hundred pounds while Peregrine is in Fleet Prison. The repayment marks the reversal of Peregrine's bad fortune.

Jennings and

Jumble, Peregrine's teachers, against whom, as a youngster, he rebels because of their hypocrisy.

Hadgi, Peregrine's valet on his travels. Peregrine befriends him after the party has returned to England and Hadgi is out of Peregrine's employ.

A PERFECT PEACE
(Menuhah nekhonah)

Author: Amos Oz (1939-   )
First published: 1982
Genre: Novel

Locale: Israel, particularly Kibbutz Granot
Time: 1965-1967
Plot: Historical realism

Yonatan Lifshitz, a citrus picker on the Kibbutz Granot in Israel, the twenty-six-year-old son of the kibbutz secretary. Born and reared on the commune, he is sensitive, lonely, and introverted, a decorated war hero who chafes under the Zionist views of his domineering father. Frustrated by his purposeless and restrictive life and his unsatisfying relationship with his wife, he flees to be by himself in the Jordanian desert and to seek the "perfect peace." Contemplating suicide, he gradually begins to accept truths about himself and his life and returns to the kibbutz to live in a family with his wife and her lover.

Rimona Lifshitz, Yonatan's wife. Elegant, subdued, unresponsive, and vague, she becomes more remote after a failed pregnancy. She has a passionless relationship with Yonatan and is unable to help him deal with his frustrations. She finds a more sympathetic relationship with Azariah Gitlin, a newcomer to the kibbutz, with whom she has a child.

Yolek Lifshitz, Yonatan's father and secretary of the kibbutz. Crafty-looking, he is shrewd, domineering, and quick-witted. He has served in Parliament and is one of the leaders of the Israeli movement. He laments the lack of idealism in the younger members of the party and his sons, and he fears that he will never see the changes he desires. As his health and hearing deteriorate, he withdraws into silence.

Azariah Gitlin (az-ah-RI-ah), who has recently been honorably discharged from the army and joins the kibbutz as a mechanic. A child of the Holocaust, he is thin and intense. Talkative and idealistic, he relies on a barrage of quotations from Baruch Spinoza to express his ideas. He longs for recognition and fantasizes about his importance. Falling in love with Rimona, he cares for her while Yonatan is gone. He becomes an admired, hardworking, and popular member of the commune.

Hava Lifshitz (KAH-vah), Yolek's wife, energetic and determinedly good-natured. She is contemptuous of Yolek, believing that he has "killed" her, as he is destroying Yonatan. She believes that her life has been sacrificed in serving Yolek.

Srulik (SHREW-lihk), the incoming secretary of the kibbutz. He is a German Jew, a bachelor who has lived on the kibbutz for thirty-six years, and a musician. Kind and patient, he is a philosophical observer of human nature who keeps a diary.

— *Millicent Sharma*

A PERFECT SPY

Author: John le Carré (David John Moore Cornwell, 1931-   )
First published: 1986
Genre: Novel

Locale: England, Switzerland, Vienna, Washington, D.C., and Czechoslovakia
Time: Early 1930's to the 1980's
Plot: Spy

Magnus Richard Pym, a British intelligence officer. Magnus is tall, handsome, and unmistakably English. Ever eager to please, Magnus calls himself "overpromised"; he has professed loyalty to too many people, to the point that he believes that there is nothing left of and for himself. It is his narrative of his life that makes up the bulk of the novel. In it, he refers to himself in the third person, differentiating himself as writer from "Pym," his protagonist.

Richard Thomas (Rick) Pym, Magnus' father. A handsome, charming confidence man who exudes righteousness despite his illegal schemes, Rick teaches Magnus the basics of betrayal: Rick promises to "see everyone right," showering them with gifts while absconding with all of their money. Magnus both loves and despises his father, feeling consumed and controlled by him, yet is always trying to please him. Magnus feels set free from his cycle of betrayal by Rick's death.

Axel H., also known as **Poppy**, **Alexander Hampel**, **Hans Albrecht Petz**, and **Jerzy Zaworski**, a Czech intelligence officer. His face betrays the hardships he has endured. Axel is a father figure to Magnus; Magnus considers him to be his oldest friend. The two first meet in Switzerland and then in Austria, when Magnus is a young military intelligence officer. Axel, playing on Magnus' guilt over betraying him while they were young in Switzerland, persuades him to betray his country. They eventually erect a network of Czech agents that passes a mixture of true and false information to the British.

Jack Brotherhood, Magnus' superior. Jack, the British intelligence officer who recruited Magnus, is one of Magnus' admired father figures. Straight-backed and blue-eyed, he embodies England for Magnus. He defends Magnus to the intelligence corps after Magnus' disappearance yet becomes convinced of his guilt and is determined to trace him.

Thomas Richard (Tom) Pym, Magnus' son. A tall adolescent, Tom is an observant boy who admires authority, especially Jack Brotherhood, and quietly seeks approval. Magnus' account of his life is meant for Tom, who he hopes will escape the destructive influence of him and Rick.

Mary (Mabs) Pym, Magnus' wife. Mary is blond, forthright, unmistakably English, and from an upper-class family with a history of government service. She was trained as an agent, but after her marriage to Magnus she leads the life of a very good diplomatic-corps wife. Her interrogation by Jack Brotherhood after Magnus' disappearance forms one of the narrative strands of the novel.

Grant Lederer III, an American intelligence agent. He and his wife befriend the Pyms in Washington and Vienna. Lederer, an overeager and overambitious agent, discovers the connection between Magnus and Axel.

Annie "Lippsie" Lippschitz, one of Rick's mistresses, who acts as a mother to Magnus. She is a beautiful German Jew who is often melancholy and guilt-ridden, both over her survival when her family perished and over her role in Rick's schemes. Lippsie loves Magnus and tries to instill a moral sense in him. In essence, she tells him that he must break from his father and be his own man.

Miss Dubber, the landlady of the beach house where Magnus goes to escape. She is a small old woman who for years has doted on "Mr. Canterbury," as she knows Magnus.

Sydney (Syd) Lemon, Rick's closest friend, a brash Cockney who understands Rick's influence over Magnus and Magnus' ambivalence toward his father.

Margaret (Peggy) Wentworth, the financially ruined widow of a man who invested in one of Rick's schemes. She gives Magnus a full account of his father's perfidy.

— *Karen M. Cleveland*

PERICLES, PRINCE OF TYRE

Author: William Shakespeare (1564-1616)
First published: 1609
Genre: Drama

Locale: The eastern Mediterranean Sea and its littorals
Time: The Hellenistic period
Plot: Comedy

Pericles (PEHR-eh-kleez), the prince of Tyre. When King Antiochus gave him a riddle to solve, the intelligent young man learned too much about the evil king's incestuous lust for his own daughter. Knowing that his life and his kingdom of Tyre are now in great danger, he flees to impoverished Tarsus, bearing shiploads of food for Cleon's people. Shipwrecked in storm-driven seas, he is cast ashore in a land governed by good King Simonides, who gives the hapless prince an opportunity to enter the lists. Pericles wins the tournament and the heart of Thaisa, the king's beautiful daughter. They marry, but he is soon separated from his bride. After many mishaps, he is reunited with his wife and child.

Thaisa (thay-IHS-uh), King Simonides' lovely young daughter. Seeing Prince Pericles, she is smitten by his charms, even though he is dressed in rusty armor that he fished out of the sea after the shipwreck. When the valiant prince wins the tourney, she is determined to marry him. Shortly after the marriage, she bears him a daughter, apparently dies on board ship, and is put afloat in a tightly caulked casket, in which she drifts to shore and is revived by Cerimon, a lord of Ephesus, skilled in healing.

Marina (mah-REE-nuh), the attractive daughter of Pericles and Thaisa. Born on a ship tossed by a raging storm, she is shortly afterward separated from her father. A good portion of her life afterward is equally tumultuous. Her life threatened because of Dionyza's hate, she is saved when pirates capture her and take her to a brothel in Mytilene, where she is the despair of Pandar and his bawd because of her unassailable virginity, a condition that drives off and purifies his prospective customers.

Helicanus (hehl-ih-KAY-nuhs), a lord of Tyre. No flatterer, he proves to be a very good friend to Prince Pericles. After the prince flees, this venerable and honorable man looks after the kingdom. He refuses to accept the crown for himself, even though pressed by various powerful lords to do so.

Simonides (si-MON-eh-deez), the king of Pentapolis. A benevolent ruler, he has no objections when his daughter wants to marry Pericles. In fact, through a genial deception, he helps to bring about her marriage to the personable young man.

Antiochus (an-TI-eh-kuhs), the king of Antioch. Because he mistrusts Pericles, this evil ruler forces the prince to leave his kingdom. Having given the prince a riddle to solve, Antiochus becomes afraid when he realizes that Pericles knows the answer—that the king has committed incest with his own daughter. Struck by fire from heaven, he is killed.

The daughter of King Antiochus, equally guilty with her father. She is killed by the same lightning.

Cleon (KLEE-on), the governor of Tarsus. This melancholy ruler is overjoyed when Prince Pericles brings corn to his starving people. A weak and cowardly man, he makes only mild objections when he learns that his wife has contrived, through jealousy, to have Marina killed.

Cerimon (SEHR-ih-mon), a charitable lord of Ephesus. A student of medicine, he revives Pericles' wife when she is brought to his house.

Dionyza (di-oh-NI-zuh), Cleon's wife. A jealous, petty woman, she attempts to have Marina killed because the young girl seems to be more talented than Dionyza's own daughter.

Dionyza's daughter, a dull girl.

Lysimachus (li-SIHM-uh-kuhs), the governor of Mytilene. Seeing Marina in a brothel, he realizes her true virtue and assures her that she will soon be freed from Pandar. It is he who unknowingly reunites Marina with her father, Pericles.

Lychorida (lih-KO-rih-duh), Marina's nurse.

Thaliard (THAL-yurd), a lord of Antioch. Antiochus sends him to kill Pericles.

Leonine (LEE-eh-nin), a servant to Dionyza.

Gower (GOW-ur), the chorus.

Pandar (PAN-dur), the master of the bawdy house.

Bault (bohlt), his servant.

A bawd, Pandar's wife.

THE PERSIAN BOY

Author: Mary Renault (Mary Challans, 1905-1983)
First published: 1972
Genre: Novel

Locale: Persia, India, Egypt, and Arabia
Time: 330-323 B.C.
Plot: Historical

Bagoas, the title character and narrator of the novel, which is based on the life of Alexander the Great. The son of a minor Persian nobleman who is betrayed to his enemies and brutally killed, he is sold because of his beauty at the age of ten, castrated, then resold to a gem dealer in Susa. Purchased at the age of thirteen by an agent of Darius, he becomes the Persian king's favorite and remains in his service until Darius is deposed and killed. A Persian lord takes Bagoas to Alexander by way of a peace offering, after which Bagoas becomes Alexander's closest personal companion and partner in love. Because he has been made a eunuch, Bagoas never reaches a man's full stature, but he is well matched to Alexander's shorter-than-average height. Although he is much resented by Alexander's squires, he makes himself useful as an interpreter of Persian customs for his Greek master.

Alexander of Macedon, later called **Alexander the Great**, the conqueror of Asia and son of Philip II. Not much more than twenty years old when Bagoas comes into his service, he already has conquered Asia Minor and is deep in Persian territory. Although he is a fearless warrior and a brilliant leader, he has, without knowing it, long needed the love Bagoas gives him. The key to Alexander's character, as interpreted by the author, is the need for love: from cities, from armies, and from captured enemies. This need lays him open to false friends but renders him a sympathetic character. Alexander may need love, but he is quick to anger and never forgives a betrayal. His role model is the romanticized Persian king Cyrus described in Xenophon's *Cyropaedia*. This penchant for Persian ways and the tutelage of his Persian boy Bagoas make Alexander sympathetic to the Persian world that he is conquering.

Hephaestion (heh-FI-stee-ehn), Alexander's Macedonian lover and companion. He is so close to Alexander at the beginning of the novel as to consider himself Alexander's other self. He yields place to Alexander's new favorite, Bagoas; it was customary for a maturing youth such as Alexander to take a younger male lover. Older and taller than Alexander, he remains his closest Macedonian friend. There is a truce between Bagoas and Hephaestion for Alexander's sake. When Hephaestion dies of fever in Ekbatana late in the novel, Alexander becomes wild with grief and gives his friend a spectacular funeral.

Artabazos, a white-haired Persian nobleman in his nineties, Darius' last loyal supporter. He surrenders to Alexander in Hyrcania and is treated as his age, rank, and loyalty merit.

Ptolemy (TAHL-eh-mee), Alexander's bastard half brother, who is some ten years his elder but who has been one of his intimates since childhood. Now one of Alexander's Macedonian generals, he will inherit the Egyptian portion of Alexander's empire and write an account of his conquests.

Krateros, a man who becomes one of Alexander's Macedonian generals and a key member of his inner circle of command. He is given charge of the Macedonian veterans to lead them home at the end of Alexander's campaigns in the East and is appointed regent of Macedonia.

Darius, the Great King of Persia, Bagoas' master until deposed and assassinated near the Caspian Gates. A man jaded with too much pleasure but unwilling to put it by, he is gracious and kindly to Bagoas but emotionally detached, neither offering nor demanding love. A cowardly leader in war, he is overshadowed in every way by his adversary and successor Alexander.

Oxarthes, the brother of the defeated Darius. He is enrolled among the Companions of Alexander. One of the fair-haired Persians, he is taller and more handsome than any of the Macedonians.

Oxhead, or **Bucephalus** (byew-SEH-fuh-luhs), Alexander's beloved black warhorse. He is a year younger than his master and lovingly cared for until his death. Alexander names a city for him (Bucephala) in India, near the place of his death.

Peritas, a tall hunting dog belonging to Alexander. Peritas is his close companion while on campaign. When he dies, Alexander names a city (Perita) in his memory.

Roxane, Alexander's Eastern wife, the daughter of Oxartes, chief of Sogdiana. Only sixteen years old when she catches Alexander's eye, she is married in part for political reasons, but her acerbity of temper suggests to Bagoas the character of Alexander's mother, Olympias. She is not often visited by Alexander, who prefers the company of Bagoas (she tries to poison him). At the time of Alexander's death, she is pregnant with his child.

— Daniel H. Garrison

THE PERSIANS
(Persai)

Author: Aeschylus (525/524-456/455 B.C.E.)
First performed: 472 B.C.E.
Genre: Drama

Locale: Susa, the capital of Persia
Time: 480 B.C.E.
Plot: Tragedy

Xerxes (ZURK-seez), the king of Persia from 486 to 465 B.C.E. The three members of the Persian Royal House who appear in this play are unique in Greek tragedy as being the only figures from actual history, as opposed to legend, to be used on the Greek stage. The Persian king is here depicted shortly after the Battle of Salamis (480 B.C.E.), in which the Persian navy was utterly destroyed by the Athenian fleet. Xerxes comes on the stage after a messenger has related to Atossa, the king's mother, and to the chorus of Persian elders a detailed account of the downfall of the Persian expedition against Athens. The account is a long and tragic recital of the names of great Persian commanders who have fallen in the battle. Xerxes finally enters as a heartbroken and ruined man who has brought about the downfall of his own kingdom. He has previously been described by the ghost of his father, Darius, as the victim of the rashness of youth, whose act of hubris consisted of chaining the Bosphorus with a bridge of boats over which his army might cross. His mother, Atossa, adds that their son had been urged on to his downfall by the counsel of evil men, who had chided him for not surpassing the great deeds of his father. Xerxes is depicted as a man so broken by misfortune that only grief is left to him; he is the ruin of a once great king.

Atossa (a-TOS-uh), the widow of Darius and the mother of Xerxes. In the early part of the play, she is an imposing figure, the widow of one great king and mother of another. While awaiting the news of her son's expedition against Athens, she eagerly asks the chorus for information about the enemy. She even has to inquire where Athens is located, for, in the eyes of so great a person, it must be a far-off, insignificant city that could not possibly withstand the might of Persia. When the news of the defeat is brought to her, she is at first incredulous; then, when the terrible truth becomes undeniable, she is so stricken with grief that she conjures up the ghost of her dead husband to seek his counsel and solace. She is a woman utterly devoted to the glory of Persia and its Royal House. On the advice of her husband, she withdraws to her palace to put on her richest attire to greet her son on his return from his defeat. She will not desert him when he most needs her.

The ghost of Darius (deh-RI-uhs), king of Persia from 521 to 486 B.C.E., the father of Xerxes and husband of Atossa. During his lifetime, he had raised Persia to its height of power; now he is summoned from the grave by his widow to hear an account of the destruction of all that he had accomplished. He is depicted as a wise and prudent ruler who, though a great conqueror, had known what limits he should put on his ambition. He had foreseen that ruin would fall on his son but had prayed that it might be postponed. Xerxes' youthful rashness and pride have brought this ruin upon him early in life. The only counsel that the ghost of the dead king can give is that Persia must never again attack Athens, for the Athenians are invincible; "their very earth fights for them." A Persian army will perish of famine on another expedition. The king knows, however, that his advice will go unheeded. With a prophecy of the second Persian defeat at Plataea (479 B.C.E.), his ghost sinks back into the tomb.

A PERSONAL MATTER
(Kojinteki na taiken)

Author: Kenzaburō Ōe (1935-   )
First published: 1964
Genre: Novel

Locale: An unnamed Japanese city
Time: The 1960's
Plot: Realism

Bird, a twenty-seven-year-old graduate school dropout who is now a cram-school teacher. Small, thin, and round-shouldered, with a pointed nose, thin lips, cold eyes, and a squawky voice, he still uses the nickname given to him in adolescence. Feeling caged, Bird resisted his marriage by indulging in a four-month drunk and dropping out of graduate school. The birth of his first son, with serious abnormalities, confronts him with a moral dilemma. Instead of killing his child, he decides to stop running away from responsibility and takes both his wife and his child home to an uncertain future.

Himiko, a former college girlfriend of Bird. Now widowed and a full-time sexual adventuress, she takes Bird in during his initial shock at the birth of his baby with two heads. She becomes smitten with his fantasy of escape to Africa and encourages him to destroy the unfortunate child. When Bird assumes full responsibility for the child, she departs for Africa.

Bird's wife, who gives birth to a malformed son later named Kikuhiko. Nameless and blameless, she is the target of Bird's intense sense of lacking and dissatisfaction in his life.

Bird's father-in-law, the retired chair of the English department at a small private college. Although he got Bird his teaching job, he also undermines Bird's success by giving him a bottle of liquor the day the baby is born.

Bird's mother-in-law, who attends her daughter at the birth. She wants to conceal the nature of the baby's deformity from Bird's wife.

— *Virginia Crane*

PERSUASION

Author: Jane Austen (1775-1817)
First published: 1818
Genre: Novel

Locale: Somersetshire and Bath, England
Time: Early nineteenth century
Plot: Domestic realism

Anne Elliot, the heroine, second daughter of Sir Walter Elliot, and the victim of persuasion. Although pretty and attractive, she has always been ignored by her family. When quite young, she had been wooed by Frederick Wentworth, then a junior officer in the Royal Navy; but because of her father's disapproval and the advice of her mother's friend,

Lady Russell, she had given him up in spite of her love. At the age of twenty-six, she meets him again; his brother-in-law and sister have leased the Elliot property. Wentworth, now a captain and rich through prize money, seems to have forgotten her, although she still loves him. He is apparently in love with Louisa Musgrove. Having joined her family at Bath, Anne receives the attentions of her cousin, William Elliot, whose charm makes some impression upon her. Through an old school friend, Mrs. Smith, she learns of William's cold, calculating, and selfish character. Although happy to be enlightened, she is still distressed by Wentworth's indifference. To her joy, he finally realizes that he is not in love with Louisa and proposes to Anne. Since William is now wealthy and a captain, Sir Walter can no longer oppose the match, and the story ends happily.

Sir Walter Elliot, of Kellynch Hall, Anne's father. Inordinately vain of his ancestry and his good looks, he is a foolish man who lives beyond his income until he is forced to lease Kellynch and live at Bath. He neglects Anne in favor of his oldest daughter, whom he wishes to marry his heir, William Elliot. He is almost snared by Elizabeth's scheming friend, Mrs. Clay, but is saved by William.

Elizabeth Elliot, the oldest daughter of Sir Walter. She is handsome but cold and selfish. Unable to make a brilliant match, she remains unmarried.

Mary Musgrove, the youngest daughter of Sir Walter and the wife of Charles Musgrove. She is spoiled and selfish.

Charles Musgrove, her husband, a typical sporting country squire.

Captain Frederick Wentworth, the hero of the novel. When a young and penniless officer, he had fallen in love with Anne Elliot and she with him, but she had given him up because of family opposition and the advice of her friend, Lady Russell. When he meets Anne again after eight years, he seems no longer interested in her; rather, he is apparently in love with Louisa Musgrove. But further association with Anne makes him aware of her real worth; he proposes again and is accepted. Since he is now a captain and a rich man, the Elliots can no longer oppose him, and the marriage can take place.

Admiral Croft and

Mrs. Croft, brother-in-law and sister of Wentworth. They lease Kellynch Hall.

William Elliot, the villain of the novel. Although heir to Sir Walter's title and estates, William, as a young man, takes no interest in his cousins. Instead of marrying Elizabeth, as Sir Walter had hoped, he married the wealthy daughter of a grazier. Being left a rich widower, he becomes interested in his family and cultivates their friendship at Bath. Having charming manners, he makes a favorable impression upon Anne until she learns from Mrs. Smith of his scheming character. He also selfishly prevents a marriage between Sir Walter and Mrs. Clay, a match that might ruin his prospects, by inducing Mrs. Clay to become his mistress.

Mr. Musgrove and

Mrs. Musgrove, of Uppercross, Charles's parents.

Louisa Musgrove, their daughter. It seems that she may marry Wentworth, especially after she is injured in an accident that he considers his fault; however, she marries Captain Benwick.

Henrietta Musgrove, her sister, who marries her cousin, Charles Hayter.

Lady Russell, a widow and an old friend of the Elliot family. She persuades Anne not to marry Wentworth because of his uncertain future.

Mr. Shepherd, Sir Walter's agent, who has the task of persuading him to lease Kellynch Hall.

Mrs. Clay, Shepherd's scheming daughter. She insinuates herself into the Elliot family in order to marry Sir Walter but in the end becomes William Elliot's mistress.

Mrs. Charles Smith, a school friend of Anne. Formerly wealthy, she is now a poor and ill widow living at Bath. She reveals to Anne the true character of William Elliot.

Captain Benwick, a melancholy widower who, after being attentive to Anne Elliot, marries Louisa Musgrove.

PEŠČANIK

Author: Danilo Kiš (1935-1989)
First published: 1972
Genre: Novel

Locale: Northern Yugoslavia
Time: During World War II
Plot: Psychological realism

Eduard Sam, a retired railroad official in Voivodina, the northern part of Yugoslavia occupied by the Germans and Hungarians in World War II. He is the only character on whom the author dwells. As a Jew, Sam is subjected to persecution, first obliquely, then openly, until he perishes somewhere in a concentration camp. The story of his tragic fate is told by the narrator, presumably the author himself. Sam is a middle-aged man, of slight build and high-strung disposition, extremely intelligent but often distraught and absentminded. His ties with his family and people around him are rather tenuous, although there is no doubt that he loves his family. Even though he once worked in a practical and exact profession, he is basically impractical and seemingly incapable of taking care of his family, despite his best efforts. The only remnant of his earlier profession is a railroad schedule, revealing a subconscious attempt on his part to bring some order into the chaotic life surrounding him. He hopes to publish this railroad schedule as a book, along with a book of his poetry, which again demonstrates that he is basically a dreamer and an eccentric. Throughout the novel, he seems to fail to grasp the gravity of situations and the ubiquitous danger in which he and many others around him find themselves. His tendency toward philosophizing renders him a grotesque Don Quixote trying desperately to stop the inexorable whirl of the windmill set in motion by the forces of evil. Sam is also a frustrated genius, and his inability to develop his full potential leads to impotence to defend himself, even to a death wish that, unfortunately, turns out to be a self-fulfilling prophecy. He offers a picture of a misplaced wanderer from some mysterious exotic land or planet, whose stay on the earth is tragically and brutally cut short. Sam's personal tragedy transcends the fate of an individual. His words of resignation notwithstanding, the fact that this intelligent, gifted, and harmless man refuses to resort to violence, even if in self-defense, speaks for his innocence and for a deep-rooted residual of goodness in humankind. Sam thus becomes a twofold symbol: of humanity's endless suffering and of its innate goodness, which is indestructible in the long run. By quoting a maxim at the end of the novel that "it is better to be among the persecuted than among persecutors," Sam expresses hope in the final victory over evil.

The narrator, presumably Sam's son. He is reduced to the role of an observer and is not a totally objective one, although at times he is as detached as possible under the circumstances. For the most part, he lets Sam tell his own story, either directly or through the police investigations.

— *Vasa D. Mihailovich*

PETALS OF BLOOD

Author: Ngugi wa Thiong'o (James Ngugi, 1938-   )
First published: 1977
Genre: Novel

Locale: The village of Ilmorog, Kenya
Time: The 1970's
Plot: Political

Godfrey Munira (mew-NEE-rah), the headmaster of a school in the town of Ilmorog, Kenya. An ordinary-looking African in his forties, the deeply religious Munira emerges as something of a saint as the story of his twelve years in Ilmorog unfolds. Even though he came from a wealthy, landowning family, he devotes his life to teaching peasant children. He describes the corruption that has dashed the dreams of those who fought for Kenya's independence. Like many a saint, though, Munira goes too far in his unbridled desire to correct injustice: When he burns a house used as a brothel, three men die, and he is charged with murder. Although Munira represents the conscience of modern Kenya and takes on symbolic overtones in his character, he still emerges as a believable, admirable, and humble man.

Wanja (WAHN-jah), a beautiful young woman with magnificent hair, a full body, and rhythmic movements. She returns from the city, where she had been a prostitute, to her native Ilmorog, where she might recapture her innocence. Soon becoming a part of Munira's circle, she wants to marry Munira, but he rejects her. The break with Munira leads her once more into prostitution, and it is her brothel that Munira burns. While ostensibly joining the nation's corrupters by catering to their sexual needs, in truth she remains faithful to Munira and to the high cause he represents.

Abdulla (ahb-DEW-lah), a shop and bar owner in Ilmorog. He is middle-aged and disabled but possesses a comic sense of life in spite of his poverty and physical condition. Once a freedom fighter in the Mau Mau, he, like Munira, deplores the rampant corruption in the newly independent Kenya, especially as Ilmorog grows and his business stagnates. Abdulla's heroic past contrasts sharply with his dreary present, made even bleaker by his arrest as an accomplice in the arson and murder at Wanja's place of business.

Karega (kah-RAY-gah), a teacher in Munira's school. Karega, a young man who has been expelled from college for leading a strike, became a political activist after an unhappy affair with Munira's sister. Like the others in Munira's group, he condemns the greed and repression practiced by the regime that has made a mockery of independence. Lacking Munira's spiritual dimensions and delusions, Karega is an angry, stubborn, and hard man who eventually becomes a loved and respected leader of the workers. Along with Munira, he is accused of the murders at Wanja's house. Even as he lingers in prison at the novel's end, he envisions the workers rising against the system, which suggests that the author sees Kenya being redeemed by practical men such as Karega, not by visionaries such as Munira.

Joseph, Abdulla's servant. At the outset, he is a skinny, pathetic seven-year-old boy who is grossly mistreated by his master. At the novel's end, he has grown into a young man determined to alter the country's destiny.

Chui (CHEW-ee), Munira's former classmate and a businessman in the new Kenya. A tall, rebellious, athletic youth who loved English literature in his school days, Chui as an adult has betrayed his earlier revolutionary beliefs and become a corrupt, greedy industrialist. He has even developed a huge stomach, one mark of success among such men. Chui is one of the brewery directors killed in the fire set by Munira.

Inspector Godfrey, an investigator of the fire and murders. The elderly Godfrey is a stereotypical civil servant, with an expressionless face. He is said to have served the colonial government as faithfully as he now conducts the new nation's nasty business. Intrigued with the workings of crime, which he considers a kind of jigsaw puzzle, Godfrey unravels Munira's story and the part that Munira, along with Wanja, Abdulla, and Karega, played in the climactic events leading to the fire and murders.

— *Robert L. Ross*

PETER IBBETSON

Author: George du Maurier (1834-1896)
First published: 1891
Genre: Novel

Locale: France and England
Time: Mid-nineteenth century
Plot: Historical

Pierre Pasquier de la Marière (pyehr pahs-KYAY deh mahr-YAY), also **Peter Ibbetson**, a confessed murderer. An English-French child living in France, afterward orphaned by the almost simultaneous deaths of his father and mother, and taken back to England for his schooling, Peter Ibbetson (as his uncle, Colonel Ibbetson, renames him) attains manhood there, joins the army briefly, and is then apprenticed to an architect. Shy, dreamy, speculative, a skeptical and rather unhappy freethinker, he often lives imaginatively in the happy world of his childhood with Mimsy. After a mystic dream, he discovers he may enter his ideal world again and be with Mimsy when he chooses, though retaining his adult identity. Enraged upon learning through Mrs. Gregory (formerly Mrs. Deane) of the colonel's malice, he kills him in a quarrel and is sentenced to a prison asylum for life. Here he again is able, through wishing, to enter his childhood world from time to time until death takes him.

Colonel Roger Ibbetson, his wealthy guardian, cousin of Mrs. Pasquier; a vain gallant and a malicious liar.

Mimsy Seraskier (seh-rahs-KYAY), his dearest friend; later the duchess of Towers. In childhood a plain, sickly, melancholy girl, she becomes a tall, beautiful woman. Visited by the same dream that changed Peter's life, she later reveals the dream when they meet and happily recall their friendship as children.

Mr. Lintot (la[n]-TOH), Peter's employer, a self-made, entertainingly egotistical, clever man; an industrious worker but a lover of drink after working hours; both amusing and sentimental when drunk.

Mrs. Lintot, his wife, older than her husband; stern, unlovely (though he thinks her beautiful), but an excellent wife and mother.

Mrs. Deane, a widow (later **Mrs. Gregory**). Deceived by Colonel Ibbetson, she long afterward reveals the colonel's villainies to Peter.

Madge Plunket, Peter's cousin, who arranges for the publication of his memoirs.

Madame Seraskier, Mimsy's mother, the tall, beautiful Irish wife of a Hungarian patriot and man of science; she dies of cholera.

Dr. Seraskier, Mimsy's father, a tall, thin, grave, benevolent man who after his wife's death takes Mimsy to Russia.

PETER PAN: Or, The Boy Who Wouldn't Grow Up

Author: Sir James M. Barrie (1860-1937)
First published: 1928
Genre: Drama

Locale: London and Never Land
Time: Late nineteenth century
Plot: Fairy tale

Peter Pan, a boy who will not grow up. He runs away on the day of his birth so that he will not have to become a man. He lives in Never Land, home of the fairies, protected by his friends the Indians against his enemy, Captain Hook. He is attracted to the Darling home by the stories the mother tells her children. He persuades the Darling children to visit Never Land and teaches them to fly.

Wendy Darling, an English girl who, with her two brothers, flies off to Never Land for a visit. She mothers Peter Pan and the lost boys, telling them stories at bedtime and tucking them in. After her return home, she goes to Never Land once a year to clean Peter Pan's house. Each year, as she grows up, she and Peter Pan drift farther apart, until at last he cannot understand her at all.

Captain Hook, a pirate captain in Never Land, named for the hook he has in place of an arm. Jealous of Peter Pan and the lost boys, he and his crew plan to kidnap Wendy so that she will be their mother. He succeeds in capturing the girl, but Peter Pan saves her. Frustrated, the captain throws himself overboard and is eaten by a crocodile who, having earlier

tasted the captain's arm, waits patiently for the rest of his victim.

Tinker Bell, a fairy in love with Peter Pan. A jealous creature, she resents Wendy, who is obviously Peter Pan's favorite. Tinker Bell tries to have the lost boys kill Wendy with their bows and arrows by telling them that Wendy is a dangerous bird.

Nana, the Darlings' dog, who acts as nurse for the children.

Mrs. Darling, Wendy's mother, who is terribly saddened by the temporary loss of her children.

Mr. Darling, Wendy's father, who welcomes the lost boys to his home when they return with Wendy and her brothers.

Michael and

John Darling, Wendy's young brothers.

Tiger Lily, an Indian princess in Never Land.

Nibs,

Slightly,

Smee, and

Tootles, other inhabitants of Never Land.

PETER SIMPLE

Author: Frederick Marryat (1792-1848)
First published: 1834
Genre: Novel

Locale: England, France, and various ships at sea
Time: Early nineteenth century
Plot: Adventure

Peter Simple, the younger son of the younger son of a viscount, who chooses the navy as a livelihood. Eventually proving the trickery of his uncle, he inherits the title and estates of his grandfather.

Old Lord Privilege, the grandfather of Peter, who unwittingly allows young Lord Privilege to cheat Peter and Mr. Simple.

Young Lord Privilege, his rascally son and Peter's uncle,

who cheats his nephew out of an inheritance from his grandfather and succeeds in having Peter committed to an insane asylum.

Mr. Simple, Peter's father, who becomes nearly insane when cheated out of his inheritance.

Terence O'Brien, an older midshipman aboard the *Diomede* who befriends Peter. He is captured with Peter during a raid on the French coast. He locates the woman who had helped dispossess Peter.

Colonel O'Brien, a French officer, not related to Terence O'Brien, who captures Terence and Peter.

Celeste O'Brien, his daughter, who frees Peter from the insane asylum and marries him.

Captain Hawkins, the illegitimate son of Lord Privilege, who has Peter court-martialed.

Ellen Simple, Peter's sister, who is rescued from poverty and married by Terence O'Brien.

PETER WHIFFLE: His Life and Works

Author: Carl Van Vechten (1880-1964)
First published: 1922
Genre: Novel

Locale: New York, Paris, and Italy
Time: 1907-1919
Plot: Religious

Peter Whiffle, a young Ohioan born to wealth and disposed to inactivity and indecision. Planning to be a writer, he goes through many stages. Believing, as a sophisticated young man in Paris, that style and form alone are important, he plans to write a book containing nothing but lists of Things. Later, dressed in rags, he haunts the Bowery in New York and plots a revolution against capitalism. Subject matter is now all-important, and Peter plans a bloody and dirty book, the heroine of which is to be clubfooted, harelipped, and hunchbacked. Later, having run away from his wedding, he lies near death in Africa and has a vision in which angels from hell and heaven wait for him to decide where he wants to go. He is relieved to realize that he need not make a decision, and he recovers. He is now convinced that it is necessary to record all aspects of his

characters, but that is also quite a task. At last, after a period in which he experiments with black magic, he returns to Toledo, Ohio. Incurably ill, he says he at last has realized that he was never meant to do anything or to make a decision, but only to appreciate the works of others and to be himself.

Carl Van Vechten, his friend, who follows the course of his career.

Edith Dale, a woman of wealth and a friend of Peter and Carl.

Mahalah Wiggins, a young woman whom Peter meets at Edith's house. After much indecision, Peter becomes engaged to Mahalah, but instead of marrying her he leaves for Africa on the day of the wedding, after deciding that marriage is too great a decision for him to make.

PETERSBURG

Author: Andrey Bely (Boris Nikolayevich Bugaev, 1880-1934)
First published: 1916; serial form, 1913-1914; revised, 1922
Genre: Novel

Locale: St. Petersburg
Time: 1905
Plot: Symbolism

Nikolai Apollonovich Ableukhov (nih-koh-LAY ah-poh-LOH-noh-vihch ah-bleh-UH-khov), a student and dissident. Nikolai's flaxen hair is so white that it looks more appropriate for an infant than for a college student. Indeed, Nikolai is still a child in many ways. He is rebellious against his father but still reliant on him for room and board. He is comically impetuous in his romantic life, but his impetuosity stems more from uncertainty than from passion. In fact, uncertainty, a wavering sense of conviction and right action, is the essential trait of his character. The novel centers on his decision whether to kill his father with the bomb delivered by his revolutionary friends. The complexity and indecisiveness of his character are further symbolized by the oriental clothing he favors in the morning, which he exchanges for more traditional (and Western) garb when he goes out of the house. Nikolai is, indeed, caught between two heritages: the oriental (Tatar and Mongol) and the White Russian (European). He cannot hope to understand his place in the world until he understands himself.

Apollon Ableukhov (ah-poh-LOHN), Nikolai's father, a high-ranking Russian bureaucrat. Apollon is small in physical stature but is impeccably dressed and proper; he is imposing because of his position of authority. He possesses little of the customary arrogance of power. He has a sense of humor, is easily wounded (especially by the memory of his wife, who deserted him), and is a caring father. He is a skilled, efficient bureaucrat, but he fears the proletariat and the faceless hordes

of the East, whom he sees as a threat to Russian civilization—forgetting that the Ableukhovs are direct descendants of these Mongol hordes. His failure to understand his son, whom he nevertheless obviously loves very much, threatens his life.

Alexander Ivanovich (ee-VAH-noh-vihch), a young revolutionary. Shabbily dressed, with a tiny black mustache, Alexander grows increasingly feverish over the course of the novel, a manifestation of his inner turmoil. He delivers the bomb to Nikolai. He seems a much more devoted revolutionary than Nikolai and is apparently firm in his convictions, but his increasingly agitated state, which culminates in psychosis and murder, belies his apparent confidence. He aptly represents the proletariat that Apollon so fears.

Lippanchenko (lih-PAN-chehn-koh), the chief of the revolutionary group. Lippanchenko's lips seem to Alexander Ivanovich to have the yellow oiliness of salmon slices, and his striped suit somehow ominously conjures up Mongol eyes—associations that tell the reader more about Alexander's paranoia than about Lippanchenko. Still, there is something innately disturbing about the head of the revolutionary group, something hypocritical about his oily unctuousness, something mendacious in the way he moves with equal ease among the fanatical extremists and the upper crust of Russian society. indeed, he has no more feeling for the Nikolais and the Alexanders whom he sends out on murderous missions than he does for their targets; in the end, he proves treacherous.

Pavel Yakovlevich (PAH-vehl yah-KOV-leh-vihch), a police detective. Pavel would seem almost a comic man if his single-minded pursuit of his quarry (Nikolai and Alexander) did not finally seem as frightening as Lippanchenko's treachery.

Sergy Likhutin (sehr-GAY lih-KHEW-tihn), an officer and a friend of Nikolai. Sergy is a robust, proper, and likable officer who is driven to the brink of suicide by his wife's flirtation.

Sophia Likhutin, Sergy's wife. Sophia is a beautiful but empty-headed flirt who spreads disaster throughout the novel.

— *Dennis Vannatta*

THE PETRIFIED FOREST

Author: Robert E. Sherwood (1896-1955)
First published: 1935
Genre: Drama

Locale: The eastern Arizona desert
Time: Early 1930's
Plot: Melodrama

Gramp Maple, the owner of the Black Mesa Bar-B-Q in eastern Arizona, near the New Mexico border. He is a dinosaur of a man, a self-styled pioneer who has lived past the age of pioneers. Gramp runs the restaurant with the help of his son, his granddaughter, and Boze Hertzlinger, who works for him. Gramp relates to Duke Mantee, an escapee from prison who lands in the Black Mesa. He looks on Duke as the kind of pioneer he would like to be and probably, despite his boasts, has never been.

Jason Maple, Gramp's son, an American Legionnaire who has spent his entire life in the desert, except for the time he served in the Army during World War I. He married a French woman, and they produced a child, Gabby. Jason's wife moved to the desert with him but, unable to stand the isolation of eastern Arizona, returned quickly to France and remarried. She left their daughter with Jason, who has little sense of purpose in life. He reflects the stereotyped patriotic jingoism typically attributed to Legionnaires.

Gabrielle (Gabby) Maple, Jason's daughter and Gramp's granddaughter, roughly twenty years old. She works in the Black Mesa but spends her life dreaming about France, reading the works of François Villon, affecting the vocabulary of a stevedore, and wishing she were in Paris. Gabby has no real memory of her mother but keeps alive an illusion of what she must have been like.

Boze Hertzlinger, a teenage boy who works at the barbecue and has romantic inclinations toward Gabby, whose fondness for poetry he utterly fails to understand. Although Gabby sometimes leads him on, they have no realistic expectation of a future together.

Alan Squier, an intelligent, sophisticated hitchhiker who appears at the Black Mesa down on his luck and unable to pay for his meal. He and Gabby are on the same intellectual wavelength. They talk about poetry and the things that matter to Gabby, who gives Alan a silver dollar and arranges for him to ride to Phoenix with a banker and his wife who are heading in that direction. Alan, who is convinced that he has no real future, concludes that he can serve humanity best by dying and leaving his five-thousand-dollar insurance policy to Gabby so that she can get away from the Black Mesa. He writes Gabby in as beneficiary of the policy, then makes a compact with Duke Mantee to shoot him.

Mr. Chisholm, an affluent banker from the East who stops at the restaurant on his way west. He, his wife, their chauffeur, and Alan Squier leave to continue to Phoenix, only to have their car stolen by Duke Mantee, who is heading for the Mexican border. They all end up back in the Black Mesa.

Mrs. Chisholm, Chisholm's long-suffering wife, who finds Duke Mantee much more attractive than her stuffy husband. After getting tipsy, she says so in no uncertain terms.

Joseph, the Chisholms' black chauffeur.

Duke Mantee, an interesting, individualistic killer who is being hunted after his escape from prison. He comes close to living up to Gramp's definition of a pioneer, and the two of them get along well despite the tenseness of the situation. Mantee gets along with everyone in the Black Mesa except Boze, whose middle-class notions of right and wrong will not permit him to judge Duke as an individual.

Ruby,

Jackie, and

Pyle, all henchmen of Duke Mantee who are helping him to escape.

Paula, the Mexican cook, one of the few people with whom Gabby can talk about her real feelings.

Two telegraph linemen, who are eating at the barbecue when the action opens. Through their conversation, they allow Gramp to reveal his pioneering spirit.

Herb, a friendly cowboy who comes into the Black Mesa to eat.

An American Legion commander,

a Legionnaire,

the sheriff, and

two deputies, all introduced to show the bloodthirsty mentality of those who are pursuing Duke Mantee.

— *R. Baird Shuman*

PHAEDRA
(Phèdre)

Author: Jean Baptiste Racine (1639-1699)
First performed: 1677
Genre: Drama

Locale: Troezen, in ancient Greece
Time: Antiquity
Plot: Tragedy

Phèdre (FEE-druh), the second wife of Thésée (Theseus) and daughter of Minos and Pasiphae, the king and queen of Crete. Phèdre is descended from a line of women of unnatural passions. When she realizes that she has fallen in love with her stepson Hippolyte, she fights the double contagion of heredity and passion with courage and in silence until, unable to resist her love, she arranges to have Hippolyte banished from Athens. She bears Thésée's children, sets up a temple to Venus, and makes sacrifices to appease the wrath of the goddess. When Thésée leaves her in Troezon with Hippolyte, Phèdre's passion feeds on her until, willing to die, she becomes exhausted and ill from her battle to suppress her illicit love. Word is brought of Thésée's death shortly after her nurse, Oenone, has forced Phèdre to confess her love aloud for the first time. In an unguarded moment, while asking Hippolyte to keep her own son safe now that Hippolyte may be heir to the Athenian throne, Phèdre rather hopefully reveals her passion to him and witnesses his contempt for her. Angry and ashamed, when Phèdre hears to her joy and to her dismay that Thésée has returned alive from his travels, she allows her nurse to accuse Hippolyte of attempted rape, mainly, Phèdre believes, to keep the stigma of her family history and its unnatural passions from falling even more heavily on her own children. Distraught because of her guilt, her love, her fear, and her fury, she confesses to Thésée that she has lied to him when it is too late to save Hippolyte and after she herself has taken poison.

Thésée (tay-ZAY), the son of Aegeus, king of Athens, traditionally faithless to women but faithful to his wives. Thésée so loves his young wife and his own honor that he believes Phèdre on slender evidence instead of trusting what he knows to be the character of his son. Thésée, in a fury, prays to Neptune to grant him the death of Hippolyte. Too autocratic to curb himself when rebuked for his cruel and misinformed curse on his son, he nevertheless begins to suspect that Hippolyte has not lied to him. As the evidence against Phèdre begins to accumulate—she is too distraught to prevent it from doing so—Thésée recovers from his jealous rage too late to save the life of his son.

Hippolyte (ee-poh-LEET), a hunter and a woodsman, the son of Thésée and Antiope, the queen of the Amazons. Like everyone about him, Hippolyte goes to extremes. Unpolished, chaste, and pure, he spurns women until he falls in love with Aricie, for whose sake he is willing to turn over Athens, which he is to inherit from his father, to Aricie, his father's enemy. Because Hippolyte is harsh in his judgment of Phèdre and uncharitable, she reacts violently against the proud boy. Thésée is also harsh in his judgment, no less an extremist than his son. Hippolyte's sense of honor prevents him from telling his father about Phèdre's indiscreet confession of her passion for her stepson, and Thésée's own outraged sense of honor makes him violent in judging Hippolyte.

Aricie (ah-ree-SEE), a princess of an older royal dynasty of Athens, held captive by Thésée. Until Hippolyte confesses his love for her, Aricie is content with her lot. Thésée has forbidden her to marry for fear that she may give birth to sons able to contest Thésée's right to rule Athens. She graciously accepts sovereignty of Athens, if Hippolyte can obtain it for her, and his offer of marriage.

Oenone (uh-NOHN), Phèdre's nurse and friend since childhood. Loyal to her mistress and determined that Phèdre shall not die from stifled passion, she is even willing to further Phèdre's love for Hippolyte. Later, after Hippolyte has spurned Phèdre, Oenone becomes the agent of his destruction.

Théramène (tay-rah-MEHN), the tutor of Hippolyte. Because of his slightly lecherous approach to life and to history, Théramène highlights the purity and aloofness of Hippolyte's views. Hippolyte, who would like to strike the love element from historical narratives, is ironically unaware that love will be the chief element in his own history.

PHILADELPHIA FIRE

Author: John Edgar Wideman (1941-   )
First published: 1990
Genre: Novel

Locale: Primarily Philadelphia, Pennsylvania
Time: The 1960's and 1980's
Plot: Social morality

Cudjoe, an aspiring writer. Having failed his first (white) wife and children and having not yet succeeded as a writer, he leaves Philadelphia to live abroad, primarily on the Greek island of Mykonos, working as a barman and dating attractive female tourists. Upon learning of the May, 1985, police attack on the MOVE headquarters that destroyed fifty-three houses and killed eleven people, he returns home, not so much hoping as needing to find the sole survivor, Simba Mintu. He needs to find the boy in part to understand the irrationality of an attack ordered by the city's black mayor and in part to atone for his own past derelictions.

Simba (Simmie) Mintu, the young boy orphaned by the police attack. His adopted African name means "Lion Man." Simba is pushed to safety by his mother, Clara/Nkisa, who dies in the conflagration. In a play on the Christian hymn "Amazing Grace," Simba first is lost, then is found (saved), but now is lost again—he has disappeared but also is condemned,

socially, politically, and economically. He symbolizes "kid power" in a double sense: literally the power to survive but figuratively the power to avenge past wrongs. Significantly, Cudjoe has no idea what he will say to Simba if he finds him.

Margaret Jones, Cudjoe's sole direct link to the fire and therefore to Simba. She met MOVE's leader, John Africa, one year earlier; three months after that, she moved into the MOVE compound, leaving behind her two children. John Africa, she says, did not brainwash her; he did not need to. He only told her what she knew: that all she had to show for all her hard work were the same sore feet that her mother had after fifty years of cleaning for white people. Although she talks reservedly to Cudjoe, she is skeptical of both his motives and his commitment.

John Africa, formerly **James Brown** and also known as **King**, MOVE's charismatic leader and the dirtiest man Margaret Jones ever saw. He taught the members of his MOVE "family" to love and respect themselves. Repelled at first by his foul smell and appearance, Margaret Jones comes to understand that his purpose is not so much to offend others as to assert himself, to lay claim to his own body in much the same way he laid claim to the abandoned row houses that the police later attack and destroy, killing him in the process.

Sam, a successful writer and editor who is Cudjoe's mentor and surrogate father. He is also Cudjoe's double, trying to live a second and better life on an island with his long-suffering wife, Rachel. In much the same way that Cudjoe stakes everything on finding Simba, Sam stakes everything, emotionally and financially, on his island home. Also like Cudjoe, Sam has failed as a father. Stricken with a fatal heart attack, his last words are "Teach me."

Timbo, a friend of Cudjoe from the 1960's, when both were part of Lyndon Johnson's Great Society "experiment." Among the best and brightest of young African Americans, they idealistically believed that change was possible. Now the cultural attaché to Philadelphia's black mayor, Timbo wonders why he, Cudjoe, and others like them ever believed things would get better. The mayor's plan for turning Philadelphia into a modern Athens would benefit only a fortunate few from the black community. Asked about the fire, Timbo offers a five-minute explanation based on the mayor's pragmatism; King is portrayed as an embarrassment to the city's black mayor and an obstacle to the city's progress. Timbo advised Cudjoe to forget about the fire and write about the 1960's instead.

KKK, not the Ku Klux Klan but the Kid's Krusade, **Kaliban's Kiddie Korps**, a new generation of disaffected black youths who communicate via graffiti and violence. Figuratively and perhaps even literally, they are the inner-city students Cudjoe taught before abandoning them to pursue his own higher education. Grown now, these children of Caliban, the monster in William Shakespeare's *The Tempest*, want their share of "Money Power Things."

John Edgar Wideman, a novelist and, in the second of the book's three parts, the narrator struggling with the telling of Cudjoe's story, that of his own writing of Simba's story. Wideman struggles to understand and support his son, Jacob Wideman, who is in prison for murder and held in solitary confinement. Jacob is caught in a judicial limbo while the courts slowly decide whether he is to be tried as a juvenile or as an adult.

J. B., a strange figure who plays a prominent but decidedly ambiguous part in the novel's final section. He is a derelict compared at one point to Frankenstein's monster.

— *Robert A. Morace*

PHILADELPHIA, HERE I COME!

Author: Brian Friel (1929-   )
First published: 1965
Genre: Drama

Locale: Ballybeg, County Donegal, Ireland
Time: Mid-1960's
Plot: Domestic

Gareth (Gar) O'Donnell (Public), who is in his early twenties and is the son of a small shopkeeper in the Ballybeg, a small village in County Donegal, Ireland. On the eve of his departure for Philadelphia, where he will live with his aunt and uncle, Gar is eager to escape the limitations of life in Ireland: the taciturn father who cannot show affection, the girl who married another man, the friends caught in a state of perpetual adolescence, and the job with little present and no future. America represents the proverbial land of opportunity for Gar, but to pursue that opportunity he will have to leave the father and the country that—however they madden him— he loves deeply. The play catches Gar at the moment of absolute and irreversible transition from one life to another, and he is intelligent enough to sense what that transition will mean.

Gareth (Gar) O'Donnell (Private), the unseen Gar, "the man within, the conscience, the alter ego, the secret thoughts, the id." Only Gar Public can see or hear Gar Private, and Gar Public never looks at him, even when they converse, because "One cannot look at one's alter ego." The two Gars are played by different actors and are always together. Gar Public is polite, quiet, and ordinary (at least while he is with others). Gar Private is sardonic, flip, irreverent, and constantly ready to identify and laugh at the attitudes and foibles of both Irishmen and Americans.

S. B. O'Donnell, Gar's father, a dour shopkeeper, a creature of habit who finds it almost impossible to put his feelings into words and so cannot frame a farewell for the son whom he probably will never see again. His sleeplessness and inability to concentrate on the newspaper are the only signs of the deep emotion that he is feeling. Gar, driven to desperation by his failure to make contact with his father, thinks of him as "Skrewballs" or "Skinflint," but Madge believes that Gar will end up just like his father.

Madge, the unmarried live-in housekeeper for Gar and his father. Kind and more an old friend of the family than a servant, she is the closest thing to a mother that Gar (whose mother died in childbirth) has known. Wise about both father and son, she tries to help bridge the gap between them, but there is little that she can do. Madge combines a sharp tongue with the warmest and most unselfish of natures; she is one of the world's givers.

Kate Doogan, the lively Irish beauty whom Gar loves and who loves him. The rosy future that they plan, with seven boys and seven girls, is destroyed partly by Gar's lack of prospects but also by his timidity. Knowing that he cannot really support a family, he is hesitant to speak to Kate's father, so she marries an older, established man. Her experience thus duplicates that of Gar's mother, who was twenty-five years younger than Gar's father, and epitomizes a typical Irish problem of the time, when economic difficulties led men to postpone marriage until their forties and made May-December unions the norm.

Senator Doogan, Kate's father. Although he is not hostile to Gar, he wants "the best" for his daughter and so encourages her to marry a man with more money.

Master Boyle, Gar's old schoolmaster. Almost a stereotype of the mind gone to waste in a stultifying atmosphere, he is pathetic in his pompous arrogance as he dispenses advice on his way to the pub, where he now spends most of his time.

Lizzy and

Con Sweeney, Gar's aunt and uncle, who have emigrated to Philadelphia and want Gar to come to live with them. Caricatures of Irish Americans, they are extravagant in their praise of all that America has to offer at the same time that they make a pilgrimage to honor the old sod. Crass and materialistic, with a propensity to drink and grow sentimental, they have combined the weaker elements of both cultures and hint at what might lie ahead for Gar.

Ben Burton, the Sweeneys' American friend, who has come to Ballybeg with them. He is the only one in the play who recognizes that a place is just a place: "Ireland—America—what's the difference?"

Ned,

Tom, and

Joe, Gar's friends, who come to bid him farewell only because Madge has invited them to tea. Poorly educated and without prospects in the stagnant economy of Ballybeg, they are what Gar might become if he stayed. Trapped in perpetual adolescence, they spend most of their time telling impossible tales of their skill on the athletic field and their prowess with women.

Canon Mick O'Byrne, the parish priest. He fails in what Gar sees as his chief priestly function—making sense of life. His regular chess games with Gar's father, complete with conversations that do not vary from night to night, are another instance of the stultifying routine that Gar is fleeing.

— *Helen Lojek*

THE PHILADELPHIA STORY

Author: Philip Barry (1896-1949)
First published: 1939
Genre: Drama

Locale: Near Philadelphia, Pennsylvania
Time: The 1930's
Plot: Comedy of manners

Tracy Lord, a strikingly beautiful young woman of twenty-four, nicknamed "Red" by Dexter Haven because of her red hair. She is a graduate of Bryn Mawr College. Divorced from Dexter Haven, who criticized her as a virgin goddess, a married maiden, and the quintessential Type Philadelphiaensis, she could be the finest woman on earth, he claims, if she could overcome an intolerance against human frailty. She insists that she does not want to be worshiped but wants to be loved. Defending herself from Mike Connor's prejudice, she argues that classes do not matter "except for the people in them" and that "there aren't any rules about human beings."

C. K. Dexter Haven, a twenty-eight-year-old formerly married, for ten months, to Tracy in an impulse marriage. He designs and races sailboats and plays polo. He drinks a bit too much and once slugged Tracy, who was a scold rather than a helpmate in their brief marriage. Urbane, witty, and with an honest if sarcastic outspokenness, he argues that occasional misdeeds are often as good for a person as the more persistent virtues. He is still in love with Tracy, thinks she is remarrying beneath her, and maneuvers to get her back. As an in-joke, he is named for the playwright's friend, professor of English Dexter Haven of The Johns Hopkins University.

Macaulay (Mike) Connor, a thirty-year-old writer from South Bend sent by *Destiny* magazine to write up Tracy's high-society wedding as part of a series on the Philadelphia story. A self-styled Jeffersonian Democrat, he dislikes the assignment, has a bias against the wealthy, and thinks the idle rich like Tracy have no right to exist. She in turn considers him an intellectual snob, but she is attracted to his sardonic iconoclasm. Tracy argues that the time to make up your mind about people is "never" and that he should follow the advice in one of his own stories, "With the Rich and Mighty Always a Little Patience." His external toughness masks a poetic sensibility that is evident in his books. Before the play is over, he has come to admire Tracy and Dexter and to see that Tracy's fiancé, who has come up from the proletariat, is really a heel. Tracy cannot understand how, when he can write so well, he

wastes his time doing cheap work for expensive magazines. His books, however, have earned practically no money for him. A drunken evening with him, involving two kisses and a nude swim, humanizes Tracy, severs her engagement to Kittredge, and helps her return to Dexter.

Elizabeth Imbrie, a twenty-eight-year-old photographer from *Destiny* who really wanted to be a painter. Divorced from a hardware salesman in Duluth, she is in love with Mike Connor.

Dinah Lord, Tracy's wisecracking thirteen-year-old sister, who prefers Dexter to George Kittredge. By chance, she witnesses Tracy's drunkenness. The next morning, she tells Tracy, who would rather forget the incident, as she claims to have forgotten a similar one during her marriage to Dexter.

Seth Lord, age fifty, Tracy's father, a banker who is separated from his wife and living in New York, where he has backed three shows for a dancer, Tina Mara. He has a controlling interest in George Kittredge's company. Tracy pretends that he is her Uncle Willie. She is unforgiving of his philandering, though he says that middle-aged philandering has nothing to do with a wife and is rather an expression of reluctance to grow old. He argues that the one thing Tracy lacks is an understanding heart and that she is a prig and a perennial spinster. Becoming reunited with Dexter also reunites her with her father.

Alexander "Sandy" Lord, age twenty-six, the brother of Tracy and Dinah, newly a father. He invited Mike Connor and Elizabeth Imbrie to stay for the wedding, in turn for their keeping Seth Lord's affair out of the news. Sandy works for *The Saturday Evening Post*.

Margaret Lord, the mother of Tracy, Dinah, and Sandy, forty-seven years old but appearing and acting younger. She is estranged from her husband, largely at Tracy's insistence.

George Kittredge, Tracy's handsome, thirty-two-year-old fiancé. He worked his way up from the bottom to become general manager of Quaker State Coal. Tracy thinks that she is in love with him, but she actually is on the rebound from Dexter, who says that "Kittredge is no great tower of strength. . . . He is just a tower." Despite his working-class origins, Kittredge is a snob. Unlike Dexter, he admires Tracy's distant, cool goddess quality. When he sees her in Mike's arms after a nude swim, he instantly concludes the worst.

William Tracy, known as **Uncle Willie**, Margaret Lord's older brother (by fifteen years) and Tracy's uncle. He is a defense lawyer. Tracy pretends that he is her father.

— *Robert E. Morsberger*

PHILASTER: Or, Love Lies A-Bleeding

Authors: Francis Beaumont (c. 1584-1616) and John Fletcher (1579-1625)
First published: 1620
Genre: Drama

Locale: Sicily
Time: The past
Plot: Tragicomedy

Philaster (fi-LAS-tur), the rightful heir to the Sicilian kingdom. Although he is popular with the people who should be his subjects and with several of his noblemen, he lacks the strength of character to attempt to regain his throne. His melancholy, poetic personality is that of a weaker Hamlet; he calls himself "a thing born without passion, a faint shadow that every drunken cloud sails over and makes nothing." He is a typical romantic hero in his longing for refuge in a pastoral world and in his distraught reaction to Arethusa when he thinks she has been unfaithful to him. He shows, in his defiance of the king and Pharamond, occasional flashes of courage that foreshadow the resoluteness with which he finally takes over his kingdom.

The king of Calabria, usurper of the throne of Sicily. He is an autocratic ruler, one quickly angered when his wishes are opposed, but he fears Philaster's popularity too much to give complete vent to his rage against the young prince. He is, like several of the fathers in the Shakespearean romances, redeemed by his recognition of his own wrongdoing and by the virtue and the love of Philaster and his daughter.

Arethusa (AR-eh-thew-zuh), the daughter of the king, betrothed by her father to Pharamond. She possesses the courage and resourcefulness of a Viola and a Rosalind, forthrightly telling Philaster of her love for him and plotting with her ladies to expose Pharamond's wickedness. She is puzzled, but not overcome, by the accusations made against her and her page, Bellario, by the king and his court, and she remains true to Philaster in spite of his cruelty to her. It is she who arranges their marriage and saves him from death at the hand of her father.

Pharamond (FAR-uh-mond), the prince of Spain, Arethusa's suitor. He is an arrogant braggart who well deserves the title, "prince of popinjays," that Philaster bestows upon him. He loses the king's favor by his seduction of Megra, Arethusa's willing lady in waiting, but almost regains it

through Philaster's mistreatment of the princess. He receives well-merited calumny from the townspeople into whose hands he falls during the rebellion, and he is saved only by the intervention of Philaster, who sends him back to Spain.

Euphrasia (ew-FRAY-see-uh), the daughter of one of Philaster's loyal lords. She disguises herself as a page, Bellario, to be near the prince, whom she secretly loves. She serves both Philaster and Arethusa loyally, and she resolves to remain with them, unmarried, after he has won his throne and his bride.

Dion (DI-on), Euphrasia's father, a Sicilian lord. He pays necessary homage to the king, but he remains a firm supporter of Philaster's claims. It is partly his loyalty to the prince that makes him too ready to believe the slanderous reports about Arethusa's love for Bellario, a misconception for which he berates himself and asks forgiveness.

Cleremont (KLEHR-eh-mont) and
Thrasilene (thra-sih-LEE-nuh), two noblemen loyal to Philaster.

Megra (MEHG-ruh), a lady in waiting to Arethusa, attracted to every handsome man she meets. She welcomes Pharamond's advances. She attempts to avenge the court's discovery of her relations with the Spanish prince by malicious slandering of Arethusa and Bellario.

Galathea (gal-uh-THEE-uh), another of Arethusa's ladies. Witty and sharp-tongued in her refusal of Pharamond's offers and in her condemnation of Megra, she helps her mistress to unveil the prince's infidelity.

Country Fellow, an honest rustic. On the way to watch the king's hunt, he finds Philaster in the act of wounding Arethusa and springs to the lady's defense. He asks to see the king as his reward, but he vows to avoid "gay sights" in the future.

A Captain, the leader of the uprising against the king. He and his followers torment Pharamond with bloodthirsty threats and insults.

PHILOCTETES
(Philoktētēs)

Author: Sophocles (c. 496-406 B.C.E.)
First performed: 409 B.C.E.
Genre: Drama

Locale: The island of Lemnos
Time: Antiquity
Plot: Tragedy

Philoctetes (fihl-ok-TEE-teez), a Greek warrior who had received as a legacy from Herakles his magical bow and arrows. As the Greek expedition sailed toward Troy, it had paused at Chrysa, where Philoctetes, approaching a shrine,

had been bitten on the foot by a serpent. The wound refused to heal. Because Philoctetes' screams of pain and the odor emanating from the wound caused acute discomfort to his shipmates, he was, at the instigation of Odysseus and the Atreidae, marooned on the barren island of Lemnos. Ten years later, the Greeks captured Helenus, a Trojan prophet, who revealed that the city would never fall without the willing aid of Philoctetes. Odysseus and Neoptolemus were sent to persuade Philoctetes to rejoin the cause of those who had abandoned him. At the beginning of the play, Philoctetes, who has endured ten years of loneliness, starvation, and hideous pain, is kept alive only by his superhuman stamina and his fierce hatred of the Greeks who wronged him. He is deceived by Neoptolemus, who, having promised to take him home, is entrusted with the great bow. When the real purpose of Neoptolemus' visit becomes clear, Philoctetes adamantly refuses to go to Troy, even though to remain on Lemnos would mean certain death for him without the weapon he uses to kill sea birds for food. There is no question but that he is morally right to resist not only Odysseus' threats but also Neoptolemus' persuasions; however, the kind of heroism to which Philoctetes dedicates himself, although grand and noble, is essentially sterile and selfish. Having triumphed over both the callous enmity of Odysseus and the spontaneous friendliness of Neoptolemus, itself a soft and subtle infringement on his will, Philoctetes can at last freely offer himself to the world again, an action symbolized by the epiphany of Herakles. With Odysseus and Neoptolemus, he sets out for Troy, where he will win glory and where his wound will be cured.

Neoptolemus (nee-op-TOL-eh-muhs), the young son of Achilles, noble and courageous but as yet untried in battle. Convinced by Odysseus that it is his duty to deceive Philoc-

tetes, he tells the outcast that he has deserted the Greek army because his father's armor had been denied him. He promises to take Philoctetes back to Greece with him and watches as Philoctetes struggles against an excruciating wave of pain brought on by his disease. When Neoptolemus at last acquires possession of the great bow, Philoctetes is made helpless. Later, in spite of Odysseus' strong protests, his sense of decency and honor and the instinctive sympathy he has felt for the sufferer cause him to return the weapon. He finally agrees truly to take Philoctetes home but is relieved of this obligation when the bowman resolves to go to Troy.

Odysseus (oh-DIHS-ee-uhs), the crafty and unscrupulous Greek leader who puts expediency over honor. His purpose is to get Philoctetes to accompany him to Troy; his means are deceit and violence. He temporarily convinces Neoptolemus that a reputation for wisdom and goodness can be won by a man willing to sacrifice personal honor for the benefit of his cause. After his experience with Philoctetes, the young man holds both Odysseus and his advice in contempt. Odysseus is not totally without dignity, and he reveals a sense of responsibility to the Greek army and its generals.

A sailor, disguised as a trader, sent by Odysseus, who cannot allow himself to be seen, to spy on Neoptolemus and Philoctetes.

Herakles (HEHR-uh-kleez), the legendary Greek hero, now deified, whose spirit informs Philoctetes that destiny requires him to leave Lemnos and go to Troy.

PHILOSOPHER OR DOG?
(Quincas Borba)

Author: Joaquim Maria Machado de Assis (1839-1908)
First published: 1891
Genre: Novel

Locale: Rio de Janeiro and Barbacena, Brazil
Time: Late nineteenth century
Plot: Psychological

Pedro Rubião de Alvarenga, a simple schoolteacher known simply as Rubião. He befriends the eccentric and dying Quincas Borba, from whom he unexpectedly inherits a substantial fortune and the obligation to care for the deceased's dog, also named Quincas Borba. While traveling to Rio de Janeiro, he meets Christiano and Sophia Palha, who introduce him into Rio's high society. He suffers from his unrequited love for Sophia. A generous man, he lends money freely, gives lavish gifts, and frequently entertains his many new friends, gradually dissipating his fortune. His rise in social status thus leads to his downfall. His descent into madness parallels his descent into poverty. He comes to believe that he is Napoleon, emperor of France.

Christiano Palha, a friend of Rubião. Christiano lives beyond his means, borrowing money from Rubião many times. He goes into partnership with Rubião and tries to restrain Rubião's impractical generosity. Christiano is particularly proud of his wife Sophia, whose beauty he displays—and uses—at every opportunity. The capital provided by Rubião gives him social mobility. As he rises up the social ladder, he leaves many old friends behind, but he does honor, to some extent, his promise to his wife to see to the care of Rubião.

Sophia Palha, the beautiful and gracious wife of Christiano Palha. Very attentive to Rubião, she manages to avoid any

indiscretion. She smooths over her husband's less graceful behavior and knows how to cultivate those of use to her while ignoring old friends no longer of import. She toys with the idea of adultery, perhaps with Carlos Maria or Rubião, but she is a chaste and faithful wife.

Carlos Maria, a pretentious young man beginning to enjoy the fruits of his mother's fortune. Narcissistic and egotistical, he finds the perfect mate in Maria Benedicta, who adores and literally worships him.

Doña Tonica, the unmarried daughter of Major Siqueira, a friend of the Palhas until they rise in social status. She is finally engaged to be married, at the age of forty, but her fiancé dies just three days before the wedding.

Doctor João de Souza Camacho, a lawyer and politician who draws Rubião into politics, using the latter's money to fund the newspaper in which he publishes his own opinions. Camacho promises Rubião a position in the ministry, thus feeding his delusions of grandeur.

Maria Benedicta, Sophia's cousin from the country. Sophia gently acclimates her to city life. Maria falls in love with Carlos Maria and eventually marries him.

Quincas Borba, a man who considers himself to be a philosopher of the school of thought he calls Humanitism, which states that above all, people must eat. Rubião takes care of him in Barbacena, but Quincas leaves for the capital, where he dies soon after writing a letter to Rubião in which he claims to be St. Augustine. His dog, also named Quincas Borba, is his constant companion. As Rubião descends into madness, he suspects that Quincas Borba, the dog, is host for the spirit of Quincas Borba, the man.

PHINEAS FINN: The Irish Member

Author: Anthony Trollope (1815-1882)
First published: 1869; serial form, 1867-1869
Genre: Novel

Locale: The British Isles
Time: Mid-nineteenth century
Plot: Political realism

Phineas Finn (FIHN-ee-uhs), a personable young Irishman with political aspirations. Elected to Parliament, he goes to London, where he makes a number of influential friends and becomes enamored, in turn, of Lady Laura Standish, Violet Effingham, and Madame Marie Max Goesler. Material and political advancement point to a promising career until passage of the Irish Reform Bill abolishes his borough. His parliamentary career over, he returns to Ireland and marries his Irish sweetheart, Mary Flood Jones.

Mary Flood Jones, a pretty Irish girl in love with Phineas Finn, whom she marries when he returns to Ireland at the end of his parliamentary career.

Lady Laura Standish, Lord Brentford's daughter, who is in love with Phineas Finn. She marries Mr. Kennedy after she exhausts her fortune on her profligate brother, Lord Chiltern.

Lord Brentford, a prominent Whig.

Mr. Kennedy, a wealthy member of Parliament who marries Lady Laura Standish.

Lord Chiltern, the profligate son of Lord Brentford and a friend of Phineas Finn. He is in love with Violet Effingham, whose hand he wins as Phineas' rival.

Violet Effingham, courted by Phineas Finn but in love with Lord Chiltern, whom she finally accepts.

Madame Marie Max Goesler, a wealthy young widow who offers her hand and fortune to Phineas Finn, who is already engaged to Mary Flood Jones.

The Duke of Omnium, the elderly suitor of Madame Goesler.

PHINEAS REDUX

Author: Anthony Trollope (1815-1882)
First published: 1874; serial form, 1873-1874
Genre: Novel

Locale: England
Time: Mid-nineteenth century
Plot: Political

Phineas Finn (FIHN-ee-uhs), a young man retired from politics. After the death of his wife, he is invited back to resume his political career. Threatened by false charges of adultery and murder, he is cleared of the charges through the efforts of his loyal friends, is overwhelmingly elected, and becomes the hero of the hour. Deeply in love with Madame Marie Goesler, he marries her and, with her fortune, is able to act independently of his party when the occasion demands.

Madame Marie Max Goesler, a wealthy young widow long in love with Phineas Finn. Through her efforts, he is cleared of the charge of murder, and later he marries her.

Lady Laura Kennedy, Mr. Kennedy's estranged wife, long in love with Phineas Finn.

Mr. Kennedy, Lady Laura Kennedy's deranged husband, who falsely accuses Phineas Finn of adultery with her.

Lord Chiltern and
Violet Chiltern,

Adelaid Palliser (AD-ehl-ayd), the niece of the duke of Omnium, and

Mr. Maule, lovers whose lack of fortune prevents their union. The marriage is finally made possible by Madame Goesler's gift of the fortune left her by the duke of Omnium.

The Duke of Omnium, a friend of Madame Goesler, to whom he leaves a handsome fortune.

Lady Glencora, later **The Duchess of Omnium**, the duke of Omnium's niece and a loyal friend of Phineas Finn.

Quintus Slide, a scandal-mongering journalist who makes public the false accusation of adultery against Phineas Finn.

Mr. Bonteen, a conniving politician of whose murder Phineas Finn is falsely accused.

Spooner, an uncouth fox hunter and a rejected suitor of Adelaid Palliser.

Mealyus (**Emilius**), the real murderer of Mr. Bonteen.

THE PHOENICIAN WOMEN
(Phoninissai)

Author: Euripides (c. 485-406 B.C.E.)
First performed: 409 B.C.E.
Genre: Drama

Locale: Thebes
Time: Antiquity
Plot: Tragedy

A Chorus of young women, maidens from Phoenicia dedicated to the service of Apollo. They have stopped in Thebes and have been detained by the war of the Seven against Thebes. They provide the historical perspective necessary to see the duel between the two sons of Oedipus as the last link in a long chain of Theban misfortunes.

Eteocles (ee-TEE-oh-kleez), the king of Thebes, the son of Jocasta and Oedipus. He and his brother Polynices had agreed to rule the city of Thebes in turn, but Eteocles has refused to give up the throne and Polynices has appeared with an Argive army to claim his right. Jocasta tries to reconcile the two brothers, but without success. Eteocles believes that might is right and will fight rather than give up his power. He is, as he admits, the typical dictator; at the same time he is young, rash, and ignorant in warfare. Creon, Jocasta's brother, helps him plan the defense of the city. In that defense he fights bravely, challenging his brother to single combat. The brothers kill each other. Eteocles' only affection, his love for his mother, is expressed in his dying moments.

Polynices (pol-ih-NI-seez), the exiled brother of Eteocles who, when Eteocles refuses to allow him his period of rule, marches against Thebes. He has justice on his side, as the Thebans and even Eteocles recognize, but he has allowed his wrongs to lead him to the unpardonable sin of attack on his homeland. Speaking to Jocasta before her attempted reconciliation between the brothers, he reveals that he still loves his country; his mother, sister, and father; and even his brother. He accepts Eteocles' challenge to single combat and is killed. Creon, following Eteocles' order, refuses burial for his body.

Jocasta (joh-KAS-tuh), the wife and mother of Oedipus. She tries unsuccessfully to reconcile her two sons by Oedipus. When she hears of their individual challenge, she calls her daughter Antigone from the house and the two leave, determined to make one last effort to prevent the conflict between brothers. She arrives in time to hear their final words; then, lamenting, she stabs herself and dies with them. Her actions and speeches are marked by restraint, except for her joy at the return of Polynices.

Antigone (an-TIHG-uh-nee), the daughter of Oedipus. She appears, accompanied by an old pedagogue, as a girl eager to observe the Argive forces assembled outside Thebes. Later, she views with Jocasta the combat between her brothers. She returns after her mother's death, rejects the proposed marriage with Creon's son, and willingly accompanies Oedipus into exile. She also swears to perform burial rites for Polynices.

Oedipus (EHD-ih-puhs), the son and later the husband of Jocasta. Although he appears only in the final scene, his presence dominates the play. Because they deposed and shut him up, he has pronounced on his sons a curse that is carried out in the action of the play. Antigone calls him forth and informs him of the death of his sons and of Jocasta. Creon, now the ruler of Thebes, orders him into exile because Tiresias has said that Thebes will not know prosperity as long as Oedipus remains within its walls. Oedipus' final speech is a lament of his fate.

Creon (KREE-on), the brother of Jocasta. He aids Eteocles in setting up the defense of Thebes and is told that he is to rule if Eteocles should be killed. When Tiresias informs him that Menoeceus, his son, must be sacrificed to ensure victory for Thebes, he tries to save his heir. At the end of the play, he appears to order Oedipus into exile and to carry out Eteocles' command that Polynices be denied funeral rites.

Menoeceus (meh-NEE-sews), the son of Creon. He hears Tiresias' prophecy that he must die to save Thebes, pretends to agree with his father's plan for his escape, and then states his intention to sacrifice himself for the city. He is the type of pure youth.

Tiresias (ti-REE-see-uhs), the Theban prophet who foresees the deaths of Polynices and Eteocles and the sacrifice of Menoeceus. He is the conventional prophetic figure but is realistically drawn.

PHORMIO

Author: Terence (Publius Terentius Afer, c. 190-159 B.C.E.)
First performed: 161 B.C.E.
Genre: Drama

Locale: Athens
Time: The second century B.C.E.
Plot: Comedy

Phormio (FOHR-mee-oh), a crafty and cynical young Athenian lawyer, a self-styled parasite who resolves to straighten out the romantic difficulties of two young cousins, Antipho and Phaedria, whose fathers are abroad. With Phormio's connivance, Antipho marries Phanium, a penniless young woman of good family. When the fathers, Demipho and Chremes, return, they bribe Phormio to marry Phanium and thus free Antipho from his imprudent union. Phormio betrays the uncles and gives part of the money to Phaedria to buy Pamphilia, a slave with whom he has fallen in love. The uncles discover that Antipho's wife is actually Chremes' daughter by a secret marriage to a woman of Lemnos. They now approve the match and demand their money back from Phormio. When they insist, Phormio tells Chremes' wife Nausistrata of the earlier marriage. She upbraids Chremes, tells Phormio to keep the money, and invites him to supper. Antipho and Phaedria are left happy with the women they love.

Geta (GEE-tuh), Demipho's shrewd servant, Phormio's accomplice in helping the young men and defrauding their fathers.

Demipho (DEH-mif-foh), Antipho's father and Chremes' brother. Pompous, class-conscious, and somewhat miserly, old Demipho wishes to revoke his son's marriage because it offers no dowry.

Chremes (KRAY-meez), Phaedria's father. Fifteen years earlier, Chremes had, while drunk and under the name of Stilpho, married a woman in Lemnos and had a daughter by her. Returning to Lemnos in search of his daughter, he learns that she has gone to Athens looking for him. He fears his Athenian wife will discover the earlier marriage.

Antipho (AN-ti-foh), Demipho's son. When his father returns, Antipho is afraid to face him until Phanium's true identity has been revealed.

Phaedria (FEE-dree-uh), Chremes' son, in love with Pamphilia, a young slave. He gets the money to purchase her from Phormio. Antipho and Phaedria are deeply devoted friends.

Nausistrata (noh-SIHS-trah-tuh), Chremes' good-hearted but nagging wife. Happy to have something to hold over her husband, she forgives Chremes for his indiscreet marriage.

Sophrona (so-FROH-nuh), Phanium's nurse. She reveals to Chremes that his Lemnian wife has died of grief and that Antipho's wife is really his daughter.

Dorio (DOH-ree-oh), a bawd who owns the young musician whom Phaedria loves. He threatens to sell her to a soldier unless Phaedria can buy her at once.

Pamphilia (pam-FIH-lee-uh), the slave girl Phaedria loves and purchases.

Phanium (FA-nee-uhm), Chremes' daughter and Antipho's wife.

Higio (HIH-gee-oh),

Cratinus (kra-TI-nuhs), and

Crito (KRI-toh), Demipho's advocates.

Davus (DAH-vuhs), a friend of Geta.

Mida (MI-duh), Phanium's servant, a young boy.

A PHOTOGRAPH: Lovers in Motion

Author: Ntozake Shange (Paulette Williams, 1948-   )
First published: 1981
Genre: Drama

Locale: San Francisco, California
Time: Late twentieth century
Plot: Poetic

Sean David, a struggling artist in San Francisco who dreams of becoming a famous photographer. He is arrogant, chauvinistic, and abusive. Before Sean's transformation, he manipulates three lovers. He tells one of his lovers that he has known only welfare, mean white folks, heroine, and whores. Although he does not deliberately set these women against one another, he does nothing to conceal his affairs. In fact, he boasts that there will always be several lovers in his life and that his sexual partners must accept his outlook on life. Sean blames his coarseness and pessimism on his father, who loved a monkey more than he cared for his son and who modeled behavior for Sean by sexually, verbally, and physically abusing women. Consequently, Sean abuses his three lovers in much the same way, by requiring sex on demand, abusing them physically, and throwing them out of his apartment when he becomes bored or wants to work. Later in the play, Sean discovers himself with the help of one of his lovers. He learns to love himself and to love someone else unselfishly. Sean metamorphoses into a determined man who truly wants to capture the unnoticed or unheralded lives of ordinary black people and who wants to share his life with the woman he loves.

Michael, one of Sean's lovers, a professional dancer who teaches him how to love. She is very nurturing and patient with Sean, even when he shouts obscenities at her and wrestles her to the floor because she tells him that she is leaving. At one point, she tells Sean that she is not jealous and will never become possessive. She tells him that all she asks of him is that he not ask her to sleep with him in the same bed where he has had other women. Michael eventually becomes the catalyst for Sean's maturation. She decides that she can no longer tolerate his womanizing or his financial dependence on women. Michael reaches back to her past to instill pride in Sean and to help him see that he is degrading himself. She uses her grand-mother as an example of a strong-willed person who protected her family from a lynch mob and who taught them about black heroes such as W. E. B. Du Bois, Marcus Garvey, Jack Johnson, and the colored horse soldiers. She tries to pass on to Sean the strength of her grandmother and the many other black people who gave their lives so that the present generation could thrive. Michael manages to instill in Sean a sense of pride in his race, himself, and his art, thereby helping him to become whole.

Claire, one of Sean's lovers, a model who seeks primarily to be an object of desire. Claire is described as a nymphoma-niac who abuses liquor and cocaine. She allows Sean to take nude pictures of her. Claire believes that Sean is a trifling person whose life has no value. She sees him solely as a means of satisfying her lust. Only for an instant is she portrayed as a hurting human being who wants to be loved and respected. She gratifies Sean's desires and rejects Earl's advances.

Nevada, one of Sean's lovers, an attorney. Nevada takes great pride in the fact that she is from an established and wealthy Carolina family. Her aim is to remake Sean in her own image, to give him class, culture, and connections. She bribes him with money, camera equipment, and the promise of art gallery exhibitions. Nevada asserts that Sean is nothing without her.

Earl, Sean's friend, an attorney. A diplomatic and refined man who was able to lift himself out of poverty, Earl unsuc-cessfully attempts to counsel Sean about womanizing. Earl's advice, however, is prompted by his spiritual and sexual yearn-ings for his boyhood friend, Sean. Like Sean's three lovers, Earl wants to take care of Sean. When Earl offers to rent a condominium in Berkeley Hills for the two of them, Sean tells him that he would be better off with Nevada. When provoked, both Sean and Claire remind Earl of his homosexuality.

— *Elizabeth Brown-Guillory*

THE PHYSICISTS
(Die Physiker)

Author: Friedrich Dürrenmatt (1921-1990)
First published: 1962
Genre: Drama

Locale: Switzerland
Time: The second half of the twentieth century
Plot: Play of ideas

Fraülein Doktor Mathilde von Zahnd (mah-TIHL-deh fon tsahnt), the founder and psychiatrist of a Swiss sanato-rium. Dr. von Zahnd, about fifty-five years old, is the last member of a prestigious family that boasted powerful figures in finance, politics, and the military. Her own love of power, masked initially by the appearance of compassion and philanthropy, emerges as the dominant force in the play. Dr. von Zahnd is "an old hunchbacked spinster" who masterminds the entrapment of a genius physicist and the exploitation of his knowledge. She heads a huge cartel that aspires to world, even universal, domination.

Johann Wilhelm Möbius (YOH-hahn VIHL-helm MEH-bee-uhs), a physicist, solver of "the problem of gravitation," discoverer of the "Unitary Theory of Elementary Particles" and the "Principle of Universal Discovery," and a patient at the sanatorium. Möbius, forty years old, has feigned madness, claiming to have visions of King Solomon, so that he would be committed to the sanatorium, where he presumes that his revolutionary findings are safe from discovery and potentially devastating misuse. When a nurse, in love with him and believing him sane, makes plans for his release, Möbius strangles her, and when two foreign agents attempt to lure him out of the sanatorium, he convinces them that it is their duty to humanity to remain with him. Möbius' passion for knowledge leads him to write up his theories in the supposed privacy of his room, where the manuscripts are discovered by Dr. von Zahnd. Möbius realizes that his sacrifices of family, career, and freedom have been for naught. A prisoner forever in the sanatorium, he assumes the identity of King Solomon.

Herbert Georg Beutler (BOYT-lehr), alias **Isaac Newton**, a physicist and patient who feigns madness, claiming to be Sir Isaac Newton. As an agent of a Western democracy, presumably the United States, he attempts to persuade Möbius to join the research team of his nation, promising "freedom of scientific knowledge." To preserve the secret of his identity and his

mission, Beutler strangles a nurse. He, too, is thwarted by Dr. von Zahnd.

Ernest Heinrich Ernesti, alias **Albert Einstein**, a physicist and patient who feigns madness, claiming to be Albert Einstein. As an agent, presumably of the Soviet Union, he urges Möbius to join the research team of his nation, calling on physicists to "become power politicians." Ernesti also strangles a nurse to protect his mission; when that fails, both he and Beutler must remain with Möbius, trapped for life in the sanatorium.

Richard Voss, a police inspector who investigates each murder at the sanatorium. After the third killing, Voss accepts Dr. von Zahnd's contention that the mad physicists are not responsible for their actions. In withdrawing from the case, he unwittingly abandons them to their fate at the hands of Dr. von Zahnd and the newly installed male attendants.

Frau Lina Rose, Möbius' former wife, who for years had supported his stay in the sanatorium. She has remarried and, after paying Möbius a final visit with her three sons, will never see him again.

Oskar Rose, a missionary. He has married Möbius' wife and is taking her, her sons, and his own six children to a mission outpost on the Mariana Islands.

Monika Stettler, a nurse who loves Möbius and believes in his sanity. When she takes steps to have him released from the sanatorium, Möbius strangles her.

Sister Marta Boll, the head nurse. She jealously defends the physicists, "my most interesting cases," from possible prosecution by Inspector Voss. When the male attendants take over, Sister Boll is dismissed.

— *Allen E. Hye*

THE PIANO LESSON

Author: August Wilson (1945-   )
First published: 1990
Genre: Drama

Locale: Pittsburgh, Pennsylvania
Time: 1937
Plot: Representational

Boy Willie Charles, who is thirty years old, with an infectious grin and a boyish charm. He is brash, impulsive, and talkative. He is proud, and he believes that he and whites occupy the world equally. Boy Willie is an independent thinker and possesses a strong sense of what he believes. His immediate goal in the play is to get a piece of land, because, as he says, when you "got a piece of land you'll find everything else fall right into place." For him, land is the key to equality, dignity, and freedom.

Berniece, Boy Willie's sister. Thirty-five years old and a widow, she still blames her brother for the death of her husband three years earlier. She now lives with her uncle, Doaker, and has come to Pittsburgh to work. She is strong, determined, serious-minded, intense, religious, and superstitious.

Doaker Charles, the uncle of Berniece and Boy Willie. Forty-seven years old, tall, and thin, he has been a railroad cook for twenty-seven years. He has retired from the world, has no fight left in him, and tries to serve as a peacemaker in

the quarrel between Berniece and Boy Willie.

Lymon, Boy Willie's companion. Twenty-nine years old, he talks little, but when he does it is with a straightforwardness that is often disarming. In his old truck loaded with watermelons, he has come with Boy Willie to Pittsburgh with the intention of selling the watermelons and remaining to find work, have fun, and find a woman.

Avery, a thirty-eight-year-old man, honest and ambitious. He wears a suit and tie with a gold cross around his neck and carries a small Bible. He wants two things: to start his own church and to marry Berniece.

Winning Boy Charles, Doaker's brother. Fifty-six years old, he tries to present the image of a successful musician and gambler, but everything about him is old.

Maretha, Berniece's eleven-year-old daughter.

Grace, a woman who goes home with Boy Willie and later with Lymon.

— *Tony J. Stafford*

PICKWICK PAPERS

Author: Charles Dickens (1812-1870)
First published: 1837; serial form, 1836-1837
Genre: Novel

Locale: England
Time: 1827-1828
Plot: Social realism

Mr. Samuel Pickwick, the stout, amiable founder and perpetual president of the Pickwick Club. An observer of human nature, a lover of good food and drink, and a boon companion, he spends his time traveling about the countryside with his friends, accepting invitations from local squires and dignitaries, pursuing Mr. Alfred Jingle in an effort to thwart that rascal's schemes, and promoting his friends' romances. The height of his development occurs at the Fleet Prison where, because of a breach-of-promise suit, he observes human suffering and learns to forgive his enemies. A rather pompously bustling and fatuous person at first, he grows in the course of events to be a truly monumental character.

Mr. Nathaniel Winkle, the sportsman of the group. Inept and humane, he finds himself involved in hunting misadventures, romances, and duels. In the end, he wins Arabella Allen, his true love, over the objections of her brother, her suitor, and his own father.

Mr. Augustus Snodgrass, the poetic member of the Pickwick Club. Although he keeps extensive notes, he never writes verses. Eventually he gains his sweetheart, Emily Wardle, after several visits to Manor Farm.

Mr. Tracy Tupman, a rotund member of the Pickwick Club, so susceptible that he is constantly falling in and out of love. Longing for romance, he finds himself thwarted at every turn. His flirtation with Miss Rachel Wardle ends dismally when she elopes with Mr. Alfred Jingle.

Mr. Wardle, the owner of Manor Farm, Dingley Dell, the robust, genial, but sometimes hot-tempered host of the four Pickwickians. A patriarch, he rescues his sister from Mr. Jingle at the cost of one hundred and twenty pounds, and he objects at first to his daughter's romance with Mr. Snodgrass. Finally, he gives the young couple his blessing.

Miss Rachel Wardle, a woman of uncertain age. She flirts coyly with the susceptible Mr. Tupman but abandons him for the blandishments of Mr. Jingle, who has designs on her supposed wealth. Mr. Pickwick and Mr. Wardle pursue the elopers, Mr. Wardle buys off the rascal, and Miss Wardle returns husbandless to Manor Farm.

Mrs. Wardle, the aged, deaf mother of Mr. Wardle and Miss Rachel.

Emily Wardle, Mr. Wardle's vivacious daughter, in love with Mr. Snodgrass, whom she eventually marries.

Isabella Wardle, another daughter. She marries Mr. Trundle.

Mr. Trundle, Isabella Wardle's suitor. Though frequently on the scene, he remains a minor figure in the novel.

Joe, Mr. Wardle's fat, sleepy young servant. He is characterized by his ability to go to sleep at any time and under almost any circumstances, a trait that both amuses and irritates his master.

Mrs. Martha Bardell, Mr. Pickwick's landlady. When he consults her as to the advisability of taking a servant, she mistakes his remarks for a proposal of marriage and accepts him, much to Mr. Pickwick's dismay. The misunderstanding leads to the breach-of-promise suit. Mr. Pickwick, refusing to pay damages, is sent to the Fleet Prison. After his refusal to pay, Mrs. Bardell's attorneys, unable to collect their fee, have her arrested and also sent to the Fleet Prison. Her plight finally arouses Mr. Pickwick's pity, and he pays the damages in order to release her and to free himself to aid his friend Mr. Winkle, who has eloped with Arabella Allen.

Tommy Bardell, Mrs. Bardell's young son.

Serjeant Buzfuz, Mrs. Bardell's counsel at the trial, a bombastic man noted for his bullying tactics with witnesses.

Mr. Skimpin, the assistant counsel to Serjeant Buzfuz.

Mr. Dodson and

Mr. Fogg, Mrs. Bardell's unscrupulous attorneys. Having taken the suit without fee, they have their client arrested and sent to prison when Mr. Pickwick refuses to pay damages after the suit has been decided against him.

Mr. Alfred Jingle, an amiable, impudent strolling player remarkable for his constant flow of disjointed sentences. He makes several attempts to marry women for their money, but Mr. Pickwick thwarts his plans in every case. He ends up in the Fleet Prison, from which he is rescued by Mr. Pickwick's generosity. He keeps his promise to reform.

Job Trotter, Mr. Jingle's cunning accomplice and servant. He is the only person whose wits prove sharper than those of Sam Weller.

Jem Huntley, a melancholy actor called **Dismal Jemmy**, Mr. Jingle's friend and Job Trotter's brother.

Sam Weller, Mr. Pickwick's jaunty, quick-witted, devoted Cockney servant. He and Mr. Pickwick meet at the inn to which Mr. Wardle has traced his sister and Mr. Jingle. Sam's aphorisms, anecdotes, and exploits make him one of Dickens' great comic creations, the embodiment of Cockney life and character.

Tony Weller, Sam Weller's hardy, affable father, a coachman who loves food, drink, and tobacco and wants nothing from his shrewish wife except the opportunity to enjoy them.

Mrs. Susan Weller, formerly Mrs. Clarke, a shrew, a hypocrite, and a religious fanatic. At her death, her husband inherits a small estate she has hoarded.

The Reverend Mr. Stiggins, called the **Shepherd**, a canting, hypocritical, alcoholic clergyman, greatly admired by Mrs. Weller, who gives him every opportunity to sponge off her husband.

Arabella Allen, a lovely young woman whom Mr. Winkle first meets at Manor Farm. Her brother, Benjamin Allen, wants his sister to marry his friend Bob Sawyer, but Arabella rejects her brother's choice. After she marries Mr. Winkle in secret, Mr. Pickwick pays his friend's debts, effects a reconciliation between the young couple and Arabella's brother, and breaks the news of the marriage to Mr. Winkle's father.

Benjamin Allen, Arabella's coarse, roistering brother, a medical student. With no regard for his sister's feelings, he stubbornly insists upon her marriage to Bob Sawyer.

Mr. Winkle (Senior), a practical man of business, much opposed to his son's romance with Arabella Allen. He changes his mind when, through the services of Mr. Pickwick, he meets his daughter-in-law. He builds the couple a new house and makes his son an assistant in the family business.

Bob Sawyer, Benjamin Allen's friend and Arabella's unwelcome, oafish suitor. He hangs up his shingle in Bristol and practices medicine there. Eventually, he and Benjamin Allen take service with the East India Company.

Bob Cripps, Bob Sawyer's servant.

Mrs. Mary Ann Raddle, Bob Sawyer's landlady.

Mr. Raddle, her husband.

Mrs. Betsey Cluppins, Mrs. Raddle's sister and a friend of Mrs. Bardell.

Mr. Gunter, a friend of Bob Sawyer.

Jack Hopkins, a medical student, Bob Sawyer's friend. He tells Mr. Pickwick the story of a child who swallowed a necklace of large wooden beads that rattled and clacked whenever the child moved.

Peter Magnus, a traveler who journeys with Mr. Pickwick from London to Ipswich. He is on his way to make a proposal of marriage.

Miss Witherfield, his beloved, into whose room Mr. Pickwick, unable to find his own, accidentally blunders at the inn in Ipswich.

The Honorable Samuel Slumkey, a candidate for Parliament from the borough of Eatanswill. He is victorious over his opponent, Horatio Fizkin, Esq.

Mr. Slurk, the editor of *The Eatanswill Independent*.

Mr. Pott, the editor of *The Eatanswill Gazette*.

Mrs. Pott, his wife.

Mrs. Leo Hunter, a lady of literary pretensions, the author of "Ode to an Expiring Frog," whom Mr. Pickwick meets in Eatanswill.

Mr. Leo Hunter, who lives in his wife's reflected glory.

Count Smorltork, a traveling nobleman whom Mr. Pickwick meets at a breakfast given by Mrs. Leo Hunter.

Horatio Fizkin, Esq., defeated in the election at Eatanswill.

Mr. Perker, the agent for the Honorable Samuel Slumkey in the Eatanswill election, later Mr. Pickwick's attorney in the suit. After his client has been sentenced to prison, Perker advises him to pay the damages in order to gain his freedom.

Serjeant Snubbin, Mr. Pickwick's lantern-faced, dull-eyed senior counsel in the breach-of-promise suit.

Mr. Justice Starleigh, the judge who presides at the trial.

Mr. Phunky, the assistant counsel to Serjeant Snubbin; he is called an "infant barrister" because he has seen only eight years at the bar.

Thomas Groffin, a chemist, and

Richard Upwitch, a grocer, jurors at the trial.

Mr. Jackson and

Mr. Wicks, clerks in the office of Dodson and Fogg.

Mr. Lowten, clerk to Mr. Perker.

Captain Boldwig, a peppery-tempered landowner on whose grounds the Pickwickians accidentally trespass while hunting.

Dr. Slammer, the surgeon of the 97th Regiment. At a charity ball in Rochester, he challenges Mr. Jingle to a duel; because Jingle is wearing a borrowed coat, Mr. Winkle is the one actually called upon to meet the hot-tempered surgeon.

Mr. Winkle, having been drunk, cannot remember what his conduct was or whom he might have insulted the night before. The situation is eventually resolved, and Mr. Winkle and the doctor shake hands and part on friendly terms.

Lieutenant Tappleton, Dr. Slammer's second.

Colonel Bulder, the commanding officer of the military garrison at Rochester.

Mrs. Bulder, his wife.

Miss Bulder, their daughter.

Mrs. Budger, a widow, Mr. Tupman's partner at the charity ball in Rochester.

Mr. Dowler, a blustering, cowardly ex-army officer whom Mr. Pickwick meets at the White Horse Cellar. The Dowlers travel with Mr. Pickwick to Bath.

Mrs. Dowler, his wife.

Lord Mutanhed, a man of fashion and Mr. Dowling's friend, whom Mr. Pickwick meets in Bath.

The Honorable Mr. Crushton, another friend of Mr. Dowler.

Angelo Cyrus Bantam, Esq., a friend of Mr. and Mrs. Dowling and a master of ceremonies at Bath.

George Nupkins, Esq., the mayor of Ipswich, before whom Mr. Pickwick is brought on the charge, made by Miss Witherfield, that he is planning to fight a duel. The mayor has recently entertained Mr. Jingle, who, calling himself Captain Fitz-Marshall, was courting Miss Henrietta Nupkins.

Mrs. Nupkins, the mayor's wife.

Henrietta Nupkins, their daughter, the object of one of Mr. Jingle's matrimonial designs.

Mary, Mrs. Nupkins' pretty young servant. She eventually marries Sam Weller, and both make their home with Mr. Pickwick in his happy, unadventurous old age.

Mr. Jinks, the clerk of the mayor's court at Ipswich.

Daniel Grummer, the constable of the mayor's court at Ipswich.

Frank Simmery, Esq., a young stockbroker.

Solomon Pell, an attorney who, to his profit, assists in settling the deceased Mrs. Weller's modest estate.

Miss Tomkins, mistress of Westgate House, a boarding school for young ladies, at Bury St. Edmunds. Mr. Pickwick, tricked into believing that Mr. Jingle is planning to elope with one of the pupils, ventures into the school premises at night and finds himself in an embarrassing situation.

Tom Roker, a turnkey at the Fleet Prison.

Smangle,

Mivins, called **The Zephyr**,

Martin,

Simpson, and

The Chancery Prisoner, inmates of the Fleet Prison during Mr. Pickwick's detention.

Mrs. Budkin,

Susannah Sanders,

Mrs. Mudberry, and

Mrs. Rogers, Mrs. Bardell's friends and neighbors.

Anthony Humm, chairman of the Brick Lane Branch of the United Grand Junction Ebenezer Temperance Association. Mr. Weller takes his son Sam to a lively meeting of the association.

PICNIC

Author: William Inge (1913-1973)
First published: 1953
Genre: Drama

Locale: A small town in Kansas
Time: A Labor Day in the early 1950's
Plot: Psychological realism

Hal Carter, a young vagabond. Hal is a powerfully built drifter, a former college athlete reluctantly aware that he must find himself a job and a place in the world or be a drifter all of his life. Hal joins a Labor Day picnic at the invitation of his former college roommate, Alan Seymour. He escorts Millie, the bookwormish younger sister of the town beauty, Madge, to the envy of Rosemary, the aging schoolteacher who rooms with the Owenses. Hal's presence creates havoc in the lives of the picnickers, especially the women.

Madge Owens, a beautiful woman. Hal's meeting with Madge, the town beauty, has an electric tension even though they are not certain of their immediate attraction for each other. Madge knows only that she is even less certain that she wants to marry Alan, even though she is being pushed into it by her mother, Flo Owens.

Millie Owens, the highly intelligent, uninhibited younger sister of Madge. Millie has won a scholarship to the state university but knows very little about attracting members of the opposite sex. Ultimately, it is Millie who gives Madge the courage to follow Hal by stating, "For once in your life, do something bright."

Flo Owens, the attractive mother of Madge and Millie. She rents rooms in her home to schoolteachers. Flo was deserted by her husband many years ago, and Hal reminds her of her husband, who could not accept life's responsibilities. She wants Madge to marry dependable Alan Seymour and live the safe, secure life that she never knew.

Helen Potts, the neighbor lady whom Hal asks if he may do some yard chores in return for breakfast. Helen is friendly and outgoing but is a resilient woman. She still cares for her invalid mother, who, years ago, had her brief marriage annulled.

Rosemary Sydney, a schoolteacher who boards at the Owenses' home and has been dating Howard Bevans, an unromantic shopkeeper whose attentions are desperately welcomed by the frustrated schoolteacher. Rosemary cannot face the obvious absorption of Hal and Madge in each other at the picnic and the breathlessness with which they dance together. Unable to share their mood, Rosemary creates a scene that forces Hal to flee the picnic. Madge follows him into the night, despite his warning that he is no good for her.

Alan Seymour, Madge's boyfriend, who is the son of a wealthy local businessman. Alan is the former college roommate of Hal, who was a football star until he flunked out. Hal comes to town as a man who is running out of options; he hopes to land a job with Alan's help, even though they have not seen each other for many years.

Howard Bevans, a mild-mannered small-town businessman who is a bachelor approaching middle age. He has been going out with Rosemary for many years without proposing marriage. After the Labor Day picnic, Rosemary abandons her feigned indifference to marriage and begs Howard to marry her. Howard gives her lame excuses, but the next morning she announces in front of other people that they are to be married, so he has little choice. Rosemary's moment of triumph occurs when she rides off with Howard for an Ozark marriage and honeymoon.

Bomber, the paperboy, who crudely lusts after Madge. Millie constantly conflicts with his adolescent desires and Madge simply tries to ignore him.

Irma Kronkite, a schoolteacher friend of Rosemary who is also an unmarried woman, just returning from a "wicked" vacation in New York. She has visited the Stork Club. She was supposed to be concentrating on a master's degree in education at Columbia University.

Christine Schoenwalder, a new schoolteacher in town who teaches "feminine hygiene."

— *Arthur F. McClure*

THE PICTURE OF DORIAN GRAY

Author: Oscar Wilde (1854-1900)
First published: 1891; serial form, 1890
Genre: Novel

Locale: England
Time: Late nineteenth century
Plot: Fantasy

Dorian Gray, a handsome young man who, while visiting the studio of an artist friend who is painting his portrait, idly wishes that the portrait would grow old while he himself remained young looking. Later, having treated a young woman cruelly, he notices the first sign of alteration in the portrait. Alarmed, he decides to repent and to marry her, but he learns that she has killed herself. He now gives himself over entirely to a life of corruption, under the tutelage of an evil friend. His crimes include murder. At last he decides to destroy the hideous portrait, which has been long locked away. He stabs it with a knife. Hearing a cry, the servants find lying before a portrait of their handsome master a withered, wrinkled body with a knife in its breast.

Lord Henry Wotton, a witty, degenerate man who deliberately tempts Dorian into a life of debauchery.

Basil Hallward, Dorian's artist friend, who paints his portrait. He asks Lord Wotton never to meet Dorian, saying that the older man's influence would be evil; but Dorian comes to the studio while Lord Wotton is there, and the friendship begins. Hallward and Dorian become estranged; but on his thirty-eighth birthday, Dorian shows Hallward the altered portrait and then, angry because he has betrayed himself, kills Hallward.

Alan Campbell, a young chemist whom Dorian blackmails into disposing of Hallward's body with fire and chemicals. Campbell later commits suicide under strange circumstances.

Sibyl Vane, a young actress who knows Dorian only as "Prince Charming." Dorian treats her cruelly, and she kills herself.

James Vane, her brother. He has sworn revenge against "Prince Charming," but he hesitates to kill Dorian, who looks years too young to be the man who ruined his sister eighteen years before. Assured that Dorian is in fact that man, he follows him to his country house and is accidentally shot and killed during a hunt on the estate.

PICTURING WILL

Author: Ann Beattie (1947-   )
First published: 1989
Genre: Novel

Locale: Charlottesville, Virginia; New York; Florida; and Connecticut
Time: Indeterminate, in the mid- to late twentieth century
Plot: Social realism

Will, the son of Jody and Wayne. At the beginning of the novel, Will is a small child living with his mother in Charlottesville, Virginia; both were abandoned by his father four years earlier. He is imaginative, loves playing with his G.I. Joe doll, and longs for a puppy. In the course of the novel, Will also becomes essentially abandoned by his mother and finds a truer parent/child bonding with his stepfather, Mel. Will, as an overriding focus of the novel, helps to define other characters as they do or do not connect emotionally with him.

Jody, Will's mother. As described in the first section of the novel, Jody is a wedding photographer who has driven randomly to Charlottesville after being abandoned by her husband. The details of her background are unstated. The first impression of her is as a remarkable single parent who is doing an admirable job of supporting herself and her son. Small details accumulate that call her moral character into question, such as the fact that she mails manila envelopes throughout the year to her former husband; they are filled with such items as pharmacy receipts, bills, junk mail, and parking tickets. After Mel introduces her photographs to the New York art world, her career takes off, and she leaves most of Will's upbringing to Mel.

Wayne, Jody's former husband. As presented in the second part of the novel, Wayne is married for the third time and is still waiting for his life to happen as he works as a landscaper and part-time grocery delivery boy. He recognizes his handsomeness and is more interested in having affairs than he is in Will's visit. Will not only makes Wayne uncomfortable, but also makes him subtly aware of his own inability to make lasting commitments in life.

Mel Anthis, Will's stepfather. He has a successful administrative position in a New York art gallery. He is desperately in love with Jody at the beginning of the novel and constantly encourages her to move to New York and become a serious artist. Although initially he might have been friendly with Will as a means to gain access to Jody, he soon comes to deeply love Will and thinks of him as a son. Mel's love for Will is the emotional core of the novel.

D. B. Haverford, an art gallery owner who is referred to throughout the work as "**Haveabud**." A heavy drinker and sexual wanderer, he spouts talk about art that he does not understand; he also serves as Jody's mentor. On a pivotal trip to Florida, he allows Will to witness a pedophiliac relationship with another young boy, the son of a former protégé.

Corky, Wayne's third wife. She is determined to see the bright side of every situation. She is idealistic, and has a good heart. She wants to have a baby with Wayne, but he refuses. She is genuinely loving and caring toward Will.

— *Laurie Lisa*

PIERRE: Or, The Ambiguities

Author: Herman Melville (1819-1891)
First published: 1852
Genre: Novel

Locale: New York City
Time: Early nineteenth century
Plot: Philosophical

Pierre Glendinning, a wealthy young easterner of the early nineteenth century. When he claims his half sister as his wife in order to shield her from the world, his decision causes him to lose his inheritance, his fiancée, and eventually his life. Having shot and killed a male cousin, he is sent to prison. During a visit from his fiancée and his half sister, he swallows poison and dies.

Isabel, Pierre's half sister, the illegitimate daughter of an alliance Pierre's father had with a young French woman. Her love for Pierre is not the typical love of a sister for a brother. She is jealous of the attention he pays another woman, and finally, after Pierre has taken his life by poison, she kills herself by drinking from the vial he had used.

Lucy Tartan, Pierre's fiancée. Though she has wealth and many friends, she follows Pierre and Isabel to New York to live with them and earn her living by painting portraits. When Pierre tells her, during the prison scene, that Isabel is his half sister and not his wife, Lucy dies of shock.

Mrs. Glendinning, Pierre's mother, a proud woman who is jealous of her influence over her son. Because Pierre claims Isabel as his wife, she drives him from home and, at her death, cuts him off without a cent.

Glen Stanly, Pierre's cousin, the relative to whom Mrs. Glendinning leaves the family fortune. Stanly is in love with Lucy. In concert with Lucy's brother, he provokes Pierre, with whom Lucy is now living. Pierre shoots and kills him during a fight.

Delly Ulver, an illegitimate farm girl befriended by Isabel and Pierre. She becomes their servant.

PIERS PLOWMAN

Author: William Langland (c. 1332-c. 1400)
First transcribed: c. 1362 (A text), c. 1377 (B text), and
  c. 1393 (C text)
Genre: Poetry

Locale: England
Time: The fourteenth century
Plot: Social

Piers the Plowman, the hardworking, sincere, and honest plowman who with each appearance in the poem becomes more clearly an incarnation of Christ. In the poet's second vision, Piers volunteers to lead the assembly of the seven deadly sins to Holy Truth and thus earns a pardon for himself and his heirs forever. The third vision of the poet concerns Piers's quests for the states of Do-Well, Do-Better, and Do-Best. Piers also explains the Tree of Charity and the nature of the Trinity of God to the poet and appears as the Good Samaritan, as the builder of the Church, and as God's champion against Satan.

William, the Poet, who has a series of visions, each concerned with human relationships to God in every aspect of medieval life. The first vision relates the contest between Lady Mede and Conscience; the next two dreams are visions of Piers the Plowman. In addition to the quest for Truth (God),

the poet also digresses on the topics of sin and virtue, the value of learning, the clergy and the laity, and Christian tradition.

Lady Mede, an allegorical character representing both just reward and bribery. She appears in the first vision as the proposed, but unwanted, bride of Conscience.

Lady Holy Church, who explains the first vision to the poet.

Conscience,

Reason, and

False, allegorical characters.

Dame-Work-While-I-Am-Able, the wife of Piers.

Do-This-Or-Thy-Dame-Shall-Beat-Thee, Piers's daughter.

Suffer-Thy-Sovereigns-To-Have-Their-Wishes-Dare-Not-Judge-Them-For-If-Thou-Dost-Thou-Shalt-Dearly-Abide-It, Piers's son.

PIGS IN HEAVEN

Author: Barbara Kingsolver (1955-   )
First published: 1993
Genre: Novel

Locale: Rural Kentucky; Tucson, Arizona; Heaven, Oklahoma; and Seattle, Washington
Time: 1989
Plot: Family

Taylor Greer, a self-reliant young woman from a long line of independent women. Born and reared in rural Kentucky by a single mother, Taylor is also determined to make it on her own. Living contentedly in Tucson, Arizona, with her boyfriend and adopted daughter Turtle, managing an auto parts store, her comfortable existence is shattered when a Cherokee lawyer claims that Turtle was adopted illegally and that the tribe has a claim on her under the Indian Child Welfare Act. Unable to bear the thought of losing her daughter, Taylor flees with Turtle, traveling aimlessly until settling in Seattle, Washington. Trying to care for and support Turtle on her own, away from family and friends, she discovers that "doing it on your own" is not necessarily an asset and that asking for and needing help can be a virtue. Taylor loves Turtle enough, finally, to face the tribe's claim on her, admitting that she needs the help of a larger community in rearing her daughter.

Turtle Greer, Taylor's six-year-old adopted Indian daughter. Turtle's alcoholic mother left her with an aunt before driving herself off a bridge, and the aunt, unable to protect the child from her abusive boyfriend, left her in the back seat of Taylor's car and fled. Named for her perpetual vicelike grip on Taylor, Turtle is painfully shy and quiet, gradually overcoming the effects of horrendous physical and sexual abuse suffered before her adoption. When Turtle finally meets her Cherokee grandfather and remembers him, Taylor realizes that Turtle cannot turn her back on her Indian heritage.

Alice Greer, Taylor's strong-minded, independent, sixty-one-year-old mother, who was reared by a tough woman who

ran a hog farm for fifty years. Deserted by her husband, Alice in turn raised Taylor on her own by cleaning other people's houses. Tiring of her television-addicted current husband and feeling that she is doomed to a solitary life, she leaves him. Visiting her cousin Sugar Hornbuckle in Heaven, Oklahoma, to learn more about the Cherokee claim on her granddaughter, she discovers that she also has Indian blood and meets and falls for Cash Stillwater, Turtle's Cherokee grandfather.

Annawake Fourkiller, an idealistic young lawyer interning on an Indian Lawyer Training Grant at the Cherokee Nation Headquarters in Heaven, Oklahoma. When her mother was institutionalized for alcoholism, Annawake stayed with her uncle, but her twin brother Gabe, adopted by a white family from Texas, turned to crime and was lost to her. Feeling strongly about children lost to the tribe and eager to right a wrong done to the Cherokee nation, she pursues Taylor and Turtle, trying to learn the details of what she suspects is an illegal adoption, after seeing them on television. In the process, she learns to temper her quest for justice with heart.

Cash Stillwater, Turtle's Indian grandfather. Fleeing his home in Oklahoma after his wife's death from cancer and his daughter's suicide, Cash settles for a time in the Rocky Mountains, working as a bag boy in a health food store. Missing his people, he returns home to Heaven, where he meets and falls in love with Alice, Turtle's grandmother.

Jax, the boyfriend Taylor leaves behind in Tucson when she flees with Turtle. Named by his alcoholic mother for her favorite brand of beer, Jax is a tall, lanky rock musician whose band, the Irascible Babies, plays local dives. Totally in love with Taylor, he is agreeable, easygoing, and eager to make a life with her and her daughter.

Barbie, a Las Vegas casino waitress who accompanies Taylor and Turtle on their travels. She styles herself after the Barbie doll. She also has strong criminal tendencies, stealing from her former employer and using a color copy machine to make counterfeit twenty dollar bills.

— *Mary Virginia Davis*

THE PILGRIM HAWK: A Love Story

Author: Glenway Wescott (1901-1987)
First published: 1940
Genre: Novel

Locale: Chancellot, a town in France
Time: An afternoon in May, 1929
Plot: Symbolic realism

Alexandra (Alex) Henry, a young, unmarried American woman who acts as hostess for the Irish Cullen family and for the novel's narrator, an American from the Midwest. She is the impressionable mind that Alwyn Tower, the narrator, most worries will be influenced by the story of disappointed love that the Cullens enact. The level-headed Alex seems less vulnerable than Alwyn fears and immune to his "grandiose theories." She is far more practical and skeptical than Alwyn and less prone to concoct stories with morals. She is also less wary of her own judgments than the self-critical Alwyn. She believes that the afternoon's events have convinced her not to marry, but she weds Alwyn's brother after she returns to the United States.

Madeleine Cullen, the owner of Lucy, the "pilgrim hawk," who means "all the world to her." The bird is to Mrs. Cullen what writing is to Alex, "an image of amorous desire." On a more literal level, her love for the bird suggests her lack of satisfaction with her husband, with his inability to satisfy her sexual and her aesthetic needs. He is too literal and down to earth to satisfy her fanciful nature.

Larry Cullen, Madeleine's husband, an Irish aristocrat who dislikes the hawk on which his wife dotes. He tries to free the creature but finds that he cannot escape either its wild clutches or his wife's obsession with it. He is a realist who cannot share his wife's devotion to this symbolic creature. He constantly advises her not to generalize so much about experience when their own is so limited. She treats him rather like a pet, and he regards her with a "captivated but uncomfortable look."

Alwyn Tower, an American novelist from the Midwest who is fascinated with the Cullens. He is an aspiring literary artist who sees in the couple a metaphor for the desire to transform nature and the environment into parables of human existence. As he points out, "humanity is histrionic, and must prepare and practice every stroke of passion; so half our life is a vague and stormy make-believe." For both the narrator and Mrs. Cullen, the hawk seems to symbolize a freedom for which they yearn, unchecked by societal restraints or the limits of their own imaginations. The self-conscious narrator compares his failures to that of a bird, "too proud and vexed to fly again." He sees the hawk as an emblem of the artist, who ought to be wild but who accepts the hospitality of hosts, who honor and support him but who simultaneously subvert his independence.

Lucy, Mrs. Cullen's hawk, who attends her mistress patiently and tamely but stands for the fierce force that Mrs. Cullen would like to unleash. Lucy fascinates Alwyn because she symbolizes pure instinct, unhindered by conscience or scruple. Mrs. Cullen admires the single-mindeness of falcons, their "painful greed," which she imitates with her own voice. She loves the bird precisely because it is not human and has needs that human beings can never feel.

— *Carl Rollyson*

PILGRIMAGE

Author: Dorothy Richardson (1873-1957)
First published: 1938
Genre: Novels

Locale: England
Time: 1893-1911
Plot: Bildungsroman

Miriam Henderson, an Englishwoman of middle-class background whose story from youth to maturity is screened through her mind in a series of discontinuous episodes, impressions, and suggestions. Forced to earn her own living after her father loses his money, she teaches in Germany and in London. She becomes a governess in a wealthy household. She nurses her dying mother. She works in a dental clinic. She interests herself in the activities of a Socialist group, the Lycurgans. She is engaged to marry Shatov, a Russian Jew, but changes her mind. She begins to write literary reviews. She rejects Dr. Densley's proposal and has an affair with a writer named "Hypo" Wilson. She goes on a vacation in Switzerland. She spends some time with a Quaker family in the country. The twelve volumes of Miriam Henderson's story represent the most extended exercise of pure stream-of-consciousness in all literature, and Miriam herself is the most completely realized character from the interior point of view. The flaw in Richardson's novel is that it offers little selectivity. The events of one woman's life, the important and the trivial, are presented on the same plane of immediate sensation, and the result is boredom as well as revelation. Reviewing Richardson's work, May Sinclair borrowed a phrase from William James and used the term "stream-of-consciousness" to describe the technique employed.

Mr. Henderson, a moderately prosperous man living on inherited income. The loss of his money throws his daughters on their own resources.

Mrs. Henderson, his wife, nursed by her daughter Miriam while she is dying of cancer.

Harriet Henderson,

Sarah Henderson, and

Eve Henderson, Miriam's sisters. Harriet marries Gerald, who also loses his money; they run a rooming house. Sarah remains with her parents until she marries. Eve moves back and forth between London and Wales, sometimes teaching, sometimes running a shop.

Gerald, Harriet's husband.

Fraulein Pfaff, the mistress of a private school in Germany where Miriam Henderson teaches for a year.

Pastor Lahmann, a friend of Fraulein Pfaff, who becomes jealous when he appears interested in Miriam Henderson.

The Misses Perne, women who conduct Wordsworth House, a school in London where Miriam Henderson teaches for a time.

Grace Bloom and

Florrie Bloom, students at Wordsworth House. They become Miriam Henderson's friends.

Ted, a young man in whom Miriam Henderson is interested. He is jealous of Max.

Max, a young man attentive to Miriam Henderson. He dies in New York.

Mr. and Mrs. Corrie, the owners of a country home where Miriam Henderson is employed as a governess.

Dr. Orly, Sr.,

Dr. Orly, Jr., and

Dr. Hancock, the owners of a dental clinic where Miriam Henderson works as a secretary and assistant. The Orlys become her friends, and Dr. Hancock introduces her to the London literary life.

Mrs. Bailey, the owner of a boardinghouse where Miriam Henderson takes lodgings.

Alma, Miriam Henderson's old school friend, now married to "Hypo" Wilson, a writer.

"Hypo" Wilson, a writer obviously modeled on H. G. Wells. He introduces Miriam Henderson to the Lycurgans, a Socialist group. Later, she has an affair with him.

Eleanor Dear, a sickly nurse who imagines that every man she meets is in love with her. Miriam Henderson nurses her through an illness. She later has an affair with Shatov, to whom Miriam is engaged.

Dr. Densley, Miriam Henderson's friend and adviser. She rejects his proposal of marriage.

Shatov, a Russian Jew, a brilliant young intellectual who also interests Miriam Henderson in Socialism and literature. They are engaged to be married, but she breaks the engagement when he becomes Eleanor Dear's lover. He eventually marries Amabel.

Selina Holland, a social worker with whom Miriam Henderson shares an apartment for a time. The two women quarrel, and Miriam returns to Mrs. Bailey's boardinghouse.

Amabel, a young girl in whom Miriam Henderson has taken an interest. She marries Shatov.

The Rescorlas, a Quaker family with whom Miriam Henderson lives for six months in the country.

THE PILGRIMAGE OF CHARLEMAGNE
(Voyage de Charlemagne à Jérusalem et à Constantinople)

Author: Unknown
First transcribed: c. 1100
Genre: Poetry

Locale: Paris, Jerusalem, and Constantinople
Time: c. 800
Plot: Folklore

Charlemagne (shahr-leh-MAHN-yeh), the king of the Franks and emperor of the West. When his wife declares that Hugo, the emperor of Greece, is the more handsome of the two kings, Charlemagne angrily sets forth, with his Twelve Peers, on a pilgrimage to Jerusalem. After the pilgrims sit in the chairs of Christ and His apostles in the great cathedral in Jerusalem and receive many relics from the Patriarch, they depart for Constantinople and are received as guests by the magnificent Hugo. In the bedchamber, the Franks drink their wine and each makes a boast concerning his host. When Charlemagne is challenged to prove the boasts true or be beheaded with his peers, he and his men, assisted by an angel, overcome Hugo and return to France, where Charlemagne forgives his wife for her unfortunate comparison.

Hugo (ew-GOH), the emperor of Greece and Constantinople.

Roland (roh-LAH[N]),
Olivier (oh-lee-VYAY),
William of Orange,
Naimes (nehm),
Ogier of Denmark (oh-ZHYAY),
Gerin (geh-RA[N]),
Berenger (beh-rehn-ZHAY),
Turpin the Archbishop (tewr-PA[N]),
Ernaut (ehr-NOH),
Aymer (eh-MAY),
Bernard of Brusban (behr-NAHR, brews-BAH[N]), and
Bertram (behr-TRAHM), Charlemagne's Twelve Peers, who boast of the ways each will overcome King Hugo. When confronted with the demand that they prove their boasts or lose their heads, they are aided by prayer and an angel, who warns them never to boast in such a way again.

THE PILGRIM'S PROGRESS

Author: John Bunyan (1628-1688)
First published: 1678 and 1684
Genre: Novel

Locale: Indeterminate
Time: Any time since the time of Christ
Plot: Allegory

Christian, an example of all God-fearing Protestants, whose adventures are recounted as events in a dream experienced by the narrator. Originally called Graceless, of the race of Japhet, Christian becomes distressed with his life in the City of Destruction and insists that his wife and four children accompany him in search of salvation. When they refuse to leave, Christian determines to set out alone. Henceforth his life story consists of hardships, sufferings, and struggles to overcome obstacles—physical, human, and emotional—that beset his path. At the outset, Christian's family and neighbors, Pliable and Obstinate, try to dissuade him from breaking away from his sins of the past. Then Evangelist appears with a parchment roll on which is inscribed, "Fly from the Wrath to Come." On his long journey, Christian finds that human beings he meets offer distractions and hindrance, even bodily harm and violence. Mr. Worldly Wiseman turns him aside from his set purpose until Evangelist intervenes. **Simple**, **Sloth**, **Presumption**, **Formalist**, **Hypocrisy**, **Timorous**, and **Mistrust** seek to dissuade or discourage Christian because of the rigors of the straight and narrow way. The Giant of the Doubting Castle and his wife beat and torture Christian and Hopeful. In the Valley of Humiliation, Christian engages in mortal combat with a monstrous creature named Apollyon for more than half a day but at last emerges triumphant. In many times of peril, Christian is fortunate in having companions who can assist him: Evangelist, who gets him out of difficulties or warns him of impending strife; Help, who assists him to get out of the Slough of Despond; Faithful, who is by his side at Vanity Fair; Hopeful, who comforts him at Doubting Castle and encourages him to give up bravely at the River of Death. In this narrative of a pilgrim's adventures, Christian must constantly overcome temptations and dangers that will thwart his goal, impede his progress toward eternal life, or prevent him from reaching Heaven; but with the aid of his religious fervor and the advice and counsel of a few true friends, he achieves salvation.

Evangelist, Christian's adviser and guide, particularly in times of danger. Evangelist shows him the way to avoid destruction, directs him to the Wicket Gate, and warns him of such people as Mr. Worldly Wiseman and of the dangers at Vanity Fair.

Apollyon (uh-PAHL-yuhn), the fiend in the Valley of Humiliation. Apollyon has scales like a fish, feet like a bear, wings like a dragon, a mouth like a lion; he spouts fire and smoke from his belly, and he discourses like a devil in his attempt to persuade Christian from honoring his religion.

Giant Despair, the giant owner of Doubting Castle. He imprisons Christian and Faithful, beats them, and threatens them with death until Christian uses a key of Promise to make their escape.

Faithful, Christian's traveling companion. Imprisoned, tortured, and put to death by the people of Vanity Fair, he is transported to the Celestial Gate in a chariot.

Hopeful, another wayfarer. He joins Christian at Vanity Fair and accompanies him through various adventures on the way to eternal salvation.

Good-Will, who tells Christian to knock and the gate that is blocking his way will be opened, so that he may see a vision of the Day of Judgment.

Ignorance, a native of the country of Conceit. Refusing to accept the beliefs of Christian and Hopeful, he continues on the journey until he is seized and thrust into Hell.

Mr. Worldly Wiseman, a dweller in the town of Carnal-Policy. He advises Christian to go to Legality and get relief from the burden of sins that Christian carries on his back.

Three Shining Ones, who clothe Christian with new raiment after his burdens fall off before the Cross.

Obstinate and

Pliable, neighbors of Christian. Both try to keep Christian from leaving the City of Destruction. Obstinate remains behind, but Pliable goes with Christian until he deserts him at the Slough of Despond.

Interpreter, who instructs Christian in the mysteries of faith.

Discretion,

Prudence,

Piety, and

Charity, virgins who arm Christian with the sword and shield of faith.

Pope and

Pagan, giants whose caves Christian must pass after reciting verses from the Psalms to protect himself from devils issuing from one of the gates of Hell.

Knowledge,

Experience,

Watchful, and

Sincere, shepherds who point out the Celestial Gate to Christian and Hopeful.

THE PILLARS OF SOCIETY
(Samfundets støtter)

Author: Henrik Ibsen (1828-1906)
First published: 1880
Genre: Drama

Locale: A Norwegian seaport
Time: The nineteenth century
Plot: Psychological realism

Karsten Bernick, a shipbuilder and a pillar of society who says that his every action is performed to help the community. Actually, Bernick is guilty of an intrigue with Mrs. Dorf, now dead, and of letting his brother-in-law, Johan Tönnesen, assume his guilt and flee to America. Because his mother's finances were in bad shape, he also permitted and helped circulate a rumor that Johan had run off with her cash box. Now he is planning to let an American ship manned with a drunken crew set sail with inadequate repairs to avoid criticism from the press. When his brother-in-law, who has returned from America, plans to sail on the vessel, the *Indian Girl*, Bernick does nothing to prevent him because Johan is the only one who can accuse him. When his own son Olaf, a boy of fourteen, plans to run away and ship aboard the *Indian Girl*, Bernick is horrified. After the son has been saved and the citizens of the town come to recognize him as a pillar of society, Bernick confesses his guilt. He had married his wife Betty because she would inherit money from her aunt, and he needed money to get his mother's business out of trouble. Betty forgives him and hopes to win him. His repentance is difficult to accept.

Johan Tönnesen, Mrs. Bernick's younger brother. Johan had taken Bernick's guilt upon himself because Bernick was willing to help him go to America and was courting his sister Betty, who would not have married Bernick if she had known he was implicated with Mrs. Dorf. Johan comes home because his half sister, Lona Hessel, insists that she is homesick. He meets Dina, Mrs. Dorf's daughter, and they plan to marry. When Dina decides to go to America with him, Johan changes his passage from the *Indian Girl* to the *Palm Tree*, a ship in good repair. Although Lona has cared for him like a mother and schemed to get him home so that he could find a wife, Johan is not aware that Karsten Bernick had been in love with Lona and she with him, but that he threw her over for Betty and her money.

Lona Hessel, Mrs. Bernick's half sister, who had gone to America to look after Johan. After some years, she returns with him and confronts Bernick with his guilt. She had loved Bernick and had boxed him on the ear when he decided to marry Betty.

Dina Dorf, a young girl living with the Bernicks. The daughter of the ill-famed Mrs. Dorf, she hates the pretense,

sham, and prudery of the proper, altruistic people about her. When Schoolmaster Rörlund asks her to marry him, she consents, but when Johan appears, she falls in love with him and seizes the chance to go to America.

Martha Bernick, Bernick's sister, a schoolteacher. Martha had been in love with Johan for years, but she sacrifices her own love to permit Dina Dorf to marry him. She had helped bring up Dina after her mother's death.

Doctor Rörlund, the schoolmaster, a leader in the community and a critic of all. He is ashamed to admit his love for Dina, but at last he decides that he will marry her to save her. Dina throws him over for Johan.

Betty Bernick, Karsten's wife. She is a passive character. Lona tells Karsten Bernick that the reason Betty has never truly shared his life is that he will not discuss his affairs with her. Betty says at the end that she will win Bernick at last.

Krap, Bernick's confidential agent, a conscientious workman who warns Bernick that the *Indian Girl* is not seaworthy. He blames Aune, the foreman of the shipyard, who is rebelling against the new machines.

Aune, the foreman of the shipyard. When Bernick orders Aune to have the *Indian Girl* ready to sail in two days, Aune protests. Bernick says that he will fire him if the ship is not ready to sail, and Aune agrees to have the work done on time. He works day and night on the job, though he knows that the ship is not seaworthy and that the whole bottom is rotten. At the end of the play, Aune issues orders, in Bernick's name, that the ship is not to sail, after Olaf has been found stowed away on the hulk destined for the bottom of the sea.

THE PILOT: A Tale of the Sea

Author: James Fenimore Cooper (1789-1851)
First published: 1823
Genre: Novel

Locale: The northeastern coast of England
Time: Late eighteenth century
Plot: Historical

Mr. Gray, the pilot, presumably the alias of **John Paul Jones**, who, betrayed by his native Britain, supports the cause of the American rebels. Picked up by an American frigate off the hazardous northeast coast of England, he gives immediate assistance by guiding the ship through the shoals during a gale. The member of a landing party dispatched to raid the homes of the gentry and to bring off political prisoners, Mr. Gray is captured and imprisoned at St. Ruth's Abbey. There, he has an unexpected visitor, an old love, Alice Dunscombe. After his escape from an intoxicated British officer he rejoins the main body of raiders and narrowly misses being captured again. In the end, he proves decisive in freeing his comrades, saving the frigate in a running fight against three enemy ships, and sailing it out of the shoals on a course toward Holland and safety. Surrounded by mystery and motivated by glory, he leaves Alice Dunscombe forever.

Lieutenant Richard Barnstable, the reckless officer of the schooner *Ariel* and the suitor of Katherine Plowden, the ward of an American loyalist, Colonel Howard. In a romantic attempt to kidnap her, he is caught but escapes a short time later. Returning to his ship, he captures the English cutter

Alacrity. His own ship is wrecked during a storm. After he assists in the rescue of his comrades from Colonel Howard's home, he and Katherine are married aboard the American frigate.

Edward Griffith, the bold yet sensible first lieutenant of the frigate, Barnstable's friend, and the suitor of Cecilia Howard, one of Colonel Howard's nieces. As the leader of the raiding party sent ashore from the frigate, he is twice captured, twice rescued, and finally married to his love. Throughout, his pride is piqued by Mr. Gray's assumptions of authority, but he comes to respect the mysterious pilot.

Colonel Howard, an exiled American Tory living in England. Wealthy and embittered, he recognizes the gallantry of the rebels but despises their purposes. After being taken from his home, St. Ruth's Abbey, as a political prisoner, he is mortally wounded during a naval engagement at sea. He dies after blessing the marriages of Katherine Plowden and Cecilia Howard.

Christopher Dillon, called **Kit**, Cecilia Howard's unsuccessful suitor, the self-seeking kinsman of Colonel Howard. Residing with Howard in England and hoping to inherit his property, he is unscrupulous in his attempts to thwart the raiders. After being captured aboard the *Alacrity* and offered as a hostage in exchange for Edward Griffith, he leads Tom Coffin into a trap. Recaptured, he drowns during the storm in which the *Ariel* is wrecked.

Long Tom Coffin, the weather-beaten, stout-hearted cockswain of the *Ariel*. Instrumental in the capture of the *Alacrity*, he proves more than equal to Dillon's scheming. When the *Ariel* is wrecked, he chooses to go down with the disabled schooner.

Katherine Plowden, Colonel Howard's ward and niece, courted by Lieutenant Barnstable. Vivacious and outspoken, she overtly sympathizes with the rebel cause. She is taken aboard the American frigate by the raiding party, and she and Barnstable are married.

Cecilia Howard, called **Cicely**, Colonel Howard's niece and Edward Griffith's love. More restrained than Katherine Plowden, she hesitates to offend her uncle, although she tacitly sympathizes with the rebels. She and Griffith are married after she has been taken aboard the American frigate.

Alice Dunscombe, Cecilia's companion and the former sweetheart of Mr. Gray. Because of her loyalist convictions, she cannot accept him, yet she wishes him well. She remains unmarried.

Mr. Merry, the spirited young midshipman of the *Ariel*. The skilled and resourceful cousin of Katherine and Cecilia, he poses as a peddler in order to get into the abbey with a message for the girls.

Captain Borroughcliffe, a clever, proud, hard-drinking British officer. Outwitted by the Americans, he challenges the American Marine captain to a duel and loses his leg. Eventually, the two become good friends.

Captain Manual, an officer of the Marine Corps and the leader of the raiding party. A tough, able soldier, he, with Edward Griffith, is twice captured by Captain Borroughcliffe.

Captain Munson, the commanding officer of the American frigate sent to harass British waters. During the fight at sea, he is killed by a broadside from an English ship.

David Boltrope, the hardy sailing master of the American frigate, who speaks in nautical tropes. He is shot in the engagement between the frigate and three British ships.

Jack Joker, a lugubrious, rather sadistic sailor aboard the frigate.

The Ship's Chaplain, who performs the two marriages after Colonel Howard has given his nieces his blessing.

Cornet Fitzgerald, a British officer.

PINCHER MARTIN

Author: William Golding (1911-1993)
First published: 1956
Genre: Novel

Locale: Mid-Atlantic Ocean
Time: During World War II
Plot: Psychological realism

Christopher Hadley "Pincher" Martin, a British navy lieutenant, called "Pincher" because that is the standard nickname for Martins in the Royal Navy. Prior to the war, he was an actor, with an eagle profile and wavy hair. Because he had no belief in anything but his own importance, he betrayed those close to him by sleeping with his producer's wife to advance his career and by raping his best friend's wife after serving as best man at their wedding. He is blown from his ship by a German torpedo. In the Atlantic Ocean, hundreds of miles from land and thirty miles from a British convoy, Martin desperately attempts to stay alive on a barren rock in the North Atlantic. Clinging to the rock, he feeds on mussels and lichens as he rationally plots his survival and rescue. In an attempt to retain touches of humanity, he names the various sections of rock, many after London locations, though he imagines the rocks to be teeth in some mighty, threatening jaw ready to devour him, and he shaves himself with his knife. Fearing to sleep, he remains exposed on the rock for four days, buffeted by the elements. When he suffers food poisoning, Martin, using parts of his life belt, performs a crude, improvisational enema on himself. Because he is still wearing his heavy boots when his corpse washes ashore at novel's end, the navy determines that he must have been drowned at sea at the time of the explosion. Essentially, the novel's main character has been a corpse, and its main action has been merely the expansion of Martin's instantaneous imaginings as he struggled all too briefly to stay alive.

Nathaniel (Nat) Walterson, Pincher's best friend. Nathaniel's spirituality and innocence contrast with Martin's self-serving sensuality, but, aboard ship, Nathaniel is a laughingstock. Extraordinarily tall, slender, and awkward, Nathaniel is thrown from the railing where he is leaning in prayer when Martin turns the ship hard starboard to evade the approaching torpedo.

Mary Lovell, the virginal woman after whom Martin lusts. Martin has introduced Nathaniel to her but, attracted by her manners and social sophistication, he wishes to ruin their happiness by sexually forcing himself on her.

Peter, the theatrical producer for whom Martin worked before the war. Peter's wife is seduced by Martin. While racing motorcycles against Martin, Peter injures his leg when Pincher delays turning into a curve, so that Peter's front wheel strikes Martin's back wheel.

Helen, Peter's wife. Martin seduces her to improve his standing in the theatrical company.

Campbell, a crofter on a small island in the Hebrides. Campbell discovers Martin's body when it washes up and reports his discovery to the Navy.

Davidson, a naval officer who comes to the island to record the death of Martin. It is Davidson who determines that Martin died almost immediately in the water, noting that Martin did not have time even to kick off his seaboots.

— *Jerry W. Bradley*

PING PONG
(Le Ping-pong)

Author: Arthur Adamov (1908-1970)
First published: 1955
Genre: Drama

Locale: Paris, France
Time: Primarily the 1950's
Plot: Absurdist

Arthur, who first appears as an impoverished young art student. A poetic and visionary neurotic—like the playwright himself, whose first name he shares—Arthur is fascinated by the creative possibilities of pinball machines, an American invention that is a Parisian craze in the post-World War II era. He constantly thinks of ways to improve pinball games to make them seem new and challenging without really changing their basic principles. His interest brings him into contact with the tycoon who manufactures and leases the machines. Over the years, Arthur becomes hopelessly entrapped by the meaningless, time-wasting contraptions, using them as an escape from the emptiness of modern existence. For a while, he makes money from his creative contributions to the company, always referred to as "The Organization," but he falls out of favor when his inspiration ceases. He is in love with Annette, but his impractical nature prevents him from earning an income that would make him a suitable husband. In the last act, Arthur, in his seventies, is an underpaid elementary school teacher who devotes his free time to playing the game of Ping-Pong with his friend Victor.

Victor, who as a young man is equally addicted to pinball machines but is more practical than Arthur. Victor is studying medicine; he later manages to get a medical license and establish a satisfactory practice. He continues to keep in touch with his friend Arthur and is still not free from pinball machines. He discovers that he can obtain patients by frequenting places where pinball machines are played. In the last act, he is an affluent retired physician whose only interest in life is playing Ping-Pong with Arthur. While overexerting himself during one of their heated, acrimonious contests, Victor suffers a heart attack and dies. In a sense, Victor is a more tragic character than Arthur because his life seems empty in spite of material success. He illustrates the playwright's existentialist view that life itself is meaningless and absurd.

Annette, a slender and pretty woman who is often cold and irritable. She dislikes having to compete with machines for male attention. At one point, she denounces pinball machines and all meretricious, dehumanizing modern toys by saying, "They're all the same in the long run, and you soon get used to them." Over the years, she tries various occupations. She begins as an usherette at a motion picture theater, works

briefly as a sales representative for the Organization, then works as a sales clerk at a shoe store, and finally becomes a manicurist. After she is killed in a traffic accident, it is revealed that she was having affairs with Arthur, Victor, and Sutter, deceiving each about the others. She symbolizes the type of calculating modern woman who uses sex to succeed but becomes another victim of the heartless, competitive socioeconomic system.

Mrs. Duranty, a small, unhappy woman in her sixties when the play opens. She exemplifies the middle-class entrepreneur who works hard and worships money but never gets ahead. She constantly complains about her aches and pains. When the play opens, she is operating a bar called, ironically, "The Good Hope," where Victor and Arthur meet to play her pinball machine. Later, she invests in a public bathhouse; still later, she appears as the owner of a small dancing school. Like most of the characters in the play, Mrs. Duranty has a horizontal career illustrating the view that capitalism wastes human lives as well as labor and resources.

Sutter, a middle-aged, self-important, high-pressure representative of the Organization. He devotes his life to promoting pinball machines and makes a good income until advancing age and dog-eat-dog commercial competition wear him out. He ends up a failure who dreams of immigrating to the United States and becoming a business tycoon in that land of opportunity. Sutter also illustrates the idea that the individual is a victim of the political and social system but is also responsible for the perpetuation of that system.

The Old Man, sometimes referred to as **Constantine**, an old-fashioned, aggressive laissez-faire capitalist who heads the Organization. He too has dreams of greater financial success but loses out to better-financed, better-organized competitors and is a senile, embittered failure on his deathbed.

Roger, the Old Man's secretary, a toady and stereotypical corporate "yes-man." He has little intelligence or imagination and is hopelessly dependent on his employer's favor. For a while, Roger makes a good income, which he spends on luxuries. He cannot adapt when the Organization flounders. He becomes yet another victim of the ruthless system.

— *Bill Delaney*

THE PIONEERS: Or, The Sources of the Susquehanna

Author: James Fenimore Cooper (1789-1851)
First published: 1823
Genre: Novel

Locale: New York State
Time: 1793
Plot: Historical

Judge Marmaduke Temple, the principal citizen and landholder of Templeton, a settlement in upstate New York. He is at once shrewd and honorable, benevolent and just. While trying to kill a deer, he shoots an unfamiliar, educated young hunter named Oliver Edwards. He has Edwards' wound dressed and

offers the man a position as a secretary. When the young man's friend, the old woodsman and hunter called Leatherstocking, is arrested for threatening to shoot an officer, the judge sentences and fines the old man but pays the fine himself. Later, he learns that Edwards is in reality Oliver Edward Effingham, the son of an old friend who had entrusted him with personal effects and family funds years before. The judge restores the property and the money to Edwards. Meanwhile, Edwards and Elizabeth Temple have fallen in love. The judge gives the young couple his blessing.

Elizabeth Temple, the judge's spirited, pretty daughter. Although she respects Oliver Edwards' abilities, she maintains a feminine independence. Grateful to Leatherstocking for saving her life when a savage panther attacks her, she assists in his escape from jail after the old man has been arrested for resisting an officer. Her romance with her father's secretary develops after the young man and Leatherstocking save her from a forest fire. When Edwards' true identity is revealed and he declares his love, she readily marries him.

Natty Bumppo, called **Leatherstocking**, a hardy, simple, upright woodsman in his seventy-first year. Although he is disgusted by wanton killing of game, he defends his right to kill game for food. He shoots a deer out of season and is arrested for resisting the magistrate who tries to search his cabin. Sentenced to jail for a month, he escapes with the help of Oliver Edwards and Elizabeth Temple. Twice he is Elizabeth's rescuer, once from a panther and later from fire. After his jail term is suspended, he moves on to a less civilized territory; he is stricken by the death of his Indian friend and companion.

Oliver Edwards, later revealed to be **Oliver Edward Effingham**, the impoverished young hunter who lives with Leatherstocking in a cabin near Templeton. Believing that Judge Temple has appropriated his inheritance, he is planning to recover it when he accepts the position of secretary to the judge. In the meantime, he falls in love with Elizabeth Temple. He quits his post when Leatherstocking is arrested and jailed, then helps the old man to escape. He aids Elizabeth during the fire and finally reveals his true identity. Judge Temple immediately restores his inheritance, and the young man and Elizabeth are married.

Indian John, an old Mohican chief called **Chingachgook** in his younger days. Lonely, aged, and grieving for the old free life of the wilderness, he rejects his Moravian Christianizing during a raging forest fire and appears in his ceremonial dress. He dies, attended by Leatherstocking, Elizabeth Temple, and Oliver Edwards, in a cave where they have taken refuge from the fire.

Hiram Doolittle, a cowardly, troublemaking, and greedy magistrate who informs on Leatherstocking for breaking the hunting law, gets a search warrant, and is roughly handled by the old hunter when he tries to force his way into Leatherstocking's cabin.

Richard Jones, a meddlesome, pompous sheriff, a frontier fop who indulges in the irresponsible killing of game, spreads rumors that Leatherstocking is working a secret mine, and leads a ragtag posse to recapture the old woodsman after his escape from jail.

Major Edward Effingham, the senile grandfather of the young man who calls himself Oliver Edwards. Years earlier, the major and Judge Temple had been close friends, and Effingham had entrusted some valuable property and a sum of money to the judge's keeping. Leatherstocking has been caring for him. His identity revealed after the fire, the old man is taken to Judge Temple's home and nursed tenderly until his death.

Mr. Grant, a sincere, eclectic minister adept at appealing to the heterogeneous frontier faiths.

Louisa Grant, his timid daughter, Elizabeth's companion. She is inept when faced with danger.

Benjamin Penguillan, called Ben Pump, a former sailor and Judge Temple's salty majordomo. Out of sympathy, he shares Leatherstocking's humiliation in the stocks and thrashes Magistrate Doolittle.

Elnathan Todd, the gigantic village doctor who dresses Oliver Edwards' wound; he is an awkward quack.

Monsieur le Quoi, the village storekeeper, a friend of Judge Temple.

Major Hartmann, a German farmer, also a friend of Judge Temple.

Billy Kirby, a good-natured woodcutter and strong man who sympathizes with Leatherstocking but takes the side of the law.

Jotham Riddel, Magistrate Doolittle's good-for-nothing deputy.

Remarkable Pettibone, Judge Temple's housekeeper.

Squire Lippet, Leatherstocking's lawyer at the time of the old hunter's trial.

Mr. Van der School, the thick-witted prosecutor.

Agamemnon, Judge Temple's silly black servant.

THE PIRATES OF PENZANCE: Or, The Slave of Duty

Author: W. S. Gilbert (1836-1911)
First published: 1880
Genre: Drama

Locale: England
Time: The nineteenth century
Plot: Comedy

Major General Stanley, the very model of a modern major general. He is laden with learned lumber, though a bit behind in his military knowledge. His numerous daughters adore him, and he loves them so much that he tells a lie to save them from the pirates. His conscience torments him. When the pirates learn that he is not an orphan, as he had told them, his life is imperiled, but he is spared, and his daughters marry the pirates, who are all noblemen gone wrong.

The Pirate King (Richard), a kindhearted but stern monarch. He does not think much of piracy as a profession but finds it comparatively honest in contrast with respectability. His piratical ventures are seldom successful, for his and his crew's tenderness for orphans has been noised abroad, and all the ships they capture turn out to be manned entirely by orphans. Also, though victorious over the policemen, he and his crew yield when charged to do so in Queen Victoria's name; with all their faults, they love their queen.

Frederic, the slave of duty. Apprenticed to the pirates because of his nurse's deafness, he serves them diligently, though he views piracy with absolute detestation. He falls in love with the general's most charming daughter, Mabel. Finding that he must serve several more decades as a pirate because of the accident of being born on February 29, his extreme sense of duty makes him betray his potential father-in-law to the pirates.

Ruth, Frederic's nurse, a piratical maid-of-all-work. She mistook the directions of Frederic's father, who wanted his son apprenticed to a pilot, and did not dare return home, so she too joined the pirates. There are the remains of a fine woman about Ruth, who has tried to convince Frederic that she is beautiful and that he loves her. After he has seen the general's daughters and found that she is, on the whole, plain, she has to bear his scorn.

Mabel, General Stanley's most romantic daughter. She feels it her duty to reclaim and reform the handsome pirate apprentice. Her sisters doubt that her sense of duty would be so keen if Frederic were homely.

Edith,

Kate, and

Isabel, three of the general's many daughters.

Samuel, the Pirate King's lieutenant. He agrees that pirates should not be merciless but is troubled by the excessive number of orphans on ships.

The Sergeant of Police, a timorous soul in a highly nervous state. A policeman's lot, he says, is not a happy one. When overthrown by the pirates, he charges them to yield in Queen Victoria's name, which they do. When Ruth explains that they are all peers, he and his fellows release them, and the general offers them his numerous daughters' hands.

THE PIT: A Story of Chicago

Author: Frank Norris (1870-1902)
First published: 1903
Genre: Novel

Locale: Chicago, Illinois
Time: The 1890's
Plot: Naturalism

Curtis Jadwin, a self-made man whose speculations in the Chicago wheat market make a fortune for him. His ruthless ambition to corner the world wheat market causes a friend's fortune to be wiped out; the friend commits suicide. Jadwin marries Laura Dearborn, but as his hectic financial career develops, he spends less and less time with his wife. His excessive greed and hunger for power at last cause his downfall. Financially ruined and broken in health, he and his wife go West to start a new life, happier in adversity than before.

Sheldon Corthell, a painter who, wooing the woman who also interests Jadwin, exemplifies the author's idea of the temperamental difference that exists between stereotyped artists and financiers.

Laura Dearborn, Jadwin's romantic young wife who, loyal to her husband, finally wins his complete devotion. She at one time is unable to decide between Corthell and Jadwin, and the fact that Jadwin wins her is significant to the author's purpose.

Samuel Gretry, an intelligent broker whose alert mind and shrewdness, manifested in professional advice, count heavily in Jadwin's initial fantastically successful maneuvers in the wheat exchange.

Charles Cressler and

Mrs. Cressler, first Laura's friends and, later, Jadwin's. Cressler, after fighting Jadwin in the exchange and losing to him—at no time does either character know the identity of his opponent—takes his own life. Knowledge of this suicide makes such a profound impression on Jadwin that he withdraws for a time from the exchange.

Page Dearborn, Laura's sister, who is a friend of the Cresslers.

Mrs. Emily Wessels (**Aunt Wess**), the aunt of Laura and Page. She also is a friend of the Cresslers.

PITCH DARK

Author: Renata Adler (1938-   )
First published: 1983
Genre: Novel

Locale: Connecticut, Ireland, and Orcas Island
Time: 1981, with flashbacks to the early 1960's
Plot: Fiction of manners

Kate Ennis, an attractive, fortyish journalist involved in an eight-year affair with Jake, a married man. Her background is revealed slowly; she appears first as "I," with her first name introduced later. She attended "a major college" and did graduate work in English. She has some knowledge of the law and was involved in a successful libel action. Kate's fractured narration of the course of her relationship with Jake reflects her disjointed state of mind: She wishes to justify and cling to the obviously deteriorating love affair, yet she simultaneously recognizes its progressively destructive effect on her psyche. Her solution is to flee temporarily from the problematic situation, and she ends up in Ireland, vacationing at the castle of an ambassador who has invited her to stay there in his absence. Her initial difficulties in finding the castle, compounded by the peculiar circumstances surrounding a car accident en route, contribute to her general nervous state of uneasiness; her subsequent indifferent treatment—which she interprets as muted hostility—by the house staff during her stay reinforces her apprehensions about the motives of other people toward her. She eventually flees the country, feeling like a criminal. Although Kate is by turns embarrassed by and self-critical of her mistrust of people and events that she deems suspicious, many of her misgivings ultimately are proved sound. Upon her return to the United States, Kate decides to retire for more contemplation to Orcas Island. Jake is still pursuing her, yet she tries to resign herself to being alone rather than suffering the uncertainties and indignities that accompany her position as the "other woman." Kate and Jake end up living together. Throughout her adventures, Kate displays a knack for capturing in only the briefest of descriptions the essence of persons and situations she encounters. She is especially perceptive in detecting others' (as well as her own) quirks and exploring their basic absurdities, which she uses as a foundation for her conclusions about the contradictoriness of life, embodied in her ambivalence toward Jake and the resolution of their affair.

Jake, Kate's married lover, a lawyer approximately fifteen years older than Kate. Jake acts selfishly and almost callously toward Kate, refusing despite her repeated requests to go away with her on a trip, even a weekend one, even though over the years he has had plenty of opportunity to do so. At the beginning of the story, he leaves Kate to spend Christmas in the Caribbean with his wife, carrying on a family tradition even though his children are grown and gone. Kate's assessment of his behavior toward her is that he has transposed the relative positions of wife and mistress: Whereas the rejected wife is supposed to experience feelings of cold isolation, the mistress should be basking in warm privilege. Jake is jolted out of his complacence and galvanized into decision only by Kate's

leaving. Repeated pleading telephone calls to her protesting his love result in their reunion as cohabiting lovers.

Diana Cummings, a Greek beauty in her early fifties who resides in Lausanne with her husband, John, a native New Englander ten years younger than she. They have three children. An activist who enthusiastically espouses radical causes with which Kate disagrees, Diana hints at possible bias inherent in Kate's German Jewish background to defend her own unsubstantiated political opinions. Kate's relationship with her is an occasion for musing on the nature of friendship.

Kathleen, the young housekeeper at the Irish castle in Cirhbradàn. She is singularly unhelpful to Kate despite the ambassador's assurance that the staff will be eager to please her. When Kate receives an invitation to dine with a neighbor, Kathleen's refusal to provide clear directions to the house results in Kate getting lost in the dark. It is largely the impassive attitude of Kathleen and Celia, the taciturn, middle-aged cook, that drives Kate from the castle.

— *Caren S. Silvester*

THE PLAGUE
(La Peste)

Author: Albert Camus (1913-1960)
First published: 1947
Genre: Novel

Locale: Oran, Algeria
Time: The 1940's
Plot: Impressionistic realism

Bernard Rieux (behr-NAHR ryew), a physician and surgeon in Oran, Algeria, where a plague is claiming as many as three hundred lives a day. Dr. Rieux, a thirty-five-year-old man of great patience, fortitude, and unselfishness, represents the medical profession during the long siege of disease and deaths that strikes rich and poor alike and from which there is no reprieve. The plague means failure to Rieux because he can find no cure or relief for the sufferers. His attitude is characterized by his regard for his fellow people and his inability to cope with injustice and compromise. Very much involved with humankind, he explains that he is able to continue working with the plague-stricken population only because he has found that abstraction is stronger than happiness. He is identified at the end of the book as the narrator of the story, and his account gives the pestilence the attributes of a character, the antagonist. Events of the plague are secondary to philosophies as he pictures the people's reactions, individually and collectively, to their plight. These run the range of emotions and rationality: escape, guilt, a spirit of lawlessness, pleasure, and resistance. During the plague, individual destinies become collective destinies because the plague and emotions are shared by all. Love and friendship fade because they ask something of the future, and the plague leaves only present moments. As the pestilence subsides, relieving the exile and deprivation, there is jubilation, followed by the stereotyped patterns of everyday living.

Madame Rieux, the doctor's wife, the victim of another ailment. Mme Rieux is sent away to a sanatorium before the town is quarantined. Her absence from Rieux points up his unselfishness in staying on in Oran.

Raymond Rambert (ray-MOH[N] rahm-BEHR), a journalist from Paris. Assigned to a routine story on Oran, he is caught in exile when the city is quarantined because of the

plague. Rambert, wanting to return to his wife, resorts to various means in attempting to escape. A nonresident, alien to the plight of the people, he personifies those who feel no involvement with the problems of others. When escape from the city becomes a reality for him, Rambert declines his freedom and accepts Rieux's philosophy of common decency, which amounts merely to doing one's job. In this instance, Rambert's job, according to Rieux, is to fight the plague. The journalist becomes a volunteer on the sanitation teams.

Father Paneloux (pah-neh-LEW), a Jesuit priest who represents the ecclesiastical thinking of people caught in the crisis represented by the plague. Preaching on the plague, he compares the present situation with pestilences of the past and tells his parishioners that they have brought the plague upon themselves through their godlessness. Placing the scientific and the spiritual in balance, Paneloux and Rieux debate whether this man of God and this scientist can consort in contending with adversities. The two men are closer in their thinking than Rieux, a self-proclaimed atheist, and Paneloux, a heretic in some of his preaching, will concede. Paneloux is among those who succumb to the plague.

Jean Tarrou (zhah[n] tah-REW), an enigma to his associates among the volunteers in fighting the plague. Addicted to simple pleasures but no slave to them, Tarrou has no apparent means of income. Little is known of his background until he tells Rieux of his beginnings. The son of a prosecutor, he had been horrified by the thought of the criminals condemned because of his father. He himself has been a political agitator. Tarrou becomes a faithful helper to Rieux, and as a volunteer he records the social aspects of the plague. In telling of the plague, Rieux borrows from these records. After the worst of the pestilence has passed, Tarrou dies from the plague.

Joseph Grand (zhoh-SEHF grah[n]), a municipal clerk. Characterized by all the attributes of insignificance, Grand has spent twenty-two years in his job, to which he was appointed temporarily. He is unable to escape from this imprisonment because he cannot find words with which to protest. He announces early in his acquaintance with Rieux that he has a second job, which he describes as a "growth of personality." The futility of this avocation, writing, is epitomized by Grand's continuing work on the first paragraph of a novel that he anticipates will be the perfect expression of love. He dies after asking Rieux to burn his sheaf of papers, manuscripts with only an adjective or a verb changed from one writing to the next.

M. Cottard (koh-TAHR), a dealer in wines and liquors, treated by Rieux after an attempt at suicide. His undercover deals and unsettled life are sublimated or furthered by his keen delight in gangster movies. He survives the plague, only to go berserk during a shooting fray with the police.

Dr. Richard (ree-SHAHR), the chairman of the medical association in Oran. He is more interested in observing the code of the organization than in trying to reduce the number of deaths.

M. Othon (oh-TOH[N]), the police magistrate. His isolation after contracting the plague shows Rieux's impartiality in dealing with plague victims.

Jacques Othon (zhahk), the magistrate's son, on whom a new serum is tried. The lengthy description of young Othon's illness illustrates the suffering of the thousands who die of the plague.

Madame Rieux, the doctor's mother, who comes to keep house for her son during his wife's absence. She is an understanding woman who reminds Tarrou of his own childhood and elicits his philosophical discussion of a man's role in life.

Garcia (gahr-SEE-ah),

Raoul (rah-EWL),

Gonzales (gohn-ZAH-lehs),

Marcel (mahr-SEHL), and

Louis (lwee), the men involved in Rambert's contemplated escape from Oran. The intricacies of illegality are shown as Rambert is referred from one of these men to another. From Garcia, an accomplice of Cottard, to Marcel and Louis, guards at the city gate, each one must have his stipend, until finally the cost of escape becomes exorbitant.

THE PLAIN-DEALER

Author: William Wycherley (1641?-1715)
First published: 1677
Genre: Drama

Locale: London, England
Time: The seventeenth century
Plot: Comedy of manners

Captain Manly, a forthright and honest man who intends to leave England for the West Indies because he hates the hypocrisy of the age that he finds at the court and in lesser social circles. He loses his ship and fortune in a sea battle with the Dutch and is forced back to England by the disaster. He discovers that Olivia, his fiancée, has married during his absence, rails at him behind his back, and will not return the small fortune he had entrusted to her. Seeking revenge for her conduct, Manly gains entrance to her chamber on two occasions. The first time, he lies with her, and the second time, he exposes her to the world as an adulteress. His trusted friend, Mr. Vernish, is the rogue who has married Olivia and plotted with her to keep the captain's money. At the end, Captain Manly is agreeably surprised to find that his supposed page is really a rich young heiress, Fidelia Grey, who loves him very much. Following this discovery, the captain and she agree to marry and go off to the West Indies to live a sober, happy life among honest people.

Olivia, a scheming, shallow woman loved by Captain Manly. She marries Manly's supposed friend, Mr. Vernish, during her lover's absence and refuses to help her fiancé when he returns penniless to England, although as his expected bride, he had given her most of his fortune before he left England. Olivia proves readily dishonest in her marriage as well, falling in love with Manly's page. She is deceived by Manly, who silently replaces the page in the darkness of Olivia's rooms and proceeds to prove his erstwhile fiancée an adulteress. When her frailty is shown to the world, Olivia, vowing revenge on Manly, stalks from the company.

Freeman, Captain Manly's lieutenant, a likable young man who tries to make the best of the world. He proves to be the captain's true friend, much to Manly's surprise, for Manly had thought the lieutenant to be a shallow, deceiving opportunist. Freeman woos the rich Widow Blackacre unsuccessfully until he works through her minor son, who accepts Freeman as his guardian upon Freeman's promise to release the lad from studying law for a more enjoyable career as a man-about-town. Freeman actually does not want to marry Widow Blackacre, and he readily releases her from her promise of marriage when she agrees to pay his debts and settle an annuity on him.

Mr. Vernish, who is supposedly Captain Manly's best friend. He betrays his trust by marrying Olivia and plotting with her to keep the captain's money. Too cowardly to admit that he is Olivia's husband, he is found out when he tries to prevent Olivia from making him a cuckold with Captain Manly's page. His true nature is displayed again when he learns the page is really a girl, for he tries to lock her in a room in his house until he can find an opportunity to ravish her.

Fidelia Grey, a wealthy young heiress who falls in love with Captain Manly and, disguised as a boy, follows him to sea. She helps Manly achieve his revenge when Olivia proposes an affair with the supposed page. Fidelia's love and service are rewarded when Captain Manly discovers her true identity and proposes marriage to her.

Widow Blackacre, a litigious woman who enjoys her status as a widow because it leaves her free to enter lawsuits in her own name. So fond is she of legal entanglements that she forces her son to study law, and she herself takes up quarters at the Inns of Court. She wastes her son's fortune until, with Freeman's help, the lad is able to escape her domination.

Jerry Blackacre, Widow Blackacre's son, a hearty young man who detests the career in law his mother plans for him; he prefers a career as a gay young blade and participation in the fashionable life of London. He readily accepts Freeman as his guardian when the lieutenant promises to help the boy live the life he desires.

Lord Plausible, a cowardly, flattering nobleman who seeks the hand of Olivia in marriage. His character serves as a foil for that of honest, outspoken Captain Manly.

Mr. Novel, a flattering coxcomb who also seeks the hand of Olivia in marriage. He derives his name from the fact that he is an ardent admirer of novelties of all kinds.

Major Oldfox, an elderly fop who seeks to marry the Widow Blackacre so that she can provide for him from her son's inheritance. He is a foolish old man and a would-be poet. His courtship of the widow descends to the utterly ridiculous when he has her kidnaped. The widow fully expects to be raped, but he astonishes her by reading his own blank-verse poetry to her.

Eliza, Olivia's cousin, who is distressed by Olivia's conduct.

PLAINS SONG, FOR FEMALE VOICES

Author: Wright Morris (1910-1998)
First published: 1980
Genre: Novel

Locale: Madison County, Nebraska, and Chicago
Time: The early 1900's to the late 1970's
Plot: Domestic realism

Cora Atkins, who is six feet tall, lean, and blonde, with an English complexion totally unsuited to the climate of the Great Plains. She moves from the East with her new husband to a farm in northeastern Nebraska. Her husband is always a stranger to her, and she to him. Firm and implacable, with her emotions always hidden, she is fenced off from others, epitomizing the isolated farm woman who finds grim satisfaction in the fact that her hard physical work is never done. Her marriage includes only one sexual act, which so horrifies her that she bites her knuckle to the bone. Cora is not a martyr, however; she is entirely self-sufficient. A limited woman with a limited life, she sets her own limits. Only once does her action go beyond her own control, when her niece Sharon outrages her so much that she strikes the girl's hand with a hairbrush. Hers is the dominant voice in the book.

Sharon Rose Atkins, Cora and Emerson's niece. Orphaned early, she is reared as a sister to her cousin Madge. Small, dark, and animated, she is almost the antithesis of either Cora or her daughter. She rebels against Cora's restrictions and feels betrayed when Madge marries. As much an egotist as Cora, she escapes the rural Nebraska life through her music, first in Chicago, then later as a professor at Wellesley. It is only when she returns at Cora's death that she understands and admires Cora for her independence and her ability to come to terms with her life.

Emerson Atkins, Cora's husband. A silent plodder, the Nebraska homesteader is usually bewildered by life and by Cora. She sets the limits in their life; he accepts them. He balks at modern mechanization; he is not sure, for example, that chickens and cows will accept electric lights. His most memorable act is to run government men off his farm during the drought of the 1930's. His daughter inherits his phlegmatic character.

Madge Atkins Kibbee, the plump, placid, sometimes flaccid daughter of Cora and Emerson. Older than Sharon, she is nevertheless her follower, the witness whom Sharon finds necessary to validate her own importance. Although her marriage is not romantic, she fulfills the role of wife and mother comfortably and relatively happily, to Sharon's bafflement.

Orion Atkins, Emerson's brother, who is unlike him. He brings a bride from the Ozarks to the farm, and he prefers hunting to farming. After his wife's death, he brings his two daughters to Cora and Emerson to rear. He has little sense of responsibility and never establishes a close relationship with the daughters. After being gassed in World War I, he suffers ill health for years, becoming more and more remote from his family. Except for his marriage, he is another isolate.

Belle Rooney Atkins, Orion's hillbilly wife. Dark, disheveled, childlike, and feckless, she scandalizes Cora with her haphazard housekeeping, her need for people, and her desire to play. Although Cora does not understand her, she is fascinated by her. Belle dies at Fayrene's birth.

Blanche Kibbee, the oldest daughter of Madge and Ned. Whereas Cora is tall and lean, Blanche is also boneless; whereas Cora's is a relatively empty, limited world, Blanche's is a crowded world of imagination. Hoping to offer Blanche a better life, Sharon takes her to Chicago but soon realizes that she cannot cope with the responsibility. When Blanche returns to Nebraska, her family accepts and rather admires her special qualities.

Caroline Kibbee, another daughter of Madge and Ned. In contrast to Blanche, she is square, brusque, opinionated, and masculine. An accusatory feminist, she startles and dismays Sharon by declaring her the role model for Caroline's generation and by blaming Cora for submitting to the rigors of her life. Sharon feels that Caroline has misunderstood both of them.

Fayrene Atkins Dickel, Sharon's sister, who is reared along with Madge and Sharon but never included in their relationship. She is a true orphan. It is only after her marriage to Avery Dickel, from the Ozarks, that she becomes a successful member of the family group.

Alexandra Selkirk, a tall, beak-nosed, conspicuous older woman whom Sharon meets and with whom she travels on her way back to Nebraska, where Selkirk is to lecture to a feminist conference. In a strange way, she recalls Cora to Sharon. She encourages Sharon to come out to watch a sunrise, thus opening new vistas for her and adding a new refrain to the female voices.

— Helen Winter Stauffer

THE PLANETARIUM
(Le Planétarium)

Author: Nathalie Sarraute (1900-   )
First published: 1959
Genre: Novel

Locale: Unspecified, but probably Paris
Time: Late 1950's
Plot: Psychological realism

Alain Guimiez (ah-LAY[N] gee-MYEHZ), an aspiring young writer, snobbish, insecure, and overly anxious to impress. At twenty-seven years of age, he has not completed his doctoral dissertation or established himself professionally, but he covets the trappings of success. Living in a tiny efficiency apartment, he envies his aunt's five-room apartment in a fashionable neighborhood. When, in a thoughtless moment, his aunt suggests an exchange, Alain first hesitates but soon greedily pictures himself entertaining friends in spacious surroundings. When his wife urges practicality and a teaching position, he sneers at "bourgeois" values and seeks solace from Germaine Lemaire. An established writer, she has praised his work and so flattered him that he has memorized her exact words. When she encourages him, she becomes the standard by which he lives. He acts ashamed of his father in her presence, questions his wife's taste, and even submits his own expertise in art to her approval. Blinded by her aura of superiority, only occasionally he glimpses her need for adulation. In rare moments, he sees her as ordinary, almost vulgar, but he cannot relinquish his faith because of his almost total lack of confidence in himself.

Gisèle Guimiez (zhee-ZEHL), Alain's wife, who clings to her husband but also is still dependent on her mother. Gisèle adores her husband but worries about their future and about Alain's lack of ambition. She tries to keep the peace between Alain and her mother, but sometimes she does not know which of the two to trust. Like Alain, she is concerned about appearances, wants his aunt's apartment for the same reasons, likes expensive antiques for their ability to impress, and is flattered by Germaine Lemaire's interest in her husband.

Aunt Berthe (behrt), Alain's aunt, an elderly, lonely woman obsessed with the details of redecorating her apartment. Until now, her major concern has been whether the oval door she has installed fits in with the rest of the decor. Now, with the apartment itself at stake, she panics, suspecting everyone. Ultimately, however, she fears losing Alain, whom she regards as a son, more than losing the apartment. As she spoiled him as a boy, she yields now, promising him her fortune as well at her death. Abandoned by her husband years earlier, she cannot bear another desertion, another enemy.

Germaine Lemaire (zhehr-MEHN leh-MAYR), an established writer and a Parisian celebrity. With aristocratic mannerisms and a false accent, she tries to replace beauty with style. A queen adored by vassals, she exults in being surrounded by young admirers. Meeting Alain's father, she exercises all of her self-control to hide her insecurity. Not a follower, he looks on her not as a writer but as a woman, and he finds her woefully lacking. In his gaze, she feels ugly and shapeless. When critics describe her work as waxlike, she rereads her favorite passage to restore her confidence. Following such attacks, she acts more imperious than ever, gloating in the power she holds over youth. When Alain accuses another writer of vanity, Germaine proclaims all authors guilty of such excesses, claiming that just such weaknesses account for their uniqueness.

Pierre Guimiez, Alain's father, a widower, proud of having early introduced his son to intellectual pursuits but considering him now led astray by the coddling of his aunt, the frivolity of Gisèle, and the superficiality of Germaine Lemaire. He intercedes with his sister in the matter of the apartment but is ashamed of appearing the villain. When Berthe ensures Alain's future, Pierre is primarily relieved to have the burden of responsibility removed from his shoulders.

— *Elizabeth A. Rubino*

PLANTATION BOY
(Menino de Engenho, Doidinho, *and* Bangüê)

Author: José Lins do Rego (1901-1957)
First published: 1966
Genre: Novel

Locale: Northeastern Brazil
Time: Early twentieth century
Plot: Social realism

Carlos de Mello (MEH-yoh), the protagonist and narrator, whose life in Recife, in the state of Paraíba, Brazil, comes to a sudden end when his father murders his mother in a rage of insanity. Carlos is only four years old when he sees his blood-covered mother dead and his father taken away to an asylum for the insane. He never sees his father again. Only three days later, he leaves the city for his maternal grandfather's sugar plantation in the country, Santa Rosa, where he learns to be a "plantation boy." At the plantation, Carlos learns a new way of life and is initiated into the mysteries of sex at an early age. First, he watches animals procreate, then he experiments with animals himself. He has a precocious relationship with a girl named Judith and develops an abiding interest in masturbation. At the age of twelve, he first has sex with a woman and promptly gets a painful case of syphilis that requires extensive treatment. He is cured in time to go away to boarding school, but he takes with him his morbid fear of death and disease, his deep pessimism, and his nervous nature—all the result of the tragic events in his early years.

Colonel José Paulino Cazuza (hoh-SEH pow-LEE-noh kah-SEW-sah), Carlos' maternal grandfather, owner of the Santa Rosa sugar plantation, which has grown abundantly under his care. A patriarch and plantation owner in the grand old tradition that is now waning, he tries to rear Carlos to follow in his footsteps as a plantation lord.

Juca Cazuza (HEW-kah), Carlos' uncle, who works the plantation for his grandfather. He is a rough and ready man. As the patriarch's son, he does and takes what he wants on the plantation with impunity.

Maria Cazuza, the aunt who reminds Carlos of his mother. She cares for him like a mother until her marriage takes her from the plantation.

Totonha (toh-TOHN-hah), a dried-up old woman who goes from plantation to plantation telling stories from folklore and modified fairy tales. Her stories are always told in verse, from memory. Totonha is a remnant of a disappearing oral tradition and is a tremendous influence on Carlos' imagination.

Sinhàzinha (seen-AH-seen-ah), called **Aunt**, though no blood relationship is clear. She is a stern taskmaster who terrorizes everyone, young and old. She screams to get her way. She once beat Carlos with little provocation; it was the

first time he had been punished physically. She is also capable of mild expressions of affection.

Zé Guedes (seh GWEH-dehs), a trustworthy plantation worker. He escorts Carlos to his reading lessons and gives him many life lessons on the way, including some about sex. He introduces Carlos to the whore with whom Carlos has his first human sexual experience.

Zefa Cajá (SEH-fah kah-HAH), the woman who finally gives in to twelve-year-old Carlos' pleas for sex. He contracts syphilis from her, and she is thrown in jail.

Chico Pereira (CHEE-koh peh-RA-rah), a plantation worker who is falsely accused of impregnating a young girl. The colonel puts him in the stocks to try to force him confess to his crime and marry the girl. After more than twenty-four hours in the stocks, Chico maintains his innocence. The colonel makes the girl tell the name of her victimizer with her hand on the Bible. Fearing for her soul, she confesses that it was Uncle Juca, and Chico is freed.

— Linda Ledford-Miller

PLATERO AND I: An Andalusian Elegy
(Platero y yo)

Author: Juan Ramón Jiménez (1881-1958)
First published: 1914; revised, 1917
Genre: Short fiction

Locale: Andalusia, Spain
Time: Early twentieth century
Plot: Elegy

Platero (plah-TEH-roh), a donkey, whose name roughly means "silver one" in recognition of his color. He is a synthesis of many such donkeys that the author knew. He has many functions in the prose poems, the most basic of which are companion, confidant, and perfect listener. He is presented as a child, an adult, and an animal. The author frequently shares Platero with the children who appear in the poems. At times, Platero is a mere donkey helping another donkey extract a cart that is stuck in the mud; at other times, he is one of the children, kicking up his heels and running around; and at others, he is a gift or toy that the author shares with children.

Darbón (dahr-BOHN), Platero's veterinarian. Descriptions of Darbón are excellent examples of literary caricature. His aged and toothless face becomes the substance of Darbón's appearance.

Don José, (hoh-SEH) **the Priest**, one of the many examples of hypocrites whom the author chastises. A man of the cloth and humble priest in church, at home Don José curses and throws stones at the children and at the poor and hungry people who try to take fruit from his orchard.

Frasco Vélez (FRAHS-koh VEH-lehs), the mayor of the town, a hypocrite like Don José. He uses the power of his office to create subterfuges that allow him to smuggle agave and fig brandy into town. Such is the case of his proclamation that unmuzzled dogs found walking the streets will be shot. This alludes to the presence in the area of rabid dogs, something that would keep people off the streets and out of the way while Vélez smuggles his goods.

Antonia (ahn-TOH-nee-ah), who is typical of the many children who interact with Platero. Dressed in her best Sunday clothing, Antonia looks for a place to cross a rain-swollen

stream. The author offers her Platero. Although initially hesitant, Antonia mounts the donkey and crosses the stream. Platero is as pleased with the experience as Antonia is with reaching the other side.

Lipiani (lee-pee-AH-nee), the schoolteacher, who enjoys taking his students on short trips into the countryside because, on these outings, he demands and gets half of each student's lunch for himself, and thus saves money on his own food.

Anilla la Manteca (ah-NEE-yah lah mahn-TEH-kah), one of the adults who enjoys playing children's games. She loves to dress up in a sheet, put white makeup on her face, and frighten the children for fun. Dressed that way, she is killed one night by a bolt of lightning.

Judas, more a custom than a specific character. The townspeople hang Judas in effigy during Holy Week for his treason to Christ. In fact, they hang many throughout the streets and then fire on them with their shotguns on Holy Saturday. The author relates that the Judas (traitor) of his time is the politician, teacher, lawyer, tax collector, mayor, or anyone else that the people hate, on whom they vent their anger in this absurd ritual.

Three old Gypsy women, One is blind; the other two are taking her to a doctor. Old, dirty, and poorly clothed, they are the nameless poor for whom society has no use. The little daughter of the charcoal vendor is drawn from the same rugged poverty. One character, "**She**," is nothing more than a blond head veiled in black that the author sees through the window of a passing train. Others are shepherds or wounded hunters, all from the poor side of life that previously had been absent from the author's writings.

— Joseph A. Feustle, Jr.

PLATITUDES

Author: Trey Ellis (1962-   )
First published: 1988
Genre: Novel

Locale: New York City and rural Georgia
Time: The mid-1980's and the 1930's
Plot: Satire

Dewayne Wellington, a recently divorced, depressed, middle-aged black writer who creates the story of Earle and Dorothy, which he calls *Platitudes*. During a correspondence with feminist author Isshee Ayam, Dewayne comes to a new self-awareness of his own ability as a writer and his attractiveness as a man, reflected in the increasing depth and sensitivity of the characters in his story. His final romantic meeting with Isshee restores his confidence in happy endings in both life and art.

Isshee Ayam, a successful middle-aged black feminist writer who criticizes Dewayne's work in progress as sexist and as being out of touch with black folk tradition. She offers Dewayne her own version of the story of Earle and Dorothy, set in the 1930's in rural Lowndes County, Georgia. Her story celebrates the clean, healthy lives of simple country folk whose sexual relations are based on the equality of men and women. Scornful of Dewayne's ability at first, Isshee comes to respect his writing and his views on romantic relationships.

Earle Tyner, the protagonist of Dewayne's story, a pudgy, awkward, and romantic sixteen-year-old middle-class black boy who acquires confidence and maturity through the course of a love affair with Dorothy LaMont. The story of his relationship with Dorothy parallels that of Dewayne and Isshee. A computer nerd excluded from the social life of the popular students at his private high school, Earle dreams that someday a beautiful girl will see past his unattractive appearance to the intelligent, sensitive, and romantic person underneath. Earle is a member of an unofficial group of computer buffs, "Trinary," along with his friends Donald and Andy.

Dorothy Lamont, a young waitress at her mother's Harlem diner. She attends St. Rita's Catholic school, where she is at the center of the popular social crowd. She cultivates a friendship with Earle that grows into a satisfying romantic relationship.

Darcelle Lamont, Dorothy's mother and owner of a Harlem diner specializing in country-style black cooking. She befriends Earle and helps to bring him together with Dorothy.

Janey Rosebloom, a pretty, white, socially popular friend of Dorothy and a schoolmate of Earle at Friends Academy. Initially, she looks down on Earle as a computer nerd and ridicules him with her friends. After learning to appreciate his kindness and intelligence, she has a sexual encounter with him during a bout of depression stemming from problems in her love life.

Captain Nat Mee, a New York City police precinct captain prominent in Harlem politics. He dates Earle's mother. As president of the Jean Toomer Democratic Club, he gets Earle a job registering voters. He later accuses the black candidate for mayor, Al Robinson, of misusing campaign funds.

Stevie, the elderly janitor and caretaker at the Jean Toomer Democratic Club. He shows Earle around and explains to him why it is important to support Al Robinson for mayor if they want the city to keep its promises to African Americans.

Richard, an elegant and rich white male model who tries to seduce Dorothy at a party. Earle catches him in bed with Dorothy.

— *Erik D. Curren*

PLAY IT AS IT LAYS

Author: Joan Didion (1934-   )
First published: 1970
Genre: Novel

Locale: Southern California and Las Vegas
Time: Late 1960's
Plot: Black humor

Maria Wyeth, an unemployed actress. She is an attractive woman in her thirties who desperately seeks love and stability, which are frustrated by the vicissitudes of her life. Separated from her husband, lovers, friends, and child, Maria consents to an abortion and then spends most of her time aimlessly driving the Los Angeles freeways. Events of the novel open after she has been committed to a sanatorium for failure to intervene in a friend's suicide. Maria, for all of her failings, is an existential heroine who comes to understand the full impact of nothingness in human existence.

Carter Lang, Maria's estranged director husband. Carter is a reasonably successful director but by no means a major influence in the film industry. Exasperated by Maria's erratic behavior, Carter leaves her but remains in touch and prevails on her to seek an abortion. A man impatient with weakness and failure and given to striking his wife and other women,

Carter seeks a rapprochement but continues to have affairs with other women.

BZ, Carter's producer and Maria's one friend. BZ is a homosexual trapped in a loveless marriage, which he cannot escape because his mother has made it financially difficult to do so. Despite all of their differences, BZ and Maria have arrived at the same psychological point but seek different solutions to their problems. BZ's despondency is so great that he eventually dies in Maria's arms of a drug overdose.

Helene, BZ's wife. Long-haired and attractive, Helene has been divorced twice and is a vicious rumor monger. Vain and self-centered, she enjoys masochism and various affairs, among them one with Carter. Although she blames Maria's selfishness for BZ's death, she is, ironically, one of the most self-centered characters in a novel rich in self-absorption.

Ivan Costello, Maria's last lover before her marriage to Carter. Adamant and manipulative, Costello is an intemperate, unsympathetic sadist who continually attempts to insinuate himself into Maria's broken life.

Les Goodwin, a married screenwriter who has a brief tryst with Maria and who is most likely the father of the aborted child. Although he is the subject of many of Maria's thoughts, he has no intention of marrying her.

Johnny Waters, a self-important young actor. After meeting him at a party, Maria sleeps with him and then steals his Ferrari and drives to Tonopah, Nevada, where she is arrested.

Freddy Chaikin, Maria's agent. After avoiding her calls, he arranges an interview for her to act in a motorcycle film and promises possible parts on television. Chaikin is instrumental in smoothing over the complications attendant to the theft of Waters' car.

Benny Austin, Maria's godfather and a business partner with her late father. Short, frail, and bald, Austin is an inveterate gambler who lives life as though it were a series of wagers at a gaming table. He is well-meaning, though irresponsible, giving Maria a false telephone number and a post office box for his address.

Kate Lang, Maria and Carter's four-year-old brain-damaged child. Deaf and mute, she is a child beyond affection or communication; nevertheless, she is Maria's single object of love and desire. Although Kate is institutionalized like her mother, Maria hopes that one day the two will be united and live in a house by the ocean.

— David W. Madden

THE PLAYBOY OF THE WESTERN WORLD

Author: John Millington Synge (1871-1909)
First published: 1907
Genre: Drama

Locale: County Mayo, Ireland
Time: Early twentieth century
Plot: Comic realism

Christopher (Christy) Mahon, the playboy of the Western World. Arriving one evening in a village on the wild coast of County Mayo, cold, tired, and hungry, he captures the imagination of the people when he tells them how he split the skull of his harsh, unimaginative old father with a loy. Timid no longer, the young man outleaps and outruns his competitors during the rigorous village sports. His reputation for bravery is tarnished, however, when his father, with a bandaged head, arrives in town. When the athletic young man attacks his father a second time, he barely escapes hanging. Even Pegeen deserts him. Like the others, she is afraid to get involved in a murder so close to home. Disgusted with the villagers, he is determined to be a playboy somewhere else.

Margaret Flaherty (Pegeen Mike), the wild, sharp-tongued daughter of publican Flaherty. Enraptured by the poetic utterances and valor of young Christy, she resists the blandishments of Shawn Keogh, her cousin whom she is to marry. After hearing of Christy's brave attack on his father and seeing his prowess on the playing field, she thinks Shawn too cowardly for her taste. She is ready to betray Christy, however, when he attacks his father again.

Widow Quin, a scheming young woman of about thirty. Hearing of the arrival of the brave young stranger, she tries to coax him away from Pegeen Mike, but to no avail. In spite of her cajolery, he is determined to remain near Pegeen. Meeting the elder Mahon in the tavern, the widow tries to send him on a wild-goose chase. Afraid the two will fight, she tells the old man that his son has left the village.

Michael James Flaherty, a fat, jovial innkeeper and the tippling father of Pegeen Mike. He is one of the drunkest men at Kate Cassidy's wake. When Christy and Pegeen tell him they intend to marry, he puts up a violent objection. He has qualms about having as a son-in-law a young man who killed his own father. Finally, however, he agrees to the wedding.

Old Mahon, a crusty, hard-bitten old squatter, Christy's father. Seemingly indestructible, he survives several painful beatings. A lesser man would have died from such repeated blows. In spite of his aching head, he advances threateningly on his young son in the tavern. Seizing a loy, Christy again batters his tough father to the floor. Rather glad that the boy has lost his timidity, the old man smilingly offers to take his son home with him.

Shawn Keogh, a cowardly young man, Pegeen's future husband. Afraid to fight Christy, he offers him numerous gifts if young Mahon will leave the village. Shawn knows that he is in danger of losing Pegeen to the stranger. In desperation, he even attempts to enlist the aid of Widow Quin, unaware of her hopes to win Christy for herself.

Jimmy Farrell, a small farmer, fat, amorous, and about forty-five years old. He is Michael Flaherty's drinking companion.

Philly Cullen, a thin and mistrusting small farmer, the exact opposite of Farrell.

Sara Tansey,

Susan Brady, and

Honor Blake, girls of the village. After hearing of Christy's arrival in the town, they rush to the inn and ask him to tell the story of how he split his father's skull. This single act has lifted the young man to a hero's level.

PLENTY

Author: David Hare (1947-   )
First published: 1978
Genre: Drama

Locale: St. Benoit, France; London and Blackpool, England; and Brussels, Belgium
Time: 1943-1962
Plot: Social

Susan Traherne, the central character of the drama, who is profoundly frustrated in her attempt to find personal and professional fulfillment in postwar England. At the age of seventeen, she served as a Special Operations Executive Courier, working with the French Resistance against the occupying Germans in 1943. After the war, she regards the future with hope and optimism but finds only frustration and boredom. Her life peaks emotionally when she meets a British agent, known only as Codename Lazar, under dangerous circumstances in France. She is courted by Raymond Brock, a career diplomat who loves her, and by a working-class lover named Mick, with whom she attempts, without success, to have a child. After she suffers a nervous breakdown, Brock marries her and attempts to care for her. Always restless and unpredictable, Susan manages to ruin Brock's career, then deserts him. Although her motives are ambiguous, Susan is meant to be a sympathetic character.

Raymond Brock, a career diplomat, forty-one years old in 1962, who first meets Susan in Brussels in 1947 and agrees to help her through a difficult situation when the married man with whom she is traveling dies of a heart attack. Brock later courts her in London and marries her after an explosive situation that results in her nervous breakdown. Brock is described as delightfully ingenuous, a man whose natural humor is eroded by years of dull, bureaucratic service at the Foreign Office, where mediocrity is valued and rewarded.

Alice Park, Susan's friend and flat mate after the war, a would-be writer, bohemian, and nonconformist. She later becomes a teacher, then a social worker, founding a home for unwed mothers. She is sprightly, optimistic, witty, and slightly younger than Susan.

Sir Leonard Darwin, a career diplomat and Brock's superior in Brussels in 1947. He distinguished himself in Djakarta. In scene 7 (October, 1956), he is disturbed because his superiors did not inform him of their policy regarding the Suez Canal. A man of high principles and old-fashioned values, he resigns in protest. When he later dies, his funeral brings Brock and Susan back to London from their post in Iran.

Codename Lazar, the man Susan meets in France in 1943 while on a military mission. They meet again years later at a shabby hotel in the seaside resort of Blackpool in 1962. Like Susan, he wants "some sort of edge" to the life he leads but has not found it in peacetime Britain. Instead, he has become a corporate bureaucrat, with a wife and a home in the suburbs. He is Susan's male counterpart.

Mick, Susan's working-class friend, whom she chooses to be the father of her child. He falls in love with her, but when he is unable to make her pregnant, she humiliates and rejects him, brutally and violently.

Sir Andrew Charleson, a man in his early fifties, the head of personnel at the Foreign Office. A cold, calculating, and ruthless man, he explains to Susan that manners and tact, not intelligence, ensure success and promotion. After he explains that "behavior is all," she threatens suicide if her husband is not advanced. Sir Andrew responds by forcing Brock into early retirement.

Dorcas Frey, a tall, heavily built seventeen-year-old blonde who attends Darwin's funeral with Susan, Alice, and Brock in 1961. Alice teaches history to her at the Kensington Academy. She desires an abortion and asks Susan for money.

Louise, a teenager from Liverpool who poses nude for Alice in 1952, when Alice is attempting to become an artist, in the scene in which Susan shoots at the rejected Mick.

M. Wong, a short, "permanently smiling" sycophantic Burmese diplomat whose obsequious manner and imperfect English create humor during the banquet the night Darwin decides to resign from the foreign service over the Suez crisis. Privately, Darwin calls him an "appalling wog."

Mme Wong, as much a caricature as her husband, who attempts to socialize by summarizing the plot of one of Ingmar Bergman's films, though she is confused about Bergman's nationality.

John Begley, a twenty-two-year-old functionary at the Foreign Office, with impeccable manners.

— *James Michael Welsh*

THE PLOUGH AND THE STARS

Author: Sean O'Casey (John Casey, 1880-1964)
First published: 1926
Genre: Drama

Locale: Dublin, Ireland
Time: 1916
Plot: Social realism

Nora Clitheroe, an Irish woman whose husband is a member of the Citizen Army. She nearly loses her sanity when he goes off to fight on the barricades and is killed.

Jack Clitheroe, Nora's husband, an Irish patriot who is killed in the fighting.

Peter Flynn, Nora's uncle, a rather pathetic, ineffectual man whose patriotism is stirred by the oratory he hears.

Fluther Good, one of the tenement dwellers. He is given to heavy drinking but makes himself generally helpful to his neighbors.

Mrs. Gogan, a neighborhood woman who engages in a barroom brawl with Bessie Burgess and disapproves of Nora buying so many new clothes.

Mollser Gogan, the small daughter of Mrs. Gogan. She dies of tuberculosis and is buried in a coffin shared with Nora's stillborn child.

Bessie Burgess, one of the tenement women. She is coarse and vigorous.

The Covey, Nora's cousin, who is the purveyor of the author's views concerning the poverty of the Irish and the problem of their independence.

Captain Brennan, an officer in the Irish Citizen Army and a comrade in arms of Jack Clitheroe.

Corporal Stoddart, an English soldier who escorts the coffin of Mollser Gogan and Nora's child.

Sergeant Tinley, of the Wiltshires.

PLUM BUN

Author: Jessie Redmon Fauset (1882-1961)
First published: 1928
Genre: Novel

Locale: Philadelphia and New York City
Time: 1900 to the 1920's
Plot: Social realism

Angela Murray or **Angèle Mory**, an art student struggling to survive in the art world. The most important fact in the life of this attractive, ambitious, and idealistic young protagonist is that she can "pass" as white, although she is approximately three-quarters black. The story follows her career from late childhood in a black ghetto in Philadelphia to relative success in the artistic world of New York City in her late twenties. By that time, she is fully accepted as white and seems well on her way to professional and financial success. Wealthy white men court her. She has made great sacrifices to attain her position: She already has been the mistress of one rich white man and has further sacrificed her moral principles by alienating herself from her younger sister, who has dark skin and would be unacceptable in the racist circles in which Angela moves. Eventually, Angela realizes that the advantages of being white are not worth the humiliation of having to lie to everyone she knows, both black and white. She publicly acknowledges her mixed blood and accepts the consequences.

Virginia (Jinny) Murray, Angela's younger sister, a music teacher. This talented, refined, sweet-tempered girl aspires to social and financial advancement like her sister but has neither the desire nor the opportunity to enter the white world. Consequently, when she follows Angela to New York, she enters the world of black artists and intellectuals active in the Harlem Renaissance; she is happy and comfortable in this world. It is mainly Jinny's example that makes Angela realize she has made a mistake in living a life of deceit and denial of her own people.

Roger Fielding, a rich white playboy. This selfish, worldly young New Yorker falls in love with Angela, whom he takes to be white, but will not marry her because his father insists on his marrying a debutante. Instead, Roger persuades Angela to become his kept mistress. The relationship deteriorates after he loses respect for her and tires of domesticity. He has a strong influence on her development. Some of his sophistica-

tion rubs off on her and enables her to move with ease in higher social circles; however, he makes her realize that true love is what she craves and what is missing in her life of deceit.

Anthony Cross, a talented portrait painter. This handsome, passionate young South American is also hiding the fact that he is a mulatto. He loves Angela but shuns her because he believes that she is pure white and would be appalled if she knew the truth about his ethnicity. He becomes involved with Jinny, which causes Angela great distress: She has realized too late that she loves Anthony and now cannot bring herself to try to win him away from her own beloved sister. Anthony serves as another example of the pain and futility involved in denying one's true racial identity. Eventually, matters resolve themselves satisfactorily when Jinny marries another man and Anthony is free to follow Angela to Paris.

Ralph Ashley, a shy, introverted young white man who falls in love with Angela and tries to persuade her to marry him after her breakup with Roger Fielding. Even though Angela does not love Ashley, she nearly accepts his proposal because of the comforts and security he can offer, an indication of how her values have been eroded by her life of deceit.

Rachel Powell, a young black woman, a fellow art student and friend of Angela. The climax of the novel comes when Rachel is denied passage to Europe on an art scholarship because she is black. Angela, outraged, publicly announces her own racial identity and abandons her life of lies.

Junius Murray and
Mattie Murray, the parents of Angela and Virginia. They die early in the novel. The father has very dark skin, but the mother can pass as white and first gives Angela the idea of doing this on a permanent basis.

— Bill Delaney

THE PLUM PLUM PICKERS

Author: Raymond Barrio (1921-   )
First published: 1969
Genre: Novel

Locale: The Santa Clara Valley, California
Time: The 1960's
Plot: Social realism

Manuel Gutierrez (gew-tee-EH-rrehs), a Chicano farmworker from Texas. Seeking to assert his Mexican heritage and its celebration of the land's potential, Manuel struggles to define himself through the value of his work. He is not ashamed of physical labor, viewing himself as the crucial link between the ripening plums that either will provide sustaining nutrition or, left unattended, will fall to the ground and rot. Unconvinced by the rhetoric of the growers that the conditions of his life are steadily improving and that he will someday reap the benefits of his labor, Manuel clings to his integrity of self-identity, even when he is reduced to the status of a caged animal.

Lupe Gutierrez (LEW-pay), Manuel's wife and the mother of his three children. She cleans their tiny shack on the compound, obsessed with providing the best possible conditions for the children's health. Although she realizes the ever-present threat of agricultural accidents and the narrowness of her children's lives, she keeps hoping to escape the probable destiny of her children of following their father into farm labor.

Ramiro Sanchez (rah-MEE-roh SAHN-chehz), a mestizo who urges the crews to claim their independence from the abuse of the growers. Cynical toward any particular ideological salvation, Ramiro pieces together various bits of revolutionary ideas while vociferously protesting any denigration of his crew or himself. He sees himself as heir to Mexico's revolutionary heritage. His strength and courage rest in his image of himself as Tenochtitlán, a god reborn to lead his people into salvation.

Frederick Y. Turner, the owner of the Western Grande migrant compound. Turner believes he is the triumph of American business and the embodiment of the self-made man. He has lied so much that he has come to believe his own lies. Eccentric in his hobbies and brash in his political manipulations, Turner has lost any recognition of the humanity of the migrants who make him rich.

Morton J. Quill, the Anglo manager of the Western Grande compound. Caught between his self-loathing and his fantastic projections of power, Quill opens the novel in fear of being attacked and closes it with his lynched corpse dangling from a tree. He never seems to grasp the fake realities that Turner constructs all around him, including that of his own importance.

Jim Schroeder, a local Anglo nursery owner. Defiant of Turner's ruthless attitude and disgusted by his exploitation, Schroeder supports the workers in their quest for labor reforms. He works beside his farmworkers, whom he pays a fair wage. Not fearful of physical work, he embodies the pastoral ideal struggling to survive in an environment of corporate indifference.

THE PLUMED SERPENT

Author: D. H. Lawrence (1885-1930)
First published: 1926
Genre: Novel

Locale: Mexico
Time: The twentieth century
Plot: Psychological realism

Don Ramón Carrasco (rah-MOHN kah-RRAHS-koh), a landowner and scholar who is convinced that only the revival of primitive religion can save Mexico. He establishes at his hacienda a meeting place for cultists who worship Quetzalcoatl, the Plumed Serpent. He is denounced by the church and is seriously wounded when his political and religious enemies attack him. Finally, having desecrated the church at Sayula by burning the holy images, he converts it into a sanctuary of the ancient Aztec gods.

Kate Leslie, the widow of an Irish patriot. Because she is restless, she goes to Mexico, where she meets Ramón and his followers, saves Ramón's life when he is attacked by his opponents, and falls in love with Cipriano. A product of a culture dominated by technology, she finds strange the masculine, atavistic culture of Mexico. Her woman's will is no match for the dark primitivism of this savage land. She marries Cipriano in a pagan ceremony conducted by Ramón. Although she wants to return to Ireland, she is impelled to stay with her husband in Mexico.

General Cipriano Viedma (see-pree-AH-noh vee-EHD-mah), a full-blooded Indian who joins Ramón to revive the ancestral gods. He comes to believe that he is a reincarnation of Huitzilopochtli, the Aztec god of war. Kate is unaccountably drawn to him and at last yields to his masculine dominance.

Doña Carlota (kahr-LOH-tah), Ramón's first wife, a devout Christian who refuses to countenance his heresies. She leaves her husband and goes to Mexico City. Returning to Sayula when Ramón opens the church there as a pagan temple, she protests her husband's blasphemy. Overcome by hysteria, she suffers a stroke and soon dies.

Owen Rhys, Kate's American cousin, who accompanies her to Mexico. He returns to the United States prior to the time Kate becomes embroiled in the ancient god movement at Sayula.

Teresa (teh-REH-sah), Ramón's second wife, the daughter of a local landowner who is deceased. Her manner toward Ramón is passive and submissive.

Mrs. Norris, the widow of a former British ambassador. She invites Kate to tea. It is at her house that Kate meets Don Ramón.

Juana (HWAHN-ah), a servant at the house Kate rents in Sayula.

PLUTUS
(Ploutos)

Author: Aristophanes (c. 450-c. 385 B.C.E.)
First performed: 388 B.C.E.
Genre: Drama

Locale: Athens
Time: The fifth century B.C.E.
Plot: Satire

Chremylus (KREH-mih-luhs), an old Athenian husbandman. Poor but honest, he has consulted the Delphic Oracle to determine whether his only son should be taught virtuous ways or the knavery and double-dealing by which successful men acquire their wealth. The god tells him to follow the first person he meets after leaving the temple. He does so, even though that person is a blind and wretched beggar. When this unfortunate reveals himself as Plutus, Chremylus conceives the idea of restoring his sight so that the God of Wealth can

distinguish between the just and the unjust. Chremylus is a simple, friendly fellow, unselfish enough to invite his neighbors to share his good fortune, but he also admits that he loves money, and he loses no time in converting the divine favor he has won into hard cash and luxuries. Like all the playwright's comic protagonists, he roundly condemns the evils of Athenian society and lashes out particularly against informers, grafters, and voluptuaries.

Cario (KAR-ee-oh), Chremylus' slave. He is a broadly

comic figure, well aware of his master's shortcomings, wryly stoical about his own lot in life, and sometimes impertinent. He is perhaps at his best in describing a night in the Temple of Aesculapius, when he had pretended to be one of the holy serpents so that he could filch some pap from an old woman.

Plutus (PLEW-tuhs), the God of Wealth. Because he had said that he would favor only the wise, the just, and the virtuous, Zeus, jealous of humankind, had taken away his eyesight so that he would be unable to tell good men from bad. He has wandered in rags, ill treated by those he benefited and, because of his fear of Zeus's anger, unwilling to have his vision restored. Chremylus convinces him that he is the source of all power, even the power of Zeus. Plutus thus accompanies Chremylus to the Temple of Aesculapius, is there cured, and afterward rewards the just and reduces the unjust to the penury they deserve.

Blepsidemus (blehp-SIH-deh-muhs), a friend who helps Chremylus to convince Plutus of his rightful place in the order of things.

Poverty, who protests that a great injustice has been done her through the rehabilitation of Plutus, as she will be banished from the land. She argues that she is the source of the public weal: Through her, artisans work, men stay fit, and politicians remain uncorrupted. Chremylus rejects her arguments because he knows the horrors that poverty can bring.

A Just Man, who brings his outworn clothes, evidence of his former wretchedness, to dedicate to Plutus.

An Informer, who accuses Chremylus of stealing his money. He is driven off by Chremylus and the Just Man.

An Old Woman, who protests that her young lover, who no longer needs her bounty, has deserted her. When she joins the celebration of the god's installation, however, Chremylus promises that her lover will be restored to her.

A Youth, formerly the Old Woman's lover.

Hermes (HUR-meez), a messenger of the gods. He complains that neither he nor the other gods are receiving sacrifices because men now realize that before Plutus' ascendancy the Olympians had governed poorly. He applies for a place in Chremylus' new establishment and is put to work by Cario washing the entrails of the sacrificial victims.

A Priest of Zeus, who also comes to seek service with Plutus, now Lord of the Universe.

PNIN

Author: Vladimir Nabokov (1899-1977)
First published: 1957
Genre: Novel

Locale: Waindell College, in New England, and a nearby mountain resort
Time: 1950-1955
Plot: Philosophical realism

Timofey Pavlovich Pnin (tih-moh-FAY PAV-loh-vihch pnihn), the protagonist, fifty-two years old in 1950, a Russian emigrant who teaches Russian language and literature at Waindell College. Bald and thick in the neck, he has a powerful torso but spindly legs. Because of his difficulties adjusting to American culture and the English language, Pnin often appears awkward and bungling, yet among his fellow émigrés, when speaking Russian, he is shown to be adroit and even erudite. Pnin is perpetually in search of "discreteness," a safe haven where he can feel insulated from both the horrible memories of his past and from the people who mock him and intrude on his privacy. Most prominent among these intruders is the narrator of the book. Pnin experiences several attacks, probably heart attacks, throughout the story. At the time of these attacks, he experiences a loss of discreteness and a feeling of melting into his surroundings and approaching death.

Vladimir Vladimirovich Nabokov (vlah-dih-MIH-rohvihch nah-BOH-kov), the narrator of the book, a front man for the author, who lends him his name and persona. He portrays himself as Pnin's friend but reveals, obliquely, that he has seduced Pnin's wife-to-be, Liza, and has meddled in his private life on other occasions. The action of the book shows how he pursues Pnin, attempting to capture images of him and transmogrify them in his fiction. His role in the book becomes more obvious as the story progresses, until, in the final chapter, he has become almost the central character. He arrives at Waindell College to replace Pnin as professor of Russian there and, in effect, to chase him out of the novel. Nabokov, an arrogant and heartless man who is dimly aware of his meretriciousness and dimly guilty about the way he has manipulated Pnin in his fiction, represents the morally tainted artist that figures prominently in many of the actual author's works.

Dr. Liza Wind, née **Bogolepov** (boh-goh-LEH-pov), Pnin's former wife, a morally bankrupt character who writes bad poetry, engages in wild Freudian psychological speculations, and frequently exchanges lovers and husbands.

Dr. Eric Wind, a onetime husband of Liza, also a psychologist, and a blockhead. The Wind couple is the focus for the author's vehement and hilarious sarcasm aimed at Freudian psychology as practiced in the 1950's.

Victor Wind, the fourteen-year-old son of Eric and Liza Wind, a young artist (painter) who demonstrates a genuine talent alien to his parents. He is used in the novel to demonstrate that individual creative genius is incompatible with the pet theories of modern psychotherapy. Victor is sort of an adopted son of Pnin.

Laurence G. Clements, the most erudite and arrogant of the Waindell professors. His most popular course is The Philosophy of Gesture. Pnin lodges for a time with Clements and his wife, Joan.

Jack Cockerell, the head of the English department. He is famous for his imitations of Pnin. By the end of the book, it is apparent that his obsession with mimicking Pnin has made him into a mirror image of the man he mocks.

Herman Hagen, the head of the German department, a patron and protector of Pnin who has to inform him that he is to be fired from Waindell.

Oleg Komarov (koh-MAH-rov), a fellow émigré but enemy of Pnin. This painter is another example of the morally tainted artist. He teaches at Waindell in the Fine Arts department.

Mira Belochkin (BEH-loch-kihn), Pnin's adolescent love. She dies during World War II in a German concentration camp. Pnin cannot bear to imagine the horrors surrounding her death.

Professor Chateau,
Professor Bolotov,
Varvara Bolotov, and
Al Cook, all Russian emigrants, friends of Pnin.

Tristram W. Thomas and
Thomas Wynn, professors of anthropology and ornithology, respectively. Pnin confuses these two men and invites one of them to his party, assuming that it is the other. This "twinning" of characters is a theme of the novel as a whole, which demonstrates that everyone is, in some way, a mirror image of everyone else.

— *Robert Bowie*

POCHO

Author: José Antonio Villarreal (1924-   )
First published: 1959
Genre: Novel

Locale: Santa Clara, California
Time: 1923-1942
Plot: Bildungsroman

Richard Rubio (RREW-bee-oh), a young man of Mexican heritage who, while growing up in the farmlands of California, aspires to be a writer. The only son of a disillusioned soldier of the Mexican Revolution who is in exile as a nomadic day laborer, he is indulged by his doting mother, eight sisters, and proud father. He is ridiculed by playmates as a "dirty Mexican" and forced by his father to accept a challenge to fight in defense of his male dignity and national pride. Richard is not a typical boy; his is a sensitive, observant, contemplative, and questioning mind that finds escape from shame, and shelter from violence and crudity, in books. When his father abandons his family for a young Mexican woman, Richard becomes the head of the household. He chooses, in self-defense, to throw off this responsibility. Only by enlisting in the Navy and heading into the unknown of World War II can he escape his mother's clutches and the captivity of her insular world. *Pocho* stands as eloquent testimony to Richard's successful escape, on the wings of language, from the poverty, lack of education, cultural oppression, and social injustices that pervade the world into which he was born.

Juan Manuel Rubio (hwahn mahn-WEHL), a fiercely passionate patriot in the Mexican Revolution who settles into family life as a migrant worker in the United States during the Depression. In his role as a soldier at the beginning of the novel, Juan is a cold, ruthless killer whose only real sentiment is dedicated to his worship of Pancho Villa and the cause of the Mexican Revolution. After the assassination of Villa, Juan escapes criminal prosecution by flight across the Rio Grande. Settled with his family in Santa Clara, California, he seems a different man, hardworking, loyal, and generous. The one aspect of his personality that remains unaltered is his fierce attachment to his native land and his intention to return. So powerful is this intention that he cannot bear seeing his family assimilate American culture, and he abandons them.

Consuelo Rubio (kohn-SWEH-loh), Juan's submissive wife and Richard's doting mother. Consuelo experiences twelve pregnancies by the age of thirty-four; she is very much a product of male-dominated Mexican tradition. In her years in America, however, she absorbs new attitudes. She finds that she does not have to acquiesce to physical abuse, and she learns that she can enjoy sexuality, not just suffer it. Although Consuelo is far from "liberated" by her discoveries, she does become more possessive of her husband and more assertive of her own needs. Refusing to get a divorce from her husband when he abandons her is consistent with her religious tenets, but it is also an act of defiance and independence.

João Pedro Manõel Alves, a forty-year-old Portuguese aristocrat. Known familiarly as **Joe Pete Manõel**, this older man is a teacher and fellow poet to the child Richard. Through him, Richard learns much of other places, other social classes, and other lifestyles. To the town's horror, however, it seems that Joe Peter Manõel has abused a twelve-year-old girl, Genevieve Frietas. Her pregnancy and Joe Pete Manõel's commitment to an asylum leave Richard shocked and disillusioned.

Richard (Ricky) Malatesta (mah-lah-TEHS-tah), a schoolmate of Richard who appears fearless and destined for great social success. Richard claims him as his best friend. Ricky is revealed as shallow, materialistic, and generally conventional as he matures, and he and Richard grow apart.

Zelda, the tough female leader of the neighborhood gang of boys. At puberty, the aggressive, battling tomboy becomes the sexual property of the males she has terrorized. Richard claims her as his steady girlfriend and commits her to sharing her sexual favors exclusively with him.

Mary Madison, a Protestant schoolgirl. Three years younger than Richard, she befriends him and shares his enthusiasm for writing. Although her family is moving away, she declares that she intends to marry him.

Marla Jamison, the daughter of the owner of a pear farm. Admired for her courage in the face of defiant laborers, the older Marla becomes a mentor for Richard, encouraging his interest in reading by sharing her interests and her library with him.

POEM OF THE CID
(Cantar de mío Cid)

Author: Unknown
First published: Early thirteenth century
Genre: Poetry

Locale: The fief of Bivar, north of Burgos, Spain
Time: c. 1075
Plot: Epic

The Cid (seed), or **Ruy Díaz** (rrewee DEE-ahs), the lord of Bivar. Banished from Christian Spain by Alfonso VI of Castile, he enters, with a company of his vassals, on a series of heroic exploits designed to impress the king and cause him to revoke the edict of banishment. The royal favor is finally won, but only after the Cid becomes powerful enough to be a threat to the throne. A period of happiness and peace lasts until the Cid is forced to subdue his treacherous sons-in-law, Diego and Fernando, princes of Carrion. When the princes are banished, the Cid is free to marry his daughters to the rulers of Aragón and Navarre. He rejoices to count among his family two kings of Spain, and he finally dies in peace as lord of Valencia.

Alfonso VI (ahl-FOHN-soh), the king of León. He banishes the Cid from Christian Spain, then reinstates the hero when his growing power becomes a threat to the throne.

Doña Elvira (ehl-VEE-rah) and

Doña Sol (sohl), the Cid's daughters, who are married to Diego and Fernando, princes of Carrion, by whom the noble ladies are robbed and beaten. They are finally married to the kings of Aragón and Navarre.

Diego (dee-A-goh) and

Fernando González (fehr-NAHN-doh gohn-SAH-lehs), princes of Carrion and the Cid's cowardly sons-in-law. Resentful of the scorn heaped on them by the Cid's vassals, they seek revenge on their lord by ostensibly taking his daughters on a triumphant tour to Carrion. On the way, they beat and rob the ladies and leave them for dead. For this deed, the princes are stripped of property and honor.

Doña Ximena (hee-MEHN-ah), the Cid's wife.

Martín Antolínez (mahr-TEEN ahn-toh-LEE-nehs), a lieutenant to the Cid.

Minaya Alvar Fáñez (mee-NI-yah AHL-vahr FAHN-yehs), the Cid's chief lieutenant and friend, who is the liaison between his banished lord and Alfonso VI.

Félix Muñoz (FEH-leeks mewn-YOHS), the Cid's nephew, who rescues his uncle's daughters after they are robbed and beaten by their husbands.

Ramón (rrah-MOHN), the count of Barcelona, who is subdued and taken prisoner by the Cid.

Bucar (BEW-kahr), the king of Morocco.

Gonzalo Ansúrez (gohn-SAH-loyh ahn-SEW-rehs), the count of Carrión and the father of Diego and Fernando González.

García Ordóñez (gahr-SEE-ah ohr-DOHN-yehs), the lord of Grañón, who is the Cid's enemy.

Raquel (rrah-KEHL) and

Vidas (VEE-dahs), moneylenders who are swindled by the Cid, after his banishment, in an effort to finance his force of loyal vassals.

POINT COUNTER POINT

Author: Aldous Huxley (1894-1963)
First published: 1928
Genre: Novel

Locale: England
Time: The 1920's
Plot: Social realism

Walter Bidlake, a literary critic in London. An essentially weak and confused man, he is unhappy in his extramarital relationship with Marjorie Carling and seeks some kind of better realization in an affair with Lucy Tantamount. The author regards Walter as an example of the emptiness of the intellectual life unsupported by sound instinctual expression.

Marjorie Carling, Walter's unhappy mistress. She has left Carling because of his perversion and yet behaves with Walter, to all effects and purposes, like a nagging wife rather than a cheering companion. Fearful of her pregnancy, she drives Walter from her. Marjorie has difficulty reconciling the needs of her body and of her soul.

Philip Quarles, a writer and diarist. He is the prime example in the novel of a man who understands everything and feels nothing. He has an encyclopedic mind and seldom fails to develop a topic in a startling way.

Mrs. Bidlake, the mother of Walter and Elinor Quarles. She is a gentle and aesthetic elderly woman who is unable to aid any of her children with their personal problems.

John Bidlake, Walter's father. Bidlake, once a successful artist and amorist, is horrified by the decline of his artistic powers and by the onset of disease. He represents the shortcomings of irresponsible sensuality.

Hilda Tantamount, a successful London hostess. Once John Bidlake's mistress and now his friend, she lives for amusement and malice.

Lord Edward Tantamount, Hilda's husband. Lord Edward is a great biologist and a failure in every personal relationship he undertakes. He represents the limitations of the scientific approach to complex human experience.

Lucy Tantamount, the promiscuous daughter of Lord Edward. Malicious and without any kind of conscience, she amuses herself with Walter Bidlake and any other acceptable male who crosses her path.

Frank Illidge, Lord Edward's laboratory assistant. He is a brilliant lower-class person who, out of hatred and socialistic conviction, allows himself to become involved in the murder of Everard Webley.

Everard Webley, a British Fascist and head of the Brotherhood of British Freemen. He is a man of tremendous physical magnetism whose thirst for power and his contempt for the masses make him a likely target for Illidge's hatred. He is also a former friend of Elinor Quarles.

Burlap, the editor of the *Literary World*. His chief critical stock in trade is religious mysticism; actually, he is a feeble sensualist who has damaged the lives of several naïve women. He is finally involved in a perverse relationship with Beatrice Gilray.

Elinor Quarles, Philip's wife. Her unsatisfactory husband drives her to consider an affair with Everard Webley. She is devastated by the death of her child, Little Philip, from meningitis.

Maurice Spandrell, a nihilist. Spandrell has been shocked into a hatred of life by the remarriage of his mother; there is nothing he can affirm, and he takes delight in destroying the dignity of other people. He pursues violent sensation even to the point of the murder of Everard Webley.

General Knoyle, the stepfather of Spandrell, a pompous military man with no understanding of the world in which he lives.

Mrs. Knoyle, Spandrell's mother. She is, in part, the innocent cause of her son's hatred of the world.

Mark Rampion, an artist. Rampion, risen from the lower class, has developed a life and a style of painting that properly express the interplay of all of life's forces; he is totally unlike Philip Quarles, who understands all of life but cannot live it.

Mary Rampion, Mark's wife. She is an upper-class woman who has married for love and life. In her cheerful enjoyment of her husband's vigor, she is an illustration of all that he preaches about the natural, spontaneous life.

Beatrice Gilray, a literary woman. She is the special friend of Burlap, from whom she learns the mingling of high thinking and sensuality.

Sidney Quarles, the father of Philip. He is engaged in a never-to-be-finished work on democracy. He is also involved with a young woman in London.

Rachel Quarles, his wife. Accepting with dignity the shortcomings of her domestic situation, she is a Christian in her devotion and forbearance.

THE POLICE
(Policja)

Author: Sławomir Mrożek (1930-   )
First published: 1958
Genre: Drama

Locale: Unspecified
Time: Mid-twentieth century
Plot: Absurdist

The Chief of Police, the quintessential bureaucrat. Faced with the fact that the last political prisoner in his state has reformed and must be released, the Chief despairs, realizing that he no longer has a function. He questions the Prisoner's sincerity, then tries to persuade him that he does not really want to reform or that he would be better off in prison. When all these efforts fail, the Chief is forced to find another way of maintaining his position. He appeals to his deputy, a sergeant who functions as an agent-provocateur, arguing that they need to find another dissenter if they are to keep their jobs. The Sergeant agrees to be imprisoned as a dissenter. When the General comes to see the new prisoner, the Chief finds himself in the difficult position of wanting to protect the Sergeant, whom he does not consider a real political prisoner, while appearing to be zealous in his pursuit of justice.

The Prisoner, a former revolutionary, later the General's aide-de-camp. When negotiating his release, the Prisoner claims vigorously that he has reformed, that he now loves his country and its rulers. So persuasive is he that he ultimately secures a position as aide-de-camp to the General and returns with the General to the prison. As an expert in dissidence, the Prisoner is asked to interrogate the Sergeant to see if he is truly a dissident. When the Prisoner concludes that the Sergeant is indeed a genuine dissident, the Chief demands that he prove his case. He does so by proposing an experiment in which the Sergeant will be given the opportunity to throw a bomb at the General, which the Sergeant does. When the Chief arrests the Prisoner for having conspired to throw a bomb at the General, the Prisoner in turn places the Chief under arrest for having failed to protect the General.

The Police Sergeant, an agent-provocateur. The Sergeant hates his work as a plainclothes officer not only because he has had no success in drumming up dissent through his provocations but also because he loves the police force so much that he is comfortable only when wearing his uniform. When he has to

work in plain clothes, he slips on his uniform at home to relax after a day on the job. Devastated at the thought of having to give up the work he loves, he agrees to the Chief's scheme and provokes dissent within himself. After being locked in prison, the Sergeant starts to lose his sense of identity and becomes confused as to whether he is a policeman pretending to be a dissenter or a genuine dissenter. The more he thinks about his country's circumstances while in his cell, the more reason for dissent he perceives. Although he says that he would never throw a bomb at the General despite his political doubts, when the opportunity arises, he does just that. At curtain, the Sergeant seems to have become a full-blown revolutionary.

The General, an archetypal military man. He comes to see the Sergeant in prison to evaluate how serious a threat he poses. After being told that there is no evidence that the Sergeant is a dissident, the General opines that he must therefore be a particularly dangerous one. He has absolute confidence in his aide, despite his past, believing that his days of dissent are behind him. While talking with the Chief, the General begins to suspect that the Chief wants to protect the Sergeant and accuses the Chief of lack of diligence. The General agrees to the bomb-throwing experiment but hides in a closet during it. When he emerges, he places both the Prisoner and the Chief under arrest for conspiring in the bomb-throwing.

The Wife of the Sergeant-Provocateur, a representative of the unthinking citizenry. She expresses her concern over her husband's state of mind to the Chief, telling him how gloomy the Sergeant has become now that no one responds to his provocations and asking the Chief to return him to uniformed duty. She also mentions that she met her husband when each reported the other to the secret police.

— *Philip Auslander*

THE POLISH COMPLEX
(Kompleks polski)

Author: Tadeusz Konwicki (1926-　　　)
First published: 1977
Genre: Novel

Locale: Warsaw, Poland
Time: The 1970's, with flashbacks
Plot: Philosophical realism

Tadeusz Konwicki (tah-DAY-uhsh kohn-WIHTS-kih), a Polish writer. He is a middle-aged man with a somewhat cynical outlook on life. On the day before Christmas, he is standing in a line outside a jewelry store in Warsaw waiting for a shipment of goods to arrive from the Soviet Union. The situation prompts his meeting a number of other people with whom he has conversations, allowing his opinions and views on a wide range of subjects to be expressed.

Tadeusz Kojran (KOY-rahn), a man standing behind Konwicki in the line outside the jewelry store. In 1951, he followed Konwicki for three weeks with the intention of shooting him. He will be taking a trip to America.

Duszek (DEW-shehk), another man waiting in line, physically large and with an outgoing personality. He loves to drink and is responsible for getting several of the men in line to a local drinking place. He also is prone to announcing generalizations about the Polish national character. He guarded Kojran in jail in 1952.

Zygmunt Mineyko (mi-NEE-koh), a young revolutionary from the 1860's. He is evoked by Konwicki in an intense flashback during which Konwicki addresses him in the first person and closely identifies with him. At the time alluded to, 1863, Mineyko is twenty-three years old, on the threshold of his first military operation. When he arrives at the designated spot, however, he finds that the hundreds of men who were supposed to be waiting for him already have gone home. In the skirmish that ensues, Mineyko finds that both his own troops and the enemy have fled at the first shot. Konwicki uses the imaginative identification to recall himself at the age of eight-

een, on the threshold of another revolutionary activity and filled with idealism for what Poland might be.

Basia (BAH-syah), a clerk in the jewelry store. A tall, good-looking young woman who is slightly taller than Konwicki, she is confident and knowledgeable about herself and her desires. When Konwicki suffers a mild heart attack, she takes him to an employee's back room, where they have sexual relations.

Anarchist, a fat, red-haired young man wearing a leather jacket. He has fled to Poland because that is where he thinks the next revolution will take place. The Poles refer to him as a terrorist, although there is no indication of violent activity in the book. He is blind and led by the French student.

The French student, the anarchist's companion, who translates for him. He defers to the anarchist.

Romuald Traugutt (roh-MEW-ahld TROW-gewt), a revolutionary from the same unsuccessful uprising as Mineyko. Konwicki imagines a rendezvous in a hotel with Traugutt's wife, speculating what it might have been like between her and Traugutt on the last night before he went off to assume leadership of the People's Government in Warsaw and to almost certain death.

Julia, a woman who manages to cut into the line. She is nearly forty years old, with a matronly face and a rough personality. She can evoke pity by pretending to be an old woman, but actually she is fairly well off. She invites Konwicki to return with her to her farm in Radosc.

— *Paula Kopacz*

POLYEUCTE

Author: Pierre Corneille (1606-1684)
First published: 1643
Genre: Drama

Locale: Melitene, the capital of Armenia
Time: 250 C.E.
Plot: Tragedy

Polyeucte (paw-lee-UHK-tee), an Armenian nobleman who is married to Pauline. Returning from a secret mission on which he has received Christian baptism, he is ordered by the Roman governor, Félix, to attend the temple sacrifices. As a traitor to the Roman gods, he is condemned to die. To those who plead with him to recant and save his life, he answers that he is through with mortal ties, and he goes to his death undismayed.

Pauline, the daughter of the Roman governor and Polyeucte's wife. When her Christian husband is condemned to death for his defilement of the Roman gods, she pleads with him to save his life by privately worshiping his God while publicly paying homage to the Roman gods. Her pleas fail, and Polyeucte goes to his death. At his execution, she feels a veil lifted from her eyes and declares herself a Christian prepared to die for her faith.

Sévère (say-VEHR), a Roman warrior. In love with Pauline before her marriage to Polyeucte, he comes as a hero to Arme-

nia ostensibly to make sacrifices of thanksgiving for victories in war; in reality, he has come to see Pauline, whom he still loves. Finding her faithful to her husband, he bids her farewell. He is later asked by Pauline to plead for Polyeucte, who is condemned to die as a Christian. Inspired by what he considers the miraculous conversions of Pauline and Félix after Polyeucte's death, he promises to beg Emperor Décie for freedom of worship for all.

Félix (FAY-lihks), the Roman governor of Armenia and Pauline's father. He condemns Polyeucte to death for defilement of the Roman gods. After the victim's execution, Félix himself is suddenly converted to Christianity.

Néarque (NAY-ahrk), Polyeucte's friend.

Stratonice (stra-toh-NIH-chay), Pauline's friend.

Albin (AHL-bihn), Félix's friend.

Décie (DAY-chee-eh), the emperor of Rome.

THE PONDER HEART

Author: Eudora Welty (1909-   )
First published: 1954
Genre: Novella

Locale: Clay, a small town in Mississippi
Time: Early 1950's
Plot: Regional

Edna Earle Ponder, a middle-aged, unmarried woman, the last of the Ponder family. She narrates the events to a guest at the Beulah Hotel, which she was given by her Uncle Daniel fifteen years ago. She is garrulous and good-humored, and she sees herself as smart. She is also perceptive regarding people's character. A "good Presbyterian" with a sense of civic responsibility (she runs the rummage sale held to benefit black people), she does not participate in small-town sectarian bickering. She sees Bonnie Dee for the "little thing with yellow, fluffy hair" that she is, and at Bonnie Dee's funeral she describes Mrs. Peacock, who wears tennis shoes, as "big and fat as a row of pigs." Generally, Edna Earle is good-natured, tolerant, and compassionate. Despite the suffering caused by the trial, she does not allow herself to become embittered. She willingly denies herself the pleasure of marriage and children to accept her role as Uncle Daniel's caretaker.

Daniel Ponder, Edna Earle's uncle, now in his fifties. He is a lovable, childlike man who enjoys being rich because he can give things away. He appears to have the mental equipment and emotional maturity of an eleven- or twelve-year-old. A big man with the large Ponder head, he has short, curly white hair and is always dressed in a white suit with a red bow tie and a large Stetson. Uncle Daniel loves to tell stories and loves having an audience. In effect, he is the ward of the town of Clay, and he is so obviously harmless that the charge of murder brought against him is comical.

Bonnie Dee Peacock Ponder, who is seventeen years old when she marries Uncle Daniel and always looks seventeen, according to Edna Earle. She comes from the country to work at the five-and-ten in Clay. Tiny (she weights ninety-eight pounds) and doll-like, with blonde hair and "coon eyes," she spends most of her time sending off for clothing and other items, some of which, like the washing machine that she buys before the house has electricity, are useless to her. She comes

from a large, poor, country family, and although she is certainly materialistic, she is perhaps not so much mercenary as she is naïve and immature. Nevertheless, she is not a sympathetic character, and she never acquires enough dimension or personality to cause the reader to lament her comical death as a result of tickling from Daniel.

Grandpa Ponder, who appears only in the early pages of the novel. He is the head of the family. Although he is devoted to his last surviving son, Daniel, and treats Edna Earle well, Grandpa Ponder manipulates the lives of those around him, in part through his wealth and local influence. When the asylum fails to be the appropriate answer for Uncle Daniel, he arranges a marriage with an acceptable matron. When that fails and Uncle Daniel marries Bonnie Dee, Grandpa Ponder dies of a stroke.

Teacake Magee, a widow and a member of the choir in the Baptist church. She becomes Uncle Daniel's first wife, but the marriage lasts only two months. He seems to have liked her, as he likes virtually everyone, but he objects to the noise of her "spool-heels" on the floor.

Narciss, the black cook who waits on Bonnie Dee and behaves more as her playmate than her servant.

Dorris Gladney, the ambitious prosecutor who talks the Peacocks into bringing Uncle Daniel to court on a murder charge. Conceited and self-important, Gladney tries to use clever ploys to trap the naïve Uncle Daniel. Although Gladney loses the case, Edna Earle speculates that he will become governor of Mississippi.

DeYancey Clanahan, Uncle Daniel's well-meaning but ineffectual defense attorney and son of an old family friend, "Judge" Tip Clanahan, who considers himself too old to take the case.

— *Ron McFarland*

THE POOR CHRIST OF BOMBA
(Le Pauvre Christ de Bomba)

Author: Mongo Beti (Alexandre Biyidi, 1932-   )
First published: 1956
Genre: Novel

Locale: Southern Cameroon, the village of Bomba, and several smaller villages
Time: The 1930's
Plot: Satire

Father Drumont, a bearded, middle-aged, archetypal Catholic missionary who founded and for twenty years nurtured the mission at Bomba. A stern but not humorless man, he is obsessed with sex and disillusioned by his failure to persuade Africans to follow church teachings on chastity and monogamy. Frustrated by the persistence of the traditional African social and religious practices that he sees on his tour of the Tala villages, he concludes eventually that he cannot successfully Christianize the Africans. At the end of the tour, he decides to return to France. By then, he is a wiser man but is dejected because he realizes that his work has functioned to

soften and prepare the Africans for an exploitative and brutal colonial system.

Denis, the fourteen-year-old narrator and Drumont's houseboy. He naïvely and ironically identifies with the Christian and European values of the missionary. Accompanying Drumont on a pastoral tour of the bush, he records, but rarely comprehends, the conversations and activities of the entourage and the villagers. Loving and admiring the priest more than his own father, Denis criticizes his fellow Africans for their failure to adhere to Christian principles and their lack of respect for Drumont. He is a sensitive and sweet adolescent who matures quickly as a result of the tour and his mentor's realizations about the brutality of the colonial mission.

Zacharia, Drumont's fun-loving, irreverent African cook. A realist, he uses his position to acquire wealth and sexual conquests. Indifferent to Christianity, he explicitly opposes Drumont's views and explains the "reality" of colonialism and African traditions to Denis and the missionary. He is a wily and independent man, unwilling to modify his behavior to please either his wife or the priest. After his wife exposes his affair with Catherine and the latter's fiancé soundly thrashes him, he flogs his wife and moves his mistress into his home. Rather than answer charges of mistreatment brought to Drumont's attention by his wife, he packs his bags and leaves the Bomba mission.

Vidal, the young, enthusiastic French colonial administrator of the region who uses forced African labor, floggings, and other brutal methods to build roads. Without training and a proper education, he feels that his best opportunities are in the colonies. Fond of Drumont for his essential "Frenchness," he tries to persuade the priest to remain at Bomba, believing that the French colonial mission is correct. Parroting colonial paternalistic arguments, he fails to persuade Drumont that Africans, if left to their own devices, would succumb to Bolshevism.

Catherine, a beautiful and playful villager who is a sexually desirable member of the *sixa*, a work camp at Bomba for the prenuptial training of young women to encourage monogamy among the traditionally polygamous Tala people. As Zacharia's mistress, she secretly accompanies the pastoral tour, spending nights with him, often in the same house as the unsuspecting Drumont. One night, she seduces Denis, who quickly falls in love with her. Before the tour's end, she is assaulted by Zacharia's wife, the opening event in Drumont's uncovering of the true nature of the *sixa*, which functions as a brothel.

Clementine, a practicing Catholic and the jealous young wife of Zacharia. In spite of having just given birth to their child, she is suspicious of her husband's activities with the *sixa*. When she discovers that one of the girls, Catherine, disappeared at the same time as Drumont's entourage departed, she follows them to catch her husband with his mistress. An angry and self-righteous Christian, she expects Father Drumont to solve her marital problem.

Raphael, a catechist and the mission assistant in charge of the *sixa*. He arranges liaisons between *sixa* women and local men. A cowardly bully who coerces the women into sexual relations by assigning brutal work to those who are uncooperative, he flees when Drumont discovers the nature of the *sixa* operation.

Father Jean-Martin LeGuen, a young, inexperienced vicar recently assigned as Drumont's assistant. He is an enthusiastic priest who speaks the local language better than Drumont but is unimaginative and dependent on his superior for instruction on most matters.

— *Kathleen O'Mara*

POOR FOLK
(Bednye lyudi)

Author: Fyodor Dostoevski (1821-1881)
First published: 1846
Genre: Novel

Locale: St. Petersburg, Russia
Time: First half of the nineteenth century
Plot: Impressionistic realism

Makar Alexievitch Dievushkin (mah-KAHR ah-lehk-SAY-eh-vihch deh-VEWSH-kihn), a government clerk or copyist whose extravagant love for a friendless orphan leaves him penniless and broken in health. A supremely noble and at the same time ridiculous aging lover, Makar, laughingly called Lovelace in his office, carries on for some months an elaborate correspondence with the woman next door. Although they see each other less than once a week, they write almost daily of their mutual respect, their penurious existence, and their calamities and minor triumphs. Makar has attached his wages to give her flowers and bonbons, driven himself mad with worry over her health, and generally devoted himself to her comfort and ease of mind. He also concerns himself with a dying clerk wronged in a scandal, a writer of penny dreadfuls, and a drunken friend in his office. His style of writing is florid; his thoughts are mostly clichés; and his feelings, though obvious, are touching. Like many of the author's great creations, the clerk welcomes suffering and forces it upon himself so that he may ask forgiveness for imagined sins, but his "dedicated" living turns out to be mostly effusions of a distraught mind and overstrained susceptibilities, dramatized for their effect rather than their feelings. Even so, within the humor there is deep pathos.

Barbara Alexievna Dobroselova (vahr-VAH-ruh ah-lehk-SAY-ehv-nuh dohb-roh-SEH-lo-vah), his beloved, a very distant relation who sensibly berates the extravagant but impoverished devotee but also thanks him for his devotion. A woman who has suffered much after a happy childhood, she is unable to adjust to the cruel world where she is lustfully sought after and generally disregarded. Loving the rural life from which she came and failing in health, she finally decides to marry a rich but irascible man who can save her, but under protest from Makar, so much her admirer that he cannot bear to see her sell herself cheaply. Her concern for the man who watches over her so tenderly and even foolishly, her deep devotion to the memory of her parents, and her cherished recollection of a dead lover who was her tutor suggest the kind of character that has allowed her to survive the insults of an aunt and the buffeting of fortune.

Thedora (teh-DOH-ruh), a cook and Barbara's companion, often her benefactress, an aging servant who loyally remains with the ailing woman. She stays on to cook for Makar when he moves into the departing bride's rooms. Often berated for her keen-eyed reporting of Makar's extravagances and misadventures, she redeems herself again and again in his eyes.

Bwikov (byih-KOHF), Barbara's betrothed, a middle-aged and wealthy but patronizing and lecherous friend of her aunt. Driven on by the embittered relative of the destitute Barbara and involved in the prostitution of Barbara's cousin Sasha, Bwikov comes to St. Petersburg supposedly to make amends for the indecent propositioning by his nephew. In reality, he intends to claim a wife and beget a legitimate heir to his fortunes.

Pokrovski (pohk-ROHV-skih), a consumptive young scholar who truly loves Barbara and dies declaring his love. A bright but shy person, he befriends Barbara and bequeaths to her his love of great books and a knowledge of good writing and good taste.

Gorshkov (gohrsh-KOHF), an unfairly indicted civil servant whose reputation is finally cleared but who dies of the shock. A victim of the bureaucratic system, the young man and his family suffer desperately and unfairly, befriended only by old Makar.

Anna Thedorovna (AHN-nah teh-OH-rov-nuh), Barbara's aunt, with whom Barbara and her mother, now dead, lived after her father's death.

Sasha (SAH-shuh), Barbara's cousin, an orphan.

Old Pokrovski, the tutor's father, devoted to his son and much impressed by the young man's learning. Apparently deranged by his son's death, he follows the funeral procession on foot, dropping a trail of books on the way to the cemetery.

POOR WHITE

Author: Sherwood Anderson (1876-1941)
First published: 1920
Genre: Novel

Locale: Missouri and Ohio
Time: 1866-1900
Plot: Psychological realism

Hugh McVey, a Midwestern American whose genius for inventing and manufacturing machinery accounts for his rise from drab poverty to material success. He is, according to many critics, Anderson's example of the force that produced the problems attendant on the impact of technology upon rural America at the turn of the century.

Steve Hunter, McVey's partner in business. He is a capable publicist who convinces the town fathers of Bidwell to invest in a plant to manufacture McVey's invention. The plant makes the town prosperous.

Clara Butterworth, a rather shy, plain, melancholy girl who in a week's time abandons her studies at the state university, returns to Bidwell, falls in love with McVey, and elopes with him. She is not suited by temperament to a man like McVey, and their marriage becomes a strained relationship. Adversity and the prospect of a child finally bring them together.

Joe Wainsworth, a harness maker who invests his savings in McVey's invention and is almost financially ruined when the money is lost. The reversal disturbs his disposition, and he becomes sullen and irritable. A trivial incident sets him off and, seriously deranged, he kills his employee, shoots Steve Hunter, and tries to strangle McVey.

Sarah Shepard, McVey's foster mother, who instills in him respect for knowledge, hard work, social success, and industrial progress.

Henry Shepard, Sarah's husband and McVey's first employer. He befriends McVey and provides a home for him.

Jim Gibson, a braggart, Wainsworth's employee. His boast precipitates Wainsworth's derangement and its concomitant violence. Gibson becomes Wainsworth's first victim.

Tom Butterworth, Clara's father, the richest man in town.

Allie Mulberry, a simple-minded workman who makes a model of McVey's invention.

THE POORHOUSE FAIR

Author: John Updike (1932-   )
First published: 1959
Genre: Novel

Locale: The Diamond County Home for the Aged, in New Jersey
Time: The 1970's
Plot: Satire

John F. Hook, a retired schoolteacher. He is ninety-four years old and has been living in the Diamond County Home for the Aged for fifteen years. He is a man of thought and reflection who delights in intellectual discourse and still feels the essential obligation of a teacher to instruct the world in terms of the values, virtues, philosophical perspectives, and cultural landmarks he sees as the structural foundation of civilization. His ideas are grounded in American history, and his continuing sense of pleasure in the infinite, intricate detail of the natural world is a source of spiritual satisfaction for him, as well as evidence of a divine shape to the universe. As his long life nears it conclusion, he is sustained by his faith in some kinds of existence beyond the earthly realm he loves. Questions concerning the dimensions of "Heaven" intrigue

him, and he is occasionally troubled by doubt, but his responsiveness to the things of the world and the social arrangements among the residents of the home revive and encourage him. He is seen as something of a wisdom figure by the others, and his gregarious demeanor—a remnant of the gallantry and charm he possessed as a younger man—makes his company welcome. The slightly artificial but captivating manner of his speech is one of his most appealing attributes.

Stephen Connor, the director or prefect of the home, a man in his middle years who has devoted his career in public service to his commitment to being of use to society. He is a rationalist who believes in the power of the state to create a kind of utopia in which human pain, suffering, and want can be reduced drastically. He believes that the limits of his present position prevent him from working toward the encompassing utopian vision he has developed, but he thinks of the residents as "his people" and tries to gauge and meet their needs. In spite of his good intentions, he is unable to understand the spiritual needs and capabilities of the residents, and his determination to keep everything organized and under control leads to frustration and disappointment as the intrinsic human tendency to strain against boundaries continually upsets his plans. He is decent and caring, if somewhat reserved. Although he often argues with Hook, there is some measure of mutual respect in their disputations. Unlike Hook, he is often fretful and troubled, because the spiritual void in his intellectual outlook has effectively removed the possibilities of love from his life.

Billy Gregg, a former electrician. He is seventy years old, small, quick, and profane. He is something of a student in Hook's loosely convened continuing education experience. He is almost constantly angry because of the emptiness of his world. He has little to show for his life and has built up a kind of perpetual grievance against anyone in authority who might be held responsible for his frustrations. His frequent expressions of profanity are a means of striking back as well as a way to keep mentally alert. In spite of his boisterous manner, he is generally ineffectual, his passion having no real outlet. His anarchist impulse is sharply in contrast with Connor's will to order and leads to a constant low level of tension between them, occasionally flaring into anger, as in the incident of the residents stoning Connor.

George Lucas, formerly a truck farmer, in the home for only three years. He is more closely connected to the outer world than most of the other residents and is still relatively young. He raises pigs and pokes at a sore in his ear as a means of maintaining the responsiveness of his body to stimuli. His wife is in the home too, and their relationship gives his life a structured partnership most of the others lack. Before entering the home, he went bankrupt in the real estate business because he knew land but "displeased people" with his stubborn, persistent nature.

Buddy Lee, Connor's assistant, a bright young man who is relatively inexperienced with the ways of the world and follows Connor's direction almost as a disciple. He is not very sympathetic about the problems of old age but is capable of stylish turns of wit and might be able to acquire the compassion he presently lacks.

Amelia (Amy) Mortis, an old woman who lives at the residence. She makes quilts that reflect the rich tapestry of the American past. She is plainspoken, direct, and perceptive, intellectually capable of conversing with Hook and Connor. Her opinions reflect the fundamental common sense of someone who has a realistic picture of life's difficulties but who is still responsive to moments of spiritual beauty and appreciates occasions of celebration.

Elizabeth Heineman, who has become blind in her old age but has developed a visionary capacity for exultation in the presence of powerful human emotion and a sensitivity to the needs and desires of others that she lacked before her loss of sight.

— *Leon Lewis*

PORGY

Author: DuBose Heyward (1885-1940)
First published: 1925
Genre: Novel

Locale: Charleston, South Carolina
Time: Early twentieth century
Plot: Regional

Porgy, an old, crippled black beggar who travels about Charleston in a goat cart. He is frail in body, but his hands are powerful. He says little but observes much. When Bess moves in and becomes his woman after Crown has fled following Robbins' murder, Porgy is transformed from an impassive observer of life to a lover of children as well as of Bess. Fearful of losing Bess to Crown, Porgy kills him, but he loses her anyway.

Crown, a stevedore, slow-witted, powerful, brutal, and dangerous, especially when drunk. He is stabbed by Porgy when he breaks into Porgy's room. Crown's body is later found in the river, but the loyalty of Porgy's friends prevents his being identified as Crown's murderer.

Bess, his woman, who lives with Porgy during Crown's absence but who returns briefly to Crown. While living with Porgy, she is less immoral than amoral; neither she nor her friends see anything improper in such conduct. Made drunk by stevedores during Porgy's absence in jail, she is taken to Savannah. Supposedly she returns to her old life.

Robbins, a weekend gambler but otherwise a good provider. He is murdered by Crown, who falsely suspects him of cheating at dice.

Serena, his wife, who adopts Jake and Clara's baby after Porgy is jailed on a contempt charge.

Peter, an old man arrested as a witness to Robbins' murder.

Sportin' Life, a flashy New York drug dealer.

Maria, Porgy's friend, operator of a small cookshop.

Jake, a fisherman drowned when a hurricane wrecks his boat.

Clara, his wife, also drowned during the hurricane. Bess and Porgy keep her baby after her death until the baby is taken by Serena.

Simon Frasier, a black "lawyer" who grants illegal divorces for a dollar.

Alan Archdale, a white lawyer, Porgy's friend.

PORNOGRAFIA

Author: Witold Gombrowicz (1904-1969)
First published: 1960
Genre: Novel

Locale: German-occupied Poland
Time: During World War II
Plot: Philosophical realism

Witold Gombrowicz (gom-BROH-vihch), a Polish writer. Although he shares the author's name and vocation, it is impossible to identify the actual Gombrowicz with the novel's passive and overly cerebral narrator. Walking proof that one's identity is determined by others and that an observer always affects the situation observed, Witold mentally orchestrates the world in accordance with his ideas, calling into question the reality of the novel's events and of the characters' motivations. Given to seeing things in terms of opposites, particularly youth and maturity, he continually ponders the mystery of the mutual seduction and wounding of these antithetical life stages. As the novel opens, Witold, eager to escape Warsaw's art circles (as insipid as ever, despite the war), visits Hippo's estate with Frederick. There, he is captivated by the youthful Karol and Henia, but while his friend contrives to bring the two together, he looks on passively, disturbed by the theatricality of events and doubting Frederick's sanity. In the end, however, he succumbs to the "sin" against the couple, believing it maturity's only access to youth and rejuvenation.

Frederick, Witold's companion and coconspirator. A middle-aged man, dark and thin, with a hooked nose, this murderous lunatic seems at first merely a parody of the intellectual; he is hyperrational and unnervingly lucid but self-consciously artificial in everything. Exciting Witold by the way he continually brings Karol and Henia together, his motives are never completely clear, even after he writes the narrator insane letters expounding his plan to undermine both religion and nature in the belief that his obscene and deadly plotting, if successful, will justify itself.

Hippolytus (Hippo) S., an estate owner. A bloated man with a pig's eyes and the habit of repeating himself, Hippo is an example of the self-satisfied and purblind Polish gentry. Never questioning his duty, he makes his estate available to the Resistance but prefers the life of the jovial squire.

Karol, a local administrator's son. An ordinary blond sixteen-year-old boy, white teeth flashing with adolescent purity and naturalness, he is seen as divine because youth, though thoughtless and unformed, transforms the crudest and cruelest actions into acts of grace (in older eyes). Dismissed from the Resistance for some silliness before the novel begins, he is staying with Hippo because he cannot get along with his father. A childhood friend of Henia, he claims to have no

romantic interest in her, but Witold senses, or projects, a passionate connection immediately. Seduced by the plotter's attentions, Karol willingly asserts his youth in their romantic and murderous schemes.

Henia, Hippo's daughter and Albert's fiancé. An ordinary young girl, she is not quite as innocent as she first appears, having slept with a Resistance fighter. In love with Albert and his adult values, she still shares a youthful sensibility with Karol that Witold and Frederick use to implicate her in their plots.

Albert Paszkowski (pahsh-KOF-skee), Henia's fiancé. Aristocratic in the best and worst senses, Albert is refined physically and spiritually to the point of nausea, in contrast to Karol's youthfulness. A handsome, well-educated lawyer and scion of a landed family, Albert is the epitome of adult values and virtues, which prove to be no match for the enticing imperfections of immaturity. Falling prey to the plotter's machinations, he lets his jealousy undermine his maturity and self-respect, which he regains at the end only through murder and useless surrender to death.

Lady Amelia, Albert's widowed mother. This elderly and saintly woman's faith calms Witold's fevered imaginings enough for normality to reassert itself momentarily. Unbalanced by Frederick's extreme rationalism, however, she loses self-control and becomes embroiled in an erotic and fatal fight with a servant. Rejecting the absolute in favor of nature, the third thing between reason and religion, she dies with her eyes on Frederick.

Olek Skuziak (SHEW-zhahk), a servant and Lady Amelia's murderer. A dirty, rustic youth with gold hair, black eyes, and white teeth, he is a crude double of Karol. Introducing a savage element into the story, his presence and bloody deed inspire the plotters to unite the fates of the other characters in a murderous conclusion.

Siemian (SHEE-mee-ahn), a Resistance leader. Elegant and charming, he comes to stay at Hippo's estate, where he suddenly loses his nerve. Realizing that this makes him a liability that must be eliminated, he begs the unmoved Witold to help him escape. The plans to do away with him culminate in a double murder intertwining the strands of death and eros that characterize the plotters' lustful fascination with youth.

— *Philip McDermott*

THE PORNOGRAPHER

Author: John McGahern (1935-   )
First published: 1979
Genre: Novel

Locale: Dublin, provincial Ireland, and London
Time: The 1970's
Plot: Satire

"I," the anonymous narrator and main character, the pornographer of the title. An attractive man, thirty years old, he keeps very close guard on his feelings. Although he seems to have no major financial worries, he works as a professional writer of pornography and is mildly successful at it. He writes well as long as he can follow a formula; his employer, Maloney, furnishes him with a new formula after each assignment. He seems content to pursue casual affairs with attractive women in whom he has no interest other than to satisfy his sexual needs. He unfortunately impregnates a woman named

Josephine who has fallen deeply in love with him; he refuses to marry her and takes little interest in the future of the child. He is cynical about the course of love, overly self-reflective, and haunted by time and the aging process. He does show genuine sympathy, though, for a beloved aunt who is dying of cancer and visits her on a regular basis. He seems to be heading toward some kind of permanent relationship at the novel's conclusion.

Josephine, a thirty-eight-year-old woman, the principal female character. Attractive, passionate, and warmhearted, she falls deeply in love with the narrator. After becoming pregnant, she insists that they marry and that they will learn eventually to live happily in spite of the awkward beginning of their conjugal life. Although she has worked at the Northern Bank for twenty years, she has pursued her own writing career at a journal called *Waterways*: She takes trips on boats and describes them in her articles. There is some suggestion that she and the narrator will marry, but as the novel concludes, she is not aware of that possibility (even though the reader is).

Maloney, a well-to-do publisher in his late fifties or early sixties. He is the narrator's employer and supplies him with the novelistic formulas for each of his pornographic works. He drinks heavily, is cynical but not hopeless about human nature, and takes the narrator to task severely for the callous way in which he treats Josephine. He enjoys the gifts that life has to offer. There are indications that he has experienced some pain in his life, but it has not taken away his basic joyful attitude.

Mary O'Doherty, the aunt of the narrator, who seems to be in her late sixties. She is an extremely intelligent, sensitive, and practical woman who is dying of cancer. She possesses no self-pity, even though she seems to know that she is dying. Unable to deal with the numbness that painkillers create, she prefers brandy to make the pain endurable. She is interested only in the welfare of her nephew (the narrator), her brother, and her selfish, alcoholic husband, Cyril. She dies at the novel's conclusion, and it is during her funeral that the narrator gets an insight that he may be able to connect with another human being in a lasting and loving relationship.

Cyril O'Doherty, Mary's husband. He is in his sixties and a functional alcoholic. He expresses no interest whatsoever in his wife's terminal illness and never goes to see her in the cancer ward in the Dublin hospital. In spite of his enormous selfishness, Mary leaves her considerable financial holdings to him and no one else.

The uncle, a hardworking farmer, the uncle of the narrator and the brother of Mary O'Doherty. The uncle visits his dying sister as often as he can and also expresses an interest in his nephew. The narrator may prove to be a mirror image of his bachelor uncle, only less sympathetic to human weakness.

Nurse Brady, a twenty-two-year-old nurse whom the narrator meets as she tends his aunt in the hospital in Dublin. They have a brief and passionate affair after meeting at one of the narrator's favorite pickup spots. Ironically, they conduct their affair just down the hall from where his dying aunt is sleeping.

Jonathan Martin, a man in his sixties who is very much in love with Josephine. He is delighted to hear that Josephine is pregnant and volunteers to support the child in spite of the terminal illness of his schizophrenic wife. After his wife dies, he proposes marriage to Josephine, who refuses because she has never been attracted to Jonathan sexually.

— *Patrick Meanor*

THE PORTAGE TO SAN CRISTÓBAL OF A. H.

Author: George Steiner (1929-   )
First published: 1979
Genre: Novel

Locale: The Amazonian jungle of Brazil
Time: Late 1970's
Plot: Philosophical

Adolf Hitler, the former leader of Germany, in his nineties and living in the Amazonian rain forest. Frail looking and barely able to speak when the Israeli Capture Team first apprehends him, he gains strength almost imperceptibly as the story progresses. As the men weaken and begin to die, Hitler becomes stronger and begins to offer suggestions and then orders on how to avoid the dangers of the jungle. By the end of the novel, he has completely regained his powerful oratorical ability, to such a degree that none of the remaining team is able to silence him or respond satisfactorily to his casuistic arguments. By the time the mysterious helicopters appear in the final scene, the team members are mute with exhaustion and confusion.

Emmanuel Lieber, a survivor of the Holocaust, an inveterate Nazi hunter and organizer of the team to capture Hitler. Lieber is the self-appointed agent to avenge Hitler's crimes against the Jews. With his incredible religious learning, he is metaphorically rearranging the sacred Hebrew texts for the demise of Hitler to be entered into them. Both historian and prophet, he views Hitler as the final enemy of the Jewish people and is in a state of visionary gratitude that Hitler has been found.

Dr. Nikolai Maximovitch Gruzdev, a physician and former medical examiner at the time of Hitler's presumed death. A man in his late sixties who is still smarting from eight years in a Siberian prison, he is terrified when called on to review his earlier findings as the one who performed the autopsy on Hitler's charred body. His initial report was that the body was not Hitler's but that of a double. After much pressure, though, he changed his report, stating that the body was Hitler's. Thirty years later, his superiors want him to revert to his first finding, which leaves the case open for a revisionist interpretation.

Dr. Gervinus Roethling, a government lawyer for the Federal Republic of Germany. A highly successful lawyer and a member of the German upper class, he has been instructed by his superiors to look into what international problems might arise if Hitler actually were alive and well.

Marvin Crownbacker, an American agent for the Central Intelligence Agency, in his late twenties. A maverick agent trying to impress his superiors with his decisive action in the Hitler affair, he attempts to coerce the radio monitor, Kulken, into giving him the information first so that the Americans can decide the fate of Hitler before any other country can act.

Sir Evelyn Ryder, a professor of history at a prestigious English university. He has written the authoritative book on the last days of Hitler in the bunker. He is keenly interested in how a living Hitler will affect his scholarly reputation and with what the sequel to his earlier work will be.

Gideon Benasseraf, the leader of the Israeli Capture Team. A scholarly man who lost his wife and two daughters in the Holocaust, he becomes a model for the four younger members of the team and, ironically, proposes that they capture Hitler and abandon him in a hotel lobby somewhere. Killing Hitler would draw a line historically and would constitute a closure to the horrors of the Holocaust. To be a Jew, he says, is to keep Hitler alive and thus to keep the issue alive forever. He dies of malaria before Hitler is delivered.

Rodriguiz Kulken, a radio monitor hired by Lieber to follow the trail of the team. He thinks that they are hunting for Martin Bormann and is severely shaken when he discovers that they have found Hitler.

Teku, an Indian guide who trails the team and reports back to some mysterious source. He objectively narrates the terrible difficulties that the team experiences and wants to intervene. He is fascinated with the growing stature of the ancient Hitler as he gradually becomes more active.

Simeon,

Isaac Amsel,

Elie Barach, and

John Asher, highly energized young Israelis who carry Hitler out of the forest and provide the stamina for the journey.

— *Patrick Meanor*

PORTNOY'S COMPLAINT

Author: Philip Roth (1933-   )
First published: 1969
Genre: Novel

Locale: Newark, New Jersey
Time: The 1930's to the 1960's
Plot: Bildungsroman

Alexander Portnoy, a Jewish man from Newark, New Jersey, who has "made good" as a bright college student and has become assistant commissioner for human opportunities in New York City. Throughout his life, however, he has been afflicted by a domineering mother, an intolerable sense of guilt, and an urgent sex drive. Intelligent and witty, he struggles to become free but succeeds mostly in engaging his family, his lovers, and himself in situations characterized by mutual vilification and sadomasochism that exacerbate rather than ameliorate his condition. He relates all of his adventures to his psychiatrist, Dr. Spielvogel, who provides the vehicle for the wild and often hilarious stories that disguise the real anguish he feels while living "in the middle of a Jewish joke," as he calls his life.

Sophie Portnoy, Alexander's mother. She cannot begin to understand her son, whom she nearly smothers with care, concern, and relentless nudging. The archetypal Jewish mother, she is the source of Alex's Oedipal complex, which he eventually recognizes but seems unable to deal with effectively. Both nurturer and devourer, she simultaneously threatens and encourages her son throughout his childhood, and she looms persistently in his life thereafter.

Jack (Jake) Portnoy, Alexander's father, an insurance salesman. He is hardworking, long-suffering, and chronically constipated; he devotes his life to his family. He frequently quarrels with Alex about getting into the bathroom (where Alex is busy masturbating) to try his luck at moving his bowels. His constipation is symbolic of his frustrations as husband, father, and Jewish American wage earner. It is the Sunday morning ball games with his father and their male friends that Alex recalls later in life as among the most pleasurable times of his boyhood.

Hannah Portnoy, Alex's older sister, who is more dutiful, if also less brilliant, than her brother. She marries Morty, a man Alex admires and emulates for his liberal socialist beliefs.

Mary Jane Reed, called **The Monkey**, a mannequin originally from West Virginia whom Alex picks up one evening in New York and with whom he has a prolonged affair. Her sexual versatility and the orgies she engages in with him are not, after all, the real goal Alex longs for, even as she satisfies all of his sexual fantasies. She truly loves Alex and recognizes the good he does and (partly) is, but she is incapable of liberating him either from his consuming sense of guilt or to a life of hedonistic abandonment.

Kay Campbell, called **The Pumpkin**, Alex's college girlfriend, a blond, full-bodied, but flat-chested Midwesterner, "always the first of the Antioch nymphs to go barefoot to classes in the spring." A true young American liberal, she astonishes Alex with her even temper and her high moral principles. She is the antithesis to everything Alex has known and still, years later, represents for him an ideal of American womanhood, though at the time of their affair he finally found her boring and ended their relationship.

Sarah Abbott Maulsby, called **The Pilgrim**, another WASP woman in Alex's life, a Connecticut aristocrat and Vassar graduate. To him, she constitutes "one hundred and fourteen pounds of Republican refinement, and the pertest pair of nipples in all New England." Her boarding school argot, Ivy League friends, and sexual finickiness finally put off Alex.

Naomi, called **The Jewish Pumpkin**, a six-foot sabra whom Alex meets in Israel and tries to seduce; he then discovers, to his amazement, that he is impotent. It is this event that at last sends him to the psychiatrist's couch.

Smolka, Alex's gentile boyhood friend, who reportedly becomes a professor at Princeton, despite his disadvantaged youth (his father is a poor tailor and his mother works all day in the shop with him, leaving her son to fend for himself).

Arnold Mandel, another of Alex's boyhood friends, whose high IQ is belied by his ducktail haircut, long sideburns, and loud dress. Orphaned at the age of ten, when his father died, he is enamored of the fast life, plays the drums, and even changes his name legally to Ba-ba-lu. He grows up, nevertheless (and much to Alex's surprise), to be a typical middle-class husband and father, working in his father-in-law's surgical supply business.

Rita "Bubbles" Girardi, an eighteen-year-old high school dropout, Alex's first sexual contact at the age of sixteen, arranged by his friend Smolka and witnessed by Mandel, with hilarious results.

Harold "Heshie" Portnoy, Alex's cousin. Alex admires him for his athletic prowess and independent mind, especially after he becomes engaged to Alice Debosky, the head drum majorette and one of the few gentiles at Weequahic High School. Heshie's father breaks up the engagement, however, and Heshie later dies as a soldier in World War II.

— *Jay L. Halio*

THE PORTRAIT OF A LADY

Author: Henry James (1843-1916)
First published: 1881; serial form, 1880-1881
Genre: Novel

Locale: England, France, and Italy
Time: c. 1875
Plot: Psychological realism

Isabel Archer, the heroine of the novel. An heiress orphaned at an early age, she uses her freedom to go to Europe to be educated in the arts of life lacking in her own country. She draws the interest and adoration of many people, all of whom feel that they can make a contribution to her growth, or at least can use her. Isabel is somewhat unworldly at the time of her marriage to Gilbert Osmond. After three years of resisting the social mold imposed on her by Osmond and his Roman ménage, Isabel faces a dilemma in which her intelligence and honesty vie with her sense of obligation. Sensitive to her own needs as well as to those of others, she is aware of the complicated future she faces.

Gilbert Osmond, an American expatriate. He finds in Rome an environment suited to his artistic taste and devotes his time and tastes solely to pleasing himself.

Madame Merle, Isabel's friend. Madame Merle was formerly Osmond's mistress and is the mother of his daughter Pansy. A clever, vigorous woman of considerable perspicacity, she promotes Isabel's marriage to Osmond.

Ralph Touchett, Isabel's ailing cousin. He appreciates the fine qualities of Isabel's nature. Distressed by what he considers her disastrous marriage, he sees to it that his own and his father's estates come to Isabel.

Caspar Goodwood, Isabel's faithful American suitor. He has the simplicity and directness of American insight that Isabel is trying to supplement by her European "education." He does not understand why he fails with Isabel.

Lord Warburton, a friend of Ralph Touchett. Like all the other unsuccessful men in Isabel's life, he deeply admires the young American woman and is distressed by her marriage to Gilbert Osmond.

Henrietta Stackpole, an American journalist and a girlhood friend of Isabel. Henrietta is, in her own right, an amusing picture of the sensation-seeking, uncritical American intelligence ranging over the length and breadth of Europe. She is eager to "save" Isabel.

Pansy Osmond, the illegitimate daughter of Osmond and Madame Merle. Pansy is unaware of her situation, and she welcomes Isabel as her stepmother; she feels that in Isabel she has an ally, as indeed she has. Determined to endure gracefully what she must, she feels increasingly the strictures of her father's dictates.

Edward Rosier, a suitor for Pansy's hand. This kindly, pleasant man lacks means sufficient to meet Osmond's demands.

Countess Gemini, Osmond's sister. She is a woman who has been spoiled and corrupted by her European experience, and she finds Isabel's behavior almost boring in its simplicity. Several motives prompt her to tell Isabel about Osmond's first wife and his liaison with Madame Merle. She does not spare Isabel a clear picture of Osmond's lack of humanity.

Mrs. Touchett, Isabel's vigorous and sympathetic aunt. Mrs. Touchett is the one responsible for the invitation that brings Isabel to Europe and the world.

PORTRAIT OF A MAN UNKNOWN
(Portrait d'un inconnu)

Author: Nathalie Sarraute (1900-　　)
First published: 1948
Genre: Novel

Locale: Paris and an unnamed Dutch city
Time: Late 1940's
Plot: Experimental

The narrator, a middle-aged man, rather neurotic, fascinated, intrigued, and finally obsessed with the relationship between his neighbors, an old man and his daughter. Like a detective, he spies on them constantly. To catch them in unguarded moments, he hides under stairways, peeks through windows, follows them in the street, and accosts them in museums and restaurants. He both delights in and shrinks from the drama between the two. He senses a love-hate relationship between them but experiences a similar, almost magnetic attraction to them followed by repulsion. Following psychoanalysis, he thinks himself cured of his obsession and travels to distract himself. When he visits a museum in Amsterdam and views the *Portrait of an Unknown Man*, the problem returns in full force. The portrait strikes him as a revelation: The eyes and face are strong and dominating, but the body is vague and indistinct. To him, it is the mirror of the old man and his daughter, seemingly dominant personalities who are actually shapeless, gluey masses of desires and passions.

As he renews his spying, he feels an undercurrent of anxiety, unconsciously recognizing a resemblance between the daughter's parasitic clinging to her father and his own dependent relationship to his parents. He too wears a mask that he calls personality.

The Father, an eccentric, miserly, self-made man, a sadomasochist, terrorizing those around him with fits of rage but considering himself a victim of his daughter's avarice. Having grown up in poverty and become successful through privation and hard work, he hates to spend a penny on his daughter, whom he thinks ought to be financially independent by now. With friends, he is usually relaxed and affable until someone mentions his daughter; he then becomes cranky and irritable, decrying her lack of gratitude. With friends from the old, poor neighborhood, he plays the role of kindly, solicitous old acquaintance, playing the part by wearing old clothes and traveling in third class on the train. With wealthy friends, he shows off, leaving big tips and spending lavishly. Alone, he reads textbooks from his school days. Only when his daughter's fiancé is ready to provide her with financial security does he relax his attitude of suspicion toward her and reflect simple fatherly solicitude.

The Daughter, who is middle-aged, unattractive, single, dependent on her father, and like him somewhat sadomasochistic. She views herself as a victim of his miserliness and will stop at nothing to wheedle money from him. She begs, cajoles, and whines, even after he pushes her out the door. She spies on him, steals household items, and requests more money than she needs; when she gets it, she deposits some in the bank. Like him, she exhibits eccentric, childish, and miserly behavior. In place of a purse, she carries a school bookbag. She wears cheap clothes and tries to use an expired ticket to gain entrance to an art exhibit. She, too, assumes a person-

ality only after her fiancé guarantees her security. Only then can she successfully play the role of middle-class matron, serene in the knowledge of being cared for.

Louis Dumontet (lwee dew-moh[n]-TAY), the daughter's fiancé, an employee of the Finance Ministry. The only character with a name, he acts as the catalyst to neutralize the anxious rage between father and daughter, thus allowing each to appear, like himself, as a personality, viewed from without. Because he ensures the daughter's future, father and daughter feel free to become the personalities they have pretended to be. His redirection of their lives gives them an opaque quality that makes only their masks visible, with no future sign of hidden emotional turmoil.

— *Elizabeth A. Rubino*

A PORTRAIT OF THE ARTIST AS A YOUNG MAN

Author: James Joyce (1882-1941)
First published: 1916; serial form, 1914-1915
Genre: Novel

Locale: Ireland
Time: 1882-1903
Plot: Bildungsroman

Stephen Dedalus, a young man who is, like his creator, sensitive, proud, and highly intelligent, but often confused in his attempts to understand the Irish national temperament. He is bewildered and buffeted about in a world of political unrest, theological discord, and economic decline. In this environment, he attempts to resolve for himself the problems of faith, morality, and art. At the end, feeling himself cut off from nation, religion, and family, he decides to leave Ireland in order to seek his own fulfillment as an artist, the artificer that his name suggests.

Simon Dedalus, an easygoing, talkative, patriotic Irishman who reveres the memory of nationalist leader Charles Stewart Parnell. During his lifetime he has engaged in many activities, as a medical student, an actor, an investor, and a tax-gatherer, among others; but he has failed in everything he has tried. Stephen Dedalus' realization that his father is self-deluded and shiftless contributes greatly to the boy's growing disillusionment and unrest. Simon is almost the stereotyped, eloquent Irishman who drinks much more than is good for him.

Mrs. Dedalus, a worn, quiet woman who remains a shadowy background figure in the novel. She is a woman of deep faith; her son's repudiation of religious belief becomes a source of anxiety and grief adding to her other cares.

Mrs. Dante Riordan, Stephen Dedalus' aunt. An energetic defender of anything Catholic, she despises anyone whose views are opposed to her own. Her special targets are certain Irish patriots, particularly Parnell, and all enemies of priests. Her violent arguments with Simon Dedalus on politics and religion make a profound impression on young Stephen.

Eileen Vance, Stephen Dedalus' childhood love. He is not allowed to play with the little girl because she is a Protestant.

E—— C——, called Emma Clery in another manuscript but in this novel more the embodied image of Stephen

Dedalus' romantic fancies and fantasies than a real person. She is the girl to whom he addresses his love poems.

Davin, a student at University College and the friend of Stephen Dedalus. He is athletic, emotionally moved by ancient Irish myth, and obedient to the Church. To Stephen, he personifies country, religion, and the dead romantic past, the forces in the national life that Stephen is trying to escape.

Lynch, an intelligent but irreverent student at University College. During a walk in the rain, Stephen Dedalus tries to explain to Lynch his own views on art. Stephen's explanation of lyrical, epical, and dramatic literary forms helps to illuminate Joyce's own career as a writer.

Cranly, a student at University College. A casuist, he serves as an intellectual foil to Stephen Dedalus. To him, Stephen confides his decision not to find his vocation in the Church and the reasons for his inability to accept its rituals or even to believe its teachings.

Father Arnall, a Jesuit teacher at Clongowes Wood School. While Stephen Dedalus is attending Belvedere College, during a religious retreat, Father Arnall preaches an eloquent sermon on the sin of Lucifer and his fall. The sermon moves Stephen so deeply that he experiences a religious crisis, renounces all pleasures of the flesh, and for a time contemplates becoming a priest.

Father Dolan, the prefect of studies at Clongowes Wood School. A strict disciplinarian, he punishes Stephen Dedalus unjustly after the boy has broken his glasses and is unable to study. The beating he administers causes Stephen's first feeling of rebellion against priests.

Uncle Charles, Stephen Dedalus' great-uncle, a gentle, hearty old man employed to carry messages. When Stephen is a small boy, he accompanies Uncle Charles on his errands.

Nasty Roche, a student at Clongowes Wood School. His mocking reference to Stephen Dedalus' name gives Stephen his first impression of being different or alienated.

THE POSSESSED
(Les Possédés)

Author: Albert Camus (1913-1960)
First published: 1959
Genre: Drama

Locale: Russia
Time: Late nineteenth century
Plot: Existentialism

Nicholas Stavrogin (stav-ROH-gihn), who is strong, intelligent, handsome, and an aristocrat by birth. He is capable of the most noble actions and the most heinous crimes. In a gesture of remarkable generosity, he has married the crippled, feeble-minded Maria Lebyatkin and supports her and her drunkard brother, Captain Lebyatkin. Later, he allows the two to be murdered by the convict Fedka, although he could have prevented the crime easily. He seduces a number of women, including Lisa Drozdov, Dasha Shatov, and Maria Shatov, each of whom he is incapable of loving. An extraordinarily charismatic man, Nicholas allows himself to be exploited as the figurehead of a local terrorist group organized by Peter Verkhovensky. Profoundly nihilistic, Nicholas is tortured by his inability to believe in any political doctrine or moral order. He hangs himself in despair at the end of the play.

Varvara Stavrogin (vahr-VAH-rah), a proud, domineering, and sensitive woman, incapable of showing love or affection, although hers is a very passionate nature. Through wealth and influence, she manipulates others to protect her son, Nicholas. Although she is in love with Stepan Verkhovensky, she arranges his marriage with Dasha Shatov as a way of keeping Dasha away from Nicholas, whom Dasha loves. Varvara confesses her love for Stepan only when the latter is dying at the end of the play.

Stepan Trofimovich Verkhovensky (steh-PAHN troh-FIH-moh-vihch vehr-khoh-VEHN-skee), an aging, ineffectual, and vain intellectual. He is generally well-intentioned, but never at the expense of his own comfort or pleasure. He abandoned his son, Peter, at an early age and spent a large part of the latter's inheritance. When the play opens, he is living off of Varvara Stavrogin. He is the former tutor of Nicholas, Dasha, and a number of the members of his son's terrorist group.

Peter Stepanovich Verkhovensky (steh-PAH-noh-vihch), Stepan's son. He is cruel, arrogant, devious, and ultimately murderous. Although he claims to be seeking equality for all, his real desire is to confirm his own power by manipulating others to commit crimes at his behest. Thus, he has Fedka kill the Lebyatkins and later has the members of his terrorist group execute one of their former comrades, Shatov. At the end of the play, when the members of the group either have gone crazy or are being punished for their participation in the execution, Peter escapes to Europe, feeling no remorse whatsoever.

Ivan Shatov (SHAH-tov), a student friend of Stavrogin and a former revolutionary. Shatov has renounced his radical leftist politics and has embraced Russia and Christianity. His refusal to submit further to Peter's authority infuriates the latter, who orders his murder on the grounds that Shatov will betray the group to the police.

Alexey Kirilov (ah-lehk-SAY kih-RIH-lov), an engineer who is obsessed with suicide as a means of proving his own freedom. He allows Peter to manipulate him into claiming responsibility, in a suicide note, for Shatov's death. The ploy fails when one of the terrorist group, Lyamshim, cracks and tells the authorities what really happened.

Lisa Drozdov (DROZ-dov), a beautiful noblewoman who loves Nicholas and gives herself to him even though she knows that he will ruin her. At the play's end, she is killed by a mob seeking vengeance against Nicholas, whom they hold responsible for the Lebyatkins' deaths.

Maria Lebyatkin (leh-BYAH-tkihn), Nicholas' wife, a virgin, cripple, and victim, along with her brother, of Fedka, the assassin.

Dasha Shatov, Ivan's sister and one of Nicholas' mistresses.

Maria Shatov, Ivan's wife and one of Nicholas' mistresses. She has his illegitimate child.

Liputin,
Lyamshin,
Shigalov, and
Virginsky, members of Peter's terrorist group.

— *Richard J. Golsan*

THE POSSESSED
(Besy)

Author: Fyodor Dostoevski (1821-1881)
First published: 1871-1872
Genre: Novel

Locale: Russia
Time: Mid-nineteenth century
Plot: Psychological realism

Stepan Trofimovitch Verhovensky (steh-PAHN troh-FIH-mo-vihch vehr-hoh-VEHN-skih), a former professor of history, a free thinker, a mild liberal, and an old-fashioned, dandified intellectual. The protégé of Varvara Petrovna Stavrogina, a wealthy provincial aristocrat, he has lived for years on her country estate, first as the tutor of her impressionable son, later as the companion and mentor of his temperamental, strong-willed friend. At times he and his patroness quarrel violently, but usually their relationship is one of mutual understanding and respect. One of the old man's claims to fame is the fact that a poem he had written in his student days was seized by the authorities in Moscow, and he still believes that he is politically suspect. Weak-willed, opinionated, hedonistic in a mild way, he has indulged his own tastes and personal comfort while allowing his only son to be reared by distant relatives. At the end, appalled by the revelation of his son's nihilistic and criminal activities, and seeing himself in the role of an intellectual buffoon in the service of Varvara Petrovna, he wanders off to search for the true Russia. Like King Lear, he is ennobled by suffering, and he dies with a deeper knowledge of himself and his unhappy country, divided between the moribund tradition of the past and the revolutionary spirit of the younger generation. Dostoevsky seems to make Stepan Trofimovitch an illustration of the way in which a generation of sentimental, theorizing, intellectual liberals bred a new generation of nihilists and terrorists who believed only in violence and destruction.

Pyotr Stepanovitch Verhovensky (PYOH-tr steh-PAHN-o-vihch), Stepan's nihilistic, revolutionary, despicable son, who has traveled widely and engaged in a number of political intrigues. Really an antihero, he is an early model of the modern, exacting, scientific, psychological fanatic and iconoclast. A monster in his capacity for irreligiosity, deception, and destruction, he undermines the moral integrity of his friend Nikolay Vsyevoldovitch Stavrogin, creates discord between his father and Varvara Petrovna, conducts a campaign of terrorism in the provincial town to which he returns after a number of years spent in study and travel, and foments criminal activities that include arson and murder. If his father's chief trait is self-delusion, Pyotr's is the ability to delude others and lead them to their ruin. He is always sure of his mission, fanatical in his single-minded belief in dissent and destruction, and convinced that the end justifies any means. Filled with a sense of his own power, he is totally wicked and corrupt, although he is not without charm to those who do not know his real nature.

Varvara Petrovna Stavrogin (vahr-VAH-ruh PEHT-rov-nuh stahv-ROH-gihn), a wealthy woman who indulges her son, befriends Stepan Trofimovitch, pays for the schooling of Pyotr Stepanovitch, and takes into her household as her companion the daughter of a former serf. Tall, bony, yellow-complexioned, she is impressive in her outspoken, autocratic behavior. Abrupt and unsentimental for the most part, she is also capable of deep feeling. Her strength of character is shown at the end of the novel, when she begins to rebuild her life after revelations of Stepan Trofimovitch's dilettantish intellectualism, her son's weakness and waywardness, and the ruthless violence of the revolutionary group. Her final blow is her son's suicide.

Nikolay Vsyevolodovitch Stavrogin (nih-koh-LI vsyeh-voh-LOH-do-vihch), the son of Varvara Petrovna. A mixture of the sensitive and the coarse, the sensual and the spiritual, he has lived abroad for a number of years. There, he has engaged in revolutionary activities and debauchery with a number of women, including Marya Timofyevna Lebyadkin, the crippled, weak-minded woman whom he married to show his mocking contempt for social conventions, and Marya Ignatyevna Shatov, who is carrying his child. His friendship with Pyotr Stepanovitch leads to the formation of a revolutionary group that he establishes in his native village. Though he is ostensibly the leader, his friend is the real power within the group, and Pyotr Stepanovitch's wild dream is to make Stavrogin a false pretender who will lead Russia back into barbarism. Handsome in appearance, Stavrogin makes his presence felt everywhere, and his reputation makes him feared. Loved by some, hated by others, he has lost all capacity for deep feeling; he tries only to experience violently contrasting sensations as a means of escaping boredom. The night Lizaveta Nikolaevna Tushin spends with him makes him see himself as a spiritually sterile and physically impotent man

aged before his time. Hoping to escape from his condition of moral torpor, he asks Darya, the sister of Ivan Shatov, to start a new life with him. She agrees, but before they can leave the village, he commits suicide.

Ivan Shatov (ee-VAHN shah-TOHF), the liberated and liberal-minded son of a former serf on the Stavrogin estate. Tutored by Stepan Trofimovitch and sent away by Varvara Petrovna for further education, he has traveled and worked in America. Disillusioned by Pyotr Stepanovitch and his revolutionary group, Shatov still worships Stavrogin for the image of idealism he evokes. He represents the emancipated, educated Russian who in spite of the disordered life about him clings to his elemental feelings for home, friends, the countryside, ideals of liberty, and passion for independence. Unable to accept the nihilism for which Pyotr Stepanovitch stands, he announces his intention to believe in a human Christ, a Christ of the people. When his wife, from whom he has been separated, returns to give birth to her child, Shatov welcomes her with joy and the child as a token of the future. Because of fears that Shatov will betray the activities of the revolutionary group, Pyotr Stepanovitch has him murdered. Dostoevski uses Shatov as a spokesman for some of his own views on politics and religion.

Marya Ignatyevna Shatov (MAH-ryuh ihg-NAH-tehv-nah), Ivan's wife, who returns to his home to bear her child, fathered, it is suggested, by Stavrogin.

Alexey Nilitch Kirillov (ah-lehk-SAY NIH-lihch kih-RIHL-of), a member of the revolutionary group. Existentialist in his beliefs, he is able neither to accept God nor to endure the human condition. He has reached a state of negation in which his only hope is to commit suicide and thus to become God by exercising his will over life and death. Before he shoots himself, Pyotr Stepanovitch persuades him to sign a false confession to the murder of Shatov, killed by the revolutionaries because they are afraid he will betray them to the authorities after the murder of Ignat Lebyadkin and his sister.

Ignat Lebyadkin (ihg-NAHT leh-BYAHT-kihn), a retired army captain, pompous in manner, ridiculous in his pride, crafty in his schemes for extorting money from Stavrogin, his brother-in-law. A would-be gallant, he makes approaches to Lizaveta Nikolaevna Tushin. Pyotr Stepanovitch sees Lebyadkin and his sister as threats to his plans for Stavrogin, and he arranges to have them killed. Their bodies are found by horrified, indignant villagers in the smoldering embers of their house.

Marya Timofyevna Lebyadkin (tih-moh-FYEHV-nah), a girl of weak mind and a cripple, Captain Lebyadkin's sister, whom Stavrogin has married in order to show his contempt for his position in society and to perpetrate a cruel joke on the girl and himself. He has kept the marriage secret, however, and the efforts to determine his relation with Marya agitate his family and friends after his return to the village. He treats her with a mixture of amused condescension and ironic gallantry.

Lizaveta Nikolaevna Tushin (lih-zah-VEH-tah nih-koh-LAH-ehv-nah TEW-shihn), also called **Liza**, the daughter of Praskovya Ivanovna Drozdov, Varvara Petrovna's friend, by a previous marriage. High-spirited and unconventional, she is strongly attracted to Stavrogin and is for a time interested in the proposed publication of a magazine by the revolutionary band. On the night that Captain Lebyadkin and his sister are killed, she gives herself to Stavrogin, only to discover that he is no more than the empty shell of a man. Stopping by to view the smoking ruins of the Lebyadkin house, she is beaten to death by the angry villagers because of her association with Stavrogin.

Praskovya Ivanovna Drozdov (prahs-KOHV-yah ee-VAHN-ehv-nah DROHZ-dof), Lizaveta Nikolaevna's mother. She and Varvara Petrovna have reached an understanding for the marriage of Liza and Stavrogin, but the young people have quarreled, possibly over Darya Shatov, possibly because of Stavrogin's friendship with Pyotr Stepanovitch, while all were living in Switzerland. Not knowing the reason, Praskovya blames Stavrogin for the disagreement and is filled with resentment against him.

Darya Paulovna Shatov (DAH-ryuh PAHV-lov-nuh), also called **Dasha** and **Dashenka**, Ivan Shatov's meek, pretty sister, who has grown up in the Stavrogin household, half companion, half servant to Varvara Petrovna. During a visit to Switzerland, her mistress leaves the girl behind as a companion to Liza. On her return, Varvara Petrovna plans for a time to marry the girl to Stepan Trofimovitch, and Darya meekly consents. When Stavrogin, with whom she is secretly in love, asks her to go away with him, she readily agrees. He commits suicide before they can arrange for their departure.

Andrey Antonovitch von Lembke (ahn-DRAY ahn-TOH-no-vihch von LEHM-kee), the new governor of the province.

Yulia Mikhailovna von Lembke (YEW-lih-yuh mee-HI-lov-nah), the governor's vulgar, ambitious wife.

Semyon Yakovelitch Karmazinov (seh-MYOHN YAH-kohv-leh-vihch kahr-mah-ZIH-nof), a pompous, foolish, elderly writer who makes a ridiculous spectacle of himself at a literary fete. He is Dostoevski's satirical portrait of Ivan Turgenev.

Liputin (lih-POH-tyihn), a slanderer and zealous reformer, **Erkel** (EHR-kehl), a youthful enthusiast, **Virginsky** (vihr-JIHN-skee), a civil clerk, and **Shigalov** (SHIH-guh-lof), his brother, members of the revolutionary group.

Lyamshin (LYAHM-shihn), the member of the group who confesses and reveals the activities of the band to the authorities.

Arina Prohorovna Virginsky (ah-RIH-nuh proh-HOH-rov-nuh), a midwife.

Artemy Pavlovitch Gaganov (ahr-TYOHM-ee PAHV-lo-vihch gah-GAH-nof), the local aristocrat with whom Stavrogin fights a duel.

Andrey Antonovitch Blum (ahn-TOH-no-vihch blohm), the assistant to Governor von Lembke.

Sofya Matveyevna Ulitin (SOHF-yuh maht-vee-YEHF-nah YEW-lih-tihn), the young widow who aids Stepan Trofimovitch during his wanderings. She goes to live with Varvara Petrovna.

Anton Lavrentyevitch G———v (ahn-TOHN lahv-REHN-tyee-vihch), the friend of Stepan Trofimovitch and the narrator of this story of violence and passion.

POSSESSING THE SECRET OF JOY

Author: Alice Walker (1944-   )
First published: 1992
Genre: Novel

Locale: California and Olinka, in Africa
Time: The latter half of the twentieth century
Plot: Social realism

Tashi Evelyn Johnson, the protagonist. She is born in Africa and reared until she is a young woman as a member of the Olinka tribe, then moves to America, where she lives for most of her adult years. She returns to Africa when she is middle-aged. She intends to murder M'Lissa, who performed a female circumcision on her. Tashi experiences a number of cultural shocks in her life, from the British takeover of her country to moving to America and trying to adjust to being an "African American." In her moves, she marries, has a slightly retarded son, learns that her husband has had a longtime affair with a white woman, and remembers a series of Olinka rituals that left her scarred for life and killed her sister. These rituals, which included genital and facial mutilation, haunt her every waking hour. In the process of making adjustments, she loses her mind.

Adam, Tashi's husband, who grew up in Olinka. He is, on the surface, a good husband and provider. Tashi's childhood scars and her ever present responses to them create a rift in their marriage. He is the adopted son of missionaries who attempted to convince the Olinkans to give up ritual mutilation.

Olivia, Adam's sister. She has been Tashi's best friend since they were prepubescent girls in Africa. She tried to convince Tashi not to allow herself to be circumcised. She understands some of the strange behavior that Tashi exhibits in her middle age and helps her deal with the medical problems that result from the circumcision.

Mzee (The Old Man), a friend to Tashi and Adam who acts as therapist, for a while, to Tashi. He has spent time among Tashi's people and tries to help her deal with her childhood trauma.

Bentu (Benny) Moraga, Tashi and Adam's son, who is slightly retarded. He responds to his limitations by keeping lists of such things as how to get to the grocery store and topics he wants to discuss with his parents. Given Tashi's medical condition, his conception and birth are miraculous.

Lisette, Mzee's niece and Adam's lover. She is the mother of Adam's son Pierre. As a white woman, she first thought her attraction to Adam had to do with his race, but later she simply fell in love with him, even though she knew and respected Tashi. She often, however, feels guilty about being the "other woman," and she often muses over the fact that both women have a son by Adam; she wonders what Tashi must think of this.

Pierre, Lisette and Adam's son. He displays the acuteness of intelligence that marks both of his parents. He studies all he can about Africa. Although he receives a Harvard University education, he is down to earth enough to seek out his half brother. During the novel, he becomes the protector of his retarded brother, Benny.

M'Lissa, the Olinkan *tsunga*, who circumcises the young Olinkan girls. In Tashi's mind, she is responsible for the death of Tashi's sister Dura and countless other African women. Tashi reasons that if M'Lissa did not carry out the ritual, the ritual might die and girls would not be sacrificed needlessly for men. M'Lissa believes that she serves her society well by performing its rituals. In her old age, she is a national celebrity.

Mbati, the young woman who is taking care of M'Lissa when Tashi returns to Olinka. She becomes a spiritual daughter to Tashi, a replacement for the daughter Tashi has aborted.

Raya, the American therapist who helps Tashi to understand herself and to accept African American women.

Dura, Tashi's older sister, who bleeds to death when the rite of circumcision is performed.

— Charles P. Toombs

POSSESSION

Author: A[ntonia] S[usan] Byatt (1936-   )
First published: 1990
Genre: Novel

Locale: London, Lincolnshire, and North Yorkshire in England and the Breton coast in France
Time: The 1980's, alternating with the 1870's and 1880's
Plot: Love

Randolph Henry Ash, a famous Victorian poet. Both his art and his life reveal a man who discovers the life of the mind first and the love of his life much later. He has hidden stories to tell to whomever can enter into correspondence with him.

Christabel LaMotte, who lives a sheltered life as a single Victorian woman, first with her friend Blanche Glover and later in the attic of her sister's home. Her art is not widely appreciated, suggesting gender attitudes that survive the Victorians and divide the modern researchers, who study them.

Ellen Ash, Randolph's wife, whose Victorian values demand that she hide the truth even in her grave.

Blanche Glover, Christabel's companion, whose death raises questions about love and gender.

Roland Mitchell, the protagonist. He has a doctorate in literature but has found only a bleak position as a research assistant. His live-in relationship with Val is equally bleak. They met as students; inertia and failure have kept them together. Roland's research keeps him buried in the London Library until he discovers evidence of a correspondence between Ash and LaMotte. His ensuing quest carries him back in touch with life and reveals him to be Ash's spiritual descendant.

Maud Bailey, a lecturer at the University of Lincoln. She is an expert on, as well as a direct descendant of, Christabel LaMotte. An icy but beautiful exterior attests her ordered single life before Roland involves her in his quest. She too will discover that the journey into the living past is a journey home to the buried self.

James Blackadder, the scholar who employs Roland in his "Ash Factory." He grows by joining the quest and sharing it with Leonora Stern.

Beatrice Nest, a diligent worker in the Ash Factory, preserving the story of Ash's wife, Ellen. She learns what happens when the buried past and the buried self are both exposed to the open air.

Leonora Stern, an American scholar who shares with Maud Bailey more than an interest in LaMotte's poetry. She learns much about British and American, and male and female, correspondences on her quest.

Mortimer Cropper, an American who deals in death. He provides an apt antagonist for the living and the dead who confront him on the quest.

— Thelma J. Shinn

THE POSTMAN ALWAYS RINGS TWICE

Author: James M. Cain (1892-1977)
First published: 1934
Genre: Novel

Locale: Southern California
Time: 1933
Plot: Detective and mystery

Frank Chambers, a drifter who is kicked off a hay truck in front of Nick Papadakis' Twin Oaks tavern. Nick offers him a job; attracted to Nick's sultry wife, Cora, Frank accepts. Engaged in a brutally passionate affair with Cora, Frank conspires with Cora to kill Nick. When an attempt to drown Nick in his bathtub fails, Frank departs, but he finds himself drawn back to Cora. Nick happily rehires Frank, who resumes his affair with Cora. A second attempt on Nick's life through a faked automobile accident is successful. Playing on the hospitalized Frank's confusion and fears, District Attorney Sackett manipulates him into signing a complaint against Cora. After the trial and Cora's release, the two return to the Twin Oaks. When Cora leaves for a week, Frank engages in a one-week

affair with a woman he meets, Madge Allen. Again, however, he finds himself drawn back to Cora. Frank has to beat Kennedy, a would-be blackmailer, into submission. Frank and Cora realize they are bound to each other. They marry and celebrate with an excursion to the beach. When Cora feels ill, Frank rushes her to the hospital, but in a foolish attempt to pass a truck, he drives into a culvert and Cora is killed. Charged with her murder, Frank is found guilty and sentenced to death. He spends his time on death row composing the narrative of these events, which he leaves in the hands of Father McConnell for publication in the event his execution is not stayed.

Cora Papadakis, born **Cora Smith**, the winner of a beauty contest in Iowa who went to Hollywood and, failing to fulfill her dreams there, escaped working in a hash house by marrying Nick Papadakis and doing the cooking for their Twin Oaks tavern. She is, however, repelled by Nick's ethnic background, and she welcomes the rough sexuality of Frank Chambers. She urges Frank to join her in killing Nick. In their first plot, Cora agrees to drown Nick in his bathtub. An accident aborts the attempt, and she agrees to abandon the Twin Oaks with Frank. She cannot, however, bear the idea of endless rambling and returns to Nick. After Frank reappears, she participates in the second, successful plot to kill Nick. When Frank seems to turn against her by filing a complaint, Cora turns against Frank by signing a full confession, which is then suppressed by her attorney, Katz, as part of his strategy to get Cora off with a conviction for manslaughter. Although Frank and Cora resume operation of the Twin Oaks and, at Cora's instigation, make improvements, they continue to mistrust each other until a crisis brings their conflict into the open. Cora informs Frank that she is pregnant. They marry, but after a brief interlude of happiness at the beach, Cora falls ill and dies in an automobile accident as Frank drives her to the hospital.

Nick Papadakis, a naïve, happy Greek immigrant who finds his American Dream in ownership of a California roadside tavern and marriage to a pretty American woman. Nick never recognizes the passion that connects his wife and his employee; he remains a benevolent admirer of both. He is unable to remember the details of their first assault on him in his bathtub, and he is singing drunkenly when Frank smashes his skull with a wine bottle prior to setting up the fake automobile accident.

Sackett, a tough district attorney with a heart of stone. He makes a wager with Katz that he can convict Cora for Nick's murder. Bested by Katz, he devotes himself to a zealous and successful prosecution of Frank for the murder of Cora.

Katz, a resourceful defense attorney who enjoys the competition with Sackett. By having Cora plead guilty to Nick's murder and then negotiating with the insurance companies interested in the case, he secures a manslaughter conviction and a suspended sentence. He prefers the hundred dollars he wins from Sackett to the ten thousand dollars Frank and Cora receive from the insurance companies. He is, however, unable to vindicate Frank when he is falsely charged with Cora's murder.

Kennedy, a former police officer who acts as Katz's agent. He attempts to blackmail Frank and Cora with the confession Cora made to Katz, but Frank beats him into submission and destroys the evidence.

Madge Allen, a trainer of big cats. A chance encounter with Frank in a parking lot leads to an intense one-week affair during Cora's absence. Madge's appearance at the Twin Oaks sparks the final crisis in which Frank and Cora confront each other and realize that they are bound ineluctably to each other. She testifies reluctantly at Frank's trial for the murder of Cora.

— *J. K. Van Dover*

THE POT OF GOLD
(Aulularia)

Author: Plautus (c. 255-184 B.C.E.)
First performed: 200-191 B.C.E.
Genre: Drama

Locale: Athens
Time: The second century B.C.E.
Plot: Comedy

Euclio (EW-klee-oh), an old miser intent on hiding from others his possession of a pot of gold hidden by his miserly grandfather but revealed to him in its hiding place by his household god. Wishing to use the gold as a dowry to help his daughter Phaedria get a husband, Euclio hides it again, pretends poverty, and suspects everyone of trying to rob him or trick him out of his treasure. Unsure of Megadorus' sincerity, he nevertheless agrees to let him marry Phaedria because of his willingness to take her without a dowry and to pay the wedding expenses. After the withdrawal of Megadorus as a suitor and the return of the stolen gold by Lyconides, Euclio accepts the young man as a son-in-law and even gives the gold to the newly wedded couple. The story of Euclio is probably based on one of Menander's lost comedies.

Megadorus (meh-guh-DOH-ruhs), Euclio's rich old neighbor. Scornful of marriage to a wealthy woman of high station who would squander his money and who might try to order him about, he is attracted to Phaedria because of her poverty, and he is willing to marry her without a dowry. For Lyconides' sake, he gives up his marriage plans so that his nephew may have her. The playwright uses Megadorus as a mouthpiece for satirizing rich women and their expensive tastes.

Eunomia (ew-NOH-mee-uh), Megadorus' sister, who wishes him to marry and father children. She later intercedes for Lyconides so that Phaedria may marry him rather than Megadorus.

Lyconides (li-KOH-nih-deez), Eunomia's son, in love with Phaedria, whom he deflowered while drunk and whom he wishes to marry. He confesses his deed to Eunomia and asks her aid in getting Megadorus to let him marry Phaedria. Thinking Euclio has discovered his guilt, he confesses and begs forgiveness, only to be thought confessing the theft of Euclio's gold. He recovers the gold from the real thief, returns it, and gets both Phaedria and the gold with Euclio's blessing.

Staphyla (STA-fih-luh), an old slave belonging to Euclio. Aware of Phaedria's pregnancy and wishing to help her, Staphyla worries about the discovery of the girl's condition.

Phaedria (FEE-dree-uh), Euclio's young daughter, who is favorably regarded by her household god because of her devotion to him and her gifts honoring him. Pregnant by Lyconides, she bears his child and marries him afterward. Phaedria does not appear in the action of the play, but her offstage voice is once heard calling for the nurse during the pains of childbirth.

Strobilus (STROH-bih-luhs), Lyconides' slave, who sees Euclio hide his gold first at the shrine of Faith and afterward in

Sylvanus' grove. He steals it to use as a bribe to acquire his freedom from slavery, but he is forced to give up the treasure without getting his freedom.

Pythodicus (pih-THOH-dih-kuhs), Megadorus' slave.

Anthrax (AN-thraks) and

Congrio (KON-gree-oh), two cooks hired for the wedding of Megadorus and Phaedria. Congrio is saucy to Euclio after being unjustly beaten and berated by him.

Phrygia (FRIH-jee-uh) and

Eleusium (eh-LEW-see-uhm), two music girls hired as entertainers for the wedding.

THE POTTING SHED

Author: Graham Greene (1904-1991)
First published: 1957
Genre: Drama

Locale: England
Time: The 1950's
Plot: Mythic

James Callifer, an employee of a provincial newspaper in central England. Although he is in his mid-forties, he is immature, self-centered, diffident, and occasionally suicidal. He is seeing a psychiatrist, who is trying to help him cope with feelings that life is meaningless, that he is a failure, that he is incapable of loving another human being, and that he has been rejected by his family for some dark deed that he has suppressed from consciousness. In this highly symbolic play, the protagonist represents modern humanity, which has lost its way because of its abandonment of religious faith.

Mrs. Callifer, an upper-middle-class housewife, the mother of James and John. At the age of seventy, she is still a handsome, dignified woman. She has devoted her life to the service of her husband, who was once an internationally noted writer of rationalist, atheistic works in the spirit of George Bernard Shaw and Bertrand Russell but has faded into obscurity. After her husband's death offstage in the first scene of the play, she realizes that he was a weak man who needed her protection and that he was not only cruel but also intellectually dishonest. She confesses to James that she has kept him away from his father for many years because H. C. Callifer's entire belief system as well as his published works and reputation had been jeopardized by a "miracle" that occurred in the potting shed thirty years earlier.

John Callifer, a prosperous banker roughly fifty years old. In striking contrast to his younger brother, James, John is pompous, self-assured, and insensitive. His main function in the play is to represent what his father must have been like in his prime. Having adopted all of his father's views, John has never troubled to have a serious philosophical thought. Like many modern men of affairs, his way of coping with existential questions is to ignore them.

Anne Callifer, a thirteen-year-old student. This pretty and precocious daughter of the widowed John is a product of enlightened views about education and child rearing. Having been taught to reject religion and believe only in facts, she has become almost too headstrong for her elders to manage. She functions as a catalyst. It is she who, entirely on her own initiative, telegraphs her Uncle James about his father's ap-

proaching death. Later, she locates Mrs. Potter, who gives James information that enables him to relive his devastating childhood trauma. Anne symbolizes the future of humanity: It can become more spiritually alienated through rational skepticism or regain its capacity for joy and love through a leap of faith.

Father William Callifer, an elderly, alcoholic Catholic priest. For many years, he has been unwelcome at his brother H. C. Callifer's home because of his conversion to Catholicism. There is a stronger reason for his rejection, however, and its revelation forms the play's climax. When James was fourteen years old, he tried to hang himself in the potting shed because his father, through scornful mockery and rationalist arguments, had destroyed his faith in God. Father Callifer prayed to God to bring James back to life and offered in exchange for the boy's life the only thing of any value he possessed: his religious faith. James revived by a seeming miracle, but William has functioned ever since as an alcoholic priest without faith in his vocation. After the loving reunion between uncle and nephew, both regain their belief in God and a meaningful universe.

Sara Callifer, James's former wife, an attractive woman of thirty-six. She resembles her former husband in being joyless and adrift. She is still in love with James but was divorced from him because he was emotionally dead. She symbolizes the death of love between the sexes that results from atheism and materialism. After James regains his religious faith, he proposes that they remarry, telling her that he is now capable of human love.

Dr. Frederick Baston, H. C. Callifer's physician and disciple. A small, fussy, pedantic man in his sixties, Baston serves as a comic figure who represents the rationalist tradition.

Dr. Kreuzer, James's elderly psychiatrist. He represents the ineffectiveness of science in resolving the deepest problems of the human soul.

Mrs. Potter, the widow of the Callifers' old family gardener. She gives James the first insight into what really happened to him in the potting shed.

— *Bill Delaney*

POWER
(Jud Süss)

Author: Lion Feuchtwanger (1884-1958)
First published: 1925
Genre: Novel

Locale: Germany
Time: Mid-eighteenth century
Plot: Historical

Josef Süss Oppenheimer (YOH-sehf sews OH-pan-hi-mur), a handsome, almost dandified opportunist, son of a German Christian marshal and a Jewish mother. He aids the countess' scheme to try to keep her hold on Eberhard, advises Karl and Marie financially, wields political power, gains a great fortune, engineers Karl's liaison with Magdalen, tricks Karl into a military fiasco, and is finally hanged. Though he could have lived by telling of his Christian father, he chooses to die proudly as a Jew.

Rabbi Gabriel (GAH-bree-ayl), his uncle, a man of melancholy demeanor and mystic ways, reputed to be the Wandering Jew.

Naemi (nah-AY-mee), Süss' daughter, who falls from a housetop to her death while escaping a sexual attack by Karl.

Eberhard Ludwig (AY-bur-hahrd LEWT-vihkh), duke of Swabia, a stout, dissipated man who deserts his mistress and returns to his wife to beget an heir.

Karl Alexander, a penniless prince who, after marrying Marie and becoming a Catholic, inherits the duchy when Eberhard dies. A despicable rake, he establishes a liaison with Magdalen and later tries to rape Naemi.

Marie Auguste (ow-GEWS-teh), Karl's duchess, daughter of Anself Franz.

Weissensee (VI-san-say), a politician who hates Süss, plots against him, and indirectly causes Naemi's death.

Magdalen Sibylle (MAHG-dah-layn sih-BIH-leh), his daughter, who becomes Karl's mistress as a result of a ruse by Süss.

Isaac Landauer (EE-sah-ahk LAHN-dow-ur), a brilliant, distinctively Jewish international banker and financial agent for the countess. He gives Süss his first opportunity to rise materially in the world.

Prince Anselm Franz von Thurn and Taxis (AHN-sehlm frahnts fon toorn oond TAHKS-sihs), father of Marie Auguste. He brings about his daughter's marriage and Karl's conversion to Catholicism.

Reb Jecheskel Seligmann (YA-shas-kehl SAY-lihg-mahn), an innocent Jew arrested for the murder of a child. He is saved by Süss.

Christl (krihstl), the countess, wife of the dullwitted Lord High Steward and Eberhard's extravagant, lampooned mistress of thirty years, deserted principally because she had grown fat, asthmatic, and middle-aged.

Johanna Elisabetha (YOH-hah-nah eh-LEE-sah-beh-tah), Eberhard's bleak, sour, neglected duchess.

THE POWER AND THE GLORY

Author: Graham Greene (1904-1991)
First published: 1940
Genre: Novel

Locale: Mexico
Time: The 1930's
Plot: Psychological realism

A Whiskey Priest who, though never named, goes sometimes under the assumed name of **Montez**. For eight years a fugitive from the anticlerical regime in a small Mexican province, the Whiskey Priest has managed occasionally to celebrate mass, to baptize children, and to say the last rites for the dying. His great failing is drink, though he has also committed adultery in the town of Concepción, where he had his last parish. Pride and slothfulness have played an equal part in making him the last cleric in the province; he feels the honor of martyrdom, and he simply exists without a plan for escape. Finally, he is humbled by the knowledge that he is loved and protected wherever he goes, and the sacrifice of hostages for his surrender fixes in his mind a plan of escape. Yet he is not a free agent, and he falls into what he knows is a trap when called upon to administer the last rites to an American gunman. Freely admitting his cowardice and lack of vision, the priest dies with the sure knowledge that he has loved and discharged his duties with a semblance of dignity.

Father José (hoh-SEH), a defrocked priest who marries and renounces his religion. Obviously a coward, he refuses any participation in the religion he so easily gave up and so much regrets. He is the laughingstock of a village as the victim of an ill-tempered wife whose sexual entreaties symbolize the degradation to which he has fallen. Without any humanitarian impulses, he refuses to hear the confession of the Whiskey Priest, even when sanctioned to do so by the government.

A Lieutenant of Police, not named, who exhibits the same fanaticism for the new state as the renegade priest does for his order. A man without formal education but with a zeal for reform that stems from his peasant childhood, the young man puts his faith in the pistol. His mind is unsettled by the Whiskey Priest's sense of destiny in a lost cause, for he cannot reconcile faith without deeds. Also, he is confused and unhappy over the means of taking and killing hostages used to the end of destroying the old priest. His tough manner hides a sentimental streak that appears in ironic contrasts.

A Mestizo, a poor half-breed who acts the part of Judas with a faltering heart. Shrewdly recognizing the Whiskey Priest when all others fail, the tenacious opportunist becomes the cleric's nemesis, waiting for the right time to strike. His whining, wheedling, ingratiating manner makes him the more deadly and sinister to the harassed father. The poor man has lived so long as a toady of the police that he lacks the will to resist, though he begs forgiveness after his betrayal of the priest.

Marcía (mahr-SEE-ah) and

Brigida (BREE-gee-dah), mother and daughter, the symbols of the priest's greatest transgression. Through boredom and alcohol, the middle-aged priest commits adultery with his parishioner Marcía, and he dies regretting that he has not loved his seven-year-old daughter enough to make any difference in her life. While the mother has a kind of inverted pride in her ghostly and human father, the poor youngster can only feel suspicion and disdain for the man who makes of her an outsider.

A Dentist,

a Trader, and

a Plantation Owner, who shelter the priest during his

pilgrimages toward escape. The daughter of the trader and the sister of the plantation owner are true humanitarians and offer solace as well as food and shelter to the priest. The dentist is as fated as the priest with whom he identifies himself, though the dramatic death outside his window seems to move him to some resolution.

THE POWER OF DARKNESS
(Vlast tmy: Ili, "Kogotok uvyaz, vsey ptichke propast")

Author: Leo Tolstoy (1828-1910)
First published: 1887
Genre: Drama

Locale: Russia
Time: The nineteenth century
Plot: Domestic

Nikíta Akímitch Tchilíkin (nih-KIH-tah ah-KIH-mihch chih-LIH-kihn), a laborer employed on the farm of Peter Ignátitch. He is engaged in an affair with his employer's wife, Anísya. Nikíta and his mistress, with the help of Nikíta's mother, Matryóna, plan Peter's murder. When their victim is dead, the guilty couple marry and Nikíta becomes master of the farm. Soon tiring of his wife, he begins an affair with Akoulína, by whom he has a child. At the urging of his wife and mother, he kills the baby. At Akoulína's wedding feast, Nikíta falls on his knees, confesses his crimes, and begs the forgiveness of all he has misused. He is then bound and led away.

Peter Ignátitch (ih-GNA-tihch), a well-to-do peasant. He is murdered for his property by his adulterous wife Anísya, at the instigation of her lover, Nikíta, and his mother, Matryóna.

Anísya (ah-NIH-syah), Peter Ignátitch's second wife. Engaged in an affair with Peter's hired man, Nikíta, she is en-couraged by her lover and his mother to poison her husband. She marries Nikíta, who soon tires of her. When he has a child by Akoulína, Anísya urges him to kill the child to force him to share her guilt in the poisoning of Peter Ignátitch.

Matryóna (mah-TRYOH-nah), Nikíta's mother. She urges Anísya to poison Peter Ignátitch so that the way will be left clear for Nikíta's marriage to Anísya and his mastery of Peter's farm. Later, she encourages her son to murder his child by Akoulína.

Akoulína (ah-kew-LIH-nah), Peter Ignátitch's daughter by his first marriage. She is seduced by Nikíta. When their child is born, Nikíta, prompted by Anísya, kills it.

Marína (mah-REE-nah), an orphan girl who is seduced by Nikíta.

Akím (ah-KIHM), Nikíta's father.

THE PRAGUE ORGY

Author: Philip Roth (1933-   )
First published: 1985
Genre: Novella

Locale: Prague, Czechoslovakia
Time: January/February, 1976
Plot: Comic realism

Nathan Zuckerman, a famous American novelist, the author of *Carnovsky*. He is approached by Zdenek Sisovsky, a Czech refugee, who wants him to help retrieve his father's unpublished short stories, which are still in Prague. Reluctantly, Zuckerman goes.

Zdenek Sisovsky, a Czech writer, the author of a single book, a mild satire that caused a scandal when published in 1967. He has therefore left his country, his wife and child, and his aging mother to go to America with his mistress, Eva Kalinova. He seeks the aid of Nathan Zuckerman, whose work he praises, to help retrieve his father's unpublished Yiddish short stories, which remain in the possession of his estranged wife, Olga.

Eva Kalinova, once the most famous actress in Czechoslovakia, now a distraught, bitter refugee with her current lover, Sisovsky. An accomplished Chekhovian, she no longer acts, because her English is poor, but she has become a salesperson for women's dresses. In Czechoslovakia, she was married to a famous folk singer, Petr Kalina, but she left him for a Jewish "parasite," Pavel Polak, and fell into disgrace.

Olga Sisovsky, Zdenek's estranged wife, herself a writer, something of a celebrity, with "the most beautiful legs in Prague." She is also famous as a drunk and a promiscuous woman, the results of her profound despair. She falls in love with Zuckerman and wants him to marry her and take her away to America. At first, out of resentment against Sisovsky, she refuses to give up his father's stories, but later, she complies.

Rudolf Bolotka, Zuckerman's guide through Prague, formerly a theatrical producer and now a janitor in a museum. Separated from his wife and children, he has many girlfriends, which is the reason (he says) he cannot leave Prague, though he has been allowed to go. He introduces Zuckerman to Olga at Klenek's house, famous for its parties, while Klenek is in France directing a film.

Oldrich Hrobek, a young student with a deep interest in American writing who visits Zuckerman at his hotel. He tries to warn Zuckerman that the government suspects him of espionage and that he should leave Prague immediately. According to Bolotka, however, it is Hrobek and his professor who are in trouble with the authorities, not Zuckerman.

Novak, the minister of culture. He escorts Zuckerman to the airport as he is being expelled from Czechoslovakia; the stories Olga has given him are confiscated. Novak lectures Zuckerman on the virtues of hardworking Czech citizens, as opposed to the "sexual perverts," "alienated neurotics," and "bitter egomaniacs" Zuckerman has chosen to meet, whom most Czechs consider "malcontents and parasites and out-casts," according to Novak.

— *Jay L. Halio*

THE PRAIRIE: A Tale

Author: James Fenimore Cooper (1789-1851)
First published: 1827
Genre: Novel

Locale: The western plains of the United States
Time: 1804
Plot: Adventure

Natty Bumppo, the resourceful, independent old woodsman, now eighty-two years old. While trapping on the plains soon after the Louisiana Purchase, he camps one evening with a clan of tough, suspicious squatters, the Bush family. Later, accused of killing Asa Bush and having helped two young men to rescue their sweethearts from the Bushes, he is forced to avoid the squatters. Meanwhile, he and his companions are captured three times by hostile Sioux Indians. Natty serves as an interpreter, pacifies their captors, and helps the captives to escape. Finally, when the Sioux have been defeated and he has acquitted himself before the Bush clan, he decides to live with a tribe of friendly Pawnees until his death. Old and weak, he dies at sundown after rising to his feet and uttering a single word, "Here."

Ishmael Bush, the huge, ferocious head of the squatters. Though he has no respect for the law, he has a rude sense of justice and honor. Enraged by Indian attacks, the murder of his son Asa, and the abduction of his niece and a female hostage, he makes a temporary alliance with the Sioux in order to capture the fugitives. When his allies betray him, he calmly helps destroy them. In a rude court of justice, he sets the two pairs of lovers free, along with an itinerant naturalist. He also frees Natty Bumppo after the old hunter reveals Abiram White, Bush's brother-in-law, as the murderer. In the end, Bush and his family move on into the unknown West.

Esther Bush, Ishmael's aging, ill-tempered, almost mannish wife. The only literate member of the family, she reads the Bible but has the instincts of a wolf. Protective toward her young and savage toward trespassers, she is a formidable Indian fighter.

Ellen Wade, called **Nelly**, Esther Bush's pretty, vivacious niece. A homeless girl of eighteen, she feels gratitude toward the Bushes for their care, even if she feels little affection for them. More genteel than others of the Bush clan, she attracts Paul Hover, a young bee hunter from Kentucky, meets him secretly, and deserts the Bushes to share his adventures. Three times captured by Indians, and retaken by Ishmael, she finally receives Ishmael Bush's permission to marry Paul.

Abiram White, Esther's cowardly, treacherous brother. He kidnaps Inez Middleton, the wife of a young soldier, shoots Asa Bush in the back after a quarrel, and blames the killing on Natty Bumppo. When his guilt is disclosed, Ishmael Bush exacts a terrible vengeance. White is placed, bound, on a rock ledge where he must either hang himself or starve. His body is found dangling from a rope tied to the limb of a tree.

Dr. Obed Battius, also called **Obed Bat**, a pompous naturalist who prefers to travel in Natty's company rather than with the rude squatters. He exemplifies a foolish, academic approach to nature that contrasts strongly with Natty's natural, pious attitudes. A rather useless person, he owns a donkey that saves the party from a buffalo stampede by braying.

Paul Hover, Ellen Wade's reckless, spirited sweetheart and a roaming bee hunter. Captured three times by Sioux Indians, along with Natty and Ellen, he is always ready to fight, but Natty's diplomatic efforts succeed in saving his neck until he is finally safe and free to marry Ellen.

Captain Middleton, a handsome young soldier, the bridegroom of Inez Middleton, the hostage kidnapped by Abiram White. Searching for the Bushes, he comes across Natty Bumppo, Paul Hover, and Dr. Battius, who help him rescue his wife. After being captured by Indians, he is set free by Ishmael Bush and happily reunited with his wife. He is the grandson of a British officer whom Natty Bumppo had known in the days of the French and Indian Wars.

Inez Middleton, his wife, a wealthy young woman held prisoner by the squatters. Having been rescued by her husband and captured by Sioux, she is in danger of becoming the wife of Mahtoree, the Sioux chief. When he is killed in single-handed combat with a Pawnee warrior, she is restored to her husband by Ishmael Bush.

Hard-Heart, the noble young chief who befriends Natty Bumppo and his comrades and is finally captured with them by a band of fierce Sioux. About to be tortured, he escapes to his tribe, challenges the Sioux chief to battle, kills him, and defeats the hostile tribe. Natty chooses to make his home in Hard-Heart's Pawnee village, where he lives until his death.

Mahtoree, the bold, fierce, cunning Sioux chieftain. A dangerous foe, he captures Natty Bumppo and the old hunter's friends three times. He is about to take Inez Middleton for his wife when Hard-Heart, the Pawnee brave, challenges him to combat and kills him.

Swooping Eagle, called **Le Balafré**, an aged Sioux chieftain who wishes to adopt Hard-Heart as his son to save the young warrior from being killed. Hard-Heart expresses respect for the old man but rejects his offer.

Weucha, a boastful, greedy Sioux brave killed by Hard-Heart.

Tachechana, Mahtoree's Indian wife, shamed when she is forced to strip herself of her finery after the chief decides to discard her and wed Inez Middleton.

Asa Bush, Ishmael's eldest son, killed by his uncle, Abiram White.

Abner Bush,

Enoch Bush, and

Jesse Bush, Ishmael's other strapping sons.

Hetty Bush and

Phoebe Bush, his strong, vigorous young daughters.

PRAISESONG FOR THE WIDOW

Author: Paule Marshall (1929-   )
First published: 1983
Genre: Novel

Locale: A Caribbean cruise ship, Grenada, Carriacou, and New York
Time: Late 1970's
Plot: Social realism

Avatara (Avey) Johnson, an affluent, determined, and headstrong African American widow in her early sixties. She is driven, as the novel opens, to escape her two friends aboard a fifteen-day Caribbean vacation cruise and return home. Feeling compelled by memory, dreams, and the ill effects of a rich peach parfait dessert, Avey has packed her six suitcases in the middle of the night and has made arrangements to leave the majestic *Bianca Pride* at its next port of call and fly home to White Plains, New York. Always a strong-willed, self-possessed woman who has known precisely where she is going and what she is doing, throughout the novel Avey finds herself suddenly out of control, confronting her past through dreams and unbidden memories that shift her between the past and the present. An aunt long dead returns to haunt her; her late husband, Jerome, also returns to stand in disapproving judgment over her current, inexplicable, actions. Once on the island of Grenada, Avey discovers that she cannot immediately take a plane to New York. After an emotionally draining night, she begins to act on whim and impulse. Yielding to an invitation, almost a command, to accompany an old man she just met on a walk up the beach, Avey is persuaded to participate in a ritual excursion to the small outer island of Carriacou. Despite her fears and suspicions, she nevertheless agrees to go with Lebert Joseph and steps into a small weathered sailboat filled with islanders returning home, all strangers to her. The channel crossing proves both physically and emotionally challenging; however, after purging her body and her spirit, Avey finds the journey redemptive. She recognizes her ties to black people from Africa, the Caribbean, and the United States.

Jerome Johnson, Avey's dead husband, a powerful presence in the novel. Jerome, called Jay in the early, warm days of their marriage, suffers a crisis and undergoes a metamorphosis during the marriage. He changes from Jay, a hardworking yet tender and playful husband and father, to the stern, driven, grimly-determined-to-succeed Jerome Johnson figure. Faced with all the economic and societal barriers raised against black men, Jerome Johnson essentially loses his identity in the struggle to overcome such racism. He adheres so closely to the American work ethic in an effort to provide material wealth for his family that he sacrifices the value of his racial identity and, equally important, denies himself any pleasure in the marital relationship. Weary of being underpaid for doing twice the work at one job, Jay holds down two jobs and attends night school to acquire training as an accountant. No white firm will hire him, so, after obtaining credentials as a certified public accountant, Jay opens his own business, catering to small black firms. Eventually, his business is so well established that he can afford to move his family from the deteriorating urban neighborhood to suburban, upper-middle-class White Plains. When Jerome Johnson dies of a stroke, his widow can find no trace of Jay, and when she looks at his face in the coffin, she sees only a laughing mask.

Lebert Joseph, the disabled but active, proud, and independent old West Indian who befriends Avey on Grenada. He owns a rum shop. He persuades Avey to go with him on the ritual journey back to his home island of Carriacou. Lebert Joseph serves as a conduit, assisting Avey. He asks her questions about the "nation" to which she belongs or the dance she can do, helping her reconnect to an African cultural heritage and to a more immediate ritual in which she formerly participated first as a child visiting her great-aunt in Tatem, South Carolina, and later as a young married woman.

Aunt Cuney, Avey's deceased great-aunt, who, when Avey was a child, required every August that she be sent to Tatem. Stern, proud, and unrepentant in her youth, Aunt Cuney gives her the name Avatara and tells her the oral narrative passed down about the Africans of Ibo Landing. They were brought to Tatem for sale as slaves. Once ashore, although still chained from their voyage in the holds of slave ships, these powerful people took one look around them and subsequently turned around and walked back across the sea to Africa. Aunt Cuney also introduces her young niece to the Ring Shout, a religious circle "dance" in which the feet must never leave the floor, practiced by the older black people of Tatem. It is Aunt Cuney's vivid appearance in Avey's dream and her insistence during the dream that Avey come with her that, in part, compel Avey to leave her vacation cruise.

Rosalie Parvay, the strong, capable, middle-aged daughter of Lebert Joseph who has remained on Carriacou despite the fact that her children and grandchildren live in the United States or Canada. After Avey is stricken by illness on the excursion boat, Lebert Joseph takes her to Rosalie's home. Rosalie assists Avey almost as a native healer, bathing and tending to her and, in a "laying on of hands," massaging her entire body to help it recover from years of encasement in long-line girdles and other unnatural garments. When not ministering to Avey, Rosalie, who is a younger image of her father, rails against Lebert Joseph's stubbornness, maintaining vigorously that he is too old to live alone in Grenada. She wants him to remain on the small island and live with her, something he has never done.

— *Sandra Y. Govan*

PRAVDA: A Fleet Street Comedy

Authors: Howard Brenton (1942-   ) and David Hare (1947-   )
First published: 1985
Genre: Drama

Locale: England
Time: Late twentieth century
Plot: Comedy

Andrew May, a twenty-nine-year-old newspaper writer and editor who, in a short period of time, shoots up to the top of his field and as quickly falls as a protégé of tycoon Lambert Le Roux. When the play opens, Andrew is fresh, in love with newspaper work, and reasonably idealistic, learning the journalist's craft at the provincial *Leicester Bystander*, at which he is unexpectedly promoted to editor-in-chief by the paper's new owner, the capricious Le Roux. As he moves up in the Le Roux organization, he becomes a willing tool, shutting his eyes to Le Roux's excesses but still trying to hold on to the shreds of his integrity. When his conscience brings him to assert himself hesitantly against the millionaire, he finds his success at an end. The plot centers on the tarnishing of his character and the breaking of his moral fiber under the influence of his employer, so that by the end he goes to Le Roux beaten, begging for a job on a scandal sheet.

Lambert Le Roux, a heavy South African millionaire in his late forties, whose building of a British media empire the play chronicles. He is completely without scruples, wrecking lives by haphazardly firing staff, corrupting politicians, and debasing the public taste. As the owner of hotels, restaurants, and clothing firms, he is a supreme manipulator whose joviality and urbanity hide savagery. He glosses his predatory exercise of power with a warmed-over existentialism, talking of his insignificance in the face of impassive nature. In a sense, he is a rebellious parvenu whose wealth gives him the ability to degrade established British institutions, such as the newspaper *Victory*, that look down on him. In another sense, he is a business anarchist, because his decisions are often impulsive and willful rather than based on bottom-line calculations. His gigantic fortune papers over his faults and lapses.

Rebecca Foley, the daughter of Sir Stamford Foley, later the wife of Andrew May. She is a recently graduated schoolteacher. She is idealistic enough to have her faith in her father hurt by his shabby treatment of his employees. She is happy about, though wary of, her husband's success and grows sickened as she sees him intoxicated and warped by his progress with Le Roux.

Eaton Sylvester, Le Roux's business manager, a tall, balding Australian with silver glasses. With his vulgarity and disdain for any value aside from monetary success, he seems to be a spokesman for Le Roux's dark side. He relishes his boss's high-handedness and gleefully participates in his underhanded tricks by pretending that he is disgruntled and willing to sell Le Roux's secrets to a rival paper. He realizes that he is always on shaky ground, because Le Roux breaks faith with everyone eventually.

Michael Quince, a member of Parliament in his late thirties who is getting fat and has thinning hair. He is conceited and fatuous, having been given a column in the *Victory* by Le Roux in exchange for political favors.

Bill Smiley, a cheerful, gangling journalist in his mid-thirties who rises with Andrew but is something of a foil to him, because he is less enamored of success and remains inspired by the standards of honest reporting.

Donna Le Roux, the proud wife of Lambert, a pampered former figure skating champion who dislikes England and yearns for her South African homeland.

Sir Stamford Foley, the owner of the *Bystander*. He is a distinguished man in his late sixties, a hunter and gambler who puts forward the pretense of high-mindedness but betrays his employees to get money to buy a racehorse.

Miles Foley, Sir Stamford's son, who is in his twenties and employed in the microchip industry. He looks disdainfully at newspapermen, whom he considers prima donnas.

Harry Morrison, a large man in his late sixties. He is the editor of the *Bystander* and a heavy drinker who is disillusioned but accepting of his disillusionment.

Hamish McLennan, a serious, dour, balding man in his early fifties who carries the real responsibility for running the *Bystander* and is resentful of Morrison for taking the credit.

Suzie Fontaine, a twenty-three-year-old writer of women's stories for the *Bystander* who rises along with Andrew.

Dennis Payne, a good-looking retired British cricketer, now working as a salesman for Le Roux.

Elliot Fruit-Norton, the editor of the *Victory*; he is tall, stooping, and polished. He is outraged that Le Roux is taking over his paper.

The bishop of Putney, an old man who is on the board of trustees of the *Victory*. He is willing to sell to Le Roux as long as he is cajoled and flattered.

Lord Ben Silk, a small, dapper man and trustee of the *Victory* who is willing to talk turkey with Le Roux.

Leander Scroop, a dandy and a *Victory* political correspondent. He is concerned with upholding professional standards, which for him means maintaining a cozy relationship with the powers that be.

Doug Fantom, the tough night editor of the *Victory*. He is unaware of how his pruning and rewriting slants the news.

Larry Punt, a young reporter on the *Victory* with liberal predilections that are rapidly being reshaped.

Hanon Spot, the editor of the *Tide*, a disgustingly vulgar tabloid owned by Le Roux.

— *James Feast*

A PRAYER FOR OWEN MEANY

Author: John Irving (1942-   )
First published: 1989
Genre: Novel

Locale: Gravesend, New Hampshire, and Toronto, Canada
Time: 1952-1968 and 1987
Plot: Bildungsroman

Owen Meany, a midget with a high, squeaky voice who always sees a clear destiny for himself. Because of his size, Owen is always lifted overhead by other children in his Sunday school. He is a bright young man with leadership qualities. He believes that all actions and objects have meaning. He processes all information, forgets nothing, and saves every-

thing. Owen believes that he is God's instrument. Although he usually is unable to hit a ball, at one little league baseball game Owen hits a foul ball that strikes and kills Tabitha Wheelwright. Owen thinks that he warded off the Angel of Death from Tabitha's room and thus later became the agent of her death. In high school, Owen, as editor of the school newspaper, becomes the voice of moral authority. As a young man living through the Vietnam era, he criticizes his country's flawed leadership. Owen sees his life as fated. As a child, he sees the date of his death on his tombstone and later has a dream vision that he will die saving Vietnamese children. While in a Phoenix airport, he indeed saves several children by hurling himself on a grenade. Owen's sacrificial death, his part as the Christ child in the Christmas pageant, and his mother's belief that his was a virgin birth mark him symbolically as a Christ figure, a hero in an age that has lost its belief in heroes.

John Wheelwright, an alienated man who holds onto his faith in God and cynically criticizes the moral laxity of the United States. As a young man, John is slow in school and depends on Owen for leadership and direction. John's mother has him out of wedlock and does not tell him who his father is. Owen's voice from beyond the grave reveals the identity of John's father to him, but his father is a disappointment. John dodges the draft during the Vietnam War by having Owen cut off his trigger finger for him. After Owen's death, John moves to Canada, where he teaches English at a girls' school. Unable to assimilate into Canadian life, John finds himself detached from his own generation, an isolated man clinging to the margins of his faith, a man never able to have sexual contact with a woman. John knows of Owen's vision and witnesses his miraculous death. This memory has haunted him; he lives in the past and wishes he had Owen back again. Symbolically,

John is Owen's disciple, writing the story of Owen as Christ figure.

Hester Eastman, John's sexually precocious cousin, labeled Hester the Molester. She becomes a part of the rebellious youth movement of the Vietnam era engaged in violent protest. In love with Owen, after his death she remains attached to his memory. Later, she becomes a famous rock singer and makes music videos that are an odd mixture of sex and political protest. Her songs, which evoke the memory of Owen, appeal to a generation of young girls who have never known suffering.

Tabitha Wheelwright, John's free-spirited mother, who had a brief fling that resulted in John's birth. Tabby loves both John and Owen, and she nurtures and protects them. She marries Dan Needham and shortly afterward is killed by a baseball hit by Owen.

Dan Needham, a Harvard graduate who teaches history at Gravesend Academy and works in amateur theatricals. He marries Tabby and becomes a father to John, teaching him the meaning of friendship. He also guides and protects Owen.

The Reverend Lewis Merrill, John's father. He is a guilt-ridden minister who had a brief affair with Tabby. As she waves at him at the fatal baseball game, he wishes her dead. Haunted by the guilt of her death, he loses his faith, but he regains it when John uses Tabby's dressmaker's dummy to fake a ghostly apparition of Tabby.

— *Paul Rosefeldt*

PRECIOUS BANE

Author: Mary Webb (1881-1927)
First published: 1924
Genre: Novel

Locale: England
Time: Mid-nineteenth century
Plot: Regional

Prudence (Prue) Sarn, the narrator of the story. Having been cursed from birth by a harelip that mars her appearance, Prue is exceptionally sensitive to the feelings of others. She agrees to work like an animal for her brother because he promises to give her the money to have her lip cured. When all his plans fail, she leaves the farm and is subsequently accused of being a witch by the village people. She is saved from their wrath by the local weaver, whom she has loved secretly for several years.

Gideon Sarn, Prue's brother. Driven by a desire to get rich, he works everyone on the farm, including himself, like an animal. Although genuinely in love with Jancis Beguildy, he will not marry her until he has made his fortune. After her father ruins his harvest, he turns her away and degenerates to the point of murdering his own mother and finally committing suicide.

Jancis Beguildy, a childhood friend of Prue and Gideon. She wants to marry Gideon and does bear him a son. When he

will have nothing more to do with her, she drowns herself and the baby.

Wizard Beguildy, Jancis' father, supposed to be able to work spells and charms. He vows that his daughter can never marry Gideon and then sets fire to Gideon's harvest to keep them apart.

Mrs. Beguildy, Jancis' mother. She approves of the planned marriage between her daughter and Gideon and tries to trick her husband into leaving home so that the wedding can take place.

Mrs. Sarn, the mother of Gideon and Prue. She is physically very weak and deathly afraid of her son, who poisons her when she can no longer work.

Kester Woodseaves, a weaver. He marries Prue after rescuing her from water torture inflicted by the villagers, who consider her a witch.

Mr. and Mrs. Grimble, Jancis' employers.

THE PRETENDERS
(I suppositi)

Author: Ludovico Ariosto (1474-1533)
First published: 1509
Genre: Drama

Locale: Ferrara, Italy
Time: c. 1500
Plot: Farce

Erostrato (EH-rohs-TRAH-toh), the son of a wealthy Sicilian. He is in love with Polynesta and gains access to her house by posing as his servant, Dulippo. Imprisoned by her father, he is released and united with Polynesta after the arrival of his father, Philogano.

Dulippo (dew-LEEP-poh), Erostrato's servant, who poses as his master to help him in his wooing. He is discovered to be Cleander's son.

Polynesta (poh-lee-NEHS-tah), a young woman in love with Erostrato.

Damon (DAH-mohn), her father.

Cleander (klee-AHN-dehr), an old doctor of law and the suitor of Polynesta, for whose hand he will give any amount of money. He is constantly fooled by the disguised Dulippo but is made happy when the latter is revealed as his long-lost son.

Because he wants to marry only to produce an heir, he gladly relinquishes his suit.

Pasiphilo (pah-see-FEE-loh), a parasite who is always hungry. Sleeping off an attack of indigestion, he overhears Damon confess that he has imprisoned Erostrato and gives this information to Dulippo.

Philogano (fee-loh-GAH-noh), Erostrato's father, who comes in search of his son. He is dumbfounded to be called, by Dulippo, either an impostor or a madman, and to find a Sienese posing as himself. Dulippo's confession clears up the confusion.

Balia (BAH-lee-ah), Polynesta's nurse and accomplice in her love affair with Erostrato.

A Sienese, who poses as Erostrato's father.

THE PRICE

Author: Arthur Miller (1915-   )
First published: 1968
Genre: Drama

Locale: A brownstone in Manhattan, New York
Time: The 1960's
Plot: Melodrama

Victor Franz, a fifty-year-old police sergeant in New York City. Frustrated and disillusioned, Victor lives almost exclusively in the past, conveniently blaming his brother for the direction that his life has taken and unwilling to accept that he alone, by his own free will, charted his own destiny. He has a strong sense of familial loyalty. Victor's self-esteem and self-worth rest solely in his belief that he did the honorable thing decades earlier by sacrificing his college studies to become a policeman so that he could support his bankrupt father. Now, sixteen years after his father's death, Victor is forced into his life's crisis and is immobilized: He lacks the courage to accept early retirement and begin a new career because that action would signify the meaninglessness of his life's work as a policeman and, by implication, the vacuity of his allegiance to his father. His confrontation with the past and the high price he paid for his choices, symbolized in his task of selling his father's possessions, reaches its climax when his brother, whom he has not seen since his father's funeral, forces him to admit that he always suspected that his father had sufficient money to support himself without need for his financial assistance. When his brother offers him both the money from the sale of their father's furnishings and a job at the hospital where he works, Victor refuses for two reasons: His acceptance would imply an admission that his life and work, his very existence, had no purpose, and indirectly it would signify his forgiveness of his brother for not helping support their father and thereby enabling Victor to attend college to pursue a career. Until the end, Victor holds tenaciously to his code of ethics, which places familial loyalty above all else, maintains the view of himself as a martyr victimized by the stinginess and callousness of his wealthy brother, and, more pointedly, sustains his belief that his life's direction was controlled by the needs and actions of others.

Walter Franz, Victor's middle-aged brother, a prominent and successful surgeon. Unlike Victor, who is a self-sacrificing sentimentalist, Walter is pragmatic, self-centered, and incapable of loving. His fear of suffering a life of poverty like that of his father made him a workaholic detached from life, but his drive for wealth and fame led to the alienation of his wife and daughter. After enduring a nervous breakdown years earlier, he has come to realize both the price he paid for his stolidity and the need to make amends for his past behavior. Now, with the hope of securing his brother's forgiveness and alleviating his guilt for not financially helping Victor to support their father, Walter meets with Victor and offers him conscience money and a job. Interpreting Victor's refusal to accept his offer as a denial of absolution, Walter leaves angrily, still unforgiven and unable, despite his rhetoric about facing responsibility for his own actions, to acknowledge openly his betrayal and sins against his father and brother.

Esther Franz, Victor's wife. Disenchanted with her middle-class existence of scraping for pennies and sacrificing her wants and needs to help support Victor's father, she has turned to alcohol to escape the realities of middle age. With Victor's retirement now imminent, Esther is angered at his unwillingness to put the past behind and get on with the life that they had planned together decades ago. She tries to reconcile the brothers, taking alternating sides as each argues his point of view about the realities of the past. At the end, however, when Walter calls Victor a failure, Esther finally becomes Victor's ally and unconditionally accepts him and the life that they have constructed together.

Gregory Solomon, an eighty-nine-year-old Jewish furniture dealer who has come out of retirement to negotiate for the Franz family's old furniture. As his surname suggests, he is a wise arbitrator-philosopher, offering words of wisdom about life with endearing charm and humor. Despite the many losses he suffers, particularly the suicide of his daughter, his indomitable will to continue an active life without blaming others for his lot affords Victor insight about coping with life's inexplicable miseries and broken dreams.

— *B. A. Kachur*

PRIDE AND PREJUDICE

Author: Jane Austen (1775-1817)
First published: 1813
Genre: Novel

Locale: Rural England
Time: Early nineteenth century
Plot: Domestic realism

Elizabeth Bennet, a spirited and intelligent girl who represents "prejudice" in her attitude toward Fitzwilliam Darcy, whom she dislikes because of his pride. She is also prejudiced against him by Mr. Wickham, whose false reports of Darcy she believes, and hence rejects Darcy's haughty first proposal of marriage. Yet Wickham's elopement with her sister Lydia brings Elizabeth and Darcy together, for it is Darcy who facilitates the legal marriage of the runaways. Acknowledging her mistake in her estimation of Darcy, she gladly accepts his second proposal.

Fitzwilliam Darcy, the wealthy and aristocratic landowner who represents "pride" in the story. Attracted to Elizabeth Bennet in spite of her inferior social position, he proposes marriage, but in so high-handed a manner that she instantly refuses. The two meet again while Elizabeth is viewing the grounds of his estate in Derbyshire, and she finds him less haughty in his manner. When Lydia Bennet and Mr. Wickham elope, Darcy feels partly responsible and straightens out the unfortunate affair. Because Elizabeth now realizes his true character, he is accepted when he proposes again.

Jane Bennet, the oldest and most beautiful of the five Bennet sisters. She falls in love with Mr. Bingley, a wealthy bachelor. Their romance is frustrated, however, by his sisters with the help of Mr. Darcy, for the Bennets are considered socially undesirable. As a result of the change in the feelings of Darcy and Elizabeth Bennet toward each other, Jane and Bingley are finally married.

Mr. Bingley, a rich, good-natured bachelor from the north of England. He falls in love with Jane Bennet but is easily turned against her by his sisters and his friend, Mr. Darcy, who consider the Bennets vulgar and socially beneath them. When Darcy changes in his attitude toward Elizabeth Bennet, Bingley follows suit and resumes his courtship of Jane. They are married at the end of the story.

Mr. Bennet, an eccentric and mildly sarcastic small landowner. Rather indifferent to the rest of his family, he loves and admires his daughter Elizabeth.

Mrs. Bennet, his wife, a silly, brainless woman interested only in getting her daughters married.

Lydia Bennet, the youngest daughter, a flighty and uncontrolled girl. At the age of fifteen, she elopes with the worthless Mr. Wickham. Their marriage is finally made possible by Mr. Darcy, who pays Wickham's debts; but the two are never very happy.

Mary Bennet and
Catherine (Kitty) Bennet, younger daughters of the family.

Mr. Wickham, the villain of the story, an officer in the militia. He had been brought up by the Darcy family and, having a certain charm, attracts Elizabeth Bennet, whom he prejudices against Mr. Darcy by misrepresenting the latter's treatment of him. Quite unexpectedly, he elopes with fifteen-year-old, flirtatious Lydia Bennet. Darcy, who has tried to expose Wickham to Elizabeth, feels responsible for the elopement and provides the money for the marriage by paying Wickham's debts. Wickham and Lydia soon tire of each other.

William Collins, a pompous, sycophantic clergyman, distantly related to Mr. Bennet and the heir to his estate, since the Bennets have no son. He proposes to Elizabeth. After her refusal, he marries her friend, Charlotte Lucas.

Lady Catherine de Bourgh, Mr. Darcy's aunt and the patron of Mr. Collins. An insufferably haughty and domineering woman, she wants Darcy to marry her only daughter and bitterly resents his interest in Elizabeth Bennet. She tries to break up their love affair but fails.

Anne de Bourgh, Lady Catherine's spiritless daughter. Her mother has planned to marry her to Mr. Darcy in order to combine two great family fortunes.

Charlotte Lucas, Elizabeth Bennet's closest friend. Knowing that she will have few chances of marriage, she accepts the pompous and boring Mr. Collins shortly after Elizabeth has refused him.

Caroline Bingley and
Mrs. Hurst, Mr. Bingley's cold and worldly sisters. They succeed for a time in turning him against Jane Bennet.

Mr. Gardiner, Mrs. Bennet's brother, a London merchant.
Mrs. Gardiner, his sensible and kindly wife.

THE PRIME OF MISS JEAN BRODIE

Author: Muriel Spark (1918-   )
First published: 1961
Genre: Novel

Locale: Edinburgh, Scotland
Time: 1930-1939
Plot: Moral

Miss Jean Brodie, an individualistic teacher of younger students at the Marcia Blaine School for Girls in Edinburgh, Scotland. Considered attractive because of her "Roman features" and brown hair coiling at the nape of her neck, Brodie is in her forties, an age that she regards as the prime of her life. She is an early admirer of Benito Mussolini, whom she credits with having eliminated unemployment and litter in the streets of Rome. She later extends her admiration to Adolf Hitler as

well and is forced into early retirement. She considers her pupils to be "the *crème de la crème*" and has devoted her life to them. Her first lover, Hugh Carruthers, died during World War I; her second lover, Teddy Lloyd, is married. Longing for romance but deprived of it, Brodie attempts to live vicariously through the affairs of her students. Her plan for one of these affairs fails, however, and the other outlets for her passion—politics and her unusual approach to education—

ultimately prove to be her undoing. Brodie dies shortly after World War II, still unmarried at the age of fifty-six and unable to understand how she could have been betrayed by one of her own students.

Sandy Stranger, one of the ten students who have become known collectively as "the Brodie set." Distinguished in the junior school for her tiny eyes and her skill at elocution, Sandy does not outwardly appear much different from the other Brodie girls; they are all dressed in the same panama hat and deep violet uniform. She is imaginative, creating stories in her mind that involve herself and the characters from whatever book she currently is reading. Sandy later enters a convent, where she becomes Sister Helena of the Transfiguration. She writes a psychological treatise titled *The Transfiguration of the Commonplace* and becomes unexpectedly famous. Her sudden betrayal of Brodie is suspected by her former mentor only shortly before Brodie's death.

Jenny Gray, Sandy's best friend. The prettiest and most graceful girl of the Brodie set, Jenny enters a school of dramatic arts during what would have been her final year at the Marcia Blaine School.

Mary Macgregor, the least intelligent of Brodie's inner circle and their scapegoat. Mary goes on to become a shorthand-typist, joins the military during World War II, and dies tragically at the age of twenty-four in a hotel fire while on leave.

Eunice Gardiner, a small but athletic girl. Eunice is both a gymnast and a swimmer. While at the senior school, Eunice alone of her set does not share Brodie's contempt for the "team spirit" and competes enthusiastically in intramural sports.

Monica Douglas, who is skilled at mathematics and famous for her hot temper. Monica is one of the least attractive of the Brodie set, having a broad and very red nose, long dark hair worn in pigtails, and fat, stubby legs.

Rose Stanley, who is known for her sex appeal even while young. Rose is a tall girl with short blonde hair, pale skin, and a huge-boned face. Although something of a tomboy when she is eleven years old, she later uses her knowledge of boys' interests to make herself even more popular. Rose is groomed by Brodie to have an affair with Teddy Lloyd, but she manages to free herself from her teacher's influence and marry a successful businessman shortly after leaving school.

Joyce Emily Hammond, a newcomer to the Marcia Blaine School, sent there because no other school could handle her. Her family is extremely rich, and she arrives at school each day in a chauffeur-driven car. Although eager to enter the Brodie set, she is a misfit and insists on being addressed by both of her first names. Joyce Emily still wears the dark green uniform of her old school and is encouraged by Brodie to go to Spain to fight for Francisco Franco. She is killed, however, when the train on which she is riding is attacked.

Miss Mackay, the red-faced headmistress of the Marcia Blaine School for Girls. Miss Mackay objects to Brodie's teaching methods and has become her implacable enemy. Intent on ending Brodie's career, she tries to win the Brodie set over to her side. After several unsuccessful attempts to obtain evidence of Brodie's sexual misconduct, Miss Mackay receives from Sandy the necessary hint that politics, not morality, will be Brodie's undoing.

Miss Gaunt, a teacher at the junior school. As gaunt and forbidding as her name implies, she insists on complete silence in her classroom. Miss Gaunt regularly wears a dark green jersey and an unfashionable knee-length skirt of a gray material like that used for blankets. Miss Gaunt's brother is the minister of the local parish, a fact that only intensifies her air of rigid and confining respectability.

Teddy Lloyd, the art master at the senior school. Although Lloyd is married, he and Brodie share a secret love for each other. On a single occasion, they have a moment of weakness and kiss. Lloyd is half English and half Welsh, with golden hair and a hoarse voice. He lost his left arm during World War I. This mark of distinction and his general air of sophistication make Lloyd seem a highly romantic figure to the girls of the Blaine School.

Gordon Lowther, the singing master for both the junior and senior schools. He is Brodie's supporter and, for a time, her lover. Brodie begins her affair with Lowther only because she is trying to free herself from her love for Teddy Lloyd. Lowther is a small, short-legged man with reddish blond hair and a mustache. He is shy but has a smiling and gentle manner that causes others to feel kindly toward him. After the death of his mother, Lowther never can regard himself as master of his own house; he becomes dependent first on his housekeeper, then on the Kerr sisters and Brodie, and finally on his wife, the former science mistress, Miss Lockhart.

Ellen Kerr and

Alison Kerr, sewing teachers at the Marcia Blaine School. With their fluffed hair, birdlike eyes, and nearly bluish skin, the Kerr sisters perfectly fit the stereotype of "spinsters." Rather than teaching, they frequently do most of the girls' sewing for them. The Kerrs become, for a time, Lowther's unofficial housekeepers.

— *Jeffrey L. Buller*

THE PRINCE AND THE PAUPER

Author: Mark Twain (Samuel Langhorne Clemens, 1835-1910)
First published: 1881
Genre: Novel

Locale: England
Time: The sixteenth century
Plot: Social satire

Edward, prince of Wales and son of Henry VIII. When a ragged waif named Tom Canty invades the royal grounds, Edward, curious about life outside the confines of the palace, invites the boy to his quarters. They change clothes as a prank and discover that they are identical in appearance. When the prince appears in the courtyard dressed in Tom's rags, guards mistake him for the intruding waif and throw him into the streets. Protesting time and again that he is the real prince of Wales, he is ridiculed and thought mad by skeptical London crowds. After many adventures and hardships that reveal to him the harsh lot of the common people, he appears as Tom Canty is about to be crowned king and proves that he himself is the rightful heir by disclosing the location of the Great Seal that his late father had entrusted to him.

King Henry VIII, his ailing father, who has entrusted to Edward the Great Seal.

Mary and

Elizabeth, daughters of the king, who think Tom is their brother.

Tom Canty, who was born the same day as the prince of Wales and is his double in appearance. He trades places with Edward.

John Canty, his father, who treats Tom and Edward cruelly. When he becomes king, Edward wants to hang Canty but can never locate him.

Miles Hendon, the disinherited son of a baronet. He befriends the homeless Edward.

Hugh Hendon, his brother, who tricks Miles in order to marry Edith.

Edith, who loves Miles but is afraid Hugh will murder him if she identifies Miles.

Hugo, a thief who tries to teach Edward his tricks.

The Lord Protector, who identifies the real prince.

THE PRINCE OF HOMBURG
(Prinz Friedrich von Homburg)

Author: Heinrich von Kleist (1777-1811)
First published: 1821
Genre: Drama

Locale: Prussia
Time: 1675
Plot: Historical

Frederick Arthur, the prince of Homburg. Exhausted from battle, he falls into a kind of half sleep during which he weaves a laurel wreath. The elector, Frederick William, takes the wreath and entwines it with his neck chain, an occurrence that later influences the prince to feel that destiny compels him into battle. In the ensuing battle with the Swedes, the prince, in ecstasy over his love for Princess Natalie, fails to hear the orders clearly and precipitously gives his own orders to advance. Later, after the battle has been won, the elector sentences the prince to die for disobeying orders. On the pleas of many, the prince's life is spared, and he is hailed as the hero of the battle.

Frederick William, the elector of Brandenburg. When he returns victorious from battle, his spirit of military discipline forces him to sentence Frederick Arthur to die for ignoring battle orders, even though the prince's forces were victorious.

After hearing many pleas for the prince's life, with charges and countercharges for placing the blame for the prince's disobedience, the elector tears up the death warrant.

Princess Natalie of Orange, the niece of Frederick William. She is loved by Prince Frederick Arthur and pleads for his life when he is sentenced to death for failing to follow orders.

Count Hohenzollern, a member of the elector's suite who pleads for Frederick Arthur's life.

Field Marshal Dörfling, a military leader from Brandenburg.

Colonel Kottwitz, an officer in the regiment of Princess Natalie of Orange. Rebuked by Frederick William for lack of fervor when he hesitates to follow the impetuous prince in his advance before the battle signal is given, the colonel, afraid of appearing unpatriotic, joins in the charge.

THE PRINCESS: A Medley

Author: Alfred, Lord Tennyson (1809-1892)
First published: 1847
Genre: Poetry

Locale: Indeterminate
Time: Indeterminate
Plot: Social

Princess Ida, a woman with a strong idea of herself and her sex. Her aim is to establish a college for women. She espouses the feminist cause, exhorting her followers to "lift up their natures." Her true self is established when she reads to the Prince from a poem: "Come down, O maid, from yonder mountain height." The poem says, "Love is of the valley." This descent forces Princess Ida to change from feminist to female. It is not, however, a reversal of her values but rather a process of discovery and discrimination leading toward selfhood. The barrier to love is more evident in Ida than it is in the Prince. She denies her femininity. Early in the poem, the Princess expresses her contempt for conventional love poems, "applying herself to the composition of 'awful odes' on more solemn subjects." When the Prince kisses her, passion is aroused and cannot be denied. She reads the erotic "Now Sleeps the Crimson Petal" and finds it to be a different sort of love poem because of her newly acquired capacity to respond to it. At the

poem's conclusion, the Princess looks to a time when she and the Prince can embrace the ideal of accepting rather than repressing sexuality.

The Prince, who makes his first appearance in women's clothing and is described as being like a girl. He is taunted by his foes as being feminine. His father simplifies the Prince's choice of garb as an issue of effeminacy; he tells the Prince to make himself a man to fight with men. The Prince is not a homosexual or a transvestite; he is a venerator of women. His beloved is Princess Ida. At the poem's end, after a series of oppositions between the Prince and the Princess, the Prince tells Ida that either sex alone is half itself, and they look to a time when men and women will take on some of the characteristics of the opposite sex. The ideal is to accept and not repress sexuality. Understanding the nature of women is the Prince's way of understanding himself and achieving true selfhood.

The King, the Prince's father. He represents traditional masculinity that rejects a woman's place in society as an equal. He berates his son for dressing in women's clothing, finding something effeminate about it and suggesting that his son may be homosexual, a charge the Prince denies. The King believes that "Man is the hunter; woman is his game."

King Gama, Princess Ida's father. He is a small old man who does not project the image of a king. He leaves the impression that Ida is a victim of having too little masculine authority, which has led her to become opinionated and outspoken, a woman with a mind of her own.

Cyril and

Florian, the Prince's friends. Cyril is impulsive and faintly disreputable; Florian is courtly. Cyril accuses the Prince of being homosexual. The Prince strikes Cyril, but the two reconcile, with the Prince seeming more manly for the reconciliation.

Psyche and

Lady Blanche, two widows who dramatize the matriarchal and maternal inclinations that are at war within Princess Ida.

Aglaia, Psyche's daughter. She functions to soften Princess Ida's heart. In doing so, Princess Ida accepts a part of her own nature that she has repressed and, in doing so, moves toward selfhood.

— *Thomas D. Petitjean, Jr.*

THE PRINCESS CASAMASSIMA

Author: Henry James (1843-1916)
First published: 1885-1886
Genre: Novel

Locale: London, England
Time: Late nineteenth century
Plot: Social realism

Hyacinth Robinson, a self-educated bookbinder in late Victorian London, England. Growing up in poverty, Hyacinth felt the callousness and violence of capitalistic society. He is easily converted to Socialism by his mentors, Anastasius Vetch and Paul Muniment. When he learns that his mother was abandoned by his aristocratic father, he swears to die for the cause of revolution, but when he meets Princess Casamassima, she introduces him to a finer, nobler world. A changed man, he becomes incapable of assassination. When the call comes, he kills himself rather than carry out his assignment.

Princess Casamassima, an American who has married into Italian nobility. Disenchanted by her husband's lack of concern for social injustice, she moves to England and, attended only by her companion Madame Grandoni, attempts to learn about—and if possible amend—the problems of late Victorian society. In her effort to uncover the "sufferings and passions" of the people, she employs a succession of guides: Captain Godfrey Sholto, who is soon discarded because he is too vulgar; Hyacinth Robinson, who is finally discarded because he becomes too noble; and Paul Muniment, who in turn discards her when the prince, appalled by the dishonor she is bringing to the family name, cuts off the allowance that has been letting her fund the revolutionary cause.

Paul Muniment, a chemist (pharmacist) who seems to embody the true nature of the revolutionary cause. A cold intellectual who sees class warfare as inevitable and necessary, he exploits the desire of the princess to make a difference in society in order to raise money. When the prince cuts off her allowance, Paul ruthlessly drops her. Paul is not wholly trusted by the underground. He diverts some of the money for his personal use, and it is implied that his relationship with the princess is not merely intellectual.

Captain Godfrey Sholto, a moneyed idler who introduces Hyacinth to the princess. As one with the money of the upper classes but the vulgarity of the lower, he is the perfect intermediary, but he cannot make even Millicent respond to his attentions.

Amanda Pynsent, a poor seamstress who rears Hyacinth after the infant's mother is imprisoned for murdering her lover when he refused to support the child. The small inheritance she leaves Hyacinth enables him to visit Paris, France, and complete his aesthetic education.

Anastasius Vetch, a violinist who is Miss Pynsent's closest friend. He teaches Hyacinth French, introduces him to Socialism, and obtains for him an apprenticeship in the bookbinding craft. He must stand by helplessly as Hyacinth is drawn into his fatal entanglement.

Millicent Henning, a shopgirl and aspiring model. Hyacinth's childhood sweetheart, she is unable to keep Hyacinth from the fatal attractions of aristocratic wealth, on one side, and revolutionary rhetoric, on the other.

Lady Aurora Languish, an upper-class woman who has dedicated her life to "doing good." Rejected by her own family and ignored by Paul Muniment, whom she adores, she accomplishes little aside from caring for Paul's crippled sister Rose.

Rose Muniment, the crippled sister of Paul. Bedridden, Rose nevertheless embraces life. She provides a moral center for the tale, which desperately needs one.

Diedrich Hoffendahl, the shadowy head of the revolutionary movement. Although he is never seen directly, Hoffendahl is a central character. Paul and the princess yearn to meet him and be taken into his confidence, but Hyacinth desperately wishes he had never met him.

— *Hartley S. Spatt*

THE PRINCESS OF CLÈVES
(La Princesse de Clèves)

Author: Madame Marie de La Fayette (Marie-Madeleine Pioche de la Vergne, 1634-1693)
First published: 1678
Genre: Novel

Locale: France
Time: The sixteenth century
Plot: Love

The Princess de Clèves (deh klehv), a beautiful young woman married to a prince of the royal household. She is a virtuous, even passionless, woman who disappoints her husband with her lack of ardor. Unlike most courtiers, she has no extramarital affairs. When she meets the duke de Nemours, she feels emotion for him but tries to put it down, even enlisting her husband's aid. After her husband's death, she refuses to marry the duke and withdraws from society, even to the point of entering a convent for a time.

The Prince de Clèves, a member of the royal family. He tries to help his wife suppress her love for the duke de Nemours. When he thinks his wife has fallen from virtue, he becomes ill of a fever and, rather than stand in his wife's way, languishes and dies.

The Duke de Nemours (new-MEWR), the handsomest and most gallant courtier in France. He is even spoken of as a possible consort for Elizabeth I of England. He falls in love with the princess de Clèves, but cannot turn her from being faithful to her husband.

The Queen Dauphine (doh-FEEN), **Mary, Queen of Scots**, who is a friend of the princess de Clèves.

The Vidame de Chartres (vee-DAHM deh SHAHRT-reh), an uncle of the princess de Clèves. He tries to bring his niece and the duke de Nemours together after the girl is widowed.

Mme de Chartres, the mother of the princess de Clèves. She is ambitious to see her daughter marry a prince.

Henri II (ah[n]-REE), the king of France.

Diane de Poitiers (dee-AHN deh pwah-TYAY), the duchess de Valentinois, King Henri's adviser. She was his father's mistress and is now the center of a court clique.

Catherine de Mèdicis, the queen of France and wife of Henri II. She leads the faction opposed to her rival, Diane de Poitiers. She seeks the friendship of the Vidame de Chartres.

THE PRINTER OF MALGUDI

Author: R. K. Narayan (1906-   )
First published: 1949
Genre: Novel

Locale: Malgudi, in southern India
Time: 1938
Plot: Comic realism

Srinivas, the protagonist, the editor of a weekly paper and later a frustrated screenwriter. Nearly forty years old, graying, and somewhat cynical, he spent years trying to fit in but found that the domestic duties with his wife and son became an extra burden. Leaving home, he ends up in the town of Malgudi, where, with his keen, questioning mind, he establishes *The Banner*, a paper in which he idealistically attacks the pigheadedness of humankind and attempts to prod humanity into pursuing some sort of perfection. When Sampath's Truth Printing Works closes, Srinivas is forced to cease publication. Without his paper, he finds himself even more lost and confused. He becomes a screenwriter for Sampath's new venture, Sunrise Pictures, but quickly becomes frustrated and disillusioned with the film industry. Attempting to search for some underlying meaning and value, he acts as a spectator of life and ends up questioning his knowledge of the self and of his own true identity. After the collapse of his friend, Ravi, and of the film company, he sets off to reestablish *The Banner* with a much more realistic concept of life and of business. He also realizes that he cannot fight the passage of time and that he must live his life as well as he can.

Sampath, the printer of the novel's title. An effusive, flamboyant, unpredictable, and eloquent man, he is the owner of Truth Printing Works and later the director of productions for Sunrise Pictures. A take-charge sort of man with a commanding presence, he, is an invaluable help to Srinivas and *The Banner*. He is also very manipulative, however, and when his press closes he not only gets Srinivas to write a screenplay but also manipulates the producers, directors, and actors of the film and even manages to convince Srinivas' miserly landlord to invest five thousand rupees in the production. Such manipulations take their toll, however, for Sampath finds himself losing control over the entire situation. Despite his wife and five children, he carries on an affair with Shanti; after the collapse of the film company, he goes away with her. He returns only to tell Srinivas of the failure of the film company and the failure of his relationship with Shanti, then disappears from Srinivas' life as suddenly as he first appeared.

Ravi, Srinivas' neighbor, a bank clerk with artistic talent. The twenty-eight-year-old Ravi is the sole provider for a rather large family and suffers from an obsessive personality. He is first obsessed with his dictatorial boss, the general manager of the bank, and then with the face of a girl whom he sees on the streets and whom he sketches afterward. He then transfers that obsession to Shanti, an actress who resembles his drawing of the girl. This obsession drives him mad, and in an insane outburst he attempts to kidnap Shanti, in the process ruining the film. Left a mumbling lunatic, he is rescued and cared for by Srinivas, who sees some hope for recovery and who plans to use his artistic talents for his new paper.

The old man, Srinivas' landlord. A widower, the old man has taken on the role of a *sanyasi*, or holy ascetic. A miserly man with few friends, he refuses to install another water tap or fix up the house at all. Becoming friendly with Srinivas, he asks his help in getting Ravi to marry his granddaughter. When this fails, he takes on Sampath as a student of Sanskrit and agrees to invest in his film company if Sampath can arrange the marriage. He dies rather suddenly, and members of his family start appearing and competing against one another for the property. The necessary repairs and improvements to the house finally are made.

Shanti, an actress. Enchanting and beautiful, with a perfect figure, rosy complexion, arched eyebrows, and almond-shaped eyes, Shanti is the object of Ravi's obsession and Sampath's desire. Posing as Sampath's cousin, she carries on a secret affair with him but eventually leaves him after Sunrise Pictures is shut down.

— *Susan V. Myers*

THE PRISONER OF ZENDA

Author: Anthony Hope (Sir Anthony Hope Hawkins, 1863-1933)
First published: 1894
Genre: Novel

Locale: The fictional kingdom of Ruritania
Time: The 1880's
Plot: Adventure

Rudolf Rassendyll, a red-bearded young English gentleman of leisure who prides himself on his red hair and large straight nose, which are reminders of an old scandal involving the wife of a Rassendyll ancestor and a visiting Ruritanian prince of the Elphberg family. To save the Ruritanian crown from Black Michael, Rassendyll impersonates Rudolf and is crowned king. He falls in love with Flavia, manages several narrow escapes from Michael and his men, rescues Rudolf, and restores the throne of Ruritania to its rightful king.

Lady Rose Burlesdon, his sister-in-law, a pretty, accomplished, and wealthy woman.

Rudolf, king of Ruritania, little known to his subjects because of his frequent and extended absences from his country. He looks like an identical twin of Rassendyll except that he has shaved off his beard, his face is a little fleshier, and his mouth less firm. He is a heavy drinker and is both drunk and drugged the day of the coronation. Imprisoned by Michael, he is freed when Michael's lodge is attacked, and he assumes his position as monarch.

Michael, duke of Strelsau, King Rudolf's villainous half brother, called **Black Michael**, who wishes to be king of Ruritania and will stoop to any deed to achieve his aim. He is killed by the treacherous Rupert.

Antoinette de Mauban, a rich, handsome, ambitious widow in love with Michael.

Princess Flavia, a pale, lovely, red-haired girl betrothed to Rudolf. Though she loves Rassendyll, she loyally becomes Rudolf's wife and queen.

Fritz von Tarlenheim, a loyal subject of Rudolf who helps to carry out Rassendyll's impersonation and later saves his life.

Colonel Sapt, another loyal subject, who first suggests that Rassendyll shave off his beard and double for Rudolf during the coronation to prevent Michael from seizing the throne.

Josef, a servant in Michael's hunting lodge. He is slain while guarding the drunken Rudolf.

Rupert Hentzau, Michael's handsome young aide, who kills him in a fight over Antoinette. In a deadly encounter with Rupert later, Rassendyll is saved by Fritz.

Detchard, another of Michael's henchmen. After attacking the king, he is slain by Rassendyll.

PRISONS

Author: Mary Lee Settle (1918-)
First published: 1973
Genre: Novel

Locale: England
Time: 1634-1649
Plot: Historical realism

Corporal Jonathan (Johnny) Church, the protagonist, a soldier during England's civil war. Tall, with autumn-colored hair and tawny eyes, the twenty-year-old Johnny is solemn and sorrowful. Coming from a strict Presbyterian family, with a cold mother and a bitter, cruel father, he is quiet, shy, and solitary. He is not, however, formally religious, though he later longs to become so. A somewhat rebellious youth who thought he would change the world, he disobeys his father and runs away to join Cromwell's army. He quickly adjusts to the life of a soldier, hiding his fear and remaining aloof. He is watchful and witty, easily led and influenced by others, especially by Robbie Lokyar, Francis White, and, of course, Oliver Cromwell. Elected an Agitator of his company, he carries on the struggle for liberty. Betrayed and disillusioned, he becomes suspicious and distrustful. Feeling abandoned, he becomes melancholy and full of despair and emptiness. His thoughts become uncontrollable as he reassesses his life from a position of being adrift and afraid yet longing for comfort and reassurance. He finally comes to terms with his life and his God. Along with his friend, Thankful, he is shot for treason.

Corporal Thankful Perkins, Johnny's closest friend and a fellow soldier. A small nineteen-year-old with a frail yet strong face and brown curls, Thankful is a gentle, loving, and compassionate friend. Angelic and pure of heart, he is deeply religious and shines with an inner light. Unfortunately, he is much too trusting; when betrayed, he is shocked and grieved. He conquers that grief, however, and meets his death with courage and grace.

General Oliver Cromwell, the leader of the Parliamentary Army that overthrew and executed King Charles I; he later became the ruler of England. A strong, imposing man with a stern and ugly pockmarked face and a very large nose, Cromwell inspires great loyalty within the army but is a rather melancholy, petulant, and preoccupied man. Operating with a strong inner voice, he is not easily swayed or weakened and is very persuasive. He knows his purpose and will do whatever is necessary to accomplish his goals. At the same time, despite his many contradictions, he always appears completely sincere in his actions. Eventually, he is faced with inevitable choices, and his decision to execute the Agitators becomes a matter of political survival.

Gideon MacKarkle, an older soldier. Extremely ugly, with a large nose, a big mouth, droopy eyes, and gray hair, the skinny Gideon becomes Johnny's first instructor on how to survive as a soldier. Gideon is bright, quick, and an excellent soldier.

Robbie Lokyar, a twenty-year-old Agitator. Not a deeply religious person, he is intelligent and interested in reason, and he has a strong sense of purpose and direction. A born leader, he imparts that direction to his fellow soldiers, especially to Johnny and Thankful, spurring them all to rise to action. Disillusioned with Cromwell's compromises and behavior, he becomes quite vehement in his criticisms and, going too far, is executed. His death makes him a martyr and a symbol for future actions. It also thrusts the burden of leadership onto Johnny and Thankful.

Cornet Henry Denne, an officer in Cromwell's army. A very religious man, with a passionate, moving voice, Denne becomes, for a short while, one of the Agitators. His loyalty is not strong, however, and he betrays the other Agitators to Cromwell. All the Agitators are sentenced to death; he is the only one to be pardoned.

Cornet Thompson, another officer. A fine, swashbuckling, stereotypical soldier, he has a sanguine character. Like the others, he too is an Agitator, but he remains loyal to their cause. Despite a last-minute appeal for pardon, he is executed.

Nell Cockburn Lacy, Johnny's aunt and mother of his son. Married at the age of fourteen to Sir Valentine Lacy, Nell is like a fairy princess. She always appears young and beautiful, and Johnny falls deeply in love with her. She conceives Johnny's child on the night her husband dies.

— *Susan V. Myers*

THE PRIVATE LIFE OF THE MASTER RACE
(Furcht und Elend des dritten Reiches)

Author: Bertolt Brecht (1898-1956)
First published: 1944
Genre: Drama

Locale: Germany
Time: 1933-1938
Plot: Social

The S. A. Man, whose name is **Theo**. He is proud of his part in the Nazi movement and enjoys kindling fear among his friends and acquaintances.

The Parlour-Maid, the S. A. Man's mistress. She fears her lover and dislikes him because he takes her money from their joint bank account.

The Worker, a man named **Lincke**. He is taunted and frightened by the S. A. Man.

The Social Democrat, a man who blames the Communists for Germany's inability to save itself politically from the Nazis.

The Old Worker, **Herr Sedelmeier**, who is forced to say over the radio that his factory is a wonderful place to work.

The Woman Worker, **Fräulein Schmidt**, who is forced to say that the factory is a pleasant place to work.

X and

Y, two German physicists who correspond indirectly with Einstein and fear discovery by the Nazis.

Judith Keith, a Jew who leaves Germany in 1934 for refuge in Holland.

Judge A, **Herr Goll**. He wants to render a verdict on a Jew but is confused as to whether the Nazis want a verdict of guilty or not guilty.

The Inspector, a man named **Tallinger**. He is too careful of his own fate to be helpful to the judge.

The Prosecutor, an ambitious man named **Spitz** who gives the judge no help because he would like the place on the bench held by Judge A.

Judge B, an elderly friend of Judge A. Judge B is too aware of the dangers in Germany to offer any advice to his friend Judge A.

The Butcher, an old-time Nazi who hangs himself when he realizes that he has been betrayed by the party.

PRIVATE LIVES

Author: Noël Coward (1899-1973)
First published: 1930
Genre: Drama

Locale: France
Time: 1929 or 1930
Plot: Comedy of manners

Elyot Chase, a handsome, thirtyish man. When the play begins, he is honeymooning at Deauville, France, with his second wife. Five years earlier, he had divorced Amanda, to whom he had been married for three tumultuous years, and then traveled around the world. When he sees Amanda again, he realizes that she is his true love. Together, they flee to Paris. Despite their bickering and fisticuffs, they remain reunited. Elyot, first performed by the playwright himself, represents the witty, irreverent, sophisticated Englishman that the playwright admired and saw himself as exemplifying.

Amanda Prynne, Elyot's first wife, newly married to Victor Prynne. She, too, is honeymooning at Deauville as the play opens. She is the most vivacious character in the work. She is

not only beautiful but also spirited, independent, and unconventional—a fit partner for Elyot.

Sibyl Chase, Elyot's blond, attractive, twenty-three-year-old bride. Conventional, unimaginative, and innocent, she is Amanda's antithesis and suggests the playwright's dim view of the "nice" English girl. She implies to Elyot that she will tailor life to suit his whims.

Victor Prynne, a handsome man a few years older than Elyot. Stuffy and stodgy, he lacks a sense of humor. Like Sibyl, he is shocked by the elopement of Elyot and Amanda; when he and Sibyl catch up with the other couple, he chivalrously offers to divorce Amanda even though he deeply loves her. He wants to make over someone's life and takes it upon himself to do so for his new wife. This drives her back into the arms of Elyot. Sibyl is his true soul mate, and their fierce quarreling at the end of the play, mirroring the battles between Amanda and Elyot, indicates that the conventional Victor will end up paired with her.

Louise, Amanda's French-speaking maid. She makes a brief appearance in the third act. Her inability to speak English and her incomprehension of the bizarre occurrences in the apartment provide a number of laughs.

— *Joseph Rosenblum*

THE PRIVATE PAPERS OF HENRY RYECROFT

Author: George Gissing (1857-1903)
First published: 1903
Genre: Novel

Locale: England
Time: Late nineteenth century
Plot: Autobiographical

Henry Ryecroft, a contemplative man, formerly a hack writer but able now through the legacy of a friend to live quietly in a comfortable cottage in rural Devon, writing only when he chooses to. He enjoys wandering about the countryside observing the common plants and learning their names. He thinks often of his hack writing days and of the conditions under which he had lived. Like Charles Lamb, he was always a lover of books and purchased them out of his meager earnings; people nowadays read newspapers, not books. He remembers also the happy excursions on which his family went along the English coast in his childhood. He contrasts the Sundays of old, when he wrote his sharpest satire, with his quiet, peaceful ones now. He thinks of the decline of English taste in food. A successful writer friend visits him, and they talk over the old days of struggle. He misses the London concerts and picture galleries. He muses on Darwinism and its effects on English thought, and he considers his own indiffer-

ence to odd fads and scientific discoveries. He finds comfort in the Stoics' views about death. He meditates on two great sources of England's strength: Puritanism and the Old Testament. One set moral standards; the other reminded the English that they were a chosen people. If in recent times conventional religion has declined and materialism grown, at least the old prudishness has been replaced by a new strength. He looks back on his varied life, which now seems fully rounded, the best life he could make it; he is content for it to end at any time.

Mrs. M., Ryecroft's excellent housekeeper, a quiet woman of discreet age who keeps an orderly house and does not obtrude on his meditations or bother about his comings and goings.

N———, Ryecroft's writer friend who pays a two-day visit.

THE PROFESSOR

Author: Charlotte Brontë (1816-1855)
First published: 1857
Genre: Novel

Locale: Belgium and England
Time: The nineteenth century
Plot: Psychological

William Crimsworth, a young English orphan who, upon leaving Eton, is faced with a decision regarding his future. He receives from his mother's aristocratic family an offer of a wife and a secure future as an Anglican clergyman. These he refuses, wanting neither his cousin for a wife nor a career as a poor churchman. He turns to his brother, a businessman, who takes him on as a junior clerk in his mill. Unhappy in his work under his brother, William travels to Brussels and becomes a teacher of English and Latin in a private school. After finding success, he marries Mlle Henri, who has been a pupil and who also becomes a teacher. Because of his hard work and his wife's, Crimsworth is able to retire and return to England while still in middle age.

Mlle Frances Evans Henri (ah[n]-REE), a pretty young woman of Swiss and English parentage who teaches lace-mending at a school where William Crimsworth is employed. She takes lessons from Crimsworth, who falls in love with her. Under his encouragement, she also becomes a teacher, and with her husband's help she opens a private school of her own. She has never seen her mother's country and yearns to visit England. Her happiness is complete when she, her husband, and their young son, retiring on the proceeds of their thrift and the sale of her school, go to England to live.

Victor Crimsworth, the son of William Crimsworth and his wife.

Edward Crimsworth, a manufacturer. He hires his young brother as a junior clerk at a very low salary. A malicious tyrant, he treats William worse than he would a stranger. He eventually goes bankrupt but is able to secure sufficient credit to start another business.

Mrs. Crimsworth, Edward's pretty but vacuous and worldly wife. She follows her husband's lead in mistreating her brother-in-law.

Hunsden Yorke Hunsden, a flippant, cynical mill owner who befriends William Crimsworth. He encourages William abroad, buys for him his mother's portrait when Edward Crimsworth's belongings are auctioned off, and later becomes William's adviser on investments. He is a confirmed bachelor, unable to find a woman who pleases him sufficiently to marry.

Mr. Brown, an Englishman living in Brussels who, at Hunsden's request, helps William Crimsworth find a teaching post.

M. Pelet (peh-LAY), the director of a private school where William is employed. Pelet is a kindly man who accepts William as an equal and becomes his friend. The friendship is strained, however, when Pelet finds that the younger man finds favor in the eyes of Pelet's fiancée. Because of his own amorous adventures with married women, Pelet is of a suspicious nature; he is relieved when William leaves the school shortly after the director's marriage.

Mlle Zoraïde Reuter (zoh-rah-EED roo-TEHR), the plump, pretty, and practical director of a school for girls next door to Pelet's school for boys. She hires William Crimsworth to teach part-time in her school and for a time is attracted to the young man, though she is engaged to M. Pelet. Because William is a poor man, she dismisses him and marries M. Pelet. Mlle Reuter is a scheming and deceitful woman.

Mme Reuter, her fat, worldly mother, who takes care of her daughter's quarters.

Mme Pelet, M. Pelet's fat, worldly mother, who looks after her son's personal life.

Lord Tynedale, the aristocratic uncle of William Crimsworth. He is highly offended when William spurns the church in favor of trade, and he refuses to have any more to do with his young relative.

The Honorable John Seacombe, another of William's maternal uncles. Offended by the young man's refusal of one of his daughters in marriage, he disclaims all responsibility for his nephew's future.

Eulalie,

Hortense, and

Caroline, three worldly and vain young girls at Mlle Reuter's school. They flirt with William Crimsworth and try to make life difficult for their teacher.

THE PROFESSOR'S HOUSE

Author: Willa Cather (1873-1947)
First published: 1925
Genre: Novel

Locale: Hamilton, a Midwestern university town
Time: A few years after World War I
Plot: Psychological realism

Godfrey St. Peter, professor of European history in a Midwestern state university. A scholar, historian, and artist, he is also a sensitive, imaginative man caught between the creativity of his middle years and the prospect of old age. His eight-volume work *Spanish Adventurers in North America* has brought him fame, the Oxford Prize, and money to build the fine new house his wife desires. Yet he is not happy in his new house or new life, and his enterprising son-in-law's exploitation of another man's invention makes him dissatisfied with material success in any form. During a summer while his family is in Europe, he stays on in the shabby old house he still rents because of its associations with all he values most: his early years as a young husband and father, his friendship with Tom Outland, a brilliant student killed in the war, the writing of his books. There, reading in Outland's diary about the discovery of ancient ruins in the Southwest, he recaptures in memory some of the passion and energy he had known as a boy and while at work on his great history. In the fall, alone in the cluttered attic study of the old house, he is almost asphyxiated by gas from a dilapidated heater. Saved by the timely arrival of the family seamstress, he realizes that his lonely summer has been a farewell to a time when life could be lived with delight. Four themes of corruption and betrayal touch upon St. Peter's story: the success that has made him the victim of his wife's ambition and his older daughter's desire for wealth and luxury; the knowledge that a frontier university, founded to stimulate scholarship of passion and vision, is becoming a refuge for immature minds, its integrity in pawn to a time-serving state legislature; the indifference of government archeologists to Outland's discovery of the mesa city and the sale of its relics to a foreign collector; and the commercialization for private gain of Outland's invention. Behind these stand the symbolic Blue Mesa and the stone city of an ancient culture. A contrast is implied. The people on the rock created a humanized world of beautiful forms and ceremonial richness. Modern America offers only the products of its materialistic concerns to eternity.

Tom Outland, professor St. Peter's former student. Orphaned as a baby, he was taken to New Mexico by foster parents. There, he worked as a railroad call boy and later, while recuperating from pneumonia, as a range rider for a cattle company. Sent to tend herd in a winter camp on the Cruzados River, he and his friend, Rodney Blake, explore the almost inaccessible Blue Mesa and find, preserved under overhanging cliffs, the stone city of a vanished tribe of cliff dwellers. The discovery, filling Outland with awe for something so untouched by time and admiration for the artisans who had built with patience and love, becomes the turning point in his life; here is evidence of the filial piety he had read about while studying the Latin poets with Father Duchene. He makes a trip to Washington in an attempt to interest government officials in excavating his find. Rebuffed, he returns to New Mexico. In the meantime, Blake, thinking that he is helping his friend, has sold most of the relics and artifacts to a German collector for four thousand dollars. Outland and Blake quarrel, and Blake leaves the region. Outland decides to continue his education and goes to see St. Peter because he has read one of the professor's articles. St. Peter takes an interest in the boy, helps him to qualify for entrance to the university, becomes his friend, and makes him almost one of the family. Outland, a brilliant young physicist, discovers the principle of the Outland vacuum, an important advance in aviation. Engaged to Rosamond St. Peter, the professor's older daughter, he wills her the patent on his invention before enlisting in the French Foreign Legion at the outbreak of World War I. He is killed in Flanders.

Lillian St. Peter, the professor's wife, a handsome, capable woman proud of her husband's success but without any real understanding of the spirit that has motivated his career. She tries to renew her youth in innocent coquetry with her sons-in-law.

Rosamond Marcellus, the St. Peters' older daughter, married to the man who has commercialized Tom Outland's invention. Still beautiful but no longer the appealing young girl with whom Outland fell in love, she is interested chiefly in her pretentious new home, her antique furniture, her clothes, and the standing of her husband in the academic community.

Louie Marcellus, an electrical engineer and a born entrepreneur. The first to realize the commercial possibilities of the patent Tom Outland had willed to Rosamond St. Peter, Marcellus has marketed it successfully and made his wife rich. Shrewd but likable, he takes delight in displaying the rare and beautiful things he buys for Rosamond. Professor St. Peter's attitude toward him is a mixture of admiration and ironic amusement.

Kathleen McGregor, the St. Peters' younger daughter, married to a young journalist. In many ways, she has been corrupted most by Tom Outland's invention, for she is unhappy with her own lot, dislikes her sister, and adds to the family tensions.

Scott McGregor, an able journalist who supplements his income by writing "uplift" editorials and a daily rhymed jingle for a newspaper syndicate. Professor St. Peter feels sorry for McGregor because he stands in second place to Louie Marcellus in family affairs, but the professor admires the young man's staunchness and independence. Rosamond dislikes her brother-in-law because she believes that he blackballed her husband when Marcellus was trying to become a member of an exclusive club.

Dr. Crane, a professor of physics, suffering from an illness that requires a series of operations. Although he had not shared in Tom Outland's experiments, he had assisted with some of the laboratory detail. He feels that he has a moral right to some of the money realized from the Outland vacuum but is too proud to demand his share.

Mrs. Crane, his wife. In a painful interview with Professor St. Peter, she asks his aid in obtaining for her husband a share of the royalties from the Outland vacuum.

Augusta, the practical, loyal sewing woman whose dress forms clutter the attic study that Professor St. Peter has shared with her for many years. Arriving to collect a set of keys so that she can open the new house in preparation for the return of the Marcelluses and Mrs. St. Peter from abroad, she finds the professor overcome by gas after the wind has extinguished the flame of the heater. She saves the life that he himself was willing to relinquish.

Professor Horace Langtry, Professor St. Peter's faculty rival. He represents the new generation of teachers, satisfied with lowered standards and active in internal academic politics.

Rodney Blake, a railroad fireman who becomes Tom Outland's friend after the boy protects him from the loss of a large sum of money won in a poker game. He nurses Outland through an attack of pneumonia and later goes with him to ride herd on the cattle range. Together they explore the Blue Mesa. Misunderstanding Outland's interest in the cliff city, he sells the relics they have collected. After the two men quarrel, Blake leaves the region and is never heard from again. Outland tries unsuccessfully to find him.

Father Duchene, a Belgian-born priest who takes an interest in Tom Outland as a boy, teaches him the classics, and helps to explore the Blue Mesa. He has great respect for anything that reveals an enduring culture.

Mr. O'Brien and

Mrs. O'Brien, Tom Outland's foster parents during his boyhood.

Sir Edgar Spilling, an English scholar interested in Professor St. Peter's historical research. At a dinner to entertain him, Louie Marcellus has the bad taste to announce that he and his wife Rosamond intend to call their new home "Outland."

PROMETHEUS BOUND
(Prometheus desmōtes)

Author: Aeschylus (525/524-456/455 B.C.E.)
First performed: Unknown
Genre: Drama

Locale: A barren cliff in Scythia
Time: Antiquity
Plot: Tragedy

Prometheus (proh-MEE-thee-uhs), a Titan, the son of Themis (Earth). In the revolt of Zeus against Kronos, he had sided with Zeus and had provided the counsel by which the older gods had been overthrown. Later, he persuaded Zeus to spare humankind, whom Zeus had planned to destroy. He has broken the command of the king of the gods by bringing to humans the gift of fire and instructing them in all the arts and crafts. For this flouting of the will of Zeus, he is carried, a prisoner, by Kratos (Might) and Bia (Force) to a rocky cliff in remote Scythia, there to be fastened by Hephaestus to the crag and to remain bound for eternity. His only comfort in his anguish is his secret foreknowledge of the eventual downfall of Zeus. His knowledge of the future remains with him. He prophesies to Io the torments that await her; tells her that her descendant, Herakles, will finally release him; and declares that Zeus himself will one day be deposed by his own son, whose future identity only Prometheus knows. This secret he refuses to divulge to Hermes, who brings the command of Zeus that Prometheus must reveal this all-important name on

pain of even worse torments. Defiant to the last, Prometheus is blasted by the thunderbolt of Zeus and sinks into the underworld as the play ends. Prometheus is depicted in this drama as the embodiment of stubborn resistance against the tyranny of Zeus, willing to bear any punishment rather than submit. To the modern mind, and especially to the writers of the Romantic period, he is the personification of the revolt against tyranny of any sort, the symbol of humanity's war against the forces of reaction and of the eternal quest for knowledge.

Io (I-oh), the daughter of the river god Inachus. She was beloved by Zeus, who changed her into a heifer to save her from the jealous wrath of Hera. Penetrating her rival's disguise, Hera sent a gadfly to torment Io throughout the world. Half-crazed with pain, Io has wandered to Scythia, where she finds in Prometheus a fellow sufferer. He prophesies her future adventures and traces her descendants down to Herakles, who will deliver him from his chains.

Hermes (HUR-meez), the messenger of Zeus, sent to wring from Prometheus the secret of the identity of that son of Zeus who will overthrow his father. In his attitude, Hermes has been called the personification of prudent self-interest. He fails in his errand, for the dauntless Prometheus reviles him as a mere lackey and refuses to divulge the secret.

Hephaestus (hee-FEHS-tuhs), the god of fire and of metalworking. He has been ordered by Zeus to forge the chains that fasten Prometheus to the rock and to drive an adamantine wedge through his breast. He performs this horrible task reluctantly, bowing only to the superior power of Zeus.

Oceanus (oh-SEE-eh-nuhs), god of the sea. He comes to sympathize with Prometheus and to preach to him the virtue of humility. He even offers to intercede on his behalf with Zeus. Prometheus warns him that, in comforting a rebel, he himself may be charged with rebellion and urges him to depart.

Kratos (**Might**) and

Bia (**Force**), brute beings who symbolize the tyranny of Zeus, for they carry out his will. They drag the captive Prometheus to the cliff in Scythia and supervise Hephaestus as he chains the Titan to the rock. Kratos taunts the fallen Titan, reminding him that the name Prometheus—the Contriver—has a terrible irony, for no contrivance can release him.

PROMETHEUS UNBOUND: A Lyrical Drama in Four Acts

Author: Percy Bysshe Shelley (1792-1822)
First published: 1820
Genre: Drama

Locale: Asia
Time: Antiquity
Plot: Allegory

Prometheus (proh-MEE-thee-uhs), a Titan punished by Jupiter for having befriended humankind. He is chained to a rocky cliff for three thousand years while eagles tear at his heart, but he will not repudiate the curse he has pronounced on Jupiter. Aided by spirits and gods, Prometheus finally is unbound. His freedom heralds an age of sweetness and light for humankind.

Jupiter (JEW-pih-tur), the chief of the gods, who has had Prometheus bound to the cliff. As Prometheus is released, Jupiter loses his power and falls, impotent, into darkness.

Demogorgon (dee-muh-GOHR-guhn), the supreme god and ruler of all gods, who finally reverses prevailing circumstances, thus causing Jupiter's downfall and Prometheus' release from torment.

Panthea (PAN-thee-ah) and

Ione (i-OH-nee), two Oceanids. Panthea and Asia, Prometheus' wife, learn from Demogorgon that Prometheus will be set free. They are Demogorgon's interlocutors as he explains what will come to pass on Earth.

Herakles (HEHR-uh-kleez), the hero famous for his strength. Herakles, before spirits friendly to Prometheus, releases the captive from his bonds and torment.

Mercury (MUR-kyew-ree), the messenger of the gods, sent by Jupiter to Prometheus to learn from the captive how long Jupiter will reign.

Earth, Prometheus' mother.

Asia, Prometheus' wife.

Phantasma of Jupiter (fan-TAZ-mah), a wraith who appears to Prometheus to repeat for him the forgotten curse he had put on Jupiter.

The Furies, agents of torment who go with Mercury to punish further the bound Titan.

The Spirit of the Hour, one of a group of Hours, figures who move in Demogorgon's realm to show the passing of time by Age, Manhood, Youth, Infancy, and Death. The Spirit of the Hour announces Prometheus' release to all of humankind and describes the pleasant things that will occur on Earth now that the Titan is free.

THE PROMISE

Author: Chaim Potok (1929-   )
First published: 1969
Genre: Novel

Locale: New York City
Time: The 1950's
Plot: Fiction of manners

Reuven Malter, an Orthodox Jew who narrates his seminary experiences as he prepares for ordination, or smicha. Reuven faces opposition to his use of his father's methods of textual criticism, especially from Rav Jacob Kalman, who is teaching Reuven the Talmud. Along with his seminary studies, Reuven struggles to help Michael Gordon. Reuven risks his chances of obtaining smicha to help Michael, whose father is under the ban of excommunication by the strict Orthodox Jewish community. Because of his bold stand of accepting his father's methods of studying the Talmud, Reuven is given smicha with the provision that he can never teach the Torah in the rabbinical school of the yeshiva, where candidates study for their ordination or smicha. Reuven is allowed, however, to teach Torah in the newly formed graduate department of rabbinic studies at Hirsch University, the very department in which his father was refused an opportunity to teach.

Michael Gordon, the fourteen-year-old son of Abraham and Ruth Gordon. Michael develops serious mental problems that resist the standard methods of counseling therapy. After being subjected to Danny Saunders' experimental silence therapy, Michael eventually begins to talk and reveals the root of his mental illness, his hatred of his parents for their controversial writings about Judaism.

Danny Saunders, a brilliant Hasidic Jew who is studying to become a psychologist while still observing Jewish law. His greatest challenge is to help Michael Gordon overcome his strong resistance to therapy. Danny employs a treatment of silence as a last effort to help Michael overcome his mental problems and thus avoid being confined to a mental institution. Essentially, Danny uses on Michael a variation on the practice of silence, which Danny's father had used on him. Danny also dates and eventually marries Rachel Gordon, a cousin of Michael. Danny's involvement with Rachel complicates his treatment of Michael and at times threatens to undermine the therapy process. In the end, with Reuven Malter's assistance, Danny succeeds and Michael makes progress toward healing.

Abraham Gordon, a nonbelieving Jewish author who often questions the substance of the Jewish faith but continues to practice its laws and traditions. Abraham's involvement in writing controversial critiques of Judaism, with the help of his atheistic wife Ruth, led to Michael's mental breakdown; Michael felt personally the animosity directed against his father.

Reb Saunders, a prominent spiritual leader of a sect of Russian Hasidic Jews and the father of Danny Saunders. Reb Saunders shows remarkable tolerance as he allows his son, Danny, to study psychology, dress like non-Hasidic Jews, and even marry Rachel Gordon, a niece of the controversial writer Abraham Gordon. Out of loyalty to his friendship with David Malter, Reb Saunders refuses to write a critical review of Malter's book on the Talmud.

David Malter, an Orthodox Jewish teacher who is known for his many articles on the Talmud and is the father of Reuven Malter. His book on the Talmud proves to be controversial within the Orthodox Jewish community because David advocates using modern, scientific methods of correcting textual problems, rather than simply resorting to the involved arguments of earlier rabbis. Throughout the novel, David struggles with a heart condition, but he is determined to promote his faith regardless of the personal price he must pay. After considerable controversy over his book, an offer of a position at Hirsch University is withdrawn, and he accepts a position at a non-Orthodox Jewish school, Zechariah Frankel Seminary, where the controversial Abraham Gordon teaches. David counsels his son to respect and love even those Jewish believers with whom he disagrees strongly, including Rav Kalman.

Rav Jacob Kalman, a harsh and demanding teacher of the Talmud who often uses ridicule and intimidation to make his students accept his ideas and methods. Rav Kalman seems to harbor bitterness over the execution of his family and over his own suffering in Russia. He is especially hostile toward Reuven Malter for daring to use modern, scientific methods to study the Talmud, and he threatens to refuse smicha to Reuven unless he recants the use of such methods. At one point, Rav Kalman enlists Reuven's help in interpreting David Malter's recently released book on the Talmud. Afterward, Rav Kalman writes several scathing critiques of this book by Reuven's father, leaving Reuven feeling betrayed and angry.

— *Daven M. Kari*

THE PROMISED LAND
(Det forjættede land)

Author: Henrik Pontoppidan (1857-1943)
First published: 1891-1895
Genre: Novel

Locale: Denmark
Time: Late nineteenth century
Plot: Social realism

Emanuel Hansted, a Danish clergyman from the upper classes of Copenhagen who throws in his lot politically with the peasants and their People's Party when he is sent to a rural pastorate. In his efforts to prove himself one of the peasantry, he marries a peasant girl and tries to farm an acreage. His efforts to farm are futile, and his rural parishioners see him only as a misfit. Though he is stubbornly sincere, he is a failure. Given a chance to visit with people of his own class, he sees his mistakes and sadly returns to Copenhagen, leaving his wife but taking his children with him.

Hansine, the minister's peasant wife. She loves her husband and presents him with three children, one of whom dies when the father neglects the child. Hansine, visited by Miss Tonnesen, realizes that her husband is still really an upper-class city man, not a peasant. She tells him he ought to return to the city and that she ought to return to her father's farm.

Miss Tonnesen, Emanuel's former fiancée. She represents all Hansted gives up, and her visit to the rectory persuades both the Hansteds of the minister's mistakes. As the daughter of the former rector in the same parish, she is horrified at the rundown condition of the rectory and the extent of Hansted's failure.

Mr. Hansted, Emanuel's father, a well-to-do conservative. He is happy when his son decides to return to the city and his old home.

Dr. Hassing, a physician in Hansted's parish. He sees the failure of the minister and gives the man an opportunity to be with people from his own class again.

THE PROPHET

Author: Kahlil Gibran (Gibran Kahlil Gibran, 1883-1931)
First published: 1923
Genre: Poetry

Locale: The city of Orphalese
Time: Harvest season in an indeterminate year
Plot: Prose poem

Almustafa, a prophet of God who has come down from the hill to embark on the ship that will take him to the land of his birth. He has dwelled among the Orphalese for twelve years, has fathered children, and has known long days of pain and long nights alone. He has acquired the love of the people, who regard him as the "Chosen," but he is a seafarer and traveler, and it is time to depart. In his demeanor, his language, and his relationship to his listeners, Almustafa bears a close resemblance to Jesus of Nazareth. By using a biblical setting, the book lends moral force to what the Prophet says. Almustafa is a mystic whose wisdom has been gleaned from much observation. In nature, he sees a revelation of all of his truths, and he takes from nature a rich array of imagery to convey his teaching. Whereas Christ spoke in parables, Almustafa employs paradoxical examples to illustrate his thoughts and find understanding and acceptance, yet his simple language makes his teachings accessible to all those who come to hear him speak. He delivers his wisdom on more than two dozen topics. The seeress Almitra asks him to speak of love and marriage. A mother wants the truth about children; a rich man, of giving; an innkeeper, of eating and drinking; a mason, of houses; and a hermit, of pleasure. Other subjects include the ordinary—clothes, talking, and buying and selling—and the lofty and timeless—freedom, good and evil, beauty, pleasure, friendship, time, and, inevitably, death. The people who seek the wisdom of the Prophet are only names of types or occupations: a ploughman, an elder, a lawyer, a weaver, an orator, a rich man, a scholar, a poet, and an astronomer. The subjects on which the Prophet speaks are but individual manifestations of the great forces that drive nature and define all things. As he speaks, he connects the everyday experiences of his audience to the powers of the Infinite, telling his listeners that he does not bring knowledge to them; rather, he shows them what they already know and feel but do not yet see. The Prophet drives home the principle that the best life is one in harmony with nature. The individual, as part of nature, partakes of its boundless forces. As it endures, so will the souls of all who open

themselves to nature and understand their affinity to it. Endless is being, he tells them, and endless is their ability to see beauty, to feel passion, and to give and receive love; endless also is their ability to receive knowledge from nature and to understand it. He assures the people that they already possess the powers of the Infinite, but because they see narrowly and see only the surface of things, they are out of harmony with the forces, interfere with them, and thereby miss the great potential of their being. Each evil thought, feeling, or action is the result of their not seeing the deeper truths. With understanding comes conversion, the Prophet implies, for people are what they think they are, and if they think they are good, they will be. One must see the truth to receive its benefits. The Prophet's final act is to give the people that understanding. Once he has conveyed this message, his mission is fulfilled, and he is ready to return to his birthplace. The implication is that he has reached the end of his days not only in Orphalese but in this world. In the beginning, the narrator speaks of the "deeper secret" that the Prophet "himself could not speak," but by the end, it has been revealed in the truths he has spoken.

Almitra, a seeress who comes from the temple and is the first to bid the Prophet speak his thoughts; she is also the last to speak to him as he departs. Through her eyes, readers see the Prophet disappear into the mist.

— *Bernard E. Morris*

PROSERPINE AND CERES

Author: Unknown
First published: Unknown
Genre: Short fiction

Locale: The Mediterranean
Time: Antiquity
Plot: Mythic

Typhoeus (ti-FEE-uhs), a Titan imprisoned under Mt. Aetna. His struggles cause Hades to fear lest the underworld be exposed to the light of day.

Hades (HAY-deez), ruler of the underworld. He comes out to inspect the entrance to his realm, sees Proserpine, and falls in love with her. He kidnaps Proserpine and makes her his queen, partly against her will.

Proserpine (proh-SUR-pih-nee), the daughter of Ceres. She is seized by the enamored Hades and carried off to be queen of the underworld. Ceres demands Jupiter's help in recovering her daughter. Jupiter decrees that Proserpine may return to the earth provided she has eaten no food in the underworld. Unfortunately, she has eaten part of a pomegranate. She is allowed to spend but half the year with her mother; during the other half, she must stay with her husband in the underworld.

Ceres (SEE-reez), the goddess of fertility and the mother of Proserpine. When she cannot find her daughter, she prevents the earth from being fruitful. After her daughter is found and Jupiter decrees that she can spend half the year with her

mother, Ceres permits the earth to be fruitful in spring and summer.

Triptolemus (trihp-TO-leh-muhs), a mortal child who is saved from death by Ceres. She then teaches him to use the plow. She would have made him immortal if his mother had not interceded. Triptolemus builds a temple to Ceres at Eleusis.

Arethusa (eh-reh-THEW-zuh), a woodland nymph changed into a fountain by Diana. She tells Ceres that Hades has taken Proserpine to the underworld.

Jupiter, the king of the gods. He decrees that Proserpine can return to her mother if the girl has eaten nothing in the underworld. Since the girl has eaten part of a pomegranate, a compromise is reached, and she is allowed to spend half her time on the earth with her mother.

Venus, the goddess of love.

Cupid (KYEW-pihd), her son.

Alpheus (al-FEE-uhs), a river god.

Diana, the goddess of the hunt.

Mercury, the messenger of the gods.

PSEUDOLUS

Author: Plautus (c. 254-184 B.C.E.)
First performed: 191 B.C.E.
Genre: Drama

Locale: Athens
Time: Late third century B.C.E.
Plot: Comedy

Pseudolus (SEW-duh-luhs), Simo's servant. When he learns that Calidorus' slave-girl sweetheart, Phoenicium, is to be sold, Pseudolus promises to trick Simo out of enough money to purchase her. The slave brazenly tells Simo of his plan and goads the old man into promising to pay for the girl if Pseudolus can get her away from her owner, Ballio. By substituting Simia for the real messenger, the wily slave succeeds in duping Ballio and wins the slave girl for Calidorus free of charge.

Simo (SIH-moh), an Athenian gentleman, Calidorus' father and Pseudolus' owner. Forewarned by his clever servant, the tightfisted old man is tricked nevertheless, but his bet with Ballio keeps him from losing any money.

Ballio (BA-lee-oh), a procurer, the owner of Phoenicium. Although he has been warned by Simo, the hard-hearted procurer is tricked by clever Pseudolus; he loses his slave girl to Calidorus and twenty minae to Simo.

Calidorus (ka-lih-DOH-ruhs), the lovesick son of Simo.

Phoenicium (fee-NEE-see-uhm), Ballio's slave girl and the sweetheart of Calidorus.

Harpax (HAHR-paks), the real messenger of the Macedonian officer who has made the initial payment for the purchase of Phoenicium.

Simia (SIH-mee-uh), the servant of one of Calidorus' friends. He impersonates Harpax and tricks Ballio.

PURGATORY

Author: William Butler Yeats (1865-1939)
First published: 1939
Genre: Drama

Locale: Ireland
Time: Early twentieth century
Plot: Fantasy

Boy, a sixteen-year-old. He has accompanied his father too long, wandering through the Irish countryside. He feels like a packhorse, burdened with his father's bundle, and is tired of listening to the Old Man's continuous talking. The boy shows only vague interest in his father's description of the ruins of an old house before them. Considering his father silly, he ignores questions about their surroundings, for these merely delay their reaching a destination. He obeys his father's command to stand in the doorway to look for someone inside the house's shell, but he cannot see what his father sees there. Arguing with the Old Man's insistence that someone is, in fact, inside, the bored boy describes what he sees: emptiness, with only a piece of eggshell, doubtlessly dropped out of a bird's nest. He dismisses as lunatic ravings the Old Man's musings about purgatorial spirits returning to their earthly homes. Only when the Old Man identifies the house as their family's does the boy show interest. He challenges his father's condemnation of his grandmother's hasty marriage choice, defending his grandfather's luck in getting both the woman and her money. His interest in the Old Man's story is not in the stormy relationships but in the bounty it evokes: a young woman, horses, a rich library, clothing, and drink. He resents the Old Man having enjoyed wealth and learning without passing any on to him. Intrigued that he is the same age as his father was when the great house burned, the boy chooses that moment to ask about whisperings he had heard on their travels that the Old Man had murdered his dissolute father. His interest in violence links him to his father and grandfather. When the Old Man is lost in a vision of the grandmother and grandfather having sex, the boy grasps the moment to steal the Old Man's bundle of money, in an obvious parallel to the grandfather who seized the grandmother's estate. Selfishly, the boy argues about his right to his inheritance, to spend on drink if he chooses, echoing the grandfather. After a violent struggle, the boy threatens to kill the Old Man and replicate the former parricide; at that moment, he can see for the first time the Old Man's ghostly vision. The sex in the nightmare and the boy's violence are linked. As he covers his eyes, he is stabbed to death by his father.

Old Man, a wanderer drawn to the scene of his childhood, a ruined old house. He tries to pass on to his young son his fond memories of the luxurious life there when he was a boy. He is easily lost in reveries about the great lives robustly and affectionately lived there. He is also furious that his own father cut down ancient trees to pay gambling debts. The Old Man declares that wasting a great house with noble history is a capital offense. He ignores his son's envy of the luxury the Old Man had as a boy; indeed, he ignores the boy's scoffing pronouncements on his shaky sanity and continues to point out the ghostly scene inside the house. Reliving his resentment of his dissolute father—his low class, drinking, whoring, squandering the estate by gambling, and refusing to educate his son—he passes on his resentment to his own son, calling him a bastard who also would probably become a drunkard. His anger flares hottest as he observes his father and mother's ghosts in the sex act. Clearly, his affection for his mother tortures him as he watches her phantom lead his father's phantom to the bedroom. Trying to enter the vision, he hopes to break the cycle of sex, betrayal, and destruction by warning his mother to flee. Even though he is disgusted, he cannot tear himself from the spectral sexual union of his parents, which suggests an oedipal fascination with his mother. When the Old Man sees the young boy steal the bag of money, repeating the cycle of the grandfather squandering the grandmother's wealth, he is livid. Blending rage at his father's callousness with fury at his son's resemblance to the wastrel parent, the Old Man wildly stabs the boy to death. Grotesquely, he sings a lullaby to the boy's body and afterward addresses his mother, excusing his violence as a release for her purgatorial reenactments. Contritely, he promises to become a harmless old storyteller in distant lands. As he hears the ghostly hoofbeats of his father's ghost again, it is clear that in spite of the Old Man's prayer for his mother's release, the eerie cycle will begin anew. Her purgatory is his also.

— Nancy A. Macky

PURLIE VICTORIOUS

Author: Ossie Davis (1917-   )
First published: 1961
Genre: Drama

Locale: A Georgia cotton plantation
Time: The 1950's
Plot: Comedy

Purlie Victorious Judson, the protagonist, an African American in his mid- or late thirties. Resentful of a beating received twenty years earlier from the owner of the cotton plantation where the play takes place, Purlie has become a preacher of the gospel, which for Purlie means freedom. Driven to acquire Big Bethel, an old barn that once was used as a church, Purlie will use any means necessary to obtain his goal. He uses a young woman to impersonate a dead cousin in order to obtain a $500 inheritance to purchase Big Bethel.

Lutiebelle Gussie Mae Jenkins, a young African American woman. Lutiebelle, from the backwoods of Alabama, has been a servant in a white household. Naïve, innocent, and good-hearted, she first met Purlie as a preacher and accompanied him back to the plantation. Purlie plans to have her impersonate the deceased Cousin Bee. Lutiebelle wishes to help Purlie, but her own desire is for a husband and family.

Missy Judson, called **Aunt Missy**, is Purlie's sister-in-law and the matriarch of the Judson clan. Missy, who is married to Purlie's brother, Gitlow, sees obstacles in Purlie's plans that he ignores, but she too is caught up in his dream of acquiring Big Bethel, which for her is also a symbol of African American freedom.

Gitlow Judson, Purlie's brother but in many ways his antithesis. He accepts the realities of plantation life. His accommodation to the white-dominated world results in the white owner selecting him as "the Deputy-For-The-Colored," to lead his fellow African Americans and ensure that they remain in their place and that the cotton gets picked.

Ol' Cap'n Cotchipee, the white plantation owner and Purlie's antagonist. An unreconstructed white Southerner, the Ol' Cap'n intends life to go on as it always has. The symbol and at times the reality of his authority is his bullwhip. His financial manipulations in his country store keep his black workers in debt and unable to leave; they must continue to labor in the fields and serve his whims.

Charlie Cotchipee, the Ol' Cap'n's son, who represents the new South. Inspired in part by the influence of his old African American nurse, he is willing to accept the court decisions that challenge the racist institutions and Jim Crow practices that have long dominated American life. The Ol' Cap'n cannot understand his son's willingness to abandon the racial practices and prejudices that have always defined the old South.

Idella Landy, a tiny, old, African American woman who was Charlie's nurse and still is his confidant. Unlike Charlie, Idella is cautious about uttering her opinions, warning Charlie that discretion is often necessary. The Ol' Cap'n' blames her for his son's attitudes and ideas, but he knows that he relies on her assistance.

— Eugene S. Larson

PURPLE DUST

Author: Sean O'Casey (John Casey, 1880-1964)
First published: 1940
Genre: Drama

Locale: Clune na Geera, Ireland
Time: The 1940's
Plot: Satire

Cyril Poges and
Basil Stoke, two English gentlemen in love with the past. With a firm conviction that life's real glories all exist in times gone by, and filled with a longing for the joys of country living, they arrive in Ireland with their mistresses, Souhaun and Avril, to take up residence in a decaying old house in the process of being renovated. Their romantic dreams of escape into the pastoral life of bygone days is interrupted constantly by a series of prosaic household crises, unromantic arguments with servants and workmen, misadventures with farm animals and machinery, and the seduction of their mistresses by O'Killigain and one of his fellow workers. Finally, as the river rises during a storm, the two gentlemen, cold, wet, and defeated, take to the roof, longing for good old England.

Souhaun and
Avril, mistresses of Cyril and Basil. Accompanying the two gentlemen to Ireland to live the country life in a decayed ruin, the ladies are soon disgusted with the discomforts of pastoral living. Beguiled by the poetic Irish charms of O'Killigain and one of his workmen, they run away with the pair.

O'Killigain, the handsome foreman of the workmen engaged in renovating the ancient ruin occupied by Cyril Poges and Basil Stoke. He is a great believer in the glories of the present. He and one of his workmen exert their Irish charms on Souhaun and Avril and run away with them.

Barney and
Cloyne, the butler and the maid to Cyril Poges and Basil Stoke.

THE PURPLE LAND THAT ENGLAND LOST:
Travels and Adventures in the Banda Oriental, South America

Author: W. H. Hudson (1841-1922)
First published: 1885
Genre: Novel

Locale: Uruguay and Argentina
Time: The nineteenth century
Plot: Adventure

Richard Lamb, a humorous, poetic young adventurer, amateur botanist, and wandering seeker of work to support himself and his wife. He briefly and unwillingly joins a revolutionary band, almost loses his life as a result, and at last returns to his wife still unemployed and facing the unpleasant prospect of a meeting with his angry father-in-law.

Paquíta (pah-KEE-tah), his olive-skinned, violet-eyed, black-haired Argentinean wife, married without her father's consent.

Doña Isidora (ee-see-DOH-rah), her aunt, a garrulous old woman.

Lucero (lew-SEH-roh), a friendly horse tamer, an old man who still possesses youthful fire and energy in his soul.

Marcos Marcó (MAHR-kohs mahr-KOH), later **General Santa Coloma** (SAHN-tah koh-LOH-mah), a tall, imposing, bronzed man whom Lamb first meets in disguise. He turns out to be a popular Uruguayan revolutionary hero.

Margarita (mahr-gahr-EE-tah), his beautiful, fair, golden-haired, sapphire-eyed young daughter.

Don Peralta (pehr-AHL-tah), an insane old landowner and former officer who thinks Lamb is his long-lost son.

Demetria (deh-MEH-tree-ah), his daughter, who wishes to marry Lamb. To save her from Hilario, Lamb abducts her and takes her to Montevideo.

Don Hilario (ee-LAHR-ee-oh), an undersized, serpentlike autocrat, the villainous supervisor of Don Peralta's estate. Demetria hates him.

Santos (SAHN-tohs), a servant who reveals to Lamb the Peralta family history.

Blas (blahs), also called **Barbudo** (bahr-BEW-doh), an insolent, black-bearded giant stabbed by Lamb in a fight.

Anselmo (ahn-SEHL-moh), a handsome gaucho, a teller of wandering, pointless tales.

Don Sinforiano Alday (seen-foh-RYAH-noh AHL-dah-ee), the owner of a large estate.

Monica, his daughter.

Anita, an orphan living with the Aldays.

Gandara (gahn-DAH-rah), a truculent, murderous man whom Lamb shoots before escaping from him.

John Carrickfergus, an amiable expatriate Scotsman who befriends Lamb.

Toribia (toh-REE-byah), a magistrate's wife, a fat slattern who takes an embarrassing liking to Lamb.

Dolores (doh-LOH-rehs), a beautiful young woman who almost makes Lamb forget Paquíta.

PYGMALION

Author: George Bernard Shaw (1856-1950)
First published: 1912
Genre: Drama

Locale: London, England
Time: c. 1900
Plot: Comedy

Henry Higgins, a linguistic scientist. A robust and handsome forty-year-old bachelor, Higgins is violently enthusiastic about anything scientific, but he is absolutely uncivilized in his relations with people. Although he firmly believes himself to be kindhearted and considerate, he is a bad-tempered and profane bully. Even so, his frankness and lack of malice make it impossible for anyone to dislike him. Higgins makes a bet with another scientist, Colonel Pickering, that he can, in six months, make a Cockney flower girl speak so well that she can be passed off as a duchess.

Eliza Doolittle, the flower girl. Dirty and ignorant, Eliza comes to Higgins and pathetically begs him to teach her to speak well enough to run a respectable flower shop. He teaches her to speak like a noblewoman. Grown fond of Higgins and grateful to him, Eliza tries to please him and is ignored. Higgins thinks it unnatural for Eliza to have feelings. He does not understand why she is enraged when, after she has successfully passed herself off as a noblewoman, he and Pickering congratulate each other and ignore her. To assert herself, Eliza threatens to go into competition with Higgins, using his own methods of teaching proper speech. Higgins rudely congratulates Eliza on her assertiveness and welcomes her as a friend and equal. Eliza marries not Higgins but Freddy Hill. They open a flower shop that, with Pickering's help, finally becomes prosperous.

Colonel Pickering, a linguist who has traveled to London from India to see Higgins. An elderly, amiable soldier, Pickering is as confirmed a bachelor as Higgins, but he is a gentleman who treats Eliza with respect and helps to moderate Higgins' mistreatment of her.

Alfred Doolittle, a dustman, Eliza's father. One of the "undeserving poor," Doolittle is distinguished by a good voice, an original mind, and a complete absence of conscience. He plans to blackmail Higgins, mistakenly thinking that Higgins has taken Eliza as his mistress. Higgins and Pickering are so delighted by the scoundrel's straightforwardness that they give him five pounds. In a letter to Ezra D. Wannafeller, an American philanthropist, Higgins calls Doolittle "the most original moralist" in England. Wannafeller leaves Doolittle an income of four thousand pounds a year. Doolittle is thus made middle class, respectable, and, at first, thoroughly unhappy. He even marries his "old woman." Eventually, Doolittle's native talents, his Nietzschean philosophy, and his odd background make him much in demand in the highest society.

Mrs. Higgins, Henry's mother, a woman of taste. She has asked her barbaric son to stay away when she is receiving guests. Her poise and competence help to bring some order into the lives of those around her.

Freddy Eynsford Hill, the uneducated and unintelligent son of an impoverished noble family. He loves Eliza and haunts the street by Higgins' house to catch a glimpse of her. He marries her at last and submits to her benevolent despotism.

Mrs. Eynsford Hill, Freddy's mother. Quiet and well-bred, Mrs. Hill is plagued by the anxieties natural to an aristocrat without money. Because of her poverty, her children have neither education nor sophistication.

Miss Clara Eynsford Hill, Freddy's sister. An ignorant, pretentious, and useless snob, Clara is at length redeemed by reading the works of H. G. Wells and becoming a critic of society. In that role, her gaucheness is an asset.

Mrs. Pearce, Henry Higgins' housekeeper, a very proper and very middle-class woman. Mrs. Pearce, by sheer force of will, enforces a semblance of order and propriety in Higgins' house.

Nepommuck, a spectacularly bewhiskered Hungarian. At the embassy reception at which Eliza is passed off as nobility, Nepommuck, a former pupil of Higgins who makes his living as a translator, testifies that Eliza is certainly of royal blood, perhaps a princess.

PYLON

Author: William Faulkner (1897-1962)
First published: 1935
Genre: Novel

Locale: Primarily New Valois, Franciana, and Ohio
Time: The 1930's
Plot: Modernism

Lazarus, a reporter, the major protagonist. He is described as tall, gaunt, and pale; often he is called the specter man or is likened to a cadaver or a corpse. Covering the air show at the dedication of the new airport, he becomes involved with a flying team, giving them lodging in his room and providing them with food, drink, and money. He is, falsely, said to have had no origin and to have no family; his mother calls on his editor on one occasion. He suffers in various ways because of his infatuation with the team. Indirectly, he causes Roger's death.

Roger Shumann, a pilot and leader of the flying team. He shares LaVerne with Jack Holmes. In the competition, he places well in his first race, crashes his plane in the second, and loses his life crashing an experimental plane in his third.

LaVerne Shumann, an attractive and desirable woman. She is the mother of young Jack; either Roger or Jack Holmes is the father. After discovering her pregnancy, Roger and Jack shot dice to see which of them would marry her: Roger won to become the lucky bridegroom. LaVerne wears coveralls and does mechanic's work with the men; she has been an exhibition parachute jumper. At the end, she leaves the boy with Roger's parents and departs with Jack Holmes. She is pregnant again.

Jack Shumann, the son of LaVerne and either Roger Shumann or Jack Holmes. He bears the first name of one and the last name of the other. He is enraged when anyone asks who his father is. The reporter buys him ice cream and candy. Jack sleeps in the reporter's bed with Roger and LaVerne. He calls team members by their first names.

Jack Holmes, a parachutist and member of the team. He is described as taller than the others. Toward the end, he has injured his leg but continues to perform. Unlike Roger, he becomes violently jealous when anyone other than Roger shows interest in LaVerne. On one occasion, he attacks the reporter while enjoying his hospitality.

Jiggs, a mechanic and member of the team. He is short and stocky. He is caught up in acquiring a new pair of boots, even though there is less than enough money for food and lodging. A former exhibition parachutist, he leaves the team and returns to his previous line of work. He is a heavy drinker, and his inability to perform his duties results in the first crash.

Hagood, the reporter's editor. He is hard-nosed and businesslike on the surface, but he relents, giving money to the reporter and reversing his decisions to fire him.

Colonel H. I. Feinman, the chairman of the New Valois Sewage Board. The airport, which is more or less the result of his efforts, is named for him. He is also the authority who decides that Roger will be permitted to fly the death plane. He utilizes all the available beds for his guests, leaving the flying teams with no lodging other than in town.

Dr. Carl Shumann, a Midwestern family physician. A good man, he makes little money, serving his patients in any place and any kind of weather. Having financed Roger's first plane, he has mortgaged and lost his home and is now living in a smaller one. He and his wife take in young Jack without knowing whether he is their grandson. He throws the reporter's money in the fire, thinking that it has come from LaVerne.

— George W. Van Devender

A QUALITY OF MERCY

Author: Paul West (1930-)
First published: 1961
Genre: Novel

Locale: Rural Connecticut, England, Italy, and Manhattan
Time: Late 1950's, with flashbacks to World War II and earlier
Plot: Black humor

Camden Smeaton, a retired schoolmaster and writer of textbooks. Articulate and cynical, he is prone to poetic tirades, which are delivered to anyone who will listen, including trees, to which he offers a passionate monologue while flailing madly at their limbs. He is fifty-seven years old and views himself as a romantic figure who utilizes his superior knowledge to remain aloof from other people. He is obsessed with incidents from his past, including the deaths of his parents and spouse. He lives in rural Connecticut, in constant turmoil, with his sister, Merula, and her unmarried daughter, Brenda. Finally, he takes his own life with a Winchester rifle.

Brenda Smeaton, a forty-seven-year-old, unmarried woman. Spurned in her attempt to consummate a sexual experience at the age of twenty-seven in a New York hotel, she is bitter and resentful toward life in general, and particularly toward men. Looking haggard beyond her years, she engages Camden in conversation but feels inferior, self-conscious, and unloved. Driven to despair by her self-loathing, Brenda murders her dog and her mother, then attempts suicide by swimming into the middle of a lake.

Merula Smeaton, the eighty-one-year-old mother of Brenda and a son who died at the age of three. Embittered and cranky, she sits in her chair and complains incessantly while delivering platitudes to Camden and Brenda. She continues to dominate her daughter's life, even to the point of disciplining her by spanking.

Huntley Fisher, a magna cum laude graduate in electrical engineering from Cornell. He is honeymooning with his wife, Wendy, in a house next door to the Smeatons. Vain and simpleminded, he is a foil to Camden's introspective brooding.

Wendy Fisher, a voluptuous blonde who becomes enraged when Brenda makes advances to her husband at a dinner party. The incident ignites Brenda's murder spree.

Linda Panton, a nurse who attends Camden during the war and, after becoming pregnant by him, becomes his wife. She dies of disease shortly thereafter, in 1946. Camden muses about whether he had ever loved her.

Camden's father, a coal miner who wanted a better future for his son. He was killed in a mining accident when Camden was a boy.

Camden's mother, who used the insurance money from the accident to send Camden to boarding school. She died shortly thereafter.

Cuthbert "Guppy" Harrison, Camden's childhood friend and fellow prankster, one year younger than Camden.

Tobacco shop girl, a seductress to whom both Camden and Guppy surrendered their innocence.

Karen, a woman with whom Camden has an ill-fated love affair that causes him to become cynical about love.

Pietro, a young Italian boy who visits Camden in the hospital. His sister is killed in a random attack by German Messerschmitts.

— *Michael Wm. Gearhart*

QUALITY STREET

Author: Sir James M. Barrie (1860-1937)
First published: 1913
Genre: Drama

Locale: An English provincial village
Time: During the Napoleonic Wars
Plot: Comedy of manners

Valentine Brown, a doctor who, through poor investments, loses the Throssel sisters' small fortune for them. He disappoints Phoebe Throssel when he goes off to the Napoleonic Wars without proposing marriage. Following his military service, during which he becomes a captain, he returns, minus his left hand. He is amazed by the alteration in Phoebe's appearance after ten years. To Phoebe's discomfiture, he does not conceal his surprise. He learns, however, to appreciate Phoebe and marries her.

Phoebe Throssel, who is in love with Valentine. When he shows dismay that ten years of schoolteaching have made a drab, mousy woman of her, she dresses as if she were twenty again. Her appearance deceives Captain Brown, and she maintains a disguise as her own fictitious niece Livvy. Her activities and popularity while in disguise convince Captain Brown that he prefers the more mature, modest, and quiet Phoebe. She accepts his proposal of marriage, and her school is closed.

Susan Throssel, Phoebe's sister. She is retiring and shy, like Phoebe. Both sisters find teaching school difficult, for they detest teaching some subjects, such as Latin and mathematics. They also fear the older boys and dare not punish them.

Ensign Blades, a former student at the Throssel sisters' school. Under duress, he asks Phoebe to attend a ball. With her pride hurt, she declines.

Patty, the Throssel sisters' maid. She discloses the identity of "Livvy" to Valentine Brown.

Livvy, the Throssel sisters' fictitious but pretty young niece, who is really Phoebe in disguise. Captain Brown is completely taken in by the ruse at first. After Patty at last reveals the secret to him, he makes Livvy disappear by taking a makeshift dummy out of town in full view of the snoopy, gossipy neighbors.

THE QUARE FELLOW

Author: Brendan Behan (1923-1964)
First published: 1956
Genre: Drama

Locale: Dublin, Ireland
Time: The 1950's
Plot: Tragicomedy

The Quare Fellow, a man scheduled for execution because he murdered his brother. He never appears on stage but is the focal point of all discussion and represents all quare fellows (prisoners scheduled for execution) everywhere.

Dunlavin, an old man who has spent most of his life in Irish prisons without becoming dulled by the experience. Often, he seems to speak for the playwright, doling out astute pieces of social criticism. His comparison of upper- and lower-class murder styles, for example, and his insistence that he prefers murderers to perpetrators of sexual crimes are comic, set pieces that focus on social pretensions and hypocrisies, which the playwright has attacked elsewhere. Dunlavin is a crafty old-timer who knows the prison system and can con authorities, cadge cigarette butts, and find access to alcohol. He is sympathetic to other prisoners, providing a practical example of how to survive an inhumane situation by using humor, but he is also hardened to the realities of his life and does not expect softness, compassion, or even justice from his world.

Warder Regan, an unusual prison guard whose humor is a match for Dunlavin's. Like Dunlavin, he uses his humor as a means of coping with a prison situation and a world that he would otherwise find unbearable. He is too familiar with the prisoners to suit prison authorities, and his clear parallels with Dunlavin prevent any implication that all virtue lies on the prisoners' side of the bars.

Neighbour, a contemporary of Dunlavin, also a prison old-timer. He is less sardonic than Dunlavin, but his presence allows the two old men to reminisce about the harshness of poverty outside the prison and to analyze prison life itself, thus voicing many of the play's social concerns. Neighbour's recognition that execution might be a kinder fate than putting a prisoner back on the streets with no real means of survival sums up major concerns of the play.

Lifer, a forty-three-year-old murderer who has just been granted a reprieve from execution and been reassigned to this ward. A member of the privileged class outside the prison, he beat his wife to death with the silver-topped cane presented to him by the Combined Staffs, Excess and Refunds branch of the late Great Southern Railways. Reprieve has brought a change from the relative comforts of the condemned cell (where he had all the cigarettes he wanted and special food) to the considerably more austere main ward. The other prisoners are more generous with him than he had been with them, and

he is a direct contrast with the Quare Fellow, who suffers a very different fate for committing a very similar crime. Thus, life inside the prison reflects the social realities of life outside the walls.

The Other Fellow, the second prisoner just reassigned to this ward. He has been convicted of an unspecified sexual crime and is timid and anxious. He is appalled by murderers, kowtows to authorities, and mouths conventional pieties.

Prisoner A, called **Hard Case**,
Prisoner B, **The Man of Thirty**,
Prisoner C, **The Boy from the Island**,
Prisoner D, **The Embezzler**, and
Prisoner E, **The Bookie**, a chorus of barely distinguishable prisoners whose general commentary climaxes in wordless howling as the Quare Fellow is executed.

Scholara and

Shaybo, referred to together as **Young Prisoners**, both seventeen years old. They are due to be released soon, and their major concern is catching a glimpse of the female prisoners. They are what the other prisoners must once have been; they are destined to become what the other prisoners are. The fact that they study Gaelic while incarcerated indicates their membership in a new generation of Irish prisoners, for whom Irish nationalism and criminal behavior frequently are linked.

Holy Healey, a representative of the Department of Justice who comes to inspect the prison. He is a stereotypical administrator and do-gooder whose membership in charitable societies and pompous piety do not conceal a general lack of compassion for everyone but himself.

Hangman, the executioner. He knows how to compute weight, height, and length of fall to plan an efficient execution and treats his job as a mere technical problem, but he is unable to perform that job without getting roaring drunk the night before.

Governor (or **Warden**) and

Chief Warder, typical prison administrators, not hostile to their prisoners but indifferent to them, seeking only to improve their own positions.

Warder Donelly and

Warder 2, older and younger versions of a typical prison guard, interested only in promotion.

— Helen Lojek

QUARTET IN AUTUMN

Author: Barbara Pym (Mary Crampton, 1913-1980)
First published: 1977
Genre: Novel

Locale: London, England
Time: The 1970's
Plot: Psychological realism

Letty Crowe, a clerical worker in a London office. Letty is a shy, lonely woman in her sixties who lives alone in an apartment. She is the typical English "spinster," a respectable woman with appropriate behaviors and attitudes. Letty survives a move to a different apartment and, after her retirement, adjusts to new routines. Her plans to move to the country and live with an old friend, Marjorie, are disrupted when the latter decides to get married. Later, after Marjorie's plans for marriage are canceled, Marjorie expects Letty to live with her as previously planned, but Letty now realizes that she has choices in life. She does not decide immediately what she will do. When her colleague Marcia dies, Letty is called on again, this time by her two male colleagues, to help resolve details of Marcia's estate.

Marcia Ivory, a clerical worker in the same London office. Unlike Letty, who is careful about her appearance, she takes little care of her appearance or health. An incurably private person in her sixties, she never recovers from the deaths of her mother and her cat. She was never married, and she lives alone in her mother's house, where she hoards cans of food and plastic bags. In a shed in the back yard, she maintains a collection of empty milk bottles, which she meticulously cleans and rearranges periodically. After a recent mastectomy, she has become obsessed with her surgeon, and she even makes surreptitious visits to his house. After her retirement, she becomes reclusive, physically frail, and increasingly demented, and she finally dies of cancer.

Edwin Braithwaite, a clerical worker in the same London office. His thin, graying hair and solemn air are appropriate to this widower in his sixties. Edwin lives alone in his house and is the only one of the four major characters who has normal family ties. He enjoys a role as grandfather, but he is obsessed with observing every special day in the church calendar. He helps Letty to find another apartment when she becomes unhappy with her new landlord, and he makes the funeral arrangements for Marcia after she dies.

Norman, a clerical worker in the same London office. He is an angry old man in his sixties who is dissatisfied with life. His conversation often is laced with sarcasm or irony. He feels most comfortable when he is at work in the office, where he even spends part of his holidays. His only family is a brother-in-law, but he visits him grudgingly. He enjoys teasing Marcia, who does not seem to mind his uncouth and often inappropriate remarks. After Marcia dies, he is surprised to learn that she has willed her house to him.

Janice Brabner, a volunteer for a local senior citizens' center. Janice is an earnest woman in her twenties who visits elderly people in their homes. She visits Marcia several times, but Marcia resents her visits as intrusions and rejects her offers of service.

Marjorie, a widow and an old friend of Letty. Also in her sixties, she has retired to the country, and she hopes that Letty will live with her after retirement. She alters those plans when she meets a new vicar at a local church and they become engaged. Eventually, these plans are dashed when her fiancé chooses to marry a younger woman.

Mrs. Pope, Letty's landlady, an aristocratic woman of age seventy-six. She has certain fixed routines, rigid attitudes about how old people should act, and definite opinions on most subjects.

Father G., the vicar of Edwin's church. He prefers evenings at the pub with parishioners to pastoral visits, which are characterized by awkward conversations and difficult moments when he must face the personal grief of a parishioner. He assists Edwin with funeral arrangements for Marcia.

The Reverend David Lydell, the new vicar at a country church. He is a tall, dark man in his mid-forties who enjoys being a priest but does not appreciate the narrow-minded attitudes of his country parishioners. He rejects Marjorie for a younger woman because the latter is an equally adept cook.

Priscilla and

Nigel, Marcia's neighbors. Both are in their thirties, and they are frustrated in their attempts to be good neighbors to her. They invite Marcia to a Christmas dinner, but she is uncomfortable in their presence.

— *Robert E. Yahnke*

THE QUEEN OF SPADES
(Pikovaya dama)

Author: Alexander Pushkin (1799-1837)
First published: 1834
Genre: Novella

Locale: St. Petersburg
Time: The 1830's
Plot: Psychological realism

Hermann, a Russian officer of German descent. A prudent, cautious man, Hermann lives frugally and modestly on his salary as an engineer. Although passionate by nature and a gambler at heart, Hermann controls his emotions. He never plays cards himself for fear of risking the essentials in life, yet he follows the card games of his friends with feverish excitement. When he learns that the Countess, Anna Fedotovna, possesses the secret of playing three winning cards in succession, his imagination is inflamed, and he coldly calculates a plan to obtain the secret by courting the Countess' ward, Elizaveta Ivanovna, thereby gaining access into the Countess' house. Exasperated when the Countess fails to reveal the secret, he threatens her, and she dies of fright. Superstitious and fearful that the Countess may take revenge on him, he attends her funeral to ask her pardon and imagines that she winks at him when he bends over her coffin. Stunned and frightened, he leaves and drinks heavily. Later that night, the ghost of the Countess appears and reveals to him the card secret. Obsessed with the thought of using the secret to win a fortune, he is taken by Narumov to Chekalinsky's gambling parlor, bets his entire patrimonial inheritance, and loses. Shocked, he imagines that the losing queen of spades playing card winks at him; he goes insane and is committed to an asylum.

The Countess, **Anna Fedotovna** (feh-DOH-tov-nah), a capricious, moody dowager, eighty-seven years old, who tyrannizes her domestic servants. A renowned beauty and vivacious socialite in her youth, she had lost a considerable sum of money while gambling at the age of seventeen. Unable to coerce her husband into paying her debt, she learned from Count St. Germain a card-playing secret that enabled her to win back her losses. She tenaciously guards the secret during her lifetime. Her ghost reveals the secret to Hermann after her death, which results from being terrorized by Hermann.

Elizaveta Ivanovna (yeh-lih-ZAH-veh-tah ee-VAH-nohv-nah), the poor ward of the Countess. Young, attractive, shy, and modest, Elizaveta is employed by the Countess as a companion and is completely dependent on her tyrannical benefactress. A respectable young lady with a sense of propriety, she initially rejects Hermann's advances but gradually succumbs to his love letters, hoping Hermann will deliver her from her unhappy dependency. She is disheartened and disillusioned when she learns that Hermann has pursued her not out of love but only as a means to secure access to the Countess and her card secret. Although horrified by Hermann's conduct, she helps him escape from the Countess' house by means of a secret staircase. Later, she marries the wealthy son of the Countess' former steward and undertakes to rear a poor relative.

Pavel Tomsky (PAH-vehl TOM-skee), the grandson of the Countess, an amiable, gregarious young army officer who leads the typical lifestyle of an aristocrat of his times, playing cards and attending fashionable balls. It is Tomsky who relates the story of the Countess' card secret, which fires Hermann's imagination, and who intrigues Elizaveta with fabricated tales about Hermann, comparing him to Napoleon and Mephistopheles.

Chekalinsky (cheh-kah-LIHN-skee), a renowned Moscow gambler, a charming, affable, and courteous sixty-year-old wealthy aristocrat. Chekalinsky plays cards with Hermann and wins the game in which Hermann unsuccessfully attempts to use the Countess' secret.

Chaplitsky (cha-PLIHT-skee), a gambler, an extravagant man who, in his youth, had appealed in desperation to the Countess when he lost money gambling. The Countess took pity on him, revealing the card secret to him, enabling him to regain his losses. Later, he died in poverty after squandering millions.

Narumov (nah-REW-mov), a cavalry officer and friend of Tomsky. He is a pleasant, friendly young man who hosts the card-playing party where Hermann hears the story of the Countess' card secret. He later takes Hermann to Chekalinsky's gambling parlor, where Hermann loses his inheritance.

Count St. Germain (sahn zhayr-MAHN), a mysterious adventurer, the French aristocrat in Paris who first revealed to the Countess the secret of the winning cards. He thus enabled her to recoup her gambling losses.

— *Jerome J. Rinkus*

THE QUEEN'S NECKLACE
(Le Collier de la reine)

Authors: Alexandre Dumas, *père* (1802-1870), with Auguste Maquet (1813-1888)
First published: 1849-1850
Genre: Novel

Locale: France
Time: The eighteenth century
Plot: Historical

Jeanne de La Motte Valois (zhahn deh lah moht vah[l]-WAH), an impoverished noblewoman who wishes to find favor at the court of Louis XVI. Although she is befriended by the queen, she plots against the queen, even to the point of forging documents and hiding a questionable necklace. She puts Marie Antoinette into a situation that makes the queen appear guilty of adultery and theft.

Marie Antoinette (mah-REE ah[n]-twah-NEHT), the queen of France and the wife of Louis XVI. She is portrayed as a charming, intelligent, and honorable woman. Her enemies victimize her so that she is made to appear an adulteress and a thief. Her enemies are Jeanne de La Motte Valois, Cardinal de Rohan, and Count Cagliostro.

Andrée de Taverney (ahn-DRAY deh tah-vehr-NAY), a female courtier who is friendly and helpful to the queen. She becomes jealous, however, when the Count de Charny is favored by Marie Antoinette. Andrée enters a convent.

Philippe de Taverney (fee-LEEP), Andrée's brother, a handsome, pleasant courtier who is helpful to the queen. He falls in love with Marie Antoinette. Later, he is led to believe sincerely that he has seen Marie Antoinette in questionable circumstances.

Count de Charny (deh shahr-NEE), a naval officer who is loved by Andrée de Taverney. He is the object of an innocent flirtation by the queen. He, like other courtiers, is led to believe that he has observed the queen in questionable circumstances.

Count Cagliostro (kahg-lee-OHS-troh), an Italian adventurer and supposed magician. He uses Oliva, a woman closely resembling Marie Antoinette, to make it appear that the queen is immoral.

Oliva (oh-lee-VAH), a young woman with a strong resemblance to Marie Antoinette. She is used by the queen's enemies to make it appear that the queen is immoral, even to being the mistress of Cardinal de Rohan.

Cardinal de Rohan (deh roh-A[N]), a churchman who wants favor at court. He loves Marie Antoinette and believes, thanks to Oliva, that the queen will take him as a lover. He tries to buy the queen's favor by purchasing for her a fabulous necklace she admires.

QUENTIN DURWARD

Author: Sir Walter Scott (1771-1832)
First published: 1823
Genre: Novel

Locale: France and Flanders
Time: 1468
Plot: Historical

King Louis XI (lwee), sometimes disguised as **Maître Pierre**, a merchant, the wily, able monarch of France, rivaled in power by the hot-headed duke of Burgundy. Gifted at Machiavellian politics, he schemes to weaken the duke by placing, through marriage, a hostile nobleman in his territory. His plan in sending Isabelle, countess de Croye, and her aunt to Liège is to have the outlawed Wild Boar of Ardennes way-lay the ladies and marry one of them. Meanwhile, he travels to Burgundy to bargain with the duke and is imprisoned when the duke learns of the uprising of his vassals at Liège. Louis barely escapes being killed, chiefly through diplomacy and luck. He assists the duke in recapturing Liège, and the two make a temporary truce.

Charles (shahrl), the duke of Burgundy, a rash, hasty-handed nobleman with bull-like courage but little intelligence in statecraft. Resentful of the assistance given by King Louis to the young countess de Croye and her aunt, the Lady Hameline, he disregards the laws of hospitality and imprisons his royal guest. His temper explodes when he learns that the Wild Boar of Ardennes has led a revolt of the citizens of Liège, a city grown mutinous under the duke's rule. Until his wrath is diverted against the outlaw, he is on the verge of killing the king. His anger abates when Louis volunteers to assist him in retaking the city. The duke vows that he will bestow the hand of the countess de Croye on the man who will bring him the Wild Boar's head.

Quentin Durward, a stalwart young Scot. Of ancient lineage, he impresses disguised King Louis but later innocently brings the law down on himself when he cuts down the body of a Bohemian hanged by order of the monarch's provost marshal. He joins the Scottish Archers, the king's bodyguard, of which his uncle is a member. After he has shown his bravery by saving the king from a savage boar, he is chosen to escort the countess de Croye and Lady Hameline, her aunt, to Liège. During the journey, he thwarts the attempt of two court gallants to kidnap the countess and an ambush set by the Wild Boar of Ardennes, and he delivers the ladies safely to the bishop of Liège. When the Liègeois revolt, Quentin rescues the countess at great risk to himself. The two are saved by a Burgundian nobleman and taken to the court of the duke, where Quentin is instrumental in saving the king's life. At the recapture of Liège, he fights with great gallantry and wins the countess as his bride.

Isabelle (ee-zah-BEHL), the **Countess de Croye** (deh kroy), a political pawn in the rivalry of King Louis and the duke of Burgundy. When Quentin sees her first, she is disguised as Jacqueline, a peasant girl. Twice he saves her from the Wild Boar of Ardennes. The angry duke offers her hand to the man who kills the outlaw. Quentin's uncle kills the Wild Boar but relinquishes his claim on the countess to his gallant nephew.

Lady Hameline de Croye (ah-meh-LEEN), the Countess Isabelle's silly, romantic, middle-aged aunt. Taken prisoner by the Wild Boar of Ardennes, she is compelled to marry him as part of his scheme to claim the estates of Croye.

William de la Marck, called the **Wild Boar of Ardennes** (ahr-DEHN), a violent, treacherous outlaw. He attempts to capture the countess de Croye, murders the bishop of Liège, and seizes power in the city. He is killed by Ludovic Lesly when the troops of King Louis and the duke of Burgundy storm Liège and put down the revolt of its citizens.

Ludovic Lesly (LEW-doh-vihk), called **Le Balafré** (leh bah-lah-FRAY), Quentin Durward's uncle, a cavalier in the king's Scottish Archers. He kills the Wild Boar of Ardennes but bestows the countess de Croye on his nephew in order to perpetuate the family line.

Hayraddin Maugrabin (i-rah-DA[N] moh-grah-BA[N]), a Bohemian adventurer, the secret envoy of King Louis, and Quentin Durward's guide while escorting the countess de Croye and her aunt to Liège. Although indebted to Quentin for cutting down the body of his hanged brother, he nevertheless tries to lead the young Scot into an ambush set by the Wild Boar of Ardennes. He also aids Lady Hameline in her attempt to deceive Quentin by disguising herself as the countess during the uprising of the Liègeois. Before he is hanged, by order of the duke of Burgundy, for impersonating a herald, Maugrabin reveals to Quentin the Wild Boar's plan to disguise his followers as French knights in order to create further dissension between the duke and the king.

Count Philip de Crèvecoeur (fee-LEEP deh KREHV-kewr), the honorable ambassador sent by the duke of Burgundy to deliver a list of that nobleman's grievances to King Louis. Later, he rescues Quentin Durward and the countess de Croye from pursuit by the Wild Boar of Ardennes and delivers them to the duke's court.

Louis, duke of Orleans, the unwilling prospective husband of King Louis' homely daughter, Joan. He tries to seize the countess de Croye while she is traveling to Liège in the company of Quentin Durward.

The Count de Dunois (deh dew-NWAH), the accomplice of the duke of Orleans in his attempt to kidnap the countess de Croye. Dunois is King Louis' most valiant soldier.

Tristan l'Hermite (tree-STAHN lehr-MEET), King Louis' provost marshal, a cruel, stupid ex-monk. He orders Quentin Durward seized and hanged for cutting down the body of Hayraddin Maugrabin's brother.

Oliver le Dain (oh-lee-VEHR leh da[n]), also called **Oliver le Mauvais** (moh-VAY) and **Oliver le Diable** (dee-AHB-leh), King Louis' barber, groom of the chamber, and trusted adviser. He is a man of unscrupulous cunning.

John, cardinal of Balue, a traitorous churchman, the secret enemy of King Louis.

Pavillon (pah-vee-YOH[N]), the syndic of Liège. He aids Quentin Durward and the countess de Croye in their escape from the city after it has been seized by the Wild Boar of Ardennes.

Gertrude Pavillon, his daughter, saved from looting French soldiers by Quentin Durward during the recapture of Liège by French and Burgundian forces.

Louis of Bourbon, the murdered bishop of Liège, killed by the Wild Boar of Ardennes.

La Glorieux (glohr-YEW), the impertinent jester of the duke of Burgundy.

Trois-Eschelles (twah-zeh-SHEHL) and

Petit André (ptee ahn-DRAY), the cruel hangmen of Tristan l'Hermite.

Carl Eberson, the son of the Wild Boar of Ardennes. Quentin Durward threatens to kill the lad in order to end the outlaw's butchery of his prisoners after the death of the bishop of Liège.

Toison d'Or (twah-ZOH[N] dohr), the herald of the duke of Burgundy. He unmasks Hayraddin Maugrabin, who pretends to be a herald dispatched to the Burgundian court by the Wild Boar of Ardennes.

Lord Crawford, the commander of the Scottish Archers, the king's bodyguard.

THE QUEST FOR CHRISTA T.
(Nachdenken über Christa T.)

Author: Christa Wolf (1929-   )
First published: 1968
Genre: Novel

Locale: East Germany
Time: The 1940's to the 1960's
Plot: Philosophical realism

The narrator, a female writer who lives in East Germany and who attempts to write a biography of her late friend, Christa T. The narrator is in her late thirties. She was very close to her friend, and, upon the latter's death, she believes that she must do something so that her memory will not be lost. She has a number of the friend's papers, letters, and notes, as well as her own and others' memories. As a writer, however, she is well aware of the distortions that writing can create and that her memories ultimately are subjective and may falsify the truth of Christa T.'s life.

Christa T., a woman who attempts to realize her sense of individual identity within the context of a socialist society. She dies of leukemia at the age of thirty-five. She was born in a small village in the eastern part of Germany and spent her adolescent years during the period of World War II. The narrator first met Christa when she was a sixteen-year-old girl at the Hermann Goering School in the town of Friedeberg. Early in life, Christa was an individualist and wanted to become a writer. After the end of the war, she chose to live in the newly created German Democratic Republic and became an idealistic socialist, committed to the creation of a just and humane society. In the course of her life, however, she came to realize that human nature is not so easily changed, and she often struggled with the problem of maintaining her individual identity within a social structure focused on group welfare. She worked as a teacher for a short time and then entered the university to study German literature. Her desire to become a writer was still with her. At the university, however, she met a young student, Justus, whom she later married and with whom she had several children. Christa devoted her life to being a good mother and wife but felt somehow unfulfilled, that her life was missing an important dimension of self-expression. She and her husband built a beautiful house in the country, and they seemed to have a happy home. Christa began to experience episodes of dizziness and chronic fatigue and was diagnosed as having leukemia. Her condition worsened, and she eventually died.

Justus, Christa T.'s husband, a rural veterinarian. A kind man, he is nevertheless sometimes insensitive to his wife's feelings and needs. As a "typical" man, he seems to believe that she should be fulfilled by her work as wife and mother.

Kostia, Christa T.'s lover during her years at the university. His knowledge and love of literature attract her to him. He later falls in love with Inge. This marks the end of his and Christa T.'s relationship and of her attempt at serious writing.

— *Thomas F. Barry*

THE QUEST OF THE ABSOLUTE
(La Recherche de l'absolu)

Author: Honoré de Balzac (1799-1850)
First published: 1834
Genre: Novel

Locale: Douai, France
Time: 1812-1832
Plot: Psychological realism

Balthazar Claes (bahl-tah-ZAHR klehs), the head of an old and respected family in Flanders who devotes his life and fortune to an attempt to discover the philosopher's stone, the substance believed to have the power of transmuting base metals into gold. When the story begins, he is roughly fifty years old but appears at least ten years older: His tall figure is stooped, his unkempt hair falls to his shoulders, his cheeks are hollow, and his face is pale and wrinkled. His eyes betray a keen intelligence and long days and nights of work in his home laboratory. He believes that he is working for the glory and enrichment of his family, but most of the time he barely acknowledges their existence. To obtain material and equipment for his experiments, he squanders three huge fortunes. He dies a broken old man, only to cry "Eureka!" with his last breath.

Joséphine de Temninck Claes (zhoh-say-FEEN deh tehm-NEENK), the adored and adoring wife of Balthazar, about forty years of age. Despite her rich, aristocratic Spanish family and her exceptional beauty, she had not expected to find a loving husband because she limps and has one shoulder higher than the other. Balthazar sees only her beautiful face and beautiful soul. Although she always has been a submissive wife and has loved her four children less than she has loved her husband, she has qualms of conscience when she realizes that Balthazar will leave the children destitute if he continues to spend his money and her inheritance so recklessly. She extracts from him a promise to give up his research. His subsequent frustration and despair induce her to absolve him from his promise; when, after heroic but vain efforts to distract her melancholy husband, she realizes their futility and gives him back his promise, she becomes gravely ill. On learning that he is raising huge sums on the strength of the children's lands, Joséphine dies slowly of despair.

Marguerite Claes (mahr-geh-REET), the beautiful oldest child of the family, sixteen years old at the time that Balthazar renounces his experiments. She has an extremely strong sense of filial duty, adores her mother, and honors her father, even though she understands that he is ruining the family. After her mother's death, Marguerite borrows money to pay the most pressing debts, but when Balthazar accidentally sees the money and demands it in vain, he attempts suicide. Marguerite gives him the ducats in exchange for his promise to abdicate his paternal authority if his experiments are again fruitless. He keeps his word. With the help of a great-uncle, Marguerite secures a post as a tax collector in Brittany for her father. In his absence, Marguerite succeeds in restoring the family fortunes, but Balthazar has run up enormous debts in Brittany. She sacrifices her savings only to discover that her father has ruined the family again while she was in Spain with her husband.

Pierquin (pyehr-KA[N]), a notary who is a distant cousin of the family. He advises Madame Claes and later Marguerite about financial matters. Marguerite understands that self-interest is his only motive at all times. When he finally offers his purse to her without interest, she allows him to marry Félicie.

Félicie Claes (fay-lee-SEE), the younger daughter, a loving, obedient young girl who manages the household in the absence of Marguerite and falls in love with Pierquin.

L'Abbé de Solis (lah-bay deh soh-LEES), Joséphine's confessor and the rich uncle of Emmanuel, whom he introduces into the Claes household.

Emmanuel de Solis, a schoolteacher who becomes a headmaster. He is a model of piety, discretion, and self-abnegation. Gradually, he and Marguerite develop an excessively chaste love for each other. Marguerite refuses to think of marriage because she does not want her father to be obliged to give an account of his stewardship of the money belonging to his children. Emmanuel offers sound, disinterested financial advice. After a number of years, he inherits his uncle's fortune and a Spanish title. He offers himself and his fortune to Marguerite and is accepted.

Lemulquinier (leh-mewl-kee-NYAY), Balthazar's uneducated valet, later his laboratory assistant, then his coworker, and finally his manager of funds. He progresses from scoffer to devoted disciple.

— *Dorothy B. Aspinwall*

THE QUEST OF THE HOLY GRAIL

Author: Unknown
First published: c. 1300
Genre: Novel

Locale: England, France, and Wales
Time: Early eighth century
Plot: Arthurian romance

Joseph of Arimathea (er-ih-muh-THEE-uh), a disciple of Jesus who was present at the Crucifixion and asked Pontius Pilate for permission to bury Jesus. He, along with Nicodemus, cleansed Christ's wounds prior to wrapping him in a shroud. While doing so, Joseph opened a wound, causing it to bleed. To prevent spilling of blood, he collected the drops in a chalice, believed to be the cup from which Christ drank during the Last Supper. For this, he was imprisoned by the Jews. While imprisoned, he was visited by the Holy Ghost. It is then that he was told of the secrets of the Grail and of its power. At this point, the quest of the Holy Grail begins.

Merlin, the illegitimate son of the devil, though he is certainly not evil. The devil, angry at the victory of Jesus, takes his revenge by raping a virgin, who, in turn, bears a son, Merlin, destined to be the wisest of all men and to oppose the teachings of Christ. He grows up to become a sorcerer in the court of Uther Pendragon, for whom he builds the Round Table. He controls the events that ultimately lead to the rise of King Arthur, son of Uther, and helps to guide the events that lead to Perceval's quest for the Holy Grail.

Perceval, a knight of the Round Table, the hero. He begins his life not knowing of his destiny to seek the Grail. At first, he is prompted by his niece to go to the court of Arthur and seek a seat at the Round Table. Young and arrogant, he enters a tournament and wins. He requests a seat at the table, and King Arthur reluctantly gives in to the knight. It is at this point that

he vows to be pure and chaste, and to take up the quest for the Grail. He remains the most powerful knight in the land, and he is never defeated. He is tempted by sin and lust but always resists. Eventually, he is led to the Holy Grail by Bron and saves Britain from its plagues and curses by learning the secrets of the Grail. He is the purest of all knights.

King Arthur, king of the Britons, a powerful and just king. He rules from the Round Table, at which all knights are equal and all is just. He is wise and at first does not like the arrogance of the young Perceval. He is well aware that there is a vacant seat at the Round Table for the purest knight in the world. When Perceval asks to sit in the seat, he argues against it. After he gives in and Perceval sits, the table and ground shake and thunder shatters the air. Arthur sees the Holy Ghost speak, and Perceval changes instantly from arrogant to pure and chaste. He then knew that the quest spoken of by Merlin would begin.

The Fisher King, the second person to possess the Holy Grail. It was passed to him by Joseph of Arimathea. He is the greatest of fisherman and is told that he cannot die, but will remain old and frail until the coming of the purest knight in the world. Only to him would he pass the Grail and its secrets. Once this was achieved, the Fisher King was allowed to die peacefully.

— *Gordon Robert Maddison*

A QUESTION OF POWER

Author: Bessie Head (1937-1986)
First published: 1973
Genre: Novel

Locale: Motabeng, Botswana
Time: Late 1960's and early 1970's
Plot: Magical Realism

Elizabeth, the protagonist and a schoolteacher, a colored émigré from South Africa. Brought up in apartheid South Africa by a woman who she thinks is her blood mother, Elizabeth is somewhat unnerved by the sudden revelation that her mother is white and has been staying in a sanatorium for the mentally ill. Once in Botswana, Elizabeth comes down with her mother's disease in the form of recurrent nervous nightmares and terrifying deliriums, making her literally a prisoner of her own tortured mind. With indefatigable willpower, the belief in the transcendence of humanity, and the sympathetic warmth of friends at the Motabeng local industries commune, however, she recovers from her illness to face life with greater resolve, independence, and optimism.

Sello, a Motabeng farmer and cattle breeder. He repeatedly appears in Elizabeth's delusions. A self-proclaimed prophet and citizen of the world, a man of seemingly profound love and compassion, he assumes the image of a benevolent white-robed monk. Beneath this immaculate veneer is a moral predator who stirs the denizens of hell to hound the soul of an innocent woman.

Dan Molomo, a cattle tycoon and millionaire. He, too, appears in Elizabeth's hallucinations, though less frequently than Sello. A demoniac sadist and a debauchee, he gloats over his endless orgies with sexually active women. A self-proclaimed king of the Underworld, a dandy, and a fop, he masks his devilry behind the charm of generosity and gaudy attire.

Eugene, an Afrikaner refugee from South Africa, the founding principal of Motabeng Secondary School. Although extremely taciturn and morose by temperament, he is at bottom a visionary and philanthropist who cares deeply about the human condition in Motabeng. As the originator of the Motabeng local industries cooperative, he works tirelessly toward the improvement of the lives of the local people. He remains one of the few men to inject a feeling of love into Elizabeth's otherwise seemingly forlorn life.

Medusa, Sello's accomplice, goddess of the infernal cesspit, and eternal dark companion to Bathsheba. Her main goal is the destruction of Elizabeth. A powerfully built woman, flat-chested and narrow-waisted, with broad hips and large, full, powerful eyes, she pursues her destructive mission with a relentlessness unmatched even in the treatment inflicted on other scapegoats of history, from Buddha to Jesus Christ.

Tom, a twenty-two-year-old white Peace Corps volunteer from America, a close personal friend of Elizabeth. He has a philosophical bent of mind, is affable, and possesses an uncommon capacity to relate to people. With a degree in agriculture, he is a leading force behind the success of the Motabeng Farmers' Youth-Development project. A pacifist, he is a conscientious objector, a believer in civil and human rights, and a promoter of rapid economic development for poorer nations of the world.

Shorty, Elizabeth's daredevil seven-year-old son. He is carefree, daft, and jaunty. A precocious and impressionable child with imaginative boldness, he is curious about everything around him. In his speech and mannerisms, he displays a sense of humor that sometimes verges on caustic wit. He remains a lovable child, however, one on whom his mother increasingly relies to stay mentally alive.

Kenosi, Elizabeth's close companion, approximately her age, a member of the wool-spinning and weaving group. Despite her austere personality, she remains at bottom a generous and selfless person, one in whose presence Elizabeth's personality comes alive. As a meticulous record keeper and a workhorse, she works with Elizabeth to make a perfect team, always dependent on each other.

Mrs. Jones, a fifty-five-year-old acquaintance of Elizabeth, a mother of three, the oldest volunteer on the Motabeng project. A former Marxist with a coarse, protrusive manner and a passion for tea, she is uninterestingly childlike, often rambling about her long life history. She often fantasizes herself as the modern English Christian good samaritan ministering to the afflicted and the lonely.

Jimmy, Eugene's sportive but mischievous child, Shorty's buddy and playmate. A wacky simulator of adult behavior, he is sometimes sassy and recklessly bold, at other times vain but lovable.

Thoko, an energetic farmer and a friend of Elizabeth with a reputation for harvesting huge, succulent pumpkins. Thoko's pumpkin growing proves to be the main motivating force behind Elizabeth's venture into agriculture. She provides an important channel of communication between the reclusive Elizabeth and the larger Motabeng village.

Mr. Grahame, the English farm manager with the Farmers' Youth-Development work group, intensely committed to the success of the Motabeng farm project. He is a Quaker and an austere moral purist for whom the Christian principle of mortification and self-abnegation is an absolute, indispensable necessity.

Birgette, Elizabeth's buddy, the confidante with whom she shares much in common. An inner-directed young girl, quiet, unobtrusive, self-effacing, and wholly reserved, she radiates charm and comeliness. She is a firm believer in the inherent worth of every human being.

Camilla, a conceited Danish instructor on the Motabeng farm, a loquacious chatterer nicknamed "Rattle Tongue." She is a prig who pries into other people's business and displays a racial bigotry that offends those around her.

Mrs. Stanley, a middle-aged acquaintance of Elizabeth, gracious and motherly, with kindly interest and goodwill. She is an optimist and a genuine source of succor to the poor and the sick. As the one who volunteers to look after Elizabeth's son while she spends time in the hospital, she is one of the few genuinely affectionate people in the dreadful perturbation of Elizabeth's life.

— Ikenna Dieke

THE QUESTIONNAIRE: Or, Prayer for a Town and a Friend
(Dotazník, aneb modlitba za jedno město a přítele)

Author: Jiří Gruša(1938-   )
First published: 1978
Genre: Novel

Locale: Chlumec, a town in Bohemia, Czechoslovakia
Time: From the onset of World War II through the early 1970's
Plot: Realism

Jan Chrysostom Kepka (HREH-soh-stohm), a self-professed time traveler (Jan Chrysostom Chrononaut) and the main protagonist of the novel, as well as its narrator. Strangely enough, Jan is present at his own carefully observed conception and, later, at his unexpected death. The nature of the narrative, however, allows him both to die and to continue living and telling. Most of the time, Jan addresses his remarks to a certain functionary named Pavlenda, usually called "Comr. Pavlenda," with the title of "Comr." signifying "friend, mate, companion, fellow member of a Communist society." For a brief portion of the novel, Jan writes directly to Monsignor Rosin, a priest and historian of his hometown.

Edvin Kepka, Jan's father, nicknamed **the Handsome** by Jan. He is, as his nickname indicates, noted mostly for his good looks. He is the weaker, or at any rate the less socially ambitious, of the two sons of a drunkard, Edvin Kepka I. The younger Edvin is content to work in the shipping department of the Largior Chocolate Factory, but his older brother, Bonek, decides that he will run the entire operation.

Bonek Kepka, Jan's uncle, a greedy and strong-willed man. After he decides that he wants to run the chocolate factory, he sets out to achieve his goal, which he eventually does, though not without difficulties. One particularly trouble-some obstacle for Bonek is the color of his sister-in-law's eyes.

Alice Vachal Kepka, Jan's mother. Jan states that "Bonek mistrusted Alice's eyes, he suspected them of being Jewish." Bonek's suspicion propels Jan into an extended explanation of his mother's "chrysoberyl" eyes, tracing them through various ancestors to the present day.

Olin Vlaciha (vlah-TSIH-hah), Jan's cousin. Olin is described by Jan as "the interpreter of [my] dreams." Olin fought the Germans in World War II as a member of the Czechoslovak legionnaires in Europe. He later serves time in a concentration camp for attempting to brew and sell his family's ancestral (pre-Communist) beer. Olin instructs Jan in astrology and advises him to continue painting and to stop sleeping with Mirena Klahn, advice that Jan follows.

Lieutenant Mikit, the officer for political affairs for Jan's unit. His most remarkable feature is the position of his eyes, which are so sunken that they are "practically gone." He indirectly encourages Jan in his artistic career by allowing him to paint pictures instead of performing regular army duties. Mikit ultimately proves psychologically unstable, however, and is removed from his post.

— *Russell Valentino*

QUICKSAND

Author: Nella Larsen (1891-1964)
First published: 1928
Genre: Novel

Locale: The United States and Copenhagen, Denmark
Time: The 1920's
Plot: Psychological realism

Helga Crane, a twenty-three-year-old teacher of mixed heritage. Born of a Danish mother and a West Indian father, she is educated by her mother's brother after the death of her mother. She is an exotically beautiful, sensuously contradictory, intelligent, sensitive lover of exquisitely beautiful clothes and things. She also is a lost, lonely, dissatisfied, alienated, dichotomous, indecisive, and spiritually and psychologically ambivalent young woman who is never at home in the world, neither in Naxos, where she teaches in an elite black school and falls in love unwittingly with the very proper and reticent Dr. Robert Anderson, nor in Harlem, where she mingles with the black bourgeoisie, attends the correct social functions and meets the correct people, and is proposed to by eligible bachelors. She does not fit into Copenhagen society, where she lives with her very proper European aunt and uncle, mingles with the artistic set, and is proposed to by a very eligible Danish artist, Axel Olsen. Ultimately, she lives in Alabama, where she is married to a most unsuitable, unlettered black minister. She sinks deeper into depression and exhaustion with the birth of each of her children.

Dr. Robert Anderson, the principal of the elite black school in Naxos where Helga first teaches. He is a tall, handsome thirty-five-year-old with gray eyes. He is a cool, reticent, controlled, and detached man, and Helga falls very passionately, though unadmittedly, in love with him. Although he is in love with Helga, he refuses to define and to act on his emotions, either in Naxos or later in New York, where he also goes to escape the provincial Naxos. It is clearly his engagement to Helga's friend, Anne, that terminates Helga's extended stay in Denmark, and it undoubtedly is his later marriage to Anne that propels Helga into the unsuitable marriage with the Reverend Mr. Pleasant Green.

Anne Grey, a socialite Harlem widow. She is an extremely beautiful, black-haired, black-eyed, madonna-like thirty-year-old. Fastidiously dressed, self-assured, selfish but gentle, and well bred, she is a hypocritically liberal, independently wealthy, well-connected, bourgeois Harlemite who has an exquisitely beautiful home filled with antiques and books that are an index to her personality. Obsessed with the race problem, she says the right thing, attends the proper social functions, and does the proper charity work for black people. Full of ambivalence and inconsistencies, she advocates social equality while living a life of social inequality. Introduced to Helga by Mrs. Hayes-Rore, her aunt-in-law, she becomes Helga's nemesis and friend; she later marries Helga's one love, Dr. Robert Anderson.

The Reverend Mr. Pleasant Green, a minister of a small black church in Alabama. He is a rather heavyset, unattractive, yellow, fattish, dirty-nailed, unlettered, uncouth, self-satisfied, dull, mild-mannered man. Helga marries him in a misguided daze to seek revenge on Dr. Anderson for marrying Anne, and with him she produces four children in rapid succession (three in twenty months) and lives in a quagmire of lost hope and disillusionment. He is an amorous man who ignites Helga's buried sexual desires. He puts his sexual desires and pleasures over his wife's needs and her health. Helga recognizes too late his character traits of selfishness, hypocrisy, and sexual self-gratification.

Mrs. Hayes-Rore, an independently wealthy, intellectually deficient, socially conscious and influential, plump, middle-aged, "lemon-colored," matronly, Chicago widow with "badly straightened hair." Although she has a false sense of her importance and gives pretentious speeches on race relations at conventions and other functions, she is a kind woman. She rescues a destitute Helga in Chicago after Uncle Peter's wife refuses her admittance, takes her to New York, and finds her both a place to stay (with Anne Grey) and a job with an insurance company. She advises Helga to conceal her white background.

Margaret Creighton, a teacher, Helga's young, attractive, unimaginative friend and colleague at the black school in Naxos. She knows how to abide by the rules and is quite at home in Naxos.

Axel Olsen, a painter. Slightly older than Helga, he has a "leonine head, broad nose, [and] bushy eyebrows." He is brilliant, elegant, and arrogant; somewhat cynical and selfish; and rather pompous. A socially prominent Danish artist, he paints Helga's portrait and proposes marriage after failing to initiate a more informal relationship with her. He is enamored not so much with Helga as with his own portrait of her and with his conception of her exotic looks. He leaves town after Helga's refusal of his marriage offer. He provides entrée into the artistic world of Denmark for Helga's Aunt Katrina.

Peter Nilssen, Helga's kindhearted and gentle uncle, brother of her mother. He is Helga's benefactor after her mother's death. He finances her education and befriends her until he marries a woman who hates black people and refuses Helga access to him. Forced to relinquish his ties to Helga, he gives her five thousand dollars and suggests that she visit her Aunt Katrina in Denmark.

Clementine Richards, a parishioner of the Reverend Mr. Green's church in Alabama and in love with him. She is a tall black beauty of great proportions. She has an obvious and open dislike for the gentle Helga.

Miss Hartley, a kindly, understanding midwife and nurse who cares for Helga during her mental and physical collapse after the birth and death of her fourth child in Alabama.

Helga's mother, a fair Scandinavian woman who is in love with life. She risks everything by marrying a black West Indian man who leaves her before Helga is born. Estranged from her family, except for her brother Pete, she remarries to a white man, who dislikes Helga but dies when Helga is very young.

James Vayle, a weak, dull, snobbish young man from the proper social stratum in Atlanta. He acquiesces to his parents' and others' ideas of what is proper. He is Helga's fiancé and fellow teacher in Naxos. He dislikes Helga for not being able to fit into the dull, smug Naxos society and dislikes himself for finding Helga attractive and desirable enough to become engaged.

Poul and
Katrina Dahl, Helga's scrupulously proper and correct, rather wealthy, and pretentious aunt and uncle in Copenhagen. In their own limited manner, they love and admire Helga because she is different and exotic and can bring them the kind of attention and acceptance they desire in the artistic world. They buy Helga beautiful and exotic clothes and set her up as an objet d'art to be admired and to be bought by the highest bidder.

— Ruth D. Fisher

THE QUIET AMERICAN

Author: Graham Greene (1904-1991)
First published: 1955
Genre: Novel

Locale: Vietnam
Time: Early to mid-1950's
Plot: Tragedy

Thomas Fowler, the narrator, a British war correspondent based in Saigon during the French-Vietnamese conflict. Middle-aged, jaded, and cynical, he takes pride in his detachment—both from the war and from life—always stressing his role as a reporter, an observer of facts, a man without opinions. Beneath his cool façade, however, he loves Vietnam and its people. Unlike other Western correspondents, he thinks of Saigon as his permanent home. As the story opens, he has lost his Vietnamese mistress of two years, Phuong, to Pyle, the "quiet American." Ultimately, Fowler's love for Phuong and his concern for her country lead him, agonizingly, to breach his code of detachment. His involvement forever alters his life and the lives of Phuong and Pyle.

Alden Pyle, the "quiet American" of the title, ostensibly employed by the American Economic Aid Mission in Saigon but covertly involved in terrorist activities conducted by the Central Intelligence Agency. Thirty-two years old and Harvard-educated, he is painfully earnest, sincere, and inexperienced. His romantic idealism about love and war is the perfect foil for Fowler's hard-bitten realism. His naïve attempts to establish a Vietnamese national democracy and his immature devotion to Fowler's mistress, Phuong, catapult him into circumstances that lead to his assassination.

Phuong, Fowler's twenty-year-old Vietnamese mistress, a fragile Asian beauty. Fowler's faithful, obedient companion, she seems simple and childlike—collecting colored scarves and poring over picture books of Europe and America—yet Fowler sees her as strong and self-possessed, as enigmatic as the Orient itself. At the urging of her sister, she leaves Fowler, a married man, for the younger Pyle, who promises her stability, marriage, and children.

Vigot (vee-GOH), a police officer at the French Sûreté who questions Fowler about Pyle's murder. An interesting man who reads Blaise Pascal and is uncommonly devoted to his wife, he suspects that Fowler is involved in Pyle's death, but he cannot prove it.

Mr. Heng, a Communist informer who links Pyle to plastic explosives and covert terrorist activities. He informs Fowler of Pyle's involvement with General Thé, and, after consulting again with Fowler, arranges for Pyle's assassination.

General Thé, the leader of a small band of Vietnamese rebel terrorists who are fighting both the French and the Communists. Pyle sees him as a possible leader for the Vietnamese national democracy that the Central Intelligence Agency is trying to establish.

Miss Hei, Phuong's cultivated, English-speaking older sister, who acts as matchmaker between Phuong and Pyle. Miss Hei has never liked Fowler, because he is too old, his wife will not divorce him, and he can never provide Phuong with a marriage and a family.

Dominguez, Fowler's faithful, hardworking journalistic assistant. Through Dominguez's political connections, Fowler learns of Pyle's terrorist activities.

Bill Granger, a crude American journalist in Saigon. His thoughtless, rude treatment of the Vietnamese people is in contrast with Fowler's caring treatment of them.

— *Karen Priest*

A QUIET LIFE

Author: Beryl Bainbridge (1933-   )
First published: 1976
Genre: Novel

Locale: Southport, England
Time: Post-World War II
Plot: Domestic realism

Alan, the protagonist. The central consciousness in this novel, seventeen-year-old Alan copes with his family's eccentric and crippling barrage of insults and recriminations. In many instances, he functions as mediator for his father and mother. He also shields his sister from his parents' unreasonable treatment, yet he often resents their random favoring of her. He tries to provide a certain stability for his family, but he faces monumental patterns of dysfunctional behavior. He is attracted to Janet, a classmate, but is unable to understand how she can accept her family as anything but destructive. Although he receives poor marks at school, Alan is attentive to his perceived duties as a son, brother, and boyfriend.

Madge, Alan's fifteen-year-old sister. Unmanageable and possibly emotionally handicapped, she sneaks into the woods to meet with a German prisoner of war. Madge's unconventional behavior at home and in the village causes Alan embarrassment and understandable concern for her safety. Madge chides her parents for their empty lives, yet she often defends their behavior to Alan.

Alan's father, a sickly perfectionist who dislikes his wife and children mainly because they intrude on his existence. He is highly excitable and unpredictable. Mysteriously self-employed, he sulks around the house and garden. He is a contemptuous yet grotesquely humorous character who often gives in to fits of rage, once burning his wife's treasured family heirloom. He does not allow his children any latitude in their

behavior even though he behaves in an infantile manner throughout the novel. Although he and his wife occasionally seems to get along, he is embittered toward her and typically wears a sneer in her presence.

Alan's mother, a dramatic and prim woman who believes in the importance of appearances. When she goes out, she appears well groomed and stylish, but when she is at home, her appearance is slovenly and unkempt. She also fancies herself to be an accomplished interior decorator. She continually rearranges the furniture and forbids anyone to use certain rooms in the house because they would be spoiled if company should come. She snaps at Alan for the least cause, but she seemingly coddles Madge. Desperate to escape her husband, she often chooses to read in the railway station in the evening rather than stay at home.

Janet Leyland, Alan's girlfriend. Shallow and inaccessible, this girl from another middle-class home represents to Alan a life of normalcy. Janet ironically is drawn to Alan's family because it seems so normal. She is frigidly possessive of Alan, who resents her easy acceptance of his mother and her shallow preoccupation with clothes and jewelry.

Aunt Nora, Alan's father's sister. Often a foil to the other family members, Nora provides a haven for Alan and his father away from home. She is a drab, unassuming woman who recognizes the dysfunctions in her brother's family.

— *Douglas A. Jones*

QUO VADIS: A Narrative of the Time of Nero

Author: Henryk Sienkiewicz (1846-1916)
First published: 1896
Genre: Novel

Locale: Rome
Time: c. 64 C.E.
Plot: Historical

Petronius (peh-TROH-nee-uhs), a wealthy Roman patrician who, because of his knowledge of poetry and music, has great influence over Nero. His discriminating taste wins him the title of arbiter of elegance, and he is highly regarded throughout Rome. Petronius tries to help his nephew, Vinitius, win the love of Lygia by having her removed from the home of her

foster parents to Nero's palace. Learning that Nero has ordered his death, Petronius commits suicide by bleeding.

Marcus Vinitius (MAHR-kuhs vih-NIH-shi-uhs), the nephew of Petronius. A soldier recently on military service abroad, he returns to Rome, where he falls in love with Lygia. After Lygia has been removed to the palace of Nero, Vinitius sees her at a banquet and tries to force his attentions on her. His efforts frighten Lygia, who flees, and Vinitius begins a search for her.

Aulus Plautius (A-luhs PLOH-shee-uhs), an old soldier who had taken part in the conquest of Britain. Lygia is his foster daughter. When she is taken from his house at Nero's command, he tries to have her returned.

Pomponia Graecina (pom-POH-nee-uh gree-SI-nuh), the wife of Aulus Plautius and the foster mother of Lygia. Pomponia, a Christian, has taught Lygia her faith.

Lygia (LIH-jee-uh), the daughter of a barbarian king. After her father's defeat, she was sent as hostage to Rome, where she became the foster daughter of a noble Roman family and was converted to Christianity. When she flees from Nero's palace, she goes to live in a community of Christians. After Vinitius locates her, she falls in love with him; through her influence, he too becomes a Christian. When Nero starts his persecutions of Christians, Lygia is captured and put in prison. There, she becomes ill with a fever and nearly dies. Still not fully recovered, she is tied to the horns of a bull and placed in the arena with her servant Ursus. After Ursus kills the bull, Nero frees them because they have won the favor of the crowd. Lygia and Vinitius are married and go with Ursus to live in Sicily.

Nero (NEE-roh), emperor of Rome. His vanity leads him to seek distinction as a poet and musician. Because Petronius is a connoisseur of fine art, Nero is always eager for his praise. Nero feels that his poetic work, the *Troyad*, describing the burning of Troy, is not authentic because he has never seen a burning city. At the suggestion of Tigellius, he has Rome set afire. Later, the Christians are accused of setting the fire and are persecuted as incendiaries.

Chilo Chilonides (KI-loh ki-LO-nih-deez), an unscrupulous and money-loving Greek hired by Vinitius to aid in his search for Lygia. Chilo later betrays the Christians to Nero and advances to a high position at court. At last, conscience-stricken, he denounces Nero's wrongdoings, becomes a Christian, and dies a martyr's death.

Poppaea (po-PEE-uh), Nero's beautiful but extremely jealous and cruel wife.

Actea (ak-TEE-uh), a Christian freedwoman who formerly had been one of Nero's favorites. Because of her amiability and modesty, she is liked by almost everyone. When Lygia is taken to Nero's palace, Actea befriends her.

Ursus (UR-suhs), the gigantic but simple-hearted slave who has served Lygia since her childhood. When Lygia becomes a Christian, Ursus is converted also. He rescues Lygia many times, remains with her while she is in prison, and saves her from death in the arena.

Glaucus (GLOH-kuhs), a Christian physician. Grievously wronged by Chilo, Glaucus forgives him.

Crispus (KRIHS-puhs), a stern, fanatical Christian who dies on the cross after denouncing Nero.

Tigellinus (tih-geh-LI-nuhs), a pretorian prefect of Rome who tries to advance his favor with Nero by suggesting that Rome be burnt. He is largely responsible for Petronius' fall from favor and death.

Chrysothemis (krih-SO-theh-mihs), a former mistress of Petronius.

Eunice (YEW-nihs), the beautiful slave who becomes the mistress of Petronius. She loves him devotedly; when Petronius falls from favor with Nero and commits suicide, she dies with him.

Miriam (MIH-ree-uhm), the Christian woman with whom Lygia lives for a time.

Nazarius (nuh-ZA-ree-uhs), Miriam's son.

Seneca (SEH-nuh-kuh), a Roman philosopher, Nero's childhood tutor.

Croto (KROH-toh), a Roman athlete of superhuman strength, killed by Ursus when he attempts to seize Lygia for Vinitius.

Paul of Tarsus (pohl, TAHR-suhs), a leader among the Christians of Rome until he is condemned to death.

Peter, the disciple of Christ who leads the Christians of Rome. After most of the Christians have been killed by Nero, Peter decides to leave the city and seek refuge elsewhere. As he walks out of the city, he sees a vision of Jesus. Peter falls on his knees and asks, "Quo vadis, Domine?" (Whither goest Thou, oh Lord?) Jesus replies, "As thou art deserting my people I go to Rome to be crucified for the second time." After Peter hears these words, he turns and goes back to Rome, where he works among the Christians until he is arrested and killed.

THE RABBIT ANGSTROM NOVELS

Author: John Updike (1932-   )
First published: 1960-1990
Genre: Novels

Locale: Mt. Judge and Brewer, Pennsylvania, and Florida
Time: 1959-1989
Plot: Domestic realism

Rabbit, Run, 1960

Harry "Rabbit" Angstrom, a former high school basketball star. Now in his mid-twenties, he is married, is a father, and holds a mediocre sales job. Plagued by feelings of boredom and alienation, he abandons his pregnant wife for a quasi-religious quest whose goal he intuits but cannot define: "something that wants me to find it." At the funeral of his second child, he flees his wife, Janice Angstrom, for the third and, he believes, final time.

Janice Springer Angstrom, a middle-class housewife. Like her husband, she is in her mid-twenties, has average intelligence, and finds her life very boring. Her escape is alcohol. In drunken grief and postnatal depression, she allows her infant daughter, Rebecca, to drown in a bath.

Ruth Leonard, a sometime prostitute. Also in her mid-twenties, she meets Rabbit shortly after he abandons Janice and allows him to move in with her because she appreciates his charm and mildness and the fact that he is searching. She

informs Rabbit that she is pregnant with his child, and he leaves her.

Jack Eccles, an Episcopalian minister. He seeks to effect a reconciliation of the Angstroms' marriage. His methods involve more psychology than theology, and he uses frequent golf games with Rabbit to make his persuasions.

Fritz Kruppenbach, a Lutheran minister. A stern man with a heavy German accent, he appears only once, in a crucial scene in which he lectures Jack Eccles and calls his counseling methods "Devil's work."

Mrs. Horace Smith, an old widow. Mrs. Smith's eight acres of gardens become Rabbit's workplace, and she shows herself to be a quick-witted woman who takes a liking to Rabbit, telling him that he has the gift of life.

Nelson Angstrom, the son of Rabbit and Janice. Two-year-old Nelson excites frequent guilt in Rabbit. During Janice's maternity ward stay, Rabbit takes care of him.

Rabbit Redux, 1971

Harry "Rabbit" Angstrom, now a linotype operator for the *Verity Press*. Thirty-six years old and fat around the middle, he has become a conservative cynic, leery (but curious) about African Americans, a hawkish defender of the Vietnam War, and resigned to his humdrum life in the Brewer, Pennsylvania, suburb of Penn Villas. When his wife, Janice, moves in with her lover, Harry allows Jill, a white teenage runaway, and Skeeter, a black fugitive, to move in with him and his son. After neighbors burn down his house, killing Jill, Harry helps Skeeter escape and reconciles with Janice.

Janice Springer Angstrom, Harry's wife, who works at her father's Toyota dealership, Springer Motors. A short, dark-eyed woman hardened by life, she has aged well during the 1960's and has acquired a stylish gypsy flair and a penchant for the latest slang. Lacking in self-confidence until her affair, she is, in her words, searching for a valid identity while harboring guilt about the death of her second child. The last time she sleeps with her lover, she saves his life.

Charles (Charlie) Stavros, a bachelor who works at Springer Motors and has an affair with Janice. A broad, hairy-shouldered Greek American with tinted glasses, a receding hairline, and prominent sideburns, he has had a heart murmur since

childhood and harbors liberal political opinions. Janice finds him sensitive and caring, whereas Harry calls him a bleeding-heart peacenik. Not entirely comfortable with long-term commitments, he willingly succumbs to the charm of Harry's sister, Mim, precipitating the termination of his relationship with Janice.

Nelson Angstrom, Harry's thirteen-year-old son. A small, dark-complexioned, delicate, impressionable adolescent with Janice's stubby fingers and shoulder-length hair, he is wary of life's unpredictable turns but anxious to learn its secrets. He, too, indiscriminately picks up the latest slang words and finds in Jill a sisterly soul mate. He blames Harry for Jill's death.

Earl Angstrom, Harry's father, who is close to retirement at *Verity Press*. A slim, thin-voiced, whiny codger with washed-out eyes and sour breath from a bad set of false teeth, he is a New Deal Democrat who admires Lyndon B. Johnson, Walt Disney, and the moon-walking astronauts. An opinionated meddler who enjoys an after-work beer with his son, he is aggrieved by his wife's illness and hopes that Harry will get his own house in order.

Mary Angstrom, Harry's sixty-five-year-old mother, who is afflicted with Parkinson's disease. She is gray-haired and loose-fleshed, like a well-cooked chicken, with hands knobbed with age. She utters epigrammatic pronouncements in partial sentences. She dislikes Janice and resents Nelson's resemblance to her, and she is the only person who understands Harry. Her advice is for him to leave Brewer and be adventurous and selfish like Mim.

Fred "Old Man" Springer, Harry's father-in-law, who owns Springer Motors. A wiry, hatchet-faced go-getter, set in his ways and angered over the tumultuous events of the 1960's, he has rosy splotches on his cheeks and a salesman's smile made timid from years of sycophancy. He takes Nelson and Harry to minor-league baseball games and bores them with commentary about his latest gripes and prejudices.

Jill Pendleton, an eighteen-year-old runaway from Stonington, Connecticut. A chalky, small-boned, thin-faced, braless prep school dropout, with tired green eyes and an elongated nose, chin, and neck, she wears hippie clothes, sunbathes clad only in bikini panties, and negligently abuses her white Porsche. She has been mentally burned out since the death of her doting father. Fleeing a destructive relationship with a drug-pushing boyfriend, she becomes Harry's mistress and homemaker, transforming the tacky Angstrom house into a consciousness-raising commune. She takes orders like a dog and is transfixed by Skeeter, who she fears (prophetically) will destroy her. She dies when Harry's house is set aflame.

Hubert H. "Skeeter" Johnson, also known as **Farnsworth**, a black junkie. A skinny-ankled, five-foot, six-inch, 125-pound, self-styled "bad niggah," he calls himself the black Jesus. After moving in with Harry, Nelson, and Jill, he proselytizes on black history and the war in Vietnam and turns them on to drugs. After informing Harry about the fire from a telephone booth, he escapes (with Harry's help) from town when authorities wrongly suspect him of arson.

Rabbit Is Rich, 1981

Harry "Rabbit" Angstrom, now the manager of the successful Springer Motors. Rabbit, gone heavy and soft in his mid-forties, lives with his wife, Janice, at the home of her mother, Bessie Springer, and marvels at the thirty-five hundred dollars that he earns each month in salary and profits at the dealership he began to run after the death of Janice's father, Fred Springer. His contentment is broken by the arrival at the agency of a young woman whom he suspects of being his daughter from his 1959 affair with Ruth Leonard and by the unexpected return home from Colorado of his son Nelson, a college student. Rabbit seeks to learn the girl's identity, while, at home, he tries to defend his safe position by lobbying for Nelson's departure.

Janice Springer Angstrom, Rabbit's wife. In her mid-forties, Janice has become a sassy and self-confident woman, seemingly more clever and more adaptable than Rabbit. Throughout this female-dominated plot, she is the center of power, because Rabbit knows that his prosperity depends on her. It is she who suggests firing Charlie Stavros, her former lover, to create a vacancy at Springer Motors.

Nelson Angstrom, now a college student at Kent State University. Nelson, bored and directionless at college, wishes to quit his studies and join the Springer Motors staff. He, like his father before him, finds himself in trouble with women and at the ultimate crisis can only flee.

Peggy Fosnacht, a false friend of Janice, estranged from her husband, Ollie. A walleyed former classmate of Harry, going to fat and aging poorly, she is sad and gropes clumsily with being a single parent. Telling Harry that he is too forgiving, she gets him to sleep with her the night his house burns down. Harry finds her sexually satisfying but rather pathetic in her needs.

Ollie Fosnacht, Peggy's husband, the owner of Chords 'n Records. Never a family man, he likes to hang out with musicians in Philadelphia and ski in Aspen. He takes his son fishing and gives him stereo equipment, a minibike, a puppy, and other presents. He comes by the house to copulate with Peggy once in a while before deciding to get back together with her.

Billy Fosnacht, Nelson Angstrom's friend, fourteen years old. A curly-haired, pimply-faced, awkward youth, he blames his mother for his father's desertion and calls her a whore. He tells her what is happening at the Angstrom house, and this gossip gets back to Janice.

Mrs. Aldridge, Jill's mother, from Connecticut. She comes to Brewer to find out why Jill died. She attacks Harry to assuage her own guilt and asks for some memento of her daughter.

Mim Angstrom, Harry's thirty-year-old sister, a would-be model and mistress to Las Vegas gangsters. Looking like a West Coast swinger, she has a pale mouth and wears Egyptian-like makeup around her eyes to match her clownish clothes and tinted hair. Coming back home, she sleeps with Charlie Stavros to patch up Harry and Janice's marriage.

Pajasek, Harry's immediate boss at *Verity Press*, a short, bald man with bristling eyebrows. When the press jettisons its antiquated linotype process, he lays Harry off.

Teresa "Pru" Lubell Angstrom, Nelson's pregnant girlfriend. Pru, formerly a secretary at Kent State, is a quiet, solid, working-class woman. She comes to Pennsylvania and marries Nelson, and her approaching childbirth creates tension for him.

Webb Murkett, a businessman and country-club friend of Rabbit and Janice. Webb's money and age—something over fifty—make him a man of stature for Rabbit, who takes his advice seriously. Webb's name and his actions, such as sanctioning the Caribbean-holiday wife-swap, suggest a sinister force.

Ruth Leonard Byer, a farmer's widow and formerly Rabbit's lover. She denies that her daughter, Annabelle Byer, is her child by Rabbit, but her story is not entirely convincing.

Lucinda R. (Cindy) Murkett, Webb's third wife. "Still smelling of high school," Cindy seems quite dull but frequently excites desire in Rabbit and represents to him a kind of bliss.

Bessie Springer, Janice's mother and half owner of Springer Motors. Her sharing of her house with Rabbit and Janice represents both her generosity and her desire for control. She favors Nelson being hired at the auto agency.

Charles (Charlie) Stavros, an auto salesman at Springer Motors. Formerly robust and now shrunk and wizened, Charles acts out Rabbit's fantasies by sleeping with Nelson's college friend Melanie and also agrees to step aside to make a job vacancy for Nelson.

Thelma Harrison, the wife of Rabbit's high school teammate, Ronnie Harrison. Thelma, who is in her forties and suffers from lupus, is the most intelligent of the wives of Rabbit's social circle. She senses and appreciates the goodness in him, and she initiates him in an ironically scatological sexual encounter.

Rabbit at Rest, 1990

Harry "Rabbit" Angstrom, now in semiretirement, spending half the year in Florida. He is overweight and cannot resist eating cholesterol-laden junk food. He has a heart attack, brought on by an attempt to rescue his granddaughter, Judy, during a boating accident. He is hospitalized and refuses a bypass operation. After a one-night sexual encounter with his daughter-in-law, he moves to his Florida condominium, where he lives a lonely life. He suffers a stroke while playing basketball with a boy he does not know. He is unable to communicate with family members when they arrive. He dies at the age of fifty-six.

Nelson Angstrom, who is embezzling from Springer Motors to support a cocaine habit. He agrees to enter a rehabilitation program, but not before Toyota withdraws its franchise. After rehabilitation, he intends to become a social worker, but he remains an unsympathetic character.

Janice Springer Angstrom, who attempts to blame Harry for Nelson's problems and leaves Nelson in charge of the auto dealership until it is too late. She and Nelson make decisions about the family business, leaving Harry out of the process. This is one of several ways in which the family prepares for life without Harry: Janice also occasionally talks about him in the past tense and takes courses in real estate.

Teresa "Pru" Lubell Angstrom, Harry's daughter-in-law. She will not let her husband sleep with her, as punishment for his drug abuse. Harry, depressed and demoralized, finds himself alone with her one night and takes her to bed. Janice finds out and demands that he confront his family; instead, he flees to his Florida condominium.

— *Kerry Ahearn and James B. Lane*

RABBIT BOSS

Author: Thomas Sanchez (1944-   )
First published: 1973
Genre: Novel

Locale: Nevada and California
Time: 1846 to the 1950's
Plot: Historical realism

Gayabuc, the husband of Painted Stick and son of the Rabbit Chief or Rabbit Boss who guides the people on the annual hunt for the rabbits that sustain their lives. He is the first to discover the presence of white people on Washo land. He witnesses the cannibalism of the Donner party on the shores of what is eventually named Donner Lake in California. His fateful encounter marks the beginning of the end of the traditional life of the Washo people. After his father's murder, Gayabuc becomes Rabbit Chief and leads his people in their last traditional rabbit hunt.

Captain Rex, the first son of Gayabuc and Painted Stick and the next to bear the hereditary title of Rabbit Boss. He is the first to bear the surname Birdsong, given to him because of his ability to sing like a bird when drunk. Though brought up in the traditional ways of the Washo, he is the first to have prolonged contact with white people. Because of his knowledge of English, Captain Rex acts as a translator for the railroad company and becomes an intermediary between the Washo and the railroad. As a result of his interaction with whites, he becomes a drunkard, petty thief, and gambler. He marries a Washo woman named Molly Moose, and they become the parents of Hallelujah Bob. Rex dies an old man, the victim of starvation and tuberculosis.

Hallelujah Bob, also known as **Ayas**, the son of Captain Rex and grandson of Painted Stick. He is the survivor of a tuberculosis epidemic in which nearly all of his family dies. Painted Stick cares for him until her death from old age. He lives with a white family, then with an elderly white dairy farmer, then at a government school. While at the school, he learns of his Washo heritage. He is reclaimed by his tribe and is taught tribal traditions and rituals. When he leaves the Washo camp because of the starvation and disease there, he works at a number of occupations, including stockyard worker, medicine show pitch man, ranch hand, and finally Christian evangelist. He returns to his people to preach the Gospel and lives with Medicine Maggie, with whom he fathers Joe Birdsong and Sarah Dick. Later in his life, he develops into a mystic, his Christianity is diluted with beliefs derived from the Ghost Dance religion, and he becomes the follower of a Paiute messiah. Ayas leads a religious rebellion that is quelled by government officials.

Joe Birdsong, son of Ayas and Medicine Maggie and last of the Rabbit Bosses. He lives in a shack on land that was given to him by his father and that white developers attempt to seize. He is employed as an exterminator, ranch hand, and hunting guide. His main employer is Mister Dixel, who owns the largest ranch in the valley. One of Joe's jobs is to kill rabbits on Dixel's ranch. Dixel informs Joe that he no longer needs his services as rabbit boss. Joe disobeys Dixel and performs his duties as rabbit boss with the help of his sister, Sarah Dick. Joe seeks to restore a tangible connection with the previous Rabbit Bosses by shooting enough rabbits to make a blanket similar to those of his ancestors. After the shoot, Joe returns to his shack to find Dixel's wife, who informs him that her husband has been murdered and that he is the prime suspect. Joe flees to the mountains and eventually dies on the edge of Donner Lake from an infected wound.

Painted Stick, the wife of Gayabuc. She blames herself for Gayabuc's lack of skill as a hunter because she allowed him to have sexual intercourse with her before she engaged in the Dance of the Woman. During her long life, she witnesses the takeover of Washo land by whites; the dissolution of her son, Captain Rex; and the tuberculosis epidemic that kills her people. She dies of old age in the company of her grandson, Ayas.

John C. Luther, also known as **The Bummer**, a greedy and cruel rascal who takes advantage of the Washo by encouraging them to drink and gamble. By threatening his life, Luther forces Captain Rex to lie concerning the location of a gold supply.

Molly Moose, the Washo mistress of Luther, the eventual wife of Captain Rex, and the mother of Ayas.

Medicine Maggie, the second wife of Hallelujah Bob and the mother of Sarah Dick and Joe Birdsong.

Sarah Dick, Joe Birdsong's sister. During her puberty rite, she is gang raped by a group of white men. She accompanies her brother on the last rabbit hunt that takes place on Dixel land.

Mister Dixel, the owner of the ranch on which Joe works. Joe is accused of his murder.

— *Pegge Bochynski*

RADCLIFFE

Author: David Storey (1933-   )
First published: 1963
Genre: Novel

Locale: Yorkshire, England
Time: Mid-1940's to early 1960's
Plot: Psychological

Leonard Radcliffe, the protagonist, the only male heir of a decaying aristocratic family, a visionary misfit, and a gifted artist. In the schematized world of this misogynist novel of ideas, Leonard represents one pole—the soul, and the aristocracy that once was England's soul—and Tolson the other. It is inevitable that the two will come together and just as inevitable that their unholy (homosexual) union will prove disastrous. He is ultimately unfathomable, fragile, passionate, and an intensely private artist. Leonard's ancestral home, The Place, functions as an extension of his mind; like him, it does not survive. He dies in a mental institution to which he has been committed after killing Tolson with his own hammer.

Victor (Vic) Tolson, the antagonist, a skilled workman. Leonard's childhood "protector" and "compensation," Tolson, a vulgar giant of a man, represents the body and the working classes. Spawned on the ugly local council housing estate that eventually will engulf the Radcliffe family home, he first meets Leonard, his "Prince," on the pale nine-year-old's first day at the council school. Tolson, the boys' favorite, is humiliated by Leonard's mental abilities and superior class. Later betrayals, when the two have met again as adults, urge Tolson to reciprocation (as his name suggests, he is both "victim" and "victor") by tricking Leonard into eating his excrement, by smashing him in the face with a hammer, by subjecting him to violent oral sexual assault, and by raping his sister (she is to bear a son with Leonard's eyes and Tolson's body).

Denis Blakeley, an obscene stand-up comic who performs in workingmen's clubs. Blakeley is a tormented self-educated workingman with grandiose ideas about art, religion, and class, looking for a way out of his predicament but trapped into pandering to the tastes of his audience. Once the would-be homosexual lover of Leonard's Uncle Austen, he is now insanely smitten with Tolson and attempts to get Leonard (to whom he provides some obvious parallels) out of the way, even offering him his daughter. After Tolson's death, he cracks up, "confesses," and slaughters his family and himself.

Uncle Austen, the elegantly dressed owner-manager of an uptown furniture shop. Somewhat ineffectual and a closet homosexual, Uncle Austen identifies strongly with Leonard and gets him his job with Ewbank.

John Radcliffe, Leonard's father, caretaker of The Place, a solitary man with religious tendencies. His marriage to a sturdy working-class woman prefigures his union with Tolson. He voices the novel's sense of encroaching philistinism and materialism, as well as its disillusionment with the postwar belief that political and economic reform could transform English society.

Ewbank, a self-made contractor of show tents. Leonard and Tolson are thrown together when he delegates to them care of the tents at a local show. He suffers a betrayal of trust, and a blow to his illusions about the upper classes, when the splendid marquee he provides for a society wedding is wrecked and soiled.

— *Joss Lutz Marsh*

THE RADIANCE OF THE KING
(Le Regard du roi)

Author: Camara Laye (1928-1980)
First published: 1954
Genre: Novel

Locale: Adramé (a city) and Aziana (a village), in Africa
Time: Unspecified
Plot: Philosophical

Clarence, a bankrupt, middle-aged white man in Africa. His previous occupation is not mentioned. Having lost all of his money and even incurred debts playing cards with his peers, he has been evicted from his hotel and landed in a miserable inn, where he also owes money. Destitute and

wholly dependent on Africans in this tribal society, he thinks that he, as a white man, will be admitted to see the king and will be taken into the king's service. His quest takes him from Adramé, a city of the North, to Aziana, a village of the South, in the company of an old beggar and two young dancing boys. Through painful, strange, and bewildering adventures, Clarence comes slowly to comprehend that his values (money, time, work, rights, and sex) carry no weight here; his color only makes him different from others. The beggar barters him to the Naba, the ruler of the South, for a donkey and a woman. Clarence is used to breed mulattoes through women from the Naba's harem under the influence of aphrodisiac scents; the discovery that this is what is happening is deeply humiliating to him. When Clarence is stripped of his false pride and values, he does come into the radiance of the king, who draws him into his embrace, the end of his quest.

The beggar, a cynical old African in rags who accompanies Clarence to the South. Abrupt in speech, contradictory, sharp, and repetitive, he responds not only to Clarence's questions and comments but also to his thoughts, interpreting events and sometimes enlightening, sometimes confusing, and sometimes irritating Clarence.

Nagoa (nah-GOH-ah) and

Noaga (noh-AH-gah), young grandsons of the ruler of the South. They are lively and mischievous boy dancers who accompany Clarence and the beggar on the journey to the South, often annoying the beggar and teasing or interpreting for

Clarence. In the last scene, Clarence sees them among the chosen who surround the king.

The Master of Ceremonies, a hard, legalistic man assigned by the king to organize festivities. It is he who reveals to Clarence that the latter has been sold into slavery and for what purpose.

Akissi (ah-KEHS-see), the African woman who is Clarence's wife. She comes and goes, waiting on him and doing what he asks. Only as part of the denouement of the story does Clarence learn that she has left their bed each night, to be replaced by a woman from the Naba's harem.

Samba Baloum (SAHM-bah BAH-lewm), a eunuch and guardian of the Naba's harem. He lets Clarence look inside briefly.

Diallo (dee-AHL-loh), the blacksmith who is trying to forge a perfect ax blade for the king. His dialogue with Clarence helps to clarify some principles.

Dioki (dee-OH-kee), an old village fortune-teller from whom Clarence tries to learn when the king will come. His contact with her and the snakes that surround her fills him with revulsion. He does not receive an answer to his question.

— *Mary Henry Nachtsheim*

THE RADIANT WAY

Author: Margaret Drabble (1939-   )
First published: 1987
Genre: Novel

Locale: London and the town of Northam in Northern England
Time: 1980-1985
Plot: Social satire

Liz Headleand, a native of Northam whose determination took her to Cambridge University and a prosperous career as a psychoanalyst on London's Harley Street. Divorced from Edgar Lintot and remarried to Charles Headleand, she learns in the novel's opening scene—a marvelous set piece of a New Year's Eve party welcoming in the Thatcher 1980's—that Charles is leaving her for the boring Lady Henrietta Latchett.

Alix Bowen, Liz's friend from Cambridge, now married to Brian Bowen, a reliable literature teacher, also from Northam. Alix teaches part-time in a reformatory for young women. Her first husband, Sebastian Manning, died not long after their marriage, and their son, Nicholas, inherits his paternal grandmother's fortune. When Brian loses his job, he and Alix move to Northam and Alix takes over the task of sorting the papers of a local poet who is somewhat famous.

Esther Breuer, who formed a triumvirate of close friends at Cambridge with Liz and Alix. Esther is an art historian who spends much of her time in Italy. Although she has remained unmarried, she has had a long relationship with a married man, an Italian anthropologist who suffers a curious obsession with werewolves. Of the three Cambridge friends, she is the most individualistic, not so much bohemian as self-reliant and inwardly directed.

Charles Headleand, Liz's second husband. Charles is a television executive who was a widower with three sons when he married Liz. When the novel begins, Charles is fifty years old and Liz forty-five. They have had two daughters of their own in their twenty years of marriage. In the 1960's, when he was a liberal, Charles made a television documentary titled

The Radiant Way exposing the British class system, but he has since swung to the political right.

Brian Bowen, Alix's husband, an earnest administrator in an adult education college who moves back home to Northam when he becomes redundant under Margaret Thatcher's austere administration. Brian is the archetypal struggling "decent" man, a faithful husband and a dutiful son to his aged father.

Shirley Harper, Liz Headleand's younger sister. When the two sisters were young, Liz's vision of a better life somewhere beyond Northam had kept her attention fixed on her textbooks, but Shirley had been the rebel with painted lips who hung around with boys and hoped for salvation through sex. Now Shirley remains in Northam, taking care of her husband, Cliff, and their three children. She sulks because the care of their reclusive mother, Rita Ablewhite, falls to her while Liz stays in London with her smart set.

Jilly Fox, a brilliant but ill-fated student at the Garfield Centre, where Alix teaches literature to delinquent girls. Jilly's affluent background and high intelligence fail her in her struggles with drugs and lesbian misalliances. She develops a crush on Alix and pursues her at home after she is released from Garfield. She turns into a problem for Alix.

Rita Ablewhite, Liz and Shirley's mother. She is comatose in her only appearances late in the novel, but she haunts Liz with guilt for neglecting to visit Northam for years on end, and she burdens the embittered Shirley, who feels that her mother's care has fallen to her unfairly.

— *Frank Day*

RAGTIME

Author: E. L. Doctorow (1931-   )
First published: 1975
Genre: Novel

Locale: New York, Massachusetts, Philadelphia, Egypt, Mexico, Alaska, and Germany
Time: 1906 to c. 1915
Plot: Historical

Little Boy, the narrator and supposed author of this story. Neither as the narrator nor as a character in the story is his age ever made known, just as it remains unclear until near the end why he is telling the story. As a character, he generally remains on the periphery of the various events that take place in the narrative; nevertheless, what he chooses to tell about reveals his changing perceptions and individual growth. His narrative begins as a retrospective account of his boyhood in New York when, according to his earliest memories, America seemed simple, clean, good, and populated only by Caucasians. Then, along with his own white Anglo-Saxon Protestant (WASP) family (composed of himself, Mother, Father, Mother's Younger Brother, and Grandfather), he chronicles the lives of two other families: a black family (Sarah, Coalhouse Walker, Jr., and their illegitimate infant) and an immigrant family (Tateh, Mameh, and The Little Girl). Although unfamiliar with one another at the beginning of Little Boy's narrative, members of these three families are joined into one uniquely American family by the story's end. The families' fates, then, all more or less shape Little Boy's life and character, as well as his perception of himself and America.

Father, a manufacturer of fireworks and flags, an amateur explorer and Little Boy's father. He is—by attitude, sentiment, and occupation—the model American patriot, and he expects his family to be the model American (WASP) family. That, at least, is the stressed norm in 1906, when he leaves with Robert Peary on the famous explorer's successful third expedition to discover the North Pole. While Father is away, however, his wife and family undergo significant changes that his absence makes possible.

Mother, who initially is a prudish creature with whom Father has had only rigidly formal sexual relations. She finds a black infant abandoned but still alive in her flower garden, and she takes upon herself the burden of caring for both the child and—after she is located—its young mother, Sarah. Not only does she take on this burden, but she also assumes all the managerial responsibilities of Father's business while he is away on his expedition with Peary, and she succeeds in making the company more profitable than Father had been able to. Mother changes in yet another way while Father is away: She

begins reading and having her attitudes shaped by feminist and socialist literature.

Mother's Younger Brother, an employee in Father's business and a resident in Mother and Father's home. Desperately in love with Evelyn Nesbit (the lover of Stanford White until her husband assassinates him), Mother's Younger Brother succeeds in briefly wooing the married woman, and in the process he becomes a political radical and revolutionary unionizer like his mentor, Emma Goldman. It is through Mother's Younger Brother that Father's family initially is connected to the immigrant family of Tateh, Mameh, and The Little Girl. Furthermore, because both Mother and her brother more or less become followers of Goldman, Father's WASP family is infiltrated by radical thought by the time he returns from his expedition, and his employees are unionizing largely as a result of the influence of Mother's Younger Brother.

Tateh, **Baron Ashkenazy**, an immigrant who travels to America to realize his dream of comfort, prosperity, and freedom from repression with Mameh and The Little Girl. Finding only abject poverty in New York, Tateh makes and sells paper silhouettes on the streets, separates from his wife because she sells sexual favors to pay the rent, gradually becomes a pioneer filmmaker, and, with newfound prosperity, changes his name to Baron Ashkenazy. As such, he marries Mother after Father drowns at sea.

Coalhouse Walker, Jr., a successful ragtime pianist and the father of the illegitimate infant whom Mother finds half-buried in her garden. Although Father is troubled by the fact that Coalhouse does not behave around whites as if he were mindful of being a black man and therefore, presumably, inferior, the pianist's self-respect and sense of honor compel him to enter Father's home in the first place. When he learns that Sarah, his former lover, is living in the home and that she has given birth to his child, he is determined to visit her as often as necessary to persuade her to marry him. After they become engaged, however, Coalhouse is victimized by violent racists, Sarah is killed trying to help him, he is killed seeking vengeance for the injustices done to him and her, and Mother is left with their baby, which—against Father's wishes—she chooses to rear.

— *David A. Carpenter*

THE RAID: A Volunteer's Story
(Nabeg: Razskaz volontera)

Author: Leo Tolstoy (1828-1910)
First published: 1853
Genre: Short fiction

Locale: The Russian Caucasus
Time: The 1850's
Plot: Love

The narrator, a young man fascinated by war, not in the sense of maneuvers devised by generals but the reality of war, the actual killing. To discover why soldiers kill, and under the influence of what feeling, he volunteers to accompany a Rus-

sian regiment on a raid into the Caucasian hills controlled by Tatar tribesmen. A thoughtful, sensitive man, the narrator wishes to grasp the meaning of bravery and discusses the issue with the captain of the regiment, whom he admires greatly.

During the action, the narrator is able to observe men risking their lives for reasons of vanity, curiosity, and greed: The truly brave man is he who, like the captain, simply and quietly "does what he ought." The narrator paints a portrait of war as often fascinating and gallant but as ultimately futile, vain, and destructive, with no clear or worthwhile goals achieved.

Captain Pavel Ivanovich Khlopov (PAH-vehl ee-VAH-noh-vihch KHLOH-pov), a gray-haired, elderly captain, severely wounded four times over the course of long years of service in the Russian army. A quiet, brave, and unassuming man surrounded by vain and loud younger officers, the captain wears a very unmartial-looking shabby coat and smokes cheap tobacco. He writes his mother dutifully once a year and, to protect her, has never revealed that he has been seriously wounded. In battle, he is calm and alert, the men under his command fighting so well and so professionally that they seldom need an order from him. A man with no illusions about war—for he has seen too many die—he serves in the army because he believes that a man must serve his country. To the narrator, it is the captain who is truly brave.

Ensign Anatol Ivanich Alanin (ah-nah-TOHL ee-VAH-nihch ah-LAH-nihn), a young and ardent soldier a month out of the Cadet Corps, killed during his first action on his first campaign, needlessly leading a charge into the woods during an orderly retreat. A beautiful, black-eyed youth with only the first indications of a mustache, Ensign Alanin is delighted to be going into action for the first time so that he can prove his bravery and devotion. As the Russian soldiers are being harassed on their retreat, Alanin keeps riding up to the captain and begging permission to charge. Not receiving permission, he disobeys orders and is killed.

Lieutenant Rosencranz, a vain, dashing, and desperate daredevil, filled with hatred, vengeance, and contempt for the human race. Tall and handsome, Lieutenant Rosencranz rides a large white horse and bedecks himself in the finery of war: swords, daggers, pistols, and Asiatic costume. An avid killer, during combat Rosencranz rides his horse up and down the cordon of soldiers, shouting out orders incessantly in his loud, hoarse voice. An extraordinarily vain man, he shapes his life on the basis of literary heroes out of the works of Mikhail Lermontov. He traces his ancestry to the Varangians, the first rulers of Russia, and thinks of himself as a pure Russian.

The general, a stylish, pompous, and vain imitator of an antiquated French chivalry. During the heat of battle, the general is fond of speaking in trivial French phrases with his junior officers.

— Michael Zeitlin

THE RAINBOW

Author: D. H. Lawrence (1885-1930)
First published: 1915
Genre: Novel

Locale: England
Time: Late nineteenth and early twentieth centuries
Plot: Psychological realism

Tom Brangwen, a substantial English farmer. He is a lonely man leading a bachelor's life, driven by his desires to sordid meetings with passing women and to frequent bouts with the brandy bottle, until his marriage to Lydia Lensky, a Polish widow whom he woos in an abrupt but successful courtship that rises above his own usual uncommunicativeness and a language barrier. Tom loves his wife, and he loves Anna, her small daughter. As the years pass, Tom becomes a kind of rural patriarch, watching his two sons, Tom and Fred, and Anna, his stepdaughter, grow to maturity and face their own problems of life and love. His good if unremarkable life ends abruptly when he drowns in a sudden flood.

Lydia Lensky, a Polish widow from an aristocratic land-owning family. She is a nurse and quite an emancipated woman for her time. Lonely for a man's love and reduced to being a housekeeper in a vicarage, she readily accepts Tom Brangwen as a husband. She becomes a passionate and devoted wife to him and bears him two sons. Although she is happily married, she sometimes misses her old life and keeps up a friendship with Baron Skrebensky, a fellow exile and an Anglican clergyman. Because her first husband, a Polish doctor, was a man driven by his enthusiasm for various causes all of his life, she appreciates all the more the phlegmatic temper of Tom Brangwen and her quiet life with him at Marsh Farm. In their early married state, she is more advanced and leads Tom in their love.

Tilly, the Brangwens' cross-eyed housekeeper, a woman with a strong affection for Tom Brangwen. Having been in the household since he was a boy, she had served his father and mother before he took over the farm.

Anna Lensky, Lydia Lensky's daughter by her first husband, a bright young child of four at the time of her mother's second marriage. Forming a deep attachment for her stepfather, she goes with him everywhere and looks on him as a real parent. Anna falls in love with her stepfather's nephew, William Brangwen, and marries him. Until her children are born, she is a fond wife and eager for love. Later, her children become her chief interest, and her husband has no place in her life except as a means to enlarging her matriarchy.

William (Will) Brangwen, Tom Brangwen's nephew, a lace designer in a factory. He marries Anna Lensky, who soon comes to dominate his whole existence. After their children are born and her interest becomes centered in them, he turns to all sorts of hobbies connected with religion. He uses his artistic talents to renovate the parish church, and he directs the church choir. Before his marriage, he had been a sculptor until he learned that his enthusiasm outran his self-discipline and his craft. Years later, he takes up sculpture again, only to find that he has lost his imagination after acquiring the necessary craft. He becomes a man driven from his home by his children, and he has little feeling for his offspring, except for his oldest child, Ursula.

Ursula Brangwen, the oldest child of William Brangwen and Anna Lensky. At an early age, she helps to take care of the four sisters and the brother added to the family. She and her sister Gudrun are given a good education, after which Ursula becomes a schoolteacher. Not wanting to marry immediately after graduation from high school, she desires a wide vista of life and continually reaches out eagerly for wider, deeper experiences. Dissatisfied with teaching, she goes to college. During her final year of college, she takes Anton Skrebensky as her lover. She has loved him many years, during most of which he has been absent in Africa, fighting in the Boer War. During his absence, Ursula's one experience in love is an affair with one of her high-school teachers, Miss Inger. Anna wants too much of love and demands too much of Anton Skrebensky, whom she sends away because she finds him spiritually inadequate. While ill with pneumonia, she also loses the infant he has fathered. Her vision of the rainbow is a promise of escape from the world of Skrebensky and the world of her parents, divided by love and conflict.

Anton Skrebensky, the son of Baron Skrebensky, a friend of Lydia Brangwen. Young Skrebensky is an intelligent young officer of engineers in the British army. Although he loves Ursula deeply, he cannot meet her demands for spiritual as well as physical fulfillment. After she sends him away, he marries the daughter of his commanding officer. He cannot understand why Ursula wants a college education; as the wife of an officer in India, she will not need one. Happy in a life of parties, golf, and riding, he fails to see Ursula's need for knowledge of the world and herself.

Winifred Inger, a schoolteacher with whom Ursula Brangwen has a brief affair. She is a practical, worldly woman who, when she has an opportunity, marries Ursula's well-to-do uncle, who manages a colliery in northern England. She bears her husband a son in exchange for a life of ease and plenty.

Gudrun Brangwen, Ursula's younger sister. A background figure in this novel, she is one of the central characters in *Women in Love*.

RAINTREE COUNTY

Author: Ross Lockridge, Jr. (1914-1948)
First published: 1948
Genre: Novel

Locale: Indiana, Tennessee, Georgia, Washington, D.C., and New York City
Time: Late nineteenth century
Plot: Historical realism

John Wickliff Shawnessy, a schoolteacher and the philosopher of Raintree County. On July 4, 1892, he looks back over his life, recalling his boyhood, his youthful loves, his two marriages, his part in the Civil War. He tries to draw out the meaning of his life, his America, from what he remembers. The day ends for him tragicomically, as he is first accused and then exonerated of committing adultery with a local widow.

Senator Garwood B. Jones, John's old friend, who makes a speech at the July Fourth celebration after John introduces him. He is a shrewd, smooth-tongued man without principles.

The Reverend Mr. Shawnessy, John's father, a doctor, a preacher, and a teetotaler.

Mrs. Shawnessy, John's mother, a gentlewoman whom he greatly loves.

Nell Gaither, John's first sweetheart, a combination of hoyden and lady. She becomes the wife of Jones after John is reported dead in the Civil War. She dies in childbirth while still a young woman.

Jerusalem Webster Stiles, the "Perfessor," a cynic and a friend of John. He establishes an academy where he teaches his charges little of the classics, much about seduction. Forced out of town because of attempted adultery, he later becomes a newspaperman in New York. It is he who proves years later that John is not guilty of adultery as charged.

Susanna Drake, John's first wife, a girl of wealth from New Orleans. She is a passionate, emotional creature who becomes demented and burns their house, killing their child. John finds that she is haunted by the fact that her mother was black. Sent back to be cared for by her relatives, she later escapes and disappears.

Esther Root, John's second wife, one of his former pupils. She and her husband elope, returning to the community to rear their family and win a respected place.

Mr. Root, Esther's father. He opposes his daughter's marriage to John on the grounds that the man is an atheist and also a bigamist, since there is no proof that his first wife is truly dead.

A RAISIN IN THE SUN

Author: Lorraine Hansberry (1930-1965)
First published: 1959
Genre: Drama

Locale: Chicago, Illinois
Time: The 1950's
Plot: Family

Lena Younger, called **Mama**, a retired domestic and the matriarch of the Younger family. In her early sixties, she is a religious, optimistic, and proud black woman. Recently widowed, she speaks of her departed husband with love and presents him as a role model for other family members to emulate. She is a self-sacrificing woman, and the well-being of her family occupies her thoughts. She does not hesitate to rebuke

family members for actions that oppose the values that she and her husband promoted. Her husband's ten thousand dollar life insurance policy gives Mama the means to purchase a house in the suburbs as a means of escaping the debilitating effects of their current slum living conditions.

Walter Lee Younger, a chauffeur and Lena's son, still living at home in Mama's crowded apartment. He is a slim, intense, thirty-five-year-old black man. Walter believes wealth to be the answer to his feelings of desperation and hopelessness as a slum resident and employee in a dead-end job. He has contempt for the women in his family, who, he thinks, do not support his aspiration to break from his working-class life to become a prosperous businessman. In such a prestigious position, Walter believes, he can finally assume his mother's role as the head of the family and have the means to leave an admirable legacy to his son. To realize his dream, he wants to use the insurance money to invest in a liquor store with two of his friends.

Ruth Younger, a domestic and Walter's wife. Thirty years old and in the first few months of pregnancy, she is a practical woman who, like Lena, cares deeply for the welfare of her family. The circumstances of her life have taken their toll: Her beauty has faded, and her spirit is almost completely broken. She realizes that her husband's feelings of inadequacy and lack of self-worth have contributed to the deterioration of their relationship. She is willing to do anything to alleviate their desperate situation, even if it means the abortion of their unborn child. Initially, she attempts to persuade her mother-in-law to permit Walter to invest the insurance money in a liquor store. When she learns of Lena's desire to move the family to the suburbs, however, Ruth becomes Mama's most ardent supporter of the change.

Beneatha (Bennie) Younger, a college student and Lena's daughter. At the age of twenty, she is an attractive, slim woman who, because of her education, speaks better English than do the other family members. She is an atheist, opinionated, and, at times, self-centered. She often speaks her mind before realizing how the expression of her beliefs will affect other people.

She quarrels frequently with her brother, who does not support her aspiration to become a medical doctor. Proud of her African heritage, she is inspired by the attentions of a Nigerian suitor to wear an Afro instead of a processed, straightened hairstyle. She adopts various interests, such as the guitar and horseback riding. Her mother accuses her of flitting from one interest to the next, but Beneatha insists that she is simply experimenting with different forms of expression.

Travis Willard Younger, Walter and Ruth's son. A handsome ten-year-old boy, he seems content with his life and enjoys the attentions of the other family members. Unlike his father, he aspires to be a bus driver and gives little thought to rising above working-class status.

Joseph Asagai (ah-sah-GI), a Nigerian student and one of Beneatha's two suitors. He is handsome, articulate, compassionate, and sophisticated. He keenly perceives the problems causing strife within the Younger household.

George Murchison, a college student, an unlikely suitor for Beneatha because of his conservative beliefs, middle-class sensibilities, and disrespect for his African heritage.

Karl Lindner, a middle-aged white man representing a homeowner's association in the suburbs where Lena has purchased a home. To prevent the Youngers from integrating the all-white neighborhood, he offers to buy the house at a profit to the family.

Bobo, a friend of Walter Lee who is to become one of the three partners in the liquor store. He and Walter Lee are taken in by a character not seen onstage, Willy Harris. Harris absconds with Walter Lee's and Bobo's money, bringing about the major crisis of the play.

— *Addell Austin*

THE RAJ QUARTET

Author: Paul Scott (1920-1978)
First published: 1976
Genre: Novels

Locale: India
Time: 1942-1947
Plot: Historical

The Jewel in the Crown, 1966

Edwina Crane, a supervisor of Protestant mission schools in colonial India. She and her colleague, Mr. Chaudhuri, are attacked on the road by a group of rebellious Indians in the wake of the "Quit India" pronouncement issued by the All India Congress Committee in August, 1942. The pronouncement was made in an effort to force England to leave the country to its own fate. Mr. Chaudhuri is killed, apparently, because he is seen riding in a car with a white woman, and Edwina is attacked when she attempts to defend him. Afterward, Edwina, dressed in a white sari, immolates herself in imitation of the traditional Indian practice of *suttee*, in which a widow follows her husband even in death by being burned alive.

Daphne Manners, the niece of a former British colonial governor. She is staying in Mayapore at the home of a family friend, Lily Chatterjee, when she becomes romantically involved with a young Indian man, Hari Kumar. After the two consummate their love one night in the deserted Bibighar Gardens, they are set upon by a group of Indian ruffians who rape Daphne and beat Hari. Afterward, Hari and five other

Indian boys are arrested, but Daphne, pregnant with what she believes to be Hari's child, refuses to give evidence at their trial. She dies in childbirth.

Hari Kumar, an Indian who was reared from the age of two in England, where he attended an elite school, Chillingborough. After his father loses his money and commits suicide, Hari is forced to return to India to live in Mayapore with an aunt. Unable to speak any language other than the king's English and utterly alienated from his country of origin, Hari is a tragic figure. While he is drunk, he comes to the attention of the district superintendent of police, who later accuses him of raping Daphne Manners. Even though there is no evidence to convict Hari of that crime, he remains in jail as a political subversive.

Ronald Merrick, the district superintendent of police for Mayapore. He is acutely aware of his lower-class British origins. He proposes to the aristocratic Daphne Manners. After she rejects him, he fixates on Hari Kumar, whom he persecutes for what he sees as the latter's more privileged existence, one he views as not befitting an inherently inferior "black" man.

The Day of the Scorpion, 1968

Sarah Layton, the elder daughter of an Anglo-Indian military family. She returns to India, where she was born, after being schooled in England. Sarah, unlike her mother and sister—and many of those around her—has a deep sympathy for India. Her complex reaction to the welter of ambiguities accompanying the last days of the Raj leads to an identification with Daphne Manners, whose orphaned child and elderly aunt, Lady Manners, Sarah visits.

Susan Layton, Sarah's prettier younger sister. She marries British army officer Teddie Bingham, who is killed in action connected with World War II shortly after their honeymoon.

The Towers of Silence, 1971

Barbie Batchelor, a retired mission school supervisor and acquaintance of Edwina Crane. She becomes a paying guest of and companion to Sarah and Susan's aunt, Mabel Layton, one of the few remaining representatives of the old, patrician Raj.

A Division of the Spoils, 1975

Guy Perron, who, after receiving an excellent English public school education at Chillingborough, refuses an officer's commission, instead becoming a sergeant in the field service in India during Britain's withdrawal. Perron, who has a deep understanding of the historical significance of the events he witnesses there, develops a relationship with Sarah Layton and, against his will, serves as an aide to Ronald Merrick, now a lieutenant colonel.

Nigel Rowan, the political aide to the British governor. He

After her elderly aunt also dies, Susan goes into early labor with the child she conceived with her husband. Events overwhelm Susan, who becomes mentally unbalanced and seemingly tries, ritualistically, to set fire to her baby.

Ronald Merrick, now a captain in military intelligence, who acts as Teddie Bingham's best man. This begins a relationship with the Laytons, particularly Sarah, who dislikes him. Merrick is revealed to be both heroic (he is badly mutilated in an attempt to save Teddie's life) and villainous (his interrogation of Hari Kumar is revealed to have been brutally sadistic).

As Barbie learns more about Edwina's fate, she comes to identify with her dead friend, and after Mabel's death, Barbie sinks into madness.

previously examined the jailed Hari Kumar and is now obliged to confront the political fallout from his case, which is being heavily exploited by forces bent on ejecting the English from India. Rowan also serves as a witness to the struggle between Hindus and Muslims that threatens to undermine Indian independence.

Ronald Merrick, who, after marrying Susan Layton, is hounded and finally assassinated by Indian fanatics.

— *Lisa Paddock*

RALPH ROISTER DOISTER

Author: Nicholas Udall (1505?-1556)
First published: c. 1556
Genre: Drama

Locale: England
Time: The sixteenth century
Plot: Farce

Ralph Roister Doister, a pompous braggart so taken with the idea of his own prowess that he believes no woman can resist him. He is gullible and is easy prey to the flattery and chicanery of Matthew Merrygreeke. His ridiculous efforts to be a romantic figure and his complete rout by the feminine forces in a pitched battle make him a laughable creation. He is a much-purified adaptation of the braggart soldier in Plautus' *Miles Gloriosus*.

Matthew Merrygreeke, a witty parasite. He makes his living by sponging on characters like Ralph, whom he flatters fulsomely for free meals. His flattery, however, usually is mixed with irony. He enjoys stirring up strife. In the pitched battle between Ralph's and the widow's forces, he pretends to help Ralph but always misses the widow and lets his blows fall on Ralph.

Dame Christian Custance, a virtuous, humorless widow betrothed to Gawin Goodluck, who is away at sea. She is infuriated at Ralph's suit. Her weapons against him do not include the laughter his behavior should arouse, and she is distressed by Gawin Goodluck's questioning about her conduct. After he has been satisfied that she is blameless, she grudgingly consents to allow Ralph to appear in her presence at the feast of general reconciliation and celebration.

Margery "Madge" Mumblecrust, Dame Christian's simpleminded nurse. She welcomes Ralph as a suitor of her mistress and greedily accepts his greeting kisses, first wiping her mouth vigorously. She readily agrees to deliver his love letter to her mistress, who scolds her severely for doing so.

Tibet Talkapace and

Annot Alyface, Dame Christian's maids. Ralph is much taken with them and looks forward to having them around the house after he marries Dame Christian. He is much more eager to exchange greeting kisses with them than with toothless Margery, but they do not cooperate. They help out Dobinet Doughty on his mission to deliver love tokens, but after their scolding by their mistress, they will have no more of the whole business. Armed with spits and other domestic weapons, they aid in the rout of Ralph and his forces.

Gawin Goodluck, a merchant betrothed to Dame Christian. Reasonable and good-natured, he listens patiently to Dame Christian's explanation of Sym Suresby's report and to Tristram Trusty's account of events. He is not angered by Ralph's foolishness and urges Dame Christian to show charity appropriate to her name. Although he finally persuades her to be courteous to Ralph, he cannot persuade her to suffer him gladly.

Sym Suresby, Gawin's loyal servant. He seems as serious as Dame Christian and misinterprets her relations with Ralph. His report to Gawin disturbs the latter and causes some difficulties.

Tristram Trusty, a reliable friend of Gawin and Dame Christian. His trusted judgment and his report of the true situation, at Dame Christian's entreaty, relieve Gawin's mind and lead to the happy reconciliation.

Dobinet Doughty, Ralph's servant-boy. He acts as Ralph's emissary to Dame Christian's house and for a time gains the confidence of Tibet Talkapace and Annot Alyface. He is one of Ralph's defeated warriors in the assault on Dame Christian's house.

Harpax, Ralph's servant. He is a member of Ralph's small defeated army.

A scrivener, who writes Ralph's letter to Dame Christian. After its unfortunate misreading and hostile reception, he and Ralph quarrel.

THE RAMAYANA
(Rāmāyana)

Author: Valmiki (fl. fourth century B.C.E.)
First transcribed: c. 350 B.C.E.
Genre: Poetry

Locale: India
Time: Antiquity
Plot: Epic

Rama, King Dasa-ratha's son, partly an incarnation of Vishnu. The handsomest and strongest of the king's four sons, he wins Sita for his bride by bending the mighty bow of King Janak. Although his aging father wishes him to become regent, he is forced by Queen Kaikeyi into a fourteen-year exile, from which he finally returns triumphant to his throne.

Sita, Rama's wife, the daughter of King Janak and the Earth Mother. She accompanies her husband into exile and is abducted by Ravan. Although she manages to remain faithful to Rama during her captivity, rumors of unfaithfulness are spread abroad and believed by her husband and the people. Finally, her virtue is proved, but the Earth Mother takes her away from those who have doubted her.

King Dasa-ratha, Rama's father, king of the Kosalas, who wishes his son to be regent but must send him, instead, into exile because of an old promise made to Queen Kaikeyi.

Queen Kaikeyi, one of King Dasa-ratha's wives and the mother of Bharat. Promised two boons by her husband, she asks that Rama be sent into exile and that Bharat be made regent.

Bharat, Rama's half brother. Although forced into the re-

gency by Queen Kaikeyi, he recognizes Rama's claim to the throne, which he holds for him.

Lakshman, Rama's loyal brother and his companion during his exile.

Satrughna, another of Rama's half brothers.

Mandavi,

Urmila, and

Sruta-kriti, Rama's sisters-in-law.

King Janak, Sita's father, who offers her as a bride to the one who bends his mighty bow.

The Earth Mother, Sita's mother, who takes her daughter back among the gods when her virtue is questioned by Rama and his people.

Ravan, the Demon King of Lanka. He abducts Sita but is finally overthrown by Rama.

Bharad-vaja,

Valmiki, and

Agastya, hermits and holy men.

Hanuman, a leader of the monkey people.

Manthara, Queen Kaikeyi's maid.

RAMEAU'S NEPHEW
(Le Neveu de Rameau)

Author: Denis Diderot (1713-1784)
First published: 1821
Genre: Novel

Locale: Café de la Régence, Paris, France
Time: An afternoon in 1761
Plot: Philosophical

I, a counterpart of **Diderot** (dee-deh-ROH), the author, who displays not only much of the author's biographical profile but also his progressive Enlightenment philosophy. The daily afternoon strolls in Paris' Palais-Royal gardens that this character takes in order to be alone with his thoughts lead him to encounter, in the Café de la Régence, the eccentric figure of Rameau's nephew, with whom he previously has had only a passing acquaintance. Their subsequent wide-ranging conversation, recorded in dialogue form by I, who occasionally steps out of character to frame a scene descriptively, is the subject of the novella. I generally acts as the levelheaded interlocutor to the younger, more impetuous nephew of Rameau, pleading for the value of reason, goodness, and virtue even as the latter argues insistently for short-term pleasures. I never ceases to marvel at the mass of contradictions present in this paradoxical figure and is particularly puzzled as to how the seemingly complete lack of morality of Rameau's nephew could be coupled with his obviously well-developed aesthetic sensibility. I mostly contents himself with allowing Rameau's nephew to hold forth on an array of topics, including why geniuses are rarely good persons; whether there are substantial differences between one's public and private selves; what constitutes a proper education for girls; whether there are higher ideals in life than mere hedonism; which musical tradition, French or

Italian, provides greater verisimilitude of emotional expression; and whether character traits are hereditary. I sits patiently through loud responses and wild gesturing by Rameau's nephew, conscious of the unwanted attention they periodically attract, and proffers some rational advice as to how Rameau's nephew might resolve his current difficulties. I buys lemonade and beer for Rameau's habitually broke nephew when he grows hoarse and feels a pain in his chest, before watching the idler set off abruptly for a performance at the opera.

Rameau's nephew (rah-MOH), identified as **He**, the ne'er-do-well nephew of famed French composer Jean-Philippe Rameau. I considers He the very model of inconsistency, because He not only seems to embody simultaneously good and evil, as well as reason and folly, but also seems to show up continually with a changed mood or physical appearance. Rameau's nephew is an unambitious shirker who schemes to maintain a high standard of living at the expense of wealthy patrons and benefactors. When He runs into I at the Café de la Régence, He is disconsolate for having just jeopardized the continued patronage of Monsieur Bertin and his mistress, the second-rate actress Mademoiselle Hus. He has fallen out of their favor because of an ill-advised off-color joke he told to an abbé at the dinner table. Although Rameau's nephew does possess some talent as a keyboard composer, He prefers to freeload off the rich, exchanging degrading services such as pet care and incessant flattery for lavish meals and invitations into the finest houses of Paris. As a foil to I's rational Enlightenment man, Rameau's nephew argues that the truth actually can be harmful. He looks to prey on the weakness of others, as this behavior also occurs in Nature; he seeks wealth above virtue and fame, because money excuses all bad behavior; he uses the writings of French playwright Molière to learn how to be a scoundrel without appearing to be one in speech; and he becomes impassioned about the future direction of music, although he neither aspires to be a great composer like his disagreeable uncle nor wishes his own son to grow up to be a musician. Given to histrionic outbursts, He chooses to squander whatever potential he may possess and to continue his irresponsible way of life unabated. At the novella's close, He is seen hurrying off to the opera to carry on his bohemian existence.

— *Gregory J. Racz*

RAMEAU'S NIECE

Author: Cathleen Schine (1953-   )
First published: 1993
Genre: Novel

Locale: Manhattan, New York
Time: Early 1990's
Plot: Bildungsroman

Margaret Nathan, the novel's protagonist. A twenty-eight-year-old Ph.D. in eighteenth century intellectual history, Margaret is known internationally for her best-selling biography, *The Anatomy of Madame de Montigny*. Despite a postdoctoral sinecure and numerous pirzes testifying to her success, Margaret is self-effacing and self-critical. She measures herself against the yardstick of her witty and effervescent husband, Edward, and focuses on her own deficient memory and social awkwardness. Once Margaret begins research for a new book, however, she embarks on an intellectual and sexual quest that fails but nevertheless leads to a better understanding of herself and of Edward.

Edward Ehrenwerth, Margaret's husband, who teaches American literature at Columbia University. An English Jew from Oxford, Edward is articulate and egotistical, but never condescending. He interlaces daily conversation with poetic quotations and literary allusions, and he thrives on bantering with colleagues and lecturing to adoring students. Edward loves Margaret and takes pride in her accomplishments. Even during her personal crisis, Edward is supportive. When Margaret first begins to find fault with their relationship and to project her own desire to commit adultery onto Edward, he meets her bad humor with good-natured tolerance. Later, when Margaret disappears and shows up naked in her editor's bedroom, Edward is more concerned than angry.

Lily, Margaret's friend from college, a feminist art critic. She views the world entirely in feminist paradigms and sees masculinist oppression even in restaurant menus. She is extremely attractive and dresses provocatively, believing that if her tight leather skirt and red lace bodice cause men to leer, it is a reflection on them, not her. Margaret is surprised to find herself leering at Lily and begins to wonder if either or both of them are lesbian. Margaret finally summons the nerve to make a sexual advance toward Lily but is interrupted when Edward, dressed only in a robe, appears in the doorway of Lily's bathroom.

Martin Court, a Belgian who sits next to Margaret on her return flight from a conference in Prague. Without knowing even his name or nationality, Margaret becomes strangely attracted to this handsome, middle-aged man and spends the flight fantasizing about him. A few days later, she is shocked to find Martin on her doorstep. Coincidentally, Margaret had met Martin's parents in Prague and had given them her name as a contact for their son who was soon to be touring the United States. Margaret accompanies Martin on his sightseeing tour in New York and later attempts to seduce him. Martin declines her advances because she is married, drunk, and nearly the same age as his daughter.

Samuel Lipi (originally Lipinsky), Margaret's dentist and the one person in the novel, other than Edward, who does not resist her sexual advances. Unable to converse on any topic but teeth, Dr. Lipi is no intellectual match for Margaret; but his physical resemblance to Michelangelo's David is enough to satisfy her temporarily.

Richard, Margaret's editor. Despite his homosexuality and attempts to keep her at a professional distance, Margaret temporarily falls in love with Richard and takes refuge in his flat when she separates from Edward.

— *Apryl Lea Denny*

THE RAPE OF LUCRECE

Author: William Shakespeare (1564-1616)
First published: 1594
Genre: Poetry

Locale: Rome
Time: 500 B.C.E.
Plot: Tragedy

Sextus Tarquinius (SEHKS-tuhs tahr-KWIH-nee-uhs), or **Tarquin**, the son of the king of Rome and a friend and fellow warrior of Collatine. He hears from the latter of the chastity of his beautiful wife Lucrece and is seized with illicit desire. Like Faustus, he is the allegorical battleground of a good and an evil influence. His good side and his evil side engage in debate, and the evil triumphs. He is hypocritical, sly, and ruthless. Part of the joy in his brutal conquest of the chaste wife stems from sheer cruelty. After his violation of Lucrece, he suffers revulsion and slinks away in the night.

Lucrece (lew-KREES), the chaste wife of Collatine, devoted to her husband. She welcomes his friend as a trusted guest. When she is helpless in Tarquin's clutches, she uses all her intelligence and persuasiveness to try to save herself from him and him from himself, but in vain. After the event, she too becomes the battleground for internal debate: She is uncertain as to whether she should kill herself without telling her hus-band of what she considers her dishonor or to tell him all that has happened. She feels guilt in that her fear may have kept her from using all defenses possible against the ravisher. After making her decision to speak, she sends for Collatine and other Roman leaders. She wears mourning to welcome them, tells her story in full, and stabs herself.

Collatinus (koh-luh-TI-nuhs), also called **Collatine** (KOH-luh-tin), a noble Roman warrior. He is stunned at Lucrece's narrative and suicide, then frantic with grief, then fiercely angry and determined to avenge her. He becomes an eager participant in the overthrow and banishment of the Tarquins (who are referred to very briefly in the final stanza of the poem).

Junius Brutus, who uses Lucrece's body and the dagger stained with her blood to foment the revolution. He accomplishes the overthrow.

THE RAPE OF THE LOCK

Author: Alexander Pope (1688-1744)
First published: 1712
Genre: Poetry

Locale: London, England
Time: Early eighteenth century
Plot: Mock-heroic

Belinda, the poetic name of Arabella Fermor, an upper-class English girl. She is a beautiful young woman and vain of her appearance. Although she is a sweet society girl who loves her spaniel and is normally quite agreeable, she flies into a horrid rage when Lord Petre snips off one of her treasured curls.

Lord Petre, a young nobleman, one of Belinda's suitors. He admires Belinda so much that he wants one of her curls as a keepsake and snips it off at a party when she bends her head over a cup. He refuses to return the curl, and it disappears to become a star.

Ariel, Belinda's guardian spirit. He tries to warn her that something dreadful may happen and sets a guard of sylphs to protect his charge, but he is unsuccessful in preventing the loss of the lock of hair.

Umbriel, a spirit who takes over when Ariel leaves Belinda. He is a melancholy gnome who receives horrible noises, tears, sorrows, and griefs from the queen of bad tempers. He pours his magic substances over Belinda, magnifying her rage and sorrow.

Thalestris, Belinda's friend, a militant girl. She fans Belinda's rage by saying that the girl's honor is at stake in the matter of the stolen curl. She demands that Belinda's brother force Lord Petre to give up the lock.

Clarissa, one of Belinda's acquaintances, who wonders openly at the vanity of women and the foolishness of men.

Sir Plume, Belinda's brother, who considers the entire affair slightly ridiculous. Prodded by Thalestris, he demands that Lord Petre relinquish the lock, but Petre refuses.

Shock, Belinda's beloved spaniel.

Spleen, the queen of bad tempers and the source of detestable qualities in human beings. She supplies Umbriel with magic substances.

Betty, Belinda's maid.

RASHŌMON

Author: Ryūnosuke Akutagawa (Ryūnosuke Niihara, 1892-1927)
First published: 1915
Genre: Novella

Locale: Kyoto, Japan
Time: Late twelfth century
Plot: Fable

An unnamed man, the former servant of a samurai; he lost his position because of a decline of his master's prosperity. Wearing a blue kimono and occasionally picking at a pimple on his cheek, the man is waiting out a rainstorm under the Rashōmon, a gate to the city of Kyoto, the ancient capital of Japan. Depressed and with no means of support, he realizes that he cannot make a living honestly, yet he cannot fully decide to become a thief. The Rashōmon is a devastated place where murderers dispose of bodies. While the man waits for the rain to stop, he sees an old woman pulling hair out of the head of a corpse. At first, he is horrified and filled with rage at the old woman, and his hatred of evil flares up. After hearing her justification for her act, however, he realizes that anything is permitted if it is done as a means of survival. He tears off the old woman's clothes, kicks her down the stairs, and runs away to sell her clothes to buy food.

A nameless old woman, described as an old hag with no more flesh on her arms than on the shanks of a chicken. The old woman plucks out the hairs of a corpse to make a wig to sell. She is not so much a horrible ghoul, however, as she is simply a poverty-stricken unfortunate. In the longest passage of dialogue in the story, the old woman justifies her actions to the unemployed servant by arguing that the woman whose hair she is pulling used to sell dried snake flesh to the barracks guards as dried fish. The old woman claims that because the dead woman did what she did to keep from starving to death, it was not wrong. Similarly, what she does is not wrong either. She makes her case too well, however; the former servant uses her reasoning as justification to tear off her clothes to sell. After being robbed, she groans and grumbles and crawls away. The story ends with the line, "Beyond this was only darkness . . . unknowing and unknown."

— Charles E. May

RASSELAS

Author: Samuel Johnson (1709-1784)
First published: 1759
Genre: Novel

Locale: Abyssinia and Cairo
Time: The eighteenth century
Plot: Philosophical

Rasselas (RAS-eh-luhs), fourth son of the king of Abyssinia. Like his brothers and sisters, he is reared in the luxury of Happy Valley, a remote mountain-rimmed vale whose only entrance is closed by a guarded gate. The royal children live a life of pleasure and entertainment, which everyone but Rasselas finds sufficient. In his twenty-sixth year, he finds his mind unchallenged by this life of pleasure, in which every want is met or anticipated. Feeling that he is something more than a beast of the field, content with sensory pleasure, he lives with his uneasiness until at last he plans to escape into the outer world where, he hopes, he will be able to exercise his choice of life. With a few companions, he finally reaches the outer world and there questions many persons in the hope of learning how to live a contented life. Though he travels great distances and talks with many people, he can find no easy solution to his problems. Everyone seems unhappy. Rasselas begins to dream of establishing a little kingdom, a utopia, which he can rule with justice; but he finally realizes that such an ideal can never be reached, and he decides to return to Abyssinia.

Nekayah (nehk-AY-yah), one of Rasselas' sisters, who is invited to join in her brother's escape. Nekayah proves a happy choice as a companion for Rasselas, for she is an intelligent and observant young woman. She takes the lower classes for her special field of study in the hope of learning how human beings may be happy. Her observations, particularly of domestic life, provide her and Rasselas with much material for thought and discussion. Nekayah finally forms the opinion that knowledge is the key to human happiness. To this end, she makes plans to learn all the sciences and then to establish a college or community of learned women, over which she will preside.

Imlac (IHM-lak), the son of a merchant. Given a chance to travel by his father, Imlac has seen much of the world, both Europe and Asia. After fourteen years of travel, he returns home to find his family dispersed and his fortune gone. Becoming a poet, he seeks to enter Happy Valley and succeeds. He realizes, however, that life in the valley is not sufficient for him. When he finds a fellow rebellious spirit in Rasselas, he offers himself as guide and mentor to the young prince. After emerging from the valley to the outer world Imlac finds that the only answer to happy life is no answer, and so he becomes content to follow life wherever it may lead him.

An Astronomer, a man Rasselas and his companions meet in Egypt, where he joins their party. His devotion to astronomy has convinced him that he controls all the elements except the winds. After he is introduced to Nekayah and the rest of the little band of searchers after wisdom and happiness, the astronomer discovers that life has more in it than the study of the heavens, and he loses his beliefs. Like Imlac, he becomes satisfied with whatever life may bring to him.

A Mechanist, one of the inhabitants of Happy Valley. He tries to invent wings that will enable him to fly. Rasselas, anxious to escape his valley prison, is quite interested in the man's experiments until the efforts prove entirely futile.

Pekuah (PEHK-oo-ah), one of the noble ladies attending Princess Nekayah; she is another of the escapees from Happy Valley. She has an extraordinary adventure in which she is kidnapped by Arabs and held for ransom. She bears this trying experience with fortitude and returns to her friends to report that Bedouin life is not a happy one for either men or women.

A Philosopher, whom Rasselas seeks out in Egypt. He seems at first to be both wise and happy. His life proves empty, however, as does his logic, when his only child, a beautiful daughter, is taken suddenly by death.

A Hermit, another of the seemingly wise and happy souls sought out by Rasselas. The hermit, at one time a military officer of high rank, renounced his worldly career to seek happiness in a hermitage. He admits to Rasselas that his life is not a happy one, and he returns with Rasselas to the society of Cairo.

An Old Man, whom Rasselas and Nekayah consult. They visit him to learn if old age is the key to happiness. They are told that it is not; the old man finds neither solace nor pleasure in having outlived his friends and rivals, as well as his capacity to work or hold office.

THE RAT
(Die Ratten)

Author: Günter Grass (1927-)
First published: 1986
Genre: Novel

Locale: Germany, Sweden, and Poland
Time: 1984
Plot: Social

Harry Liebenau, the narrator, a writer employed by video producer Oskar Matzerath. Liebenau, obviously representing the author himself, is a writer from Danzig who was a character in Grass's *Dog Years* (1963).

Oskar Matzerath (MAH-tseh-raht), a three-foot-tall, humpbacked drummer who also appeared in Grass's *The Tin Drum* (1959). He is now a prosperous, bald, sixty-year-old video producer who wears too many rings and dresses in suits with large checks. Oskar agrees to the narrator's suggestion to produce a film that would utilize a fairy tale motif to depict the unwillingness of the government to confront the destruction of Germany's forests by acid rain. As the production goes forward, Oskar is driven to Poland in his Mercedes to attend the 107th birthday celebration of his grandmother, Anna Koljaiczek. His surprise gift to her is a video produced by his company, which had foreseen and recorded in advance everything that would happen at the birthday celebration. In the She-rat's version of events, the video predicts the destruction of humanity in the midst of the party. Oskar's grandmother survives for a while after the holocaust, but, after her death, she and a desiccated Oskar become objects of worship for the rats. In the narrator's alternate version of events, the nuclear holocaust does not occur and Oskar, though afflicted with an enlarged prostate, survives to celebrate his sixtieth birthday and learn of his grandmother's death.

The Rat, a gray-brown female rat, which the narrator receives as a Christmas present. The She-rat invades the narrator's dreams in a vision of the nuclear destruction of humanity and its replacement by rats. Rats, foreseeing humanity's suicidal bent, retreat underground when their warnings go unheeded. They survive the Armageddon, which they regard as inevitable and trigger by gnawing the microchips in the controlling computers of the superpowers. The She-rat shares with the narrator the rats' efforts to construct a posthuman society and their final victory over a race of mutant rat-men, called Watsoncricks and manipples, the products of late human genetic engineering. Banding together under the slogan "Solidarity," the rats of Danzig exterminate the parasitic and authoritarian rat-men and free themselves of the last vestiges of human exploitation and aggressiveness.

Damroka, the narrator's wife, a tall blonde with flowing hair. Damroka, an organist, purchases and refits an old sailing barge, which she christens *The New Ilsebill*. She recruits four fellow feminists to join her on a research voyage to sample the levels of jellyfish infestation in the Baltic. Damroka's actual goal is the sunken Wendish city of Jumne, or Vineta, which had once been governed by a matriarchy. She is counseled in her quest by the talking Flounder from Grass's novel *The Flounder* (1977). In the She-rat's story, the endlessly knitting and regularly contentious women find the city but, before descending to it, are incinerated in the nuclear catastrophe. In the narrator's version of reality, the scientific mission is completed and Damroka, having failed to find her Vinetan utopia, returns home.

Hansel, also called **Johannes**, and

Gretel, also called **Margarethe**, the "punk" children of the West German chancellor. The boy is fifteen years old and resembles Störtebeker, the teenage gang leader from *The Tin Drum*. The thirteen-year-old girl is similar to the thin and malicious Tulla Pokriefke of *Dog Years*. Hansel and Gretel, in rebellion, run away from the chancellor and his materialistic and corrupt society. They join forces with Jacob Grimm (the Federal Republic's minister for forests, rivers, lakes and fresh air), his brother Wilhelm, his undersecretary, and an array of Grimm characters in an effort to reverse the ecological destruction of Germany. The military and the industrialists, however, with the blessing of the clergy, ruthlessly crush the fairy tale so that their version of reality might prevail.

Lothar Malskat, a painter from Königsberg who, when hired to restore remnants of Gothic murals, replaces the unsalvageable originals with his own brilliant but eclectic work. His forgeries are universally touted as glorious examples of northern Gothic. Oskar wants to produce a film about Malskat, who had publicly admitted the hoax. In Oskar's opinion, the true forgers of postwar Germany were Konrad Adenauer and Walter Ulbricht, who had opportunistically crafted the façades of their new German states to win the support of their respective occupying powers.

— *Bernard A. Cook*

RAT MAN OF PARIS

Author: Paul West (1930-)
First published: 1986
Genre: Novel

Locale: Paris and Nice, France
Time: 1944 and 1983
Plot: Psychological

Etienne Poulsifer (ay-TYEH[N] pewl-see-FEHR), the eponymous "Rat Man of Paris," a Parisian boulevardier famous for accosting strangers and flashing, from beneath his coat, a rat (later only a decrepit fox fur that once belonged to his mother). He is an emaciated, haunted figure in his fifties

who lives on the meager sum that he extorts from strangers. Orphaned when the inhabitants of his childhood village were exterminated by the Nazis, Rat Man has spent his adulthood trying to forget the war. When he sees in a newspaper that a Nazi war criminal is to return to France and stand trial for his crimes, Rat Man creates elaborate street spectacles to awaken the nation's conscience. After being shot and convalescing, Rat Man fathers a child and arrives at a new sense of meaning in his existence.

Sharli Bandol (shahr-LEE bahn-DOHL), a grammar school teacher, an attractive woman in her thirties. She meets Rat Man at a café and essentially adopts him. As she comes to love Rat Man, he is also her obsession, someone she wants to civilize and nurture with her love. In many ways, Rat Man appears to be her opposite, yet they are significantly alike in their desperate emotional need to love and be loved. After his injury, she removes Rat Man to Nice, France, where she becomes pregnant, and the two settle down to an eccentric experiment in parenthood.

Boche (bewsh), initially an anonymous Nazi war criminal whom Rat Man believes responsible for killing his parents and neighbors. Except for a description of his picture in the newspaper, Boche is present only in Rat Man's fevered mind. Eventually, the reader learns that this is not the man stationed in Rat Man's village, but Klaus Barbie.

The Spanish novelist, an anonymous figure who is described as thin, dark, and hook-nosed. Rat Man believes that this figure follows him for the purpose of later using him in a novel. Although Sharli and the reader doubt his existence, the narrator eventually reveals that he is an actual person who contemplates but then rejects Rat Man as a subject for fiction.

Madame R., a large, impatient, insensitive native of Rat Man's village who shelters him for a few years. Loud and unaffectionate, she would tie the boy to a bed for days, then berate him for soiling the sheets and hose him off with cold water.

Alphonse (ahl-FOHNS), a janitor at the Paris jail where Rat Man erroneously believes that Boche is incarcerated. For payment in brandy, Alphonse pretends to smuggle personal effects of Boche's (used tissues and clippings of hair) to Rat Man. The latter soon realizes that these effects are a hoax.

Charles De Gaulle Poulsifer (shahrl deh gohl), Rat Man and Sharli's infant son. Rat Man begins feeling jealous of the child but grows to have a sense of cool affection for him. He resolves to protect the child from the horrors that have blighted his life.

— *David W. Madden*

RATES OF EXCHANGE

Author: Malcolm Bradbury (1932-   )
First published: 1983
Genre: Novel

Locale: Eastern Europe
Time: 1981
Plot: Parody

Angus Petworth, a British professor of linguistics on a cultural visit to Slaka (the capital of an imaginary Eastern European country), where he is to give a series of lectures on the English language. Middle-aged, somewhat lonely, and vaguely dissatisfied with his staid life, Petworth is a hesitant adventurer in the overwhelmingly foreign world of Slaka. Pensive and observant, he interprets much of what befalls him in terms of the theories of communication, which are his field. Partly because of his difficulty with the constantly changing language of Slaka, Petworth is taciturn and passive under the direction of his several guides.

Marisja Lubijova, Petworth's official guide. Tense and white-faced in a mohair hat, Marisja studies at the university in Slaka. Humorous, sarcastic, efficient, and knowledgeable, she is also extremely protective and (it appears) somewhat infatuated with Petworth. She is frequently outspoken and opinionated and is suspicious of the other Slakans who vie for Petworth's attention.

Katya Princip, a free-spirited, confident, and uninhibited magical-realist novelist with whom Petworth has a brief affair. Adventurous and emotional, beautiful Katya lives life to the fullest. Beneath her charming and exuberant exterior, there is a certain hard-edged and practical self-interest. She is aware of the risks that she takes in getting involved with Petworth, and there is a suggestion that she has used her several husbands and lovers for her own advancement. Impulsive and strong-willed, she effectively whisks away a willing but passive Petworth on her escapades.

Felix Steadiman, the meticulously attired British cultural attaché in Slaka. With a stammer that seems to result mostly in puns of a sexual nature and a careless disregard for the various restrictions placed on him by the Slakan government, Steadiman seems singularly unsuited to a diplomatic career. An atrocious driver, he runs over and kills a peasant while traveling through a part of the country that is off-limits to foreigners, thereby effecting his expulsion from Slaka. Rather inclined to stray himself, he is unconcerned by his wife's nymphomania.

Budgie Steadiman, Felix's wife. She seeks to alleviate the oppressive boredom and monotony of life in Slaka with a kind of determined sexual adventurism. Sexually aggressive and incredibly indiscreet, she virtually attacks Petworth on several occasions, necessitating some rough if good-natured manhandling by Felix to separate them.

Doctor Plitplov, a small, tidy, bird-eyed man with a neatly trimmed beard and a large, curving pipe. He is vague and obsequious, and he seems to turn up everywhere that Petworth goes. Connected with the university, Plitplov is pompous and always insists that he is correct in everything, from his English usage to his opinions on Ernest Hemingway to his assessment of the workings of the Slakan political and social machine. He hints at a connection with Petworth's wife while he was a summer student at the University of Cambridge, and he may be Katya Princip's current "useful" lover. Sly, suggestive, and always appearing to know more than he tells, Plitplov subtly claims responsibility for many of the events of Petworth's visit.

Lottie Petworth, Petworth's small, dark wife. She does not actually appear in the novel but is spoken of often enough to afford some insight into Petworth. He senses that she is unhappy and longs for some sort of fulfillment that he cannot provide, but he understands little more than this. The impression is of a loveless yet comfortably secure marriage that leaves both members seeking satisfaction elsewhere but not willing to give up an established domesticity that provides a measure of secure regularity in an uncertain world.

Professor Rom Rum, a respected Slakan academic. He writes articles in the state-run newspaper on literary subjects, specializing in Anthony Trollope. He is possibly Katya Princip's lover and "protector."

Tankic, a high official in the Ministry of Culture. He speaks very little English. By the end of the novel, after an undefined coup or shift of power, he appears to have become the minister of culture.

— *Catherine Swanson*

A RAT'S MASS

Author: Adrienne Kennedy (1931-   )
First published: 1968
Genre: Drama

Locale: A house called "Rat's Chapel"
Time: The 1960's
Plot: Surrealism

Brother Rat, also known as **Blake**, who is in conflict between his need to protect his sister and his love for Rosemary. He believes that he and Sister Rat are damned unless Rosemary saves them. A light black man with a human body but the head and the tail of a rat, Blake wants to return to the innocent time before, at Rosemary's urging, he copulated with his sister on the playground slide to prove his love for Rosemary. His sister's dead child and her return from a mental institution, as well as the secrecy that both have promised on Rosemary's Holy Communion prayer book and their own father's Bible, culminate in synaesthetic imagery of attic worms, gnawing attic rats, Nazis, and communion wine of all sisters' blood. Blake recognizes that his obsession for Rosemary betrays both him and his sister. Brother Rat believes that he and his sister will be murdered but hopes that new life can come after the battle.

Sister Rat, also known as **Kay**, Blake's sister. On her first day home from the mental institution, she believes that she has been betrayed by her mother, God, and Blake. A light black woman with the head of a human but the stomach and the tail of a rat, she cries constantly and wants Blake to protect her from herself as well as the gnawing rats, the Nazis, and the Procession but does not trust that he will. Desperately lighting candles with her brother against the invading battle sounds, she remembers their adoration of Rosemary's Italian ancestry and her Catholic practices. Kay longs for the return of the holy time, before she was sent to Georgia to bear her brother's baby. Kay is on constant guard against others who may be eavesdropping. She wants to forget but knows that neither she nor her brother ever will.

Sister Rat also believes that she and Brother Rat will be murdered.

Rosemary, the most beautiful child in school, jealous of Brother Rat and Sister Rat's family bond. A proud Italian Catholic who wears a white First Communion dress and who attends catechism classes, Rosemary "has worms in her hair." She wishes to destroy Brother Rat and Sister Rat's allegiance to each other. Rosemary entices Blake into initiating sexual intercourse with his sister and then watches. She forces them to swear an oath of secrecy. Later, Rosemary denies Blake's plea to save them and suggests instead that he shoot himself in the head with his father's shotgun. While Sister Rat prays, Rosemary asks Blake to come with her, but Blake refuses because he realizes that he cannot recover the innocence of spring with Rosemary. Rosemary, too, hears the Nazis, but she interprets their approach as her wedding to Blake, a wedding that climaxes in the shotgun murder of both Brother Rat and Sister Rat.

The Procession, made up of **Jesus**, **Joseph**, **Mary**, **Two Wise Men**, and a **Shepherd**. The Procession serves as the connection between past and present. Watching and marching with malignant potential, the characters in the Procession represent the approaching Nazis. Aware of the Procession's malevolent power, Kay and Blake threaten to hang its characters to gain their own freedom. The Procession believes the time to have been Easter. With no place in a resurrection scenario, they exit, only to return with shotguns. The Procession does not allow Brother Rat and Sister Rat to escape; its members shoot until both are dead.

— *Kathleen Mills*

RAVENSHOE

Author: Henry Kingsley (1830-1876)
First published: 1862
Genre: Novel

Locale: England
Time: Early nineteenth century
Plot: Domestic

Father Mackworth, the resident priest at Ravenshoe, who engages in nefarious schemes to prevent Ravenshoe from becoming the property of a Protestant heir. He dies after confessing his plots and begging forgiveness of the heir he has dispossessed.

Charles Ravenshoe, the second son of Densil Ravenshoe and his Protestant wife. When Charles's mother dies in childbirth, Densil promises her that her son will be reared as a Protestant. He is reared by Norah, the gamekeeper's wife, along with her own son, William. To prevent Charles from inheriting Ravenshoe, Father Mackworth says that Norah switched the babies in her care and that William, a Catholic, is the true heir. Charles then becomes a servant and later enlists in the army to fight in the Crimea, where he is wounded. Charles finally learns that he is the true heir to Ravenshoe. He then marries and shows great leniency to William.

Densil Ravenshoe, Charles's father, who as a young man goes off to London and falls in with Lord Saltire, an atheist. He finally returns to the church but marries a Protestant woman.

Adelaide Summers, the ward of Lady Ascot. Charles falls in love with Adelaide, but she runs away with Lord Welter, Charles's cousin. She is a vain young woman and not worthy of Charles's love.

Lord Welter, Charles's cousin, a wild and dissolute young man with whom Charles carouses when they are both at Oxford. He becomes Adelaide's lover, and she and Welter live by gambling. Eventually, they are married.

Mary Corby, the daughter of the captain of a ship that goes down in the bay at Ravenshoe, leaving her an orphan. A good and sweet girl, she becomes the ward of the Ravenshoes. She falls in love with Charles and eventually marries him.

William Horton, Norah's son, who is reared with Charles. Father Mackworth says that William is the true heir to Ravenshoe and William takes over the estate when Cuthbert, the elder son, dies. In the end, William and Charles become good friends.

Lord Saltire, an atheist and a good friend of Densil Ravenshoe. Later, he meets Charles and becomes fond of him. When Lord Saltire dies, he leaves a large sum to Mary. Thinking that Charles has died in the Crimea, he leaves the rest of his fortune to Lord Welter and Adelaide.

Cuthbert Ravenshoe, Densil's elder son, reared as a Catholic. He dies by drowning.

Ellen Horton, William's sister who, it later turns out, is really Charles's sister. Ellen runs away to become a nun, taking with her the evidence that Charles is truly the heir of Ravenshoe. She later produces this evidence and then returns to her nursing duties.

THE RAVISHING OF LOL STEIN
(Le Ravissement de Lol V. Stein)

Author: Marguerite Duras (1914-1996)
First published: 1964
Genre: Novel

Locale: The resort towns of South Tahla and Town Beach
Time: The 1950's and early 1960's
Plot: Antistory

Lol Valerie Stein, a young woman who is jilted by her fiancé. At the age of nineteen, Lol, a beautiful blue-eyed blond, is engaged to Michael Richardson, who later, at a ball, abandons her for another woman, Anne-Marie Stretter. Lol, led home by her mother, suffers a mental collapse and is secluded. Lol's apparent madness stems not from the rejection but from her lack of emotional depth, which has been evident since childhood. Her distress at leaving the ball is caused not by the pain of losing a lover but by not being able to follow Michael and Anne-Marie to witness their intense passion, thus experiencing love vicariously. Later, after briefly meeting John Bedford, she marries him and moves away from South Tahla. After her return ten years later, she takes long walks; renews her acquaintance with Tatiana Karl, a friend from her school days; and acquires a lover, Jack Hold, one of Tatiana's conquests. Her greatest pleasure, however, is derived from watching for glimpses of Jack and Tatiana through a hotel window as she lies in a field of rye.

Michael Richardson, a young, wealthy heir with no vocation. Cultured and brilliant, Michael, at the age of twenty-five, is engaged to Lol Stein. At a ball, however, he becomes infatuated with a stranger, Anne-Marie Stretter, and leaves at dawn with her. Rumors circulate that they separate after a few months and that he liquidates his large landholdings in the vicinity of South Tahla so that he can follow her to Calcutta.

Anne-Marie Stretter, the wife of the French consul to India. Elegant but older than Michael Richardson, she enthralls him to the point where he rejects Lol Stein. After they have a short affair, she chooses not to leave her husband.

John Bedford, Lol's husband, a talented musician. After a single chance encounter with Lol during an evening walk, he proposes marriage, intrigued by her vacuity. During their marriage of more than ten years, he is content, pleased with Lol, with their three children, and with their home and garden, meticulously ordered and arranged by Lol and patterned after displays and examples she discovers in stores and magazines. He never questions her lack of interest in common social activities but prefers her blankness.

Tatiana Karl, Lol's best friend, sensuous, with long black hair. Tatiana, although married to Peter Breugner, chooses to amuse herself with a series of lovers. She is as close as anyone can be to Lol, having known her as a schoolgirl, having comforted her the night of the ball, and, most recently, constituting part of Lol's plan to be, surreptitiously, with a pair of lovers.

Peter Breugner, a successful doctor who is married to Tatiana. Unknown to his wife, he is aware of and tolerates her many affairs.

Jack Hold, the narrator of the novel, a thirty-six-year-old doctor who is a friend of Peter Breugner and a lover of Tatiana Karl. Jack is enchanted with Lol, mystified by the enigma that she is. After falling in love with her, he pieces together the story of her teenage years, her madness, and her life with her husband. At first unknown to him, he is part of Lol's voyeuristic interests, but later he knowingly complies with her wishes.

— *Barbara Wiedemann*

A RAW YOUTH
(Podrostok)

Author: Fyodor Dostoevski (1821-1881)
First published: 1875
Genre: Novel

Locale: St. Petersburg, with flashbacks to Moscow
Time: The 1870's
Plot: Psychological realism

Arkady Makarovitch Dolgoruky (ahr-KAH-dee mah-KAH-roh-vihch dol-goh-REW-kee), the narrator and "raw youth" of the title. He is a boy of some talents but no social polish, and his attempts to strike a course for himself in life are hampered by his confusing social position and his unorthodox family situation. He is the legal son of a servant, the natural son of an aristocrat, and a volatile character, even by the standards of Russian literature. He is an exemplar of the dual nature, combining in himself a craggy, low selfishness with high principles and a warm, effusive love of others. The personality built on this cracked foundation is unformed and ill-directed. He is as likely to break out in shouted insults, or to remain haughtily silent, as to be gushingly affectionate. Arkady has a powerful talent for solitude. His ambition is to become a "Rothschild," a man of immeasurable wealth and influence. Like his natural father, he is neither good nor bad but has a double nature and can be pulled both ways. Although he has this dual nature, he is good, because he understands that he is divided and must struggle to support his better self. The knowledge that he is divided, that he has no true strength over his own soul, gives him humility, which, in the eyes of the author, is close to true holiness.

Andrei Versilov (ahn-DRAY vehr-SIH-lov), Arkady's natural father, a nobleman. He is a figure in society, with a questionable reputation. In the first section of the novel, Arkady, in the bitterness of adolescence, is misled by a number of coincidences and, jumping to conclusions, denounces Versilov as an evil and degraded man. When Arkady finds out his mistake, he comes to love and esteem Versilov. He is revealed, through Arkady's eyes, as a true cosmopolitan, endowed with the noblest progressive European spirit and committed to a utopian vision. Behind this truth, Versilov has a baser nature, a second self, that has an equal claim on him. He brings it out in a symbolic act: He breaks an icon, showing his rejection of religion. By the book's end, he has changed for the better and come to terms with his other self. He does so, however, with the knowledge that he has not overcome it, that he lives with it still.

Makar Dolgoruky (mah-KAHR), Arkady's legal father, a religious pilgrim. In the many years since he lost his wife to Versilov, he has spent his time wandering across Russia, begging, going from shrine to shrine. His religion is not at all ideological but something more than an attitude. He is infinitely resigned, to the point of refusing to take pride even in his piety and obedience. This beatific disposition has a profound effect on Arkady's extended family, particularly on Arkady himself. Enfeebled by age and his travels, he comes to stay with them. While Arkady is recovering from an illness, sunk in his worldly concerns, Makar distracts him, changing his own joy in the mystery of the world for Arkady's dreadful, scientific certainties. Although Makar, desperately ill himself, dies soon afterward, it is his vision of the world that survives after Versilov's own weaknesses have shown themselves.

Sofia Dolgoruky, Makar's wife, the mother of Arkady by Versilov. She takes little part in the action of the book but remains its domestic center, perhaps because of the calming effect she has on her two random and rampant men, her lover and her son. She had had a passionate affair with Versilov when she was his servant. Now that she is past middle age, he still has an emotional attachment to her (at least when his better self is dominant) and to her kind nature and selflessness. This attachment is perhaps not so surprising as that this pious woman had a passionate affair. She does not renounce it, although she feels that she must atone for it. This affair is her dual nature, and her humility in the face of her sin is, again, the author's true piety.

— *Fritz Monsma*

THE RAZOR'S EDGE

Author: W. Somerset Maugham (1874-1965)
First published: 1944
Genre: Novel

Locale: Chicago, Paris, and India
Time: 1919-1944
Plot: Psychological realism

Larry Darrell, a young American who flew with the Canadian Air Force in World War I. He is twenty years old at the beginning of the novel and in his forties by the end of it. Experiencing the horrors of war changes Larry: He becomes solemn and introspective, restlessly seeking answers to the ultimate age-old questions about life, death, God, and the nature of evil. Turning down the offer of a lucrative job, Larry spends several years in Paris reading anything he hopes may contain an answer to his questions. He works in a mine in France and a farm in Germany, lives in an ashram in India, and enters a Benedictine monastery in Bonn. At the end of the novel, he gives away all of his money and sails to New York to become a taxi driver.

Isabel Bradley Maturin, who is engaged to Larry Darrell at the beginning of the novel. She marries Gray Maturin when Larry refuses to return with her to Chicago. She is nineteen years old when the novel opens. She genuinely loves Larry but cannot think of marrying a man who will not work for a living. She has been brought up in luxury and has no intention of living without it. She adapts well to losing her fortune in the stock market crash, but that is easy to do, because she spends the Depression in her uncle Elliott Templeton's fashionable Paris apartment. Selfish and materialistic, she contributes to Sophie Macdonald's suicide by offering her liquor, knowing that Sophie is a recovering alcoholic.

Gray Maturin, a rising young stockbroker, Isabel's husband, twenty years old at the start of the novel. His father started him at the bottom of his brokerage firm, but by the end of the novel, Gray is running it. Like his father, Gray takes pride in looking out for his clients and believes that he is doing his part to make America prosperous and powerful. Gray loses everything in the stock market crash, however, and suffers a nervous collapse, which Larry Darrell cures with a technique he learned from an Indian yogi.

Elliott Templeton, Isabel's uncle, a social climber in his late fifties at the beginning of the novel. A snob who made his fortune dealing in art, Elliott sneers at his social inferiors, having finally climbed above them. Taking pride in his impeccable taste in fashion, cuisine, manners, and art, Elliott gives advice on all four throughout the novel. His only purpose in life is to hobnob with the European aristocracy, but as he ages, Elliott finds himself less and less in demand at their parties. His last act, while on his deathbed, is to send a haughty answer to a princess who snubbed him by not inviting him to her fancy ball.

Sophie Macdonald, a quiet, introspective girl, tall and thin, who grew up with Larry Darrell in Marvin, Illinois, and dies in debauched squalor in France near the end of the novel. She appears in the first chapter as a young adult, a friend of Isabel Bradley, at a dinner given by Isabel's mother. A few years later, she marries a lawyer, Bob Macdonald, and bears him a child who is killed with Bob in a car crash. Sophie, crazed with grief, flees to Paris, where she drowns her pain in alcohol, opium, and indiscriminate sex. Larry helps her to put aside this decadence for a while and plans to marry her, but jealous

Isabel returns Sophie to her squalor by tempting her to drink again. Sophie disappears until the police find her dead, half-naked body in the river in Toulon, her throat cut.

W. Somerset Maugham, the author and narrator, who appears as a character in the novel. Maugham plays only a peripheral role in the lives of the other characters, but he is able to piece together their stories from conversations. Because he is a writer, the other characters trust him with their most intimate secrets, making him an ideal narrator. He possesses insight into human nature, and especially into Larry Darrell, that other characters lack: He is the first to realize the nature of Larry's search for answers, he comforts Elliott Templeton when others abandon him, and he identifies Sophie Macdonald's body and pays for her funeral in Paris. As narrator, Maugham is able to present the foibles of other characters without being judgmental.

— John R. Holmes

THE REAL LIFE OF SEBASTIAN KNIGHT

Author: Vladimir Nabokov (1899-1977)
First published: 1941
Genre: Novel

Locale: Europe, primarily London and Paris
Time: The 1890's-1936
Plot: Biographical

Sebastian Knight, a Russian émigré writer of dubious artistic talent and merit. His untimely death at the age of thirty-six from congenital heart disease prompts the investigation into his life by his half brother, V., that is the subject of the novel. Beginning with his college years at Cambridge, Sebastian takes great pains to affect English manners and tastes, although ample evidence exists that he never quite masters his adopted language. Occasional ham-handed quotations from his five published books of fiction, bearing such improbable titles as *The Prismatic Bezel* and *The Doubtful Asphodel*, attest this (disputed) shortcoming. A difficult, aloof, even contemptuous man, Sebastian pens three early works under the "inspiration" of Clare Bishop, whom he meets during his student days. A second mystery woman encountered while at a sanatorium in Blauberg, Germany, may have exerted even more influence over his final writings, as well as his physical and psychological well-being. Sebastian's sometimes stilted and cumbrous prose ultimately belies his avowed pretensions to high art, and nagging suspicions persist as to just how autobiographically his fiction ought to be read.

V., Sebastian's younger half brother and arguably the novel's main character. His confessed lack of literary understanding hampers his attempt to write Sebastian's biography two months after the latter's demise. V. is at best a biased and unreliable interpreter of Sebastian's life and works. His various assessments often are debatable, if not laughably inaccurate, because they frequently are colored by his personal relationships with the writer and his circle of acquaintances. V.'s most common error is to assume a direct connection between life and art in Sebastian's oeuvre as he proceeds with his chronological research into the elusive life of this sibling, who barely took notice of his existence while alive. V.'s hasty character judgments and notable discomfort around the two most influential women in Sebastian's life render his literary biography even more suspect.

Mr. Goodman, Sebastian's invaluable secretary after his breakup with Clare, and the author of the critically acclaimed *The Tragedy of Sebastian Knight*, which scoops V.'s less reliable volume in the making. The disorganized and impractical Sebastian relies heavily on Goodman until the latter is discovered to have made an unauthorized deletion in one of his reissued works, after which Goodman is promptly dismissed. Although potentially as biased and unreliable a biographer as is V., Goodman generally paints a more accurate picture of the writer as distant and uncongenial. He suffers V.'s unwarranted ridicule for his apparently sound historical thesis depicting Sebastian as a modern idealist out of sync with his times. Goodman tries to dissuade V. from completing his planned rival biography; it becomes clear that his own work is rife with errors and omissions.

Clare Bishop, the attractive English art student who is for a time Sebastian's secretary, live-in lover, and muse. Clare remains with Sebastian until her literary ambitions for the author clash with his abhorrence of the bohemian circles and artsy soirees in which she foresees them mingling. An increasingly bored and surly Sebastian unceremoniously banishes her from the train platform when she tries to accompany him as a surprise on his trip to Blauberg. Clare later marries a man who refuses to allow V. to interview her about her relationship to Sebastian. She dies, possibly by her own hand, beside an empty cradle.

Mr. Silberman, a former toy salesman and detective of unknown origin, and a current hawker of leather goods. Silberman's chance encounter with V. on a train during the latter's return from unproductive inquiries in Blauberg concerning the mystery woman of Sebastian's last few months leads Silberman to promise that he will acquire the names of those women whose stay at the sanatorium coincided with Sebastian's. In exchange for the four possibilities he uncovers, Silberman asks only a minuscule fee and one copy of V.'s forthcoming biography.

Madame Lecerf, the unhappily married Parisian friend of Helene von Graun who invites V. to meet her constantly traveling former schoolmate at the Lecerf summer residence in Lescaux, France. V.'s suspicion that Helene is the most probable candidate to have been Sebastian's mystery woman in Blauberg leads him to conduct various interviews with Lecerf concerning what Helene has told her about the snobbish intellectual with whom she once carried on an affair. The fact that V. never meets Helene, that Lecerf volunteers to have Helene communicate to V. through her, and that Lecerf herself fits the personality description of the woman he believes ruined Sebastian leads V. to conclude, perhaps incorrectly, that Lecerf actually is Helene.

— *Gregory J. Racz*

THE REAL THING

Author: Tom Stoppard (Tomas Straussler, 1937-   )
First published: 1982
Genre: Drama

Locale: England
Time: The 1980's
Plot: Comedy

Henry, a successful playwright in his forties for whom writing about love is difficult. His play, *A House of Cards*, has just opened. Its first act is the first act of *The Real Thing*. Henry, a partially autobiographical character, changes in the course of the play as he is educated in what love is by the three women in his life: his former wife, his current wife, and his daughter. Acknowledging to his precocious teenage daughter the verity of her perception of him as an ironist in public and a prig in private, he reluctantly accepts modern attitudes toward marriage as the result of his wife's affairs and his daughter's colorfully honest appraisal of him. As a husband, he takes his wives for granted and leaves them with unfulfilled needs. His belief in the artist's removal from personal emotions and political causes creates tensions with Annie, as it had with his first wife. As an artist, he believes in the innocence, neutrality, and precision of words as the means for building "bridges across incomprehension and chaos" and regards his short-lived rival in love, Brodie, as a writer of rubbish. Even so, he finally admits that in love, unlike art, "dignified cuckoldry, although difficult, can be done."

Annie, Henry's second wife, a twenty-five-year-old actress and activist in political marches. She is Henry's mistress at the start of the play. Like her predecessor, Charlotte, in Henry's real life, she takes lovers and argues with Henry about her needs. Her roles bring her into close contact with Billy, another actor, and her activism in liberal movements involves her with a politically committed dramatist, Brodie, who is boorish and artistically inferior to Henry. She reacts angrily to Henry's jealousy of Brodie with a reference to Henry's "fastidious taste."

Brodie, a twenty-five-year-old loutish dramatist who has spent time in prison as a result of his protests against nuclear missiles and other political injustices. He meets Annie on a train en route to a demonstration and interests her in a role in his television play. As a dramatist committed to causes, he writes with his "guts" and is incensed when he discovers that Henry, at Annie's request, has rewritten a television play that Brodie wrote.

Charlotte, Henry's former wife, roughly thirty-five years old, who serves as a double character—in Henry's play and in *The Real Thing*. In both, she is the unfaithful wife. She informs Henry that he cannot write plays about women and that she has had a number of lovers, the most recent of whom was an architect. In the play within the play, Charlotte is married to Max, who is also an architect. Charlotte, as Henry's former wife, educates him regarding his erroneous view of marriage as a commitment that is finished when made, insisting that it needs daily renewal.

Debbie, Charlotte and Henry's very modern seventeen-year-old daughter, who has her own advice for Henry in regard to his marital problems. She states that free love is free of the old propaganda and that exclusive rights to a person "isn't love, it's colonization." Her father's own daughter, she is as articulate about her views on free love as Henry is about his love of language.

Billy, an actor, about twenty-two years old, with whom Annie rehearses love scenes from August Strindberg's *Miss Julie* and John Ford's *'Tis Pity She's a Whore*. Both rehearsals become metaphors for Annie's affair with Billy. Billy likes the content of Brodie's plays even as he recognizes that Henry is a much better writer.

Max, who is about forty years old, also an actor and a double character who appears in both plays. In *The House of Cards*, he is the architect, and in *The Real Thing*, he is in love with Annie and, consequently, despondent at the news of her affair with Henry. He eventually falls in love again and calls at the end to inform Henry that if it were not for Henry, he would not be currently engaged. His roles in both the play and the play within the play are minor.

— *Susan Rusinko*

REBECCA

Author: Daphne du Maurier (1907-1989)
First published: 1938
Genre: Novel

Locale: England
Time: The 1930's
Plot: Gothic

Maximilian (Maxim) de Winter, middle-aged owner of Manderley. He is detached, moody, mysterious, at times gracious, friendly, and apologetic for his seeming rudeness, only to return unaccountably to his reserve. This reserve is finally removed with the lifting of the burden on his conscience.

Mrs. de Winter, Maxim's young wife, the narrator. A shy, sensitive orphan, she first meets Maxim through her older traveling companion, Mrs. Van Hopper. Deeply in love with him, she happily accepts his proposal and marries him. Puzzled and troubled by Maxim's strange shifts of mood and his abstracted manner and by Mrs. Danvers' obvious dislike of her, she thinks herself unwelcome, an inferior successor to Rebecca at Manderley. Desiring Maxim's love, she yet remains aloof because of her brooding insecurity and thus hinders his revealing his painful memories to her.

Rebecca de Winter, Maxim's dead wife, a very beautiful woman who charmed many people but who tortured her husband with flagrant infidelities. When she learned that she would soon die of cancer, she taunted her husband with a false story of her unborn child by another man until she drove him to murder her.

Mrs. Danvers, the housekeeper at Manderley. Tall, gaunt, with a face like a death's head, she is cold, formal, and resentful of the new Mrs. de Winter, who has replaced the Rebecca she adored. She is the first to reveal to Mrs. de Winter what Rebecca really was like with men. After the closing of the inquiry into Rebecca's death, Mrs. Danvers apparently sets fire to Manderley and disappears.

Frank Crawley, estate manager at Manderley. A thin, colorless bachelor, he is a devoted friend of Maxim.

Jack Favell, Rebecca's cousin, tanned and good looking, but flashy, with hot, blue eyes and a loose mouth. He is a heavy drinker who attempts to blackmail Maxim after the discovery of Rebecca's sunken boat.

Colonel Julyan, a magistrate who suspects the truth about Rebecca's death but keeps it to himself.

Mrs. Van Hopper, an overbearing American social climber who forces herself upon Maxim at Monte Carlo.

Beatrice Lacy, Maxim's sister, tall, broad-shouldered, handsome, tweedy, inquisitive, blunt, and chatty.

Major Giles Lacy, Beatrice's fat and genial husband.

Dr. Baker, a London physician visited by Rebecca (under Mrs. Danvers' name) the day of her death. He reports that she was dying of cancer, though she appeared in good health.

Frith, Maxim's elderly butler.

Clarice, Mrs. de Winter's young maid.

Ben, a simple-minded old man.

THE REBEL ANGELS

Author: Robertson Davies (1913-1995)
First published: 1981
Genre: Novel

Locale: Toronto, Ontario, Canada
Time: Early 1980's
Plot: Psychological

Maria Magdalena Theotoky, a graduate student. The beautiful Maria is studying the works of François Rabelais in preparation for her doctoral thesis under the direction of Professor Clement Hollier, whom she loves. Maria comes to understand that her Gypsy heritage, her "root," is as important as her university persona, her "crown" (as of a tree). She marries Arthur Cornish. She narrates the chapters collected under the title "The Second Paradise," which form approximately half of the novel.

The Reverend Simon Darcourt, a professor of classics. He is one of the three faculty members who are executors of Francis Cornish's will. The kind, somewhat overweight Darcourt narrates the chapters titled "The New Aubrey," so called because he wants to limn the personalities of those at the university, following the spirit of John Aubrey's *Brief Lives* (1898). He loves Maria and proposes marriage to her, telling her that she is his Sophia, a feminine personification of God's wisdom. Maria in turn calls him her "Rebel Angel," a teacher of some of the secrets of heaven.

Clement Hollier, Maria's dissertation director and the second of the three executors from the university. Hollier's field is paleopsychology, which examines folk beliefs and customs to understand the thought processes of people of the Middle Ages. His special area of research is filth therapy: He examines such beliefs as the one that binding a child's legs with camel dung will cure rickets. Hollier is another of Maria's rebel angels. Hollier becomes obsessed with a manuscript that he believes Urquhart McVarish to have stolen; he begins to hate McVarish and cannot see that his obsession and hatred are destructive to himself.

John Parlabane, a skeptic philosopher and failed monk. Parlabane, an old friend of Hollier and a former star at the university, cadges money and favors from virtually everyone.

He tries to live life by the code of his skeptical philosophy, which postulates that nothing is certain, yet he appears to believe in God. Hollier warns Maria that Parlabane is an evil man. Parlabane murders McVarish and commits suicide in the hope that the sensation will help get his (unreadable) novel published. He, too, is one of Maria's rebel angels, teaching her to pay attention to her "root."

Urquhart McVarish, a professor of Renaissance history and the third executor of Francis Cornish's will. A narcissist and a braggart, McVarish is a very unpleasant man who is fascinated by pornography. He is always trying to bait people. McVarish employs Parlabane to satisfy his unorthodox sexual tastes; Parlabane murders him at the end of one encounter.

Arthur Cornish, a banker. Not yet thirty, Arthur is self-composed and confident. He is the overall executor of his uncle's will. He knows quite a bit about music, art, and literature, yet has not attended a university; his goal is to become a patron. He asks Maria to marry him because she is the most splendid friend whom he has ever had.

Oraga "Mamusia" Laoutaro, Maria's mother. A luthier, Mamusia fixes stringed instruments using the *bomari*, an old procedure involving horse dung that fascinates Hollier. Mamusia, after the death of her non-Gypsy husband, has reverted to her Gypsy ways and wisdom. She reads the tarot cards for both Darcourt and Hollier. She has a very strong personality.

Yerko Laoutaro, Maria's uncle and Mamusia's brother. He is a skilled smith and also follows Gypsy ways.

Ozias (Ozy) Froats, a biology professor. Froats is, in the spirit of pure science, examining human excrement for clues to health, personality, and physical type. He is a possible contender for a Nobel Prize. Maria calls him a magus, a man who serves the forces of nature.

— *Karen M. Cleveland*

THE REBEL GENERATION
(De opstandigen)

Author: Johanna van Ammers-Küller (1884-1966)
First published: 1925
Genre: Novel

Locale: Leyden, Holland
Time: 1840-1923
Plot: Social

Louis Cornvelt, an upper-middle-class Hollander. An ultraconservative, orthodox Calvinist, he expects from his family complete adherence to his way of life and submission to his will.

Katie Cornvelt,
Nicholas Cornvelt,
Sarah Cornvelt, and
David Cornvelt, Louis Cornvelt's children. After a brief youthful rebellion, each finds himself or herself too accustomed to parental domination to break the habit of obedience and finally bows submissively to the father's will.

Marie Elizabeth (Lysbeth) Sylvain, sometimes called Sylvia, Louis Cornvelt's orphaned niece, who comes to live in her uncle's home. She brings new ideas that inspire Louis' children to a brief rebellion. When her uncle refuses to allow her to earn a living, she runs away to France. Later, with an inherited fortune, she returns to Holland to work for the emancipation of women.

Doctor William Wiseman, Katie Cornvelt's husband, whom she marries in obedience to her father's will, even though the young doctor is repugnant to her.

Doctor Eliza Wiseman, the daughter of Katie Cornvelt and William Wiseman. She scandalizes her parents by wishing to become a doctor and receives help and encouragement from Marie Elizabeth Sylvain.

Louis Cornvelt, David Cornvelt's rebellious son, a political radical.

Clara Cornvelt, David Cornvelt's daughter, who gives in to her father in matters of love, though she persists in continuing as a social worker among the lowest classes.

Stephen Cornvelt, Dr. Eliza Wiseman's nephew. Infatuated with Millicent Cornvelt, he asks his wife Dorothy for a divorce.

Dorothy Cornvelt, Stephen Cornvelt's wife, a lawyer and member of Parliament. Her life is empty because of her family's indifference to her success and her husband's infatuation with Millicent Cornvelt.

Millicent Cornvelt, the great-granddaughter of Louis Cornvelt, Sr.

Kitty and
Puck Cornvelt, the daughters of Stephen and Dorothy Cornvelt. They are unhappy in the insecurity of their unstable home.

REBELLION IN THE BACKLANDS
(Os Sertões)

Author: Euclides da Cunha (1866-1909)
First published: 1902
Genre: Novel

Locale: The backlands of Northeast Brazil
Time: The 1870's through the 1890's
Plot: Historical

Antonio Vicente Mendes Maciel (vee-SEHN-teh MEHN-dehs mah-see-EHL), also called **Antonio Conselheiro** (kohn-sehl-HA-roh), the fanatic religious leader of the backlands rebellion. Quiet and withdrawn, this former store clerk vanishes into the backlands in the aftermath of a disastrous marriage, only to reappear, years later, transformed into an ascetic and emaciated anchorite. Roaming from town to town, Maciel, now known as Conselheiro (the counselor), preaches an apocalyptic religious message and is asked to settle disputes. In the process, he attracts an increasingly large following of the dispossessed poor, including numerous outlaws, who eventually settle with him in Canudos in 1893. Threatened by what they perceive as Conselheiro's antirepublican message, the state and federal governments organize four different expeditions to destroy the rebel town. Conselheiro dies two weeks before the final surrender of Canudos. His body is later exhumed so that his brain can be studied scientifically.

Pajehu (pah-heh-EW), the guerrilla leader of the *sertanejos*. A notorious bandit, this tall and athletic man of mixed race exhibits extraordinary bravery and superb tactical skills in leading the rebels against the government troops. He dies in July, 1897, in one of the many fierce battles during the government's fourth expedition against Canudos.

Lieutenant Manuel da Silva Pires Ferreira (PEE-rehs feh-RA-rah), the leader of the government's doomed first expedition. He sets out from Bahia with roughly one hundred troops. Before they are able to reach Canudos, they are ambushed by the rebels in Uauá. Although casualties are relatively few, Pires Ferreira's troops must face a demoralizing retreat.

Major Febronio de Brito (feh-BROH-nee-oh deh BREE-toh), the leader of the government's doomed second expedition. A major in the Ninth Battalion of Infantry in Bahia, de Brito departs for Canudos in late 1896. Ambushed by the backlanders, de Brito's troops are completely disabled and, like Pires Ferreira's, forced into a humiliating retreat.

Colonel Antonio Moreira Cesar (moh-RA-rah SEH-sahr), the leader of the government's doomed third expedition. Diminutive in stature, with bandy legs and a weak chest, Moreira Cesar has a physical appearance that belies his ruthless, ambitious, and vengeful personality. After one of his frequent epileptic seizures, Moreira Cesar makes a sudden decision to leave for Canudos earlier than planned. His overconfidence and impetuosity prove to be his downfall. Displaying downright contempt for the backlanders, Moreira Cesar sees his victory as certain. After some initial success, his exhausted and hungry troops eventually are driven back by the crafty and resilient backlanders. Moreira Cesar is wounded in combat and dies. As his discouraged troops retreat, they are attacked repeatedly by the backlanders, who inflict considerable casualties. In the confusion, Moreira Cesar's body is left by the roadside.

General Arthur Oscar de Andrade Guimarães (ahn-DRAH-deh gee-ma-RAYNSH), the leader of the government's doomed fourth expedition. A highly respected officer with a knightly conception of the military career, the general sees his expedition as a crusade to save the young republic from the supposedly antirepublican rebels of Canudos. Although known for his restless, bold character and for his incomparable tactical skills, Oscar has his mind so set on completely destroying Canudos that he uncharacteristically fails to act soon enough. As his troops are encircled and immobilized by the rebels at Favella, Oscar decides simply to hold out and wait for reinforcements.

General Claudio do Amaral Savaget (ah-mahr-AHL sah-vah-ZHEH), the leader of the second column of the fourth expedition. More flexible than all the other commanders, Savaget, although attacked on his way to Canudos, is able to reach Oscar's entrenched forces, to free them from their precarious position, and to force the rebels to retreat into Canudos. After he is wounded at Cocorobo in June, 1896, he leaves the front.

Marshal Carlos Machado de Bittencourt (mah-CHAH-doh deh bee-tehn-KOHRT), the war minister and eventual commander of the fourth expedition. Cold, quiet, calculating, and practical, he lacks the disastrous overconfidence of his predecessors. He plans the final attack on Canudos in an organized and methodical way. He is in command when Canudos finally surrenders on October 5, 1897.

— *Luiz Fernando Valente*

RECKLESS EYEBALLING

Author: Ishmael Reed (1938-   )
First published: 1986
Genre: Novel

Locale: New York City and the fictional Caribbean island of New Oyo
Time: The 1980's
Plot: Satire

Ian Ball, a black playwright in his late twenties or early thirties. Ian was born and reared by his mother on the fictional Caribbean island of New Oyo. Ian misses the easy lifestyle and predictable character of what he calls the South. Ian's first play produced in Manhattan, *Suzanna*, was a great success, but it was heavily criticized as sexist by feminist critics. Ian is staging his second play, *Reckless Eyeballing*. After Ian's friend and director, Jim Minsk, is viciously killed by a group of white racists and anti-Semites, Ian weathers the complex adversities of rewriting and restaging his play; in the process, he undergoes an identity crisis. The conflicting demands of the theater world complicate Ian's initial impressions of his talent and his fellow writers. Antagonistic male and female relations force Ball to re-examine some of his sexual attitudes. He changes his play drastically to make it conform to politically correct criteria, and his honesty is questioned.

Tremonisha Smarts, a playwright and a black feminist. Tremonisha is the first victim of the Flower Phantom, a mysterious masked man who attacks prominent feminists and shaves their heads. Tremonisha is enlisted to help Ian rewrite his play, although she balks at certain arch revisions insisted on by the white feminist producer, Becky French. Tremonisha undergoes a last-minute anticonversion from feminism to rehabilitated black mother figure after successfully changing and directing Ian's play.

Becky French, a director and white feminist. Becky refuses to produce Ian's play after the death of Jim Minsk, Ian's supporter. Finally, she enlists Tremonisha to rewrite the play and gets Ian to agree to having it staged in a much smaller venue.

Jake Brashford, a black playwright. Jake's first and only play, *The Man Who Was an Enigma*, caused a sensation when it was produced many years before. Since that time, Jake has lived off gifts and prizes and has been unable to complete his second play. Jake cautions Ian against giving in to whatever theatrical philosophy is prevalent at the time.

Lawrence O'Reedy, a white detective with the New York police force. O'Reedy is known as "Loathsome Larry" for his violent attacks on criminals, particularly Hispanics and blacks. O'Reedy is put on the case of the Flower Phantom, which he believes he solves. It proves to be his last case, as he dies giving a speech during his police retirement party.

Randy Shank, a black playwright. His play *The Rise and Fall of Mighty Joe Young* is described as satire. Because of its premise that American women crave to be raped by a beast, he was put on a feminist blacklist in the 1960's. Randy now works as a doorman at Tremonisha's apartment complex. Rabidly anti-Semitic, Randy also criticizes Ian for changing his play and working with women. Randy is killed by O'Reedy, who believes he is the Flower Phantom.

— *Stephen F. Soitos*

THE RECOGNITIONS

Author: William Gaddis (1922-   )
First published: 1955
Genre: Novel

Locale: New York City, Paris, Spain, and Rome
Time: 1910-1946
Plot: Social morality

Wyatt Gwyon, an artist who forges imitations of the paintings of old masters. An enormously talented painter in his early thirties, with a genius for reproducing the works of

others, he is in despair over the lack of authenticity in art as in life. Wyatt produces imitations that fool all but the most discerning art critics. After the death of his mother when Wyatt was only four, he was reared by his father, a minister interested in anthropology and mythology, and his father's aunt, a Calvinist for whom creativity was evil. Drawn toward both religion and art, Wyatt goes first to seminary for a year, then to Germany and Paris to study art. Repulsed by the decadence and avarice of the art world, he rejects his own original paintings, moves to New York City, and turns his talents first to restoring paintings and then to forgery. Both his marriage and an affair with a model fail for a lack of genuine feeling. Tormented by the lack of any apparent relationship among art, truth, and reality, Wyatt determines to expose the forgery ring and moves to Spain, where his mother is buried. He changes his name to Stephen. Again he becomes involved with women and in forgery, this time in faking a mummy. Wyatt/Stephen flees to a monastery, where he restores paintings to the original canvas. Eventually having achieved some reconciliation with himself, his art, and his life, he leaves the monastery, apparently in search of his daughter by one of the Spanish women.

The Reverend Gwyon, Wyatt's father and the town minister. His interest in anthropology and mythology and subsequent dissatisfaction with Christianity lead him to worship the sun. He instills in Wyatt a love of learning and a passion for a spiritual context for the details of life. When his wife dies aboard ship in transit from New England, he buries her in Spain and seeks solace in a Franciscan monastery in Spain before returning to his young son. The introduction to Catholicism impels his rejection of Calvinism and his increasing mysticism, culminating in his sun worship.

Aunt May, Wyatt's Calvinist aunt, who helps to rear Wyatt until her death, when he is twelve years old. She has a major effect on Wyatt. She condemns creativity as blasphemy because when humans create, they imitate God. She makes Wyatt, as a child, feel guilty about his drawing, leaving him deeply ambivalent about art.

Esther, Wyatt's wife and the author of books about art. Intelligent, knowledgeable about art and literature, and analytical, but emotionally dependent, she is frustrated by Wyatt's absorption in himself and his work. She begins an affair with Otto that precipitates Wyatt's leaving her. About a year later, Otto abandons her, and she takes up Ellery, an adman. Each man distances her further from genuine art.

Esme, a poet and an art model. Her ethereal beauty makes her a good model for Wyatt's virgins and madonnas. Her promiscuity and drug habits reflect her lack of concern for the details of life. In both her poetry and her actions, she looks for the principles behind details. Believing that she is only an object for Wyatt, she attempts suicide, surviving, but in a state of schizophrenia in which she refers to herself in the third person. In her search for the transcendental, she accompanies Stanley to Italy, where she dies of an infection.

Otto Pivner, an aspiring playwright. Newly out of Harvard University and with an undeveloped personality, Otto carries with him everywhere a draft of what he hopes will become his first play. It consists of dialogue consisting of conversations he has overheard; its main character, Gordon, is simply a version of Otto as he wishes he were: witty, intelligent, and debonair. Otto has no vision of his own and therefore cannot make these collected words cohere. Even his emotions seem borrowed. He likes to hear others, especially Wyatt, talk about art and phi-

losophy, but he has nothing to say. He even becomes involved with Esther and Esme, Wyatt's wife and girlfriend, respectively. Otto's lack of any viable identity is expressed in his vain attempts to meet his father. After a trip to Barbados to work on his play, he returns with his arm in a sling to dramatize himself. His play is rejected, Esme rejects him, and he goes back to the banana plantation. Disoriented after a fall from a horse, identifying himself as Gordon, he remains a patient of the doctor at the plantation.

Basil Valentine, an art critic and a former Jesuit. Exceptionally sophisticated, self-assured, homosexual, and decadent, he authenticates Wyatt's forgeries to make money. The most intelligent character in the novel, Basil is fascinated by Wyatt's genius and despair. To stop Wyatt from exposing the forgery ring, Basil destroys evidence that Wyatt needs to clear himself. He tells Wyatt that spiritual ideals are irrelevant and that style is all that matters, prompting Wyatt to forsake New York for Spain.

Rectall Brown, an art collector. A complete cynic and corrupter of art and people, believing only in money, fame, and power, he involves Wyatt in the forgery scheme. Brown sells the paintings Wyatt forges after Valentine authenticates them. Brown's cruelty to his man Fuller is avenged when he is killed by a falling suit of armor.

Frank Sinisterra, a master forger of money and government documents. An artist in his own way, dedicated to his craft, precise, thorough, and technically close to perfect, Sinisterra is always something other than what he appears. Masquerading as a doctor, he is responsible for the death of Wyatt's mother; he operates on her for appendicitis. Otto mistakes him for the father whom he has never seen when Sinisterra appears at the scheduled meeting place. Sinisterra mistakes Otto for a messenger to whom he is supposed to give some counterfeit money. Otto uses the money to go to Barbados. Sinisterra goes to Spain, calls himself Mr. Yak, and involves Wyatt in a scheme to forge a mummy. He provides Wyatt with a passport of a man named Stephen.

Stanley, a composer of religious music. A devout Catholic and a talented musician, Stanley tries to make converts through his musical compositions. He helps Esme after the disappearance of Wyatt and takes her to Europe. He wants to play his organ composition at an Italian church. He loses track of Esme but finally gets to play in the church on Easter Sunday. The old church, shaken by the loud music, collapses on Stanley.

Anselm, a lapsed Catholic. A drunken, bitter member of the pseudoliterary/artistic group, Anselm acts as if he has no morals at all. When most of the others go to Europe, he goes to a monastery in the western United States and attacks them in his memoirs.

Agnes Deigh, a literary agent. Agnes, another lapsed Catholic, also suffers from the disparity between her childhood faith and the life she leads. She, rightfully, rejects Otto's play. She reports to the police what she thinks is a case of child abuse but is apparently only a father disciplining his daughter. Her guilt over this interference drives her to attempt suicide by jumping out her hotel window.

— *William J. McDonald*

THE RECRUITING OFFICER

Author: George Farquhar (1678?-1707)
First published: 1706
Genre: Drama

Locale: Shrewsbury, England
Time: Early eighteenth century
Plot: Comedy

Captain Plume, a recruiting officer in the Queen's army who goes into Shrewsbury to recruit for a French campaign. His chief endeavor, however, is winning Sylvia Balance for his wife. Blatant and ribald, he declares he will not marry, to spend his entire life with a woman, until he knows premaritally whether he will like her company for half an hour. Winning Sylvia after trickery against him has failed, he quits the service to raise recruits in a matrimonial way. His men's conduct in the town is well described by the accusation that they leave as many recruits in a town as they take away.

Sergeant Kite, his sergeant. He tries to lure recruits by offers of money and gay living. Ineffectual in these efforts, he disguises himself as a conjurer, predicting for men brilliant futures, according to their vocations, if they will enlist. Through his "predictions," he also brings the principals of the play together, foretelling the plot. Kite procures other enlistments as he cajoles the justices in court to declare men needy, without means of support, and therefore wards of the Crown.

Sylvia Balance, a young woman who spends the greater part of the play dressed as a man, young Mr. Willful. Suspecting Plume of being attentive to Rose, Sylvia, disguised as a recruit, courts Rose to learn of Plume's relations with other women. She learns that Plume is not the philanderer he is reputed to be. As a result, she disregards her father's admonition to break off with Plume and becomes his wife. Her handsome income is no small factor in Plume's love for her.

Melinda, Sylvia's cousin, a lady of fortune. She adds to the plot with her attitude toward Sylvia and by her attractiveness to Brazen and Worthy. Melinda's ill temper causes her to be suspected of writing letters to Sylvia's father, maligning Plume. Melinda's comment that the confounded captains do more harm by debauching at home than they do good by their defenses abroad epitomizes the tone of the play.

Mr. Worthy, a gentleman of Shropshire who wins Melinda. Never sure of Melinda's temperament at a given time, Worthy assumes she is in love with Brazen. Easily influenced, Worthy takes Plume's advice to win Melinda's affections by ignoring her. The ensuing misunderstandings make for some rollicking scenes of dispute before Worthy succeeds with Melinda.

Captain Brazen, one of the recruiting officers, whose name fits him well. He is an arrogant coxcomb whose sole goal in life is woman or women. He is impetuous and approaches any woman familiarly, undaunted by her resistance. Plume, who sides with Mr. Worthy in the contest for Melinda, sends Brazen packing with the twenty recruits raised by Kite and without the benefit of Melinda's twenty thousand pounds, which Brazen hoped to gain along with Melinda's hand.

Rose, a pretty, buxom country girl who is taken in by Sylvia's disguise as a soldier. Caught in the middle in more than one piece of chicanery, Rose is finally taken as Sylvia's charge, at Plume's suggestion. Sylvia assumes the responsibility, telling Plume that she will take care of Rose because Plume will have job enough to take care of a wife.

Bullock, Rose's oafish brother. He sells grains in the market as Rose sells poultry. Bullock is the butt of many a bawdy joke. His commonness, however, is little different from the sensual behavior of the other, better-bred men. Naïve and bold, Bullock, having become a recruit, has the last word with Plume, telling him that he will desert if he is ever mistreated.

Lucy, Melinda's maid, actively involved in the forgeries that sustain the plot. Finding papers with Melinda's signature, Lucy writes to Brazen, criticizing Worthy. Lucy stops the duel between Brazen and Worthy that is instigated by the letters.

Costar Pearmain and
Thomas Appletree, two recruits who resist Kite's appeals to honor and patriotism, only to be tricked into the army. Kite hands them coins, saying that they are pictures of the Queen. When the two bumpkins plead with Plume, claiming they have not enlisted, Kite tells the captain that the two men have accepted money from him, implying payment for going into the service.

Justice Balance, Sylvia's father and a justice of the peace. He sits in judgment on the men brought in as vagrants whom Kite would have as recruits. Among those appearing before him is Sylvia, in her brother's uniform. Balance recognizes Sylvia, shows his recognition indirectly by telling her that she should go home to her father, and gives her to Plume in marriage.

Justice Scruple and
Justice Scale, justices of the peace who add to the burlesque of the country courts by their inane handling of cases.

A constable, who brings Kite before the justices. He is introduced to point up the treatment civil authorities suffer at the hands of the military at a time of recruitment. Kite goes unpunished for his misdemeanors, and the constable is sentenced to get four recruits for Plume or to enlist himself.

Pluck, a country butcher. Kite, impersonating a conjurer, tells Pluck that he will be surgeon general of the Queen's army for his part in the battle of Flanders.

Thomas, a smith in Shropshire who Kite predicts will be made captain of the forges in the grand train of artillery. In his soothsaying, Kite advises Pluck and Thomas that they will, in a given time, be approached by gentlemen who will lead them to their good fortunes. The gentlemen are, of course, Kite's accomplices in recruiting.

THE RECTOR OF JUSTIN

Author: Louis Auchincloss (1917-   )
First published: 1964
Genre: Novel

Locale: Primarily New York City and New England
Time: 1887-1947
Plot: Social

Francis (Frank) Prescott, the rector, or headmaster, of Justin Martyr Academy. He is the central figure of the novel. Although orphaned, he is able to attend good schools because of family trusts; by the time he is seventeen years old, he has determined to create his own Christian preparatory school. Short of stature, he is imposing in a broad-shouldered, bullnecked way, with a large, handsome head. Educated at Harvard University and the University of Oxford, Frank temporarily loses the faith essential to his ambition and goes to work for the New York Central Railroad. His faith returns, and he goes to divinity school, is ordained, and founds his school thirty miles west of Boston. It flourishes. His methods, progressive when introduced, appear old-fashioned by the time he retires in 1941. Boys are required to attend daily chapel, to wear blue suits on Sunday, and to enter the dining room in marching order. Discipline is strict, and planned activities, chiefly schoolwork, rugged sport, and worship, keep the boys occupied and usually out of mischief. The rector, an inspiring teacher to thousands of boys, becomes a legend. In retirement, though, he has moments of doubt about his life's work.

Brian Aspinwall, who comes to Justin in 1939, replacing a teacher who has departed for military service. Slight, timid, sensitive Brian has been rejected because of a heart murmur. He wants to be a minister but lacks self-confidence. Frank admires Brian's ability to please his dying wife. He consents to Brian's writing his biography. Much of the story is in the form of Brian's entries into his diaries; the rest is from memoirs gathered from others.

Harriet Winslow Prescott, a member of an old Boston family. She meets Frank during his days at divinity school. She marries him following his ordination and works with him to found and run Justin Martyr. She dies shortly before Frank's retirement. Tall, large-nosed, and plain, she is also intelligent, cultivated, and independent in mind and spirit.

Cordelia Prescott Turnbull, the youngest of Frank and Harriet's three daughters, the rebel in the family. She tells Brian her story. After eloping at the age of seventeen with a confused Catholic boy, she soon left him but could not, for several years, secure a divorce. Cordelia lives with Charley Strong in Paris after World War I; later, she marries Guy Turnbull, a rich industrialist. In middle age, divorced again but with plenty of money, she lives alone and collects art.

Horace Havistock, Frank's oldest friend. He meets Frank in preparatory school. Determined to live a bachelor life of ease, elegance, and refinement, Horace is an altogether different type of man from Frank but can admire, instruct, and entertain him. Their friendship flourishes at Harvard, at Oxford, and in New York City. Horace supplies Brian with his memoir of Frank's—and his own—early years.

David Griscam, who enters Justin in 1891, burdened with the knowledge that his father has ended his life a swindler. Frank inspires David to erase a bad reputation by creating good one. A successful lawyer, David becomes the first Justin graduate to serve as a trustee; he becomes its leading fundraiser and donor. His career and his avocation—the school—do very well; his family proves less satisfactory.

Eliza Dean, a hazel-eyed, auburn-haired beauty from California who seeks a man with whom she can reach the top of society, culture, and politics. Frank Prescott of the New York Central seems exactly that man. They become engaged. After the renewal of Frank's faith, however, she concedes Horace's point: She would not do well as the mistress of a boys' school. She breaks the engagement.

Charley Strong, one of the finest of Justin's graduates and a participant in World War I. His wounds promise an early death. Cordelia meets him in Paris, becomes his lover, and encourages him to nihilistic views. Frank Prescott appears and captures Charley's attention. Charley dies with his faith restored, causing Cordelia to seethe.

Jules Griscam, the youngest child of David Griscam. He grows up detesting what his father most admires: the rector of Justin and his school. A clever and resourceful rebel in his years there, Jules finally goes too far, and Frank expels him. Later, Jules, in a drunken rage, drives back to Justin and hurls a rock through the chapel window. Now Harvard expels him. He goes to Europe and dies, along with a French mistress, in an auto accident caused by his own, possibly deliberate, recklessness.

Duncan Moore, who becomes the new rector of Justin in 1941. His mild relaxation of discipline, changes of curriculum, and liberalizing of admissions stir up several older faculty members, alumni, and trustees. Frank almost puts himself at the head of this rebellious old guard, but, warned by Brian Aspinwall, David Griscam prevents him from doing so.

— *Robert McColley*

THE RED AND THE BLACK
(Le Rouge et le noir)

Author: Stendhal (Marie-Henri Beyle, 1783-1842)
First published: 1830
Genre: Novel

Locale: France
Time: Early nineteenth century
Plot: Psychological realism

Julien Sorel (zhew-LYAH[N] soh-REHL), the son of a lawyer, an opportunist whose brilliant intellect, great ambition, and self-pride elevate him for a time, only to defeat him in the end. The youthful protégé of a local priest in the French town of Verières, Julien becomes the beloved tutor of the mayor's children and the lover of that aristocratic official's wife. Brazen, hypocritical, but shrewd, this contradictory hero espouses Napoleonic sentiments yet believes that his own salvation is through the church. Pushed by scandal into a seminary, he proudly stands aloof from its politics and manages to become a secretary to one of the first men in France. Though he is insensitive to all feelings, his intellect again raises him in esteem to the point where he seduces as well as is seduced by the nobleman's daughter, a lively, intellectual young woman. Playing both ends against the middle—the middle being a respected position and a respectable income—he brings about his own downfall through attempted murder of his first mistress after she has revealed his villainy to his noble benefactor.

Madame de Rênal (deh reh-NAHL), Julien Sorel's first mistress and greatest love, a beautiful, compassionate, though bigoted woman. Although she vacillates always between religiosity and passion, she truly loves the ascetic-looking younger man and dies shortly after he has been executed for his attempt to kill her. Her allegiance to the tutor is the more remarkable because of her clever deceptions, necessary to prevent an immediate tragedy brought about by her husband's vindictiveness. In the end, religiosity predominates; she is torn by anguish, remorse, and guilt and dies while embracing her children three days after the death of her lover.

M. de Rênal, the miserly mayor and village aristocrat, who desperately seeks status by hiring a tutor for his children. Vulgar and greedy to an extreme degree, this boorish landowner is elevated by the marquis de La Mole, who later becomes Julien's employer. He loses his wife to a commoner's love and his position to his republican enemy.

Mathilde de La Mole (mah-TEELD deh lah mohl), a proud, intelligent aristocrat destined to become a duchess but fated to love out of her class. Desirous of the unexpected and bored with the conventionality of her life, she at first seeks distraction in lovemaking with Julien Sorel. When he pretends boredom, she pursues him shamelessly. Her pregnancy sets off a chain of tragic events that will leave her unborn child without name or father. After Julien's execution, her romantic nature causes her to imitate the deed of a famous ancestress; she buries her lover's head with her own hands and decorates his cave tomb with marble so that it resembles a shrine.

The Marquis de La Mole, a peer of France and the wealthiest landowner in the province. He is a subtle, learned aristocrat who through caprice gambles on a young man's genius, through kindness makes a gentleman of him, and through pride in family negotiates his downfall. Although he admires his brilliant secretary, the marquis can never rid himself of his social ambitions for his beautiful and intelligent daughter, and to bring about Julien Sorel's downfall, he conspires to gain incriminating evidence against the young man.

The Marquise de La Mole, aristocrat proud of her noble ancestors.

The Comte de La Mole, their son, a pleasant young man conditioned to fashionable Parisian life, in which ideas are neither encouraged nor discussed.

Fouqué (few-KAY), a bourgeois but devoted friend of Julien Sorel. Acting as ballast for his mercurial friend, he offers Julien a good position in his lumber business, financial support for his studies, and finally his whole fortune to free him after his arrest.

The Abbé Chélan (ah-BAY shay-LA[N]), the local parish priest, who teaches and advances the fortune of Julien Sorel. The first to discover the tragic duality of his protégé's nature, he nevertheless supports him in his ambitions and grieves over his misadventures.

The Abbé Pirard (pee-RAHR), the director of the seminary at Besançon, where Julien Sorel studies. He obtains for his brilliant pupil the post of secretary to the marquis de La Mole. An irascible Jansenist among Jesuits, this learned priest sees in Sorel genius and contradiction. In spite of these contradictions, Pirard helps to elevate the youth to the munificence of courtly Paris.

M. Valenod (vah-leh-NOH), a provincial official grown prosperous on graft. Jealous because M. de Rênal has hired a tutor for his children and because his own advances to Madame de Rênal have been unsuccessful, he writes an anonymous letter that reveals the love affair between Julien Sorel and his employer's wife.

THE RED BADGE OF COURAGE: An Episode of the American Civil War

Author: Stephen Crane (1871-1900)
First published: 1895
Genre: Novel

Locale: A Civil War battlefield
Time: 1861-1865
Plot: Psychological realism

Henry Fleming, a young recruit under fire for the first time in an unnamed battle of the Civil War, possibly Chancellorsville. A farm boy whose struggle with his emotions might be that of the eternal recruit in any battle of any war, Henry has dreamed of fighting heroically in "Greeklike" battles. Irritated and unnerved by his regiment's inactivity, he tortures himself with the fear that he may run away when the actual firing begins. He does so. Sheepishly rejoining his regiment, he learns that his cowardice is not known to his fellow soldiers. In the next attack, he keeps firing after the others have stopped. When a color-bearer falls, he picks up the flag and carries it forward. Later, he hears that the colonel has complimented his fierceness. Henry's psychological battle with himself is now ended; it has gone from fear to cowardice to bravery and, finally, to egotism.

Jim Conklin, "the tall soldier," a veteran who comforts Henry and squabbles with the braggart Wilson. He predicts that the regiment is about to move into battle. When it does so, he is mortally wounded. Henry and "the tattered man" find him stumbling to the rear, still on his feet, fearful of falling under the wheels of an artillery wagon. He wanders into a field, as if it were a place of rendezvous with death. Henry and the tattered man follow him, trying to bring him back. He brushes them off and, with a great convulsion, drops dead.

Wilson, "the loud one." At first, he seems confident, absolutely sure of his courage. As the battle begins, he suddenly thinks he may be killed, and he turns a packet of letters over to Henry Fleming. After the first attack, he asks for the return of the letters. Some of his loudness and swagger is now gone. He and Henry struggle to get the flag from the fallen color-bearer. Henry seizes it, but Wilson aids him in going forward and setting an example to the wavering troops.

"The Tattered Man," a soldier encountered by Henry Fleming just after he has run away. The man embarrasses the recruit by asking where he is wounded. Later, he and Henry follow Jim Conklin into the field. The soldier is so impressed by the manner of Jim's death that he calls the dead man a "jim-dandy." Then he cautions Henry to "watch out fer ol' number one."

Lieutenant Hasbrouck, a young officer of Henry Fleming's company. He is shot in the hand in the early part of the battle but is able to drive a fleeing soldier back into the ranks and tries vainly to stop the disorganized retreat. He later compliments Henry and Wilson by calling them "wild cats."

Colonel MacChesnay, the officer who also compliments Henry Fleming and Wilson. He is berated by the general, shortly after Henry's advance with the flag, for not forcing the partial success of the charge to a complete one.

THE RED PONY

Author: John Steinbeck (1902-1968)
First published: 1937; expanded, 1938
Genre: Short fiction

Locale: Salinas Valley, California
Time: Early 1900's
Plot: Pastoral

Jody Tiflin, a young boy (ages ten through twelve over the four stories) growing up on an isolated California ranch. He is a normal kid—dreamy, sometimes irresponsible, and not above childish pranks—who loves the other members of his ranch family and learns something from each of them in the different stories of this novella: practical sense from his father, sensitivity from his mother, courage and caring from ranch hand Billy Buck, and a feeling for the past from his grandfather. Jody is at the center of each story. It is his red pony, Gabilan, that is "The Gift" that dies in the first story. In the second, Jody learns about life and death from Gitano, who returns to the ranch to die; in the third, Jody watches as Billy Buck saves Nellie's colt but has to kill the mare to do it; and in the last story, Jody learns from Grandfather's stories of "westering" in the nineteenth century about the importance of human history and human kindness.

Carl Tiflin, Jody's tall, stern father, who runs their Salinas Valley ranch. Carl is a disciplinarian who can be mean and cruel and who does not like to see weakness in others. A large part of his character clearly has been formed by the harsh environment that he is trying to control, yet he is not totally insensitive to Jody's problems and growth.

Mrs. Tiflin, Jody's mother, a sensitive and sympathetic woman who defends her son and her father to her husband. She works as hard as the male characters do in the struggles of

California ranch life in the years around the beginning of the twentieth century.

Billy Buck, the Tiflins' middle-aged ranch hand and a significant part of the boy's life. He teaches Jody much about the world, both by what he says and by what he does. Billy tries everything he can to save Jody's pony, Gabilan, in the opening story and then to ensure that Nellie's colt lives in the third, but in both cases he is only human. Jody learns from Billy's fallibility, however, as well as from his own, and this knowledge is an important part of his own development over the course of the novella.

Grandfather, Mrs. Tiflin's father, a former wagon train leader. Grandfather is a garrulous old man who teaches Jody something about heroism and history. Jody's father has tired of the old man's stories, but both Jody and Billy Buck look up to this pioneer.

Gitano, an elderly Chicano laborer who returns to the ranch, his birthplace many years ago, to die. Gitano's rapier holds special significance for the young boy.

Gabilan,
Nellie,
Doubletree Mutt, and
Smasher, animals that figure prominently in this rural life as well as in the author's naturalistic prose.

— David Peck

THE RED ROOM
(Röda rummet)

Author: August Strindberg (1849-1912)
First published: 1879
Genre: Novel

Locale: Stockholm and X-köping, a provincial Swedish town
Time: The 1870's
Plot: Satire

Arvid Falk, a would-be poet. Unable to find a publisher for his poems, he takes a job on a newspaper. His poems are finally published, and he becomes, to all appearances, a successful journalist. Disillusioned, however, because he is never allowed to report the news honestly as he sees it, he moves from paper to paper and eventually suffers a mental breakdown. After his recovery, he becomes a conventional schoolmaster and marries a schoolmistress.

Charles Nicholas Falk, Arvid Falk's brother, a businessman. He emerges unscathed from a financial disaster to go on to further material successes.

Mrs. Charles Nicholas Falk, Charles Nicholas Falk's self-indulgent, socially ambitious young wife.

Levin, a clerk, and
Nystrom, a schoolmaster, fawning cronies of Charles Nicholas Falk.

Sellen, a painter. For reasons having nothing to do with art, he becomes celebrated as a painter and, to all appearances, a highly successful young man.

Lundell, a practical painter who earns money by illustrating magazines.

Rehnhjelm, a young man who ardently desires to be an actor. As a member of a theatrical company, he falls idealistically in love with Agnes. When he learns that she is Falander's mistress, he threatens suicide, but he recovers from the affair and returns to the security of his wealthy family.

Olle Montanus, a philosopher and sculptor. Finally, unable to work except as a stone mason, he takes his own life.

Ygberg, a philosopher who argues with the artists and writers in the Red Room.

Falander, an elderly fellow actor of Rehnhjelm and Agnes' lover.

Borg, a cynical young doctor who is Arvid Falk's friend and benefactor. Expecting nothing from life, he alone remains unchanged among the changing fortunes and ideals of Arvid's friends and associates.

Agnes (**Beda Petterson**), who, as Agnes, a sixteen-year-old ingenue and the mistress of Falander, inspires the idealistic love of Rehnhjelm. As Beda Petterson, a worker in a Stockholm café, she is loved by Arvid Falk.

Smith, a publisher.

Struve, a journalist.

RED ROSES FOR ME

Author: Sean O'Casey (John Casey, 1880-1964)
First published: 1942
Genre: Drama

Locale: Dublin, Ireland
Time: 1913
Plot: Expressionism

Mrs. Breydon, a woman of the working class, roughly fifty years old, whose face and hands show the marks of hard work and the bitter struggle to maintain dignity and respectability in the lower-middle-class world of Dublin on the eve of World War I. Despite patched clothes and some scars from the effort to make a living and rear her son, Mrs. Breydon is still a woman of spirit and shows some signs of the handsomeness that she once possessed. Her chief concern in life is her son, whom she has reared virtually on her own; where his interests are involved, she displays a surprising shrewdness. She supports his commitment to the labor movement but fears for his safety in the coming strike. She also displays skepticism about Sheila Morneen's willingness to make sacrifices for his causes.

Ayamonn Breydon, her son, a twenty-two-year-old idealist and visionary. Breydon, handsome and dramatic in his gestures, has talents in many areas: politics, the theater, writing, and painting. He aspires to be a Renaissance man, though some suggest that he may diffuse his energy by spending it on too many diverse enterprises. A railroad worker with high aspirations, Breydon hopes to awaken the working class to its cultural heritage while supporting efforts to better its economic condition. In the third act, Breydon's dream vision of a Dublin transformed from dispirited poverty into an enchanted realm of beauty and dance provides a key to his character. Breydon lacks the experience to understand how much jealousy his courtship of Sheila, a Catholic girl, arouses in Inspector Finglas, or how much resentment the workers' demand for an extra shilling increase in wages creates among their employers. As a result, Breydon's involvement in the strike and, in particular, his willingness to speak in support of it at a public meeting lead to his tragic death.

Sheila Morneen, Ayamonn's sweetheart, a beautiful but somewhat timid and conservative young lady who has been reared as a devout Roman Catholic. Because Breydon is a Protestant, his attraction for her is counterbalanced by a realization that he is not an acceptable suitor in the eyes of her parents. Although Sheila is fascinated by Breydon and considers his idealism attractive, she is frightened by his readiness to flout convention. She is also attracted to the fine uniform and authority of Inspector Finglas, and Mrs. Breydon shrewdly predicts that Sheila will never be content with a life of poverty. Sheila implores Breydon to disengage himself from the striking railroad workers and win the gratitude of his employers; she threatens to end their relationship if he refuses. After his tragic death, she has the spirit to denounce his murderers and those—like Inspector Finglas—whose indifference and neutrality allowed his murder to occur.

Brennan O' The Moor, an elderly man who is a friend of the Breydons, the owner of some old houses and tenements in their neighborhood. A retired working man of seventy-six, Brennan is conservative and full of anxiety about social change and unrest. A kindly man beneath a gruff exterior, Brennan has known the Breydons for years. He has misgivings about Ayamonn's participation in the strike, and he constantly wonders if even the Bank of Ireland is a stable institution. He looks forward to singing in Ayamonn's minstrel show, however, and despite a theological hostility to Catholics, he secretly removes the statue of Our Lady of Eblana, a neighborhood icon, and buys new clothes for it.

Tim Mullcanny, another friend of Ayamonn, known in the Breydons' neighborhood as a mocker of religion and an iconoclast in almost the literal meaning of the word because he ridicules the icons of the local Catholics. Ayamonn tolerates Mullcanny's opinions, though Mullcanny is on the level of the village atheist and Ayamonn is in his own way a believer in the Protestant faith in which he was reared. Mullcanny's lack of humor and his intensity come close to the fanaticism that he ridicules and make him unpopular. He manages to bring both Brennan and the Catholic Roory together against him in argument, and in the second act, he enters in flight from several men who have physically attacked him for his opinions.

The Reverend E. Clinton, a handsome man of forty, the Protestant rector of St. Burnupus and a sympathetic friend of the Breydons. Although Inspector Finglas is his churchwarden, he feels more respect and friendship for Ayamonn, and he comes to warn Ayamonn that it would be unwise to speak at the public meeting in support of the strike.

Roory O'Balacaun (oh-BAL-ah-kon), a fervent Catholic and a patriotic Irishman, a likable but quarrelsome fellow worker of Ayamonn. Roory believes in the strike, but he believes more strongly in the Fenians and Irish nationalism, and he voices an unswerving loyalty to the Roman Catholic church. Although he is a friend of Ayamonn, Roory would cheerfully burn books and suppress the free expression of opinion. Although he argues with Brennan over theology, his particular anathema is Mullcanny and the latter's espousal of evolution.

Dowzard and

Foster, members of St. Burnupus' select vestry. They condemn the strikers as "papists" and pretend to be scandalized that their fellow vestryman, Ayamonn Breydon, is supporting the labor movement. During the rally, they are forced to flee from angry workers because they are considered "scabs." After Breydon's death, they are angry that his body is taken to St. Burnupus.

Eeada (ay-AD-nah),
Dympna (DIHM-nah), and
Finoola (fa-NEW-lah), poor flower sellers and Mrs. Breydon's neighbors in the tenement. Eeada is old, Dympna middle-aged, and Finoola young, but they play their role as a stylized trio. Except in the third act, they display stiff looks of depression on their faces, and their dress is dark and somber. They embody the wan hopelessness of Dublin's poor, providing a type of background chorus to the conflict engendered by the strike. In the third act, their faces and their clothes are transformed miraculously in Breydon's vision, and they dance and sing songs of joy to celebrate a revitalized Dublin.

Inspector Tom Finglas, an officer of the Metropolitan Mounted Police, also the churchwarden of St. Burnupus. Proud of his authority and his blue uniform with silver braid, the inspector is an arrogant man who views the poor of Dublin as moral failures and a blot on the city's image. He sees the railroad workers' strike as a threat to the established order of titles and property owners, which it is his duty to protect. He also feels jealousy of Breydon because of the latter's relationship with Sheila, whom he longs to possess for himself. Finglas leads his mounted police in a charge to disperse the strikers at their rally and helps to create the violent conflict between workers and authority in which Breydon is killed by a soldier. Then he begins to console Sheila while Breydon's body is being brought to St. Burnupus.

Samuel, the elderly verger of St. Burnupus, who warns the Reverend Clinton that two of his vestrymen are plotting mischief against Breydon.

— Edgar L. Chapman

THE RED ROVER

Author: James Fenimore Cooper (1789-1851)
First published: 1827
Genre: Novel

Locale: Newport, Rhode Island; and the Atlantic Ocean
Time: Mid-eighteenth century
Plot: Historical

The Red Rover, a pirate who is really a good man in many ways. He saves the lives of Harry Wilder, Dick Fid, and Scipio Africa when his crew demands their deaths. Later, he fights for the colonists' cause in the American Revolution against the British. Just before his death, it is revealed that he is a patriot and the long-lost uncle of Harry Wilder. His pirate ship is the *Dolphin*.

Harry Wilder, a young British naval officer who is sent on a secret mission to capture the Red Rover. He is a brave young man who makes his way into the pirates' confidence, but he is unsuccessful in capturing the men. While a prisoner of the Red Rover, after a sea battle, Harry Wilder's identity as **Henry Ark**, a naval officer, is revealed. Then, unexpectedly, he is discovered to be **Henry de Lacy**, the long-lost son of Paul de Lacy and Mrs. Wyllys.

Gertrude Grayson, the daughter of a British general. She is befriended by Harry, who tries to warn her against traveling aboard the *Royal Caroline*, for he knows that the ship is slated to be a victim of the Red Rover.

Mrs. Wyllys, the governess and companion to Gertrude Grayson. Mrs. Wyllys is finally revealed to be the mother of Harry Wilder. She has thought her child, born of a secret marriage to Paul de Lacy, dead for many years. She pleads for her newly found son's life before the Red Rover when the young man is revealed as a spy against the pirates. She succeeds in her pleas, and it is later learned that the Red Rover is really Mrs. Wyllys' long-lost brother.

Dick Fid, a sailor and faithful friend of Harry Wilder. He found Wilder as a baby aboard an abandoned ship at sea.

Scipio Africa, a black sailor. He is Dick Fid's companion and helped rear Harry after the latter was found as a baby at sea.

Captain Bignall, the commanding officer of the *Dart*, a British warship sent after the Red Rover. He is Harry's superior officer. The captain is killed and his ship captured in a battle with the *Dolphin*, the Red Rover's vessel.

Roderick, a cabin boy to the Red Rover who actually is a woman.

REDBURN: His First Voyage

Author: Herman Melville (1819-1891)
First published: 1849
Genre: Novel

Locale: New York, the Atlantic Ocean, and England
Time: Mid-nineteenth century
Plot: Bildungsroman

Wellingborough Redburn, a young American who leaves his widowed mother and his brothers at home on the Hudson River in New York to go to sea. He learns, during a voyage from New York to Liverpool and return, that a sailor's life is a good but rugged one, that each generation makes its own world, and that true joy and sorrow are components of the human condition.

Harry Bolton, a young English prodigal son of good family who becomes Redburn's friend during the voyage from Liverpool to New York. Bolton is a misfit aboard ship, thus belying the stories he tells of his voyages as a crew member on other vessels. His pride is so injured when the captain pays him a dollar and a half as wages at the voyage's end that he throws the money back on the captain's desk.

Captain Riga, the tough, shrewd master of the *Highlander*, Redburn's first ship. He pays Redburn three dollars a month for his work on the voyage, but when the ship returns to New York, he dismisses Redburn without a penny because he says Redburn had left the ship for a day at Liverpool and, furthermore, had lost tools overboard.

THE REDSKINS: Or, Indian and Injin, Being the Conclusion of the Littlepage Manuscripts

Author: James Fenimore Cooper (1789-1851)
First published: 1846
Genre: Novel

Locale: Upstate New York
Time: 1842
Plot: Historical

Hugh Roger Littlepage, the narrator and heir to Ravensnest, and

Hugh Roger Littlepage, called **Uncle Ro**, his uncle. While traveling abroad, they receive word that they are in danger of losing their estate, Ravensnest, which is threatened by a terrorist group of anti-rentist tenants greedy for land. Disguised as a watch peddler and an organ grinder, Hugh and Uncle Ro return to Ravensnest and assess the situation. With the help of a band of friendly Indians, they subdue the terrorists and see the rights of the landlords upheld by the Supreme Court.

The Reverend Mr. Warren, a clergyman living at Ravensnest. He is a friend and ally of Hugh Roger Littlepage and Uncle Ro.

Mary Warren, the daughter of the Reverend Mr. Warren. An ally of Hugh Roger Littlepage in his fight against the anti-rentists, she finally becomes his wife.

Seneca Newcome, a demagogue lawyer and the leader of the anti-rentist tenants at Ravensnest.

Tom Miller, a farmer who is hostile to the anti-rentist factions at Ravensnest.

Joshua Brigham, Tom Miller's greedy farmhand and an ally of Seneca Newcome.

Jack Dunning, Hugh Roger Littlepage's business agent.

Susquesus, an old Onondaga Indian living at Ravensnest. He is honored in a ceremony by a band of Indians from Washington who help subdue the anti-rentist terrorists at Ravensnest.

Jaap (Jaaf), an old black servant living at Ravensnest.

Patt Littlepage, Hugh Roger Littlepage's sister.

Mrs. Ursula Littlepage, Hugh Roger Littlepage's grandmother.

Opportunity Newcome, Seneca Newcome's sister and ally.

Hall, a mechanic hostile to the anti-rentist faction at Ravensnest.

Henrietta Coldbrook and

Anne Marston, wards of Uncle Ro.

REFLECTIONS IN A GOLDEN EYE

Author: Carson McCullers (1917-1967)
First published: 1941
Genre: Novel

Locale: A Southern military base, probably Fort Bragg, North Carolina
Time: The 1930's
Plot: Psychological realism

Private Ellgee (L. G.) Williams, a soldier at an army post in the South. He lives a clean life, never smoking, drinking, gambling, or fornicating. He has neither friends nor enemies. He is assigned to stable detail because of his skill with horses. Williams becomes enamored of Leonora Penderton after he accidentally sees her naked; she is the first naked woman he has ever seen, as he was reared by his father in an all-male household. His father, a Holiness preacher, had told him that women carried deadly diseases. He had not willingly interacted with a female person since he was eight years old. After seeing Mrs. Penderton, whom he thinks of as "The Lady," naked, he begins squatting by her bedside at night to watch her sleep.

Captain Weldon Penderton, a cowardly sort of man who is torn between cruelty and tenderness and who falls in love with his wife's lovers. He is thirty-five years old and about to be promoted to major. Reared by five unmarried aunts, he had never really been loved. He constantly fights the desire to steal. After Private Williams sees him beat a horse, Penderton reacts violently but ambivalently toward the young man. He begins to follow Williams. When he sees the soldier beside his wife's bed, he shoots him dead.

Leonora Penderton, the thirty-one-year-old wife of Captain Penderton. She is not an intelligent woman (she cannot add her card values when she plays blackjack, for example), but she is beautiful. Because her husband is not attentive, she has a succession of lovers, the latest of whom is Major Morris Langdon. She is a devoted horsewoman and a tough person who likes to hunt.

Major Morris Langdon, Leonora Penderton's lover. He thinks of women as weak and morbid; for example, he disdains his wife's weeping over a quail he shoots and then brains because it falls but is not dead. He is disgusted by his wife's attachment to the odd and effeminate Anacleto. When Alison threatens to leave him, he decides that she is insane and sends her to a mental institution. After her death, he grieves.

Alison Langdon, Major Langdon's wife, an ill woman of twenty-nine. Mrs. Langdon's sickness is both physical and mental; it is exacerbated by her husband's philandering. A few months before the beginning of the book, she had gone home from a get-together at the Pendertons' and cut off both her nipples with gardening shears. Part of her distress comes from the fact that her baby, Catherine, had died three years before. She reportedly has a beautiful singing voice, but no one has heard her sing for years. She knits sweaters and frets, feeling constantly like weeping. She sees Private Williams sneaking into the Penderton's house and goes to see what is happening, but everyone thinks she has completely lost her mind. After her husband sends her to a mental institution, she dies of a heart attack.

Anacleto, Mrs. Langdon's twenty-three-year-old Filipino

houseboy. He has been with his employer since he was seventeen years old and is absolutely devoted to her; he had even helped her through labor when Catherine was born. Anacleto paints in watercolors and dances around the house, catering to himself. After his mistress's death, he disappears.

Lieutenant Weincheck, a company commander and a friend of Alison Langdon. Because of eye trouble, he is about to be retired.

Susie, the Pendertons' servant, on whom Mrs. Penderton is quite dependent.

— *M. Katherine Grimes*

REFLEX AND BONE STRUCTURE

Author: Clarence Major (1936-   )
First published: 1975
Genre: Novel

Locale: New York City
Time: Late 1960's or early 1970's
Plot: Experimental

The narrator, who functions as a screening device for the novel as well as being a primary character. Although nameless and never described, the narrator self-reflexively manipulates the plot and characters of this episodic novel. Through repeated references to the act of writing, the narrator playfully deconstructs the text while in the process of composing it. The narrator is whimsical, forgetful, and unreliable. The other characters are seen exclusively through the narrator's eyes. The narrator refuses to tell a consistent story that follows traditional discursive conventions. Little is known of the personal history of the narrator other than that he lives in Manhattan. The narrator exists through the act of writing, and his identity is inextricably tied to that process. Throughout the novel, the narrator remains aloof, detached, and fearful of his advancing age.

Cora Hull, an African American actress who lives in Greenwich Village in Manhattan. At various times, she has intimate relationships with the three other characters in the novel. She is often in rehearsal for plays but never seems to

have any long-term commitments, either to the stage or the other characters. She may have been killed in a mysterious bombing episode that occurs in the beginning of the novel, but because of the convoluted time frame of the plot, the reader cannot be sure. She is described as being twenty-five years old and as having been born and brought up in Atlanta.

Canada Jackson, an African American who may be part of a black revolutionary group. He is a serious suitor of Cora and in this way is a rival of both Dale and the narrator. Canada collects weapons and keeps a gun in the silverware drawer in the kitchen of his apartment. He is also an actor in New York.

Dale, an Off-Broadway actor who flits in and out of the text and remains largely undefined. The narrator professes to have the most difficult time constructing Dale. Furthermore, Dale threatens the narrator's sense of self. As another suitor of Cora, Dale causes more problems than Canada. The narrator is very jealous of Dale and often sends him on long journeys.

— *Stephen F. Soitos*

LA REGENTA

Author: Leopoldo Alas (Clarín, 1852-1901)
First published: 1884
Genre: Novel

Locale: Vetusta, Spain
Time: The 1870's
Plot: Psychological realism

Ana Ozores (oh-SOH-rehs), the judge's wife. She is a beautiful, sensitive woman of twenty-seven who has endured eight years of a childless marriage. A tireless reader of mystical and romantic literature, she longs to escape the suffocating world of the provincial capital in which she lives, the imaginary city of Vetusta. Her fabled virtue as a model wife is imperiled as she finds herself alternately torn between the promise of sexual fulfillment offered by the libertine Don Alvaro and the hope of spiritual communion with the priest Fermín de Pas. Ultimately, she succumbs to an adulterous affair with the former, which concludes with her husband's death and her own complete ostracism by the community.

Victor Quintanar (keen-tah-NAHR), the chief stipendiary magistrate of the provincial court, now retired. Already in his fifties, he behaves more as a father than as a husband to his young wife, Ana. He encourages the nervous Ana to socialize more and thus inadvertently propels her into the arms of another man. Among his passions are hunting, fencing, and the reading of Spanish seventeenth century honor plays. When cuckolded, he is ironically unable to commit the murderous

vengeance prescribed by the literature he so avidly consumes. He demands a duel of Alvaro but is killed unheroically by a single shot that ruptures his bladder.

Fermín de Pas (fehr-MEEN deh pahs), a canon theologian and vicar-general of the Diocese of Vetusta. He is, at thirty-five years of age, a man of superior intelligence, physical strength, and worldliness. Once a lowly cowherd, he has risen to the position of the most powerful churchman in his city and as such is an object of both admiration and envy. As Ana's new confessor, he initially views her as a kindred soul, spiritually superior to the mediocrity of Vetusta; later, he falls prey to a purely human love based on his physical attraction to her.

Alvaro Mesía (AHL-vah-roh meh-SEE-ah), the president of the Gentlemen's Casino and leader of Vetusta's liberal Dynastic Party. A fashionable dresser whose superficial elegance is much imitated, he is Vetusta's aging Don Juan. A pragmatist in matters of love and politics, he considers his seduction of Ana both a challenge to Fermín de Pas' power and a reaffirmation of his own masculine prowess, now in slow decline. After killing her husband, he abandons Ana and flees to Madrid.

Tomás Crespo (toh-MAHS KREHS-poh), or **Frigilis** (free-HEE-lees), Victor's close friend, distinguished by his lack of social pretentiousness and his professed tolerance of human frailties. His chief avocations are hunting and botany. Responsible for first introducing Ana to her future husband, he stands alone in continuing to look after her once she is widowed and disgraced.

Petra, an opportunistic servant in the household of Ana and Victor. Resentful of her mistress, she resets Victor's alarm clock so that he will awaken early and discover his wife's infidelity.

Marquis of Vegallana (veh-gah-YAH-nah) and

Marchioness of Vegallana, wealthy and dissolute aristocrats whose son Paco is one of Alvaro's confidants. Ana, Victor, Fermín, and Alvaro frequently come together at their home in town and at their country estate, which are governed by the most relaxed of moral standards and known to be a haven for all manner of sexual escapades among their social intimates.

Doña Paula (POW-lah), Fermín de Pas' tyrannical, conniving mother. Born into poverty in a small mining village, she finds economic salvation as housekeeper to a local parish priest and thereafter devotes her formidable energies and ambitions to furthering her son's ecclesiastical career.

Doña Petronila Rianzares (peh-troh-NEE-lah ree-ahn-SAHR-ehs), nicknamed "Constantine the Great," a widow now devoted to the management of charitable organizations. Her home provides a place where Ana and Fermín may meet away from the watchful eye of Vetustan society.

Santos Barinaga (bah-ree-NAH-gah), a drunkard who has repudiated the Church, blaming the financial ruin of his shop, which sells religious articles, on the monopolistic trade practices of a competing store run by Doña Paula and her son Fermín. Barinaga's refusal of the sacraments and civil burial are rallying points in the campaign waged by de Pas' enemies to discredit him.

Pompeyo Guimarán (pohm-PA-yoh gee-mahr-AHN), a friend of Barinaga and a onetime atheist whose unexpected deathbed conversion and confession help restore Fermín de Pas' reputation as a man of miraculous pastoral powers.

Cayetano Ripamilán (kah-yeh-TAH-noh rree-pah-mee-LAHN), the canon and archpriest of the cathedral. At seventy-six years of age, the birdlike Ripamilán passes the responsibility of serving as Ana's confessor to Fermín de Pas and instead spends his time composing bucolic and epigrammatic poetry.

Visitación Olías de Cuervo (vee-see-tah-see-OHN oh-LEE-ahs deh KWEHR-voh) and

Obdulia Fandiño (ohb-DEW-lee-ah fahn-DEEN-yoh), two previous mistresses of Alvaro, the former known for her habit of sucking on caramels and pastries, the latter for her brassy mode of dress and comportment. Both encourage Alvaro in his attempts to seduce Ana, wishing to see her equally dishonored as they are.

Celedonio (seh-leh-DOH-nee-oh), the adolescent homosexual acolyte whose kiss at the conclusion of the novel signifies Ana's moral fall and punishment.

— *Hazel Gold*

THE REIVERS: A Reminiscence

Author: William Faulkner (1897-1962)
First published: 1962
Genre: Novel

Locale: Fictional Yoknapatawpha County, Mississippi, and Memphis and Parsham, Tennessee
Time: May, 1905
Plot: Psychological realism

Lucious Priest, an innocent eleven-year-old. When his parents and grandfather leave town to attend a funeral, he goes with Boon on a wild adventure to Memphis. Boon takes him to Miss Reba's brothel and then to Parsham and a racetrack. He becomes terribly sad, hungry, desperate, and homesick while waiting to return home. He tells this story in 1961, as a man of sixty-one years who does not feel the confusion and pain he felt at the time. He gives an incredible and detailed account of the events that transpired. The boy learns many things during this adventure, at the heart of which are the forces of good and evil. He learns that nothing is entirely good or bad, but that everything contains strains of each. In the process of his adventure, he passes out of childhood and becomes an adult. Throughout the dilemmas and trials he faces, he always wonders what he should do and what a gentleman would do. No matter how homesick he becomes, it is his point of honor to act like a man and not show that he wants to cry. He is at odds with the things he has been taught as a child as he sees older people who do not act reasonably. The one thing Lucious knows with certainty is that a person should never lie or make promises he is unable to keep. His confession in the end is not about the trip to Memphis or risking the safety of the automobile; it is that he lied about helping Aunt Callie keep the other children. He intends to take the punishment he deserves from his father, but

when the time comes, his father knows that a whipping is no longer in order for Lucious. He has been through a greater ordeal than a whipping could cover. The grandfather breaks the impasse between boy and father by sending Lucious' father away. The grandfather then tells Lucious that his punishment will be that he has to live with his guilt for the rest of his life. This, Lucious learns, is the meaning of being a gentleman.

Boon Hogganbeck, a fun-loving sportsman without much intellect. He is innocent in his own way. When Lucious' parents leave for a funeral, Boon uses keys to the family car to take Lucious on an adventure to Memphis. He is boyish and wild, heroic in his spirit and his sense of virtue, but not a born gentleman. He makes advances toward Everbe that are refused, but they eventually decide to marry.

Ned McCaslin, a rough and unsavory man. Meeting Boon and Lucious at a private racetrack, he manages to barter away their automobile. He is a gentleman in a sense, but holding only the qualities that are useful to him; he lacks the virtue and morality that normally accompany a person of noble spirit. He has seen much and been many places. He knows right from wrong but does not attempt to keep to the right, as Lucious aspires to do. He values beauty and simple truths, and he despises Otis, who speaks crudely. He tries to prevent Lucious from having to hear Otis. At his most righteous, he strives to take from the rich and give to the poor. He does this with the help of a racehorse who runs in rigged races.

Uncle Parsham Hood, a farmer who is a bastion of gentle wisdom and virtuous spirit. He is an upstanding member of the church and community and fits the sincere definition of "gentleman."

Butch, the brash deputy sheriff. He respects Uncle Parsham, but this alone is not enough to redeem his poor taste and general unkindness. He makes advances toward Everbe, which she accepts.

Everbe, a prostitute. Lucious fights for her. She falls in love with Boon but refuses to have sex with him on the grounds that she loves him and it would therefore be wrong to have sex if they were not married. She has sex with Butch, which causes Boon to hit her.

— *Beaird Glover*

THE RELAPSE: Or, Virtue in Danger

Author: Sir John Vanbrugh (1664-1726)
First published: 1696
Genre: Drama

Locale: England
Time: The seventeenth century
Plot: Social satire

Loveless, a gentleman living quietly in the country after a period of marital troubles. He goes to London frequently, however, to test his reform. He finds little difficulty in suffering a relapse.

Amanda, his wife. She remains chaste in spite of the combined efforts of her would-be lover and a friend who plays on her jealousy.

Berinthia, a comely widow and Amanda's friend. Loveless is attracted to Berinthia and succeeds with her easily.

Worthy, a gentleman of the town who was formerly Berinthia's lover. He enlists her aid in his pursuit of Amanda. Although Amanda admits him to her house, she retains her virtue.

Sir Novelty Fashion, Lord Foppington, a London fop who makes advances to Amanda and is repulsed by her and slightly wounded by Loveless. He is engaged to wealthy Miss Hoyden and marries her, only to learn afterward that she is already the wife of his younger brother.

Young Fashion, the brother of Lord Foppington. Unsuccessful in getting his brother to pay his debts, young Fashion pretends to be Lord Foppington and is admitted to Sir Tunbelly Clumsey's house as Miss Hoyden's fiancé. He persuades her to marry him secretly. Before the marriage is made known,

the real Lord Foppington arrives, and young Fashion is forced to flee.

Miss Hoyden, a nubile heiress. On the real Lord Foppington's arrival, she decides to say nothing of her earlier wedding but to play safe and marry again. When the prior wedding is disclosed, however, and she learns that her husband is Lord Foppington's brother, she is content.

Sir Tunbelly Clumsey, a country squire, the father of Miss Hoyden. At first thunderstruck at young Fashion's disclosure, Sir Tunbelly accepts him as his son-in-law when it is revealed that he is Lord Foppington's brother.

Bull, the chaplain. He marries Miss Hoyden and young Fashion secretly. Fortunately, young Fashion has at his disposal the recently vacated Fat-goose Living. He promises it to Bull in return for Bull's admitting the truth about the recent marriage.

Lory, young Fashion's servant.

Coupler, the matchmaker who had arranged the engagement of Lord Foppington to Miss Hoyden. Fearing never to see Lord Foppington's promised two thousand pounds, Coupler plots with young Fashion and is to receive in return five thousand pounds.

REMEMBRANCE OF THINGS PAST
(À la recherche du temps perdu)

Author: Marcel Proust (1871-1922)
First published: 1913-1927
Genre: Novel

Locale: France
Time: Late nineteenth and early twentieth centuries
Plot: Psychological realism

Marcel (mahr-SEHL), the narrator, who tells the story of his life from unsettled childhood to disillusioned middle age. Dealing with time lost and time recalled, Marcel says, as he looks back to a crucial childhood experience when his mother spent the night in his room instead of scolding him for his insomnia, that memory eliminates precisely that great dimension of time that governs the fullest realization of our lives. Through the years, from his memory of that childhood experience to his formulation of this concept of time, Marcel sees the principals of two social sets spurn each other, then intermingle with the change of fortunes. He experiences love in various forms: an innocent affair with a friend's daughter, an adolescent passion for the friend's coquettish wife, an intermittent love affair with a lesbian. He develops friendships and ani-

mosities among individuals in the different social levels on which he moves. Reminded, by seeing the daughter of his childhood sweetheart, that he is old, he realizes the futility of his life and senses the ravages of time on everyone he has known.

M. Swann, a wealthy broker and aesthete, a friend of Marcel's parents. Swann, having known the comte de Paris and the prince of Wales, moves from level to level in the social milieu. Having married beneath his station, he knows that wealth sustains his social position and keeps his fickle wife dependent on him. Jealous and unhappy in courtship and marriage, he manipulates social situations by cultivating officers and politicians who will receive his wife. He dies, his life having been as meaningless as Marcel sees his own to be; in fact, Marcel sees in his own life a close parallel to that of his sensitive friend.

Mme Swann, formerly **Odette de Crécy**, a courtesan. A woman whose beauty is suggestive of Botticelli's paintings, she is attractive to both men and women. Stupid and uncomprehending, Odette continues affairs with other men after her comfortable marriage. She introduces Swann to the social set below his own. Despite her beginnings, she moves to higher levels and becomes a celebrated, fashionable hostess when she remarries after Swann's death.

Gilberte Swann (zheel-BEHR), the Swanns' daughter and Marcel's playmate in Paris. Their relationship develops into an innocent love affair, and they remain constant good friends after Gilberte's marriage to Marcel's close friend, Robert de Saint-Loup. The sight of Gilberte's daughter, grown up, reminds Marcel that he himself is aging.

Mme de Villeparisis (deh veel-pah-ree-SEE), a society matron and the friend of Marcel's grandmother. It is said that her father ruined himself for her, a renowned beauty when she was young. She has become a dreadful, blowsy, hunched-up old woman; her physical deterioration is comparable to the decline of her friends' spiritual selves.

Robert de Saint-Loup (roh-BEHR deh sah[n]-LEW), her nephew, whom she introduces to Marcel. Their meeting is the beginning of a friendship that lasts until Robert's death in World War I. In his courtship and marriage, Robert suffers from the same insecurity, resulting in jealousy, that plagues Swann and Marcel in their relations with women. He marries Gilberte Swann.

M. de Charlus (deh shahr-LEW), another of Mme de Villeparisis' nephews, a baron. The baron, as he is usually called, is a sexual "invert" who has affairs with men of many different stations in life. In his aberration, the baron is both fascinating and repulsive to Marcel, who makes homosexuality a chief discussion in the volume *Cities of the Plain*. The baron's depravity leads to senile old age.

Mme Verdurin (vehr-dew-RA[N]), a vulgar person of the bourgeoisie who, with her husband, pretends to despise the society to which they have no entrée. Odette introduces Swann to the Verdurins. Mme Verdurin crosses social lines as she comes into money and marries into the old aristocracy after her first husband dies. The middle-class Verdurins seem to surround themselves with talented individuals, and many of their guests become outstanding in their professions and arts.

The Prince de Guermantes (deh gehr-MAH[N]T) and

The Princess de Guermantes, members of the old aristocracy, the family used by Proust in the volume *The Guermantes Way* to delineate the social classes. The Guermantes represent the aristocratic group, as opposed to the moneyed society described in *Swann's Way*. After the princess dies, the prince, ruined by the war, marries widowed Mme Verdurin. Their union is further evidence of social mobility.

The Duke de Guermantes and

The Duchess de Guermantes, members of the same family. After Odette's rise on the social scale, the duchess is received in Odette's salon. In earlier years, the duchess left parties to avoid meeting the vulgar social climber.

Albertine (ahl-behr-TEEN), a lesbian attracted by and to Marcel. Over an extended period of time, their affair takes many turns. Marcel seeks comfort from her when his grandmother dies; he is unhappy with her and wretched without her; his immaturity drives her from him and back to her home in Balbec. A posthumous letter to Marcel, after Albertine is killed in a fall from a horse, tells of her intention to return to him.

Marcel's grandmother, a woman known and revered in both the aristocratic and the merely fashionable social sets. Marcel loves and respects her, and her death brings into focus for him the emptiness in the lives of his smart, wealthy friends.

M. Vinteuil (va[n]-TOY), an old composer in Combray. He dies in shame because of his daughter's association with a woman of questionable character. Unhappy in his own life, Vinteuil's music brings pleasure to many. Among those affected is Swann, moved to marry Odette, his mistress, because he associates the charm of Vinteuil's exquisite sonatas with the beauty of the cocotte. Marcel, also captured by the spirit of Vinteuil's music, senses its effect on various listeners.

Rachel (rah-SHEHL), a young Jewish actress who becomes famous. Although she is Robert de Saint-Loup's mistress, she despises him because of his simplicity, breeding, and good taste. Rachel likes the aesthetic charlatans she considers superior to her devoted lover.

Dr. Cottard (koh-TAHR), a social boor because of his tiresome punning and other ineptitudes, a guest at the Verdurins' parties. He becomes a noted surgeon, professionally admired.

Elstir (ehl-STEER), a young man Marcel meets at the Verdurins'. He becomes a painter of genius.

Mme de Saint-Euverte (deh sah[n]-tew-VEHRT), a hostess whose parties attract both the old and new friends of Swann, to his displeasure at times.

The Princess des Launes (day lohn), a longtime friend of Swann and a guest in Mme de Saint-Euverte's salon. She is distressed at her friend's unhappiness, caused by lowering himself to Odette's level.

Morel (moh-REHL), the musician who, at the Vendurins' party, plays Vinteuil's compositions. Morel is a protege of the baron de Charlus.

Jupien (zhew-PYAH[N]), a tailor. After becoming the object of de Charlus' affection, he establishes a house for affairs among men.

M. de Norpoie (deh nohr-PWAH), an ambassador who, as Marcel finally realizes, has been Mme de Villeparisis' lover for many years.

Aunt Léonie (lay-oh-NEE), Marcel's aunt. At the end, he likens himself to her as he recalls her from his childhood, when she had become an old hypochondriac.

REMEMBRANCE ROCK

Author: Carl Sandburg (1878-1967)
First published: 1948
Genre: Novel

Locale: England and America
Time: 1607-1945
Plot: Historical

Orville Brand Windom, affectionately called Bowbong by his grandson. A former Supreme Court justice, he is an independent, idealistic, and whimsical man with a deep interest in the American past and future. In his yard, he keeps a huge boulder surrounded by earth representing the crises of American culture. The fictitious author of the novel's three stories, he wills his manuscript to his grandson.

Raymond Windom, his intelligent and sensitive grandson.

"The First Comers"

Oliver Ball Windrow, a middle-aged woodcarver and philosopher in Stuart England, a man much like Orville Windom. Rejected in his suit for Mary Windling, he marries his housekeeper.

Matilda Bracken, Oliver Windrow's mute, devoted housekeeper. She marries him and bears him two children.

Mary Windling, a lovely, spirited young friend of Oliver Windrow. She marries a Puritan, moves with him to Holland, and then sails to America on the *Mayflower*. She dies during the first winter.

John Spong, her sturdy, affectionate, and pious husband. In America, he becomes stern and solemn, disapproving of all his daughter's suitors.

Remember Spong, the daughter of John and Mary, a lively,

"The Arch Begins"

Ordway Winshore, a Philadelphia printer, a man of character similar to Orville Windom. He loses two sons in the Revolutionary War.

Robert Winshore, his older son, a dashing, idealistic young man who loses his love because of his commitment to the Revolution. He dies at Valley Forge.

John Locke Winshore, the more prudent younger son, a tradesman who joins the Revolutionary cause, becomes a military courier, marries Ann Elwood, and dies soon afterward.

Marintha "Mim" Wilming, a lovely young woman who rejects Robert's love because of his political convictions. Later, she becomes a nurse for the rebels.

"The Arch Holds"

Omri Winwold, a gambler, a manly, amiable, and prophetic man somewhat like Orville Windom. He moves West, settles on an Illinois farm, loses three wives, and sees his sons killed or maimed in the Civil War.

Brooksany Wimbler, his distant cousin and friend, a charming woman who moves with her husband and daughter to Illinois and dies there during the Civil War.

Joel Wimbler, her hardy, sensible husband, a harness maker and abolitionist who becomes an officer and dies in the war.

Millicent "Mibs" Wimbler, their beautiful, spirited daughter. Though wooed by two other suitors, she swiftly decides, without her parents' consent, to marry a cattle buyer and has a child by him. She goes to meet him when he is released from the military prison on Johnson's Island.

Rodney Wayman, her gay, intelligent, and manly husband, a former miner and cattle buyer who becomes a Confederate captain and is twice captured by Union troops. Embittered by the war, he nevertheless feels compassion when he

A pilot in World War II, he returns home exhausted and cynical, but his grandfather's manuscript tends to restore his faith in the nation's possibilities.

Maria "Mimah" Windom, his attractive, spirited wife. She shares her husband's and Orville's concern for America.

Joseph Stilwell Windom, their infant son, a symbol of the future.

pretty young Puritan who attracts several suitors but loves Resolved Wayfare, a Separatist, and finds herself torn between orthodox and independent piety.

Orton Wingate, her middle-aged friend and suitor, a kind man with audacious opinions, much like Orville Windom.

Peter Ladd, her gay, handsome suitor, a sailor and gambler who settles down under her influence but returns to the sea when she refuses him.

Resolved Wayfare, an idealistic young man who follows Roger Williams and eventually wins Remember's love. The two lovers part with vows of fidelity.

Roger Williams, a rebel of conviction and integrity, a friend of the Indians and the founder of the Rhode Island Colony.

Ann Elwood, a sensitive, pretty young woman involved in a fraudulent marriage. She later marries John Winshore and has a child by him.

Oates Elwood, Robert Winshore's rough, good-hearted, and patriotic friend.

Lieutenant George Frame, Marintha's suitor, a cultured British officer wounded in the war and sent back to England.

Sapphira Reggs, a Tory who recognizes Robert Winshore while her father is being tarred and feathered by patriots. She reports him to the British.

Mary Burton, the warm, attractive widow who marries Ordway Winshore.

learns of Omri Winwold's losses.

Hornsby Meadows, a teacher, Millicent Wimbler's keen but bigoted abolitionist suitor.

Danny Hilton, a farmer and contractor, Millicent Wimbler's husky, lighthearted suitor.

Nack Doss, Rodney Wayman's business associate and friend, a rough, honest Southerner killed in a Civil War engagement in Mississippi.

Bee Winwold, Omri's first wife, a wild, flashy, and promiscuous woman whom he deserts.

Andrew Marvel Winwold, Omri's son by Bee. He becomes an officer and loses an arm in the Civil War.

Henry Flack, Bee's second husband, a rather pathetic man who is attracted to prostitutes. After Bee deserts him and Anne Winwold dies, he and Omri become friends.

Anne Moore, a widow, and

Sarah Prindle, two affectionate farm women and sisters, Omri's second and third wives. They bear him seven children.

THE REMOVALISTS

Author: David Williamson (1942-   )
First published: 1972
Genre: Drama

Locale: Australia
Time: The 1960's or 1970's
Plot: Social

Sergeant Dan Simmonds, a senior policeman of a small, inner-suburban two-man branch station in Australia. An overweight bully and lecher in his fifties, he possesses an uneasy self-esteem dependent on his self-image as a tough, authoritative cop, which he must constantly demonstrate. Anyone challenging his authority challenges his private concept. Consequently, he effectively strives to dominate the rookie constable, Ross, through humiliation and false paternalism. Simmonds is the pivotal figure of the action. His expectation of sexual favors from two sisters, Kate and Fiona, motivates him to execute their request to remove the belongings of the younger sister from her abusive husband's home. The later frustration of those expectations, augmented by the husband's refusal to accept Simmonds' authority with its attendant self-image of manliness, prods Simmonds into vilifying one of the women, brutalizing the husband, and goading his young partner to violence that proves fatal.

Constable Neville Ross, a new policeman, twenty years old, just assigned to the branch station as his first duty out of training school and eager to prove his competence. His idealistic conception of his new role as a law enforcement officer is cunningly broken down by his superior, Simmonds, who denigrates his family background and religion and undermines his belief in proper police procedures. Continually taunted by Simmonds' dominating authoritarianism, Ross becomes a reluctant participant in the action of the furniture removal but treats the fiercely resisting homeowner, Kenny, far more fairly than does his superior. When he finds himself the butt of demeaning insults to his competence by Kenny, as well as by Simmonds, Ross uncontrollably attacks the former (as a displaced attack on his bullying partner). Panic-stricken at Kenny's consequent death, he desperately forces the now-frightened Simmonds to share the blame. Victimized by the sergeant, and with his self-esteem proved equally precarious, Ross descends to the brutish level of his superior.

Kenny Carter, the young husband of Fiona, a feisty and unpretentious working-class Australian whose image of himself as a great lover and fighter makes him a counterpart to Simmonds. He chauvinistically sees nothing amiss in thumping his wife to keep her in line and feels unjustly betrayed by her desertion. Surprised and outraged by the invasion of his home, he resists aggressively, provoking repeated beatings by Simmonds by hurling foulmouthed insults at the women and the police. These insults topple the latter's self-esteem and self-control and ultimately result in Kenny's death. His irreverence toward authority and his graphic ego-maintaining assertion of sexual prowess play on both Simmonds' repressed sexuality and demand for dominance and Ross's fear of incompetence. In a play focusing on the interplay of three men, Kenny emerges as a scapegoat sacrificed to the repressed frustrations and violence of the two policemen.

Kate Mason (**Kate le Page** in the original text), a snobbish and expensively dressed suburban dentist's wife who has persuaded her abused younger sister, Fiona, to leave her working-class husband after a beating and to register a complaint with the police. Dominating her sister, she uses her as a pawn to arouse Simmonds' prurient expectations falsely as a means of enlisting his aid in removing Fiona's furniture. Kate and her sister act as a catalyst in the play's action, which comes to expose her weakness for infidelity. Her dominance of Fiona is a counterpart to that of Simmonds over Ross.

Fiona Carter, a young married woman and mother, far less sophisticated than her older sister in dress and appearance. Reflecting an attractively innocent sensuality, she has a passive and casual nature, in sharp contrast to Kate's calculating dominance and cold tenseness. Although frequently physically abused by her husband, Fiona is somewhat reluctant to leave him, despite Kate's forceful advice. Appalled at Simmonds' brutality toward her husband and vilification of Kate, she doubtless regrets having been the instrument for police interference.

Rob, the Removalist, a single-minded young furniture mover bent on completing a job with as little effort and explanation as possible and brooking no interference. Grateful to the police for removing Kenny as an obstructing force, he is indifferent to the sergeant's brutality toward Kenny and refuses to risk involvement or delay by making a telephone call at Kenny's desperate request. He exploits Ross's aid in moving furniture. He represents the public indifference to violence.

— *Christian H. Moe*

RENÉE MAUPERIN

Authors: Edmond de Goncourt (1822-1896) and Jules de Goncourt (1830-1870)
First published: 1864
Genre: Novel

Locale: France
Time: The nineteenth century
Plot: Naturalism

Renée Mauperin (reh-NAY moh-peh-RAH[N]), a French girl. She is a sensitive, lively girl and her father's favorite child. She is in no hurry to settle down in marriage. Like her friend Naomi, Renée is horrified when she learns that her brother Henri is his prospective mother-in-law's lover. In revenge, Renée notifies M. de Villacourt that her brother is taking the man's name. When she thinks her action has been discovered, she has a heart attack and then wastes away to death.

M. Mauperin, Renée's father and a veteran of the Napoleonic Wars. Once a scholar and interested in politics, he is now a middle-class businessman. He is grief-stricken when all three of his children die within a short time.

Mme Mauperin, Renée's mother. She is a very proper woman who wants her family to be respectable above all else. She dotes on her son and cannot see his selfishness. Like her husband, she is grief-stricken at the deaths of her children.

Henri Mauperin (ah[n]-REE), Renée's brother. He is a political economist and a lawyer, a cold, calculating, and extremely selfish man. He becomes the lover of his fiancée's mother in order to further his marriage to the daughter. When his fiancée learns of the affair, he tells her it is none of her business. He fights a duel with the real de Villacourt, whose name he has officially taken, and is killed.

Mme Davarande (dah-vah-RAHND), Renée's sister. She is a quiet, respectable woman who has married dutifully. She dies in childbirth, not long after the deaths of her brother and sister.

Naomi Bourjot (nay-oh-MEE bewr-ZHOH), Renée's friend and Henri's fiancée. She is from a rich family, and her father wants her to marry a man with a title. She is horrified when she discovers that her mother has taken Henri as a lover.

Mme Bourjot, Naomi's mother and Henri's mistress.

M. Denoisel (deh-nwah-ZEHL), a family friend who acts as Henri Mauperin's second at the duel.

M. de Villacourt (deh vee-lah-KEWR), the last member of his family. He fights a duel with Henri Mauperin in order to keep Henri from assuming the family's name.

M. Bourjot, Naomi's father. He is a middle-class man of wealth who wants his daughter to marry higher in the social scale.

REQUIEM FOR A NUN

Author: William Faulkner (1897-1962)
First published: 1951
Genre: Novel

Locale: Mississippi
Time: The 1930's
Plot: Psychological realism

Mrs. Gowan Stevens, née **Temple Drake**, the central character of William Faulkner's earlier work *Sanctuary* (1931), a novel in which Temple is abducted by a petty criminal, Popeye Vitelli, and forced to live in a Memphis brothel. She is both repulsed by and attracted to the evil and sexually strange outlaw and even provides perjured testimony to protect Popeye from a murder charge. At the end of *Sanctuary*, Temple is taken abroad by her father for a long rest cure. By the opening of *Requiem for a Nun*, she has married and is the mother of two children: a son, Bucky, and an infant daughter who is smothered in her crib by Nancy Mannigoe. The dramatic episodes in the novel explore the lingering connection between Temple's past life of degradation and obsession with her current one of guilt and remorse. She still experiences some lingering attraction for the sexual license released during her captivity, and she agrees to run away with one of her captor's brothers in the backstory at the beginning of the novel.

Gowan Stevens, who in *Sanctuary* was responsible for placing Temple in Popeye's control by getting drunk and smashing his car on a back road in search of more bootleg liquor. What began as a college spree turns increasingly ugly. Unable to control his drinking, Gowan is unable to help Temple, and he eventually runs away, leaving her in the control of the criminal. Gowan feels responsible for destroying Temple's reputation, and by the time of *Requiem for a Nun*, he has married her and assisted her in living down the perfidy of her past. Unfortunately, the consequences of that past reappear and cost him the life of his baby daughter.

Gavin Stevens, Gowan's uncle and the lawyer who defends the murderer of his nephew's daughter. Gavin is a recurring character in Faulkner's fiction and appears as the representative of the law, a law that transcends, or at least tries to transcend, the local prejudices and suspicions of Jefferson, Mississippi, Faulkner's mythical Southern community. In spite of Nancy's guilt and conviction, Gavin tries to get a last-minute stay of execution for his client by having Temple visit the governor of Mississippi to recount the details of her kidnapping and subsequent behavior that led to the circumstances surrounding the death of her child.

Nancy Mannigoe (or Mannihoe), the nurse Temple hired to act as babysitter for her daughter. Nancy is a local African American woman of questionable reputation who has been both a drug addict and a prostitute. In spite of the fact that Temple repeatedly refers to her as a "dope-fiend nigger whore," she is the only one with whom Temple can talk about her past life and who understands the kind of compulsions that the white, upper-middle-class Temple has experienced. Nancy kills Temple's child in order to force Temple to stay with her husband and not abandon both him and her family to run away with Pete, the brother of the man with whom she tried to escape the degraded life she lived under the control of Popeye in Memphis.

Mr. Tubbs, who runs the Yoknapatawpha County jail in Jefferson. He is a typical Faulknerian poor white Southerner who displays an awkward deference to the upper-class Stevens through the manners and civilities of faded gentility he thinks appropriate in social meetings between the classes.

The governor of Mississippi, who hears Temple's late-night confession of her guilty complicity in the death of her daughter at the hands of Nancy. Although moved by the story, he does not commute the sentence.

Pete, the brother of Alabama Red, who was Temple's lover and who was killed when he tried to help her escape Popeye's control in *Sanctuary*. In *Requiem for a Nun*, Pete comes to Jefferson to blackmail Temple with some incriminating letters she wrote to his brother, and she agrees to run away with him. This event precipitates the death of her child.

— *Charles L. P. Silet*

RESTLESS HEART
(La Sauvage)

Author: Jean Anouilh (1910-1987)
First published: 1938
Genre: Drama

Locale: France
Time: The 1930's
Plot: Naturalism

Thérèse Tarde (tay-REHZ tahrd), a twenty-year-old violinist engaged to Florent France. Honest and innocent, she attempts to overcome the moral and cultural deprivation she inherited from her parents. Her beauty and personality attract two opposing characters: Gosta, her mother's lover, and Florent, a wealthy, socially prominent musician. Despite Gosta's demonstrations of affection, she loves Florent for his musical talents, sensitivity, and correctness. Oblivious to her parents' pleas for marriage on materialistic grounds, she is attracted to his noble character. Her honesty induces guilt for her degenerate and sordid background, thereby alienating her from Florent's upright, affluent world. Shame impels her to reveal this division. During her engagement to Florent, she invites her father to Florent's house. His obscenity and pettiness demonstrate the obstacles between her and Florent. She decides to leave Florent, who, overcome by the pain of unrequited love, acknowledges their differences but, through this suffering, identifies with Thérèse. After hearing of Florent's remorse, Thérèse believes that she has reconciled her degenerate background with Florent's noble world. Traces of her "race" intrude: The seamstresses and maids do not belong in these surroundings and contrast with Florent's aunt, Madame Bazin, and his sister Marie. Gosta arrives to assassinate Florent. Although Thérèse prevents the killing, hope in the uniting of the two contrary realities dissolves into a self-understanding of her alienation. Morally, she is separated from the society of her parents; socially, she cannot adapt to Florent's world. Maturity and a realistic look at the situation incite her departure from both worlds and lead her to solitude and despair.

Florent France (floh-REH[N] frahns), a wealthy pianist and Thérèse's fiancé. Morally upright and sensitive, he is attracted to Thérèse's purity, beauty, and disdain of materialistic values. Blind to the realities of her economic deprivation and degenerate background, he does not perceive the tensions dividing them. After hearing of Thérèse's decision to leave, he suffers a rejection that coincides with Thérèse's pain. With Thérèse's departure, he is left alone in his affluent world and musical creativity.

Monsieur Tarde, Thérèse's sixty-year-old father, the director of, and double-bass player in, an orchestra. Weak and cowardly, he knows the reality of impoverishment and the necessity of survival. He is obsequious to the proprietor of the cheap café, and he permits his wife to have an adulterous relationship with Gosta. He is aware of Gosta's attraction to Thérèse but, afraid of Gosta's departure, refuses to inform him of her intention to marry Florent. During his daughter's engagement, he accepts Thérèse's invitation to stay at Florent's mansion, thereby allowing her to use him as a foil to express her deprived background. His vulgarity surfaces in his obscene remarks and overindulgence in food and drink. Eventually, cowardice, hypocrisy, and moral degeneration separate Thérèse from him. When Gosta arrives to kill Florent, he hides behind Thérèse. Unlike his daughter, he never recognizes the social, cultural, and moral deficiencies that distinguish his world from Florent's.

Madame Tarde, Thérèse's mother, a cellist in her husband's orchestra. Unlike her daughter, who aspires to moral integrity, she enjoys a thirteen-year adulterous relationship with Gosta. Mercenary and self-serving, she intends to profit financially from her daughter's marriage to Florent. Her singing of obscene songs reflects her low cultural standard. To ensure marriage, she advises Thérèse to be docile and false, thereby revealing a hypocrisy and cynicism that contrast with Thérèse's honesty and innocence.

Gosta (goh-STAH), the orchestra's pianist and Madame Tarde's lover. Although a generation older than Thérèse, he falls in love with her. Violent and impulsive, he becomes enraged and sullen when he learns of Thérèse's planned marriage to Florent. He weeps passionately over Thérèse's violin cover. Despite his thirteen-year relationship with Madame Tarde, the frustration of his unrequited love for Thérèse produces an anger resulting in his near-fatal beating of Madame Tarde. He attempts to kill Florent. Listening to Thérèse, however, he recognizes the differences dividing his situation from Florent's world and Thérèse's maturing vision. His hatred, Thérèse notes, results from his incapacity to attain nobility. Fatalism imposes on him a resignation to his social and moral place.

Jeannette, a violinist in the orchestra. Self-serving, she sees only economic security in marriage. Loyal to Thérèse, she conveys an untruth, fabricated by Thérèse, that reveals her friend's background.

Hartmann, a friend and adviser to Florent. Recognizing the cultural and economic differences between Thérèse and Florent, he describes to both of them the barriers dividing their worlds.

— Donald Gilman

THE RESURRECTION

Author: John Gardner (1933-1982)
First published: 1966
Genre: Novel

Locale: Batavia, New York
Time: Early 1960's
Plot: Metaphysical

James Chandler, a forty-one-year-old philosophy professor at Stanford University. Influenced by R. G. Collingwood, especially his idea that the process that destroys also creates, Chandler is at odds with the philosophical fashions of his time—positivism and existentialism. This quixotic as well as meditative and usually cheerful academic thus begins writing an "apology for contemporary metaphysics," then learns that he is suffering from aleukemic leukemia and has only a few months to live. Rather than stay in the hospital in order to prolong his life slightly, he decides to return, with his wife and three daughters, to the hometown he has visited only rarely during the past twenty years, Batavia, in western New York. Batavia, however, has declined or at least changed, as, of course, has Chandler. His disease weakens his body, troubles his sleep (in his dreams, he is unable to protect his children from a strange old woman), and affects his thinking and writing. Desperately, he tries in the little time he has left to work out on paper his insight into Immanuel Kant's mistake, his failure to see the disinterest in moral affirmation. Although he believes that one's goal should be to make life into art, the dying (and still quixotic) Chandler ends up looking like "an image out of some grim, high-class Western."

Marie Chandler, James Chandler's wife, formerly a high school English teacher and more recently a full-time mother. Her self-control and especially her practical-mindedness contrast with her husband's character, yet she too is an idealist, albeit "mute."

Karen,

Susan, and

Annie, Marie and James Chandler's daughters, ages eight, six, and two.

Rose Chandler, James's mother, a widow for thirty years. She has a goiter, walks with a cane, and is nearly blind, but she nevertheless seems as indomitable and unthinking as nature itself. In a way, she resembles her meditative, scholarly son, using lists to order her life in much the same way that he uses his lectures and writing.

George Chandler, James's father, now dead. Owner of a novelty shop, he spent much of his time dabbling in magic and pseudoscience and tinkering with, among other gadgets, a perpetual motion machine that he believed he eventually would get right with just a little more work. It was a beautiful machine, not unlike his wife's lists and more especially his son's philosophical writings.

Emma Staley, one of three aged sisters whom Chandler remembers from his youth and visits upon his return. She formerly was a painter in the Romantic style and is now virtually a cliché from gothic fiction, a "madwoman locked in the attic" who spends her days waiting.

Maud Staley, another of the sisters, a singing teacher.

Elizabeth Staley, the third sister, a piano teacher who, it turns out, is deaf.

Viola Staley, the Staley sisters' nineteen-year-old relative and ward. She may not be evil, as Rose Chandler claims, or "impure" and "unfit for nature," as she herself thinks, but Viola certainly is strange, in part because she was orphaned at an early age; in part because she has lived thirteen years with her aunts, who are as odd as they are old; and in part because she has directed all her anger inward. When James has a seizure, she comes to his aid, and during the time he is hospitalized, she stays with his family. She believes herself to be profoundly changed by her four days with the Chandlers, by their interest in books and, more important, by their existence as a family. Wanting to come to life, for a time at least, she leaves Emma alone and goes to visit Chandler, the father figure to whom she feels herself romantically drawn. It is an act that will have dire if not quite tragic consequences for all concerned.

John Horne, an attorney specializing in more or less pointless legal research and, like Chandler, a patient in the local hospital. Badly scarred, foul smelling, and enormously fat, he is a caricature of the human condition, not a participant in life but merely a spectator, less a human being than a "sad clown." He is grotesque, childishly demanding, frantic, and violent, and he is well aware of his condition. His endless prattling parallels James Chandler's philosophical musings.

— *Robert A. Morace*

RESURRECTION
(Voskreseniye)

Author: Leo Tolstoy (1828-1910)
First published: 1899
Genre: Novel

Locale: Russia
Time: Late nineteenth century
Plot: Social realism

Prince Dmítri Ivánovitch Nekhlúdoff (DMIH-tree ee-VAH-noh-vihch neh-KHLEW-dov), a gentleman. At a trial in which he is serving as a juror, he is astonished to see that the defendant is the falsely accused Katúsha Máslova, whom he had seduced in the past. When Katúsha is sentenced to hard labor in Siberia, his pity for her in the life to which he has driven her leads him to a period of self-examination, from which he emerges regarding his life as empty and degenerate and feeling a need to cleanse his soul. Determined to follow the prisoner to Siberia and marry her, he feels himself purged when her sentence is lightened to exile and she elects to stay with Valdemar Símonson, who loves her.

Katerína Mikháelovna Máslova (kah-teh-REE-nah mih-KHAH-ih-lohv-nah MAH-sloh-vah), called **Katúsha** (kah-TEW-shah), an illegitimate girl. Seduced at sixteen by Prince Dmítri Ivánovitch Nekhlúdoff, she becomes a prostitute and later is falsely accused of complicity in murder. At her trial, she is recognized by her seducer, a juryman, who, in remorse for his past treatment, wishes to marry her. When, through Dmítri's efforts, her sentence is commuted to exile, she elects to remain with Valdemar Símonson rather than jeopardize her benefactor's happiness by his marriage to a woman like herself.

Valdemar Símonson (VAL-deh-mahr SIH-mon-son), a political prisoner who falls in love with Katúsha Máslova as they are on their way to exile in Siberia.

Véra Doúkova (VEH-rah doh-EW-khoh-vah), a political prisoner interested in the welfare of Katúsha.

Lydia Shoústova (SHEW-stoh-vah), Véra Doúkova's friend.

Selénin (seh-LEH-nihn), a public prosecutor and an old friend of Prince Dmítri. Fundamentally an intelligent, honest man, he has come to make society's standards his own.

Sophia Ivánovna (ee-VAH-nohv-nah) and

Mary Ivánovna, aunts of Prince Dmítri and childhood guardians of Katúsha.

Katerína Ivánovna Tchársky (CHAHR-skee), an aunt of Prince Dmítri.

Matróna Khárina (mah-TRYOH-nah CHA-rih-nah), Katúsha's aunt.

Princess Mary Korchágin (kohr-CHA-gihn), the prospective fiancée of Prince Dmítri.

RESUSCITATION OF A HANGED MAN

Author: Denis Johnson (1949-   )
First published: 1991
Genre: Novel

Locale: Cape Cod, Massachusetts
Time: 1980-1981
Plot: Psychological

Leonard (Lenny) English, a drunk in his early thirties with an unstable past. The story is told in the third person, from his point of view. He is troubled by his lack of faith and seeks absolution for his sin of attempted suicide, which occurred in the year prior to the beginning of the novel. One of his first acts after arriving in Provincetown, on Cape Cod, is to go to confession, but he finds himself unable to confess his sin to the priest. He has been unable to tell anyone why he tried to kill himself. Leaving church, he meets Leanna Sousa and is immediately attracted to her, but she says that she is "strictly P-town," meaning that she is gay. Leonard is in Provincetown because he was hired by Ray Sands to work two part-time jobs, as a disc jockey and as a private detective. His first assignment is to tail Marla Baker and find out where she moved. She is a middle-aged divorcée with a lesbian lover named Carol. One night, Leanna visits Marla; she soon begins sleeping at Marla's apartment. Leonard meets Leanna again and tells her about his unstable past, then admits to getting worked up about unimportant things and tells her that the only real question is whether God really killed himself. Leonard wonders about the propriety of spying on Marla and sends her a letter telling her that she is being followed; she leaves town shortly thereafter. Ray later assigns Leonard to find Gerald Twinbrook, Jr., a painter. After Ray's death, Leonard takes over the case. He is kidnapped in a case of mistaken identity and begins to think that he has stumbled into some kind of conspiracy. In his increasing paranoia, he begins to draw connections between unrelated events, fearing that the kidnapping might have something to do with the Truth Infantry and his search for Gerald Twinbrook. He moves into Leanna's hotel because he is afraid to go home and renews the search for Twinbrook. After Marla returns to Leanna as a lover, Leonard becomes less mentally stable and makes appeals to Leanna over the air while working at the radio station. He becomes obsessed with the Twinbrook case and suspects that Twinbrook may have been kidnapped by the Truth Infantry. Eventually, Leonard finds Twinbrook's body, in a forestry camp in New Hampshire. After he returns to Provincetown, he goes to Leanna's hotel, dresses in her clothes, steals a rowboat, and joins other boats in a procession for the annual Blessing of the Fleet. Using Leanna's gun, he attempts to shoot Bishop Andrew, who is officiating at the blessing. He is imprisoned for this crime and reveals that he likes being hungry and in prison.

Leanna Sousa, Leonard's lover, the owner of a hotel in Provincetown. When Leonard first sees her, in church, she has scarlet fingernails and black bangs, and Leonard is attracted by her legs. She dismisses Leonard at their first meeting but later admits that she fell in love with his leather jacket. During their first long talk, Leanna says that Leonard does not really want women to know him. After they have dated several times, and after Ray's death, she reveals that she is tired of the gay life and takes him to her hotel. The next morning, Leonard does not remember what happened there. Leonard stays with her more often and they sleep together, but he is impotent. The night of his kidnapping, they discuss his attempted suicide, and she asks if it felt sexy to hang himself. He says that it did and gets an erection from the conversation. They make love, and she reveals that she had one other male lover, whom she paid to have sex with her in an attempt to get pregnant so that she and Marla could have a baby. Later, Marla returns as her lover. Leanna says that she can handle having both a male and a female lover, but Marla's return troubles Leonard.

Ray Sands, a former police detective who hires Leonard to work as a disc jockey and private investigator. He is about sixty-five years old and owns a radio station as well as running his investigation agency. He is usually rather cheerless but shows a human side when he invites Leonard to his house on the day of New Year's Eve. He shows Leonard his model trains and exhibits tenderness toward his wife, Grace, who is senile or at least eccentric. He ignores her when she does not make sense or she responds inappropriately. He has a photo studio in his house, and Leonard discovers fake passports there. It is in Ray's office that Leonard finds a note saying "Kill the Bishop."

Phil, a local taxi driver. He is the first person Leonard meets in Cape Cod. Leonard crashes his Volkswagen on his way there, and Phil stops to see that he is all right. Phil smokes marijuana as he drives Leonard to a rooming house owned by a cousin. He appears several times in the novel, providing facts to Leonard. He tells Leonard a little about the Truth Infantry and reveals that Ray Sands was the head of the local branch. He admits that he was Leanna's first male lover.

Gerald Twinbrook, Jr., a missing artist whom English is hired to find. He had tried to get information about various corporations from the government, under the Freedom of Information Act, and had been researching a case of attempted resuscitation of a hanged man. He hangs himself in a forestry camp, and Leonard finds his body. Leonard takes his sketchbook from the camp and has conversations with his ghost on the bus back to Provincetown, but he never finds out why Twinbrook committed suicide.

Berryman, a reporter for Ray Sands's radio station. He is fired because Ray does not like his report on Agent Orange, which involved an interview of a Vietnam veteran. Berryman's interview mentioned the Truth Infantry, introducing Leonard to that group.

— *A. J. Sobczak*

THE RETURN

Author: Walter de la Mare (1873-1956)
First published: 1910
Genre: Novel

Locale: England
Time: The nineteenth century
Plot: Ghost

Arthur Lawford, a middle-aged Englishman who, while resting in an ancient churchyard, finds himself strangely turned into the shape of Nicholas Sabathier, an eighteenth century Britisher who had committed suicide on the Eve of St. Michael and All Angels in 1739. Lawford keeps his own mind and has strange feelings about himself, as well as difficulties with his family and friends. On the anniversary of Sabathier's death, however, he is returned to his own shape once again.

Sheila Lawford, Arthur's wife. Though she believes the stranger she sees is really her husband in a different shape, she refuses to stay with him at night as a wife and insists on leaving the house. She finally leaves him alone in the house for several days to wrestle with his problems.

Herbert Herbert, a stranger in the neighborhood, a bookish recluse. He identifies Lawford's new shape as that of Nicholas Sabathier. During his transformation, Lawford spends a great deal of time with Herbert and his sister Grisel, both of whom are quite sympathetic.

Grisel Herbert, Herbert's sister. She and Arthur come to realize that in another life they have previously loved. She gives Lawford the feeling when he is with her that he is fighting some strange spirit, and yet he takes great comfort in her company.

Alice Lawford, Arthur's teenage daughter. While she faints from shock when first she sees her transformed father, she goes to him in secret, against her mother's wishes, to tell him that she sympathizes and hopes that all will turn out well.

The Reverend Mr. Bethany, rector of the parish. Although he is horrified at what happens to Lawford, he remains sympathetic. On the night that Lawford returns to his own shape, the rector arrives at the Lawford home to keep vigil.

THE RETURN OF THE NATIVE

Author: Thomas Hardy (1840-1928)
First published: 1878
Genre: Novel

Locale: Egdon Heath, in southern England
Time: The 1840's
Plot: Tragedy

Clement Yeobright, called **Clym**, a native of Egdon Heath who returns to visit with his mother and cousin after having made a career for himself as a successful diamond merchant in Paris. His success and his education make him an outstanding figure among the humble people who live scattered about the wild heath, and his return for a visit is a great occasion for them. During his stay, he decides to remain, finding that the heath and its people mean far more to him than worldly success in Paris; his intention is to become a teacher and open a school to educate the people among whom he grew up, a superstitious and ignorant, if lovable and kindly, set. A sensitive and somewhat rash young man, he falls in love with Eustacia Vye, a beautiful and passionate woman. In her, Clym sees a perfect helpmeet for a schoolmaster, but she sees in him only a chance to escape the heath and to live abroad. Clym and Eustacia Vye are married, over the protests of his mother. These protests arouse the anger of Clym, who after his marriage does not communicate with her. Disaster, in the form of partial blindness, strikes Clym, but he accepts his plight philosophically and turns to the homely task of furze-cutting to earn a living. Unhappy in her lot, Eustacia turns against him. On one occasion, she refuses to let his mother into the house, an inhospitable act that indirectly causes the death of the older woman. Stricken by his mother's death and, a short time later, by his wife's suicide, Clym becomes a lay preacher to the people of the heath.

Eustacia Vye, the self-seeking and sensuous young woman who marries Clym Yeobright. Unhappy on the heath, bored by life with her grandfather, she tries to escape. First she seeks an opportunity to do so by marrying Clym. When he cannot and will not leave the heath, she turns to a former fiancé, now a married man. At the last, however, she cannot demean herself by unfaithfulness to her husband; instead of running away with her lover, she commits suicide by plunging into a millpond.

Damon Wildeve, a former engineer, still a young man, who settles unhappily upon the heath as keeper of the Quiet Woman Inn. Selfish and uninspired, when he loses Eustacia Vye to Clym Yeobright, he marries Thomasin Yeobright, Clym's cousin, out of spite. The marriage is an unhappy one, for Wildeve still pursues Eustacia, who is also unhappy because her husband cannot give her the life she wishes. Wildeve's pursuit of illicit love ends in his own death, for he drowns while trying to save Eustacia's life after she throws herself into a pond rather than elope to Paris as his mistress.

Thomasin Yeobright, called **Tamsin**, Clym's cousin,

reared with Clym by his mother. A simple and faithful girl who loves Damon Wildeve despite his treatment of her, she is also faithful to the conventions and clings to her marriage even after it turns out badly. At her husband's death, she inherits a small fortune left by his uncle shortly before Wildeve's end. She finds happiness eventually in a second marriage and in her little daughter.

Diggory Venn, an itinerant young reddleman in love with Thomasin Yeobright. Once of good family and some little fortune, he has fallen upon evil days. His lonely existence gives him opportunity to act in his love's behalf, and he tries to circumvent Wildeve's pursuit of Eustacia Vye. Having saved up a little money, he becomes a dairyman and presents himself, after a decent time, as Thomasin's suitor, following her husband's death. His patience, love, and understanding are rewarded when she accepts him.

Mrs. Yeobright, Clym Yeobright's mother and Thomasin Yeobright's aunt. In her good sense, she opposes both their marriages, although the young people misinterpret her motives as selfish. Being of a forgiving nature, she tries to be reconciled with her son and his wife, as she became with Thomasin and her husband. Yet Eustacia refuses her overtures and is indirectly the cause of the older woman's death; Mrs. Yeobright dies of exposure and snakebite after having been refused admittance to her son's home.

Captain Vye, Eustacia Vye's grandfather, a retired seaman who brings his granddaughter to live on the heath with no thought of how such a place will affect her. He is a self-contained old man with little knowledge of the intense personality of his charge; therefore, he makes no effort to prevent her tragedy.

Johnny Nunsuch, a little boy who plays upon the heath and unwittingly becomes involved as a witness to the fate of the Yeobrights, Eustacia Vye, and Damon Wildeve. His testimony concerning Mrs. Yeobright's last words brings about the separation of Clym Yeobright and his wife.

Mrs. Nunsuch, Johnny's mother. Convinced that Eustacia Vye is a witch who has cast a spell upon the child, Mrs. Nunsuch, an uneducated, superstitious woman, resorts to black arts to exorcise the spell. On the night of Eustacia Vye's death, she forms a doll in the girl's image and destroys it in a fire.

Granfer Cantle, an ancient,

Christian Cantle, his elderly youngest son,

Olly Dowden,

Sam, a turf-cutter,

Humphrey, a furze-cutter, and

Timothy Fairway, residents of Egdon Heath. They voice much of the rural wisdom and observe the folk customs of the region.

THE RETURN OF THE SOLDIER

Author: Rebecca West (Cicily Isabel Fairfield, 1892-1983)
First published: 1918
Genre: Novel

Locale: Southern England
Time: During World War I
Plot: Psychological realism

Chris Baldry, a thirty-five-year-old English country gentleman who is attractive and fair-complected, with brown and gold hair. Charming, honorable, and amiable, he has left his wife and cousin Jenny home at Baldry Court in the south of England to become a soldier in France during World War I. Fifteen years earlier, after the death of his father, Chris was given a large estate, along with the "responsibility of" his many female relatives. He married a beautiful but ostentatious woman and, several years later, suffered the death of their only child, a two-year-old boy named Oliver. The story begins when Chris is fighting in the trenches during the war. He suffers an injury that results in a memory loss that erases everyone from his mind save the woman whom he loved as a young man fifteen years earlier and whom circumstances had caused him to lose. From a military hospital, he writes to her; consequently, she informs his family of his whereabouts. When he returns home to Baldry Court, he demands to see her. Her subsequent periodic visits are his only joy and reality, and their love for each other remains fresh and genuine. It is her generous spirit and his sense of duty to his family that ultimately bring back his memory and the end of their relationship, if not their love. His return to the trenches of Flanders is ensured.

Margaret Allington Grey, the first and only real love in Chris's life. Thirty-three years old, she is plain, with tender gray eyes and fair, curly hair, and she has aged considerably since her love affair with Chris fifteen years earlier. For the past ten years, she has been living a life of dreary poverty with

a nondescript husband in an ugly working-class town. Like Chris, she has suffered the death of a two-year-old son, and later she notes that both she and Chris were unable to have a "complete child." It is she to whom Chris writes of his war injuries. After she informs Chris's family of his condition, her love and concern motivate her to visit Chris at Baldry Court. When she was eighteen years old, she had been living on Monkey Island with her father, where the two of them had kept an inn. When Chris rowed by one day, they were attracted immediately to each other; both loved the sights and scents and sounds of nature. Similarly, fifteen years later, when they are reunited on the lawn of Baldry Court, they often commune with one another wordlessly. Margaret brings this series of visits to an end by suggesting and carrying out the plan that ends Chris's amnesia and thereby forces his unwilling return to his wife and worldly responsibilities.

Kitty Baldry, the wife of Chris Baldry, who lost her son five years earlier. Beautiful and gentle but vain and materialistic, Kitty spends her days improving the quality of Baldry Court with elegant touches. The degree of her sensitivity to her son's death is seen in her use of his sunny nursery as the room where she dries her hair. Her first encounter with Margaret is marked by disdain for the latter's shabby appearance and lower-class address. Her response to her husband's amnesia is one of annoyance rather than concern for his well-being. When his memory finally returns after Margaret's intervention, her response is not joy or relief but mere satisfaction.

Jenny, a thirty-five-year-old, unmarried cousin of Chris and friend of Kitty. She lives at Baldry Court and narrates the story. Jenny was the childhood playmate of Chris and has loved and revered him ever since. More perceptive and high-principled than Kitty, she comes to love and admire the saintly Margaret as the story progresses, while her opinion of Kitty deteriorates.

— Vicki K. Robinson

RETURN TO REGIÓN
(Volverás a Región)

Author: Juan Benet (1927-1993)
First published: 1967
Genre: Novel

Locale: Región, Spain
Time: The 1920's to the 1960's
Plot: Antistory

Aurelio Rumbal (oh-REE-lyoh rewm-BAHL), or **Rombal**, or **Rubal**, or **Robal**, a revolutionary who has been to America and has come back to Región. He is a teacher in a high school, an intellectual who, with his wife, prepares the intellectuals of Región for a confrontation with conservative forces. The multiple names by which he is known provide a clue to the nature of all the characters: The author is giving a blurred picture of men and women seen through the veil of memory.

The Intruder, a newcomer to Región. He appears with a golden coin; he is representative of the outsiders who will dispute the rights of the natives of Región to their land. He has been working in a mine, and on most nights he goes to play with the young people in town, among them Gamallo.

Gamallo (gah-MAH-yoh), one of the players at the game of cards with the Intruder. He loses all of his wealth and, ultimately, his fiancée, María Timoner. She accepts her fate and goes with the Intruder.

Marré Gamallo (mah-RAY), Gamallo's daughter, now a commander of the Nationalist Army trying to reconquer the territory of Región. She is a hostage of the Republicans, and she becomes the lover of Juan de Tomé, one of the leaders on the Republican side.

Doctor Daniel Sebastián (seh-bas-TYAHN), a physician who established a clinic in Región. He devotes all of his care to only one patient, the Boy.

The Boy, a mentally retarded youth who has been left to the care of Doctor Sebastián and Adela, his maid. The Boy will spend the period of the Spanish Civil War waiting for the return of his mother; at the end, after Adela has died, he will kill Doctor Sebastián.

The Numa (NEW-mah), a mythical guardian of the region, a figure whom no one has seen but who nevertheless dominates the imagination of the people. The legends that surround him explain that nobody is safe in his territory because he hunts and kills trespassers. The fact that he has killed his father enhances his mythical leadership among the people, who incessantly recount his exploits, feeling that they are safe under this vigilante.

— Jaime Ferrán

THE REVENGE FOR LOVE

Author: Wyndham Lewis (1882-1957)
First published: 1937
Genre: Novel

Locale: Andalusia and Navarre, Spain, and London, England
Time: 1936-1937
Plot: Social satire

Percy Hardcaster, a fat Englishman of forty; he is five feet, eight inches tall and is a propagandist for the Communists in the Spanish Civil War. He has a little mustache, and he wears silver-rimmed spectacles. He is shot in the leg while trying to escape from a Spanish prison; infection sets in, and the leg must be amputated. He disputes the truth of Marxist politics with Gillian and is beaten by Jack Cruze. He runs guns into Spain with Victor Stamp; he is captured and returned to prison there.

Victor Stamp, a big Australian painter, twenty-six years old. A decent man, he recognizes his limitations as an artist, but this awareness robs him of any sense of purpose. He loans pictures to the People's Art League but cannot sell them. He tries working for Freddie Salmon, faking paintings by Vincent van Gogh, but he destroys his work. He goes with Percy and Margot to the Spanish frontier, where he is used as bait in smuggling guns to Communists. He and Margot die from a fall during a mountain storm while trying to escape from the Spanish Civil Guard.

Margaret (Margot) Stamp, Victor's common-law wife, twenty-four years old. Devoted to Victor, she retains faith in him despite his failures. She accompanies him to the Spanish frontier, where she tries to prevent him from running guns for the Communists. She dies with Victor while trying to escape from Spain to France through the mountains.

Tristram (Tristy) Phipps, a painter and friend of Victor Stamp, six feet, two inches tall. He lives with Gillian in a basement flat near the Thames. A dedicated Communist, he quarrels with Gillian over politics, and she leaves him. He accepts work for Freddie Salmon making counterfeit paintings.

Gillian (Jill) Phipps, Tristy's wife, a Communist who was born in privileged circumstances. A self-consciously liberated woman, she enjoys toying with men. When a dalliance with Percy Hardcaster turns into a quarrel in which he dismisses her as a pampered intellectual who gets a thrill from her association with the working class, she watches with complicity as Jack Cruze gives him a brutal beating. Later, she moves in with Jack.

John "Jack" Cruze, a stocky man of forty, five feet, eight inches tall, and an inveterate chaser of women. His father was a country constable, but he is an actuary in the London offices to which Tristram Phipps goes for help with tax matters. Jack pursues Gillian, who treats him with a mixture of seductiveness and condescension that both angers and arouses him.

Don Alvaro Morato (AHL-vah-roh moh-RAH-toh), a prison guard. He shoots Percy Hardcaster and kills Percy's accomplice during Percy's attempted escape. Black-mustached and cynical, he despises the English Communists fighting in the Spanish Civil War.

Serafin (seh-rah-FEEN), a prison guard subordinate to Don Alvaro, about thirty years old, with a hanging underlip, a squinting and winking left eye, a small mustard mustache, bad gums, and amber eyes. He is shot and killed by Don Alvaro when he attempts to help Percy escape.

Don Agustin (ah-guhs-TEEN), a Communist imprisoned with Percy in Spain.

Pascual (pahs-KWAHL), the Communist who arranged Percy's escape. He visits Percy in the hospital and rails against the brutality of Serafin's death.

Sean O'Hara, an Irish-born Communist leader, dwarfish and dark. He and his wife give a party in honor of the heroic Percy after his return to England from the Spanish prison. According to rumors that he denies, he is guilty of serious betrayals. He and Abershaw send Percy and Victor to smuggle guns into Spain.

Eileen O'Hara, Sean's English wife, thirty years old and of middle-class background. She is disturbed by the rumors about her husband despite her desire to disbelieve them.

Peter Wallace, born **Reuben Wallach**, a Communist art critic who writes about pictures and sculpture. He discusses modern painting with Victor and Tristram at O'Hara's party.

"Abb" Abershaw, an accomplice of Sean O'Hara and a business partner of Freddie Salmon. He is six feet, three inches tall, with the face of a crook and a small mustache. He forges Victor's name and sets Victor up as a decoy in the smuggling operation in Spain.

Freddie Salmon, the owner of a "factory" for counterfeiting paintings. He dislikes Victor and provokes him into destroying a fake self-portrait of van Gogh.

Isaac Wohl, a painter who works for Freddie Salmon, specializing in faking paintings by Marie Laurencin.

Agnes Irons, a friend of Margot, deeply suntanned from a golfing trip to Malaya. She has large teeth and laughs constantly. She listens to Margot's troubles.

Don Mateu (Mat) (mah-TEH-ew), the Spanish proprietor of a hotel on the French side of the Spanish frontier. He works with Percy to smuggle arms to the Communists in the Civil War.

— *Richard D. McGhee*

THE REVENGE OF BUSSY D'AMBOIS

Author: George Chapman (c. 1559-1634)
First published: 1613
Genre: Drama

Locale: Paris, France
Time: The sixteenth century
Plot: Tragedy

Clermont d'Ambois (klehr-MOH[N] dahm-BWAH), the brother of Bussy d'Ambois and his sworn avenger. He is the playwright's ideal hero, brave, learned, and stoic, resolved to preserve inviolate "a good mind and a name" through whatever changes in fortune destiny brings him.

Charlotte, his intensely emotional sister, who spurs Clermont and her husband to avenge Bussy with the cold-blooded forcefulness of a Lady Macbeth.

Baligny (bah-leen-YEE), Charlotte's husband, a timeserving courtier. He professes allegiance to Guise and virtue while he is conspiring with King Henry to overthrow the duke.

Henry III, the king of France. No longer portrayed as the just, if slightly susceptible, ruler of *Bussy d'Ambois*, he surfeits himself with sensual pleasures and plots the destruction of virtuous men around him.

The duc du Guise (dewk dew geez), Bussy's enemy, who has become a "tenth worthy," the exemplar of all virtue, and

Clermont's friend and patron.

Montsurry (moh[n]-sewr-REE), Bussy's slayer. His refusal to accept Clermont's challenge marks him as weak and cowardly until the last moments of his life, when he summons enough courage to defend himself valiantly against his opponent.

Tamyra (tah-MEER-rah), his countess. Forsaking her resolution to wander until her death, she is again living with her husband and simultaneously plotting with Charlotte to avenge her lover.

Renel (reh-NEHL), Clermont's friend, an astute critic of the corruption at court.

Maillard (mi-YAHR), Baligny's lieutenant. He defends his ambush of Clermont on the grounds that the public good and the will of the king justify private treachery.

The countess of Cambrai (kahm-BRAY), Clermont's mistress, who literally cries her eyes out grieving over his arrest.

THE REVENGER'S TRAGEDY

Author: Cyril Tourneur (c. 1575-1626)
First published: 1607
Genre: Drama

Locale: A city in Italy
Time: The Renaissance
Plot: Tragedy

Vendice (vehn-DEE-chay), a young Italian who broods over the skull of his dead sweetheart while plotting revenge on the duke, her murderer. Well-versed in the corruptions of the court, he disguises himself as Piato, a crafty, lascivious old man, and offers his services to Lussurioso. After his diabolical

murder of the duke, who is poisoned when he kisses the lips of the skull that Vendice has dressed as a masked lady, he appears in his own person, assuming a melancholy spirit to deceive his young prince again. Although he successfully dispatches his enemies and places the dukedom into the hands of just men, he is himself executed; he condemns himself out of his own mouth and receives justice from the man to whom he has given the right to dispense it.

Hippolito (ee-POHL-ee-toh), his brother, who supports him in his plots to purge the court of its corruption.

The duke, a despicable old lecher who governs more by personal desires than by any notion of right and wrong. The few honest men of his court deeply resent his staying of the sentence of his wife's youngest son, who had raped the virtuous wife of one of his lords. There is a strong element of poetic justice in the manner of his death. Vendice's lady was executed for refusing to yield to him; her lover traps her murderer by promising to procure a young woman for his pleasure.

The duchess, his second wife, a fitting mate for the duke. Enraged by her husband's refusal to release her youngest son absolutely, she takes her vengeance by having an affair with Spurio, the duke's bastard son.

Lussurioso (lews-sew-ee-OH-soh), the duke's heir, whose character is aptly expressed in his name. He hires Vendice, disguised as Piato, to seduce Castiza for him, cynically suggesting that he try the mother first if the daughter is recalcitrant. He has some lingering remnants of honor with regard to the behavior of his stepmother and Spurio, and his first act as duke is to order her banishment and Spurio's execution.

Ambitioso (ahm-BEE-tee-oh-soh) and

Supervacuo (sew-pehr-VAH-kew-oh), the duchess' sons. Each is eager to destroy Lussurioso and seize the dukedom for himself; mutually ambitious, they are extremely envious of each other. Their treacherous plot to have the legal heir executed fails, and they succeed only in causing the death of their own brother.

Spurio (SPEW-ree-oh), the duke's bastard son, ambitious, like his stepbrothers, for power. He resents his father and chooses a peculiarly damnable mode of revenge for his birth, that of becoming his stepmother's lover. His greed brings him a fitting death: He and Ambitioso stab each other in a quarrel over the possession of the dead Lussurioso's dukedom.

Gratiana (grah-tee-AH-nah), the mother of Vendice, a weak-spirited woman who is persuaded by her son, disguised as Piato, to encourage her daughter to submit to Lussurioso's lust. She is won over chiefly by his offer of money. Confronted by Vendice with her betrayal of Castiza, she repents and once again recognizes the inestimable value of virtue.

Castiza (kahs-TEE-zah), Gratiana's daughter and Vendice's sister. She violently rejects her mother's insistence that she submit to Lussurioso and boxes the ears of the ducal emissary, Piato, who rejoices at his sister's lively virtue. She seems for a few moments to have given in to her mother's arguments, but when she sees that Gratiana has been convinced again of the value of honor, she confesses that she was only testing her; her own allegiance to virtue is unchanging.

Antonio (ahn-TOH-nyoh), a just nobleman who becomes duke after the mass murder of the old ruler's family. He, like Vendice, had just cause to hate the ducal family, for his wife died after she was attacked by one of the duchess' sons. He recognizes, however, the necessity for law, and he orders Vendice's immediate arrest when he reveals himself as the avenger of wrongs committed by the old duke.

Piero (pee-EH-roh), Antonio's friend, one of the group of masquers who kill Lussurioso and his nobles.

Dondolo (DOHN-doh-loh), a pompous gentleman usher.

THE REVOLT OF THE ANGELS
(La Révolte des anges)

Author: Anatole France (Jacques-Anatole-François Thibault, 1844-1924)
First published: 1914
Genre: Novel

Locale: France
Time: Early twentieth century
Plot: Fantasy

Arcade (ahr-KAHD), an angel who plans to lead a revolt against God (Ialdabaoth). He gathers together hundreds of thousands of rebel angels but is disappointed when Satan quashes the revolution.

Monsieur Julien Sariette (zhoo-LYAH[N] sahr-YEHT), the meticulous librarian in charge of the extensive collection that Arcade uses to educate himself for the revolution. Sariette is confounded and frustrated because Arcade scatters the books. When a volume of *Lucretius*, a very rare work, is lost, Sariette's mind snaps.

Maurice d'Esparvieu (moh-REES dehs-pahr-VYEW), a wealthy, lazy young man whose guardian angel is Arcade. After an attempt to dissuade Arcade from his plans, d'Esparvieu regards him with quiet amusement and shares his clothes and his mistress with the angel.

Madame Gilberte des Aubels (zheel-BEHR day-zoh-BEHL), Maurice's mistress, who also bestows her favors on Arcade.

Satan, a sympathetic prince who, petitioned by Arcade and his army of rebels to lead the revolution against God, refuses.

The rebel forces accept his reasons for not making war: If the revolution succeeded, Satan and his forces would become as God and the heavenly hosts; that is, they would lose their sympathy for humanity. War begets war, and the vanquished always seek to regain what they have lost. The real duty of the revolutionary army of angels is to stay on Earth to spread the doctrine of love and compassion because only by doing so can God be defeated and peace come to the universe.

Prince Istar, a rebel angel who specializes in chemistry. He supports the revolutionary cause by manufacturing bombs.

Théophile (tay-oh-FEEL), an angel, approached by Arcade, who refuses to fight God. He is ashamed because he has satisfied his lust with a mortal woman, but he still respects God's authority.

Sophar (soh-FAHR), an angel who has become a Jewish banker named **Max Everdingen**. He will not join the rebel forces, but he offers to sell them munitions, the cost of which he would finance at his bank.

Zita (zee-TAH), a hostile female angel who wishes to join the ranks and fight as a man in the revolution.

REYNARD THE FOX

Author: Unknown
First transcribed: c. 1175-1250
Genre: Short fiction

Locale: Europe
Time: The Middle Ages
Plot: Satire

Reynard, the fox. So crafty and persuasive a liar is he, that he is at last made high bailiff of the country, though he has flagrantly cheated and injured all of the animals, including the king. Thus is craftiness set above mere strength.

Noble, the lion, king of beasts. He listens to the animals' grievances against Reynard, and even sentences the fox to death, but Reynard lies so cleverly about hidden treasure and treachery on the part of the others that the king frees him. Noble is similarly gulled a second time and on this occasion even makes Reynard high bailiff.

Isegrim, the wolf, whose children have been made blind by Reynard. Convinced of Isegrim's treason, the king gives the wolf's shoes to Reynard. After this, when the wolf and the fox are engaged in combat, Reynard persuades Isegrim to let him go with promises of rewards.

Tibert, the cat. He defends Reynard before the others until he has been tricked by the fox into jumping into a trap.

Bruin, the bear. Reynard's promises of honey lure him into a trap, and he is badly beaten before he escapes. Later, Reynard convinces the king that Bruin is plotting to replace him as ruler. Noble gives Bruin's skin to Reynard.

Grimbard, the brock (a badger). He defends Reynard before the court and even warns the fox of a plot against him.

Panther, who complains of Reynard to the king.

Chanticleer, the cock. His complaint is that Reynard deceived him into relaxing his vigilance by pretending to have given up eating flesh; Reynard then eats Chanticleer's children.

Kyward, the hare. He accompanies Reynard on a "pilgrimage" and is eaten by him.

Bellin, the ram, who goes with Reynard and Kyward. Deceived into thinking he is carrying a letter, he brings Kyward's head to the king. The furious king then gives the stupid ram and all his lineage to the wolf and the bear to atone for his misjudgment of them.

RHADAMISTUS AND ZENOBIA
(Rhadmiste et Zénobie)

Author: Prosper Jolyot de Crébillon (1674-1762)
First published: 1711
Genre: Drama

Locale: Artanissa, the capital of Iberia
Time: c. 60 C.E.
Plot: Tragedy

Rhadamistus (rah-dah-MIHS-tuhs), the king of Armenia, the son of Pharasmanes but reared by Mithridates as his own child. When Mithridates turns against him, Rhadamistus attacks his foster father's kingdom, murders him, and, in a rage, throws his own bride Zenobia into a river, from which she is rescued without his knowledge. Later, as Roman envoy at the court of Pharasmanes, he learns that Zenobia is alive. He begs for and receives her forgiveness and is mortally wounded as he attempts to flee with her.

Zenobia (zee-NOH-bee-ah), also called **Ismenia**, Mithridates' daughter and the wife of Rhadamistus. To protect her father from Rhadamistus, she marries him, only to be thrown by her husband into a river and left for dead. Rescued, she becomes a prisoner of Pharasmanes, who desires to marry her. She, in turn, is in love with Arsames, to whom Pharasmanes

finally relinquishes her in his remorse over his killing of his son Rhadamistus.

Pharasmanes, Rhadamistus' father. His jealousy and lust for power lead him into conflict with his son Rhadamistus, whom he kills. In remorse, he sacrifices his throne and the widowed Zenobia to Arsames.

Arsames, another of Pharasmanes' sons, in love with Zenobia.

Mithridates (mihth-rih-DAY-tees), Zenobia's father and Rhadamistus' foster father.

Phenice, Zenobia's confidante.

Hiero, Rhadamistus' companion.

Hydaspes, Pharasmanes' confidant.

Mithranes, the captain of Pharasmanes' guard.

RHINOCEROS
(Rhinocéros)

Author: Eugène Ionesco (1912-1994)
First published: 1959
Genre: Drama

Locale: A small provincial town in France
Time: Indeterminate
Plot: Absurdist

Berenger, an average man who grew up in the small town where he now lives and works in a government office. Occasionally lazy but sometimes conscientious, he never seeks to distinguish himself. Although he is accused by his friend Jean of having slovenly habits (such as never shaving or wearing a tie and always arriving late), Berenger would like to fit into the

conventional provincial society in which he grew up, to marry his coworker, Daisy, and to live a normal life. His inability to discount what his senses tell him ultimately puts him in the difficult position of being the last person on Earth not to go along with the crowd. Beneath his seemingly ordinary exterior, Berenger is basically decent, though insecure. In spite of his timidity and self-doubt, he is capable of enormous courage in resisting the rhinoceroses who have taken over the town. He is the only character in the entire play who is developed in three dimensions. As the "Everyman" protagonist of the play, he fights a brave but doomed battle against the pressure for him to give up his humanity.

Jean, Berenger's coworker and best friend. Determined to succeed, he frequently notices how others (especially Berenger) do not come up to the highest standards of conduct or professional behavior. A perfectionist with ambition, Jean will perhaps do more than most in order to succeed.

Daisy, another of Berenger's coworkers and the object of Berenger's affection. Although he constantly addresses her as Miss Daisy, out of respect, she seems to share in Berenger's warm feelings. Daisy tries hard to resist the rhinoceros invaders and puts up a good fight, but ultimately she is attracted to them and abandons (and repudiates) Berenger.

Dudard, another of Berenger's coworkers and, at the age of thirty-five, the man most likely to be promoted next. Diplomatic and eager to advance, Dudard tries to ignore the threat of the rhinoceroses until he serves as an accessory to them and then becomes one of them.

The Logician, a professional philosopher who prides himself on his ability to think logically. His attempts at rational thought, although they seem to make sense, are ultimately without value to the townspeople confronted by the irrational threat of the rhinos.

The Waitress, a young woman who works in the town's café. She is shocked by the sudden appearance of a rhino in the main street.

The Housewife, who comes out to shop and is overcome by sadness when her cat is killed by a rhino.

The Old Gentleman, a skeptical bystander who is seated at the café when the first rhino appears in town.

Mrs. Boeuf (BEUF), the wife of one of Berenger's coworkers. She comes to the office to explain her husband's absence that day but is shocked when he arrives a few minutes later, because he has become a rhinoceros. Her loyalty to him, even in his changed form, never waivers.

Mr. Papillon (pah-pee-YOH[N]), the head of Berenger's department. As supervisor, he tends to be an authority figure who orders around the office workers.

— *Kenneth Krauss*

RICEYMAN STEPS

Author: Arnold Bennett (1867-1931)
First published: 1923
Genre: Novel

Locale: Riceyman Steps, a suburb of London
Time: 1919
Plot: Social realism

Henry Earlforward, a miserly bookstore owner. He marries a neighboring confectioner whom he believes as miserly as he. He refuses to spend money for electricity, a wedding ring, even for food and medical advice. When he becomes ill, he refuses to enter a hospital because of the expense. He dies the victim of his own parsimony.

Mrs. Violet Arb, thrifty owner of a confectionery shop. She discovers too late that her husband Henry is miserly. Although a doctor sees to it that she goes to the hospital for a needed operation, she has become so weakened by malnutrition that she dies.

Elsie, the Earlforwards' maid. Because she is half-starved, she steals food from her employers. In order to have sixpence to send a messenger to inquire about her mistress, she has to steal the money from her miserly master. After the Earlfor-

wards' deaths, she goes to work, along with her sweetheart, for Dr. Raste.

Joe, Elsie's sweetheart. He turns up at the bookstore shabbily dressed, sick, and just released from jail. Elsie nurses him back to health while concealing him in the Earlforwards' quarters. He goes to work for Dr. Raste. He and Elsie plan to marry.

T. T. Riceyman, the dead uncle who left the bookstore to Henry.

Dr. Raste, the medical doctor who tries to save the life of Earlforward's wife and befriends Elsie and Joe.

Mr. Belrose and
Mrs. Belrose, the couple who buy Mrs. Arb's shop when she marries Henry. They try to be helpful to the Earlforwards when the latter become ill.

RICH IN LOVE

Author: Josephine Humphreys (1945-   )
First published: 1987
Genre: Novel

Locale: Mount Pleasant and Charleston, South Carolina
Time: Mid-1980's
Plot: Domestic realism

Lucille Odom, the protagonist and narrator. "Lulu" to her mother and sister, she is a seventeen-year-old high school senior during the events of the novel but is narrating from two years later. When her mother, Helen, abruptly disappears, Lucille tries to keep the family together. As it becomes clear that her mother will not be returning, Lucille tries out some new relationships and eventually learns to redefine "family." Her telling of the story emphasizes the joy she takes in her world rather than the sadness of a disintegrating family. Indeed,

Lucille's coming together, opposed to her family's coming apart, makes the novel life-affirming.

Warren Odom, Lucille's father, called "Pop." A sixty-year-old retired demolition expert, his distinguishing characteristic is his innocence, according to Lucille, but Lucille no doubt sees herself reflected in him. Lucille thinks he will be heartbroken by Helen's departure, but in fact his heart is remarkably resilient. Troubled by memories of poverty during the Depression, he uses his memories to help him move forward. Gradually, he comes to accept his wife's disappearance and begins a relationship with another woman in which he finds a new happiness. In the end, all that holds him to Helen is memory.

Helen Odom, Lucille's mother. Forty-nine years old, she and Warren have been married for twenty-seven years. She leaves the family suddenly and disappears. Lucille eventually reunites with her mother, but by then major changes have taken place in both their lives. According to Lucille, Helen's distinguishing characteristic is absent-mindedness, which suggests her need to make herself present outside marriage.

Rae Odom McQueen, Lucille's sister. Twenty-five years old, she is beautiful, with brown eyes and blonde hair. When she was growing up in South Carolina, she was a singer with a black band. Later, she graduated from Sweet Briar and worked in Washington, D.C., for a senator. When Lucille calls her about Helen's disappearance, Rae leaves Washington and surprises Lucille by bringing home a new husband.

Billy McQueen, Rae's husband. An Illnois Yankee among Southerners, he was working on a Ph.D. in history at George Washington University before he and Rae headed south. He made Rae pregnant by using deliberately punctured condoms; in his view, this was the only way he had a hope of getting her to marry him. Living with the Odoms, he gets a job teaching history and coaching soccer at Wando High School. He is deeply in love with Rae, who appears to be bored with him, perhaps because, as she says, he wants only a normal life.

Wayne Frobiness, Lucille's friend. Close to Lucille's own age and the child of divorced parents, he works as a counselor at a crisis center. He desires Lucille.

Rhody Poole, a black friend of Rae. Rhody has a daughter, Evelyn, who was born when Rhody was fourteen. Rhody provides an ironic link between Lucille and Helen.

Vera Oxendine, Warren Odom's hair stylist. She and Warren begin dating after Helen leaves. Lucille sees Vera as the exact opposite of Helen, which implies that Warren is changing.

— Thomas Lisk

RICHARD II

Author: William Shakespeare (1564-1616)
First published: 1600
Genre: Drama

Locale: England
Time: The fourteenth century
Plot: Historical

King Richard II, a self-indulgent and irresponsible ruler. He neglects the welfare of his country and brings on his own downfall. He is insolent in his treatment of his dying uncle, John of Gaunt, and greedy in his seizure of the property of his banished cousin, Henry Bolingbroke. To his lovely young queen he gives sentimental devotion. Being forced to give up the crown, he wallows in poetic self-pity, playing with his sorrow and theatrically portraying himself as a Christ figure. He dies well.

Henry Bolingbroke (BOL-ihn-brook), the duke of Hereford (afterward **King Henry IV**), the son of John of Gaunt. Able and ambitious, and roused to anger by Richard's injustice and ineptitude, he forces the latter to abdicate. Although as king he desires the death of his deposed and imprisoned cousin, he laments the death and banishes the murderer permanently from his presence.

John of Gaunt (gahnt), the duke of Lancaster, the uncle of King Richard. Grieved by the banishment of his son and his country's decline, he delivers a beautiful and impassioned praise of England and a lament for its degradation under Richard. Angered by Richard's insulting behavior, he dies delivering a curse on the young king that is carried out in the future.

Edmund of Langley, the duke of York, the uncle of the king. Eager to do right and imbued with patriotism and loyalty, he is torn and troubled by the behavior of Richard as king and Bolingbroke as rebel. As protector of the realm in Richard's absence, he is helpless before Bolingbroke's power and yields to him. He bestows his loyalty on Bolingbroke when he becomes King Henry IV.

Queen to King Richard, a gentle, loving wife. Grief-stricken, she angrily wishes that her gardener, from whom she hears the news of Richard's downfall, may henceforth labor in vain. She shares with the king a tender and sorrowful parting.

The gardener, a truly Shakespearean creation, unlike any character in Christopher Marlowe's *Edward II* (1594), the source of much in Shakespeare's play. A homely philosopher, he comments on the king's faults and his downfall and is overheard by the queen. Tenderly sympathetic, he wishes the queen's curse on his green thumb might be carried out if it could give her any comfort; however, confident that it will not be, he memorializes her sorrow by planting flowers where her tears fell.

The duke of Aumerle (oh-MEERL), the son of the duke of York. One of Richard's favorites and scornful of Bolingbroke, he is accused of complicity in the murder of the duke of Gloucester. His father discovers a document linking him to a plot to assassinate King Henry IV. Aumerle outrides his father to King Henry and gains a promise of pardon, which is confirmed after the duchess pleads for her son.

The duchess of York, the indulgent mother of Aumerle. She is frantic at her husband's determination to report their son's treason, and she pleads to King Henry on her knees.

Thomas Mowbray, the duke of Norfolk, an enemy of Bolingbroke. Accused of plotting the duke of Gloucester's death, he and Bolingbroke are prepared for combat when Richard breaks off the combat and banishes both. Mowbray dies in exile.

The duchess of Gloucester, the widow of the murdered duke. She pleads with John of Gaunt to avenge his dead brother and prays that Bolingbroke may destroy Mowbray as part of the revenge. York receives news of her death.

Bushy and

Green, unpopular favorites of King Richard. They are captured and executed by Bolingbroke's followers.

Bagot (BAG-eht), another of the king's unpopular favorites. At his trial before Bolingbroke, he declares Aumerle guilty of having Gloucester murdered.

The earl of Northumberland, a strong supporter of Bolingbroke. He aids in the overthrow of Richard.

Henry Percy (**Hotspur**), the son of Northumberland. At Bagot's trial, he challenges Aumerle to combat, but nothing comes of it.

The Lord Marshall, who officiates at the abortive duel of Mowbray and Bolingbroke.

The bishop of Carlisle, a supporter of King Richard. Objecting to Bolingbroke's seizure of the crown, he is accused of treason and banished.

The abbot of Westminster, a conspirator against King Henry IV. He dies before he can be tried.

Sir Stephen Scroop, a loyal follower of King Richard. He brings to the king unwelcome tidings of Bolingbroke's success.

A keeper, King Richard's jailer, who angers the king and is beaten by him.

A groom, a devoted servant of King Richard who visits the deposed monarch in prison.

The earl of Salisbury, a follower of Richard executed by Northumberland.

The duke of Surrey, a Yorkist and a friend of Aumerle.

Lord Berkeley, a follower of the duke of York.

Lord Fitzwater,

Lord Ross, and

Lord Willoughby, supporters of Bolingbroke.

Sir Pierce of Exton, a savage and ambitious knight. He kills King Richard in the hope of a splendid career under King Henry IV but is disappointed, cast off, and banished by the king.

RICHARD III

Author: William Shakespeare (1564-1616)
First published: 1597; revised, 1623
Genre: Drama

Locale: England
Time: The fifteenth century
Plot: Historical

Richard, the duke of Gloucester, afterward **King Richard III**, the sinister and Machiavellian brother of King Edward IV. A fiendish and ambitious monster, he shows the grisly humor of the medieval Devil or the Vice of the morality plays. An effective hypocrite, he successfully dissembles his ambition and his ruthlessness until he has won his kingdom. His character in this play is consistent with that established in *King Henry VI*. The role furnishes great opportunities for an acting virtuoso and has long been a favorite with great actors.

King Edward IV, the eldest son of the deceased duke of York. An aging and ailing monarch with a sin-laden past and a remorseful present, he struggles futilely to bring about peace between the hostile factions of his court. Tricked by Gloucester into ordering the death of his brother Clarence, he tries too late to countermand the order. His grief over Clarence's death hastens his own.

George, the duke of Clarence, the brother of King Edward and Richard. Guilty of treachery and perjury in placing his brother Edward on the throne, he is bewildered by his imprisonment and death. In prison, he is troubled by terrible dreams, partly begotten by his guilty conscience, and he fears being alone. He has no idea that his fair-seeming brother Richard is responsible for his miseries until his murderers tell him so at the moment of his death.

Queen Margaret, the maleficent widow of the murdered King Henry VI. Her long curse delivered near the beginning of the play, in which she singles out her enemies, is almost a scenario of the play.

The duke of Buckingham, Richard's kinsman and powerful supporter. A cold and masterful politician, he is instrumental in placing Richard on the throne. Unwilling to consent to the murder of the helpless young princes, he loses favor, flees the court, rebels, and is captured and executed. As he goes to his death, he recalls the curses and prophecies of Queen Margaret, whose warning to him he ignored.

Edward, prince of Wales, afterward **King Edward V**, the older son of King Edward IV. A bright and brave boy, he furnishes pathos by his conduct and by his early violent death.

Richard, the duke of York, King Edward's second son. Impish and precocious, he bandies words even with his sinister uncle. He dies with his brother in the Tower of London.

Henry Tudor, the earl of Richmond, afterward **King Henry VII**, King Richard's major antagonist. A heroic figure, he leads a successful invasion against King Richard and kills him in hand-to-hand combat at the Battle of Bosworth Field. His concluding speech promises the healing of the wounds of civil war and the union of the houses of York and Lancaster by his forthcoming marriage with Elizabeth, the daughter of King Edward IV.

Lord Thomas Stanley, the earl of Derby, the stepfather of Richmond. Suspicious of Richard of Gloucester from the beginning, he remains a token supporter through fear. His heart is with Richmond. At the Battle of Bosworth Field, he risks the life of his son George, a hostage to Richard, by failing to bring up his troops against Richmond. George Stanley's death is prevented by the killing of King Richard.

Lord Hastings, Lord Chamberlain under Edward IV. He is devoted to King Edward and his sons, though an enemy to Queen Elizabeth and her family. His loyalty prevents his becoming a tool of Richard in the campaign to set aside the claims of small Edward V. He trusts Richard to the point of gullibility and pays for his trust and his loyalty to Edward with his life.

Queen Elizabeth, the wife of King Edward IV. A haughty and self-willed woman during her husband's reign, she has powerful enemies at court, including Hastings and Richard of Gloucester. After the murder of her small sons, she is a grieving, almost deranged mother. Her terror for her daughter's safety drives her to appear to consent to Richard's monstrous proposal for the hand of her daughter, his niece. The horrible match is prevented by Richard's death.

The duchess of York, the mother of Edward IV, Clarence, and Richard III. A loving grandmother to the children of Edward and Clarence, she hates and despises her son Richard, whom she sends to his last battle with a heavy curse, prophesying and wishing for him a shameful death.

Cardinal Bourchier, the archbishop of Canterbury. He enables Richard to gain possession of the little duke of York to confine him in the Tower of London with his brother.

Thomas Rotherham, the archbishop of York. He conducts Queen Elizabeth and the little duke of York to sanctuary, but his kind action turns out to be in vain.

John Morton, the bishop of Ely. His gift to King Richard of strawberries from his garden is in grim contrast to the immediately following arrest and execution of Hastings.

The duke of Norfolk (**Jockey of Norfolk**), a loyal follower of Richard III. In spite of a warning that Richard has been betrayed, Norfolk remains faithful and dies in battle.

Anthony Woodville (**Earl Rivers**), the brother of Queen Elizabeth. An enemy of Hastings, he becomes reconciled with him at King Edward's entreaty. He is arrested and executed at Richard's commands.

The marquess of Dorset and

Lord Grey, Queen Elizabeth's sons by her first husband. Dorset escapes to join Richmond, and Grey is executed by Richard's orders.

Sir Thomas Vaughan, one of Richard's victims. He is beheaded with Earl Rivers and Lord Grey.

Sir Thomas, Lord Lovel,

Sir Richard Ratcliff, and

Sir William Catesby, Richard's loyal henchmen. Catesby remains with the king almost to his death, leaving him only to try to find a horse for him.

Sir James Tyrrel, a malcontent. Ambitious and haughty, he engineers for Richard the murder of the little princes in the Tower. He is later remorseful for his crime.

Sir Robert Brackenbury, lieutenant of the Tower. He resigns the keys to the murderers of Clarence when he sees their warrant. He is killed at Bosworth Field.

The keeper in the Tower, a kind man. He does his best to ease Clarence's captivity.

Christopher Urswick, a priest. He acts as a messenger from Lord Derby to Richmond to inform him that young George Stanley is held as a hostage by the king.

The Lord Mayor of London, who allows himself to be used by Richard and his followers to help replace Edward V with Richard III.

Edward Plantagenet, the earl of Warwick, the young son of Clarence.

Margaret Plantagenet, the young daughter of Clarence.

The earl of Surrey, the son of the duke of Norfolk. He remains with King Richard's army.

The earl of Oxford (**John De Vere**), one of the lords who join Richmond in his rebellion.

The sheriff of Wiltshire, who conducts Buckingham to execution.

Tressel and

Berkeley, gentlemen attending Lady Anne and the body of Henry VI.

Sir William Brandon,

Sir James Blunt, and

Sir Walter Herbert, supporters of Richmond.

Ghosts of Richard's victims, who include, in addition to the characters killed in this play, King Henry VI and his son Edward, prince of Wales. All appear to both Richard and Richmond. They rouse uncharacteristic terror in Richard and give refreshing encouragement to Richmond.

THE RIDE ACROSS LAKE CONSTANCE
(Der Ritt über den Bodensee)

Author: Peter Handke (1942-   )
First published: 1971
Genre: Drama

Locale: The stage
Time: Unspecified but probably the 1960's
Plot: Surrealism

Emil Jannings, who is described only as quite fat, heavily made up, and wearing the hints of a costume. His closest relationship, which vacillates between friendliness and animosity for no apparent reason, is with Heinrich George. During the course of the play, Jannings learns and increasingly adopts the poses of the role of boss, in particular in his interactions with George. More than any other character, he epitomizes power and understands the mechanisms of instituting it: Individual desires must be subordinated to the laws of an order naturalized by means of repetition, ritual, and custom. In spite of the apparent ease with which Jannings plays his role, he nevertheless undergoes moments of uncertainty and confusion when events do not correspond to his imagined order, as for example in the final scene, when Alice Kessner does not, contrary to expectations, wear a watch.

Heinrich George, the closest person to Jannings, described in a similar manner. Characterized above all by a somewhat childlike naïveté, George frequently does not comprehend the language of a particular system and accordingly experiences more difficulties than any other character in acting out his various parts. This means that at isolated moments George questions the established order and even contradicts it, although unwittingly, by expressing his own needs and desires. George's difficulty in learning the rules of the game excludes him from ever holding the reins of power himself: He becomes subordinate to Jannings, and eventually his identity is reduced to that of servant.

Erich von Stroheim (fon SHTROH-him), an impressive figure who, like the other two male characters, wears the hints of a costume. As the master gamesman, von Stroheim plays a variety of parts, including those of magician, actor, and teacher. He serves Jannings as mentor, instructing him and George in the ways of the master-servant relationship. Most important, however, von Stroheim assumes the role of a lover caught between two women. At first appearance, he and Henny Porten belong together, but during the course of the play, he and Elisabeth Bergner go through the motions of a love affair. Von Stroheim accompanies his lover's role with the appropriate stance, occasionally strumming some softly sentimental chords on a guitar.

Elisabeth Bergner, a beautiful and elegant woman wearing a long dress. Involved in a love affair with von Stroheim, she eventually becomes tired of the role and impassively breaks off the relationship. Dreamy sleepiness, characteristic of all the characters to some extent, typifies Bergner as she glides across stage as if in a trance or merely sits silently with closed or half-closed eyes. The natural ease with which she functions, indicative of an unquestioning acceptance of the order and her place within it, is destroyed periodically by moments of total confusion and disorientation, terrifying reminders of the precariousness of her balance.

Henny Porten, who is described only as wearing an evening dress with a velvet stole. She arrives on stage with von Stroheim as the third member of the love triangle. She is not at all upset at von Stroheim's vacillation and at times even encourages his relationship with Bergner. Of all the characters, Porten is the most difficult to identify. The distinction between her and Bergner, for example, becomes blurred so that one of the women reacts in the other's place. Similarly, she is the subordinate member of the partnership with von Stroheim and accordingly sometimes becomes interchangeable with George.

Alice and

Ellen Kessler, identical twins who walk onstage toward the end of the performance as if by mistake. The entrance of first Alice and then Ellen is a shock to the other characters, because the twins have no assigned role within this drama. Initially, Alice and Ellen allay the fear and confusion they have caused by reciting lines and performing actions so common that they could belong in any play. Gradually, their actions begin to contradict themselves, and they run off the stage, leaving the remaining actors in a state of helplessness in which neither words nor actions follow logically or naturally. The twins epitomize the tendency noted for the other characters toward interchangeability and loss of individuality.

Woman with white scarf, in blackface. The woman opens the play by cleaning the set and removing most of the dust-clothes from the props. She appears once again in the final scene with a big doll representing a child. The child cries when confronted with disorder and reaches for the women's breasts and between the men's legs. The woman exits, with her doll, leaving the characters immobile and speechless until Bergner awakens, recognizes von Stroheim, and begins to smile.

— *Linda C. DeMeritt*

RIDERS IN THE CHARIOT

Author: Patrick White (1912-1990)
First published: 1961
Genre: Novel

Locale: Sarsaparilla, a suburb of Sydney, Australia
Time: Post-World War II
Plot: Parable

Mary Hare, the homely, unmarried daughter of an aristocratic Australian family. Despised by her father because of her awkwardness and lack of beauty, and ignored by her mother, who found the child a bother, Mary survived "what passed for childhood." She has grown into a peculiar adulthood and lives alone in the dilapidated family mansion called Xanadu. Mary cannot relate to her fellow humans, so she turns to birds and animals, at times even to plants, for companionship as she wanders about the overgrown grounds of Xanadu, performing religious rites among nature. After gaining wholeness through her union with the other riders in the chariot, she simply disappears into the natural setting, which had become her refuge. As one rider of the chariot, Mary is thought to represent the quality of instinct.

Mordecai Himmelfarb, a Jewish refugee from Germany who settled in Australia after World War II. Himmelfarb loses his wife in a concentration camp but manages to escape death himself, going first to Israel, then to Australia. He works on an assembly line in a suburban Sydney factory, and there on Maundy Thursday of Passion Week some of the other workers subject him to a mock crucifixion. Early the next morning, on Good Friday, he dies in a fire. After his headlong confrontation with evil in Nazi Germany and his subsequent wanderings, Himmelfarb (whose name in German suggests "ascension") questions the existence of God. During his ordeal on the makeshift cross he becomes conscious of a stillness and clarity, at the center of which his God is reflected. As another rider in the chariot, Himmelfarb is considered to represent intellect.

Ruch Godbold, a washerwoman with six daughters who has been deserted by her husband. Mrs. Godbold, whose name

is certainly suggestive, displays an undeniable goodness and has the ability to love without measure. Those qualities have made her overly possessive in her relationships with others, finally driving away her husband, who was not strong enough to suffer the full force of his wife's love. Just as the meeting of the other riders in the chariot changes each one, so does it alter Mrs. Godbold. Her fierce love and forceful goodness undergo revision to become tempered and restrained. This refining process allows her to express unfettered love, free of obsessiveness, and true friendship, untainted by consciously charitable acts. Mrs. Godbold, another chariot rider, may represent the quality of emotion. But only one of the riders alive at the novel's conclusion, she surveys the ruins of Xanadu.

Alf Dubbo, an Aboriginal painter. As the fourth rider in the chariot, Alf is thought to represent imagination. He was reared by a white clergyman and the minister's sister, Mrs. Pask. The Reverend Calderon seduced the adopted boy, and Mrs. Pask encouraged his artistic talent but did not approve of what he painted. Alf wants to believe the Gospels' truths but fails because "the duplicity of the white man prevented him considering Christ." Although he is a brilliant painter, Alf is unable to locate and evince himself in his art until he meets the other riders in the chariot. Before his death from tuberculosis, Alf completes his two greatest paintings, *Deposition* and *Chariot*, which give visual representation to the spiritual discoveries propelling the chariot and its four unlikely riders.

Mrs. Jolley, Mary Hare's housekeeper, who is drawn in sharp satirical tones. Mrs. Jolley belies her name, for she emerges as a gossipy, cruel, and pretentious woman. She represents the side of humankind that seeks no understanding beyond the immediate and material world.

Mrs. Flack, an acquaintance of Mrs. Jolley who shares her love of gossip and expression of cruelty. Like her counterpart, Mrs. Flack lacks any sense of the spiritual fulfillment the chariot riders seek. She lives in a world full of pretension and falseness.

Blue, Mrs. Flack's illegitimate son. The ignorant, insensitive, and prejudiced Blue leads the mock crucifixion of Himmelfarb.

Harry Rosetree (born **Haim Rosenbaum**), the manager of the factory where Himmelfarb and Blue work. Formerly a Jew, Harry Rosetree has forsaken his inherited religion for the more fashionable and acceptable Christianity of mainline Australia. He denies Himmelfarb when he arrives at the Rosetree home but later hangs himself in remorse and guilt.

— *Robert L. Ross*

RIDERS TO THE SEA

Author: John Millington Synge (1871-1909)
First published: 1903
Genre: Drama

Locale: An island off the western coast of Ireland
Time: Late nineteenth and early twentieth centuries
Plot: Tragedy

Maurya (MOY-ruh), an old peasant woman living on one of the Aran Islands at the mouth of Galway Bay on the western coast of Ireland, a wild, desolate, impoverished area. She has reared six sons, four of whom are known to be dead, as are her husband and her husband's father—all from the ravages of the sea, whose fierce tides and winds make life difficult and dangerous. She is afraid that Michael, the next from youngest son, who has been absent unexpectedly for some time, is drowned also, and she tries to dissuade her last son, Bartley, from crossing over the tumultuous sea to sell two horses at the fair on the mainland. Twice unable to give him a journey's blessing, she has a vision foretelling his death. When her two daughters, after identifying as Michael's some clothes found on a drowned body, inform her of Michael's death, she recites the list of the others' deaths and the circumstances. As she is being persuaded that he is dead, villagers enter to announce the death of her last son, Bartley, who was knocked into the sea by his pony. Instead of becoming bitter and angry, Maurya recognizes that the sea can do no more to harm her, because she has lost all her men. There is an end to anxiety and a beginning of peace for her, though there will be little to eat. She realizes that she will not long survive these deaths. Maurya's nobility and maturity of spirit enable her to see the good in all of her men now being together. She sprinkles Holy Water over the dead Bartley and asks God's mercy on the souls of her men, on her own, and, generously, on the souls of everyone left living in the world.

Bartley, the youngest of six sons, now the sole support of the household. He earns income by riding horses into the sea

to the steamer anchored far offshore, so that they can be sold at the mainland fair. Preoccupied with practical exigencies, he ignores his mother's request that he not go to sea, being the last surviving male of the family. He nevertheless asks God's blessing on the family and rides off on the red mare, leading the pony. His mother foretells his death and omits the giving of a blessing to him, an omission considered bad luck. When his mother subsequently stands on the path trying in vain to say the blessing, he gives her his blessing.

Cathleen, a daughter about twenty years old. As the older of two sisters, she takes the lead in expressing concern and making arrangements. She sympathizes with her brother's need to go to sea and criticizes her mother for repeatedly trying to stop him and for not giving him a blessing. She sends Maurya with some bread to give him. Cathleen is effective in dealing with practical details, as when she identifies some clothes as belonging to her other brother, Michael, drowned nine days earlier. Cathleen is matter-of-fact and impatient with her mother's lamentations and visions, telling Maurya of the evidence of Michael's death. Filled with life herself, she sees her mother as old, broken, and lamenting excessively. Cathleen stands in sharp contrast to her mother's deep, powerful, and mature emotions.

Nora, a young girl, another of Maurya's daughters. Her main function in the play is to talk with Cathleen and enable the exposition of background and commentary on the action. She speaks more respectfully to her mother than does Cathleen and with pity about her dead brother.

— *E. Lynn Harris*

THE RIGHT STUFF

Author: Tom Wolfe (1931-   )
First published: 1979
Genre: Novel

Locale: The United States
Time: 1947-1963
Plot: New journalism

John Glenn, the best known of the Mercury astronauts, the first American to orbit the earth. A freckle-faced country boy with reddish blond hair and a winning smile, he flew combat missions in both World War II and Korea and was one of the Marines' best-known pilots. The oldest of the original seven astronauts and the only Marine, he sets the moral tone for the astronauts at their first press conference by invoking God, country, and family. He is ambitious, hard-working, a bit self-righteous, and a great favorite of the press and public. After the

flight of *Friendship 7*, he becomes a hero like few others in the history of the United States.

Chuck Yeager, the first pilot to break the sound barrier. The short, wiry, tough-looking Yeager had a successful career as a fighter pilot and went on to win every major decoration and honor available to test pilots. He set the standard by which members of the flying community measured themselves, and his Appalachian drawl was imitated by fliers from commercial airline pilots to astronauts. Lacking a college education,

Yeager is not eligible to be an astronaut, but he has no interest in abandoning flying to serve as a "lab animal" in a space capsule.

Gordon Cooper, who pilots the last and longest orbital flight of Project Mercury, becoming the most celebrated of the astronauts since John Glenn. The thin, handsome, confident son of an Army Air Force officer, he neither flew combat missions nor distinguished himself as a test pilot, but instead flew for the less prestigious engineering corps. So relaxed that he falls asleep on the top of the rocket before liftoff, he handles problems with the electrical system during the flight with equanimity. Forced to operate the capsule manually during the last orbit and reentry, he still manages to land nearly on target.

Scott Carpenter, who makes the second orbital flight. He is high spirited, outgoing, good looking, athletic, and the only astronaut with "the touch of the poet" about him. Although trained as a test pilot, he is not in a league with most of the others and is something of an outsider among them. By most accounts a success, his flight nevertheless is denigrated by the other astronauts because he concentrated on the science experiments he was given to perform during his flight at the expense of operational efficiency. Carpenter's vision of the astronaut as a man of science in space does not please the other astronauts.

Alan Shepard, who is chosen to be the first of the original seven astronauts in space and becomes an American hero after his suborbital flight. The son of a career officer and a graduate of the Naval Academy, he is considered to be one of the Navy's best test pilots. Able to be both "one of the guys" and a leader, he sets the standard for coolness and competence under pressure for the other astronauts to follow.

Gus Grissom, who is assigned to the second suborbital flight. He is best known as the astronaut who lost both his cool and his capsule by blowing the hatch too soon after touching down. A short, compact, dour-faced man with a black crew cut and bushy eyebrows, he is uncommunicative except around fellow pilots. Reared in Indiana and the son of a railroad worker, he earned the Distinguished Flying Cross in Korea and tested fighter planes before being chosen as an astronaut.

Deke Slayton, who was supposed to man the second orbital flight but is grounded after doctors discover he has a slightly irregular heartbeat. Rugged, handsome, witty, charming and intelligent, he has no patience for small talk. He is crushed and humiliated by being grounded, but after being given the title of coordinator of astronaut activities, he becomes a power to be reckoned with in NASA.

Wally Schirra, the fifth of the Mercury astronauts to orbit the earth. His six-orbit flight is nearly perfect, a "textbook flight" during which he conserves fuel and lands nearly on target. A relaxed, joking prankster, Schirra is a leader of men who insists on running his own show.

Annie Glenn, John Glenn's wife. She is terrified to talk to the press because of a severe stuttering problem but has the courage to stand up to Vice President Lyndon Johnson and refuse to let him into her home the morning of her husband's flight.

Betty Grissom, Gus Grissom's wife. She hates the life of the military wife and is outraged when she is cheated out of her share of the "goodies" after her husband's flight.

— *Mary Virginia Davis*

THE RIGHT TO AN ANSWER

Author: Anthony Burgess (John Anthony Burgess Wilson, 1917-1993)
First published: 1960
Genre: Novel

Locale: A London suburb, Ceylon, and Tokyo
Time: After World War II, probably the late 1950's
Plot: Social satire

J. W. Denham, the central character and narrator, a forty-year-old, well-to-do, upper-level manager for a British trading company, currently posted to Tokyo. Returning to England on one of his biennial four-month vacations, he finds himself bemused by the social and moral decline characteristic of life in Britain. He considers the deterioration of standards to be brought about by postwar democratic leveling to the lowest common denominator. On this visit to his aging father, now retired in a suburb of a Midlands city, he becomes even more aware of this omnipresent venality. At the local pub, the Black Swan, he observes that casual wife-swapping has become almost acceptable, the fling to which everyone is entitled; the only other recreations are tasteless, imported American television and drinking to the point of senselessness. He much prefers the elite life still available to commercial agents overseas.

Mr. Raj, a student from Ceylon whom Denham meets after he puts in a period as emergency representative for his firm there. Raj is charming, effusive, and insistent, a descendant of the stock oriental sidekick of British colonial fiction now become the colonial beneficiary of imperial enlightenment. Insinuating himself into Denham's friendship, he proves mas-

terful in handling some embarrassing situations once they return to England, where he is supposed to be researching a graduate thesis on interracial relations. He assumes, as a student of the British patriarchal system—the tradition of sweet reasonableness—that in Britain interracial harmony should prevail. He determines in his own small ways to promote that cause. One way in which he follows this course is by falling in love with and pursuing Alice Winter. Another is by moving in with Denham's father, Bert, when Denham has to return to Tokyo. Raj determines to restore the elder Denham to vitality by cooking curries for him as only an Asian can. Unfortunately, as Arden's cables to Denham eventually reveal, Raj's cooking overwhelms Bert's system; he dies of heart failure before Denham can get back. To compound the error, Raj, after defending his conduct to Denham, goes to see Alice, whose husband has just returned to her. Alice and her husband tumble into bed in an ecstasy of reunion. Raj, assuming that Alice is being assaulted, kills Winter with a pistol that he has stolen from Arden. Confronted by Denham, he kills himself just before the police arrive. As a result, Denham realizes that his own way of life is morally defective.

Ted Arden, the middle-aged owner of the Black Swan. Arden is the ideal publican, dispensing libations and personal philosophy in equal measure. An evening at the Black Swan normally includes the bestowing of gifts on Arden by appreciative customers returning from trips abroad. As his name indicates, he is descended from the family of William Shakespeare's wife.

William Winter, or **Winterbottom**, a printer whom Denham meets at the Black Swan. Winter discloses that he is a victim of sexual liberation; his wife flagrantly makes a public cuckold out of him with an electrician. Denham urges him to retaliate by confronting her. Instead, Winter sets up an adulterous liaison of his own with Imogen Everett in London, where they expect Denham to subsidize them.

Everett, a poet and friend of Denham's conventional suburban sister, Beryl. Because Denham refuses to underwrite the publication of his poems, he lampoons the visitor in a newspaper column. Later, he continues to ask Denham for support.

Imogen Everett, his daughter, a foulmouthed, tough-minded "modern" woman who becomes Winter's mistress in London. Because Winter has trouble finding work there and Denham is reluctant to finance his unorthodox lifestyle, she decides to make money by running a confidence game. Setting up as a prostitute, she extracts the fee from her clients in advance, then slips out without performing the stipulated act.

Len, a racketeer of sorts whom Denham meets in Colombo and again in Tokyo. During the first encounter, Denham tells about losing money while in London to a woman running Imogen's game. Len promises to avenge the deed. Before their next meeting, Denham's Japanese mistress is attacked and nearly raped by a teenage gang from the American armed forces settlement at Washington Heights; she subsequently leaves him. Len reports that Denham's swindling has been avenged but includes details that reveal the victim to be Imogen. She has been beaten, after which four teeth were extracted. She then returns to live with her father, repudiating Winter. Len justifies this action by asserting the necessity of balancing good and evil.

— *James L. Livingston*

RIGHT YOU ARE (IF YOU THINK SO)
(Così è [se vi pare])

Author: Luigi Pirandello (1867-1936)
First published: 1918
Genre: Drama

Locale: A small Italian town, the capital of a province
Time: Early twentieth century
Plot: Parable

Signora Frola (FROH-lah), an old woman and the mother-in-law of Ponza. She causes talk by living alone in a fine apartment rather than with Ponza and her daughter, by never exchanging visits with her daughter, and by not allowing the neighbors to pay a social call. When she finally confronts the neighbors, she explains that Ponza is mad and must be humored into believing that his wife is, indeed, a second wife taking the place of the one he is convinced he has lost.

Ponza (POHN-zah), the secretary to the provincial councilor. He causes talk by living with his wife, whom no one ever sees, in a fifth floor tenement, and by visiting Signora Frola every day, alone. When he finally confronts the neighbors, he explains that Signora Frola is mad, that her daughter is dead but that she refuses to believe it, and that his second wife humors her in this belief by pretending to be her daughter and fostering the illusion by communicating with the old lady from the fifth floor balcony.

Signora Ponza, who, veiled, confronts the gossiping neighbors and informs them that she is the daughter of Signora Frola, that she is the second wife of Ponza, and that, for herself, she is nothing. She is, in short, the person she is believed to be.

Commendatore Agazzi (ah-GAHZ-zee), the provincial councilor.

Amalia Agazzi (ah-MAH-lee-ah), his wife.

Dina Agazzi (DEE-nah), his daughter.

Centuri (chehn-TEW-ree), a police commissioner. The Agazzis and Centuri are gossiping fellow townsmen bent on solving the mystery of the Ponza-Frola domestic arrangements.

Lamberto Laudisi (low-DEE-see), Commendatore Agazzi's brother-in-law, who insists that the Ponza-Frola domestic arrangements are their own business. When Signora Ponza gives the solution to the mystery, he laughs and says that now everybody knows the truth.

THE RIME OF THE ANCIENT MARINER

Author: Samuel Taylor Coleridge (1772-1834)
First published: 1798
Genre: Poetry

Locale: At sea
Time: Late medieval period
Plot: Allegory

The Ancient Mariner, a somewhat mysterious figure. The poem deals with two separate times, the time of the voyage and the time of the Mariner's retelling. Facts helping to date the time of the voyage are that the Mariner uses a crossbow rather than a firearm and that his ship is the first ever to sail into the Pacific Ocean, thereby preceding Ferdinand Magellan's voyage of 1520. He is evidently a Catholic, because he twice calls on the Virgin Mary and also invokes other saints. As for the time of the retelling, there is only a general sense that the Mariner is perceived as belonging to an earlier generation. There is not enough information about the wedding to know whether it was Catholic or Protestant, and the vesper bell toward the end of the poem could belong to either faith. The bassoon mentioned toward the beginning, however, would not have been possible before the sixteenth century. In a fragment of conversation recovered in the twentieth century, Samuel Taylor Coleridge once remarked that the Mariner was in fact a young man while on board the ship and that he was retelling the story fifty years later.

The Wandering Jew, a traditional figure in European literature. He is a blasphemer condemned to wander the earth until the second coming of Christ because he had mocked Christ while He was bearing the Cross on his way to Calvary. The legend was believed in late medieval Europe, and several accounts of supposed meetings with the Wandering Jew were published, beginning in the sixteenth century. Several writers of the Romantic period then took up the idea, making it central to their theme of social and spiritual alienation, a burden felt by Coleridge also. Coleridge was himself known to be an incessant talker.

The Wedding Guest, one of three "gallants," or fashionable young men particularly attentive to women, whom the Mariner accosts while they are on their way to the wedding. He is apparently the bride's brother. Throughout the poem, the Wedding Guest (when allowed to speak) represents a normal but naïve view of reality. Eventually, he is decisively influenced by the Mariner's extraordinary revelations. Members of the wedding include the bride, the bridegroom, the guests, and the musicians.

The ship's crew, at the beginning numbering some two hundred men, including a helmsman and the Mariner's nephew. The crew is later joined by an albatross of uncertain dimensions and color who is obviously more than just a bird. The poem does not say so, but there was a common superstition among sailors at this time that albatrosses were reincarnations of sailors who had died at sea. If so, then it was in fact "a Christian soul"; if not, then it was (like the water snakes) to be cherished simply because it was a living thing and therefore an example of God's creative power. By wantonly killing the albatross, the Mariner affronts God.

The spirits, who include the mysterious Pole Spirit. The spirits resemble angels in being wholly immaterial but have no regular place in Christian cosmology. These are the "invisible beings" referred to in the poem's epigraph. They illustrate that however much one may come to know about the material world, the spiritual one is far more varied and more significant; it remains unknowable and elusive.

The Ghost Ship's crew, two hideous characters, **Death** and **Life-in-Death** (of whom additional details are given in the 1798 version of the poem). They play at dice for the ship's crew, and Death wins all of them except the Mariner. He is won by Life-in-Death and thereby condemned to the eternal wanderings that follow. It is important to note that the Mariner's fate is decided by a vehicle of random chance, not by any kind of divine judgment. Having denied God's continuous governance of the world by blaspheming against His chief manifestation, life, the crew and Mariner find themselves in a world without Providence, exemplified by the failure of the winds, which are not simply forces of nature but part of the divine plan to sustain life on Earth. Before he is allowed to leave the ship, the Mariner must learn that life in all forms is sacred.

The Pilot,

the Pilot's Boy, and

the Hermit, who rescue the Mariner in a small boat. The crew are dead, the Ghost Ship and the angelic spirits have disappeared, and the ship has gone down like lead. It is not clear how they fit into the poem, and few critics are able to say more about them than that the Hermit in part resembles poet William Wordsworth. Though the Mariner asks the Hermit for spiritual cleansing, it is the judgment of Life-in-Death that prevails.

— Dennis R. Dean

THE RIMERS OF ELDRITCH

Author: Lanford Wilson (1937-   )
First published: 1967
Genre: Drama

Locale: Eldritch, a small town in the American Midwest
Time: The 1960's
Plot: Poetic

Robert Conklin, an eighteen-year-old, average in most ways but quieter and more serious than most of his contemporaries. Robert is sensitive and thoughtful. He is almost the opposite of his popular and adventurous brother, who died in an automobile crash. He chooses to spend his time with a fourteen-year-old girl rather than with his schoolmates. It is his "out of character" behavior that creates the situation around which the play revolves.

Eva Jackson, a fourteen-year-old girl. Although she is physically disabled and therefore something of an outsider, Eva is in many ways a typical young girl. She is intelligent but given to quick shifts of mood. The willingness of Robert and Eva to indict another person for their own wrongdoings is one of the major issues that this play raises.

Evelyn Jackson, Eva's mother. Protective and suspicious, Evelyn is a devout Christian who can find fault with her own daughter but will not allow a word of criticism to be spoken by anyone else.

Mary Windrod, a senile old woman. Berated frequently by her daughter, Nelly, Mary is tolerated by the people of Eldritch. She was once known as "the first registered nurse in Des Moines," but now most people consider her harmlessly crazy. Despite her mental state, Mary is observant and aware, and she tends to see the truth of most situations. She also has dreams that seem to predict the future. Her testimony at the trial is ignored, even though she knows what actually occurred.

Nelly Windrod, Mary's middle-aged daughter. A dominating person, Nelly is strong-minded and enduring. It is Nelly who responded to her mother's shouting and who shot Skelly, and it is she who is on trial during the play.

Skelly Manor, the town hermit. Sixty years old, disheveled, and unkempt, Skelly is regarded by the townspeople with a mixture of fear and contempt. Boys and men taunt him for a prior act of bestiality with a sheep, whereas women are frightened by his wild ways and sudden appearances. A loner, Skelly serves as the scapegoat for the town's own evil.

Cora Groves, the owner of the local diner, the Hilltop Cafe. A strong-willed, independent woman, she is also passionate and vulnerable. Considered an outsider by the townspeople because she has been living with Walter, a young drifter, she remains fair-minded and befriends even Skelly. When she discovers the truth of the murder, she is castigated as a whore. She is hurt deeply when Walter leaves her.

Walter, a young, handsome drifter and Cora's lover. Easygoing and friendly, Walter has worked hard to help Cora improve the restaurant. He is not interested in long-term commitments, however, and is seduced easily by a pretty young girl.

Patsy Johnson, who is sixteen years old and the prettiest girl at Centerville High. Patsy is bright and a flirt. Hypocritical and shallow, she becomes pregnant by Walter and forces a boy from town to marry her.

Peck Johnson, a farmer and Patsy's father. Peck is careful, pragmatic, and fair. He is interested in his farm and not given to gossip or undue alarm.

Mavis Johnson, Patsy's mother. Prim and proper, Mavis is almost always sure that the worst will happen, and her reaction to that is to worry.

Josh Johnson, Patsy's brother, a typical young boy with high spirits but no ill will.

Lena Truit, Patsy's best friend and Josh's girlfriend. She is utterly loyal to Patsy and easily influenced by her.

Martha Truit and

Wilma Atkins, town gossips.

— John C. Watson

THE RING AND THE BOOK

Author: Robert Browning (1812-1889)
First published: 1868-1869
Genre: Poetry

Locale: Italy
Time: The seventeenth century
Plot: Dramatic

Count Guido Franceschini (GWEE-doh frahn-chehs-KEE-nee), the oldest male member of a destitute noble family of Arezzo. Knowing that he is the last hope for continuing the family name, because his two brothers are priests, Guido seeks a wife to bear him a son. Impoverished, he needs a woman with an attractive dowry. His brother finds a likely prospect, and Guido's family name attracts the girl's mother. Inept as a husband and angered by denial of the dowry after the wedding, Guido abuses his wife. To retain the last vestige of honor as a husband, after he has driven her to extramarital affections, Guido, with four men from his village, kills his parents-in-law and fatally wounds his wife. The court hearings and the gossip relating to the affair, presented from various viewpoints, point to Guido's instability, he representing an old family without means of sustenance or continuation—no wealth, no prestige, no progeny. He is sentenced to be hanged, by rulings of both church and state.

Pompilia Comparini (pohm-PEE-lee-ah kohm-pah-REE-nee), his seventeen-year-old wife. Bought as a newborn infant from a prostitute, Pompilia was brought up by aged foster parents. Trapped in an incompatible marriage not of her choice, she flees to Rome with Caponsacchi, a priest. Overtaken, she and the priest disavow that they are lovers. After hearing that Pompilia, who has returned to her foster parents, has given birth to a son, Guido returns to Rome with four ruffians and attacks the Comparinis. Pompilia, mortally wounded, lingers for four days, time enough for her to identify her attacker.

Violante Comparini (vee-oh-LAHN-teh), her foster mother. Violante's warped sense of values leads to bizarre behavior. She feigns pregnancy, presents Pompilia to her husband as his child, negotiates Pompilia's marriage, and convinces her husband, who has objected to the marriage, that the status achieved by the union will be worth the promised dowry. Realizing her bad bargain and attempting to keep Guido from profiting by the marriage, Violante divulges Pompilia's parentage and disqualifies her from inheriting Comparini's money.

Pietro Comparini (PEE-eh-troh), Violante's husband. Naïve and browbeaten, he is governed by his wife's whims and desires.

Giuseppe Caponsacchi (jee-ew-SEHP-peh kah-pohn-SAHK-kee), a handsome priest, Pompilia's gallant lover. Excommunicated for his part in the affair, Giuseppe wishes himself dead but looks forward to the day when he will be returned to the grace of the church.

Margherita (mahr-geh-REE-tah), Pompilia's maid, who advises and encourages Pompilia to throw off the drudgery of her life with Guido by responding to Giuseppe's attentions.

Paolo (PAH-oh-loh), Count Guido's brother, a priest in Rome, who makes the initial contact with Violante for the marriage of Guido and Pompilia. His description of his brother makes Guido sound more attractive than the Comparinis find him.

Doctor Johannes-Baptista Bottinius (yoh-HAHN-ehs-bahp-TEES-tah boht-TEHN-yuhs), familiarly called **Giovambittista o' the Bottini**, who defends Pompilia at the hearings and for her behavior in the affair and persecutes her, as the gossips of Rome cried, by ordering her money given to a sisterhood rather than to her child.

Dominus Hyacinthus de Archangelis (DOHM-ih-nuhs HI-ah-SIHN-thuhs day ahr-KAN-jee-lihs), familiarly called **Don Giacinto of the Archangeli**, the procurator of the poor in Rome. He defends Guido and his hired companions at the hearings.

Pope Innocent XII, who condemns Count Guido to die in the presence of the populace; however, before his death, he prays that the condemned man may be forgiven his sin.

Gaetano (gah-eh-TAH-noh), Pompilia's two-week-old son, who, she says in her dying moments, "nor was, nor is, nor yet shall be/ Count Guido Franceschini's child at all—/ Only his mother's born of love not hate!"

Tommati (tohm-MAH-tee) and

Venturini (vehn-tew-REE-nee), judges at the hearings.

RING ROUND THE MOON
(L'Invitation au château)

Author: Jean Anouilh (1910-1987)
First published: 1953
Genre: Drama

Locale: The Auvergne, France
Time: 1912
Plot: Comedy

Hugo, a young man without a heart and the identical twin of Frederic. Not realizing that he, himself, is in love with Diana Messerschmann, he plots to end Frederic's infatuation for her by hiring Isabelle to masquerade as an invited guest to the ball where she is to draw Frederic from Diana to herself. As his scheme goes awry, Hugo realizes that he and Diana are made for each other and that he has wanted her all along.

Frederic, a young man with a heart and the identical twin of Hugo. Engaged to Diana Messerschmann, he blindly follows where love leads until Hugo plots to end his infatuation by hiring Isabelle to lure him away from Diana. Finally, he sees Diana for what she is and finds in Isabelle a tender heart to match his own.

Diana Messerschmann, a young lady without a heart. Engaged to Frederic, whom love has blinded to her true nature, she finally is led to see that she and the heartless Hugo are meant for each other.

Isabelle, a ballet dancer hired by Hugo to masquerade as an invited guest at the ball and to win Frederic away from Diana. She succeeds by revealing to Frederic a heart as innocent and gentle as his own.

Madame Desmermortes, the aunt of Hugo and Frederic and the hostess at the ball. Shrewd and worldly-wise, she sets to right the confusion brought about by Hugo's hiring of Isabelle to masquerade as an invited guest.

Messerschmann, Diana Messerschmann's millionaire father, in love with Lady Dorothy India.

Lady Dorothy India, Madame Desmermortes' niece and Messerschmann's mistress.

Romainville, a guest gently blackmailed by Hugo to pass off Isabelle as his niece and, hence, an invited guest at the ball.

Patrice Bombelles, Messerschmann's secretary, engaged in a secret love affair with Lady Dorothy India.

Capulat, Madame Desmermortes' companion.

RIP VAN WINKLE

Author: Washington Irving (1783-1859)
First published: 1819
Genre: Short fiction

Locale: The Catskills, New York
Time: Mid-eighteenth century
Plot: Fantasy

Rip Van Winkle, a figure based on a character from a German folktale. His name is still used to refer to anyone who is content to sleep his life away or who spends much of his time in sleepy idleness. As a character, he is not so much an as-if-real person as he is the embodiment of a common human desire—to sleep through all the trials and tribulations of adulthood and thus to move painlessly from childhood to the second childhood of old age. Diedrich Knickerbocker describes Rip as a simple, good-natured man who is a kind and considerate neighbor. Although he is a favorite among the neighborhood wives, who defend him, and the village children, with whom he is always willing to shoot marbles or fly kites, he is henpecked by his wife at home. Because of Rip's aversion to work, his fences are always in ruins, his yard is filled with weeds, and he has the worst farm in the neighborhood. His one faithful companion, to whom his wife's nagging becomes too much to bear, is his old dog, Wolf. After Rip's twenty-year sleep in the Catskills, he returns to a changed world, having slept through the turbulent beginnings of the American republic. Now that he is an old man with a long white beard, he can enjoy his old age as a respected patriarch who can be idle with impunity. Thus, he lives out his life as a storyteller, entertaining the children of the village with the fantastic tale of how he went into the mountains and bowled nine pins with the spirits of Hendrick Hudson and

his men, who cast him into a twenty-year sleep.

Dame Van Winkle, who has become the stereotype of the nagging wife in American literature. Although Rip certainly needs to be prodded to do any work around the house, she is presented as a hateful scold who finally drives Rip out of his house.

Nicholas Vedder, the patriarch of the village and landlord of the village inn in the first part of the story. He communicates his opinion by puffing rapidly on his pipe when displeased and slowly and lazily when pleased.

Rip Van Winkle (the son), a lazy, ragged counterpart of Rip Van Winkle. When Rip first sees his son on his return from his long sleep, he thinks, "I'm not myself—I'm somebody else—that's me yonder—no—that's somebody else got into my shoes."

Diedrich Knickerbocker, an old gentleman, familiar with the history of old Dutch New York, who tells the story of Rip Van Winkle.

Hendrick Hudson, the explorer who discovered the Hudson River. Along with the crew of his ship, the *Half Moon*, he keeps a vigil in the mountains every twenty years.

Peter Vanderdonk, the oldest inhabitant of the village when Rip returns. He is well versed in the history of the neighborhood and thus is the only one who recognizes Rip.

— *Charles E. May*

THE RIPENING SEED
(Le Blé en herbe)

Author: Colette (Sidonie-Gabrielle Colette, 1873-1954)
First published: 1923
Genre: Novel

Locale: A summer house on the coast of Brittany
Time: One summer in the early 1920's
Plot: Social realism

Vinca Ferret (feh-RAY), a fifteen-year-old girl who has always spent her summers in Brittany with her family and their friends, the Audeberts. Vinca is a beautiful young girl whose periwinkle-blue eyes are her most striking feature. She is a girl/woman whose behavior moves between naughty, rebellious outbursts and coquettish charm. She is in love with Philippe Audebert, and during the summer when the action of the novel takes place, she is confused about the changes in each of them, changes that affect their relationship and cause a rift in what has been a long-standing and fast friendship. She is particularly bewildered by her own newly discovered sexual desire and by Philippe's affair with an older woman. She cannot understand why he would choose to have his first sexual encounter with someone else.

Philippe Audebert (fee-LEEP oh-deh-BEHR), a sixteen-year-old boy who spends his summers in Brittany with his family and their friends, the Ferrets. He is slender, with a beautiful young body of firm flesh molded over taut, unobtrusive muscles. During this particular summer, he is aware of the awakening of his sexuality and of his sexual desire for Vinca, his childhood friend and the girl he knows he is destined to marry one day. He is frustrated and impatient to possess Vinca when he meets an older woman, dressed entirely in white, on the Brittany beach. Camille Dalleray introduces him to sexual pleasure, and he becomes sexually addicted to her, although he continues to love Vinca. He makes comparisons between the older woman and his inexperienced young girlfriend; these comparisons create conflicts for the young protagonist in the summer of his coming of age.

Madame Camille Dalleray (kah-MEEL dahl-REE), the **Lady-in-White**, who spends her summers vacationing in Brittany. She is a mythic figure, appearing entirely in white: white dress, white diamonds, and white skin. She is experienced in seduction; it is her vocation. She particularly desires boys with bodies like Greek statues. She has a dizzying effect on Philippe when they meet. When he returns to find her, she quickly and deftly seduces him, and when she decides that the affair must end, she leaves Ker-Anna, her villa in Brittany, just as quickly.

— *Anne Callahan*

RISE AND FALL OF THE CITY OF MAHAGONNY
(Aufstieg und Fall der Stadt Mahagonny)

Author: Bertolt Brecht (1898-1956)
First published: 1929
Genre: Drama

Locale: The mythical American West
Time: Mid-nineteenth century, during the gold rush
Plot: Epic

Jimmy Gallagher, also known in different versions of the opera as **Jim Mahoney** or **Paul Ackermann**, a lumberjack from Alaska. He is a hedonist who entangles himself in the nets of Mahagonny, a city in which one can buy all pleasures. During the approach of a hurricane that threatens to destroy Mahagonny, Jimmy proclaims his new principle, that henceforth everything is permitted. After the city has been saved miraculously, and as the people of Mahagonny continue to indulge in excessive eating, lovemaking, fighting, and drinking, to the point at which some people begin to die, Jimmy is arrested and tried in an ad hoc court. Although he is acquitted of most of the charges, he is sentenced to death for what is considered the capital offense of Mahagonny: to be without money.

Ladybird Begpick, known in different versions as **Leocadia Begbick** or **Leokadia Begpick**, a fugitive from justice who becomes the cofounder of Mahagonny in a desolate place on the road to Alaska. Like her namesake in another of Bertolt Brecht's plays (*Man Equals Man*, 1926), Begpick uses men for her profit by catering to their pleasures. In Mahagonny, she runs the As-You-Like-It Tavern (Hotel Rich Man in the more literal translation from German) and also performs the function of judge in the trial scene.

Jenny, known in different versions as **Jenny Jones** or **Jenny Smith**, a prostitute. She lures men on their way back from Alaska into Begpick's tavern and becomes Jimmy's lover. She sings the most lyrical passages of the opera, including the "Alabama Song," "Let Me Tell You What My Mother Called Me," and (together with Jimmy) the love duet "See there two cranes veer by one with another." Jenny abandons Jimmy in his critical situation and refuses to loan him money according to his (and her own) principle, "[I]f someone must kick, why, that's my part."

Trinity Moses and
Fatty the Booky (who is known in a different version as **Willy the Booky**), both social outcasts who are on the run from justice and who help Begpick with the founding of the city of Mahagonny. Like Begpick, they survive both the pleasures and the accusations of Mahagonny. In the trial scene, Fatty is the defense attorney and Moses the prosecutor. At the end of the opera, they proclaim, together with Begpick, a new price hike and the fight of everyone against everyone as the most extreme form of capitalism.

John Jacob (Jake) Smith, known in different versions as **Jack O'Brian** or **Jakob Schmidt**,

Alaskawolf Joe, known in a different version as **Joseph Lettner**, and

Bookkeeping Billy, known in a different version as **Heinrich Merg**, all former lumberjacks who worked with Jimmy in Alaska but who refuse to help him out of his financial debt in Mahagonny. Jake dies of overeating, and Joe is killed by Trinity Moses in a boxing match. Bill takes over Jenny from Jimmy when the latter is executed in the electric chair (or hanged, in another version).

— *Helmut F. Pfanner*

THE RISE OF SILAS LAPHAM

Author: William Dean Howells (1837-1920)
First published: 1885
Genre: Novel

Locale: New England
Time: The nineteenth century
Plot: Domestic realism

Silas Lapham, a millionaire paint manufacturer in Boston. He is respected in business circles, but his family is not accepted socially. Garrulous, bourgeois, burly, and brusque, he reflects traits of the self-made man who loves his maker, yet he is compassionate with outsiders and loving to his family. Babbitt-like, he emulates men he has admired for their savoir faire. Bankrupt after a series of business reverses, he gladly leaves the material comforts of Boston to return with his family to the modest living of their earlier days. Lapham is called "Colonel," his rank when he was injured at Gettysburg during the Civil War.

Persis Lapham, his wife. Like her husband, she has kept the ways of the country. More aware of present social conduct than is her husband, she is no more capable of observing the proprieties. Interested in marriage for her daughters, as well as prudent and self-effacing in social matters, she restrains herself in advising them. As an influence in his affairs, she goads Lapham into business dealings, to her involving morality, only to regret later the action taken. When uninformed of his activities, she becomes suspicious; she is remorseful and self-reproaching when she senses her unfounded jealousies. To Persis, returning to the country is an escape from the rigors of Boston's social life and her inability to cope with status.

Irene, the Laphams' younger daughter. Quiet, reserved, beautiful, and domestic, she infers that Tom Corey is interested in her, only to learn that he is in love with her sister. She escapes the sympathy and questioning of her family and the trials of the family's financial reverses through a month-long visit with relatives in the Midwest. Returning to Boston to let the family know that her cousin's evident interest in her is another misleading affair, she becomes a virtual recluse other than for visits to the Midwest.

Penelope, the Laphams' older daughter. She is satirical, humorous, and droll. Inferring that Tom Corey is in love with Irene, but being secretly in love with him herself, Penelope is guilt-stricken when Corey reveals his affection for her. She refuses Corey's attentions, thinking her father's financial adversity would imply the wrong motivations for her accepting Corey. Ultimately, they are married and go to Mexico and Central America, where Corey will be in business.

Tom Corey, the son of a proper Bostonian family. Shaking off the effects of hereditary stratification, he displays considerable business acumen. In his attentions to Irene, he hopes to attract Penelope to him. This indirection misleads the Laphams and the Coreys. His stability, self-reliance, and graciousness in personal affairs, as well as removal from their families, ensure marital happiness for him and Penelope.

Milton K. Rogers, Silas Lapham's former business partner. His recurrent appearances for assistance create situations to point up Lapham's character and the attitudes and rapport between the Laphams. Unsuccessful in appeals to Silas, Rogers turns to Persis, who intercedes with her husband.

Anna Corey, Tom's mother. In her seemingly innocuous role of an aristocrat whose chief occupation is the comfort of her husband and children, she is likable. In protecting her son from questionable associations, as with the Laphams, she is protective in a genteel way.

Bromfield Corey, Tom's father. A rich young painter in Rome at the time of his marriage, he has never changed his pace. Sedentary, he remains unassuming in social matters. Nothing surprises him, nothing shocks him, and nothing upsets him. In his self-imposed isolation, he views life as an amusing process and expresses his ready opinions on happenings accordingly.

Zerilla Dewey, a typist in Lapham's office, the butt of Mrs. Lapham's jealousy.

Mrs. James "Moll" Millon, Zerilla's mother. Moll Millon is the ne'er-do-well widow of the man who was killed by a bullet intended for Lapham in an early labor dispute.

Lily and

Nanny, Tom Corey's young sisters. Their behavior toward the Laphams and Tom's marriage reflects their mother's influence.

Walker, the Laphams' younger daughter. Quiet, reserved, beautiful, and domestic, she infers that Tom Corey is interested in her, only to learn that he is in love with her sister. She escapes the sympathy and questioning of her family and the trials of the family's financial reverses through a month-long visit with relatives in the Midwest. Returning to Boston to let the family know that her cousin's evident interest in her is another misleading affair, she becomes a virtual recluse other than for visits to the Midwest.

Bartley Hubbard, a journalist who writes Lapham's biography.

Mr. Sewell, a minister, the adviser to the Laphams in their dilemma after Tom's indirection with Irene and Penelope.

James Bellingham, Mrs. Corey's brother and a business adviser to Lapham at the time of Lapham's financial losses.

THE RISING OF THE MOON

Author: Lady Augusta Gregory (1852-1932)
First published: 1905
Genre: Drama

Locale: Ireland
Time: Late nineteenth or early twentieth century
Plot: Protest

Sergeant, an officer in the Royal Irish Constabulary, a force recruited from native Irishmen by the British authorities. The Sergeant reveals the ambiguities and divided loyalties of his professional role. He is a slow, cautious, and somewhat unimaginative character. Although he is not particularly enlightened, he is also not outside the range of patriotic sentiment's appeal. His discovery that this is the case is as much of a surprise to him as it is to the audience.

The Man, a character conceived of as the Sergeant's antithesis. As a ballad singer, he is as identifiable a presence in the society of the time as a police officer. This populist disguise covers the character's more subversive activities. Ballads provide a medium through which the Man's political activities may be seen as legendary. His ability to win over the Sergeant's collusion is an argument in favor of the innate appeal of his presence and his cause.

Policeman B., one of the play's minor characters, who constitutes the search party with Policeman X. He is intent on little more than doing his duty. His speech at the end of the play reveals his lack of interest in the world of history and culture. His behavior indicates that he needs the Sergeant to issue orders to him in order to function.

Policeman X., who is as one-dimensional and minor a character as his colleague, Policeman B. He is a little more committed to doing his duty in pursuit of the escaped prisoner. The play does not develop what this commitment means either to the character or to the play's depiction of the powers that be. Together, the two policemen make up a framework of orthodoxy, within which the complications of the Sergeant's loyalties may be perceived.

— *George O'Brien*

RITES OF PASSAGE

Author: William Golding (1911-1993)
First published: 1980
Genre: Novel

Locale: Aboard a ship, en route from England to the Antipodes
Time: Early nineteenth century
Plot: Moral

Edmund Talbot, the epistolary narrator of the novel. He is writing to his godfather and patron, an influential aristocrat who has not only acquired a government position for him in one of the new British colonies in Australasia but also has instructed him to write a full account of how he progresses. Edmund takes the task seriously, not only to please his godfather but also because he sees himself egotistically as the central character in a drama played out on board the ship taking him to his destination. He defines "central" as "highest born" at first, but the voyage becomes a learning process. His eyes are opened over a number of things, and he has to revise values and attitudes by, for example, realizing that his patron and his journal do not have the manipulative influence with the ship's captain that he thinks they do. Above all, he learns, in the tragedy of the Reverend James Colley, that with rank comes responsibility and not power. Edmund is sensuous and full of himself, yet frank and eager to do well.

The Reverend James Robert Colley, a young, poor Church of England clergyman going to the colonies. He has no official position on board and becomes isolated, partly as a result of his own inept behavior and perceptions and partly because of the hostility of the captain, crew, and passengers, Edmund included. Colley takes over as epistolary narrator for a period when Edmund discovers an unfinished letter of Colley to his sister and includes this in his own account. Quite a different view of Colley is thereby rendered. Whereas Edmund portrays him at first as clumsy, inept, and obsequious, Colley's own account shows him to be naïve and almost saintlike in his attempt to establish a religious presence on board ship, to forgive his detractors, and to be patient in suffering. Edmund concludes that Colley died of shame over the fact that his naïveté had led him to be maneuvered into drunken behavior and finally into a homosexual orgy with crew members.

Captain Anderson, a man overtly hostile to Colley and to all forms of religion. He isolates himself fiercely from the crew and passengers, seeking to maintain both his inner psyche and his authority by such isolation. He is reactive in his leadership, which is why he twice fails to stop the crew from persecuting Colley and ultimately causing his death. His cover-up of the death points most clearly to the moral failure of his authority.

Lieutenant Summers, who has risen from the ranks to become one of the three lieutenants serving under Captain Anderson. He is the only person on board who understands what is happening to Colley. In the end, he confronts Edmund with his irresponsible behavior toward Colley, even though such intervention could lead to his dismissal. Although he convinces Edmund, he is nevertheless involved, along with Edmund, in the captain's inquest and the subsequent cover-up of Colley's death.

Lieutenant Deverel, the lieutenant with the most polished manners, which immediately attracts Edmund. As the novel proceeds, Deverel becomes involved in a covert affair with Zenobia and, more seriously, becomes a leader in the persecution of Colley. In comparison with Summers, he is a moral lightweight, which Edmund finally realizes.

Mr. Brocklebank, who is by far the most obnoxious of the middle-class passengers. He calls himself a painter, but the fact that he is accompanied by two younger women, his "wife" and his "daughter," leads to speculations that he is a procurer. He has no moral sense, is full of himself, and has gross manners.

Zenobia Brocklebank, Mr. Brocklebank's "daughter." Edmund describes her as "approaching her middle years"; she is an actress and a wanton. Despite Edmund's perception of her coarseness, her sexual availability soon infatuates him, even though he then realizes that a number of the officers are also seeking, and acquiring, "commerce" with her.

Miss Granham, a woman traveling as a governess. She is "of uncertain years" and is the daughter of a ranking English clergyman, but she shows herself to be hostile to religion. At the end of the novel, she becomes engaged to Mr. Prettiman, an avowed atheist.

Mr. Prettiman, a printer by trade but obviously aiming to export his revolutionary ideas to the colonies. He argues, with anyone willing to engage him, for his rational atheism against religion and superstition. In his ridiculous style, he is even prepared to shoot an albatross to prove that Samuel Taylor Coleridge was wrong.

Wheeler, one of two servants assigned to the better class of passengers. He serves Edmund, nursing him through his bouts of seasickness. He is aware of all that goes on (for example, with Zenobia and Colley). At the end of the novel, he is mysteriously washed overboard, but unlike Colley's death, his causes hardly a ripple.

— *David Barratt*

THE RIVALS

Author: Richard Brinsley Sheridan (1751-1816)
First published: 1775
Genre: Drama

Locale: Bath
Time: The eighteenth century
Plot: Comedy of manners

Captain Jack Absolute (Ensign Beverley), a young aristocrat who poses as a penniless ensign to win the love of Lydia Languish. After many problems—among them relatives who oppose his marriage, rivals who challenge him to duels, and misunderstandings with his fiancée—Jack wins fair Lydia.

Lydia Languish, Jack Absolute's beloved, a girl whose head is so stuffed with the fantastic adventures of popular fictional people that she cannot bear to marry anyone in her own class. She spurns Jack Absolute when she learns that he is not the penniless Ensign Beverley, but she is greatly impressed when she learns that he is to fight a duel because of her, and he wins her hand.

Sir Anthony Absolute, Jack's strong-willed father, who insists that Jack marry the woman Sir Anthony selects. Jack refuses to obey his father's edict until he learns that Sir Anthony has chosen Lydia to be his son's wife.

Mrs. Malaprop, Lydia's aunt, whose eccentric treatment of the English language spawned the word "malapropism." She opposes Lydia's intention to marry Jack, but she drops her objections at last to bask in the high spirits of those whose problems have found happy solutions.

Bob Acres, an affable country squire who challenges Ensign Beverley to a duel. When he learns that Beverley and his friend Jack are the same person, the timid squire is greatly relieved that no duel will be necessary.

Sir Lucius O'Trigger, a brash Irishman who is hoodwinked into believing that he is corresponding with Lydia when, actually, Mrs. Malaprop and he are exchanging letters. He challenges Jack to a duel but withdraws when he learns that Lydia never has been interested in him.

Faulkland, Jack's friend, who is in love with Julia Melville, Lydia's cousin. Faulkland's avocation is worrying about the welfare of his suit for Julia, thus creating obstacles where there are none. Finally, however, he banishes care and generously accepts Julia's love.

Julia Melville, Lydia's cousin, who marries Faulkland.

THE RIVER BETWEEN

Author: Ngugi wa Thiong'o (James Ngugi, 1938-   )
First published: 1965
Genre: Novel

Locale: Kameno and Makuyu, in Kenya
Time: The 1890's-early 1930's
Plot: Social realism

Waiyaki (way-YAH-kee), a dedicated teacher. His father, Chege, rears him to appreciate his African heritage so that when he is sent to the missionaries to learn the white man's magic, he acquires knowledge without repudiating his inheritance. Waiyaki urgently seeks to educate his people through schools that, being locally sponsored, will increase literacy but not undermine tradition. His determination to maintain a balance between old and new beliefs is suspect to those who prefer the extremes of total rejection and eager acceptance of colonial ways. Waiyaki joins Kiama, a secret society dedicated to maintaining the old principles, but he is uncomfortable with the restrictions it imposes. His dissatisfaction increases when he falls in love with Nyambura, because his relationship with her violates tradition. At the height of his achievement, he wonders whether he may not be the savior who is anticipated in local legend. He is given a people's trial and although he pleads for moderation, he is defeated by Kabonyi's bitter prosecution. When forced to admit his love, he is accused of treachery against the people. Guiltless but condemned, he sees fanaticism triumph and all of his dreams for reconciliation and education collapse.

Chege (CHAY-gay), Waiyaki's beloved father, a distinguished elder, a Kikuyu seer deeply committed to the beauty and significance of tribal traditions.

Joseph, a self-righteous convert to Christianity who has established a church in Makuyu. His adoption of a non-African name indicates his determination to make a complete break with the traditions in which he was reared. As a minister, he develops an extreme ardor for rigid religious conformity, damning his own people as pagans. When his daughter Muthoni, though a devout Christian, follows the ancient custom of female circumcision, he rejects her utterly.

Muthoni (mew-DHOH-nee), Joseph's daughter. She is converted to Christianity and has a deep commitment to the creed, but she also feels an obligation to follow to some degree the rites of her tradition. She undergoes the cruel ritual of circumcision and, in spite of Waiyaki rushing her belatedly to the hospital, dies of the resulting infection even while expressing her commitment to a belief in Jesus, as she has been taught.

Nyambura (NYAHM-bew-rah), Joseph's other daughter. She reciprocates Waiyaki's love but rejects his first proposal because of her obligation of obedience to her father and her realization that marriage will raise antagonisms that will destroy them. Her father disowns her for immorality, yet as his daughter, she is too Christian for the traditionalists: She shuns the circumcision ritual that killed her sister. Waiyaki's continuing love for her is the cause of his tragic downfall.

Kabonyi (kah-BOH-nyee), the tribal seer after Chege's death. Kabonyi has none of his predecessor's gentle reasonableness. He is an angry, bitter man, and although his beliefs are diametrically opposed to Joseph's, the two have much in common. Kabonyi engineers the persecution of Waiyaki because he fears the changes that will result from Waiyaki's sensible moderation.

Kamau (kah-MOW), Kabonyi's son. He follows the principles of his father without question but is constantly criticized for having achieved less distinction than Waiyaki. Kamau supports his father's attack on Waiyaki only partly out of principle: He sees Waiyaki as his rival for Nyambura, and the religious issue becomes the means of confronting him.

Kinuthia (kee-new-DHEE-ah), a young man who is brought up with Kamau. In the novel's schematic action, Kinuthia is Kamau's opposite; he grows up to develop complete loyalty to Waiyaki and respect for his principles.

— *John F. Povey*

RIVER OF EARTH

Author: James Still (1906-   )
First published: 1940
Genre: Novel

Locale: Kentucky
Time: Early 1930's
Plot: Regional

Brack's Oldest Boy, the narrator. The events in this story of poverty-ridden Kentucky mountaineers are seen through the eyes of this young boy, who is observant but too young to comprehend some of what he observes.

Brack Baldridge, his father. Poverty and depression are not Brack's only enemies in his struggle to keep his family from starving. He is too humane to deny food to miners out of work and begging for their families, or to send sponging relatives away.

Alpha Baldridge, Brack's wife. In desperation, she moves her furniture and children to the smokehouse and sets fire to the house, so that the sponging relatives, having no place to sleep, will then leave her family in possession of their meager supply of food.

Grandmother Middleton, Alpha's brisk mother, who lives on a small farm. The boy is sent to help her with her harvesting and ends by staying more than a year. When she dies, her body is taken to the boy's home in Blackjack prior to burial. As the wagon takes her body away for the last time, the boy hears the first cry of his mother's new baby.

Uncle Jolly, Alpha's brother, who spends much of his time in jail. Once he is pardoned by the governor for his bravery in helping fight a prison fire, which he admits to his mother he started.

Uncle Samp, who never worked and does not intend to start. Evicted once from the Baldridge home by Alpha's fire, he shows up later at their coal camp house. He finally marries a fortune-teller.

Euly Baldridge, the sister of the narrator. Wanting to be educated, the children go to school until the schoolmaster is shot by an angry mountaineer whose loutish son had been punished by the teacher.

Harl Logan and

Tibb Logan, cousins also evicted by Alpha's fire. They return to work in the mine and live with the Baldridges. Laid off, they dynamite one of the veins and, having been kicked out by the mine boss, leave the Baldridge home.

Uncle Luce, who is supposed to replace the boy as Grandmother Middleton's helper on the farm; however, he arrives after the harvest.

Uncle Toll, who fetches the boy from his grandmother and leaves him to sleep outside Jolly's jail cell so that lack of companionship will not drive Jolly to break out. Knowing that a jailbreak will get him a long prison term, Jolly puts temptation out of reach by stealing the keys and sending the boy home with them to his family.

Grandpa Middleton, who was killed some time before the time of the story by Aus Coggins; no Baldridge has avenged the death. The narrator has a fistfight with a neighbor boy who says the Baldridges are cowards.

Aus Coggins, who is tormented by Uncle Jolly, who cuts Coggins' fences and breaks his dam. It is said that Uncle Jolly is avenging his father's death.

THE RIVET IN GRANDFATHER'S NECK

Author: James Branch Cabell (1879-1958)
First published: 1915
Genre: Novel

Locale: Litchfield, not to be found on the map of Virginia
Time: 1896-1927
Plot: Social satire

Colonel Rudolph Musgrave, the head of the Musgrave family. A thorough Southern gentleman, he is aristocratic and scholarly, a lover of many women, and a less than successful businessman. Having loved and lost Anne Charteris in the past, he falls in love with and marries his cousin, Patricia Stapylton. After a deterioration in their relationship, Patricia dies of a heart attack, but he feels too deep a loyalty to her to marry the now free Anne Charteris.

Patricia Stapylton, Colonel Rudolph Musgrave's young cousin, later his wife. Happy at first in their marriage, she gives her husband a son at the risk of her life and with permanent damage to her health. As tensions develop between husband and wife, she becomes enamored of John Charteris. After he is killed, she dies of a heart attack.

John Charteris, a novelist. Having been involved in many affairs, he is easily persuaded by Patricia Stapylton to run off with her. The runaways are stopped by Colonel Musgrave, and a few days later Charteris is killed by a jealous husband.

Anne Charteris, John Charteris' adoring wife. She refuses to recognize that her husband is a scoundrel until the knowledge is forced on her after his death. Even then, however, her loyalty prevents her marriage to Colonel Rudolph Musgrave.

Agatha Musgrave, Colonel Rudolph Musgrave's sister, whose resentment of her brother's wife, Patricia Stapylton, is part of the cause of their growing marital tensions.

Roger Stapylton, Patricia Stapylton's father, formerly an overseer, now a wealthy businessman.

Joe Parkinson, Patricia Stapylton's rejected suitor.

Virginia, a servant in the Musgrave household.

Lord Pevensey, Patricia Stapylton's rejected fiancé.

Mrs. Clarice Pendomer, a former mistress of John Charteris.

THE ROAD

Author: Wole Soyinka (1934-)
First published: 1965
Genre: Drama

Locale: Nigeria
Time: The 1950's or 1960's
Plot: Mythic

Professor, a forger of driver's licenses and the proprietor of a rest stop for truckers and of a used-parts store for all sorts of vehicles. He was removed from his position as lay reader and Sunday school teacher because a naïve, naturalistic explanation that he gave to his class was deemed blasphemy. He spends much of his time looking for the "Word" in places as diverse as the betting sheet of the local newspaper and traffic signs, all of which he collects and saves. His establishment is within sight of the church, against which he speaks cryptically of going to "war." During the climactic appearance of the *egungun* (the mask of an ancestor), he fuels the frenzy of celebrants with palm wine. In the following confrontation, he is stabbed fatally by Say Tokyo Kid.

Kotonu (koh-TOH-new), the driver of the passenger vehicle "No Danger No Delay." Foreseeing an accident on an approaching bridge, he allowed another truck to pass; it broke through the rotten boards and crashed, killing all aboard. Unlike other drivers, Kotonu does not happily run over dogs; he avoids them even at some risk, thus depriving the bloodthirsty god, Ogun, of his appointed sacrifice. This continued sacrilege is repaid when a drivers' festival celebrating the feast of Ogun crosses in front of the truck and Kotonu runs down the mask. When the drivers, whips in hand, come seeking their mask, Samson persuades Kotonu to don the costume and become the mask. Kotonu is horrified to discover that the costume is full of the blood of its former owner.

Samson, a companion and "tout" for the driver, Kotonu. Because he could not master the skills of driving, he paid Kotonu's license fee with his own savings, and he works now to find and take care of passengers for Kotonu's passenger-truck runs. When a near accident convinces Kotonu to quit, Samson tries unsuccessfully to change his mind. To recoup some of the lost income, he negotiates with Professor to sell Kotonu's license, but even this business venture is swept away by the violence at the play's end.

Say Tokyo Kid, a driver of timber trucks and chief of a gang of unemployed drivers. He is proud of driving timber (a clean but dangerous load) and contemptuous of passengers, whom he finds inconvenient and filthy. At one point, he hires his men out for a political rally. When, inflamed by Professor's palm wine and the dance, his men are beyond his control, Say Tokyo confronts and grapples with the *egungun*. As a result of this encounter, he stabs Professor and is lifted up and smashed with deadly force on a bench by the *egungun*, which then swirls and collapses like an empty costume.

Salubi (sah-LEW-bee), a driver trainee. He cannot find a driving job without a license and cannot get a license unless he has a job. When Kotonu announces his intention of quitting, Salubi steals his driver's uniform and negotiates with Professor for a forgery based on Kotonu's old license. During Say Tokyo's fight with the *egungun*, Salubi slides a knife to him, thus precipitating the stabbing of Professor.

Murano (mew-RAH-noh), a mute, Professor's palm-wine tapper and bodyguard. Professor, who found him half dead from an accident and nursed him back to health, considers Murano to be living in the shadow of death.

Particulars Joe, a local policeman. He is aware of Professor's forgeries and makes regular and companionable visits to collect his bribe. His present visit is to investigate the apparent abduction of a mask during the drivers' celebration of Ogun's feast.

Chief-in-Town, a politician who hires Say Tokyo's gang.

— *James L. Hodge*

THE ROAD TO MECCA

Author: Athol Fugard (1932-)
First published: 1985
Genre: Drama

Locale: South Africa
Time: 1974
Plot: Play of ideas

Miss Helen Martins, an elderly South African widow and an artist. Miss Helen lives alone in the town of New Bethesda, where her eccentric sculptures have served to isolate her from her neighbors. Since her husband's death, her work has become the spiritual center of Miss Helen's life, bringing her a sense of fulfillment that was missing earlier, when she lived as a conventional member of society. Now that she is becoming increasingly unable to manage on her own, her wellspring of creativity seems at an end, and she is faced with a sense of darkness and despair that threatens at times to overwhelm her.

Elsa Barlow, a teacher in her thirties. Elsa is Miss Helen's closest friend and the only person who treats the older woman's work with respect and interest. Concerned for her friend's well-being, Elsa arrives from Cape Town for an unannounced visit and urges Miss Helen to resist local attempts to persuade her to enter a retirement home. Elsa herself is in many ways confused and troubled; fearing commitment in her life, she has recently had an abortion and is now questioning that decision. Miss Helen has long served as a source of inspiration for her, and her reaction to the older woman's growing inability to cope is tied to her need for Miss Helen to remain a strong role model.

Marius Byleveld, a pastor and longtime friend of Miss Helen. Marius and Miss Helen are contemporaries, and it is he who is urging her to enter a retirement home. A far more complex character than he initially appears, he seems at first to represent simply the repressive elements in conventional society that see Miss Helen's work and lifestyle as a dangerous break with the status quo. It becomes clear as the story progresses, however, that although there are indeed aspects of that outlook in Marius, his concern for Miss Helen's welfare is entirely genuine and is in fact motivated largely by the long-cherished love he feels for her.

— Janet Lorenz

THE ROADS TO FREEDOM
(Les Chemins de la liberté)

Author: Jean-Paul Sartre (1905-1980)
First published: 1945-1949
Genre: Novels

Locale: France and New York City
Time: 1938-1940
Plot: Existentialism

The Age of Reason, 1945

Mathieu Delarue (mah-TYEW deh-lah-REW), Marcelle's lover, a philosophy teacher in Paris. During a visit to Marcelle, he learns that she is pregnant. He decides to raise the money to pay for an abortion, which is illegal in this place and time. Mathieu asks both his friend Daniel and his brother Jacques for the money, but they refuse. He meets his old friend Brunet, who asks him to become a communist. Mathieu refuses. He is enamored of Ivich, a young woman. He takes her to an art gallery to view the paintings of Paul Gauguin. Later, he meets her, her brother Boris, and his mistress Lola in a nightclub. After Ivich stabs herself in the hand, Mathieu repeats her gesture. The following day, he meets with Boris, who thinks Lola has died, and agrees to retrieve Boris' letters from Lola's apartment. He is tempted to steal Lola's money, but she awakens. Later that night, however, he returns and steals the money, which he then gives to Marcelle for her abortion.

Boris Serguine (sehr-GEEN), the brother of Ivich, lover of Lola, son of Russian emigrants, and protégé of Mathieu. He hangs out in nightclubs where Lola, a much older woman, sings. After spending the night with her in her apartment, he wakes up and mistakenly concludes that she is dead; she is only in a deep sleep induced by drugs. He flees, meets Mathieu, and persuades Mathieu to retrieve his letters from Lola's apartment.

Daniel Sereno, a homosexual friend of Mathieu. When Mathieu visits him and asks for money for Marcelle's abortion, he refuses, although he can afford it. After cruising an arcade that serves as a meeting place for homosexuals, he visits Marcelle and persuades her to keep the baby. When Mathieu refuses to marry Marcelle, Daniel marries her. He then returns Lola's money.

Ivich Serguine (ee-VEECH), Boris' sister, a student. She believes she has failed her final examination. Sitting in a nightclub with Mathieu, she stabs herself in the hand to shock a nearby couple.

The Reprieve, 1945

Mathieu Delarue, who is now a reservist in the French army. He is vacationing on the French Riviera with his brother and sister-in-law when the Munich Crisis of 1938 begins. Although he is called up to serve in the army, he delays reporting so that he can see his friend Gomez. They meet in Marseilles. Mathieu then returns to Paris for one night and has a fling with a woman he meets on the street. The morning afterward, he departs to join his army unit and partially reads a letter from Daniel before destroying it.

Boris Serguine, who has returned to Lola and is traveling with her while she tours the country singing at various nightclubs. He follows the events of the Munich Crisis on the radio and makes friends with the patrons of the clubs. He looks forward to the war as a way of getting rid of Lola.

Daniel Sereno, who is vacationing in the countryside with his bride Marcelle but is still attracted to young men.

Ivich Serguine, who marries a rich young man she despises.

Gomez, a Spanish painter and general in the Spanish Loyalist army. He is on leave in France. After visiting his family in Paris, he stops in Marseilles to see Mathieu. He is back in Spain when the Munich agreement is announced and declares that they have lost the war.

Troubled Sleep, 1949

Mathieu Delarue, who is now serving with the army as a meteorologist. He and his comrades see their officers desert them when the French army collapses in the spring of 1940. He joins up with an infantry unit and kills a German soldier in an inconsequential fifteen-minute firefight.

Boris Serguine, who is wounded in the first week of fighting in the invasion of France and is evacuated to Marseilles. He decides to flee to England, although that would mean abandoning Lola. When she reaches Marseilles, Lola does not tell Boris that she is pregnant and allows him to go in good conscience.

Daniel Sereno, who awaits the Germans in Paris. He prevents a young Frenchman, who had deserted from the army, from committing suicide and then attempts to seduce him.

Ivich Serguine, who travels in a chauffeur-driven limousine provided by her in-laws and visits Boris in Marseilles. She complains about her unhappy marriage.

Brunet (brew-NAY), an old friend of Mathieu, a Communist organizer, and a soldier. He is captured by the Germans and placed in a prisoner-of-war camp. He organizes a secret Communist cell.

Gomez, who is now a refugee from the Spanish Civil War. He lives in New York City and tries to earn a living as an art critic.

— *Tom Feller*

ROADSIDE PICNIC
(Piknik na obochine)

Authors: Arkady Strugatsky (1925-1991) and Boris Strugatsky (1933-   )
First published: 1972
Genre: Novel

Locale: Harmont, a town in Canada
Time: Late 1990's and early 2000's
Plot: Science fiction

Redrick (Red) Schuhart, the protagonist, a daring, competent, and roguish "stalker" from the Visitation town of Harmont. He is nicknamed "Red" because of his bright red hair. A laboratory assistant at the Harmont Institute for Extraterrestrial Cultures at the age of twenty-three, with time he deals more and more in illegal Visitation Zone contraband. By the age of twenty-eight, he has only his illegal career. He remains insatiable in his desire to face the hidden terrors of the Zone and to find value (both material and spiritual) among the alien remains, despite being imprisoned twice for illegal activities and despite many brushes with death. He frequents the Borscht, a stalker bar, where he finds oblivion in drink. He is contemptuous of priggish authority, talkative greenhorns, and stalkers who break the code. He is hot-tempered but can be calm and cool when necessary. He has quick reflexes, a basic instinct for survival, and a knowledge of the peculiarities of the Zone that comes only from experience, but he is always a physical wreck after his excursions there. A loner who talks tough and acts tough, he has a soft heart for friends and family; beneath his protective shell and surface hate is a deep-seated, though intermittent, humanism. After sacrificing his companion to his quest, he requests from the hard-earned magical Golden Ball "Happiness for everybody, free, and no one will go away unsatisfied."

Buzzard Burbridge, an infamous, avaricious old stalker, a survivor known for his desertion of companions in trouble. Schuhart rightly calls him "a rat." He is a wife-beater and a sadist. Buzzard loses his legs on one trip (they melt) and thereafter tries to bribe Schuhart (who brought him back alive) into going after a booby-trapped Golden Ball, reputedly an Aladdin's lamp that will grant any truly wanted wish. His only redeeming quality is his love for his two handsome children: an idealistic, innocent son and a beautiful but vicious daughter. His greed forces him to share the secret of the Golden Ball and send Schuhart on his final trip into the Zone.

Kirill Panov, a friend and employer of Schuhart, a Russian scientist with the United Nations team at Harmont. Worn out, gray, and silent at the beginning, he becomes radiant and grinning from his clandestine trip to the Zone with Schuhart, for he needs the excitement of discovery to give his life meaning and truly believes that the Zone will bring peace and harmony. His inexperience, however, results in his blind step back into a silvery web whose alien force leaves him dead shortly thereafter.

Dr. Valentine Pilman, a wry Canadian Nobel Prize winner, the senior physicist at the Zone. His tongue-in-cheek discussions of the "Visitation" mock the pretensions and vanities of his fellow mortals. Dr. Pilman is small, delicate, and neat, with a low, broad forehead and a bristly crewcut. He shares with a schoolboy credit for the Pilman Radiation theory of Deneb visitors; he describes the extraterrestrial visit as a "roadside picnic" and the curious, incomprehensible, ofttimes destructive materials left behind as the waste discards. He speculates that humanity may be superfluous, that human definitions of reason are meaningless, and that the universe is basically an absurdist one on which humans try to impose unrealistic theories that fit their preconceptions and prejudices. Pilman's comments provide the philosophical base of the novel.

Richard (Dick) Noonan, a lazy, complacent bureaucrat, out to stalk the stalkers but blind to the daily dealings of even his longtime friend, Red Schuhart. Short, plump, and pink, at the age of fifty-one he dashes around town in his Peugeot, supposedly supervising electronic equipment supplies for the Harmont branch of the IEC. In actuality, he is an incompetent spy, making contacts and trying to stop the flow of Zone materials out of the area but duped by his informer and ignorant of the intricacies of the illegal trade. He adores Guta and Monkey (to whom he takes candy and toys) and threatens the neighbors who pester them. Dr. Pilman shares his theories with Noonan over drinks.

Guta Schuhart, Redrick's mistress and then devoted wife, beautiful, energetic, strong, and proud, with a long neck "like a young mare's." Guta is committed to life and to family. She defends her mutant child against human cruelty and provides the solid family security her husband needs, but the strain takes its toll.

"Monkey" Schuhart, Redrick's mutant daughter. Her nickname results as much from her nonstop chattering as from the long, silky golden fur that covers her body, her hairy paws, and her huge, dark eyes with no whites at all. As an infant, she is warm and affectionate, but growth produces terrible and pathetic regression. She develops a sullen face, coarse brown fur, and limited responses.

— Gina Macdonald

ROAN STALLION

Author: Robinson Jeffers (1887-1962)
First published: 1925
Genre: Poetry

Locale: Carmel Coast, California
Time: The 1920's
Plot: Symbolism

California, a young farm wife, the daughter of a Scottish sailor and a Spanish and Indian mother. She is graceful, lithe, strong, and darkly beautiful but soiled by her life with Johnny and his associates. Her passionate offering of herself to the stallion on a hilltop on an April night symbolizes her turning from her sordid relationships with men and her submission to the majestic strength and clean beauty of God. When, filled with hatred the next night, she flees from the drunken Johnny to the stallion's corral, she is followed by Johnny and his dog Bruno. The frightened Christine brings her mother a gun to kill the raging stallion. California shoots Bruno and watches the stallion crush Johnny with his hoofs and rend the lifeless body with his teeth. Then, faithful to her own race after all, she shoots the stallion and in stark agony turns toward her daughter like a woman who has killed God.

Johnny, her husband, an outcast Hollander. He has a pale face and burned-out blue eyes, and his still-young body is shriveled from debauchery.

Christine, their small blonde daughter, blue-eyed like her father, wizened of forehead and sickly in body.

The roan stallion, a symbol of the rejection of man and the embracing of natural life.

Jim Carrier, the owner of a bay mare bred to the roan stallion.

ROB ROY

Author: Sir Walter Scott (1771-1832)
First published: 1817
Genre: Novel

Locale: Northumberland and Glasgow
Time: 1715
Plot: Historical

Frank Osbaldistone, a young man who has been sent abroad to learn his father's mercantile business and whose progress has not been satisfactory. He is sent to his uncle's home to find his replacement among his uncle's sons. He and his cousin Rashleigh, who takes the position, dislike each other immediately. On the way to his uncle's house, Frank meets Rob Roy, an outlaw, without knowing who he is. He also falls in love with Diana Vernon, whom he meets on the way to his uncle's home. After the Jacobite revolt, Frank inherits all of his uncle's lands and marries Diana, in spite of the fact that she is a Catholic and he is a Presbyterian.

Rashleigh Osbaldistone, Frank's cousin, who takes a position with Osbaldistone and Tresham and proceeds to embezzle funds from the firm. He betrays the Stuart cause and is disinherited.

William Osbaldistone, Frank's businessman father. He does not like the idea of Frank marrying a papist, but at last he consents.

Sir Hildebrand Osbaldistone, Frank's uncle and one of the plotters in the Jacobite uprising. He dies at Newgate after willing Frank all of his property.

Diana Vernon, Sir Hildebrand's niece, with whom Frank falls in love. She is a Catholic and an outspoken girl.

Rob Roy (**MacGregor Campbell**), a Scottish outlaw. He befriends Frank and helps him discover that Rashleigh is embezzling funds from Osbaldistone and Tresham. When Frank is arrested while on the way to meet him, Rob Roy's wife Helen leads an attack on the arresting soldiers and frees Frank. Meanwhile, Rob Roy has been captured, but he escapes by throwing himself into a river. After the Jacobite revolt, Rob Roy kills Rashleigh when that turncoat comes to arrest Diana and her father.

Sir Frederick Vernon, Diana's father and a Jacobite.

THE ROBBER BRIDEGROOM

Author: Eudora Welty (1909-   )
First published: 1942
Genre: Novel

Locale: Along the Natchez Trace in Mississippi
Time: Pioneer days
Plot: Satire

Clement Musgrove, an innocent backwoods planter. After his son and wife are killed by Indians, Clement escapes with Salome and his daughter. He marries Salome to look after his child and becomes a planter on the Mississippi River. Although he is rich, he is not greedy; in fact, he does not even know how much he is worth. After Rosamond is kidnapped, he and Jamie Lockhart search for her in the forest, but in vain. When he hears Goat shouting "Jamie Lockhart is the bandit,"

Clement becomes so disillusioned that he wanders aimlessly in the forest, where he is captured by Indians. After Salome dies, the Indians release him. Convinced that Rosamond has been eaten by a panther, he is overjoyed when he accidentally meets her in New Orleans.

Salome, Clement's second wife. After being captured by the Indians, this ugly woman is consumed by greed and ambition, which drive her to encourage Clement to plant more profitable crops, build a finer house, and increase the size of his plantation. Even though Clement constantly buys her gifts, she is envious of the ones that he buys Rosamond, especially a fine green dress. She sends Rosamond out to the woods every day to collect herbs in the hope that an animal or an Indian will kill her, but to no avail. In desperation, she hires Goat to spy on Rosamond, but he is unable to turn up any hard evidence against the girl. Eventually, Salome's jealousy leads to her own destruction. She persuades her Indian captors to choose her instead of Rosamond as their sacrifice, and she drops dead during a ritualistic dance to the sun.

Rosamond, Clement's beautiful daughter. Haunted by the opinion that her dead mother would have of her, she blindly obeys her stepmother. Contrary to Salome's accusations, Rosamond is not vain, but she is an inveterate liar. Even though Jamie Lockhart steals her dress, rapes her, and abducts her, she falls in love with him and devotes herself to cleaning his house and making him happy. After removing the berry stains from his face with her stepmother's potion, she discovers his identity and, thinking that he has no honor, leaves him. Having escaped from the Indians by promising to marry Goat, she becomes lost in the woods while looking for Jamie and eventually tracks him down in New Orleans. They are married shortly before she gives birth to twins.

Jamie Lockhart, a gentleman bandit. After helping Clement elude Mike Fink, Jamie is invited to Clement's house. Although Rosamond serves him dinner, Jamie does not recognize her as the girl he raped in the woods. After Jamie abducts Rosamond, Clement asks him to find his daughter, but Jamie brings Clement the wrong girl by mistake. After he escapes from the Indians, Jamie mistakes the bones of an Indian maiden for those of Rosamond and runs wild through the woods. Just as he is boarding a boat in New Orleans, he is reunited with Rosamond. He marries her and becomes a rich merchant.

Mike Fink, a legendary river boatman. Standing six and a half feet tall, this boasting giant tries to murder Clement Musgrove and Jamie Lockhart at an inn at Rodney's Landing so that he can steal their gold. He beats the sugarcane that the two men have substituted for their bodies in bed. When they reappear from the wardrobe, he escapes through the window and becomes a mail rider. Still thinking that Jamie is dead, he tells Rosamond at the end of the novel that he has seen Jamie's ghost in New Orleans. Afterward, he returns to the river and is restored to his former glory.

Goat, Salome's assistant and Clement's neighbor. Driven by his desire to help his mother marry off his six virgin sisters, he agrees to spy on Rosamond for Salome, and he takes his oldest sister to Little Harp, who he thinks is rich. After rescuing Rosamond from the Indians, he takes Big Harp's head to the authorities, who believe the head to be Jamie Lockhart's, and receives a bag of gold, which he plans to give to his sisters when they marry.

Little Harp, an ugly bandit. Having talked Goat into working for him, he persuades Goat to give him his hen, his pig, and his sister, but he loses Goat's sister to Jamie, who punches him in the stomach. To get even with Jamie, Little Harp tries to take over his gang and even murders an Indian maiden who he thinks is Jamie's girl. After he and the bandits are captured by the Indians, he is stabbed in the heart by Jamie Lockhart.

— *Alan Brown*

ROBERT ELSMERE

Author: Mary Augusta Ward (Mrs. Humphry Ward, 1851-1920)

First published: 1888

Genre: Novel

Locale: Westmoreland, Oxford, Surrey, and London, England

Time: 1882-1886

Plot: Social realism

Robert Elsmere, an eager young clergyman who combines strong intellectual interests, particularly in history, with a drive for social reform, particularly improvements in the conditions of the poor. He is swept away by Catherine Leyburn's saintliness and purity and determinedly pursues her, although she has little tolerance for the wide-ranging thought that engages him. As part of his ministry in Surrey, Elsmere creates educational programs for his parishioners and confronts the region's leading landowner, Squire Wendover, with the miserable state of the housing he provides his tenants. Not until Wendover witnesses children dying in a diphtheria epidemic does he agree to improve the tenants' living conditions. Despite their political differences, Elsmere is grateful for the use of Wendover's magnificent library for his historical studies, and their discussions of the cultural mechanisms that shaped Christian beliefs lead Elsmere to doubt some central tenets of Anglican faith and to resign his ministry, though this nearly destroys his marriage. Elsmere's subsequent work in the London slums enables him to move beyond his religious crisis by developing a form of religious devotion and social service modeled on the life of Christ. The New Brotherhood of Christ, the religious community he founds, seems strong enough to flourish even after the strains of his work there cause his early death.

Catherine Leyburn, a young woman who longs for a sanctified life. At the beginning of the novel, she seems to have found it in selfless service to the people of her beautiful Westmoreland valley and hills. With marriage to Elsmere, partnership in his work as a clergyman, and the birth of a daughter, she hopes she has found a worthy equivalent of the Westmoreland life she gave up, but this hope is shattered by Elsmere's resignation from the ministry. Catherine's beliefs in the religious tenets Elsmere abandons are so absolute that she can never fully accept her husband's changed views, and as he dies she still hopes he will return to his old faith.

Rose Leyburn, Catherine's volatile younger sister. She sees the model of service to others Catherine holds up to her as dull and constricting. She succeeds in breaking away to study the violin, first in Manchester and eventually in Germany. Rose is troubled by an involvement with Edward Langham, but she eventually attributes it to her immature romanticism and agrees to marry Hugh Flaxman, who is both eminently eligible and sufficiently freethinking to seem a reasonable match for her.

Edward Langham, Elsmere's tutor at Oxford, a brilliant scholar and aesthete who in his twenties already has burned out and lapsed into a languid skepticism. His attachment to Elsmere is the strongest feeling he maintains, but even it weakens. Though for a while Rose's beauty, vitality, and talent seem to rouse him, he is unable to commit himself to a relationship with her.

Henry Grey, an Oxford don whose powerful effect on Elsmere contributes to his decision to become a clergyman. That Grey himself does not subscribe to Anglican orthodoxies but preaches as a layman foreshadows both Elsmere's religious crisis and the nature of his work in London.

Squire Wendover, the chief landowner in Murewell, Elsmere's Surrey parish, and a historian whose work challenges fundamentalist religious beliefs. Wendover and Elsmere clash over Wendover's disregard for his tenants' welfare, a disregard connected both to political conservatism and to his insistence that he not be bothered with the affairs of his estate so he can devote himself to scholarship. Elsmere's friendship becomes crucial to Wendover, and Wendover is desolate when his own intellectual influence results in Elsmere's decision to resign from the church and move to London. Wendover dies emotionally isolated and fearing the madness that had overtaken his father.

Hugh Flaxman, a wealthy young widower who all his life has exasperated some members of his aristocratic family with his democratic sympathies. He meets the Elsmeres through his sister, Lady Helen Varley, a supporter of their work with the poor in Surrey, and his aunt, Lady Charlotte Wynnstay, a socialite who takes Rose Leyburn under her wing in London. Although he is not particularly religious, he shares Elsmere's socialist sympathy with the working classes, and he becomes a major financial benefactor of the New Brotherhood of Christ. In love with Rose Leyburn, Flaxman has to keep himself on the sidelines while he watches the progress of her infatuation with Edward Langham. After giving her time to recover, he appears at the Leyburns' house in Westmoreland, where Rose has retreated. By the time Elsmere dies, Rose and Flaxman are engaged.

— *Anne Howells*

ROBIN HOOD'S ADVENTURES

Author: Unknown
First published: c. 1490
Genre: Short fiction

Locale: England
Time: The thirteenth century
Plot: Adventure

Robin Hood, actually the young **earl of Huntingdon**, whose father has been wrongly dispossessed of his estates. Robin Hood becomes an outlaw when he kills one of the king's stags after being taunted by foresters to show his skill with a longbow. Under sentence of death for killing the animal, the young nobleman flees to Sherwood Forest, where he gathers together a band of outlaws known as the Merry Men. Robin earns his place of leadership by outfighting and outshooting his comrades, all of whom become intensely loyal followers. Robin enjoys playing tricks on the authorities sent to capture him and gains support by helping the poor. Although eventually he is pardoned by Richard the Lion-Hearted and given back his title and estates, Robin becomes homesick for his old ways and returns to life in Sherwood Forest and outlawry. He eventually is killed by a cousin, the prioress at Kirkley Abbey, who bleeds him to death under the guise of giving him medical treatment.

Little John, a huge man who joins the Merry Men after being bested by Robin in a shooting match. As a lark, Little John spends six months in the service of the sheriff of Nottingham, Robin Hood's enemy. Little John is with Robin at the time of the hero's death, though he arrives too late to save him. He buries Robin under the ancient oak where his last arrow fell.

Friar Tuck, a hedge priest who joins the Merry Men after a fight with Robin precipitated by the friar's ducking of Robin in a stream.

Will Scarlet, one of the Merry Men. He participates with Robin and Little John in an archery match against the king's men. In the match, the outlaws appear as the queen's men and win for her.

Richard the Lion-Hearted, the king. He bests Robin in a fight and then pardons the outlaws, returning the rightful title and estates to their leader.

King John, who is infuriated when Robin Hood reverts to outlawry. He sends a force of men to capture Robin and his men.

The sheriff of Nottingham, a crown officer who tries for years to capture Robin Hood. He is killed in a battle just before the death of Robin himself.

Sir Richard of the Lea, Robin Hood's friend, a knight whom Robin once helped.

The Tinker,
the Cook,
Allan-a-Dale, and
George-a-Greene, faithful followers of Robin Hood.

Maid Marian, a young woman vaguely associated with the Robin Hood cycle. Her importance in the story grew as the morris dance developed.

ROBINSON CRUSOE

Author: Daniel Defoe (1660-1731)
First published: 1719
Genre: Novel

Locale: An island off the coast of South America and the Several Seas
Time: 1651-1705
Plot: Adventure

Robinson Crusoe, a self-sufficient Englishman who, after several adventures at sea and on land, is cast away on a small, almost uninhabited island. A practical, farsighted man of talents, he sets about making his island home comfortable, utilizing all his knowledge. His prudence and industry, aided by an imaginative insight, enable him to pass twenty-four years on the island, providing for himself in every way from the resources of the island itself and what he is able to salvage from the shipwreck that puts him in his predicament. A God-fearing man, he reads his Bible and gives thanks each day for his delivery from death. Eventually, he is rescued and returns to England after an absence of thirty-five years, only to go traveling again.

Mr. Crusoe, Robinson Crusoe's father, a middle-class Englishman. He wants his son to go into business and remain at home, rather than go to sea.

Friday, a native of a nearby island rescued from cannibal captors by Robinson Crusoe. He proves to be an apt pupil and learns how to participate in his rescuer's life and labors. He learns to speak English and becomes a friend and companion, as well as a fellow laborer.

THE ROCK CRIED OUT

Author: Ellen Douglas (Josephine Haxton, 1921-   )
First published: 1979
Genre: Novel

Locale: Homochitto County, Mississippi
Time: The 1960's and the 1970's
Plot: Realism

Alan McLaurin, the narrator of the story. Alan is twenty-nine years old in 1978, the year he records the events of two earlier years, 1964 and 1971. At the time of the main action of the novel, 1971, Alan is twenty-two, a conscientious objector, a college dropout, and a would-be poet. He has returned to Mississippi to take up residence on his family's land at Chickasaw Ridge. Haunted by the death of his older cousin, Phoebe, Alan has left behind Miriam, the girlfriend who reminds him of his lost love. During the course of a few months spent in the remoteness of Chickasaw, Alan is reunited with several people connected with the fateful summer of 1964. After Miriam and his aunt join him at the farm, he learns the truth about his cousin's death. The narrative he creates seven years after the events of 1971 records his reactions at the time and his more mature reflections several years later.

Phoebe Chipman, Alan's beautiful and gifted cousin. Her death in a fiery automobile accident in the summer of 1964 has been a constant burden for Alan, who thought that Phoebe was destined to achieve great things.

Dallas Boykin, a pulp wood cutter. Dallas, a Vietnam veteran who says that he learned to enjoy killing during the war, has returned to Chickasaw, married a young woman from a nearby town, fathered a child, and, from all appearances, settled down. Dallas feels oppressed because he cannot achieve a religious experience that will bring him peace. He finally makes his spiritual breakthrough by confessing his role in Phoebe's death: He fired the shot that caused the accident that took her life.

Miriam West, Alan's Northern girlfriend. After she arrives at Chickasaw, she becomes romantically involved with Alan's boyhood acquaintance, Lee, and eventually deserts Alan to accompany Lee to New Orleans.

Lindsay Lee Boykin, Dallas Boykin's younger brother. He has also returned to Chickasaw in the winter of 1971. Lee, as he now prefers to be called, has been living in New Orleans, where he has become a hippie. His long hair and flamboyant clothing, as well as his attempts to interview and photograph the country people of Chickasaw for a projected newspaper article, bring him trouble. After he learns the truth about his mother's origins, he flees back to the city, taking Miriam with him.

Sam Daniels, a middle-aged black man. Sam, who taught the youthful Alan about life in the country, lives on the McLaurin farm as a caretaker. He is at the wheel the night that the fatal accident involving Phoebe and Timmie, his wife, takes place. Later, despondent over civilization's encroachments on his beloved woods, Sam attacks a satellite tracking station. Sentenced to a prison term, he attempts to escape and is shot by the sheriff. Now paroled, he seems to Alan to be diminished both physically and spiritually from the strong personality he once was.

Timmie Daniels, Sam's wife. She is killed with Phoebe in the accident near Mercy Seat Church.

Leila McLaurin, Alan's aunt. She comes to Chickasaw to serve as chaperon for Alan and Miriam. A free-spirited woman who has created a new life and business for herself after her divorce, she reveals to Alan and Miriam that she and Sam once had an affair.

Noah Daniels, Sam's father and patriarch of the black community at Chickasaw. Noah provides information to Alan about the McLaurin family's past.

Lorene Boykin, Dallas Boykin's young wife. Lorene is an intensely religious woman who believes that she is possessed by the Holy Spirit. She urges her husband to give up his life to the Spirit, and her insistence that he "come through" pushes him into making his confession about Phoebe's death.

Lester Chipman, Phoebe's father and Alan's uncle. A conservative and conventional man, he still grieves for his lost daughter. His refusal to listen to Dallas Boykin's confession contributes to Dallas' choosing to admit his guilt on a citizens band radio broadcast.

Calhoun Levitt, a black man whose family has owned land at Chickasaw for many years. His story about the Boykins, told to Alan, Miriam, and Lee during a taping session for Lee's projected newspaper article, causes Lee to leave Chickasaw.

Gene Hamm, Dallas and Lee Boykin's maternal grandfather. Calhoun Levitt relates the story of Hamm's arrival at Chickasaw in December, 1933. Hamm, an idealistic preacher with progressive ideas, envisions a racially mixed South. He is killed after discussing his ideals with a pair of local white men.

Frances Hamm, Gene Hamm's wife. She dies of a fever shortly after her husband's murder. Before her death, she delivers her little girl to Calhoun Levitt for safekeeping.

Mrs. Mac Boykin, the daughter of Gene and Frances Hamm and the mother of Dallas and Lee Boykin. After being orphaned, she is adopted by the Boykin family. Eventually, she marries one of her stepfather's sons, Mac. Shortly before her death in the summer of 1964, she informs the Federal Bureau of Investigation about Ku Klux Klan activity in the Chickasaw area.

Mac Boykin, the father of Dallas and Lee Boykin. During the summer of 1964, Boykin is active in the Ku Klux Klan. He carries his sons to Klan meetings and assigns them to spy on a civil rights meeting at Mercy Seat Church; as a result of his involvement, Dallas causes the deaths of Phoebe and Timmie.

Henry Levitt, the brother of Calhoun Levitt. While drunk, Henry encounters Lee Boykin in a country store at Chickasaw. Alan is forced to intervene to save Lee, who has been surreptitiously photographing Henry and his brother, from violence.

— Michael P. Dean

RODERICK HUDSON

Author: Henry James (1843-1916)
First published: 1876
Genre: Novel

Locale: Primarily Rome, Italy; also Florence, Italy, and Switzerland
Time: The 1870's
Plot: Psychological realism

Roderick Hudson, who lives with his widowed mother in Northampton, Massachusetts. He is studying in a law office, reluctantly and ineptly. He is not stupid, but he dislikes the law and has artistic aspirations; in his spare time, he produces some promising sculpture, but he has no hope of becoming an artist. He meets Rowland Mallet, a rich young man who admires Hudson's work and offers to help him financially. Mallet takes Hudson to Rome to work as a sculptor. Hudson proves to be a very good artist with the possibility of a major career. He is confident of his gift, but he can be erratic, arrogant, and, more seriously, occasionally tempted by expensive pleasures. Mallet is willing to help Hudson with his financial difficulties, but he finds it more difficult to keep Hudson focused on his work. Hudson becomes fascinated with Christina Light, a beautiful American girl who seems to encourage him. Her mother, however, has plans to marry her into the moneyed classes of Europe. Hudson, a vain man, thinks that Christina will renounce everything for him. His failure to win her eventually destroys him.

Rowland Mallet, a rich young New Englander. He is intelligent, handsome, and generous, but lacking in ambition and talent. He decides to live in Rome, perhaps permanently. Before he leaves America, he meets Roderick Hudson and sees a chance to put his fortune to good use, supporting the artist. While getting to know Hudson, however, he falls in love with Hudson's cousin, Mary Garland. He keeps his feelings to himself, but he has hopes for the future. On the voyage to Europe, Hudson informs Mallet that shortly before they left, he became engaged to Mary. Mallet, always the gentleman, decides to repress his feelings for Mary. He is an excellent friend and mentor to Hudson. He is drawn, despite himself, into Hudson's pursuit of Christina, an American fortune hunter. Mallet is prepared to despise her, both because of her ambitions and because she distracts Hudson from his work. Mallet is an open-minded man, and he becomes, despite his reservations, a confidant of Christina, whom he finds hates the idea of what she is doing. Mallet convinces Hudson to bring his mother and Mary Garland to Italy, but the infatuation with Light continues. Mallet is torn between his concern for Hudson and his reemerging love for Mary. Hudson openly ignores Mary in his determination to possess Christina. Mallet finds that despite his help and his concern for playing fair, the matter gets out of hand, and in the end, his hopes are thwarted.

Christina Light, a stunningly beautiful American girl who has lived in Europe all her life. She has been groomed to make a rich marriage. The girl is intelligent and entirely aware of the dubious moral nature of her quest, but she seems unmoved by any reservations in the search for a suitable partner. She is not without interest in men, but she makes it clear that a moneyed marriage is her object. She presents a disdainful, self-absorbed visage to the social world of Rome. Her encounter with Hudson and Mallet is complicated by the fact that her mother is arranging a marriage for her to a rich Italian nobleman, Prince Casamassima. She begins to understand the personal and moral sacrifice she is expected to make, and she reveals to Mallet that she has serious doubts, which are not caused by feelings for Hudson, who is determined to think that they are. At the last minute, she attempts to get out of her betrothal, but her defiance of her mother is short-lived. What convinces her to do as she is told is not entirely clear, but it is suspected that her mother, frantic to escape the chancy life they have been leading, has told her that she is, in fact, illegitimate, and that she had better do what is planned or face the possibility of social ruin. She marries the prince, whom she openly despises, and lives a life of material luxury.

Mary Garland, a distant cousin of Hudson's mother who becomes her companion at the time of his departure of Rome. She is a young, attractive, and sensible woman who inspires deep affection in both Hudson and Mallet, although she is unaware of Mallet's feelings. She constantly thinks the best of Hudson and often expects too much of Mallet when Hudson goes wrong.

— Charles Pullen

ROGER'S VERSION

Author: John Updike (1932-   )
First published: 1986
Genre: Novel

Locale: An unnamed city in New England
Time: 1984
Plot: Philosophical realism

Roger Lambert, a university professor of divinity. A former minister, Roger lost his pulpit when he became involved in an adulterous relationship with Esther, who later became his second wife. Now in his early fifties, Roger seems also to have lost his faith. Roger is an adherent of the reforming Protestant theologian Karl Barth, and his academic specialty is the Skeptics. His skeptical approach to religion is challenged by Dale Kohler, a graduate student who enters Roger's life seeking funding for a project that will attempt a mathematical proof of God's existence.

Dale Kohler, a computer expert and perennial student who has both a profound belief in God and an ambition to provide Him with an opportunity to speak to humanity through Dale's digital manipulation of data. Dale serves as Roger's "Inquisitor" as the two engage in lengthy debates about the import of God and the meaning of faith. Dale also serves as Roger's foil when he becomes a tutor to Roger's son and, consequently, Esther's lover. By reintroducing Roger to his niece, Verna Ekelof, whom Dale meets in a church group, Dale provides a means for Roger to reconnect, if not with God, at least with the more mundane import of his own existence.

Esther Lambert, Roger's wife. Now in her late thirties, Esther has grown weary of her relationship with her husband and concerned with her own midlife crisis. In an attempt to seize the day and recover some of the excitement that has gone out of her life, Esther seduces Dale, who soon falls hopelessly in love with her sexual daring. She later tires of the affair. Her rejection proves to be the catalyst for Dale's loss of religious faith.

Verna Ekelof, the daughter of Roger's half sister, Edna, with whom Roger had a love-hate relationship during their midwestern childhood. Verna is a young white woman who, at the age of nineteen, is the single mother of a half-black toddler, Paula, whom she regards with a mixture of affection and loathing. Fleeing her disapproving parents in Ohio, Verna moved to the city where Roger, her uncle, lives. She ekes out a living on welfare. Roger, who seems at first to feel no obligation to help Verna, is goaded into action by Dale. Verna, for her part, proves singularly intransigent. Verna expresses less interest in pursuing a high school equivalency diploma than in seducing Roger, whose own motivations in attempting to tutor her are not unblemished. Roger does help Verna, giving her money occasionally and assisting her through an abortion and an unpleasant encounter with the authorities that follows an episode of child abuse. Verna, who finally manages to get Roger into her bed, seems to help him let go of some of the fears and inhibitions that have contributed to his rigidity and disaffection with life.

— Lisa Paddock

ROGUE HERRIES

Author: Sir Hugh Walpole (1884-1941)
First published: 1930
Genre: Novel

Locale: England
Time: 1730-1774
Plot: Historical

Francis "Rogue" Herries, so called because of his notorious escapades. In 1730, he takes his family and his mistress to live in the long-deserted family house of Herries; there he continues to earn his reputation as the family black sheep. After the death of his wife, whom he had married more for pity than for love, he becomes attracted to a gypsy-like girl whom he meets under strange circumstances. He pursues her and finally marries her. She runs away but later returns to him. His oldest child is fifty-five years old when Francis again becomes a father. He and his wife both die on the night of their daughter's birth.

Margaret Herries, Francis' first wife, who is never able to command her husband's love. When she is dying, however, she feels that he will be at a loss without her and makes her son promise never to leave his father.

Mirabell Starr, a woman living with thieves. They kidnap Francis to give him a cross and chain left to him by Mirabell's mother, whom he had once befriended. Mirabell agrees to marry Francis, in return for food and protection, but he cannot succeed in making her love him. She leaves him for several years but eventually returns to him. She dies in childbirth.

David Herries, the son of Francis and Margaret. His wife is hated by Mirabell. David and his wife move from Herries and become well established in their new community.

Sarah Denburn, a friendly, handsome girl whom David meets and falls in love with on a business trip. Her uncle-guardian intends her for another man, but David kills his rival, carries her off, and marries her.

Deborah Herries, the daughter of Francis and Margaret. She marries a clergyman.

Alice Press, ostensibly the governess to Francis' children but in fact his mistress. He tires of her and tries to get rid of her, but she refuses to leave. Encountering her at a fair, Francis creates a scene and makes a show of selling her to another man.

Osbaldistone, who in the course of a duel with Francis slashes him from temple to chin. The scar marks Francis for life.

Harry, Mirabell's only true love, who is killed before her marriage to Francis by a jealous and ugly older man. Francis witnesses the attack, but his warning comes too late.

ROLL OF THUNDER, HEAR MY CRY

Author: Mildred D. Taylor (1943-   )
First published: 1976
Genre: Novel

Locale: Rural Mississippi
Time: October, 1933-August, 1934
Plot: Historical realism

Cassie Logan, age nine, the narrator and central character, a bright rebel who wants fairness and justice in this world. As an African American child in the South, she learns instead about injustice and discrimination. By getting sweet, subtle revenge for her humiliation at the hands of Lillian Jean Simms, Cassie proves her successful passage through childhood innocence by the end of the novel.

Stacey Logan, her twelve-year-old brother, the Logan family's eldest child, who is itching to become the man of the family while his father is away. Stacey's growth to maturity matches Cassie's when he proves himself a loyal friend and as resourceful as his father.

Christopher-John Logan, another brother, age seven.

Clayton Chester Logan, called "**Little Man**," the youngest Logan, age six.

David Logan (**Papa**), who works on the railroad in Louisiana for part of each year in order to make money to pay the mortgage on the Logan land. David Logan is a man of compassion and reason; his quick thinking at the end of the novel saves his family.

Mary Logan (**Mama**), the seventh-grade teacher at the school the four children attend. She is sensitive and loving and has a strong physical and spiritual bond with her husband. Their love spills over onto others beyond the circle of their family.

Big Mar, Cassie's grandmother (Papa's mother), a woman in her sixties who helps to teach Cassie the importance of the family and their land.

Uncle Hammer, Papa's hot-tempered older brother, who lives in Detroit and who must sell his car to help the family.

Mr. Morrison, the huge "human tree" Papa brings back from Louisiana to help protect the family against night riders.

— *David Peck*

THE ROMAN ACTOR

Author: Philip Massinger (1583-1640)
First published: 1629
Genre: Drama

Locale: Rome
Time: The first century
Plot: Tragedy

Domitian (duh-MIHSH-ee-ehn), the emperor of Rome. Cruel and self-indulgent, and convinced of his own godhood, he has no fear of the laws of the gods or men. Infatuated with Domitia, he forces her husband to divorce her, then has him killed. He is shaken when two stoic senators scorn his tortures and die calmly. In his own mind, he performs a kindness by killing the actor, Paris, while taking part with him in a play, rather than having him executed. Eventually, he gathers the nerve to have his faithless wife killed, but he is assassinated before he can have his sentence executed.

Domitia (duh-MIHSH-ee-uh), the beautiful and ambitious wife of Aelius Lamia. Willingly divorcing her husband, she uses the emperor's power to dominate the noblewomen. Becoming madly infatuated with the handsome actor, Paris, she indiscreetly orders him to a private meeting and attempts to seduce him. The emperor surprises them together, but Domitia's voluptuous power over him keeps him from killing her. After the emperor kills Paris, her hatred leads her to join the conspirators. She is sentenced to death by the Tribunes after Domitian is killed.

Paris, the Roman actor. A dignified defender of the stage and a loyal servant of the emperor, he has political enemies. Domitia's infatuation destroys him. He acts roles in three plays within the main play, his final role ending in real, not mimic, death.

Parthenius (pahr-THEH-nee-uhs), the emperor's toady, a freedman. He arranges the divorce of Domitia and her marriage with the emperor. He suffers Domitian's fiendish cruelty, even the death of his own father, Philargus, but after finding his name listed in the emperor's death book, he joins the conspirators and tricks the emperor to his death.

Aretinus (ay-reh-TI-nuhs), an unprincipled informer. His spying leads to the deaths of Aelius Lamia, Junius Rusticus, and Palphurius Sura. He informs the emperor of the secret meeting of Paris and Domitia and receives the reward of being strangled for his trouble.

Philargus (fih-LAHR-guhs), Parthenius' miserly father. His avarice is not cured by Paris' play but is cured by Domitian, who has him killed.

Latinus (lah-TI-nuhs) and

Aesopus (ee-SOH-puhs), actors in Paris' company.

Aelius Lamia (EE-lee-uhs LA-mee-uh), a senator, Domitia's husband. He despises Domitian.

Junius Rusticus (JEW-nee-uhs RUHS-tih-kuhs), a virtuous senator. At the moment of his death, he prophesies the destruction of Domitian.

Palphurius Sura (pal-FEWR-ee-uhs SEW-ruh), another stoic senator, who is tortured and murdered with Rusticus.

Ascletario (as-kleh-TA-ree-oh), a soothsayer. Prophesying that his body will be devoured by dogs just before the emperor's death, he rouses Domitian to fury. Subsequent events reduce the fury to fatalistic despair.

Domitilla (do-mih-TIHL-luh), Domitian's cousin, whom he has violated.

Julia, Domitian's niece, with whom he has committed incest.

Caenis (SEE-nihs), the former mistress of the dead Titus.

Sejeius (seh-JAY-yuhs) and

Entellus (ehn-TEHL-luhs), conspirators who, with Domitilla, Julia, and Caenis, help kill the emperor.

THE ROMANCE OF A SCHOOLMASTER
(Il romanzo d'un maestro)

Author: Edmondo De Amicis (1846-1908)
First published: 1890
Genre: Novel

Locale: Italy
Time: The nineteenth century
Plot: Social

Emilio Ratti (RAHT-tee), a young Italian schoolmaster. He learns the tribulations of teaching school in a small community. Badgered by the pupils and the patrons of his schools, he finds that everyone—even the priests—seems to use the teachers as scapegoats. After several years of teaching in rural communities, he passes the examination that permits him to obtain a much better teaching position in the city of Turin.

Faustina Galli (fah-ews-TEE-nah GAHL-lee), a pretty young schoolteacher loved by Emilio Ratti. She learns that she is regarded as fair game by petty village officials who solicit her favors with cajolery and threats. She cannot return Emilio Ratti's love because she has the responsibility of caring for a crippled father. Like Ratti, she is a devoted and successful teacher.

Professor Megari (meh-GAH-ree), one of Emilio Ratti's professors at the normal school. At the request of Emilio's dying mother, the professor encourages the young man and, at one point, saves him from drunkenness.

Giovanni Labaccio (jee-oh-VAHN-nee lah-BAHK-kee-oh), an insinuating young man who tries to please everyone. He marries a rich widow and thus escapes from the drudgery of teaching. Although he marries the widow, an older woman, only for her money, he reviles his former fellow teachers as persons interested in money and advancement, rather than teaching.

Carlo Lerica (leh-REE-kah), a former corporal of grenadiers who turns to teaching school as a better life than that of an enlisted man in the Italian army. Like Emilio Ratti, he becomes a good schoolteacher.

THE ROMANCE OF LEONARDO DA VINCI
(Voskresshiye Bogi: Leonardo da Vinci)

Author: Dmitry Merezhkovsky (1865-1941)
First published: 1901
Genre: Novel

Locale: Italy and France
Time: 1494-1519
Plot: Historical

Leonardo da Vinci (lee-oh-NAHR-doh dah VEEN-chee), the famous artist and inventor of the fifteenth century. He serves the duke of Milan, then Cesare Borgia. He also serves the city of Florence by using his talents as an artist and as inventor. In Florence, he enjoys the friendship of Raphael and earns the enmity and jealousy of Michelangelo. He returns to Milan and the service of Louis XII of France, that city's conqueror. He ends his life in the service of Francis I of France, living in France and dying there. Although he is rumored to be a disciple of the Antichrist, he dies a Christian.

Duke Moro, the ruler of Milan, the benefactor of Leonardo and Leonardo's patron. Leonardo leaves Milan when it is threatened by French forces.

Cesare Borgia (cheh-ZAH-reh BOHR-jee-ah), the son of Pope Alexander VI, a hated man but a patron to Leonardo.

Niccolò Machiavelli (neek-koh-LOH MAH-kee-ah-VEHL-lee), a friend of Leonardo who helps him get a commission from the city of Florence to plan a system of waterways.

Michelangelo (mee-keh-LAHN-jeh-loh), the famous artist. He is a jealous rival of Leonardo.

Pope Leo X, an artistically minded pontiff who is Leonardo's friend and patron.

Louis XII, the king of France, who is also one of Leonardo's patrons.

Monna Cassandra, a beautiful Milanese girl who is loved by Beltraffio, Leonardo's pupil. She is burned as a witch.

Giovanni Beltraffio (jee-oh-VAHN-nee behl-trahf-FEE-oh), a pupil of Leonardo. He commits suicide after the death of Monna Cassandra.

Francesco Melzi, a favorite pupil of Michelangelo and the artist's friend in his old age.

Andrea Salaino (sah-lah-EE-noh), a student of Leonardo.

Zoroastro da Peretola (zoh-roh-AHS-troh dah peh-reh-toh-lah), a student of Leonardo who is killed while trying to use the artist's unfinished flying machine.

Monna Lisa Gioconda (joh-KOHN-dah), the model for Leonardo's famous portrait. She and the artist fall in love, and her death is a great shock to Leonardo.

THE ROMANCE OF THE FOREST

Author: Ann Radcliffe (1764-1823)
First published: 1791
Genre: Novel

Locale: France and Savoy
Time: The seventeenth century
Plot: Gothic

Pierre de la Motte (pyehr deh lah moht), a fugitive from the law, a passionate man who has run through a sizable

fortune. He rescues Adeline from ruffians. He takes refuge with his household in an ancient abbey. He tries to rob the marquis de Montalt and falls into the man's power. La Motte is finally exiled to England for his misdeeds.

Mme de la Motte, a faithful, patient wife. She takes pity on Adeline until she thinks that her son loves the girl; then her manner becomes cold.

Louis de la Motte (lwee), Pierre's son, a soldier stationed in Germany. He traces his parents to the ancient abbey, drawn by his love for them. He falls in love with Adeline but loses her to Théodore Peyrou.

Adeline (ah-day-LEEN), a sweet, lively young woman rescued by Pierre de la Motte. She shares the family's hiding place in the ancient abbey. Actually an heiress, she has been cheated by her evil uncle, the marquis, but comes into her rightful inheritance when he is executed. She falls in love with Théodore Peyrou, whom she marries after many adventures.

Théodore Peyrou (tay-oh-DOHR peh-REW), a young officer. He tries gallantly to rescue Adeline from the marquis de Montalt because he loves her. Théodore turns out to be the son of Armand La Luc, a clergyman. He is innocent of charges brought against him by the marquis de Montalt, and he marries Adeline.

The marquis de Montalt (moh[n]-TAHL), a villainous nobleman, the owner of the abbey in which Pierre de la Motte takes refuge. He desires Adeline until he learns that she is his murdered brother's daughter; then he hates her and wants her killed so that she cannot claim the estates he has inherited after killing her father. He is condemned and put to death for his crimes.

Peter, de la Motte's coachman. He helps Adeline escape from the wicked marquis.

Arnaud la Luc (ahr-NOH lah lewk), a scholarly clergyman who befriends Adeline after her escape from the marquis.

Clara la Luc (klah-RAH), the clergyman's daughter and Adeline's friend. She marries a distant kinsman of Adeline.

M. Verneuil (vehr-NOO-yeh), a good man who marries Clara la Luc.

Du Bosse (dew bohs), one of the ruffians hired to do away with Adeline. His testimony reveals the crimes of the marquis.

ROMANCE OF THE THREE KINGDOMS
(San kuo chih yen-i)

Author: Lo Kuan-chung (c. 1320-c. 1380)
First published: The fourteenth century
Genre: Novel

Locale: China
Time: c. 180-c. 280
Plot: Historical

Liu Pei, the legitimate heir to the Han Dynasty, the founder of one of the Three Kingdoms, and the exalted lord of a great people. His deeds are legend. Although history does not altogether bear out his nobility, in this involved tale he is a patriarchal warrior, noble and amiable, loyal to his friends, and terrible in battle. These attributes lie under a calm exterior, a dignified carriage, and eyes that supposedly can see from the back of his head. He is commonly called **Liu Yuan-te**. His rise from protector of a widowed mother, shoemaker, and able scholar to a leader in the rebellion occurs before he is twenty-eight years old. Wherever he goes, he inspires confidence, and with the help of his two friends, he conquers two of the Three Kingdoms and makes it possible to fuse the three before his death and the passing of his reign to a weakling son.

Kuan Yü, a clear-headed strategist; he is handsome, dignified, and somewhat aloof but awe-inspiring. So daring and resourceful a leader is he that he is revered as a war god and his deeds are still passed along in oral tradition. Determined to defend his sworn brother Liu Pei, he becomes second in command. A learned man, quick of wit, and austere, Kuan, or Yun-ch'ang (meaning "long as a cloud"), is the idealized Chinese scholar-gentleman-warrior. He antagonizes a rival leader, however, when he is recalled from the wars and made governor of a province; hence, he is killed. Liu Pei and Chang Fei avenge his death as they had sworn to do but thereby weaken the alliances.

Chang Fei, the first to recognize Liu but the least learned and most blunt of the triumvirate. He is an extremely elemental and realistic man. Rather short, with a bullet head, raucous voice, and bristling mustache, he is called I-te and is a wine seller and butcher by trade. He is the best soldier, the most daring in hand-to-hand combat, and surprisingly energetic and resourceful. One of his stratagems is the appearance of drunkenness to surprise his enemy. When Kuan is killed, Chang swears vengeance and is assassinated in the attempt.

Chu-ko Liang, more often known as **Chuko K'ung-ming**, the prime minister, whose abilities include conjuring, enchantment, magic, and sorcery. He is a remarkable man, talented in duplicity and stratagems, led by an ascendant star. It is he who finally unites the kingdoms. He is the only one of the original group to survive the first stages toward building a coalition. Liu is largely unsuccessful until this brilliant recluse is called out of his hermitage. Tragically worn out from the extreme labors of his loyalty, he dies, but he leaves a valuable book of strategy in warfare and a number of occult secrets.

Chiang Wei, Chu-ko's successor, the last of the great heroes of legend and fact, the carrier of a wooden image of his mentor to frighten men in battle. A young and brilliant scholar, loyal and filial, he is much esteemed as a warrior. Chu-ko Liang chooses him from among all others after testing his abilities.

Ts'ao Ts'ao, the king of Wei, the greatest single leader, although unscrupulous and cruel. Much more successful than his adversaries, at least in the beginning, Ts'ao is especially gifted in the art of government. Portrayed in later Chinese drama as the stereotyped villain, he is herein a master strategist, wily conspirator, and forceful administrator. To achieve his ambitions, he resorts to trickery and cunning more diligently than all the others. A seer thinks him able to rule the world but too wicked to manage it.

Chou Yü, another of the brilliant young scholar-warriors, the antagonist of the wizard, and the great defender of the opposition forces of Sun Ch'uan.

Ssü-ma I, the ultimate in rulers, a composite of the other heroes, who successfully establishes the kingdom.

Sun Ch'uan, the founder of the Wu Kingdom. He and Liu Pei form an alliance and defeat the forces of Ts'ao Ts'ao.

Chao Yün, a brave general of the Shu Han Kingdom.

Lü Po, a great warrior but one without principles. He is famous for his romantic involvement with Tiao Shan.

THE ROMANTIC COMEDIANS

Author: Ellen Glasgow (1873-1945)
First published: 1926
Genre: Novel

Locale: Richmond, Virginia
Time: The 1920's
Plot: Fiction of manners

Judge Gamaliel Bland Honeywell, a wealthy widower, sixty-five years old. He is tall, dignified, and well preserved but spindle-legged. His hair and beard are silvery, his mustache is dark, his eyebrows are beetling, and his nose is Roman. His views are conservative, Southern, nineteenth century ones. Especially interested in young women, he is chivalrous toward all women. Unless he is careful of his diet, he suffers from dyspepsia. Retired from the bench, he now practices law and enjoys respect for his legal ability. Lacking a common-sense knowledge of human nature, he enters a marriage that is doomed from its beginning. Although he is kind and generous to Annabel, he is nevertheless chained to his habits and his enjoyment of physical comfort, and he is unable to perceive her urgent need for the kind of love he cannot give. He accepts the blame for Annabel's leaving him because, as he says, he is older and should have known that marriage to him would not be enough for her.

Annabel, his second wife, twenty-three years old. Appealingly fragile in body, she has a freckled, heart-shaped face, nut-brown hair with coppery glints, and gray-green eyes. She is a frank and somewhat selfish realist but much more naïve than she thinks. Bitter and filled with hatred over Angus Blount's deserting her, she resents the genteel poverty in which she and her mother live, and she accepts the judge partly to forget Angus and partly to escape the atmosphere of her home. Vivacious, impulsive, and extravagant, she is cold and hardly appreciative of what the judge does for her. The judge is drawn by her elusive charm, but he cannot conquer her aversion to him, her fear and resentment of his being affectionate. Insisting that she has no desire to live without love, she is

determined to attain her goal regardless of consequences.

Mrs. Bella Upchurch, Annabel's mother, a widow, brisk, cheerful, plump, pretty, and talkative.

Edmonia Bredalbane, the judge's twin sister, large, raw-boned, and heavy-bosomed. She is a woman of liberal views and unorthodox behavior, the mate of four husbands and reputedly (though she denies it) the mistress of many rich lovers. She is a gaudy dresser with tinted brown hair. To the judge, she appears to flaunt her past instead of being ashamed of it. Having more worldly perception than her brother, Edmonia attempts to keep him from making a fool of himself and tries in vain to promote a marriage to Amanda.

Amanda Lightfoot, the judge's childhood sweetheart, fifty-eight years old, unmarried, handsome, tall, willowy, regal, blue-eyed, and silver-haired. She dresses in an old-fashioned manner in the colors that Gamaliel used to like on her many years earlier. She has accepted her plight in an excessively ladylike manner, remaining pious and chaste through the years, tediously faithful to the man she lost but never ceased to love.

Dabney Birdsong, Annabel's childhood playmate, now a successful architect. He becomes her lover, and she deserts the judge for him.

Angus Blount, Annabel's false lover, who married a French woman after deserting Annabel.

Dr. Buchanan, the judge's physician.

Cordelia Honeywell, the judge's deceased first wife, to whom he was peacefully and unexcitingly married for thirty-six years. He continually remembers Cordelia's tastes and ways and contrasts them with Annabel's.

THE ROMANY RYE

Author: George Henry Borrow (1803-1881)
First published: 1857
Genre: Novel

Locale: England
Time: The nineteenth century
Plot: Autobiographical

The Romany Rye, known previously as **Lavengro**, **George**, and **Shorsha**, all terms of respect for his linguistic accomplishments among the Gypsies. The young wanderer is alert, perceptive, friendly, and resourceful. He is traveling to acquire a better understanding of language differences. Not content with knowing meanings and sounds, the tinker turned horse trader wants to know reasons, folkways, mores, and rituals; in short, everything interests him, especially the nomadic life of the Romany groups, the Armenian Gypsies. Like an errant Don Quixote, the hero rights wrongs, sets things straight, and always extracts life histories from those he encounters. He irritates many with his questions, but this Rom-

any Rye (Gypsy gentleman) almost always wins respect and admiration.

Isopel (Belle) Berners, an Amazon of the open road. Although she is not a Gypsy, she goes her independent way without interference. The flaxen-haired and handsome young woman has laid out numerous travelers who made untoward remarks, but she respects and admires the hero. She refuses to marry him, however, on the basis that she believes him to be mad because of his philological curiosity. Finally, to maintain her independence and be true to her vision, she leaves for America alone.

Jasper Petulengro, the Gypsy who more than anyone else

helps the Romany Rye with his research. Jasper not only aids Lavengro with introductions to interesting and important leaders in the encampment but also buys his adopted brother a fine horse. Although known to cheat in business and misrepresent the truth, he is a true friend and a natural gentleman.

Ursula, Mrs. Petulengro's sister, a young widow intended for the hero; instead, she marries within her group. Through this beautiful young woman, the young semanticist learns shades of meaning, particularly the ways and words of brushing off an advance. Although nothing comes of the romance, Ursula occupies a warm spot in the heart of the hero.

Francis Ardry, the hero's associate from his London publishing days, who reappears and brings his adventures up to date. This handsome, wealthy, and resourceful man has dissipated his energies and destroyed his character through frivolity. Charming as he is, the hero does not lament parting from him for the last time.

The Man in Black, who appears briefly, proselytizing the hero and his landlord for the Roman Catholic church. The contrast of this cynical and learned churchman and the simple, direct Methodist evangelist forms one of the most controversial arguments of the author's autobiographical books. Both the landlord and the linguist turn down the monk's overtures.

Jack Dale, the confidence man who has become an honest trader in spite of the underworld connections of his family. Proud to a fault, Jack will not permit a word against him or his character, nor will he allow the hero to interrupt his lengthy discourse of his life's adventures. Independent and honest, he has made a good living, reared a fine family, and earned the respect of his constituents in a most dishonest trade.

Murtagh, the Irish boyhood friend of the adopted Gypsy. He has given out many secrets of the old language and folktales of the ancient Irish. Irrepressible and humorous to the point of being ridiculous, Murtagh regales the tavern with his stories of card sharping. He is a generous and pleasant companion whose reunion with the hero brings the series of sketches to a close.

The Chinese Scholar, an old man who has spent what would otherwise have been an indolent life in transcribing ideographs and symbols from pottery. He befriends the hero and tells his sad story. He lives the life of a Chinese sage because of his translations.

ROME HAUL

Author: Walter D. Edmonds (1903-   )
First published: 1929
Genre: Novel

Locale: The Erie Canal
Time: 1850
Plot: Regional

Dan Harrow, a tall, stooped, broad-shouldered young man. He is a naïve newcomer on the canal who, after brief jobs on two canal boats, becomes captain of the *Sarsy Sal* after Samson Weaver's death. At last, feeling that the canal is not the place for him, he returns to farm life.

Molly Larkins, his tall, strapping, amoral cook, blowsy looking but attractive. She formerly cooked for Jotham. Although she likes Dan and remains with him for a time, she pities Jotham after he is beaten by Dan, and she returns to the chastened bully.

Fortune Friendly, an old, red-faced, skinny canal character and rascal, a former divinity student who still preaches occasionally when he needs money.

Joseph P. "Gentleman Joe" Calash, a cruel-faced canal highwayman for whose capture a large reward is offered. He aids Dan in a fight with Jotham and rescues him after a second fight. He is at last caught and killed.

Jotham Klore, a big, black-bearded, tobacco-chewing canal bully who is knocked out twice by Calash and who knocks out Dan in a fight over Molly. In a final fight, Dan wins a great victory.

Jacob Turnesa, a hook-nosed, pale-faced Jewish peddler who picks up Dan and gives him a volume of William Shakespeare's plays.

Hector Berry, a henpecked canal boatman.

Penelope, his nagging, dictatorial wife.

Solomon (Sol) Tinkle, a bald, diminutive canal boatman.

Mrs. Gurget, Sol's fat, good-natured cook and mistress, addicted to rum noggins.

Julius Wilson, the owner of the canal boat *Xerxes*.

Benjamin (Ben) Rae, the big Jewish steersman of the *Xerxes*.

William Wampy, the cook and fiddler on the *Xerxes*.

Lucy Cashdollar, the operator of an agency supplying women as cooks for lonely canal men.

Samson Weaver, the captain of the *Sarsy Sal*. He dies shortly after hiring Dan.

Mr. Butterfield, the agent for whom Samson and Dan work.

ROMEO AND JULIET

Author: William Shakespeare (1564-1616)
First published: 1597
Genre: Drama

Locale: Verona, Italy
Time: The fifteenth century
Plot: Tragedy

Romeo (ROH-mee-oh), the only son of old Montague, a nobleman of Verona. A romantic youth, inclined to be in love with love, he gives up his idealized passion for Rosaline when Juliet rouses in him a lasting devotion. His star-crossed young life ends in suicide.

Juliet (JEW-lee-eht), the only daughter of old Capulet. Little more than a child at the beginning of the play, she is quickly matured by love and grief into a young woman of profound grace and tragic dignity. Unable to find sympathy in her family and unable to trust her nurse, she risks death to avoid a forced marriage, which would be bigamous. Awakening in the tomb to find Romeo's body, she too commits suicide.

Montague (MON-teh-gyew), Romeo's father, head of the house of Montague. An enemy of the Capulets, he is a good and reasonable man and father. In the family feud, he seems more provoked than provoking. After the deaths of Romeo and Juliet, he becomes reconciled with the Capulets.

Lady Montague, Romeo's gentle mother. Tenderhearted and peace-loving, she breaks down under the fury of the clashing houses and the banishment of her son and dies of grief.

Capulet (KAP-yew-leht), Juliet's fiery father. Essentially good-hearted but furiously unreasonable when thwarted in the slightest thing, he destroys the happiness and the life of his dearly loved daughter. He joins his former enemy in grief and friendship after her death.

Lady Capulet, Juliet's mother. Dominated by her husband, she fails to offer Juliet the understanding and affection the girl desperately needs.

The nurse, Juliet's good-hearted, bawdy-tongued mentor. She aids the young lovers in consummating their marriage but, lacking in moral principle, she urges Juliet to marry Paris after Romeo is banished. Hence, Juliet has no one to turn to in her great distress and need.

Friar Lawrence, a kindly, timorous priest. He marries the young lovers and tries to help them in their fearful adversity, but he fails, thwarted by fate.

Benvolio (behn-VOH-lee-oh), old Montague's nephew, the friend of Romeo and Mercutio. Less hotheaded than Mercutio, he tries to avoid quarrels even with the irreconcilable Tybalt. His account of the deaths of Mercutio and Tybalt saves Romeo from execution but not from banishment.

Mercutio (mur-KYEW-shee-oh), Romeo's volatile and witty friend. Poetically fanciful and teasing, he can be a savage foe. His angry challenge to Tybalt after Romeo has behaved with humility leads to various deaths and the final catastrophe. He has a superb death scene.

Paris, a young nobleman in love with Juliet. The hasty marriage planned by the Capulets between Paris and Juliet forces her to fake death to avoid a bigamous union. The false death becomes real for her as well as for Paris and Romeo.

Escalus (EHS-kuh-luhs), the duke of Verona, a kinsman of Mercutio and Paris. A just, merciful ruler, he tries to arrange a peace between the feuding families. He joins them at the tomb that holds their dead children and presides over their reconciliation.

Peter, Capulet's stupid servant. Unable to read, he asks Romeo and Mercutio to help him with Capulet's invitation list, thus bringing about the meeting between Romeo and Juliet.

Friar John, a friend of Friar Lawrence. Caught in a home visited by the plague, he is delayed too long to deliver Friar Lawrence's letter to Romeo informing him about Juliet's counterfeit death. This is another of the fatal events that work against the young lovers.

An apothecary, a poverty-stricken old wretch. He illegally sells Romeo poison.

Balthasar (BAL-theh-zahr), Romeo's servant. He brings Romeo news of Juliet's supposed death and actual internment in the Capulet vault. He accompanies Romeo to the tomb and remains nearby, though ordered to leave the area by Romeo. His testimony, added to that of Friar Lawrence and Paris' page, enables Duke Escalus and the others to reconstruct the events.

Samson and

Gregory, servants of Capulet who begin the street brawl at the play's opening.

Cousin to Capulet, who joins old Capulet in reminiscences at the dance.

Tybalt (TIHB-ahlt), a fiery member of the Capulet clan. He challenges Romeo at the Capulet feast, but the fight is prevented by old Capulet. Still bearing a grudge, he meets Romeo's friend Mercutio in the street and kills him in a duel. Romeo then takes up the fight and kills Tybalt.

ROMOLA

Author: George Eliot (Mary Ann Evans, 1819-1880)
First published: 1862-1863
Genre: Novel

Locale: Italy
Time: 1492-1498
Plot: Historical realism

Tito Melema (TEE-toh meh-LEH-mah), an adventurer and pleasure-seeking young Greek who arrives in Florence in 1492. He quickly acquires a fortune through his talents, his charm, and the fact that he sells a number of gems that rightfully belong to his benefactor, Baldassare Calvo. He impresses the famous blind scholar, Bardo, so much that the latter willingly gives his daughter to Tito for a wife. At the same time, Tito is connected with a peasant woman with whom he has made a mock marriage in a carnival ceremony. Becoming powerful in Florentine politics, he carefully avoids aligning himself with either the Medici or the reformer, Savonarola. Because of his double dealing, he is both personally and politically discredited. He is chased by a mob and then strangled by Baldassare Calvo, the benefactor whom Tito had deceived, stolen from, and left confined in prison.

Romola de' Bardi, Bardo's daughter and Tito's wife. A sheltered young woman, she easily falls in love with handsome, charming Tito. Disillusioned when Tito attempts to sell her father's library and antiquities, she leaves him, but Savonarola convinces her that her duty is to return to her husband. At first, she is strongly attracted to Savonarola's moral reforms. Later, when her godfather, a supporter of the Medici, is executed, she loses faith in the evangelical government. She also discovers that her husband has betrayed Baldassare Calvo and that he has been keeping a peasant woman named Tessa and her two children. Saddened, she leaves Florence and goes to Viareggio. After Tito's death, she returns and makes a home for Tessa and Tito's two children.

Bardo de' Bardi, Romola's father, a famous scholar to whom she is devoted. Deceived by his secretary's knowledge, charm, and apparent interest in scholarly studies, he encourages the marriage of Tito and his daughter; he regards Tito as a substitute for the lost son he believes dead, a young man who abandoned scholarship for mysticism. Bardo dies in 1494, before Tito's crimes are revealed.

Baldassare Calvo (BAHL-dahs-SAH-reh), Tito Melema's

scholarly foster father and benefactor. He had given Tito some gems to sell in Florence, to raise money to ransom Baldassare from the Turks. Tito uses the gems to advance his own fortune and tries to forget Baldassare entirely. When Baldassare is brought, as a prisoner, to Florence, Tito rejects him. After a mob frees him from his fetters, Baldassare encounters Tessa and realizes her connection with Tito. By this time, Baldassare's desire for revenge on Tito is implacable. He later denounces Tito's deceitful ingratitude at a dinner party of the rulers of Florence, but Tito calls him mad and has him cast into prison. Released, Baldassare tells Romola the whole story. He pursues the fleeing Tito and strangles him.

Dino de' Bardi (DEE-noh), Bardo's lost son, supposed dead, who has disguised himself as **Fra Luca**, a Dominican friar. He first carries a note from Baldassare to Tito requesting help, but Tito ignores the note. Later, when ill, he is reunited with his sister Romola, and he tells her of a vision he has had, a dire warning that she should not marry Tito. Dino dies before he can explain his specific and nonmystical reasons for not wanting her to marry Tito.

Tessa, a peasant woman, the daughter of a milk vendor, who falls in love with Tito after he rescues her from drunken revelers at a carnival. At a later carnival, she goes through a mock marriage ceremony with him. She then bears him two children and remains entirely loyal to him, even though he visits her only infrequently. She is a simple woman of generous nature and loving heart.

Bernardo Del Nero, Bardo's friend and Romola's godfather. Disliking Tito, he tries to delay the marriage between Tito and Romola. Later, he remains friendly with Romola and tries to help her. A strong supporter of the Medici, he is executed by followers of Savonarola.

Monna Brigida (BREE-jee-dah), Bardo's loquacious cousin. She reveals to Romola that her brother is not dead but is living as Fra Luca, a Dominican friar. At the end of the novel, she makes her home with Romola and Tessa.

Fra Girolamo Savonarola (jee-roh-LAH-moh sah-voh-nah-ROH-lah), the prior of the Dominican convent of San Marco, a reformer who bitterly assails the corruption of the Medici and becomes the leader of a strong Florentine faction. In addition to his political activity, he also befriends Dino and persuades Romola to return to her husband. He and Romola are spiritually attracted to each other.

Piero di Cosimo (pee-EH-roh deh KOH-zee-moh), a famous painter, friendly with Tito, who puts his friends into his pictures. He uses Tito and Romola as models for Bacchus and Ariadne, and he paints Bardo as Oedipus. He also helps to reveal Tito's duplicity to Romola.

Bartolomeo Scala (BAHR-toh-loh-MEH-oh SKAH-lah), the powerful secretary of the Florentine Republic. He buys many of Tito's gems and helps start him on his spectacular career in Florence.

Alessandra Scala, the beautiful daughter of Bartolomeo Scala.

Marullo (mah-REWL-loh), her husband, a Greek soldier and poet.

Nello, a barber and town gossip who helps to introduce Tito to important people.

Bratti Ferravecchi (fehr-rah-VEH-kee), a rag merchant and tradesman whom Tito meets after arriving in Florence. He buys Tito's ring.

Bernardo Rucellai (rew-CHEHL-lah-ee), the wealthy Florentine and political leader who orders Baldassare arrested when the latter accuses Tito at the dinner party.

Lorenzo Tornabuoni (tohr-nah-BWON-ee), a wealthy citizen friendly with Tito. He is at the dinner when Baldassare is arrested. He is imprisoned later for his support of the Medici.

Niccolò Ridolfi (neek-koh-LOH ree-DOHL-fee) and

Giannozzo Pucci (jee-ahn-NOHZ-zoh PEW-chee), Florentine aristocrats and supporters of the Medici, imprisoned and executed.

Maestro Vaiano (vah-ee-AH-noh), an astrologer and mountebank from whom Tito rescues Tessa at the carnival.

Dolfo Spini (SPEE-nee), a false and conniving Florentine with whom Tito deals.

Niccolò Machiavelli (MAH-kee-ah-VEHL-lee), a young Florentine thinker and man of ideas.

Niccolò Caparra, an iron worker who makes a thick coat of mail for Tito to wear after the latter encounters Baldassare in Florence.

Fra Salvestro Maruffi (mah-REWF-fee), Savonarola's friend, a Dominican friar who aids Romola.

Menico Cennini (meh-NEE-koh CHEHN-nee-nee), a Florentine goldsmith and moneylender.

Maso (MAH-soh), Bardo's old servant, always loyal to Romola.

Politan (POH-lee-tahn), a scholar, the rejected suitor of Alessandra Scala.

Monna Ghita (GEE-tah), Tessa's mother, a fierce milk vendor in the market.

Piero de' Medici (deh MEH-dee-chee), the rash and ineffectual son of the famous Lorenzo de' Medici. He rules Florence after his father's death in 1492.

Giovanni de' Medici (jee-oh-VAHN-nee), the luxury-loving younger son of Lorenzo de' Medici. He becomes **Pope Leo X**.

Alamanno Rinuccini (ree-new-CHEE-nee), a scholar friendly with Bardo. He is Romola's suitor before her marriage to Tito Melema.

Monna Lisa, a deaf old woman whom Tito hires as a servant to Tessa.

Lillo, Tessa's sturdy son by Tito.

Ninna, the baby daughter of Tessa and Tito.

ROMULUS THE GREAT
(Romulus der Grosse)

Author: Friedrich Dürrenmatt (1921-1990)
First published: 1958
Genre: Drama

Locale: The villa of Emperor Romulus in Campania
Time: March 15-16, 476
Plot: Tragicomedy

Romulus Augustus, the emperor of the Western Roman Empire and a chicken breeder. Romulus is an imperturbable man quite capable of focusing his full attention on his breakfast even as the empire collapses around him. At first, he appears to be a humorous fool whose sole interest is his chicken raising. In the course of the play, however, he reveals that his do-nothing attitude has been calculated carefully to destroy an empire that he believes has become tyrannical and corrupt. Rome's conquest by the Germans is, for him, a just punishment. At the same time, he expects to die in sacrificial atonement for his actions. Ironically, fate intervenes, and he must suffer a humiliating retirement instead.

Odoaker (oh-doh-AY-kur), a Teutonic chieftain, conqueror of the Roman Empire, and chicken breeder. A man very much like Romulus, he had hoped to contain the warlike tendencies of his people by making them subjects of Rome. He views an execution of Romulus as pointless, but he accepts the transfer of power, expecting to rule only a short time before his nephew assassinates him.

Emilian, a Roman patrician and Rea's fiancé. Captured by the Germans and having spent three years as their prisoner, he is gaunt and pale and shows evidence of having been tortured. He is willing to sacrifice Rea for his country and revolts against the emperor for refusing to act to save Rome. Because of his suffering (caused by Romulus' action), he is the one person to whom Romulus feels he owes an accounting.

Julia, the emperor's wife. An ambitious woman who married Romulus so that she would become empress, Julia does not understand his attitude and condemnation of the empire. As the Germans approach, she attempts to escape with members of the household but drowns in a storm before they can reach safety.

Rea, the emperor's daughter, who spends her days studying drama and declaiming tragic verses. She is willing to sacrifice herself for her country by marrying Rupf, but, convinced by her father that love is more important than this meaningless gesture, she agrees to escape with her fiancé.

Caesar Rupf, a wealthy manufacturer of trousers and a parody of the modern capitalist. He offers to pay the Teutonic chieftain to leave Italy on condition that trousers become obligatory dress and that the emperor's daughter become his wife.

Zeno, the Isaurian, the emperor of the Eastern Roman Empire, who seeks sanctuary with Romulus. Bound by Byzantine tradition, he is required to recite prescribed formulas in pleading for sanctuary—at least if there are any witnesses, because appearance is all-important. Romulus spares him this tedious routine by locking his two chamberlains in the chicken coop.

Spurius Titus Mamma, the captain of the cavalry, who brings news of the impending collapse of the Roman Empire. With an exaggerated sense of patriotism, this officer believes that it is his duty to sacrifice his life for Rome, regardless of whether this sacrifice achieves anything. Although he is exhausted and wounded when he arrives at the palace, he resists sleep with a superhuman effort until the end of the play, when, ironically, he sleeps through the moment in which Romulus yields power to Odoaker and the Roman Empire ceases to exist.

Apollonius, an art dealer who buys Roman art treasures from Romulus, who must sell them to pay household expenses.

Tullius Rotundus, the minister of state, a comic figure whose name indicates his physique. The minister tries to convince Romulus to act. When he does not, the minister joins in the unsuccessful plot to assassinate him.

Mars, the minister of war. Like the minister of state, he does not understand Romulus' refusal to fight and joins the conspiracy to assassinate him.

Theoderich, Odoaker's nephew, a warlike person who believes in conquest and subjugation of other nations. He temporarily follows Odoaker's orders but is impatient with his uncle's desire for peace.

Achilles and

Pyramus, the emperor's chamberlains, who refuse to let anyone see him without an appointment. They represent a bureaucracy that makes quick action on any problem virtually impossible.

Phosphoridos and

Sulphurides, Zeno's chamberlains with matching, intentionally comical names.

Phylax, an actor and Rea's drama instructor. He appears absurd in instructing her in the high-sounding verses of classical tragedy as the empire crumbles.

— *Susan L. Piepke*

ROOM AT THE TOP

Author: John Braine (1922-1986)
First published: 1957
Genre: Novel

Locale: Warley, an imaginary town in Yorkshire, England
Time: 1947
Plot: Social realism

Joe Lampton, an ambitious twenty-five-year-old accountant who takes a job in the municipal treasury of the City of Warley, in the northern English county of Yorkshire. The physical move from his hometown to Warley allows Joe to make a social move away from his working-class background. He tries to dress in a middle-class manner, and through the Warley Thespians, a theater group that he joins when he gets there, he learns more middle-class ways. He also faces a moral dilemma. Determined to get the best for himself, Joe is cold-blooded and calculating in his will to rise. For example, he used his time in a German prisoner-of-war camp during World War II to study accounting instead of planning heroic or patriotic deeds. The will to rise collides with his personal relationships. He meets two women at the Warley Thespians, Alice Aisgill and Susan Brown. He is attracted to Alice, and they have a passionate affair, but marriage with Susan, the daughter of Warley's most powerful industrialist, would further his career. Joe chooses Susan, and Alice commits suicide. Joe knows that he is responsible for Alice's death, but no one else blames him and he accepts marriage with Susan.

Alice Aisgill, the thirty-four-year-old wife of a local businessman. She is unhappy and frustrated. She had given up an acting career in provincial repertory theater for marriage to a man who proved to be interested only in business. As an outlet for her frustration, she gets involved in the Warley Thespians. She also has affairs with younger men. Alice loves Joe but recognizes that he is self-centered and ambitious. She almost believes him when he talks about marriage, but her more realistic view of their relationship ultimately prevails. Still, when he abruptly dumps her for Susan, she is devastated. After going on a drinking binge, she misses a curve while driving too fast and is killed. Her friends think it was an accident, but it really was suicide.

Susan Brown, an attractive nineteen-year-old woman, active with the Warley Thespians as a way of filling time until marriage. Daughter of the town's most powerful economic and political figure, she has little education, few skills, and few interests. She is empty-headed and superficial. She is attracted to Joe because of his good looks and aura of sexuality, and because her parents (especially her mother) disapprove. Although she breaks off the relationship when she learns of Joe and Alice's affair, she really wants him back and allows him to persuade her to meet. They make love, and she becomes pregnant. The two eventually marry.

Jack Wales, Joe's rival for Susan's affections. He is a war hero from a rich business family. While Joe was studying accounting, Jack plotted a heroic breakout from the prisoner-of-war camp. While Joe drudges in his office, Jack drives a sporty car and attends an elite university. Joe sees Jack as the symbol of how the English class system weighs him down, blocking his rise. Jack turns out to be a lightweight, unable to maintain Susan's interest.

Mr. Brown, Susan's father. He is Warley's leading industrialist and an important member of the town council. He, like Joe, came from a working-class background. His main concern is to keep fortune hunters away from Susan. He tests Joe's resolve by offering to set Joe up in business if the latter promises to leave Warley and Susan. When Joe refuses to be bought, Mr. Brown agrees to the marriage and reveals that his daughter is pregnant. Mr. Brown sees in Joe the same determination and lack of scruples that he himself had shown in his rise, so he welcomes Joe into the family.

— *D. G. Paz*

A ROOM ON THE HILL

Author: Garth St. Omer (1931-   )
First published: 1968
Genre: Novel

Locale: St. Lucia, West Indies
Time: c. 1950
Plot: Psychological realism

John Lestrade (leh-STRAHD), a drifter who was once ready to study abroad. A twenty-five-year-old black man from St. Lucia, John is traumatized by the recent death of his mother and the suicide of his best friend, Stephen, two years ago. Extremely thoughtful, meditative, withdrawn, and full of intense memories of the past, John crosses his native island, where he quietly observes the people and the limitations life has imposed on them. After two more untimely deaths, John feels confirmed in his decision to live alone on a day-by-day basis.

Anne-Marie D'Aubain (doh-BAY[N]), a civil servant. Her extremely light-colored black skin led her father to deny her illegitimate birth and pass her off as white. Devastated by discovering this fraud, her tragedy continues when Anne-Marie is abandoned by her boyfriend, Derek, whom she meets again on the beach of the island shortly before her death in a car driven by her new lover. The Catholic church refuses to bury her, so the service is performed by friends.

Stephen, a young black man on St. Lucia. He haunts the life of John, who stood helplessly at the beach while Stephen drowned himself because his father had squandered the money for his studies. He had dreamed that as an engineer he could leave behind something of permanence.

Miriam Dezauzay (deh-zoh-ZAY), Stephen's fiancée, level-headed and seemingly recovered from his death. She had fought with his mother over Stephen, the lover who postponed college for her sake. Left behind and alone, she nevertheless cannot love John.

Harold Montague (MON-tah-gew), a pushy young black lawyer who came back from England to his native St. Lucia to get rich. Perhaps a homosexual, he is bright and self-confident but ashamed and resentful of his lower-class parents. John and his friends dislike him for this, yet they appear at his homecoming party.

Derek Charles, another young lawyer. He leaves his native girlfriend for a white Englishwoman with whom he has two babies and whom he brings back to his island. His welcome party occurs after Anne-Marie's burial and closes the novel.

Rose, a high school pupil on Grenada when John first meets her, a girl of exceptional attraction. Afraid of the "solidity" that her determined love and intact family background represent to him, John refuses her offer to wait for him. Her last letter still speaks of a chance that he might find his way to her; she goes to live in England.

Lena Lestrade, John's mother. She dies, perhaps of grief over her son's emotional withdrawal, and is buried in the same Catholic churchyard where Anne-Marie will be put to rest.

Dennys (DEH-nihs), a radical nonconformist painter and lover of Anne-Marie, whom he kills in a crash caused by his drunken, reckless driving. Generally refusing to integrate, he escapes after the accident and is picked off a rock by fishermen after grieving privately for his dead lover.

Agnita (ag-NEE-tah), a twenty-two-year-old mother (with one child) from Martinique, tall, with flashing teeth and dressed in too-tight outfits. She is a casual acquaintance of John. After a passionate night, John comes back to see her the next evening, but she is dead.

— *R. C. Lutz*

A ROOM WITH A VIEW

Author: E. M. Forster (1879-1970)
First published: 1908
Genre: Novel

Locale: Florence, Italy, and Surrey, England
Time: Early 1900's
Plot: Social realism

Lucy Honeychurch, a young Englishwoman. As a traveler in Italy, she is disappointed that her room at the pension has no view. Unwillingly, she changes rooms with Mr. Emerson and his son, George, whom she regards as ill bred. For the rest of her stay abroad and back at home in England, she tries to stifle her attraction to George. Finally, she is led by Mr. Emerson to acknowledge her love for his son, and she starts to live the truth she has learned, by marrying him.

Mr. Emerson, an Englishman. Aware of Lucy Honeychurch's love for his son George, he draws from her an admission of her love and inspires her to acknowledge and to live the truth she has learned.

George Emerson, Mr. Emerson's son, who is in love with Lucy Honeychurch, whom he finally marries.

Charlotte Bartlett, Lucy Honeychurch's cousin and chaperon in Italy.

The Reverend Arthur Beebe, Lucy Honeychurch's friend and rector.

Cecil Vyse, Lucy Honeychurch's fiancé. She breaks her engagement with him when George Emerson tells her of his love but before she has acknowledged, even to herself, her love for George.

Mrs. Honeychurch, Lucy Honeychurch's mother.

Miss Eleanor Lavish, a novelist,

Miss Catherine Alan, and

Miss Teresa Alan, guests at the Italian pension, later neighbors of Lucy Honeychurch.

Freddy Honeychurch, Lucy Honeychurch's brother.

ROOTS: The Saga of an American Family

Author: Alex Haley (1921-1992)
First published: 1976
Genre: Novel

Locale: The Gambia, West Africa; and the southern United States
Time: 1750-1967
Plot: Historical realism

Kunta Kinte (KEWN-tah KIHN-tay), "the African," progenitor of the American line of Haley's family. Kunta, a member of the highly respected Kinte clan of the Mandinka people of Gambia, is captured at the age of seventeen, transported to Annapolis, Maryland, and subsequently sold into slavery. A man of immense courage and spiritual fortitude (he remains a devout Muslim in Christianized America), he never relinquishes his dream of returning to his homeland. He instills in his daughter Kizzy a strong sense of self-worth and dignity, as well as the desire to be free. Kunta teaches his young daughter the Mandinka words of *ko* (a kora is a stringed instrument resembling a guitar) and *Kamby Bolongo* (the Gambia River), which eventually is transmitted orally down through seven generations.

Kizzy, the daughter of Kunta and Bell. She keeps her father's dream alive, even after she is sold to the wretched Tom Lea. After being raped by Lea, she gives birth to their son, whom Lea names George after "the hardest-working nigger I ever saw." Despite her baby's sordid conception, light skin, and undignified naming, Kizzy resolves to see him only as the grandson of Kunta Kinte. She perpetuates the dreams and teachings of her father in the rearing of her son.

Chicken George, Kizzy's clever and resourceful son. Chicken George earns his unusual moniker while successfully serving as Massa Leas's gamecocker. Although he shares some of the vices of his white father, he never forgets the teachings of Kizzy, especially the importance of knowing who

he is and who his people are. He is the first of Kunta Kinte's descendants to become free.

Tom Murray, the son of Chicken George. A stolid, forthright man, Tom fervently believes in the traditions passed on in the family narrative. He expresses his concern with racial purity and pride, refusing to allow his daughter Elizabeth to marry the "high yaller" John Tolan.

Cynthia Murray Palmer, the daughter of Tom Murray and grandmother of Alex Haley. After her husband's death, she invites the female Murrays to spend summers with her in Henning, Tennessee. These "graying ladies" retire after dinner to the front porch and retell the family narrative. Over her daughter Bertha's objections to "all that old-time slavery stuff," Cynthia persists in maintaining the oral tradition. The porch talk leaves an indelible impression on Cynthia's young grandson.

Georgia Anderson, the sole survivor of the "graying ladies" who perpetuated the family narrative on Cynthia Palmer's porch. Characterized as a cherished, yet feisty, member of the community, the elderly Cousin Georgia encourages Haley on his quest to discover the ancestral roots. Almost mystically, Cousin Georgia dies within the very hour that Haley enters Juffure to meet with the griot.

Alex Haley, the great-great-great-great-grandson of Kunta Kinte. A professional writer, Haley spent twelve years researching and writing the family narrative passed down from Kunta Kinte.

— Anita M. Vickers

THE ROPE
(Rudens)

Author: Plautus (c. 254-184 B.C.E.)
First performed: Late third or early second century B.C.E.
Genre: Drama

Locale: Cyrene, in Libya
Time: Late third century or early second century B.C.E.
Plot: Comedy

Daemones (DEE-muh-nehz), an elderly and kindly Athenian spending his last years in exile because of debts incurred through his excessive generosity. His sorrows are increased by the absence of his daughter Palaestra, stolen from him years before and sold to the procurer Labrax. A series of coincidences finally brings father and daughter face to face, reveals their identities to each other, and unites all in a joyful celebration.

Palaestra (pah-LEHS-truh), Daemones' daughter, who had been kidnapped and sold to the procurer Labrax. On the way to Sicily to be resold by her master, she is shipwrecked and cast ashore near the house of Daemones. Seeking shelter in the temple of Venus, she is set upon by Labrax, who has been washed up from the sea and is determined to recover his slave. After her rescue by Daemones, her identity is established by

trinkets from Labrax's wallet. She is received with joy by her long-lost father and betrothed to Plesidippus.

Labrax (LA-braks), a procurer who buys the kidnapped child Palaestra. On the way to Sicily to resell his slave, he is shipwrecked and loses sight of her when she gets ashore in a boat. Later, when her identity is established by trinkets from his wallet, he is forced to relinquish her on the grounds that she had been born free.

Plesidippus (pleh-sih-DIH-puhs), a young man in love with Palaestra and finally betrothed to her.

Charmides (KAHR-mih-deez), a cohort of Labrax.

Ampelisca (am-peh-LIHS-kuh), a slave girl shipwrecked and rescued with Palaestra.

Trachalio (truh-KAY-lee-oh), Plesidippus' servant.

Gripus (GRI-puhs), Daemones' servant.

RORY O'MORE: A National Romance

Author: Samuel Lover (1797-1868)
First published: 1837
Genre: Novel

Locale: Southern Ireland
Time: 1798
Plot: Adventure

Rory O'More, an Irish peasant who suffers through his unselfish efforts for Irish freedom and has to escape to America with his wife Kathleen.

Mary O'More, his sister, who is to marry Horace de Lacy in America.

Shan Regan, who is refused marriage to Mary and therefore forbids his sister Kathleen's marriage to Rory. After many crimes, he is killed by the police.

Kathleen Regan, Shan's sister. Shan refuses her to be married to Rory, so they marry in secret.

Horace de Lacy, an Irish patriot who brings Napoleon's offer of aid in the rebellion of 1798. He contracts smallpox and is nursed by Mary. The family is proud to have this gentleman

of good bloodlines share their home. He returns to France to find that his sweetheart has married another man and that Napoleon has withdrawn his promised support of Ireland. He returns to Ireland, then travels to America, where he will marry Mary O'More.

De Welskein, a smuggler to whom profit means more than political liberty. Although he is saved by Rory and de Lacy, he betrays them and ships them to France.

Scrubbs, an English tax collector. Rory is charged with his murder. Scrubbs reappears at the trial, but even so, Rory is convicted. The judge sets the verdict aside.

The Colonel of the Police, who is outwitted by Rory.

ROSENCRANTZ AND GUILDENSTERN ARE DEAD

Author: Tom Stoppard (Tomas Straussler, 1937-   )
First published: 1967
Genre: Drama

Locale: Denmark
Time: The Elizabethan period
Plot: Existentialism

Rosencrantz, a well-dressed Elizabethan courtier, with hat, cloak, stick, and all, carrying a large leather moneybag and waiting for something, or someone, for reasons that he does not seem to understand. He and his comrade, Guildenstern, are enough alike to be confused with each other. In fact, he introduces himself as Guildenstern, not noticing the error until his companion calls a brief conference with him. In part, he, with Guildenstern, seems to mark time while waiting for a messenger who will advise him as to his function in the plot of William Shakespeare's *Hamlet*. A favorite pastime is witty word games, but they are played with an urgency that suggests

that, rather than being fun, they are more a way of avoiding despair. Commissioned by Claudius, he only understands that his job, along with Guildenstern, is to learn something about Hamlet's strange behavior. He, practicing with Guildenstern, arrives at one approach by which to confront Hamlet and to inquire why he is behaving so oddly. As a result of a trick by Hamlet, whom Claudius meant to have executed, Rosencrantz is condemned to die.

Guildenstern, another Elizabethan courtier, well dressed with hat, cloak, and stick, and also carrying a large leather moneybag and waiting for something, or someone, for reasons that he does not seem to understand. He and Rosencrantz are so much alike that no distinguishing characteristics can be described for either. He pretends to be Hamlet so that Rosencrantz can try out an approach of inquiry into the reasons for the prince's odd behavior. Like Rosencrantz, as the result of a trick by Hamlet, whom Claudius meant to have executed, Guildenstern is condemned to die.

The Player, a spokesperson for the tragedians. His conversations with Rosencrantz and Guildenstern expose him (and,

by proximity, all the tragedians) as having few principles, a lack not shared by the two gentlemen. Guildenstern sees him as a "comic pornographer and a rabble of prostitutes."

The Tragedians, a troupe of six traveling actors, including Alfred, a small boy, and the Player. There is a drummer, a horn player, and a flutist; one other moves the cart of props. They are on the way to the royal court, where they will be commissioned by Hamlet to play a drama of his design.

— *Cynthia Jane Whitney*

ROSMERSHOLM

Author: Henrik Ibsen (1828-1906)
First published: 1886
Genre: Drama

Locale: A small coastal town in Norway
Time: Mid-nineteenth century
Plot: Social realism

Johannes Rosmer, a former clergyman who has become a freethinker. He wants to work for the liberal cause in politics, but he is denounced by both sides. The conservatives believe that he has forsaken his class, and the liberals think he will be a political liability. Both sides also accuse him of forcing his wife to commit suicide so he could marry Rebecca West. When Rosmer asks West to die to prove her love for him, he commits suicide with her, as punishment for loving a woman other than his wife.

Beata Rosmer, Johannes' dead wife. She kills herself before the action of the play to make way for Rebecca West in her husband's affections, after being told falsely by the other woman of the imminent birth of a child by Johannes.

Rebecca West, a freethinking woman who uses her charms to try to claim Rosmer for the liberal cause. She also wants him as a man and drives his wife to suicide. She comes to love

Rosmer deeply and commits suicide to prove her love for him.

Rector Kroll, Beata Rosmer's brother, the local schoolteacher. He is an ardent conservative who tries to encourage Rosmer to forget the liberals. When he is rebuffed, he accuses Rosmer of adultery with Rebecca West and of driving his wife to suicide. Kroll is a bitter, narrow man.

Peter Mortensgard, a liberal newspaper publisher. He solicits Rosmer's help until he learns that Rosmer, a former pastor, has left his church and become something of an outcast. Then, like Kroll, he accuses Rosmer of adultery. He is a practical politician and an amoral one.

Ulric Brendel, a liberal. He goes penniless and unrewarded, but happy, until he becomes disillusioned by the actions of his fellow liberals.

Mme Helseth, Rosmer's housekeeper.

ROSSHALDE

Author: Hermann Hesse (1877-1962)
First published: 1914
Genre: Novel

Locale: A manor house near Berne, Switzerland
Time: Early 1900's
Plot: Bildungsroman

Johann Veraguth (FEHR-ah-gewt), a successful artist with an international reputation. Despite assurances that he is known for exhibitions of his work all over Europe, Veraguth is clearly not involved in the world of fame. Two passions visibly affect him: the intellectual and aesthetic content of his paintings and love for his youngest son, Pierre. He is largely indifferent to his wife, who inhabits the main manor house of Rosshalde, leaving Veraguth to his own domain in his studio. The painter has another son, Albert, who returns to Rosshalde during school vacations. Veraguth shows few open feelings for him; those he shows are negative. Veraguth's main concern seems to be to obtain legal custody of Pierre, even to the point of being willing to give up any other claims if Adele will agree to a discreet divorce. Gradually made conscious of the need to break with this world of constant tensions, Veraguth is about to agree to leave Rosshalde to sojourn abroad with his lifetime friend Burkhardt.

Adele Veraguth (ah-DEH-leh), the wife of the painter, a proper woman, strongly built and fit but missing any traces of her youth. She maintains all the outward signs of decency in

dealing with her estranged husband but, without showing any outward emotion, harbors muted regrets that their relationship has failed. Adele is a protective mother; given the age difference between her two sons by Veraguth, however, this protectiveness is manifested in different ways. When Albert, the older son, loses patience with little Pierre's fits of jealousy at the thought of his brother receiving attention normally reserved for him alone, Adele excuses him for his childishness. She tries very hard to convince Albert of the value of acknowledging what is good and right, without trying to understand or worry about hereditary tendencies that cannot be changed.

Pierre Veraguth, an extremely sensitive seven-year-old who would like to understand why his father, despite outward signs of affection, never allows himself to share his emotions fully. Pierre is too young to understand the emotional effects that the estrangement has worked on both his mother and his father. To vent his own emotions, Pierre sometimes retreats, either literally or in his mind, to secret hiding places. Pierre's fatal bout with meningitis infuses the plot with a high degree of tension in the last section of the book, bringing his two parents together in anxiety and then grief (but not reconciliation) when he dies.

Albert Veraguth, the older of the Veraguth sons. Albert already shows signs of becoming an accomplished pianist. It is his mother who shows appreciation of his talents; Albert has practically no communication with his father. Albert occasionally resents his younger brother, who is clearly preferred by Veraguth, and is definitely disturbed by the mixed blessing of having a famous father. Although Albert generally maintains an image of self-assurance and maturity, his relations with his mother reveal occasional weaknesses. At Rosshalde during a school break, he expresses regret that he could not stand the pressure of bringing a schoolmate with him, for fear of exposing the true situation of his family's existence. His irrational wishes—that he had no father, that the family had no estate, and that his mother would find herself reduced to earning a modest income through sewing and music lessons—reveal the extent to which Albert is tied to the image of Adele as an injured woman.

Otto Burkhardt, Veraguth's lifetime friend, tall and somewhat stout, who imparts a feeling of sociability and a natural enjoyment of life. Burkhardt is a man of material substance, having established himself as a planter in South Asia. He maintains frequent contact with his home country. There seem to be two main elements underlying his relationship with Veraguth during one of his annual home leaves. One is to relive the experiences of the two men as youths. The other, which remains incompletely developed at the end of the novel, is Burkhardt's need for the completion—through Veraguth's companionship and the proposed voyage of the latter to India for an extensive sojourn—of his own, apparently only outwardly successful, life.

— *Byron D. Cannon*

ROXANA

Author: Daniel Defoe (1660-1731)
First published: 1724
Genre: Novel

Locale: England and Europe
Time: The eighteenth century
Plot: Picaresque

Roxana, a woman left penniless by her husband at the age of twenty-two. To support herself and her children, she becomes her landlord's mistress and bears him a child. After his death, she becomes the mistress of a prince, out of vanity rather than need. She bears the prince a child during the eight years of their alliance. She then takes other lovers, receiving riches from them, until she is fifty years old. She finally leaves her role as a courtesan to marry and become a respectable wife.

Mr. ———, Roxana's landlord and first lover. He helps Roxana when her husband leaves her, becoming a boarder in her house and then her lover, treating her generously during their five years together. He wants children badly and, when Roxana does not at first bear him a child, Roxana's maid does so. Mr. ——— is robbed and murdered. He leaves his wealth to Roxana.

The Prince de ———, Roxana's second lover. He protects her after her first lover's untimely death in Paris. He remains her lover for eight years and rewards her with rich gifts. Upon his wife's death, however, he repents his sinful life and leaves Roxana.

A merchant, who takes care of Roxana's wealth for her during the years after she parts from the Prince de ———. Roxana bears the merchant a son, after a brief affair. Later, he and Roxana are married, legitimize their son, and settle down to respectability in Holland.

Amy, Roxana's faithful maid. She serves her mistress without pay while Roxana is poor. She even bears a child for Mr. ——— when it seems that Roxana cannot. Loyal to the end, she is finally dismissed by Roxana when she threatens to murder Roxana's legitimate daughter to quiet her tongue about Roxana's past.

THE ROYAL HUNT OF THE SUN

Author: Peter Shaffer (1926-   )
First published: 1964
Genre: Drama

Locale: Primarily Ecuador and Peru
Time: 1529-1533
Plot: Livre à clef

Francisco Pizarro (pee-ZAH-roh), a sixty-three-year-old soldier of fortune who sets out to conquer Peru, the land of gold. He starts out with a neat uniform and a trimmed beard, but his appearance deteriorates as the play progresses. A bastard, born of peasant stock, he joined the army to seek glory and escape poverty, but he was never rewarded for his valor. At one time, he would have been satisfied with a title and a pension, but now he wants immortal fame. A disillusioned man, he no longer believes in the honor of war, loyalty to country, or the power of riches. Haunted by the ravages of time and faced with the inevitability of his death, he is looking for a god to replace his youthful hope and his lost faith. He forms a bond with Atahuallpa, the Inca ruler, who promises to rise from the dead especially for Pizarro. When the Indian fails him, the Spaniard is left in despair.

Atahuallpa (ah-tah-HWAHL-pah), the sovereign Inca of Peru, son of the Sun God, a tall, thirty-three-year-old Indian dressed in ceremonial garb, complete with a gold crown and a jeweled mask. A bastard who killed his brother to gain the Inca throne, he rules with godlike power. Believing that Pizarro is a white god come to bless him, he eagerly greets the Spaniards, who eventually capture him. With his ransom set at a room full of gold, he is held prisoner by Pizarro and forms a fraternal relationship with the old man, teaching him how to dance and celebrate life. Compassionately aware that Pizarro has lost faith in God and confident in his own immortality, Atahuallpa promises to rise from the dead after the Spaniards strangle him.

Old Martin, a grizzled old man in his mid-fifties, dressed in the traditional black costume of a mid-sixteenth century Spanish hidalgo. He is a lifetime soldier who has earned a fortune fighting and plundering for his country. As a weary and disillusioned warrior, he sadly recollects the conquest of Peru and his own adulation for Pizarro. As narrator, he describes the scenes, explains the actions of the men involved, and tries to come to terms with himself as a young boy. After narrating the story of the conquest, he is left with a sense of despair at the waste and ruin of an entire nation.

Young Martin, Pizarro's fifteen-year-old page, who can read, write, and later translate. As a naïve young man full of dreams of glory, honor, and chivalry, he worships Pizarro. After the slaughter of the Incas, he vomits as he begins to see that fighting is not as chivalrous as he thought. In the end, he cries and walks away defiantly when Pizarro is ready to break his promise to set Atahuallpa free unharmed. To Pizarro, Young Martin represents the hope that the old soldier has lost and can never regain.

Hernando de Soto, Pizarro's second in command, a dependable soldier in his forties who has freely chosen to fight for God and king, even if it means killing for the sake of Christ. Born into wealth and status, he is a man of honor, loyalty, and faith. As a friend and confidant to Pizarro, he urges his commander to keep his promise to set the Inca free, for he truly understands Pizarro's feelings toward Atahuallpa.

Miguel Estete (mee-GEHL ehs-TEH-teh), the royal veedor or overseer, arrayed in his official black uniform. Haughty and pretentious, he takes great pride in flaunting his status as the official representative of the crown in order to challenge Pizarro's power. Behind his façade as an official bureaucrat, he hides his own personal greed and ambition. Sly and politic in his actions, he tries to get de Candia, the Venetian, to kill the Inca so that the crown can save face, and he plays on Pizarro's desire to be an absolute ruler by telling him to kill Atahuallpa out of sheer willfulness.

Pedro de Candia (KAHN-dee-ah), a Venetian captain and commander of the artillery. He wears a pearl in one ear and swaggers when he walks. As an outsider who is blunt in admitting his selfish motives, he mocks the Spanish officials and priests who try to hide their rapaciousness behind official language and missionary zeal. Volatile and quick to act, he treats the Indians roughly and is ready to kill Atahuallpa himself rather than risk the safety of the army.

Fray Vincente de Valverde (vee-SEHN-teh deh vahl-VEHR-deh), the chaplain of the expedition, a Dominican priest of peasant heritage. He is a self-righteous zealot who believes naïvely that he can convert the Indians by a mere declaration of his creed. Not only does he condone and forgive murder and violence in the name of Christ, but he also treats the Indians as less than human. In his typical fashion, he advises Pizarro to break his promise and kill Atahuallpa because promises given to pagans are not binding.

Fray Marcos de Nizza (NEE-sah), a Franciscan friar who is more severe and intelligent than Valverde. For him, Christianity is a matter of free choice, and he condemns the socialist society of the Incas as evil because it prevents individual enterprise, personal ambition, and free choice.

Felipillo (feh-lee-PEE-yoh), a thin Ecuadoran with gold ornaments who acts as a translator for Pizarro. Converted to Christianity in name only, he is a treacherous Indian driven by lecherous desires for Peruvian women. He is replaced by Young Martin, who catches him deliberately mistranslating Atahuallpa.

Rodas (RROH-dahs), a peasant tailor who disparages Pizarro's recruiting efforts in Spain, renounces his share of the gold because he is afraid to follow Pizarro into Inca territory, and deliberately starts a fight after the gold is shared.

Vasca (VAHS-kah), a rugged peasant. His lust for gold, accompanied by his weariness with his impoverished state, not only impels him to venture into Peru but also spurs him to risk his life. He often motivates others to follow Pizarro.

Domingo (doh-MEEN-goh), a peasant cooper recruited to serve in Pizarro's army. Both doubtful and fearful, he is weak and indecisive both about joining Pizarro and about following him into risky situations.

— *Paul Rosefeldt*

THE ROYAL WAY
(La Voie royale)

Author: André Malraux (1901-1976)
First published: 1930
Genre: Novel

Locale: French Somaliland, French Indochina, and Siam
Time: The 1920's
Plot: Adventure

Claude Vannec (klohd vah-NEHK), an ambitious young archaeologist. He sets out to explore the Royal Way in the jungles of Cambodia and to profit professionally and financially from his discoveries. Intense, impatient, and in revolt against the banality and conformity of bourgeois existence, Claude is also intent on affirming his own manhood on the journey. Obsessed with nonconformist, virile men, whom he wishes to emulate, Claude meditates on his father and grandfather and is drawn to Perken, whom he meets in a Djibouti brothel. It is Perken who shapes Claude's ideas about women,

sensuality, and, finally, the meaning of death. Under Perken's influence, Claude comes to consider the journey less an archaeological mission than a voyage of self-discovery.

Perken (pehr-KAH[N]), an experienced, graying, Danish-German adventurer who accompanies Claude on his archaeological treasure hunt along the Royal Way. It is Perken who insists on continuing the journey into the jungle to seek out the Dutch adventurer's former comrade, Grabot. Perken is an extraordinarily complex individual, combining energy, endurance, and a will of steel with an acute and flexible intelligence capable of understanding individuals and cultures very alien to him. This unique combination of qualities makes Perken a compelling and powerful figure. In the past, it had allowed him to gain ascendance over the native tribes and establish a personal empire in the jungles of Indochina. Perken's empire-building made him a living legend among his fellow Europeans, especially Claude, who considers him to be everything that a man should be. In the jungles with Claude, Perken proves himself to be courageous as well as resourceful, but these qualities ultimately fail to protect him. Perken accidentally wounds his leg on a poisoned stake put in the ground by the natives. The leg becomes gangrenous; because there is no one available to amputate it, Perken ultimately dies of his wound.

Grabot (gra-BOH), an army deserter and, like his friend Perken, an adventurer intent on creating his own empire in the jungle. At the outset of the novel, Grabot has disappeared.

Perken and Claude resolve to find him after completing their journey along the Royal Way. When they locate him, he is the captive of Moi tribesmen. Blinded and no longer able to speak, he has been reduced to the status of a beast of burden, endlessly working a treadmill.

Albert Rameges (ahl-BEHR rah-MEHZH), the director of the French Institute in Saigon, an intellectual who is interested in Claude's work but who suspects the young man's mercenary motives. He warns him of the dangers of the journey and attempts to dissuade him from making it. Rameges also informs Claude that he is not to remove any statuary from the jungle, an order the latter chooses to ignore.

Xa (zhah), Claude's native manservant on the journey. He has just been released from prison and has a bad reputation with the colonial authorities.

— *Richard J. Golsan*

RUBYFRUIT JUNGLE

Author: Rita Mae Brown (1944-   )
First published: 1973
Genre: Novel

Locale: Pennsylvania, Florida, and New York City
Time: Early 1950's to late 1960's
Plot: Social realism

Molly Bolt, an aspiring film director. As an illegitimate child, a lesbian, and a feminist, Molly feels that she is different for most of her life. She grew up poor and was a bright child. She was the first person in her family to go to college but was expelled for having an affair with her roommate. Now a thin, very attractive young woman, Molly expends much of her energy resisting labels; she demands the freedom to have any career she wants, love whomever she wants, and live the way she wants without interference. She is not tolerant of anyone who thinks differently and seems rather cruel and selfish at times. She is true to herself, however, and never compromises her values. She faces the difficulties of trying to break into a traditional man's career squarely and unflinchingly. When a job or a relationship begins to sour, she moves on without regrets.

Carrie Bolt, Molly's sharp-tongued stepmother. Carrie and Molly rarely agree on anything. Having no patience for Molly's independence and mischief, Carrie uses bullying and scolding to try to force her to be more ladylike. When she learns of Molly's homosexuality, Carrie throws her out of the house. Years later, when Molly is twenty-four years old and in film school, Molly returns home, and she and Carrie reach a shaky truce.

Carl Bolt, Molly's good-natured stepfather. Carl works hard all of his life, and his muscular body shows it, but he dies of a heart attack at the age of fifty-seven, a discouraged man who never accomplished anything he could be proud of. Before he dies, he tells Molly to pursue her dreams and to live her life the way she wants to.

Leroy Denman, a redneck, Molly's cousin and closest childhood friend. Fat and not very bright, Leroy admires Molly and is always ready to help her pull a prank or to listen open-mindedly as she thinks things through. He is Molly's first male lover. After a tour in Vietnam as a Marine, he marries and has children and dreams of running away, as he and Molly had dreamed when they were children.

Leota B. Bisland, a sixth-grade classmate of Molly. Tall and thin, with beautiful green eyes and lovely skin, she experiences her first kiss with Molly, and the two begin to spend afternoons in the woods kissing. Just before Molly moves away at the end of sixth grade, they become lovers. Years later, when both women are twenty-four years old, they meet again. Leota, married and a mother, denies ever having been attracted to Molly.

Carolyn Simpson, the captain of the high school cheerleaders and school chaplain. An all-American girl with deep blue eyes and dark hair, she holds very traditional values until Molly and another friend encourage her to drink and to have sex with her boyfriend. She and Molly become lovers, but Carolyn resorts to labels and insults, denying her own sexuality when they are found out.

Faye Raider, a pre-med major at the University of Florida and Molly's roommate. A Southern belle with black hair, porcelain skin, and hazel eyes, Faye is wealthy, irreverent, and an alcoholic. She and Molly fall in love, and Faye becomes the first woman in Molly's life who does not deny their relationship. The two are reported to the administration by the other women in the dorm, and Faye's father pulls her out of college.

Calvin, a hustler living in a car in New York City. A gay man in his twenties, Calvin has long eyelashes and brown skin, eyes, and mustache. Before meeting Molly, he left his Philadelphia home rather than marry a woman he impregnated. He becomes Molly's guide for her first days in New York, teaching her how to get around the city, how to steal food, and how to earn money for sex. He leaves to hitchhike to San Francisco.

Holly, the kept woman of a film actress, a waitress working with Molly, and Molly's lover. Almost six feet tall, black, and with a spectacular body, she is impressed by clothes and money and cannot understand why Molly will not become a kept woman herself as a way of obtaining these things. The daughter of wealthy parents, she does not take Molly's ambitions for a career seriously.

Polina Bellantoni, a Columbia University professor, author of a book on the Middle Ages. She is forty-one years old, her black hair is beginning to gray, and her brown eyes are softly wrinkled. Married, and with a sixteen-year-old daughter, she is educated, witty, and charming. She has a lover, Paul, with whom she shares complicated sexual fantasies, and she is equally attracted to and ashamed of Molly.

— *Cynthia A. Bily*

RUDIN

Author: Ivan Turgenev (1818-1883)
First published: 1856
Genre: Novel

Locale: A provincial estate in Russia
Time: The 1840's
Plot: Psychological realism

Dmitri Nikolaich Rudin (DMIH-tree nih-koh-LA-ihch REW-dihn), an impecunious former civil servant, roughly thirty-five years old, "tall, slightly round-shouldered, curly-haired, swarthy, with irregular, but expressive and intelligent features, and a liquid brilliance in his lively, dark blue eyes." He is an enthusiastic intellectual and makes the rounds of various country estates, moving on when he ceases to entertain his hosts. He has progressive ideas and arouses sympathy in many of his hearers, but, given the social structure in the novel, he is very much a superfluous man. As the plot of the novel unfolds, he joins the group of characters at the country estate of Darya Mikhaylovna Lasunskaya and sparks their interest with his conversation. Darya Mikhaylovna's daughter, Natalya, falls in love with Rudin and offers to run away with him, but he "submits" to the will of her mother and society, refusing to return her affections.

Darya Mikhaylovna Lasunskaya (mih-KHAH-ih-lohv-nah lah-sewn-SKAH-yah), a wealthy widow, the mother of three children (including Natalya). Darya Mikhaylovna possessed good looks in her younger days but has lost most of her charms in her old age. Her wealth and impressive country estate, however, attract the local people and various hangers-on; it is where the only intellectual stimulation in the area is available. Snobbish and egotistical, she values Rudin at first for his conversation but exiles him from her "salon" when she learns of his attentions to her daughter.

Natalya Alexandrovna Lasunskaya (nah-TAHL-yah ah-lehk-SAN-drohv-nah), the seventeen-year-old daughter of Darya Mikhaylovna. Thin, swarthy, and a bit round-shouldered, she is not attractive at first glance. She has a handsome face, however, and is described as having potential. She is a good listener who does not talk much. Although immature and under the thumb of her mother, she has independent ideas and is a relatively deep thinker under her silent exterior. She falls in love with Rudin and offers to run away with him. When he rejects her advances, she marries Volyntsev.

Mikhaylo Mikhaylych Lezhnev (mih-KHAH-ih-loh mih-KHAH-ih-lihch LEH-zhnehv), a phlegmatic former school friend of Rudin, a neighboring landowner. He is described as "a sack of a man." He voices most of the criticism of Rudin in the early part of the novel, having had a falling out with his former friend. He later marries Alexandra Pavlovna Lipina, a childless, fairly wealthy widow who is Volyntsev's sister.

Sergey Pavlych Volyntsev (sehr-GAY PAV-lihch voh-LIHN-tsehv), a retired staff captain who lives with his widowed sister, Alexandra Pavlovna Lipina, and manages her estate. He has fallen deeply in love with Natalya Alexandrovna. During her brief infatuation with Rudin, he retreats, because he is no match for the enthusiastic rhetorician. After Rudin rejects her, Volyntsev marries Natalya.

Afrikan Semyonych Pigasov (AH-frih-kan sehm-YOH-nihch pih-gah-SOV), a failed academic who entered government service. He is "of medium height, with dishevelled grey hair, a swarthy face, and active dark little eyes." Self-educated and ambitious, born of poor parents, he was forced into retirement because of shady deals. Pigasov is very much a misogynist but, before Rudin's arrival, is a valued conversationalist at Darya Mikhailovna's.

Konstantin Diomidych Pandalevsky (kon-stan-TIHN dih-oh-MIH-dihch pan-dah-LEHV-skee), a civil servant. He is a dandy who lives off the philanthropy of others, including Darya Mikhailovna, who is the latest of a series of widows to take him under their wings. He speaks with an accent, and there is "something Asian about his features." He minces and speaks with a slight lisp around women but acts differently when he is out of their company. He entertains the company at Darya Mikhailovna's by playing the piano.

— *John P. Turner, Jr.*

THE RUINED MAP
(Moetsukita chizu)

Author: Kōbō Abe (1924-1993)
First published: 1967
Genre: Novel

Locale: An unnamed Japanese metropolis
Time: 1967
Plot: Detective and mystery

The narrator, a private investigator. A heavy smoker and drinker, and an observant and cynical man as befits his profession, this nameless character combines an obsessive attention to detail with a curious passivity. He worries about justifying his expense reports yet does little to prevent two deaths. Separated from his own wife, he is increasingly fascinated by his client, Nemuro Haru; he refers continually to the lemon-yellow curtains in her home. He is also an imaginative man, proud of the investigative technique he has thought up, that of mentally re-creating a subject. Eventually, he loses his own identity and seems to become the man whom he is seeking.

Nemuro Haru, the wife of the missing man. Short, slender, and with a husky voice and a freckled face, she drinks beer often and seems to live in an alcoholic daze, often talking to herself. She initiates the search for her husband.

Nemuro Hiroshi's brother, also nameless. He is a mysterious character who appears to be involved in homosexual prostitution, blackmail, protection rackets, and other shady projects. He carries a blue and silver badge, apparently a gang insignia. He is insistent about the search for his brother and trails the private detective around until he himself is killed. The detective questions the true relationship of this character to the wife throughout the novel.

Tashiro, a young clerk in Nemuro Hiroshi's company. He is an unattractive man with a bad complexion, shifty eyes, and thick glasses that he is constantly pushing up. A man who feels inferior and ignored, he confuses the investigation by suggesting that the missing man photographed nude models, then confesses that he himself is a compulsive liar. His suicide forces the narrator to resign as a detective.

Nemuro Hiroshi, a fuel dealer who has been missing for six months. A photograph of him shows a long, asymmetrical face with a sad expression. His employer describes him as a serious, steady, and honest worker. He has a sideline as a car mechanic and a mania for collecting professional licenses— for example, as a film projectionist, a secondary school teacher, and a radio operator. He is never found, but the search for his whereabouts drastically changes the lives of the other characters.

The chief, the narrator's boss. As head of a private investigation agency, he is extremely careful not to let his agency get entangled with the police and warns his operatives to give their clients only what they want and not to invade their privacy. The narrator eventually gives up his job and loses his purpose in life because he realizes that his chief's priority is to stay detached from cases and make money.

Toyama, a taxi driver. He bought a car from Nemuro Hiroshi, and he enters the investigation because he returns a raincoat that he found in the trunk of the car. His answers in the interrogation by the narrator provide important narrative and thematic information.

— *Shakuntala Jayaswal*

RULE A WIFE AND HAVE A WIFE

Author: John Fletcher (1579-1625)
First published: 1647
Genre: Drama

Locale: Spain
Time: c. 1600
Plot: Comedy

Leon (leh-OHN), a young Spanish gentleman. Pretending to be a cowardly soldier and a stupid oaf, he is married by Margarita in expectation of his being a tame husband; however, he tames his wife and overcomes his rivals.

Margarita (mahr-gahr-EE-tah), a rich and unprincipled young woman. Wishing to indulge her romantic passion indiscriminately but desiring to protect her reputation, she marries Leon. His cleverness and strength reform her and make her a faithful wife.

Don Juan de Castro (hwahn de KAHS-troh), a colonel and a successful, battle-proved veteran. A fair-minded man, he delights in Leon's actions and encourages them.

Michael Perez (PEH-rehs), a fellow soldier of Don Juan. He pretends to be wealthy to marry the attractive Estifania, whom he thinks wealthy. Their marriage, based on mutual deceit, is a rocky one, but it reaches a reasonable level of stability and happiness.

Estifania (ehs-tee-FAH-nee-ah), Margarita's wily maid. Living as a caretaker in Margarita's house, she pretends to be a wealthy lady. She cheats and steals from her masculine victims, including her husband, Michael. Finally, she and Michael settle down as dependents of Leon and Margarita.

The duke of Medina (meh-DEE-nah), Margarita's projected lover. At first thwarted in his amorous attempts by Leon, he is finally completely discomfited by Margarita herself.

Cacafogo (kah-kah-FOH-goh), a fat, drunken coward. Thinking himself irresistible to women, he is cheated by Estifania and fooled by Margarita.

Altea (ahl-TEH-ah), Margarita's companion. Unknown to Margarita is the fact that Altea is Leon's sister. Her successful matchmaking gives her brother a rich and beautiful bride and her friend a stabilizing and redeeming husband.

THE RULING CLASS: A Baroque Comedy

Author: Peter Barnes (1931-   )
First published: 1969
Genre: Drama

Locale: England
Time: The 1960's
Plot: Satire

Jack Arnold Alexander Tancred, the fourteenth earl of Gurney. Declared a paranoid-schizophrenic by the medical profession, he has been institutionalized for seven years because he believes that he is God, the God of love who deals in compassion and justice. As the gentle **J. C.**, he is the object of contempt and victimized by his family, who hope to inherit his estate. After a "cure," which involves his meeting another mental patient who thinks he is the Messiah, he becomes Jack the Ripper, a malevolent and murderous man ruling with ruth- less absolute authority. As a sadistic autocrat, he is regarded as a perfectly normal member of society, eventually taking his seat in the mummified House of Lords. As Jack, he represents in the extreme the attitudes of the ruling class about themselves and those below them in rank and in gender.

Daniel Tucker, the Gurney manservant. A would-be lower-class revolutionary who despises the upper classes that he serves, he nevertheless remains with them, although he is incredibly insolent after he receives a sizable inheritance from the thirteenth earl of Gurney. His habit of servility accounts for the perpetuation of an unjust and dangerous class system. It even leads to his accepting a conviction for a murder that Jack commits.

Sir Charles Gurney, the brother of the thirteenth earl of Gurney and uncle to Jack. Disappointed by not being named Jack's guardian, which would have given him control of a substantial estate, he plots with his wife to marry Jack to his mistress, who would bear an heir. Charles is a pompous, self-righteous member of the upper classes.

Lady Claire Gurney, the wife of Charles. A bored, self-indulgent, totally amoral woman, she beds many men, including Herder, right under her husband's nose. She is tremendously attracted to Jack, responding sexually to the danger that she senses in him after his cure. In the middle of her seduction of him, he kills her, associating her in his mind with the prostitutes who were the victims of Jack the Ripper.

Grace Shelley, the mistress of Charles and the wife of J. C. A lower-class actress, she assumes the role of Marguerite Gautier, Alexandre Dumas' Lady of the Camellias, to whom

J. C. has pledged his love. An acquisitive and conniving woman, she uses their child to cement her own fortunes and not those of the other Gurneys. At the chilling conclusion of the play, Jack murders her in the middle of a passionate kiss.

Dr. Paul Herder, a thin, cold-mannered German psychiatrist. He prostitutes himself professionally and sexually to obtain a grant for his research on the brains of laboratory rats. He takes part in Charles's schemes to delude Jack, and he seduces Claire. He is also a buffoon: He spouts psychological and medical jargon, all the while completely misdiagnosing Jack's mental state and the horrendous outcome of his cure.

McKyle, the demented, self-proclaimed Electric Messiah. Claiming to exert his will on others through electrical charges, he is like an electroshock treatment for Jack, who is forced to give up his delusion about a God of love existing in this world.

Kelso Truscott, Q. C., the Master in Lunacy and an Old Boy Etonian. Cleverly complimented and reminded of his class loyalty, he declares Jack as the Ripper recovered and totally sane.

— *Lori Hall Burghardt*

RUNAWAY HORSE
(Ein fliehendes Pferd)

Author: Martin Walser (1927-   )
First published: 1978
Genre: Novella

Locale: A resort town on Lake Constance, in Germany
Time: The 1970's
Plot: Psychological realism

Helmut Halm (hahlm), a teacher at a reputable *Gymnasium* in Stuttgart, now on vacation at Lake Constance. Forty-six years old, with a middle-age paunch, he is an introverted intellectual bourgeois who cherishes his privacy, detests familiarity, and desires to remain incognito as much as possible. He reads Søren Kierkegaard and is fond of heavy red wines, good food, cigars, and, above all, escape and seclusion from the world in the company of his wife of many years, Sabina. He is troubled by his loss of sexual desire only to the extent that he is not entirely sure whether his wife has also reached that stage in her life. In the presence of Helene Buch, he experiences a mild erotic reawakening, but, tired by life, alienated and even repulsed by his own body, and fully resigned to his own inertia, he merely registers these stirrings vaguely and without any active interest in Helene. More an observer of life than a participant in it, he is thoroughly annoyed by Klaus Buch's intrusion into his placid vacation and by the threat that his former schoolmate poses to his way of being and his tranquillity. Most of all, Helmut would like to flee but is pressured by the others into submitting to the heartiness and joviality of a renewed, if imposed, friendship. All the while pretending—something that he has not only learned to do well throughout his life but also thoroughly enjoys—he plays along. Finally, during an outing on the stormy lake, out of either an instinct for self-preservation or murderous fury—he himself does not know which—he causes Klaus to fall overboard and disappear in the waves.

Klaus Buch (klows bewkh), a freelance journalist specializing in ecological topics. Although also forty-six years old, he is slender, athletic, and virile looking, with blond hair, white teeth, and bronzed skin. He is garrulous—full of vitality, en-

thusiasm for life, and courage in the face of danger—and seems to be the very opposite of Helmut Halm. In conformity with his professional interests and the trend of the times, he is a health enthusiast who abstains from alcohol and tobacco, plays tennis, sails, hikes, runs, and wears blue jeans and shirts unbuttoned to his waist; he also unabashedly boasts of his sexual accomplishments. He energetically undertakes to draw Helmut out, to convert him to his way of life. In reality, however, Klaus is an insecure, frequently sullen, hardworking, and not very successful man who only pretends to be dashing through life with ease and adroitness. He resents his dependency on his publishers and editors and has become bitter and even mean-spirited. In desperate need of confirmation and affection, he clings to his former classmate and does not recognize the latter's rejection of him until the very last moment before falling into the lake.

Helene (Hella) Buch (heh-LEH-neh), the attractive, charming, and vivacious wife of Klaus Buch. She writes books on herbs and is presently collecting old grandmothers' sayings in the region of Lake Constance. Eighteen years younger than her husband, she seems happy in her role of the loving and devoted wife, always ready to support and reassure him and to join him in his adventures. Just as she is the one who in the end discloses her husband's true nature, she also reveals that she is not what she seems to be. Once an aspiring pianist who had to give up her hopes to follow the dictates of her husband, she is in reality unhappy with the existence imposed on her, including her present profession, and has been dissembling all the while. When she believes that her husband has drowned, she is less sad than curiously relieved. At the Halms', she drinks excessively, smokes, and tells of her pitiful lot; in her husband's presence, she abhorred alcohol and tobacco and constantly pointed out his superior qualities. When Klaus miraculously reappears, it is with irritation rather than joy that she welcomes him.

Sabina Halm (zah-BEE-neh), the loving and motherly wife of Helmut Halm. She has no profession, is childless, and is

devoted to her husband. Although the same age as he, she has not yet entirely lost her interest in sex and becomes mildly infatuated with Klaus Buch. At the conclusion of the story, it is she who initiates the attempt to rekindle the dormant sex life in her marriage.

— *Stella P. Rosenfeld*

RUNNER MACK

Author: Barry Beckham (1944-   )
First published: 1972
Genre: Novel

Locale: Various locations in the United States
Time: A time resembling the Vietnam War era of the 1960's
Plot: Absurdist

Henry Adams, a black baseball player. A wiry, athletic, and relatively short young man, Adams has come north from Mississippi with a clear goal: to become a baseball star. Instead, he is hit by a truck, employed in a meaningless job, terrorized by police, humiliated by the baseball team that had called him to a tryout, drafted and sent to a war in Alaska, and finally taken back to the northern city for a revolution that fails to materialize. As the novel ends, another truck is bearing down on him.

Beatrice Mark Adams, Henry's wife, another native of Mississippi. She is young, light-skinned, graceful, and charmingly seductive. A much-loved child, she insisted on marrying Henry, despite her father's conviction that he could never support her. In the northern city where Henry takes her, she spends most of her time in their inadequate apartment, troubled by the air pollution, which makes it impossible for her to breathe, and by the maddening level of urban noise. Just as Henry is about to leave for Alaska, she tells him that she is pregnant. When he returns, he finds that she can no longer hear what he says: The noise has made her deaf.

Runnington (Runner) Mack, a black soldier and revolutionary. A tall, mustached man from the West whose every other word is profane, he is a natural leader. When Henry encounters him in an Alaska barracks, Mack is already organizing black and white soldiers for the invasion of Washington. His confidence is illustrated by the fact that he shows no hesitation in seizing and piloting a helicopter, even though he

admits that he has had no training. After a successful trip from Alaska in various conveyances, ranging from limousine to train, Runner Mack arrives at the union hall to lead the revolution that will change the country. When he finds only eight participants present, he hangs himself in the men's room.

Mr. Boye, Henry's supervisor at Home Manufacturing Company. A man in late middle age, he has a pimpled forehead and a tendency to spill saliva while he is talking. An employee of the company for forty years, he has risen from messenger boy to supervisor; however, he is frustrated because he has been stopped at that level for thirty years, when someone decided that he should rise no further. In an effort to establish himself as a friend of the black workers, he shows Henry pornographic photographs of a black woman. When Henry later asks about the meaning of his job, Boye admits that he has never known what he himself is doing or even what the plant is making. Later, he is reprimanded for that confession.

M. A. Peters, the personnel manager at Home Manufacturing Company, where Henry Adams works. A tall man with bushy brows and closely clipped hair, he wears the corporate pinstriped suit and a meaningless smile. At the Christmas party, he is the typical toady, leading the employees in applause for the decrepit company president.

— *Rosemary M. Canfield Reisman*

R. U. R.

Author: Karel Čapek (1890-1938)
First published: 1920
Genre: Drama

Locale: An unnamed island
Time: The future
Plot: Social satire

Harry Domin, the general manager of Rossum's Universal Robots (R.U.R.). He is dedicated to the idea that humans ought to be completely free from the slavery of work.

Helena Glory, the daughter of the president of R.U.R. and later the wife of Harry Domin. Concerned both over the robots' living conditions and over the millions of people out of work, she believes that the robots should be given souls. When this plan proves disastrous, she burns the formula for making robots.

Dr. Gall, the scientist who is persuaded by Helena to give souls to the robots.

Mr. Alquist, the head of the R.U.R. works department. He

recognizes that human idleness is not the perfect goal Domin thinks it to be. Because, like the robots, he works with his hands, he is the only human being in the world spared after the uprising of the robots. He is, however, unable to duplicate the formula for robot manufacture.

Primus, a robot.

Helena, a robot made in Helena Glory's image. In some miraculous way, Helena loves and is loved by Primus. With humankind destroyed and robot manufacture no longer possible, these two completely human robots remain as the only hope for the reproduction of new life.

RUSLAN AND LYUDMILA
(Ruslan y Lyudmila)

Author: Alexander Pushkin (1799-1837)
First published: 1820
Genre: Poetry

Locale: Russia
Time: Late tenth century
Plot: Mock-heroic

Vladimir, the grand prince of Kiev from 980 to 1015. The ruler, an actual figure from history, is best known for bringing Christianity to Kievan Russia, the territory that eventually would expand into the Russian Empire. He was also the hero of legends and tales. In this poem, he is featured merely as the father of the bride, Lyudmila.

Lyudmila, the younger daughter of Vladimir. Whisked away from her bridegroom Ruslan on their wedding night and held captive by the sorcerer Chernomor, she is no languishing damsel in distress. The high-spirited young woman almost succeeds in outwitting her would-be-ravisher. Only by using her love for Ruslan to trick her is Chernomor able to snare her and put her into an enchanted sleep.

Ruslan, a member of Vladimir's famed warrior retinue and Lyudmila's betrothed. True-hearted and brave in the face of danger, despair, and humiliation, he must pass through a number of trials to rescue his bride.

Rogday, the first of Ruslan's three human challengers. Genuinely brave but dour and pugnacious, he intends to fight his way into Vladimir's favor by doing away with Ruslan and rescuing Lyudmila.

Ratmir, a young Khazar khan who is another of Ruslan's rivals. Quick and passionate, and excited by the prospect of wedding and bedding Lyudmila, he too sets out to rescue her. He is soon distracted from the chase by the more immediate pleasures of an enchanted castle inhabited by twelve beautiful maidens.

Farlaf, Ruslan's third and deadliest challenger. Long on talk and short on deeds, Farlaf also sets out on the quest but soon conspires with the sorceress Naina to slay Ruslan once the true knight does the dangerous work of retrieving Lyudmila.

Chernomor, the evil dwarf who kidnaps Lyudmila. Although he is a powerful sorcerer, his physical charms are far inferior to his magic ones, and she finds him too grotesque and ridiculous to truly fear.

The Finn, a hermit-sorcerer who aids Ruslan in his quest. In his youth, he had been desperately in love with the beautiful peasant Naina and went off seeking wealth and glory as a pirate-raider. When she continued to spurn him, he turned to sorcery and spent decades learning the magic arts. He succeeded in bewitching Naina only to realize that forty years had passed and the woman who now passionately desired him was a hideous crone. Rueful and wise, he has retreated from the world.

Naina, the vengeful witch who takes up the mischief making where Chernomor leaves off. Her late, thwarted passion for the Finn has turned to malice toward him and anyone close to him, and she helps Farlaf plot the betrayal of Ruslan.

The Enchanted Head, all that remains of a giant and warrior whose body is slain by his brother Chernomor. His head is doomed to remain alive to guard the magical sword that can cut off the dwarf's beard and render him powerless. Although its encounter with Ruslan begins on a comic note, the Head does have an air of tragedy that the other characters lack.

— *Jane Ann Miller*

RUTH

Author: Elizabeth Gaskell (1810-1865)
First published: 1853
Genre: Novel

Locale: England and Wales
Time: Approximately the 1830's
Plot: Moral

Ruth Hilton, later called **Mrs. Denbigh**, who as a girl of sixteen is on her own, working long hours in a seamstress's shop with many other girls. With no living family, she is often lonely. Her life changes for the worse when she meets Mr. Bellingham, a young noble. He eventually lures her off to London and North Wales, and she becomes pregnant. When he becomes ill in Wales, his mother comes to nurse him and sends Ruth away. Her rescue by Mr. Benson takes her to Eccleston and a life as Mrs. Denby, a model "widow" and loving mother. She works as the governess to two daughters of a rich local family. When her secret is discovered, her son is about six years old. The Bensons—a minister and his sister—stand by her, and she stays to become a nurse for the ill. She dies as a revered and beloved woman after working during an epidemic.

Mr. Bellingham, later known as **Mr. Donne**, who seduces Ruth because she is attractive. He does not try to find her after his illness. He later appears as a friend of Mr. Bellingham, running for political office as Mr. Donne, having changed his name to acquire a legacy. He proposes to Ruth, but she spurns him, and he goes on to have a questionable political career. He is a weak and self-serving man.

Thurstan Benson, a beloved and generous minister with a humpback. He is in his forties when he and his sister meet Ruth in North Wales and befriend her. He depends for his income on his small congregation in Eccleston. They are Dissenters from the official English church. Keeping Ruth's secret is difficult for him, especially when she goes as nurse/governess to the daughters of the local gentleman, Mr. Bradshaw. His generosity and nobility of spirit define him.

Sally, a beloved elderly retainer of the Bensons. She believes that she is responsible for Mr. Benson's humpback, having dropped him when she was a teenager and he was a baby. She stays with the Bensons, has a mind of her own, and at first is very harsh with Ruth. She becomes as devoted to Ruth as she is to the Bensons, and money she has saved for them from her salary goes to help Ruth.

Mr. Bradshaw, a proud man who is an important parishioner in Mr. Benson's church. He is morally upright but puts little effort toward that, and he neither understands nor will tolerate the weaknesses he sees in others. He is inclined to be judgmental and condescending; as a result, he holds at a distance his eldest daughter and badly misunderstands his son. He hires Ruth as a governess but is cruel to her concerning her illegitimate child, making it more difficult to tolerate the weaknesses and crimes of his son. He disowns his son but gradually reconciles himself to the Bensons and to Ruth. His wife and children have more sympathy for Ruth and for his erring son than he is capable of showing.

Richard Bradshaw, Mr. Bradshaw's son, who grows up to be a solicitor like his father and works in his father's office. He is dishonest with investors' money. This is discovered long after Mr. Bradshaw has made Ruth's shame public and humiliated her son. Richard stole the money invested for Mr. Benson by his father. He is sent to Scotland, where he reforms and does well, but he has shamed his father.

Jemima Bradshaw, Mr. Bradshaw's eldest daughter, who is attractive, and energetic. As a young woman of sixteen, she is courted by Mr. Farquhar, who is favored by her parents, especially her father. She is somewhat rebellious. She wants to marry Mr. Farquhar and eventually does, but she cannot abide his "correction" of her faults and becomes impatient with him. She is characterized by jealousy, contrariness, and a good heart.

Mr. Farquhar, who is moral by nature. As a man of forty, he is attracted by Jemima's beauty and her good family background. He tries to make her more appropriate as a candidate for his wife. His strictness is tempered, so that he is able to satisfy Jemima, help Richard in his difficulties, and, as Mr. Bradshaw's business partner, keep Richard and his father from destroying each other.

Leonard Denbigh, Ruth's son, a sober boy who is very fond of his mother. When, at the age of six, he finds out that he was born out of wedlock, he hates her, but only for a short time. He lives with her and the Bensons and is dear to Miss Benson and Sally as well as to Ruth. He is portrayed as largely noble and naturally sweet and good.

— *Janice M. Bogstad*

S

SACRED FAMILIES
(Tres novelitas burguesas)

Author: José Donoso (1924-1996)
First published: 1973
Genre: Short fiction

Locale: Spain
Time: Early 1970's
Plot: Psychological symbolism

Chattanooga Choo-Choo

Sylvia Corday, a tall, slender professional model with the perfect artificial beauty of a mannequin. While her husband is away, she enters Anselmo's room without eyes, mouth, or arms. After they make love, Sylvia asks Anselmo to give her a mouth by cutting one out of red paper. She then directs him to draw in the rest of her face on her head, which resembles a featureless egg. After they make love a second time, Sylvia removes Anselmo's penis with vanishing cream. She becomes a friend of Magdalena, Anselmo's wife. Sylvia teaches her how to disassemble her husband, pack him into a suitcase, and reassemble him at will. She also initiates the swapping of their husbands' penises.

Anselmo Prieto (pree-EH-toh), the narrator and Magdalena's husband. He is obsessed with the need to control women. He becomes attracted to Sylvia when he finds her incomplete and helpless in his room. Giving Sylvia a mouth and creating her face with makeup demonstrates to him that a woman's being depends on man's will. When he realizes that

his penis is gone, he attacks Sylvia and removes her face with vanishing cream. He considers psychiatric treatment to restore his virility, but guilt and fear of revealing his impotence make him decide against it. He ignores Ramón's warnings and is disassembled by Magdalena without his knowledge. After she reassembles him, he discovers that he is whole again but still does not realize that his wife can disassemble him again at will.

Magdalena Prieto (mahg-dah-LEHN-ah), the seemingly timid and submissive wife of Anselmo. She learns from Sylvia the technique for dismantling Anselmo. She packs the pieces of Anselmo's body in a suitcase, safeguarding his penis in a small velvet bag in her purse. She takes the suitcase with her when she meets Sylvia for coffee.

Ramón del Solar (rrah-MOHN dehl soh-LAHR), an architect and Sylvia's husband. He tries to warn Anselmo about what Sylvia is teaching Magdalena.

Green Atom Number Five

Roberto Ferrer (feh-REHR), a middle-aged dentist, the husband of Marta Mora. He fancies himself to be a talented amateur painter. He has just bought a new apartment, built and decorated to reflect his marriage to Marta and their identity as a couple. When Marta shows indifference to the disappearance of Roberto's best painting, *Green Atom Number Five*, he confronts her with her major shortcoming: She is barren. As their possessions disappear from their apartment, he fears that if he leaves the apartment he will be unable to find it again. He no longer attempts to hide his dissatisfaction with his marriage, and his relationship with his wife deteriorates rapidly. His final

effort to recover their missing possessions fails, as does all hope of saving the marriage.

Marta Mora, Roberto's wife, who cannot have children. She admits to Roberto that she does not think highly of his artistic talent when his favorite painting disappears. She despises Roberto for his love of the art objects in the apartment. She runs into traffic and is hit by a car while trying to retrieve her mother's cabinet from a moving van. After her hospitalization, the condition of the apartment deteriorates in pace with her relationship with Roberto.

Gaspard de la Nuit

Sylvia Corday, a model who did not want motherhood to interfere with her professional life. Mauricio's rejection of her maternal overtures of friendship greatly upset her. She wants to become a part of his life and acquire his affection by giving him material things. When he finally warms up to her and wants to have the things she wants him to have, she is overcome with joy.

Mauricio (mow-REE-see-oh), Sylvia's thin, pale, adolescent son. He resists his mother's attempts to make him a part of her freethinking, materialistic lifestyle. He walks the streets of Barcelona whistling tunes from Maurice Ravel's *Gaspard de la Nuit*, hoping his music will connect him with someone on the street and give him an identity. In the Vallvidrera forest, he meets a street urchin who looks just like him. They change places. The urchin puts on Mauricio's clothes, returns to Sylvia's apartment, and obliges her in everything. Mauricio puts on the urchin's clothes to start a new, independent life, free of the adults who have been trying to mold him in their image.

— Evelyn Toft

THE SACRED FOUNT

Author: Henry James (1843-1916)
First published: 1901
Genre: Novel

Locale: Newmarch, a British country estate, and on board a train
Time: The 1890's
Plot: Psychological realism

The narrator, a novelist who goes with a group of friends for a weekend to Newmarch, a country resort outside London. He is not named in the novel. Naturally inquisitive and an astute observer of human nature, he notices changes in several of his friends for which he can find no immediate explanation: Grace Brissenden seems younger than when they last met, Guy Brissenden older, Gilbert Long more lively, and May Server more withdrawn and worn. He becomes determined to observe everyone carefully, looking for clues that will explain why these character changes have taken place. Over the course of the weekend, he formulates an elaborate theory that the power of love is the source for rejuvenation in some and deterioration in others. He is especially interested in confirming his notion that May and Gilbert are lovers, and he enlists the aid of Grace Brissenden and Ford Obert to help gather evidence in support of his idea. He is devastated when, at the end of the weekend, Grace disabuses him of his notions and pokes holes in his carefully constructed theory about these people's relationships.

Grace Brissenden, a woman of middle age who has been married to a younger man for some time. In the view of the narrator, her marriage seems to have made her younger. Throughout the weekend, she schemes with the narrator to determine if Gilbert Long and May Server are lovers. Eventually, however, she turns on her coconspirator and accuses him of being needlessly inquisitive. She finally offers him an explanation for everyone's behavior that does not match his interpretation of the events and insinuations he has witnessed or overheard during the weekend.

Guy Brissenden, a young man who married an older woman. He seems to have aged considerably during the years of his marriage, so much so that the narrator becomes convinced there must be some cause for this physical change. He befriends May Server and is generally pleasant with other members of the company, especially Lady John, though it is never clear that they have any more than a platonic relationship.

Gilbert Long, a friend of the Brissendens and the narrator, long thought to be rather dull by those who know him. His rejuvenation with no apparent cause sets the narrator to thinking that he must be having an affair. His conversations with May Server, seen from afar by the narrator, give some indication to others that she may be the woman who has made him seem younger and more aesthetically sensitive.

May Server, a woman who seems to be especially drained emotionally by some recent experience, but who keeps her own counsel, sharing little information about her private life with the narrator. She spends time with Gilbert Long and with Guy Brissenden, piquing the narrator's curiosity and causing him to believe that a secret affair with Long has led to her physical deterioration.

Ford Obert, an artist who travels to Newmarch with the narrator and the Brissendens. Like the narrator, he is a student of human nature, and he has tried to capture the human spirit in his paintings. His portrait of a figure holding a mask catches the attention of the entire group at Newmarch, setting them to discussing the difficulty of interpreting character from outward appearance. He engages the narrator in long conversations about the difficulty of reading motive into the actions of others.

Lady John, a guest at Newmarch who spends time with Gilbert Long. Her association with him leads the narrator to surmise that they are more than casual acquaintances, and for some time he entertains the notion that they are lovers. Lady John has only brief contacts with the narrator, whom she seems not to trust.

— Laurence W. Mazzeno

THE SAFETY NET
(Fürsorgliche Belagerung)

Author: Heinrich Böll (1917-1985)
First published: 1979
Genre: Novel

Locale: West Germany
Time: c. 1978
Plot: Social

Fritz Tolm (tohlm), a wealthy newspaper owner in his mid-sixties who has just been elected president of the Association. As president of this organization, which represents the conservative interests of the West German business establishment, Tolm is catapulted into public prominence and is more vulnerable than ever as a symbolic target for the terrorists wishing to strike a blow at the West German system. Tolm, who experienced poverty in his youth, inherited a newspaper from his godfather toward the end of World War II. Although Tolm had a Ph.D. in art history and had no interest in newspapers, his paper, under the direction of its financial manager, Amplanger, consumed competing papers and became an empire. Reluctantly maneuvered into accepting the presidency of the Association because of his positive public image as a cultured and kindly gentleman, Tolm is mentally and physically weary. He lacks true independence and does not even control his own paper. He is surrounded by elaborate police protection and has no privacy. With the support of his wife, Käthe, he repudiates his public position to bury the dead terrorist, Heinrich Beverloh, whom he loved as a son. He and Käthe decide to leave their mansion, Tolmshoven, and to move into an empty vicarage to be accessible to their children.

Käthe Tolm (KAY-teh), Fritz Tolm's attractive, warmhearted, and generous wife. She, like Fritz, comes from a humble background, and she has little tolerance for self-important or stupid members of the economic elite; she much prefers common people. Her life centers on her family, and she longs to regain privacy and family intimacy.

Rolf Tolm, a son of the Tolms, a brilliant and talented economist whose promising career as a banker was aborted when he was jailed for throwing stones and setting cars on fire during a violent political protest. Still a radical, he has repudiated violence and lives on the grounds of a Catholic parish with his common-law wife, Katharina Schroter, an intelligent and sensitive communist, and their son, Holger II.

Herbert Tolm, the Tolms' other son. Opposed to violence, he, too, rejected the artificiality and mindless development of West German society. He has refused to go to Tolmshoven, where his family has moved after selling their former home to a strip-mining coal corporation. He nevertheless welcomes his parents' visits to his apartment in Cologne, where he plans protest demonstrations with his lively fellow bohemian proponents of an "alternate society."

Veronica Zelger (ZEHL-gehr), the former wife of Rolf Tolm and the mother of his son Holger I. She has become the lover of the terrorist Heinrich Beverloh and has been underground with him in the Middle East for three years. She telephones the warning that the terrorists will launch an attack using booby-trapped bicycles. Placed in charge of planting an explosive bicycle, a disenchanted Veronica turns herself over to the police.

Sabine Fischer (zah-BEE-neh), née **Tolm** the beautiful, golden-blonde, quiet, and religiously devout daughter of the Tolms. She married the insensitive, materialistic, playboy scion of an exploitative textile conglomerate, Erwin Fischer. Sabine, under elaborate police protection against terrorism, has fallen in love and had a furtive affair with one of her protectors, Hubert Hendler.

Hubert Hendler, a tall, blond, serious, and morally upright security guard who joined the police because he loves order.

Hubert has become infatuated with Sabine, whom he is guarding. After prolonged and agonized soul-searching, Hubert decides to leave his wife and son for Sabine.

Helga Hendler, Hubert's noble and long-suffering wife. More concerned for Hubert and his happiness than for herself, she tells him to go and live with Sabine, hoping that Hubert eventually will return to her and their son, Bernhard.

Holger I, the son of Rolf Tolm and Veronica Zelger. Veronica persuaded Heinrich Beverloh to send him back home. Holger I has been carefully trained not to divulge any information that might betray the terrorists and has been programmed, as Veronica has attempted to warn the Tolms, to wreak havoc. During Beverloh's funeral, he sets fire to Tolmshoven, which Fritz and Käthe have already decided to leave.

Holzpuke (HOHLTS-pew-keh), the officer in charge of security for the Tolm family. He is an extremely efficient technician but attempts to be as sensitive to the feelings of the Tolms as his professionalism will allow.

Heinrich "Bev" Beverloh (HIN-rihkh BAY-vehr-loh), a brilliant economist who has grown up with the Tolm children. After earning his doctorate in the United States, he has become a radical and a terrorist. He was masterminding a terrorist attack against the Association, from his hiding place in the Middle East, when he was located by the German security forces. Holzpuke, through electronic surveillance of a conversation between Käthe and Fritz, learns of Beverloh's obsessive interest in shoes; by tracking the purchases of a specific size and brand of expensive shoes in Istanbul, he locates Beverloh. In surrendering, however, Beverloh deliberately sets off an explosive device that kills him and two of his captors.

Bleibl (BLI-behl), a dominant German industrialist, a coarse man who Fritz believes is out to destroy him. Bleibl, although he was a Nazi, was favored by his American captors at the end of the war. With an American officer, Bangors, Bleibl looted the vaults of destroyed banks; the loot served as the foundation for a financial and industrial empire. During one of the thefts, however, Bleibl was startled by a young woman, who had been sleeping in the rubble. Without thinking, he shot her, and her corpse became a specter that destroys his marriage to his attractive, talented, and industrious wife, Hilde. Unable to find satisfaction in a succession of women and wives, a sixty-five-year-old Bleibl exorcises the ghost by a confessional reconciliation with his antagonists, the Tolms, and becomes determined to attempt a reconciliation with Hilde.

— Bernard A. Cook

THE SAGA OF GRETTIR THE STRONG
(Grettis Saga)

Author: Unknown
First transcribed: c. 1300
Genre: Novel

Locale: Iceland, Norway, and Constantinople
Time: The eleventh century
Plot: Folklore

Grettir the Strong, a folk hero of Iceland. Outlawed at fourteen after killing a man, he goes to Norway, where he routs a party of berserk raiders. Acclaimed as a hero, he becomes increasingly involved in murderous feuds, particularly after his return to Iceland. At last, able to trust no one because of the price on his head yet tormented by a growing fear of the dark

that makes it impossible for him to live alone, he settles with a brother and a servant on an island accessible only by rope ladders. Several years later, he is overcome by witchcraft and killed.

Onund, his ancestor, a Viking who fled Norway to escape injustice and settled in Iceland.

Aesa, the wife of Onund.

Ofeig, the father of Aesa.

Thrand, a great hero who accompanied Onund to Iceland.

Asmund Longhair, the father of Grettir. During Grettir's youth, father and son quarreled constantly.

Skeggi, whom Grettir kills in the course of a quarrel. Thus begins Grettir's long outlawry.

Thorfinn, a Norwegian landman with whom Grettir makes a home after being shipwrecked.

Thorir and

Ogmund, the leaders of a band of raiders who come to lay waste to Thorfinn's district during his absence. Grettir kills both.

Karr-the-Old, the long-dead father of Thorfinn. After Grettir kills the raiders, Thorfinn gives him an ancient sword from the treasure hoard of Karr-the-Old.

Bjorn, who is jealous of Grettir's strength and bravery. Grettir kills him.

Jarl Sveinn, before whom Grettir is summoned after killing Bjorn.

Thorgils Maksson, Asmund's kinsman, slain in a quarrel. Asmund takes up the feud against the murderers.

Glam, a shepherd possessed by a fiend. Grettir fights him and kills him, but before his death, Glam predicts that Grettir will come to fear the dark.

Thorbjorn Slowcoach, an enemy killed by Grettir.

Thorbjorn Oxmain, a kinsman of Slowcoach. He gets revenge for Slowcoach's death by killing Grettir's brother. Grettir then kills Oxmain and his son.

Atli, Grettir's brother, who is killed by Oxmain.

Thorir of Gard, whose sons are having a drunken feast in an inn to which Grettir has swum for coals to make a fire. In the ensuing fight, the inn and Thorir's sons are burned. Thorir later puts a price on Grettir's head.

Thorodd, a kinsman of Thorbjorn Oxmain. He also puts a price on Grettir's head.

Einar, on whose lonely farm Grettir lives for a time. Grettir falls in love with Einar's daughter, but he knows that his suit is hopeless because of his reputation.

Snaekoll, a wild, lawless man who comes to Einar's farm. Grettir kills him.

Thorsteinn Dromund, the half brother of Grettir. Grettir goes to stay with him after giving up his suit for Einar's daughter. Thorsteinn swears to avenge Grettir if he should be slain. Years later, after Grettir's death, Thorsteinn pursues the murderer to Constantinople, where he kills him with the sword of Karr-the-Old.

Thorbjorg, a wise woman who releases Grettir after he is captured by some farmers.

Grim, an outlaw whom Grettir kills because Grim is intending to kill him for the reward money.

Redbeard, an outlaw hired by Thorir of Gard to kill Grettir but who is killed by Grettir.

Hallmund, Grettir's friend. He prevents Grettir's capture by helping him against a force of eighty men led by Thorir of Gard. Later, Hallmund is treacherously slain for the aid he gave to Grettir.

Steinvor of Sandhauger, who gives birth to a boy whom many call Grettir's son. The boy dies at seventeen.

Illugi, Grettir's youngest brother, who lives with him in an almost inaccessible island. He dies with Grettir when they are attacked.

Thorbjorn Angle, who overcomes Grettir with the aid of witchcraft and kills him. Outlawed, Thorbjorn goes to Constantinople, where he is pursued and killed by Grettir's half brother, Thorsteinn Dromund.

Steinn the Lawman, who decrees that Thorbjorn Angle cannot collect the reward because of his use of witchcraft.

THE SAILOR WHO FELL FROM GRACE WITH THE SEA
(Gogo no eikō)

Author: Yukio Mishima (Kimitake Hiraoka, 1925-1970)
First published: 1963
Genre: Novel

Locale: Yokohama, Japan
Time: After World War II, perhaps the late 1950's
Plot: Psychological realism

Ryuji Tsukazaki, a sailor and Fusako Kuroda's lover. Having crossed the seas countless times on a freighter, Ryuji is thoroughly at home on the ocean and enjoys his work but lately has had passing thoughts of settling permanently on land. He also sees himself as destined for some kind of glory, although he cannot yet define in his own mind what kind of glory he will receive. He meets Fusako Kuroda and her son Noboru and becomes her lover, as well as a hero figure for the son, who is fascinated with his strength. Ryuji and Fusako decide to get married; he further determines to retire from the sea and work for her in the fashion boutique that she owns. Ryuji's determination to retire from the sea enrages her son, Noboru, who wants Ryuji to retain his hero status by remaining primarily at sea. Ryuji finally receives his ironic "glory" by means of a painful death at the hands of Noboru and his friends, who seek to punish him.

Noboru Kuroda, a thirteen-year-old boy and the son of Fusako Kuroda. Noboru, like his friends, is a nihilist who

believes that there is little meaning in life; nevertheless, he is fascinated with the strength and vastness of the sea and with Ryuji, who lives on and in the sea. Noboru believes that Ryuji partakes of the sea's strength. When Ryuji becomes Fusako's lover, Noboru is delighted, seeing direct links between himself and his mother, his mother and the sailor, and the sailor and the sea. Through this linkage to the sea and his general fascination with the strength of the sailor, Noboru begins to see some significance in his own life. When the sailor retires from the sea and exhibits "weak" behavior, such as working in a dress shop, he is no longer of heroic stature in Noboru's eyes, and the psychic linkage of the boy to the sea is broken. He is infuriated and decides to punish Ryuji for "falling out of grace" with the sea. The punishment is a ritualistic murder of Ryuji.

Fusako Kuroda, Noboru's mother, a widow and owner of a clothing boutique. A very lonely woman since the death of her husband, Fusako occupies herself at her shop. When the sailor, Ryuji, comes into her life, the vacuum is filled, and she happily looks forward to marriage and a classic suburban domestic life with her new mate. She is completely unaware of her son's strange, nihilistic bent, and she unwittingly draws her intended husband to his death by attracting him to a domesticated but unheroic existence on land. She reflects the author's own distaste for the unimaginative middle-class mentality, and she is left a pitiful figure at the end, unaware of what will become of her fiancé and of the awful deed perpetrated by her son and his friends.

The Chief, a thirteen-year-old boy, Noboru's friend and leader of their six-member gang. The Chief is the instructor in nihilism for the boys. He spends his time at their meetings enlightening them on the meaninglessness and chaos in the world, directly reflecting the author's own views. He makes Noboru kill a kitten and then proceeds to dissect it to show the gang that there is nothing sacred or magic about a living being. It is the Chief who suggests to Noboru that killing the sailor would be an appropriate way to punish him and to return the sailor to his heroic status.

— *James V. Muhleman*

THE SAINT
(Il Santo)

Author: Antonio Fogazzaro (1842-1911)
First published: 1905
Genre: Novel

Locale: Italy
Time: Late nineteenth century
Plot: Religious

Piero Maironi (pee-EH-roh mah-ee-ROH-nee), who previously left his wife in an insane asylum to take Jeanne Dessalle as his mistress. Later, at the time of his wife's death, three years before the time of this story, he had a prophetic vision and renounced the world. He left Dessalle to pursue a holy life and is now called **Benedetto the Saint** for his many good works. He speaks out against the corruption of the church, even traveling to Rome to speak with the pope.

Jeanne Dessalle (dehs-SAHL-leh), who hopes that Piero will renounce his holy life and come back to her now that her husband has died. She travels across Italy trying to find him and persuade him to come back to her before he takes his final vows as a monk. She finds him and manages to speak to him

alone, and she tells him honestly that she still does not believe in God. Her conversion comes just in time to give him delight in his dying moments.

Noemi d'Arxel (noh-EH-mee d'ahr-ZHEHL), her friend, who scours Italy with her in search of Piero.

Giovanni Selva (jee-oh-VAHN-nee), Noemi's saintly brother-in-law, a philosopher whose writings Benedetto keeps off the Catholic Church's Index of forbidden books.

Don Clemente, a Benedictine monk who is the instructor of Benedetto at the monastery of Santa Scholastica.

The pope, who summons Benedetto to discuss ideas about the needs of the church. He begs Benedetto to be patient in waiting for correction of the church's problems.

SAINT JACK

Author: Paul Theroux (1941-   )
First published: 1973
Genre: Novel

Locale: Singapore, at an unnamed American college
Time: 1953-1971
Plot: Social morality

Jack Flowers, born **Jack Fiori** in North Boston, fifty-three years old and living in Singapore at the opening of the novel, which is a first-person memoir of his misadventures. His voice is comically candid but consistently underscored by a poignant thoughtfulness. He is a rascal with compassionate inclinations; a pragmatic panderer and a shameless poser, he secretly entertains very romantic illusions. He has lived with an energetic restlessness for imagined possibilities, and now he suddenly confronts the probability that his life will end in pathetic anonymity. The mundane death of William Leigh—whom Jack had very recently met and to whom he took an almost immediate dislike, although he would develop a reflexive understanding of him because of their comparable delusions—prompts Jack to establish a record of his life, not to impose meaning on it but to lend to it whatever permanence exists in the public expression of private experience.

William Leigh, a British accountant from Hong Kong, sent to audit Hing's books. He assumes a transparently superior attitude toward Jack, who is supposed to see to his accommo-

dations and entertainment. Despite his pretensions, William is clearly waiting out his retirement pension. In an uncharacteristic moment, he confides to Jack that he and his wife cherish the notion of retiring to a cottage in the English countryside. When William dies of a heart attack while sitting on an open toilet in the back room of a seedy bar where Jack hangs out, Jack feels a deep pathos. Jack telephones William's wife, to whom he describes a more dignified death, and arranges William's cremation in Singapore.

Edwin (Eddie) Shuck, a U.S. government official who is probably connected in some way to the Central Intelligence Agency. He meets Jack by posing as a tourist who needs Jack's assistance in discovering the wilder diversions that Singapore has to offer. This deception tries Jack's patience, but after Eddie offers Jack the job of managing Paradise Gardens, Eddie seems to exhibit a more agreeable and personable side to his character. He and Jack have few difficulties with each other until the abrupt closing of that establishment. In that situation and in his hiring of Jack to gather blackmail material on the general, he finally demonstrates that his position and his ambition have corrupted his sense of values in a more sinister way than pimping has corrupted Jack.

Chop Hing Kheng Fatt, the Chinese ship chandler who employs Jack. He presents an impervious demeanor to Cauca-sians, but he is very proud and volatile and is likely to kick his dog or abuse his Chinese employees when he thinks that his doing so will not be noticed.

— Martin Kich

SAINT JOAN

Author: George Bernard Shaw (1856-1950)
First published: 1924
Genre: Drama

Locale: France
Time: The fifteenth century
Plot: Historical

Joan of Arc, a farmer's daughter from the village of Dom-rémy. Joan's imagination is so vivid that her inspirations seem to come to her as visions in which the voices of the saints direct her to raise the siege of Orleans and crown the Dauphin at Rheims. By sheer force of personality and a ge-nius for leadership, the seventeen-year-old Joan does these things. Ignorant of the complexities of politics, Joan is un-willing to defer to the experience and advice of ordinary men. She oversteps herself and is tried by the Inquisition for heresy. Her trial is an eminently fair one by the standards of the age, but Joan condemns herself by insisting that the in-structions of her "voices" take precedence over the instruc-tions of the Church. Sentenced to be burned and fearing pain, she recants. When she finds that her recantation simply commutes her sentence to perpetual imprisonment, she reaf-firms her innocence and is burned. In an epilogue, Joan's ghost appears and learns that she has been canonized. Her allies and enemies alike bow down and worship her, but when Joan offers to bring herself to life again, they all demur and drift away. Joan wonders when Earth will be ready for God's saints.

The Dauphin (doh-FA[N]), later **Charles VII**. Although physically weak and bullied by everyone, he is intelligent and more refined than most nobles of his time. Once he is crowned, Charles tells Joan to be content with what she al-ready has won. He warns her that he cannot protect her if she continues her fight. After Joan is executed, Charles himself becomes a successful warrior.

The Inquisitor, **Brother John Lemaître** (leh-MEHTR), a Dominican monk. A mild, elderly, and highly intelligent man, he believes that Joan's heresy is the most heinous one of all: the Protestant heresy of believing that God speaks directly to an individual through one's conscience. Realizing that Joan is innocent of evildoing, he believes she must be sacrificed for the welfare of Christian society.

Peter Cauchon (koh-SHOH[N]), the bishop of Beauvais, the co-judge, with the Inquisitor, at Joan's trial. An honest believer in the grossness of Joan's heresy, the bishop wishes to save Joan's soul and, if possible, her life.

Richard de Beauchamp (boh-SHAH), the earl of Warwick, the English commandant. Warwick wants Joan put to death because she represents the new spirit of nationalism that threatens the power of his social class.

John de Stogumber (STAH-guhm-buhr), Warwick's chap-lain. A bigoted and fanatical English patriot, he howls for Joan's death at her trial. He is so horrified by her execution, however, that, half mad, he retires to a small country parish and becomes an exemplary priest.

Dunois, Bastard of Orleans (dew-NWAH), the rugged and pragmatic commander of the French forces. He admires Joan's military ability, but he abandons her when she ignores his advice.

Brother Martin Ladvenu (mahr-TA[N] lahd-veh-NEW), a young priest who takes pity on Joan at her trial and tries to persuade her to save herself.

The archbishop of Rheims (ram), a member of the Dau-phin's court. The archbishop, a rich and worldly administrator, is struck by Joan's saintliness. He tries to warn Joan of the dangerousness of her contempt for all authority.

Gilles de Rais (zheel deh ray), a flippant and cynical young courtier who affects a blue beard. He is contemptuous of Joan.

Captain la Hire (lah eer), a tough French soldier who becomes fanatically devoted to Joan.

Canon John d'Estivet (dehs-tee-VAY), the prosecutor at Joan's trial, so captious and vindictive that the Inquisitor must repeatedly censure him.

Canon de Courcelles (kewr-SEHL), a young priest who, with de Stogumber, draws up the indictment against Joan. He is stupid, petty, and contentious.

Robert de Baudricourt (boh-dree-KEWR), a loudmouthed but weak-willed French gentleman-at-arms. Against his better judgment, he provides Joan an escort to the Dauphin's court.

Bertrand de Poulengy (pewl-lehn-ZHEE), a knight under Baudricourt's command. Convinced of Joan's holiness, he es-corts her to see the Dauphin.

The executioner of Rouen (rew-AH[N]), who puts Joan to death.

An English soldier, who gives Joan a cross of twigs while she is at the stake. For this action, he is given each year one day's vacation from Hell.

A gentleman of 1920, an English priest who, in the epi-logue, announces Joan's elevation to sainthood.

SAINT MANUEL BUENO, MARTYR
(San Manuel Bueno, mártir)

Author: Miguel de Unamuno y Jugo (1864-1936)
First published: 1931
Genre: Novel

Locale: Valverde de Lucerna, Spain
Time: Late nineteenth and early twentieth centuries
Plot: Philosophical realism

Don Manuel (mahn-HWEHL), a Catholic priest in Valverde de Lucerna, a small village in Spain. A tall, slender, erect man in his middle years, he is wholly devoted to the service of his parishioners despite the fact that he has lost his ability to believe in life after death. His service takes many forms, all practical: helping children with schoolwork, promoting joyous social interaction, mediating quarrels, and caring for the poor, the sick, and the dying. His reputation as a healer and spiritual teacher spreads beyond the village, and people come to regard him as a living saint. Don Manuel carefully guards the secret of his loss of faith, not wanting to jeopardize the faith of his people. Only Angela and Lázaro Carballino are aware of the priest's private agony.

Angela Carballino (AHN-heh-lah kahr-bah-YEE-noh), an educated village woman who becomes a confidante of Don Manuel and narrates his story. Orphaned as a child, she has known Don Manuel since girlhood and has been aware that others regard him as a saint since her years at convent school. At Don Manuel's urging, she decides to make the village her convent rather than become a nun, sequestered from everyday life. Angela has collected numerous instances of Don Manuel's effective ministry to the villagers, his words of wisdom, and his acts of compassion. In revealing Don Manuel's lack of faith, Angela takes the risk of destroying his reputed sainthood; however, she does so in the belief that Don Manuel, by living a life of service to others without hope of an eternal reward, is even more worthy to be called a saint. Thus, her narrative becomes a brief in support of his canonization.

Lázaro Carballino (LAH-zah-roh), Angela's older brother, a freethinker. After a sojourn in America to make his fortune, Lázaro returns to Valverde de Lucerna, intending to move his family to a city to escape the intellectual suffocation of rural life. Blaming Don Manuel's influence for his mother's and sister's resistance to the move, he begins a campaign of anticlerical propaganda; however, the priest gradually wins him over, and in the process Lázaro guesses Don Manuel's secret. Like Angela, he comes to respect the priest's selfless efforts on behalf of the villagers, and he gives up all appearance of nonconformity. The support of the Carballinos measurably aids Don Manuel in carrying out his mission.

— *Marian Price*

SAINT MAYBE

Author: Anne Tyler (1941-   )
First published: 1991
Genre: Novel

Locale: Baltimore, Maryland
Time: The 1960's to the 1980's
Plot: Domestic realism

Ian Bedloe, the protagonist, the son of Bee and Doug Bedloe, optimistic parents of the ideal American family. Ian cannot reconcile life's reality with his family's rosy views. He tells his elder brother Danny that Danny's wife Lucy is being unfaithful and that "their" new baby is no more Danny's than are Lucy's other two children, by her first husband. When Danny dies in a car wreck immediately afterward, followed quickly by Lucy's death by an overdose of sleeping pills, Ian blames himself for Danny and Lucy's "suicides" and orphaning of three small children. Ian becomes the "Saint Maybe" of the novel's title, torn between his fear of making more mistakes and his human desires. He is a flawed hero who must come to terms with his own and others' humanity.

Lucy Dean Bedloe, Danny's wife and Ian's sister-in-law. A traditional American housewife, Lucy depends on men to support herself and her children. Impoverished in youth, when she developed the habit of shoplifting items she could not afford, undereducated, and untrained for work, Lucy marries early, is deserted, and divorces her immature husband, becoming totally responsible for the welfare of her two children. Drawing on her youthful energy and sexual attractiveness, Lucy wins the hand of Danny Bedloe in marriage. Initially, Ian secretly admires her. After Danny's sudden death, Lucy finds it difficult to locate work or attract another man to help take care of her new baby and two older children. The unfairness of Danny's death and the harsh reality of single parenthood overwhelm her. Lucy uses sleeping pills to keep reality at bay.

Agatha Bedloe, Lucy's oldest child. Agatha is a serious, unattractive girl who "mothers" her own frightened mother and younger siblings, taking on responsibilities far beyond her years. She becomes the antithesis of her mother as a dedicated California physician and career wife with no children of her own.

Thomas Bedloe, Lucy's second child, Agatha's loyal follower and family protector. He is a gregarious boy who becomes an inventor for a New York software company, engaged to a bossy woman like his sister Agatha.

Daphne Bedloe, Lucy's youngest child. She is carefree but scolds Ian for his tentative sainthood and worries with the others about Ian's happiness. Daphne follows in Ian's footsteps, remaining in Baltimore, living in her family home long past the ages when Thomas and Agatha left, staying single, and spurning college for nonprofessional jobs. Like Ian, Daphne searches for work that will not be too personal; she needs to keep human intimacy at one remove.

The Reverend Emmett, pastor of the Church of the Second Chance. The reverend tells Ian that he must atone for his sins to win God's forgiveness and advises him to drop out of college to take care of Danny and Lucy's children. Later, he suggests that Ian return to college in mid-life to become his assistant pastor.

Rita di Carlo, who becomes Ian's wife. Rita is the neighborhood "clutter counselor," a competent, decisive woman the Bedloes hire to help clean the house after Bee's death. Rita's youthful sensuality and resourcefulness spark Ian's interest; she seems both safe (she will not need to be taken care of) and unsafe (vibrant and sexual) at the same time. She surprises Ian into mid-life marriage and subsequent fatherhood.

— *Susan S. Kissel*

ST. PETER'S UMBRELLA
(Szent Péter Esernyöje)

Author: Kálmán Mikszáth (1847-1910)
First published: 1895
Genre: Novel

Locale: Hungary
Time: Second half of the nineteenth century
Plot: Comic realism

János Bélyi, a priest. He arrives, as a young man, in Glogova. His prospects for a pleasant life in the forlorn village are extremely remote until he comes into possession of a red umbrella, the miraculous powers of which change his fortunes from bad to good.

Veronica Bélyi, János Bélyi's sister, who is left, as an infant, on her brother's doorstep. When János returns from a walk in the rain, he finds her protected by a mysterious red umbrella that the townspeople decide is a gift from St. Peter. As a young woman, she falls in love with and marries Gyury Wibra, the heir of the red umbrella's real owner.

Pál Gregorics, a wealthy bachelor, the father of Gyury Wibra and original owner of the red umbrella. He is reputed to have carried secret documents in its handle. On his death, the umbrella is sold. It disappears until his son traces it to the home of János Bélyi.

Gyury (György) Wibra, Gregorics' illegitimate son. Embarrassed during his father's life by the red umbrella, he hears rumors after Gregorics' death that the umbrella is a repository of valuable documents. He sets out to find the umbrella and traces it to the home of János Bélyi, where he finally comes into possession not only of the treasured relic but of Veronica Bélyi as well.

Jónás Müncz, a Jewish merchant who buys the red umbrella after Gregorics' death and is seen placing it over the infant, Veronica Bélyi.

Frau Müncz, Jónás Müncz's wife.

Anna Wibra, Gregorics' housekeeper and mistress. She is the mother of Gyury Wibra.

The Widow Adamecz, János Bélyi's housekeeper.

János Sztolarik, Gregorics' lawyer.

ST. RONAN'S WELL

Author: Sir Walter Scott (1771-1832)
First published: 1823
Genre: Novel

Locale: Scotland
Time: Early nineteenth century
Plot: Social

Francis Tyrrel, a young Englishman posing as an artist. He is a half brother of the earl of Etherington. He returns to St. Ronan's in an effort to prove his legitimacy and the treachery of his illegitimate half brother. He succeeds, but too late for any happiness to come from the revelations.

The earl of Etherington, the illegitimate half brother of Francis Tyrrel and the usurper of his title. As a young man, he had treacherously substituted himself for Tyrrel and had married Clara Mowbray for the fortune that went with her hand. Forced to leave before the consummation of the marriage, he had vowed never to see her again, but he returns later, again disguised, to attempt to force another marriage. His betrayal is finally revealed, and he is killed by John Mowbray.

Clara Mowbray, the daughter of a Scottish laird. Because of a fortune that goes with her hand, she was coerced into a marriage with the earl of Etherington, who was forced to flee before the marriage was consummated. Later, he returns, disguised, hoping to force another marriage and acquire the fortune. His treachery is revealed too late for Clara, who, in an effort to escape, flees, wanders about distractedly, and finally dies.

John Mowbray, Clara Mowbray's brother, who attempts to force her marriage to the earl of Etherington, whom he later kills when he learns of the earl's treachery.

Mr. Touchwood, an elderly gentleman, the son of the man who left the estate coveted by the earl of Etherington. He is in possession of and reveals the proof of Francis Tyrrel's legitimacy.

Meg Dods, the proprietress of the inn at old St. Ronan's.

Lady Penelope Penfeather, a leader of society at St. Ronan's Well.

Captain Harry Jekyl, a friend and correspondent of the earl of Etherington.

The Reverend Josiah Cargill, a clergyman who knows the secret of Clara Mowbray's forced marriage to the earl of Etherington.

Hannah Irwin, Clara Mowbray's former maid and the ally of the earl of Etherington.

Solmes, the earl of Etherington's servant.

Sir Bingo Binks, a boorish young man who challenges Tyrrel to a duel.

Captain MacTurk, Sir Bingo's second.

ST. URBAIN'S HORSEMAN

Author: Mordecai Richler (1931-   )
First published: 1971
Genre: Novel

Locale: London and Montreal
Time: Late 1960's, with flashbacks
Plot: Impressionistic realism

Jacob (Jake) Hersh, a Canadian film and television director in his late thirties, living and working in London. He is

"modishly ugly" and obsessed with the deterioration of his body and an exaggerated fear of death and disease. He is happily married and has three children. His guilt, induced in large measure by a stereotypical "Jewish mother" and by his realization that, as a Canadian, he escaped the Holocaust and other miseries of World War II, causes him to become involved, against his better judgment, with Harry Stein. Guilt and the need for a hero motivate his fascination with his cousin, Joey, whom he imagines to be the Jewish avenger, St. Urbain's Horseman, named for the main street of the Jewish immigrant neighborhood in which Jake grew up. In London, Jake is often mistaken for Joey or asked to repay money that Joey has borrowed or stolen, including the life savings of Ruthy Flam, whom Joey had promised to marry. Pressured by Ruthy and her fiancé, Harry Stein, Jake settles Joey's debts and takes Joey's saddle and rifle, which he keeps in his attic studio. Jake returns from his father's funeral in Montreal to find Harry and a German girl he has picked up in a coffee bar using his home for an uninhibited sexual encounter. Incensed that they have used Joey's saddle as a prop and offended by the woman's nationality, Jake throws her out. Picked up by the police naked and obviously under the influence of drugs, the woman charges both Harry and Jake with rape. Jake is acquitted of all but the most minor of the charges and fined.

Joseph (Joey) Hersh, who is seen only through the memories and stories of other characters. He is the handsome, daring black sheep of the Hersh family. He is admired by the younger family members for his looks, his varied career as a professional baseball player and a movie extra, and his success with women, but he is feared and mistrusted by the more conventional, older Hershes. There is much evidence that Joey is a con man and a thief, but his mother, Hanna, and cousin Jake continue to believe that he is a hero on the trail of escaped Nazis. At the novel's end, word reaches Jake that Joey has died in a plane crash in Paraguay while smuggling cigarettes, but Jake recalls that Paraguay is the reputed hideout of Dr. Joseph Mengele, a notorious war criminal.

Harry Stein, an accountant in the offices of Oscar Hoffman, who specializes in show business accounts. Harry is small in stature and unattractive, with thin, dry hair, splotchy skin, and bad teeth. He is hostile, jealous, and resentful, blaming his lack of success in business and personal relations on a social system that discriminates against the poor. He is ob-

sessed with sex but unable to establish a relationship. He spends his time with pornographic books and in sexually explicit "photo studies," where he photographs live models. Harry has been in trouble with the law for attempted extortion and attempted murder, both crimes motivated by his resentment of more fortunate people. Harry uses his inside information about Jake's finances and Jake's guilt about Joey's mistreatment of Ruthy to force himself into Jake's life, finally involving him in the trial for rape that is the central crisis of the novel. Harry's only legitimate accomplishment is his membership in Mensa, an organization for the intellectually gifted. He challenges Jake to take the test for admission to the group, and Jake's sense of insecurity is enhanced when he fails.

Luke Scott, a playwright, fashionably slender and handsome. He is the son of a Canadian senator. He and Jake left Canada together to seek success in London. Luke is more successful than Jake both commercially and artistically. Although the two remain close friends and Luke is especially supportive during Jake's trial, the unspoken rivalry between the two forms an important subplot in the novel.

Ruth (Ruthy) Flam, a plump woman in her forties who works in a dress shop to support her children after being deserted by their father. She is a natural victim, seduced and abandoned by Joey and used by Harry to get money from Jake. She enters contests compulsively, and Jake guiltily buys products that he cannot use so that he can give her the labels to use in contest entries. After Harry is sentenced to jail for rape, she finds a new and equally unsatisfactory man.

Nancy Croft Hersh, Jake's beautiful, dark-haired, longlegged wife. Her upper-middle-class Protestant background intrigues Jake but also adds to his sense of insecurity, as do the innocent attentions of his friend Luke Scott. Jake's father broke off all contact with his son because of his marriage to a non-Jew, adding to Jake's sense of guilt.

Duddy Kravitz, another St. Urbain's Street boy, a crude, self-made millionaire with a shrewd understanding of human nature and a generous heart. He appears at important moments to give Jake confidence. His freely given check for $10,000 to tide Jake over after the trial inspires Jake to take up his life again.

— *Katherine Keller*

ŚAKUNTALĀ
(Abhijñānaśākuntala)

Author: Kālidāsa (c. 100 B.C.E. or 340 C.E.-c. 40 B.C.E. or 400 C.E.)
First performed: c. 45 B.C.E. or c. 395 C.E.
Genre: Drama

Locale: India
Time: The Golden Age of India
Plot: Love

Dushyanta, the king of India and hero of this poetic drama. Falling in love at first sight with Śakuntalā, he persuades her to marry him secretly. In fulfillment of a curse, he forgets about her thereafter until a ring he gave her is shown to him. Reunited first in heaven and then returned to Earth, they live happily for many years.

Śakuntalā, the daughter of a Brahman and a water nymph. She returns the king's love and marries him but remains in her sacred grove after his departure to await her foster father's

return. After her husband fails to recognize her, she is taken away to heaven by a strange winged being. She gives birth to a son before she and her husband are reunited.

Kanwa, a wise hermit and Śakuntalā's foster father. Having the gift of omniscience, he knows all about the secret wedding. Informed by a supernatural voice that Śakuntalā's son is destined to rule the world, he blesses the union and sends Śakuntalā off to her husband. Her premonitions of evil prove true when Dushyanta fails to recognize her.

Mathavya, the king's jester. To be near Śakuntalā, the king breaks off his hunting, pretending that his motive is to humor a wish of Mathavya.

Bharata, the son of Śakuntalā and Dushyanta. Carried to

heaven for a reunion with his wife, Dushyanta finds a young boy playing with a lion. The boy proves to be his son, who accompanies him and Śakuntalā back to Earth.

SALAMMBÔ

Author: Gustave Flaubert (1821-1880)
First published: 1862
Genre: Novel

Locale: Carthage
Time: The third century B.C.E.
Plot: Historical

Hamilcar (ah-meel-KAHR), the suffete of third century Carthage. A great feast is given, in his absence, for his thousands of mercenaries. He arrives home to find them in rebellion, and after several reversals, he conquers and destroys them.

Salammbô (sah-lahm-BOH), the daughter of Hamilcar and the priestess of the Carthaginian moon goddess, Tanit. She utters a curse on the angry barbarians who, after their defeat by the Romans and the delay with their back pay, begin pillaging the palace of Hamilcar. When Mathô later invades the sacred temple, she screams for help, though she is attracted to him. To regain the sacred veil of Tanit, which he has stolen, she goes in disguise to his tent and submits to him. The broken chastity chain between her ankles betrays her to her father, who angrily offers her to Narr' Havas. At the wedding, she contrasts drunken Narr' Havas with gentle Mathô, who is tortured by the Carthaginians. She drinks a cup of poison and dies with Mathô.

Narr' Havas (nahr ah-VAHS), a Numidian chief sent by his father to learn warfare under Hamilcar. He falls in love with Salammbô after she appears on the palace balcony. He deserts the rebellious barbarians to help Hamilcar and is promised marriage with Salammbô after Hamilcar finally defeats the mercenaries.

Mathô, a gigantic Libyan chief of mercenaries, also in love with Salammbô. Following the payment by the Council of

Elders of a gold piece to each soldier, he leads his followers out of Carthage to Sicca to await the return of Hamilcar. Guided by Spendius, he then returns to Carthage and sacrilegiously goes into the Temple of Tanit, to Salammbô's sleeping quarters. Although he is discovered, none dares hinder his escape because he wears the sacred veil. He is finally captured by Hamilcar's army, tortured and lacerated, and taken to the nuptial dais of Salammbô, who joins him in death by drinking poison.

Hanno (ah-NOH), a fat, suppurating member of the Council of Elders who appears in Sicca in his costly litter and, in unintelligible Punic, tries to persuade the barbarians to go home and there await their back pay. He is almost killed by the soldiers, who are aroused by Spendius as he falsely translates Hanno's words.

Spendius (spah[n]-DYEWS), a former Greek slave who is now shrewdly and craftily serving Mathô. Because Spendius has lived for many years in Carthage, he is able to tell his master of the delightful possibilities of Salammbô. He stirs up the mercenaries with a false translation of Hanno's speech, and they accept him as a chief; he then leads them toward Carthage. He guides Mathô into the city through the aqueduct to the Temple of Tanit, the goddess in whom the Carthaginians put their trust.

Gisco (zhees-KOH), a famous warrior sent by Carthage to turn back the barbarians at the gate of the city.

SALAR THE SALMON

Author: Henry Williamson (1895-1977)
First published: 1935
Genre: Novel

Locale: The English coast and rivers in the West Country
Time: The 1930's
Plot: Pastoral

Salar the Salmon, whose name means "the Leaper," a five-year-old salmon in his prime. For two years, he had been a smolt, living in the river of his birth. For three years after that, he lived in the ocean, feeding on its richer food and growing in strength as a grilse. At the start of the novel, he is about to obey the salmon's instinct to return from the sea to spawn in the river where he was born, after which, exhausted, he will die. Salar faces many dangers in the course of his journey to the river's headwaters: seals, porpoises, conger eels, and killer whales in the sea; men's hooks and lines in the river; and otters and poison algae. His greatest obstacle, however, is the weirs that people have built. He must leap up them against the current. Salar surmounts all these difficulties and succeeds in fertilizing the eggs of the grilse Gralaks. Humans would call his behavior instinctive and therefore devoid of individual character, but the reader comes to admire the unfailing courage

and drive of the fish, beautifully expressed in the salmon leaps that give him his name. The world he lives in, however, is presented remorselessly as one of continuous savage conflict, in which few live to breed and species prey on one another just as much as they are preyed on by other species and by humans.

Shiner, a poacher, the only named person in the book. As with the fish, humans live in a state of constant conflict with one another. The lower-class fishermen are preyed on by the water-bailiffs, who allege that their job is to conserve fish stocks but who are seen by the netters as class enemies, dedicated only to preserving salmon so that they can be taken on rod and line by rich sport fishermen. Shiner is opposed to netters, anglers, and bailiffs alike, and he seems driven by a reverence for life that makes him immobilize a poaching gang's car and at one point open a vital sluice to give Salar the chance to swim upstream. He takes fish in the same way the animals do: one at a time, without sport or ritual, and only for his own needs.

Petromyzon, a lamprey, one of Salar's potentially deadliest enemies. His hunting mode is to clamp onto a fish and then slowly drain it of blood like a giant leech. Salar is saved from his attack only by the intervention of the even more repulsive Myxine, or sea-hag, a creature that clamps onto Petromyzon in his turn and sucks at him from inside. The two creatures present a dramatic allegory of the constant struggle for survival.

Trutta, a great spotted pug-trout who accompanies Salar on his journey, with the same intention of spawning. Trutta, like all trout, is a cannibal who eats his own kind, but he shows a kind of loyalty in his dogged following of the larger salmon. At the end, Trutta harasses hunting otters as they try to catch the weakened Salar. He is trapped and killed by the otters.

Gralaks, a female grilse salmon who functions in the novel as an image of young beauty. She is the counterpart of Salar in her urge to lay her eggs in the headwater of her birth, to be fertilized indiscriminately by the milt of Salar or other salmon, or eaten by cannibal fishes. Gralaks shows that if there is no love in this animal world, there is nevertheless desire and yearning.

— *T. A. Shippey*

SALLY HEMINGS

Author: Barbara Chase-Riboud (1939-   )
First published: 1979
Genre: Novel

Locale: Albemarle County, Virginia, and Paris, France
Time: 1787-1835
Plot: Historical realism

Sally Hemings, the protagonist, based on a female slave owned by Thomas Jefferson. She is characterized as Jefferson's mistress and mother of seven children by him. Sally grows up at Monticello, the daughter of the slave Elizabeth Hemings and John Wayles, Jefferson's father-in-law; she is thus the half sister of Martha Wayles Jefferson, who dies at the age of thirty-four. When she is fourteen years old, Sally is sent to France as servant and companion to her niece, Jefferson's daughter Maria (Polly). For love of Thomas Jefferson, she resists her brother James's urging to remain in France, where she is legally free, and returns, pregnant, to Monticello as Jefferson's unacknowledged "wife." Although Jefferson frees her sons, Sally herself is not freed until after his death, by his daughter Martha Jefferson Randolph (Patsy). Once free, she is permitted to remain in Virginia only by a special dispensation of the state legislature.

Thomas Jefferson, who is based on the historical author of the Declaration of Independence, ambassador to France, and third president of the United States. Jefferson, having promised his dying wife that he would not remarry, retains possession of her image in her half sister Sally, who is doubly bound to him by slavery and love. When published allegations about his relationship with Sally create a scandal, the Jefferson family denies the charges, but Jefferson himself remains silent, and his political stance on slavery is fraught with ambivalence.

Nathan Langdon, a fictional character, a white Southern lawyer educated in the North. While working as census taker in Albemarle County in 1830, he becomes fascinated by Sally and records her and her sons in the census as white. That action is recorded in actual history.

James Hemings, Sally's older brother, based on the historical son of John Wayles and Elizabeth Hemings. James accompanies Jefferson to France and becomes a master chef. James is determined to be free but equally determined that Jefferson should take the responsibility of freeing him. He returns, like Sally, to Monticello. James's recurring nightmare of retribution for his sister's concubinage haunts him for the rest of his life. Eventually freed by Jefferson, James has a complex love-hate relationship with his former master. His ambivalent feelings about his family prevent his attaining a satisfactory independent identity.

Elizabeth Hemings, a historical character, the slave mother of twelve children, including James, Sally, and three others by John Wayles. She was sent with her children to Monticello when Martha Wayles married Thomas Jefferson; she was part of Martha Wayles's dowry. She insists that her children be addressed by their own family name, Hemings. Working as best she can to secure their freedom, she advises her daughters, "don't love no masta if he don't promise in writing to free your children." Having chosen Sally to accompany Polly to France, she is angry when Sally returns to slavery.

Martha Jefferson Randolph, called Patsy, who is based on the historical daughter of Thomas Jefferson and Martha Wayles. She wages a lifelong battle with Sally for the love of her father and role of mistress of Monticello, with combined feelings of affection and jealous arrogance. Tall, red-haired, and freckled, she is trapped in an unhappy marriage to an alcoholic. Martha carries out her father's unwritten request to free Sally after his death, though the rest of the slave family, along with Monticello itself, are auctioned off to pay Jefferson's debts.

— *Carol E. Schmudde*

THE SALT EATERS

Author: Toni Cade Bambara (1939-1995)
First published: 1980
Genre: Novel

Locale: Claybourne, Georgia
Time: The 1970's
Plot: Fable

Velma Henry, a committed civil rights activist and the center of the activist work in her community. When she is

away from the Academy of the Seven Arts, a school run by her husband, he reflects that it takes seven people to replace

Velma. She is also the talented pianist for The Seven Sisters, a performing arts group, and keeps the group's political and spiritual factions from splitting to pieces. She becomes "uncentered" and falls to pieces herself, however, culminating in a failed suicide attempt.

Minnie Ransom, a community healer, Earth Mother, and vehicle for spiritual forces. Minnie fought the acceptance of her spiritual gift when she was young, as Velma, who has a similar gift, does now. Minnie ate dirt and was called "batty, fixed, possessed, crossed," but she has come to accept her spiritual powers and use them to heal others.

James "Obie" Henry, Velma's husband, the head of the Academy of the Seven Arts and The Brotherhood. Frightened by the change in Velma, he has been unfaithful to her. Now he misses her in his life and in his work. He feels that he is losing control of his groups and of himself.

Sophie Heywood, also called **M'Dear**, Velma's godmother. Despairing of Velma being healed, she thinks of her

dead husband, Daddy Dolphy, and her son Smitty, left paraplegic from an injury in a civil rights protest. She tries to become the medium through which Velma recenters herself in African goddess traditions.

Fred Holt, a bus driver who takes The Seven Sisters to Claybourne for the festival and waits to take visiting medical people back to the city. He thinks of his dead friend, Porter; he also thinks about his first wife, Wanda, who left him because of her involvement with the Black Muslims, and of his present white wife, who does not understand him. On the way to Claybourne, he thinks about driving the bus off the road into the swamp ooze so that he can see Porter again.

B. Talifero "Doc" Serge, the owner of the Southwest Community Infirmary. He has had many occupations, including those of pimp and numbers man.

— *Katherine G. Lederer*

SAMSON AGONISTES

Author: John Milton (1608-1674)
First published: 1671
Genre: Drama

Locale: Palestine
Time: c. 1100 B.C.E.
Plot: Tragedy

Samson, the great Hebrew champion, who has been blinded and imprisoned by the Philistines. When the Chorus first greets him, he is deeply depressed, for he feels that he has betrayed God and himself by his own weakness. His successful resistance of Dalila's temptations and his defiance of Harapha's taunts restore his sense that he has a mission to perform. He goes to the Philistines' feast in honor of their god, Dagon, with strong consciousness that he will find there a task to do in God's service, and he "quit[s] himself like Samson" by pulling the hall down on the heads of his enemies and himself.

Manoa, Samson's kind old father. He seeks to ransom his son and offers to devote the rest of his life to caring for him. Although he mourns Samson's death, he rejoices at the grandeur and heroism of his end.

Dalila (dah-LI-lah), Samson's treacherous Philistine wife. She cajoles her husband, avows her repentance, and tries to excuse her betrayal of him by pleading her duty to her country, as a means of winning him back. Realizing that he will not fall prey to her hypocrisy, she departs in anger, consoling herself with the thought that she will be regarded as a heroine by her own countrymen.

Harapha, a boastful Philistine warrior. He insults Samson and challenges him to defend his God against Dagon, when he believes his enemy to be weak. He exits quickly when he realizes that Samson has recovered his strength and his willingness to fight.

A Chorus of Hebrew elders, a group of old men who sympathize with Samson and comment on the action as it takes place.

THE SAMURAI
(Samurai)

Author: Shūsaku Endō (1923-1996)
First published: 1980
Genre: Novel

Locale: Japan, New Spain, Spain, and Italy
Time: 1612-1624
Plot: Historical realism

Rokuemon Hasekura (roh-KEW-eh-mon), a rural samurai (military knight) with the rank of lance-corporal (*yari-gochō*) in His Lordship's gun corps. He is the master of the family fief in the marshland of northeastern Japan, a feudal vassal of the most powerful *daimyō* (feudal nobleman) of the region. A short, well-built man in his early thirties, he has sunken eyes, high cheekbones, a flat nose, and long black hair tied up with white ribbon. Unprepossessing in appearance, he seems more a peasant than a samurai. Although he is a man of feeling, he never allows his face to register his emotions. Politically naïve, he is a simple man of few words and trusts his feudal superiors implicitly, granting them unquestioning obedience. Appointed

by His Lordship to serve as an envoy to the Spanish viceroy of Nueva España (New Spain, modern Mexico), he functions as a heroic but gullible scapegoat, or "holy fool," in the game of national politics. A confirmed Buddhist, he becomes an insincere Christian.

Lord Ishida, Hasekura's immediate feudal superior and patron, a plump, dignified nobleman given to smiling.

His Lordship, **Masamune Date** (DAH-teh), the *daimyō* ruling the region in which Ishida and Hasekura live.

Padre Vrais Luis Velasco (VRAH-ees lew-EES veh-LAHS-koh), a Spanish Catholic priest from Seville and provincial of the Franciscan order of missionaries at Edo (modern Tokyo).

He is also an interpreter for and an adviser to the Japanese government. Ambitious (he wants to be bishop of Japan), vainglorious, arrogant, condescending, scheming, deceitful, and basically unprincipled, he is a religious fanatic who is ruled by an intense passion, one that is often lustful. He rules and manipulates—by concealment and deceit—the four samurai envoys on their mission to Nueva España.

The Naifu, a Chinese title assumed by **Ieyasu Tokugawa** (eeih-YAH-sew toh-kew-GAH-wah), the first Tokugawa *shōgun*, after naming his third son, Hidetada (hee-deh-TAH-dah), the second *shōgun*, thus remaining the real ruler of Japan.

Lord Shiraishi, the houseman of His Lordship.

Yozō, Hasekura's faithful servant and companion, several years older than he, who becomes a sincere Christian convert.

Nishi Kyūsuke, the youngest samurai among the four envoys. Boyish, high-spirited, and unreserved, he is curious about anything "new" and eager to learn about it.

Tanaka Tarozaemon, the oldest of the envoys. His body is plump. Stubborn and inclined to anger when frustrated, he seeks always to maintain the dignity appropriate for a samurai.

Matsuke Chūsaku, a pale, gloomy samurai of slender build and grave and thoughtful expression. He is of quick intelligence and acute perception, with political savvy, but is always skeptical and cynical. He is contemptuous of his role as an envoy and returns to Japan rather than journeying to Europe with the others.

The man in Tecali, a Japanese Christian convert and former monk. Disenchanted with Catholic clerics and the church, he lives among the Indians in Nueva España and follows a Jesus of his own making.

— *Richard P. Benton*

SANCTUARY

Author: William Faulkner (1897-1962)
First published: 1931
Genre: Novel

Locale: Mississippi and Memphis, Tennessee
Time: 1929
Plot: Melodrama

Popeye, a cruel, passionless killer who is symbolic of the ruthless, sterile, and materialistic exploitation that destroyed the antebellum social order of the South. Ironically, he is executed for a murder he did not commit.

Temple Drake, a college girl of good family who is attacked by Popeye and then sent to live the life of a prostitute in a bawdy house in Memphis. Her family removes her from the house of ill repute, but her life has been ruined.

Lee Goodwin, a moonshiner who tries to protect Temple from a group of bootleggers and who is accused of murdering Tommy, a gang member actually shot by Popeye. He is convicted, but before he can be sentenced, he is burned to death by a mob that storms the jail to take him.

Gowan Stevens, a college student whose irresponsible conduct causes Temple to become Popeye's victim.

Ruby Lamar, Goodwin's common-law wife, who helps the officers locate Temple in Memphis.

Horace Benbow, a lawyer who defends Goodwin and who is symbolic of the early Southern historical tradition.

Tommy, a bootlegger whom Popeye kills, and of whose death Goodwin is accused.

Miss Reba Rivers, the madam of the Memphis bawdy house.

Red, a young customer of Temple who is killed by Popeye's gang because Temple hopes to escape from Popeye and run away with Red.

Judge Drake, Temple's father, a wealthy, old-fashioned Southerner.

Senator Clarence Snopes, a corrupt Southern politician.

Van, a moonshiner who fights with Goodwin over Temple.

SAND MOUNTAIN

Author: Romulus Linney (1930-   )
First published: 1985
Genre: Drama

Locale: The southern Appalachian Mountains
Time: Late nineteenth century
Plot: Fantasy

Sand Mountain Matchmaking

Rebecca Tull, an attractive widow in her early twenties. Her first marriage was not very successful, though she did not wish for her husband to die. Other inhabitants of Sand Mountain, including her father (who is a preacher) and her mother, believe that it is her duty to remarry quickly so that she does not provide too much temptation for the men of the area. Rebecca, however, is too particular to settle for what she has mercifully escaped. Rebecca seeks some sort of equality and respect in her ideal partner, characteristics that are not abundant in the men of Sand Mountain. She has her own wealth; she does not need to marry for any reason except to please herself.

Clink Williams, Rebecca's first suitor. Clink Williams is a young man about Rebecca's age. He views any future relationship with Rebecca on a purely physical plane. He sees himself as the man to fill Rebecca's physical needs; he is very conceited and arrogant—though arrogance is a quality shared equally with his first two rivals. His cocksureness does not endear him to Rebecca. Despite his emphasis on sex, he is offended when Rebecca says Lottie's charm ("A man's horn is times three the size of his nose") to him; hypocrite that he is, he says that she is now not "delicate" enough for him.

Slate Foley, Rebecca's second suitor, a man in his forties. He also sees any partnership with Rebecca in physical terms.

More insidious, however, is his stated determination to break her spirit. He is as arrogant as Clink Williams and also cruel. His reaction to Lottie's charm is to take offense and leave because he thinks that Rebecca is making fun of him.

Radley Nollins, Rebecca's third suitor. He presents a different face from the previous suitors, that of a God-fearing, Bible-quoting, respectful man. His respect, however, is more for the Bible than for any person. When Rebecca uses Lottie's charm on Radley, he is offended because her words do not come from the Bible.

Lottie Stiles, an old woman who serves as a sort of medicine woman on Sand Mountain. Lottie knows a cure for anything, and she uses all the plants and animals on Sand Mountain to effect her cures. Lottie understands why Rebecca is not interested in any of her suitors and gives her a spoken charm to get rid of the unwanted suitors and to find the right husband for herself.

Vester Stiles, Lottie's grandson, a young boy. He does not have much to say in the play, but his words reveal an early wisdom.

Sam Bean, Rebecca's final suitor, a man in his thirties. Sam Bean is the successful suitor because he is honest with Rebecca. He does not make impossible promises but seems to say that if they both put in the effort, they could have a successful marriage. He comes because he hears about what Rebecca has been saying to her other suitors; rather than being driven away by the words, he is attracted by them. It is her boldness that intrigues him, instead of scaring him as it did the other men.

Why the Lord Came to Sand Mountain

The Sang Picker, a mountain woman who picks ginseng to make her living. When the Lord stops to ask directions, the Sang Picker is elusive in her answers, but he does not seem to mind. Her key to a long and happy life is to "chew Gen Sang" and "ponder Bible Tales." The Sang Picker has had three husbands, all of whom are dead by the time of the play. The Sang Picker is the narrator of this part of the play.

The Lord, a mountain traveler. He is dressed like an "outlander" but with a mountain hat and a kerchief as well as a small pack on his back. The Lord has come to Sand Mountain for a specific reason, as unfolds in the play, so he does not let Saint Peter deflect him from going up to the top of Sand Mountain. The Lord does not look like a miraculous figure, though people sometimes see halos on him and on Saint Peter. He carries a long stick, which he uses to keep the fire going in Jack and Jean's cabin.

Saint Peter, the Lord's friend and traveling companion. He does not see the goodness in the simple Appalachian mountain people and instead wishes to spend his night with the more prosperous people, who can offer good food and comfortable lodgings. Saint Peter realizes that he is the butt of the play, but the Lord shows his love for Peter.

Prosper Valley Farmer, a well-to-do man who lives in the valley below Sand Mountain. A large, stout, and greedy man, he tries to get the Lord and Saint Peter to come stay with him. When he sees what the Lord has blessed Jack and Jean with, he mindlessly demands equal treatment. His greed then ruins his plans.

Jack, an old drunken man. He lives in a squalid cabin on top of Sand Mountain with his common-law wife and their fourteen children. He is a sage man whose life has gone wrong through outside events such as the cow dying. He and the Lord take a liking to each other as they tell tall tales.

Jean, the thin, pale, drunken wife of Jack. Though poor, she and her husband do their best to make the Lord and Saint Peter welcome. Jean seems to understand why the Lord has come, and she and her husband help him by telling the one "Jesus Tale" that the Lord needs to hear.

Fourteen children, Jack and Jean's children, played by one actor. They are a fractious group, constantly squabbling with one another, until the Lord quiets them by telling a story and making the fire so warm that it puts them to sleep. They wake up after a while, though, and help Jack and Jean tell "Joseph the Carpenter," the story the Lord has come to hear.

— *T. M. Lipman*

THE SANDCASTLE

Author: Iris Murdoch (1919-   )
First published: 1957
Genre: Novel

Locale: England's Surrey and Dorset counties, and London
Time: Mid-1950's
Plot: Philosophical

William Mor, a teacher and housemaster at St. Bride's. He is the husband of Nan, father of Felicity and Donald, and friend of Demoyte and Tim Burke. William is submissive to his wife, estranged from his son and daughter, and at a standstill in his work. As an agnostic, he is unable to succeed Demoyte as headmaster. He wishes to enter politics, but Nan opposes this. William falls in love with Rain Carter. Nan discovers the affair, but William decides to leave her and writes to tell her so. When his son disappears, he postpones his departure and loses Rain. William believes that goodness cannot exist where there is tyranny but that freedom is not an end in itself. His story, his indecisiveness, his loss of love, and his adherence to duty illustrate this statement. The Mor family members are together at the end of the novel, and William, Felicity, and Donald are all embarking on work that they wish to do.

Nan Mor, the wife of William and mother of Felicity and Donald, a determined, complacent, limited, and limiting woman. Nan lacks the imagination to see any point of view but her own and systematically defeats her husband's desires. Shaken by the prospect of losing him, genuinely concerned about her son, and jealous of Rain Carter, Nan breaks up William and Rain's relationship by stating, falsely, that she and William have jointly agreed that he will stand in a safe Labour seat next election. The events leave her with her family intact but committed to her husband's new career and with her attitude somewhat changed.

Rain Carter, a young and attractive woman hired to paint

Demoyte's retirement portrait. Rain falls in love with William, but his children discover their meetings. When William's wife hears of the affair, she returns home unexpectedly from Dorset and discovers her husband and Rain together. Although William finds his hidden glimpse of Rain's professional life attractive, she believes that he has too much to leave. This is confirmed when, at the dinner to celebrate the portrait's completion, Nan reveals William's political plans, of which Rain knew nothing. Deeply hurt but unselfish, she decides to return alone to France and her career.

Demoyte, the former headmaster, a lover of oriental rugs and rare books. He is a tyrannical but generous old man. He is attracted by Rain, the enemy of Nan, and a friend of William. Demoyte is on the side of possibility: He encourages William's love for Rain, offers to pay for Felicity's education, and encourages William in a political career.

Felicity Mor, William and Nan's daughter, a believer in witchcraft. She is a secretive, difficult girl, devoted to her brother and eager to keep the family together. Her mother thinks that she should be a secretary. Felicity decides that she will attend a university. Through Felicity, Nan learns of William's love for Rain.

Donald Mor, William and Nan's son, who is less than successful as a scholar. His father intends for him to go to a university. After a forbidden climbing attempt on the school tower, Donald hides out until the entrance examinations are over. He then takes refuge with Tim Burke and decides to become a jeweler. Donald's disappearance leads William to delay, crucially, his leaving Nan.

Tim Burke, an Irish jeweler who is a Labour Party official, friend of William, and admirer of Nan.

Bledyard, the art master at St. Bride's, a Christian who is critical of Rain's work and of William's conduct. Bledyard is a comic figure, but his views are to be taken seriously.

— *Jocelyn Creigh Cass*

SANINE
(Sanin)

Author: Mikhail Artsybashev (1878-1927)
First published: 1907
Genre: Novel

Locale: Russia
Time: 1906
Plot: Philosophical

Vladimir Petrovitch Sanine (vlah-DIH-mihr peh-TROH-vihch SAH-nihn), a young man who believes only in himself. Following his inclinations wherever they take him and claiming the same freedom for others, he influences several people to take actions with tragic consequences, for which he refuses to accept any moral responsibility. Finally, at Yourii Svarogitsch's funeral, he horrifies the townspeople with his insensitivity and hardness of heart. Soon afterward, he leaves the town on a train, from which he jumps to his death.

Lidia (Lida) Petrovna (peh-TROHV-nah), Sanine's sister. Although fearful of her brother's ideas, she is nevertheless attracted to them and, under their influence, gives herself to Captain Sarudine. Expecting her lover's child, she learns that he is through with her. She attempts suicide, from which she is dissuaded by Sanine, who urges her to live and to marry Dr. Novikoff.

Maria Ivanovna (ee-VAH-nohv-nah), Sanine's mother.

Captain Sarudine (sah-REW-din), an insensitive, lascivious officer who seduces Lida Petrovna with no opposition from her free-thinking brother Sanine. When he is ordered from the house by Sanine, he challenges the young man to a duel, but his challenge is refused. Later, when he is knocked down on the street by Sanine, the additional blow to his pride and honor is so great that he hangs himself.

Dr. Novikoff (NOH-vih-kov), Lida Petrovna's sincere but awkward suitor.

Sina Karsavina (SIH-nah kahr-SAH-vih-nah), a young schoolteacher who is in love with Yourii Svarogitsch but is strangely attracted to Sanine, to whom she briefly gives herself. She immediately regrets her surrender.

Yourii Nicolaijevitsch Svarogitsch (YEW-ree nih-koh-LAH-yeh-vihch svah-ROH-gihch), a young student in love with Sina Karsavina. Although his need for her is great, the problems with which marriage confront him are so much greater that he takes his own life.

Soloveitchik (soh-loh-VAY-chihk), a Jewish friend of Sanine. He takes his own life.

SAPPHIRA AND THE SLAVE GIRL

Author: Willa Cather (1873-1947)
First published: 1940
Genre: Novel

Locale: Southwestern Virginia
Time: 1856 to c. 1881
Plot: Historical realism

Sapphira Colbert, a slave owner and mistress of Mill House, Back Creek, Virginia. An invalid now confined to a wheelchair, Sapphira is still the mistress of her home. Her cultivated and seemingly placid outward self-esteem masks cruelty and selfishness. Although she holds great affection for some of the slaves, she maintains the right to control their lives regardless of the consequences. Suspicious of the growing but innocent affection between her husband and Nancy, she tries to sell Nancy. When Henry blocks that attempt, she seeks another way to rid herself of Nancy. She invites Henry's nephew, Martin, a known rake, for a visit. Martin's blatant attempts to seduce Nancy, combined with Sapphira's obvious displeasure with the slave girl, compromise Nancy's position in the household and her relationship with the other slaves. Sapphira's long-strained relationship with her daughter, Rachel, is further damaged when Rachel aids Nancy in fleeing to Canada. Although Sapphira often displays uncompromising cruelty, she is also capable of unexpected, solicitous concern for others. When Rachel's daughter dies of diphtheria, Sapphira's love for her daughter and grief over the child's death overcome her feelings of betrayal, and she welcomes Rachel back to Mill House.

Henry Colbert, the miller of Back Creek, Virginia, and Sapphira's husband. Henry is a solid, powerful man whose quiet yet unquestionably fair nature allows him to be trusted, but not liked, by the community. Troubled by slavery, he cannot find a way to resolve his own feelings with his wife's ownership and treatment of slaves. Honest affection for Nancy, which is misinterpreted by Sapphira, is tested by Martin's lecherous pursuit of the girl. Warned by the slave Sampson that Nancy is in grave danger, Henry does little to dissuade Martin. Not until Rachel forces the issue and asks for money does he actually take any stand; then his help is only a feeble gesture. Although he agrees to leave the money in an overcoat, he refuses to have anything more to do with the situation. His guilt at betraying his wife is his greatest concern.

Nancy, a mulatto slave owned by the Colberts. Good manners and pleasing ways instilled by her mother once garnered her much favor with Sapphira. Nancy's honest affection for Henry, which he returns, and her eagerness to please him raise Sapphira's suspicions, which are confirmed in her mind when Henry refuses to allow her to sell Nancy. Sapphira's mistreatment of Nancy and Martin's lecherous and relentless pursuit make Nancy's position in the household precarious. With Ra-

chel's help, Nancy flees for Canada with the assistance of the Underground Railroad. She returns twenty-five years later as a handsome, successful, and free woman.

Rachel Blake, the daughter of the Colberts and an abolitionist. Her views against slavery, formed at an early age, serve to make her reserved and introverted in the wake of her mother's ownership of slaves. At the age of sixteen, she marries Michael Blake, whose election to Congress rescues her from her family and life in Back Creek. The happiest time of her life is spent in Washington making a home for her husband. The deaths of Michael and their son Robert leave her with little money and force her to move back to Virginia. Taking up a new life in Back Creek, she provides what healing and support she can for the poor people of the area. Her opposition to slavery comes to a head with Martin Colbert's attempted seduction of Nancy. When Nancy appeals for her assistance, Rachel helps Nancy flee to Canada, thus incurring her mother's wrath. Rachel is secure with the righteousness of her conviction and her subsequent action to save Nancy.

Martin Colbert, Henry's nephew, a miscreant seeking to hide from his creditors. He accepts Sapphira's invitation for a long visit. His air of impudence and insolence amuses Sapphira and livens up the Colbert household but leaves his uncle speechless. Nancy's fresh prettiness catches his eye, and he unknowingly falls into Sapphira's plan to ruin Nancy. His lecherous attempts to compromise her catch the eye of Sampson, another slave, who appeals to Henry for help. Although he helps Nancy to leave, the master does nothing to discourage Martin. Twenty-five years later, at Nancy's return, it is revealed that Martin was killed in the army during the Civil War.

— *Geraldine L. Hutchins*

SAPPHO
(Sapho)

Author: Alphonse Daudet (1840-1897)
First published: 1884
Genre: Novel

Locale: Paris, France
Time: The nineteenth century
Plot: Naturalism

Fanny Legrand (leh-GRAH[N]), an intelligent, shrewd, and completely feminine prostitute. She is fifty years old and has been mistress to many men of various occupations and professions. She ends her days with one of her first lovers and their child.

Jean Gaussin (zhah[n] goh-SA[N]), a student from the south of France who has come to Paris to prepare himself for a diplomatic career. He meets the experienced courtesan Fanny Legrand and, attracted by her sophistication, falls in love with her despite the great difference in their ages. After they have lived together for a time, Fanny's hold on Jean is so strong that his naïve fiancée has little attraction for him. When he is awarded a post in South America, he breaks his engagement and begs Fanny to go with him. Unwilling to leave Paris, she declines his offer.

Déchelette (daysh-LEHT), a wealthy engineer who spends most of his time on construction projects far from France. For two months of the year, however, he lives in Paris, where he hosts lavish parties and enjoys the society of his native city.

Fanny has been his mistress, and he has shared his wealth with her.

Flamant (flah-MAH[N]), an engraver who goes to prison for counterfeiting bank notes. Fanny and Flamant have had a child. After Flamant is released from prison, the three settle down to live as a family.

Caoudal (kah-ew-DAHL), a sculptor with whom Fanny lives for a short time. He does a figure of Sappho for which Fanny is the model.

La Gournerie (lah gewr-neh-REE), a poet who keeps Fanny for several years. It was he who taught Fanny the colorful language she uses on occasion.

Césaire Gaussin (say-ZAHR), Gaussin's ne'er-do-well uncle, who comes to Paris to collect an old debt of eight thousand francs to pay off Gaussin's parents' indebtedness resulting from a crop failure. When Césaire gambles away the money he has collected, Fanny, out of her love for Gaussin, gets eight thousand francs from Déchelette, gives it to Césaire, and sends him back home.

Rosario (Rosa) Sanches (roh-SAH-ree-oh SAHN-chehs), a wealthy composer's mistress for whom Fanny manages an apartment for a short time.

Tatave de Potter (tah-TAHV deh poh-TAY), Rosa's lover, a famous composer. He is hated by his wife and unknown to his children because he is obsessively attracted to Rosa. His story profoundly impresses Gaussin.

Bouchereau (bew-sheh-ROH), an eminent physiologist who befriends Gaussin.

Irène (ee-REHN), Bouchereau's niece and Gaussin's innocent, naïve fiancée. Irène's simple charm, however, is not sufficient to attract permanently a man who has loved the sophisticated Fanny, and Gaussin breaks the engagement.

SAPPHO

Author: Franz Grillparzer (1791-1872)
First published: 1819
Genre: Drama

Locale: Lesbos, Greece
Time: The sixth century B.C.E.
Plot: Tragedy

Sappho (SA-foh), the Greek poet. Wearing the laurel wreath of victory from the Olympian contest of poetry and song, she returns to her island home bringing Phaon, with whom she has fallen deeply in love. When the young man falls in love with Melitta, Sappho, offended and troubled, accuses him of being a deceiver in love. Phaon's reply that he now realizes it was her genius he loved rather than herself causes Sappho to reflect on her gifts. Deciding that her genius bars her from meeting the demands of ordinary mortal existence, she calls on the gods to receive her as she hurls herself into the sea.

Phaon (FAY-on), a young charioteer. Having a great admiration for the poems of Sappho, he falls in love with the poet when they meet at Olympia. He returns with her to Lesbos where, in spite of her love and consideration, the simple young man is uncomfortable in her luxurious surroundings. When he falls in love with Melitta, he realizes that it was Sappho's genius he had loved at Olympia, not the woman herself.

Melitta (meh-LIH-tuh), Sappho's beautiful young slave, who brings to Phaon the realization that it is the poet's genius and not Sappho herself that he has loved.

Rhamnes (RAM-neez), Sappho's elderly slave.

SARAGOSSA: A Story of Spanish Valor
(Zaragoza)

Author: Benito Pérez Galdós (1843-1920)
First published: 1874
Genre: Novel

Locale: Spain
Time: 1808-1809
Plot: Historical

Don José de Montoria (hoh-SEH deh mohn-TOH-ree-ah), who is in charge of the defense of Saragossa in the siege of 1808-1809. By force, he seizes grain hoarded by Candiola. The death of his son, Manuel, brings about a change in him, and he asks for Candiola's forgiveness, which is not granted.

Augustine (ow-gews-TEEN), Montoria's son, who is preparing for the priesthood, though he is in love with Mariquilla. He fights side by side with Araceli in the front lines. He tells Araceli of his love for Mariquilla. When he is put in charge of the firing squad that is to execute Mariquilla's father, she breaks completely with him. After her death, he asks Araceli to help him bury her. Don José tells him to forget her, but he says that he intends to enters a monastery as soon as she is buried.

Manuel (mahn-HWEHL), the older brother of Augustine. He is killed in the siege.

Mariquilla (mahr-ee-KEE-yah), Candiola's daughter. She speaks disparagingly of Don José when Augustine comes to see her; earlier, Don José hit her father for his refusal to sell his

wheat. She does not realize at first that Augustine is Don José's son. She later begs Augustine to save her father from execution, then finds out that he is to be on his firing squad. Don José then appears, and she realizes their relationship. She begs Augustine to spare her father; he breaks his sword and walks away. She dies of grief.

Candiola (kahn-dee-OH-lah), Mariquilla's father, a miser and grain hoarder. He does nothing to help the city during the first siege. His house is destroyed by a bomb. He refuses to leave it for fear that looters will steal something from the rubble. He later helps the French tunnel into the city and is condemned to death as a traitor.

Manuela Sancho (mahn-HWEH-lah SAHN-choh), a heroine who battles the French at a breach in the wall. Her action inspires the Spanish soldiers to hold their position against the French.

Araceli (ahr-ah-SEH-lee), a friend of Augustine who goes to Sarogossa to help defend the city.

SARAH PHILLIPS

Author: Andrea Lee (1953-   )
First published: 1984
Genre: Novel

Locale: Paris and the French countryside; Philadelphia, Pennsylvania; and Cambridge, Massachusetts
Time: 1963-1974
Plot: Domestic realism

Sarah Phillips, the protagonist and narrator, a pretty twenty-one-year-old black woman, who grew up in an affluent Philadelphia suburb. She went to a private school and to Harvard University, and now, after her graduation, has gone to live in Paris. When she realizes that she cannot break off with her family or her heritage, Sarah thinks back over the past in an attempt to find her own identity before her inevitable return home.

The Reverend James Forrest Phillips, her late father, who until his recent death was minister of the New African Baptist Church in Philadelphia. An outgoing, likable person and a natural leader, he is highly respected both as a superb preacher and as an activist in the Civil Rights movement.

Grace Renfrew Phillips, Sarah's mother, a teacher in a Quaker school. A polished, witty, and cultivated woman who plays the role of minister's wife flawlessly, she nevertheless has a fascination with the grotesque and the outlandish, which delights her daughter.

Matthew Phillips, Sarah's older brother, a law student. Matthew plays an important part in Sarah's recollections, first as a smug, superior thirteen-year-old boy who unlike his sister has agreed to be baptized, then later as a rebel who breaks his ties with the church and scandalizes his family by falling in love with a white Jewish girl.

— *Rosemary M. Canfield Reisman*

SARRASINE

Author: Honoré de Balzac (1799-1850)
First published: 1831
Genre: Novella

Locale: Paris, France
Time: The 1820's
Plot: Psychological realism

The narrator, a young Parisian who frequents the Parisian salons, where powerful, ambitious men and beautiful, desirable women entertain themselves at lavish soirées. He is set apart from the other guests by his awareness of the superficiality of his life and by his desire to discover the forms of beauty that will lead to truth. Each of the other characters possesses a type of beauty, on which he reflects. He tells his companion, the Marquise de Rochefide, the story of one of the guests, Zambinella.

Madame de Rochefide (rohsh-FEED), a beautiful marquise who possesses pure, transparent beauty. She has accompanied the narrator to a soirée at the Paris townhouse of the Lanty family. She is fascinated by a painting she sees there, and the narrator agrees to tell her the story of the model for the nude Adonis of the painting. After hearing the story, she decides that she will become the most chaste woman of her generation and will keep her ravishing beauty only for herself, thus closing the door on the possibility of an erotic experience with the narrator.

Ernest-Jean Sarrasine (ehr-NEHST-zhah[n] sah-rah-SEEN), a young sculptor with an impetuous nature and wild genius. He is rather ugly and always badly dressed, and he has had little experience with women. He began his career in poverty but became famous when he won a major sculpture prize. His prize money took him to Italy, where he attended an operatic performance in Rome and fell in love with a singer, Zambinella. His love for her is obsessive and as impetuous and wild as his general behavior. Again and again he returns to the opera to wonder at her perfection. He spends the intervening hours composing one drawing after another of her in every conceivable form. He sees her as absolute female beauty embodied. When he discovers that she is a castrato, he tries to kill her and is himself killed instead. His obsession for Zambinella thus leads to insanity and death.

La Zambinella (zahm-bee-NEHL-lah), a castrato who sings soprano roles at the opera in Rome. She is exquisitely beautiful, with an expressive mouth; heavy, voluptuous eyelids framed by dark curved lashes; a perfect oval face; and a dazzling white complexion. She is protected by Cardinal Cigognara, who was responsible for having transformed a beautiful young man, a member of the Lanty family, into this beautiful woman. Zambinella is at the Lanty party and is now a grotesque old man whose decrepitude is concealed beneath a blond wig and a mask of carefully applied makeup; he is bedecked with sparkling jewels. This bizarre figure is the subject of the story that the narrator tells to Madame de Rochefide—Zambinella was the model for the Adonis of the painting. The character is a constantly changing figure in the novella, a beautiful young Italian boy who is castrated and transformed into Zambinella, who creates the illusion of a beautiful female singer. The singer is the model for a statue created by the sculptor Sarrasine, who was madly in love with Zambinella; finally, the statue becomes the model for the painting of a perfectly beautiful Adonis.

The Count de Lanty (lahn-TEE), a wealthy resident of Paris at whose home the narrator and his companion see Zambinella, a relative of the Countess de Lanty. The source of the Lanty fortune is a mystery.

The Countess de Lanty, the wife of the Count de Lanty. She is thirty-six years old and possesses a vibrant beauty. Her face is marked by an extraordinarily intelligent expression; she is a coquette and a powerful siren at the same time. Her beauty has been inherited by her children and is the type that fires Sarrasine's irrational passion for Zambinella.

Marianina de Lanty (mahr-yah-NEE-nah), a sixteen-year-old girl whose beauty is like that of a sultan's daughter in an Eastern tale. She has her mother's beauty, which is also shared by her mother's relative, Zambinella. She shares a beautiful singing voice as well with Zambinella, a voice that embodies secret poetry. Marianina sings in the room where the guests are gathered at the Lantys' party, and her voice draws the grotesque old man who fascinates the narrator and his companion.

Filippo de Lanty (fee-LEE-poh), Marianina's brother, who shares his sister's marvelous beauty. He resembles Antinous, the paragon of youthful beauty, but is even more slender. His primary role in the novella is to represent the mother and sister's beauty in male form.

— *Anne Callahan*

SARTORIS

Author: William Faulkner (1897-1962)
First published: 1929
Genre: Novel

Locale: Jefferson, Yoknapatawpha County, Mississippi
Time: 1919
Plot: Psychological realism

Colonel John Sartoris, a Civil War hero, an entrepreneur, and progenitor of the Sartoris family. Colonel Sartoris led a Confederate regiment during the Civil War and returned from the war to found a railroad and become a community leader in Jefferson. He shot and killed two carpetbaggers who were enrolling African Americans to vote, and he was shot and killed in 1876. To his descendants, he represents a code of honor that has become unfashionable in the twentieth century. At the time of the action of the novel, he has been dead for many years, but he remains a vital force in the lives of his descendants.

Bayard Sartoris, the son of Colonel Sartoris, a banker known as **old Bayard**. He worships the memorabilia of the colonel's wartime exploits and deplores modern inventions such as the automobile. He rides in a fast car with his grandson, young Bayard, only to try to keep him from going too fast, but in the end this leads to a near-accident and old Bayard's fatal heart attack. Nothing he does can stem the tide of modernization.

Bayard Sartoris, known as **young Bayard**, the grandson of old Bayard. A fighter pilot during World War I, he comes home obsessed with the death in combat of his twin brother, John Sartoris, feeling guilt for not saving John but also for not dying heroically as his twin did. He continually flirts with danger, driving a powerful car at high speeds over crude country roads, riding an unbroken stallion while drunk, and taking other risks even after swearing that he will not. His first wife and child having died, he reluctantly marries Narcissa Benbow and gets her pregnant, but he is no more restrained in his behavior. After old Bayard dies in his car, he flees. He takes sanctuary with the McCallums, a clan of yeoman farmers who were friends of his brother John, but eventually he leaves. Young Bayard tries to live up to the code of bravery and honor typified by the original Bayard, who died in an impossibly romantic raid as a junior officer in J. E. B. Stuart's cavalry, but the postwar world provides no fitting arena for such heroics. He is killed in Dayton, Ohio, in the crash of a rickety airplane he was told was not airworthy.

Virginia Sartoris DuPre, known as **Aunt Jenny**, a widow from the Carolina branch of the Sartoris family. She rules the domestic side of the Sartoris household. She bosses the black servants with a fatalistic acceptance of their laziness, and her attempts to control old Bayard and young Bayard meet with a similar lack of success. She encourages the match between young Bayard and Narcissa Benbow.

Narcissa Benbow, Horace Benbow's sister, a self-absorbed, twentyish resident of the town of Jefferson. She professes a hatred for men, preferring romantic dreams, but she is fascinated by a series of semiliterate letters she receives from an unknown admirer expressing his love for her. She fears young Bayard but eventually agrees to marry him and bears him a son, born at the time of young Bayard's death, before falling into a grateful widowhood. Jenny suggests that the son be named John, but Narcissa names him Benbow.

Horace Benbow, who served in the war with the Red Cross instead of with the armed forces. He returns to Jefferson after the war. Back in Jefferson, he carries on a desultory affair with a married woman, Belle Mitchell, and pursues a dilettantish interest in glass blowing. His major accomplishment is a glass vase that he addresses as Narcissa and that he worships as a surrogate for his sister. Horace is the representative of the false aestheticism that the author despised.

Mr. McCallum, the progenitor of a clan of sons and grandsons who live the life of simple yeomen who have never been slaveowners. They distill moonshine whiskey, hunt foxes, and raise subsistence crops. They offer refuge to young Bayard and represent a more solid and earth-related set of values than do the more aristocratic Sartorises.

Simon, a black coachman and butler of the Sartorises. He tries to uphold the values of the family while his own descendants, after experiencing a kind of equality during the war, go bad. After one hair-raising ride in young Bayard's car, he refuses to go near the vehicle again.

Byron Snopes, a bookkeeper in Bayard Sartoris' bank and member of the rapacious Snopes clan, which has begun to take over the town of Jefferson and most of Yoknapatawpha County. Byron is a Peeping Tom who writes the admiring and vaguely suggestive letters to Narcissa Benbow. Like most of the Snopes clan, he represents the degradation of the modern world.

— *John M. Muste*

THE SATANIC VERSES

Author: Salman Rushdie (1947-   )
First published: 1988
Genre: Novel

Locale: India, London, Jahilia
Time: Late twentieth and early seventh centuries
Plot: Fantasy

Odd-numbered (contemporary) chapters

Gibreel Farishta (GEE-bree-EHL fah-REESH-tah), a forty-year-old actor, formerly named Ismail Najruddin. Poor and orphaned, Farishta escapes his poverty and becomes India's most significant film star. When an Air India jumbo jet is sabotaged over the English Channel by Sikh terrorists, Farishta is one of two survivors. Rescued from the sea, he dresses in the clothes of his host, Rosa Diamond's late husband. The authorities permit him to go free. He falls into an affair with

Alleluia Cone (née Cohen), who scaled Mount Everest and whom he had met several months previously following a near-fatal illness that preceded his mysterious disappearance from Bombay. Finally, Farishta's fortunes suffer a reversal. His films fail to attract audiences. He shoots his well-meaning film producer, Whisky Sisodia, and throws Alleluia off the roof of a high-rise building, then ends his own life.

Saladin Chamcha (sah-lah-DEEN CHAM-chah), an actor, master mimic, and costar of a popular English television series. Estranged son of a prominent Anglophile Bombay businessman, Chamcha (formerly Salahuddin Chamchawala) is one of two survivors of an Air India jumbo jet that is destroyed by Sikh terrorists over the English Channel. Pulled from the sea by racist police officers, Chamcha, unable to prove his identity or citizenship and having assumed a goatlike appearance, is thrown into an immigrants' mental hospital and held until his British citizenship is verified. Released from his confinement, he returns home to find his wife, Pamela Lovelace, in bed with Jamsheed Joshi. He also learns that the government of British prime minister Margaret Thatcher has demanded that his role in the television series be cut, so he is jobless. He finds temporary lodgings in the sort of immigrant section of London that he has spent his life trying to avoid.

Even-numbered (early seventh century) chapters

Abu Simbel (ah-BEW SIHM-behl), the leader of the seventh century Jahilia (pre-Islamic Arabia), who appears to Farishta in a dream in which Abu attempts to bargain with Mahound, offering to accept the new monotheism if Mahound will grant divine status to three local goddesses.

Mahound (mah-HEWND), a pejorative Christian variation of Mohammad, who appears in Farishta's dream in which Farishta, disguised as an angel, counsels him to accept Abu Simbel's offer. Mahound finally concludes, however, that the

Then, surrealistically, he begins to grow, reaching eight feet and being transformed into a satanic-appearing satyr, able to resume his form only after he has vented his rage. He nearly dies trying to save the Bangladeshi couple who had earlier taken him in. Finally, he suffers a heart attack and returns to India, where he is reconciled with both his father and his country, but not before he, transmogrified as Shaitan, has avenged his decline by wrecking Farishta's life and bringing him one step closer to the mental breakdown that precedes his suicide.

Pamela Lovelace, whose name suggests Samuel Richardson's eighteenth century heroine, was Chamcha's wife. He caught her in bed with another man when he arrived home unexpectedly following his release from the mental hospital where he was confined after surviving the destruction of the Air India jumbo jet in which he was a passenger.

Alleluia Cone (AL-lay-LOO-yah), formerly Cohen, a woman who scaled Mount Everest and shortly thereafter became Farishta's lover. Chamcha destroyed their relationship and led Farishta to the point of killing Cone by throwing her from the top of a high-rise building to die in much the way his former mistress, Rekha Merchant, had committed suicide two years earlier.

concession is the work of the satanic Shaitan and the revelatory verses are satanic in origin. Mahound completes his conquest of Jahilia, ordering the closing of the brothel and the execution of its prostitutes.

Ayesha (i-EE-shah), a young woman who leads a group of pilgrims to the sea and finally to Mecca. An angel had told her that the sea would part. When it failed to do so, several of the pilgrims drowned.

— *R. Baird Shuman*

SATANSTOE: Or, The Littlepage Manuscripts, a Tale of the Colony

Author: James Fenimore Cooper (1789-1851)
First published: 1845
Genre: Novel

Locale: New York State
Time: 1751-1758
Plot: Historical

Cornelius (Corny) Littlepage, the narrator. As the son of a landed proprietor, he travels, on business for his father, between Albany and New York City, and, later, into the forests of New York State, where he engages in the battle of Ticonderoga and subsequent forays against Indian raiders.

Anneke Mordaunt, the beautiful daughter of Herman Mordaunt. Courted by Major Bulstrode, her father's choice as a husband, and Corny Littlepage, she finally confesses her love for Corny, whom she marries.

Major Bulstrode, a British officer and the rival of Corny Littlepage for the hand of Anneke Mordaunt.

Guert Ten Eyck, Corny Littlepage's friend, who is in love with Mary Wallace. After many difficulties, he finally wins her hand, only to be mortally wounded in an Indian raid before they can be married.

Mary Wallace, Anneke Mordaunt's friend, who falls, too late, in love with Guert Ten Eyck.

The Reverend Thomas Worden, Corny Littlepage's tutor and companion in his travels.

Herman Mordaunt, Anneke Mordaunt's father, a wealthy landowner.

Dirck Van Valkenburgh, called **Dirck Follock**, Corny Littlepage's friend.

Abraham Van Valkenburgh, called **Brom Follock**, Dirck Van Valkenburgh's father.

Jason Newcome, a schoolmaster.

Jaap, Corny Littlepage's black servant.

Mr. Traverse, a surveyor.

Susquesus, called **Trackless**, and

Jumper, Indian guides and runners.

Musquerusque, a Canadian Indian captive taken by Jaap at Ticonderoga.

Mother Doortje, a fortune-teller who warns Guert Ten Eyck that he may never marry.

Hugh Roger Littlepage, Corny Littlepage's elderly grandfather.

Lord Howe, a British general killed at Ticonderoga.

THE SATIN SLIPPER: Or, The Worst Is Not the Surest
(Le Soulier de satin: Ou, Le Pire n'est pas toujours sûr)

Author: Paul Claudel (1868-1955)
First published: 1928-1929
Genre: Drama

Locale: Various countries in Europe, Africa, and Central and South America
Time: Late sixteenth century
Plot: Play of ideas

Don Rodrigo (rrohd-REE-goh), a Spanish nobleman who loves Doña Prouheze, who is married to an elderly judge, Don Pelagio. Rodrigo's desire to sleep with her is frustrated when she leaves for the African city of Mogador to represent Spanish interests there. As the years pass, Rodrigo becomes an amoral colonial administrator who ruthlessly exploits Indians in Central America. He travels to Mogador just before Prouheze dies. She tells him that religion has brought her extraordinary joy. Her stoic acceptance of death transforms Rodrigo into an altruistic Christian. When he is offered a high governmental position near the end of the play, Rodrigo politely informs the king that he can accept this appointment if Spain ends its exploitation of the New World. Rodrigo believes that Christ's teachings are incompatible with colonialism. Rodrigo's remarks offend the king of Spain, who has him arrested on the charge of treason. Rodrigo will end his life in slavery.

Doña Prouheze (proo-EH-seh), an attractive and young Spanish noblewoman who marries an elderly judge, Don Pelagio. Bored in her arranged marriage, she falls in love with Rodrigo, but they never sleep together. She is lonely, and Pelagio seems incapable of understanding her feelings. He does not even accompany her to the harsh African fortress of Mogador. She marries Camillo, an army officer, after Pelagio's death, and at his hand she endures physical and psychological abuse. She and Camillo have a daughter, Doña Sevenswords. Despite or perhaps because of her unjust suffering, Prouheze grows spiritually in Mogador. She experiences great religious happiness, and she accepts her death with profound dignity. She and Rodrigo are the only two characters who change significantly.

Prouheze's Guardian Angel, who is clearly a supernatural character, possibly representing her conscience. The Guardian Angel assists Prouheze in her spiritual development and also helps her to prepare for death.

Don Pelagio (peh-LAH-hee-oh), an elderly and influential Spanish judge who clearly understands that Prouheze would have preferred not to marry him. Marriages in Spain were then arranged, and Prouheze was not truly free. Pelagio seems obsessed with preserving appearances. He asks his friend Balthazar to accompany Prouheze to Mogador, not to protect her from pirates but to prevent her from seeing Rodrigo. He is afraid of what others may think if they learn of Prouheze's love for Rodrigo. He never sees his wife after she leaves Spain for Africa. Pelagio dies while Prouheze is in Mogador.

Don Camillo (kah-MEE-yoh), a violent and unpredictable Spanish army officer who hates Spain and Christianity. While in Mogador, he converts to Islam for reasons that are never explained. After his marriage to Prouheze, he begins to beat and humiliate her. Their daughter, Doña Sevenswords, develops an intense hatred of her father. Camillo has no positive qualities; his amorality represents the moral corruption and spiritual apathy against which Rodrigo and Prouheze eventually will revolt.

Doña Sevenswords, the only child of Camillo and Prouheze. She resembles Rodrigo, to whom the dying Prouheze entrusts her. Like her father, however, she is prone to violence. She entreats Rodrigo to lead a military attack against Mogador to punish Camillo for the death of Prouheze. When Rodrigo declines her request because of his new commitment to pacifism, she sails for Mogador herself, but her boat sinks. As the play ends, Rodrigo learns that she survived this accident.

A Jesuit Priest, Rodrigo's only brother, who is dying as the play begins. He appears only in the opening scene, in which he predicts correctly that Rodrigo's physical desire for Prouheze eventually will be transformed into a desire for spiritual values.

Daibutsu, a Japanese artist who paints huge religious banners, which Rodrigo displays on his boat. After his conversion, Rodrigo meets Daibutsu in a Japanese prison. Rodrigo believes that Daibutsu's paintings, which reveal European, Asian, African, and American influences, will communicate to others the universal nature of Christianity. Rodrigo hopes that Daibutsu's colorful banners will encourage religious tolerance.

The king of Spain, a consistent admirer of Rodrigo's administrative skills. He is angered when Rodrigo argues that Christianity and colonialism are incompatible. The king orders Rodrigo's arrest on the questionable charge of treason.

— *Edmund J. Campion*

SATIROMASTIX: Or, The Untrussing of the Humourous Poet

Author: Thomas Dekker (c. 1572-1632)
First published: 1602
Genre: Drama

Locale: England
Time: c. 1100
Plot: Satire

William Rufus, the king of England, a lustful, treacherous tyrant. He tricks and taunts Sir Walter into promising to send his beautiful wife alone to the palace, intending to violate her.

When Sir Walter brings him her apparently dead body, the king is seized with remorse; he repents, and on her revival he gives her back to her husband unharmed.

Sir Walter Terrill, the king's loyal follower. He agrees to let his wife take poison rather than become the prey of the king.

Caelestine, Sir Walter's beautiful bride. She too prefers the poison to the loss of her virtue.

Sir Quintilian Shorthose, Caelestine's father. Deceiving both Caelestine and Sir Walter, he pretends to poison her but actually gives her a sleeping potion that causes her to appear dead.

Mistress Miniver, a foolish wealthy widow. Her hand is sought by Sir Quintilian, Sir Vaughan, Sir Adam, and Captain Tucca. She yields to the aggressive Tucca and rejects the three knights.

Sir Vaughan ap Rees, a Welsh knight, one of the widow's suitors.

Sir Adam Prickshaft, another of the widow's suitors.

Horace, the humorous poet, an amusing caricature of Ben Jonson. A specialist in satires and epithalamiums, he writes satirical pieces on his fellow poets and others and on invitation works on a marriage song for Sir Walter and Caelestine. He is forced by Tucca to wear a laureate crown of nettles and to swear to give up satirical writing against his fellows.

Asinius Bubo, Horace's admiring follower, perhaps a caricature of Michael Drayton.

Crispinus, a poet, probably a representation of John Marston.

Demetrius, another poet, probably a representation of the playwright himself.

Captain Tucca, a roaring roisterer, loudmouthed and vulgar, given to fantastic figures of speech. He is the instrument of Horace's humiliation at court. He wins the hand of the widow in spite of her knightly suitors.

SATURDAY NIGHT AND SUNDAY MORNING

Author: Alan Sillitoe (1928-   )
First published: 1958
Genre: Novel

Locale: Nottingham, England
Time: The 1950's
Plot: Psychological realism

Arthur Seaton, a lathe operator in a bicycle factory in Nottingham, England. The blond, muscular twenty-one-year-old fights to remain independent of society, employers, and marriage. He dates married women—first Brenda, then Winnie—and engages in boisterous drinking bouts. After a beating by Winnie's soldier husband, he settles for the single Doreen, deciding that he need not reject all that life offers to remain independent.

Brenda, Jack's wife and Arthur's lover. A young mother of two, she is bored with Jack and finds romance and excitement with Arthur. She is part of the dangerous "Saturday Night" life of the first half of the novel. After having an abortion, and after Arthur, discovered by Jack, has been beaten, she fades from the action.

Doreen Greatton, a factory worker. Nineteen years old and single, she is eager to be married but seeks to curb Arthur's excesses. She represents marriage and settling down to Arthur in the "Sunday Morning" half of the novel. She fails to get him

past every pub but has won commitment from Arthur at the end.

Winnie, nicknamed "**Gyp**," Brenda's sister. She is livelier and more reckless than her older sister. She, too, has an affair with Arthur. Her husband, Bill, is a soldier stationed in Germany. He returns on leave with a friend and, tipped off to the affair by Jack, beats Arthur. By dating Winnie, Arthur hastens an end to the dangerous life that he is finding to be a strain.

Jack, Brenda's husband and Arthur's foreman at the factory. He is steady but dull. Rather than confront Arthur, he betrays him to Bill, Winnie's husband.

Aunt Ada, Arthur's widowed aunt, a large, boisterous, and nurturing mother figure whose house teems with family at Christmas. Following his beating by Winnie's husband, Arthur becomes withdrawn and cautious. It is in her house, under her vital influence, that Arthur breaks out of his withdrawal and returns to life, but with new attitudes.

— *Peter J. Reed*

THE SATYRICON

Author: Petronius (Gaius Petronius Arbiter, c. 20-c. 66)
First transcribed: c. 60
Genre: Short fiction

Locale: Italy
Time: The first century
Plot: Satire

Encolpius (ehn-KOHL-pee-uhs), the narrator, who despises the artificiality of rhetoric and the poor preparation of his students. He goes off on a series of roguish adventures.

Agamemnon (a-guh-MEHM-non), a teacher who agrees with Encolpius that students are ill-prepared. He places all the blame on parents who do not force their children to study.

Gito (GI-toh), Encolpius' young slave. A handsome boy, he is by turns upset and happy because of the amorous attentions of Ascyltus. He deserts his master for Ascyltus' service for a time.

Ascyltus (as-KIHL-tuhs), Encolpius' friend and companion on many of his adventures.

Lycurgus (li-KUR-guhs), a rich man and a friend of Ascyltus.

Lichas (LI-kuhs), a rich friend of Lycurgus. Completely taken with Encolpius, Lichas invites him and Gito to his house.

Doris, Lichas' beautiful wife, to whom Encolpius makes love.

Tryphaena (tri-FEE-nuh), a beautiful, amoral woman of Lichas' household who makes love to both Encolpius and Gito. When they tire of her, she spitefully accuses them of making improper advances to her, and they have to flee from Lichas' house.

Trimalchio (trih-MAHL-kee-oh), a former slave who is now rich. He is unused to wealth and is very vulgar. He makes a great show of his riches to impress both himself and other people. He gives an elaborate, ostentatious banquet for which his name is still remembered.

Niceros (NI-seh-ros), a freedman who tells a tale about a man who turns into a wolf.

Eumolpus (yew-MOHL-puhs), a poet who becomes Encolpius' friend and shares in some of his escapades.

Circe (SUR-see), a woman to whom Encolpius tries to make love.

SAUL

Author: Vittorio Alfieri (1749-1803)
First published: 1788
Genre: Drama

Locale: Gilboa, Israel
Time: Eleventh century B.C.E.
Plot: Tragedy

Saul (SAWL), the aging king of Israel who, influenced by his cousin Abner and the priests of Nob, becomes paranoid and turns against David, hero of the battles with the Philistines following David's defeat of the giant, Goliath. Saul's mental faculties are rapidly deteriorating, so his feelings regarding David fluctuate from moment to moment. Saul exiles David from his kingdom under threat of execution should he return. When David finally does return to Gilboa to humble himself before the deranged king and beg his forgiveness, Saul's cousin, Abner, urges Saul to kill David, insisting that he was the cause of various misfortunes that had befallen Saul. Yet, in a dream, David's loyalty to Saul is revealed, and the ambivalent relationship between Saul and David becomes more solid although no more stable. Ultimately, however, Saul's kingdom is defiled by the king's irrationality and violence. The Israelites are defeated in the battle against the Philistines in which Saul's son Jonathan also dies. Saul, wholly defeated, falls on his sword, a suicide.

David, the play's protagonist. Small of stature, he has defeated the mighty giant Goliath and afterward has won a victory over the Philistines. Saul honors and values him. He is the closest friend of Jonathan, Saul's son, and eventually marries Saul's daughter, Michal. Influenced by evil priests and by a conniving cousin, Abner, Saul begins to feel threatened by David and exiles him. Eventually, David returns to humble himself before Saul and to beg his forgiveness even though there is nothing to forgive. Saul fluctuates between loving and valuing David and fearing and suspecting him. David proves that his motives are pure by demonstrating to Saul that he had the opportunity to kill him but did not. Back in Saul's good graces, David urges the king to allow the deceitful and dangerous Abner to continue in his post as commander. Finally, a distraught Saul, clearly insane, flies into a tirade against David, which brings him and his kingdom to ruin. The Israelites are defeated by the Philistines and Saul kills himself by falling on his sword.

Jonathan, Saul's son and David's closest friend. Jonathan remains loyal to David but cannot convince his deranged father of David's loyalty and trustworthiness. Jonathan finally meets his end in the last battle of the Israelites against the Philistines.

Michal (mee-SHAWL), Saul's daughter, Jonathan's sister, and David's wife. Michal suffers separation from her husband when Saul exiles him. When David steals into Gilboa at night following his exile, she and Jonathan inform him of Abner's treachery, which has turned Saul against David. As the Philistines approach in the Israelites' last battle against them, Michal seeks out her father but finds that he is hallucinating, confusing her with his old enemy Samuel. He appeals to her for David's return even if this signals his own death, which occurs by suicide shortly afterward.

Abner (AB-ner), Saul's vicious and deceitful cousin, who, along with the priests of Nob, poisons the king's mind against David. Abner commands Saul's forces and, even after David's reconciliation with the king and his return to the kingdom, is retained as commander at David's behest.

Ahimelech (AH-ee-MEE-lehk), a cunning priest of Nob who plants suspicions about David in Saul's failing mind. Surrounded by counselors like Abner and Ahimelech, Saul's paranoia proliferates. Eventually, however, when he is reconciled with David, Saul orders Abner to kill Ahimelech and the other priests of Nob.

— *R. Baird Shuman*

SAVE ME THE WALTZ

Author: Zelda Fitzgerald (1900-1948)
First published: 1932
Genre: Novel

Locale: Alabama, New York, France, and Italy
Time: Primarily the 1920's
Plot: Autobiographical

Alabama Beggs Knight, the daughter of Millie and Judge Beggs, wife of David Knight, and mother of Bonnie. She stands in for the author and is the author's fictional counterpart to Nicole Diver in F. Scott Fitzgerald's novel *Tender Is the Night* (1934). The wildest of three sisters, she is well bred. The youngest of the three, and fourteen years old at the start of the novel, she envies the social life of her older sisters. After she marries David, a handsome military officer and painter from the North, they live a glamorous, but increasingly unsatisfying, life during the Roaring Twenties. They escape to Connecticut, New York, Paris, the Riviera, and Italy, then finally back to Alabama for the final illness and funeral of her father. Each escape seems to begin with an attempt by Alabama to define herself, only to leave her with a sense of emptiness. Even the birth of her daughter, Bonnie, cannot fill that void. She eventually takes up ballet and a lover, only to find those experiences palling on her. The novel ends with her return home for the funeral of her father. She thinks to herself that she will always return "to seek some perspective on ourselves, some link between ourselves and all the values more permanent than us . . . in our father's setting." In her search for some direction in her own life, however, Alabama reflects about her father: "He must have forgot to leave the message."

David Knight, Alabama's husband, based on F. Scott Fitzgerald. His very name suggests the romantic escape he represents to Alabama in her flight from her mother's suffocating weakness and her father's entrapping sternness. Although he is a "knight" to whom she is wildly attracted and later a painter whom she admires, he also evokes in her envy of his art and fame. Their glamorous life is filled with free-wheeling parties, intoxication, and debts.

Judge Austin Beggs, the father of three socially frivolous daughters. His "detached tenderness" serves as a center of gravity in the emotional volatility and dizzyingly paced life of his youngest daughter, Alabama. Disappointed by the loss of an only son in infancy, he is stern, and sometimes cruel, in providing financial and moral security for his family. His presence hovers in the background of Alabama's glamorous life, particularly when the shifting sands of experience seem constantly to dislocate her values.

Mrs. Beggs, often called **Miss Millie**, the wife of Judge Beggs and mother to their three daughters. She is as accessible as her husband is inaccessible. Her "wide and lawless generosity" contrasts sharply with her husband's "irrefutable logic." Of limited intellectual capacity, she spends her life avoiding problems and fights her major battles over dresses remade for one daughter from an older sister's clothes. Miss Millie is incapable of making decisions or understanding complexities, so that when Alabama decides to leave school, she saves her mother the trouble of attempting to understand her explanation by merely switching the subject.

Bonnie Knight, the daughter of Alabama and David. As a child, she experiences increasing unhappiness with her mother and increasing admiration for her father. When she returns from visiting her mother in Italy, she is described as a princess and David as a knight. She is, indeed, her mother's daughter.

Dixie and

Joan Beggs, Alabama's older sisters. The former writes society columns for the local newspaper.

Madame, a Russian ballet mistress. She provides temporary direction to Alabama, countering Alabama's sense of aimlessness in life, in her role as Alabama's ballet teacher.

Jacques Chevre-Feuille, a French aviator with whom Alabama falls in love. She meets him during the Knights' stay at a Riviera villa, Les Rossignols (The Nightingales). Bored while David paints, Alabama sees Jacques as another "knight." Their relationship ends on a note of irresolution when he leaves for duty in Indochina.

Gabrielle Gibbs, an attractive film actress with whom David flirts. When Alabama returns to Paris from Italy, she increasingly feels "excluded by her lack of accomplishment," and Gabrielle's elegance only serves to make Alabama feel inelegant.

— *Susan Rusinko*

SAVED

Author: Edward Bond (1934-   )
First published: 1966
Genre: Drama

Locale: South London, England
Time: Early 1960's
Plot: Naturalism

Len, a twenty-one-year-old working-class lodger. Described as "naturally good" in spite of the brutalizing environment in which he lives, he is an outsider both in regard to the home in which he lives and to the gang of unemployed toughs who congregate in the park. As he moves between the violence of the family and that of the gang, he functions as a theatrical device, highlighting the parallels between the public and the private displays of senseless violence and empty, cliché-littered language. He is the only character in the play who displays nurturing, caring capabilities, and he remains ineffectual in affecting or moderating the actions of the other characters.

Pam, the twenty-three-year-old mother of an illegitimate child, to whom she refers only as "it." Numbed by the constant arguments in her home, by poverty, by drink, and by watching television, she is filled with a kind of hopeless cynicism that is in sharp contrast to Len's seemingly unwarranted optimism about making things better. She can feel only lust and not love, reacting to Len's affection with hostility and to Fred's abandonment with desperation. Even the death of her child does not touch her. She is as much a victim of society as her child is, and her inability to feel is a product of that influence rather than of any innate difficulty.

Mary, the fifty-three-year-old mother of Pam, trapped in a loveless, empty, and trivial marriage with a husband who rarely speaks, and then never to her. She assuages her sexual frustration by openly going out to meet other men and by flirting with Len. Like Pam, she has no maternal feelings. The years she has spent in this environment have left her with a simmering rage, which she directs against Harry.

Harry, the sixty-eight-year-old father of Pam. An older version of Len, he is also on the outside looking in. He spies on all the sexual encounters in the house, never interfering or reacting until he catches Mary trying to seduce Len. Generally a taciturn character, he does explain to Len why he puts up with everything: He will allow neither his wife nor his daughter to drive him from his home, the only secure place that he has. It is little enough, but it is all he has.

Fred, Pam's present lover, a good-looking twenty-one-year-old. As one of the leaders of the gang of unemployed young men, he is goaded into throwing the first stone at the baby, a crime for which he spends time in jail. Although he demonstrates more feeling than the other men in his gang—for example, he has a tenuous friendship with Len, he is reluctant to tell Pam directly that he is sick of her constant pleas for attention, and he initially defends the baby—eventually he reacts with violence and cruelty. He also is a victim of a society that robs him of his manhood by denying him work and dignity.

Pete,
Colin,
Mike, and
Barry, a gang of young "roughs," ranging in age from

eighteen to twenty-five. Filled with rage against society and totally lacking abstract moral qualities, they redirect their hostility by stoning Pam's baby to death. These are clearly the least sympathetic characters in the play, yet they, too, are driven to this act by the economic and material deprivations of their class.

— Lori Hall Burghardt

SAWBONES MEMORIAL

Author: Sinclair Ross (1908-   )
First published: 1974
Genre: Novel

Locale: Upward, Saskatchewan, Canada
Time: April 20, 1948
Plot: Psychological realism

Doc Hunter, a seventy-five-year-old who is retiring after forty-five years of practice. His birthday party also celebrates the opening of the Hunter Memorial Hospital in the town of Upward. Through the conversations of the characters with and about him, counterpointed with Doc's own thoughts, his character is created. Doc always attended patients, through the worst of winters, whenever he was summoned. The druggist remembers him as a "salt and aspirin man"; he bluntly advised patients to keep their bowels open and "pots" off. Many townsfolk regret that, now that the adequate hospital has come, Doc, who had to manage without modern aids and with only the nursing care provided by Maisie, the local madam, is now leaving Upward. Doc knows that new medicines and techniques bewilder him; he recognizes, without self-pity, that only a younger doctor will make proper use of the new facilities. No one in Upward knows that the new doctor is Doc's illegitimate son. The need to provide for Nick was part of the reason for Doc's hard-nosed determination to be paid in cash or in kind. Chickens and eggs often went to Big Anna, Nick's mother. Nick has obviously—though surreptitiously—been central to Doc's life. Upward residents suspect that he did abortions. He has doubts about only one that he refused to do. He has also—and without qualms—helped some patients out of the world. The townspeople saw Doc's wife as a snob, humiliated by her husband's womanizing, especially with Maisie; Upward residents know nothing of the significant relationship with Big Anna, and Doc keeps to himself the frigidity of his wife, his lack of understanding of her, and the aridity of his marriage.

Edith, Doc's genteel, superior, frigid wife.

Big Anna, the Ukrainian cleaning woman, Nick's mother.

Duncan Gillespie, the only school friend of Nick Miller, inheritor of the family grocery business, and chairman of the hospital board. As Upward's chief citizen, he is considerably responsible for Nick's return.

Caroline Gillespie, Duncan's English war bride, who is learning her place in a new society.

Maisie Bell, a friend of Doc. She is the local madam, a symbol of the narrow hypocrisy prevalent in Upward. She nurses the sick, who, when well, shun her in the street.

Benny Fox, a homosexual musician, the son of a woman to whom Doc refused an abortion. She married a man she despised, made life miserable for her family, and committed suicide. If his homosexuality is discovered, Benny will have to leave Upward.

Nick Miller, Doc's unrecognized, "Hunky" son, the new doctor. He is big and brilliant. When Anna died, Doc arranged for Nick's education. Having suffered from the attitudes in Upward, Nick is returning only to lay his past to rest.

Mr. Harp and

Mrs. Harp, who are both racist, conformist, and spiteful, representative of the worst small-town minds. They are opposed to the new doctor; they fear that Nick will remember Harp's persecution of him at school. They resent his success.

The Reverend Grimble, a good, poor pastor. He ignores Doc's unorthodoxy and appreciates his goodness. Grimble suffers from yet another Upward attitude: Religion is respectable and, therefore, necessary, but not worth financial support. Christianity receives only lip service.

— Jocelyn Creigh Cass

THE SCAPEGOAT

Author: Mary Lee Settle (1918-   )
First published: 1980
Genre: Novel

Locale: West Virginia
Time: June 7-8, 1912
Plot: Historical realism

Beverley Lacey, the proprietor of the Seven Stars coal mine in Lacey Creek, West Virginia, and descendant of the family that originally settled and controlled this entire mining district. During his lifetime, he has seen his family give up first the mineral rights and then the land itself to wealthy entrepreneurs who in turn have remitted it to faceless corporations and holding companies. He has also seen the relationship between owner and laborer deteriorate from cooperative to adversarial. He has been broken by the process, physically and emotion-

ally. Although merely forty-two years old, he is on his deathbed; he will not survive the year. He also believes that he has failed his wife and family; he has not maintained the aristocratic ideals that he inherited from his parents, and he fears that his family members will not be able to protect themselves in this altered world after his death. Furthermore, he is aware of both the injustice inflicted on the mine workers by the managerial class and the propaganda manipulation of the union organizers. Although he would like to rise above the pettiness and stupidity of what he perceives as a staged conflict, he feels compelled to install a Gatling gun on his front porch to protect his family. Worst of all, he feels intensely about nothing.

Ann Eldridge Lacey, Beverley's wife, around forty years old. From a relatively common background, she "married up" when she wed Beverley, and she is determined to maintain the family eminence, even when everything is crumbling around her and her dreams of grandeur are evaporating. She attempts this task by bullying Beverley into taking stands on preserving the status quo. Because these stands are basically ineffectual, he resents her interference and has withdrawn from her emotionally. To compensate, she has developed migraines that she doses with laudanum. She is aware that her husband is dying, although he has not told her so, and she is desperate to secure her future and that of her daughters.

Lily Lacey, who at nineteen years of age is the eldest daughter of Beverley and Ann. Idealistic and intellectual, she commits herself completely to the concept of social reform and the elevation of the working class. This makes her see everything as either black or white and people as either heroes or villains. For example, as a typical gesture she "adopts" one of the sons of a family of migrant Italian laborers, a young man her own age but lacking her privileges. She is determined to compensate for his disadvantages by educating him herself: She reads her textbooks from Vassar to him every day of her vacation. Well versed in her ideas of the evils of capitalism, she attempts to join the miners' strike but is rebuffed. Later, she serves as a military nurse during World War I.

Althea Lacey, who is sixteen years old, the second daughter of Beverley and Ann. The antithesis of Lily, Althea is carnal and sensual, driven by her body and her selfish urges. Completely self-centered, she is incapable of appreciating any motives larger than personal ones. Thus, during a period that subjects family, neighborhood, community, economy, and society to unprecedented tests, she remains preoccupied with her romance of the moment. Although she marries well—from a conventional social point of view—she ends up a drunken degenerate.

Mary Rose Lacey, the third Lacey daughter, who is fifteen years old. Recognizing the shortcomings of both of her sisters, she is able to avoid their extremes, but that does not necessarily result in success. She has a practical focus that both of her sisters lack, but she is without either Lily's sophisticated understanding or Althea's intuitive insight into personal motives. She has the resilience of a young girl, but this resilience is sorely tested by the events to which she is exposed, and she is not able to grow through them.

Jake Catlett, a friend from boyhood of Beverley and a descendant of another founding family; he is in his early forties. Because he lost out in an earlier round of mineral-right transactions, he is on the side of the striking miners in this labor dispute and is their leader. Like Beverley, he is uncomfortable with this new world of impersonal negotiation; unlike Beverley, he recognizes and accepts that things change. Both men remain good at heart and do what they can to avert the impasse that will result in tragedy, but their sense of futility shows that the situation is beyond their control, or that of any individuals. He differs most from Beverley in his holding some hope for the future and for the role of individuals.

Essie Catlett, Jake's wife, in her early forties. Although she is from the same background as Ann Eldridge, she has experienced a very different adulthood. To make ends meet, she has spent twenty years "helping out" in the Lacey family's kitchen; originally, she was Ann Eldridge's closest friend. She deeply resents this social differentiation. Plain and practical, she knows trouble is at hand and also knows which side she is on.

Eduardo Pagano, the twenty-year-old son of an immigrant Italian family. The Italians, brought in to work the mines when the native population balked, have been segregated, like the other minorities, until the present strike. Now solidarity is drawing them together, but Eduardo, inspired by Lily's dreams, is determined to rise above them. Accordingly, he is singled out for retaliation by the thugs hired by the mine owners.

Neville St. Michael Roundtree, an English-born superintendent of the Mark Hanna Coal Company, in his early thirties. Appointed by the directors to run the operation as efficiently as possible, Roundtree finds that his duties include a confrontation in which he has to deny his sympathies for the men. His only alternative is to quit, which is equivalent to giving up his career.

Daniel Neill, a descendant of another founding family, in his early twenties. Forced to leave Princeton after his father kills himself and after his grandfather, a U.S. senator, is convicted of fraud, Neill is attempting to retrieve the family fortunes by serving as captain of the army of guards that is securing the mines and locking out the strikers. He sees himself as a leader, but he does not understand the situation, and his frustration leads him to take rash actions.

Mother Jones, the famous labor organizer, who at eighty-two years of age is on one of her last missions. Long experienced in such confrontations, she single-mindedly choreographs the actions of the laborers and their families for greatest emotional impact. Tough, clever, and articulate, she knows the legal limits of her position and attempts to avoid bloodshed, though she is willing to use it—or anything—to her advantage.

— *James L. Livingston*

THE SCARLET LETTER

Author: Nathaniel Hawthorne (1804-1864)
First published: 1850
Genre: Novel

Locale: Boston
Time: Mid-seventeenth century
Plot: Psychological realism

Hester Prynne, an attractive young woman living among the Puritans of Boston during the 1650's. She becomes a martyr because she, presumably a widow, bears a child out of wedlock; this sin results in her being jailed and then publicly exhibited on a pillory for three hours. After she is released from jail, she must wear for a lifetime a scarlet "A" upon her bosom. She becomes a seamstress, stitching and embroidering to earn a living for herself and for Pearl, her child. After her one act of sin, Hester behaves with such uncanny rectitude that she seems an American Jeanne d'Arc, battling not against opposing armies and bigotry but against bigotry alone, the most formidable of antagonists. Hester refuses to name the child's father, who is the Reverend Arthur Dimmesdale, her minister; she does not quail when her supposedly dead husband, Roger Chillingworth, comes from out of the forest to witness her appearance on the pillory; and without complaint or self-pity, she fights her way back to respectability and the rights of motherhood. Her situation is made more poignant and heroic by Dimmesdale's lack of sufficient moral courage to confess that he is Pearl's father. Hester seems to need no partner to share her guilt. Tragedy befalls her when Dimmesdale dies, but the reader feels that Hester will stoutly and resolutely make her way through life.

The Reverend Arthur Dimmesdale, a minister in Boston. Emotionally, he is drawn and halved by the consequences of his sin with Hester, and he is pulled apart by responsibility. Should he confess and thus ruin his career, or should he keep silent and continue the great good resulting from his sin-inspired sermons? Outwardly, Dimmesdale is a living man, but inwardly he is the rubble and wreckage resulting from a Puritan conscience. One night, he drags himself (along with Hester and Pearl) up to the pillory where he feels he should have stood long ago, but this confession is a sham, for only Roger Chillingworth, hidden in the darkness, observes the trio. Finally, at the end of his Election Day sermon, he takes Hester and Pearl by the hand, ascends the pillory, confesses publicly, and sinks down dead. When his clothing is removed, Puritans see the stigma of an "A" on the skin of his chest. Hawthorne takes no stand on Dimmesdale's weakness or strength; he says simply, "This is Dimmesdale."

Roger Chillingworth, a "physician" who might better be called "Evil." Thought to have been killed by Indians, he reenters Hester's life when she first stands on the pillory. Pretending to minister to the physically ailing Dimmesdale, he tries only to confirm his suspicion that the minister is Pearl's father. When Arthur and Hester, in a desperate act of hope, book passage on a ship to England, Chillingworth also signs up for the voyage, and Hester knows she can never escape him. Although motivated by the fact of his wife bearing another man's child, Chillingworth nevertheless seems inordinately twisted toward vengeance. Conniving, sly, and monomaniacal, he is more a devilish force than a man.

Pearl, Hester's elfin, unpredictable daughter. She refuses to repeat the catechism for the governor and thus risks being taken from her mother. At a meeting of Hester and Arthur in the forest, she treats the minister as a rival; when he kisses her on the brow, she rushes to a stream and washes away the unwelcome kiss.

Governor Bellingham, the leader of the Massachusetts Colony. He thinks Hester is unfit to rear Pearl but is persuaded to allow them to remain together by the plea of Dimmesdale.

The Reverend John Wilson, a stern divine. Early in the story, he exhorts Dimmesdale to force Hester to reveal Pearl's father.

Mistress Higgins, the bitter-tempered sister of the governor. She is simply and literally a witch.

SCENES FROM AMERICAN LIFE

Author: A. R. Gurney (1930-   )
First published: 1970
Genre: Drama

Locale: Buffalo, New York
Time: The 1930's to the near future
Plot: Satire

Father, from the first and last scenes, the wealthy father of Snoozer. Depicted first as a young father and later as a family patriarch, he represents the established upper class. In concert with Snoozer's godparents, he expresses class fears of Franklin Roosevelt and the impact of the Depression while enjoying a lifestyle aloof from the suffering around him. The family members swill bootlegged gin and give exotic, costly gifts while preaching responsibility to self and country from the hypocritical pulpit. In the last scene, Father officiates at the family's traditional tennis ball toss and canoe burning, a sunset ritual that suggests the fate of his class.

Mother, Snoozer's mother. Like her husband, she is basically insensitive to the misery of others. She is frivolous, playfully demanding that those at the post-christening party give her son his nickname. She herself comes up with "Snoozer" because the infant sleeps through a second baptism when his godmother spills her drink on him. In the final scene, she explains the family tradition to Ray, the prospective son-in-law.

Mother, from the third scene. She voices dubious concern for her child's welfare when, after chastising the child's nurse for inviting a male friend to her room and thereby neglecting child-tending duties, she reveals that she is planning an assignation with her lover.

Snoozer, a character alluded to often but encountered only in the final scene. Although he plays only a minor role when he actually appears, he is a reference point for many of the other characters throughout the play. He is notable only for his nickname, given to him by his mother.

Nellie, the nurse. She is polite, acquiescent, and lonely, an Irish immigrant forced to be thankful for her position. Her efforts to defend her actions are squelched by her charge's mother.

Uncle John, a blunt, sarcastic spectator at a tennis match in the fifth scene. Although he hates the sport, he is forced to watch by his nagging wife.

Aunt Helen, Uncle John's wife. She promotes sportsmanship to their nephew while maligning her husband and his opinions. She discusses her relationship to Uncle John in analogies to the doubles match but is ridiculously one-sided in her thinking.

Wife, from the eighth, futuristic, scene. She is pregnant and wants to have the child because she feels left out of things. When her husband insists on an abortion, she claims that the child is not his, then recants and capitulates to his demands.

Husband, from the same scene. He is uninterested in having another child, envisaging a future free from parental responsibility to his children (and stepchildren). Given the civil unrest, his dream of future tranquillity seems at best delusional.

Father, from the tenth scene. When his daughter is arrested for hitchhiking, he bails her out of jail in time for a family Christmas. He cannot comprehend her odd behavior but accedes to her wishes to bail out her friend Mark and invite him home, even though she does not know Mark's last name.

Mr. Van Dam, the **Dancing Master** from the sixteenth scene. A stiff martinet with a German accent, he insists on strict discipline in his dance class. He uses a cane to threaten his wayward students, but his most effective weapon is mortification: He makes disobedient boys dance with him.

Mother, in the twenty-third scene. A stickler for class proprieties, she opposes her daughter's desire for a serious education because it would interfere with the obligations of a true debutante.

Daughter, called **Pookins**, who appears in the same scene. Somewhat light in mental acuity, she is unsure of what she really wants and does not put up much of a struggle against her mother's insistence that her coming out is more important than a higher education.

Father, in the twenty-fourth scene, a man devastated by his son's decision to skip bail and run from the law. He is bitter about self-sacrifices made to provide the best for his son.

Son, the father's eldest scion. He is unyielding and unresponsive to his father's arguments. His firmness merely antagonizes the father, who, venting frustration and anger, verbally assaults him as a loser.

Bucky Kratz, referred to as **Colonel**, the district commander in the futuristic, thirty-fifth vignette. Under martial law, he has the authority to interfere in civilian business. A graduate of Dartmouth, he is unsympathetic to the plight of the Yale graduate who comes to him for help.

Phil Ramsey, a discharged banker. Approaching the colonel for help in getting reinstated, he tries to trade on their shared Ivy League background. When stymied, he destroys his chances by insulting the colonel with absurdly snobbish and petty remarks.

— *John W. Fiero*

A SCHOOL FOR FOOLS
(Shkola dlia durakov)

Author: Sasha Sokolov (1943-   )
First published: 1976
Genre: Novel

Locale: Moscow and a nearby summer cottage settlement
Time: Early 1960's
Plot: Psychological realism

The narrator, also known as **Nymphea alba** and **Those Who Came**, a schizophrenic adolescent. His mental illness is diagnosed as hereditary, though his family situation probably has aggravated it. He has spent some time in a mental hospital but is later enrolled at a special school for students unable to meet the demands of a regular education. The peculiarities of his affliction most obvious in his narrative are his complete lack of a sense of time and his inability to delineate completely the characters of others. The novel is, for the most part, a dialogue between the two selves of his personality. One self yearns to become an engineer, whereas the other is interested in entomology.

The narrator's father, the town's chief prosecutor, a large, impatient man who perhaps aggravates, by his lack of tolerance, his son's affliction. He cannot stand disorder or drunkenness and is forever suspicious of freeloaders, including musicians and sponging in-laws. He owns a dacha in the suburbs of Moscow where much of the action takes place.

The narrator's mother, a housewife who has not worked since her mentally disturbed son first went off to school. She constantly tries to reconcile the son and his father. Goodhearted, though lacking in imagination, she is the only character in the novel whose physical attributes are described. She is "almost grey-haired," with green eyes and glasses with thin gold frames.

Pavel Petrovich Norvegov (PAH-vehl peh-TROH-vihch nohr-VEH-gov), also known as **Savl** (SAHV-ehl), a geography instructor at the narrator's special school. He is "the most prominent turner of the cardboard globe." He is an eccentric dresser: The narrator describes him as barefoot and wearing a laboratory coat both at the dacha and at the school. The narrator considers him his mentor and idolizes him.

Veta Arcadievna Acatova (VEE-tah ahr-kah-DIH-yehv-nah ah-KAH-toh-vah), a strict teacher of biology, botany, and anatomy at the special school. The narrator imagines that she is his beloved and fantasizes a happy future with her. Aside from his claim that she was the inspiration for Leonardo da Vinci's Mona Lisa, the narrator does not describe her further.

Arcady Arcadievich Acatov (ahr-KAH-dee), Veta's father, a retired, world-renowned entomologist. His early work was challenged by the Soviet government for reasons unspecified by the narrator. He apparently was put in prison or an asylum and physically abused. Later released, he was allowed to continue his research. Now an old man, he is stooped, weary, and hard of hearing.

Nikolai Gorimirovich Perillo (nih-koh-LAY goh-rih-MIH-roh-vihch peh-RIH-loh), the principal of the special school. Middle-aged, gloomy, and punctilious, he has instituted meaningless regulations that oppress both faculty and students.

Sheina Solomonova Trachtenberg (SHAY-nah soh-loh-MOH-noh-vah), also known as **Tinbergen**, the assistant principal and curriculum director at the special school. She is the nemesis of Norvegov. A Jewish widow, she is confused with a Moscow neighbor of the narrator and his family.

Mikheev (mih-KHAY-yehv), the postman in the dacha district, also known as **Medvedev** (MEHD-veh-dehv) and called **The Sender** and **The Sender of Winds** by Norvegov and the narrator. He is a pensioner who delivers the mail by bicycle.

Doctor Zauze (ZOW-zeh), the psychiatrist at the mental hospital who treats the narrator's schizophrenia.

— *John P. Turner, Jr.*

THE SCHOOL FOR HUSBANDS
(L'École des maris)

Author: Molière (Jean-Baptiste Poquelin, 1622-1673)
First published: 1661
Genre: Drama

Locale: Paris, France
Time: The 1660's
Plot: Comedy of manners

Sganarelle (zgah-nah-REHL), a gentleman entrusted with the guardianship of Isabelle, who was orphaned by the death of her father. Scorning his brother Ariste's leniency in the upbringing of Léonor, Isabelle's sister, Sganarelle attempts to govern his ward by severity and keeps her confined at home in preparation for marriage to him. In spite of his surveillance, Isabelle manages to fall in love with Valère and to trick her guardian into arranging a marriage ceremony for her and her lover.

Ariste (ah-REEST), Sganarelle's brother and the guardian of Isabelle's sister, Léonor. Disapproving of his brother's strictness in bringing up his ward, Ariste governs by affection and allows freedom to Léonor, whom he loves enough to leave to her the choice of a husband. Returning from a ball, she declares that she loves only her guardian and wishes to marry him immediately.

Isabelle (ee-zah-BEHL), Sganarelle's ward. Confined at home and strictly guarded by her guardian, she manages nevertheless to fall in love with Valère. By a series of deceptions, the lovers trick Sganarelle into arranging meetings and, finally, their marriage.

Léonor (lay-oh-NOHR), Isabelle's sister and Ariste's ward. Allowed the freedom to come and go at will by her lenient guardian, she learns to love him and confesses her willingness to marry him whenever he wishes.

Valère (vah-LEHR), Isabelle's lover, with whom she deceives Sganarelle.

THE SCHOOL FOR SCANDAL

Author: Richard Brinsley Sheridan (1751-1816)
First published: 1780
Genre: Drama

Locale: London, England
Time: The eighteenth century
Plot: Comedy of manners

Sir Oliver Surface, a gentleman whose problem it is to discover which of two nephews is more worthy of the Surface fortune. Posing once as Mr. Premium, a moneylender, and also as Mr. Stanley, a poor relation, Sir Oliver is finally able to decide that Charles Surface is the worthier nephew.

Joseph Surface, the unworthy nephew. He is a double dealer and in the famous screen scene is discovered in several falsehoods by people upon whose influence his future depends. Joseph is one of two people who are left unhappy when the denouement takes place.

Charles Surface, Sir Oliver's worthy nephew. Charles' only real fault seems to be extravagance with money. He is well-intentioned and even kind and honest. Discovered by Sir Oliver to be the better of the two nephews, he wins the girl of his choice and receives his uncle's inheritance.

Sir Peter Teazle, an elderly nobleman and Sir Oliver's friend, whose lot in life it is to be married to a young wife who almost plays him false with Joseph Surface. Sir Peter is pleased at his part in helping to expose Joseph.

Lady Teazle, Sir Peter's young, country-bred wife, who relishes the pleasure of living in London. She treats her long-suffering husband with disdain until she learns that Joseph has simply been toying with her affections. Her lesson learned, she is a better wife to Sir Peter.

Lady Sneerwell, Lady Teazle's friend, who ruins women's reputations to make them more closely match her own. Her plan to expose Joseph for the person he is, wreck Charles' love for Maria, and gain Charles and the family fortune goes awry when her confederate, Snake, sells her out.

Maria, Sir Peter's ward, who is a girl with a good head on her shoulders. Her guardian selects Joseph to be her husband but, loving Charles, she keeps putting Joseph off, biding her time. Her patience is rewarded when Joseph overreaches himself; with his downfall, she gains Sir Peter's permission to marry Charles.

Snake, Lady Sneerwell's intimate, who takes money from two factions, thus aiding Sir Oliver by exposing Lady Sneerwell's plan to ruin Joseph, scandalize the Teazles, and win Charles and his uncle's money.

Sir Benjamin Backbite, a slanderer, Lady Sneerwell's friend.

Rowley, Sir Peter's servant, who believes from the beginning that Charles has a better character than Joseph.

Lady Candour, a lady whose defense of a reputation is certain to ruin it.

Moses, a Jew who concerns himself with Sir Oliver's money matters.

THE SCHOOL FOR WIVES
(L'École des femmes)

Author: Molière (Jean-Baptiste Poquelin, 1622-1673)
First published: 1663
Genre: Drama

Locale: France
Time: The seventeenth century
Plot: Comedy of manners

Arnolphe (ahr-NOHLF), also known as **M. de la Souche** (deh lah sewsh), a man who is convinced that, to avoid being disgraced by an unfaithful wife, he must marry a very innocent girl who has been sheltered and kept from the world. He decides to marry Agnès, his ward. He sends her to a convent and then keeps her in seclusion in a small cottage on his estate. He plots to keep her apart from Horace, the young man she loves, but eventually is foiled in his plan.

Agnès (ahn-YEHS), Arnolphe's ward, a young and very innocent girl who knows nothing of love affairs but is very much in love with Horace. She is so ignorant that she once asked if babies came from the ear. In spite of Arnolphe's plotting, she is united with her lover.

Horace (oh-RAHS), the young man who is in love with Agnès. He does not know that Arnolphe, her guardian, and the man named de la Souche, who is supposed to marry Agnès, are one and the same person. He considers Arnolphe to be his friend, consults him, and asks for his aid in winning Agnès. Arnolphe attempts to betray him but fails, and Horace and Agnès are united in spite of Arnolphe's plots against them.

Chrysalde (kree-ZAHLD), Arnolphe's friend and confidant. He is the recipient of Arnolphe's declarations about how a wife should be trained.

Enrique (ehn-REEK), Chrysalde's brother-in-law. Horace's father is determined that Horace must marry Enrique's daughter, and Arnolphe encourages this plan. When he learns that Enrique's daughter is really Agnès, his discovery comes too late.

Oronte (oh-ROHNT), Horace's father and Enrique's friend. He insists that Horace must marry Enrique's daughter.

THE SCORCHED-WOOD PEOPLE

Author: Rudy Wiebe (1934-   )
First published: 1977
Genre: Novel

Locale: Canada, the northeastern United States, and Montana
Time: 1869-1885
Plot: Historical

Louis Riel, a visionary, the leader of the Métis people and founder of the province of Manitoba. Born in the Canadian West in 1844, Riel is educated in Montreal by priests. Despite his desire to enter the priesthood, Riel returns to his people, determined to improve their lot. He finds the Métis living in poverty, their way of life threatened and their plight ignored by the greedy Hudson's Bay Company. Riel is a complex man: Devout, pious, and solitary, he is also clever, charismatic, and an impassioned speaker. In 1869, with the help of Gabriel Dumont and his army, Riel captures Fort Garry from the company, proclaims a Provisional Government of the North-West, and declares himself its president. Like many idealists, Riel is also naïve. One of his first mistakes is to execute a white man, Thomas Scott, in 1870. The act brands him as an outlaw. Despite the fact that Riel is elected as a member of Parliament for his region, a bounty is put on his head, and he is obliged to seek exile in the United States. He settles in Montana, marries and has children, and teaches there until Dumont arrives in 1884 to entice him to Saskatchewan. A quiet, introspective man given to seeing visions, Riel believes that God is calling him to return, and he goes. The Métis arm themselves but are defeated at Batoche, Saskatchewan, by the Canadian army. Riel gives himself up, is tried, and is hanged in Regina on November 16, 1885.

Gabriel Dumont, a buffalo hunter, friend of Riel, and military leader of the Métis. Dumont is a great, burly man, uneducated and accustomed to leading a rough, simple life. Although not himself religious, Dumont respects Riel's devoutness and willingly follows his spiritual leadership. It is he who persuades Riel to return to Canada from exile in Montana, and it is he who organizes and leads the small band of Métis against the Canadian army at Batoche. Following the defeat of his people and the capture of Riel, Dumont flees to the United States, where he joins Buffalo Bill's Wild West Show. To the end, he never doubts Riel's vision or his sanity.

Pierre Falcon, the narrator of the novel and singer-poet for the Métis, born in 1793. Falcon relates events that occur well outside the range of his own lifetime. He manages to be everywhere, both a participant in and reporter of the action. Falcon displays an uncanny knack for delving inside the heads of many characters, from Riel to the prime minister of Canada. Still, his is a decidedly biased view of people and events: The English and Scottish settlers usually appear dry, inhumane, and dishonest, whereas the Métis are presented as vital, emotional, and straightforward people. Falcon reveals their contrasting ways of life with extraordinary skill and some humor; he also excels at describing battle scenes. He triumphs in bringing the complex Riel to life. Falcon's idiosyncratic mode of narration gives the novel its fluid structure. His binary vision, which moves seamlessly between past and future, allows events to appear in the light of their inevitable, tragic end.

Sir John Alexander Macdonald, the first prime minister of Canada. He is the main force behind the Confederation of Canada in 1867 and the building of its national railroad. More than a little concerned about Riel's influence on the Métis, Macdonald orders him into exile and, years later, bows to English Protestant pressure to have Riel tried and executed.

Thomas Scott, who is court-martialed and executed by Riel's provisional government in 1870. He becomes a martyr, and his death increases the hostility of the English Protestants toward the French Catholic Métis.

Marguerite,

Jean, and

Sara Riel, respectively Riel's American-born wife and son and his sister. Sara shares Riel's vision, becomes a nun, and dies as a martyr to her religion. She is idealized by Riel.

Donald A. Smith, the chief representative of the Hudson's Bay Company in Canada.

William McDougall, the lieutenant-governor of the North-West in 1869.

Edgar Dewdney, the Indian commissioner for the North-West Territories from 1879 to 1888 and lieutenant-governor from 1881 to 1888.

Lief Crozier, an inspector in the North-West Mounted Police. He leads the attack against the Métis at Batoche.

— *Susan Whaley*

THE SCORNFUL LADY

Authors: Francis Beaumont (c. 1584-1616) and John Fletcher (1579-1625)
First published: 1616
Genre: Drama

Locale: London, England
Time: Early seventeenth century
Plot: Comedy of manners

The Scornful Lady, a headstrong, independent young woman. Cursed with a streak of perversity, she heaps scorn and indignity on the man she loves whenever he is present. She is disturbed by this and frequently resolves to reform, but she constantly lapses. Only the fear that she is about to lose him forever brings her to accept marriage with him.

Martha, the Lady's sister. She joins in jeering and flouting her sister's lover, but he later triumphs by tricking her into marrying one of the Lady's other suitors.

Elder Loveless, the Lady's true lover. Angered at being banished by her for kissing her in public, he tries various tricks to make her revoke the banishment and marry him. He is several times outwitted by her but finally overcomes her reluctance by producing an apparent bride-to-be.

Young Loveless, his trifling and prodigal younger brother. In spite of his scapegrace behavior, Young Loveless finds a wealthy and attractive widow for his wife.

Savil, Elder Loveless' steward. When the elder brother is reported dead, Savil panders to the younger's scandalous behavior. On the master's return, Savil is discharged for failing in his responsibility; he is later forgiven.

Morecraft, an unscrupulous moneylender. His projects for gaining possession of Loveless' land fail, and he loses his fiancée to Young Loveless; as a result, he decides to turn prodigal, hoping that the dividends will be as high in his case as in Young Loveless'.

Abigail (Mrs. Younglove), the Lady's elderly waiting woman. Highly susceptible, she pursues several men, finally marrying Sir Roger, the curate.

Welford, a suitor for the Lady's hand. After a quarrelsome first meeting, he and Elder Loveless join forces. He disguises himself as Elder Loveless' supposed bride-to-be, thereby helping his former rival to win the Lady and winning Martha for himself.

The Widow, Morecraft's fiancée, who will not consent to marry him until he gains a knighthood. She deserts him for Young Loveless.

Sir Roger, the Lady's curate, whom aging Abigail snares for a husband.

A SCOTS QUAIR

Author: Lewis Grassic Gibbon (James Leslie Mitchell, 1901-1935)
First published: 1946
Genre: Novel

Locale: Northeastern Scotland
Time: 1911 to the Great Depression
Plot: Social

Sunset Song, 1932

Chris Guthrie, a crofter's (farmer's) daughter, crofter's wife, farmer, mother, and minister's wife, twice a widow, and the principal character of the trilogy. With her high cheekbones, long, finely spun red-brown hair, and bright, piercing brown eyes, Chris is a striking Scotswoman who catches the attention of men and women alike. From childhood, Chris feels like two people: one an English Chris who loves books and genteel culture and the other a Scottish Chris who eschews English bourgeois pretensions and believes only in the immortality of the Scottish land and sky. Chris's early recognition that nothing human lasts becomes a lifelong conviction and provides comfort to her in the worst times of her life. By the end of the third volume, the thirty-eight-year-old Chris seems herself to be an extension of the Scottish countryside she has lived on and loved.

John Guthrie, Chris's father, a crofter. Hardy, firm, red-haired, and red-bearded, John Guthrie strives with the beautiful but harsh farmland of Kincardineshire with undying energy. The incessant struggle finally embitters this fiercely independent man, who dies enraged, paralyzed by a stroke.

Jean Murdoch Guthrie, Chris's mother. By nature blithe and vigorous, Jean is lovely and sensual with her fine, long, golden hair. Worn down by childbearing, a farm wife's duties, and an unexpected seventh pregnancy, the despondent Jean takes her own life as well as those of her young twins.

Will Guthrie, the oldest of the Guthrie children. Resembling his mother in his natural temperament and full head of red-gold hair, Will is the too-frequent recipient of his dour father's stern, even vicious, discipline. Hating his father and unwilling to endure him any longer, Will runs away to Argentina. Will visits Chris several years later, on his way to the trench warfare of World War I. He is killed in action.

Ewan Tavendale, Chris's first husband, a farmer from the Highlands. Tall, agile, and powerful, Ewan is depicted with his dark features and black hair as one of the ancient Scots, the Picts, older than the Celtic peoples who later came to Scotland. The natural energy and harmony of Ewan's life as a farmer is perverted by the violence of World War I. Ewan enlists in a Highland regiment and returns only briefly to Chris and his son, Ewan; he is now drunk, coarse, and corrupted. He is executed in France when he comes to his senses and deserts, trying to return to Scotland, the land, and Chris.

Robert (Rob) Duncan, called **Long Rob of the Mill**, a miller, wit, horse lover, and neighbor of the Guthries. Tall and sinewy, with flaxen-gold hair and mustache and smoky blue eyes, Rob strikes his neighbors as coming from Viking stock.

Rob exhibits the Scots independence and self-reliance exalted in the novel: He goes to jail rather than be conscripted into the military. He helps Chris tend the crops in Ewan's absence, and they become one-time lovers when he tells her that he will enlist in the army. Capitulating to the societal bloodthirstiness of the war, Rob joins a Highland regiment. He dies a hero and is posthumously awarded a medal for bravery.

Charles "Chae" Strahan, another crofter, a neighbor of the Guthries and later of Chris and Ewan. Tall, broad-shouldered, and ruggedly handsome with his prominent nose, fair hair, and waxed mustache, Chae combines personal strength and a crofter's independent mind to stand as one of the pillars of the farm community. Like Rob, Chae is reminiscent of the traditional Scots, who both define and are defined by the land and the tilling of it. A favorite with Chris, Chae is a loyal friend and neighbor. He too is killed in battle in France, one hour before the armistice is effected.

Cloud Howe, 1933

Robert Colquohoun (ka-HEWN), Chris's second husband, a veteran of World War I and minister of the Kirk. He is fair-haired and fair-complexioned, tall, and thin. Although his lungs were injured by mustard gas during combat, he still possesses athletic skills. He attempts to rekindle civic compassion and duty among the complacent middle class of Segget. He becomes involved with local labor leaders and organizers, but his dream of a revivified new world after the upheaval of World War I is shattered by the postnatal death of his and Chris's newborn son, Michael, and by the horrible suffering of laborers and their families. Robert dies in the pulpit, alienated from Chris, his health broken and his dream shattered.

Young Ewan Tavendale, Chris's son, who grows from early childhood to adolescence. Ewan bears a startling resemblance to his father: He is dark-haired and dark-complexioned, intense, self-possessed, and mysterious. Intelligent and inquisitive, Ewan distinguishes himself academically and intellectually, immersing himself in the history and archaeology of the ancient Picts and Scots. At times, Chris worries that Ewan is too aloof, disinterested in and disconnected from his fellows. Her concern is warranted: By the end of the third volume of the trilogy, Ewan has become a cold, vindictive, and ruthless Communist labor organizer and agitator.

Else Queen, Chris and Robert's housekeeper, also an employee and mistress of a local landowner. Large, buxom, hearty, and vigorous, Else comes to love the Colquohouns after working for and living with them. When she is fired after Robert catches her with her lover in the manse kitchen, she moves in with her lover and bears him an out-of-wedlock child. When Chris's life is threatened by premature childbirth, Else comes back to nurse her back to health and remains with the Colquohouns until Robert's death.

Grey Granite, 1934

Ma Cleghorn, Chris's partner and boardinghouse co-owner, a widow. Large, brisk, competent, and plain-spoken, she comforts the recently widowed Chris and earns her affection. When Mrs. Cleghorn dies toward the end of the novel, Chris imagines her declining the passive Heaven of which the ministers speak, choosing instead the Scottish mountaintops.

The Reverend Stuart Gibbon, the minister of the Kirk at Kinraddie. With his booming voice, large physique, red face, and black hair, Gibbon looks the role of minister of the Kirk. He proves, however, to be vain, hypocritical, and lecherous. He fights the war ferociously from his pulpit, wearing a military chaplain's dashing uniform. Others hating the war discredit Gibbon by marching off quietly to die in the trenches.

McIvor, Ewan's best man at his wedding and a fellow Highlander. A towering man, redheaded and red-faced, McIvor is a haunting, enigmatic figure. He disappears from the narrative until the end, when he reappears in kilts to play a Highland dirge on bagpipes as he paces slowly around a memorial commemorating the battle deaths of Ewan, Long Rob, Chae, and another man from Kinraddie. McIvor contributes a powerful sense of ancientness and continuity to the dramatic ending of the novel.

Dalziel of Meiklebogs, a local landowner, Else Queen's lover and, for a time, her common-law husband. Dalziel acts shy in public and speaks quietly, but his burly size, red features, and unshaven face remind Chris of a deceptive Highland bull. Dalziel reveals his true nature by allowing a mortally injured draft horse to suffer so that he can collect insurance money, and by refusing to acknowledge his natural son, born to Else Queen.

Stephen Mowat, the owner of the local textile mills, a libertine and dilettante. In his early or mid-twenties, Mowat is short, curly haired, bespectacled, and ingratiating. Mowat plays at being the laird (lord) of Segget, talking of what he will do for the local mill economy. In fact, however, he is but one more profligate aristocrat, squandering money gotten from mistreated workers. Mowat secures a bank loan under false pretenses and flees Segget, knowing that the bank will seize and shut down the mills, thus leaving Segget's workers destitute and desperate.

Alec "Ake" Ogilvie, a joiner (carpenter), World War I veteran, amateur poet, and Chris's third husband. Another big Scotsman, Ake has twinkling green eyes, a long mustache, and unapologetically country mannerisms that cast him as one more ancient Scot, so much so that his age is indeterminate. Chris marries Ake in the third volume of the trilogy, but when Ake cannot awaken Chris's passionate nature, he abruptly leaves her to become a ship's carpenter.

Sim Leslie, nicknamed "**Feet**," a constable in Segget, later a police sergeant in Duncairn in the third volume. Dull-witted, large, and oafish, Leslie is one of the police officers who hound and then persecute striking laborers. Leslie arrests Chris's son, Ewan, and is involved in his torture in jail.

Neil Quaritch, a boarder in the rooming house, a newspaper copy editor and book reviewer. Although he is small and dominated by red features (beard, hair, eyes, and nose), Quaritch is spunky, skeptical, and urbane. At the end of the novel, after Ake has left Chris, Quaritch makes a halfhearted proposal to Chris, which she rejects.

Meg Watson, a maid at the boardinghouse, the sister of

Alick Watson. Thin, pale, and sly, Meg combines the general unhealthiness of the laborers with their survivors' cunning. She becomes pregnant out of wedlock by one of the Communist organizers.

Alick Watson, a foundry worker, initially Ewan's enemy, then his friend and follower. As with most of the laborers in Duncairn, Alick is pale, sour-looking, and violent, tall but not healthy. Alick becomes Ewan's friend after the two have a bloody fistfight. After betraying Ewan to the police on false charges, the despondent Alick joins a Highland regiment, whose harsh discipline prompts Alick to lead an uprising of enlisted men. For this act, he is court-martialed and severely disciplined, a final degradation in a brutish life.

Ellen Johns, a middle-class teacher, Socialist, and activist. She is Ewan's lover. Pretty and fair-skinned, catlike, and blue-eyed like Ewan, Ellen strikes Chris as being almost a natural mate of Ewan with her ancient Scots appearance and air of mystery. Ellen's love supersedes her social activism and is rebuked by Ewan's "grey granite" commitment to his Communist Party responsibilities. Ewan ends the relationship.

Big Jim Trease, a key Communist organizer in Scotland and, eventually, Ewan's mentor. Large and plump, with small twinkling eyes, forbearing of laborers' suspicions, patient, and cunning, Trease bides his time, making what use he can of police violence, whether provoked or premeditated, to advance his cause. Trease combines steely purpose with delayed gratification, smiling at laborers' fearful insults, confident that eventually workers will rise against their masters, united and ready for vengeance.

Bailie Brown, an elected official of Duncairn's Labour Party. An object of satire, Brown represents the muted voice of laborers, toned down by being assimilated into the power structure. The irony is that Brown has as much vested interest in maintaining the status quo as do the Conservative members of the council. For all intents and purposes, he is merely one more ineffectual bourgeois gentleman, unsupportive and unsympathetic to the plight of the workers.

Jimmy Speight, the lord provost of Duncairn, a childhood sidekick of Ake Ogilvie. Long-faced and big-nosed, wizened, and small-statured, Speight has learned the grand airs to accompany his gains in power and status. Goaded by Ake's recollection of a rape Speight committed in his youth, however, the lord provost agrees to two favors Ake needs in exchange for Ake's promise of secrecy about the rape.

The Reverend Edward MacShilluck, a prominent Duncairn minister, a lecher, and a hypocrite. Pompous and vain, this complacent minister of the Kirk appears intermittently, preaching only what his affluent congregation wishes to hear and practicing venality at home with his intimidated working-class housekeeper. Although not much developed as a character, MacShilluck adds to the satirical tone that builds as the narrative develops. Significantly, at the end of the novel, MacShilluck preaches a sermon defending the actions of the police, the attitudes of his affluent congregation, and the useful discipline of wartime. He returns to the manse only to find that the housekeeper has taken money and silver (as partial payment for her forced sexual favors) and left. One working-class character thus has her revenge at last.

— *David W. Pitre*

THE SCOTTISH CHIEFS

Author: Jane Porter (1776-1850)
First published: 1810
Genre: Novel

Locale: Scotland, France, and England
Time: 1296-1305
Plot: Historical

Sir William Wallace, a Scottish patriot of the thirteenth century. He seeks to free Scotland from the domination of the English. He is a courageous leader and becomes regent of Scotland. His success is envied by other Scottish nobles, and he is delivered into the hands of the English, who execute him as a traitor.

Robert Bruce, a claimant to the Scottish throne. He joins Wallace's patriots and after Wallace's death assumes leadership, freeing Scotland by defeating the English at Bannockburn. During the wars, he calls himself the Count de Longueville. He becomes king of Scotland after Bannockburn.

Sir John Monteith, a Scottish nobleman who gives Wallace a mysterious box that is not to be opened until Scotland is free. Monteith later turns against Wallace and betrays him to the English.

The earl of Mar, an elderly Scots nobleman and patriot who is Wallace's friend. He is killed while fighting the English.

Lady Mar, the earl's wife, who wants to marry Wallace when she is a widow and he a widower. He refuses her and wins her enmity. It is her false accusation of treason that

causes Wallace's death. She disguises herself for a time as the Knight of the Green Plume.

Lady Wallace, Sir William Wallace's wife. She is killed by the English when she refuses to betray her husband.

The abbot of St. Fillan, a loyal Scot who keeps the mysterious iron box through the war. The box contains the Scottish crown and royal vestments.

Edwin Ruthven, a faithful adherent to Wallace who dies defending his leader.

The earl of Gloucester, an English nobleman who sides with the Scots, believing his father-in-law, Edward I, to be wrong in claiming Scotland as his.

Lady Helen Mar, a daughter of Lord Mar. She loves Wallace and marries him on the eve of his execution.

Lord de Valence, an English nobleman held as a hostage by Wallace.

Lord Cummins, a Scottish nobleman who distrusts Wallace's ambitions. He becomes regent after Wallace resigns.

Isabella Mar, a daughter of Lord Mar. She becomes Robert Bruce's queen.

Edward I, the king of England.

THE SCREENS
(Les Paravents)

Author: Jean Genet (1910-1986)
First published: 1961
Genre: Drama

Locale: Algeria
Time: The twentieth century
Plot: Existentialism

Said (sah-EED), an Arab thief and a traitor, uncommitted to any person or cause. Indigent and unwed, twenty-year-old Said acquiesces to marrying Leila, the ugliest girl in the village. He dreams of going to France to purchase a new wife but until then spends time at the bordello. Requiring money to fulfill his dreams, he begins to steal from his fellow workers in the orange groves and is thrown in jail. After his release, Said is ostracized by the farmworkers but protected by the French colonial bosses. When the rebellion gains momentum, he is given an assignment but sells out to the French Legion for money. After returning to the village, he is executed. Said does not appear in the land of the dead but disappears into nothingness.

The Mother, Said's impoverished mother. She is caustically humorous and fond of impersonating the sounds of barnyard animals. She derides her daughter-in-law, Leila, for being ugly and idiotic. She is ostracized by her peers for her son's thievery and is forced to wander from village to village, residing in public dumps. She accidentally kills a soldier before dying and is thus revered by the revolution. She arrives in the land of the dead to find her peers and the soldier she murdered all very amiable. She warns her son not to serve any facet of the rebellion or any purpose whatsoever.

Leila, Said's hideously ugly wife, who wears a black hood over her face. She readily accepts her plight in life. To be with Said, who she knows detests her, she takes up stealing. When she is not on the run with her mother-in-law from village to village, she is in prison with Said. Said puts out one of her eyes, and she accepts this as a good thing. Like Said, she has no passion for the rebellion. When Leila dies, she, like her husband, disappears into nothingness.

Warda, a prideful whore in her forties. She views prostitution in a shroud of glamour and mystery. She does not undress before her clients as the French whores do but instead makes the men undress. Her time is spent more on clothes and makeup than in the art of sex. During the revolution, façades are stripped away, and Warda is disgraced by becoming a commercial sex toy. Her only joy is that she is murdered by a group of jealous village housewives.

Djemila (jeh-MEE-leh), an Algerian whore who arrives from France. She brings with her the French custom of undressing for her patrons, which soon becomes the standard.

Malika, a young, inexperienced whore under Warda's wings.

Kadidja (kah-DEE-jeh), a gamy, base, sixty-year-old Arab woman. She organizes the rebellion, draws the men into it, and eventually dies for the cause. She leads the village women to ostracize Said's mother for her son's crimes. After venting her hatred at Sir Harold, she is killed by his son. Her death manages to stir up more trouble. Kadidja arrives in the land of the dead and is infuriated that the conquering revolutionaries are becoming like their European foes.

Sir Harold, a narcissistic French colonist. He is prideful and obsessed with his self-image. He employs Arabs in his orange groves and keeps a close tab on them, even leaving behind his glove—stuffed with straw—as a symbol of his presence. Because he views all Arabs as thieves, he is not pleased when they take it on themselves to isolate Said for stealing. Sir Harold is killed in the revolution and retires to the land of the dead.

Mr. Blankensee, an arrogant Dutch colonist who has the finest rose garden in Africa. He wears a pad on his stomach and one on his buttocks to project an image of power. Soon after the deception is discovered, he is assassinated.

The Lieutenant, a vain leader obsessed with his self-image. To him, surfaces and façades are all-important. He believes that warfare should be clean and seductive. He is given an unbecoming funeral.

The Sergeant, a cold-blooded warrior who finds beauty in cruelty. Although heavily decorated, he dies with his pants down. In the land of the dead, he is pleasant and friendly.

Ommu, a blasphemous, indigent, and squalid sixty-year-old Arab woman. She becomes the passion behind the revolution following Kadidja's death. She despises the glossy façades of the French soldiers, including their uniforms, discipline, and military marches. To her, war is without scruples, and she even poisons the drinking wells with arsenic. Ommu plans to have Said killed for his betrayal but, after being repulsed by the revolution's adoption of European façades, she turns to bless Said instead for his baseness.

The Son, Sir Harold's son. He is sixteen or seventeen years old and in love with a vamp. He kills Kadidja when she insults his father.

Si Slimane, a dead Arab who no longer has any passion for anything.

— *Steven C. Kowall*

SEA GLASS

Author: Laurence Yep (1948-   )
First published: 1979
Genre: Novel

Locale: Concepcion, California
Time: Late 1950's
Plot: Bildungsroman

Craig Chin, a Chinese American eighth-grader, the focal character. Until the year in which the novel takes place, he and his parents lived in Chinatown in San Francisco. He now must adjust to a new environment, a smaller Chinatown in a small city on the California coast and a high school in which most of the students are "Western people," or non-Chinese.

His two Chinese cousins also attend the high school, but they think of themselves as Americans first. Craig has to adjust to life in a much smaller city than San Francisco. He also copes with a father whose expectations for him include standard sports such as football and basketball; he has neither the talent nor the physique to be good at either, being a little overweight. He negotiates an identity as a Chinese and an American. He changes during this year under the influence of his mother, his father, and Uncle Quail, an old friend of the family. Craig's suppressed artistic and aesthetic interests, discounted by his father as impractical, emerge gradually.

Calvin, Craig's father, in his thirties. He moved from Concepcion to San Francisco with his father when he was twelve years old. He had a small grocery store there but now has taken over operation of a store owned by a friend, known to Craig as Uncle Lester. Craig's father, who had been a good athlete in high school and had won acceptance by "Westerners" that way, pushes Craig toward sports.

Jeannie, Craig's mother, who seems beyond reproach in every way. She is about the same age as Calvin and was also a sports champion in her youth, winning many awards in Ping-Pong tournaments. She is less obsessive about sports and seems to understand her husband's frustrations well enough to help Craig deal with them. She is a retiring person, and her own personality does not often come forward.

Uncle Quail, a lonely man in his seventies. He lives on a stretch of beach near Concepcion that he owns, and he has fenced it off to preserve his privacy. He lost his wife and his fishing business during World War II as a result of racial prejudice. He is still bitter and stays away from people, Western people in particular. Craig brings him groceries once a week, and they slowly become friends over the fall. Uncle Quail teaches Craig how to snorkel and about sea life in the shallow waters off his beach. Uncle Quail's unwillingness to forgive any Western people for his losses causes a major conflict for Craig when Craig becomes friendly with a Western classmate named Kenyon. Uncle Quail finally is persuaded to have both Craig and Kenyon swim at his beach. Uncle Quail asks Calvin to allow Craig to pursue his own interests and activities.

Kenyon, an eighth grader in Craig's class. Her mother, Dory, and her father, Archie, are separated. Dory is an artist and Archie a poet. Kenyon tries to be as normal as possible to compensate for her parents' oddness. She is unfriendly to Craig at first, making up names to call him and prompting others to tease him. She becomes his friend as he tries to listen to her problems concerning her parents. She becomes interested in his snorkeling with Uncle Quail. She wants to participate, but Uncle Quail at first refuses to allow a Westerner to swim on his beach.

Uncle Tim and

Auntie Faye, Craig's aunt and uncle, Stanley and Sheila's parents. Both of their children are athletic and strive to be Westernized. Uncle Tim and Auntie Faye are inclined to judge other Chinese by these standards. Uncle Tim is an engineer, and Auntie Faye is a registered nurse. They do not live in Chinatown but in a big house in the Western part of town. They are portrayed more as problems for Craig to overcome than as characters in their own right.

Sheila, Tim and Faye's daughter and Craig's cousin. She is his age and is eager to differentiate herself from her Chinatown cousin. Sheila participates in teasing Craig about being too Chinese at school and about his physical appearance and city clothes.

Stanley, Craig's cousin, who is in the ninth grade. Stanley takes every opportunity to demonstrate Craig's physical ineptness. Craig describes Sheila and Stanley as "All American," citing how they demand soft drinks and silverware when they come to dinners with the extended family in Chinatown.

Bradley, another eighth grader, who starts out as Craig's nemesis playing basketball and football but turns into a friend. Bradley is courted for some positions in these team sports because he is large and strong, but he is not terribly coordinated. By the end of the book, he and Craig have become friends.

— *Janice M. Bogstad*

THE SEA OF FERTILITY
(Hōjō no umi)

Author: Yukio Mishima (Kimitake Hiraoka, 1925-1970)
First published: 1969-1971
Genre: Novels

Locale: Japan, Thailand, and India
Time: 1912-1975
Plot: Psychological realism

Spring Snow, 1969

Shigekuni Honda, the protagonist, a young Japanese man who is studying to become a lawyer. A natural leader, he is exceptionally mature, sometimes appearing to be almost pompous. He is already committed to governing his life by the rule of reason instead of being controlled by his emotions. When he is at the deathbed of his friend Kiyoaki Matsugae, he realizes somewhat regretfully that he can never give himself fully to any passion.

Kiyoaki Matsugae, the best friend of Honda. At the age of eighteen, he is handsome, with dark eyes and an elegant air. The descendant of a distinguished samurai family, he lacks the vigor of his forebears. Instead, he drifts aimlessly, enthusiastic about nothing. Even though he knows that a childhood companion loves him deeply, he rejects the possibility of marriage to her until she has become engaged to a member of the Imperial Household. Then he falls passionately in love with her, and although he cannot persuade her to run away with him, he has an affair with her. His walk through the snow in a vain attempt to see her results in his getting pneumonia. He dies at the age of twenty.

Satoko Ayakura, the childhood companion and, later, the lover of Kiyoaki. A beautiful, graceful, bright-eyed girl of twenty, she has loved Kiyoaki hopelessly for years. When her secret meetings with Kiyoaki result in a pregnancy, she has an abortion, breaks off her engagement to a prince, and retires to a convent.

Runaway Horses, 1969

Shigekuni Honda, who is now a judge in the Osaka Court of Appeals. Thirty-eight years old and happily married but childless, he lives a tranquil life until his encounter with Isao Iinuma, whom he believes to be the reincarnation of his dead friend Kiyoaki Matsugae. Defeated in his attempt to persuade Isao to lead a reasonable life instead of an unreasoned, passionate one, he resigns his judgeship to become Isao's defense lawyer, hoping to save his life.

Isao Iinuma, a kendo champion, the son of Shigeyuki Iinuma. A dark boy whose eyes reveal his intensity and determination, he becomes obsessed with the samurai tradition and desires only to die a pure death for an ideal. Gathering a small group of young men around him, he formulates a plot to kill a number of Japan's leading capitalists. The plot is discovered, and the students are arrested. Eventually, Isao is freed. When he finds out that his betrayers were his lover and his own father, Isao kills Japan's most powerful

The Temple of Dawn, 1970

Shigekuni Honda, who is now a middle-aged, successful lawyer and, eventually, a wealthy man. He now appears cheerful and outgoing. On a trip to India, however, he comes to surrender his previous dedication to reason and begins to indulge his emotions, if only as a voyeur. He falls in love with Princess Chantrapa (Ying Chan), but she eludes him.

Chantrapa, also called **Ying Chan**, a Thai princess, the youngest daughter of Honda's schoolmate Prince Pattanadid. When Honda first meets her as a seven-year-old, she is considered mad because she insists that she is the reincarnation of a Japanese. When she comes to Japan ten years later, she has

The Decay of the Angel, 1971

Shigekuni Honda, who is now in his seventies. Polite and quiet, he is, however, very strong-willed. Convinced that a sixteen-year-old signalman is the reincarnation of Kiyoaki, Isao, and Ying Chan, Honda adopts him, hoping to teach him to live rationally and thus to avoid an early death. After being exposed as a voyeur, Honda loses his reputation and control of his estate. At the end of the novel, Honda is shocked when the abbess who was once supposedly the mistress of Kiyoaki denies any knowledge of him, thus suggesting that the successive reincarnations that have ruled Honda's life may themselves be illusory.

Tōru Yasunaga, a sixteen-year-old harbor signalman. A handsome boy with beautiful dark eyes, he is actually malevo-

Shigeyuki Iinuma, Kiyoaki's tutor, in his middle twenties. He is reserved and bitter. After he becomes involved with a maid in the Matsugae household, she is dismissed.

capitalist and commits suicide.

Shigeyuki Iinuma, Isao's father and the former tutor of Kiyoaki, now the headmaster of the right-wing Academy of Patriotism. A man in his forties, he is no longer reserved but talkative and outgoing. To keep his position, he has had to take money from the very capitalists against whom his son is plotting. His motives for betraying the plot are mixed. He cannot lose the support of the capitalists, his school, and his position, but he is also eager to save his son's life.

Makiko Kito, the daughter of a general and poet. A beautiful woman of thirty who is always perfectly dressed, Makiko is gentle and kind. Although at first she is drawn to Isao because of his idealism and supports his plan to assassinate the capitalists whom she despises, she is eventually overcome by her love for Isao and betrays the plot to his father so as not to lose her lover.

forgotten that obsession. A graceful, lithe, golden-skinned woman, she regularly breaks her appointments with the infatuated Honda and rejects the advances of a young man he has provided for her, only to become involved in a lesbian affair with Honda's neighbor. At the age of twenty, Ying Chan dies of a cobra bite.

Keiko Hisamatsu, a divorcée and a neighbor of Honda. A chic, Westernized woman, she is bisexual and amoral. She offers her nephew to Honda as a seducer of Ying Chan but later herself has a sexual relationship with her.

lent. When he is adopted by Honda and elevated from the station of a poor orphan to that of a wealthy man's son, he wishes only to injure others, especially his new father. He torments Honda mentally and physically, eventually having him declared incompetent and seizing control of his estate. After reading the "dream diary" of Kiyoaki, however, Tōru realizes his own inadequacy and kills himself.

Momoko Hamanaka, Tōru's fiancée and the first of his victims. A mediocre girl from a well-to-do family, she continues to love Tōru even while he behaves sadistically toward her. Finally, the engagement is broken off by Honda, through Tōru's contrivance.

— *Rosemary M. Canfield Reisman*

THE SEA OF GRASS

Author: Conrad Richter (1890-1968)
First published: 1936
Genre: Novel

Locale: The U.S. Southwest
Time: 1885-1910
Plot: Regional

Colonel Jim Brewton, a pioneer rancher. He stages a bitter but losing fight against the encroachment of homesteaders

who come west to fence and farm the free range. A proud man, the colonel claims his range as his empire, and he has only contempt for the "nesters" who would destroy it with wheat crops. He marries a vivacious young woman from St. Louis who brightens his home and his life for a time. After bearing three children, one not his, she tires of her rough, monotonous existence on the ranch and deserts her husband for a period of fifteen years. Although aware that one of her children is not his, the colonel rears the boy as his own and buries him as a full-fledged member of the family.

Hal Brewton, the colonel's nephew, who deplores the inevitable changes he sees taking place all around him. He detests the homesteaders who spoil the range, and he resents Lutie's "Eastern ways," which mean new furniture, flowers growing in the yard, and frequent guests and visitors. Returning home from medical school to establish his practice, he finds that the sea of grass of his youth is gone forever.

Lutie Cameron, a charming young woman who comes to Salt Fork from St. Louis to marry Colonel Brewton. She soon turns the ranch house into a center for gay parties and distinguished guests, and for a while she seems to adjust satisfactorily to her new way of life. She bears three children, one by her favorite dancing partner, a young lawyer named Brice Chamberlain. Eventually tiring of the harsh ranch life, she leaves the colonel, expecting Brice to go away with her. Nothing is heard from her for fifteen years. One day, she unexpectedly returns, without explanations, and the colonel takes her back as though she had never been away. Meanwhile, he has reared her illegitimate son and with the force of his personality has kept local gossip to a minimum.

Brice Chamberlain, who as a young lawyer takes the homesteaders' side in a trial. Although he loses the trial, he continues to fight the free-range policy of Colonel Brewton and eventually sees the "nesters" win out. He becomes Lutie's lover and fathers a son by her. Being a cowardly man, he lacks the courage to leave town with her as planned when the colonel appears at the station wearing a gun.

Brock Brewton, Lutie's son by Brice Chamberlain. Realizing as a youth that he is illegitimate, he grows up bitter and resentful; to avenge himself, he turns to drinking, gambling, cheating at cards, and, eventually, outlawry. When he is trapped by a posse and shot, the colonel defiantly claims the body as that of his own son and buries it on the Brewton ranch.

Jimmy and

Sarah Beth Brewton, the children of Lutie and the colonel.

THE SEA WALL
(Un Barrage contre le Pacifique)

Author: Marguerite Duras (1914-1996)
First published: 1950
Genre: Novel

Locale: The Pacific coastal plain of French Indochina and the city of Kam
Time: The 1920's
Plot: Psychological realism

Ma, a widowed, eccentric settler in French Indochina who has struggled for seven years to make a worthless tract of coastal land profitable amid the annual assaults of the Pacific Ocean. Much of her strength, resolve, and sanity was broken when her attempt to build a wall to hold back the sea failed. Following the collapse of the dikes, Ma's life has been a routine of planting rice in vain and finding some person, object, or institution on which to place the blame for her misfortunes. Ma's hope lies in her two children. She worships her son, Joseph, and continually entertains the dream that one day she will be able to marry her daughter, Suzanne, to a wealthy planter. That wish comes nearest to being realized in the person of Monsieur Jo, the son of a wealthy planter who wishes to take Suzanne as his mistress.

Joseph, Ma's idle, angry, twenty-year-old son, whose one desire is to find a way off the plain. There exists a strong bond between Joseph and Suzanne, and they spend much of their day together doing what they can to avoid the oppressiveness of the heat and of their mother's ranting. Joseph is a hunter whose record with both animals and women is unmatched by the other men of the area. He does not approve of Monsieur Jo's advances toward Suzanne and does nothing to mask his disdain for the man's appearance, wealth, and lust.

Suzanne, Ma's youngest child, a pretty girl who, like her brother, is waiting for a means to escape the hopelessness of their lives on the plain. Although Suzanne is still a virgin, she is not innocent; her life has been harsh and has shown her that she can manipulate men to survive. She loathes Monsieur Jo but allows him to call on her every afternoon because in him she sees the possibility for the money that the family needs to escape its present condition. She eventually persuades Monsieur Jo to give her a valuable diamond ring as a down payment for sex. After the ring is delivered, Suzanne reneges on the agreement, dismisses Monsieur Jo, and begins with the family a journey to sell the ring. Suzanne leaves the plain with Joseph and his girlfriend following Ma's death.

Monsieur Jo, the only son of a wealthy planter, a man of little worth other than his fortune. He is not a businessman, is not socially adept, and has no ambition other than to sleep with Suzanne, whom he sees in a bar in the provincial town of Ram. The extent of Monsieur Jo's inadequacies is seen in the way that he is manipulated initially by Ma and Suzanne to promise to marry Suzanne and to subsidize the family. Ma entices him through promises of sex with Suzanne. Suzanne receives his gifts and then provides few rewards. His gift of a diamond ring is met with jeers and confessions of the extent to which his presence is detested by all the family, including, by this time, Ma.

— *Eric H. Hobson*

THE SEA-WOLF

Author: Jack London (1876-1916)
First published: 1904
Genre: Novel

Locale: The Pacific Ocean and the Bering Sea
Time: Early twentieth century
Plot: Adventure

Wolf Larsen, captain of the *Ghost*, a ship used in hunting seals. Larsen is a fierce, satanic figure, driving his men relentlessly and beating them brutally when they disobey him. He calls himself a materialist who does not believe in morality, ethics, or religion. He is contemptuous of anyone who believes in a spiritual dimension to existence. Although he is a monster, he is also courageous and curiously intellectual. He loves debating his views of life and earns the admiration of the novel's narrator, Humphrey Van Weyden, who learns from Larsen a code of self-reliance and honest self-scrutiny.

Humphrey Van Weyden, a writer and gentleman rescued from the sea by Larsen. At first, Van Weyden is revolted at Larsen's cruelty and physical violence, and he refuses to believe that such an intelligent man could really believe completely in the doctrine of "might makes right," no matter what the circumstances. Van Weyden confesses that he is soft and unused to physical labor and that he was called a sissy at school. He gradually comes to admire Larsen's independence and lack of sentimentality. He cannot accept Larsen's philosophy, but he is grateful for the opportunity to test himself against the elements and to discover reserves of energy and pluck that he did not realize he possessed.

Thomas Mugridge, the ship's cook, who is assigned the task of teaching Van Weyden his tasks. Mugridge, a Cockney, despises Van Weyden for his gentlemanly ways and for the privileges that Mugridge has never enjoyed. He bullies Van Weyden and even threatens to kill him, but Van Weyden rebels and eventually masters Mugridge.

Johnson, one of two hunters aboard ship who mutiny against Larsen. Johnson is a courageous rebel who fights Larsen, even though Johnson knows he cannot best the stronger man. Losing his battle against the captain, Johnson and his accomplice, Leach, escape the ship. Larsen catches up with the men and then toys with them, allowing them to drown in their small boats.

Leach, John's fellow mutineer, whose implacable hatred of Larsen causes him to risk everything to subdue the captain. He escapes from the ship when the mutiny fails.

Maud Brewster, a writer who also is rescued at sea by Larsen. Like Van Weyden, she despises Larsen's vicious amorality, but also like Van Weyden, she is mesmerized by his titanic will and strength. She is shocked by the inhumanity aboard ship. Although she is frail in health, she confederates with Van Weyden in plotting an escape. The couple succeed and are washed ashore on an island they call Endeavor. Through their struggles, Brewster supplies the inspiration and the grit that sustains Van Weyden. Their respite is short lived: The *Ghost* also washes up on shore. Although its crew is gone, Larsen remains as the couple's nemesis. They discover that Larsen is dying, possibly suffering from a brain tumor that has blinded him and is slowly numbing other parts of his body. The couple, now in love, fight desperately to oppose Larsen's efforts to thwart their escape in a rerigged *Ghost*. Contrary as ever, Larsen tries to burn the ship, but the couple prevails. Largely at Brewster's instigation, they nurse Larsen until he dies, evincing an admiration of his indomitability even as they reject his antihumanist philosophy.

— *Carl Rollyson*

THE SEAGULL
(Chayka)

Author: Anton Chekhov (1860-1904)
First published: 1904
Genre: Drama

Locale: Russia
Time: The nineteenth century
Plot: Impressionistic realism

Irina Arkadina (ihr-IHN-uh ahr-kah-DIH-nuh), an aging, famous Russian actress who is vain, egotistical, and selfish. Living only for public acclaim of her art, Irina is neither willing nor able to establish a warm human relationship with her lover, Boris Trigorin, or with her son, Constantine Treplieff. Her disregard for her son helps to drive him to self-destruction.

Constantine Treplieff (kohn-stahn-TIHN trehp-LYEHF), a struggling young writer, the son of Irina Arkadina. He is an extreme idealist, both in his love for Nina Zarietchnaya and in his art. Constantly seeking new forms in his writing, he ignores literary conventions and believes that life must be represented not as it is but as it ought to be. In a moment of despair over his work, he shoots a seagull (which symbolizes human aspiration) and then makes an unsuccessful attempt on his own

life. Near the end of the play, deserted by Nina, misunderstood by his mother, and ignored by more successful literary men, he finds himself unable to believe in anything, and he commits suicide.

Boris Trigorin (boh-RIHS trih-GOH-rihn), a successful author and Irina Arkadina's lover. Although his writing has brought him fame, he has no real satisfaction in his work or his honors. He finds that writing is a tyrant forcing him to produce new works. Unlike Constantine, he uses established forms and writes prolifically on every subject. His restlessness drives him to use people and then to discard them, and his weakness of character leads him to marry and then to desert Nina Zarietchnaya. Some critics believe Trigorin's comments on writing embody the playwright's own ideas.

Nina Zarietchnaya (NIH-nuh zah-REHCH-nuh-yah), an aspiring actress, the young daughter of a rich landowner. Deserted by Trigorin after their marriage, she continues her unsuccessful attempt at a career in the theater. She calls herself a seagull and aspires in the face of failure, but she does not expect honor and glory as she did when she was younger. Believing in her abilities, she can diminish her suffering; she is the only character in the play who learns that what is important in life is the strength to endure, like a seagull.

Peter Sorin (PYOH-tr soh-RIHN), Irina Arkadina's brother, on whose country estate the action of the play occurs. Like those of the other characters, all of his youthful wishes and dreams are shattered, and he ends his days wishing to escape his boredom.

Ilia Shamraeff (ihl-YAH shahm-RAH-ehf), the manager of Sorin's estate, a gruff, surly man dissatisfied with his status.

Paulina Shamraeff (poh-LIH-nuh), Ilia's wife, frustrated in her love for Eugene Dorn. She is bored with her lot and yearns for the unattainable.

Masha Shamraeff (MAH-shuh), their daughter. Hopelessly in love with Constantine Treplieff, she settles for marriage to a dull, impoverished schoolmaster.

Simon Medviedenko (seh-MYOHN mehd-VEHD-ehn-koh), a provincial schoolteacher married to the nagging, dissatisfied Masha. He is overwhelmed by responsibilities and debts.

Eugene Dorn (ehv-GEH-nihy dohrn), a doctor fifty-five years old and unwilling to change his ways of living by eloping with Paulina Shamraeff. In spite of his long and meaningful practice, he is penniless, but he has no fear of death because he has joy in life.

Jacob,

a maid, and

A cook, servants in the Sorin household.

A SEARCH FOR AMERICA: The Odyssey of an Immigrant

Author: Frederick Philip Grove (Felix Paul Greve, 1879-1948)
First published: 1927
Genre: Novel

Locale: Toronto and various U.S. locations
Time: Early 1900's
Plot: Bildungsroman

Philip Branden, the protagonist, a young Swedish immigrant to America. Tall and thin, with blue eyes and fair hair, Philip is educated, well-traveled, wealthy, cultured, and a bit pretentious; he speaks five languages fluently, knows fine wine, and has an eye for good clothing. When his money runs out and he travels to the United States at the age of twenty-four, he finds that none of these accomplishments is of any value to him in making his way in the New World. As he wanders from Toronto to New York, through the Midwest and into the Dakotas, he works as a waiter, a door-to-door salesman, a factory worker, and a harvester. He quickly learns that he is better suited for intellectual than manual labor. As he searches for work and for the America of Abraham Lincoln, he reflects on nature, art, education, and American and European values.

Frank Carral, a waiter in a Toronto restaurant and Philip's first real friend in America. Frank is a small young man with a pleasant voice, dancing eyes, and a laughing manner, and he is the most successful waiter on the staff. Philip learns, however, that Frank is successful because he steals, and Frank defends his petty graft on the grounds that it is simply the way things are done in the United States. As it turns out, Frank is living under an assumed name, hiding from the wife he abandoned in Buffalo. He encourages Philip to try New York City and provides him with the names and addresses of contacts there. All the names turn out to be phony.

Mr. Ray, a fellow book salesman in New York and Philip's second friend. Like Philip, Ray was born for a different sort of work, and his great desire is to be an artist. A tall, slender man with graceful movements and dark flowing hair, he begins to read great works under Philip's guidance. When he and Philip meet again after going their separate ways, just before Philip heads west, Ray is working in Harlem as a sign painter, one big step closer to his dream of creating art.

Dr. Goodwin, a generous country doctor who puts Philip back on his feet after he becomes ill in his travels. Goodwin has gnarled fingers, coarse features, and ill-fitting clothes, but he is one of the finest men Philip will ever know. Treating Philip's illness without any consideration for his fees, finding him a home and a job, and staking him enough money to get a few necessities, Goodwin acts purely from a sense of humanity. He is the first important contact Philip makes in what he soon comes to consider the "real America," the rural America of good-hearted laborers.

The Hermit, a recluse in the tobacco belt who gives Philip another perspective on life. A tall, gaunt man with long, braided hair and shaggy brows, he resembles a portrait Philip has seen of Mark Twain. When Philip saves the Hermit from drowning, the Hermit takes him in for a few days, sharing his meager home and food with Philip. The two work side by side. The Hermit is Philip's first human company in three months, although he never speaks, except for two words as Philip leaves. From this experience, Philip learns that advancing in America depends on give and take, and that he does have something to give.

Ivan, a thirty-five-year-old Russian immigrant who teaches Philip the life and methods of a hobo. A sallow-skinned man with a dark, curly beard, he reminds Philip of Titian's paintings of Christ. His nickname at some of the farms where he works is "Jesus." Ivan speaks perfect English and has delicate and refined manners, but he is as physically strong as Philip is weak and often does the work of two men when Philip cannot do his share. No idle drifter, Ivan rides the rails from town to town finding work and saving money, hoping one day to buy a small farm and settle down with a wife and children.

— Cynthia A. Bily

THE SEARCH FOR SIGNS OF INTELLIGENT LIFE IN THE UNIVERSE

Author: Jane Wagner (1935-   )
First published: 1986
Genre: Drama

Locale: Los Angeles and New York
Time: The 1980's, with flashbacks to the 1970's
Plot: Comedy

Lily, the actress (that is, **Lily Tomlin**, for whom the play was written). Addressing the audience directly, with respect and gratitude, Lily wonders and worries about the quirks of modern life.

Trudy, a New York City bag lady. Trudy has been certified as "crazy" and is proud of it. She communicates directly with aliens, whom she calls her "space chums," helping them to evaluate the signs of intelligent life on earth. She is carefree and playful, with a deep sense of irony. Survival on the streets has sharpened her perceptions and blunted her sensibilities: She unabashedly acknowledges the vulgar realities of urban life and confronts anyone who gets in her way. Trudy ranges the streets, talking to Tina and Brandy or organizing the paradoxical scientific data she records on Post-it notes. While penetrating society's delusions and questioning its idiocy, Trudy is beyond searching for answers or meaning; she simply loves the mystery.

Judith Beasley, a suburban housewife who once sold Tupperware products but recently discovered sexual freedom and now markets erotic products that guarantee orgasms for suburban housewives.

Chrissy, an unskilled but energetic aerobics fanatic. Chrissy is a jumble of conflicts and rationalizations. Virtually unemployable, obsessively self-aware, and potentially suicidal, she is searching for easy answers to all of her problems and finds false hope in ironic sayings, conventional wisdom, and self-help formulas.

Paul, a young divorcé. Between sex, drugs, and bodybuilding, Paul is tired of living on thrills. He philandered and ruined his marriage, and now he misses his son. Paul has difficulty adapting to modern mores.

Kate, a rich and beautiful socialite. Kate is bored—with her husband, her boyfriend, and her entire life. Obsessed with appearances, she needs to be in control and demands attention. A stranger's (Chrissy's) suicide note, a violin concert by a teenage virtuoso, and a moment of joyful understanding anonymously shared with Trudy, Tina, and Brandy combine to reawaken Kate's awe for life.

Agnus Angst, a punk rocker. Agnus is an angry teenager ready to fight for both strong leftist politics and petty personal grievances. Exiled from her father's house and abandoned by her globetrotting performance-artist mother, Agnus flees to her grandparents. She expresses her detachment, contempt, and alienation in the fevered outpourings of her own performance art. She desperately longs not to care; her tragedy is that she cares too deeply.

Lud and
Marie, Agnus' grandparents. Lud and Marie are an old-fashioned suburban couple who bicker endlessly and cannot begin to understand their radical granddaughter.

Tina and
Brandy, Times Square prostitutes and Trudy's friends. Tina and Brandy are strong, brassy women of the street who take pride in their lives and have compassion for the suffering of others.

Lyn, a Los Angeles divorcée. Lyn's personal history includes the women's rights movement in the 1970's, a lesbian relationship with Janet (Agnus' mother), participation in numerous self-help programs, marriage to Bob, the birth of devilish twin sons, a promising position in public relations, and, finally, a career change and a divorce. Lyn lacks direction and searches everywhere for security and fulfillment. She finds in Bob the perfect mate but has no time for him. She has professional aspirations but finds her job frustrating and unsatisfying. Having worked all of her life to "have it all," Lyn finds that it is all too much. She ends up holding a big yard sale, appraising and selling the mementos of her life.

Bob, Lyn's husband. A modern man, Bob reconciles capitalism with a holistic lifestyle by marketing New Age products. He attends myriad seminars and classes, including male sensitivity training and aikido, where he has an affair that ends his marriage.

Marge, a plant store owner. Marge is a tasteful, fashionable woman whose feminism seems less committed than Lyn's and Edie's. Striving for propriety and perfection, she goes through a series of unhealthy romances. One of her disco affairs was with Paul, whom she persuaded to provide the sperm for Edie and Pam's child. Marge becomes an alcoholic, suffers a traumatic rape, and finally, desperately, hangs herself from a macramé planter.

Edie, a left-wing journalist. Edie is a lesbian happily married to Pam, with whom she has a son, Ivan, a violin prodigy. The most radical among her friends, Edie has a strong identity and a healthy sense of humor about herself. She hates pretensions, though she can be trendy in her radicalism. Outspoken, skeptical, critical, and even vindictive at times, Edie openly expresses her needs and feelings.

Pam, Edie's lover, a psychologist who leads male sensitivity seminars.

— *B. P. Mann*

SEASCAPE

Author: Edward Albee (1928-   )
First published: 1975
Genre: Drama

Locale: A beach on the East Coast of the United States
Time: The 1970's
Plot: Comedy

Nancy, a middle-aged, well-to-do woman with an immeasurable love for life, adventure, and romance. Acutely aware of the time lost rearing a family, she views the remainder of her life positively and wants to fill those years by embracing all life has to offer, preferring to enjoy the beautiful expanse of the outdoors by trekking from beach to beach rather than staying in the stultifying confines of a retirement home. In conflict with her husband, who refuses to take part in any of her suggested recreations, Nancy, to no avail, takes various tacks (cajolery, mockery, and anger) against him to force him into activity. Her opportunity for excitement and purpose materializes with the arrival of Leslie and Sarah. She is able to share with them her innate inquisitiveness, ebullience, and compassion as she eagerly and openly explains to them the vagaries of the human condition.

Charlie, Nancy's retired middle-aged husband. The antithesis to Nancy, Charlie resists change and wants nothing of adventure. His lifelong propensity for isolation, evident in his childhood memories of sinking to the sea's bottom and relishing its peace and solitude, now reaches a crisis as he, painfully aware of his own mortality and cynically viewing his active life as passed, prefers spending his retirement doing absolutely nothing as if stoically awaiting inevitable death. His self-imposed detachment from life is ended abruptly, however, with the intrusion of the two anthropomorphic sea creatures. He is initially frightened and prepared to fight these strange saurians, but by the play's conclusion he reaches an epiphany. Brought out of his moribund state through his interaction with the reptiles, Charlie not only transforms into a vibrant, compassionate, and active man but also unites finally with his wife in the humane and extraordinary task of teaching the childlike creatures how to survive and exist in humankind's world.

Leslie, an anthropomorphic male lizard who, inexplicably, speaks fluent English and is conversant in metaphysics. Like Charlie, he is suspicious of strangers and always on his guard. Unlike Charlie, however, his dissatisfaction with a static and familiar life had forced him into action; he came out of the sea to explore the unknown in search of a better world. Leslie symbolizes primordial humanity with all of his animal instincts but lacks both knowledge of self and an awareness of loss and death. Leslie acquires this self-knowledge by the end of the play, when Charlie goads Sarah into crying so that he can explain the experience of human emotions; Leslie flies into a rage for the first time in his life, crossing the boundary between brute beast and human. This transformation, this acquired knowledge of human experience and emotions, mandates that Leslie (like Charlie in his childhood) can never return to the peace and safety at the bottom of the sea and must, for better or worse, continue on land in life's evolutionary process.

Sarah, Leslie's reptilian spouse. She shares Leslie's feelings of displacement in the sea and longing for something better, but she has none of his cynicism. More akin to Nancy, Sarah is open, candid, and eager to learn and share experiences. Although at times she is a satire on the domineering wife, she is kind, gentle, and the more childlike of the two reptiles. It is her keen sensitivity that enables her, when asked by Charlie what she would do if Leslie disappeared and never returned, to be the first of the two to experience human emotion. The humanlike tears that she sheds kindle Leslie's wrath and take them both to the symbolic threshold of humanity's first and cardinal evolutionary step: self-enlightenment.

— *B. A. Kachur*

A SEASON IN RIHATA
(Une Saison à Rihata)

Author: Maryse Condé (1937-   )
First published: 1981
Genre: Novel

Locale: Rihata and Farokodoba, two towns in Africa
Time: Late twentieth century
Plot: Psychological realism

Zek, a husband and father to seven children, who may not all be his own because his wife had a long-term affair with his half brother Madou. Zek has always resented his half brother because he believed that their father, Malan, loved Madou and Madou's mother (Malan's first wife) more. His brother's arrival in Rihata disturbs him, but once Madou promises to help him obtain a position as an embassy attaché, he hopes that this could be the beginning of a new life for them all. After Madou's death, he feels a sense of guilt because much of his sadness derives from the fact that Madou can no longer help him obtain a better-paying position with the government.

Marie-Hélène, Zek's wife. A native of Guadeloupe, she went to Africa with her husband in search of a sense of self, identity, and connection with her racial heritage that has eluded her. She is haunted by guilt over the suicide of her sister Delphine in France as well as her affair with Madou. She is extremely disenchanted with Rihata and its political and social corruption and oppression. She is also dissatisfied with her personal life and feels a sense of alienation and loneliness. Although she once thought Africa would give her a sense of rootedness, she still feels unconnected to her racial heritage.

Madou (MAH-dew), Zek's brother. He negotiates on behalf of President Toumany with representatives from the government of the neighboring country in order to obtain their aid in moving his country toward self-sufficiency. He travels around Rihata in a Mercedes, which represents his power and affluence. He is married to Mwika (MWEE-kuh). He convinces himself, on his death bed, that he was a good husband to her despite the possibility that he may have fathered several of Marie-Hélène's children.

Victor, a member of the opposition to Toumany's dictatorship. He is concerned that the reconciliation between Lopez de Arias and President Toumany will lead to further oppression and domination of the common people. He travels to Rihata and kills Madou for his involvement in Muti's arrest. He despises Madou because of the power and wealth he represents.

Kunta (KEWN-tah), the wife of a freedom fighter and Victor's aunt. She castigates Victor for robbing and drugging Inawale, Madou's chauffeur. She believes that President Toumany's reconciliation with Lopez de Arias will lead to more bloodshed. Her nickname, "**Muti**" (MEW-tee), means "mother" in her native language. She symbolizes the resistance of the common people to political social oppression.

President Toumany (tew-MAH-nee), the leader of the African state of which N'Daru is the capital and Rihata is an important city. When Madou dies, President Toumany declares a national period of mourning and appoints Madou as prime minister, knowing that a dead man cannot exercise political power. His reconciliation with Lopez de Arias is a ploy to make himself appear to be benevolent and peace-loving. He symbolizes the political corruption in his country.

Sory, a singer who is disgusted by the greed and abuse of power among public officials. He uses his son's name-giving ceremony as a way of ridiculing the materialistic leaders in the county. As a consequence, he is arrested and imprisoned as a political dissident. On his way from Rihata to N'Daru, he sings "Epic of Bouraina," a song that calls attention to the feats of a valiant and courageous African man of the past before the present corruption.

Dawad (dah-WAHD), a regional secretary who is corrupt and greedy. He is determined to succeed in his post of authority and will not allow anyone to speak out against the government. He has Sory arrested and imprisoned for singing a song that criticizes the greedy and materialistic government officials in Rihata.

Christophe (kree-stawf), the adopted son of Zek and Marie-Hélène. He constantly seeks information about his mother, Delphine. He feels a sense of emptiness because he knows little about his parentage. Frustrated by his unsuccessful attempts to find information about his mother and father, he dreams of going to Haiti, the land of his father.

Sia (SEE-ah), the eldest daughter of Zek and Marie-Hélène. She is two years younger than her cousin Christophe. Detached and dreamy, she is fond of historical romances such as *Anna Karénina* and *Gone with the Wind* because she desires to experience passion and adventure.

— *Sharon Lynette Jones*

SEASON OF ADVENTURE

Author: George Lamming (1927-   )
First published: 1960
Genre: Novel

Locale: San Cristobal, a Caribbean island
Time: In the third year of postcolonial independence
Plot: Social

Fola Piggott, a recent graduate of an exclusive girls' college on the Caribbean island of San Cristobal. The beautiful eighteen-year-old mulatta is established in a well-to-do middle-class family. Initially, she is inquisitive and sincere but unsure of herself. In her attempt to link with her private and cultural past, she seeks knowledge of her unknown father. This quest leads her to form relations with the peasant community, embodied in a tract of land called the Forest Reserve. Her "backward glance" in affirmation of the past estranges her from her stepfather and mother's set, who would "wipe out" much of their Afro-Caribbean ethnic roots. Having taken her stand with the Forest Reserve community, she becomes more determined and plans to become a teacher.

Chiki, a rebel artist and painter with a battered body; he is missing an ear. Thirty-one years old but looking much older, he serves as a mentor and guide to Fola as she seeks connections with her past. A son of the Forest Reserve who bought the land with money earned in the United States, he casts his lot with the peasant populace and with its resolve to retain natural ethnic cultural ties in a stance of truth.

Police Commissioner "Piggy" Piggott, Fola's stepfather, an insecure official of Forest Reserve origins. "Made" by his wife's urgings and promptings, he has risen from the low ranks of the colonial constabulary to a high position in independent San Cristobal. Attempting to escape the past, he is inspired by materialism and privilege. He is a prime agent of the attempt to suppress the steel drum bands. He loves his stepdaughter and is unable to have children of his own.

Agnes Piggott, Fola's mother, who lives a life of leisure. A proud beauty with a sharp tongue, married for twelve years to Piggy Piggott, she has been a steering force in her husband's rise in the island's political hierarchy. She is envious of Fola's close relationlship with her stepfather; it is closer than that between Fola and Agnes. She claims that Fola's natural father is dead; in fact, she does not know who he is because she had sexual relations with the bishop's nephew, then was raped by Chiki's brother.

Gort, a master drummer, a Forest Reserve confidant of Chiki and Powell. Gentle yet strong, he leads the revolt of the drums in successful challenge of the proclamation banning the steel bands.

Powell, the leader of a steel drum band, a self-educated son of the Forest Reserve. Often perplexed by curious paradoxes that confuse his thinking, he clings sullenly to peasant roots. He kills Vice-President Raymond as a despicable class enemy, and he attempts to kill Fola from a similar motivation. He is able to keep his role in the assassination hidden from the authorities.

Charlot Pressoir, a history teacher at San Cristobal's most exclusive girls' college. Until six months ago, Fola had been his pupil. Of European and Chinese descent, he is about thirty years old. He comes to accept that the past has an inescapable effect on people of the present. He returns to England.

Lady Carol Baden-Semper, a wealthy society matron, a pretentious but candid stalwart of the island's elite class. Freckled and apparently in her sixties, she is a kind of seer to the younger generation of Fola's class. Her wealth is built on a foundation of counterfeit money.

Dr. Kofi James Williams Baako, a college professor of science and technology and an old college friend of Chiki. A reformist, he becomes president of the Second Republic of San Cristobal two months after peasant demonstrations prompt the fall of the First Republic.

Veronica Raymond, the image-conscious daughter of the vice-president and Fola's close friend. Grief-stricken over her father's murder, she betrays Fola's confidence.

Therese, a maidservant to the Piggotts. In starched blue uniform and stiff, white cap, she is austere with strangers and contemptuous of surbordinates and guests not of equal status with her employers.

Vice-President Raymond, a man who, like Police Commissioner Piggott, has risen from the colonial clerical ranks to a lofty position in independence. Powell, spurred on by an incident involving Raymond's haughty contemptuousness, later kills Raymond.

Liza, a child of the Forest Reserve. About six years old, she is precocious and has a lively gift of gab. She is one of several children who flock around Gort and in whom he glories.

Bobby Chalk, called **Old Magdala**, a proud, now blind, elderly Englishman, a former engineer and longtime resident of the island. Gort and others call him Old Magdala, a name derived from the bridge spanning the river that divides the island in half. He is a drinking companion of Gort in the Moon Glow Bar.

Eva Bartok Turnstyle, a vivacious young office worker of quick wit and acerbic tongue. A girl of the lower class, she owes her position in part to her clandestine meetings with Vice-President Raymond. She is envious of Veronica and Fola's higher social status. Used and jilted by Dr. Camillon, Eva dies from complications surrounding an abortion.

Belinda, a short, thick woman with fuzzy hair and large copper earrings. She plies the trade of prostitution to buy books for her son, who has won a scholarship to a government college.

Dr. Camillon, a young surgeon. His name is suggestive of his deceitful character. He attempts to seduce Fola, but he exposes himself as dispassionate and self-centered.

The Houngan, a voodoo priest. He officiates over the *tonelle* in which Fola has a troubling visionary experience as a medium of possession in a voodooistic Ceremony of Souls.

— *James H. Randall*

SEASON OF ANOMY

Author: Wole Soyinka (1934-   )
First published: 1973
Genre: Novel

Locale: An African country
Time: After 1960
Plot: Social

Ofeyi (oh-FAY-yee), a chief promotions man for the Cocoa Corporation, also called the **Coordinator** because he organizes the campaign to sell cocoa products. Sent on a trip to study other methods because he is showing signs of insubordinate thought, he is fascinated by the power of backwater Aiyero to reclaim its youth after they study or work abroad. By placing Aiyero emigrants in key places throughout the country and lacing his advertising campaign with subtly antigovernment and anticorporation images, he undermines the ruling combination of white industrialists and native government and military men represented by the Cartel.

Pa Ahime (ah-HEE-may), the chief minister to the Founder of Aiyero and its breakaway cult. Ahime recruits Ofeyi as next Founder (Custodian of the Grain) and assists him in his plan of subversion. Later, he helps to organize and protect those who have escaped the Cartel's bloody counterstroke.

Iriyise (ee-ree-YEE-say), also called **the Celestial**, **the Iridescent**, and **the Cocoa Princess**, Ofeyi's volatile lover and the cynosure of his advertising campaign. She is kidnapped by Cartel forces and found in a coma by Ofeyi. Both are rescued from Temoko Prison by the combined efforts of Zaccheus, the Dentist, and the Doctor.

Zaccheus (ZAHK-ee-uhs), a bandleader who arranges and performs Ofeyi's songs. He witnesses Iriyise's kidnapping and accompanies Ofeyi on his many adventures to find and rescue her.

Taiila (ti-EE-lah), the Indian friend and lover of Ofeyi. She intends to become a nun, arguing with Ofeyi over their differing perceptions of the world. She meets him when he has an established relationship with Iriyise and sees him after a long separation in the home of her brother.

The Doctor, Taiila's brother, who ministers to victims of the Cartel pogrom, only to see those whom he saves killed by relentless soldiers. After Ofeyi and Zaccheus have failed to

find Iriyise in his morgue, he takes them home, where they meet his mother and Taiila.

Isola Demakin (ee-SOH-lah deh-MAH-kihn), **the Dentist**, an Aiyero native who has studied dentistry abroad and meets Ofeyi when the latter is creating his subversive network. The philosophically diametric opposite of Taiila, the Dentist expands beyond systematic extermination of lower-level functionaries to planned assassination of Cartel leaders.

Chief Batoki (bah-TOH-kee), one of the four most powerful members of the Cartel, known as the Big Four. He is the "brains" of the group, adept at behind-the-scenes maneuvering and setting one party against another.

Zaki Amuri (ZAH-kee ah-MOO-ree), another of the Big Four and the tyrant of Cross-river, where the whites do their mining and many Aiyero agents have settled. He launches the pogrom against proponents of economic and political freedom.

Karaun (kah-RAH-ewn), the governor of Temoko Prison, so nicknamed because of his physical handicaps. He has opened the prison to people fleeing murderous mobs. On Cartel orders, he has also kept Iriyise in the "lunatic" section of the prison, and he has Ofeyi placed there with her.

Semi-dozen, the Doctor's immensely obese neighbor, who drinks exactly six beers every evening. He is a token native officer of the mining company. When the pogrom and attendant mob action begin, he puts his family on a passenger truck going to the "South." When the driver and passengers are massacred, he makes his house into a bomb and himself into bait to attract and destroy some of those who killed his family.

Biye (BEE-yay), the daughter and fanatical supporter of Chief Batoki, often defending him against the verbal assaults of Ofeyi and her mother.

The Chairman of the Cocoa Corporation. He is deceived

into helplessness by Ofeyi's campaign. The Corporation therefore becomes known as "The Headless Corpse."

Suberu (sew-BAY-rew), a giant trusty devoted to Karaun. He has refused release so that he can serve Karaun. After listening to Ofeyi, he is last seen walking purposefully away, perhaps to leave the prison, perhaps to confront Karaun about his treatment of prisoners.

The Trouble-shooter, who is appointed by Cartel headquarters and approved by the government to investigate Ofeyi's treachery and deal with him. Ofeyi resigns on the spot and leaves without being detained as planned.

Mrs. Batoki, the Chief's large and overbearing wife. She never lets him forget that he owes his success to her family's prestige.

Spyhole, a malicious newspaper columnist in league with Zaccheus and Ofeyi.

Chief Biga (BEE-gah), another of the Big Four. He had once kidnapped Iriyise to fix a beauty contest.

Commandant, the other member of the Big Four, representing the military.

Elihu and

Aliyu (ah-LEE-yew), the self-appointed priest and guardian, respectively, of many refugees from the Cartel persecution.

IQ, the Chairman's intelligence officer, who interprets the hidden messages in Ofeyi's advertising material.

— James L. Hodge

THE SECOND COMING

Author: Walker Percy (1916-1990)
First published: 1980
Genre: Novel

Locale: Linwood, North Carolina
Time: Late 1970's
Plot: Philosophical

William (Will) Barrett, a middle-aged Wall Street lawyer, now retired and living in North Carolina, playing a considerable amount of golf. He seems to have spent his life trying to escape the memory of his bitter, neurotic father, who committed suicide and once tried to kill Will in a hunting "accident." Will is recently widowed, having married a rich, pious, and crippled woman who was devoted to good works. He is vaguely dissatisfied with his financial success, sensing that everything has been a mistake. Only in moments of distress or emergency does he feel that he knows exactly what he should be doing. He has periods of disorientation, sometimes falling down like someone having a mild epileptic seizure. Eventually, he "goes mad" and crawls into an obscure cave under the golf course to wait until God gives him an unambiguous sign of His existence—or to die of starvation if God does not make Himself known. He finds, however, that an acute toothache effectively renders his search for truth irrelevant. In his rush to escape from the cave, he loses his way, falls precipitously through a side tunnel, and crashes through a ventilator shaft into an old greenhouse occupied by a disturbed young woman who shares his alienation from society. Although his mysterious malady eventually is diagnosed in quasi-scientific terms, it still seems to be a psychological ailment rooted in unsatisfied emotional and religious needs.

Allison (Allie) Huger, a young woman who escapes from a mental institution where she was confined by her parents because she stopped talking. Although her memory has been partially wiped out by repeated electroshock treatments, she is intelligent and quite capable of solving complex problems, especially when they do not require communication with other people. She has been intimidated by her opinionated father and a mother who reinterprets anything he says to fit her own notions of reality. Allie's ability to listen sympathetically endeared her to an old woman who subsequently died and left her some property, including the greenhouse into which Will falls and a small island that the Arabs want to buy. This puts her in danger of being found and declared incompetent by her greedy parents, in collusion with her psychiatrist, so that the parents can manage her financial affairs. Allie has a peculiar

but uniquely expressive manner of speech that puzzles most people. Will, however, is charmed by her direct, yet poetic, language. They seem to complement each other: He is her interpreter and she his "hoister"; that is, she manages to pick him up (with the help of a block and tackle) when he is wounded or unconscious and take care of him. She remembers too little about the past, and he remembers too much.

Katherine (Kitty) Vaught Huger and

Alistair Huger, Allison's parents. Alistair is a dentist. Kitty knew Will briefly in their college days and implies that they had a love affair. She wants to enlist him as a lawyer to help her to declare Allison incompetent. She is horrified and self-righteous when she finds out that Will spent some time with her daughter in Allison's greenhouse. She still seems receptive to going to bed with Will herself.

Dr. Duk, Allie's foreign-born psychiatrist. He is inadequately trained (possibly in Pakistan), having an imperfect understanding of American psychology and using outmoded shock treatments as a kind of cure-all.

Jack Curl, a chaplain in an old folks' home. Knowing little about religion, he is ambitious to manage the charities endowed by Will's deceased wife.

Lewis Peckham, an unhappy golf pro who writes poetry in secret and thinks that Great Books can tell him how to live. Lewis says that he and Will suffer because they are once-born in a society of the twice-born. He shows Will the secret entrance to the cave.

Ewell McBee, a swinish country lout turned small-time businessman. He bullied Will as a child. In Will's somewhat unbalanced mental condition, he seems like a dark alter ego representing the lustful, materialistic common denominator of fallen man—or perhaps Mephistopheles, the spirit that denies that human goodness is possible.

Leslie Barrett, Will's self-righteous, Fundamentalist daughter, who tries to get her father committed to a sanatorium to "save him" from his involvement with Allison and to acquire control of her mother's money.

— Katherine Snipes

THE SECOND MAN

Author: S. N. Behrman (1893?-1973)
First published: 1927
Genre: Drama

Locale: New York City
Time: The 1920's
Plot: Comedy of manners

Clark Storey, a struggling writer of fiction and poetry. At the age of thirty-one, he is a cosmopolitan master of the bon mot who cheerfully admits to being selfish and devoid of passion and genuine talent. His self-deprecation, however, is more the posturing of a wit than a reflection of his true nature or creative ability. An early, ill-fated marriage has left him distrustful of love, and he assumes the role of foppish cad to avoid facing his inner emptiness, or his lack, as Monica Grey puts it, of soul. Fundamentally, he is a decent fellow who, if short on love, is long on affection, loyalty, and kindness. Because he values the lifestyle that wealth affords, he unblushingly accepts money from Mrs. Frayne and, further, despite not loving her, plans to wed her. Although Storey's dormant passion is rekindled momentarily by Grey, his cynical self, the second and stronger man within, represses it. As the decent thing to do, with a studied, ironic detachment, Storey does his best to foster the relationship of Austin Lowe and Grey.

Mrs. Kendall Frayne, a wealthy widow who is a friend of Storey. She is a charming, sophisticated, and extremely gracious lady who, temperamentally, seems ideally suited to the writer. At the age of thirty-five, she is a bit older than Storey and considerably more experienced and cultured than the effusive and ingenuous Grey. She is also handsome and stylish. She has a keen intelligence and a good sense of humor, both of which Storey values greatly. She, in turn, is in love with him, perceiving the man's fundamental generosity of spirit behind his selfish mask. She is no fool and senses that Storey, despite his disavowals, has a good heart. Her faith in him is only momentarily tested by Grey's deceitful claim that she is pregnant with Storey's child.

Austin Lowe, a wealthy chemist and friend of Storey. Lowe is twenty-nine years old and on the fat side, a stolid and basically humorless and plodding fellow, in notable contrast to Storey. Although a genius in matters scientific, he lacks the facile wit of Storey and Mrs. Frayne, who finds him a bore. Lowe is a man of feeling, however, and is painfully in love with Grey, whose flighty and capricious behavior leaves him morose and tongue-tied. Despite Lowe's inarticulateness, Storey admires his genius and does his best to convince Grey of Lowe's promise as a husband. Believing Grey's lie about her pregnancy, Lowe makes a comic attempt on Storey's life.

Monica Grey, a friend of Storey and Lowe. At the age of twenty, she is something of an ingenue. She is radiant and charming but very poor, which, for Storey, is worse than a character flaw. He claims that she is as "shallow as a platter," but in truth she is simply inexperienced and uncertain of what she wants. She is drawn to Storey by his urbane style and, at first, attempts to discourage the sincere but clumsy advances of Lowe. Her reckless lie about being pregnant, however, results in some sobering and maturing reappraisals when Storey forces her to face the mordant side of his nature.

— *John W. Fiero*

THE SECOND MRS. TANQUERAY

Author: Arthur Wing Pinero (1855-1934)
First published: 1895
Genre: Drama

Locale: London and Surrey, England
Time: The 1890's
Plot: Social realism

Aubrey Tanqueray, a wealthy English widower. He is resolved to marry a second time, to a young woman from a lower class. The marriage is disappointing, because he finds the young wife's boredom perplexing and her humor and cynicism embarrassing. He finally learns that his young wife has been his daughter's suitor's mistress.

Paula Ray Tanqueray, a younger woman of somewhat questionable character, loved by Aubrey. She is unsure of herself but glib. After her marriage, she finds she is bored and lonely in the country. She intercepts a letter from Ellean Tanqueray to her father, is discovered, and promises to try to be a better wife. When she learns that her former lover is her stepdaughter's suitor and that she stands in the way of her stepdaughter's marriage, she commits suicide.

Ellean Tanqueray, Aubrey's teenage daughter by his first wife. She is highly religious and considers becoming a nun. When she thinks her mother's spirit has told her to do so, she returns home for a time. She falls in love with an army officer who proves to have been her stepmother's former lover.

Captain Hugh Ardale, an army officer who courts Ellean and wins her love. His marriage to her is delayed, however, because he was at one time Ellean's stepmother's lover.

Cayley Drummle, Aubrey's good friend, who tries to counsel him against a marriage with a woman from a lower class.

Mrs. Alice Cortelyou, Aubrey's longtime friend and neighbor, the first of his set to call after his marriage to Paula Ray.

Sir George and

Lady Orreyed, friends of Paula Ray before her marriage. She invites them to the Tanqueray home after the marriage, despite her husband's objections. They prove to be coarse, boorish, and even insulting to guests.

Mrs. Tanqueray, Aubrey's dead wife, who had not made her husband happy. When she died of a fever, one of Aubrey's friends observed that it was the only warmth ever to have come to the woman's body.

THE SECOND SHEPHERDS' PLAY
(Secunda Pastorum)

Author: The Wakefield Master (c. 1420-c. 1450)
First transcribed: The fifteenth century
Genre: Drama

Locale: Bethlehem and the surrounding country
Time: The Nativity
Plot: Mystery and miracle play

Coll, the first shepherd. He complains to his companions of the cold winter, poverty, and the oppression of husbandmen by the gentry. It is his kindly thought of leaving a present for Mak's child that leads to the discovery of the sheep.

Gyb, the second shepherd, who is plagued by a shrewish wife as well as by the weather and his masters. He urges the others on to Bethlehem to worship the Christ Child after they have heard the song of the angels.

Daw, the third shepherd, a boy. He is suspicious of Mak from the moment he appears, and he first recognizes Gill's new baby as the lost sheep.

Mak, a rogue and a well-known sheep stealer who attempts to gull the shepherds and nearly succeeds in convincing them that their ram is his child. He finally wins a tossing in a blanket for his trouble.

Gill, his sharp-tongued wife. She complains incessantly of his failings as husband and provider, but she is happy to aid in his deception of the shepherds and suggests that he dress the sheep in swaddling clothes while she pretends to be lying in childbed.

An angel, who sings to the shepherds of the birth of Christ.

Mary, the mother of Christ. She greets the shepherds and accepts their simple gifts for her child.

SECOND TRILOGY

Author: Joyce Cary (1888-1957)
First published: 1952-1955
Genre: Novels

Locale: England
Time: c. 1860-1926
Plot: Domestic realism

Prisoner of Grace, 1952

Chester Nimmo, a Radical Liberal politician and Methodist lay preacher, the first husband of Nina Woodville. While a clerk in a real estate office, Nimmo meets and woos Nina Woodville, the niece of his clients. He saves her from scandal by marrying her despite her pregnancy by Jim Latter. After their marriage, he uses her inheritance and social connections to launch his political career. A pro-labor and pro-Boer member of the Liberal Party, he eventually wins a seat in Parliament. After the 1905 election, he becomes under-secretary for mines. He survives a scandal caused by his buying shares in a company about to benefit from a government contract. After World War I breaks out, he repudiates his antiwar position and becomes minister of production. He loses his seat in the election of 1924. Although Nina has left him and married Jim Latter, he visits their home. During the visit, he has a heart attack (or feigns one) and becomes their houseguest.

Nina Woodville, the wife of Chester Nimmo and later of Jim Latter, her cousin. Orphaned at the age of four, she grows up in the household of Aunt Latter. As a child, she has a nearly

fatal sailing accident when Jim sails into a storm. At the age of seventeen, she becomes pregnant by Jim. Not wanting to ruin Jim's army career, Aunt Latter persuades Nina to marry Chester. Nina's son, Tom, is brought up as Chester's. She becomes a political wife and is active in Chester's campaigns. When Jim returns from the Boer War, they meet and fall in love again. The result is a daughter, Sally. Chester arranges a settlement for Jim's gambling debts in return for Jim joining the colonial service in Africa. Nina tries to leave Chester but returns after he meets her at a railway station. Later, she attempts to commit suicide by jumping from her bedroom window. After Tom commits suicide following World War I, Nina leaves Chester and eventually divorces him. When Jim returns to England for good, she marries him. They have another son, Robert.

Jim Latter, Nina's cousin, lover, and second husband. The younger son of a baronet, Jim joins the army and becomes an officer. He is wounded in the Boer War. Disgusted with the British Army, he resigns his commission. He eventually joins the colonial service in Africa.

Except the Lord, 1953

Chester Nimmo, the son of Tom Nimmo. Nimmo dictates this "memoir" to Nina during the last year of his life as a form of final lovemaking and as a chastisement for her behavior before their divorce. As the son of small farmer turned Methodist preacher, he grows up poor. His mother and one sister die of tuberculosis when he is still a boy. When Chester is six years old, his father loses his own farm and becomes foreman of a larger one. Chester earns money as a farm laborer. He sneaks into a melodramatic play during a fair and is entranced

by the experience. Nimmo meets Dr. Dolling, a French refugee and leftist philosopher who settled near Nimmo's home. Dolling tutors Nimmo in political and economic theory. Nimmo seeks union leaders and tries to organize farm workers. He meets Pring, a Communist who becomes his mentor. He finds the violent and dishonest tactics of the Communists deplorable and leaves them. Eventually, he regains his Christian faith and finds employment as a clerk.

Not Honour More, 1955

Chester Nimmo, who, having been the uninvited houseguest of Jim and Nina Woodville for two years, leaves only when Jim Latter threatens him at gunpoint. The direct cause of the incident was Chester's attempt to seduce Nina. During the General Strike of 1926, he becomes the chairman of the Emergency Committee.

Nina Latter, who leaves Jim after his confrontation with Nimmo and becomes Nimmo's personal secretary and mistress. She helps Nimmo suppress evidence in an incident involving a special constable and a Communist leader.

Jim Latter, who discovers Chester making advances toward Nina and tries to shoot him with a rifle. He eventually chases Nimmo out of his house. During the General Strike of 1926, Jim finds himself serving under Nimmo, who appoints him head of a team of special constables. He does his best to keep order and defends one of his men accused of using excessive force in the arrest of a Communist leader. He discovers that Nina and Chester suppressed evidence in the case to placate labor leaders. After chasing Chester into the bathroom, where Chester has a heart attack, Jim cuts Nina's throat with a razor.

— *Tom Feller*

THE SECRET AGENT: A Simple Tale

Author: Joseph Conrad (Jósef Teodor Konrad Nałęcz Korzeniowski, 1857-1924)
First published: 1907
Genre: Novel

Locale: London, England
Time: The 1880's
Plot: Psychological realism

Mr. Verloc, an agent provocateur assigned to spy on anarchists in London; he poses as a shopkeeper. He is indolent and unkempt. Under pressure from his superiors at a foreign embassy, he plans to bomb Greenwich Observatory, a deed he believes sufficiently irrational and anarchistically shocking enough to stir up the London police in a campaign against the anarchists. His feebleminded brother-in-law, whom he enlists to carry the explosive, stumbles in Greenwich Park and is himself blown to bits. Because he uses her half-witted brother as his dupe, Winnie Verloc murders her husband.

Winnie Verloc, a motherly woman who married Verloc mainly to provide security for Stevie, the half-witted brother whom she loves protectively. When she learns that her husband was instrumental in having her brother blown up, she murders him with a knife and attempts to escape to the Continent with Comrade Ossipon. Under great stress after Ossipon deserts her, she commits suicide by jumping from the steamer on the way to Calais.

Chief Inspector Heat, an investigator of the Special Crimes Department of the London police. A methodical man, he wishes to follow conventional and routine procedures in trying to solve the mystery of the bombing, the motive for which he can in no way understand. He arrests Michaelis, the most harmless of the anarchist propagandists, whom he knows to be but slightly involved but against whom he can make a case. Because of the insistence of the new assistant commissioner, his superior, and the finding of a scrap of an overcoat collar with an address on the label, he is forced to approach Verloc, whose information to the police has been helpful many times before.

The assistant commissioner, an official of the London Police who has only recently come to his position from service in the tropics. He realizes the dangers of depending on routine and on conventional police rules and procedure. He questions Chief Inspector Heat's methods and finally feels compelled to take an active part in the investigation of the bombing episode.

Privy Councilor Wurmt, of the foreign embassy in London. He orders that Verloc be called in for reprimand and instructions.

Mr. Vladimir, the first secretary of the embassy. He accuses Verloc of indolence and deliberately pressures him into the bomb attack on Greenwich Observatory as a means of waking the British people to a sense of their European responsibilities.

Comrade Ossipon, "the Doctor," the unprincipled sensualist among the anarchists. He escapes with Winnie Verloc after she murders her husband. He is willing to share Verloc's bank account, but he deserts Winnie when he realizes the possibilities of suspicion that his relationship with her may incur.

Michaelis, called the **Apostle**, an idealistic anarchist who has been in prison and who has written a book about his experiences. This harmless man is cared for by Lady Mabel, his patroness. To save face, Inspector Heat arrests him.

Professor X, the perfect anarchist. Small and deformed physically, he has grandiose ideas and dreams of making the perfect detonator. For protection, he carries explosives, fastened to his body, that can be detonated immediately to destroy himself and anyone near him. He supplies Verloc with the explosive to blow up the Greenwich Observatory.

Karl Yundt, an old "terrorist." Skinny, bald, malevolent, and pitiless, he is a man of much talk but little action.

Stevie, the half-witted brother of Winnie Verloc. Because of his doglike devotion to his brother-in-law, Verloc plans to have him plant the bomb. It explodes accidentally and Stevie is killed.

Sir Ethelred, the home secretary, the great personage to whom the assistant commissioner reports progress of the investigation.

Lady Mabel, the patroness who supports Michaelis.

Toodles, the young secretary to Sir Ethelred.

THE SECRET HISTORY OF THE LORD OF MUSASHI
(Bushūkō hiwa)

Author: Jun'ichirō Tanizaki (1886-1965)
First published: 1935; serial form, 1931-1932
Genre: Novel

Locale: The Mount Ojika and Mount Tamon castles in Japan
Time: 1549-1559
Plot: Historical

Terukatsu, a daring, clever, and ambitious warrior, a vassal and hostage of the lords of Tsukuma, Ikkansai, and Norishige. As a boy of twelve, he experiences the siege of Ikkansai's castle, is sexually stirred and twisted by seeing the dressing of dead warriors' heads, and kills the leader of the besieging forces, taking his nose as a prize. He becomes a cruel lord who uses others to advance his career and to satisfy his masochistic and sadistic desires.

Teru, the daughter of Lord Ida of Suruga. The young girl calmly dresses the heads of dead warriors, including the "woman's head," that of a warrior who has lost his nose. Her cruel smile sets alive Terukatsu's masochistic desire first to be a "woman's head" himself and, failing that, to create a "woman's head" by taking a warrior's nose.

Yakushiji Danjō Masataka, an aristocratic general who attacks the castle of the Tsukuma clan. He is killed, and his nose is sliced off and taken away, by Terukatsu. His death ends the war against the Tsukuma clan but creates Lady Kikyō's desire for revenge.

Lady Kikyō, the daughter of Yakushiji Danjō Masataka, who is ordered by her brother to marry the heir of the Tsukuma clan, Oribenshō Norishige. She is beautiful and is intent on avenging the insult to her father. She conspires with her servants, the Matoba family, to take the noses of Ikkansai, her father-in-law, and Norishige, her husband. She fails to achieve her first goal but succeeds in the second with the aid of Terukatsu, with whom she has an affair. She becomes a devoted wife, to Terukatsu's dismay, after her husband loses his territories.

Oribenshō Norishige, Ikkansai's heir as head of the Tsukuma clan. Deeply in love with his wife, Kikyō, he provides weak leadership to his clansmen, especially after suffering attacks that take his ear and nose. Much happier reading and writing poetry and making love to his wife than in waging war, he loses his territory.

Lady Oetsu, Terukatsu's gentle and kindly wife, who becomes the main audience for Terukatsu's bizarre and masochistic stunts of entertainment. She is ashamed of her participation in her husband's treatment of Dōami, and they become increasingly estranged.

Dōami, Terukatsu's court fool, used by his master to relive the dressing of dead warriors' heads that he witnessed at Ikkansai's castle. Dōami is required to pretend that he is a dead warrior's head, and Terukatsu even wants to cut his nose off to show his women a "woman's head." Dōami suffers repeatedly from Terukatsu's cruel desires for satisfaction. Dōami's "Confessions" tell of the true character of Terukatsu that is ignored in the official histories.

— *Joseph Laker*

THE SECRET SHARER

Author: Joseph Conrad (Jósef Teodor Konrad Nałęcz Korzeniowski, 1857-1924)
First published: 1910
Genre: Novella

Locale: The Gulf of Siam
Time: 1880
Plot: Adventure

The Captain, the narrator and protagonist of the story, a young man who is beginning his first command. The nameless young Captain not only feels like a stranger to his ship but also feels like a stranger to himself. Being the youngest man on board, with the exception of the second mate, he doubts his abilities, and he wonders if on this first voyage he will turn out to be faithful to his own ideal conception of his personality, something that he believes all men secretly set up for themselves. His first real challenge comes with the arrival of the escaped murderer, Leggatt. He believes Leggatt's story of a justified and accidental killing and makes every effort to conceal him from the rest of the crew, even though this leads his men to suspect his abilities even more than they might have ordinarily. At the end of the story, he ignores the warnings of his chief mate and takes the ship dangerously close to shore to allow Leggatt to escape. Through his concealment of Leggatt, he gains the authority and confidence necessary for command.

Leggatt, the chief mate of the *Sephora*, who has killed a man aboard his own ship and has swum to the young Captain's ship to escape being taken back home to face trial. The character of Leggatt is not as clear-cut as those of the other characters in the story. For one thing, the only person who sees him in the story is the narrator. For another, he not only looks very much like the Captain but also went to the same school. Throughout the story, the narrator continually refers to him as his "double," his "secret self," his "secret sharer," and other terms that suggest that Leggatt is not so much a real person as he is a psychological reflection of the Captain himself. This does not mean that Leggatt does not exist, for it seems quite clear that he actually did kill a man aboard his own ship, one who would not do his duty and who was endangering the lives of others. Because Leggatt has dared to act on his own individual initiative in spite of authority, however, he seems to represent in some ways the "ideal conception" that the Captain has in mind of himself. Furthermore, he provides the opportunity for the Captain himself to act independently and to assert his own authority to his crew.

The chief mate, an elderly man, simple in his perceptions. He is a painstaking sort who likes to "account" for everything.

He has little confidence in the Captain and challenges him at the crucial climactic point of the story, when he is afraid that the Captain will crash the ship into the rocks.

The second mate, a taciturn young man who is younger than the Captain but who is given to sneering at him.

Archbold, the captain of the *Sephora*, the ship on which Leggatt was chief mate. His treatment of Leggatt makes it clear that he is not only obstinate but also that he is a stickler for a strict interpretation of rules. When he comes aboard the narrator's ship looking for Leggatt, it is clear that he is timid and fearful and that he can make no decisions on his own without the backing of the law and of the authorities.

— *Charles E. May*

SEDUCTION BY LIGHT

Author: Al Young (1939-   )
First published: 1988
Genre: Novel

Locale: Southern California
Time: The last decades of the twentieth century
Plot: Psychological realism

Mamie Franklin, the protagonist, a former rhythm and blues singer and minor screen actress from Hattiesburg, Mississippi. Hailed in the 1950's for her roles as a domestic in Hollywood films, Mamie is, until her death in her forties, employed as a housekeeper for an eccentric white couple in Beverly Hills. Mamie's psychic ability allows her to communicate with the dead.

Burley Cole, Mamie's common-law husband, father of Kendall, stepfather to Mamie's son, Benjie, and an avid junk collector. Burley dies of a heart attack early in the novel but remains an important character after his death. Lost in a netherworld between heaven and Earth, he exists as a ghost who reports to Mamie on important events in her life such as the meeting between Benjie and Harry Silvertone.

Benjamin (Benjie) Franklin, the son who was conceived out of wedlock by Mamie and Harry Silvertone. Named after the American patriot and inventor, Benjie is a young, talented screenwriter who is completing his master's degree at the prestigious University of California, Los Angeles, film school.

A comedy script cowritten by Benjie and his friend Nono is accepted as a literary property by Benjie's natural father, Harry, after their relationship is revealed to Benjie.

Harry Silvertone, the agent and film producer who helped Mamie start her film career in the 1950's. Harry's love affair with Mamie, whom he employed as a housekeeper, resulted in the birth, out of wedlock, of Benjie. Harry eventually accepts his responsibility for his son by helping him to get a script produced and helping to free him from legal troubles.

Theo, a handsome young man who waits tables at the Railroad Croissant café. He is decades younger than Mamie. The two sleep together after a dinner date at Mamie's Santa Monica apartment on the night of the great earthquake.

Brett Toshimura, the news reporter for a Los Angeles television station whose report on the aftermath of the Santa Monica earthquake leads to a massive show of public support for Mamie.

— *Daniel Charles Morris*

SEIZE THE DAY

Author: Saul Bellow (1915-   )
First published: 1956
Genre: Novella

Locale: New York City
Time: The 1950's
Plot: Domestic realism

Tommy Wilhelm, born **Wilhelm Adler**, an unemployed salesman living at the Gloriana Hotel in New York City. Middle-aged and separated from his wife and sons, Tommy is mired in a professional and personal slump. Almost broke, he seeks financial help but longs for spiritual solace as well, and he appeals to those around him for any help they can offer. His pleas to his father, not simply for money but for compassion or even a kind word, are met with scolding and impatient sighs of disgust. Down on his luck and reeling from some recent mistakes, Tommy is largely innocent of the selfishness and irresponsibility of which he is accused. Although misguided at times, he emerges as the most forgiving character in the story, compassionate even toward the father who has rejected him and torn inside at the thought that he might not be able to provide for the needs of his own two sons. Tommy's struggles and his search for a humane response to his need underscore the novel's major themes—suffering, compassion, and the blindness of greed.

Dr. Adler, Tommy's father, a retired physician. Elderly and somewhat frail, Dr. Adler also lives at the Gloriana Hotel, but his substantial wealth allows him to indulge his taste for the luxuries the hotel offers—fine dining, saunas, and massages. It is not merely in his financial status, however, that he provides a stark contrast to his son. Tommy's sufferings, though not enviable, are at least evidence of a rich inner life, and the pain that he feels is rooted in a concern for others as well as for himself. Dr. Adler, on the other hand, is moved to no emotion save anger, and even that he suppresses. He complains that the needs of others, even those of his own son, are an unwelcome burden on his hard-earned self-sufficiency. His sympathies, though never visible, are allegedly reserved for "real ailments"—fatal illness, injuries, and other physical hardships. He exudes a certain hardness, not only in his harsh assessment of Tommy's pain as self-indulgent melodrama but also in his narrow concern for tangible, "skeletal" problems, such as the bone disease from which a retired business acquaintance suffers. His hard-hearted refusals not only add to his son's misfortune but also serve to define Tommy further as a caring and generous man despite his limitations.

Dr. Tamkin, a self-proclaimed psychologist, poet, and healer, also a resident of the hotel. After Dr. Adler refuses to help his son, the eccentric and enigmatic Tamkin becomes the only alternative Tommy has in his search for a way out of his troubles. Dr. Tamkin (whose credentials are never established) allegedly "treats" a diverse clientele that seems to include a disproportionate number of attractive young women. Although he pays more attention to Tommy than does Dr. Adler, his behavior and his use of psychological jargon to deflect Tommy's questions suggest ulterior motives, a suspicion that is confirmed at the novel's end. Because there is wisdom and sense in much of what he says, he is able to exploit Tommy's desperation and emotional vulnerability and divert attention from his own decidedly ungenerous actions. Tamkin speculates in the commodities exchange market, claiming that this market is driven by a collective guilt/aggression cycle that he understands and thus can predict. He persuades Tommy not only to invest with him as a partner but also to put up most of the front money. While at the exchange, he pressures Tommy,

nervous about the downward turn in their investment, to escort an ill-natured old "friend" out on an errand. When they return, Tommy becomes frantic about their heavy losses, only to discover that Tamkin has cashed out what little money they had left and fled.

Mr. Rappaport, an elderly man who spends his days at the commodities exchange. The former owner of a commercial chicken farm and slaughterhouse, he is now a frail, bony old man and is nearly blind. He ignores those around him except to demand service or attention and is secretive and miserly while plotting his investment strategies. Tommy is coerced by Tamkin into accompanying the old man in and around the exchange.

Margaret Wilhelm, Tommy's former wife. Still bitter over Tommy's decision to leave, Margaret extracts vengeance by refusing him a divorce and by using their two sons, ages ten and fourteen, as bargaining chips in negotiating for money. She maintains a calm, polite exterior but seems to enjoy adding unmerciful demands to Tommy's already considerable difficulties.

— *William LaHay*

THE SEIZURE OF POWER
(Zdobycie władzy)

Author: Czesław Miłosz (1911-   )
First published: 1953
Genre: Novel

Locale: Warsaw and elsewhere in Poland
Time: 1944-1950
Plot: Political

Peter Kwinto (KWIHN-toh), a young intellectual and journalist who writes for the Polish Workers' Party. Although he is of Italian descent, Peter was reared in Poland under his mother's guidance, and he is in Warsaw when the Polish underground rebels against the Nazis. Peter is disillusioned when the Soviet army fails to support the Warsaw uprising, and he watches, helpless and in shock, as the Germans obliterate his hometown. After World War II is over, the Soviet Union is allowed to occupy Poland, and Peter becomes angry with himself for succumbing to the new Communist government, which he despises. Finally, by interpreting a recurring nightmare, Peter understands his apparent powerlessness against the new party by associating it with his father's death. When Peter was a young boy, his father was killed in a war against Russia; as an adult, Peter realizes that he has the same fear for himself. That insight causes him to leave Poland and flee to France.

Stefan Cisovski (sih-SOV-skih), a cadet officer in the Home Army of the Polish underground. He is nicknamed **Seal** because of his swimming expertise. He eventually escapes from Warsaw by crawling through the sewer system. Although he manages to survive the war, he is guilt-ridden for abandoning a wounded friend and for having a brief affair. He believes that everything comes too late, when it is no longer valuable, but he nevertheless helps his commander escape to freedom and decides to remain in Poland to aid in rebuilding his hometown. He is arrested by the Communist regime and given a sentence of eight years of imprisonment because of his Socialist tendencies.

Professor Gil, a scholar of classical literature. He appears only in two brief scenes during the body of the text, once when he refuses to leave his dying wife and a second time when he searches for his daughter's corpse. Despite the brevity of his appearances, his musings set the framework for the novel. The opening pages reveal him at work, translating Thucydides' writings about the Peloponnesian War. A link with history helps Gil to comprehend his own experience during World War II. The transition between parts 1 and 2 offers some of his personal history. Born a peasant's son, he had to fight for the right to attend a university. With the Soviet occupation, he has lost his department chairmanship and feels his life ending because he can no longer encourage the youth to pursue truth. The closing pages show him gleaning information from a newspaper and pondering how people can survive sadness and indifference.

Wolin, the head of the Security Department of the NKVD (police force). Reared in an upper-class family, he feels oppressed by the unreality of that lifestyle and runs away from home when he is fifteen years old. Experiencing poverty, manual labor, and prison as a result, he develops a keen class consciousness and strongly supports Communism. Fanatic about mystery stories, Wolin himself is enigmatic, and he is excellent at playing political mind games.

Josiah Winter, a man who supports the communization of Poland not because he believes in communist theories but because he is afraid of the power of communism. Described as apelike, with small, black eyes, he wants desperately to be accepted by the Communist Party. When the NKVD questions him about Peter Kwinto, he provides enough information to sentence his intellectual acquaintance to the Urals for five years.

Michael Kamienski (kah-mee-EHN-skih), the publisher and editor of an underground newspaper in Poland that advocates the combination of Fascism and Catholicism. He is viewed by the Communists as one of the blackest reactionaries in the country. Eventually, Kamienski agrees to recognize their political power if they will allow him to practice spiritual resistance.

— *Coleen Maddy*

SEJANUS HIS FALL

Author: Ben Jonson (1573-1637)
First published: 1605
Genre: Drama

Locale: Rome
Time: The first century
Plot: Tragedy

Lucius Aelius Sejanus (LEW-shee-uhs EE-lee-uhs seh-JAY-nuhs), the corrupt favorite of Emperor Tiberius. Willing to use bribery, seduction, unnatural vice, and murder to gain power, he overreaches himself by underestimating the sinister emperor and receives his death at the hands of an enraged mob manipulated by the emperor's damnable tool, Macro.

Tiberius (ti-BIH-ree-uhs), the devious and ruthless emperor of Rome. Given to self-indulgence and many vices, he allows Sejanus to assume his duties and much of his power. His suspicion aroused by Sejanus' proposal to marry Livia, he sends the Senate a letter that undermines Sejanus and leaves him helpless before Macro's machinations.

Lucius Arruntius (a-RUHN-shee-uhs), a righteous and indignant Roman citizen. Throughout the play, he delivers a running satirical and moral commentary on people and events. Although he despises Sejanus and his parasites, he sees no hope for better things after the overthrow of Sejanus.

Marcus Lepidus (MAHR-kuhs LEH-pih-duhs), a grave and honest Roman admired by Arruntius. These two and Terentius, at the end of the play, comment on the downfall of Sejanus and the survival of Rome's evils.

Marcus Terentius (teh-REHN-shee-uhs), another noble Roman. He delivers the final exemplary warning to all those greedy for power and insolent in its use.

Drusus Senior (DREW-suhs), the son of Tiberius. A blunt, angry, and immature man, he strikes Sejanus in public for his insolence. Sejanus has him murdered for personal revenge as well as to acquire political power.

Livia (LIH-vee-uh), Drusus' corruptible wife. She yields to Sejanus' temptations, becomes his mistress, and helps in plotting the murder of her husband. Her crimes are exposed by Apicata.

Apicata (a-pih-KAY-tuh), the divorced wife of Sejanus. She never appears onstage, but her agony at the death of her children and her exposure of Livia, Eudemus, and their accomplice are reported.

Eudemus (ew-DEE-muhs), an unscrupulous barber and physician. Sejanus corrupts him and uses him in the seduction of Livia and the murder of Drusus.

Sertorius Macro (sur-TOH-ree-uhs MAY-kroh), an inhumanly clever and cruel instrument of the emperor. Instructed by Tiberius to undermine Sejanus, he destroys the favorite and has the latter's innocent children horribly executed.

Agrippina (a-grih-PI-nuh), the widow of Germanicus, Tiberius' nephew, in whose death Sejanus and Tiberius had a hand. A proud woman and indiscreet, she is the center of a group of Romans suspicious of the emperor and hostile to Sejanus.

Caligula (kuh-lihg-yuh-luh), the son of Agrippina and Germanicus. On the advice of Macro, he seeks sanctuary from Sejanus with Tiberius himself, thereby inflaming still more the emperor's suspicions of Sejanus.

Drusus Junior or **Drusus Caesar** (SEE-zur), another of Agrippina's sons.

Nero (NEE-roh), the third son of Agrippina. When Caligula flees to Tiberius, Nero is arrested on Sejanus' orders.

Gaius Silius (GAY-yuhs SIHL-yuhs), a noble Roman of Agrippina's circle. When unjustly accused of treason in the Senate, he recalls his worthy services to Rome and stabs himself, choosing a stoic death rather than falling victim to Sejanus and Tiberius.

Sosia (SOH-see-uh), Silius' wife and a friend of Agrippina. After her husband's suicide, she is proscribed and executed.

Cremutius Cordus (kreh-MEW-shee-uhs KOHR-duhs), an annalist of the Roman history of Julius Caesar's time. He is executed, and his books are condemned to be burned. Hearing of this sentence, Arruntius delivers a savage denunciation of book-burning.

Titius Sabinus (TIH-shee-uhs seh-BI-nuhs), another of Agrippina's friends. Tricked into making critical statements against the emperor before witnesses, he is executed. When his body is cast into the water, his faithful dog leaps in after it and drowns.

Asinus Gallus (eh-SEE-nuhs GA-luhs), another of Agrippina's friends struck down by Sejanus' plots.

Latiaris (la-shih-AY-rihs), a senator, a cousin of Sabinus. He betrays Sabinus to Sejanus' spies but is himself crushed in the fall of Sejanus.

Domitius Afer (doh-mih-shee-uhs A-fur), an orator. He is the tool of Sejanus, speaking against Silius and Cordus in the Senate.

Varro (VAY-roh), a consul. He joins in the accusation of Silius in the Senate.

Pinnarius Natta (pih-NAY-ree-uhs NA-tuh),
Satrius Secundus (SA-tree-uhs seh-KUHN-dehs),
Rufus (REW-fuhs), and
Opsius (OP-see-uhs), spies employed by Sejanus.
Cotta (KO-tuh),
Haterius (heh-TIH-ree-uhs),
Sanquinius (san-KWIH-nee-uhs),
Pomponius (pom-POH-nee-uhs),
Julius Posthumus (JEW-lee-uhs POS-chuh-muhs),

Minutius (mi-NEW-shee-uhs), and
Fulcinius Trio (fuhl-sih-nee-uhs TREE-oh), fair-weather supporters of Sejanus.
Regulus (REHG-yuh-luhs), a consul, unfriendly toward Sejanus.

Gracinus Laco (gruh-SI-nuhs LAY-koh), the commander of the guards. Well-meaning but confused by the shifts in policy and power, he arrests Nero for Sejanus. He also brings the guards into the Senate to prevent Sejanus from escaping and to arrest his active followers.

SELF CONDEMNED

Author: Wyndham Lewis (1882-1957)
First published: 1954
Genre: Novel

Locale: London and Rugby, England, and Momaco (Toronto) and Windsor, Canada
Time: 1939 and the early 1940's
Plot: Psychological realism

René Harding, an English professor of history, formidably handsome, bearded, broad-shouldered, brown-eyed, and somewhat dark, revealing his French lineage on his mother's side. In his late forties, he has established himself as a thinker of considerable, if eccentric, proportion. His books are well known, and he has been made a member of the French Legion of Honour. At the end of the 1930's, disgusted with the way in which politicians have allowed the world to slip inevitably toward war and believing that historians are partly responsible because of their praise of political leaders, he resigns his professorship and leaves for Canada with no prospects of employment. He is very intelligent, irascible, and somewhat intolerant of contrary opinion.

Hester Harding, René's wife, called **Essie** by him. She is a very pretty younger woman, with gray-blue eyes and ash-gold hair. She is not an intellectual and has little interest in her husband's work, but their sexual life is happy and seems to keep them together. She accompanies her husband to Canada, but she is not happy about it and ultimately finds it much more difficult to adjust to what she considers the stupidities and intellectual vapidities of that country than does René, with severe consequences for their marriage. She is a kind, sweet-natured woman who is much taken for granted by her husband.

Percy Lamport, René's brother-in-law, an insurance executive in his early fifties. Financially successful, he is inclined to left-wing enthusiasms in politics and to following fashionable artistic trends. Despite his liberal leanings, he is still a man of commerce, as his rimless glasses seem to reveal to René, who despises him and his split public personality. Percy nevertheless supports René when René resigns and gives him a large check to help him on his way.

Robert "Rotter" Parkinson, a free-lance scholar of history who makes his living as a reviewer. He is square-headed and square-bodied, and he constantly smokes a pipe. He is René's best friend from college days and something of a disciple of René's ideas of history. His nickname, "Rotter,"

picked up while attending a university, is misleading because he is a thoroughly respectable and thoroughly loyal supporter of René. He is intellectually quite as solid as René, though not of comparable intelligence. They have great affection for each other, and René's departure is difficult for both of them.

Mrs. McAffie, called **Affie** by the Hardings, the over-rouged, skinny manageress of the Blundell Hotel in Momaco (probably Toronto, Canada), where the Hardings, very hard up, live for some time after their arrival in Canada. She is in late middle age and is the widow of an Ottawa attorney. She has fallen on difficult times but is determined to retain her fading gentility. She is cheerful, if nosy, and her former respectability does not restrain her from happily providing rooms for itinerant prostitutes, busy at their trade.

Herbert Starr, a social confidence man in his forties who affects smartness in a soiled silk scarf and a close-fitting overcoat; he pursues wealthy old women. He writes advertising copy and sometimes passes himself off as "Lord Herbert." He promises to introduce René to the right people, but he never does.

Cedric Furber, a tall, bearded, and elegant man with large, dull brown eyes, in his forties. He is a wealthy book collector particularly interested in books of questionable sexual interest, and he probably is a homosexual. He supplies René with a modest job as his part-time librarian. He is often kind to the Hardings when they are badly in need of money, but he never tries to get René anything very substantial, and he seems to get pleasure out of treating him as a servant.

Professor Ian McKenzie, a Scottish philosophy professor who comes to the University of Momaco sometime after the Hardings' arrival in Canada. He is easygoing, modest, and open-minded, and he takes the place of Parkinson as René's intellectual confidant. He makes a serious effort to get René back into university work, and he succeeds in getting him work at the school, which relieves the years of hardship but will have consequences that no one can imagine.

— *Charles Pullen*

THE SELF-TORMENTOR
(Heautontimorumenos)

Author: Terence (Publius Terentius Afer, c. 190-159 B.C.E.)
First performed: 163 B.C.E.
Genre: Drama

Locale: The countryside near Athens
Time: The fourteenth century B.C.E.
Plot: Comedy

Antiphila (an-TIH-feh-luh), the daughter of Chremes and Sostrata. Given, at birth, to a Corinthian woman, she grows up

unknown to her parents. In love with Clinia, she lives with him as his wife. She becomes involved in a plot designed to assist

Clitipho in his affair with the prostitute Bacchis, but he is finally persuaded to renounce his mistress. When Antiphila's identity becomes known, she receives permission to marry Clinia.

Clinia (KLIH-nee-uh), the son of Menedemus. In love with Antiphila but fearing the disapproval of his strict father, he lives with her as her husband. When his father discovers the affair, his harshness drives Clinia to the wars, from which he returns in secret because of his longing for Antiphila. Involved in a plot to aid his friend, Clitipho, in his infatuation for Bacchis, he learns of his father's regret over his former severity and receives Menedemus' permission to marry Antiphila.

Menedemus (meh-nuh-DEE-muhs), Clinia's father. Because of his unjust severity, he drives his son to the wars.

Finally, seeing the error of his way, he repents of his harshness and grants permission for Clinia to marry Antiphila.

Clitipho (KLI-tih-foh), the son of Chremes and Sostrata. In love with the courtesan Bacchis, he becomes a party to a plot to deceive his father about the true state of affairs. Finally, when he is found out and threatened with disinheritance, he decides to mend his ways and marry a virtuous woman.

Chremes (KRAY-meez), an old Athenian, the father of Antiphila and Clitipho.

Sostrata (SOH-strah-tuh), his wife, the mother of Antiphila and Clitipho.

Bacchis (BA-kihs), a courtesan loved by Clitipho.

Syrus (SIH-ruhs) and

Dromo (DROH-moh), Clitipho's servants.

EL SEÑOR PRESIDENTE

Author: Miguel Ángel Asturias (1899-1974)
First published: 1946
Genre: Novel

Locale: Guatemala
Time: Early twentieth century
Plot: Social

El Señor Presidente (sehn-YOHR preh-see-DEHN-teh), a dictator partially modeled on Manuel Estrada Cabrera, a ruler of Guatemala during the author's lifetime. His government runs on webs of political intrigue and corruption involving rumors, rigged elections, spies, secret police, hired assassins, false imprisonment, and torture. Since childhood, he has enjoyed tormenting weaker beings. Now he takes brutal revenge on all those who oppose or hinder him, including his former associates. He initiates a plot to frame his rival, General Canales, for murder. He at first appears to accept the relationship between Miguel and Camila, but he steadily works against them in secret.

Miguel Cara de Ángel (mee-GEHL KAH-rah de AHN-hehl), the handsome protagonist, called "as beautiful and as wicked as Satan," who serves as aide and favorite adviser to the dictator. His character changes when he falls in love with and later marries Camila Canales, whom he had earlier kidnaped while engaged in the dictator's plot against her father. His efforts to protect her lead him deeper into conflict with the regime and into a web of deception that the dictator suspects and eventually unravels, causing disaster for the young couple. Arrested while supposedly leaving on a foreign mission for the government, Miguel is tricked, betrayed, tortured, and finally thrown into prison, where he eventually dies in anonymity and despair after hearing lies about his wife's involvement with the dictator.

Camila Canales (kah-MEE-lah kah-NAH-lehs), the innocent young daughter of an influential general. During a plot against her father, she is kidnaped by Cara de Ángel, who wants her for himself. He is charmed by her and comes to pity her situation. They soon fall in love and marry, despite obstacles. She is separated from her husband and relatives through the dictator's deceits. She and her son finally leave the city to live in seclusion in the countryside, believing that Miguel abandoned them after he supposedly goes abroad on a secret mission for the dictator.

General Eusebio Canales (eh-ew-SEH-bee-oh), an opponent of the dictator who is falsely accused of murder. He flees,

learns of more abuses by the government, organizes a failed revolution, and finally dies of shock after hearing lies about his daughter's connections with his enemies.

Lucio Vásquez (LEW-see-oh VAHS-kehs), a low-level employee of the secret police. His killing of Pelele, under orders, causes a series of events culminating in the downfall of Cara de Ángel. He is eventually imprisoned.

Genaro Rodas (heh-NAHR-oh RROH-dahs), a misguided friend of Vásquez who wants to join the secret police. He witnesses the killing of Pelele without understanding all of its implications. Beaten and imprisoned by the authorities, he agrees to spy against Cara de Ángel and is involved in his eventual arrest.

Fedina de Rodas (feh-DEE-nah), the wife of Genaro and a friend of Camila. Thought to know too much about the plot against General Canales, she is tortured by the authorities. After her baby dies of neglect, she is sold into prostitution and driven to madness.

Pelele (peh-LEH-leh), meaning **Zany** or **Idiot**, one of several unfortunate beggars found around the cathedral early in the novel. His demented killing of one of the dictator's officers sets the plot into motion, as the dictator tries to blame the crime on General Canales. Pelele is aided by the unwitting Miguel but eventually is killed by Vásquez under the pretext that he is a public danger infected with rabies.

El Auditor General de Guerra (GEH-rrah), the Judge Advocate General, a military counselor, one of several powerful, brutal, and corrupt officials. He is successful in undermining Cara de Ángel, thus fulfilling his own political ambitions and gaining favor with the dictator.

Doña Chon (chohn), a brothel madam who knew the dictator in the old days. She bargains with the Judge Advocate General to buy Fedina de Rodas for her establishment.

Abel Carvajal (ah-BEHL kahr-vah-HAHL), a lawyer summarily executed for supposedly aiding General Canales. His wife tries desperately to save him but cannot.

Major Farfán (fahr-FAHN), a minor officer who is aided by Miguel but who eventually betrays and arrests him.

SENSE AND SENSIBILITY

Author: Jane Austen (1775-1817)
First published: 1811
Genre: Novel

Locale: England
Time: Early nineteenth century
Plot: Domestic realism

Elinor Dashwood, a young woman representing the "sense" of the title. She is much attracted to Edward Ferrars, Mrs. John Dashwood's brother, and believes him to be attracted to her. His seeming indifference puzzles her until she learns from Lucy Steele that the two are engaged but cannot marry because of Mrs. Ferrars' opposition. Elinor arranges for a living for Edward when he shall have taken Holy Orders so that he and Lucy can be married. Elinor is led to believe that the marriage has taken place but soon learns that Lucy has jilted Edward in favor of his brother Robert, because Edward has been disinherited. Edward is forgiven by his mother, and he and Elinor are married.

Marianne Dashwood, Elinor's younger sister, representing the "sensibility" of the title. She is emotional and impulsive, with highly romantic ideas of love and marriage. Beloved by Colonel Brandon, she considers him too old for her and falls in love with John Willoughby, an attractive young man. When the sisters visit London, Willoughby ignores Marianne, and this rejection makes her emotionally ill. While stopping at a country estate on her way home, she becomes physically ill as well. Willoughby, having heard of the illness, comes to confess to Elinor that his family, incensed at his seduction of Colonel Brandon's ward, had cut off his allowance, and, having no money, he had been compelled to marry a rich wife. Cured of her infatuation, Marianne learns to appreciate Colonel Brandon's good qualities and marries him.

John Willoughby, the villain of the story, a handsome and fashionable but dissipated young man. He encourages Marianne Dashwood to fall in love with him. It is revealed that he has seduced Colonel Brandon's ward and, rejected by his family, been forced into a loveless but wealthy marriage.

John Dashwood, the half brother of Elinor and Marianne and owner of Norland Park. Because he is wealthy both by inheritance and by marriage, he had been urged by his father to provide for his stepmother and his half sisters; being cold, selfish, and easily influenced by his wife, he does nothing for his relatives.

Fanny Dashwood, his wife, the daughter of the rich Mrs. Ferrars. She is even colder and more selfish than her husband and persuades him not to carry out his plan of settling three thousand pounds on his half sisters and stepmother.

Mrs. Dashwood, the stepmother of John and mother of Elinor and Marianne. She is a warmhearted, impulsive woman, not endowed with much practical sense.

Mrs. Ferrars, the mother of Mrs. John Dashwood, Robert, and Edward. She is rich, ill-tempered, and domineering, using her money to coerce her children.

Robert Ferrars, her older son. He marries Lucy Steele.

Edward Ferrars, her younger son. He wishes to take Holy Orders. When young, he had become engaged to Lucy Steele and thus cannot woo Elinor Dashwood, whom he really loves. His mother, learning of his engagement, disinherits him, and Lucy jilts him for his brother. Thus freed, he is able to marry Elinor.

Lucy Steele, a vulgar, mercenary young woman, engaged to Edward Ferrars. When he is disinherited, she marries his brother Robert.

Anne Steele, her equally vulgar sister.

Colonel Brandon, a quiet man of thirty-five, in love with Marianne Dashwood. She considers him too old. When his ward is seduced by Willoughby, Marianne, horrified by the latter's conduct, finally appreciates the colonel, and they are married.

Sir John Middleton, a wealthy and hospitable man who befriends his Dashwood cousins.

Lady Middleton, his wife, who also is kind to the Dashwoods.

Mrs. Jennings, her mother, a kindly but silly old lady.

Mrs. Palmer, Lady Middleton's sister, good-natured and rattlebrained.

Mr. Palmer, her husband, sensible but cold and sarcastic.

A SENTIMENTAL EDUCATION
(L'Éducation sentimentale)

Author: Gustave Flaubert (1821-1880)
First published: 1869
Genre: Novel

Locale: France
Time: The nineteenth century
Plot: Naturalism

Frederic Moreau (fray-day-REEK moh-ROH), a young student who, in 1840, has graduated from the College of Sens and is returning by boat to Nogent, along the Seine. In the fall, he will begin his law courses, but now he is more interested in studying human nature. After a talk with M. Arnoux, he goes to the upper deck, where he is attracted by the sight of lovely Mme Arnoux. Not until he retrieves her ball of yarn does he learn that she is married and has a small daughter. Later, in Paris, he is so infatuated with her that he fails in his final law examinations. He decides to give up thoughts of her and go into politics under the sponsorship of M. Dambreuse. He plans with Deslauriers to found a paper with wealth inherited from his uncle; instead, he gives the money to M. Arnoux. When Mme Arnoux fails to appear for a rendezvous, he seeks out Rosanette, her husband's mistress, to get revenge. He and Rosanette live together in the country for a time. Frederic is never able to find a really permanent love.

M. Jacques Arnoux (zhahk ahr-NEW), a sophisticated businessman who meets Frederic on a boat trip and invites him to call when in Paris. Primarily because Frederic is greatly attracted to Mme Arnoux, the older man becomes well acquainted with him. In an effort to save the failing Arnoux business enterprises, he eventually borrows a large sum of money from Frederic, which is never repaid. He goes bankrupt and begins to neglect his wife for his mistresses, but because of her innate honesty, she remains faithful.

Mme Marthe Arnoux (mahrt), his wife, an honest woman who likes Frederic but remains faithful to her fickle and unsuccessful husband. Her plan to spend an afternoon with Frederic has to be changed because of the illness of her child, a situation that she takes as a judgment on her; she then breaks with Frederic. Years later, she convinces him that they were right not to love carnally.

Rosanette (roh-zah-NEHT), called **La Maréchale** (lah mahr-eh-SHAHL), an attractive woman whom Frederic meets at a masquerade ball. He guesses correctly that she is the mistress of M. Arnoux. She goes to the country with him to stay during the riots accompanying the overthrow of the monarchy in 1848. Later, she has a child who, she claims, is Frederic's. The boy dies. She brings trouble on M. Arnoux and his wife out of revenge.

Mme Moreau, the mother of Frederic, who had hoped to see her son become a diplomat. She loses most of her money because of the troubled politics of monarchical France and cannot finance him.

Deslauriers (day-lohr-YAY), Frederic's friend, with whom he plans to found a newspaper. They room together in Paris. When Frederic lends his money to Arnoux, Deslauriers breaks with his friend and goes back home to practice law. Many years later, he visits Frederic and they decide that love, like life, is capricious.

Louise Roque (lweez rohk), a neighbor of Frederic who becomes his special friend during his summer vacation. She later follows him to Paris, but she realizes that he no longer cares for her. She marries Deslauriers later, back in Nogent, only to desert him for a singer, Anténor Delamarre.

Anténor Delamarre (ahn-tay-NOHR deh-lah-MAHR), sometimes **Delmas**, a singer-actor.

M. Roque, who gives Frederic a letter of introduction to M. Dambreuse, a wealthy banker in Paris.

M. Dambreuse (dahm-BREWZ), who offers to get Frederic started in public life. Suspicious of his wife, he leaves his wealth to his niece.

Mme Dambreuse, his wife, who is attracted to Frederic and becomes his mistress. Her hopes of marriage to him following her husband's death are spoiled when she does not inherit his wealth.

Frederic's uncle, a rich man of La Havre. He announces that he will not leave his wealth to his nephew, thus forcing the boy to spend three years in idleness in Nogent. Then he dies intestate, without other heirs, and Frederic gets the money to go to Paris.

Vicomte Cisy (sih-ZEE), a coward who quarrels with Frederic over a woman's reputation and challenges him to a duel. He falls in a faint and skins himself on a twig; this blood satisfies the requirements.

Pellerin (peh-leh-RA[N]), an artist who paints Rosanette's portrait.

A SENTIMENTAL JOURNEY: Memoirs, 1917-1922
(Sentimental'noye puteshestviye: Vospominaniya, 1917-1922)

Author: Viktor Shklovsky (1893-1984)
First published: 1923
Genre: Novel

Locale: Petrograd, Persia, Galicia, Ukraine, and Berlin
Time: 1917-1922
Plot: Autobiographical

The narrator, a Russian novelist, literary theorist, and soldier modeled on the author. In the narrative of his experiences during critical periods of Russian history, the narrator reveals his character. The image of a highly intelligent, sensitive, and humane artist bitter with grief at the painful events of war and revolution in his country emerges by means of artistic devices that depend on detachment, irony, and distancing. The narrator shows his reaction to the ingrained hatred, inhumanity, and stupidity he observes by means of telling detail that is kaleidoscopic, vivid, dramatic, and terrifying in its routineness. The ability to see steadily and to represent objectively the awful reality of a country torn apart are major elements of his character. The digressions and disruptions in his narrative suggest his broad view of human understanding and the connectedness of widely separated moments of reality. The man behind the detached observer is revealed in the course of the deliberately fragmented narrative. Numberless other characters, quickly sketched, make brief appearances in the account of these turbulent years, but no other character emerges in depth. Major officers in the White Army and the provisional government, ordinary soldiers, literary figures such as Maxim Gorky, and leaders and members of ancient hostile ethnic groups in Persia all appear in momentary vividness in the narrative, then are gone.

— *Martha Manheim*

A SENTIMENTAL JOURNEY

Author: Laurence Sterne (1713-1768)
First published: 1768
Genre: Novel

Locale: France
Time: The 1760's
Plot: Sentimental

Mr. Yorick, the Sentimental Traveler. He reacts with exaggerated sensibility to the many, mainly humorous sentimental adventures of which he is a collector in his travels.

La Fleur, Yorick's servant, a boy accomplished at flute playing and lovemaking.

Madame de L——, a fellow traveler whom Yorick

meets in Calais. He hopes that she will travel to Paris with him and is heartbroken that she must return to Belgium.

Madame de R———, a lady living in Paris. Madame de L——— gives Yorick a letter of introduction to her.

Count de B———, a Frenchman enthusiastic about everything English. He mistakes Yorick for the character in *Hamlet, Prince of Denmark* and, greatly pleased to meet so famous a person, presents him with a passport naming him the King's

Jester. Later, the count and his friends entertain Yorick at many parties while he is in Paris.

Count L———, the brother of Madame de L———. He comes to take her back to Belgium, just as Yorick's acquaintance with her is ripening.

Maria, an unhappy girl who wanders about the country grieving for her dead father. Yorick sees her in Moulines and sheds a few tears with her.

A SEPARATE PEACE

Author: John Knowles (1926-   )
First published: 1959
Genre: Novel

Locale: The Devon school in New Hampshire, and Boston
Time: 1942 and 1957
Plot: Psychological

Gene Forrester, a Southern teenager attending Devon, a preparatory school in New Hampshire. A highly sensitive, studious, and intellectual sixteen-year-old, he experiences maturation, goes through a dark night of the soul, and conquers adolescent angst during this short novel. Primarily, he is a keenly perceptive youth struggling to establish his identity at a time when World War II interferes with any peaceful and meaningful attempt to do so. He is capable, popular, boyish, and somewhat daring. The main action of the novel centers on his relationship with Finny, who is in most ways his physical, emotional, and intellectual opposite. At first, the two boys have a rather carefree existence as complementary halves of a friendship. This ends when Gene intentionally jolts the limb of a tree on which Finny is standing. His friend falls, crippling himself for life and ending his athletic endeavors. After this event, Gene spends his life accepting this fact of his guilt and trying to reconcile it to human nature and activity. The opening and ending chapters of the novel are narrated by Gene when he is thirty-one years old, now mature, yet still groping with the implications of what he had done years earlier as a teenager.

Phineas, called **Finny**, Gene's friend, roommate, rival, and intimate companion at Devon School. Rambunctious, daring, winsome, popular, and athletic, he takes Gene as his best friend and other self in this intensely emotional, adolescent, and male relationship. Finny constantly breaks the school rules only to get away with doing so; he organizes sports, activities, and games among the boys; and he repeatedly causes Gene to take chances and mature by becoming more like him. After Gene is responsible for crippling him for life,

Finny is able to forgive him and accept the implications of his friend's action. Late in the book, at a mock trial of Gene orchestrated by other boys at Devon, Finny leaves the room in haste, anger, and frustration, only to fall down a flight of stairs. His death occurs when the surgeon anesthetizes him to set the leg.

Elwin "Leper" Lepellier, an obtuse, offbeat student at Devon. He is freakish and unstable, the boy who never quite fits into either the athletic or the academic camp at the private school. Before finishing his course of studies, he leaves Devon School to enlist in the military and fight in the war. He quickly goes crazy and returns to his mother's home in Vermont, to which he summons Gene for a visit. He stands as a foil to the other boys, an indication of the cost of the war and of life. He is also the only witness to Finny's fall from the tree and is a witness at the mock trial of Gene.

Brinker Hadley, a fellow student at Devon, the closest to Gene and Finny. He is described as being "straight" in every respect—a word applied to his physical features, psychological makeup, and political beliefs. He understands many of the aspects of the relationship between Gene and Finny, and he misguidedly organizes the mock trial that leads to Finny's second fall and death. Toward the end of the novel, he is identified as Gene's best friend.

Cliff Quackenbush, the senior crew manager and leader of the Devon boat team. Cranky and bullyish, he starts a fight with Gene after Finny's fall from the tree. Gene, in Finny's absence, successfully defends himself.

— Carl Singleton

SERAPH ON THE SUWANEE

Author: Zora Neale Hurston (1891-1960)
First published: 1948
Genre: Novel

Locale: Rural Florida
Time: Early twentieth century
Plot: Psychological realism

Arvay Henson Meserve, the protagonist, a woman whose insecurities and irrational fears dominate the novel. A lissome, delicately formed woman, Arvay fails to recognize that what she sees as faults are really indicative of her innate superiority over her "cracker" family. Unable to reconcile her initial sexual attraction to her brother-in-law, Arvay allows her feelings of sexual guilt and social inferiority to affect her marriage even though she truly loves her husband.

Jim Meserve, Arvay's husband, an enterprising, rakishly

handsome man of aristocratic, but impoverished, stock. He sees a fineness and goodness in Arvay not apparent to most of the people in Sawley and courts her relentlessly. After raping her under the mulberry tree, he marries her the same evening. Jim gauges his manliness by his ability to take care of his wife, believing that all women are unable, physically and mentally, to take care of themselves.

Earl David Meserve, the genetically deformed firstborn child of Arvay and Jim. Earl is prone to violence and beastlike behavior. As he enters puberty, he becomes obsessed with one of the Carreigo girls and brutally attacks her. Pursued by a posse, he hides in the swamp and eventually is ambushed and killed.

Angeline (Angie) Meserve, the beautiful and sensual daughter of Arvay and Jim. More like her father than like her mother, Angie is self-assured and secure in her role of wife and mother.

Kenny Meserve, the youngest son of Arvay and Jim. Kenny is an amalgam of the best traits of both parents. He inherits his mother's talent and inclination for making music. He leaves the University of Florida, Gainsville, to seek a career as a musician. Kenny becomes a success, both financially and critically. His blues-based music represents a successful fusion of black and white culture.

Joe Kelsey, an African American whose unswerving loyalty to Jim Meserve serves him in good stead. Eventually, Arvay's resentment of her husband's relationship with Joe causes Joe to move his family off the Meserve orchard.

Dessie Kelsey, Joe's wife, a woman whose common sense and wisdom are appreciated by Arvay and sorely missed when she and her family move into town.

Lorraine (Raine) Henson Middleton, Arvay's jealous older sister. Her voluptuous, flamboyant looks are highly prized by her lower-class family and the Sawley community. She and her father, the shiftless Brock Henson, recognize a quality in Arvay that they both lack, and they resent it. Through her underhanded manipulations, she thwarts the budding romance between fifteen-year-old Arvay and a young, eligible preacher, the Reverend Carl Middleton, and marries him herself. Her life deteriorates into a series of petty scramblings for money and favor.

Carl Middleton, a preacher who, like Jim Meserve, recognizes Arvay's fineness. Tricked into a marriage with Arvay's gross, petty older sister, he eventually loses both his position as minister and the town's respect. By the end of the novel, he is as gross, fat, and slovenly as his wife.

— *Anita M. Vickers*

SERIOUS MONEY: A City Comedy

Author: Caryl Churchill (1938-)
First published: 1987
Genre: Drama

Locale: England and New York
Time: Mid-1980's
Plot: Satire

Scilla Todd, a London International Financial Futures Exchange (LIFFE) dealer, a job that is out of keeping with her sex and her upbringing. An initially caring but also highly ambitious young woman, she undertakes a quest to find Jake's murderer that ends in her corruption; she becomes greedy, amoral, and cunning. She is a victim of a paternalistic and capitalistic British society in which gender and class lines are being challenged in ways that promise a future that is even bleaker, devoid of any sense of morality or responsibility toward others. She gives up on finding Jake's killer, cuts herself in on his action, and is named as Wall Street's rising star by *Business Week*.

Jake Todd, Scilla's brother and a commercial paper dealer who has the whistle blown on him for dealing in insider information in the stock market. He is killed before he has a chance to talk, and almost every character in the play, including his father, has sufficient motive to be under suspicion. A public-school boy, he is typical of the new generation of young Brits who are challenging the old class system and succeeding. He bases his power on money and threats.

Greville Todd, Scilla and Jake's father and a stockbroker. Part of the English "good old boy" system, he is a pompous hypocrite who is concerned with appearances and with protecting his class and his female family members from the new breed of traders. He sells out to these very people, however, to obtain more money. Consequently, he is the only trader sacrificed by the Tories to avert a further scandal.

Zac Zackerman, a brash Jewish banker from New York who supplies various methods of creative financing so that companies can succeed in hostile takeovers. Representing everything that the British establishment hates, he is nevertheless invited to hunts and homes because the upper class is in such need of money that it will tolerate those who can provide it.

Jacinta Condor, a Peruvian tin mining heiress who goes to London to convert her family's ill-gotten wealth into Eurobonds. Probably the most intelligent character in the play, she uses her wit and attractiveness to swindle every British and American male of every class that she encounters, except for Zac. They are equals in their predatory natures, which results in a comic sexual scene in which each is turned on by the wheeling and dealing of the other. They eventually marry.

Billy Corman, called **William the Conqueror**, a corporate raider who is out to take over and break up Albion, an old-fashioned company with an excellent record of social involvement and management. After being accused in the papers of being a "profiteering robber," he is advised by his public relations person to cultivate the arts and indulge in a sex scandal because then the British public will become sympathetic. He becomes a lord.

Marylou Baines, an American risk arbitrageur, a person who buys and sells large amounts of stock, keeping the market liquid and making takeovers much easier. She is a woman who succeeds in a man's world by being tougher and more ruthless than they are. She responds to news of Jake's death by ordering her personal assistant to shred any documents from him. She runs for president in 1996.

Frosby, the oldest friend of Greville Todd and a member of the City, London's financial center. A choral figure, he is nostalgic about the way the class and financial system used to be. He is the one who informs on Jake, setting off the chain reaction of financial manipulations that almost results in a stock market crash akin to the one in the United States. He commits suicide because his "way of life is at an end."

Nigel Ajibala, an importer from Ghana. Like Jacinta, he swindles and robs his own people to make himself rich. He tricks Corman and disappears with a large amount of money.

Mrs. Etherington, a stockbroker with a reputation for integrity. She is used as a front for notorious raiders such as Corman in exchange for considerable profit.

Duckett, the chairman of Albion, known for fair and effective management and a commitment to the community. He is ruined by the government's blocking of the Corman takeover. He suffers a nervous breakdown.

Ms. Biddulph, a white knight for Duckett. In exchange for a company of her own, she will step in and guarantee the security of his job when Corman takes over.

Soat, the president of Missouri Gumballs. In a counterplay by Klein and Merrick, a stockbrokerage firm, this small-town entrepreneur acquires Corman Enterprises and "a dangerous reputation."

Gleason, a cabinet minister. Concerned about an upcoming election and the fate of his party—and, by implication, Margaret Thatcher—he forces Corman to give up the takeover bid because it makes the City and the government look "greedy."

Merrison and

Durkfeld, co-chief executives of Klein and Merrick.

— *Lori Hall Burghardt*

SERJEANT MUSGRAVE'S DANCE: An Unhistorical Parable

Author: John Arden (1930-   )
First published: 1960
Genre: Drama

Locale: Northern England
Time: c. 1879
Plot: Protest

Serjeant Musgrave, called **Black Jack**, the leader of the small band of army deserters and a prime mover in the violent, ill-fated stratagem to denounce British colonialism in the home community of one of his murdered compatriots. Part prophet and part madman, he is obsessed with his mission. He seethes with a quiet, self-righteous fury that he struggles to suppress with an insistence on order and what he calls logic. Although at times aloof and distant from his men, he commands their loyalty and respect. He is humorless, tough, acrid, intimidating, and severe. Like many pious visionaries, he is spiritually myopic, and he badly miscalculates the impact of his bloody scheme.

Private Sparky, one of Musgrave's men. Youthful and insecure, he masks his doubt behind a stream of songs, idle chatter, inane stories, and card tricks, irritating his comrades. His plan to defect and run off with Annie leads to his accidental, violent death, prefiguring the play's somber conclusion.

Private Hurst, another of the band. Seemingly more mature and dedicated than Sparky, he is bloody, resolute, handsome, and vain. Although distrustful of Musgrave's piety, he follows him for his own cynical reasons. As an atheist, anarchist, and murderer, gratuitous violence suits him perfectly. Although prevented from doing so, he is willing to fire on the crowd after Musgrave falters in purpose. His shooting ends the threat to the townspeople.

Private Attercliffe, the oldest, at about fifty years, of the soldiers and a self-proclaimed cuckold. On the staid and morose side, he is far less mercurial than the other soldiers and is a stabilizing influence. Ironically, it is Attercliffe who fatally stabs Sparky.

Joe Bludgeon, a hunchbacked bargee (barge man) prone to intrigue. He is cringing and obsequious before the town dignitaries, with an unfailing instinct for self-preservation. Like the morality vice figure, he makes trouble for its own sake, squirming free from all responsibility. Quick, cunning, and

without honor, he senses the town's mood and adapts to it. In the climactic scene, "as a kind of fugleman" he incites the emotions of the unseen crowd of townspeople.

The Parson, a town magistrate and dignitary whose arrogant, class-conscious snobbery fans the fire of the workers' discontent.

Mrs. Hitchcock, the widowed landlady at the public house where Musgrave and his followers stay. At about fifty years of age, she is an intelligent and acute observer of her fellow citizens. In a mysterious, almost motherly way, she is drawn to Musgrave.

Annie, a barmaid in the public house. Although large-boned and hardly pretty, she attracts men through her forwardness. Her former lover was the soldier whose death prompted Musgrave's crusade. She attempts to seduce Hurst, then settles for Sparky. Their elopement plans end with his death.

The Constable, a loud, crude, and ineffective official who bullies those he can but is deferential toward his betters.

The Mayor, the owner of the local coal mine. He has a narrow entrepreneur's perspective. Although outwardly affable, he is rather bossy and uncompromising. He hopes to rid the town of the principal agitators by having Musgrave recruit them into the army. He unwittingly sets up the ill-fated confrontation of the citizenry and Musgrave and his men.

Slow Collier,

Pugnacious Collier, and

Earnest Collier, called **Walsh**, the striking union members who, in desperation, are planning an insurrection. Musgrave's hopes of enlisting their support are dashed when the reality of violence confronts them and they back down.

A Trooper of Dragoons and

an Officer of Dragoons, representatives of the military contingent that arrives in timely fashion to arrest Musgrave and Attercliffe and abort the threatened violence.

— *John W. Fiero*

THE SERPENT AND THE ROPE

Author: Raja Rao (1908-   )
First published: 1960
Genre: Novel

Locale: Aix-en-Provence, Paris, India, and London
Time: Late 1940's and early 1950's
Plot: Philosophical

K. R. Ramaswamy, or **Rama**, the narrator and protagonist. He is a South Indian Brahmin, a research scholar and historian who is living in France while writing his doctoral dissertation on the Albigensian heresy. Twenty-six years old, this handsome, consumptive, gentle, sensitive, and self-conscious intellectual leisurely recounts the story of his family background, his stay in Europe from 1946 to 1954, his marriage with a Frenchwoman at the age of twenty-one, his two trips to India, his discovery of a soul mate in a young Hindu woman studying at Cambridge, his subsequent estrangement from his French wife resulting in divorce, and his determination to go back to India to seek truth under the spiritual guidance of his guru. Deeply rooted in Indian culture and tradition and equally conversant with the philosophies of the West, Rama has chosen the abstract dialectical path in his quest for truth. He revels in abstruse thinking, metaphysical analysis, aphoristic sayings, and mythological ramblings. His two trips to India have reinforced his spiritual heritage. At the end of the novel, having finished his thesis, he is ready to embark for India to fulfill his spiritual destiny.

Madeleine (Mado) Roussellin (rew-seh-LAHN), Rama's French wife, a teacher of history. Five years older than Rama, this shy, beautiful, golden-haired intellectual is attracted to Rama's spiritual heritage and falls in love with him. After marriage, she tries to be a devoted wife and learns to venerate everything that is sacred to him. Although she is a self-avowed atheist, she turns to Buddhism to understand India and her Brahmin husband. After the death of her two infant children, however, she becomes cold, withdrawn, and aloof, absorbing herself in meditation and other Buddhist rituals. Unaware of Rama's emotional involvement with Savithri and his brief sexual encounter with Lakshmi, she initiates divorce proceedings through her cousin Catherine to release him from the bondage of marriage.

Savithri Rathor (sah-VIHT-ree), a young modern Hindu woman, the daughter of a ruling prince, studying at Cambridge. Endowed with natural grace and intelligence, this idealistic, restless, and unconventional nineteen-year-old princess is a heavy smoker and attracted to communism. Having an aversion to British rule in India, she defies her betrothal to Pratap, because as a civil servant he had served the British government faithfully. She betrays her fiancé by becoming interested in a young Muslim in London. When she meets Rama, she is dazzled by his intellectual brilliance and metaphysical knowledge. She falls in love with him, solemnizes a ritualistic and symbolic marriage, and becomes his true spiritual bride. Eventually, at Rama's persuasion, she marries Pratap and promises to be a good wife to him.

Vishalakshi, or **Little Mother**, Rama's stepmother, widowed at the age of twenty-six. A simple, loving woman of meager education, she spends her time in religious ceremonies and in taking care of the large household. She provides Rama with an opportunity to accompany her to Benares and other holy places to perform his father's last rites and thus to rediscover his ancient cultural heritage.

Oncle Charles, Madeleine's uncle, a notary public. Fifty-seven years old and always dressed meticulously, he exudes vitality and looks much younger than his age. A paternal figure, he pays annual visits to Rama and Madeleine and looks after Madeleine in Rama's absence.

Georges Khuschbertieff (khewsh-BYEHR-tih-yehf), a brilliant and pious Russian refugee teaching Latin at the College de Garcons. Thirty-two years old, he has a grave face, a deep voice, a twisting arm, and gray-blue flashing eyes that give him the appearance of an inspired prophet. A devout Catholic, he manifests deep interest in India in his frequent discussions of Christianity and Vedanta philosophy with Rama. Once fascinated by Madeleine, he finally discovers his marital bliss with her cousin Catherine.

Lakshmi (LUHK-shmee), a married Indian woman with whom Rama has a brief adulterous relationship during his two-week stay in Bombay. Neglected by her husband, this sad, unfulfilled, round, and fine-looking woman hungers for male attention and spends several nights of amorous enjoyment in bed with Rama with the connivance of her husband and children.

Pratap Singh, an Indian civil servant betrothed to Savithri. When he learns of Savithri's interest in a young Muslim in London, he solicits Rama's help to persuade her to keep her marital commitment to him.

Catherine (Cathy) Roussellin, Madeleine's cousin, the daughter of Oncle Charles. Shy, jovial, maternal, and five years younger than Madeleine, she marries Georges. Rama adopts her as his sister, and she helps him obtain the divorce from Madeleine.

Lezo, a young Basque refugee studying linguistics at Aix University. Deeply interested in Buddhism, he initiates Madeleine into Buddhist studies and teaches her Pali, Chinese, and Tibetan so that she can understand the various forms of Buddhism. Although he is a close friend of Georges, he flirts with Catherine before her marriage.

— *Chaman L. Sahni*

SET THIS HOUSE ON FIRE

Author: William Styron (1925-   )
First published: 1960
Genre: Novel

Locale: Sambuco, Italy
Time: Mid-twentieth century
Plot: Psychological realism

Cass Kinsolving, an expatriate, struggling American painter in the throes of alcohol addiction. A Southerner who helped destroy the furnishings in a black family's house years earlier, Cass is guilt-ridden and depressed, conditions that led to his alcoholism. He struggles, with little success, to comprehend the symbolic implications of his dreams and fantasies, such as being locked away for a horrible crime that he cannot remember and being constantly surrounded by black people. By playing "trained seal" to Mason Flagg in Sambuco, Italy, however, Cass assumes the slave's role and thus does penance for his racial oppression, as he does by helping an Italian peasant, the odor of whose dwelling he directly connects to the odor of the dwellings of impoverished black families in the United States. Finally, by killing Mason for his rape (and, Cass believes, murder) of a peasant girl, Cass overcomes his guilt and oppression: Mason represents the excesses of "Yankee" American materialism and sexual violence. Cass, who is symbolic of the American South, can then disavow alcohol and achieve spiritual peace and artistic success.

Mason Flagg, a millionaire American obsessed with pornography and sexuality. His name suggests America (Flagg), particularly the North (Mason, as in Mason-Dixon Line). He is abusive of women but not capable of murder. In Cass's words, he is not "evil . . . just scum." Presented only through the descriptions of Peter Leveritt and Cass Kinsolving, Mason develops as a victim of an uncaring, distant father (devoted only to making films and attending parties with celebrities) and of an excessively doting mother who becomes alcoholic because she is neglected as a spouse. Mason is dismissed from high school for seducing a thirteen-year-old imbecile. He buys and controls women and male friends via his wealth. In Sambuco, Mason conflicts with and manipulates Cass, an obsessive Southern artist who hates Mason's greed, superficiality, and abusiveness. After Mason rapes Francesca, Cass's girlfriend, the North-South conflict represented by the characters erupts, and Cass kills Mason in the mistaken belief that Mason killed Francesca. Never a sympathetic character, Mason serves as an illustration of the excesses produced by the corruption of the values and culture of the North.

Peter Leveritt, an American lawyer originally from Virginia but practicing in New York. He observed some of the events in Sambuco. Peter visited Mason, a school friend of years before, when Mason was in Sambuco, arriving the evening before Mason was killed. Uncertain of the reality of what happened (officially, Mason raped an Italian peasant, Francesca Ricci, and killed her, then killed himself out of guilt), Peter visits Cass in Charleston, South Carolina, several years later, to try to resolve his doubts about the official account of the Sambuco events and end his own sense of guilt about Mason's death. Cass explains the truth about the events

in Sambuco, allowing both characters to finally accept the tragic unavoidability of Francesca's death at the hands of the village idiot, Saveria; of Mason's guilt of rape; and of Cass's understandable errors of believing that Mason killed Francesca and of then killing Mason.

Luigi Migliore (lew-EE-jee meè-lee-OH-reh), a Fascist humanist policeman/philosopher who meets and befriends Cass. Luigi saw his younger brother killed by a British bomb during World War II, and he has never since stopped questioning the nature of a universe in which such a thing could happen. Highly educated by individualized reading, particularly in philosophy, Luigi has had to accept a policeman's status and thus identifies with Cass's professional frustration, as well as sharing his spiritual suffering and questioning. Thus, when Cass kills Mason, Luigi is philosophical (existential) enough to believe that human existence is a prison anyway, and he successfully contrives to save Cass from an actual Italian prison. He also learns from Cass, realizing the essential humanity of the peasants whom, in his Fascist assumptions, he previously had ignored. Cass learns from Luigi to endure more stoically the absurdities of a seemingly meaningless universe.

Francesca Ricci (frahn-CHEHS-kah REE-chee), a peasant whose beauty captivates Cass and who thus helps to save him from self-destruction, but who loses her life in the process. After Cass hires her as a maid, Mason sees her and begins immediate pursuit. Interested only in Cass, she rebuffs Mason, but at Cass's prompting, she does steal from Mason in order to help her family survive. After Mason rapes her, she is traumatized and reacts in horror when the idiot Saverio later casually touches her. Frightened, confused, and angered, Saverio attacks her. Before she dies, she explains the truth to Luigi, who is thus able to conceal quickly the evidence of Cass's mistake-driven killing of Mason. Thus, Francesca is an essential, very positive character, reflecting the author's powerful sympathy for the oppressed and for the true victims in human society.

Saverio (sah-veh-REE-oh), a mentally deficient Italian who kills Francesca.

— *John L. Grigsby*

SETTING FREE THE BEARS

Author: John Irving (1942-   )
First published: 1969
Genre: Novel

Locale: Primarily Austria and Yugoslavia
Time: 1967, with flashbacks to 1938-1955
Plot: Comic realism

Hannes Graff (HAHN-nehs grahf), a failed university student who narrates the first ("Siggy") and third ("Setting Them Free") sections of the novel. A naïve, easygoing young man, Hannes first encounters Siggy Javotnik eating salted radishes on a bench in Rathaus Park, then later sees him in Herr Faber's motorcycle shop. Hannes initially is a follower, a student in search of order; his experience with Siggy forces him to act according to his own conscience, though his actions cause harm, suffering, and loss.

Siegfried (Siggy) Javotnik (ZEEG-freed yah-VOT-nihk), a university dropout and motorcycle salesman named for his father's alias, Siegfried Schmidt, under which his father successfully eluded Yugoslav partisans and German soldiers to return to free Vienna in the last days of the Third Reich.

Siggy always wears a corduroy duck hunter's jacket and affects a pipe. A carefree and footloose adventurer who entices Hannes into a cross-country tour of Austria on a Royal Enfield motorcycle, Siggy narrates the second section, "The Notebook," divided between his "Pre-History" and twenty-two "Zoo Watches." The "Pre-History" chronicles his mother's family's flight from Vienna ahead of the Nazis and their subsequent misfortunes and his father's adventures hiding out from the war in Yugoslavia. The "Zoo Watches," logged during a night of clandestine after-hours reconnoitering, form the core of a plan to liberate all the animals from the Heitzinger Zoo. On his way back to rejoin Hannes, Siggy crashes his motorcycle into a trailer of beehives and is stung to death on the road.

Gallen von St. Leonhard (GAH-lehn fon zahnt LAY-ohn-hahrt), a pretty country girl whom Hannes and Siggy meet on the road. After Siggy's death, she and Hannes become lovers, and she assists him in setting free the zoo animals, with calamitous results. Guilty and upset, she leaves Hannes and returns to Vienna alone.

Vratno Javotnik (VRAT-noh), Siggy's father, an apolitical linguist who runs afoul of the terrorist Slivnika family during the war and heads into the mountains on a motorcycle, accompanied by Gottlub Wut, a German soldier. Vratno later is killed by Todor Slivnika in Vienna.

Hilke Marter (HIHL-keh MAHR-tehr), Siggy's mother, who abandons him in Kaprun when he is ten years old.

Gottlub Wut (GOHT-lewp vewt), the leader of Motorcycle Unit Balkan 4 during the German occupation of Yugoslavia. A scarred and practical former champion racing mechanic, he teaches Vratno how to ride his 1939 Grand Prix racer, and the two hide out together in the mountains of Yugoslavia until Gottlub is killed by his old Balkan 4 comrades, stuffed head-first down the toilet in a men's room in Maribor.

Ernst Watzek-Trummer (VAHT-zehk TREWM-mehr), a chicken farmer who, as a patriotic gesture, goes to Vienna on the eve of the Nazi invasion wearing an eagle suit fashioned from chicken feathers, lard, and pieplates. After Hilke's abandonment and Grandfather Marter's death, he becomes guardian to the young Siggy. An autodidact, he records everything, becoming a kind of self-appointed family historian.

Grandfather Marter, Hilke's proper father, who organizes the family's flight, in Zahn Glanz's stolen taxi, from Vienna to Kaprun to escape the Nazis. In 1956, after Hilke disappears in search of long-lost Zahn Glanz, he dies suicidally, sledding down the Catapult trail wearing the shopworn and heavily symbolic eagle suit.

Grandmother Marter, Hilke's mother. She is machine-gunned to death while standing in the kitchen window of her Vienna home, boldly announcing to the neighborhood the birth of her grandson, Siggy.

Zahn Glanz (tsahn glahnts), a spirited student of politics and journalism and Hilke's boyfriend before the war. On the day of the Austrian plebiscite against German annexation, he wears Watzek-Trummer's eagle suit and in a series of reckless mishaps becomes a fugitive from the police. When Hilke's family flees Vienna, he stays behind to arrange for bank drafts to be sent to Kaprun, then disappears.

Keff, the driver of the tractor and trailer loaded with beehives with which Siggy fatally collides. Though once in love with Gallen, he now engineers her escape with Hannes.

O. Schrutt (shrewt), the second watchman at the Heitzinger Zoo. He wears jackboots, carries a truncheon, and routinely tortures the small mammals at night. Apparently a former concentration camp guard, he is left trussed up in a cage when Hannes and Gallen free the animals.

— *Philip Gerard*

THE SETTING SUN
(Shayō)

Author: Osamu Dazai (Tsushima Shūji', 1909-1948)
First published: 1947
Genre: Novel

Locale: Tokyo and a country house in Izu
Time: Shortly after World War II
Plot: Psychological realism

Kazuko, the narrator, a twenty-nine-year-old woman living with her mother. She is from an aristocratic family whose fortunes are dwindling, and she is well-educated in Western culture. She sees herself as a victim. After her marriage ended in divorce, she returned home to live with her mother. She idolizes her mother's elegant manners but, like her mother, is helpless in handling finances. After leaving their Tokyo estate and servants for a humbler life in the country, Kazuko and her mother await the return of Naoji, Kazuko's brother. Kazuko becomes hysterical over her mother's waning health and favoritism of Naoji. She sends frantic love letters to a dissolute writer, Uehara, and eventually pursues him in Tokyo to achieve her purpose of becoming pregnant.

Naoji, her brother, a frustrated writer. He is fearful of everyone. As a student, his aristocratic background was a burden. As a soldier in a losing war, he felt despair that led him to opium. He rationalized that under the effects of drugs he could become friendly and brutal like the common people. The pose of being coarse never won people's approval and never quelled his innate sensibilities. He ruthlessly impoverishes his mother and sister to pretend to start a publishing business. He even fails at declaring his love for a married woman. His mother's death overwhelms him with guilt. In the end, he commits suicide.

The mother of Kazuko and Naoji, an aristocratic lady. A creature from an obsolete society, she knows only how to comport herself; she understands nothing of finances or survival in the postwar world. She is dependent on her brother, Wada, to make important decisions about how and where she will live. She never questions the actions of her brother or her son, Naoji, whom she favors over Kazuko. When she falls ill, she abandons the fight to keep on living and dies docilely and quickly.

Uehara, a debauched novelist who becomes Kazuko's lover. He is a friend of Naoji and transmits money from Kazuko to her brother. Uehara leads a dissolute life but criticizes Naoji for not substituting alcohol for drugs, as he himself has done. He is a farmer's son who became educated but is cynical about life. Although he does not reply to Kazuko's love letters, he cannot resist her when she seeks him out in Tokyo.

Uncle Wada, the mother's younger brother who manages the family finances. He is a miser who shows little sympathy for his dying sister or her children. He will not even observe his sister's death with the traditional mourning ceremony, yet he feels righteous in his stern lecture to Kazuko on how she should live.

— *Lila Chalpin*

SETTLERS OF THE MARSH

Author: Frederick Philip Grove (Felix Paul Greve, 1879-1948)
First published: 1925
Genre: Novel

Locale: The Canadian prairies
Time: Late 1890's or early 1900's
Plot: Regional

Niels Lindstedt, a pioneer farmer from Sweden. Niels likes to conceive a plan and then carry it out. Remembering his mother's poverty, he makes his dreams come true by clearing a homestead near Minor and Balfour, in the marsh area of Manitoba. His first sight of Ellen inspires his visions of a wife and children in a comfortable home. He makes a plan to be ready to have Ellen accept his proposal of marriage. This vision motivates Niels, who is ever ready to help neighbors, a steady worker even in winter, and a fair employer who pays his help well. When Ellen makes it clear that she does not want to be married, he leaves and works even harder, even though he is despondent. His lapse with Mrs. Vogel causes him, for the rest of his life, to be plagued by a strong sense of sin because he gave way to his passion. Once out of prison, he goes to Ellen to say that he would accept being a brother to her but is quietly overjoyed with her outpouring that she would attempt to be a wife. Both are very happy, for now they share the same vision.

Ellen Amundsen, the daughter of a neighboring pioneer farmer. Ellen actively works like a man for her father, but she had observed her mother lifting and working too hard, efforts that brought on many miscarriages. Others see Ellen as unusual because after her father's death she continues to farm. She even issues neighbors permits to take off hay and, alongside men, plows a fire break. Although always correct and conservative in her behavior, Ellen loves Niels. She expresses a freer spirit in a pastoral romantic scene: They go through the woods and fields to share a vista from the top of a haystack, then huddle together in a hollowed-out niche during a downpour. She refuses Niels's offer of marriage, however, unable to overcome her memories of her mother's grief at having to leave two children in Sweden to be reared by grandparents, of her mother's hard life with her father, and of her own promise to her mother never to marry. That she loves Niels is very evident, because she wants him to continue to be her one and only friend. Years later, she still loves him, and she attends to his house until he returns from prison. When he calls, she finally tells him that she was wrong: She will try marriage and wants his children.

Clara Vogel, a widow who marries Niels. Clara had inherited a farm near his homestead. Portrayed as a well-dressed woman whose eyes look for men and whose voice is ready with repartee, Clara first meets Niels at the Lunds' Sunday gatherings. She chances on Niels and intercepts him in the hall of the hotel. Just refused by Ellen, he succumbs to Clara's advances. The next morning, he proposes, and Clara, with only a slight hesitation, accepts. In the farmhouse, she gets meals for several months but eventually keeps to her room, which is furnished with her boudoir frills. Niels tolerates her laziness and primping. Although Clara might have responded to being ordered about by Niels, he treats her too well. When she ignores his best friend, Nelson, and his family during their visit at Christmas, she no longer restrains her disinterest and isolation. Later, she lets herself be found in compromising situations with men, until Niels finally shoots her.

Bobby, Niels's faithful employee and friend. At first, Bobby worked for his foster father, Mr. Lund. His brother-in-law Nelson, married to his sister Olga, then paid Bobby to work for him, until Niels offered full regular pay. Bobby, still in his teens, is happy when his steady work with Niels earns wage increases for him as time and circumstances warrant. On Sundays, he goes visiting, especially after Niels marries Clara, whose presence makes Bobby blush. Young, hardworking, and faithful, Bobby eventually not only takes care of Niels but also establishes his own farm. He marries a capable wife, and they have five children. Although he is poor, Bobby looks after Niels's farm during the six and a half years that Niels is in prison and banks its profits. His honesty and reliability are rewarded by the fair Niels, and Bobby is given comfortable affluence.

— Greta McCormick Coger

SEVEN AGAINST THEBES
(Hepta epi Thēbas)

Author: Aeschylus (525/524-456/455 B.C.E.)
First performed: 467 B.C.E.
Genre: Drama

Locale: Thebes
Time: Antiquity
Plot: Tragedy

Eteocles (ee-TEE-oh-kleez), the son of Oedipus and grandson of Laius. Long ago, Laius, the king of Thebes, was warned by the oracle of Apollo that, should he beget a son, this act would bring ruin on his ancestral city. Laius disregarded the warning and became the father of Oedipus, thus bringing a curse upon his house. Oedipus, exposed by his parents on Mount Cithaeron, was rescued by a shepherd. Grown to manhood, Oedipus unknowingly slew his father and then solved the riddle of the Sphinx, thus rescuing Thebes from the monster. Made king of Thebes, he—again unknowingly—married Jocasta, his mother. Of this incestuous union were born four children. When Oedipus finally learned what he had done, he blinded himself, and Jocasta took her own life. It was agreed that Eteocles and Polynices, his sons, should rule Thebes in alternate years. They mistreated their blind father, who, dying, put on them the curse that they should die by each other's hands. Eteocles refused to allow his brother his turn at ruling and drove him from Thebes, whereupon Polynices enlisted the aid of six warriors from Argos and, with himself at the head of their forces, besieged his native city. At the beginning of the play, Eteocles is informed by a scout that each Argive champion has been chosen by lot to attack one of the seven gates of Thebes. Having calmed the fears of the terrified Thebans, Eteocles sends a warrior to defend each of the gates, choosing to defend in his own person the gate that Polynices will attack. The chorus warns him of the mortal danger that he risks, but, driven almost insane by hatred of his brother, he takes his post. In the encounter, the brothers kill each other. The other Argive champions having been slain, Thebes is saved. The body of Eteocles is brought back to the city, and the senate declares honorable burial for it, because, although guilty of fratricide, Eteocles had saved his native city. The curse on the house of Laius is fulfilled.

Polynices (pol-ih-NI-seez), the twin of Eteocles and son of Oedipus. Deprived by his brother of his rightful term as king of Thebes and exiled, he goes to Argos, where he raises an army against his own city. The gate of Thebes that he has been chosen to attack is revealed to Eteocles by a scout, and brother fights against brother. In the struggle, they kill each other, and Polynices fulfills his grim name, which means "much strife." His body is brought into Thebes with that of Eteocles. The senate decrees that because he fought against his own city, he cannot have honorable burial and that his body must be thrown to the dogs. His sister Antigone defies the decree of the senate and declares that she will give her brother a burial befitting his rank.

Antigone (an-TIHG-uh-nee), the daughter of Oedipus and sister of Eteocles and Polynices. After the brothers kill each other at the gate of Thebes and Polynices is denied burial by decree of the Theban senate, she defiantly announces that she will bury him herself with rites befitting a king of Thebes.

Ismene (ihs-MEE-nee), the sister of Eteocles, Polynices, and Antigone. She has a silent part in the tragedy.

THE SEVEN AGES

Author: Eva Figes (1932-   )
First published: 1986
Genre: Novel

Locale: A village in Great Britain
Time: The 1980's, with flashbacks
Plot: Social

The narrator, a midwife retired after a thirty-five-year practice, the mother of Kate and Sally, and the grandmother of Emily and Adam. After years spent dedicated to women in her work as a midwife and in her role as a single mother, the narrator feels newly aware of her solitude. In the quiet darkness of the country, she is visited by memories, by women's voices, and by tales from far history.

Granny Martin, a pioneer in family planning, the grandmother of the narrator. In Granny Martin, the narrator finds precious knowledge, a clever mind, and the example of a woman who has "done things" with her talents. Before the Great War, the young Granny Martin works in a family planning clinic begun by Dora, a granddaughter of The Matriarch. Although the clinic is scorned and attacked by men, it is a valuable resource for women dying piecemeal from undergoing childbirth too often.

Sophie, called **The Matriarch**, the mistress of the manor house and an astute manager of family businesses. As Sophie, she is a lonely, timid, and delicate heiress who is restrained by her various guardians. Later, as the black-robed Matriarch, she is respected and feared by her household. When Sophie meets a man who laughs at her strict and dour housekeeper, she marries him. Life with the "Master" ruins her health; in the first seven years of marriage, she bears seven children. It is also ruinous to her manor, because the Master sells her meadows and home farm without her knowledge. The semi-invalid Sophie suffers from the local doctor's ignorance, enduring his leeches and bleedings, his Victorian outrage, and his mistaken ideas about the female reproductive system. Freedom and The Matriarch are born together when the doctor and the Master die in a train and carriage collision.

Lady Lucy, a notable descendant of Lady Aethelfrida and mistress of the manor. A capable and resilient woman, Lady Lucy has abilities and family loyalties that prove to be great. During the seventeenth century, Lady Lucy and her sister, Lady Sarah, are caught on opposite sides during the Civil War. Colonel Francis is busy levying troops for Parliament, so Lady Lucy must manage the manor, collect rents, send provisions to her husband, and maintain a constant preparation for siege. Seven months pregnant, she worries about the three younger children trapped with her in the manor house. She miscarries when she learns that her eldest son, Edward, has left the University of Oxford to become a captain of horse. Colonel Francis is purged from the House and imprisoned, later returning to the manor as a ghostly figure.

Lady Sarah, Lady Lucy's sister. Pregnant and penniless, Lady Sarah realizes the folly of a civil war and is shaken by constant, hysterical laughter. Lady Sarah's husband supports the royal cause and flees to France. Her home burned, Lady Sarah takes refuge with her sister.

Alice, a nun and later a mother, a great-great-granddaughter of Judith, and an inheritor of the family's skill in healing. The simple, hardworking, and unlettered Alice labors for the nuns. After the dissolution of nunneries and monasteries under Henry VIII, she is sent home. She marries a priest and bears six children. After the death of King Edward and the coming to power of his sister Mary, Alice's husband is deprived of his benefice for falsely marrying a nun. Under Queen Elizabeth, her husband returns to her, confused and old.

Judith, a midwife and healer in feudal Britain, the granddaughter of Emma-of-the-caul (who was a granddaughter, in turn, of Moriuw). Black-haired and blue-eyed, Judith is as beautiful as Bedda, her wild mother who was drowned for practicing witchcraft. She is the successor in herbal medicine to her grandmother Emma. Fearless of danger, she attempts to defend herself from a series of rapes but in turn gives birth to six children, all of whom die during a pestilence. Half-crazed by grief, she succumbs willingly to the advances of a friar and conceives again.

Moriuw (MOHR-ew), a midwife and healer in pre-Christian Britain. Regarded by many as a witch because of her skill with herbs, Moriuw is under the protection of the Lord Edwin and the Lady Aethelfrida because she oversees the birth of their first living child. Her female descendants learn Moriuw's skills and, like her, show signs of magical abilities: visionary dreams, cauled birth, and healing powers.

— *Marlene Youmans*

THE SEVEN DAYS OF CREATION
(Sem dnei tvoreniia)

Author: Vladimir Maximov (Lev Samsonov, 1930-1995)
First published: 1971
Genre: Novel

Locale: Russia
Time: The Russian Revolution through the 1960's
Plot: Social

Pyotr Vasilievich Lashkov (pyohtr vah-SIH-leh-vihch LASH-kov), an elderly Communist Party functionary who becomes a Christian. In the winter of his life, Pyotr, a self-righteous autocrat and a faithful Communist, realizes that he is isolated from his relatives and from other people, without any meaningful relationship, and facing bleak emptiness. Deciding to renew his neglected family ties, after all of his six children have abandoned him, he visits one close relative after another, only to discover that most of them have not fared much better. His daughter Antonina fills the void in Pyotr's later life with her religious zeal and with renewed faith in the future, symbolized by her newborn son. Pyotr belatedly realizes that being an honest but stern Communist, without a genuine rapport with fellow human beings, leads to alienation and general resentment by others. With the help of several people (Antonina, Gupak, and his two grandsons), he enriches his empty existence through love and caring for other people. He is finally able to reconcile his Communist beliefs with an active and loving religion. The final words of the novel symbolize his spiritual rebirth: "He went, and he knew. He knew, and he believed."

Andrei Lashkov, his brother, a warden in the Kurakin forest. Although driven by the same urge as all the Lashkovs—to bring honor and justice into life and to do what is best for everybody—Andrei chooses a different path. Instead of wielding political power, he opts for forest service, for only in closeness to nature and in communion with the forest does he feel at peace. He thus escapes the silent agony endured by his older brother.

Vasilii Lashkov (vah-SIH-lee), another brother, a janitor in Moscow. Vasilii escapes the tutelage and domination of Pyotr by moving to Moscow, but at the price of a drab, joyless life and of his being alienated from everyone and everything. Even though he is his own man, he is so embittered that even a belated visit by Pyotr fails to restore a good relationship that may have brought happiness.

Antonina Lashkov, Pyotr's daughter, whose return home with an infant son reinforces Pyotr's belief in religion. A middle-aged woman who has become an alcoholic, she finds happiness and peace late in life, not so much through actual happenings as through a religious awakening. She is able to convey that message to her influential but frustrated father. Together, they find a new meaning in life through love and genuine concern for each other and for fellow human beings, finally realizing that they are not alone in this world but a part of the unity of all things.

Vadim Lashkov (vah-DIHM), Pyotr's grandson, a debauched variety artist. At times, Vadim reflects the author's own experiences as a young man. Finding himself in the spiritual and moral desert of Soviet society, Vadim gropes in the dark for a long time. He, too, finds peace with himself and fulfillment through his art, though not before he suffers through a painful period of heartache, misunderstanding, and alienation. Always surrounded by strangers and always doing the wrong things, constantly on the move and never having time to get attached to things, Vadim finally becomes reconciled with his grandfather (who needs him more than Vadim needs him, as the only male offspring of the family until Antonina's son is born). More important, he, like Antonina and Pyotr, is helped by the religious soul-healer Gupak. Even though the results are not visible yet, Vadim is on his way to total recovery.

Gupak (gew-PAK), an elderly friend of the Lashkovs. A religious fanatic, in a positive sense, Gupak is able to spread his beneficial influence and help several people searching for salvation. His belief in traditional Christian values parallels those of the author himself; such belief indicates the resurgence of a religious life among the Soviet populace thirsty for spiritual rebirth. His stoic acceptance of his impending death from cancer underlines the strength of his faith, which he is able to convey to others.

— *Vasa D. Mihailovich*

THE SEVEN MADMEN
(Los siete locos)

Author: Roberto Arlt (1900-1942)
First published: 1929
Genre: Novel

Locale: Buenos Aires, Argentina, and its suburbs
Time: The 1920's
Plot: Magical Realism

Augusto Remo Erdosaín (ow-GEWS-toh RREH-moh ehr-doh-sah-EEN), the protagonist, a hapless dreamer who, at the beginning of the novel, loses both his wife (to a virile military captain) and his low-paying job as a bill collector for a sugar company in Buenos Aires (because he has embezzled funds). Frustrated, humiliated, and emotionally overwrought, Remo surrenders himself to fantasies of amorous and financial success, as well as to the crackpot schemes of a subversive group that he joins. He fancies himself an inventor, and his desire to fortify his precarious existence is reflected in his project of coating roses with copper to preserve them. Out of resentment, he plans to kill his wife's obnoxious cousin, Barsut, who turned him in for embezzlement.

The Astrologer, a charismatic charlatan who leads a pseudorevolutionary cell of down-and-outers and plans to take over Argentina in a *coup d'état*. With his rhombus-shaped face and broken nose, his hulking frame, and his kinky, tangled hair, the Astrologer has looks that are as bizarre as his ideas. His plan for revolution is elitist in intention: The happy few will benefit from the labor of the masses, who will be regimented for maximum productivity. The Astrologer's subversive society meets at his house in a wooded suburb of Buenos Aires.

Arturo Haffner (ahr-TEW-roh), called the **Melancholy Ruffian**, a pimp and member of the Astrologer's activist cell. Haffner despises women, seeing only potential earnings in them. He befriends Erdosaín at the Astrologer's house and gives him the money he needs to pay back the funds he embezzled.

Elsa, Erdosaín's wife, a woman brought up in some luxury who has sacrificed herself to live with Erdosaín but reaches the end of her patience with the poverty and hopelessness of his life. She goes off with Captain Belaunde after a tense scene with Erdosaín at his apartment. Elsa still loves Erdosaín and promises to return to him. She leaves the Captain almost immediately, after he makes an offensive pass at her, and ends up in a nervous crisis at a hospital, unbeknown to Erdosaín.

Eduardo Ergueta (eh-DWAHR-doh ehr-GEH-tah), a corpulent pharmacist who is a compulsive gambler, religious fanatic, and member of the Astrologer's group. A deluded small-time prophet, Ergueta has married a prostitute, Hipólita, so that he can save her. He refuses, however, to save Erdosaín

from his predicament by lending him money to pay back the sugar company. Ergueta's ravings eventually land him in a mental hospital.

Hipólita (ee-POHL-ee-tah), a redheaded prostitute married to Ergueta and befriended by Erdosaín. Hipólita is not physically impaired, but she is called the **Lame Woman** or **Lame Whore** by Ergueta because she has, as he says, gone astray. This sobriquet sticks to her. Formerly a domestic servant, Hipólita made a calculated decision to become a prostitute and thereby take greater control of her life. She has a prostitute's cynical view of men but seems to adopt an almost motherly attitude toward Erdosaín. She plans, however, to betray his confidence—Erdosaín has told her about the proposed murder of Barsut—by blackmailing his accomplice, the Astrologer.

Gregorio Barsut (greh-GOH-ree-oh bahr-SEWT), Elsa's cousin, who is locked into an ongoing contest of wills with Erdosaín. Barsut's rapacious personality is mirrored in his shaven head, his bony nose like the beak of a bird of prey, and his pointed wolf's ears. He punches Erdosaín upon learning of Elsa's departure and then confesses that it was he who denounced Erdosaín to the sugar company. Erdosaín resolves to have Barsut killed, and the revolutionaries kidnap Barsut on Erdosaín's suggestion. Barsut is saved from death by the Astrologer, who arranges with him to simulate the execution in front of Erdosaín.

The Gold Seeker, a young member of the activist group whose incongruous physical makeup combines aspects of a cardsharp, a boxer, and a jockey. He mesmerizes the group with (mainly fictional) tales of his expeditions in southern Argentina, and he suggests a southern region for the subversives' training camp. The Seeker makes friends with Erdosaín, whom he impresses with his cult of violence and adventure.

The Major, an army officer affiliated with the Astrologer's group who plans to use the revolutionary movement as a provocation for a military coup.

— *John Deredita*

THE SEVEN WHO FLED

Author: Frederic Prokosch (1908-1989)
First published: 1937
Genre: Novel

Locale: China
Time: c. 1935
Plot: Exotic

Dr. Liu (lyew), a Chinese merchant who permits six men and a woman, all Europeans, to join his caravan as a means of escaping civil disturbances in Sinkiang Province. He agrees to take them to Shanghai, two thousand miles away. Along the way, two of the party are imprisoned, two are detained as hostages, serious illness befalls another, and a sixth member leaves the caravan to visit Tibet. When Dr. Liu finds himself left with only the beautiful Mme de la Scaze, he tries to make her a prisoner at his sumptuous villa in Lu-chow, but she escapes and makes her way to Shanghai.

Hugo Wildenbruch (VIHL-dehn-brewkh), a young German geologist who is imprisoned by the authorities at Aqsu. He passes his time in prison counting passersby and keeping a journal. He falls ill with tuberculosis and becomes despondent while hoping wildly to return to his native land.

Joachim von Wald (yoh-AH-khihm fon vahlt), a young Austrian geologist who is imprisoned by authorities at Aqsu. High-spirited and hopeful, he enjoys his adventures, becomes enchanted by the Orient, and decides upon arriving in Shanghai to stay in the East.

Serafimov (seh-rah-fih-MOF), a Russian exile, a huge, powerful man. He is held as a hostage at Aqsu. He tires of being tormented by his fellow hostage, Goupillière, and kills him. He makes his way to Shanghai, where he meets a prostitute, the ill-fated Mme de la Scaze.

Goupillière (gew-pee-LYEHR), a Belgian criminal, held as a hostage at Aqsu. An evil man who has robbed and murdered women, he is a fugitive from punishment. He torments the Russian, Serafimov, who murders him.

Mme Olivia de la Scaze (duh lah skahz), a beautiful young

Spaniard. She continues on the journey with Dr. Liu toward Shanghai from Aqsu. She escapes from Dr. Liu at Lu-chow, only to fall into the hands of Chinese rivermen who place her, feverish and listless, in a brothel in Shanghai. She resigns herself to her fate.

M. de la Scaze, a wealthy Frenchman who falls ill and is forced to remain at Aqsu because of his illness. He loses his sense of purpose there, simply enjoying life as he finds it. His life ends when he contracts cholera from a beautiful dancer.

Layeville (lay-VEE), a handsome English explorer who is accustomed to hardships. He turns off with another caravan to travel to Tibet, seeking the distant and unattainable. Dying in the Himalayan peaks, he finally realizes that he has sought death.

Mme Tastin (tahs-TAN), a friend of Goupillière.

Mordovinov (mohr-DOH-vih-nof), an old Russian exile who befriends Wildenbruch and von Wald in Mongolia.

THE SEVEN WHO WERE HANGED
(Rasskaz o semi poveshannykh)

Author: Leonid Andreyev (1871-1919)
First published: 1908
Genre: Novel

Locale: Russia
Time: Early twentieth century
Plot: Social realism

Ivan Yanson (ihv-AHN yahn-SOHN), a vicious murderer convicted of stabbing his master. Repulsed by all who know him, he responds to his frustrations by drinking and by beating animals entrusted to his care. He is terrified by the prospect of death and must be carried to the scaffold to be hanged.

Tsiganok Golubets (tsih-GAH-nehk goh-LOO-behts), a professional robber and murderer. In more lucid moments, he takes pride in his inhuman deeds. At other times, he falls to all fours and howls like an animal. Although frightened at times by the prospect of death, he finally mounts the scaffold arrogantly.

Tanya Kovalchuk (TAHN-yuh koh-VAHL-chook), the bravest of the five persons condemned to die as political conspirators. She concerns herself with the six persons who must die with her, thinking of them instead of herself. Only she of the seven goes to her death alone, the others going in pairs.

Musya (MEWS-yah), another woman condemned as a political conspirator and sentenced to hang. She believes in a life after death and views her hanging as a martyrdom. At the appointed time, she takes the professional criminal by the hand and mounts the scaffold with him.

Sergey Golovin (sehr-GAY goh-LOH-vihn), a young man sentenced to hang for political conspiracy. Because of his youth and vitality, he finds death hard to face. He and Vasily Kashirin are the first to be hanged.

Vasily Kashirin (vah-SIH-lihy kah-SHIHR-ihn), another young man found guilty of political conspiracy. Unloved and unloving, he goes to his death with no show of fear.

Werner, the fifth of the condemned political conspirators. Although tired of life and contemptuous of his fellow human beings, he learns in his last two days of life to have sympathy for others.

SEVENTEEN

Author: Booth Tarkington (1869-1946)
First published: 1916
Genre: Novel

Locale: A small Midwestern town
Time: A summer in the early 1900's
Plot: Comic realism

William Sylvanus Baxter, a seventeen-year-old suffering the relentless self-consciousness of that awkward age. The story begins on the day that William ("Willie" to his family, "Silly Bill" to his friends) falls in love at first sight with Lola Pratt, a beautiful summer visitor. As the one-sided romance unfolds, he must endure much from the world. His peers do not seem to realize that Miss Pratt is his girl, not theirs. His parents persist in treating him like a child, his little sister embarrasses him at every opportunity, and the general population—children, adults, and even dogs—seems to him positively obsessed with being rude and disrespectful. He tries manfully to show the world a façade of "lofty and uncondescending amusement," but he makes a fool of himself in the attempt.

Jane Baxter, William's ten-year-old sister, an intelligent, inquisitive, and not particularly tidy girl whose primary occupations are eating applesauce sandwiches and making William's life miserable. Jane keeps a close watch on her brother's attempts to appear more dashing and grown-up. She dutifully informs their mother when he borrows their father's dress suit,

and she is faithful in reporting other incriminating incidents. She also takes every opportunity to intrude on William's outings with Miss Pratt. In so doing, Jane does not endear herself to the young lady, and the feeling is mutual. Worried about William's attraction to the stranger, Jane discusses romance with various acquaintances. The neighborhood gardeners convince her that marriage is not unheard of for seventeen-year-olds, and she naturally passes this information on to her parents, giving them several uncomfortable moments. Jane has many friends in town, from gardeners to elderly businessmen to other mischievous young girls, and somehow her relationships always seem to bring trouble to William.

Lola Pratt, William's love interest, who is beautiful, coquettish, and entirely self-centered. Miss Pratt carries an obnoxious little dog and affects a syrupy baby talk, even to adults. Not only William but nearly every other young man in town finds her irresistible. She pits them against one another and obviously is delighted with being the center of attention. She is merely trifling with their affections, however; as she confides to another young woman, she "would never dream of getting engaged to any man who didn't have seven hundred and fifty thousand dollars."

May Parcher, a plain young woman who supposedly is the object of Miss Pratt's visit. Miss Parcher is ignored by all, even by her parents. Her only function seems to be talking to boys who are unable to crowd close enough to Miss Pratt to get the exalted visitor's attention.

Mr. Parcher, May Parcher's father, a high-strung businessman who becomes increasingly disturbed by the young men who swarm about his house day and night, paying court to Miss Pratt. Their constant adolescent crooning and "serious" discussions of love drive him near to a nervous breakdown. Jane's informing on William gives Mr. Parcher some relief, and because they both despise Miss Pratt, he forms a sympathetic partnership with Jane.

Mrs. Baxter, William's mother, who dimly understands his teenage angst and tries to help him through his trials. She even rescues him from hard labor at a construction site, a job he has taken to pay for a secondhand dress suit of dubious heritage. Her assistance is unappreciated.

Genesis, the neighborhood gardener. His race, attire, and familiar demeanor are a constant source of embarrassment to William, but this amiable African American, either on his own or in league with Jane or Mr. Parcher, seems always to be on hand to ruin William's attempts to appear as a young gentleman about town.

George Crooper, a large, supremely self-confident young man from out of town who almost succeeds in distracting Miss Pratt from her local admirers. To William and his friends' amazement, she does not see that for all of his bragging of race cars and riches, he is merely, according to them, a "big, fat lummox," entirely unworthy of her attention.

Rannie Kirstead, a ten-year-old girl who moves to town and becomes friends with Jane on the last day of Miss Pratt's visit. William finds his new neighbor even more unkempt and obnoxious than Jane, and Rannie seems more direct in her desire to puncture his affected pomposity. In the glimpse of the future that ends the novel, the author reveals that in ten years, Miss Kirstead will be William's bride.

— *Richard A. Hill*

A SEVERED HEAD

Author: Iris Murdoch (1919-   )
First published: 1961
Genre: Novel

Locale: London, Cambridge, and Oxford, England
Time: Early 1960's
Plot: Psychological realism

Martin Lynch-Gibbon, the forty-one-year-old, oversensitive, intellectual narrator, a wine tradesman by vocation, having taken over the family business. He has acquired a reputation as a morose and reclusive cynic. The neurotic, misguided, and generally naïve narrator tells his story of love, romance, lust, incest, and adultery in an aura of 1960's liberalism toward these matters. At the beginning, he is happy and in love with both his wife, Antonia, and his mistress, Georgie Hands. This stability ends when Antonia reveals her affair with and coming marriage to Palmer Anderson, Martin's best friend. Martin tries to convince himself that he loves and must have both women, and he pursues this end by complacently and placidly accepting the situation. Meanwhile, Honor Klein, Palmer's half sister, appears on the scene; consequently, Martin falls in love with her to lose his infatuation for his wife and mistress. Thwarted by Klein, he attacks her physically though not sexually, only shortly thereafter to realize that he has homosexual inclinations for Palmer. After Antonia and Palmer decide not to marry, she returns home for a short-lived period of peace and reconciliation, until she announces that she will marry Alexander, Martin's brother and her lover of many years. At the end, Martin is left alone, but with some great though ambiguous hope of capturing Honor Klein.

Antonia Lynch-Gibbon, Martin's forty-six-year-old wife, graceful, accomplished, and sophisticated. Her overriding characteristic is her beauty. Her emotions rule her conduct to blunt her efforts to know and to keep stability and happiness. Antonia, intense and passionate, always professes love for her husband, particularly so on the two occasions when she informs him of her lovers, Palmer and Alexander. After her relationship with Palmer disintegrates, her reunion with Martin is short-lived; at the end, she is to marry Martin's brother, Alexander.

Georgie Hands, Martin's twenty-six-year-old lover, an instructor at the London School of Economics. Martin loves her for her nature, which is antithetical to Antonia's in many ways: She is tough, independent, and witty, and she possesses a dryness and lack of intensity. During the novel, she becomes the lover first of Palmer, then of Alexander. She is insecure because she had aborted Martin's child, and she sees this as contributing to her attempted suicide midway through the novel. She is last seen at the London airport, headed to America and Palmer.

Alexander Lynch-Gibbon, Martin's older brother, a sculptor, the lover of Antonia and of Georgie. Artistic, flamboyant, cunning, and manipulative, Alexander has a history of seducing Martin's lovers and taking them away from his brother. Alexander is sculpting a head that has "imagination" rather than an actual head as its model. At the end of the novel, Alexander is paired with Antonia.

Palmer Anderson, a psychoanalyst to Antonia, best friend to Martin, and lover to Antonia, Georgie, and Honor Klein, his half sister. Professionally astute and prone to using jargon, he assumes superiority over all other characters except Honor. He copes with reality by changing it. Like the other characters, he cannot succeed—as a lover, a husband, or a person. The most constant thing in his life seems to be his affair with Antonia.

Honor Klein, an anthropologist who spends about half of her time in Germany. She is a half sister and lover to Palmer and is the final object of Martin's desire. Martin first describes her as a "middle-aged Germanic spinster," and he is repelled by her until he realizes that he loves her rather than Antonia or Georgie. She is dark, short, and unattractive, with greasy black hair and narrow black eyes. Shrewd, perceptive, and effectual, Honor repeatedly functions so as to prove disconcerting to other characters, particularly to Martin. She is a woman of intellect and accomplishment, a character never wrong yet never the better for her astuteness about the motivations of others.

Rosemary, Martin's sister and an emotional eunuch. Rosemary, always stable yet alienated from the other characters, stands in contrast to those who would perpetually love and lose. She is divorced, at once blissfully and bitterly so.

— *Carl Singleton*

SEXING THE CHERRY

Author: Jeanette Winterson (1959-   )
First published: 1989
Genre: Novel

Locale: London, England
Time: 1630-1666 and the late twentieth century
Plot: Fable

Jordan, one of two alternating narrators. His earliest memory begins the tale, and his romantic heroism buoys it. As an infant, he is fished from the Thames in 1630 by the Dog-Woman, who christens him for a more redemptive river, rears him as her own, and reluctantly relinquishes him to the quest that drives the narrative. Inspired at the age of three by the sight of the first banana brought to England, the young Jordan spends his youth sailing handmade boats and dreaming of exotic lands. At the age of ten, he is discovered by the famous explorer and royal gardener, John Tradescant, who, as his mentor, provides him with passage to the uncharted world. He journeys in search of Fortunata, the fleet, dancing princess he once glimpsed, in the hope that she will lead him to himself.

The Dog-Woman, the independent giantess who shares narration duties with her adopted son. She breeds fighting and racing dogs for a living. Heavier than an elephant but capable of melting into thin air, the Dog-Woman is the earthier reporter of the two, providing historical context to Jordan's more fanciful and philosophic descriptions. A staunch Royalist, she uses her fabulous size and considerable courage to both protect and nurture the boy and to battle the intolerant Puritans. Self-sufficient and murderous (her father was her first victim), the Dog-Woman is vulnerable to a mother's anxiety over the heartbreak of her son.

John Tradescant, who is based on the historical figure Tradescant the Younger. He spent his twenties exploring exotic places and collecting rare plants for his father's museum and garden at Lambeth. After his father's death in 1637, the post of gardener to the king fell to him, but his heart remained at sea.

Enchanted by one of Jordan's vessels, he sees in him his chance to voyage anew. Loyal, cultured, tolerant, and worldly, Tradescant represents the virtues of the monarchy in contrast to the ignorance, repression, and hypocrisy of the Puritans.

Fortunata, the youngest of the Twelve Dancing Princesses whose stories make up a section in the first half of the novel. She is the object of Jordan's affections and so light she may be merely an essence. After escaping her arranged wedding and traveling the world, she opened a dancing school in Barbados where the pupils spin so quickly that they become harmonic points of light. By the time Jordan finds her, she no longer wants to be rescued, but she reveals enough of herself for him to navigate by her.

The Dog-Woman's neighbor, a woman so filthy she is mistaken for a side of saltbeef. She counts clairvoyance among her occult powers and predicts heartache for both Jordan and his mother.

Preacher Scroggs and

Neighbour Firebrace, opportunists who join the Puritan uprising and denounce the king. Later, they are discovered at the brothel, and the king is avenged.

Nicholas Jordan, a modern counterpart to Jordan. He gives up a career in the Navy to join the ecological protest of the pretty chemist he sees in a newspaper photograph.

A chemist, the unnamed modern recipient of the Dog-Woman's prodigious outrage and Fortunata's charisma. She is an ecological terrorist and takes up the feminine narration when the novel jumps to the late twentieth century.

— *Susan Chainey*

SEXUAL PERVERSITY IN CHICAGO

Author: David Mamet (1947-   )
First published: 1977
Genre: Drama

Locale: Chicago, Illinois
Time: The 1970's
Plot: Comedy

Danny Shapiro, an insecure twenty-year-old assistant office manager who seeks the acceptance of others. He simply wants to belong. Toward that end, Danny listens with awe to Bernie's tales of sexual prowess and asks questions that feed Bernie's ego. To please Bernie, his replies are generally nondirective reflections of Bernie's statements. Danny is a loyal friend to both Bernie and Deb. He defends Bernie against their coworkers' verbal assaults, and he refuses to discuss the details of his relationship with Deborah. Danny is unable to open himself to others, however, and retreats from his own emotions into the safety of patterned communication. Consequently, he

rejects Deb when she wants to know more about his inner being, and he returns to Bernie. Danny is sensitive enough to recognize the one point at which Bernie appears to have lost himself as well as to accept Bernie's hurried masking of that one vulnerable moment.

Bernard (Bernie) Litko, Danny's friend and coworker, a 1970's heterosexual American male stereotype locked into exaggerating his sexual prowess to validate his masculine identity and desirability. He is homophobic. Bernie showers his speech with obscenities to prove his superiority and believes that females should be subordinated and mistreated. He, too, is insecure. Bernie lies about his occupation to attract women, deals ineffectively with a confrontive female, and is envious of Danny and Deb's relationship. He has centered his life on genitalia, female seductiveness and willingness, and male size and endurance. Bernie focuses on appearance and blames women both for his sexual arousal and for his sexual rejections. Although he once questions the meaning of his words, Bernie immediately reverts to the security of his ritualistic behaviors.

Deborah (Deb) Soloman, an attractive, twenty-three-year-old professional illustrator who wants to be loved but habitually feels misunderstood. She enters into a sexual, then cohabitative, relationship with Danny in an effort to establish emotional security but alternates a desire for closeness with alienating behaviors to protect herself. Deb blames herself for

their eventual dissolution and uses her friend Joan as her primary psychological support. Deborah is a dependent person in conflict between what she believes that she wants and what she is willing to risk.

Joan Webber, a kindergarten teacher who lives with Deb. She is a bitter woman who views sexual intercourse as mutually destructive behavior from which she has withdrawn. She is predominantly hostile toward men (for example, she sees premature ejaculation as a consequence of the man's desire to punish her). As a dramatic foil for Bernie, Joan could be described as a 1970's American castrating female stereotype. Intelligent and witty, Joan uses negative philosophical patter (that she herself interrupts for practical considerations) to fuel her own sense of depression, alienation, and helplessness.

— *Kathleen Mills*

THE SHADOW BRIDE

Author: Roy A. K. Heath (1926-   )
First published: 1988
Genre: Novel

Locale: British Guiana
Time: The 1930's
Plot: Psychological realism

Betta Singh, a young medical doctor of East Indian descent. He has studied in England and come home to his native British Guiana with the intention of helping the many impoverished people there who suffer from tropical diseases and malnutrition. His scientific training has left him skeptical about religion, yet he yearns to find some higher meaning in life that would explain the misery he sees all around him. His idealism brings him into conflict with the selfish, materialistic people who dominate the economy.

Mrs. Singh, Betta's wealthy widowed mother. She evinces a strange combination of strength and weakness. She tries to dominate her son and everyone else in her household yet yearns to have a strong man dominate her completely. The author refers to her as "the shadow bride" because she seems to have left her soul in India when she went to British Guiana as a young bride.

Meena Singh, the beautiful, sensual woman whom Betta marries when she is sixteen. She becomes devoted to her husband and shares in all of his misfortunes and occasional triumphs. She is the innocent cause of a serious rift between Betta and his mother, because the older woman does not approve of her son's undistinguished marriage.

Aji, an ancient female family retainer who tyrannizes the Singh household until she becomes so feeble that she has to be cared for like an infant. She is the only person in the household who dares to stand up to Mrs. Singh, who mildly accepts Aji's verbal abuse. Aji can behave as she does because she alone knows Mrs. Singh's terrible secret: that she murdered her own husband.

Mulvi Sahib, a Muslim religious teacher who was brought to live in the Singh family home when Betta was a child to give the boy private tutoring. He remains Betta's friend and coun-

selor, a sort of father substitute, until his death. Mulvi Sahib also exercises a strong influence over Betta's mother but ultimately is replaced in her esteem by the Pujaree.

The Pujaree, a Hindu religious teacher who assumes such powerful influence over Betta's mother that he eventually becomes her lover and finally her husband. In spite of his sincere belief in nonattachment and self-effacement, the Pujaree cannot help coveting power and material possessions. After replacing Mulvi Sahib and Betta in Mrs. Singh's affections, the Pujaree manages to drive away all of her household retainers so she is totally dependent on him.

Rani, an orphan adopted by Mrs. Singh as a little girl. She is in love with Betta and is heartbroken when she is given away to another man and Betta marries Meena. She eventually becomes Meena's best friend and confidante.

Lahti, another orphan adopted by Mrs. Singh as a child. It is revealed late in the story that Lahti actually is an illegitimate daughter of Mrs. Singh's deceased husband. Although Mrs. Singh supports the girl, she cannot help hating her as a reminder of her husband's infidelity. Lahti develops a self-hatred as a result of Mrs. Singh's attitude. Because of her self-hatred, Lahti allows herself to be physically and sexually abused by Sukrum.

Sukrum, a vicious, scheming opportunist who insinuates his way into Mrs. Singh's household. He eventually becomes Lahti's lover and then her husband. Temporarily fallen out of Mrs. Singh's good graces, Sukrum and Lahti becomes vagrants living from hand to mouth. Lahti dies from the privations of their homeless existence. Later, Sukrum worms his way back into Mrs. Singh's household and becomes her sole retainer and her virtual jailer.

— *Bill Delaney*

THE SHADOW OF A GUNMAN

Author: Sean O'Casey (John Casey, 1880-1964)
First published: 1925
Genre: Drama

Locale: Dublin
Time: May, 1920
Plot: Tragicomedy

Donal Davoren, an aspiring poet who shares a tenement room with Mr. Shields. He is a man of about thirty with a strong romantic streak. Davoren evinces a mixture of weakness and strength. When a rumor begins that he is a "gunman" on the Republican side of the civil war, Davoren proves susceptible to the admiration and flattery that his new reputation brings him. This seemingly innocent deception is the foundation of his romance with Minnie Powell. When it threatens to bear serious consequences and the British authorities appear, Davoren weakens and proves unable to face danger.

Seumas Shields, a peddler of shoddy goods, a lazy and superstitious man who loudly voices both nationalist sentiments and condemnation of the Republican gunmen. Shields has pretensions to literary and political ideals, but his ideals are merely catchphrases inserted into his conversation. His chief enemy, in reality, is his landlord, who demands payment of rent past due. Like Davoren, he proves cowardly in the face of British military authority.

Tommy Owens, a resident of the tenement, a small, unexceptional man about twenty-five years old. He is a hero worshiper who breaks into patriotic song at any opportunity and who vows that he would die for Ireland. Owens is primarily responsible for creating the false public image of Davoren as a gunman.

Minnie Powell, a working woman who resides in the tenement. She is self-assured, good-looking, and carefully dressed. She is twenty-three years old. Despite her lack of education, she is intelligent and poised. Davoren is attracted as much by these qualities in her as he is flattered by her admiration for the "gunman." She is flirtatious, even frivolous, with Davoren, but ultimately she is the only one who acts bravely and idealistically in the final crisis of the play.

Adolphus Grigson, a resident of the tenement, a well-fed clerk of about forty-five with a tendency to drink. He is a domestic tyrant who bullies his wife. Grigson is avowedly anti-Republican. He is, nevertheless, ruthlessly terrorized and humiliated by the British auxiliaries who raid the building, but he denies this fact, claiming to have faced them bravely.

Mrs. Grigson, a worn-out woman looking much older than her forty years, who is in a constant state of worry or panic. It is she who brings the news of Powell's arrest and death.

Mr. Malone, a business associate of Shields and a genuine Republican gunman who appears only briefly in the play. He leaves in the room of Shields and Davoren a bag that proves to contain bombs, and that Powell attempts to hide. That action leads to her arrest and death.

Mrs. Henderson, a neighbor and local authority on any topic of conversation. A large, good-natured woman, she helps to spread the rumor of Davoren's political activities.

Mr. Gallogher, a neighbor and friend of Mrs. Henderson. He is a small, nervous man. He is harassed by disorderly neighbors. At Mrs. Henderson's request, he writes a letter to the Irish Republican Army asking for assistance; he gives the letter to Davoren. The possession of this letter becomes a source of danger during the raid.

— *Heidi J. Holder*

SHADOWS ON THE ROCK

Author: Willa Cather (1873-1947)
First published: 1931
Genre: Novel

Locale: Quebec, Canada
Time: 1697-1713
Plot: Historical

Euclide Auclair (ew-KLEED oh-KLAR), a temperate, humane, and philosophical apothecary living in Quebec at the end of the seventeenth century. Although loyal to his patron and friend, the Count de Frontenac, whom he accompanied to Canada in 1689, he feels that he has lived in exile for eight years, and he makes little effort to adjust his thinking or habits to life in a new land. At night, when he draws the curtains of his shop and sits down to dinner with his daughter Cécile, he likes to imagine that he is back in his beloved home on the Quai des Célestins in Paris. When he learns that the count expects to be recalled by King Louis, Auclair looks forward to returning with his benefactor. The count, neglected by his monarch, dies in Quebec, and in the end, Auclair stays on. His daughter has married a Canadian, and to the old apothecary it seems that the future may after all be better in Quebec, a place where change comes slowly, remote from the designs of kings and their ministers.

Cécile Auclair (say-SEEL), the apothecary's thirteen-year-old daughter, who has taken over the household after her mother's death. She is an appealing child because of her quaint mixture of youth and maturity. She is deeply pious but with no sense of a religious vocation; instead, she resembles a household vestal guarding domestic rites that stand for the order and grace of a transplanted culture. Unlike her father, she is a Canadian; the river flowing below the rock, the mountains to the north, and the dark pine forests stretching away as far as one can see frame everything that is familiar and dear to her. She grows up to marry Pierre Charron, her father's friend, a famous hunter and scout.

Pierre Charron (pyehr shah-ROH[N]), Euclide Auclair's young friend from Montreal, a wilderness runner and hunter. Disappointed in love when the daughter of his employer became a religious recluse, he had taken to the woods; now he has made a name for himself among the traders and Indians all along the Great Lakes. Whenever he is in Quebec, he visits the Auclairs. The apothecary admires him because the young man combines the manners and tradition of the Old World with the bravery and resourcefulness needed to survive in the new. Cécile loves him first as a child, then as a woman. They marry and have four children to make the apothecary satisfied with his growing family in his old age.

The Count de Frontenac (deh froh[n]-teh-NAK), the governor of Canada, a stern but just man who has alienated many civil authorities and churchmen in France and Canada through his tactless actions. An able administrator and soldier, he dies neglected by the king he has served faithfully.

Bishop Laval (lah-VAHL), the first bishop of Quebec, now succeeded by Monseigneur de Saint-Vallier. The old prelate is unsparing of himself, devoted to the poor, and ambitious for the church. Gruff in manner, he is capable of great generosity and kindness to the deserving. In the past, he and the Count de Frontenac had clashed on many matters of policy, and he carries on a feud with his ambitious young successor.

Monseigneur de Saint-Vallier (deh sah[n]-vahl-YAY), the young bishop of Quebec, who since his appointment has spent most of his time in France. Clever and ambitious, he often acts more like a courtier than a churchman; Euclide Auclair thinks that he looks like an actor. He appears determined to undo the work of his predecessor, old Bishop Laval. After having been captured and imprisoned by the English and later detained in France, he returns, a much chastened man, to Quebec in 1713.

Jacques Gaux (zhahk goh), a street waif befriended by Cécile Auclair. He grows up to become a sailor. Between voyages, he stays with the old apothecary.

'Toinette (twah-NEHT), called **La Grenouille** (greh-NEW), meaning "the frog." She is an unsavory, shrewish woman, the mother of Jacques Gaux and the keeper of a sailors' boardinghouse.

Nicholas Pigeon (nee-koh-LAH pee-ZHYOH[N]), a baker and a neighbor of the Auclairs.

Noel Pommier (noh-EHL poh-MYAY), a cobbler.

Madame Pommier, the cobbler's mother. A woman of great piety, she is responsible for the location of her son's shop on Holy Family Hill.

Jules (zhewl), nicknamed **Blinker**, a disfigured, cross-eyed man who tends the fires of Pigeon and the baker and empties the Auclairs' refuse in repayment for a bowl of soup and a small glass of brandy each night. He tells Euclide Auclair a strange story. Apprenticed to the king's torturer at Rouen, he had brutally compelled a woman to confess to the murder of her son. A short time later, the young man reappeared. Unable to sleep at night because of the burden on his conscience, Blinker asks the apothecary for a drug that will allow him to rest.

Mother Juschereau de Saint-Ignace (zhew-sheh-ROH deh sah[n]-teen-YAHS), the superior of the Hotel Dieu, who tells Cécile Auclair many tales of miracles and saints. She regrets that the girl shows no signs of a vocation in religious life.

Father Hector Saint-Cyr (ehk-TOHR sah[n]-SEER), a Jesuit missionary to the Indians, Euclide Auclair's friend.

Jeanne Le Ber (zhahn leh behr), the daughter of a wealthy merchant in Montreal. Rejecting all suitors for her hand, including her old playmate, Pierre Charron, she becomes a religious recluse.

SHAKESPEARE'S DOG

Author: Leon Rooke (1936-)
First published: 1983
Genre: Novel

Locale: Stratford-upon-Avon and its vicinity
Time: 1585
Plot: Fantasy

Hooker, a mongrel dog. He has a long nose, a whitish smear behind the ears, lean haunches, and a sturdy tail. Inquisitive, aggressive, and lecherous, he gets aroused by any bitch, including his twin sister Terry, and even by Anne Hathaway Shakespeare. Adopted by William Shakespeare, Hooker saves him from drowning in the Avon River and provides him with phrases that will become famous in his plays. Considering dogs to be as intelligent and important as humans, Hooker despises Shakespeare's acceptance of conservative beliefs, such as the chain of being, his lack of compassion, and his exaltation of body over soul. Having killed a deer in Sir Thomas Lucy's park at Charlecote, and therefore being in danger of severe punishment, Hooker is overjoyed when his master decides to leave Stratford for London.

William Shakespeare, an aspiring writer. Highbrowed and balding at the age of twenty-one, he has been married for three years to the former Anne Hathaway, whom he impregnated. Now he attempts to write in an upstairs room, but domestic affairs continually interrupt him, and he frequently comes to blows or bed with his wife. He chafes at small-town life but aspires to buy New Place if he can escape to make his fame and fortune in London, seat of the queen, about which he fantasizes.

Anne Hathaway Shakespeare, who is eight years older than her husband, a stocky, lusty, and earthy woman oppressed by the chores of motherhood and unalterably suspicious of and opposed to her husband's plans to leave her in Stratford while he goes to London.

John Shakespeare, William's father. Now white-haired and bloated with dropsy, he used to be a citizen of importance in Stratford, but quarrels and debts have driven him into staying at home. There he drinks Warwickshire brown ale, deplores contemporary trends such as the spread of enclosures and the increase in Hathaways under his roof, and reminisces about his wooing Mary Arden thirty years ago.

Wolfsleach, a dog. He lusts after Marr, Hooker's steady bitch, and is defeated by him in a fight. Apparently dead, he eventually recovers and runs off with Terry, Hooker's twin sister.

— *Christopher M. Armitage*

SHAME

Author: Salman Rushdie (1947-)
First published: 1983
Genre: Novel

Locale: Pakistan
Time: c. 1920 through the early 1980's
Plot: Magical Realism

Omar Khayyam Shakil, a physician friend of Iskander Harappa and son-in-law of General Raza Hyder. Omar is an antihero who describes himself as peripheral to his own life. He grows up in a secluded, crumbling palace on what seems to him like the edge of the world, in an unnamed country that has all the attributes of Pakistan. His mother is one of three sisters who reveal to no one, including Omar, which of the three gave birth to him or who his father is. At the age of twelve, he leaves home for school. He becomes a physician and engages in a life of debauchery with Iskander Harappa. He becomes obsessed with and marries Sufiya Zinobia Hyder, the retarded daughter of General Hyder. His life is always shaped by other actors—by his three mothers and by Iskander, Raza, and Sufiya. He is finally executed when he is about sixty-five years old, accused, wrongly, of having killed General Hyder.

Chhunni (CHEW-nee),

Munnee, and

Bunny Shakil, Omar's three mothers. They live walled off from the world, receiving supplies into their mansion through a dumbwaiter. After Omar leaves, they have another son, Babar. Babar is killed by General Raza Hyder. Years later, the three women execute General Hyder, an act that results in Omar's death.

Iskander Harappa, the prime minister, a character based on Prime Minister Zulfikar Ali Bhutto. Iskander is a rich playboy until his friends and relatives begin to gain high positions in society. Out of competitive sense, not social concern, he becomes serious, giving up his playboy life. He uses his charm and a radical program of "Islamic socialism" to gain power, based on mass support. Cynical and ruthless, he becomes prime minister and places his friend and competitor, General Raza Hyder, in command of the army. Iskander rules for four years, is jailed for two, and is then executed after Raza takes over. He returns as a ghostly adviser to General Hyder, reading to him from Niccolo Machiavelli's works.

Raza Hyder, a general and president. Raza, based on Pakistani president Zia-ul-Haq, is a short, mustachioed, proud man with impeccable manners and a deceiving air of humility. His forehead is marked by the *gatta*, a permanent bruise stemming from fervent praying with his forehead on the floor. After he overthrows Iskander, he rejects the prime minister's social program and creates an Islamic theocratic state. When he loses power, he flees, dressed as a woman, with Omar. Omar's mothers kill him.

Sufiya Zinobia Hyder, the daughter of General Raza Hyder and wife of Omar Shakil. Sufiya, called Shame by her mother, is retarded, symbolizing purity and innocence. She is a saintly figure who absorbs the shame of those around her who commit brutal acts. Shame, internalized, emerges as rage and violence, in nations or individuals. At the age of twelve, the shy, quiet girl kills 218 turkeys, pulling their heads off and their entrails out. After Omar marries her, she erupts in violence again, killing several men, pulling their heads off after having sex with them. Omar keeps her sedated and chained for months before she breaks free and turns into a legendary white panther, killing people all over Pakistan, creating part of the uproar that leads to the overthrow of her father and, indirectly, leads to his and Omar's deaths. The white panther then disappears, never to be heard from again; it is perhaps, the narrator says, a collective fantasy of an oppressed people.

Maulana Dawood (mah-LAHN-ah), an Islamic divine, a serpent, the narrator says, who becomes a spiritual adviser to General Hyder. When Dawood dies, he joins Iskander as a ghostly presence sitting on General Hyder's shoulders. He pours Islamic fundamentalism into the general's right ear while Iskander reads Machiavelli into his left.

Bilquis Hyder and

Rani Harappa, the wives of Raza and Iskander. Both are publicly honored but privately ignored as their husbands begin their rise to power. Both accept their subordination quietly. Bilquis sinks into eccentricity and madness. Rani knits shawls, recording the memory of her husband, who achieves quasi-sainthood after his death. Her shawl shows him as he really was: a philandering, authoritarian, ruthless man, determined to obliterate his opponents rather than merely defeat them. The wives symbolize their husbands' failures as statesmen. Men cannot create democratic societies, as Iskander wanted, or moral theocracies, as Raza wanted, if they cannot tolerate freedom and justice in their personal lives.

— *William E. Pemberton*

THE SHARPEST SIGHT

Author: Louis Owens (1948-   )
First published: 1992
Genre: Novel

Locale: California and Mississippi
Time: Late 1960's
Plot: Detective and mystery

Ramon (Mundo) Morales (rah-MOHN MEWN-doh moh-RAH-lehs), a twenty-five-year-old deputy sheriff in Amarga, California. This Vietnam veteran and conscientious law enforcer was a friend of Attis McCurtain, a mixed-blood Indian, in high school and during the Vietnam conflict. The Morales' vast ranch, given to them by the Spanish king in the 1700's, has been taken over by Dan Nemi, the richest, most powerful rancher in the valley. When Attis McCurtain, suffering from shell shock after Vietnam, is reported to have escaped from a mental hospital, Mundo is certain that Attis was murdered and that he had seen Attis' body floating in the floodwaters of the Salinas River. Although Mundo is under suspicion from Federal Bureau of Investigation (FBI) agents and local police for perhaps having helped Attis to escape and hide, he is determined to find Attis' killer, whom he suspects to be one of the Nemi family, and to prevent Attis' father, Hoey, from killing Dan Nemi.

Cole McCurtain, a mixed-blood Choctaw-Cherokee-Irish, the son of Hoey McCurtain and the younger brother of Attis. He returns to the cabin in a Mississippi swamp where he and his father were born. He is being sheltered by his Chactaw great-uncle, Luther, in order to avoid being drafted and becoming another Indian sacrificed in a white man's war. At first, he is immature and uncertain of his identity, but through Uncle Luther's teachings and by getting back to his own family's connections with the Mississippi land, Cole comes to know himself as Indian. He returns to California to find Attis' bones and take them back to Uncle Luther's place so that Attis' spirit can continue on its way. In affirming his Indian identity and heritage, Cole discovers his own story and can live it.

Hoey McCurtain, the widowed father of Cole and Attis. He begins to think according to the old ways of his Choctaw childhood in Mississippi. He has taught his sons the Indian skills of trapping, fishing, and hunting. Patient and determined, he waits for a chance to shoot Dan Nemi to avenge Attis' murder. Upon discovering Diana Nemi, hurt and abandoned after being raped by Jessard Deal, Hoey reveals a compassionate nature in carrying out a sweat lodge ceremony to help Diana heal and purify.

Diana Nemi, the wealthy, spoiled, and seductive eighteen-year-old daughter of Dan and Helen Nemi. She also is the sister of Jenna Nemi, whom Attis had stabbed to death; that crime sent him to the mental hospital. Diana is beautiful and troubled. She barters her sexuality to gain power and adulation. She is abducted and raped by Jessard, who suspects her of being Attis' murderer and sees her seductive power as a challenge.

Uncle Luther Cole, a Choctaw medicine man. He lives in a Mississippi swamp in a one-room cabin with only his dogs and his friend Onatima as companions. With the gift of second sight and knowledge of the future, he knows, from the start, how the story ought to turn out. Gentle, wise, and crusty, he teaches Choctaw traditions and beliefs to his nephew Cole. Luther uses his spiritual powers to ward off the black panther—"Soul-eater"—that is stalking Attis' spirit. Using extra-sensory perception, Luther inspires Cole to find Attis' body and monitors the progress of the story being played out in California.

The Viejo, the ghost of Mundo's dead grandfather, Antonio Morales. He appears to Mundo, urging him to confront Diana and her seductive wiles directly and on his terms so that Mundo will not become another of Diana's victims. He also appears to Diana to tell her to let go of her pursuit of power through sexuality.

Jessard Deal, who owns and manages the toughest bar in Amarga. Although he is noted for truthfulness and knows poetry by heart, he is insensitive, brutal, destructive, and cynical, caring only for power obtained through physical violence.

Onatima (Old Lady Blue Wood), Luther's friend and lover. Although she is college educated, she has returned to the remote swamp and the Indian way of life. She is the keeper of stories, both indigenous and in Western literary traditions. She loans Luther books and helps him interpret the story he now finds himself involved in through his California relatives.

— *Diane Brotemarkle*

THE SHAWL

Author: Cynthia Ozick (1928-   )
First published: 1989
Genre: Short fiction

Locale: Germany and Miami, Florida
Time: The 1940's and early 1980's
Plot: Psychological realism

"The Shawl," 1980

Rosa Lubin, a young Polish refugee in a Nazi concentration camp with her infant, Magda, and her fourteen-year-old niece, Stella. They have been so brutalized that they are hardly recognizable as human. Rosa feels no hunger or pain, but rather light, as if she were an angel in a trance. Her only concern is to keep Magda concealed and thus alive. When Magda is discovered and her life is in danger, Rosa can do nothing but watch in horrified silence.

Magda, Rosa's infant daughter, who has the swollen belly of the starving. Because she can get no nourishment from Rosa's dried-up breasts, she sucks on the corner of a shawl, which seems to have some sort of magic power to comfort and sustain her. Because of her Aryan appearance, it seems clear that Magda is the result of Rosa being raped by one of the Nazi guards. Rosa loves her nevertheless and tries desperately to hide her. Magda maintains absolute silence until Stella steals her shawl to warm her own body; Magda stumbles into the open camp yard crying out for it. In a horrifying poetic passage, with Rosa watching in anguish but unable to do anything, a Nazi guard throws Magda into an electrified fence. She dies instantly.

Stella, Rosa's fourteen-year-old niece, the indirect cause of Magda's death when she takes away her shawl. She is so close to death from starvation and exposure that she can think of no one but herself.

"Rosa," 1983

Rosa Lubin, now a fifty-eight-year old woman. She smashes the contents of the secondhand furniture store she ran in New York City and moves to Miami, Florida, to live alone in a tenement hotel. More than thirty years after the death of her infant daughter Magda in the concentration camp, Rosa tries to stay isolated from others. Her only communication is with the imagined Magda and the hated Stella, to whom she still refers as the "Angel of Death." After a nightmarish journey in Miami, looking for a pair of underpants lost when doing her laundry, she, with the help of the elderly Mr. Persky, tries to free herself of her fantasies about Magda and the magic shawl and begin human relationships again.

Magda, Rosa's infant daughter, who was killed by a Nazi prison guard in "The Shawl." Rosa imagines that she is still alive and a professor of philosophy at Columbia University in New York.

Stella, who is now forty-nine years old. She remains unmarried and lives and works in New York. She sends money to Rosa and tries to make her give up her fantasy of Magda still being alive and her conviction that the shawl is somehow magical. At Rosa's request, Stella mails the shawl to her.

Simon Persky, a seventy-one-year old interested in Rosa. He flirts with her and tries to bring her out of her isolation. At one point, Rosa mistakenly thinks he has stolen a pair of her underpants from a laundromat. At the end of the story, in a gesture of new communication, Rosa allows Simon to come to her hotel room. This gesture drives away the fantasy of Magda.

Dr. James Tree, a sociologist who wants to interview Rosa for a study he is doing of survivors of the Nazi camps.

— *Charles E. May*

SHE

Author: H. Rider Haggard (1856-1925)
First published: 1887
Genre: Novel

Locale: Africa
Time: Late nineteenth century
Plot: Adventure

She, also known as She-who-must-be-obeyed and as **Ayesha**. She is a white queen who has lived for two thousand years in the hidden city of Kor, deep in the African interior, awaiting the reincarnation of the man she loved but murdered. Trying to prove to Leo Vincey that she can make him her immortal lover, she walks into a pillar of flame and is consumed by it, though previously it had given her protection from all the ravages of age.

Leo Vincey, a young Englishman, a descendant of Kallikrates, the man She loved and killed. Following instructions in documents left by his father, Leo travels to Africa to find the Pillar of Life. He meets She, who loves him, and he falls in love with her. After her death in the pillar of flame, he returns, gray-haired from shock, to England.

Mr. Vincey, Leo's father. When he dies, he places his five-year-old son in the hands of Ludwig Holly, a fellow student at Cambridge, to be reared. He also leaves an iron chest that is not to be opened until the boy's twenty-fifth birthday.

Ludwig Horace Holly, Leo's guardian. After his ward is grown, Holly accompanies him to Africa on his incredible adventure.

Job, Holly's servant. He dies of shock when he sees She die in the pillar of flame.

Ustane, a woman of the savage Amahagger tribe who falls in love with Leo and marries him according to tribal rite. She is killed by a look from the jealous She.

Billali, an Amahagger chief who befriends the white men and helps them escape to the African coast after their adventures with She.

Mahomed, an Arab who accompanies Leo and Holly into Africa. He is shot accidentally when his companions try to rescue him from cannibals.

SHE STOOPS TO CONQUER: Or, The Mistakes of a Night

Author: Oliver Goldsmith (1728 or 1730-1774)
First published: 1773
Genre: Drama

Locale: England
Time: The eighteenth century
Plot: Comedy of manners

Mr. Hardcastle, a landed English gentleman. Sometimes grumpy, he is more often a hearty old squire with the habit of retelling the same jokes and stories to his guests. At first excited by the prospect of having Marlow as his son-in-law, he finds his patience severely strained by the apparent impudence of the young man, who is the son of Hardcastle's old friend, Sir Charles Marlow. When he receives incivilities in return for his hospitality, the old gentleman loses his self-control and orders Marlow and his party from the house. Finally, however, he realizes that he is the victim of a hoax and willingly accepts the young man as Kate's suitor.

Mrs. Hardcastle, his formidable wife. Her strongest desire, other than having her son Tony marry Constance Neville, is to have an annual social polishing in London. For a time, she manages to thwart the romance of Hastings and Constance. Seeing that they are in love, she tries to circumvent their plans by taking Constance to Aunt Pedigree's. This stratagem fails when her undutiful son Tony merely drives them around Mrs. Hardcastle's home for three hours, finally landing the unsuspecting old lady in a horsepond near her home. Finally, she is forced to acknowledge the fact that her beloved Tony has only one desire—to get his inheritance.

Tony Lumpkin, her son by her first marriage. He is a roistering young squire completely spoiled by his doting mother. In return for her parental laxness, the lazy, hard-drinking prankster, when he is not singing bawdy songs in low taverns, plagues the Hardcastle household with practical jokes. Although he is uncommonly healthy, his mother is certain that he is dying of some dread ailment. When he meets Hastings and Marlow, he gives them some wrong information, thus creating his masterpiece among tricks. By telling them that Mr. Hardcastle's home is an inn, he causes them to think Hardcastle is an innkeeper and, what is worse, a windy, inquisitive old bore who takes unseemly social liberties with his guests. Hardcastle, on the other hand, is certain of their being impudent, cheeky young scamps.

Kate Hardcastle, Hardcastle's lovely young daughter. Like her stepmother, she also has social pretensions. Because of her stubbornness and desire to be a woman of fashion, her father makes her agree to wear fine clothes part of the day and ordinary clothes the rest of the time. Aware that Marlow is often improper with ordinary working girls, she disguises herself as a servant. Only then does she realize that he has qualities other than modesty and timidity. Liking this impetuous side of her suitor, Kate is now determined to have him as a husband.

Constance Neville, Kate's best friend. Early in the play, she learns of the joke that Tony has played on Marlow and Hastings, the man she loves. Entering into the spirit of the prank, she and Hastings plot their elopement. Unfortunately for their hopes, Mrs. Hardcastle is keeping a fortune in family jewels for Constance. To outwit the old lady, Constance acts out a part: She convinces Mrs. Hardcastle of her love for Tony, who actually dislikes Constance strongly. Finally, with the help of Kate's father, she is free to marry Hastings.

Young Marlow, Kate's reluctant suitor. Timid in the presence of ladies, Marlow is quite different with working girls. After mistaking Kate for a servant, he is mortified to learn her true identity. In his wounded pride, he plans to leave the house immediately; instead, she leads him away, still teasing him unmercifully.

Hastings, Marlow's best friend. With the help of Tony and Mr. Hardcastle, Hastings, a far more impetuous lover than Marlow, wins Constance as his bride.

Sir Charles Marlow, Mr. Hardcastle's old friend, the father of young Marlow.

THE SHEEP WELL
(Fuenteovejuna)

Author: Lope de Vega Carpio (1562-1635)
First published: c. 1619
Genre: Drama

Locale: Spain
Time: 1476
Plot: Social realism

Commander Fernán Gómez de Guzmán (fehr-NAHN GOH-mehs deh gews-MAHN), the feudal lord of the village of Fuente Ovejuna (Sheep Well or Watering Place) in 1476. Lusting after the village girls, he has his servants, Flores and Ortuño, seize them and bring them to his palace for his pleasure. The girl he desires most is Laurencia, the prettiest girl of the village, but she manages to elude his servants. One day, the commander does seize her, but she is saved by Frondoso, a courageous young peasant. To further his political ambitions, the commander persuades the young master of Calatrava to attack the city of Ciudad Real, in the possession of King Ferdinand and Queen Isabella. He intends to turn the town over to the king of Portugal. His career of tyranny and treachery ends when he is overthrown and killed by the people of Fuente Ovejuna after he has halted the marriage of Laurencia and taken the girl to the citadel.

Pedro Téllez Girón (PEH-droh TEH-yehs hee-ROHN), the youthful head of the military and religious Order of Calatrava. Urged by the older Commander Gómez, he captures Ciudad Real, but he is later defeated by the royal Spanish army. His appeal to King Ferdinand for clemency is accepted, and he is restored to honor.

Laurencia (low-REHN-see-ah), a charming peasant girl in love with Frondoso. She eludes the commander's men by staying in the fields as much as possible. One day, she is found by Gómez. Only the bravery of Frondoso, who seizes the commander's crossbow and threatens to kill him, saves her. She agrees to marry Frondoso, but the commander breaks up the wedding, has the groom jailed for attempting to murder him, and carries Laurencia off to his citadel. Escaping, she arouses the village, including the women, to storm the citadel and kill the cruel tyrant. She is pardoned by Queen Isabella.

Frondoso (frohn-doh-soh), a handsome young peasant who is in love with Laurencia. He earns the enmity of Gómez but escapes death when the commander's servants kill the wrong man. He is arrested on the eve of his marriage to Laurencia and is sentenced to be hanged. The revolt of the villagers saves him.

Flores (floh-rehs) and

Ortuño (ohr-TEWN-yoh), servants of the commander who try to supply Gómez with girls. They are finally routed by the aroused peasantry.

Esteban (ehs-TEH-bahn), an alcalde, the father of Laurencia, who provides a dowry of 4,000 maravidis for her marriage to Frondoso. He refuses to surrender his daughter to the commander.

Alonso (ah-LOHN-soh), another alcalde.

Juan Rojo (hwahn rroh-hoh) and

Cuadrado (kwah-DRAH-doh), regidores of the village.

Jacinta (hah-SEEN-tah), a peasant girl, the friend of Laurencia, who is seized and raped by Commander Gómez.

Pascuala (pahs-KWAH-lah), another pretty peasant girl.

Mingo (MEEN-goh), a peasant whose attempts to save Jacinta from the attentions of the commander result in his being flayed by Spanish soldiers.

Barrildo (bah-RREEL-doh), another peasant. He argues humorously with Mingo and Frondoso over the nature of love.

Juan Chamorro (chah-MOH-rroh), a sacristan.

A judge, who is sent by King Ferdinand and Isabella to investigate the happenings at Fuente Ovejuna. Although he tortures and questions some three hundred villagers to discover the murderer of the commander, he gets the same reply from all: "The executioner was Fuente Ovejuna."

King Ferdinand and

Queen Isabella, the Catholic monarchs of Spain.

The villagers of Fuente Ovejuna (FWEHN-teh oh-veh-HEW-nah), the real protagonist of this proletarian drama. Collectively, they assume guilt for the execution of the tyrant, and collectively they are pardoned and taken under the protection of the Crown.

THE SHELTERED LIFE

Author: Ellen Glasgow (1873-1945)
First published: 1932
Genre: Novel

Locale: Richmond, Virginia
Time: 1906-1914
Plot: Psychological realism

General David Archbald, an old Southern gentleman whose life is dominated by the needs of his daughters, his daughter-in-law, and his granddaughter. He is tall, spare, and very erect, with silver-gray hair and mustache, dark beetling eyebrows, and an eagle nose. Though a rebel at heart since childhood, he has throughout his long life been largely a conformist. He often muses on the past, on what might have been, and on the insoluble puzzles of human nature.

Jenny Blair Archbald, his spirited granddaughter, a pretty girl who from her childhood on listens to conversations and closely observes the older people about her. Fascinated by George, who at first regards her only as a charming child, she is the half-innocent cause of his murder.

George Birdsong, the general's neighbor, a handsome and romantically attractive but improvident attorney who loves his wife but cannot remain faithful to her. He tries to control his weaknesses, especially after Eva's illness, but nature is too strong within him. Ironically, he dies after being discovered impulsively kissing Jenny Blair, to whose pursuit he had previously paid very little attention.

Eva Howard Birdsong, George's beautiful wife, who, like a lady, affects a happiness she does not feel with her husband. She has smiled through her married life, realizing both George's love and his inconstancy. She also endures her severe illness valiantly. Finding George and Jenny Blair in an amorous embrace in the Birdsong home is too much for her, and she shoots him.

Etta, the general's frail, plain, and sickly daughter who desperately and vainly longs for love and must settle for its substitute by reading French novels.

Isabella, the general's other daughter—strong, handsome, and magnetic—whose marriage to a man socially beneath her disappoints her father. The marriage, however, is a happy one.

Joseph Crocker, a carpenter whom Isabella marries after breaking two engagements.

Bena Peyton, the plump girlhood friend with whom Jenny plans to go to New York.

Cora Blair Archbald, Jenny's mother, whose husband Richard died while fox hunting. She and Jenny live with the general.

John Welch, Eva's cousin, a doctor, whom Jenny hates because he seems to understand her better than she does herself.

Delia Barron, one of George's passing fancies.

Memoria, the Birdsongs' mulatto laundress and one of George's mistresses.

Erminia, the general's dead wife, whom he married without love and with whom he lived faithfully but without real love for thirty years.

Erminia Crocker, Joseph and Isabella's young daughter.

THE SHELTERING SKY

Author: Paul Bowles (1910-   )
First published: 1949
Genre: Novel

Locale: Oran, Algeria; various outposts in the Sahara desert; and a remote Bedouin village
Time: After World War II
Plot: Psychological realism

Port Moresby, an independently wealthy American. Fascinated by maps, he defines himself as a traveler rather than a tourist, feeling that he has no permanent home but instead journeying continuously from one place to another. Married to Kit Moresby for twelve years, he realizes that they are experiencing difficulties and arranges an excursion to Africa with the hope of sorting through their problems. At the last instant, he panics about the trip and invites Tunner, one of his close friends, to join them. Both husband and wife come to wish that Tunner would leave them alone, Port because he longs for intimacy with Kit and she because Tunner continually makes advances toward her. Because of their lack of communication, neither expresses that desire clearly to the other. Instead, Port turns to prostitutes out of frustration, and Kit eventually is seduced by Tunner. Ironically, Port contracts typhoid and dies, alone, while Kit has a rendezvous with Tunner.

Kit Moresby, Port's wife, an attractive, small blonde with an intense gaze. Her white skin draws attention from African men and envy from African women. Quite superstitious, she is excellent at interpreting everyday occurrences as good or bad omens. Tunner's presence during the trip bothers her, but she tolerates him because of his friendship with Port. After she is seduced by the young man, the remorse she experiences causes her to refrain from voicing her disgust with the various traumatic circumstances the threesome undergo. After Port's death, she appears to reject Western civilization and hides out in the desert.

Tunner, Port's friend and Kit's paramour. Handsome, sturdy, and young, he is a proud and persistent individual who

refuses to acknowledge the hints dropped by both Port and Kit that his companionship is no longer desired. When he and Kit are separated from Port, he offers her several glasses of champagne and then sleeps with her. Kit is overcome by guilt, but Tunner sees the encounter simply as another conquest. After Port's death, however, Tunner becomes greatly distressed by Kit's disappearance.

Mrs. Lyle, a photographer and writer from Australia. Belligerent and boisterous, she is large and sallow-skinned, with expressionless black eyes. Described by Port as the loneliest woman he has ever met, she seems to be motivated primarily by fear of relationships. Even with her son, Eric, she communicates mainly by shrieking at him. Her favorite topics of conversation include the stupidity of the French, the laziness of the Arabs, and her own ill health.

Eric Lyle, Mrs. Lyle's spoiled and greedy son. Allusions are made to his probable homosexual tendencies, but one witness claims that he has seen mother and son together in bed. Always running low on financial resources, Eric tries to befriend the Moresbys by offering to drive them to their next destination so they will not have to travel by train. In the process, he manages to borrow three hundred francs and to steal Port's and Tunner's passports.

Belqassim (behl-kah-SEEM), Kit's second husband. Finding Kit alone in the desert, he rapes her, kidnaps her, and then marries her, much to the dismay of his three other wives.

— *Coleen Maddy*

THE SHEPHEARDES CALENDAR

Author: Edmund Spenser (c. 1552-1599)
First published: 1579
Genre: Poetry

Locale: The English countryside
Time: The sixteenth century
Plot: Pastoral

Colin Clout, a shepherd who falls in love with Rosalinde, who treats his affection rudely and thus causes him to become depressed and melancholy. Frustrated by Rosalinde's lack of response, Colin breaks his pipe, on which he had sought to play songs of love that would win her approval. His friend Hobbinoll notices his distress and composes a song about Colin's plight, recalling to his friend Thenot a song that Colin composed in honor of the queen. Colin's poetic gifts are celebrated by Hobbinoll, and at the urging of his friend, Colin seeks to fulfill his lyric potential, especially because he is nearing the age of thirty and sees his window of opportunity vanishing. Colin also feels the pull of more sedate and conventional pastoral moods. Colin's love continues to plague him, especially because he is no longer physically even in contact with Rosalinde. His poetry continues to excite the admiration of his fellow shepherds, who see his as the one truly talented voice among them. As the seasons pass and the year comes to a close, Colin transcends the personal limits of his feelings for Rosalinde. He gives voice to the collective desires and sorrows of his fellow men, especially in his great elegy for the mysterious lady Dido. Colin, close to death himself, has matured into a poet of true magnitude.

Rosalinde, a country girl beloved by Colin. Rosalinde is disdainful of Colin. She becomes the object of his poetry but eventually is set aside by him.

Thenot, an old shepherd who is no longer attractive and lacks interest in worldly lusts and pleasures. Taunted by the younger Cuddie for his senescence, Thenot retorts by telling the younger man the fable of the Oak and the Brier. Thenot listens attentively to Hobbinoll's tale of Colin's love. Thenot

admires Colin's talent but scorns his captivity to romantic feelings.

Cuddie, a young shepherd who teases old Thenot about his age. Later, he engages in discussions with Piers concerning Colin's poetic abilities and referees a dispute between two rival shepherd-singers. Cuddie is admired as a poet, but he knows that he is not as talented as Colin.

Hobbinoll, a shepherd and a friend of Colin who seeks to appreciate and stimulate Colin's poetic talents. Hobbinoll's affection for Colin leads him to tolerate his friend's complaints, though he seeks to steer Colin toward a calmer and more relaxed attitude. Hobbinoll condemns Rosalinde as the source of Colin's unhappiness yet also understands Colin's devotion to her. Hobbinoll represents ideals of rural stability, peace, and contemplation.

Piers, a shepherd representing Protestantism. Piers engages in a debate with Palinode in which he appears to prevail. Piers calls for clergy to live simpler, more disciplined, and more responsible lives. Piers later attempts, in vain, to convince Cuddie that he should aspire to be a poetic rival of Colin.

Palinode, a shepherd representing Catholicism. He engages in a debate with Piers that, at least on the face of it, he appears to lose.

Morell, a shepherd-clergyman accuses by Thomalin of being overly proud and self-admiring.

Thomalin, a shepherd who accuses Morell of excessive pride and attempts to back up his assertion in sung debate.

Diggon Davie, a well-traveled shepherd who contrasts his worldly wisdom to Hobbinoll's preference for uncomplicated ease and the simple life.

— *Nicholas Birns*

SHIKASTA

Author: Doris Lessing (1919-   )
First published: 1979
Genre: Novel

Locale: Shikasta (Earth) and surrounding planes or zones
Time: Primarily the twentieth century, but far into the past and into the near future
Plot: Science fiction

Johor, incarnated as **George Sherban**, a representative of the galactic empire Canopus to the planet Earth, which is named Shikasta in the novel. Shikasta is Johor's worst assignment, for he must watch its decline from the golden age when it was named Rohanda to its low point in the twentieth century. Rohanda/Shikasta/Earth once had two races: the Giants, who live twelve to fifteen thousand years and are sixteen to eighteen feet tall, and the Natives, who live five hundred years and are half the height of the Giants, with the former acting as benevolent guides and teachers to the latter. Johor witnesses and reports on the degeneration of both races as a mystical flow of goodwill called "the Lock" between Canopus and Shikasta breaks down and chaos replaces an idyllic pastoral life. He travels about in various incarnations, including that of a "shaggy" Native, attempting to salvage what he can and

opposing the influence of Shammat, a criminal planet allied with the evil empire Puttioria. Johor ultimately resurfaces as George Sherban, a young man tutored by a remarkable series of Canopean influences as he lives with his family in Nigeria, Kenya, Morocco, and Tunisia. George, though basically Scotch-Irish, has an Indian grandfather; he is tall, with ivory skin, black hair, and black eyes, easily passing for an Indian or an Arab. He becomes an international youth leader, helping to organize both Children's Camps, for refugees and orphans, and Youth Armies, which attempt to maintain civilization under the Chinese socialist overlordship now controlling Europe. George's greatest achievement is in his role as prosecutor at the Mock Trial of the white race sponsored by the Combined Youth Armies of the World. George's artful defusing of the hostility against the whites by admitting their culpability for colonial and other misdeeds circumvents a planned genocide of all remaining Europeans by the newly resurgent black, brown, and "golden" races. After the trial, George continues his work for human betterment, developing geometrically organized cities in the Andes in South America and siring his family. When his work is finished, he dies.

Benjamin Sherban, George's fraternal twin, who is always contrasted to George. Benjamin is heavy, tending toward fat, with curly brown hair, blue-gray eyes, and reddish-brown skin, the result of perpetual sunburn in the North African climate. As an adolescent, he is cynical, sarcastic, surly, and in constant conflict with his sister, Rachel. Benjamin, as a boy, clearly is made to feel inferior by the near perfection of Johor/George; as he grows up, he comes to accept his second-class status, takes on the supervision of the Children's Camps, and makes his peace with George and Rachel. He acts as an assistant to defense counsel Taufiq/John Brent-Oxford in the Mock Trial of the white race. He ends up on a remote Pacific island in a settlement committed to starting life anew.

Rachel Sherban, George and Benjamin's younger sister. Her journal, which composes a substantial part of the middle of the book, gives a quirky, rather earthy perspective on George and Benjamin through the eyes of a somewhat spoiled and petulant teenage sister. Like Benjamin, Rachel is intimidated by George's casual success in all of his many endeavors and by his enormous influence on all around him. Rachel's jealousy is complicated by her schoolgirl crush on George, but she learns tolerance and responsibility, finally sacrificing herself for her brother. Rachel's rich description of life in a tenement in Morocco is a high point in the novel.

Taufiq, like Johor a secret agent of Canopus, born on Earth as **John Brent-Oxford**. He attains success as a lawyer and politician but is corrupted by the malign influences of Earth/Shikasta and begins to live only for his own pleasure, in complete contradiction to the Canopean ideal of service. His neglect of his duties leads to failure and disaster for a number of people, whose unhappy stories are listed by Johor. Taufiq/John Brent-Oxford, at the end a frail, white-haired old man, redeems himself at the Mock Trial by acting as defense counsel for the white race and behaving with wisdom and decency. He is killed by a falling rock when an unidentified airplane bombs the Greek amphitheater where the trial is held.

— *Andrew Macdonald*

THE SHINING

Author: Stephen King (1947-   )
First published: 1977
Genre: Novel

Locale: Sidewinder, Colorado
Time: The 1970's
Plot: Horror

Jack Torrance, a former preparatory school teacher in his early thirties who has taken the job of winter caretaker for the isolated Overlook Hotel, high in the Colorado Rockies. He hopes to use this time to restore intimacy to his relationships with his wife, Wendy, and his young son, Danny, and also to renew his earlier successes as a writer. These intentions are complicated and threatened by the darker elements in Jack's character: a history of alcoholism, a background of child abuse (learned from his father and already manifested in one episode against Danny), an uncontrolled temper, and self-destructive thoughts and tendencies that, in the past, have led to a serious contemplation of suicide. These flaws make Jack especially vulnerable to the malevolent powers of the Overlook, and he is led eventually to betray loyalties to wife and son. In the final moment of his life, the strength of his love for Danny overpowers even the evil persona with which the hotel has endowed him. A final glimpse at Jack's almost lost humanity materializes and then is destroyed in a climactic explosion and conflagration.

Wendy Torrance, Jack's pretty wife, also in her early thirties. Despite past problems, she is committed to her husband, but only when this commitment does not conflict with her loyalty to her young son. She joins Jack at the Overlook with the highest hopes, but when the vicious ghosts of the hotel begin to absorb Jack's personality, she finds unforeseen strength to protect Danny and to survive their encounter with the Overlook.

Danny "Doc" Torrance, Jack and Wendy's five-year-old son, gifted with "the shining," a telepathic ability to read the thoughts of other people and to visualize future events. It is Danny's presence and his special abilities that seem to activate the stored-up evils of the Overlook. Danny inspires great love in his father, a love that is Jack's strongest claim to respectability and, ultimately, to his own humanity.

Dick Hallorann, a single black man in his sixties, the summer-season cook at the Overlook Hotel. When he meets the Torrances in the autumn, on closing day, he feels an instant affinity with Danny; Hallorann, too, has a touch of "the shining." An urgent telepathic message from Danny eventually summons the kindly Hallorann to return from Florida to the Overlook in the depth of winter to rescue Wendy and Danny.

Albert Shockley, a shadowy character, a single man of independent, and perhaps illegally obtained, wealth. During Jack's days at Stovington Prep, Shockley, a board member, was Jack's drinking buddy and fellow alcoholic. More recently, as a part owner of the Overlook, he is responsible for Jack finding employment as caretaker. By telephone, he later discourages Jack's interest in researching and writing the history of the Overlook and its unsavory background.

Stuart Ullman, the short, plump, officious manager of the Overlook. He gives Jack Torrance the caretaker's job, against his better judgment, because of Shockley's influence.

Delbert Grady, the ghost of an earlier Overlook caretaker who murdered his wife and two young daughters many winters before, apparently in a fit of cabin fever. He is one of Jack's hallucinations during the period when the hotel seduces and overpowers Jack's personality.

— *Laura Stone Barnard*

SHIP OF FOOLS

Author: Katherine Anne Porter (1890-1980)
First published: 1962
Genre: Novel

Locale: Aboard the *Vera*
Time: August 22-September 17, 1931
Plot: Allegory

Jenny Brown and
David Scott, young American painters living together in a tortured, on-again, off-again relationship, unable even to agree whether their first destination after landing in Europe will be Spain or France.

Dr. Schumann, the ship's doctor. He has a serious heart condition. More than any other character, he is remote from common prejudices, tensions, and jealousies, but he becomes enamored of La Condesa.

La Condesa (kohn-DEH-sah), a dissolute noblewoman being deported from Cuba to Tenerife.

Siegfried Rieber (REE-behr) and
Lizzie Spöckenkieker (SHPEH-kehn-kee-kehr), a couple on board the ship. He is the publisher of a ladies' garment trade magazine, and she is in the ladies' garment trade. He is short and round, and is separated from his wife. She is taller, scrawny, and long divorced. Their bumptious and never quite consummated courtship lasts almost the whole voyage.

Professor Hutten and
Mrs. Hutten (HEWT-tehn), who are returning to Germany after his long tenure as head of a German school in Mexico. When they are not concerned with polishing his image as a deep thinker, they are taking care of their continuously, messily, and embarrassingly seasick bulldog, Bébé.

Wilhelm Freytag (FRI-tahg), who is returning to Germany to fetch his beloved but Jewish wife, Mary, and her mother. He plans to relocate permanently to Mexico, where he works for an oil company. His roving eye falls on Jenny, and he becomes the focus of David's jealousy and Jenny's gamesmanship.

Karl Baumgartner and
Greta Baumgartner (BOWM-gahrt-nehr), who are traveling with their eight-year-old son, Hans. Karl is a clown and a drunk, Greta is a long-suffering wife, and Hans is a thoroughly repressed and timid boy.

Mrs. Rittersdorf, who prefers to observe others and record her often acid opinions in a voluminous diary.

The Lutzes, a couple traveling with their ungainly eighteen-year-old daughter, Elsa. They are returning to Switzerland after Mr. Lutz has spent fifteen years as a hotelkeeper in Mexico.

William Denny, a crude, hard-drinking American chemical engineer who is going to Berlin. His fruitless pursuit of the Spanish dancer Pastora culminates in a befuddled confrontation with Mary Treadwell.

Mary Treadwell, a decorous and bitter American divorcée, returning with hope and fear to Paris and her youth.

Julius Löwenthal (LEH-wehn-tahl), a Jewish maker and seller of Catholic religious objects and a devout anti-Gentile.

Arne Hansen, a large, strong, slow Swede. He is fascinated by the dancer Amparo and prone to depressing and inchoate philosophizing.

Karl Glocken (GLOK-kehn), a hunchback who has sold his tobacco stand in Mexico to return to Germany.

Captain Thiele (TEE-leh), a stern, autocratic, and extremely class-conscious Junker.

Ric and
Rac, six-year-old twins—male and female, respectively—of two of the members of the Spanish singing and dancing troupe. Their antics cross the line from prankishness to malice.

The Spanish troupe, who provide an impudent and criminal counterweight to the Germanic order on the ship.

— *James L. Hodge*

THE SHIPYARD
(El astillero)

Author: Juan Carlos Onetti (1909-1994)
First published: 1961
Genre: Novel

Locale: Santa Maria and its hinterlands
Time: Late 1950's
Plot: Existentialism

E. Larsen, the antihero, a stout, balding, late-middle-aged former pimp with a swagger to match his former trade. He wishes to reintegrate himself legitimately into the area of Santa Maria, the Argentine or Uruguayan river city from which he was exiled five years before for establishing a brothel there. Larsen is named general manager of a bankrupt shipyard nearby at Puerto Astillero. Feeding self-delusion to justify his vitiated existence, he tries to make something out of its rusting plant, which has not received an order or paid its managers in years. He even courts the boss's mentally defective daughter in the hope of possessing the seignorial house where she and her father live. Larsen's end comes when he realizes fully, at long last, that his quest for upward mobility has been a farce. Apparently dying, he rides upriver on a ferryboat.

Jeremías Petrus (heh-reh-MEE-ahs PEH-truhs), the elderly owner of the defunct shipyard. Petrus, too, is self-deluded. He keeps up the role of willful pioneer of industry with his bustling gait, heavy eyebrows, and sideburns. When he is jailed for forgery, Petrus ages further overnight, calls the cell his office, and continues to make empty plans for the business with his visitor, Larsen.

Angélica Inés Petrus (ahn-HEHL-ee-kah ee-NEHS), the idiot daughter of the shipyard owner. Tall, blonde, and childlike, she emits involuntary bursts of laughter from her perpetually open mouth and is generally incapable of making coherent conversation. Larsen courts her with comic formality at their proper meetings in the summerhouse of the Petrus estate, but Angélica Inés barely comprehends what is happening.

A. Gálvez (GAHL-vehs), the bald young administrative manager of the shipyard. Receiving no salary in his purely nominal job, with nothing to do but occasionally sell off spare parts from the plant, he lives in poverty with a wife and dogs in a shack on the shipyard grounds. When Larsen first meets him, Gálvez acts the role of the perfect cynic, mimicking Petrus' pomposity and the irony of the nonexistent activities and salaries of the shipyard. He then becomes increasingly humorless, denounces Petrus to the police for forgery, and commits suicide, as if he were no longer able to live the lie of the shipyard.

Gálvez's wife, a tall and pretty but unkempt woman who wears a man's overcoat and shoes. At the time of the action, she is pregnant. Larsen is attracted to her, considering her a real woman, perhaps by comparison with the childish Angélica Inés. She is kind and patient, but Larsen realizes that she is spent by her wretched existence. Their relationship is not intimate, although Larsen spends many evening hours alone with her at the shack. He leaves Puerto Astillero after looking through the window of the shack and seeing the woman alone, struggling in labor.

Kunz (kewnz), the older, corpulent, hairy technical manager of the shipyard, a German immigrant. Like Gálvez, Kunz is cynical and sarcastic about the phantom enterprise and spends his supposed work time looking over his stamp album. He simply yawns and professes ignorance when Larsen asks him about past operations. Kunz is the source of a story about a visit Larsen receives at the shipyard from Angélica Inés, who presumably accuses her aging beau of infidelity with Gálvez's wife.

Dr. Díaz Grey, a middle-aged bachelor physician from Santa Maria, formerly acquainted with Larsen. Díaz Grey lives a life of dull routine: evenings of solitaire, an unvarying program of recorded sacred music, and drugs to put him to sleep. He is happy to break the monotony when Larsen visits him one evening. Díaz Grey's impressions of Larsen and recollections of the string of Larsen's predecessors at Petrus Limited provide another perspective on things. When he is informed of Larsen's absurd engagement to Angélica Inés Petrus, Díaz Grey soberly recommends that they avoid having children.

Josefina (hoh-seh-FEE-nah), Angélica Inés' servant, a short, dark, and sturdy country girl whom Larsen bribes and romances to get access to Petrus' daughter. He spends his last night in Puerto Astillero with Josefina in a kind of sentimental replay of his past, which, nevertheless, is faceless: Anyone could have had the experience.

— *John Deredita*

SHIRLEY

Author: Charlotte Brontë (1816-1855)
First published: 1849
Genre: Novel

Locale: Yorkshire, England
Time: Mid-nineteenth century
Plot: Psychological

Shirley Keeldar, the mistress of Fieldhead, a young woman of wealth who owns estates in Yorkshire. A spirited, independent woman of great sense, she finds marriage difficult to contemplate because she does not wish to put herself into the hands of a man who is after her money or a weakling who has no moral fiber of his own. Most of all, she fears submitting to someone who might be a domestic tyrant. Beneath her independent spirit, Shirley is a good-hearted, warm person eager to help anyone who needs assistance. She has a social conscience and tries to organize in the surrounding parishes a system of giving charitable aid to the families of unemployed millworkers. She eventually falls in love with Louis Gérard Moore, her former tutor, and marries him.

Louis Gérard Moore, a young man of Belgian and English ancestry who, because of his family's straitened circumstances, becomes a tutor in the family of Mr. Sympson, Shirley's uncle. Moore, a quiet, intelligent man, loves Shirley deeply. Through his patience and wisdom, he comes to understand her and to help her understand herself. He wins her for his wife despite his impecunious circumstances and the opposition of Shirley's uncle, her former guardian.

Robert Gérard Moore, a textile manufacturer and Louis Moore's brother. The mill he operates is rented from Shirley Keeldar. Robert Moore is a man with two sides to his nature. He is a hard-headed businessman for whom his mill and financial success are paramount. Under the domination of this side of his character, he battles ruthlessly with unemployed work-

ers to try to prevent modernization of his factory. Politically, he opposes the embargo of British ports caused by the Napoleonic wars. Once removed from the scene of business and politics, however, he becomes a different man, loving, thoughtful, and kind. Influenced by the harder side of his character, he tries to marry Shirley Keeldar, but she refuses his suit because she realizes that he is more interested in her wealth than in her. Later, he woos and marries Caroline Helstone, whom he truly loves.

Caroline Helstone, a distant cousin of Louis and Robert Moore. She is reared by a widowed uncle, the rector of the parish, who treats her as kindly as his austere nature allows. Caroline, a beautiful, sweet, and reticent young woman whom everyone likes, becomes Shirley Keeldar's close friend. In love with Robert Moore, she keeps her love to herself when she thinks that Robert Moore and Shirley are in love, for she believes a match with Shirley would be better for her beloved. Eventually, Moore and Caroline discover their love for each other and are married on the same day as Shirley and Louis Moore.

Mr. Helstone, the rector of Briarfield parish, Caroline's uncle. He is a clergyman who would have been better fitted for a career as a military officer. In the conflicts between the workers and the mill owners, he is a great help to the manufacturers, even to participation in a pitched battle. He is liberal with his money to his niece, but he is not capable of giving her warmth and understanding.

Mr. Malone, the bumptuous Irish curate to Mr. Helstone.

Mrs. Pryor, Shirley Keeldar's companion and former governess, a quiet, reticent woman of charm and fading beauty. She takes a great liking to Caroline Helstone and becomes her close friend. After nursing Caroline through a serious illness, she reveals herself as Mrs. James Helstone, Caroline's mother and the rector's sister-in-law. She had changed her name because she feared that her late husband, then living, would find her and force her to live with him under desperate circumstances.

Sir Philip Nunnely, a young peer given to writing bad poetry. He falls in love with Shirley Keeldar but his suit is rejected.

Mr. Sympson, Shirley Keeldar's uncle and former guardian. He is a weak but tyrannical man who takes his family to Fieldhead in hopes of dominating Shirley, even though she is of age and can make her own decisions. He tries to force Shirley to accept each of several suitors in turn and is horrified when she announces her love for Louis Moore.

Sympson is ejected by Moore for insulting his former ward.

Mrs. Sympson, his patient, well-bred wife.

Henry Sympson, their only son, who is crippled. He is Louis Moore's pupil.

The Misses Sympson, their prim and proper daughters, older than Henry.

Hortense Moore, the sister of Louis and Robert Moore. She keeps house for Robert during his bachelorhood. More Belgian than English, she is unhappy in Yorkshire.

Michael Hartley, a crazed and drunken millworker who shoots Robert Moore from ambush and seriously endangers his victim's life. Himself a victim of drink, Hartley dies a few months after the shooting.

Miss Mary Ann Ainley and

Miss Margaret Hall, two spinsters who perform deeds of charity among the poor of Briarfield parish. Shirley Keeldar gives them three hundred pounds to distribute among the needy unemployed.

THE SHOEMAKER'S HOLIDAY: Or, The Gentle Craft

Author: Thomas Dekker (c. 1572-1632)
First published: 1600
Genre: Drama

Locale: London and the nearby village of Old Ford
Time: c. 1413-1422
Plot: Comedy

Simon Eyre (ayr), the blustering, "madcap" shoemaker who becomes lord mayor of London. One of the kindliest of men, he watches over the welfare of his journeymen while he berates them vigorously; it is his intercession with the king that reconciles Sir Hugh and Sir Roger to the marriage of Rose with Eyre's sometime Dutch assistant, Lacy. He is not overawed by his high-ranking position, and he rejoices more at feasting those who were once apprentices with him than at entertaining the king. Loyal to his trade, he asks for one royal boon, the privilege of selling shoes twice a week at Leadenhall Market.

Rowland Lacy (**Hans**), a gallant, spendthrift young nobleman who learned the shoemaker's trade when he arrived penniless in Germany on his Grand Tour. Forbidden by his domineering uncle to marry his sweetheart, Rose Otley, he abandons his military command, disguises himself as a Dutch journeyman named Hans, and joins the workshop of Simon Eyre. He proves to be an excellent businessman and vastly increases his master's wealth by introducing him to an old skipper with a ship full of spices to sell. With persistence and fidelity, he at last wins his bride, wooing her while he pretends to be fitting new shoes.

Sir Hugh Lacy, the earl of Lincoln, his overbearing uncle. Adamant in his opposition to his nephew's proposed marriage, he tries to engineer Sir Roger's disapproval. He is somewhat disgruntled to find that the mayor scorns the match, which would be a fine one for his daughter, without Sir Hugh's persuasion.

Sir Roger Otley, lord mayor of London. He is astute, if not oversubtle, in his dealings with Sir Hugh and resents any suggestion of patronizing in the earl's behavior toward him. His independent young daughter infuriates him by refusing the hand of a wealthy citizen he has chosen for her, and

he shuts her up at home to keep her away from Lacy.

Rose Otley, the lord mayor's daughter. She is agreeable and devoted to Lacy but perversely sarcastic to the suitor she rejects.

Sybil, her witty, voluble maid.

Askew, another of Sir Hugh's nephews, a kindly young man who helps his cousin Rowland escape their uncle's close surveillance.

Dodger, Sir Hugh's servant.

Firk and

Hodge, Eyre's journeymen, industrious workmen who cheerfully exchange insults with their master and mistress.

Margery, Eyre's wife, who is, on occasion, bawdy and sharp, but basically is good-hearted and fond of her husband. After Simon becomes lord mayor, she worries that his manners are not proper for entertaining the king, and she gives voice to her concern about her wardrobe.

Rafe Damport, another of Eyre's journeymen, gentler and quieter than his fellows. In spite of his master's efforts to keep him at home, he is drafted and sent to France soon after his marriage. He is heartbroken to find his wife missing when he returns wounded from his campaign, yet he resigns himself to accept her second marriage when she does not recognize him. Happily reunited with her through the efforts of Firk and Hodge, he proudly rejects Hammond's offer of money for her.

Jane, his wife, who mourns his loss but finally allows herself to be partially consoled by Hammond. She shows her tender heart in her generous gift to the unknown shoemaker who reminds her of her lost husband.

Hammond, a London citizen who pays court to Rose. Rejected by her, he turns to Jane, whom he has admired in her shop.

SHORT LETTER, LONG FAREWELL
(Der kurze Brief zum langen Abschied)

Author: Peter Handke (1942-   )
First published: 1972
Genre: Novel

Locale: The United States
Time: Late 1960's
Plot: Philosophical realism

The narrator, an Austrian writer almost thirty years old. As the novel begins, he has just arrived in the United States (in New England). His journey across America makes up the external plot of the novel. The narrator is a strange and introspective figure, often overcome by mood swings that range from pure horror almost to euphoria. He believes that he has a very exaggerated sense of time. He is not very tolerant of other people and does not like to look at them up close. When people tell the narrator stories, the narrator is annoyed because he thinks that "one look at me must have told them I wouldn't like it." He also thinks that people can see at a glance that he is the kind of person who will put up with anything. Throughout the novel, the narrator reads works of American and German literature and reflects on his past and his anxieties about death.

Judith, the narrator's estranged wife. Although little is said of her, she seems obsessed with taking revenge on her former husband.

Claire Madison, an American instructor of German and friend of the narrator, with whom she had an affair on one of his previous trips to the United States. She is a single parent and travels with the narrator to St. Louis. Claire is genuinely concerned about the narrator and, in the course of various conversations, helps him to clarify his feelings.

Delta Benedictine, the two-year-old daughter of the narrator's friend Claire. She is obsessed with having things in order and becomes extremely upset when objects are misplaced. The child seems out of touch with nature and the environment and is interested only in the artificial products and imitations that make up much of modern American life.

John Ford, a seventy-six-year-old American film director. He lives in his Bel Air estate and is visited by the narrator and his wife at the end of the novel. The romantic and optimistic images of nature and America found in the director's films (such as *Young Mr. Lincoln*) have been highly significant for the narrator in his coming to terms both with modern America and with his own life.

— *Thomas F. Barry*

SHOSHA
(Neshome Ekspeditsyes)

Author: Isaac Bashevis Singer (1904-1991)
First published: 1974
Genre: Novel

Locale: Warsaw, Poland, and Tel Aviv, Israel
Time: 1914-1952
Plot: Historical realism

Aaron Greidinger, nicknamed **Tsutsik**, a vegetarian writer who narrates the events of the novel from his humble beginnings as a rabbi's son on Krochmalna Street in Warsaw to post-World War II New York. Young and idealistic despite his poverty and the growing menace of Nazism in Poland, Aaron must grapple with recurring bouts of despair that naturally result when he, his friends, and his country cannot live up to his high illusions. He nevertheless maintains his belief in a Supreme Power. Red-haired, balding, and sexually attractive to women of all classes, he engages in a series of brief affairs, finally marrying his childhood sweetheart even though he risks his career and very life to do so. After a temporary stint as an aspiring playwright supported by a wealthy patron, he makes a meager living writing articles and serialized biographies for a Yiddish newspaper, thereby acquiring a measure of fame. He escapes from Poland before the Holocaust and relates at the end of the novel the fate of the other characters.

Shosha Schuldiener, Aaron's childhood sweetheart, who becomes his wife. A blonde, blue-eyed beauty, she is physically and mentally stunted. An academic failure, she still manages to attract the intellectual boy Aaron with her total acceptance of and devotion to him, and he has never forgotten her, despite their early separation. When they meet as adults, he reaffirms his love for her, and they marry in the face of others' incredulity at this seeming mismatch. She matures in the mar-riage, displaying unusual insight in her philosophical discussions with Aaron and eventually disarming and winning over his friends with her simple charm. She remains compulsively dependent on Aaron, continually voicing fears of separation from him and her family. She dies while fleeing Poland, having lost her will to live as a result of this violent upheaval.

Morris Feitelzohn, a writer and philosopher who takes an interest in Aaron and whom Aaron greatly admires. Stocky and square-faced, with bushy eyebrows and thick lips, he is witty, debonair, and chronically unemployed, constantly borrowing money from his friends. At the Writers' Club and various other meeting places, he engages Aaron in lengthy conversations that explore almost every known philosophy, though he subscribes to none of them. He introduces Aaron to several of the novel's major characters and thus initiates much of the plot. He dies in Warsaw in 1941.

Betty Slonim, an American actress in her early thirties. She is in Poland with her wealthy lover to find a play for the Yiddish stage in which she can star. Red-haired and extremely attractive, she is immediately drawn to Aaron, with whom she shares the story of her Russian Jewish background and generally hard life. Aaron is hired to write a play for her, but she sabotages his work by demanding that he spend his time accompanying her around Warsaw; they soon become lovers. Her constant suggestions concerning the play and revisions of it render it a disaster before it can even open. Far from abandoning Aaron, she wishes to marry him and thus ensure his safety in America. He rejects her, though, for Shosha. Brittle, cocky, and with little self-esteem, she ends up married to an American officer who is instrumental in smuggling Aaron out of Poland. She eventually commits suicide, which she has threatened throughout the story.

Sam Dreiman, an American millionaire who is Betty's lover. A vigorous old man with a shock of white hair and a broad face and body, he is essentially a father figure to Betty. He is alienated from his wife and children, who have disappointed him. The fortune he has made in construction is now devoted to Betty's happiness. He finances the writing of Aaron's play. When it dissolves into chaos, he is incensed at Aaron for Betty's sake. When he falls gravely ill in Warsaw, it is he who proposes that Betty marry Aaron and that they become joint heirs in Sam's will.

Celia Chentshiner, a wealthy, sophisticated intellectual who is an avowed atheist and with whom Aaron has a brief affair. She is severely proper in her appearance but warmly gracious as a hostess.

Haiml Chentshiner, Celia's childlike and independently wealthy husband, who survives the war and remarries several years after his wife's death. Aaron meets him in Israel at the story's end, and Haiml delivers the poignant and philosophical last words of the novel.

Dora Stolnitz, Aaron's first mistress. A fanatic communist, she persists in her ideology even when presented with evidence of its treachery.

Tekla, Aaron's buxom housemaid and mistress, a peasant who serves him devotedly and for whom he finds a job at the Chentshiners'.

— *Caren S. Silvester*

SHROUD FOR A NIGHTINGALE

Author: P. D. James (1920-   )
First published: 1971
Genre: Novel

Locale: Heatheringfield, England
Time: January, 1971
Plot: Detective and mystery

Adam Dalgliesh, the protagonist, chief superintendent of New Scotland Yard. He is as renowned for remaining dispassionate as for solving cases rapidly. A reserved, introspective man who has published two books of poetry, he nevertheless insists that all considerations of privacy must cede before a criminal investigation. His moral indignation over murder does not undermine either his judicious examination of witnesses and evidence or his confident bearing in the alien world of John Carpendar Hospital. Eventually, weakened but undeterred by a serious head wound received in an ambush, Dalgliesh confronts the nurse he believes to be guilty, even without proof. The end of the case leaves him disheartened rather than triumphant.

Charles Masterson, Dalgliesh's handsome subordinate, a complacent and ambitious detective sergeant who resents his superior's self-discipline and aloofness. Crassly calculating in his sexual pursuit of Julia Pardoe, one of the nurses, he also earns Dalgliesh's reproof for cruelty toward an elderly female witness he interviews in London. Masterson ably backs up Dalgliesh, whose experience and intuition win his grudging respect.

Mary Taylor, the matron of John Carpendar Hospital's nurse training school. Enjoying the same confidence and excellent reputation in her field as Dalgliesh does in his, the attractive Mary Taylor impresses Dalgliesh from the first as an intellectual equal, one who reflects his own dedication and cool detachment. The night of the second murder, she is abroad at a conference. When she returns to find the police on the scene, she acts quickly and efficiently to facilitate the investigation.

Sister Ethel Brumfett, the second in command at Nightingale House. This stolid, shrewd-eyed woman obsessed with her supervision of the private ward is also—to Dalgliesh's considerable surprise—the matron's intimate friend of twenty years. Her eventual confession to double murder leaves some troubling loose ends.

Sister Hilda Rolfe, the principal tutor, a discontented, abrasive senior nurse who stays at Nightingale because of her unrequited love for the student Julia Pardoe.

Sister Mavis Gearing, a clinical instructor, the third senior nurse. She is a naïve, effusive woman who regularly entertains the married pharmacist and is flirtatiously cooperative with Dalgliesh.

Dr. Stephen Courtney-Briggs, the senior consultant surgeon, an arrogant, worldly man who condescends to everyone, including Dalgliesh, and resents the police inquiry.

Heather Pearce, an unpopular student nurse who dies horribly during a demonstration of intragastric feeding; her stomach is burned with carbolic acid. A hypocrite and a would-be blackmailer, Pearce was about to make the most of her discovery that one of the Nightingale personnel had been a Nazi war criminal.

Josephine Fallon, an intelligent loner, older than the other students, who originally was scheduled to receive the intragastric feeding. The autopsy after her death from nicotine poisoning reveals that she was three months pregnant, perhaps by Dr. Courtney-Griggs.

Madeleine Goodale, an efficient, sensible student nurse whose brightness appeals to Dalgliesh and whose friendship with Fallon made her heir to sixteen thousand pounds, providing possible motive for murder.

Julia Pardoe, the attractive student who juggles the attentions of Hilda Rolfe and Charles Masterson.

Morag Smith, a backward maid who feels persecuted by the local police but responds to Dalgliesh's courtesy. She eventually saves him from an assailant.

—*Margaret Bozenna Goscilo*

THE SHROUDED WOMAN
(La amortajada)

Author: María Luisa Bombal (1910-1980)
First published: 1938
Genre: Novel

Locale: The southern part of Chile and the realm of Death
Time: The first half of the twentieth century
Plot: Surrealism

Ana María, a dead woman who alternately views her mourners, the memories they arouse, and the dramatic landscape of death. A passionate woman and mother of three children, Ana María finds that in death her perceptions are amplified; her emotions are fully realized. Her early beauty returns, and she sees herself as pale, slender, and unwrinkled by time. In life she was imaginative, sensitive, intense, and playful. She journeys through the past and relives her adolescent love for Ricardo, his betrayal, and her subsequent herbally induced abortion; her marriage to Antonio, his love for her and the loss of that love, and her passion for him; the adoration of the luckless Fernando in her later years; and the unhappy loves of her three children. Following heart attacks and a stroke, Ana María dies and witnesses her wake, a journey to the family vault, and her fall to surreal subterranean landscapes. Flowing back to the surface, she roots herself to the world and longs for immersion in death.

Ricardo, Ana María's adolescent lover and neighbor. As a young man, Ricardo is clear-eyed, tanned, and wiry. A trickster tyrant, he teases Ana María. He is willful, rebellious, and impetuous. Ana María is a childish lover; she does not share his passion but desires his strong arms and the "wild flower" of his kisses. Ricardo deserts Ana María when he goes to study agricultural farming in Europe. On his return, he fails to approach her, then says that he is not to blame for her pregnancy. From this time on, each avoids the other; when he enters her room of death, Ana María understands that her love for him was a hidden core and that his love for her is the same.

Antonio, Ana María's rich, handsome, and charming husband. For a year, Antonio spies on Ana María from the wild black forest adjoining her father's hacienda. After marriage, his young bride feels lost in his sumptuous, labyrinthine house; she resists both his home and the pleasure that Antonio arouses in her. Antonio allows her to visit her father's home, but when she returns, he is indifferent to her presence. Fated now to love a man who seems only to tolerate her, Ana María suffers from Antonio's constant pursuit of other women, just as he suffers from her long, vicarious bond to Ricardo. Antonio weeps for the dead Ana María, who discovers that she neither loves nor hates him.

Fernando, an older man who woos Ana María and becomes her confidant in her later years. Fernando—ill, luckless, unhappy, swarthy, and lean—repulses Ana María, although she needs to confide in him. His dispassionate attitude toward his wife's suicide disturbs Ana María; requited love, he says, eludes him. Fernando, tormented by his love, finds that he can admire, understand, and forgive Ana María after her death. The death releases him to return to his interests in politics, farming, and study.

Alberto, the son of Ana María and Antonio. Handsome and taciturn, he loves only life on his southern hacienda until he meets María Griselda. Her overwhelming beauty and appearance of self-containment drive him to agony and drink. Jealous, he walls her up in the family hacienda, deep in the dark forest.

María Griselda, Alberto's wife. The swanlike María Griselda is lovely, and her beauty causes her to suffer from early childhood. Green eyes, pale skin, black hair, and harmonious gestures draw the adoration of men and women, children, and nature. Left lonely by her husband's searching love, she remains solitary. Only Ana María can forgive her great beauty.

Fred, the son of Ana María and Antonio. Ana María dearly loves this child, who fears mirrors and talks an unknown language in dreams. As a robust young man, he falls in love with blond Silvia, but it is dark María Griselda who awakens his poet's soul.

Silvia, Fred's wife. Tiny, graceful, and golden, Silvia makes the tragic decision to spend her honeymoon at the forest hacienda. The new bride shoots herself in the temple when Fred confesses that he has been transformed by the presence of María Griselda.

Anita, the daughter of Ana María and Antonio. Anita is arrogant, private, haughty, and brilliant. When her good-natured sweetheart, Don Rodolfo, falls under the spell of María Griselda, Anita seduces him and becomes pregnant.

Sofía, the estranged wife of Ricardo. Lively Sofía envies Ana María's intensity; the two are bound by friendship until Ana María comes to think that Sofía has betrayed her.

Alicia, Ana María's sister. Sad, pale, and religious, Alicia has suffered her husband's brutality and the death of her son.

Luis, Ana María's brother. Commonplace values separate Luis from Ana María, especially after he rejects the vivacious Elena for a conventional woman.

— Marlene Youmans

SHUTTLECOCK

Author: Graham Swift (1949-   )
First published: 1981
Genre: Novel

Locale: London, England
Time: Early 1980's
Plot: Detective and mystery

Prentis, the narrator, a senior clerk in a London police bureau that handles information on closed and unsolved cases.

In his early thirties, secretive, and self-consciously prickly—almost paranoid—with a tyrannical and sadistic streak, he also has a capacity and craving for affection that leave him hurt by his sons' lack of interest and respect and his wife's quiet withdrawal. He has been unable to live up to his own father's heroic image after reading his wartime memoirs at the age of eleven. Prentis' confused adult relationship to "Dad," whom he visits religiously every Wednesday and Sunday at a mental home (visits that his family resents), talking to him even though he cannot talk back, is one reason for his own familial failures. His obsession with the past and his father's role in it, especially his father's daring escape from the Gestapo, ultimately dovetails with his professional suspicions about the C-9 case, missing files, and his boss, Quinn. At the opening of the novel, he is surprised to hear that he is to get Quinn's job; at the close, his promotion and his decision quietly to suppress police information that may hurt the innocent allows his rehabilitation as husband and father.

Quinn, the bureau chief, another problematic father figure with a suspect military background, unsmiling and curt. Quinn is plump and bespectacled, with none of the physical attributes of power, but his position (literally) elevates him above his clerks at work in their semibasement. An internal window allows him to spy on them unseen. His silent removal of files, assignment of projects that cannot be completed, and sudden takeovers of cases generate an aura of mystery and turn his subordinates' jobs into a guessing game. His revelation that "Dad" cracked in the hands of the Gestapo and stooped not only to betrayals but to perpetuating his impostures in print releases Prentis from his obsessions—the files are "lost" and the past rewritten. Quinn's retirement

and naming of Prentis as his successor ensure Prentis a large chair in a large office, like his father's. He finds the status he needs.

Prentis, Sr., referred to frequently as **Dad** and codenamed **Shuttlecock**, a World War II espionage agent. He is a retired partner in a successful firm of consultant engineers and now resides in an institution. He is a silent and seemingly noble figure whose apparent mental breakdown a few years ago has left him unable or unwilling to talk to his son, in whom he lost interest when, as a boy of eleven, Prentis withdrew from him. His terse, brisk memoirs of daring wartime operations in France made him something of a public figure in the late 1950's. Pages of them fill Prentis' narrative.

Marian, Prentis' wife. Slightly dull but still sexually attractive, pliant of limb and compliant by disposition, Marian withdraws from domestic battles into caring for her plants. She seems set to transfer her affection from husband to sons.

Martin, Prentis' ten-year-old son. On the verge of growing up, with a rebellious streak and considerable courage, Martin has taken to spying on Prentis from a distance as Prentis goes to and from work. When his father gets rid of the television set, resentful of both sons' addiction to "heroes" like the Bionic Man, Martin provokes a confrontation and a beating by removing Grandpa's book from the shelves.

Peter, Martin's younger brother. An instinctive conformist with a tendency to snivel, Peter submits to his father's whims and temper.

— *Joss Lutz Marsh*

THE SIBYL
(Sibyllan)

Author: Pär Lagerkvist (1891-1974)
First published: 1956
Genre: Novel

Locale: Delphi
Time: Probably the second century A.D.
Plot: Philosophical

The Sibyl, an old woman who occupied the position of pythia, or oracle, at Delphi. She was given by her parents into the service of the Delphic god of prophecy, who, in this story, is a combination of Apollo (represented by serpents) and Dionysus (represented by goats). Having spent her adolescence and much of her young womanhood as the bride of the god, she violates her office by having sexual union with a man whom she loves. The man very shortly meets his death, and the Sibyl gives birth, not to his son, as she had expected, but to the son of the Delphic god. She listens to the story of a male visitor to her mountain hut and then relates her own story, while her son, now an aging idiot, sits silent and perpetually smiling in her presence.

The Sibyl's visitor, a man with the features of early middle age who is recognizable in the story of himself that he relates to the Sibyl as **Ahasuerus** (ah-hah-sew-AY-ruhs), **The Wandering Jew**. He had had a wife and son in the city of his birth. One day, he refused to let a man, who was carrying a cross, rest against his house. The man, whom people later identified as God's son, laid on Ahasuerus the curse of eternal life without rest. Ahasuerus seeks from the Sibyl advice and an answer to the mystery of life and the inscrutability of the deity. Her

story impresses him but does not lessen his perplexity, and he departs from her to continue his endless wandering.

The Sibyl's son, who is to be understood as a son of God. He was conceived by the Sibyl during one of her prophetic trances, when she was invaded by the temple god in the form of a goat. The Sibyl, expelled from the temple for her infidelity to the god, later gives birth to her son in a mountain cave. She is attended by protective goats, who lick clean the newborn boy and his mother. While his mother tells the visitor her story, the son disappears. The Sibyl and her visitor track him by his footprints in the snow. The footprints come to a stop in an open space, and the conclusion is that this son of God has ascended to his Father.

The Sibyl's lover, a man of twenty-five or thirty who has lost one arm as a soldier and has returned to do his family farming. His inability to complete an embrace and his shock at the Sibyl's excessive sensuality combine to indicate the Sibyl's destiny never to live with a human mate. After he and the Sibyl have entered into their affair, he is found dead in the rapids of a river; he is drained of blood but without visible wounds, and he is clutching a twig of the tree sacred to the Delphic god, the laurel.

The Sibyl's parents, simple farming people. Both die—first the mother, then the father—while the Sibyl serves as the pythia.

The little servant of the oracle, the custodian of the temple and its precinct and the Sibyl's only true friend.

The priest of the temple, an unpleasant man. He is often impatient with the Sibyl in her duties as the pythia.

— *Roy Arthur Swanson*

SIDDHARTHA

Author: Hermann Hesse (1877-1962)
First published: 1922
Genre: Novel

Locale: India
Time: Approximately the sixth century
Plot: Bildungsroman

Siddhartha, a Brahman's son, tall and handsome. He decides in his youth to seek enlightenment. As a result of this quest, he and his friend Govinda leave their comfortable homes and join a group of wandering ascetics, the Samanas. Later, they go to hear the Buddha. Although Siddhartha admires the man, he feels that the life of this monk is not what he is seeking, so he leaves. In his wanderings, he sees a beautiful courtesan and decides that he must know her. She sends him to a merchant to learn a trade. While she teaches him about love, the merchant teaches him about business. By the time he reaches the age of forty, he realizes that he has not found enlightenment. He wanders into the forest, where he meets a ferryman. He stays with him and finally achieves enlightenment by listening to the songs of the river.

Govinda, a monk. A childhood friend of Siddhartha, he insists on accompanying him and joining a group of wandering ascetics. When he hears the Buddha speak, he decides that he must remain with this man, and the friends part. Much later, he encounters a wealthy man sleeping in the woods and stands guard over him until he awakes. It is only then that he discovers that it is his old friend Siddhartha. He is surprised at the changes he finds but makes no judgments. In old age, after the death of the Buddha, he hears of a ferryman who is considered a sage and a holy man, and he goes to see him. Again he finds that it is his old friend, who has since found enlightenment, but he does not understand the words Siddhartha uses to try to explain what has happened to him. It is only when Govinda kisses his forehead that he realizes that Siddhartha sees and partly understands.

Kamala, a courtesan. An extraordinarily beautiful woman, she is wealthy and experienced. She teaches Siddhartha the ways of love, but she realizes that neither of them is capable of love as they are. After Siddhartha leaves, she discovers that she is pregnant. She closes her house and no longer receives visitors. Eventually, she turns her house over to the followers of the Buddha, and when she hears that he is dying, she takes her son and sets out to see him. On the journey, she is bitten by a snake while near the river, and Siddhartha and his friend find her. She dies in Siddhartha's arms.

Vasudeva, a ferryman. A poor old man, he has found enlightenment listening to the river. He takes Siddhartha in after Siddhartha leaves his wealth. Vasudeva becomes Siddhartha's friend and adviser. Already an old man, during Siddhartha's stay he begins to lose his strength and can no longer operate the ferry. After Kamala's death, he counsels Siddhartha to allow his son to leave and live his own life. It is only after Siddhartha finally takes his advice that he reveals the river's entire message to his friend. After he is sure that Siddhartha understands, he walks off into the woods to die.

Gotama, the Buddha. He is a wise man living an ascetic life whose words and manner of living have a profound effect on those around him. From all over India, people flock to hear him; many remain as his followers. Siddhartha goes to hear him speak in the hope that he will find enlightenment. Although he recognizes the Buddha as a very holy man, he does not find the path he seeks.

— *C. D. Akerley*

THE SIEGE OF KRISHNAPUR

Author: J. G. Farrell (1935-1979)
First published: 1973
Genre: Novel

Locale: Northeastern India
Time: 1857
Plot: Historical

Mr. Hopkins, called "**the Collector**," the chief administrator of the East India Company in the Krishnapur district of the Bengal Presidency in northeastern India. A large, handsome, brown-haired man with carefully trimmed, low sideburns, he is a fastidious dresser, complete with high collars. Possessing a public sense of dignity and duty, Hopkins is privately moody and often overbearing toward his family. His wife leaves for England, ostensibly after the death of a child, but it seems that the marital relationship was less than happy, for "the Collector" has an eye for the ladies, including a fondness for Miriam Lang. Through Hopkins' rov-ing eye and commentary, the life and position of women in mid-nineteenth century India is illuminated. Hopkins is a well-rounded character capable not only of the highest duty and courage but also of showing grief and fear. Early in the novel, he demonstrates foresight by preparing for the revolt that he believes is coming and fortitude by continuing his actions amid scoffs and general disdain. Hopkins is in command of the defensive operations at Krishnapur once the sepoy revolt. As the British ominously retreat to their second line of defenses, Hopkins symbolically falls ill with cholera but later returns to lead the final retreat and the last stand. Hopkins' character strikes a balance between emotionalism and human spirit versus materialism and scientific progress, a conflict that runs through the novel. By the end of the book, however, Hopkins' faith in both emotionalism and the human spirit seems shattered.

George Fleury, the son of Sir Herbert, who is a director of the East India Company. He has only recently come to India. George is fashionably dressed, but his personality is serious, even somber. He stands in contrast to Louise's other, more carefree, suitors. A musician, a purported writer, and a poet in the Romantic vein, Fleury originally adopts a strident antimaterialistic tone but, by the end of the novel, acquires an almost unqualified appreciation of modernist ideas and gadgetry. Described as slightly fat and perpetually perspiring, Fleury presents a vulnerable and sometimes humorous character. Fleury is capable of cowardice yet also capable of heroism. He is a secondary protagonist; when the main stream of the novel diverts from Hopkins, it is carried along primarily by Fleury. In the end, he marries Louise.

Tom Willoughby, called "**the Magistrate**," the chief judicial officer for the Krishnapur district. Somewhat younger than Hopkins, he sports red hair and ginger-colored whiskers. Cold, rational, cynical, and pessimistic concerning human nature, Willoughby has no discernible human attachments. Addicted to the science of phrenology (which asserts that the shape of a person's skull reveals his or her personality), Willoughby makes himself generally detested or, at best, tolerated. Hopkins' decisions are frequently at odds with what Willoughby recommends; the men are antagonists, each being content not to be the other man.

Louise Dunstaple, the local beauty and a target for aspiring suitors; she is blonde, fair, pale, and remote. She is the daughter of Dr. Dunstaple and the sister of Harry. Originally insipid and self-occupied, she learns willpower and how to help others, even the unfortunate Lucy, during the siege.

Dr. Dunstaple, the civilian surgeon, a fat, energetic man with a rosy complexion and a good-humored face. He is also stubborn. His hatred for Dr. McNab becomes so pathological that he drinks cholera-infested water to prove a medical point and, subsequently, dies.

The Reverend M. Hampton, called "**the Padre**," a lightly built, unassuming man with a healthy manner (a former rower at Oxford) who becomes sickly with cholera during the defense and has his faith tested during the trials. At times, he

appears half crazy in a humorous way that contrasts with the grim surroundings.

Dr. McNab, the Scottish military surgeon, at odds with Dr. Dunstaple over methods of medical treatment. McNab's practices, though unorthodox for his time, are in fact more correct. He is a young widower with a middle-aged air and is also described as gloomy, formal, and reticent. He eventually marries Miriam Lang.

Harry Dunstaple, the brother of Louise and son of Dr. Dunstaple. He is a young lieutenant of a sepoy infantry regiment who is a "manly" opposite of Fleury, at least originally, but both become friends during ensuing adventures and behave with equal gallantry. Harry falls for Lucy, and, despite gossip that her reputation will damage his future, several years after the siege he makes the rank of general.

Miriam Lang, the widowed elder sister of George Fleury. She often embarrasses her brother in front of Louise and others by referring to him by the childhood nickname of "Dobbin." She represents the more sensible and sure side of feminine nature when compared with the relatively more naïve Louise, who respects her.

Lucy Hughes, a lovely woman "fallen" because of a sexual indiscretion and broken engagement. After contemplating suicide while drunken, Lucy gradually makes herself acceptable to some polite company, including Hopkins, Louise, Miriam, and Harry, although she never wins respectability with the majority of ladies at Krishnapur.

Hari, the son of the local maharaja. The fat-cheeked, black-eyed, and pale-faced Hari, having been educated by English tutors, is the bridge between native Indian and English colonial society. Hari and Fleury are ironical opposites, Hari embracing all the materialism and scientific advances of the West that Fleury views as irrelevant to human progress; each fails to understand the other.

General Jackson, the commanding officer of the garrison at Captainganj, a small, fat, and very forgetful man. At well over seventy years of age, Jackson was appointed by circumstance of seniority rather than by virtue of competence. Because of his behavior, confidence in the ability of the military to handle the uprising is diminished. He represents an obstacle for Hopkins to circumnavigate, for Hopkins intends to take precautions, whereas Jackson supports the alternative opinion that precautions will merely incite the Indians to rebel.

— *David L. Bullock*

THE SIEGE OF RHODES

Author: Sir William Davenant (1606-1668)
First published: 1663
Genre: Drama

Locale: The fortress at Rhodes and the nearby coast of Caria
Time: 1522
Plot: Historical

Alphonso, the young duke of Sicily, whose life is shaped by his love for his wife Ianthe and by his sense of honor. His fleeting jealousy of the attentions lavished by the sultan on Ianthe does not impair the happiness of his marriage, and he fights valiantly to save his wife and Rhodes.

Ianthe, his beautiful wife, who bravely travels from Sicily to join her husband in Rhodes. Captured by the Turks, she wins the sultan's admiration with her fidelity and devotion to

her husband. She thus can later intercede with him on behalf of the besieged island. She is as conscious as Alphonso is of the value of honor, and she encourages his refusal to fly to Sicily under the sultan's protection.

Solyman II (SAHL-uh-muhn), called **Solyman the Magnificent**, the magnanimous sultan of the Ottoman Empire. He values virtue and love above military victory and offers aid to Ianthe and her husband. He contrasts the patience and calm of the Christian wife with the fury directed at him by his beloved sultana and contrives to win her back by letting her witness Ianthe's devotion to Alphonso.

Roxalana (ROKS-ah-lan-ah), his tempestuous queen. Jealous for the future of her son, the sultan's younger child, she rails at her husband and passionately resents his favors to Ianthe. She is, however, so much touched by Ianthe's patience

and love that she arranges Ianthe's reunion with Alphonso. She is herself happily reconciled with the sultan, who welcomes this sign of tenderness in her.

Villerius, Philip Villiers de L'Isle Adam (vihl-LEHR-ee-ews), the brave grand master of Rhodes, another upholder of "love and honor."

Pyrrhus (PIHR-uhs), a Persian general.

SIGISMUND: From the Memories of a Baroque Polish Prince
(Sigismund: Ur en polsk barockfurstes minnen)

Author: Lars Gustafsson (1936-   )
First published: 1976
Genre: Novel

Locale: West Berlin; Västmanland, Sweden; Cracow, Poland; and East Berlin
Time: 1973
Plot: Magical Realism

Lars, the narrator, a Swedish writer. He has a wife and children, as well as an alter ego named Sigismund III, the king of Poland. Lars apparently writes the novel titled *Sigismund* under direction from the Polish king. In fact, the entire book is made up of the narrator's attempts to describe his writing process and the rationale for the text he produces. The novel encompasses various styles and genres, including science fiction, fantasy, pornography, and realism.

Sigismund III, the king of Poland from 1587 to 1632, the narrator's alter ego, who calls Lars his "stand-in." The narrator supposedly writes for this king, who, at the end of the novel, shows up at the narrator's door complaining about the book's composition.

Laura G., a friend of the narrator and of his wife. This artist becomes the subject of some of Lars's fanciful writing. Drawing his inspiration from her comment that she would sell her soul to the devil for perfection in her paintings and wealth, Lars creates a narrative in which Laura descends into hell to determine whether she would care to spend eternity there. In Lars's fiction, she requests of hell the opportunity to become another person for one day. The boundary between fantasy and reality breaks down when Lars sees Laura as a young man on a street in Berlin. Apparently, she has signed a contract with the devil.

Uncle Stig, the narrator's uncle, a Marxist and a member of the Sophia Bicycle Club. He is an inventor, and one of his inventions is a bicycle that can go as fast as sixty miles an hour and possibly faster. He believes that he is always "swindled

out of" the patents on his inventions. After an accident on his newly crafted bicycle, he gives up inventing altogether.

Aunt Clara, the narrator's mother's sister. She is beautiful and charming; her voice is particularly melodic. As a telephone operator for a government office, she falls in love with a government official. When jilted by him, she is momentarily crushed but then falls madly in love with the neighborhood's blind beggar. The two of them wander off together and become a romantic legend in the area. Aunt Clara dies of lung disease shortly thereafter.

Gottwold, a blind beggar who makes small cloth dolls to sell. Children either love him or hate him. Aunt Clara falls in love with him, and the two of them run off together. He has also written two novels, which he has wrapped in waterproof cloth and carries in a wagon filled with various pieces of junk. One of these novels imitates Homer's the *Iliad*; the other mirrors the *Odyssey* and is an expression of Gottwold's love for Clara.

Baal B. Zvuvium, one of the emissaries from hell who seek to convince Laura G. to sell her soul to the devil. He is charming and handsome, but Laura realizes that although he is very skilled in rhetoric, he is not truly interested in her well-being. Originally bemused by the painter's request to become another person for one day, he later comes to understand her reasoning. Consequently, these two individuals develop a mutual empathy.

— *Sally Bartlett*

THE SIGN IN SIDNEY BRUSTEIN'S WINDOW

Author: Lorraine Hansberry (1930-1965)
First published: 1965
Genre: Drama

Locale: Greenwich Village in New York City
Time: Early 1960's
Plot: Play of ideas

Sidney Brustein, a cynical, disillusioned intellectual living in a Greenwich Village apartment with his wife, Iris. An idealist in his youth, Sidney had been involved with all manner of causes and was active on various committees advocating social change. Now in his early thirties, he epitomizes the alienated white intellectual searching for meaning in his life. As the disappointed, disinterested dreamer, Sidney has withdrawn from social and political action to run a failed coffee house and, subsequently, to attempt running a community newspa-

per. As a newspaper owner, he helps to elect a local reform candidate, whom he then discovers is in the pay of the crime syndicate. Both the coffee house and the newspaper reflect his efforts to escape to an ideal world. Circumstances force Sidney to realize that his mask of cynical detachment prevents him from seeing life realistically and allows others to manipulate his political naïveté. He learns, as well, that in the absence of committed involvement by responsible individuals, chaos, disintegration, and failure may well result.

Iris Parodus Brustein, Sidney's wife, an aspiring but unsuccessful actress. She is a young and pretty woman, with long, flowing hair that Sidney is always letting down. Iris is several years younger than Sidney and is the realist of the two. She feels stifled in their marriage. The pressure of trying both to conform to and yet escape from Sidney's image of her as a rustic, naïve, and unsophisticated woman-child whom he has educated has worn on her nerves. Her own inability to overcome her fear of auditions has also taken its toll. Iris is capable of rebellion, of making changes, and of taking control of her life back into her own hands.

Mavis Parodus Bryson, Iris' traditional, matronly older sister and the family conservative. She is married to a wealthy businessman and has three sons. Although she is almost a stereotype of the staid, meddling, racist, and parochial elder sister who cannot understand the lifestyle of her younger sister or her Jewish husband and their bohemian friends, Mavis manages to escape her limitations by raising challenging questions. She is also a more honest person, a more caring person, and a far stronger person than either her sister or her brother-in-law realizes.

Gloria Parodus, the youngest of the three Parodus sisters, who, collectively, function something like a chorus annotating the play's action. Although Gloria is not introduced until the third act, her presence colors the attitudes and actions of several characters. A beautiful, wholesome-looking young woman, Gloria makes her living by prostitution. Because of her line of work, she has been physically abused by clients and is involved in substance abuse, taking a variety of pills and drinking far too much to enable her to face her life. Gloria resolves to leave prostitution and marry, attempting to escape from a brutal life to an idealized one. When her fiancée learns of her profession, however, he finds that he cannot marry her, and she commits suicide.

Alton Scales, a black American intellectual, part of Sidney's bohemian circle, and the man Gloria plans to marry.

Alton is the lone African American character (except perhaps for Max) in the play. He is a fair or light-skinned African American whose color permits a discussion of interracial relationships and racism. He is light-skinned enough to be taken for white but insists on proclaiming his black heritage. Serving initially as a goad forcing Sidney to reorganize his obligation to become involved in the political affairs of the community, Alton accuses Sidney of "ostrich-ism" and intimates that hiding his head will not make the problems of the world disappear. Later, however, Alton bungles his own moral problem of individual responsibility and integrity. He had been willing to love and cherish Gloria, despite a rebuff by Mavis, until he discovered that she was not a fashion model as he had believed but a prostitute. Unable to accept her as a "commodity," he rejects her without speaking to her and vanishes.

David Ragin, a young and struggling but successful playwright living upstairs from the Brusteins. As an artist, an intellectual, and a homosexual, David serves as a catalyst for many of the issues in the play. He provides shock value for Mavis, who does not realize that "gay" implies homosexuality; he helps debate the function of art, the role of the artist, and the integrity of the artist. His lifestyle illustrates yet another dimension of societal prejudice, and he proves without question that being an artist or intellectual does not necessarily mean that an individual possesses sensitivity.

Wally O'Hara, the corrupt local politician who uses Sidney's idealism to his own advantage. Wally convinces Sidney to get involved and to raise his voice, via editorials in his newspaper, against machine politics. Wally, however, is owned by the political machine he attacks.

Max, a middle-aged, gravel-voiced, scruffy, egotistical, comic type. Max, an artist who may be played by a black or white actor, believes that the sole responsibility of the artist is to reflect himself. He designs an obscure masthead for Sidney's newspaper.

— *Sandra Y. Govan*

THE SIGN OF FOUR

Author: Sir Arthur Conan Doyle (1859-1930)
First published: 1890
Genre: Novel

Locale: London, England
Time: 1888
Plot: Detective and mystery

Sherlock Holmes, the famous detective known for his powers of observation and deduction.

Dr. John Watson, Holmes's friend and assistant. In this story, he is attracted to Mary Morstan, proposes to her, and is accepted.

Mary Morstan, Holmes's client. She is a young Englishwoman whose father, an officer with an Indian regiment, failed to meet her, as he had sent word he would, at a London hotel. Her father has been missing for ten years.

Major Sholto, a friend and brother officer of Miss Morstan's father. He reveals to his two sons that Morstan died accidentally as they argued over some jewels that had been handed over to them for transportation from India to England. He refuses to relinquish the fabulous jewels and is relentlessly hounded by The Four. He dies strangely before he can reveal their hiding place to his sons.

Dr. Thaddeus Sholto, an art collector, one of the major's twin sons. Trying to share his wealth with Mary Morstan, he sends her a pearl each year. He learns that his twin brother has located the treasure chest, and he so informs Mary Morstan and Holmes.

Bartholomew Sholto, Dr. Sholto's twin brother. After having located the jewels in his dead father's attic, he is found murdered.

Jonathan Small, Holmes's key to the mystery. When captured, he tells that he is one of The Four, four men who accidentally discovered the jewels in India. Imprisoned after an uprising, they gave the secret of the treasure to Major Sholto and the now dead Morstan. Small and one of the other men sought to regain the treasure, committing murder in doing so. About to be captured, Small dumps the jewels in the river.

SILAS MARNER: The Weaver of Raveloe

Author: George Eliot (Mary Ann Evans, 1819-1880)
First published: 1861
Genre: Novel

Locale: England
Time: Early nineteenth century
Plot: Domestic realism

Silas Marner, a weaver of Raveloe. As a resident of Lantern Yard, he had been simple, trusting, and religious until falsely accused of theft. He then lost his faith in religion and people. Turning away from humanity, he directs his stunted affections toward his steadily increasing pile of coins. When Eppie enters his life, he regains his belief in the fundamental goodness of humanity. In his bewildered fashion, he accepts help from his Raveloe neighbors and decides to rear the motherless child who has captured his heart; under her influence, he no longer despairs because of the stolen money.

Eppie (**Hephzibah**), Marner's adopted daughter. Fair-haired and blue-eyed, she captivates everyone who meets her, including young Aaron Winthrop, her future husband. After years of loneliness, Silas is sustained and his spirit nurtured by having her constantly near him. Even after she marries Aaron, she is determined to care for Marner, now frail and bent from years of unremitting toil at the loom.

Godfrey Cass, Eppie's real father and the weak son of Squire Cass, a prominent Raveloe landowner. Blackmailed by his brother Dunstan, he lacks the moral courage to acknowledge to the public that Eppie is his daughter. Instead, fearing disinheritance, he keeps silent for many years, with his guilt gnawing at his soul. Later, however, when Dunstan's skeleton is found in the Stone Pits, he finally confesses to Nancy his previous marriage to Molly, dead for sixteen years. Belatedly, he wants, with Nancy's consent, to accept Eppie as his daughter. Thinking she will be overcome by his generosity, he is shocked by her determination to remain with Silas.

Dunstan (Dunsey) Cass, Godfrey's dull-minded, spendthrift brother. Drunken and dissolute, he forces Godfrey to give him money by threatening to reveal the secret of Godfrey's marriage to Molly, a low-bred, common woman. After

stealing Silas' gold, he falls into the Stone Pit. Years later, his skeleton, the gold still beside it, is found wedged between two huge stones.

Nancy Lammeter, Godfrey's second wife, a lovely, decorous, and prim young woman. Although she lives by a narrow moral code, she surprises her husband, who has underestimated her, by courageously accepting the knowledge of his marriage to Molly.

Squire Cass, a prominent Raveloe landowner. Often lax in his discipline, he can be unyielding when aroused. At times, this inflexibility of character makes both his sons and tenants fear his anger.

William Dane, Silas Marner's treacherous friend in Lantern Yard. While mouthing religious platitudes, he steals money from the church and implicates Marner, thus forcing the latter's exile from the village. By planting Silas' pocketknife at the scene of the crime, Dane can steal the money with impunity, knowing that his friend will receive the blame.

Aaron Winthrop, a sturdy young Raveloe citizen. For many years, he has worshiped Eppie; when she promises to marry him, he is overjoyed. He promises Silas security and love in the old man's increasing feebleness.

Molly Cass, Godfrey's first wife, a drug addict who marries him when he is drunk. She is walking to Raveloe to expose him as her husband. Fortunately for Godfrey, she takes an overdose of laudanum and freezes to death in the snow, leaving her baby to toddle into the warmth and security of Silas' cottage.

Dolly Winthrop, Aaron's mother, the wife of Raveloe's wheelwright. She and her little son often visit Silas, and it is she who defends his right to keep Eppie when the villagers question Silas' suitability as a parent.

SILENCE
(Chimmoku)

Author: Shūsaku Endō (1923-1996)
First published: 1966
Genre: Novel

Locale: Japan
Time: 1632-1644
Plot: Historical realism

Sebastian Rodrigues (seh-bahs-tee-AHN rrohd-REE-gehs), a young Portuguese seminarian. Rodrigues, with two other priests, acquires permission to journey to Japan to track down his former mentor to learn why he has renounced his faith. Because the novel is essentially the spiritual odyssey of Rodrigues told through his correspondence, his character is discerned through his sensitive and candid portrayal of the events around him, which are filtered through the eyes of one seeking to understand and exonerate his beloved teacher from his ostensible apostasy. Rodrigues begins as a naïve young priest with textbook theories about cross-cultural evangelism and with his own vague aspirations toward martyrdom neatly submerged. As he matures in his understanding of the com-

plexities of the Japanese setting, he confronts Ferreira in his supposed sin and, eventually, undergoes his own apostasy by trampling the *fumie*, or image of Christ. In this act, he comes to reinterpret his actions and those of his fellow apostates as renunciations of only an institutionalized form of Christianity that had no roots in Japan or the original gospel and deserves no allegiance. In his apostasy, Rodrigues has learned to love the unlovely, to forgive and embrace his fallen mentor and the formerly outcast Kichijiro, whom he once rejected as a betrayer.

Christovao Ferreira (krees-toh-VOW feh-RRA-rah), a Jesuit missionary priest to Japan. Ferreira, held in the highest respect by his peers, is an intellectual and theologian who attains the high position of provincial. Having spent thirty years building the church in Japan, Ferreira has written glowingly back from Japan to his Portuguese colleagues, telling of the indomitable courage of his converts and the steadfastness of his fellow priests undergoing intense persecution. Inexplicably, a report comes back that he has apostatized, sending his colleagues into a quandary. Ferreira remains a shadowy, noncompelling figure in the story; until his confrontation with Rodrigues, he is known only through his reputation and the rumors about him. He emerges as a pragmatist who has renounced his faith not so much to save the Japanese from martyrdom as to salve his own theological conscience for bringing a faith unsuitable to the Japanese psyche. Ultimately, Ferreira is more anthropologist than missionary, ironically sharing this rather momentous conclusion with the one man presumably most at odds with his vision of Christian faith and love: Inoue, the chief persecutor of Japanese converts.

Kichijiro (kee-chee-hee-roh), Rodrigues' Japanese guide during his search for Ferreira. Kichijiro is a lapsed Christian convert whose drunkenness and shifty, mercenary spirit mark him initially as the "chief of sinners" in Rodrigues' eyes. Despite his slovenly character and apparently loose moral standards, Kichijiro emerges as a maternal, forgiving creature, moved in compassion for the suffering of his fellow Japanese converts to betray the foreign priests who have come to his native shores. At the novel's end, Kichijiro has returned to find absolution at the hands of Rodrigues, re-embracing the faith he had intermittently denounced previously.

Yuki, a Christian convert in Japan. Yuki demonstrates her courage and bravery by willingly interposing herself between her non-Christian lover and his captors when they demand that he step on the *fumie* to demonstrate his contempt for the faith of Christianity. As a result of his refusal to step on her or the *fumie*, both are condemned and executed.

Inoue, the fierce Japanese magistrate who pursues and compels the Japanese Christians, under torture, to apostatize. Cool, calm, and relentlessly detached from the human suffering about him, Inoue unwittingly raises the key issues of the confrontation between East and West in his piercing intellectualized questions about the appropriateness of Christianity for the Orient.

Francisco Garpe (GAHR-peh), Rodrigues' fellow seminarian and traveling companion to Japan. Garpe drowns while swimming after a boat from which bound Christians will be cast into the sea to their deaths.

— *Bruce L. Edwards*

THE SILENT CRY
(Man'en gan'nen no futtoboru)

Author: Kenzaburō Oē (1935-   )
First published: 1967
Genre: Novel

Locale: The Okubo village in Shikoku, Japan; and Tokyo
Time: Early 1960's
Plot: Psychological realism

Mitsusaburo (Mitsu) Nedokoro, a young academic aristocrat. A stoic man, he is depressed by two events: the suicide of a friend and the birth of his first child, who is mentally retarded. He notes the details of his wife's depression and her consumption of alcohol, but he feels powerless to change their situation. After the return to Japan of Taka, his younger brother, he consents to a return to their native village to begin life anew. There they are both swept up in research on a peasant revolt in 1860, led by an ancestor. They are also overwhelmed by an awareness of their two dead siblings—an older brother named S. and a young retarded sister. Mitsu tries to balance Taka's romantic versions of their family's deaths through logic and cynicism.

Takashi (Taka) Nedokoro, a reformed student activist. A charismatic young man in his twenties, Taka returns from the United States determined to seek his roots in his native village. Along with a small band of followers, and with his brother and sister-in-law, he completes the arduous journey. Once there, Taka sells the homestead and unilaterally decides to invest the money in a football team. Prone to violence and distortion of events, both past and present, he seduces Natsumi without remorse, murders a young woman senselessly, and finally confesses to his brother his incestuous relationship with their sister. He feels responsible for her death and commits suicide.

Natsumi Nedokoro, Mitsu's wife, who has become an alcoholic since the birth of her retarded son. Natsumi is an intelligent, sensitive young woman who is suffering from her thwarted motherhood and collapsing marriage. She becomes an ardent follower of Taka and eventually becomes pregnant with his child.

Paek Sun-gi, called **The Emperor**, a Korean former laborer and now owner of a supermarket chain. He buys the Nedokoro homestead and outbuildings. Although Taka paints him as a villain, he appears to be civilized.

Great-grandfather's younger brother, the leader of a peasant revolt in 1860. Thought to have been a deserter and to have brought shame on the clan, he is finally exonerated through Mitsu's research.

Momoko, a young woman who becomes a follower of Taka. At first, she is an enthusiastic follower, but when Taka organizes the riot at the supermarket, she becomes disenchanted.

Hoshio, a young boy who becomes a bodyguard of Taka. In the course of Taka's treachery and violence, Hoshio tells Mitsu that Taka has seduced Natsumi. He, too, is disenchanted and wants only to leave the village and return to normal life.

Jin, a grossly overweight family retainer. Because of her uncontrollable appetite, her husband and children are undernourished. Both Mitsu and Taka respect her and make provisions for her shelter even though they sell the homestead. After the riot, Jin's appetite decreases markedly.

— *Lila Chalpin*

THE SILENT WOMAN

Author: Ben Jonson (1573-1637)
First published: 1616
Genre: Drama

Locale: London, England
Time: Early seventeenth century
Plot: Satire

Morose, an unbalanced man with a horror of any noise except the sound of his own frequently exercised voice. He is given to outbursts of violent temper when disturbed. His servants are trained to wear tennis shoes, answer as much as possible in sign language, and to speak—if speak they must—in a whisper through a trunk to deaden the sound. A constant victim of noisy practical jokes, he believes his nephew to be the cause of many of the disturbances; consequently, he determines to disinherit him and to marry a silent woman found for him by a silent barber. After the wedding, harassed to the limit by his far from silent bride and her stentorian companions, he signs over his property to his nephew in return for rescue and goes into disgruntled retirement.

Sir Dauphine Eugenie, Morose's nephew, a pleasant and intelligent young man. He succeeds, in spite of complications brought on by his friends, in tricking his uncle first into marriage with the supposed silent woman, then into signing over his estate to the nephew. He is somewhat bashful with the ladies collegiate but is later overwhelmed by their attentions.

Truewit, an officious, argumentative, and witty friend of Sir Dauphine. He argues with his friends about the propriety of the use of all possible beauty aids by ladies. He stoutly defends a lavish use of cosmetics. He sets up a series of small plots to annoy Morose, whom he finds both ridiculous and irritating. He also maneuvers the three collegiate ladies into their love of Sir Dauphine, arranges the discomfiture of Sir John and Sir Amorous, and provides the divine and the canon lawyer for the further torment of Morose.

Ned Clerimont, another of Sir Dauphine's friends. Opposing Truewit, he holds that unadorned simplicity is woman's greatest charm; he therefore objects to all use of cosmetics and elaborate coiffures. Although he is more moderate and reliable than Truewit, Sir Dauphine maintains reserve and does not take him completely into his confidence.

Cutbeard, Morose's quiet barber. Actually in the service of Sir Dauphine, he arranges the meeting of and the marriage between Morose and Mistress Epicoene. Then, in disguise, he enacts the role of a voluble canon lawyer, engaging in legal argument with a supposed divine, to the torment of Morose.

Captain Tom Otter, the henpecked husband of a wealthy wife. He is a ceremonial drinker, having three mugs (a bear, a bull, and a horse) from which he drinks in turn, carrying on elaborate dialogues with himself in different roles. When he thinks his wife is not around, he speaks boldly and contemptuously of her; when she is present, he grovels obsequiously. He falls in with Sir Dauphine's plans and acts the part of the noisy divine, first to tantalize Morose with hope of divorce, then to drive him frantic with disappointment.

Mistress Otter, the captain's overbearing wife. Demanding that he treat her like a princess, she nags him mercilessly. Planted by Truewit where she can overhear her husband's rebellious comments on her shortcomings, she charges out and beats him thoroughly.

Sir John Daw (**Jack Daw**), a ridiculous, cowardly boaster. His affectations include the writing and criticism of verse. He is given to boasting of the amorous favors bestowed on him by the fair sex. His testimony of having had Epicoene as his mistress gives Morose temporary false hope that a divorce is possible. He is variously discomfited by the machinations of the witty young men, beaten, and discredited.

Sir Amorous La-Foole, a foolish kinsman of Mistress Otter. He is prodigal, fantastic, and cowardly. The young men make him think that Sir John thirsts for his blood. He and Sir John are both so terrified of each other that they tamely submit to blindfolding and personal indignities like nose tweaking, each thinking the other is the aggressor. He also belies Mistress Epicoene's morals.

Mistress Epicoene, the supposed silent woman. Actually a clever boy and a gifted actor, he fools Morose with his well-acted silent modesty, then plays a strident termagant. All are taken in by his performance except Sir Dauphine, whom he aids. At his unmasking, which releases Morose from his immediate torment, embarrassment descends on Sir John, Sir Amorous, and the three ladies collegiate. Even Clerimont and Truewit are astounded.

Lady Haughty, the "autumnal" leader of a group of "collegiates" who live separated from their husbands in a constant social whirl. She takes on the supposed bride as her protégée, graciously condescending to teach her how to handle her husband and how to act in the collegiate society.

Lady Centaure and

Mistress Mavis, ardent followers of Lady Haughty in the so-called college. They become her rivals (and each other's) for Sir Dauphine's favors. Each backbites her two colleagues to him.

Mute, Morose's well-trained servant. Bound to complete silence, he rarely breaks the taboo.

Parson, who is chosen by Morose to perform his wedding ceremony because he has lost his voice with a terrible cold and cannot be heard six inches away.

Mistress Trusty, Lady Haughty's maid and confidential emissary.

THE SILESIAN TETRALOGY

Author: Horst Bienek (1930-   )
First published: 1975-1982
Genre: Novels

Locale: Gleiwitz, Upper Silesia, and Dresden and Berlin, Germany
Time: 1939-1945
Plot: Realism

The First Polka, 1975

Irma Piontek (pee-ON-tehk), the daughter of Valeska and Leo Piontek. She marries a German soldier, whom she had met a few days before, in a civil ceremony. The reception is held in the most exclusive hotel in town.

Leo Maria Piontek, a photographer, husband of Valeska, and father of Irma and Josel. Spurning commercial success, he has concentrated his work on photographing old castles and other landmarks. He also produced anti-Nazi political leaflets. He dies after returning home from the reception.

Josel Piontek (YO-zehl), the fifteen-year-old brother of Irma, a member of the Hitler Youth and the Bosco Bund, a religious organization. He rents a shed to German soldiers where they can take their women. The soldiers are in the area because they are preparing for the invasion of Poland. He leaves town on a freight train on Irma's wedding night. He believes he has killed a German army sergeant who tried to rape Ulla Ossadnik, his girlfriend.

Ulla Ossadnik (EWL-lah os-SAHD-nihk), a piano student and admirer of Frédéric Chopin. On her way to the reception, she witnesses the staged attack on the Gleiwitz radio station by the Nazis. This was Hitler's excuse for invading Poland. She later becomes a famous pianist.

Georg Montag (GAY-ohrg MOHN-tahg), a Catholic-Jewish magistrate who lives in the Piontek's garden cottage. He commits suicide after finishing his biography of Wojciech Korfanty, a Polish politician. The suicide is prompted by hearing German soldiers in his yard.

September Light, 1977

Valeska Piontek (vah-LEHS-kah), a widow and piano teacher. Her husband had died on the same night as Irma's wedding. She arranges the funeral, including playing Chopin on a gramophone at the cemetery. She also arranges the funeral of Georg Montag, who is buried as a Catholic.

Josel Piontek, who learns that the sergeant lived but cannot identify his assailant. He returns for his father's funeral. During the funeral, he slips a note to Ulla expressing his love for her. Afterward, he stops a gang of boys from abusing a boy from another part of town.

Irma Piontek, who reveals to her mother after the funeral that she is pregnant, not by her husband but by Kaprzik, the local "village idiot." Irma had seduced the man to learn what sex was like.

Anna Ossadnik, the mother of Ulla and husband of Franz. Despite rearing a large family, she spends most of her time reading escapist novels. She wishes her husband was something more than a locomotive engineer. She and her family attend Leo's funeral, but they are almost late because Ulla cannot find black stockings.

Arthur Silbergleit (ZIHL-behr-glit), an old Jewish/Catholic writer, a friend of Herman Hesse and Stefan Zweig, and husband of Ilse. Although he is a native of Gleiwitz, he now lives in Berlin with his younger Aryan wife. While his wife is at work, he is visited at home by two government officials who inspect their apartment and hint that they will soon be thrown out. He decides to flee Berlin and take refuge with old friends, such as Georg Montag, in Gleiwitz. He stops by the Piontek house after Leo's funeral to ask about Georg. Valeska agrees to accompany him to Georg's grave the next day. Finally, Silbergleit meets his old friend Kochmann, also a Jew, who introduces him to Gleiwitz's remaining Jewish community.

Time Without Bells, 1979

Irma Piontek, who has married again and is the mother of two children. She is accused of consorting with a Russian soldier.

Valeska Piontek, who makes a fortune in real estate speculation.

Franz Ossadnik, who now transports Jews to the death camps every day in his job as a locomotive engineer. He wants to quit, but Anna persuades him to continue because they have never been so prosperous.

Josel Piontek, who has been drafted into military service.

Arthur Silbergleit, who has been arrested and is transported on Franz's train to a death camp.

Earth and Fire, 1982

Valeska Piontek, who flees with her family to Dresden to escape the advancing Russian army. They survive the firebombing of Dresden.

Josel Piontek, a soldier in the German army. While in Dresden, he is recuperating from wounds suffered in combat.

Franz Ossadnik, who is arrested by the Russians. He objects to being called a Fascist because he has never been to Italy.

— *Tom Feller*

THE SILMARILLION

Author: J. R. R. Tolkien (1892-1973)
First published: 1977
Genre: Novel

Locale: Valinor and Middle-earth, in the world of Arda
Time: A mythical past
Plot: Fantasy

Ilúvatar, also known as **Eru** (the one), his name meaning "father of all." He is the creator of Ea (the universe) and of Arda (the earth). He first sang into being the Ainur, a race of angelic beings who then helped him to sing into existence the universe and finally the earth. Although all the Ainur (except Melkor the rebel) know part of his thoughts, no single Ainu knows them all; their amazement at his creativity and compassion never ceases, and they love best his newest creation, the Children of Ilúvatar: humanity. All things involving Arda are woven into the ultimate design of Ilúvatar; nothing, not even

Melkor's rebellion, happens without Ilúvatar's foreknowledge or permission.

Manwë, the chief of the Valar (those Ainur who came to dwell on earth either permanently or temporarily) and ruler of Arda. His special delights are winds, clouds, and the regions of the air. He takes no kingly power in the sense of forcing humans or Elves (created before humans on earth and therefore called the Firstborn) to serve him, but he is the wisest of the Valar, so they seek his counsel. He submits always to the will of Ilúvatar. From his mountaintop home, he can behold almost everything that occurs in Arda.

Varda, Manwë's spouse, also called **Elbereth** (lady of the stars), one of the Valar. She knows all regions of Ea and loves light above all creations of Ilúvatar. With his blessing, she creates the stars and is often invoked by both Elves and humans, who revere her above all other Valar. She creates the mighty lamps that first light Middle-earth (where humans and Elves dwell) and places several especially bright constellations in the sky when those lamps are thrown down by Melkor. He fears her power above that of her peers because his strength lies in darkness.

Melkor (he who arises in might), originally the mightiest and most favored of the Ainur, renamed **Morgoth** (dark enemy) after his theft of the Silmarils. Lucifer-like, he turns his power to selfish ends and eventually loses his surpassing beauty, rebelling against Ilúvatar and seeking to destroy the Music. After eons of undermining and perverting the works of the Valar, he is taken captive and imprisoned for centuries in the halls of Mandos, the realm of Namo, keeper of the houses of the dead. When he eventually "repents," he is paroled by Manwë, who is incapable of understanding evil; eventually he escapes, enlists the aid of the ferocious spider-creature Ungoliant, and destroys the Two Trees that light the Blessed Lands of Valimar. After he steals the Silmarils, jewels of incredible beauty in which the light of the Trees is preserved, the Valar join forces with Elves and humans to overthrow his kingdom at tremendous cost: Ainur, Maiar, Elves, and men die, and the earth itself is rent and twisted by the tremendous forces unleashed in the battle. Melkor has corrupted others of the Ainur and multitudes of the Maiar, a lesser order of angelic beings, in addition to seducing many humans, so his evil cannot be fully eradicated from Arda. Able only to pollute or to imitate, he perverts captured Elves into Orcs, which become some of Sauron's most terrible servants. His most terrible "creations" are the ferocious demons called Balrogs, which may be twisted Maiar. His most powerful and deadly convert is Sauron.

Sauron, one of the Maiar perverted by Melkor. Originally the lieutenant of Morgoth (the Valar refuse to call Melkor by any other name), he becomes a Dark Lord himself after the downfall of Melkor, taking the Black Land of Mordor for his own and building the mighty Barad-dur (Dark Tower) as his chief fortress. Desiring to rule all Middle-earth, he seduces many humans and a few Maiar, as well as drawing to himself sundry dark creatures devised by Melkor in imitation of Ilúvatar's true powers. Sauron's deadliest weapon is the One Ring, which he forges in the fires of Orodruin (Mount Doom), pouring into the ring much of his own power. It controls the nine rings, which he gives to mortal men to enslave them, and exerts some power over the seven rings of the Dwarves and the three rings of the Elves. Cut from his hand by Isildur during the Last Alliance of Elves and Men, it is lost for an age in the river Anduin, then found by Gollum and taken by Bilbo Baggins, and finally destroyed by Frodo, Bilbo's heir, thus casting down Sauron and bringing the Third Age to an end.

Ulmo, one of the Valar, the lord of waters. Close to Manwë in might, he seldom goes to the councils of the Valar, preferring to roam the seas, streams, lakes, fountains, and rivers of Arda. Because water is ubiquitous, all the news, needs, and griefs of earth come to Ulmo, who conveys what might be otherwise hidden to Manwë. Earth dwellers say that the sound of his great horns, the Ulumuri, can be heard during storms and high tides; once heard, it implants the sea-longing forever in the heart of the hearer.

Aule, one of the Valar, the lord of all substances of which earth is made. He is a smith and master of all crafts. Melkor, envious of his skill, takes special delight in marring his works. Weary of battling Melkor and desiring to make something marvelous, Aule creates the hardy race of Dwarves, unwittingly usurping the prerogative of Ilúvatar. When he humbly submits his creation to Ilúvatar and repents of his audacity, offering to destroy his creations, Ilúvatar forgives him and casts the Dwarves into a deep sleep until their proper time to join the other races.

Yavanna, also called **Kementari** (queen of the earth), the spouse of Aule. She loves all growing things, especially trees. She sings into being the Two Trees that light Valinor until Melkor destroys them. At her request, Ilúvatar creates the Ents, giant shepherds of trees, to protect the forests.

Fëanor (spirit of fire), the son of the Elven king Finwë and Miriel, who fades into death soon after his birth. He is greatest among the race of Elves called Noldor, skillful craftsmen whom he later leads into rebellion. He creates the Silmarils, the three most beautiful jewels in the universe, and the Palantiri, the "seeing stones" of Numenor. Corrupted by Melkor, he is used to destroy the bliss of the Elves who have migrated from Middle-earth to Valinor.

Thingol (grey-cloak), also called **Elwë**, an Elven lord who marries the Maia Melian, the father of Luthien. His Hidden Kingdom of Doriath is one of the few refuges for Elves in Middle-earth during the depredations of Melkor.

Luthien Tinuviel (nightingale), the daughter of Thingol, the most beautiful of Elvenkind. She relinquishes immortality for love of Beren, a human, so that she can join him in the afterlife. They help to overthrow Melkor and rescue one Silmaril from his iron crown.

Beren One-hand, a mortal, the husband of Luthien Tinuviel. After helping to overthrow Melkor, he loses a hand to Carcharoth, a demon-wolf from Angband, who bites it off to devour the Silmaril, which Beren holds. Eventually slain by the same wolf, which has been driven mad by the power of the Silmaril (and from whose body the Silmaril is recovered), he alone of mortal men is allowed to return from the dead to help in later battles. He and Luthien are the ancestors of Elrond, Elros, and the Kings of Numenor.

Eärendil (lover of the sea) **the Mariner**, a half-elven who weds Elwing, the granddaughter of Beren and Luthien. His doom is to sail the heavens forever with the one remaining Silmaril on his brow, as a light and a hope for earth dwellers.

Ar-Pharazôn (the golden), the last king of Numenor, a great island within sight of Valinor prepared by the Valar to be the dwelling of the Edain (men of the west) as a reward for their struggles against Sauron. Captor of Sauron, by whom he is seduced, he leads a great fleet in rebellion against the Valar, seeking eternal life. At the moment when his fleet touches the Blessed Lands, it is removed forever from the confines of earth; the fleet is swallowed by a huge abyss. Numenor is destroyed by a gigantic tidal wave from which only nine ships of loyal Numenoreans, led by Isildur, escape.

Elrond Half-elven, a descendant of Beren and Luthien who chooses to belong to the Elven kindred. Wise and revered, he rules Imladris (Rivendell), in which the heirs of Isildur dwell until the time for the final battle with Sauron. He is the keeper of Vilya, the Ring of Air, bequeathed to him by Gilgalad the Elven king, and is the father of Arwen Undomiel, the "Evenstar" of her people, in whom the likeness of her great-grandmother, Luthien, has come again to Middle-earth. To Elrond's grief, she also chooses mortality to marry Aragorn, heir of Isildur.

Gandalf, also called **Mithrandir** (the grey pilgrim), a Maia, one of the Istari (wizards) sent by the Valar to battle Sauron. Ancient, wise, and fearless, he is the keeper of the Elven ring Narya, the Ring of Fire, which he wields in his long struggle against Sauron. Long aware that the One Ring resides in the Shire with Bilbo Baggins, he is instrumental in preserving it until Frodo can undertake the quest to destroy it.

Cirdan, the Lord of the Havens, from which homesick Elves may depart Middle-earth for Valinor. A shipwright, he was keeper of the Elven ring Narya, which he surrenders to Gandalf for use in the war against Sauron.

Elendil (star lover), who is descended from Eärendil and Elwing but not of the direct line of the Kings of Numenor. He leads the fleet of the faithful who escape the downfall of Numenor and founds the realms of the Numenoreans in Middle-earth. Although he is slain in the overthrow of Sauron at the end of the Second Age, the shards of his sword, Narsil, which broke beneath him when he fell, are preserved by his heirs throughout the Third Age until the time for their reforging for the final battle against Sauron.

Isildur, the son of Elendil. He cuts the One Ring from Sauron's hand at the end of the Second Age and keeps it as weregild for his father and brother instead of throwing it into the fires of Orodruin to destroy it.

Aragorn, called **Elfstone** and **Estel** (hope) by the Elves, the son of Arathorn. Disguised as a Ranger of the North, he has been reared in Rivendell, where he falls in love with the Elven maiden Arwen Evenstar. Isildur's heir through generations unbroken, he inherits the shards of Narsil and bears the sword reforged into the final battle against Sauron to inherit his kingship and earn his right to wed Arwen. He becomes the first king of the Fourth Age, the age of humans.

Frodo Baggins, a Hobbit, who inherits the One Ring from Bilbo. He and his servant Samwise help to bring about the final downfall of Sauron as well as the fading of the three Elven rings. As a reward for valor, he is allowed to join the last Elves who sail from the Havens.

— *Sonya H. Cashdan*

THE SILVER DOVE
(Serebryanny golub)

Author: Andrey Bely (Boris Nikolayevich Bugaev, 1880-1934)
First published: 1909-1910
Genre: Novel

Locale: Tselebeyevo and Likhov, Russia
Time: c. 1900
Plot: Symbolism

Pyotr Daryalsky (pyohtr dahr-YAL-skee), a poet who makes a summer visit to the small Russian village of Tselebeyevo. The handsome young Daryalsky, who has no obvious intellectual gifts or notable background, soon falls in love with Katya Gugolevo, who lives nearby with her grandmother, the Baroness Todrabe-Graaben. The dreamily impractical Daryalsky is an innocent romantic weakling who is soon identified by the revolutionary leader Kudeyarov as an appropriate potential father of the messiah who will lead the hoped-for overthrow of the government. Thus, Daryalsky is paired off by Kudeyarov with Matryona, a peasant woman whose earthiness contrasts with the vaguely spiritual beauty of Katya Gugolevo. His plight—torn between the two women—represents allegorically the plight of Russia at the turn of the century, looking West to European culture while looking East at its Asian heritage.

Katya Gugolevo (gew-GOH-leh-voh), a lovely young aristocrat who lives with her grandmother and falls in love with Daryalsky. Katya has no special qualities; she is an allegorical embodiment of what many Russian intellectuals at the time saw as a waning European civilization. She contrasts physically and spiritually with Matryona.

Matryona (may-TRYOH-nah), the peasant woman chosen to be the mother of the messiah of the revolution. The earthy Matryona is Mother Russia, a clichéd incarnation of the vitality of Russia's Tolstoyan peasantry. She is cloaked in a mystique that is aptly symbolized by the hypnotic appeal she exerts on Daryalsky, the same kind of mythic force that the peasantry represented for European Romantic intellectuals throughout the nineteenth century. She is also apparently Kudeyarov's common-law wife.

Kudeyarov (kew-deh-YAH-rov), a carpenter who lives with Matryona and leads the group of political revolutionaries known as the "Doves." Kudeyarov is the most interesting of the four characters who carry the story. His face is described as split into opposed halves, a peculiarity that suggests the ambivalence of his personality. He is eager to pander for Daryalsky in inciting an affair with Matryona, but he is at the same time distressed by jealousy. The response is understandable enough on the simplest level, but his jealousy perhaps also betrays his envy of the role he sees Daryalsky playing in the revolution. His heavy allegorical burden is further weighted by the New Testament allusions that enrich his role: his carpenter's occupation, his anticipation of a messiah, and the ritual sharing of bread and wine that introduces the meetings of the Doves. Matryona and Daryalsky produce no child, and the disappointed Kudeyarov has Daryalsky murdered by the Doves when the poet realizes how he is being used.

— Frank Day

THE SILVER TASSIE

Author: Sean O'Casey (John Casey, 1880-1964)
First published: 1928
Genre: Drama

Locale: Dublin, Ireland, and the front lines in France
Time: During and after World War I
Plot: Tragicomedy

Harry Heegan, a boisterous and athletic young man. He is established as a local hero early in the play, winning the cup, the "silver tassie," for his football club while he is on leave from the army. In love with Jessie, Harry is a rather unthinking man, devoted to the senses. He takes for granted his own strength and health and the adoration of others. After he is wounded in battle and his legs are paralyzed, he loses his standing at home as well as Jessie's love, and he becomes a bitter outcast, haunting his former friends and ultimately renouncing them.

Teddy Foran, a neighbor and comrade of Harry who is married to a woman who prefers to have him away at war. He is large and powerful and is first seen chasing his battered wife into the Heegans' home. Physical dominance over others is his most notable trait: He breaks all the crockery in his home before his leave is ended. He is rendered powerless, and dependent on his wife, when he is blinded in battle.

Barney Bagnal, a friend and comrade of Harry, a pleasant, unexceptional young man. He is clearly in Harry's shadow when they are home on leave, and he is tied to a gunwheel throughout the entire second act as punishment for stealing a chicken. Despite his unheroic character in much of the play, it is Barney who is the hero at home after the war. He has come home unscathed and decorated; he is the latest hero of the football club and Jessie's new lover. He comes to represent all that Harry has lost and finally rejects.

Jessie Taite, a spirited, young local woman who is in love with Harry. When he is injured, she refuses even to visit him in the hospital. Her attachments are based on physical attraction and public esteem, and she easily transfers her love to Barney after the war. Although at first other characters disapprove of her, she comes to represent the prevailing ethos—selfish and utilitarian—of the community.

Sylvester Heegan, Harry's father, a retired dockworker who spends his free time drinking and bragging about his son's exploits. He is a strong, stocky man of a humorous and argumentative temper. Ultimately, he cares little for his son, and his comic exploits with his friend Simon Norton begin to appear grotesque when they are removed from their earlier, jovial context.

Mrs. Heegan, Harry's mother, a nervous, worn-out woman. Her conversation tends to revolve around money. Her worries that Harry might miss his boat after his leave-time is ended mask a concern that the family might then lose money from the government. She is oblivious to Harry's pain after he is disabled, and she reproaches Jessie not for her betrayal of Harry but for the money that he had spent on her when courting.

Simon Norton, a friend and former colleague of Sylvester Heegan. He is a slightly less robust and loud man than Sylvester. A caricature of a petty, self-centered man, Simon maintains a running debate with his friend, intent on preserving an air of authority. Their trivial wrangling endures throughout the play, in increasing contrast to the situation around them.

Susie Monican, an attractive young woman who is in love with Harry and extremely jealous of Jessie. She hides her infatuation behind a rigid sense of propriety and loud religious fervor. A stint as a wartime nurse ironically liberates her, and she enters a romance with Harry's doctor while treating Harry with impersonal pity.

Mrs. Foran, Teddy's wife. She is indifferent to her husband, who beats her when she appears to be pleased to see him return to war. She is heartbroken over Teddy's destruction of her household goods and less concerned over his blindness.

— Heidi J. Holder

A SIMPLE HONORABLE MAN

Author: Conrad Richter (1890-1968)
First published: 1962
Genre: Novel

Locale: Pennsylvania
Time: Early and mid-twentieth century
Plot: Pastoral

Elijah Morgan, a Lutheran minister who finally gives Harry Donner, his son-in-law—in his late thirties—his blessing to enter the ministry.

Harry Donner, the main character, a storekeeper who later pastors the town of Mahanoy. When the church resents his work at Lost Run, he takes a position in Wetherill. He finds a rift there and resigns, even though he does not have another

position. He finds work at Paint Creek and also serves Chadd's Cove. He serves others after retiring at the age of seventy.

Oliver Piatt, the treasurer of the Wetherill church. He always requires Harry Donner to ask for his small salary. Piatt wants a big, new church.

Phillip Rodery, who opposes Piatt. He keeps a stray pig, is arrested, and is later injured in two falls. Church meets on his farm after a fire. Later, Piatt helps Rodery and others replace their church.

Isaac Gottschall, a one-armed miner who loses his other arm. Donner helps him purchase a home with a store.

Shelby Bashore, who is dying and wants to live. Donner tells him that life can never be put in the ground, that every seed rises, and that the ground is comforting: warm in winter and cool in summer.

Cal Harmon, a ninety-four-year-old man who wants to die.

Jake Schneck, who promises to shoot anyone who comes to his room. He shoots Tom Staller, his best friend, when Tom 3comes upstairs. Donner convinces Jake to allow him to enter after Jake shoots himself. Donner takes Jake downstairs to die.

Dave Mace and

Sheba Mace, two residents of Chadd's Cove. This couple thinks that Donner is preaching about them when they hear that he spoke of David and Bathsheba.

Valerie Morgan Donner, Elijah Morgan's daughter and Harry Donner's wife. She bears three sons: Gene, Johnny, and Tim. She dies before Harry does.

Mimm, who preaches a trial sermon in another church on Donner's recommendation. Although almost eighty years old, Donner drives one hundred miles to hear Mimm, whom he helped to educate. Because Mimm wants to return for a funeral, Harry drives him. Mimm does not even invite Donner to rest, though it is close to 2:00 A.M. Donner spends the night in the cold car and later dies of pneumonia. It is significant that this character, to whom Donner has given much and who indirectly causes the death of the old man, has no first name; others whom Donner meets become friends with him on a first-name basis.

John Donner, the narrator and the son of Harry Donner, the main character. John discovers that his father has few possessions. His father has groaned much in his sleep but has praised God much in his life. John sees his father's life as wasted on a log church in a little-known valley—his father's final resting place.

Tilly, an in-law but still a family member. She senses Harry Donner's death about the time that it occurs.

— *Anita P. Davis*

A SIMPLE STORY
(Sipur pashut)

Author: Shmuel Yosef Agnon (Shmuel Yosef Czaczkes, 1888-1970)
First published: 1935
Genre: Novella

Locale: Szybusz (Poland) and Galicia
Time: The late nineteenth and early twentieth centuries
Plot: Psychological

Hirshl Hurvitz (HUR-shuhl), the weak-willed son of a wealthy shopkeeper. He falls madly in love with the family servant, Blume, who is also his cousin. His domineering mother manipulates him into a more suitable marriage, which he spinelessly accepts. His feelings for his wife range from detached tolerance to hatred. In the first year of his marriage, he falls into a deep depression that culminates in insanity. With the help of Dr. Langsam, he slowly returns to health and is able to find a measure of happiness within the conventions of family life and the traditions of the Jewish community.

Blume Nacht (BLEW-meh nahkt), Hirshl's beautiful, penniless cousin, who becomes a servant in his household after the death of her parents. She is a paragon housekeeper and cook, yet quiet and retiring and as mysterious as her name, meaning "night flower," suggests. She secretly returns Hirshl's love, but when she learns of his betrothal, she leaves her employment with the Hurvitzes. Deeply hurt, idealistic, and proud, she remains loyal to her secret love, although two other men want her. By the novel's end, she has faded from sight.

Mina Ziemlich (ZEEM-lihk), the daughter of a wealthy tavern keeper of a nearby town. She has been educated in a city boarding school and is considered cultured and fashionable. Although her betrothal to Hirshl is a product of matchmaking and misunderstanding, she admires her groom and is attracted to him. She knows in her heart that her husband does not love her, however, and although she tries to make the best of their joyless and uncommunicative marriage, her pregnancy debilitates her, and she gives birth to a sickly child. Her second child, conceived after Hirshl's return to mental health, is a healthy product of her newly happy marriage.

Tsirl Hurvitz (TSUR-ehl), Hirshl's mother, clever, determined, forceful, and a consummate diplomat. She is able to implement her will in her business dealings, her social relationships, and her family. She steers Hirshl in the direction she wants in everything—his diet, his occupation, even his exercise habits—and she chooses Mina to be his wife.

Baruch Meir Hurvitz (bah-REWK mah-YEHR), Hirshl's father, a completely conventional man who wants nothing more from life than that it run smoothly. He performs his duties, and somewhat more than his duties, to his family, his community, and his business. He quarrels with no one. Although he is always ready to help his son in any way he can, he finds his son's unhappiness and depression to be beyond his understanding.

Gedalia Ziemlich, Mina's father, a wealthy innkeeper and manager of the count's estate. He worries continuously that his good fortune will be reversed, plunging him back into his former destitution. His daughter's marriage to a Hurvitz seems an undeserved stroke of good luck, and his son-in-law's insanity seems one piece of expected catastrophe.

Bertha Ziemlich, Mina's mother, an industrious woman who continues to work hard and prides herself on putting on no airs, although her husband has attained a high place in their town. She and Hirshl's mother form a bulwark of tradition for the young couple. At the end of the novel, she nurses her sickly infant grandson back to health while her daughter and Hirshl begin to be happy.

Yona Toyber, the matchmaker who arranges the marriage of Hirshl and Mina. For himself, long after the death of his first wife, he chooses a no-longer-young, ill-tempered hunchback who, after their marriage, becomes a good-natured angel of domesticity.

Getzel Stein, a clerk in the Hurvitz store, a political activist,

idealist, and ambitious founder of the local chapter of Workers of Zion. He is in love with Blume.

Dr. Langsam, a neurologist who uses no drugs and administers no psychological tests. He nurses Hirshl back to health with gentle conversations and a peaceful environment.

— *Lolette Kuby*

SIMPLICISSIMUS THE VAGABOND
(Der abenteuerliche Simplicissimus)

Author: Hans Jacob Christoffel von Grimmelshausen (1621-1676)
First published: 1669
Genre: Novel

Locale: Germany
Time: 1618-1648
Plot: Picaresque

Simplicius Simplicissimus, a simple lad reared in Germany's Spessart Forest. At the age of twelve, when taken by soldiers to Hanau, he knows only that he has been reared by peasants and a hermit. He pretends to have lost his wits and becomes the governor's fool. Later, he becomes a great soldier known as the Hunter of Soest and has many adventures. He learns eventually that he is really the son of a German nobleman and that his real name is Melchior Sternfels von Fuchsheim, but he still remains an adventurer, traveling all over the world.

A peasant, Simplicissimus' foster father, a good man. He

turns up later to inform Simplicissimus of his true identity.

A hermit, who befriends Simplicissimus when, at the age of ten, he is separated from his foster parents during the Thirty Years' War. He is really a nobleman, Simplicissimus' father, who became a hermit because he was sick of war. His name is **Herr von Fuchsheim**.

Ulrich Herzbruder, a young German who becomes Simplicissimus' friend and aids him many times.

Oliver, an erstwhile friend of Simplicissimus who mistreats Ulrich Herzbruder.

THE SINGAPORE GRIP

Author: J. G. Farrell (1935-1979)
First published: 1978
Genre: Novel

Locale: Singapore
Time: 1938-1942 and 1976
Plot: Historical

Walter Blackett, the protagonist, the ambitious co-owner and acting director of the Singapore firm of Blackett and Webb. Walter is a commanding figure, with pale blue eyes and white hair and mustache; his large head looms over a compact body and short legs. An entrepreneur convinced of his own worth, for years Walter has greedily exploited the native economy to advance company interests and has used the law and corrupt officials to undermine local competition. As the Japanese invade and Singapore falls, he remains contemptuous of Asians in general and is more concerned with his company's simple-minded allegorical Jubilee pageant and with his rivals, the Langfields, than with historical inevitability. A prototype of the uprooted British imperialist, he is held tightly by the "Singapore grip," the dream of greater and greater financial coups, and is blind to the realities of his and the British position in Malaya. He considers collaborating with the Japanese more acceptable than forgoing his long-held tyrannical power.

Monty Blackett, Walter's spoiled and insensitive thirty-year-old son and heir apparent. With blue, bulging eyes and poor judgment, he is clearly his father's son. Amoral and mindlessly exuberant, Monty thinks of the natives only in terms of sexual encounters and amusement potential. As a second-generation colonial convinced of British superiority and native inferiority, he implements his father's plans for

exploitation with self-assured aplomb, no matter how injurious to the locals.

Joan Blackett, Walter's bumptious, headstrong, and coldly calculating daughter, a femme fatale who toys with the sensitive Ehrendorf and who then tries to capture Matthew and his half of the business. A product of a Swiss finishing school, healthy and solidly built in the English manner, Joan is contemptuous of provincial Singapore. Her youthful, rebellious affairs are a trial to her parents, though her pursuit of Matthew wins their blessing. Having forced him, while weak from fever, to consent to her marriage proposal, she is affronted by his later forceful rejection of the engagement. She and her brother share an unquestioning belief in their own superiority and in their right to manipulate and exploit those around them. They are both overwhelmingly materialistic; matters of the soul and conscience are unknown to them. Joan relies on sexual allure to grip the men under her spell; she is self-serving, predatory, grasping, and ruthless, as confirmed by her attempts to escape from Singapore with her unexpectedly acquired husband, Nigel Langfield.

Matthew Webb, the conscience-ridden son and heir of Walter Blackett's deceased partner, whom Joan and Walter pursue as a marital alliance. He is stooped and shortsighted, with rounded shoulders and an unhealthy complexion. At the age of thirty-three, he is an otherworldly Oxford innocent who believed in and worked for the League of Nations and who arrives in Singapore eager to apply socialistic solutions easily and painlessly. Matthew is bothered deeply by racial abuse and by his own ineffectuality. Stricken with a tropical disease that he imagines is the "Singapore Grippe," he finds Singapore a surreal nightmare and, throughout half the book, sees and hears life swirl around him through the veil of high fever and possible hallucination. Through Vera Chiang, he sees a Malay that many foreigners do not, and his incredulous and then horrified reaction to traditional colonial attitudes and behavior provides the moral cornerstone of the book. He is an idealist amid opportunists, a slightly comic, muddled figure made sympathetic by good intentions. Refusing to believe that the "Singapore Grip" is the sexual technique certain Singapore prostitutes use to improve trade, he asserts that it is the European stranglehold on the Orient.

Vera Chiang, Matthew's mistress and his father's protégée, an exotic Eurasian (the reputed daughter of a Russian princess and a Cantonese tea merchant). She is a social activist who fled Shanghai police oppression. Initially befriended by a thrill-seeking Joan, she becomes Joan's rival for Matthew, with her stunning Asian beauty and sexuality proving more intoxicating. Following the elder Webb's program of strenuous acrobatic nude exercise, she lives in the Webb home and nurses Matthew until forcibly removed. She is enigmatic but human, visiting and sympathizing with the aged and dying, giving English lessons, and nursing those injured by the Japanese invasion.

Major Brendan Archer, a well-meaning and kindly retired British officer, an ineffectual liberal sympathetic to the natives and appalled at their racist exploitation. Major Archer is always in the background, listening to Blackett's theories and plans, helping with civil service war preparation, sympathizing with refugees (in pidgin), caring for the castoff people and animals of his associates, and indignantly protesting tragedy, disgrace, and injustice. A cynic and an optimist, the major, like Matthew, provides an outsider's critical commentary on Singa-

pore insiders. "What fools those men are!" he exclaims at one point, but then adds humbly, "Of course, they may know things that we don't."

François Dupigny (frahn-SWAH dew-peen-YEE), an old friend of Major Archer from World War I days, a cynical French rationalist who is continually appalled at the inanities and rudeness of the local British and who has watched his friend become more private and eccentric in his habits. He longs for prewar days in Hanoi or Saigon but instead finds himself fleeing Japanese bombers. Dupigny debates Major Archer on the nature of humanity and concludes that self-interest negates any possibility of brotherhood and a community of races.

Captain Jim Ehrendorf, an American officer from Kansas City, longtime school chum of Matthew, and rejected suitor of Joan. Ehrendorf contradicts all the British stereotypes of Americans: He is a Rhodes scholar, soft-spoken, cultured, well-educated, well-mannered, tactful, polished, and well-informed. He is pale and handsome, with an attractive smile. He is hopelessly in love and suffers Joan's torments without complaint, throwing himself fully clothed into a pool or thrusting his hand into an open fire at her whim. He becomes introspective and quiet, then finally yields to his friend, Matthew. As the Japanese advance, he provides an American perspective on British defense and is practical and commonsensical about war in a way the British are not. He observes the confirmation of Ehrendorf's Second Law: "In human affairs things tend inevitably to go wrong. Things are slightly worse at any given moment than at any preceding moment."

Cheong, an embittered Blackett family servant whose father and uncles had been shipped to Singapore as indentured coolies under appalling conditions and who incarnates their anger and sense of outrage. He finds the strange mixture of exploitation, general cruelty, and personal kindness of whites inscrutable. Attuned to the Chinese grapevine, he always has news before his masters and fears the worst.

— *Gina Macdonald*

SIR CHARLES GRANDISON

Author: Samuel Richardson (1689-1761)
First published: 1753-1754
Genre: Novel

Locale: England
Time: The eighteenth century
Plot: Fiction of manners

Sir Charles Grandison, an English baronet and the hero of a novel whose author, after writing two novels concerned with men who are rakes, was trying to present a picture of a truly virtuous character. The honorable Sir Charles rescues Harriet Byron from the clutches of Sir Hargrave Pollexfen and takes her to his country house as his sister. Although his family and friends favor his marriage to Harriet, he feels honor bound to Lady Clementina della Porretta, who has a claim on his affection. When Lady Clementina finally refuses him, he feels free to ask for Harriet's hand.

Harriet Byron, a virtuous young woman of modest expectations. On a visit to London, she is pursued by and refuses the attentions of Sir Hargrave Pollexfen. The enraged suitor attempts to abduct her and force a marriage. She is rescued by Sir Charles Grandison and taken to his home, where she falls

in love with him. Realizing that Sir Charles regards her as a sister, she tries to subdue and hide her affection for him until he becomes free to declare his love for her and to win her hand.

Sir Hargrave Pollexfen, Harriet Byron's libertine suitor, from whom she is rescued by Sir Charles Grandison. After Sir Charles rescues him from the enraged family of a woman he tried to seduce in France, Sir Hargrave begins to realize the evil of his ways. He reforms, and upon his death he leaves his fortune to Sir Charles and Harriet Byron.

Lady Clementina della Porretta, an Italian beauty who is so in love with Sir Charles Grandison that his departure from Italy robs her of her reason, thus putting Sir Charles under an obligation that leaves him bound to her until a cure is effected and she finally refuses to marry him.

Charlotte Grandison and
Lady L., Sir Charles Grandison's sisters, on whom he bestows the benefits their late father was reluctant to give.

Mrs. Oldham, the paramour of Sir Charles Grandison's late father.

Lady Olivia, an Italian woman who is enamored of Sir Charles.

Emily Jervois, Sir Charles's young ward.

Mr. Greville, a suitor of Harriet Byron.

SIR GAWAIN AND THE GREEN KNIGHT

Author: Pearl Poet (fl. late fourteenth century)
First transcribed: The fourteenth century
Genre: Poetry

Locale: England
Time: The sixth century
Plot: Arthurian romance

Sir Gawain, the bravest, most virtuous of the Knights of the Round Table. He accepts the Green Knight's challenge to uphold the honor of Arthur's court and sets out in autumn on the quest that is essentially a test of his virtue. Temptation awaits him at the castle of Bercilak de Hautdesert, where he must resist the amorous attentions of his hostess without violating the courtesy he owes her as her guest and, at the same time, keep his bargain with his host to exchange whatever he receives at home for the game Bercilak kills while he hunts. Gawain is faithful for two days, but on the third he succumbs to his fear for his life and accepts from the lady a green girdle that protects its wearer from injury. This very human lapse brings him a mild wound from the Green Knight, and he returns to Arthur's court a chastened, shamefaced hero.

King Arthur, the merry young ruler of Britain who is prepared to fight for his own cause if none of his knights will challenge the Green Knight.

Guenevere (GWEHN-eh-veer), his beautiful young queen, the object of Morgan le Fay's hatred.

Sir Bercilak de Hautdesert, the good-humored knight who is Gawain's host. An avid sportsman and lover of good entertainment, he proposes to Gawain an exchange of the gains of each day as amusement for both of them; the bargain is in reality a part of his test of the knight's virtue, for it is he who is disguised as the Green Knight by the arts of Morgan le Fay.

The Lady, his charming wife and accomplice in the temptation of Gawain.

Morgan le Fay, Arthur's half sister, who had learned her skills in magic from Merlin. She is said to have plotted the appearance of the Green Knight at Arthur's court to frighten her enemy Guenevere.

SIR JOHN VAN OLDEN BARNAVELT

Authors: John Fletcher (1579-1625) and Philip Massinger (1583-1640)
First published: 1883
Genre: Drama

Locale: The Netherlands
Time: 1618-1619
Plot: Historical

Sir John van Olden Barnavelt, the aging advocate of Holland and West Friesland. Filled with growing pride, he resents the power and the excellent reputation of the prince of Orange, and he conspires to arouse sedition to regain the control he thinks he has lost. Brought before the senate, he defends himself against charges of treachery by reiterating his real contributions to his nation, and he pathetically tries to console himself for his fall by recalling the esteem in which he was held by many monarchs in his younger days. He swears, even as he stands on the scaffold awaiting execution, that he has not committed treason, and he dies praying for his prince and casting "honour and the world" behind him.

Leidenberch, his fellow conspirator, secretary of the States of Utrecht. He is notoriously a smooth-tongued flatterer and a man who will promise anything; one soldier complains that no suitor ever left him dissatisfied, yet none ever received what he wanted. Lacking the strength to remain silent after the defeat of his forces, he confesses his part in Barnavelt's plot before he is imprisoned. Convinced by Barnavelt that suicide is the only way to preserve some semblance of honor, he resolves to die, then delays a few moments to speak of the pain of leaving his beloved young son, who sleeps nearby.

Modesbargen, another of Barnavelt's followers. He is at first wary of the old statesman's plans and counsels him bluntly not to risk destroying the effects of his forty years of service to the state by giving vent to his ambition. He eventually joins Barnavelt's campaign and is forced to flee to Germany to escape imprisonment. There he grows to love country living and calls himself a fool for participating in political schemes.

Grotius, another of Barnavelt's followers. He, with Hogerbeets, vows to defend the old man against the prince of Orange, but the discovery of their plot makes their efforts futile.

Hogerbeets, a leader of the Arminians, the sect Barnavelt makes pawns in his attempt to gain power.

Maurice, the prince of Orange, a just and wise ruler who shares his responsibilities with his council. He restrains his followers, who are eager to vent their justifiable anger against Barnavelt, yet he is strong-willed enough to exert military force when it is necessary to put down rebellion in Utrecht. Although his natural inclination is to be merciful, he finally orders Barnavelt's death to show that law and order are stronger than the corrupt policies of even the wisest of men.

Bredero and

Vandort, senators and members of the prince's Council of State. They listen sympathetically to Barnavelt's initial plans, but they soon recognize his ambition for what it is and remain loyal supporters of order and the prince.

William and

Henry, loyal supporters of Prince Maurice.

Rockgiles, Barnavelt's chief ally among the burghers.

A captain, who makes an impassioned defense of soldiers, whose only honor lies in their obedience and loyalty to their ruler.

Holderus, a scholar, held firmly under control by a group of domineering Dutch women. He supports Barnavelt and flees the advancing army of the prince in terror.

William, Barnavelt's son, who acts as his aide. He brings his father word of Leidenberch's suicide.

Leidenberch's son, a precocious, sensitive boy who looks after his father in prison. He is rather like Christopher Marlowe's Prince Edward and several of William Shakespeare's bright young children.

Boisise and

Morier, French ambassadors who go to the prince to protest the death of Barnavelt, whom they have known only as a wise statesman.

Harlem,

Leyden, and

Utrecht executioners, grotesque humorists. They throw dice to see who is to have the privilege of executing Sir John.

THE SIR ROGER DE COVERLEY PAPERS

Authors: Joseph Addison (1672-1719), Sir Richard Steele (1672-1729), and Eustace Budgell (1686-1737)
First published: 1711-1712
Genre: Short fiction

Locale: London and Worcestershire
Time: Early eighteenth century
Plot: Social

Sir Roger de Coverley, a fifty-six-year-old bachelor, the benevolent autocrat of a large Worcestershire estate. The knight's humaneness, according to his own opinion, is the result of his love for a beautiful widow whom he has wooed for thirty years. His kindness is equaled by his rigid control of his servants, whose morals, finances, and behavior are the assumed responsibility of Sir Roger. In London, he presides over "The Club," an informal but close-knit group of men of divergent interests and personalities. Sir Roger's every thought seems marked by affability, his every act by broad knowledge and understanding.

Mr. Spectator, the anonymous first-person narrator of the articles describing customs and personalities of eighteenth century London. The writer sets the tone of the journal with the editorial pronouncement that any faulty character described in the journal fits a thousand people and that every paper is presented in the spirit of benevolence and with love of humankind.

Captain Sentry, Sir Roger's nephew, who leaves a successful naval career to assume his position as heir to Sir Roger in The Club, as well as in his uncle's financial holdings. The captain's great courage, keen understanding, and gallantry in naval sieges are quietly balanced by an invincible modesty, qualities that make him a liked and admired individual.

Sir Andrew Freeport, a club member whose eminence as a merchant and personal frugality speak for the differences between Sir Andrew's and Sir Roger's political and economic philosophies. Those differences provide the basis for many hours of debate between the two devoted friends. Among Sir Roger's last acts is making the gift of a book to Sir Andrew, a collection of acts of Parliament.

Will Honeycomb, a beau and fop in the decline of life. Despite his age, he remains youthful, he says, because of his many attempts to marry. His contributions to club discussions stem from various aspects of the female world. His ultimate marriage at an advanced age bears out his claim to gallantry.

William Wimble, a bachelor neighbor of Sir Roger de Coverley. The youngest son of an ancient family, born to no estate and bred to no business, Will lives with an older brother and acts as gamekeeper on the family estate. Resigned to his lot in life, amiable Will is the darling of the countryside.

Moll White, a slatternly recluse who lives near Sir Roger's estate. Known as a witch by her neighbors, she is blamed for any untoward event or incident. Her death is said to have caused winds violent enough to blow off the end of one of Sir Roger's barns. Sir Roger tells Mr. Spectator of the coincidence of the two events but professes no belief in any relationship between them.

Kate Willow, a witty, mischievous wench in Sir Roger's neighborhood. Kate's value of her beauty over love has kept her unmarried. To the consternation of many, she tries to influence young girls in love to be as indiscreet as she has been.

Laertes (LAY-ur-teez) and

Irus (I-ruhs), men of the countryside. Their economic practices, both based on poverty, are opposites. Because he is ashamed to appear poor, Laertes spends unthriftily, moving always closer to poverty. Irus' fear of poverty causes him to save, moving him from it.

Tom Touchy, the selfish neighbor of Sir Roger. At every meeting of the court, he sues someone for poaching on his land. Touchy, generally disliked for his littleness, incurs the wrath of the countryside when he sues Will Wimble for taking hazel sticks from his hedge. Good-natured Will has taken the sticks to make tobacco-stoppers for his friends.

A minister, a club member whose visits add to every man new enjoyment of himself.

The Templar, another member. His interest turns from poetry to law, and he leaves The Club.

Edward Biscuit, Sir Roger's butler. From Biscuit's correspondence, Mr. Spectator learns the details of the baronet's death and burial.

THE SIRENS OF TITAN

Author: Kurt Vonnegut, Jr. (1922-   )
First published: 1959
Genre: Novel

Locale: Earth, Mars, Mercury, and Titan (the ninth moon of Saturn)
Time: The Nightmare Ages, between World War II and the Third Great Depression
Plot: Science fiction

Malachi Constant, called **Unk**, the world's richest and luckiest playboy, whose name means "faithful messenger." Having inherited from his father, Noel, a previously infallible system for stock investment, Malachi is told by Winston Niles Rumfoord that he will lose his money, marry Rumfoord's wife (Beatrice), have a child, and move to Saturn's largest moon. Despite all of his efforts to the contrary, these events occur. Lawsuits deplete his capital; he is impressed into the army of Mars and fitted with a radio control; he rapes Mrs. Rumfoord while drunk; he engenders a son, Chrono; he is lost on Mercury; he returns to Earth, where he is vilified by Rumfoord's new Church of God, the Utterly Indifferent; and he is forced to retreat with Beatrice and Chrono to Titan.

Winston Niles Rumfoord, a former millionaire, member of the social elite, and explorer. He is now, with his dog Kazak, a collection of particles that materialize at regular intervals. Stylish, elderly, and possessing a winning smile, Rumfoord has had the power to foresee the future ever since he drove his spaceship into a time tunnel, or "chrono-synclastic infundibulum." In an attempt to manipulate Earth's history, he creates a suicidal army on Mars, whose destruction engenders global remorse and the formation of a new religion. All of this is done to force his wife and Malachi to marry and create a son whose good-luck piece must be transported to Titan, where it is needed by a visiting alien.

Beatrice (Bee) Rumfoord, the reserved, privileged, and too-proper virgin wife of Winston. A tall and beautiful woman in her late thirties at the story's start, her central desire is to remain chaste and so frustrate her husband's predictions. Her rape by Malachi defeats both wishes and makes her the mother of Chrono. During the story's forty years, she loses her affec-

tation as well as teeth and one eye. In the end, she loves both Malachi and her son.

Chrono, the son of Malachi and Beatrice. This juvenile delinquent unknowingly carries the secret of Earth's history. Born on Mars as the product of his mother's rape, Chrono, a dark and sociopathic player of German bat ball, picks up a piece of scrap metal in a flamethrower factory. This good-luck charm is the key to the story. As the reader discovers in the end, all the plot's involutions serve to take Chrono's talisman to Titan, where it is needed as a replacement part for an alien spaceship.

Salo, an interstellar robot from the small Magellanic Cloud. A sentient and ultimately caring machine, the orange Salo has a head on gimbals, three inflatable feet, no arms, and three eyes. He carries the single word "Greetings" across the galaxy. His spaceship's breakdown has forced the members of his home planet, Tralfamadore, to use their "Universal Will to Become" to influence Earth's history such that it would produce, in the form of Chrono's good-luck charm, the piece needed for the spaceship's repair. In the end, Salo learns to love Rumfoord more than his robot mission, and it is this emotion more than the absurd machinations of planetary fate that becomes his triumph.

Stony Stevenson, Malachi's only friend and one of the commanders of the army of Mars. Stony is an admirer of Unk because Unk resists the brainwashing to which he is repeatedly subjected. Ironically, Unk (or Malachi) strangles Stony to death after a final and effective mind cleansing. This execution takes place under radio control and in Malachi's complete ignorance. It demonstrates yet again how little human wishes have to do with personal or collective fate.

— *Daniel D. Fineman*

SISTER CARRIE

Author: Theodore Dreiser (1871-1945)
First published: 1900
Genre: Novel

Locale: Chicago and New York City
Time: 1889
Plot: Naturalism

Caroline Meeber, called **Sister Carrie**, a young Midwestern girl who rises from her small-town origins to success as an actress. Her story illustrates one part of the author's division of humankind between the Intellectual and the Emotional. Members of the latter division he calls "harps in the wind," hopelessly seeking to satisfy an inexplicable yearning for beauty, accomplishment, and the good life. Caroline Meeber belongs to this second group, which performs its sad, forsaken quest in the manner of dancers after a flame. Although Carrie is not capable of much rationalization, she is capable of sensing an ideal, and she has a tenacious energy to bend toward its realization. The key to Carrie's apparently simple character is that she is a rather complex person. Moved by desires that at first

she sees as ends in themselves—to have money, to own fine clothes, to be socially accepted—she enters into an affair with Hurstwood and contributes to his degeneration while remaining virtually untouched herself. Her restlessness and seeming disregard for others are really manifestations of her inability to recognize anything outside of concrete representation. Throughout the book, she is never given to reflection. Although she uses Drouet and Hurstwood to her advantage, she is no gross country girl grasping at opportunity. There is something monolithic in her nature, and certain gifts or curses of sensitivity and pluck combine to give her an appeal that her fellows recognize as representative of themselves. As Carrie Madena, she scores a success on the stage by acting in flimsy, superficial parts. What is sad about Carrie is that each time she steps up to the much prized rung that has been just above, her ideal eludes her and she becomes vaguely disillusioned with still another symbol of happiness and success. Thus, she becomes the author's commentary on people's pathetic reach for the ideal on the distant peak; reality is the intractable stuff they have to work with to achieve it.

George Hurstwood, the manager of a Chicago saloon, a man who has worked his way into a carefully balanced niche of the social order. In the class just below the luxurious rich, he has created for himself an air of success made substantial by good food, good company, and comfortable living. When he encounters Carrie, Hurstwood has fallen into the practice of maintaining only the semblance of marital order; he denies himself little in the way of pleasures that he genuinely covets, but he has the saving grace of discretion on his side. He begins to fancy himself as quite clever, something of a commander on the field of life, and this self-deception brings about his eventual collapse. With Carrie, he imagines nothing can stay his success, and in a weak moment he discards the last shreds of caution. Because he never fully understands Carrie, a pall of reality weights their relationship. Hurstwood has betrayed his place of trust by stealing money from his employers and has hoodwinked Carrie into running off with him, and these conditions prove insufferable. Faced with a much lower status in society, Hurstwood, now using the alias of Wheeler, is unable to reconcile himself to fact and begins to indulge in living in the past. One by one, his carefully structured conceptions of himself and his flamboyance crumple, and he learns that he is no match for grubbiness. The painstaking chronicle of Hurstwood's decline into apathy becomes the signal merit of this novel. Hurstwood is incapable of checking his downhill slide because, even to his end, a desolate, grimy suicide in a flophouse, the granules of former pride remain with him, actually sapping his powers of adaptation.

Charles Drouet (drew-AY), a traveling salesman and a superficial egotist, Carrie Meeber's first lover. Drouet has no real depth to his nature. He has no wish to inflict harm on others and tries, while pleasing himself, to bring them happiness. He serves as Carrie's first introduction to a form of the good life, but she quickly outgrows him as she passes on to George Hurstwood. At the end of the novel, Drouet is shown essentially as he was at the beginning: handsome, flashy, gay, boylike, effervescent, and entirely without scope or perspective.

Bod Ames, a young man intellectually inclined. He is the only character who really understands or genuinely moves Carrie. Ironically, he causes the most painful reawakening of the quest for the "ideal" in Carrie's nature.

Minnie and

Sven Hanson, Carrie's sister and brother-in-law, with whom she lives when she goes to Chicago. They live a sterile, plodding life that Carrie earnestly wishes to avoid.

Mrs. Hurstwood, a deceived and deserted wife who has watched her marriage deteriorate steadily, even before her husband's affair with Carrie Meeber. Cold and social-minded by nature, she ends up in possession of all the property accumulated by Hurstwood over the years.

Jessica and

George Hurstwood, Jr., the Hurstwood children, rather selfish offspring, without depth, who conform to their mother's way.

Mr. and Mrs. Vance, a couple who live next to Carrie and Hurstwood in New York. They impress Carrie with their sophistication and put her life with Hurstwood under a shabbier light.

SISTER MARY IGNATIUS EXPLAINS IT ALL FOR YOU

Author: Christopher Durang (1949-   )
First published: 1980
Genre: Drama

Locale: The United States
Time: Late 1970's
Plot: Satire

Sister Mary Ignatius, a nun and fifth grade teacher at what she calls Our Lady of Perpetual Sorrow School. Sister Mary appears in an old-fashioned nun's habit; her age is uncertain, but she might be anywhere from forty to sixty. Although she displays many human characteristics, Sister Mary is a caricature of an earnest but oppressive parochial school teacher, more concerned with doctrine than with truth. One of her chief assertions is that God answers all prayers, but that sometimes the answer is no. She lectures directly to the audience, occasionally answering questions that she has on file cards, but the information she presents is often confused. When questioned, Thomas, her assistant, gets the commandments wrong, but Sister Mary nevertheless approves his answers and rewards him with cookies. She claims to come from a large family, some twenty-six children, of whom five became priests, seven nuns, and three brothers. The others, as well as her mother, she says, were placed in institutions. When four students from her 1959 fifth grade class arrive and perform a Christmas pageant, she becomes even more confused. The pageant, presumably written by Mary Jean Mahoney, a fifth grade student from 1948, clearly reflects Sister Mary's teachings and marks the turning point of the play. After the performance, Sister Mary questions her former students and discovers that they have all abandoned her teaching and that each has sinned in some way. Sister Mary immediately dislikes Diane, who has had two abortions. When Diane accuses Sister Mary of being insane and threatens her with a gun, Sister Mary tricks her and, drawing her own gun from beneath her habit, kills her. After learning that Gary, a homosexual, has been to confession just that morning, Sister kills him, too, so that he may go directly to Heaven. She allows Philomena to leave quietly but finally takes Thomas on her lap and directs him to keep the gun aimed at Aloysius while she naps.

Thomas, a seven-year-old boy, in the second grade at Our Lady of Perpetual Sorrow School. He serves as Sister Mary's assistant and is an example of her latest victim. He wears a tie and a school blazer. When he first enters, Sister Mary explains that, having achieved the age of seven, he is capable of choosing to sin or not to sin. In reciting his lessons and his catechism, Thomas illustrates Sister Mary's warped teaching. He remains loyal to her when she is attacked by her former pupils and in the end happily recites his catechism.

Diane Symonds, a student in Sister Mary Ignatius' 1959 fifth grade class who plays the Blessed Mother in the pageant. At the age of eighteen, on the same day that her mother died of cancer, Diane was raped by a maniac who broke into her house, and she subsequently had an abortion. Depressed for many years afterward, she had a second abortion after she was raped by her psychiatrist. She organizes her classmates to present the Christmas pageant as a means of getting even with Sister Mary for having instilled in her a false view of the world. Her death at the hands of Sister Mary illustrates the sister's continuing strength and Diane's own ineptitude.

Gary Sullavan, another member of Sister Mary's 1959 fifth grade class, a homosexual who joins with Diane to em-barrass their former teacher. Seduced when he was in the seminary, Gary afterward went to New York, where he reports having slept with five hundred different people. Gary, who portrays St. Joseph in the pageant, lives with Jeff Hannigan, another of Sister Mary's former fifth grade students.

Philomena Rostovitch and

Aloysius Busiccio, who together perform the role of the camel, Misty, in the pageant. Philomena is an unwed mother with a three-year-old daughter. She was beaten by Sister Mary for being stupid. Aloysius is married and has two children but recently has become an alcoholic and has taken to beating his wife. He attributes his bladder problems to Sister Mary never having allowed him to go to the bathroom.

— *Robert M. Bender*

SISTER PHILOMÈNE
(Sœur Philomène)

Authors: Edmond de Goncourt (1822-1896) and Jules de Gon-court (1830-1870)
First published: 1861
Genre: Novel

Locale: Paris, France
Time: The nineteenth century
Plot: Naturalism

Marie Gaucher (mah-REE goh-SHAY), who becomes **Sis-ter Philomène**. Orphaned as a child, she is sent to a convent orphanage. After a period of adjustment, she is led, through her friend Céline, to a state of religious agitation that finally threatens her health. Her aunt is permitted to take her home. After an unhappy time as servant to Henri de Viry, she begins her novitiate to the Sisters of St. Augustine, who send her to work in a hospital. There, she wins the hearts of doctors and sufferers by her compassionate tenderness. She falls in love with Barnier but punishes herself by remaining in the hospital and enduring love's torments until his death.

Barnier (bahr-NYAY), a young doctor loved by Sister Phi-lomène. Haunted by memories of the dead Romaine, his for-mer mistress, he deliberately exposes himself to disease and dies as Sister Philomène is having prayers for unbelievers said for him.

Céline (say-LEEN), Sister Philomène's friend at the orphan-age, who later becomes Sister Lawrence. She dies of typhoid.

Madame de Viry (deh vee-REE), the employer of Sister Philomène's aunt, with whom the child Marie goes to live after the death of her parents. When she begins to assume equal footing with Henri de Viry, Madame de Viry sends her away to an orphanage.

Henri de Viry (an-REE), Madame de Viry's son.

Romaine (roh-MEHN), Barnier's former mistress, who had left him for a life of dissipation. Her death leads the grief-stricken Barnier to expose himself to a fatal disease.

Malivoire (mah-lee-VWAHR), a doctor and a friend of Barnier.

Marguerite (mahr-geh-REET), a sister who befriends young Marie at the orphanage.

SIX CHARACTERS IN SEARCH OF AN AUTHOR
(Sei personaggi in cerca d'autore: Commedia da fare)

Author: Luigi Pirandello (1867-1936)
First published: 1921
Genre: Drama

Locale: The stage of a theater
Time: The twentieth century
Plot: Comedy

The Father, who, during preparations for the rehearsal of a play, appears on stage with five members of his family, in search of an author who will put them, already living charac-ters, into a drama. The manager finally agrees to hear their story and allows them all to rehearse their parts as their illu-sions cause them to believe them to be.

The Mother, who years ago was provided with a lover by her husband. After the lover tires of her, she returns, destitute, with her three illegitimate children and is again received into her husband's home. She watches, sorrowing, as she sees her husband act out his visit to Madame Pace, from whom he attempts to purchase a replacement for his wife. Unknown to him, the girl he desires is the illegitimate daughter of his own wife.

The Stepdaughter, who, while playing her part in Madame Pace's establishment, is approached by her stepfather, who does not recognize her. She is abruptly pulled from him by her horrified mother, who rushes in from offstage.

The Son, who, when urged by the manager to play his part, insists that he simply walked in the garden. He violently accuses the father of displaying the family shame to the world and of dragging him onstage. He finally admits finding the body of the little girl in the fountain.

The Little Girl, who, placed by the stage manager beside a fountain, is found dead in its waters.

The Boy, who is placed by the stage manager behind some bushes, from which comes the sound of a pistol shot. In the resulting confusion, the rehearsal ends in a frantic discussion about whether or not the boy's death is real or pretended.

Madame Pace, a procuress. Scandalized at having to play her part before the mother, she leaves the stage.

The Stage Manager,

the Leading Lady, and

the Leading Man, the professional company interrupted in rehearsal by the six characters in search of an author.

62: A MODEL KIT
(62: Modelo para armar)

Author: Julio Cortázar (1914-1984)
First published: 1968
Genre: Novel

Locale: Paris, London, Vienna, Arcueil, and an imaginary city
Time: The 1950's or the 1960's
Plot: Psychological

Juan, an Argentine interpreter who works for an international agency. He has a humorous and unprejudiced character and an almost surrealist vision of the world, which he shares with most of the characters, all of whom are among a group of friends who meet habitually in the café Cluny. Juan is interested in metaphysical matters, especially in the ways in which reality is perceived. He has much imagination and looks for secret keys or symbols to understand the universe or what happens to him. He shares the keys, the dreams, and the imaginary realms ("the city," "the zone") with his friends. He usually travels with his partner, Tell, but he is desperately in love with Hélène. During his stay in Vienna, as he works at an international conference and shares his life with Tell, he is obsessed with the story of a bloody countess, the Basilisk House, and an old and disgusting woman, Frau Marta, who vampirizes an English girl who is touring Vienna. Always mixing fantasies with real life, he tries to save the English girl from an imaginary danger. Everything becomes a metaphor of his relationship with Hélène. Back in Paris, he has an intense encounter with Hélène but is unable to keep her after she tells her story of a dead patient who resembled Juan and her affair with Celia. He desperately intends to reach her and to follow her, but he loses her in a scene in which dreams and symbols are mixed and become real.

Hélène, a young French anesthetist, aloof and distant but a sensible and tender person. Unlike Juan, she is unable to share everything with her friends in the Cluny. She is touched when a young man, almost a boy, with a close resemblance to Juan dies without awakening from anesthesia. She leaves the hospital very disturbed, goes to the Cluny, and meets Celia, who has just run away from her parents' home. She invites Celia to her small apartment and, that night, having no control of her feelings and senses, forces Celia to make love with her. After this disturbing experience, she has a sexual encounter with Juan, but she cannot forgive herself for the disgraceful incident of the night spent with Celia.

Marrast, a French sculptor with an extraordinary sense of humor who travels to London to get a stone to carve a statue of Vercingetorix, commissioned by the mayor of Arcueil. To forget that his lover, Nicole, has revealed to him her love for Juan, he invents absurd situations in a museum, situations in which almost all the members of the group, now in London, are engaged. He teaches French to Austin but then, when Nicole betrays him with Austin, goes back to Paris and works on the sculpture. All the members of the group are together in the inauguration of the Vercingetorix statue. He continues to love Nicole and tries to get her back.

Nicole, a French illustrator of children's books. She has a good relationship with Marrast, but their happiness is destroyed when she confesses that she is in love with Juan. They live together for a while, but she decides to go to bed with Austin to destroy Marrast's love. She is not able to gain another's love, forget Marrast, or destroy his affection for her.

Tell, Juan's lover. She is a young, beautiful, and independent Danish woman. She shares Juan's friends and travels with him, trying to enjoy their relationship even when she knows that Juan is in love with Hélène. She participates joyfully in the surrealistic games in which Juan is engaged, such as following Frau Marta and the English girl in their wanderings across Vienna and trying to protect the girl from impending danger.

Calac and

Polanco, two Argentines, the first a writer and critic, the second a worker in unusual jobs. Both have a ludicrous sense of life and are always engaged in absurd dialogues, in which they have nothing to say. Sometimes, they use a language of their own, which irritates conformist people. They are, in some respects, as Juan is in others, the alter ego of the author.

Celia, the youngest member of the group. She is rich and spoiled and decides to leave her parents' home. She runs into Hélène in the Cluny. They are alone because Juan and Tell are in Vienna and the others are in London. She has no place to spend the night and accepts Hélène's invitation to her place with curiosity, because Hélène is a mystery to most members of the group. She suffers a tremendous shock when she accepts Hélène's sexual assault, and she decides to go to London to join the others. She meets Austin and falls in love with him.

Austin, a young English lute player who receives French lessons from Marrast and joins the group. He is handsome and self-confident. He has a casual affair with Nicole and initiates Celia into the delights of heterosexual love. He meets the group in London and travels to Paris, attending with them the inauguration of Marrast's statue in Arcueil.

The paredros, abstract entities that sometimes function as alter egos of the main characters.

Feuille Morte (fweh mohrt), an indefinite entity, a feminine voice that says only "bisbis bisbis."

— Leda Schiavo

THE SKIN OF OUR TEETH

Author: Thornton Wilder (1897-1975)
First published: 1942
Genre: Drama

Locale: Excelsior, New Jersey, and the boardwalk at Atlantic City
Time: All of human history
Plot: Phantasmagoric

George Antrobus, a citizen of the world. He wants to believe in the goodness of humankind and the survival of the race, but often his faith is shaken. A kind and generous man, he insists that starving refugees from the cold then enveloping the world be admitted to the house and fed, whereas his practical wife does not want to take them in. A good provider, he obtains a boat so that he can save his family during the big flood. After the great war, he decides to try to live in peace with his vicious son Henry. Striving to regain his confidence in humankind, he takes comfort in his books, his home, and the good people of the world.

Mrs. Antrobus, George's wife. She is a typical middle-class mother who loves her family and willingly sacrifices herself to their needs. Her typically female responses enable her to hold her husband, survive catastrophes, and perpetuate the race. When she is about to lose George to Sabina, she takes advantage of the coming great flood to bring him back to duty and family. When the great war comes, she finds safety in the basement for herself, her daughter, and, most important of all, her new grandchild.

Gladys Antrobus, their daughter, a wholesome girl much like her mother. Content to remain within the security of the family circle, she survives the great flood. By hiding in the basement, she and her new baby survive the great war as well.

Henry Antrobus, formerly called Cain, the Antrobuses' son, a nonconformist. When he hits his brother with a stone and accidentally kills him, his parents change his name from Cain to Henry and thereafter make every effort to hide his past. In another fit of hate, he kills a neighbor with a stone. In the great war, his aggressive temperament enables him to rise from the rank of corporal to that of general.

Sabina, the maid in the Antrobus household. She is the former mistress of George, who had brought her back from the Sabine rape. She leaves the Antrobuses and, as Miss Lily-Sabina Fairweather, wins a beauty contest at Atlantic City, after which she tries unsuccessfully to win back George.

Moses, a judge,

Homer, a blind beggar with a guitar,

Miss E. Muse,

Miss T. Muse, and

Miss M. Muse, refugees from the killing cold who stop at the Antrobus house hoping to find food and warmth.

SLAUGHTERHOUSE-FIVE: Or, The Children's Crusade, a Duty-Dance with Death

Author: Kurt Vonnegut, Jr. (1922-   )
First published: 1969
Genre: Novel

Locale: Dresden, Germany, and Ilium, New York
Time: 1922-1976
Plot: Science fiction

Billy Pilgrim, a conservative, middle-aged optometrist living in upstate Ilium, New York. Born in 1922, Pilgrim leads a very bland life, except for the facts that at the end of World War II he came "unstuck in time" and began to jump back and forth among past, present, and future, and that in 1967 he was captured by a flying saucer from the planet Tralfamadore. The novel's jerky structure mirrors his interplanetary and time travel. Pilgrim is thus a schizophrenic character: An apathetic, almost autistic widower in the present, he is also a crackpot visionary who claims to have visited another planet and to speak as a prophet. The cause of Pilgrim's schizoid behavior, as the author makes clear, is the horror he witnessed in Dresden as a prisoner of war when that beautiful old German city was systematically incinerated by American bombers.

Kurt Vonnegut, Jr., the author of the novel and a character in it, living on Cape Cod, Massachusetts. The first and last chapters of the novel form a frame around the narrative proper. In them, Vonnegut describes his trip with his wartime buddy, Bernard V. O'Hare, back to Dresden, Germany, where they were imprisoned during World War II, as well as current events (for example, the assassinations of Martin Luther King, Jr., and Robert Kennedy). The persona of this narrator is naïve,
idealistic, and fixated on World War II, especially on the fire-bombing of Dresden, a city of no apparent military significance. As he tells readers, Vonnegut himself was one of the few survivors of the destruction of Dresden, when he and other prisoners of war—including Pilgrim in the novel itself—were entombed in a slaughterhouse below the city and thus survived the holocaust above. Vonnegut surfaces several other times in the narrative, so history, fiction, author, and fictional characters intermingle freely.

Montana Wildhack, a voluptuous film star who is captured and put in a zoo on Tralfamadore along with Billy Pilgrim, and who becomes his lover and bears his child while they are living in captivity there.

Valencia Merble Pilgrim, Pilgrim's wife, a rich, overweight woman who is later killed rushing to his aid after a plane crash in which he is the only survivor.

Howard W. Campbell, Jr., an American collaborator working for the Nazis who tries to convince Pilgrim and his fellow prisoners to defect to the German side.

Edgar Derby, an older, idealistic American soldier and former high-school teacher who stands up to Campbell but then is executed at the end of the war for the trivial act of stealing a teapot.

Roland Weary, a pathetic and tiresome comrade of Pilgrim who dies in the boxcar taking the prisoners to Dresden.

Paul Lazzaro, a mean and ugly member of the band of prisoners being shipped to Dresden who vows to kill Pilgrim after the war in revenge for the death of Weary. He eventually fulfills his threat, in 1976.

Kilgore Trout, a science-fiction writer living in Ilium.

— *David Peck*

THE SLAVE
(Der Knekht)

Author: Isaac Bashevis Singer(1904-1993)
First published: 1961
Genre: Novel

Locale: Poland and Palestine
Time: Mid- and late seventeenth century
Plot: Historical

Jacob, a devout, scholarly Jew, twenty-nine years old as the novel opens. A survivor of a massacre, he is sold as a slave to Polish peasant Jan Bzik, who uses him as a cowherd. He is tall, with brown hair and blue eyes, and he is descended from rabbis. He resists the temptation to commit adultery with Wanda, Jan's daughter, in a mountain village in which diseased sexuality is rampant, but he finally succumbs and is tormented by shame and desire. After five years, Jacob is ransomed by fellow Jews. Their account of Cossack atrocities in his village and of the death of his wife and children increases his guilt. He returns to Wanda after seeing her in a dream. It is Jacob's faithful nature that makes him return to Pilitz twenty years after her death, and there he dies, faithful to the last.

Wanda Bzik, the widowed daughter of Jan. She is almost pagan but comparatively civilized, a fair-haired, good-looking, capable, and healthy woman. Managing her father's household, she falls in love with Jacob and helps him by bringing him food and treating a snakebite. She pursues him passionately and is eager to learn his doctrine. When he is ransomed, she falls sick; she is in this condition when he rescues her. She accompanies him to Pilitz, pretending to be a deaf-mute, Dumb Sarah, and trying to behave as a Jewish married woman should. She dies giving birth to a son and reveals, in her agony, the truth about her origins. She appears to Jacob in dreams for the rest of his life.

Adam Pilitzky, the fifty-four-year-old overlord of the village of Pilitz, whose youth was spent in the West. He is ruthless with his peasantry but is a poor manager, with corrupt bailiffs. Against his declared intent, a Jewish community forms in Pilitz. He hangs himself when Pilitz passes to a creditor.

Theresa Pilitzky, Adam's wife. She is small, plump, sprightly, and as loose-living as her husband. For her own amusement, she tries to tempt Jacob. She dies alone after giving her remaining wealth to an impoverished nobleman, her last lover.

Jan Bzik, Wanda's father and Jacob's master. He has a certain innate intelligence that prevents him from ridiculing Jacob. Once a man of importance in the village, he is now old, sick, and morose, so that his wife wishes him dead. He dies, leaving Wanda, his favorite daughter, unprotected.

Gershon, a powerful man in Pilitz who has leased the manor's fields. A cunning dealer and a leader of the Jewish community who collects (and embezzles) their taxes, he dresses like a rabbi, looks like a butcher, and dislikes Jacob and all scholars. He is a stickler for the forms of religion and is loud in condemning Jacob when the truth emerges.

Dziobak, a Catholic priest in the mountain village, where pagan superstitions prevail. He is short, broad, clumsily built, lame, dirty, and often drunk. He is the father of many children.

Miriam, Jacob's sister, who survived the massacre. Formerly handsome and well-to-do, she is now toothless and ragged. She shrilly enumerates the atrocities.

Tirza Temma, a Jewish woman forced into marriage with a Cossack. Hearing that her first husband will be allowed to be divorced from her, she berates the community in Cossack, having forgotten her Yiddish.

— *W. Gordon Cunliffe*

SLEEPLESS DAYS
(Schlaflose Tage)

Author: Jurek Becker (1937-   )
First published: 1978
Genre: Novel

Locale: East Berlin and Hungary
Time: The 1970's
Plot: Social

Karl Simrock, an East Berlin high-school teacher. Soon after his thirty-sixth birthday, he examines his past life and finds it wanting. His marriage is empty, and his work as a teacher is governed by authoritarian regimentation. He leaves his wife, Ruth, and daughter, Leonie, and enters into a relationship with Antonia Kramm. At work, he starts to measure the difference between East German ideology and reality. He tries to teach his students to question and doubt, not merely to accept. This emphasis causes him to lose his position, and he takes work as a bakery truck driver with Boris.

Ruth Simrock (rewt), a part-time insurance agent and Karl's wife. Karl complains that she will not accept certain matters as "women's business." Very controlled, she never cries, even when her husband suddenly leaves her. She admits that marriage to him has been "hellish." She accuses him of leaving her because school authorities "broke his back."

Kabitzke (kah-BITS-keh), the vice principal at Simrock's school. A timid sycophant, he cannot understand Karl's rebelliousness and warns him that it is self-destructive. He refuses to support Karl publicly.

Antonia Kramm, a former physics student, now a freelance typist at the age of twenty-eight. When younger, she was a textbook socialist; she became embittered by the hypocrisy of her society. Accepted at a university, she studies physics to avoid politics, but after three semesters she is nevertheless exmatriculated for political reasons. She attempts to create the greatest possible independence for herself, dreaming of "islands of solitude" in a society of enforced community. On vacation in Hungary with Simrock, she attempts, without first informing him, to escape to Austria. She is caught and imprisoned for at least nineteen months.

Boris, a physically strong, twenty-two-year-old bakery truck driver with "charming long hair." His dream is to see Liverpool. No heroic worker, he believes that anyone who claims to derive satisfaction from delivering bread is a liar or a fool. He goes through the notions of political commitment, not out of conviction but to be left in peace. He thus destroys Karl Simrock's remaining illusions about his society.

— *Thomas C. Fox*

SLEEPLESS NIGHTS

Author: Elizabeth Hardwick (1916-   )
First published: 1979
Genre: Novel

Locale: New York
Time: Primarily the 1940's to the 1970's
Plot: Psychological realism

Elizabeth, the self-conscious narrator, who describes her story as a record of "transformed" and "distorted" memory. Born in 1922 in Lexington, Kentucky, she was one of nine children. Feeling misplaced and uneasy in the South, she moves from Kentucky to New York at the age of eighteen to study at Columbia University. She is the author's fictional persona.

Alex, an intellectual friend of thirty years, a "dubious Casanova" and Elizabeth's first lover. Following years of separation, he returns to Elizabeth for comfort and understanding when jilted by Sarah, his fiancée.

Dr. Z., "the eternal husband" to Madame Mevrouw Z.; "fervent romancer" to Simone, the painter; and "faithless" lover of his nurse employee. Elizabeth, in retrospect, attributes his insatiable desire for love from women to his Jewish identity and the ghastly memories of experiences in a concentration camp in Germany.

J., Elizabeth's childhood friend from Kentucky. The homosexual jazz enthusiast is Elizabeth's roommate in New York in the 1940's.

— *Roland E. Bush*

THE SLEEPWALKERS
(Die Schlafwandler)

Author: Hermann Broch (1886-1951)
First published: 1931-1932
Genre: Novel

Locale: Germany
Time: 1888-1918
Plot: Philosophical

Joachim von Pasenow (yoh-AH-khihm fon PAH-zeh-noh), a young German lieutenant who feels comfortable only in a uniform. He has odd ideas about his wife as a kind of madonna. By the end of World War I, he has become a major in the German army.

Bertrand, Joachim's friend. He leaves the army to become a businessman. He becomes Esch's enemy. He hires agents to provoke Martin, the Socialist, into trouble with the authorities.

Herr von Pasenow, Joachim's father, a funny, fat old man who embarrasses his son. He wants Joachim to marry Elisabeth and retire from the army to manage the family estates.

Ruzena (rew-ZEH-nah), a sensitive Bohemian girl who becomes Joachim von Pasenow's mistress. She shoots Bertrand, wounding him in the arm, when she thinks he is coming between her and her lover.

Elisabeth, Joachim von Pasenow's wife.

Martin, a Socialist. Bertrand has him harassed by the police and by hired baiters.

Esch (ehsh), a German bookkeeper who becomes a theatrical manager and, later, a newspaperman. During a workers' revolt in 1918, he is murdered by Huguenau, who stabs him with a bayonet.

Frau Hentjen (HEHNT-yehn), a restaurant keeper. She becomes Esch's mistress and, later, his wife. She is raped by Huguenau shortly before he murders her husband.

Helmuth von Pasenow (HEHL-mewt), Joachim's brother, killed in a duel.

Korn, a customs inspector. He is Esch's friend and landlord.

Lohberg, a tobacconist and Esch's friend.

Erna Korn, the customs inspector's sister, desperate to be married.

Teltscher (TEHLT-shehr), a Hungarian knife thrower.

Ilona (ee-LOH-nah), a flashy blonde. She is Teltscher's human target in his act.

Gernerth (GEHR-nehrt), a theatrical manager who becomes Esch's partner.

Huguenau (HEW-geh-now), an Alsatian businessman who looks after himself and takes what he wants.

Marie, a Salvation Army girl attracted to a Talmudic Jew.

Hanna, a lawyer's wife.

SLEUTH

Author: Anthony Shaffer (1926-   )
First published: 1970
Genre: Drama

Locale: England
Time: The 1970's
Plot: Detective and mystery

Andrew Wyke, a writer of detective stories. A tall, well-built man of fifty-seven, he has written many old-fashioned mystery novels featuring the fictional detective Inspector Merridrew. Disdaining the modern detective shows one sees on television, he favors the golden age of mystery fiction, the 1930's, with stories featuring complex plots and elaborate puzzles. In the first act, Andrew amicably invites Milo Tindall over to his home to discuss Milo's plan to marry his wife, Marguerite. Andrew's real intention in inviting Milo over is to teach him a lesson in humility. He persuades Milo to participate in a game to steal Marguerite's jewels from a safe in the house; Milo can fence the jewels and keep the money to support Marguerite. The game turns nasty, however, when Andrew pulls a gun and threatens to shoot Milo. He explains that he will tell the police that he heard a burglar in the house and shot and killed the man. Andrew has no intention of letting Milo marry Marguerite. When he points the gun at Milo's head and shoots, the bullet is a blank. When Milo faints at the shot, Andrew wins the game; he has humiliated Milo.

Milo Tindall, Marguerite Wyke's lover, a slim, handsome man of thirty-five, of medium height, with a Mediterranean complexion inherited from his half-Italian, half-Jewish father. Milo is in the travel business in Dulwich. Humiliated in An-

drew's game, Milo seeks revenge by disguising himself and reappearing at Andrew's house as Inspector Doppler, pretending to investigate the possible murder of Milo Tindall. Much to Andrew's surprise, Milo, as Inspector Doppler, discovers clues that incriminate Andrew in the so-called murder. Milo wins his game as he tells the horrified Andrew that the most time he will serve is seven years for manslaughter. When Milo finally unmasks himself, Andrew knows he has found a worthy opponent. Milo, however, has not yet completed his revenge. Milo tells Andrew that he gained access to the house with the help of Andrew's lover, whom, Milo says, he raped and strangled and then buried in the yard. Furthermore, Milo planted evidence in the house that will incriminate Andrew in the murder. Through a series of riddles, Andrew finds the evidence before the police come to arrest him. In fact, the police do not arrive, because there has been no murder: Milo has humiliated Andrew a second time. When Milo tells Andrew that he plans to take Marguerite away and marry her, Andrew is desperate. Believing that he can make the burglar plan work in reality, and not simply as a hoax, he shoots Milo. As Milo dies, however, he achieves his ultimate revenge on Andrew: As the play closes, the police do arrive.

— *Dale Davis*

SLOW HOMECOMING
(Langsame Heimkehr, Die Lehre der Sainte-Victoire, *and* Kindergeschichte)

Author: Peter Handke (1942-   )
First published: 1985
Genre: Novel

Locale: The United States, France, and Germany
Time: The 1970's and 1980's
Plot: Philosophical realism

The Long Way Around, 1979

Valentin Sorger, an Austrian geologist working in Alaska, above the Arctic Circle. He is in early middle age. His work consists of making geological sketches of the Alaskan terrain. Sorger begins to feel estranged from existence and decides to return to Austria. He flies to San Francisco and spends time with a married couple he knows. The colors and forms of

nature become the object of his meditations, and he longs to find some kind of spiritual law, an experience of salvation, that will redefine his existence. He then flies to Denver and, finally, to New York, where he engages in a long and intense conversation with a stranger. Ultimately, he takes a plane for Europe.

The Lesson of Mont-Sainte-Victoire, 1980

The narrator, a writer who wanders in the South of France to see the various scenes that had been painted by artist Paul Cézanne, especially the Mont-Sainte-Victoire. The narrator reflects on the shapes of nature and the artist's task of transforming these landscapes into the transcendent forms of art.

After a bizarre encounter with a half-crazed guard dog in a Foreign Legion camp, he realizes the extent of the hate and violence that permeate the world, and he longs even more for the existential salvation of art.

Child Story, 1981

The adult, an Austrian man, a simple parent living in Paris with his young daughter. He is in his late thirties. After the birth of his child, the parents' marriage breaks up, and the man and his daughter move to Paris. The adult constantly reflects on his relationship to his child and often tends to view her as a kind of symbol of the innocence and spontaneity that he has lost in his own life. One night, he loses his temper

and strikes the child. He feels great guilt over his act.

The child, a girl around six years old. She is an average child and must deal with the consequences of her father's move to Paris. She attends a special school and must learn to make new friends.

— *Thomas F. Barry*

SMALL CHANGES

Author: Marge Piercy (1936-)
First published: 1973
Genre: Novel

Locale: The U.S. Northeast and Cleveland, Ohio
Time: Late 1960's through early 1970's
Plot: Social

Beth Phail Walker, a high-school graduate who works as a secretary in Boston. Slight, quiet, and introverted, she is an omnivorous reader and a perceptive observer of her surroundings. Made to feel inferior by the traditional expectations of her family and husband and trapped in an early marriage with no possibility of attending college, she runs away, finds a job and room of her own, and audits classes at the Massachusetts Institute of Technology. Encounters with Miriam Berg and communal life lead to a series of "small changes." She becomes a vegetarian, forms a women's commune, gets a divorce, and works intensely in women's theater. In her liaison with its leader, Wanda Rosario, she acquires political awareness, speaks out, and discovers her sexuality and the joys of physical labor. Forming a lesbian family with Wanda brings her fulfillment.

Miriam Berg, a graduate student and researcher in computer science. She is an intelligent young Jewish woman with glossy black hair; she is full-bodied, vivacious, and outgoing. She pours her considerable energies equally into her academic studies and her stormy love relationship with Phil. Her search is for the love and support missing during her Flatbush years as a fat teenager with braces and thick glasses. The experiences of college in Wisconsin, the ordeal of her mother's slow death, and her sexual awakening with Phil and Jackson give her self-confidence and new goals. Frustrated, however, by the transitory nature of communal life and the sexism that impedes her academic life and professional work at Logical Systems Development, she finds temporary security in marriage to Neil Stone and motherhood. That role fails to satisfy her energy. Her desire to reenter the job market and maintain her ties with Phil, Beth, and friends in local communes creates tension and misunderstanding with her husband.

Phil, a Vietnam veteran, woman chaser, and would-be poet. He is extremely handsome, with blue-green eyes and an ingratiating manner especially attractive to women. He works at a series of menial jobs to support his constant use of drugs. Rejecting the alcoholic father and battered mother who scarred his Boston childhood, he finds primary support in the strong friendship forged with Jackson during their war service. He is Miriam's first lover and constant friend. Only after a jail term

does he find a vocation, as a carpenter, as well as finding a partner, Dorine.

Jackson, an older, long-haired, fringe academic, Phil's roommate and mentor. A lined, sad face characterizes the complex, sardonic loner who never mentions his cultured background and later misfortunes. Shielding himself with constant banter, he manipulates human beings as if they were pawns in his favorite game, chess. Only Miriam and Beth penetrate his reserve briefly. He is finally graduated and teaches political science at the University of Massachusetts.

Neil Stone, a director of Logical Systems Development, a small research corporation in Cambridge. He is a precise, methodical, and attractive man with traditional family values. As Miriam's husband, he encourages her role of model homemaker and pressures her to have children, but he resents her attempts at financial and social independence. At the novel's end, he seeks companionship with a lonely female colleague and considers divorce.

Wanda Rosario, a chunky, gray-haired, Italian-Polish woman in her late thirties who is married to Joe, a radical political organizer who deserts her and their two young sons. She is a hardworking, wise, and earthy woman who finds a new vocation as director of a traveling women's theater troupe and is joined by Beth, who becomes her lover. A political activist before her marriage, she is jailed for refusing to testify against former comrades. After her release, she steals her children from custody and begins a new life, disguised and fugitive, with Beth in Ohio.

Dorine, a frizzy-haired, timid girl who performs the role of maid, doormat, and bedmate for Phil and Jackson's circle of friends. Finally tiring of their ridicule and insensitivity, she moves to a women's commune. Through the support and love of her friends, she acquires respect for herself, attends graduate school, becomes a strong leader in the women's movement, and works out an equal relationship with Phil.

Jim Walker, Beth's hard-drinking and sports-loving young husband, who expects his wife to cater to his demands and uses physical force to keep her in line.

— Jo C. Searles

THE SMALL HOUSE AT ALLINGTON

Author: Anthony Trollope (1815-1882)
First published: 1864; serial form, 1862-1864
Genre: Novel

Locale: London and the fictional county Barsetshire
Time: Mid-nineteenth century
Plot: Domestic realism

Lilian (Lily) Dale, the younger daughter of widowed Mrs. Dale and niece of the squire of Allington. She falls in love with Adolphus Crosbie, and they become engaged. Adolphus asks her uncle for a dowry. Refused, he still intends to marry Lily, but later, at a house party at De Courcy Castle, he suddenly becomes engaged to the more wealthy Lady Alexandrina, whom he marries. Lily stays at home, refusing a steady suitor

whom her family wishes her to marry. She helps to arrange a match between her sister Bell and a young doctor.

Christopher Dale, the squire of Allington, a dour but well-meaning member of the country gentry. He allows his widowed sister-in-law to live rent-free in the small house at Allington. His kindness is finally appreciated when he does all he can to help Lily after she is jilted. He also tries to arrange a marriage between his heir and Lily's sister, his favorite niece. At the end, he settles money on both nieces.

Mrs. Mary Dale, the widow of Philip Dale, the squire's youngest brother. She has accepted the squire's offer of a house for the sake of her daughters. She insists that both her daughters be able to choose their husbands freely, despite pressure from the squire to have Bell marry his heir. Mrs. Dale prepares to move into a small cottage in Guestwick, a neighboring town, so as not to be dependent on the generosity of a man whose advice she will not take; however, when the squire treats Lily kindly, the family decides not to move.

Isabella (Bell) Dale, the older daughter of Mrs. Dale and the beauty of the family. She is in love with Dr. Crofts, the young Guestwick physician, who thinks himself too poor to marry her. She refuses the proposal of her wealthy cousin, Bernard Dale, and waits until Dr. Crofts finally offers her marriage.

Adolphus Crosbie, the senior clerk in the General Committee Office in Whitehall, an attractive and impetuous young man. He really loves Lily when he proposes to her at Allington, but his weak selfishness leads him into a bad marriage with Lady Alexandrina. Shortly after his marriage, he realizes his mistake and is relieved when Lady Alexandrina joins her mother in Baden-Baden.

Captain Bernard Dale, an officer in the Corps of Engineers, the nephew and heir of the squire of Allington. He is an undemonstrative young man, willing to follow his uncle's wishes in proposing to Bell Dale.

John Eames, a clerk in the Income Tax Office in London. He has always loved Lily Dale. He saves Lord De Guest, the principal local aristocrat, from a bull, an event that helps his career. He also thrashes Adolphus Crosbie in a London railway station after the jilting of Lily.

Lord De Guest, the local aristocrat who becomes John Eames's benefactor.

Lady Julia De Guest, the kind, unmarried sister of Lord De Guest. She reports the engagement of Adolphus Crosbie and Lady Alexandrina to Lily's uncle.

Dr. Crofts, the physician who becomes Lord De Guest's doctor and finally marries Bell Dale.

Mrs. Roper, a widow who runs the London boardinghouse where John Eames lives.

Amelia Roper, her daughter, who schemes unsuccessfully to marry John Eames but later marries Cradell.

Joseph Cradell, a friend of John Eames and a fellow clerk in the Income Tax Office.

Mr. Lupex, a drunken scene painter who boards at Mrs. Roper's.

Mrs. Lupex, his blowsy wife, intimately involved with Joseph Cradell.

Earl De Courcy, a misanthropic aristocrat.

Countess Rosina De Courcy, the earl's scheming wife, who gets her daughter engaged to Adolphus Crosbie.

Lady Amelia De Courcy Gagebee, the oldest De Courcy daughter.

Mortimer Gagebee, the attorney and son-in-law to the De Courcys. He succeeds in acquiring for Lady Alexandrina a settlement that is ruinous to Adolphus.

Lady Alexandrina De Courcy, a selfish beauty, the youngest daughter of the De Courcys. She marries Adolphus but leaves him after a few months.

THE SMALL ROOM

Author: May Sarton (1912-1995)
First published: 1961
Genre: Novel

Locale: A New England women's college
Time: The 1950's
Plot: Realism

Lucy Winter, a twenty-seven-year-old Harvard graduate who has recently experienced the collapse of her engagement and is beginning her first year of teaching American literature at Appleton, a small New England college for women. She is abruptly initiated into the twisting relationships of academe when she accidentally discovers indisputable plagiarism in the paper of an outstanding student who is the protégée of one of the most powerful and respected professors on campus. Confronted with issues of honesty, loyalty, pride, confusion, and commitment, Winter maintains her integrity during the ensuing arguments about the situation and grows steadily in respect from and for her colleagues and students. Simultaneously, she sharpens her awareness of teaching as a challenging profession and a demanding art.

Carryl Cope, a brilliant, indomitable scholar and professor of medieval history. Totally devoted to her profession and the college, she cares little for appearances and is passionately committed to academic excellence. After discovering the dishonesty of a student in whom she has invested countless hours and enormous energy, Cope at first hopes to cover up the incident. When it becomes clear that exposure is inevitable,

she maintains her self-respect and that of others by admitting her mistakes in pressuring the student and concentrating exclusively on cultivating the mind. In the painful resolution, Cope not only faces her own pride directly but also risks the dissolution of her intimate twenty-year friendship with Olive Hunt.

Harriet (Hallie) Summerson, a secure, honest, well-liked woman and a superb teacher of British literature. A generation older than Winter and unfailingly generous, Summerson welcomes Winter into the college community and consistently offers her valuable advice and support. In her characteristically unselfconscious way, Summerson also models for Winter, a teacher accomplished in her art.

Olive Hunt, a wealthy, influential, and generous trustee of Appleton College. Once elegant but now somewhat faded with age, she is proudly rigid in her ideas and beliefs. Convinced that people are responsible for managing their own lives independently, she violently opposes the college's hiring a resident psychiatrist and vows to withdraw her financial support if her views are dismissed. An irreparable consequence of her adamant resolve is alienation from Cope, whom she has loved for years.

Jennifer Finch, an apparently unassuming but wise professor who inserts a quiet objectivity and compassion into frequently heated discussions of campus affairs. Bound tightly to an extraordinarily dominating mother, she still maintains an inner freedom that gives her unique influence among her peers and students.

Jane Seaman, a brilliant student whose plagiarized essay on Homer's the *Iliad* is published in the college magazine. When Winter confronts her, Seaman admits that the pressures to excel academically and to fulfill the demanding expectations of Cope drove her to dishonest scholarship. Softened by Winter's genuine, loving concern, Seaman eventually agrees to see a psychiatrist for assistance in dealing with her problems.

Blake Tillotson, the president of Appleton College. He maintains an honest, intelligent, and compassionate attitude throughout debate over the plagiarism incident, despite conflicting demands, including those from Cope; from Hunt, whose financial support depends on his decisions; from students who are angered that their governing councils were ignored in handling a student's dishonesty; and from faculty members who express opposing views on both the Seaman case and the proposed mental health committee.

Jack Beveridge, an intense and seasoned professor of Romance languages whose ironic, cynical attitude masks a deep kindness and compassion. His defense of Cope and Hunt leads him to unaccustomed anger and alienates him from his wife.

Maria Beveridge, an ample, commanding, straightforward woman, the wife of Jack and mother of three young boys. Disagreements with several of her husband's views, and particularly her jealousy of Cope and Hunt, move the couple close to divorce.

Henry Atwood, a young assistant professor who is completing his dissertation on Henry Fielding. Initially naïve about the complexities of the college scene, he grows into a new sense of himself and his profession during his first semester at Appleton.

Deborah Atwood, Henry's wife, a somewhat immature young woman. She also develops as she finds her way in a new academic environment.

Pippa Brentwood, a student who especially needs encouragement and affirmation following the death of her father. She questions Winter about the plagiarism issue and tests the young teacher's developing, ambivalent convictions about the nature of teacher-student relationships.

— *Sara McAlpin*

SMALL SOULS
(De kleine zielen)

Author: Louis Couperus (1863-1923)
First published: 1901
Genre: Novel

Locale: The Hague
Time: The nineteenth century
Plot: Social

Constance van der Welcke, a daughter of the respectable van Lowe family. After several years of a loveless marriage to the respectable Dutch envoy at Rome, she has an affair with Henri van der Welcke, whom she marries after divorcing her husband. After twenty years away, she returns to Holland with her second husband, hoping that time will have healed the scars caused by the old scandal. In spite of the outward appearances of forgiveness, Constance becomes aware that she is still condemned by a society of small souls quick to criticize others while engaged, itself, in an interplay of gossip, scandal, and fear.

Henri van der Welcke, Constance van der Welcke's second husband. His political career ruined by his affair with and marriage to Constance, he returns with her to Holland and the condemnation of Dutch society.

Adriaan (Addie), Constance and Henri van der Welcke's thirteen-year-old son. Disturbed by the shreds of gossip he hears about his family, he becomes so melancholy that his

father tells him the story of the scandal of his parents' marriage. Addie accepts the truth in a mature fashion that marks the end of his childhood.

Mrs. van Lowe, Constance van der Welcke's mother.

Bertha van Voorde, Constance's socially prominent sister, through whose influence she hopes to become accepted in higher circles.

Van Naghel van Voorde, Bertha van Voorde's husband, who refuses to accept Constance and Henri van der Welcke.

Adolphine, Constance's petty and envious sister.

Jaap, Adolphine's young son, who taunts Addie about his parents.

Gerrit van Lowe,
Paul van Lowe, and
Karel van Lowe, Constance van der Welcke's brothers.
Cateau van Lowe, Karel van Lowe's wife.
Van Vreeswijck, Henri van der Welcke's friend.

SMALL WORLD: An Academic Romance

Author: David Lodge (1935-   )
First published: 1984
Genre: Novel

Locale: Primarily England and the Continent
Time: 1979
Plot: Fiction of manners

Persse McGarrigle, a poet and lecturer in English literature at Limerick University, Ireland. A "conference virgin," he is as ignorant of the structuralist and poststructuralist theories, which have come to dominate literary criticism in the twenti-

eth century, as he is of sex. At his first conference, this "hopeless romantic" falls in love with the elusive Angelica Pabst. He uses the poetry prize he wins to finance his international, conference-to-conference quest for her hand in marriage. He finally catches up with her at a mammoth meeting of the Modern Language Association (MLA) in New York. At the meeting, Persse, playing the part of grail knight, asks the question that frees the small world of academic critics from their sexual and intellectual impotence. He saves them but loses Angelica; ever hopeful, he is last seen about to set off in pursuit of yet another grail/girl, Cheryl Summerbee.

Angelica Pabst, a brilliant and beautiful graduate student, twenty-seven years old, who is the object of Persse's chaste desire. Adept in the field of contemporary literary theory, she is writing a dissertation on romance from Heliodorus to Barbara Cartland. A foundling, she has been reared by a KLM executive who has bestowed on her the gift of unlimited air travel.

Lily Papps, Angelica's twin sister. Their only distinguishing feature is birthmarks high on one thigh that, when they stand together in their bikinis, make them look as if they are inside quotation marks. Not knowing that Angelica has a twin sister, least of all one who works as a stripper and porn star, Persse mistakenly believes that the face he sees outside Soho clubs, in porn theaters, and in Amsterdam's red-light district is Angelica's. Only after he has made love to Lily (believing that she is Angelica) does Persse learn that Angelica has not only a twin but a fiancé, named Peter McGarrigle.

Philip Swallow, the head of the English department at Rummidge University and author of *Hazlitt and the Amateur Reader*. He is a recurring character in the author's work; since his initial appearance in *Changing Places* (1975), Swallow has become professionally and sexually more assertive. During one of his lecture trips, he resumes his affair with Joy Simpson, whom he believed to be dead. He loses her later as a result of his very British preoccupation with appearances. At the MLA session devoted to literary theory, Swallow is asked at the last minute to stand in for Rudyard Parkinson and represent the naïvely conventional approach.

Morris Zapp, a professor of English at Euphoric State in California. He exemplifies the new international scholar, jetting from conference to conference. His latest book is appropriately titled *Beyond Criticism*. After being kidnapped by an Italian terrorist group, which mistakenly believes that his former wife will pay ransom, he decides to give up Deconstruction (and his "Textuality as Striptease" lecture) to pursue the more domestic pleasures of life with Thelma Ringbaum, who is about to be divorced from a former colleague.

Fulvia Morgana, a professor of cultural studies at the University of Padua and, with her husband, a well-to-do supporter of Marxist radicals, including the ones who kidnap Zapp. She seduces Zapp, mistakenly confusing him with the sexual animal that his former wife, Desiree Byrd, vilifies in her best-selling book about their marriage.

Siegfried von Turpitz, a former Panzer commander and currently a German scholar specializing in reception theory.

He is caught plagiarizing Persse's unpublished dissertation and mystifying one of his perfectly normal hands by concealing it inside an enigmatic black glove.

Michel Tardieu, a homosexual professor of narratology at the Sorbonne.

Rudyard Parkinson, a South African who has turned himself into the quintessential English academic, the Oxford don, stuffy, conventional, celibate, snide, and malicious. He damns Zapp's book and praises Swallow's in a *Times Literary Supplement* review solely to promote his own name and position among the possible candidates for the newly created UNESCO chair of literary studies.

Rodney Wainwright, an instructor at the University of North Queensland whose efforts to get beyond the opening of his paper for Zapp's Future of Criticism conference in Jerusalem repeatedly fail. At the moment of truth, he is saved by an outbreak of Legionnaire's disease.

Arthur Kingfisher, the major literary theorist of his time. He has had no new ideas and no new erections in years. At novel's end, this fisher king is freed from his sterility by Persse, confers the coveted UNESCO chair of literary studies on himself, and announces his intention to marry his Korean assistant, Ji-Moon Lee. Kingfisher is also exposed as the natural father of Angelica and Lily.

Ronald Frobisher, the British novelist who has been blocked ever since, six years earlier, Robin Dempsey showed him a computer analysis of his style. He has a brief affair with Desiree Byrd.

Desiree Byrd, Zapp's former wife and author of *Difficult Days*, a book about her marriage. Currently blocked in the writing of *Men*, she has an affair with Ronald Frobisher at the Reception Theory conference in Heidelberg.

Miss Sibyl Maiden, a retired professor and former pupil of Jessie Weston. Twenty-seven years earlier, when she was forty-six, she bore Arthur Kingfisher's twin daughters, Angelica and Lily, then abandoned them in the restroom aboard a KLM airliner.

Robin Dempsey, who is demoralized professionally and sexually. He carries on a lengthy, obsessive conversation with Eliza, a computer program modeled on the psychiatric interview, never realizing that a colleague is manipulating Eliza's responses.

Cheryl Summerbee, a blonde and cheerful checker for British Air at Heathrow who livens up her job by making seat selections according to her perception of passengers' characters. She is responsible for Zapp meeting Fulvia Morgana and for Frobisher missing the MLA meeting. She loses her job but unknowingly gains Persse's love.

Peter McGarrigle, the McGarrigle with whom Angelica is in love and to whom the Limerick University thought it was offering the job that mistakenly went to Persse.

— *Robert A. Morace*

SMILEY'S PEOPLE

Author: John le Carré (David John Moore Cornwell, 1931-)
First published: 1980
Genre: Novel

Locale: England, Germany, Russia, France, and Switzerland
Time: The 1970's
Plot: Spy

George Smiley, who is known as a "case man" for British intelligence. He is called out of retirement when one of his agents, General Vladimir, is murdered. Oliver Lacon, the foreign office liaison with the intelligence service, wants Smiley to wrap up the case quickly, but the dogged Smiley scents a trail that leads directly to his arch nemesis, Karla, the head of Soviet intelligence. Twenty years earlier, Smiley had caught Karla and had tried to convince him to defect, but Karla had refused and was later sent back to the Soviet Union in a deal between the intelligence services. One by one, Smiley calls on his old contacts, braving considerable danger to penetrate to the core of Karla's spy network. A weary Smiley does so more out of loyalty to General Vladimir and others who have risked their lives for British intelligence than out of any zeal for Britain. Smiley realizes that his time is over, and he is left with considerable doubt about the value of his efforts. His personal code of integrity drives him toward a final showdown with Karla.

Peter Guillam, Smiley's right-hand man, who has to fight Smiley's rivals within the intelligence service to preserve his chief's plans. Smiley often keeps Guillam in the dark.

Connie Sachs, a dying alcoholic researcher for British intelligence. Retired and embittered, she nevertheless provides Smiley with crucial data that help him to unravel Karla's spy network.

Mostyn, a new British intelligence officer who first takes the call from General Vladimir asking for Smiley. Because Smiley has retired, Mostyn follows standard procedures, referring the case to his superior, who fails to follow up on it. As Mostyn relates the case background to Smiley, he is watched carefully by his superiors, who want Smiley to know only those details that are absolutely necessary to learn who murdered the general. Smiley, uncomfortable with Mostyn's hero worship of him, later learns that Mostyn has been sacked, his career sacrificed because he knew too much.

Oliver Lacon, a foreign service officer who makes sure that the actions of case men such as Smiley do not contradict British government policies. The British cabinet is attempting a rapprochement with the Soviet Union, and it does not wish to have any embarrassing disclosures of Soviet intelligence agents. Lacon asks Smiley to investigate the murder of General Vladimir, but Lacon's job includes ensuring that Smiley does not exceed the boundaries of his assignment.

Saul Enderby, head of the intelligence service. He respects Smiley's prowess but also wants to control his case man. He makes it clear that, if necessary, he will spy on Smiley. Enderby is most interested in protecting his power base, not in following every lead that the tenacious Smiley may turn up.

Sam Collins, Enderby's second in command, a "yes man" whom Smiley and Guillam despise and try to ignore. Collins often articulates policies that Enderby himself would not care to make explicit.

Maria Andreyevna Ostrakova, a Russian émigré living in Paris. When she is approached by a Soviet agent who demands that she become a spy, she writes to General Vladimir, setting in motion the chain of events that lead to the general's murder and Smiley's quest to find the murderers and to expose Karla.

Otto Leipzig, one of General Vladimir's agents. British intelligence distrusts him because much of the information he has passed on to the West has proved worthless. Smiley insists on searching for him because his data on Moscow Central (the headquarters of Karla's spy network) always has been reliable.

Herr Kretzschmar, Otto Leipzig's shady friend, whom Smiley convinces to help him. Through Kretzschmar, Smiley is able to piece together events that lead him to Karla.

Anton Grigoriev, a Soviet embassy official in Bern, Switzerland. He is the last link in the chain that takes Smiley to Karla. Smiley has an old intelligence hand, Toby Esterhase, kidnap Grigoriev and threaten him with exposure if he does not cooperate with the plan to smoke out Karla.

Toby Esterhase, a British intelligence agent near retirement. General Vladimir had gone to Esterhase claiming to have information that would finally destroy Karla. Esterhase distrusted this old émigré and concluded that the risk to himself and to British intelligence was too great to pursue the lead. Smiley works on Esterhase, promising him that there will be no retribution for his part in denying the general. Smiley gets Esterhase to reveal everything he knows about the general's last days. Esterhase, sensing a chance to redeem himself and to participate in the greatest intelligence coup of his time, that of capturing Karla, becomes Smiley's enthusiastic accomplice.

— *Carl Rollyson*

SMOKE
(Dym)

Author: Ivan Turgenev (1818-1883)
First published: 1867
Genre: Novel

Locale: Germany and Russia
Time: 1862-1865
Plot: Social realism

Grigóry Litvinov (grih-GOH-rihy liht-VEE-nof), a farmer's son. Wishing to farm progressively on his father's estate, he has tried to learn scientific agriculture by studying modern practices in several European regions. His plans for marriage to Tatyana and for modernizing his father's estate are interrupted by the temporary resurrection at Baden of his former love for Irina and the breaking off of his engagement to Tatyana. Observant and thoughtful, he is repelled by the impractical windiness of the group of liberals who associate with Gubaryov at Baden and likewise by the shallow, aimless, and bored existence of Irina, her husband, and their aristocratic friends. His break with Tatyana pains him because he is ashamed of casting her off so unexpectedly and hurting her so deeply. Although his passion for Irina consumes him until he is willing to give up everything for her, his pride will not let him live as one of her hangers-on. Irina's refusal to leave with him brings him such grief as he had earlier brought Tatyana, but it is combined with shame over being rejected a second time by Irina and by guilt over his treatment of Tatyana. Hard work enables him to make some progress in improving conditions on the estate that he inherits on his father's death. His abject plea for forgiveness after more than two years is accepted by the generous Tatyana, and they are married at last.

Tatyana Petrovna Shestov (tah-TYAH-nah peht-ROHV-nuh shehs-TOHF), called **Tanya** (TAH-nyuh), his fiancée, plump, blonde, heavy-faced, brown-eyed, kind, and good. Intuitively, she guesses that Irina is the cause of her rejection by Litvinov. She is shocked and hurt, but she does not attack him with angry abuse; she accepts her fate with quiet dignity and leaves Baden, the scene of her humiliation. When Litvinov later goes to her home and, kneeling, begs her to forgive him, she is at once surprised, frightened, and happy.

Kapitolina Markovna Shestov (kah-pih-toh-LIH-nuh mahr-KOHV-nuh), Tanya's maiden aunt. Talkative and completely provincial in outlook, she is both fascinated and morally shocked by the gambling and other evidences of dissolute life at Baden. Litvinov thinks her absurd but appears to respect her piteous but vain attempts to make him change his mind about breaking his engagement to Tanya.

Irina Pavlovna Osinin Ratmirov (ih-RIH-nuh PAHV-lov-nuh oh-SIH-nihn raht-MIH-rof), the oldest daughter in a family of noble ancestry but straitened circumstances. In her youth, Litvinov was infatuated with and informally engaged to Irina, a tall, slim girl with a willful, passionate nature and a cold heart. After throwing over Litvinov to live in Count Reisenbach's home, she inspired many rumors and much gossip before she married General Ratmirov. When Litvinov meets her ten years later, she has become a truly beautiful woman, and he is captivated again. Although she declares her love and means it, she is unwilling to do as Leo Tolstoy's Anna Karenina did and forsake all that she has to go with her lover; at the same time, aware of her power, she will not let him go. Litvinov is finally strong enough to compel her to make a choice. Her decision to continue the life she must have to survive brings him temporary misery but eventual freedom and salvation. Irina moves in a social world of luxury and evil yet somehow seems above and apart from that evil. Her ironical intellect stirs fear in the men and the women who know her, as if they, like her, recognize her superiority to them.

General Valerian Vladimirovitch Ratmirov (vah-leh-rih-AHN vlah-DIH-mih-ro-vihch), Irina's youthful-looking, elegant, and dandified husband, who appears unconcerned about Litvinov's visits to his wife and the time she spends with other men. As a military man, he symbolizes the combination of cruelty and aristocratic indifference to the masses that helped to bring about the Russian Revolution.

Sozont Ivanitch Potugin (soh-ZOHNT ih-VAH-nihch poh-TEW-gihn), a retired clerk who becomes Litvinov's friend; he is broad-shouldered, short-legged, curly-haired, mournful-eyed, and potato-nosed. Soft-voiced and philosophical, he enunciates the author's own views of Russia and the Russians, whom he both loves and hates. He loves the culture and civilization of the West and foresees that the Russia of the future will develop out of a borrowing from and an assimilation of Western ideas and technical advancements. A kind of errand boy used by Irina in the past, he warns Litvinov against an involvement with her.

Rostislav Bambaev (rohs-tihs-LAHF bahm-BAH-ehf), a good-natured, good-for-nothing Muscovite, flabby-nosed, soft-cheeked, greasy-haired, fat, crude, impecunious, exclamatory, and enthusiastic. When Litvinov meets him on his trip to see Tatyana, he has become a butler for the Gubaryov brothers.

Stepan Nikolaevitch Gubaryov (steh-PAHN nih-koh-LAY-eh-vihch gew-bahr-YOHF), Bambaev's friend at Baden, a nervous strider and beard-twitcher who stimulates his liberal-thinking friends but remains silent himself. A theorizer rather than a doer, when he occasionally talks he spouts dirty stories at which he guffaws.

Bindasov (bihn-DAH-sof), a surly, repulsive sponger to whom Litvinov lends money he knows will not be returned. He is killed in a tavern brawl.

Prince Pavel Vassilyevitch Osinin (PAH-vehl vahs-SIH-lyeh-vihch), Irina's father, an opportunist who willingly exploits his daughter's charms.

Count Reisenbach (RI-zehn-bahkh), a wealthy, middle-aged, and childless chamberlain, bloated, wrinkled, haughty, and evil-mouthed, who in effect buys Irina as a pretty ornament for his home. It is not clear whether she became his mistress before her marriage to General Ratmirov.

Semyon Yakovlevitch Voroshilov (seh-MYOHN YAH-kov-leh-vihch voh-roh-SHIH-lof), a good-looking, fresh-faced, and dignified follower of Gubaryov, showily sophisticated and esoteric at times and sententiously silent at others.

Matrona Semyonovna (maht-ROH-nah seh-MYOH-nov-nuh), a childless, frail, and middle-aged widow. She is a convulsively intense talker and capricious theorist.

THE SNAIL ON THE SLOPE
(Ulitka na sklone)

Authors: Arkady Strugatsky (1925-1991) and Boris Strugatsky (1933-   )
First published: 1966-1968
Genre: Novel

Locale: A forest on another planet
Time: Near future
Plot: Science fiction

Pepper, the central figure, a linguist who tries to escape the Kafkaesque bureaucracy of the Directorate and seek illumination from a distant contemplation of the primal forest that the Directorate strives to contain and destroy. Intellectually superior, he is nevertheless treated with condescending tolerance as a bumbling, naïve incompetent. He flees one nightmarish situation after another: wrestling with the illogic of a Forest Study Group bent on eradication and with the jargon-ridden nonsense of Directorate communications, encountering blindfolded men seeking a lost classified machine the sight of which is forbidden, being caught up in meaningless bureaucratic processes (such as room repairs scheduled at midnight), overhearing machines debating when they should demonstrate their dominance over humans, and finally finding himself inexplicably supplanting the old Director. Faced with the mechanistic, he feels compelled to exercise reason and to seek explanations. For him, hope lies in the human decency of "considerate" and "hospitable" people, but his peregrinations never reveal any. After a lifetime of senseless activities performed at the bequest of nonsensical directives, Pepper so accommodates himself to the system that, when he can bring change, he is trapped by a historical accumulation of absurdities that determine the course of his own directives, ones as cruel, chaotic, and meaningless as those of his much deplored predecessors. Pepper is the prototype of the intellectual who theorizes about life (the Forest) from a distance, is repulsed by closer contact with it, and is, in the end, content to be seduced by power. His "yearning for understanding" (what he calls "his sickness") is cured at the cost of his humanity.

Kandid, Pepper's counterpart, a scientist who, after ejecting from his crashing helicopter, finds himself trapped in the alien and ever changing forest among primitive villagers. Assumed to be dead by his colleagues, Kandid spends his time seeking a way back to "civilization." Kandid, like Voltaire's Candide, travels amid alien peoples and, while seeking vainly to comprehend the incomprehensible, furthers the authors' satiric purpose. Unlike Pepper, Kandid is immersed in the Forest and lives amid the chaos and disorder of nature, facing bandits and organic anomalies (faceless men, disappearing villages, mermaids and Amazonian Maidens, "Swampings," "Harrowings," and "deadlings"). Nicknamed "Dummy" by the narrow-minded villagers, who find him eccentric and slightly mad, he is later feared for his power to wield a scalpel to destroy "deadlings," odd forest creatures whose touch burns. Kandid is metaphorically too close to the trees to see the forest (he is at the other extreme from Pepper) and, consequently, suffers from a strange inability to retain ideas or to find meaningful patterns or relationships. With heart and head in conflict, Kandid refuses to succumb to his situation. His conclusions that annihilating populations for the sake of some nebulous theory about progress is wrong, that nature may be outside the concepts of good and bad but that humans are not, and that one must look at the Authority and the Forest both

"from the side" seem to voice the authors' views.

Nava, Kandid's chattering, clinging child-wife, who pressures him to accept the monotonous "vegetable way of life" of her village and who complains of the dangers inherent in escape. Her mother, kidnapped by "deadlings," has become one of the matriarchal Maidens, whose generative power is responsible for the peculiarities of the Forest. Although she saves Kandid's life, clearly Nava will join the Maidens as a parthenogenetic power, a regenerative and reproductive force methodically directing the burgeoning growth and change of the Forest in its progress toward a future clear to the Maidens but not to others.

Claudius-Octavian Hausbotcher, the quintessential bureaucrat, ignorant and narrow-minded. With dark, piercing eyes and a long, stony face, Hausbotcher records deviant statements and actions and is obsessed with paperwork, permits, and regulations. He meets chaos with regimen, dismisses the unfamiliar as mysticism, and supports the party line as inviolate. He intimidates subordinates and toadies up to superiors.

Acey, a sexually obsessed Directorate driver convicted of passport violations and theft, a Neanderthal who guzzles yogurt and speculates on the peculiar characteristics of the Forest. He has a darkly handsome, Italianate face, with bushy eyebrows, lively eyes, and flashing teeth. His feet smell, and his narrations focus on sexual exploits. His hairy arms are tattooed with the phrases "What destroys us" and "Ever onward," cryptic comments on Directorate goals. As Pepper's driver, Acey provides a sense of how much Pepper has capitulated to power when Pepper regrets not being able to castrate him for his own good.

Alevtina, a photo lab worker determined to become Pepper's mistress, despite his aversion to sex. She helps Pepper take over as Director and becomes the guiding power behind the scenes, suggesting the direction his orders should take, theorizing about the historical continuity of bureaucratic power, and praising his new measures (such as orders to the Eradication Group to self-eradicate).

— *Gina Macdonald*

THE SNAKE PIT
(Olav Audunssøn i Hestviken *and* Olav Audunssøn og hans børn)

Author: Sigrid Undset (1882-1949)
First published: 1925-1927
Genre: Novel

Locale: Norway
Time: Late thirteenth and early fourteenth centuries
Plot: Historical

Olav Audunsson, the master of Hestviken. Now married to Ingunn and returned, for the first time since the age of seven, to his home of Hestviken, he finds that the concealing of his murder of Ingunn's lover Teit, which is necessary to protect Ingunn from shame, becomes increasingly burdensome. After her death, Olav must still keep her reputation spotless for the sake of his daughter.

Ingunn Steinfinnsdatter, Olav's wife, once beautiful but now frail and sickly. After she has four stillborn children, Olav brings to Hestviken from a foster home her son Eirik, whom he claims as his. Olav regrets the decision when Ingunn gives birth to a boy, Audun, now defrauded of his birthright. Audun is sickly and lives only a short time. Ingunn

herself dies after giving birth to another child, a daughter.

Eirik, Ingunn's son by Teit. At first fond of his supposed father Olav, Eirik comes to dislike him after Olav's manner becomes harsh and aloof.

Cecilia Olavsdatter, the daughter of Olav and Ingunn.

Audun Olavsson, the short-lived son of Olav and Ingunn.

Torhild Björnsdatter, the housekeeper at Hestviken. After she bears Olav's son, Olav gives her a farm for her own.

Björn, the illegitimate son of Torhild and Olav.

Olav Half-Priest, an aged kinsman of Olav Audunsson. Hestviken deteriorated somewhat under his stewardship during the years before Olav Audunsson's return.

Tora, Ingunn's sister, now widowed.

Jon Steinfinnsson, Ingunn's brother. After his death, Olav goes north to collect Ingunn's share of Jon's goods. Olav brings Eirik back to Hestviken on his return.

Arnvid Finnsson, an old friend of Olav and Ingunn. He is about to enter the order of the Preaching Friars. Olav unburdens his guilt to Arnvid, who can say little to comfort his friend.

SNOOTY BARONET

Author: Wyndham Lewis (1882-1957)
First published: 1932
Genre: Novel

Locale: New York, London, Provence, and Persia
Time: c. 1930
Plot: Social satire

Sir Michael Kell-Imrie (known as **Snooty** or **Snoots**), the author-narrator, who is almost forty years old. Although he is poor, he is the seventeenth baronet of his Scottish family. He was wounded five times during World War I. His artificial leg is removed by his mistress before they have sex; afterward, he suffers illness resulting from head wounds. A writer of scientific books about behaviorism, he is celebrated most for his fictional skills. He developed his interest in animals after catching a huge fish and reading *Moby Dick*. Persuaded to pretend to be captured by a Persian bandit while researching Mithra religious cults, he reads D. H. Lawrence's work on animal worship. Although he despises Persia, he cooperates with Humph, allowing Val to pay his passage and accompany him; finally, he shoots Humph to death for pleasure, abandons Val to smallpox, and finds solace in the arms of a Persian harem girl on the Bosphorus.

Captain Humphrey (Humph) Cooper Carter, Snooty's literary agent in London. He has a big head, a large chin, and short legs. He met Snooty in the Scots Guards during World War I. He held a desk job for most of the war, while Snooty was in the trenches. He concocts the scheme for Snooty to be kidnapped by a Persian bandit to extract ransom money and attract publicity. He is shot and killed by Snooty during the rendezvous with Mirza Aga's bandits.

Mrs. Valerie (Val) Ritter, Snooty's first girlfriend, whom he visits in Chelsea as soon as he returns to London from America. She is between thirty and forty years old and already has a double chin, thinning hair, and pocked skin. She has the annoying habit of giggling constantly, but she knows how to please Snooty in bed. She writes pornographic novels that are never published, and she pays for Snooty's passage to Persia so that she can accompany him and Humph. Although she dislikes Humph, she is appalled when she sees Snooty shoot him, and she tries unsuccessfully to blackmail Snooty into marrying her. When she contracts smallpox while a guest of Mirza Aga, she is abandoned by Snooty. She recovers and sends him a telegram of indignation.

Lily Tayle, Snooty's second girlfriend. She works at a tobacco kiosk at Victoria Station, London. She is two months past her twenty-fourth birthday. She does not know that Snooty is a baronet until she reads it in the gossip columns of newspapers while he is in America. She writes him letters while he is in Persia.

Rob McPhail, a poet and a close friend of Snooty. He has lived for four years with his wife and children on the French coast near Marseilles, at Faujas de Saint Riom, where he fishes and sometimes fights bulls. He was born in China, where his father was employed by the Chinese government. A tall man dressed in white, he drinks heavily. After he tells Snooty that he will go to Persia with him, Rob is killed by a bull during the prefight sticking ceremony.

Pat Bostock, a source of information about Persia. He causes Humph to think of the kidnapping caper.

Mirza Aga, the Persian bandit contracted to kidnap Snooty for ransom. He speaks perfect English with a Chicago accent. When he discovers that Snooty shot Humph, he thinks it was done so that Snooty would not have to share the ransom. He orders his men to kill all the muleteers and guides who accompanied Snooty, Humph, and Val. Acting as host to Snooty and Val, he waits in vain for the ransom but escorts Snooty back to civilization, while Val lingers with smallpox.

Ali Akbar, the leader of the Persian muleteers who carry Snooty, Humph, and Val to the point of the kidnapping. He is impressed with Snooty's skill with a rifle and is indignant when he sees Snooty shoot Humph. He and his men are slaughtered by Mirza Aga's bandits.

Mortimer, who pays rent for Val's Chelsea rooms.

Mr. Willis, a forty-one-year-old tobacconist whom Lily introduces to Snooty as her uncle.

Vieuxchange (vyew-CHAHNZH), Rob McPhail's brother-in-law and fishing partner. He is a big, leonine former marine who leaps with Rob into the bullfighting arena to stick the bulls.

Laura McPhail, Rob's wife. She has black-violet eyes and talks to Snooty of her Communist brother in Leningrad.

Juanito, the Spanish manager/owner of the bullfight at Faujas de Saint Riom. He dresses as Charlie Chaplin for prefight entertainment.

Shushani (shew-SHAH-nee), Snooty's Persian harem girl, who helps him hide from Humph and stays with him at the Bosphorus.

Kafi, a Persian harem girl. Her name means "enough."

Hasan, a Persian muleteer who sneezes at Humph to frighten him.

— *Richard D. McGhee*

SNOW-BOUND: A Winter Idyl

Author: John Greenleaf Whittier (1807-1892)
First published: 1866
Genre: Poetry

Locale: Haverhill, Massachusetts
Time: Early nineteenth century
Plot: Idyll

The Poet, who remembers a great snowfall of his boyhood, with all its beauty and attendant pleasures.

Our Father, the poet's father, a man of action. To the snow-bound group collected around the fire, he tells stories of adventures with Indians, of fishing trips, and of witches reputed to have inhabited the land long ago.

Our Mother, who, while turning her wheel, tells of Indian raids, of her happy girlhood, and of stories read in books by famous and revered Quakers.

Our Uncle, who is innocent of books. He shares his knowledge of nature: moons and tides, weather signs, and birds and beasts.

Our Dear Aunt, a selfless unmarried woman of simple faith.

The Elder Sister, who is impulsive, generous, truthful, and sternly just.

The Youngest Sister, the dearest, a sweet and loving girl.

Brother, the only one of the happy group, besides the poet, now living.

The Schoolmaster, a boarder in the Whittier home. A poor man's son, he learned independence as a boy. Seemingly carefree and boyish, he is an earnest shaper of youthful minds. The cause of freedom should have many young apostles like him.

Another Guest (**Harriet Livermore**), a strange, half-feared, half-welcome woman, violent of temper, eccentric, cultured, and intense. Later, she will go to Europe and the Near East, prophesying the imminent second coming of Christ.

SNOW COUNTRY
(Yukiguni)

Author: Yasunari Kawabata (1899-1972)
First published: 1947; serial form, 1935-1937
Genre: Novel

Locale: A hot-spring resort in Niigata Prefecture, Japan
Time: Mid-1930's
Plot: Psychological realism

Shimamura, an idle man from Tokyo, perhaps in early middle age, who makes a series of visits to a village in Japan's "snow country." There, he takes advantage of the hot springs and breathtaking scenery. He also strikes up an ambiguously spiritual and sensual relationship with Komako, a young apprentice geisha. Married with children, Shimamura is unable to make a lifetime commitment to Komako. More to the point, he is unable to invest himself emotionally in their affair, such as it is, or, it seems, in any aspect of his life. An amateur writer on classical Western dance, which he experiences only through books, Shimamura notes the "wasted effort" of Komako's life but seems unaware of his own emptiness until the novel's final scene.

Komako, a young geisha with whom Shimamura has a relationship stretching over several years. Komako begins the novel as something less than a full geisha, though in ways she seems older than her years. By the novel's end, the example of another geisha has been used to suggest that Komako will age quickly in her role as a professional entertainer of men. In addition, Komako's personality undergoes change. She becomes cynical and acutely sensitive. Komako's life has been sad. She is forced by financial necessity to give up her interest in dance and work as a geisha. Aside from Shimamura, she has no lover for whom she feels deeply. In addition, a man to whom she may have been engaged becomes ill and dies

young. These difficulties never kill Komako's spirit. She faithfully keeps her diary and hones her musical skills. She also has a tendency to drink too much sake and is often confused in her feelings, particularly regarding Shimamura.

Yukio, the son of Komako's music teacher, rumored to have been Komako's fiancé (a rumor she vehemently denies). Yukio returns to the village to die. As he is about to expire, he calls for Komako to be at his side. Komako is seeing Shimamura off at the train station and refuses to return when Yukio's request is brought to her, even though Shimamura urges her to be at the dying man's side. Yukio dies before Komako's return.

Yoko, Yukio's nurse and Komako's friend. Yoko is much younger and more innocent than Komako. She remains devoted to Yukio until his death. Afterward, she spends considerable time mourning at his grave. Shimamura is captivated by Yoko's voice and her apparent purity. Yoko is considering a trip to Tokyo so that she might be trained as a geisha. Komako refuses to answer Shimamura's questions about Yoko, and relations between the two women become strained after Yukio's death. In the final scene, Yoko dies in a fire. Komako rushes forward to carry her lifeless body from the ruins. This display of naked passion brings Shimamura face to face with his own emptiness.

— *Ira Smolensky*

THE SNOW WAS BLACK
(La Neige était sale)

Author: Georges Simenon (1903-1989)
First published: 1948
Genre: Novel

Locale: An unnamed Central European city
Time: 1940-1945
Plot: Psychological realism

Frank Friedmaier, an idler, robber, and killer. The son of a former prostitute (now a madam) and of an unknown father, Friedmaier is short and boyish. He is nineteen years old when the story begins. His outward lack of emotion, disconcerting to others and terrifying to his mother, conceals an intense desire

to find a stable place in the chaos of Nazi-occupied Europe. Although he craves attention, he despises those who demonstrate affection for him. He bullies his mother, who fears him, even while he lives off of her earnings; he is contemptuous of the source of his money, of his mother's pliable morality, and of himself for taking advantage of both. He kills a woman who had befriended him in his childhood; he assaults Sissy Holst, who adores him; and he loathes the prostitutes who satisfy his physical needs. Imitating his wealthy and obviously criminal friend, Fred Kromer, Friedmaier decides on murder as a method of self-assertion. Even as he kills, he realizes that what he is really trying to do is attract the attention of his respectable neighbor, Gerhardt Holst, who is, for Friedmaier, a father figure. In prison, Friedmaier finally finds the structured life he craves. When Holst and Sissy visit him, the former treats him with paternal affection despite his abuse of Sissy, and Sissy, despite his cruel tests of her, asserts her lasting love. Now fulfilled, Friedmaier is ready to die; he confesses his two murders and is shot.

Lotte Friedmaier, Frank's mother, a former prostitute, now a madam. A blowsy, reddish-blonde, overweight woman with a youthful face, Lotte runs a manicure parlor on the third floor of a boardinghouse; it actually is a brothel. She hires young girls, trains them to wait on her, and fires them rapidly, to be replaced by new excitements for jaded appetites. Her job provides the luxuries that others lack during the German occupation. Well fed, warm, and amply clothed, Lotte and Frank are hated by most of their neighbors except for the Holsts.

Gerhardt Holst, a former art critic forced under the occupation to be a streetcar conductor. Despite his quiet, colorless appearance, Holst possesses unmistakable integrity. Although he is thin, weak, and prematurely aged from hunger and cold, he neither hates Lotte and Frank nor envies them their comforts, although he lives across the hall from them and can smell them cooking food. After Friedmaier and Kromer assault his daughter, Sissy, Holst gives up his job to do bookkeeping at home and to nurse his daughter. Aware of Sissy's love for Friedmaier, he takes the girl to visit Friedmaier in prison, where Holst admits that Friedmaier reminds him of his own lost son, who was first a thief and later a suicide.

Sissy Holst, the sixteen-year-old daughter of Gerhardt Holst. She adores Friedmaier despite his clear contempt for her efforts to attract him. She senses, or Friedmaier fears she does, the unhappiness he is unwilling to admit to anyone. As a result of her childish flirtatiousness, she is sexually assaulted by Kromer, with Friedmaier's help. After this attack, she falls seriously ill but does not renounce her love for Friedmaier. When she visits him in prison, she voices this love, with her father's consent.

Annie Loeb, an elegant prostitute. As lazy and insolent as Friedmaier himself is, Annie attracts him by the way she refuses to do Lotte's housework. She demands service and reads and smokes her days away. Unknown to Friedmaier, she is waiting for death. The daughter of a captured Resistance worker, she is serving as a prostitute to spy on German officers.

Fred Kromer, a twenty-two-year-old drug dealer, bull-like in his corrupt sensuality. Boasting a fur-lined coat and expensive cigars, Kromer is Friedmaier's pipeline to occupation forces. Kromer enjoys pursuing the young, hungry, miserable girls made vulnerable by the occupation and thus is attracted by Sissy and cooperates in Friedmaier's desire to contaminate her innocence.

The "Old Gentleman," a professorial man in glasses who smokes constantly, carefully rolling his own cigarettes. Another father figure to Friedmaier, although he represents the occupying forces, he questions Friedmaier repeatedly in prison, moving him toward the confession and death that are precipitated by Holst and Sissy's visit.

— *Betty Richardson*

SO BIG

Author: Edna Ferber (1885-1968)
First published: 1924
Genre: Novel

Locale: Illinois
Time: Early twentieth century
Plot: Social realism

Selina Peake DeJong, a female schoolteacher turned truck farmer outside Chicago. To support herself after her gambler father is murdered, nineteen-year-old Selina accepts a teaching job in the Dutch community of High Prairie. Her exclamation that the fields of cabbages are beautiful elicits guffaws from the pragmatic, work-worn Dutch, but her ability to seek and find beauty in the most unlikely of circumstances pervades her entire life, bringing zest and adventure to her and success to the dilapidated farm she inherits from her husband. Becoming physically scarred by the backbreaking farm work does not eradicate Selina's fun-loving spirit, indomitable courage, and shrewd ability to judge character and values. Even as an old woman, her son Dirk's secretary claims, she has an air about her that is better than style. Although she loves Dirk above all else, she considers herself a failure because he has compromised his desire to become an architect for more immediate financial success as a banker. She is not despondent over the partial blame she accepts for her son's choices. She receives joy from life on the farm itself and from the work of a former student, Roelf Pool, an artist and son of the first family with whom she lived. She experiences life as "velvet," the legacy her father gave her by encouraging her to live life richly whether it brought good or bad.

Dirk "So Big" DeJong, nicknamed as a baby, the son of Pervus and Selina DeJong. He is intelligent, charming, and appreciative of those around him. Unlike his mother, however, whose character never wavers, Dirk makes choices within relatively easy circumstances that determine who he will become. He leaves the new university in Chicago, where he had given up a natural friendship with a farm girl for fraternity life, to study architecture at Cornell because he despises the buildings the newly moneyed were able to build. When he cannot make a living at his new trade shortly before World War I, he turns to selling bonds and adopts the lifestyle of the rich, which he had formerly questioned. Later, unable to give up his habits, he will not return to architecture. It is then that his mother can argue that he has sold the love of beauty that he had inherited from her for a mess of pottage-success measured only by money. He must also settle for a liaison with the fabulously wealthy married daughter of his mother's old friend instead of the love he would have preferred, that of Dallas O'Mara, an artist who is much like his mother. His choices stunt his life to only "so big."

Pervus DeJong, a kindly but ineffective Dutch farmer who marries Selina. He buys the beautifully arranged but scanty boxed supper that Selina prepared for an auction, paying an exorbitant ten dollars he cannot afford. Pervus then asks Selina to teach him to read and figure. His is the least successful farm in the community, but even so Selina falls in love with the gentle giant. He refuses to initiate any of the farming changes she suggests, however, and in his own stubborn way persists in doing things as they had always been done, hastening his death from pneumonia.

Paula Arnold Storm, the granddaughter of a meatpacking magnate, August Hemple; daughter of Selina's schoolfriend, Julie; and wife of a Chicago businessman far older than she. She also is in love with Dirk. Paula knows Dirk from their teenage days, but when it looks like he will only be a struggling architect, unable to give her the lifestyle she craves, she marries an extremely wealthy man instead. Later, she controls Dirk's financial career by possessive manipulation. She is a slim, dark, vivacious, slinky socialite. Her unhappiness is betrayed by her hot, nervous, twisty hands. She is a natural contrast both to Selina and to Dallas O'Mara, the artist with whom Dirk falls in love to no avail.

— *Barbara J. Hampton*

SO FAR FROM GOD

Author: Ana Castillo (1953-)
First published: 1993
Genre: Novel

Locale: Tome, New Mexico
Time: The last two decades of the twentieth century
Plot: Farce

Sofía (soh-FEE-ah), the protagonist, the mother of four daughters. She was born into an old and respected family in New Mexico that was heir to Spanish land grants. Sofía elopes at the age of eighteen with Domingo, a handsome young gambler. She gives birth to four daughters at three-year intervals, is abandoned by her husband (after she asks him to leave), and supports her family in her rural home by butchering pigs and lambs to sell at her "Carne Buena Carniceria" (Good Meat Butcher Shop). At the age of fifty-three, she becomes the titular mayor of Tome by developing and organizing sheep and cattle cooperatives to improve the economic condition of the town's people. She survives all four of her daughters.

Esperanza (ehs-pehr-AHN-sah), Sofía's eldest daughter. A radical Chicana activist during her college years, she earns a master's degree in communications and becomes a TV news journalist.

Caridad (kah-ree-DAHD), Sofía's second daughter. The beauty of the family, she marries her high school sweetheart, but his infidelity moves her to leave him shortly after the wedding. She drowns her sorrow in alcohol and men until her nightly bar adventures are cut short by a savage attack that leaves her mutilated and near death. After a miraculous recovery, she becomes clairvoyant and an apprentice *curandera* (medicine woman) to Doña Felicia, an older healer woman.

Fe (fay), Sofía's third daughter, a methodical, hardworking and reliable bank clerk. Her ambition is to marry her boyfriend and buy a house. When he jilts her shortly before their planned wedding, she suffers a nervous breakdown that results in her emitting a continuous scream that does not stop for a year. Fe

subsequently marries her cousin and becomes a well-paid factory employee working with deadly chemicals. She dies from exposure to chemicals.

La Loca (LOH-kah), Sofía's fourth daughter; her name means "the crazy one." At the age of three, La Loca appears to die from convulsions, but at her burial she apparently "resurrects." Repelled by people and human touch, she lives surrounded by animals. She possesses extraordinary (and sometimes miraculous) powers, including foresight.

Domingo (doh-MEEN-goh), Sofía's errant husband. A charming, handsome man and a confirmed gambler, he leaves his wife and daughters and later returns to them after many years of absence. He gambles away the family's remaining land and their house. Sofía divorces him.

Doña Felicia (DOHN-yah feh-LEE-see-ah), Caridad's ancient, eccentric landlady and mentor. She is instrumental in helping Caridad learn to recognize, accept, and use her healing gifts.

Francisco el Penitente (frahn-SEES-koh ehl peh-nee-TEHN-teh), Doña Felicia's godson. His obsession with Caridad leads to her death. He later takes his own life.

Ruben (REW-behn), Esperanza's activist boyfriend. Afraid to commit to a relationship with her, only after her death does he finally admit that he loved her.

Esmeralda (ehs-meh-RAHL-dah), a mysterious woman who becomes romantically involved with Caridad. Their relationship leads to Esmeralda's abduction and rape by the obsessed Francisco.

— *Irene Campos Carr*

SO RED THE ROSE

Author: Stark Young (1881-1963)
First published: 1934
Genre: Novel

Locale: Mississippi
Time: 1860-1865
Plot: Historical

Malcolm Bedford, the owner of Portobello plantation in Mississippi. He becomes a Southern patriot during the Civil War and falls ill of dysentery while serving at Vicksburg. He

returns home to die, prophesying that the fall of Vicksburg dooms the Confederate cause.

Sarah Tait Bedford, Malcolm's second wife, who is the

gracious hostess and mistress of Portobello plantation. After the war, she succeeds in keeping it for the family and making it successful.

Duncan Bedford, the oldest of Malcolm's children, a student at Washington College. He enlists in the Confederate cause and fights valiantly until captured. He returns home after the war to work with Mrs. Bedford in reclaiming the family plantation. He long loves Valette, a girl adopted by the Bedfords, and eventually marries her.

Hugh McGehee, the owner of the Montrose plantation and a neighbor of the Bedfords.

Agnes McGehee, the wife of Hugh and a sister of Malcolm Bedford.

Edward McGehee, the oldest son of Hugh and Agnes. He enlists in the Confederate army and is killed in the battle at Pittsburg Landing.

Shelton Taliaferro, a distant relative of the McGehees.

Charles Taliaferro, Shelton's son. He becomes a great friend of Edward McGehee during visits at Montrose. Like his friend, Charles is killed at Pittsburg Landing.

Lucinda (Lucy) McGehee, the daughter of Hugh and Agnes. She falls in love with Charles Taliaferro, who does not pay any attention to her, and is heartbroken at her beloved's death.

Zach McGehee, Hugh's nephew.

Amelie Balfour, Zach's fiancée. She persuades Valette Bedford to marry Duncan Bedford, her foster brother.

Valette Bedford, a coquettish girl loved by Duncan Bedford. After some misunderstandings, they are married, following the Civil War.

Mary Hartwell and
Frances Bedford, younger children of Malcolm.

Middleton Bedford, the orphaned nephew of Malcolm.

SOHRAB AND RUSTUM

Author: Matthew Arnold (1822-1888)
First published: 1853
Genre: Poetry

Locale: Western Asia, on the banks of the Oxus River
Time: Antiquity
Plot: Historical

Sohrab (SOH-rahb), the champion of the Tartar army. Little more than a boy but the mightiest warrior of the Tartar hosts, Sohrab, restless and dissatisfied, seeks Rustum, a Persian, the father he has never seen. Hoping that his fame will reach his father's ears, he asks Peran-Wisa to challenge the Persians to a single combat, with each side choosing a champion for the duel. Sohrab, the Tartar, faces Rustum, the Persian, on the field of battle, and Sohrab is transfixed by Rustum's spear. Before Sohrab dies, father and son become known to each other.

Rustum (REWS-tuhm), a Persian chieftain and champion of the Persian army. Meeting the challenge of the Tartars for a

duel between a chosen warrior from each side, Rustum, unknowingly, faces his son, Sohrab. He transfixes and mortally wounds the youthful champion with his spear. As the victim's life ebbs away, Rustum learns the identity of his son. In an agony of grief and remorse, he promises to bear Sohrab's body to the palace of his fathers.

Peran-Wisa, the commander of the Tartar army.

Ferood, the leader of the Persians.

Gudurz, a Persian chieftain.

Zal, Sohrab's grandfather.

SOLARIS

Author: Stanisław Lem (1921-   )
First published: 1961
Genre: Novel

Locale: A space station above the planet Solaris
Time: The distant future
Plot: Science fiction

Kris Kelvin, a scientist in his early thirties who has just arrived at the Solaris station. Kelvin descends from space to find that the experimental work station he has reached is in chaos. He feels fearful and disoriented when he discovers that his former teacher, Gibarian, has just committed suicide and that the station's two other scientists appear to be insane: Snow and Sartorius often hide in their rooms and speak in a cryptic and paranoid fashion. After waking from a much-needed sleep, Kelvin finds himself confronted with the reincarnation of his girlfriend, Rheya, who committed suicide ten years earlier, after he had left her. Although he is repulsed by this replica of a past love, he also appreciates the opportunity to expiate his guilt over her death and continue, if only in a sham, the experience of their relationship. As he talks to the other scientists, reads books in the station's library, and performs experiments, he gradually comes to understand that she is a projection of his own memories created by the planetary entity he has come to study. When she dissolves at the novel's end,

he is left with the desire to get her back again but has little hope that this will occur.

Solaris, the protoplasmic creature that covers the planet of the same name. For more than a hundred years, Earth missions have attempted to understand this multibillion-ton gelatinous oceanic entity. Although the myriad shapes that form on this global creature suggest sentience, no previous attempts at communication have been successful. Hundreds of theories have attempted to account for this blob, but each is flawed. At the time of the story, an illegal dose of X rays has caused the mass to express itself in a new way. Reaching into the minds of the station's occupants, it has created, out of neutrinos, perfect replicas of remembered or imagined people. Although these models, called phi-creatures, are palpable, they are no more intelligible to the crew than any other phenomenon exhibited by Solaris. Although Solaris' human simulacra are destroyed at the story's end, neither they nor the planet itself is understood.

Rheya, the most important of the phi-creatures. Rheya is an almost perfect duplicate of Kris's girlfriend, who was nineteen years old when she committed suicide ten years before the time of the novel. She has no self-consciousness of her own artificiality and differs mentally from the original woman only in her knowledge of some facts she should not know and in an undeniable compulsion to stay in Kris's proximity. Physically, she is exactly the same, except at the subatomic level: Because she is composed of neutrinos, she heals rapidly. As she gradually comes to understand that she is not who she thinks she is, she, like the original, attempts suicide. This effort fails, but with the help of two other scientists, she is able to dissolve herself and leave a suicide note that unintentionally parodies that of the original.

Snow, called **Ratface**, a cybernetics expert and Gibarian's deputy. Drunk and half mad from his recent experiences on Solaris, Snow tries to help Kelvin understand the situation without appearing to be crazy. His mental struggles have left him haggard, gray, and sunken. He is reticent and only semifunctional. He understands the situation to some degree and aids Kelvin.

Sartorius, the most reclusive and yet insistently professional scientist at the station. Tall, thin, and distracted, Sartorius attempts, despite his own phi-creature, to maintain the scientific method. It is largely through his efforts that the scientists attempt direct communication with Solaris, and it is he who develops the antineutrino device that dissolves the replicas, including Rheya.

Gibarian, Kelvin's former teacher. At the story's start, Gibarian has just committed suicide because of his inability to deal with the Solaris projections. He is still active in the narrative, however, through Kelvin's memories, through his publications, and, finally, in an embodiment that may be a dream or another phi-creature.

— Daniel D. Fineman

A SOLDIER OF THE GREAT WAR

Author: Mark Helprin (1947-)
First published: 1991
Genre: Novel

Locale: Rome, Bologna, and the Appenines, in Italy
Time: Early 1900's to August, 1964
Plot: Bildungsroman

Alessandro Guiliani (ah-leh-SAHN-droh gwee-lee-AH-nee), a professor of aesthetics in Rome, Italy. At the age of seventy-four, he travels to Monte Prato, seventy kilometers from Rome. He meets Nicolo Sambucca and recounts his life during World War I. His experiences show him to be a man of unfaltering resolve, individuality, and honesty. As the son of an attorney, he acquires his father's sense of justice. He attends university in Bologna, studying aesthetics and protesting Italian involvement in the Turkish War. In 1914, he enlists in the navy despite his father's discouragement. His tour of duty begins in the Nineteenth River Guard, stationed on the border between Austria and Italy. Alessandro and his friend Guariglia barely escape death after Austrian advances; they are both reassigned to a covert unit ordered to capture deserters in Sicily. Understanding the deserters' motivations, he leaves his post and journeys back to Rome. He returns to an ailing father and the reality of his mother's recent death. Although he fears arrest, he remains at his father's bedside until apprehended by Italian troops and taken to Stella Maris. During his imprisonment, his father dies. A firing squad executes Alessandro's comrades from the River Guard, but he escapes this fate through an unexplained reprieve. He begins to recognize his remarkable ability to sidestep death and his inability to save the individuals he loves. After his imprisonment, he is sent to the front lines. As Alessandro recovers from an arm wound, he falls in love with his nurse, Ariane. Austrians bomb the clinic, and his fear that she has died steals his passion for life. Although he accepts dangerous assignments, he survives. Eventually, he is captured by Austrian soldiers; he travels to Vienna as a prisoner of war. Overwhelmed by his desire to return to Rome, Alessandro escapes before his official release. He believes that Ariane might be alive and begins a diligent search. He is reunited with her and his son one year later. Sharing these memories with Nicolo comforts Alessandro and enables him to accept his own death.

Alessandro's father, an attorney in Rome. He believes in truth, the rewards of hard work, and the importance of the family. He also advocates calculated risk-taking and sells the family garden in order to buy a plot of land in Rome that he predicts will later benefit his children. He tries to dissuade his son from joining the navy but realizes that Alessandro must live beyond his father's wishes. He suffers through reports of Alessandro's death but believes that he lives. As the older Guiliani dies, Alessandro returns to his bedside, and belief becomes truth.

Nicolo Sambucca (nee-KOH-loh sahm-BEW-kah), a young worker at a propeller-making factory in Rome. He misses his train to Sant'Angelo and runs doggedly after it. The train stops, but he is denied entrance, and Alessandro leaves the compartment in protest. Nicolo walks the sixty kilometers to visit his sister, enjoying the old man's company. When Alessandro reaches the end of his account, Nicolo realizes that he has passed his destination. Although reluctant to leave Alessandro, he agrees to do so, taking with him the concrete memories of his companion's loves and losses.

Orfeo Quatta, (ohr-FEH-oh KWAHT-tah), an old, misshapen scribe who works for the attorney Guiliani until the introduction of the typewriter. Unable to stomach subordination to a machine, he leaves the attorney's employment, becoming a scribe for the ministry of war. Embittered by powerlessness, Orfeo manipulates transcribed military orders. His changes protect Alessandro in certain instances. Eventually, he succumbs to eccentricities and dies in an explosion of his own making.

Guariglia (gwah-REE-lyee-ah), a Roman harness maker and soldier in the Nineteenth River Guard. Fellow soldiers name him the toughest among them, but that toughness is tempered by his devotion to his children. He survives the River Guard massacre and is reassigned to a unit bound for Sicily. When separation from his family becomes overwhelming, he deserts his post. Italian troops arrest him soon afterward, sending him to Stella Maris for execution.

Ariane, the daughter of an Italian doctor and a French woman. She becomes a nurse at the Greunsee Clinic and treats the wounded Alessandro. They fall in love and conceive a child. Austrians bomb the clinic, and Ariane believes that Alessandro is dead. She returns to Rome, where she is reunited with Alessandro three years later.

Luciana Guiliani (lew-CHEE-ah-nah), Alessandro's sister. As a young woman, she falls in love with her brother's univer-sity friend, Rafi Foa. She comforts both her dying father and Alessandro, as he awaits execution. After she believes that she has lost her entire family, she immigrates to America.

Rafi Foa (RAH-fee FOH-ah), a Jewish law student in Bologna when he befriends Alessandro. He falls in love with Luciana, although her youth prevents their marriage. Rafi joins the war effort and perishes on the front lines as Alessandro struggles to save him.

— *Elizabeth Vander Meer*

THE SOLDIER'S FORTUNE

Author: Thomas Otway (1652-1685)
First published: 1681
Genre: Drama

Locale: London, England
Time: c. 1680
Plot: Comedy

Captain Beaugard, a military officer. Returning from a campaign, he is approached, through the offices of Sir Jolly Jumble, by Lady Dunce, who claims to have been in love with him long before he went off to the wars. A meeting with the lady reveals her as his old love, Clarinda, now married to the elderly and distasteful Sir Davy Dunce. There follows a series of machinations designed to blackmail Sir Davy into acknowl-edging Captain Beaugard as his wife's lover.

Lady Dunce (**Clarinda**), Captain Beaugard's beloved. De-spairing of her lover's return from the wars, she marries the wealthy but unattractive and elderly Sir Davy Dunce. When the captain does return, she finds herself still in love with him. She and the captain engage in a series of ruses designed to fool her husband into being cuckolded and finally forced to ac-knowledge his wife as the captain's mistress.

Sir Davy Dunce, Lady Dunce's cuckolded husband. Jeal-ous and thick-witted, he is used by his wife in the furtherance of her affair with Captain Beaugard. Manipulated into becom-ing a party to a conspiracy to assassinate the captain, he is forced, to escape the extreme penalty for attempted murder, to acknowledge his wife as Beaugard's mistress and free her from his unwanted attentions.

Courtine, Captain Beaugard's companion-in-arms, who wins and marries Sylvia.

Sylvia, Sir Davy and Lady Dunce's niece, who rejects the idea of matrimony because of her observations of her aunt and uncle. She is finally prevailed upon to marry Courtine.

Sir Jolly Jumble, an elderly rake and the ally of Lady Dunce in her amorous adventures.

SOLDIERS' PAY

Author: William Faulkner (1897-1962)
First published: 1926
Genre: Novel

Locale: Charlestown, Georgia
Time: April and May, 1919
Plot: Impressionistic realism

Donald Mahon, a flyer dying of wounds suffered in World War I. Wild like a faun in his youth, he was shot down and now is going blind, has lost most of his memory, is not fully conscious, and says little. His face is so dreadfully scarred that it shocks people, revealing their natures. He brings out the best in some and the worst in others. As the novel begins, he is coming back from the war by train to his home in a small town in Georgia, where he is engaged to a prominent Southern belle. At the end, his death, like the war, significantly changes the lives of some characters while not affecting others at all.

Margaret Powers, a young war widow on the train who nurses and, shortly before his death, marries Mahon. Tall, slim, dark, and pallid, with a mouth like a red scar, she is an independent woman of twenty-four, self-contained, unconven-tional, and the most intelligent, perceptive character in the novel. Some intend to insult her by calling her a black woman. Her compassion for Mahon is motivated to some extent by guilt about the way she broke off with her first husband, also a young officer, shortly before he was killed at the front by one of his own men. At the end, she declines a marriage proposal from Joe Gilligan and sets out on her own.

Joe Gilligan, a discharged American soldier who serves as Donald Mahon's guardian throughout the novel, regarding him as the kind of son he would have liked to have. An easygoing, talkative man of thirty-two, with a sense of humor and a capacity for self-sacrifice, he is almost the only person to whom Mahon speaks. He is a strong, mature man, and when Margaret Powers declines his proposal, he is not wounded for long.

Julian Lowe, an air cadet whose anticipation of glory as a flyer is disappointed by the armistice. On the train with Mahon and Gilligan, traveling back to his home in San Francisco, he naïvely envies Mahon. He is infatuated with Margaret Powers, whose feeling toward him is maternal, and throughout the novel he writes her ungrammatical love letters. His expecta-tion of marrying her is frustrated, like his equally absurd dream of becoming a hero in the war.

Joseph Mahon, the rector, an Episcopalian priest who is Donald's father. A hopeful clergyman inclined to illusion, he sustains a faith that his son will recover and rise again. He grows increasingly realistic as Donald's condition wors-ens, but he transcends disappointment. In the end, after the death of Donald and the departure of Margaret, he consoles Joe Gilligan and leads him to some inspiration from black culture.

Cecily Saunders, the local belle engaged to Donald Mahon. A shallow flirt with reddish dark hair and green-blue eyes, she has a conventional perfection but is spoiled and petulant. She is jealous of Margaret (she calls her a black woman) and forces herself to kiss Mahon on the side of his face that is not scarred, but she cannot go through with the marriage. She consorts with other men and finally elopes with George Farr.

George Farr, an ordinary, gullible young man in love with Cecily Saunders. Duped by the superficial, he suffers from jealousy and at last succeeds in eloping with Cecily, who continues to make him miserable.

Emmy, the housekeeper at the rectory. She is in love with Donald Mahon. A poor, loyal, and passionate young woman with a wild face and dark eyes, she gave her virginity to Mahon before he became engaged to Cecily and went to war. She is distraught that, as a result of his wounds, he has forgotten her. In wounded pride, she declines the opportunity to marry him offered her by Margaret after Cecily runs away.

Januarius Jones, a fat, coldhearted Latin teacher who pursues women like a satyr. Baggy in gray tweeds and the antithesis of Donald Mahon, he has eyes the color of urine and the morals of a goat. Margaret rejects him, whereas Cecily, to some extent his moral counterpart, teases him, and Emmy, as an escape from grief, submits to him.

— *Michael Hollister*

A SOLDIER'S PLAY

Author: Charles Fuller (1939-   )
First published: 1982
Genre: Drama

Locale: Fort Neal, Louisiana
Time: 1944
Plot: Detective and mystery

Captain Richard Davenport, a black lawyer and military officer attached to the 343d Military Police Corps Unit. Davenport investigates the murder of Tech/Sergeant Vernon C. Waters. Ignoring the prejudiced statements and threats of Captain Charles Taylor, Davenport dispassionately fulfills his job and discovers that Private First Class Melvin Peterson murdered Waters while Private Tony Smalls watched. After the discovery, Davenport returns to his unit while the other men prepare to go to the front.

Captain Charles Taylor, a white man in his mid-to late thirties who resents Davenport's assignment and rank. Taylor wants Davenport taken off the murder investigation because he does not believe that a black man can accuse white men or solve the case. After interrogating white soldiers Byrd and Wilcox, Taylor orders that they be arrested; however, Davenport proves that they are not guilty. When Davenport discovers the truth, Taylor admits that he was wrong about African Americans being able to be in charge.

Tech/Sergeant Vernon C. Waters, a well-built African American with light brown skin who manages the baseball team and is disliked by his men. Waters believes that black men must overcome their ignorant status and harasses his men who match the stereotype of being foolish. Waters belittles C. J. Memphis until Memphis attacks Waters. Feeling guilt after Memphis' death, Waters drinks too much; he is beaten by Byrd and Wilcox after insulting them, but the two men leave him alive. Peterson and Smalls find Waters lying in the road, and after beating him, Peterson murders him.

Corporal Bernard Cobb, a black man in his mid-to late twenties who defends Memphis when he hits Waters. Cobb relives the scene between Waters and Memphis. He visits Memphis in the brig, and after Memphis' death, he helps throw the last baseball game. Cobb reports that Peterson and Smalls were on guard duty and the last ones in the barracks the night of Waters' death.

Private Louis Henson, a thin black man in his late twenties or early thirties who does not like to talk to officers and is the pitcher on the baseball team. Henson tells Davenport about the shooting at Williams' Golden Palace and that he saw someone run into the barracks and put something under Memphis' bed.

Private James Wilkie, a black man in his early forties, a career soldier. Wilkie reveals his anger over losing his stripes. Waters removed his stripes after Wilkie drank on guard duty. Wilkie was ordered to place the murder weapon under Memphis' bunk. Davenport places Wilkie under arrest.

C. J. Memphis, a young, handsome, and superstitious black man from Mississippi who plays an excellent game of baseball. A likable man and the best hitter on the team, Memphis also plays the guitar and works harder and faster than anyone else, but Waters does not approve of him because he thinks that Memphis represents the honky-tonk side of the black man. When Memphis hits Waters and is put in the brig, he decides that he will not be caged like an animal. He commits suicide.

Private Anthony Smalls, a black career soldier in his late thirties who is afraid of Peterson. Accused and arrested for going absent without leave (AWOL), Smalls claims that he did not go AWOL but got drunk and fell asleep in the bus depot. After Davenport's interrogation begins, Smalls admits that he did go AWOL and that he watched Peterson shoot and kill Waters.

Private First Class Melvin Peterson, an angelic looking black man and model soldier in his late twenties who calls Waters "ole Stone-ass." From Hollywood, California, by way of Alabama, Peterson plays shortstop on the baseball team. He joined the Army because he thought he might have the chance to fight. Peterson does not hesitate to talk back to Waters, and after a confrontation, the two men fight. Even though Waters beats Peterson, he later does not badger Peterson as much. Peterson discovers Waters lying on the ground in a drunken stupor. After kicking him, Peterson shoots him twice, once in the chest and once in the head.

Byrd, a spit-and-polish soldier in his twenties who works in Ordnance. Byrd fights with Waters outside of the NCO Club the night of the murder. Byrd orders Waters to shut up and starts shoving him. Byrd beats and kicks Waters and threatens to blow his head off.

Wilcox, a medical officer who keeps Byrd from killing Waters. More sympathetic to Waters' condition, Wilcox tries to help. Wilcox attempts to keep Byrd from beating Waters, but Byrd breaks free of his grasp. Wilcox finally restrains Byrd and pulls him away.

— Patricia T. Cheves

THE SOLID MANDALA

Author: Patrick White (1912-1990)
First published: 1966
Genre: Novel

Locale: Sarsaparilla, Australia, and its suburbs
Time: c. 1900-1960
Plot: Psychological

Arthur Brown, the fraternal twin brother of Waldo Brown. Arthur is a huge, simpleminded, kindly man who is entirely devoted to his brother Waldo. He considers himself Waldo's protector, although Waldo is always trying to dissociate himself from his dull-witted brother. Arthur lives by intuition and instinct; he is a noble primitive who sees into the essence of people and things. He is also capable of building meaningful, platonic relationships with women such as Mrs. Poulter and Dulcie Feinstein, both of whom value his innate wisdom. Despite his apparent handicap, Arthur proves himself capable of reading classics such as Fyodor Dostoevski's *The Brothers Karamazov* and of writing symbolic poetry. Although he loves dogs and simple things such as tables and chairs, Arthur prizes his collection of glass marbles most of all. In particular, he considers four to be his solid mandalas, or symbols of totality and wholeness. Arthur keeps these with him always, until he decides to give them to the people who mean the most to him: Waldo, Dulcie, and Mrs. Poulter. Waldo refuses his mandala, a rejection that makes Arthur ineffably sad. In the end, though, it is Arthur who endures.

Waldo Brown, the fraternal twin brother of Arthur. Waldo is Arthur's opposite in every way. Thin, moody, and self-centered, Waldo is capable of great anger and cruelty toward his well-meaning sibling. Arthur is an embarrassment to Waldo, and Waldo is burdened with him throughout their lives. Waldo considers himself an intellectual: He has some schooling and works for years in the local library. He also has literary ambitions and actually starts work on a novel. Waldo's writing is uninspired because his mind is so disconnected from his emotions. He remains half a man, and that is why Arthur's unwitting successes so infuriate him. Waldo, like Arthur, pursues both Dulcie and Mrs. Poulter, not because he loves them but because he believes that they should love him. Waldo never succeeds in getting close to another human being; he cannot even enjoy the dogs that he and his brother adopt. Waldo's resentment of his twin increases as the two of them grow up and grow old together in their parents' house. He is particularly incensed because Arthur always seems to know so much about him: Waldo despairs that he can never have secrets from his blundering, perceptive brother. Finally, Waldo's murderous resentment builds to the point where it explodes.

Mrs. Poulter, the Browns' neighbor from across the street. Mrs. Poulter and her husband move into the suburb of Sarsaparilla shortly after the Browns become residents. An uneducated, nosey sort, she is well-meaning enough to take an interest in Waldo and Arthur after their parents die. Having lost a baby herself, she bonds with Arthur in a maternal way. He spends a good amount of time with her, until her husband objects, after which Arthur and Mrs. Poulter see each other only infrequently. In the end, it is Mrs. Poulter who takes Arthur in; because of his simplicity, goodness, and innocence, he comes to seem a kind of savior to her, and she comforts him in his misery. She also remains a keeper of one of his solid mandalas.

Dulcie Feinstein, a Jewish girl, a friend to both Arthur and Waldo. Despite Arthur's eccentricities, the Feinsteins invite him into their home and enjoy his surprising insights. Waldo meets Dulcie by chance at a party and is most annoyed to find his brother already ensconced in her home the first time he goes to call on her there. The Feinsteins are a cultured family but somewhat adrift emotionally because Dulcie's father rejects Judaism. Eventually, World War II has a profound effect on the Feinsteins. Dulcie ends up marrying a Jewish carpet merchant named Leonard Saporta and having two children, one of whom she names for Arthur. Dulcie is also a keeper of one of Arthur's solid mandalas.

George Brown and
Anne Brown, the father and mother of Waldo and Arthur. Anne marries below herself when she chooses George. They set out from England for Australia with their two boys and end up in an ugly house in a drab suburb named Sarsaparilla. They still possess ideas of grandeur; for example, George has a classical pediment built onto the front of the house. The incongruous addition makes the domicile something of a curiosity on Terminus Road and keeps others at a distance from the Brown family. George works in a bank. It is said that he is sadly disappointed in Arthur, the son for whom he had high hopes. Anne stays on in the house following her husband's death, frequently indulging in flights into the past and declining into an alcoholic end.

— Susan Whaley

SOLSTICE

Author: Joyce Carol Oates (1938-   )
First published: 1985
Genre: Novel

Locale: Bucks County, Pennsylvania
Time: The 1980's
Plot: Psychological realism

Monica Jensen, the protagonist and viewpoint character. Nearly thirty years old and recently divorced, she bears a tiny scar on her jaw as a reminder of her failed marriage of nine years. She has undergone an abortion. To obliterate her past, she takes a position teaching English at an elite preparatory school, the Glenkill Academy for Boys in rural Pennsylvania. She rents an old farmhouse that she plans to refurbish, just as she seeks to remake her life. Cherishing her solitude, she works to the point of exhaustion, preparing courses and helping students while devoting weekends to household repair. Monica is self-absorbed, diffident, conscientious, and sensible. The blonde woman was once called a "golden girl," an epithet that reverberates throughout the novel but one she often questions. Her desire is to recover her calm and stability.

Sheila Trask, a nonrepresentational painter of minor renown and widow of a famed sculptor. One of many artists scattered in Glenkill, Sheila lives at Edgemont, her country estate a few miles from Monica's farmhouse. Physically and emotionally in contrast to Monica, Sheila is tall and lanky with olive skin, black hair, and gypsy eyes. Her temperament is stormy; she is given to manic mood swings. She is rumored to experiment with drugs and alcohol. She suffers bouts of artist's block and depression, but when energized, she paints with compulsive fury. Often she appears untidy and soiled. Sheila sends ambiguous gender signals. Stalking about in boots and smelling of horses and sweat, cigarettes, and turpentine, she exudes an air of swaggering masculinity, but she can also present herself as seductively feminine. Sheila makes the first overtures to Monica, brusquely invading her privacy. Against her will, Monica finds Sheila's eccentricity, talent, and aggressive bids for attention to be irresistible.

Harold Bell, Monica's former husband. He pushed her during a quarrel, and she cut her jaw. With shame and embarrassment, Monica reflects on his fussy self-importance. He does not appear in the novel, but twice he sends her letters, which she ignores.

Morton Flaxman, Sheila's deceased husband, who had been a sculptor. He exists as a remembered presence and is the novel's only appealing male character. His cryptic sculpture *Solstice* stands on the Glenkill campus. Monica studies his photograph, noting his strength, sensuality, and fatherliness and envying what she assumes was Sheila's exciting marriage.

Keith Renwick, a lawyer who takes Monica to dinner. Athletic and courteous, he shows a sinister side with his library on weaponry and survivalist techniques.

Jackson Winthrop, a sketchily drawn guest at a party hosted by Sheila. He invites Monica out and rapes her.

Jill Starkie, the meddlesome wife of Glenkill's chaplain. Comically portrayed, Jill dresses like a teenager to play a sisterly role to her daughters. She provides Monica's chief link to the social community, inviting her to parties where guests ridicule the quirks of local artists, notably Sheila. Jill patronizes Monica at first but drops her when Monica persists in her friendship with the bizarre Sheila.

— *Marcelle Thiébaux*

SOME PREFER NETTLES
(Tade kuu mushi)

Author: Jun'ichirō Tanizaki (1886-1965)
First published: 1936; serial form, 1928-1929
Genre: Novel

Locale: Osaka, Awaji, Kobe, and Kyoto, Japan
Time: March-June, 1929
Plot: Psychological realism

Kaname, a sinecurist in his father's company, a quiet, unassuming man in his mid-forties. He and his wife, Misako, agree that their marriage has ended in all but name (they still live together), but neither has the necessary decisiveness to obtain a divorce. Although the basic reason for the marriage's failure is Kaname's lack of sexual interest in his wife, he is equally put off by her modern ways and extreme interest in the latest fads of Western culture. Kaname, though somewhat Westernized himself, becomes increasingly interested in traditional Japanese culture, as evidenced by his growing enthusiasm for the Osaka puppet theater and in the model provided for him by the apparently satisfying relationship his father-in-law has with a young but old-fashioned mistress. The concluding implication is that he will turn away from his wife and become more interested in "doll-like" women, but it is uncertain if he can overcome his indecisiveness.

Misako, Kaname's wife. Estranged from her husband but still living with him, Misako is a woman who has turned her back on traditional culture and ideals and tries to make herself a modern, Westernized woman. She shares her husband's indecisiveness about her marriage, partly for the sake of their ten-year-old son, and for solace has been having an affair for the past two years. It is her interest in shallow and insubstantial Western objects and fads, as much as her sexual unattractiveness, that propels Kaname toward his increasing interest in traditional Japanese culture and women. Kaname becomes aware that Misako's lover is not permanently committed to her, which increases his anxiety about divorcing her and setting her adrift.

Hiroshi, the ten-year-old son of Kaname and Misako. Hiroshi is a sensitive boy who has been living in a constant state of anxiety because his parents have concealed their marital problems from him, forcing him to guess their intentions. He thinks, for example, that his parents may be intending to abandon him and lives in a constant state of torment until he is finally informed by a relative that his parents are getting a divorce (supposedly) and that he will not be abandoned by them. This news apparently serves to calm his fears.

Misako's father, a man in his early sixties. He is a conservative, old-fashioned man interested in all aspects of traditional Japanese culture, especially the Osaka puppet theater. He has a mistress in her mid-twenties, a traditional-looking and -acting woman who resembles one of the theater puppets. Kaname grows to admire the older man and his style of living, especially his interest in traditional Japanese arts and his successful relationship with his doll-like mistress.

O-hisa, the mistress of Misako's father, a woman in her mid-twenties. She is the opposite of Misako, the modern woman. O-hisa not only is young and pretty but also is old-fashioned and docile, quite content to wait hand and foot on Misako's father. She serves as the model for the type of woman to whom Kaname may be beginning to turn; in fact, she serves as a living counterpart to the Osaka puppets to which Kaname increasingly finds himself attracted.

Hideo Takanatsu, a divorced businessman who is a cousin of Kaname. While on a visit to Kaname and his wife, he tries to talk them into going ahead with the divorce and is astonished to discover that they have procrastinated and never

gotten around to saying anything to their son. He takes it upon himself to inform their son, who is relieved to get some hard facts.

Louise, a Eurasian prostitute who is Kaname's sometime lover. She is a sex object for Kaname and also satisfies his woman-worshiping tendencies and flirtation with Western erotica. He loses interest in her as he becomes more interested in Japanese culture.

— *James V. Muhleman*

SOME SOUL TO KEEP

Author: J. California Cooper
First published: 1987
Genre: Short fiction

Locale: The United States
Time: Late twentieth century
Plot: Social realism

Superior, the heroine of "Sisters of the Rain," a big, strong, homely girl. Although she has below-average intelligence, she has acquired from her mother an abiding faith in education as a means of salvation from her impoverished existence. She is shy, quiet, industrious, patient, and generous. She ends up with four successful children who all enjoy supporting her in luxury. Her virtues set her off from Jewel and Glenellen, her two "sisters of the rain."

Jewel, who in contrast to Superior is a sexy girl who "goes all the way" with boys in high school and believes in having fun while avoiding hard work and family responsibilities. She has what appears to be an exciting life with lots of male friends, but she ends up penniless, childless, and alone. Her sterile lifestyle serves as a contrast to Superior's industry and foresight.

Glenellen, the only major character in this collection of stories who is white. She is a spoiled, selfish girl.

Molly, the narrator of "The Life You Live (May Not Be Your Own)." She lives as an enemy of her next-door neighbor, Isobel, for twelve years, believing that Isobel hates her. Only after Isobel's husband dies and Molly's husband leaves her do the two women realize that they have been deceived. Realization of this deception leads Molly to resolve to lead her own life and never to trust men or to become financially or emotionally dependent on them.

Isobel, Molly's childhood friend who becomes her neighbor and is deceived into becoming her enemy.

Birdie, the narrator of "Red-Winged Blackbirds." As a twelve-year-old, she is almost raped by the son of her father's white employer. Her parents are murdered by members of the Ku Klux Klan when her father accuses the young man of attempted rape. Birdie grows up an orphan and later achieves financial success as the owner of a bordello. She is so trauma-

tized by the rape attempt that she remains a virgin until the age of forty-six, but she longs for a child of her own. Eventually, she adopts Reva.

Reva, who is industrious, patient, kindhearted, and loving. She is described as a "Cinderella." Reva is abused by her mother and forced to do all the dirty work. Birdie meets the girl by accident when she is fifteen years old and brings out her hidden beauty, talent, and joy of living through love and understanding.

Bessie, the protagonist of "About Love and Money." She begins life with the handicaps of being poor, black, and ignorant. She becomes an orphan at the age of eleven and is reared by an older sister who exploits her. She learns kindness from being treated with cruelty, and she learns the virtue of hard work from being forced to lead a life of drudgery. She wins the affection of a wealthy black dentist who appreciates her strength of character and homemaking talents.

Mavis, who serves as Bessie's foil to illustrate the moral of "About Love and Money." Mavis, Bessie's opposite, is lazy and self-indulgent. She does not even have the sense to satisfy her wealthy husband's sexual needs and consequently loses him to Bessie, her housemaid, through her own negligence. Mavis, like many of the other failures in the author's stories, never develops to her potential because she believes that the world owes her a living.

Christine, the heroine of "Feeling for Life," the most unfortunate of all the abused and unhappy women in these five stories. She is born blind and has no one to care for her after her mother dies. Christine acquires spiritual strength from her handicap. When she becomes an unwed mother, she stubbornly refuses to give up her child and learns to do all the caretaking in spite of her blindness.

— *Bill Delaney*

SOMETHING HAPPENED

Author: Joseph Heller (1923-   )
First published: 1974
Genre: Novel

Locale: New York City and a Connecticut suburb
Time: Late 1960's or early 1970's
Plot: Psychological

Robert (Bob) Slocum, a middle-level corporate executive in his early forties. He works in New York City and lives with his wife and three children in Connecticut. At his office,

Slocum is fearful and cynically prudent in dealing with his superiors. At home, he is often competitive and abrasive with his two older children, or he retreats from them to the isolation of his study. He recalls with enthusiasm his earlier, insatiable lust for his wife, but he feels threatened by her increasing sexual assertiveness, and he scrutinizes her carefully for signs of alcoholism and marital infidelity. Slocum himself is a philanderer who is joyless and emotionally numb with prostitutes and his girlfriends. He is preoccupied with death, disintegration, and fear of the unknown, and he ruminates obsessively on unresolved emotional experiences, such as his adolescent flirtation with a girl who later committed suicide and his neglect of his mother before her death in a nursing home. At the end of the novel, following the death of his nine-year-old son, Slocum is promoted to the head of the sales department.

Slocum's wife, unnamed, four years younger than Slocum, a tall, slender, well-dressed woman. She is bored and unhappy, and she has recently become a secretive drinker. In the years since marrying Slocum, she has lost self-confidence. She feels unloved by Slocum and their children, and she is beginning, awkwardly, to use obscenities and to flirt with other men at parties.

Slocum's daughter, unnamed, an unhappy fifteen-year-old high school student. Overweight and anxious about her appearance, she both fears and provokes arguments between her parents. Rebellious in her use of obscenity and her insistence on smoking cigarettes, she expresses fear of her parents' dying

or divorcing through her abrasive assertions of indifference. Her eagerness to have a car and her delight in the prestige of a new house express her pleased participation in the economic upward mobility of the family.

Slocum's older son, unnamed, a bright and agreeable nine-year-old. As a young child, he had exasperated and delighted his parents by giving money to other children and by his lack of competitiveness. This family peacemaker has numerous irrational fears, however, and he is physically delicate. Slocum loves and identifies with this boy but inadvertently suffocates him after he is injured in a minor, freak auto accident.

Derek Slocum, Slocum's brain-damaged younger son. This child is a focus of concern and conflict among the characters. A major issue is deciding whether to keep Derek at home or send him to an institution.

Andrew (Andy) Kagle, the head of the sales department at the unnamed company for which Slocum works. A middle-aged man with a limp, Kagle wears the wrong clothes for his executive position, and he is not comfortable dealing with his superiors or the salespeople who work under him. He trusts Slocum and has been good to him. At the end of the novel, Slocum is promoted to sales manager, and Kagle is shunted into special projects.

— *Donald Vanouse*

SOMETHING TO BE DESIRED

Author: Thomas McGuane (1939-   )
First published: 1984
Genre: Novel

Locale: Deadrock, Montana
Time: 1958 to the 1980's
Plot: Psychological realism

Lucien Taylor, the main character, a man who is unsure of where to find meaning in his life. As a boy, Lucien witnesses his father with a prostitute and later hitting his mother. She admits to having had an affair, and Lucien's father leaves the family. Lucien grows up in Deadrock, Montana, with his mother, who becomes a tippler. While in college, he meets Suzanne and gets to know Emily. He marries Suzanne, and his work in the foreign service takes them to Latin America. They have a child, James. Five years after marrying, they hear that Emily has murdered Eric, her husband. Lucien feels a lack of high romance in his life and announces to Suzanne that he is not going back to work. He returns to his hometown in Montana without her and makes bail for Emily, then moves into Emily's home. He feels a sense of mission in helping Emily and begins to paint, for the sense of peace that it gives him. He and Emily make love in the mineral springs on the ranch, but the next morning, she leaves, giving him the ranch and asking if she can come back. He has no sense of purpose gradually realizes that he is becoming lonely. He tries to paint and realizes that he has no talent; the solutions to his problems seem to him to be womanizing and alcohol. From being a loner, he becomes a town fixture and barfly. He realizes that he wants Suzanne back and discovers that he wants to accomplish something big. He takes out a loan against the ranch to construct a spa around his hot mineral springs, where he has taken a succession of lovers, beginning with Emily. The spa is a success, and Lucien uses that as a lever to persuade Suzanne to

bring James to see him. When she arrives, he realizes that he has never been more in love, and throughout her visit he tries to persuade her to return to him.

Emily, a raving beauty with electrifying dark eyes. She makes Lucien think of himself as a painter and a rancher. She went to high school with Lucien but had no idea who he was; nevertheless, she sleeps with him on their first date in college. He continues to sleep with her and is almost caught with her by Eric, another boyfriend who is a medical student and who later marries her. She later shoots Eric to death, a fact that she admits to Lucien. Emily agrees to give Lucien her ranch should she skip bail; when she leaves with her hired hand, he takes over the ranch. She returns after killing the hired hand and admits that she gave Lucien the ranch only so that it would not be seized by the government when she skipped bail. Lucien sends her away.

Suzanne, a brown-haired, brown-eyed beauty whom Lucien meets in college. She makes Lucien think of himself as an intellectual. When Lucien meets her, she has the easygoing nature of a 20-year-old with many suitors; she gradually rejects them. Lucien is then a bookish, curiously distracted type who will not shut up about Emily, who has abandoned him to marry Eric. Suzanne courts Lucien, rather than the other way around. After they marry, she becomes tough and smart but stays beautiful. She knows that Lucien uses prostitutes while they are married but chooses not to make an issue of it because she is afraid that she will drive him back to Emily. After they separate, she refuses to see him and to let him see James, but her position gradually softens. She sees the progress Lucien has made and allows him to make love to her when she visits his spa, but she is disappointed when Emily returns. She leaves the spa with James after Emily leaves.

Dee, an unhappily married woman from Deadrock with whom Lucien has an intermittent and never very serious affair. She is pretty, but Lucien sees minor faults. At one point, after they have dated several times and made love, she asks him to say her name; he cannot remember it. She continues to see him, however, and eventually her husband discovers the affair. He threatens Lucien at rifle point and forces him to buy seamless rain gutters from him; he seems more concerned about saving his failing business than with saving his marriage. Eventually, Dee leaves her husband and plans to leave town.

James, Lucien and Suzanne's son. He wears thick glasses and is unsure of himself when he arrives at the spa. Lucien encourages him to try new things, such as fishing, and gradually wins him over.

Wick Tompkins, Emily's lawyer, a heavy man with the hands of a laborer. He knows that Eric beat Emily but that he had not done so near the time of her death; even Emily describes the murder as premeditated. All Tompkins hopes for is a reduced sentence and to string out the judicial process so she stays free for as long as possible. After Emily skips bail, Wick and Lucien become friends. Wick aids Lucien in his negotiations to spend more time with James. He also relays information from and about Emily.

W. T. Austinberry, Emily's hired hand. He tells Lucien that Eric had it coming, but that a jury might not understand. He leaves with Emily when she skips bail, and she later murders him.

— *A. J. Sobczak*

SOMETHING WICKED THIS WAY COMES

Author: Ray Bradbury (1920-   )
First published: 1962
Genre: Novel

Locale: Green Town, Illinois
Time: Early 1930's
Plot: Fantasy

Will Halloway, a boy of almost fourteen, born one minute before midnight on October 30. He is the best friend of Jim Nightshade. The less adventuresome of the two, he is frightened by the hypnotically attractive carnival that appears in Green Town, Illinois, just before Halloween. He is still very much a young boy, in contrast to Jim. His experience with the evil Cooger and Dark's Pandemonium Shadow Show helps to teach him about the value of friendship, the importance of his father, and the nature of evil. He brings down the wrath of Cooger and Dark by jamming the carousel's controls in the forward position while Cooger is riding the machine, thus turning the man into an ancient, dying being. Will eventually acquires the courage necessary to fight off the sideshow freaks and help his father save Jim Nightshade.

Jim Nightshade, Will Halloway's best friend, born one minute after midnight on October 31. His father has died. In contrast to Will, Jim is the dark side of youth and is very much attracted to the carnival and its mysterious and threatening sideshow and rides. Jim is eager to grow up and falls under the spell of the promise of adulthood held out to him by the carousel, which ages a person one year for every one of its forward revolutions. By the novel's conclusion, he has learned that growing up takes time, and he is content to let time run its course naturally.

Charles Halloway, Will's father. He married late in life and considers himself an unworthy man. He works as a janitor in the Green Town library and is a man of tremendous intellectual curiosity and learning. Despite his negative self-image, he loves his family and wants to protect his son from the dangers he perceives in Cooger and Dark's carnival. Halloway discovers that the carnival is as old as time and that it has kept itself alive by feeding on others' dissatisfactions, hopes, and foolish wishes. It is Halloway who discovers how to defeat the dark forces of the carnival: by means of laughter and love.

G. M. Dark, a man covered in sinister tattoos and one of the owners of Cooger and Dark's Pandemonium Shadow Show. Dark is intent on capturing as many gullible persons as he can because the people of the carnival feed on human suffering. Dark and Cooger depend on people's fear of death and suffering to bring them willing victims. He, like his followers, fears death; he exists in a perpetual limbo between living and dying. He manages to entice Miss Foley into meeting her demise on the carousel and nearly captures Jim.

J. C. Cooger, the other carnival proprietor. He first rides the carousel in reverse to become Robert, the phony nephew of Miss Foley. Eventually he rides the carousel forward and is trapped in the body of a dying old man because Will prevents him from getting off the machine. He becomes a grisly parody of old age, kept alive by G. M. Dark's black electric chair. He serves as a horrible example of what results from falling prey to the carnival's dark promise of eternal life.

Tom Fury, the enigmatic lightning rod salesman. He sells Jim a lightning rod just before the carnival appears in town.

Miss Foley, Will and Jim's unhappy, unmarried seventh grade teacher, in her fifties. She is a well-intentioned woman who is kind to the local children. Because she has no family, she is empty and dissatisfied with her life. Cooger and Dark's carnival holds out to her the promise of recapturing her lost youth and another chance to lead a fulfilled life. Because she is so intent on attaining her goal, she betrays Jim and Will to the carnival owners and to the police. She becomes lost in the carnival's mirror maze and is trapped as a member of the carnival, an adult woman in the body of a young child.

— *Melissa E. Barth*

SOMETIMES A GREAT NOTION

Author: Ken Kesey (1935-   )
First published: 1964
Genre: Novel

Locale: The coast of southwestern Oregon
Time: 1961
Plot: Realism

Hank Stamper, the head of a small family logging operation in Oregon. He has all the virtues of the traditional hero: self-reliance, physical strength, endurance, courage, determination, and the ability to do the job. His strength of character, in particular his emphasis on independence, creates conflicts not only with the local community but also within his family, especially with his wife and younger half brother. He lives by the motto his father nailed over his bed: "Never Give an Inch." His independence has been fostered by his lifelong struggle with nature, which he sees as his principal opponent. An element of rivalry is present in all of his relations with people as well. Hank's determination to fulfill the contract to deliver logs to the mill in spite of a strike by local loggers puts him at odds with the town. Time is running out: The river is rising, not enough men are available to cut the trees, and the machinery is breaking down, as usual. Moreover, dissension from a variety of sources breaks out within the family. Hank perseveres.

Leland (Lee) Stamper, a graduate student at Yale who returns to help the family fulfill the logging contract. Lee is Hank's younger half brother, the son of Hank's father's second wife, who took Lee to the East after having an affair with Hank. Moody, apprehensive, self-destructive, self-conscious, and willing to play on his own weakness, Lee returns to Oregon with hopes of getting revenge on Hank, on whom he blames his sense of alienation. Lee seduces Hank's wife. In the meantime, he is initiated into the logging business. He has to prove himself as a logger. The rivalry with Hank is conducted in the woods and in the house.

Henry Stamper, the patriarch of the Stamper family. An independent, stubborn old man, he is the living link with the pioneer spirit of the Stamper past. When Henry's father, Jonas, gave up the battle with nature in Oregon and abandoned the family, Henry dug in his heels and made the family business a success. His toughness is his heritage to Hank; however, his intolerance of the weakness of others contributes to Lee's alienation. Only age defeats Henry Stamper. He loses his arm in the desperate attempt to deliver the logs and dies in the hospital. His death is a major source of suffering for Hank and thereby a contributing factor to Hank's development of tolerance.

Vivian (Viv) Stamper, Hank's attractive, spirited wife, a woman with a will of her own, a great capacity for love, dreams of her own self-realization, and the ability to manage the houseful of cantankerous men. Viv's vulnerability to Lee derives from their mutual sense of alienation. Hank brought her to Oregon from Colorado, and she has never felt at home. Their inability to have children contributes to her lack of fulfillment. She believes that Lee needs her more than Hank does, because Hank is unable to express his needs and is unable to see that she has needs of her own. After the two men fight over her, she leaves them both, in spite of her love for them, to seek an identity of her own.

Joe Ben Stamper, Hank's cousin and fellow logger, Hank's friend since childhood. Joe Ben's spirit is one of the positive aspects of the family struggles. He is cocky, optimistic, and full of humor and fun. Married, with two young children, Joe Ben remains Hank's principal ally amid all the controversies and problems in the woods. His accidental death by drowning during the fight to fill the contract is another strong blow to Hank's spirit.

Jonathon Draeger, the union president, an outsider sent to direct the local strike. Draeger believes in communal action and values. He thinks that any man will give up his principles to protect someone he loves. He cannot understand the independent values of Hank but eventually comes to appreciate him. Draeger is in conflict with Hank because if Hank delivers the logs, the strike will be jeopardized.

Floyd Evenwrite, the local union representative. Floyd fancies himself a rival of Hank and resents Draeger's presence. Unlike the rationalist Draeger, Floyd operates by his emotions. He is ambivalent about Hank's success because that means Draeger's failure. In the face of Hank's determined independence, Floyd—and with him the strikers—is finally reduced to passivity.

— *William J. McDonald*

THE SON AVENGER
(Olav Audunssøn i Hestviken *and* Olav Audunssøn og hans børn)

Author: Sigrid Undset (1882-1949)
First published: 1925-1927
Genre: Novel

Locale: Norway
Time: The fourteenth century
Plot: Historical

Olav Audunsson, the master of Hestviken. Accumulating family tragedies seem to him part of the retribution for his great unconfessed crime. He suffers a stroke that makes it impossible for him to confess, despite his great and constant remorse. At last, he dies.

Cecilia Olavsdatter, the daughter of Olav and Ingunn. She makes an unhappy marriage to a wastrel who becomes a thief. After he is killed, she marries the man who was her first choice.

Eirik, the illegitimate son of Ingunn, whom Olav has accepted as his heir. Feelings of guilt after the girl he has been pursuing dies cause him to decide to become a monk. A poor novice, he is sent home and settles down. A planned advantageous marriage is called off, and he marries a fallen woman. At last, both go into holy orders.

Jörund Rypa, a young squire who marries Cecilia and proves to be dishonest. Discovery of his part in a robbery causes the breaking off of Eirik's engagement. When Jörund is found stabbed in his bed, guilt-ridden Olav believes to his horror that Cecilia is the murderess, but this is not true.

Liv and

Arnketil, a husband and wife who keep a house of thieves and gamblers. To avenge the ruin of a daughter, Arnketil kills Jörund. Arnketil's body is found long afterward in a swamp.

Bothild Asgersdatter, Olav's foster daughter. Trying to evade Eirik's pursuit, she falls and vomits blood; thus he first learns that she is ill with the wasting sickness. In remorse, he leaves Hestviken for a short while. He returns to make amends by asking for her hand in marriage but finds that she has died.

Gunhild Bersesdatter, to whom Eirik is betrothed.

Guttorm, Gunhild's rich uncle, of Draumtop. Some of the proceeds of a robbery against him are found in Jörund's chest. Eirik's efforts to cover up the crime prove unsuccessful.

Berse, of Eiken, Gunhild's father. He forbids the marriage between Eirik and Gunhild after Jörund's part in the robbery is disclosed.

Aslak Gunnarsson, a young man with whom Olav fought in Duke Eirik's war. An outlaw, he is sheltered by a reluctant Olav. When he leaves Hestviken after his family has paid atonement for his crime, he begs to return with his kinsmen to ask for Cecilia's hand, but Olav gives him no hope. He marries Cecilia after her widowhood.

Eldrid Bersesdatter, Gunhild's older sister. She caused great scandal and is living alone. Eirik goes to her house as part of a plan of Gunhild's, but Gunhild is prevented from getting away to meet him there. Eirik finds Eldrid kind and marries her. She enters a convent later.

Björn, the illegitimate son of Olav, who is married and happy. Visiting the pair, Olav feels that family troubles cannot touch this son whom he cannot claim.

SON OF MAN
(Hijo de hombre)

Author: Augusto Roa Bastos (1917-   )
First published: 1960
Genre: Novel

Locale: Itapé, Sapukai, and the site of the battle of Boquerón
Time: 1910-1935
Plot: Social realism

Miguel Vera (mee-GEHL VEH-rah), the narrator of the odd-numbered chapters, a member of the educated upper middle class in Paraguay. Characterized by his utter lack of direction in life, he can never seem to make a commitment to any cause. He joins the military at an early age and becomes an officer but later sneaks away to help a group of rebel peons whom he subsequently betrays. Later, when fighting in the Chaco war, he and his men become stranded and are dying of thirst. When, after a treacherous journey, Cristóbal Jara arrives with a water truck, Vera, delirious with thirst, shoots him. In the end, Vera is killed by a bullet from his own gun in an apparent suicide.

Cristóbal Jara (krees-TOH-bahl HAH-rah), a rebel leader of the Paraguayan *campesinos*. A brave and silent young man, he works selflessly to better the lives of the peons, of which he is one. He organizes a peon rebellion to fight for their rights in the Chaco war. After Vera's betrayal, he ingeniously escapes the persecution of the military. He later embarks on a final selfless mission of carrying water across the enemy lines to a group of isolated soldiers, one of whom is Vera, who shoots at the water truck, killing Jara.

Casiano Jara (kah-see-AH-noh), an indentured worker. Weakened from abuse, he and his wife Nati escape with their infant son, Cristóbal, from their forced labor. They flee to their hometown of Sapukai, where they make their home in an old train car. Demented by their harrowing experiences, they con-

tinue their flight by pushing the car up and down old and forgotten rails.

Gaspar Mora (GAHS-pahr MOH-rah), a leper who has isolated himself in the woods so as not to contaminate them with his disease. To assuage his loneliness, he busies himself by carving a life-size wooden image of himself. After his death, this statue is cherished by the townspeople as a Christ-like symbol of Mora's sacrifice for his fellow people.

Alexis Dubrovsky, an exiled Russian doctor. He comes to live in the town of Sapukai and establishes a ranch for the lepers of the town. He begins caring for the sick, from whom he rarely accepts payment until one day, when he discovers a coin in the neck of an ancient image he receives from a patient. He begins demanding these images from his patients and ultimately breaks them all open, goes on a drinking spree financed with the coins from within the images, and disappears from the village, never to be seen again.

Crisanto Villalba (kree-SAHN-toh vee-YAHL-bah), a soldier who fought in the Chaco war. After the war, he returns to his hometown of Itapé a broken man. Although he is reunited with his son and is now able to return to his ranch, he is depressed and dejected. He no longer wants to be a farmer. He had found his identity and his purpose in life as a soldier. He returns to his ranch with his son and blows it up with hand grenades.

— *Gaston F. Fernandez*

SONG OF A GOAT

Author: John Pepper Clark (1935-   )
First published: 1961
Genre: Drama

Locale: Deinogbo, Delta Province, Nigeria
Time: 1960
Plot: Tragedy

Zifa (ZEE-fah), the protagonist, a fisherman and ship's pilot who is a proud man unable to accept his impotence. He

blames his inability to father a child on his wife, Ebiere, and on everyone else. He consults experts, but to no avail. When his younger brother, Tonyá, replaces him as surrogate father, Zifa, in a rage, ritually slaughters a goat, which foreshadows Tonyá's suicide and Zifa's act of atonement—his own suicide.

Tonyá (TOH-nyah), Zifa's younger brother. He attempts to take Zifa's place in fathering a child, a tradition accepted by Nigerian people, but finds that he cannot live with what he has done in good faith and commits suicide. Tonyá is, therefore, a victim of tragic circumstances.

Ebiere (ay-bee-AY-ray), Zifa's wife. She is told by the Masseur that she should have a child by Tonyá, Zifa's younger brother, because Zifa is impotent. Ebiere follows this advice, thinking that Zifa would believe the child to be his. After Zifa's violent reaction to the act, Ebiere loses her child in a miscarriage, but she accepts the child's death as punishment for her sin. This incident takes place in a sequel to *Song of a Goat* titled *Masquerade* (1964).

The Masseur, the most important person in the community. The Masseur is the symbol of strength and stability to the people of the village. He serves as the family doctor, the confessor, and the oracle. The Masseur acts as the sage. He attempts to convince Zifa that infertility will bring ruin to a family and that Zifa must accept Tonyá as a surrogate father. Zifa, in his pride, refuses to follow the Masseur's advice.

Orukorere (OH-rew-koh-RAY-ray), Zifa's half-possessed aunt. When she hears of Ebiere and Tonyá's plan to conceive a child without Zifa's knowledge, she makes a prophecy of tragic consequences. Her warning, however, is disregarded by all; Orukorere, because of her half-crazed personality, is not taken seriously by the members of her family. Her warnings of disaster, which become reality, echo the myths and superstitions that have been a large part of the people's consciousness. Throughout the drama, she acts as chorus and conscience.

— *Robert J. Willis*

THE SONG OF BERNADETTE
(Die Lied von Bernadette)

Author: Franz Werfel (1890-1945)
First published: 1941
Genre: Novel

Locale: Lourdes, France
Time: 1858-1875
Plot: Religious

Bernadette Soubirous (behr-nah-DEHT sew-bee-REW), a young girl of Lourdes, growing up in grinding poverty and generally regarded as hopelessly slow and stupid. One day, she goes alone into the Grotto of Massabielle. A beautiful lady, shining with a brilliant light, appears to her. Bernadette's story becomes known, and she is reviled both as mad and as a fraud. People go with her on her repeated visits, but they see nothing. The lady bids Bernadette to ask Dean Peyramale to build a chapel on the sight of the grotto. He insists that only a sign will convince him: a blooming rosebush in the cave in February. The lady bids Bernadette dig with her hands; to the following crowd, Bernadette's actions seem mad. A spring flows from the spot, and the soil applied to a blind man's eyes cures his blindness. Roses bloom in the cave, and at last the authorities agree that Bernadette has seen the Blessed Virgin. She becomes a nun, remaining calm and humble until she dies, more than seventeen years later, after a painful illness. Canonized, she is now a saint of the Roman Catholic church.

François Soubirous (frah[n]-SWAHZ), Bernadette's father. Fallen into pitiful poverty, he and his family are dependent on the odd jobs he can beg from the prosperous citizens of Lourdes.

Louise Soubirous (lweez), his wife. She takes in washing, but this income added to her husband's is insufficient to take care of the family.

Sister Marie Thérèse (mah-REE tay-REHZ), Bernadette's teacher, who regards the girl as impossibly stupid, even in her study of religion. Sister Marie Thérèse remains skeptical even after Bernadette becomes a nun; it is only on Bernadette's deathbed that Sister Marie Thérèse admits her error and her belief in the miracle.

Dean Peyramale (pay-rah-MAHL), who refuses to build a chapel on the site of the grotto until he has evidence of a miracle in a blooming rosebush. Later, he becomes disappointed and saddened because he has been ignored by the church authorities in the establishment of a shrine.

THE SONG OF HIAWATHA

Author: Henry Wadsworth Longfellow (1807-1882)
First published: 1855
Genre: Poetry

Locale: Around Lake Superior
Time: The aboriginal period
Plot: Folklore

Hiawatha, an Indian with magic powers who grows up in the Lake Superior region and becomes a prophet and guide. From the body of a stranger he conquers, Hiawatha gets corn. He defeats disease-bearing Pearl-Feather with the help of a woodpecker, whose feather tuft he streaks with red. He invents picture writing. Following the death of Minnehaha and the coming of the white man, Hiawatha leaves his tribe to travel through the Portals of the Sunset to the Land of the Hereafter.

Nokomis, who falls to Earth from the full moon to become the mother of Wenonah and the counselor of Hiawatha.

Wenonah, who, despite her mother's warning, listens to the wooing of faithless Mudjekeewis and bears him a son, Hiawatha. When Mudjekeewis deserts her, she dies of grief.

Mudjekeewis, the immortal and fickle West Wind. He battles his vengeful son for three days, then sends him back to his people, as the prophet promised by the Great Spirit, to teach and unite them.

Minnehaha, the lovely daughter of a Dacotah arrowmaker, whom Hiawatha sees on his journey to avenge his mother's death, and whom he marries despite Nokomis' advice to chose a woman of his own tribe. She dies of fever during a winter famine.

Pearl-Feather, the evil magician who sends fever, pestilence, and disease to the Indians and is vulnerable only at the roots of his hair.

Kwasind, the strong friend of Hiawatha who helps him dredge the rivers of roots and sandbars and rid the lake of its greatest menace, the sturgeon.

Chibiabos, a singer of love songs.

Iagoo, the teller of fanciful tales who entertains at Hiawatha's wedding feast.

THE SONG OF ROLAND
(Chanson de Roland)

Author: Unknown
First published: The twelfth century
Genre: Poetry

Locale: Western Europe
Time: c. 800
Plot: Romance

Emperor Charlemagne (shahr-leh-MAHN-yeh), also called **King Charles** and **Carlon**, represented as being two hundred years old, with a flowing white beard, regal bearing, and undiminished vigor. He presides democratically over his court in an orchard near Cordova and accepts the majority view in favor of what proves to be a false peace pact with the Saracens. His militant zeal for Christianizing pagans is offset by his humble submission to fate when his beloved nephew Roland and twenty thousand of his troops are killed by Moorish forces in the Pass of Roncevaux. He laments the deaths of his men before taking terrible vengeance on their conquerors, but he is completely unmoved by the pleas of Ganelon, the traitor knight.

Roland, the duke of the Marches of Brittany and nephew of Charlemagne. The favorite of his uncle, he glories in his post as leader of the emperor's rear guard, the exposed flank of the French army, on its homeward march from Spain. Roland is the most outspoken of the Twelve Peers, a hater of all pagans, and the enemy of Ganelon, his stepfather. His suggestion that Ganelon be sent to negotiate the truce proposed by the Saracens seems designed as a test of that knight's loyalty and honor. Brave in battle, Roland is also rash to the point of folly and lacking in foresight. He is the owner of the famous sword Durendal and the horn called Oliphant, both possessing supernatural powers. When Saracens attack the French force in the Pass of Roncevaux, he refuses to blow his horn and summon the main army until it is too late. Relying on his own Durendal and Christian supremacy over pagan knights, he dies by his simple chivalric code after facing the enemy and performing prodigious feats of valor.

Oliver, Roland's friend and fellow Peer. His prudence balances Roland's impetuosity, but his warnings are unable to save the day when the Saracen army attacks the French forces at Roncevaux. After estimating the enemy's strength, he urges Roland to blow his horn, Oliphant, to summon Charlemagne and the chivalry of France riding ahead. Dismounted, he dies with honor, a ring of dead enemies piled about him.

Ganelon (gah-neh-LOH[N]), also called **Guènes** (gehn), the traitor knight who nurses so deep a grudge against his stepson Roland that he conspires with Marsilion, the Saracen king of Saragossa, to betray the rear guard of the French army to the enemy. When Charlemagne hears the blast of Roland's horn, blown to summon aid of the emperor, Ganelon derides his ruler. Later, he is arrested and charged with treason. After his champion has been defeated in an ordeal by combat, he is tied to four stallions, who tear his body apart as they pursue a galloping mare.

Archbishop Turpin (tewr-PA[N]), the militant churchman of Rheims, killed at Roncevaux. He absolves Charlemagne's host of sin before the battle and urges all to die like Christian soldiers. It is he who finally persuades Roland to blow his horn, Oliphant, a blast that bursts Roland's temples and helps to cause his death. It also is he who survives long enough to arrange the bodies of the Twelve Peers so that Charlemagne will find them, avenge them, and give them Christian burial. Charlemagne orders his heart, like those of Roland and Oliver, preserved in an urn.

Gerin (zheh-RA[N]),

Gerier (zhehr-YAY),

Ives (eev),

Ivor (ee-VOHR),

Othon (oh-TOH[N]),

Berenger (beh-rah[n]-ZHAY),

Anseis (ahn-SAY),

Samson (sam-SOHN),

Gérard of Roussillon (zhay-RAHR, rew-see-YOH[N]), and

Engelier of Bordeaux (ehn-gehl-YAY, bohr-DOH), Charlemagne's Peers, also slain with Roland and Oliver.

Pinabel of Sorence (pa-nah-BEHL, soh-REHNS), the knight who defends Ganelon, accused of treason, in an ordeal by battle.

Thierry (tyeh-REE), the younger brother of Duke Geoffrey of Anjou. He fights with and defeats Pinabel of Sorence in the ordeal by battle that decides Ganelon's guilt.

Duke Naimon (nay-MOH[N]),

Geoffrey, the duke of Anjou,

Ogier the Dane (oh-ZHYAY),

Count Jozeran of Provence (zhoh-zay-RAH[N], proh-VEHNS), and

Antelme of Mayence (ahn-TEHLM, may-YEHNS), Charlemagne's loyal vassals and trusted advisers.

Walter de Hum, a valorous French knight killed at Roncevaux.

Marsilion (mahr-see-YOH[N]), also called **Marsile**, the Saracen king of Saragossa. Acting on the advice of one of his nobles, he sends envoys to Charlemagne with promises that he will sign a treaty of peace and receive Christian baptism if the emperor will withdraw his army from Spain. He leads the Saracen host against the French rear guard at Roncevaux. After Roland severs his sword hand as they struggle in hand-to-hand combat, Marsilion leaves the battle. Later, he dies in his castle at Saragossa.

Blancandrin (blahn-kah[n]-DRA[N]), the crafty Saracen knight who suggests the treacherous proposal that King Marsilion makes to Charlemagne. Ganelon plots with Blancandrin the destruction of the Twelve Peers and the French host at Roncevaux.

Adelroth (ah-dehl-ROHT), the nephew of King Marsilion,
Duke Falsaron (fahl-sah-ROH[N]),
King Corsablis (kohr-sah-BLEE),
Malprimis of Brigale (mahl-pree-MEE, bree-GAHL),
the emir of Balaguet (bah-lah-GAY),
the lord of Moriana ,
Turgis of Tortelosa (tewr-ZHEE, tohr-teh-LOH-sah),
Escremiz of Valterne (ehs-kreh-MEEZ, vahl-TEHRN),
Estorgan (ehs-tohr-GAH[N]),
Estramarin (ehs-trah-mah-RA[N]),

Margaris of Seville (mahr-gah-REE, seh-VEEL), and
Chernubles of Munigre (shehr-NEWBL, mew-NEEGR), King Marsilion's Twelve Champions killed by the Twelve Peers at Roncevaux.

Baligant (bah-lee-GAH[N]), the emir of Babylon and the ally of King Marsilion. He brings a mighty army to attack the French under Emperor Charlemagne. After a fierce battle that lasts from early morning until dusk, the emir and Charlemagne engage in single combat. Charlemagne, wounded, is heartened by Saint Gabriel. His strength renewed, he strikes with his sword the helmet of his enemy and cleaves him to his beard. The Saracens, seeing their leader dead, flee.

Aude (ohd), the damozel betrothed to Roland. Hearing that her lover is dead, she falls at Charlemagne's feet and dies.

Bramimond (brah-mee-MOH[N]), the widow of King Marsilion. Charlemagne takes her with him when he returns to France. She is baptized and given a Christian name, Juliana.

SONG OF SOLOMON

Author: Toni Morrison (1931-   )
First published: 1977
Genre: Novel

Locale: Detroit, Michigan
Time: 1869-1963
Plot: Bildungsroman

Macon Dead III, also known as **Milkman**, the protagonist, a black man in his twenties who grows up when he discovers his connection with his ancestors, especially the founder of his family, his great-grandfather, Solomon. At first, Milkman is a spoiled, self-centered, confused, and immature boy affected greatly by the tense atmosphere of his unhappy home and family. Milkman's family is ruled by his domineering and unsympathetic father, who has no interest in his past and his family heritage. Milkman, however, with the help of his aunt, Pilate, and his friend, Guitar, manages to complete his journey of cultural, historical, and personal discovery with satisfaction even though it puts his life in jeopardy at the conclusion of the novel.

Macon Dead II, Milkman's materialistic and unsympathetic father. He is the richest black man in town and cares nothing for people in general, including his wife, daughters, and sister. He rules his household autocratically. His primary interest is in obtaining money and land, and he admonishes Milkman to make this his primary goal.

Ruth Foster Dead, Milkman's mother. She is dominated first by her father and then by her husband, Macon Dead II, who rejects her and abuses her physically and mentally. She is spiritually frail and weak. She focuses her life on a water mark on her dining room table and clandestine visits to her father's grave. She is the reason that her son acquired the nickname Milkman—from her extended nursing of him in an attempt to hold on to her son in some way.

Pilate, Milkman's aunt and Macon Dead II's sister. Her outstanding physical feature is the absence of a navel, supposedly because her mother died before Pilate was born. She lives with her daughter and grandmother in complete absence of all the material things that her brother finds so necessary. Her value system is in complete opposition to all that her brother and her nephew, at first, find important. She represents family and folk values and aids Milkman in his quest for identity. She

also symbolizes humanistic values in that she aids Ruth before the birth of Milkman, enabling her through folk charms to achieve a third pregnancy in spite of the past rejection of her husband. She also aids Ruth in bringing about Milkman's safe birth.

Reba Dead, Pilate's daughter, a lesser version of her mother. Unlike her mother, Reba has little strength of character and no folk wisdom. Like her mother, she has little regard for materialist things and is unselfish and giving. In the household of Pilate, Reba, and Hagar, Milkman finds warmth, love, and a safe harbor until he can begin his quest.

Hagar Dead, Pilate's granddaughter and Milkman's cousin, who becomes Milkman's lover. Like her mother and grandmother, she is unmaterialistic. She gives Milkman her complete love and devotion. She is finally spurned by Milkman and attempts to kill him several times, but she can never carry out her murderous intentions. She believes that Milkman rejects her because her hair and skin are too dark. Finally, she becomes insane and dies of unrequited love.

Guitar Baines, a young black man who is a bit older than Milkman and befriends Milkman as a young boy. Guitar and Milkman become best friends, and their friendship grows throughout their youth and young adulthood. Guitar becomes a member of the Seven Days, a racial consciousness group that takes revenge for the unjust murder of African Americans by killing white people. He and Milkman become enemies during their search for gold that they believe was hidden by Milkman's ancestor. At the conclusion of the novel, Guitar is trying to murder Milkman.

Magdelena (Lena) Dead and
First Corinthians Dead, Milkman's boring and dominated sisters. Lena eventually rebels and leaves her parents' household.

— *Betty Taylor Thompson*

THE SONG OF SONGS
(Das hohe Lied)

Author: Hermann Sudermann (1857-1928)
First published: 1908
Genre: Novel

Locale: Germany
Time: Early twentieth century
Plot: Naturalism

Lilly Czepanek (TSHAY-pah-nehk), an attractive and capable young woman. Deserted at the age of fourteen by her music-master father, she is left entirely alone after the subsequent insanity of her mother. She makes an unhappy marriage, takes a lover, and is divorced by her husband. Gradually, she sinks deeper into vice. Falling truly in love, she lies frantically about her past in her desire to keep the young man's friendship. The projected marriage is broken off by his uncle, and Lilly, in despair, unsuccessfully attempts suicide. She does, however, throw into the river a musical composition by her father, "The Song of Songs," which she has kept for years as a symbol of the fine and good in her life. At last, she agrees to marry a man she does not love but with whom she has lived in the past.

Fritz Redlich (REHD-lihkh), a high-minded young student whom Lilly admires before her first marriage. Misunderstanding her overtures of friendship, he spurns her. Years after her divorce, she finds him destitute, looks after him, and secures a job for him. She wants to devote her life to his regeneration, but he still misunderstands her and again spurns her friendship.

Walter von Prell, a young lieutenant interested in Lilly. After her marriage, he becomes her lover.

Colonel von Mertzbach (MEHRTS-bahkh), Lilly's elderly, well-to-do, and jealous first husband. She marries him to gain security; in turn, she is to him little more than his chattel. Discovering her infidelity, he divorces her.

Richard Dehnicke (DAY-nih-keh), a friend of von Prell living in Berlin. Lilly goes there after her divorce and becomes Dehnicke's mistress. He is much under the influence of his mother, who wants him to marry an heiress. At last, his mother, like Lilly, resigns herself to the inevitable, and his marriage to Lilly takes place.

Kellermann, a glass painter to whom Lilly goes to learn the art. She resists his advances until Dehnicke's temporary desertion at his mother's insistence. When Dehnicke returns, she resumes her old way of life with him.

Konrad Rennschmidt, a young art history student with whom Lilly finds true happiness. When the lies she has told him are exposed to his uncle, she is forced to give him up.

Miss von Schwertfeger (SHVEHRT-fay-gehr), Colonel von Mertzbach's housekeeper. Because she hates the colonel, who for years forced her to be a party to mad orgies in his castle, she keeps secret Lilly's infidelity when the colonel almost discovers the affair with von Prell.

Mrs. Czepanek, Lilly's mother, who loses her mind and, after attacking Lilly with a bread knife, is committed to an asylum.

Mrs. Asmussen (AHS-mews-sehn), in whose circulating library Lilly works as a clerk after her mother is committed and until her first marriage.

Lona Asmussen and

Mi Asmussen (mee), the worldly daughters of Lilly's employer. They coach her in the ways of catching men and are then envious of her success in attracting them.

THE SONG OF THE LARK

Author: Willa Cather (1873-1947)
First published: 1915
Genre: Novel

Locale: Colorado, Chicago, and New York City
Time: Late nineteenth and early twentieth centuries
Plot: Impressionistic realism

Thea Kronborg, the daughter of the Swedish Methodist pastor in Moonstone, Colorado. She is a grave, shyly awkward girl in whom a few perceptive people see qualities of imagination and desire still without shape or direction. A down-at-the-heels German pianist finds in her the promise of great talent as a musician and tries to explain to her that beside the artist's vision of fulfillment, the world and all life are petty and small. Dr. Howard Archie, a physician poorly adjusted to the community in which he practices, hopes that she will realize in her life the things he has missed in his. Her eccentric Aunt Tilly claims that the day is coming when Moonstone will be proud of Thea. Ray Kennedy, a young railroad conductor, has fallen in love with Thea and is waiting to marry her when she grows older. The German musician teaches her all he can before he leaves town after one of his drunken sprees. When Ray Kennedy is killed in a wreck, he leaves Thea six hundred dollars in life insurance. She uses that money to go to Chicago to study piano under Andor Harsanyi, who discovers that her true talent is in her voice. She then takes lessons from Madison Bowers, a celebrated voice teacher. He introduces her to Fred Ottenburg, the heir to a brewery fortune and an enthusiastic art amateur. The young beer baron takes an interest in Thea and arranges singing engagements for her. When she reaches a point of physical and spiritual exhaustion, he sends her to his father's ranch in Arizona for a rest. There, exploring the ruins of an ancient civilization, she has an almost mystic vision of art as the discipline of form imposed on raw materials, as in Indian pottery. Accepting Ottenburg's proposal of marriage, she goes to Mexico with him, only to learn that he already has a wife from whom he is estranged. With money borrowed from Dr. Archie, she goes to Germany to continue her studies. After her first success abroad, she returns to make a triumphant career as an opera star, and she marries Ottenburg after his wife's death. Harsanyi declares that the secret of Thea's success is passion. Thea's story is based in part on the career of Olive Fremstad.

Herr A. Wunsch, Thea Kronborg's piano teacher in Moonstone. Formerly a distinguished musician and now ruined by drink, he drifts into Moonstone and is temporarily reclaimed from his sodden ways by Fritz Kohler, a German tailor, and his wife. They give Wunsch a home and look after him while he resumes his career as a teacher. He is the first to discover Thea's musical talent. Eventually, he relapses into his old habits, goes on a wild drunken spree, and leaves town. His parting gift to Thea is the tattered score of Christoph Gluck's *Orpheus*, which he had saved from his student days.

Dr. Howard Archie, an imaginative, sympathetic doctor who becomes interested in Thea after he attends her during an attack of pneumonia. Hoping to save her from the mediocrity of Moonstone life in which he himself has been trapped, he suggests that she use the insurance money from Ray Kennedy to continue her musical studies. Later, his own affairs prosper from the development of some mining property, and he becomes active in business and political life in Denver. He follows Thea's career with interest and lends her the money to study abroad. Better than anyone else, he understands the miracle of chance and endeavor that carries Thea from the crudeness and vulgarity of a Colorado mountain town to her great career as a singer.

Belle Archie, the doctor's wife, a fanatical woman engaged in a constant campaign against dust. She dies as the result of her passion for cleanliness, when gasoline she is using to clean furniture explodes, burning her and the house.

Fritz Kohler, a German-born tailor, one of the first settlers in Moonstone. He has never forgotten his earlier years in his homeland. He rescues Herr Wunsch, the broken-down German music teacher, from his dirty room over a saloon, gives him a proper home, and for a time turns the old drunkard into a respectable citizen and competent teacher. Kohler has three grown sons who work and live away from home; they are ashamed of their father's broken English, his European ways, and his sentimental memories of the past.

Paulina Kohler, his wife, a woman dedicated to making her husband comfortable and her garden grow. Indifferent to the town's opinion, she wears the same clothing summer and winter, prefers men's shoes to women's, and cultivates plants instead of friends. Her garden resembles a small corner of the Rhine Valley set down in an expanse of sagebrush and sand. Generous and warmhearted to those she likes, she welcomes Thea into her home. Through her friendship with the Kohlers and Herr Wunsch, Thea catches a glimpse of a different world, of older, more cultured, and less materialistic European life as illustrated by the older generation of immigrants.

Johnny Tellamantez, called **Spanish Johnny**, a temperamental musician living in the Mexican settlement on the outskirts of Moonstone. A painter by trade, he is given to periodic spells of restlessness during which he suddenly leaves home and travels through the West and Mexico. On these trips, from which he usually returns exhausted and ill, he earns his way by singing and playing his mandolin in bars and cafés. Thea Kronborg scandalizes the proper citizens of Moonstone by going to Mexican Town to hear Johnny and his friends play their folk songs.

Ray Kennedy, a freight train conductor on the run between Moonstone and Denver. Older than Thea Kronborg, he has fallen in love with her and hopes to marry her when she grows up. He is fatally injured in a railroad wreck. After his death, it is learned that Thea is the beneficiary of his six hundred dollar life insurance policy.

Philip Frederick Ottenburg, the younger son of a wealthy family of brewers, a lover of music, and a patron of the arts. Years before, barely out of college, he had made an unfortunate marriage, and he now lives apart from his violently hysterical and mentally deranged wife. Meeting Thea Kronborg at the studio of Madison Bowers in Chicago, Ottenburg is immediately attracted to the reserved yet intense young girl from Moonstone, both as a woman and as an artist. When Thea, exhausted by intense study and hard work, seems on the verge of a breakdown, he sends her to his father's ranch in Panther Canyon, Arizona, to recuperate. When he sees her again, she has been revitalized by her summer in the hot sun and dry air, and he asks her to marry him. Hating himself for his deception but able to rationalize his act, he takes Thea to Mexico, only to lose her when she learns that he is already married. He tries to lend her money for study in Europe, but she rejects his offer and asks her old friend, Dr. Archie, for a loan. Thea and Ottenburg resume their friendship when she returns from Europe, and she marries him after his wife's death.

Andor Harsanyi, the brilliant young musician under whom Thea Kronborg studies piano in Chicago. Like Herr Wunsch, he is baffled by the combination of talent, intelligence, and ignorance in her nature, her stubborn secrecy, and her determined resolve. After working with her for a time, he discovers that she possesses an untrained but magnificent voice.

Madison Bowers, the teacher under whom Thea Kronborg studies voice. She admires him as a teacher but dislikes him as a man because of his fashionable following. Bowers is cynically amused when Fred Ottenburg begins to take an interest in Thea and her career.

Pastor Peter Kronborg, Thea's father, an unimaginative but sincerely dedicated minister.

Mrs. Kronborg, his wife, a practical woman who shows instinctive common sense. Although she never understands her daughter Thea, she sees in Thea traits possessed by none of her other children, and she respects the girl's reserve. She dies while Thea is on a concert tour in Germany.

Axel,

Gunnar,

Gus,

Charley,

Thor, and

Anna, Thea Kronborg's brothers and sister. During the last summer she spends in Moonstone, she realizes that they are like the other citizens of the town: commonplace, smug, and narrow-minded.

Tilly Kronborg, Thea's well-meaning but garrulous and silly aunt, always confident that her niece is marked for greatness. The last Kronborg left in Moonstone, she takes innocent delight in Thea's fame and basks comfortably in that reflected glory.

Lily Fisher, Thea Kronborg's girlhood musical rival. Lily represents Moonstone's idea of culture, a pretty song sung by a pretty girl.

Mrs. Livery Johnson, a Baptist, a member of the Women's Christian Temperance Union and the arbiter of culture in Moonstone.

Mrs. Lorch, the motherly landlady with whom Thea Kronborg lives during her first winter in Chicago.

Mrs. Andersen, Mrs. Lorch's daughter, who tries to interest Thea Kronborg in art museums and other cultural centers in Chicago. Acting on her advice, Thea goes to the Art Institute, where she finds a picture that moves her subtly; it is titled *The Song of the Lark*.

Oliver Landry, a musician, Thea Kronborg's friend and for a time her accompanist.

THE SONG OF THE WORLD
(Le Chant du monde)

Author: Jean Giono (1895-1970)
First published: 1934
Genre: Novel

Locale: The Basses-Alpes region, France
Time: Early twentieth century
Plot: Impressionistic realism

Danis (dah-NEE), the red-haired son of Sailor, who fatally wounds Médéric in a quarrel over Gina. Enraged by his father's murder, he burns Maudru's property; then, in the excitement, he is able to escape Maudru's men.

Sailor (say-LOHR), Danis' woodcutter father, who goes searching for him. While drunk, he is stabbed by two drovers, who are Maudru's men.

Junie (zhew-NEE), Sailor's wife and Jérôme's sister.

Antonio (ah[n]-toh-NYOH), a semi-primitive man of the river, called "**Goldenmouth**," who accompanies Sailor in his search for Danis.

Maudru (moh-DREW), a wealthy ox-tamer whose word is law in the Rebeillard region of France.

Gina (zhee-NAH), his daughter, who is supposed to marry her cousin Médéric but is carried off by Danis.

Clara (klah-RAH), a blind unmarried woman found in childbirth in the woods by Sailor and Antonio. Antonio loves her and takes her back home with him.

Jérôme (zhay-ROHM), Junie's brother, a hunchbacked healer called **Monsieur Toussaint** in the village. He hides Danis, his nephew, and Gina in his house, and he tries unsuccessfully to heal Médéric's wound.

Médéric (may-day-REEK), the nephew of Maudru. He is shot by Danis, who then abducts young Gina.

Gina, Médéric's mother and Maudru's sister, a hard, capable woman.

SONS AND LOVERS

Author: D. H. Lawrence (1885-1930)
First published: 1913
Genre: Novel

Locale: England
Time: Late nineteenth and early twentieth centuries
Plot: Psychological realism

Walter Morel, an English collier in many ways typical of the literary image of the lower-class workingman. He is not interested in the arts, in matters of the intellect, or even greatly in his work, which for him is merely a source of income. He is a creature who lives for whatever pleasures he can find in eating, drinking, and his bed. At first a warmly vital man, he later becomes rough and brutal to his family and fights with them verbally and physically. His wife, after the first glow of marriage fades, means little to him because of her puritanical attitudes and regard for culture, and he becomes alienated from his children. His one creative joy is mending odd bits of household equipment and his work clothing. He has been a coal miner since boyhood, and a coal miner he is content to be.

Gertrude Morel, Walter Morel's wife, who married beneath her class and who soon regrets her action. She is quickly disillusioned by her husband, and the glamour of their courtship soon fades. She discovers that her husband has debts, which he tells her he has paid, and that he constantly lies about the little money he brings home. He always keeps aside some money for his drinking, regardless of how little he earns at the mine. In her disillusionment, Mrs. Morel turns to her children for understanding and affection, as well to protect them from their father's brutality when drunk. As the sons and daughter appear on the scene, each becomes a focal point for the mother's love. She tries to help them escape the little mining community, and she succeeds. She places a blight on her second son, Paul, by centering her affections on him and loving him too well, making him the recipient of love that should have been given to her husband. Her affection and attentions cause him to be stunted emotionally. She never realizes what she is doing to the talented young man but always believes that she is working in his best interest by keeping him at home and governing his affections. Her life is cut short by cancer; Paul ends her terrible pain by giving her an overdose of opiates. Even after her death, her influence lingers in his life, so that he shows little evidence of developing into an individual, fulfilled personality.

Paul Morel, the second child of Walter and Gertrude Motel. After his older brother goes off to London to take a job, Paul receives the bulk of his mother's affection; she helps him find work as a clerk close to home so that he can continue to live with his family. He receives encouragement to study art and becomes a successful part-time painter and designer. Paul's mother and her influence keep him from growing up. Although he fights against her ruling his life, he is trapped. He readily understands how she forces him to give up his love for Miriam Leivers, whom he courts for many years, but he fails to see that his ability to love any woman as an adult man has been crippled by his emotional attachment to his mother.

William Morel, Paul's older brother. When he leaves his family to go to London, his mother transfers her obsessive affections to Paul. William falls in love with a shallow, pseudo-sophisticated woman who takes his money readily, even for her personal clothing, and treats his family as her servants. Although he sees through the girl, William feels trapped into marrying her. A tragic marriage for him is averted only through his sudden and untimely death.

Miriam Leivers, a young farm girl with a highly spiritual yet possessive nature. She and Paul Morel are companions until their late teens, at which time Miriam falls in love with the young man. She spends a great deal of time with him, for he undertakes to educate her in French, algebra, and other subjects, but his mother objects strenuously to her, especially when Paul seems to return her love. Of a highly romantic nature, Miriam is at first repelled by the physical aspects of love but is slowly persuaded to give herself to her lover, who later breaks off his engagement to her, saying that in her need for a committed love she wants too much from him.

Clara Dawes, a handsome married woman, physically emancipated and living apart from her husband. She becomes Paul Morel's mistress and comes as close as anyone can to helping him achieve the ability to love as an adult. At last, even she despairs of him; with his help, she is reconciled to her husband, from whom she has been separated for many years.

Mrs. Radford, Clara Dawes's mother.

Baxter Dawes, Clara Dawes's husband. Although he and Paul Morel are bitter enemies for a time and have a fight in which Paul is badly beaten, Paul's mother's final illness drives the young man to feel sympathy for his rival, the wronged husband. Dawes, who is recuperating from typhoid fever, is helped financially and morally by Paul, who eventually brings the man and his wife together.

Anne Morel, Paul Morel's sister. She escapes her home by becoming a schoolteacher. She achieves a happy, successful marriage and goes to live in Sheffield.

Arthur Morel, the youngest of Mrs. Morel's children, much like his father. He enlists in the Army, but later Mrs. Morel buys him out of the service. He is trapped into marriage with a young woman he does not love.

Louisa Lily "Gipsy" Denys Western, William Morel's shallow fiancée.

Mr. Leivers, a silent, withdrawn man, the owner of Willey Farm and Miriam's father.

Mrs. Leivers, his good, patient, and meek wife. Her philosophy is that the smitten should always turn the other cheek.

Agatha, a schoolteacher,

Edgar,

Geoffrey,

Maurice, and

Hubert Leivers, Miriam's sister and brothers. Edgar is Paul Morel's good friend. The Leivers boys display a brooding, almost brutal nature in contrast to Miriam's romantic spirituality.

Thomas Jordan, a manufacturer of surgical appliances in Nottingham. Paul becomes a clerk in his factory.

Miss Jordan, Paul Morel's patroness. She encourages his interest in art.

Mr. Pappleworth, a senior clerk, in charge of the spiral department, in Jordan's factory. When he leaves to set up a business of his own, Paul Morel becomes the spiral overseer.

Fanny, a hunchback, a "finisher" in the spiral department at the Jordan factory. She sympathizes with Paul Morel in his adolescent moodiness and unhappiness.

SOPHIE'S CHOICE

Author: William Styron (1925-   )
First published: 1979
Genre: Novel

Locale: Brooklyn, New York
Time: 1947
Plot: Psychological realism

Stingo (STIHN-goh), a twenty-two-year-old transplanted Southerner and would-be novelist living in New York City, where he struggles to find himself and write. He is oversensitive, intellectual, and astute. The novel is a record of Stingo's pursuits in the big city, which primarily include his employment at the McGraw-Hill publishing company, his attempts to write, and his relationship with Sophie Zawistowska and Nathan Landau. Stingo, who in many ways resembles the author, becomes more and more involved with these two characters to the extent that he becomes the third point of a love triangle. As the plot unfolds, the reader learns of Sophie's history. Concurrently, Stingo falls in love with her. After Nathan goes violently insane, Stingo takes Sophie to the South, to his home region, for one night of passionate lovemaking. Subsequently, Sophie and Nathan commit suicide, leaving Stingo unable to comprehend evil in human nature, primarily embodied in Auschwitz but more immediately in these two deaths.

Sophie Zawistowska (zah-vih-STOV-skah), née **Biegań-ska** (bi-GAHN-skah), a stunningly beautiful Polish survivor of Auschwitz who becomes a lover to Nathan Landau and later to Stingo. The essential aspect of her character is that, although she is a survivor of the worst atrocities of World War II, she remains a victim of the war. In terms of the immediate plot, Sophie is the object of Stingo's infatuation turning to love, a fact that presents problems to all because of her longstanding affair with Nathan Landau. More important, though, Sophie is the focus of the novel in that the gradual revelation of her history is the main thrust of the work. She feels guilty for having survived Auschwitz, a circumstance with which the demented Nathan repeatedly taunts her. In fact, Sophie had been complicit in the terrors of Auschwitz because her father and husband had favored the Nazi cause. Sophie had been arrested in Poland and sent to the prison camp because, out of depression, she smuggled meat and was caught. In the prison camp, she survived as private secretary to the camp director. Sophie, on her arrival at Auschwitz, had been given a choice: One of her two children would live; the other would die. She saved her son, who later disappeared. Finally, Sophie chooses death over life when she kills herself.

Nathan Landau, Sophie's Jewish lover and Stingo's New York friend. He is extremely manipulative and cruel, vainly intellectual and accomplished, perceptive, and articulate. Nathan's two main characteristics are his Jewishness and his dementia. Seemingly, he can exist only in love-hate relationships: He persecutes Sophie for being a Gentile and a survivor of Auschwitz; at the same time, he persecutes Stingo, making him feel guilty for Southern slavery in the past and racism in the present. Nathan is vain, moody, and violent. Nathan entices Sophie into the suicide pact that ends the novel.

Zbigniew Bieganski (ZBIHG-nyehv), Sophie's father and a law professor. Dictatorial and authoritative, he had abetted the Nazis by writing a political tract arguing for the extermination of the Jews. As a result of her father writing that tract, Sophie feels guilt for what happened even though the Nazis later arrested and imprisoned her father in a concentration camp, where he eventually died.

Rudolph Franz Höss, Sophie's employer, the director of the prison camp/extermination center at Auschwitz. An actual historical figure, Höss tried to maintain his humanity (particularly his family relations) even while supervising the atrocities at Auschwitz. As camp commandant, he was the object of Sophie's sexual advances while she worked as his secretary and translator (she would sell herself for survival). The advances failed, and Höss returned Sophie to work camp.

Fritz Jemand von Niemand (YEH-mahnd fon NEE-mahnd), an SS officer at Auschwitz, totally devoid of compassion or morality. Niemand determined which new arrivals at Auschwitz would survive temporarily as workers and which would proceed to immediate death. As Sophie confronted him, she professed herself a Roman Catholic and not a Jew. Niemand was the agent of evil who afflicted her with the heinous crime of choosing which of her children would live and which would die. (*Jemand von Niemand* is German for "somebody from nobody," a phrase that has several applications in this situation.)

— *Carl Singleton*

A SORROW BEYOND DREAMS
(Wunschloses Unglück)

Author: Peter Handke (1942-   )
First published: 1972
Genre: Novel

Locale: A small Austrian village, Berlin, and Frankfurt
Time: Early 1920's to early 1970's
Plot: Philosophical realism

The narrator, a young Austrian writer whose mother has recently committed suicide. He is in his early thirties. His mother's death comes as a shock, and he deals with his grief by attempting to write a memoir, a chronicle of her life. He struggles with the problems of writing this difficult book, that is, with both his own painful feelings and the inherent tendency of all language to fictionalize—and therefore distort—its subject. He is committed to trying to write the most honest and authentic account of her life and death that he can. He reflects on the various strategies that he might pursue in composing this work; finally, he decides to look at the kind of language used to describe a woman's life—a typical woman's biography—and to see the ways in which his mother's life is both similar to and different from that of the prototypical woman. He composes a sensitive and touching portrait of his mother but is unable, in the end, to overcome the horror of her death. He is left with his guilt and anxiety.

The narrator's mother, an Austrian woman born in the early 1920's. She is an intelligent and good-looking woman with a winning smile. Her existence is, in certain crucial ways, dictated by the traditional expectations and limitations imposed on a female's life by the rural and conservative society into which she is born. Although she does well in school, she is not supposed to continue her education because a woman's "place" is to get married and have children. Her grandfather finally allows her to study cooking, because this is useful for a "girl." When the Nazis annex Austria in 1938, she, like many others, embraces the festive spirit engendered by the propaganda machine of the Germans. She falls in love with a married German soldier and gives birth to an illegitimate child, the narrator. To fulfill her duty as a "mother," she marries another German, who does not really love her. He eventually becomes an abusive alcoholic and repeatedly beats her. Their marriage becomes a prolonged war of silence, and the mother's friendly smile is slowly—and literally—beaten out of her. Her life becomes more solitary and desperate, and she becomes chronically depressed. Despite the narrator's efforts to renew her interest in life through literature, she grows worse, and one night, she takes an overdose of sleeping pills.

— *Thomas F. Barry*

THE SORROWS OF YOUNG WERTHER
(Die Leiden des jungen Werthers)

Author: Johann Wolfgang von Goethe (1749-1832)
First published: 1774
Genre: Novel

Locale: Germany
Time: Mid-eighteenth century
Plot: Bildungsroman

Werther, a well-educated young man who, corresponding with his friend Wilhelm, tells his story. He loves, but cannot marry, the woman of his choice because she is promised to another man. He talks with her, walks with her, and accompanies her to call on the parson but fails to win her. He tries to forget her by taking a government post away from Walheim. It is useless. He returns to her—now living with her husband—and, finally, forces his attentions on her. Crushed and humiliated by his erratic behavior, he shoots himself and dies. Werther's heart invariably rules his head, and he is the victim of unrequited love who uses Nature as a model for peace of mind.

Albert, Werther's rival in love, a respectable and well-mannered young man who sympathizes with Werther but can do little to help him. It is, ironically, Albert who supplies the pistol with which Werther commits suicide.

Charlotte (Lotte) S., Werther's beloved, a German eighteenth century study in femininity. She is faithful, she is kind, and she does good work among the sick and the poor. Her conduct is a model of deportment for wives. She is compassionate but not passionate. She is genteel: When confronted by a distraught, practically incoherent Werther who one night stumbles into her house while her husband is away, to profess his absolute love for her, she asks the wild hero to read to her from the poems of Ossian. Her reaction to the news of Werther's suicide is predictable: She falls into a swoon so profound she nearly dies.

THE SOT-WEED FACTOR

Author: John Barth (1930-   )
First published: 1960
Genre: Novel

Locale: England and colonial Maryland
Time: Late seventeenth and early eighteenth centuries
Plot: Picaresque

Ebenezer (Eben) Cooke (EH-beh-nee-zur), the main character, who moves from the position of naïve fool to wounded and wise sophisticate during this novel, which describes his adventures as he learns the difference between his romantic view of the world and cruel reality. Eben and his twin sister Anna were born in 1666 in Maryland, on Malden, a tobacco plantation owned by their father, Andrew. Eben's mother died giving birth to the twins. Andrew returned to England for the children's education, hiring Henry Burlingame III as their tutor. Eben attends Cambridge University. While there, he meets a prostitute, Joan Toast. He does not have sex with her; he vows eternal love to her and promises to maintain his virginity as a tribute to her. He has been adrift in his life; she inspires him to be a poet. His father asks him to return to Maryland to run the plantation. At about the same time, he has an interview with Lord Baltimore, a former governor of Maryland, who appoints Eben poet laureate of the colony and asks Eben to help him regain his former post as governor. The man posing as Lord Baltimore is really Henry Burlingame III in disguise. This episode is the first of many tricks played on Eben by a person he thought he could trust like a member of his family, and before long his head is spinning, and he no longer knows what to believe. Fearing trouble from those plotting against Lord Baltimore, Eben exchanges identities with his servant, Bertrand Burton. They travel to Maryland (after being taken by pirates and thrown overboard), where he mistakenly gives away his estate and is forced to work on it as a common servant. After further misadventures, the worst of which is his capture by murderous Indians, Eben regains the plantation, marries Joan Toast, and writes a bitter, cynical poem, *The Sot-Weed Factor*, which is very different from the romantic epic he had first planned.

Henry Burlingame III, Eben's friend and teacher, a master of disguises. As a baby, he was found by Andrew Cooke floating in Chesapeake Bay with a note reading "Henry Burlingame III" pinned to his clothes. Burlingame adopts many roles and disguises as he pops in and out of the story, always one step ahead of the befuddled Eben. His goal is to recover the lost journal of Captain John Smith, which he hopes will reveal his true identity. He finally discovers that he is one of three brothers descended from a priest and an Indian maiden. Burlingame marries and has a child with Anna, but at the end of the novel, he disappears, perhaps off on another of his many escapades. He acts as a contrast to Eben because, unlike the poet, he sees the world as it really is and adapts to it to get what he wants.

Joan Toast, Eben's love. She travels to the New World with a group of whores. Their vessel is attacked by the same pirates who take Eben prisoner, but she arrives at Malden. She is stricken with smallpox, but Eben follows through on his vow of love for her and marries her.

Bertrand Burton, Eben's servant, who acts as Eben's master for most of the story. While he is pretending to be Eben, he gets a landowner's daughter pregnant and gambles away much of Eben's estate. Bertrand is always looking to save his own skin, no matter what the consequences for others.

John McEvoy, Joan Toast's pimp, who pursues Eben because the poet never paid for his meeting with the prostitute. He also goes to Maryland, where he becomes another irritation for Eben.

Captain John Smith, an early explorer of Maryland and Virginia. He appears as a character in his own journal, which reveals that his friendship with Pocahontas was very different from the traditional legend.

Henry Warren, a scoundrel who, in Andrew Cooke's absence, turned Cooke's tobacco plantation into an opium farm. He is Eben's adversary as Eben attempts to take back the land.

Drepacca, also known as **Drakepecker** and **Dick Parker**, the king of a band of runaway slaves. When Eben, Bertrand, and McEvoy are captured by hostile Indians, he remembers his friendship with Eben and helps them out of this desperate circumstance.

— *James Baird*

SOTILEZA

Author: José María de Pereda (1833-1906)
First published: 1884
Genre: Novel

Locale: Santander, Spain
Time: 1880
Plot: Regional

Silda (SEEL-dah), an orphan called **Sotileza** (soh-tee-LEH-zah) because she is as dainty as a fishing-line leader. Attractive to men, though not beautiful, she is a paragon of virtue and rejects all advances until faithful Cleto proposes.

Mocejón (moh-seh-HOHN), her guardian, who dislikes her.

Carpia (KAHR-pee-ah), Mocejón's nineteen-year-old daughter, who is jealous of Sotileza.

Cleto (KLEH-toh), Mocejón's son, who marries Sotileza after being drafted into the navy.

Andrés Bitadura (ahn-DREHS bee-tah-DEW-rah), a friend of Sotileza. Kept away from the sea by his frightened mother, he reveals his father's blood by saving a boat during a storm.

Captain Pedro Bitadura (PEH-droh), the father of Andrés and the captain of the SS *Montañesa*.

Padre Apolinar (ah-poh-lee-NAHR), who puts Sotileza into Mechelín's care.

Mechelín (meh-cheh-LEEN), a crippled fisherman who becomes Sotileza's foster father.

Muergo (MWEHR-goh), Mechelín's son, who is drowned in an accident at sea.

Venancio Liencres (veh-NAHN-see-oh lee-EHN-krehs), a merchant to whom Andrés is apprenticed.

Luisa (lew-EE-sah), his daughter, who loves Andrés.

Tolín (toh-LEEN), her brother.

Reñales (rehn-YAH-lehs), a friend of Andrés.

SOULS AND BODIES

Author: David Lodge (1935-   )
First published: 1980
Genre: Novel

Locale: England
Time: 1952-1978
Plot: Social

Adrian, one of nine characters whose fortunes and growth are traced from late adolescence to early middle age. They are representative not of English youth in general but of young Anglo-Catholics. Collectively, they are sexually ignorant and quite accepting of church doctrine. Their development is influenced profoundly by the changes then sweeping through Western society and more specifically through the Catholic Church as a result of Vatican II. Adrian is a particularly repressed, unquestioning young man. During his military service, this dogmatist of the political and religious right becomes disillusioned with British foreign policy (the Suez crisis). He marries Dorothy ("of course" a virgin) and later continues to move leftward, eventually becoming the chairman of Catholics for an Open Church.

Angela, a shopkeeper's daughter and devout Catholic who has been "conditioned" to do all the right things. She and Dennis are the last of their college set to marry and the first to experience tragedy (one daughter is afflicted with Down syndrome, another is struck and killed by a van). Their marriage begins to dissolve.

Dennis, who is not a devout Catholic; he is, however, devoted to Angela. After a long and ardent but entirely chaste courtship, they marry and, as dutiful Catholics, multiply. Domestic tragedies lead Dennis to break first with the church and then with his wife. After a brief affair with his secretary, Lynn, Dennis returns to Angela.

Edward, a medical student with large ears and a funny face. He marries Tessa, an Anglican willing to convert to Catholicism to have a Catholic nuptial mass. Ignorance and inexperience rather than promiscuous intention account for her being pregnant with their first child at the time of the wedding. As a Midlands general practitioner, Edward counsels his patients to use the church-approved rhythm method until he comes to realize its negative consequences. Shunned by his Catholic colleagues and in need of some support, the conservative Edward finds himself joining Catholics for an Open Church despite its liberal ideas.

Michael, who is obsessed by sex and eventually falls in love with Miriam, a Protestant. Despite her doubts concerning certain Catholic doctrines, she becomes a convert. He becomes

a lecturer in English literature at a Catholic college, finds himself shocked yet fascinated by the new sexual openness, participates in the 1960's counterculture, moves on to a more liberal Catholic college, and publishes a book titled *Moving the Times: Religion and Culture in the Global Village*. He worries that he may have cancer, and when he learns that he does not, he almost has a heart attack as he tries too hard to participate in the liberated lifestyle of Polly and her husband, Jeremy Elton.

Miles, who is tall and thin, effeminate in appearance, and homosexual in orientation. A graduate of an English public school, he knows considerably more about sex than any of the others. A recent convert to Catholicism when the novel begins, this religious conservative (and later Cambridge don) rejects the liberalizing of the Catholic Church and eventually returns to the Church of England.

Polly, who is cheerful, sexy, and considerably less chaste than the others. After numerous affairs, she marries a philandering television producer, Jeremy Elton, in a civil ceremony. She later writes an advice column for a women's magazine (at first as "Ann Field"). Sexually liberated and financially well off, she remains at least superstitiously Catholic, baptizing her children when one of them becomes seriously ill. She divorces Elton when she discovers his infidelities.

Ruth, a plain girl who becomes a nun, later questions her calling as well as the church's authority, goes to the United States as part of her research on changes in the convents, and in the middle of a spiritual crisis recovers her faith at a meeting of charismatics in California.

Violet, who is small, dark-haired, and neurotic. Easy prey for several men who take advantage of her sexually and emotionally, she suffers several nervous breakdowns. Desperately, she turns from Catholicism to psychoanalysis, which she in turn gives up to become first a Jehovah's Witness and later a Sufist.

Austin Brierley, a young curate and unofficial chaplain of the University of London Catholic study group to which all the above characters belong and on whom he depends for human contact. Theologically naïve, he gradually realizes and attempts to overcome his ignorance. He is suspended for questioning the wisdom and validity of the papal encyclical on birth control, *Humanae Vitae.* While on leave, he studies sociology and psychology. After saving Dennis and Angela's marriage, he leaves the priesthood and marries Lynn, Dennis' former lover.

The narrator, an anonymous professor of English at a redbrick university who writes novels in his spare time. He interrupts the story to comment on it, to acknowledge its fictiveness, to provide background information, to refer to relevant literary theories (especially those of Gerard Genette), and to point to his own limited omniscience—indeed, to his own inability to keep pace with a reality that changes so swiftly.

— *Robert A. Morace*

THE SOUND AND THE FURY

Author: William Faulkner (1897-1962)
First published: 1929
Genre: Novel

Locale: Mississippi
Time: 1900-1928
Plot: Stream of consciousness

Jason Lycurgus Compson (III), the grandson of a Mississippi governor, son of a Confederate general, and father to the last of the Compsons. Like his illustrious ancestors, his name suggests his passion, the classics. Unlike his forebears, he is unable to make a living or to fulfill his deepest ambition, the study of the Greek and Latin epigrammatists, but his stoic philosophy, culled from his reading, stands him in good stead. He speaks wisely, does little, drinks much, and is weary of his complaining wife, his wayward daughter, and his bickering sons.

Caroline Bascomb Compson, his wife, who resents the Compson lineage and feels that hers is more glorious. A neurotic woman with psychosomatic symptoms, she complains constantly of her grievances and ills. Reluctant to face reality and rejoicing that she was not born a Compson, she indulges her fancies and pretends to be an antebellum Southern gentlewoman. Her fortitude in tragedy is even more remarkable for all her complaining, but she victimizes her children and devoted servants to maintain her resentment and illnesses.

Candace Compson, their only daughter, affectionate, loyal, and libido-driven. She is called Caddy, a name that results in great confusion for her idiot brother, whose playground is the pasture sold to a golf course. She is devoted to her dead brother, her weak-minded brother, her own illegitimate daughter, and her loving father. She is at odds with her mother, her vengeful brother Jason, and several husbands. So promiscuous is she, even urging her sensitive brother Quentin to abortive intercourse, that she does not really know who is the father of her child. As an adventuress, she travels widely, and in the postlude to the novel she appears as the consort of a Nazi officer in Paris.

Quentin Compson, her beloved brother for whom she names her child even before the baby's birth. Obsessed by a sense of guilt, doom, and death, he commits suicide by drowning in June, 1910, two months after his sister's marriage to a man he calls a blackguard. Because he is deeply disturbed by family affairs—the selling of a pasture to pay for his year at Harvard, the loss of his sister's honor, the morbid despair he feels for his idiot brother, his hatred of the family vices of pride and snobbishness—his death is predictable and unalterable.

Jason Compson (IV), the only son to stay on in the Old Compson place, loyal to his weak and querulous mother, determined to gain his full share of his patronage, and bitter over his deep failures. His tale is one of petty annoyances, nursed grievances, and egotistic aggressiveness in his ungenerous and self-assertive mastery of his niece and the black servants. This descendant of aristocrats is more the type of small-town redneck, wily, canny, cunning, and deceitful. Not without his reasons for bitterness, he finally rids himself of his enervating responsibilities for a dying line by himself remaining a bachelor and having his idiot brother castrated.

Quentin, the daughter of Candace and her mother's own child. Reared by Dilsey, the black cook, Quentin is the last of anything resembling life in the old Compson house. As self-assertive as her uncle, she steals money he calls his but which is rightfully hers, and she elopes with a carnival pitchman. Beautiful in the wild way of her mother, she has never had affection from anyone except her morbid old grandmother and a brokenhearted servant. She is possibly Caddy's child by a young man named Dalton Ames.

Dilsey Gibson, the bullying but beloved black family retainer, cook, financier (in petty extravagances), and benefactress who maintains family standards that no longer concern the Compsons. Deeply concerned for them, she babies the thirty-year-old Benjamin, the unfortunate Quentin, and the querulous old "Miss Cahline," though she resists the egocentric Jason. A woman whose wise and understanding nature goes beyond limits of race or color, she endures for others and prolongs the lives of those dependent on her shrewdness and strength.

Benjamin (Benjy) Compson, at first named Maury after his mother's brother. He is an idiot who observes everything, smells tragedy, and loves the old pasture, his sister Caddy, and firelight but cannot compose his disordered thoughts into any coherent pattern of life or speech. Gelded by his brother Jason, he moans out his pitiful existence and is finally sent to the state asylum in Jackson.

Maury L. Bascomb, Mrs. Compson's brother. A bachelor, a drunkard, and a philanderer, he is supported by the Compsons. Benjy Compson was christened Maury in honor of this uncle.

Roskus, the Compsons' black coachman when the children were small.

T. P., a black servant who helps to look after Benjy Compson. He later goes to Memphis to live.

Luster, a fourteen-year-old black boy who is thirty-three-year-old Benjy Compson's caretaker and playmate.

Frony, Dilsey's daughter.

Sydney Herbert Head, a young banker, Caddy Compson's first husband. He divorces her after he realizes that her daughter Quentin is not his child. The divorce ends young Jason

Compson's hope of getting a position in Head's bank.

Shreve McCannon, Quentin Compson's Canadian roommate at Harvard.

THE SOUND OF THE MOUNTAIN
(Yama no oto)

Author: Yasunari Kawabata (1899-1972)
First published: 1954; serial form, 1949-1954
Genre: Novel

Locale: Kamakura, Tokyo, and Shinshu, Japan
Time: Early 1950's
Plot: Psychological realism

Shingo, a businessman. At roughly sixty-three years old, he is a year younger than his wife and preoccupied with some of the principal concerns of aging. His unreliable memory at one point makes him forget momentarily how to knot his tie, whereas his longing for his beautiful, long-dead sister-in-law is disturbingly fresh. It is right before her death that he first hears the sound of the mountain. Concerned that the problems of his son and daughter point to his failure as a father, he feels inept trying to straighten out their lives as adults. Unable to sleep soundly, he dreams frequently and is forced to remember his old friends as they pass away. A man sensitive to the beauty of nature, especially of flowers, he takes refuge in a subtly erotic but platonic friendship with his daughter-in-law, who seems to care more about him than do his own children.

Yasuko, Shingo's wife of some forty years. She is a plain woman who grew up in the shadow of her beautiful sister. When her sister died, Yasuko, in love with both her sister and her brother-in-law, went to live in her sister's home, willingly becoming a maid. Rescued from this domestic slavery by her marriage to Shingo, Yasuko has settled into a comfortable matronly role. She annoys her husband with her snoring and her habit of collecting newspapers for several days before reading them, sometimes aloud, to her family. Her relationship with her daughter is strong, but her long marriage has made her indifferent to her husband.

Shuichi, Shingo's son and a coworker in the same office. He appears to be suffering from his traumas as a soldier during the war, and perhaps it is for this reason that, though married to the beautiful and loving Kikuko, he finds a mistress soon after the wedding. With his mistress, he drinks excessively and

becomes violent, but with his wife he seems to show his softer, hurting side. He and his wife share a love of French songs.

Fusako, Shingo's daughter and the mother of two children. Only thirty years old, she has left her husband and come to live with her parents but appears to be in touch with her abusive failure of a husband until he commits suicide with another woman. Somewhat defensive about her plain looks, she perceives her father's attraction to her sister-in-law and is jealous.

Kikuko, Shuichi's wife. The youngest of eight children, she retains a delicate, fragile, and childlike quality about her, a quality that her father-in-law describes as "clean." She is the only beautiful woman in Shingo's household but is childless. Although she is an ideal daughter-in-law and a loving and forgiving wife, she quietly rebels against her husband's philandering by aborting her long-awaited pregnancy.

Tanizaki Eiko, a secretary in Shingo's office for three years, a slight, petite woman recommended to Shingo by an acquaintance. Eiko has a passing fling with Shuichi and has to leave her job. She visits Shingo briefly but regularly and is the chief go-between who brings the father together with the son's mistress to negotiate a breakup.

Kinuko, also called **Kinu**, Shuichi's mistress. A large woman with a round and cheerful face, she is a war widow resentful of women whom she perceives to be pampered wives, those who still have their husbands. She is determined to have a child, even illegitimately. Although Shuichi beats her in his attempts to get her to have an abortion, she is determined to carry her pregnancy through and breaks up with him. She soothes everyone's conscience by avowing that the baby is not Shuichi's.

— *Shakuntala Jayaswal*

THE SOUND OF WAVES
(Shiosai)

Author: Yukio Mishima (Kimitake Hiraoka, 1925-1970)
First published: 1954
Genre: Novel

Locale: The Japanese island of Uta-Jima (Song Island)
Time: Approximately the 1950's
Plot: Pastoral

Shinji Kubo, a bashful eighteen-year-old fisherman. He is well built and sunburned, with clear, dark eyes. He is level-headed for his age but is sometimes conscious of his poverty, especially when confronted with the wealth and social status of Hatsue, the young woman he loves. Before meeting her, he had led a peaceful, contented life. His only driving ambition in life, other than winning Hatsue's hand, is to acquire his own fishing boat and do coastal fishing with his younger brother. Basically unselfish and thoughtful, he has a "haphazard" re-

spect for morality. When he finally gets a job on a fishing vessel, Shinji, unlike his rival, shows courage during a typhoon at sea and proves to himself that his own strength kept him safe through the perilous night. His efforts are rewarded: Despite an ugly rumor of Shinji having slept with his daughter, Hatsue's father relents and allows Shinji to court her.

Hatsue Miyata, the daughter of Terukichi Miyata, the wealthiest man on the island. Her three sisters left the family through marriage, but she was adopted out to another family.

Later, however, her father decides that she should return and marry Yasuo Kawamoto. On returning, she finds that she prefers Shinji Kubo, even though there is little likelihood that he could provide the kind of life to which she has been accustomed. Hatsue herself, however, works hard. Her healthy, glowing skin and cheeks suggest a wholesome country girl. She is a kindred spirit to Shinji.

Yasuo Kawamoto, the son of a leading family in the village. He is Hatsue's suitor. Fat and red-complexioned, he seems both naïve and crafty. He knows how to make others follow him, and he takes pride in speaking with no trace of the local dialect. By the age of nineteen, he has become hypocritical. Something of a bully, he boasts of being able to seduce a girl and know that she would never tell anyone about it. His laziness, shown in his work on a fishing vessel, leads to his downfall as a contender for Hatsue's hand, for he is unable to prove himself superior to Shinji.

Mrs. Kubo, Shinji's mother. She is a widow, her husband having been killed during World War II. Until her son finishes school and can work, she must support the family by diving for abalone. Neither a complainer nor a gossip, Mrs. Kubo is naturally cheerful and is proud of her good health. She has never worried about unknown things. When a rumor spreads that her son Shinji has been less than honorable with his girlfriend, Mrs. Kubo trusts her son's honesty when he denies having slept with Hatsue. Although a simplehearted woman, she is sensitive to the feelings and motives of others, especially when Hatsue presents her with a purse that she won in a competition. She respects the girl's gesture to make amends for an earlier time when unpleasant words had passed between them.

Terukichi Miyata, Hatsue's father, a widower and the wealthiest man on the island. With some justification, he is proud of having raised his family from nothing to wealth in a single generation, and he is highly respected in the community. After changing his mind about having had Hatsue adopted out, he sends for her and plans for her to marry someone of equal station. He is no fool, however; when Shinji proves himself to be more worthy than his rival Yasuo, he is willing to admit that Shinji, though poor, is more deserving of his daughter's hand than is the wealthier Yasuo.

Chiyoko, the daughter of the lighthouse keeper. She left the island to go to a university in Tokyo. After a long absence, she returns home for a visit. She is decidedly unsociable. Her plain dress is accented by the fact that she never wears makeup. Even more characteristic, however, is her gloomy demeanor. She is obsessed with the notion that she is unattractive, an idea underscored in her presence by her father, who blames it on fate. She excels in being able to memorize material by rote, even to the point of recording her professor's sneezes. When Chiyoko sees that Shinji is interested only in Hatsue, she circulates a hurtful rumor that he has been dishonorable with Hatsue. Chiyoko longs to be told that she is pretty. When she finally elicits from Shinji an assurance that she is attractive, her unhappiness is lifted, and she repents having caused trouble with her rumor. A virtue is her honesty in recognizing beauty in another woman.

— *Victoria Price*

SOUR SWEET

Author: Timothy Mo (1950-   )
First published: 1982
Genre: Novel

Locale: Central and South London
Time: The 1960's
Plot: Social

Chen, a Chinese émigré to England, a stocky, pale, unprepossessing man with a round, bunlike face and a chubby torso atop short legs. He is only modestly ambitious and works his way up from menial jobs to the ownership of a tiny restaurant in a rundown suburb, where he settles down to create the perfect vegetable garden and to hide from a Triad family. Earlier, Chen had turned to the Triad society of the Chinese underworld for help in paying off his father's debts; in return, he has "helped" the society as a drug runner. His whereabouts are revealed to the society as a result of his wife's stubbornness, and Chen is murdered.

Lily, Chen's strong-willed and ambitious wife. Taller than the average Chinese woman (and possessing large hands and feet), Lily was trained by her father as a temple boxer and a traditional herbalist. Very much a traditionalist, she clings to her Chinese ways, arrogantly assuming that anything unfamiliar to her is inferior. She insulates herself from English culture with both ridiculous and disastrous results. When her son obeys her instructions to kick and bite the bullies at school, he is reprimanded for fighting dirty; worse, her refusal to learn about English law gets her into trouble with the district tax office. Her arrogance is Chen's death sentence: Refusing to obey his request that she omit their address on her monthly check to his father, she inadvertently informs the Triad society of Chen's location. She never finds out what happened to Chen and never discovers that she sent her husband to his death.

Mui, Lily's older sister, initially very much the dutiful, submissive, and compliant traditional Chinese woman. Paralyzed by culture shock when she is brought to England to help Lily and Chen, Mui learns English quickly and adjusts rapidly to English ways. Eventually, Mui bears a daughter out of wedlock (she refuses to identify the father), and later she marries Lo, a friend of the family.

Man Kee, the young son of Chen and Lily, educated in both English and Chinese schools. His ambition to be a gardener when he grows up infuriates Lily, who dreams of more impressive careers for her son.

Mrs. Law, a rich widow who takes an interest in Lily and Mui, whom she entertains frequently at lavish teas and dinners in restaurants. An old-fashioned Chinese woman, she views home hospitality as inferior to restaurant meals.

Lo, a barbecue chef who is Chen's only friend. The quiet and withdrawn Lo (whose wife ran off with another man) becomes a regular guest at the Chen home; eventually, he marries Mui.

Red Cudgel, the leader of a Triad gang that functions in London, a short, ugly, harsh-voiced man whose face is pockmarked, whose knuckles are calloused, and who is missing some fingers. He prefers expensive clothes and a chauffeured car. He believes in Chinese tradition (he insists on eating peasant food) and in the use of force.

White Paper Fan, Red Cudgel's deputy leader. A mild, scholarly man, White Paper Fan speaks French, English, and four Chinese dialects—all of which he learned in his travels around the world.

Grass Sandal, a former jet-setting model, now a Triad officer. Born to wealthy parents as Miranda Lai, she speaks a heavily accented English learned in convent and finishing schools. She is highly ambitious and single-minded; her only real interests are money, power, and sex.

Night Brother, once a foundling and street urchin, now the Triad officer in charge of public relations. He is amiable and cheerful, and he possesses abundant self-confidence.

— *E. D. Huntley*

THE SOURCE

Author: James A. Michener (1907-1997)
First published: 1965
Genre: Novel

Locale: Tell Makor, in western Galilee
Time: 1964, with flashbacks
Plot: Historical

Dr. John Cullinane, a forty-year-old Irish American archaeologist from a museum in Chicago, the leader of an expedition to excavate one of the mounds in Galilee known as Tell Makor. He is exceptionally well educated for the job, having learned to read Aramaic, Arabic, and ancient Hebrew script, as well as Mesopotamian cuneiform and Egyptian hieroglyphs. He is also trained in ceramics, metallurgy, ancient coins, and problems of biblical research. Although he is Catholic, his religiosity is not so much a matter of ardent participation as another intellectual interest. He is moved by some of the Jewish religious ceremonies he observes in Israel. Cullinane's easy religious tolerance and ecumenical spirit contrast with the religious passions that emerge in the history of this area, particularly the fanatical devotion to Jewish law that survived multiple disasters.

Jemail Tabari, an Arab trained at Oxford, a first-rate scientific archaeologist. When the Jews threatened to capture Palestine from the Arabs, young Jemail, then twenty-two, fought the Jews vigorously. After his army was crushed, however, he chose to stay in Israel and work with the Jews to rebuild the war-torn area. He is the last of an unbroken line of the ancient family of Ur, which originally occupied Makor. He and his Jewish friend Eliav are the ones who make the final breakthrough to the ancient, long-buried well that was the source of water for Makor, a Hebrew word meaning "source."

Dr. Ilan Eliav, a Jewish statesman and archaeologist, the official watchdog of the dig, whose job is to see that the valuable tell is not mutilated. Cullinane finds out early that Eliav is Bar-El's fiancé, but this fact does not prevent the rivals from enjoying mutual respect. The former history of Eliav is not revealed to either Cullinane or the reader until the last flashback, dated 1948, when the Jews drove the Arabs from the area, then called Safad. Eliav had been a German Jewish immigrant named Isidore Gottesmann. His father had shipped him to Amsterdam during the rise of the Nazis, and he became part of the Jewish underground operating along the German border. English agents spotted his abilities and turned him into an excellent soldier. They then sent him to Syria with a secret unit to keep Damascus out of German hands. There, he met members of the Jewish Brigade from Palestine and acquired their vision of a free Israel. When the British left Galilee, virtually handing over power to the Arab majority, Gottesmann and a small band of Jews rose up and took over the town,

fighting against great odds. Gottesmann's seventeen-year-old wife died in this action. The bitter Gottesmann, worn down by many years of warfare, changed his name to the Hebrew Ilan Eliav and vowed to devote his life to the new Israel.

Dr. Vered Bar-El, a Jewish archaeologist and Israel's top expert in dating pottery. She is an extremely attractive, thirty-three-year-old widow, about whom the reader knows little of a personal nature. She was a young girl in those fateful days when Jewish men, women, and even children launched their desperate assault against the Arabs. Later in that war, she, with gun blazing, rescued Eliav when he was captured. Few details emerge, however, about her attachment to Eliav. When legal complications in traditional Jewish marriage law concerning widows threaten to endanger Eliav's political career, Vered surprises everyone by marrying the rich American Jew Paul Zodman, who financed the dig.

Paul J. Zodman, a Chicago businessman and thoroughly Americanized Jew who has little patience for the old rigid religious laws of Orthodox Judaism. He still considers the State of Israel as the source and preserver of Jewish heritage, however, and willingly pours money into projects that confirm the Jewish homeland.

Ur, a caveman and hunter of the prehistoric period that first saw some attempts to domesticate plants and animals. Ur himself would never have deviated from the familiar hunting pattern of his ancestors had it not been for his wife, who was responsible for gathering wild plants. She conceived the idea of planting seed near the cave and, later, tricked Ur into neglecting the hunt so that he could protect their wheat fields. She is also credited with the beginnings of religion, and her daughter first domesticated a wild dog.

Urbaal, Ur's descendant, a farmer who, in 2202 B.C.E., prayed to a father-god El, as well as Baal-of-the-Storm, Baal-of-the-Waters, Baal-of-the-Sun, and the love goddess Astarte. In spite of the vehement objections of his second wife, Timna, he dutifully allowed her firstborn son to be sacrificed to Melak, god of death and war. Ultimately, however, unruly passions overcame the law-abiding farmer. He fell in love with a priestess of Astarte and killed a herdsman who was a rival for the privilege of lying with her in the temple for seven days and nights as part of an institutionalized fertility ritual. He fled from the city and took refuge at the altar of Joktan, an approaching desert nomad.

Joktan, a desert nomad who was thought to be the forerunner of the Hebrews and was the first Habiru to see Makor. He worshiped only one god, El. After the death of Urbaal, Joktan married his widow, Timna. Urbaal, Joktan, and Timna became parts of later religious myth. Joktan was a heavenly stranger who arrived from the east. Urbaal became the god Ur-baal, the principal god of Makor, and Timna became an aspect of Astarte. Amalek, the herdsman Urbaal killed, was transformed into Melak, the god of war. Timna/Astarte rescued Baal from the realm of darkness by killing Melak and scattering his fragmented body over the fields. This ritual brings the wheat to germination and the olive trees to blossom. In later times, Ur-Baal became simply Baal, the dying and resurrected earth god of the Canaanites.

Uriel, the astute Canaanite governor of Makor in 1419 B.C.E, also a descendant of Ur. He allows a large group of Hebrews led by an old man, Zadok, to settle outside the town.

Zadok, a man who calls himself "the right arm of El-Shaddai," the god of "the mountain that no man ever sees." Although both Zadok and Uriel were men of integrity and generally tolerant of each other's religion, Zadok was shocked by the temple prostitution involved in the worship of Astarte. When Zadok's daughter married Uriel's son and began to worship the fertility goddess, Zadok declared the town an abomination. El-Shaddai spoke to Zadok and ordered him to kill every man of the town, take the children as his own, and distribute the women among his men. Zadok objected to this cruel assignment, but his hot-blooded sons slaughtered the Canaanites, as well as their sister, and burned Makor.

Jabaal, called the **Hoopoe**, a man who, in 963 B.C.E., accepts Yahweh as the great deity of the outer heavens while continuing to worship the earth god Baal as the local deity. Hoopoe is a descendant of Governor Uriel but a rather ridiculous figure—a short, stocky man with an oversized bottom that wiggles as he walks and a large, bald head covered with freckles. Children and most other people call him Hoopoe, the name of a common bird that seldom flies, instead running from place to place poking into holes for insects. The man is an excellent architect who rebuilds the walls of Makor and creates a remarkable tunnel to the well, which is vulnerable to attackers because it is outside the city walls. He then buries the well in an underground chamber so that no one could see the source of water. This chamber is the hidden well found by Tabari and Eliav.

Jehubabel, a pudgy, middle-aged wise man living in 171 B.C.E. Mediocre in talent, Jehubabel is a master of commonplace knowledge. He is tediously prone to quoting old Jewish proverbs but is neither forceful nor particularly religious. He does, however, confront the Canaanite Governor Tarphon, though Tarphon is not very impressed by Jehubabel's objections to the ban against circumcision. Driven by forces that he does not understand, Jehubabel risks his life to perform the circumcision ritual in secret. His greatest trial, however, is when his son Benjamin has his foreskin reconstructed so that he can participate in the Greek games. Appalled at his son's betrayal and heresy, Jehubabel crushes his son's skull with the knotted walking stick of a nearby cripple.

Abd Umer, a man born a slave but now a servant of Muhammad in 635 C.E. He achieves an almost bloodless conquest of Makor. Neither Jews, Christians, nor pagans offer any resistance.

Rabbi Laki, the shoemaker, the most beloved of three rabbis who come to Safad in 1559 C.E. He is short and grossly fat, neither brave nor learned, but full of goodwill. He is a buffoon of the spirit. His people had fled the Inquisition from Spain to Portugal, then from Lisbon to Italy. Rabbi Laki senses the hatred of the Christians there as well and foresees a Jew-burning in a vision. Years later, after he had become a beloved leader in Safad, his vision came to pass, and he returned to the congregation he had abandoned. He was honored thereafter as a martyr.

Rabbi Eliezer bar Zadok, the leader of the Jewish community of Gretz, Germany, where his ancestors had come from Babylonia a thousand years before. When both Catholics and Protestants were castigating Jews as well-poisoners, ritual murderers, and practitioners of black magic, Rabbi Eliezer started on the long and dangerous journey to Turkey. In Safad, he became famous for codifying Jewish law.

Dr. Abulafia, a distinguished medical man in Avaso, Spain, whose Jewish ancestors had become Christian in 1391. The Avaro Inquisition had begun ferreting out thousands of persons of Jewish background who had accepted baptism, claiming they were secret Jews. They tortured and burned some six thousand on flimsy evidence. After watching a personal friend die in the fire, the sickened Abulafia circumcised himself with a pair of scissors, cried "I am a Jew," and fled Spain. He became a noted Kabbalist scholar in Safad.

— *Katherine Snipes*

SOUTH WIND

Author: Norman Douglas (1868-1952)
First published: 1917
Genre: Novel

Locale: The island of Nepenthe
Time: Early twentieth century
Plot: Social satire

Bishop Heard of Bampopo, an English clergyman who goes to the Isle of Nepenthe to meet his cousin and escort her to England, where he is going from Africa.

Don Francesco, a Roman Catholic priest who introduces Bishop Heard to Nepenthean society.

The duchess of San Martino, an American-born woman who married a title. She is being converted to Catholicism.

Mr. Keith, an ardent, aging hedonist. He believes people ought to do what they wish.

Denis Phipps, a college student who confides in Bishop Heard. He finally learns how to make a decision for himself.

Mr. Eames, an elderly scholar.

Count Caloveglia, an antiquarian and a dealer in fake antiques.

Freddy Parker, the proprietor of a café. He sponsors a religious procession in an effort to end an eruption of the local volcano.

Miss Wilberforce, an American who drinks heavily and undresses in the streets.

Mr. Van Koppen, an American millionaire. He is something of an eccentric. When cheated by Count Caloveglia, he pays the outrageous price, pleased that the count has fooled an expert.

Mrs. Meadows, the bishop's cousin. She kills Retlow because, as her first husband, he tries to blackmail her.

Retlow, alias **Muhlen**, a blackmailer and former. Mrs. Meadows murders him because he tries to blackmail her.

Signor Malipizzo, the local magistrate and a Freemason. He hopes to discredit the church by showing that a cousin of Don Francesco committed the murder of Muhlen.

Commendatore Morena, the lawyer who defends the boy accused of murdering Muhlen.

THE SOUTHPAW

Author: Mark Harris (Mark Harris Finkelstein, 1922-   )
First published: 1953
Genre: Novel

Locale: New York City and fictitious locations
Time: 1952
Plot: Social morality

Henry Whittier Wiggen, a left-handed pitcher for the New York Mammoths. The twenty-one-year-old rookie is an innocent who is reluctant to be corrupted by a cynical world, cocky about his pitching prowess, and unashamedly cowardly when confronted by violence. Henry grows up in Perkinsville, New York, believing that he will be the greatest pitcher of all time. He wins twenty-six games in his first season, is named the league's most valuable player, and leads his team to the world championship. His controversial year includes taunts for having a black roommate, back pain caused by the tension of the pennant race, refusal to take a postseason tour to Korea because of his opposition to the war, and an obscene gesture at hecklers during the World Series.

Holly Webster Wiggen, Henry's wife. Before they are married, she is a rebel unable to live with her parents in Baltimore; she lives with her uncle next door to Henry, seduces him, and reads him poetry. As Henry's moral conscience, Holly finally accepts his fourth proposal, once he has proven that he is an individual.

Pop Wiggen, Henry's father. Despite great promise, he quits professional baseball after two years in the minor leagues, never explaining why. He drives a school bus, is caretaker at Aaron Webster's observatory, pitches semiprofessional baseball, and rears his son alone after his wife dies when the boy is two years old.

Aaron Webster, Holly's uncle. An eighty-year-old intellectual, he runs an observatory that he refuses to allow the government to use during World War II. He also declines to pay taxes that promote war. Aaron convinces Pop, his best friend, not to force the young Henry to become a right-hander.

Mike Mulrooney, Henry's minor league manager. He wins Henry's admiration by treating all his players as human beings and teaches the youngster more about baseball than even Pop has.

Herman H. "Dutch" Schnell, the Mammoths' manager. Alternately a stern disciplinarian and a kindly grandfather, Dutch will do anything to motivate his players, though he resents that they have different personalities.

Samuel Delbert Yale, called **Sad Sam**, the Mammoths' longtime star pitcher. Soured on life, Sam does not enjoy baseball, money, or sex. As a boy, Henry worships Sam, talking to his photograph and rereading his autobiography, only to discover years later that his idol is a phony.

Berwyn Phillips "Red" Traphagen, the Mammoths' catcher. The smartest player in professional baseball, Red is a Harvard graduate, an atheist, and a pacifist. He helps guide Henry's development as a pitcher, worrying that the youngster will hurt his arm by throwing the screwball.

Robert Stanley "Ugly" Jones, the Mammoths' shortstop. Unattractive because of a misaligned jaw, Ugly is nevertheless a ladies' man, married to a film actress. He ends his salary holdout only when Patricia Moors goes to bed with him. His jaw is fixed after it is broken in a fistfight.

Perry Garvey Simpson, a rookie second baseman. The only African American on the team for most of the season, he is not allowed in hotels and restaurants during spring training in Florida. A hustler and student of the game, he is Henry's roommate until a second black player joins the Mammoths.

Bruce William Pearson, Jr., the third-string catcher and Henry's second roommate. Unsophisticated and slow-witted, he is the butt of his teammates' jokes. He gets drunk once a year, en route to spring training, because he knows he will play less than he desires.

Patricia Moors, the vice president of the team owned by her father. Beautiful, bored, and an alcoholic at the age of thirty, she will do anything for the good of the Mammoths, including sleeping with the players, but she resists Henry's schoolboy advances.

Krazy Kress, a sports columnist. Grossly overweight, self-serving, and opportunistic, he attacks Henry as an ungrateful, unpatriotic, and obnoxious whiner, giving the young pitcher the impetus to write an honest book about baseball.

John Llewellyn "Coker" Roguski and

Earle Banning "Canada" Smith, other Mammoth rookies. With Henry and Perry, they form a locker room quartet invited to sing on television.

Lester T. Moors, Jr., an automobile manufacturer who owns the Mammoths.

— *Michael Adams*

1824 / *The Space Trilogy*

THE SPACE TRILOGY

Author: C. S. Lewis (1898-1963)
First published: 1938-1945
Genre: Novels

Locale: Earth, Mars, and Venus
Time: The mid-twentieth century
Plot: Fantasy

Out of the Silent Planet, 1938

Elwin Ransom, the protagonist, a middle-aged scholar who is kidnapped while on a walking tour of the English countryside. His abductors take him aboard a spacecraft bound for Mars, where he is to be given to the Martian natives. Assuming he is to be sacrificed as part of an alien ritual, Ransom escapes from his captors once they reach the planet's surface. Wandering the Martian landscape, he encounters the planet's other intelligent life-forms—the hrossa, the sorns, and the pfifiltriggi—as well the eldils, luminous spiritual beings of a higher order. The Martians easily defeat the schemes of Ransom's captors, and the humans are returned to Earth; Ransom is enjoined to keep an eye on the future actions of his kidnappers.

Dick Devine, one of Ransom's captors, a former schoolmate. He is glib and outwardly sociable; in reality, he is a crass, selfish con artist who is primarily interested in the gold to be found on Mars. He and his accomplice, Weston, erroneously regard the sophisticated Martians as primitives who can be bought with trinkets or cowed by technology.

Professor Weston, Ransom's other captor, a brilliant physicist who has managed to build a working spacecraft. Imperious and arrogant, he is at once more noble and more sinister than Devine. He seeks to dominate the Martians as a first step in a program of interplanetary imperialism.

Hyoi, a hrossa, a member of a species of large, graceful, otterlike creatures who are supremely talented artists, singers, and communicators. He becomes Ransom's first acquaintance among the intelligent Martian species. Hyoi is shot and killed by Devine and Weston.

Augray, a sorn, a member of a species of tremendously tall, thin humanoids who are learned in the physical sciences.

Kanakabera, a pfiffiltriggi, a member of a subterranean race of dwarflike creatures who serve as the planet's builders and sculptors.

Oyarsa, the chief eldil and guardian spirit of the planet, an ageless, bodiless, and extraordinarily powerful entity. The Martian oyarsa explains the cosmic dynamic to Ransom: Because of the ancient rebellion of its own guardian spirit, the Earth, or Thulcandra, is the one fallen planet in the solar system, which is otherwise utterly harmonious under the rule of Maledil, the eldilic name for God. The Martian oyarsa humbles Weston and Devine and returns all three Earthmen to their own planet.

Perelandra, 1943

Elwin Ransom, the protagonist of the first novel, who is again embroiled in an interplanetary struggle between good and evil. In the second volume, Ransom is transported to Venus, or Perelandra, by the "light" eldils of the solar system. He learns that the "dark," or fallen, eldils of Earth, which are responsible for the planet's suffering, are meditating an attack on Perelandra. Because he has learned the language of the unfallen planets, Ransom is sent to the emergent paradise of Perelandra to contest Weston in an intellectual and spiritual contest for the souls of the planet's first humanoid inhabitants.

Professor Weston, also known as **The Un-Man**, whose spirit is possessed by the dark eldils. He tries to persuade the Green Lady—the Eve of the new world—to repeat the earthly Fall by breaking the one commandment she has been given by Maledil: not to leave the planet's idyllic floating islands to reside on its "fixed land." Empowered by his possessors, he is tireless and relentlessly persuasive. When Ransom senses that the Green Lady is on the verge of succumbing, he attacks the Un-Man and kills him in a brutal physical combat.

The Green Lady, also known as **Tinidril**, the entirely innocent foremother of Perelandra, who is targeted for corruption by the dark eldils and who must be educated and protected by Ransom.

The King, also known as **Tor**, the Adam of Perelandra. He is separated from the Green Lady during a storm, leaving her alone and vulnerable to Weston's approach.

Lewis, the narrator, who assists Ransom upon his departure for Perelandra and his return to Earth.

Humphrey, a doctor friend of Ransom and Lewis who treats Ransom's wounds upon his return.

That Hideous Strength: A Modern Fairy-Tale for Grown-ups, 1945

Elwin Ransom, now known as **The Director**, the protagonist of the earlier books, who has been vested with spiritual powers since his return from the paradise of Perelandra. He gathers about him a cadre of believers to contest the efforts of the dark eldils and their dupes to attain control of England.

Mark Studdock, a young sociologist who is inveigled into the inner councils of the National Institute for Co-ordinated Experiments (N.I.C.E), a quasi-governmental organization that serves as a front for the dark eldils' plans. Obsessed by the desire to "belong," Mark is at first deceived by the N.I.C.E.'s blandishments; eventually, he comes to oppose the organization's goals and is imprisoned.

Jane Studdock, Mark's wife. Unhappy in her marriage, she begins to have dream visions that prove to be true. The N.I.C.E. covets her as a source of intelligence, but she gravitates to Ransom's group. At the novel's end, she and Mark are reunited and recommitted to their marriage.

Dr. Dimble, an elderly professor at Edgestow, the fictional university at which Mark also works. Jane's former tutor and a devout Christian, he is one of Ransom's principal followers.

Mrs. Dimble, Dr. Dimble's pleasant, motherly wife.

Grace Ironwood, another of Ransom's followers, a psychologist.

Ivy Maggs, a servant in Ransom's household whose husband is jailed by the N.I.C.E.

Camilla Denniston and

Arthur Denniston, a likable young couple allied with Ransom.

MacPhee, another member of Ransom's household, a rationalist and skeptic.

Merlin, the sorcerer of Arthurian legend, who wakes from a state of suspended animation to help destroy the N.I.C.E., kill its leaders, and liberate its prisoners.

Lord Feverstone, known as **Dick Devine** in the first novel, a corrupt opportunist who introduces Mark into the N.I.C.E.

Professor Frost, one of the N.I.C.E.'s directors, a cold, precise man controlled by the dark eldils.

Professor Wither, the N.I.C.E.'s other director, a master of verbal misdirection, also controlled by the dark eldils.

Professor Filostrato, an eminent anatomist who directs the N.I.C.E.'s most secret project, the effort to animate a severed human head.

Miss Hardcastle, also known as **The Fairy**, a sadistic, vulgar woman who directs the N.I.C.E.'s secret police.

Professor William Hingest, an internationally renowned scientist who attempts to leave the N.I.C.E. and is murdered by its police; Mark is subsequently accused of the crime.

The Head, the severed head of a criminal guillotined for murdering his wife. Filostrato and the others believe it is their technical prowess that keeps the head alive; in reality, it is animated by the dark eldils, who use it as a mouthpiece.

Horace Jules, the N.I.C.E.'s figurehead, the pompous, uncomprehending author of trite but popular philosophical and political tracts.

Curry, Feverstone's toady at the University of Edgestow.

Steele, Mark's early colleague and rival in the N.I.C.E.'s sociology section.

Straik, a defrocked minister and religious fanatic employed by the N.I.C.E.

THE SPANISH FRIAR: Or, The Double Discovery

Author: John Dryden (1631-1700)
First published: 1681
Genre: Drama

Locale: Aragon, Spain
Time: The fifteenth century
Plot: Tragicomedy

Torrismond (TOHR-ihs-muhnd), the reputed son of Raymond but actually the son of the deposed King Sancho of Aragon. This gallant young warrior has just saved the kingdom from the Moors. Returning, he valiantly declares his love for Queen Leonora in the presence of his rival, Bertran, the duke who has been defeated three times by the Moors but who is betrothed to the queen. Torrismond, true to the dictates of his conscience, weds the queen without knowing that there is a plot to murder the imprisoned King Sancho. Turning first toward, then away from, his wife, he is urged to join the loyalists led by Raymond, exiled since the usurper king and then the usurper's daughter, Queen Leonora, came to power. Torrismond remains loyal to his wife. He is overjoyed when he learns that Bertran had merely spread the rumor that King Sancho was dead. Further, he feels that as prince regent he can successfully rule the kingdom.

Queen Leonora (lay-uh-noh-rah), the successor to her father's usurped throne, betrothed to Bertran but actually in love with Torrismond, the savior of Aragon. Beautiful yet benevolent, Leonora is overwhelmed with love for the warrior hero, a sense of obligation to the people of her kingdom who suffer invasion because she had turned down the marriage proposal of a Moorish king, and guilt for not loving as her father directed. She craftily tests Bertran, who offers to kill Sancho, the rightful king, but she regrets her actions when she discovers that the old king is in reality her father-in-law. Her penitence brings tears to the eyes of her worst enemies, and her love for Torrismond is deeply returned.

Duke Bertran (behr-TRAHN), a peer of the new realm and the betrothed of the queen. Although he is inept in battle and envious of the conquering hero, Bertran shows himself to be a diplomat by neither protesting his fate too loudly nor resorting

to the villainy he espouses. Finally forgiven his duplicity, he is called brother by his rival, Torrismond.

Raymond, the foster father of Prince Torrismond and an emissary to the deposed king. Returning after some years in exile to find that the boy he reared is the defender of the kingdom, Raymond is forced to tell Torrismond that King Sancho is his true father and that the young man must therefore expose his bride as a usurper who disloyally schemed to murder the old king. He is finally moved to mercy after leading an insurrection.

Father Dominic (DOM-ih-nihk), the Spanish friar who serves self before God and who humorously plays pimp in the name of the church. A Falstaffian priest, the imbibing and blackmailing Dominic scorns money except for charity, charity being his own immense belly. He cozens miserly Don Gomez to bring a young gallant to the ancient man's young and desirous wife. Although constantly on the brink of disaster, the brazen friar weathers every storm through his quick tongue and merry wit.

Lorenzo (loh-REHN-zoh), the young soldier who has designs on Elvira, the wife of a moneylender. Extremely volatile, Lorenzo presses a licentious suit through the good offices of his loved one's ghostly confessor, the fat friar. He is on the point of winning her by kidnaping the husband when he discovers that Elvira is really his sister.

Elvira (ehl-VEE-rah), the coquettish young virgin bride who seeks a handsome soldier. Roguish and waggish to an extreme, the beautiful Elvira agrees to the licentious proposal presented by Lorenzo through the importuning of Friar Dominic. The elopement is discovered in time to prevent incest, and the witty young sister passes off the affair as the natural affection she felt toward her brother.

Don Gomez, an elderly usurer who is wed to Elvira.

THE SPANISH GIPSY

Authors: Thomas Middleton (1580-1627) with William Rowley (1585?-1642?)
First published: 1653
Genre: Drama

Locale: Madrid
Time: Early seventeenth century
Plot: Tragicomedy

Fernando de Azevida (fehr-NAHN-doh deh ah-zeh-VEE-dah), corregidor of Madrid. A good man, strict in his morality, he is horrified to learn that his son has violated a noble virgin. Feeling that his son is worthy of death, he labors to right the wrong; however, he is able to bring about a happy marriage between the reclaimed son and the forgiving girl. He is also rewarded by the recovery of his daughter, long believed lost at sea.

Roderigo (rroh-deh-RREE-goh), Fernando's wild son. Borrowed from a novel by Cervantes and much like that author's Ferdinand in *Don Quixote de la Mancha*, he is pitiless when he captures and ravishes Clara, but he is eaten by remorse and love afterward. He disguises himself and joins the Gypsies, but his father recognizes him. His vicious behavior modified by repentance, he gains a true and lovely wife in Clara.

Clara (KLAH-rah), the beautiful daughter of Pedro and María. Kidnapped and violated by Roderigo, she pleads piteously with him to marry her and save her good name. Failing in this entreaty, she does succeed in gaining his promise to conceal his act. She takes a crucifix from the room and notes other objects in it before leaving. Later, when she faints and is carried into the corregidor's house, she recognizes the room. She tells Fernando of his son's crime and bears out her story with the crucifix. She refuses her suitor Louis, forgives the repentant Roderigo, and marries him.

Pedro de Cortés (PEH-droh deh kohr-TEHS), an old don, the father of Clara. Deeply grieved by his daughter's wrong, he tries to comfort her, meanwhile encouraging her to marry Louis. At Fernando's pleading, he gives his consent to the marriage of Roderigo and Clara.

María, the wife of Pedro and mother of Clara. She is a counterpart to her husband and is not sharply individualized.

Álvarez de Castilla (AHL-vah-rehs deh kah-STEE-yah), an old lord, brother-in-law of the corregidor. Having killed old Castro, the father of Louis, he has fled and lives in banishment disguised as the leader of a band of Gypsy entertainers. To save the life of John, living with the Gypsies as Andrew, he reveals himself to Louis and offers the latter revenge for the slaying of his father.

Guiamara (gee-ah-MAHR-ah), the wife of Álvarez and sister of Fernando. As **Eugenia** (eh-ew-HEH-nee-ah), she lives with her husband as queen of the Gypsies. She reveals herself to her brother and returns his lost daughter Constanza to him.

Constanza (kohns-TAHN-sah), the daughter of Fernando, called **Pretiosa** (preh-tee-OH-sah). She is a pert young girl in her early teens living with her aunt among the Gypsies. She leads her lover John on a merry chase and makes him join the Gypsies. When his life is imperiled by a false accusation, she pleads strenuously for him and claims him as her husband-to-be. When he is released and both are recognized by their relatives, they are betrothed.

Cardochia (kahr-DOH-chee-ah), a young hostess with whom the Gypsies stay. She is seized with an ungovernable passion for John (Andrew). When he rebuffs her because of his love for the supposed Pretiosa, she falsely accuses him of theft to her lover Diego, who attacks him and is dangerously wounded. She finally confesses that her accusation is false, and John is freed.

John de Carcomo (**Andrew**), the son of Francisco. In love with Constanza, he disguises himself and lives with the Gypsies. She gives him little encouragement until he is in peril. He behaves with nobility under his false accusation and unjust imprisonment.

Francisco de Carcomo (frahn-SEES-koh deh kahr-KOH-moh), the father of John. He is disturbed by the unexplained absence of his son. When the latter is saved from unjust execution, he rejoices in his return and consents to his marriage with Constanza, after her noble birth has been revealed.

Louis de Castro (lew-EES deh KAHS-troh), a young nobleman dedicated to revenge for his dead father. He is an unwilling but nevertheless guilty participant in the kidnapping of Clara, whom he does not recognize at the time. Later, he woos her with the consent of both her parents but cannot get her consent. He does not understand her reluctance, because Roderigo, in keeping with his promise to her, has assured Louis that he released her unharmed. The nobility of Álvarez rouses his own nobility, and they become reconciled.

Diego (dee-EH-goh), the third of the young men involved in the kidnapping of Clara. He is in love with Cardochia and believes her false accusation of John de Carcomo. This belief leads him to attack John and nearly costs both of them their lives. He recovers, pleads for forgiveness for Cardochia, and takes her back.

Sancho (SAHN-choh), the foolish, self-satisfied ward of Don Pedro. He too lives for a while with the Gypsies, offering gold and self-composed verse.

Soto (SOH-toh), Sancho's servant. He is his master's companion in the Gypsy venture.

Carlo (KAHR-loh) and
Antonio (ahn-TO-nee-oh), pretended Gypsies.
Christiana (krees-TYAH-nah), a gentlewoman disguised as a Gypsy.

THE SPANISH TRAGEDY

Author: Thomas Kyd (1558-1594)
First published: c. 1594
Genre: Drama

Locale: The Spanish and Portuguese courts
Time: The sixteenth century
Plot: Tragedy

Revenge, the master of ceremonies, forming a chorus with the Ghost of Andrea.

The Ghost of Andrea (ahn-DRAY-ah), Bel-Imperia's slain beloved. He complains bitterly at the delay of the revenge of his death. He still loves Bel-Imperia and his friend Horatio, who succeeds him as her lover. At the end, he is satisfied with the vengeance accomplished.

Hieronimo (ee-ehr-OHN-ee-moh), the marshal of Spain and father of Don Horatio. A proud and devoted father, he pleads for his son's rights in the capture and ransom of Don Balthazar. He is driven almost to madness by the murder of his son (in the later additions to the play, he suffers actual insanity). To avert suspicion from his planned revenge, he feigns madness, thus foreshadowing Hamlet. Despairing of justice for himself, he still acts as a just judge. He is gifted as a dramatic writer and actor, furnishing a pageant for the triumph at the beginning of the play and executing his plan for revenge in a play written and acted by himself with Bel-Imperia and the murderers of his son as supporting actors.

Bel-Imperia (behl eem-PEHR-ee-ah), the daughter of Don Cyprian and sister of Lorenzo. She is a somewhat enigmatic character, devoted to the memory of Andrea and apparently capable of love, even passion, for Horatio, but cold-bloodedly using her love to further her revenge. She scorns her suitor Balthazar, and after the murder of Horatio, she joins forces with Hieronimo and acts a bloody part in his play within the play.

Horatio (hoh-RAY-shee-oh), the best friend of the slain Andrea. Courageous and noble, he has captured the slayer of his friend. He loves Bel-Imperia, and because of this love he is trapped and murdered.

Lorenzo (loh-REHN-zoh), Don Cyprian's Machiavellian son. A cold-blooded, ambitious, and treacherous man, he tries to promote a marriage between his sister and the Portuguese prince. Finding that Horatio is in the way of this match, he engineers his murder; then, for security, he has one of his murdering tools kill the other and go to the gallows for the second death. He keeps Hieronimo from the king's ear and undermines the old man with lies, but he underestimates him. Hieronimo arranges the play within the play so that his own hand can cut down Lorenzo.

The king of Spain, Don Cyprian's brother. He is a fair and just ruler, but he does not learn of the truth in time to help Hieronimo.

Don Cyprian (SEE-pree-ahn), the duke of Castile. He marvels at the realism of the action in Hieronimo's play, not realizing that the deaths of his two children are real. At the end of the play, Hieronimo stabs him, too, before killing himself.

Balthazar (bahl-TAH-sahr), the young prince of Portugal, killer of Andrea, and captive of Horatio. Released into Lorenzo's custody by the king, he woos Bel-Imperia sedulously in spite of her obvious distaste for him. He is involved in the murder of Horatio and plays into Lorenzo's hands by insisting on the hanging of Pedringano. By so doing, however, he helps destroy both Lorenzo and himself, for Pedringano's death leads to Hieronimo's discovery of the murderers.

The viceroy of Portugal, the father of Don Balthazar. Grieved over the supposed death of his son and deceived by Viluppo, he almost has his innocent follower Alexandro executed; however, he learns the truth in time to release Alexandro and executes Viluppo.

Viluppo (vee-LEW-poh), an envious, treacherous villain in the Portuguese court.

Pedringano (peh-dreen-GAH-noh), Bel-Imperia's servant. Terrified by Lorenzo, he betrays to him the secret meeting of Bel-Imperia and aids in the murder of Horatio. At Lorenzo's instigation, and with a written commission from him, he kills Serberine, his partner in the murder. He foolishly believes that Lorenzo has procured a pardon for him and insults his judge Hieronimo and the hangman. At the height of his self-confident impudence, he is hanged; however, he leaves behind evidence incriminating Lorenzo in the murder of Horatio.

Serberine (SEHR-behr-een), Balthazar's servingman. He shares in the murder of Horatio and is killed by Pedringano on Lorenzo's orders. The watch, having been alerted by Lorenzo, apprehends Pedringano immediately after the murder of Serberine.

Isabella (ihz-uh-BEHL-uh), Hieronimo's wife. An adoring mother, she is driven mad by the murder of Horatio and cuts down the arbor in which he has been hanged.

A general, the commander of the Spanish forces against Portugal. He gives to the king the account of the death of Andrea and the capture of Balthazar by Horatio.

Christophil (krees-toh-FEEL), Bel-Imperia's custodian during her imprisonment by Lorenzo.

The Portuguese ambassador, who returns from Spain with news of Balthazar, thus saving Alexandro's life.

Bazulto (bah-SEWL-toh), an old man whose son has been murdered. Hieronimo shows compassion for him as a fellow sufferer.

A hangman, a simple man who is amazed at Pedringano's impudence in the face of death, later fearful of the consequences of the hanging. He delivers Lorenzo's commission for the murder to Hieronimo.

Perseda (pehr-SEH-dah), an Italian lady (acted by Bel-Imperia).

Soliman (sohl-ee-MAHN), the Turkish emperor (acted by Balthazar).

Erasto (eh-RAHS-toh), the **Knight of Rhodes**, Perseda's lover (acted by Lorenzo).

The Bashaw (bah-SHOH), the sultan's treacherous follower (acted by Hieronimo). He, Perseda, Soliman, and Erasto are characters in Hieronimo's play within the play, in which he gets revenge and discloses the murder of Horatio.

SPECULATIONS ABOUT JAKOB
(Mutmassungen über Jakob)

Author: Uwe Johnson (1934-1984)
First published: 1959
Genre: Novel

Locale: East Germany
Time: Mid-1950's
Plot: Psychological realism

Jakob Abs (YAH-kohp ahps), a calm and competent young man who seems to be at ease with himself. His demeanor shows a casualness that is genuine. He is respected by his coworkers. He also believes in socialism, which is the reason for the communist government's interest in him; Rohlfs considers Jakob to represent the ideal of a worker in a socialist state. Although he has a kind of working relationship with Rohlfs, he is very much his own man, caught between two countries where he is not allowed to be himself. When he went to Jerichow at the end of World War II, Cresspahl's daughter, Gesine, looked up to him as an older brother. He began an apprenticeship with the railroad and became a dispatcher for the state-owned East German railroad in Dresden, a position for which he needs security clearance. He visits Gesine in West Germany, and they become lovers. He decides to return to East Germany and has an accident the next morning. He is twenty-eight years old when he is struck by a train engine and dies.

Gesine Cresspahl (gay-ZEE-neh), a highly independent and self-sufficient woman. She is deeply in love with Jakob, who is five years older than she is. In contrast to Jakob and in spite of her independence, she does not appear rooted in her own being because she suffers from her isolation. Not only has she left the social environment in which she grew up, she also has left the social system of communism in East Germany for the capitalist social system of West Germany, where she works as a translator for NATO. Although it is not an easy choice, she feels that she has to stay in West Germany, even after she and Jakob become lovers.

Herr Rohlfs, a levelheaded and efficient agent of the East German secret service. He is never identified by his first name, but always by his last name preceded by "Mr.," or "Herr" in German. He has a little daughter. In the novel, his primary goal, which he ultimately fails to achieve, is to convince Ges-

ine to work as an East German spy. He talks with her relatives and friends about the ideals of socialism. He seems to genuinely like Jakob and takes considerable risks, allowing Jakob to visit Gesine in West Germany. Ironically, although he personally sees in each person an individual, his job forces him to look at each individual as a number.

Jonas Blach (YOH-nas blahkh), a somewhat arrogant intellectual. He has a Ph.D. in English and teaches English linguistics and literature at the university in East Berlin. His involvement in the reformist movement eventually leads to his arrest by Rohlfs.

Heinrich Cresspahl, Gesine's father, a man in his late sixties with an endearing stubbornness. A widower since 1938, he is caring and considerate to his family and friends and can be relied on in many ways. He emerges as one of the truly human characters of the novel. He took Jakob and his mother into his household when they came to Jerichow at the end of World War II. He respects Jakob for his integrity and becomes a father figure to him.

Marie Abs, Jakob's mother, who looks old for her age (fifty-nine). Although the relationship between Marie and her son seems a little distant, Gesine feels as though she has found in Marie a mother for all times. After the encounter with Rohlfs, Jakob's mother is so scared that she decides to leave East Germany.

Sabine (zah-BIH-neh), Jakob's girlfriend in Dresden. She works in the administration of the East German railroad. She and Jakob split up in an unemotional manner sometime after his mother left for West Germany. They remain on friendly terms.

Jöche (YEH-kheh), a friend of Jakob who lives in Jerichow and works for the East German railroad. He is one of the people with whom Jonas talks.

— *Ingo R. Stoehr*

SPEED-THE-PLOW

Author: David Mamet (1947-   )
First published: 1988
Genre: Drama

Locale: A Hollywood film studio office
Time: The 1980's
Plot: Comedy

Bobby Gould, the number two man in a Hollywood production office. At almost forty years of age, he is still immature, guided by the "street smarts" learned in his youth. Gould has earned his position by honoring the principle that a film is good only if it makes money. By following this standard, he has been rewarded with an office redolent of success. Gould is concerned primarily with his own self-image, his maleness, and the appearance of success. He dresses expensively and uses special, irreverent, and vulgar insiders' language with ease and fluidity. For a brief period, because he is starving for love and affection, he tries to impress a good-looking girl, his temporary secretary, Karen. He allows himself to pretend that scruples were always important to him. He almost produces an "art for art's sake" film, seemingly abandoning Hollywood's "money rules" credo. His lack of faith in his ability to sustain a caring relationship proves justified when Karen is found to have been interested in him only for what he could do for her career. A misogynist from the start, Gould has no

qualms or thoughts about what will happen to her when he dumps her.

Charlie Fox, who is about Gould's age and is an old pal of his. Fox is a hanger-on in the film industry, continually flattering all those in a position to help him while waiting for his big break to come along, which occurs when a hot property (film star or director) agrees to sign on his team, thereby making him a producer. Using friendship as motivation, he presents his new deal to his old buddy, knowing that his friend will remain faithful to him. Fox uses language riddled with clichés. He has no pretensions to intelligence, charm, or wit, and he seems proud of his coarseness. He will stop at nothing and let nothing get in the way of his success, which is defined by Hollywood's rules. He will even use the street behavior learned as a child, physically bullying others to get his way. Fox probably lacks a family, as indicated by his own sense of mistrust, impotence, and misogyny. Suspecting that everyone is, like himself, motivated by self-interest, Fox will use and abuse, all the time pretending long-term affection and trust for those who have been more monetarily successful than he.

Karen, a good-looking, seemingly sweet, temporary secretary in her twenties who has the makings of an opportunist. While working for Gould, Karen sees a chance to make a difference in the type of film produced while furthering her career. Using earnestness as a cover, she is unfortunately honest enough to admit that she had sex with her boss only to get ahead; she did not care for him as a person. Although she pretends a certain amount of naïveté, she nevertheless relies on the stereotype that a man will take care of her, ironically proving herself to be actually naïve as well as stupid, manipulative, plotting, power-hungry, and whorish.

— *Marjorie J. Oberlander*

SPEEDBOAT

Author: Renata Adler (1938-   )
First published: 1976
Genre: Novel

Locale: Primarily New York City
Time: Primarily the 1970's
Plot: Ironic

Jen Fain, the thirty-five-year-old narrator and protagonist of a novel that is, like her life, at once highly discontinuous and yet all of a piece. Currently living in New York and working as a reporter on a tabloid, the *Standard Evening Sun*, she has held a variety of jobs—speechwriter, grants rewriter, investigative reporter, gossip columnist, member of a congressional select committee, teacher, librarian, and worker at a university infirmary. She has also traveled extensively and in fact describes her life as a series of idle periods interspersed with travel. She grew up in the country in, or near, a New England mill town (her account is not entirely consistent) and has been educated in progressive schools as well as American, English, and French universities. Neither her education nor her psychoanalysis, however, has prepared her either to order her life or to overcome her fears. She has, she says, led several lives, successively but also to a degree concurrently. She is attracted to situations that involve risk and have a "moral edge." This is true of her writing and, more especially, of her relationships with the men with whom she lives intermittently. At the end of the novel, Jen, uncertain whether to tell her lover that she is pregnant, looks for reassurance, including whatever reassurance that illusions and clichés can provide. She is, however, too self-conscious not to realize how false such a position would be.

Aldo, a "gentle, orderly, soft-spoken" writer from St. Louis who lives with Jen when he is not living alone. They attended graduate school together in England and have visited Venice and a Caribbean island together. He is currently back in New York "doing a political essay."

Jim, a lawyer from Atlanta who used to work for the Office of Strategic Services (OSS) but who now runs a political campaign for a man whom Jen has never liked and who dies near the end of the narrative. Jim has known Jen for a long time and lives with her occasionally. He remains uncommitted, to the point that any calls he makes from her apartment are made collect or on his credit card. He does not know what Jen knows: that he has begun to talk like a politician. He is the father of the child she is carrying.

Will, a lawyer at the foundation where Jen once worked rewriting grant applications. Although they have slept together on occasion, he is presently "gone."

Stewart, a thirty-two-year-old tennis instructor from whom Jen takes lessons on her weekends in the country. "A good, confused," and quiet man, he considers himself both a humanitarian and a bohemian.

Jen's group, people who, like Jen, wanted to live safely and successfully but who now find themselves quietly and desperately "fighting for their lives." Collectively, they are urban, ambitious, financially well off, international, well-meaning (or at least meaning no harm), and capable of issuing "a qualified no." They have had their share of breakdowns, divorces, abortions, homosexuality, and long, sad affairs. Although they exercise and do yoga, they are, Jen says, "really a group of invalids, hypochondriacs, and misfits."

Ned, a representative member of Jen's group. He is a young uptown doctor who, until the change in the abortion law, made an extra two thousand dollars per week, tax-free, performing illegal abortions in his office. He now finds himself in a financial bind. His wife is in analysis and his daughters are in therapy; he prefers not to talk about his son.

— *Robert A. Morace*

THE SPELL
(Die Verzauberung)

Author: Hermann Broch (1886-1951)
First published: 1976
Genre: Novel

Locale: The Austrian Alps
Time: The twentieth century
Plot: Allegory

The narrator, a country doctor, formerly an obstetrician and deputy director on the staff of a large urban hospital. This aging physician has settled in Kuppron, a remote Alpine village, to get over a failed love affair with a fellow doctor named Barbara (about whom he reminisces at length) and in search of a purer lifestyle. He is fascinated by the archaic mountain madness that he witnesses and by the atavistic surfacing of primal drives and delusions among the inhabitants. In various ways, the doctor attempts to atone for a certain guilt incurred by allowing himself to get caught up in the mass hysteria.

Marius Ratti, a mysterious stranger in his thirties whose appearance one spring marks the beginning of something sinister, barbaric, and demonic in the isolated mountain community. The embodiment of a malevolent mysticism, this Pied Piper with Italianate curly hair and mustache is a curiously charismatic catalyst as he inveighs against the corrupt capitalistic cities and preaches a primordial purity, chastity, misogyny, metaphysical machismo, and regressive social structure based on hate-filled power. Ratti urges the abandonment of such devilish devices as radios and assures the impoverished villagers that gold may once again be mined from the mountain. After civilization reasserts itself, Ratti extends his triumph by becoming a member of the municipal council.

Wetchy, a weak and ineffectual insurance agent and salesman of agricultural machinery and other merchandise, including radios. He is the quintessential outsider and a scapegoat for the villagers' frustrations and problems. Wetchy becomes the chief target of Ratti's hatred. Wetchy, his wife, and their two children are attacked in their home and hounded out of the village. In a final encounter with his persecutor, Wetchy temporarily abandons his downtrodden and obsequious stance.

Irmgard Miland, called **the Mountain Bride**, who believes that she is in love with Ratti and has premonitions of her doom. During the bacchanalian revelry of the mountain kermis, the murder of this young woman marks the climax (or nadir) of the rustic frenzy. This expiatory ritual sacrifice is intended to appease the earth and provide the villagers with strength-giving knowledge of death. Irmgard's killer, the innkeeper Theodor Sabest, perishes among the rocks.

Mother Grisson, Irmgard's grandmother and the guardian of the earth spirit. This matriarch of the community is securely rooted in her this-worldly faith and provides a counterpoise of sanity. Her warnings having gone unheeded, Ratti's triumph leads to her mystically experienced death, but first she imparts her "knowledge of the heart" to Agatha, a young woman expecting a child.

Wenzel, a clownish dwarf, a "wenching runt," and Ratti's henchman. This Joseph Goebbels (Nazi propagandist) figure compensates for his small size by affecting an aggressive virility. Concentrating on the harassment of Wetchy, he becomes the leader of a band of young lads. Wenzel almost loses his life in a mining mishap.

— *Harry Zohn*

SPERANZA

Author: Sven Delblanc (1931-   )
First published: 1980
Genre: Novel

Locale: A slave ship crossing the Atlantic Ocean
Time: 1794
Plot: Philosophical

Count Malte Moritz von Putbus (MAHL-teh MOH-rihtz fon POOT-buhs), known as **Mignon** (mee-NYOHN), a callow Swedish aristocrat who both relates the story and serves as its protagonist. A self-professed idealist and political visionary, this naif has embraced the liberal creed of the Enlightenment and dedicated himself to extending the effects of the French Revolution. The novel consists entirely of his diary, which, after summarizing the inept radical activism and erotic misadventure that have led his parents to exile the young man to the New World, reflects on events during his journey aboard the *Speranza*, a slaver vessel. In effect, Mignon's mind, not the ship itself, is the story's stage, and the drama is defined through his transition from the presumption of his own goodness and a delusive faith in humankind to the realization that human corruption is complete and unredeemable.

Roustam (rew-STAHM), the count's black valet. Dressed in European finery and displaying European manners, he is regarded as no more than an entertaining clown by the court at Putbus, but on the *Speranza* he quickly tests his master's egalitarian posture and eventually emerges as the leader of the slaves during their insurrection. The diary's last entries, in relating Roustam's execution, indicate the terrible secret that impels Mignon to wish him dead: a homosexual liaison that occurred the night the former valet called on the aristocrat to side with the slaves once they rebelled.

Hoffman, Mignon's tutor, who has reveled in Putbus' pleasures of the flesh while pretending to covet the superior rewards of the liberated intellect. After boarding the slave ship, however, he drops his philosopher's pose and shamelessly tries to satisfy his base appetites. To the extent that the novel alludes

to Voltaire's *Candide* (1759), Hoffmann is a grim elaboration of Pangloss.

Doctor Rouet (rew-AY), an embittered humanist who pitches his charity and solidarity with the oppressed in futile defiance of civilization's rampant depravity. The ship's physician assumes the role of tutor to Mignon that Hoffmann has abandoned; instead of the philosopher's hypocrisy, however, the severe truths of reality issue from Rouet's instruction. If he represents the best qualities that Europe has developed since the Renaissance, his retreat into cynicism bespeaks the failure of society to act according to the very virtues it has exalted.

Abbe Marcello (mahr-CHEHL-loh), who was appointed by the Jesuits to oversee their financial investment in the human cargo of the *Speranza*, the opposite of Dr. Rouet. A man wholly without emotion, he perverts reason to justify any cruelty or any injustice as an instrument of the soul's salvation.

The Black Aphrodite, later called **Eve**, the beautiful slave whose erotic appeal shatters Mignon's illusions about himself as an apostle of the Age of Reason. Once he sees her in her naked voluptuousness, he will resort to any means to ravish her. The Aphrodite's blackness is not only a mark of her race but also, and more profoundly, a manifestation of the dark powers that mock the faculties emphasized by the Enlightenment.

Grethel, the parish clerk's daughter, whom Mignon seduced. Her lover promises liberation from outmoded strictures, but it is the gratification of an adolescent's itch that motivates his arguments, not the logic of political freedom.

— *Frank Gado*

SPIDERTOWN

Author: Abraham Rodriguez, Jr. (1961-)
First published: 1993
Genre: Novel

Locale: South Bronx, New York City
Time: The 1990's
Plot: Bildungsroman

Miguel (mee-GEHL), a sixteen-year-old crack cocaine delivery boy. At one time in his life, he wanted to become a writer, but he abandoned this dream when he realized that there were no famous Puerto Rican writers. In the seventh grade, his English teacher asked him to compose an essay about his father, but he could only think of negative things to say; he then dropped out of school. On the streets, he turned to Spider for support, regarding the crack czar as a surrogate father. Miguel is well read, intelligent, and uncommonly sensitive, but he is also self-deluded. He misconstrues money and power as success and considers himself to be an adult. His relationship with Cristalena forces him to see the perversion and ugliness of his life. Gradually, through a process of self-analysis, he redeems and defines himself. By the end of the novel, he has attained considerable self-awareness and crossed the threshold of maturity.

Amelia, a twenty-one-year-old crack user and psychology major at City College (though she has taken a brief respite from her studies). She is Firebug's girlfriend and Miguel's best friend. Miguel describes her as "funny and twisted and sometimes sad." She has sex with Spider in exchange for crack. Although she suffers from low self-esteem, she is intelligent, sensitive, and independent. She reads books by Charles Dickens and Jean-Paul Sartre, whose existential philosophy appeals to her. She describes herself as a "Latino girl with brains." Unlike her two older sisters, obsequious husband-hunters, Amelia has set her sights on a career as a therapist and a marriage of equality, but the men in her life discouraged her, treated her contemptuously, and drove her to society's fringe, where she lives with junkies, prostitutes, and outcasts. As she counsels Miguel to self-awareness, she undergoes a parallel transformation, finds herself again, and returns to college.

Cristalena (krees-tah-LEH-nah), Miguel's sixteen-year-old girlfriend, a preacher's daughter. She is rebellious, sexually repressed (though not a virgin), and intelligent. Her parents are oppressive religious fanatics. To dress fashionably and date boys, she must resort to subterfuge, changing clothes at school and pretending to spend her evenings at her aunt's apartment. She pursues Miguel aggressively, initiating their first sexual encounter. Miguel is fond of saying that she has a name like a poem, and Amelia describes her jealously as a "Latino Barbie Doll." Her father's fiery sermons on sin continue to haunt her, causing her occasional pangs of guilt. Although naïve and pristine, Cristalena is extremely sensible, a planner by nature. She rejects Miguel's suggestion that they move in together because she knows that they will not be able to support themselves. She is realistic about her age and education and recognizes the necessity of staying in school. Her ambition is to become a dress designer and work in Paris.

Spider, an ambitious crack czar who is both a "Streetwise Patton" and a latter-day Fagin. To dissociate himself from his boring father, who worked for years as a postal employee and then retired to a life of dominoes, Spider entered the exciting, lucrative world of drugs and staked his claim aggressively. Now he considers himself to be an important crime boss. He loves corporate paraphernalia such as business cards, which in his organization are appropriately vague. He boasts that he can "grab a ten-year-old kid and turn him into a successful businessman faster than IBM or ITT." He talks like a successful entrepreneur drunk on the American Dream, yet he dresses poorly and smells bad. Through flattery, bribery, and lies, Spider lures children into his web and devours them.

Firebug, Miguel's roommate, a teenage arsonist. Abused by his father, who used to burn him as punishment, he grew extremely fond of fire. In school, he would throw fiery "scrunchballs" at the teacher, and once he set a girl on fire. He makes a living by burning down tenement buildings for businessmen. He requires his friends to attend his "wienie roasts" to witness his art; he depends on their accounts of the fires to inflate his ego. Because he wants to be ready to move at a moment's notice, he shuns possessions, keeping his few belongings in a gym bag. He seldom displays emotion and may be incapable of genuine emotion.

THE SPIRE

Author: William Golding (1911-1993)
First published: 1964
Genre: Novel

Locale: An English city resembling Salisbury
Time: The fourteenth century
Plot: Symbolism

Jocelin, the dean of the Cathedral Church of Our Lady, somewhere in England. He obtained the position through the influence of his aunt, who was mistress to a previous king. Despite this connection, Jocelin appears a spiritual man, full of visionary faith, feeling called by God to construct a tower and spire for the cathedral. At first, the vision is seen by Jocelin as an act of faith over material impossibilities, such as inadequate foundations. He feels tremendous joy and love as this act of faith begins to take shape. He sees his vision as providing the willpower to motivate those who doubt the feasibility of the project. As opposition and difficulties mount, however, he finds that his will becomes more naked. He realizes that self-sacrifice may not be cost enough; he starts to "sacrifice" those around him, for example, making no move to protect Goody Pangall or her husband. Eventually both die. He also learns to shut difficult people and situations out of his consciousness, to become indifferent to them. This enables him to remain totally uncompromising, whatever the consequences. His will becomes all-consuming and obsessive, and he neglects all of his other duties as he drives the workmen.

Roger Mason, the master builder, the only person, as far as Jocelin is concerned, who has the skill and the workers to build so ambitiously. Roger cannot respond to Jocelin's faith. When he discovers how insufficient the foundations are, he tries to compromise with merely a tower. In this battle of wills, Roger loses, undermined by his own infatuation with Goody. He also fears heights. In the end, he is broken by the tensions, becomes alcoholic, walks off the job, and ultimately attempts suicide, unsuccessfully.

Rachel, Roger's wife and one of the four "pillars," people around him whom Jocelin views as equivalent to the four pillars supporting the new building. Her unconsummated marriage to Roger is a complex affair, full of power struggles yet held together by a brother-and-sister compatibility. Under the growing tensions, she talks incessantly and hysterically. She is left at the end to look after an imbecile husband.

Pangall, another of Jocelin's "pillars." He is the church caretaker and odd-job man, a position held by members of his family since the first building of the cathedral. He has a limp and is impotent. He is made the workmen's scapegoat to ward off bad luck, is persecuted, and is finally ritually murdered, his pleas to Jocelin for protection having remained unanswered.

Goody Pangall, the last of Jocelin's "pillars." She was married to Pangall by Jocelin, to keep her nearby. Her youthful innocence and dutifulness are finally destroyed by Roger Mason's lust for her. She may or may not know the manner of her husband's death. She dies in a sordid childbirth, just as Jocelin is bringing her money to go to a convent to have Roger's child. Jocelin has allowed the affair to go on to keep Roger working on his project, and she dies feeling both accused and betrayed by the church.

Father Anselm, the Lord Sacristan of the cathedral and one of its "Principal Persons." Previously, he was master of novices, one of whom was Jocelin. He is embittered by Jocelin's rise to power and the masterful way in which Jocelin squashed his opposition to the spire. He ceases to be either Jocelin's friend or his confessor, claiming never to have wanted those relationships in the first place.

Father Adam, or **Father Anonymous**, as Jocelin calls him, a cathedral chaplain. He neither supports nor opposes Jocelin. As Jocelin lies dying, he tries in his patient, orthodox way to minister to him, without ever understanding the complexities of Jocelin's mind or motivation.

— *David Barratt*

THE SPLENDORS AND MISERIES OF COURTESANS
(Splendeurs et misères des courtisanes)

Author: Honoré de Balzac (1799-1850)
First published: 1838-1847
Genre: Novels

Locale: Paris, France
Time: The 1820's and 1830's
Plot: Social realism

The Way That Girls Love, 1838, 1844

Jacques Collin (zhahk koh-LA[N]), called **Dodgedeath**, a cold-blooded former convict. Collin murders the Spanish priest **Don Carlos Herrera** and assumes his identity. He then uses the money entrusted to him by other prisoners to install his protégé Lucien in Parisian society.

Lucien Chardon de Rubempré (lew-SYAH[N] shahr-DOHN deh rew-behm-PRAY), a handsome but weak young man of modest background. Rescued from despair by the supposed Don Carlos, Lucien becomes his creature, assumes a title, and, as a wealthy young dandy, sets about to marry an heiress. He falls desperately in love with Esther.

Esther Gobseck, called **The Torpedo**, an illiterate, eighteen-year-old prostitute. Once she has given her heart to Lucien, she abandons her profession. After being insulted in public, Esther attempts suicide, but she is saved by Don Carlos, who sends her to a convent school. Unable to live without Lucien, she is brought back to Paris, and for four happy years, she is his mistress. when Baron Nucingen notices her, she is ordered to become his property instead.

Prudence Servien, also called **Europe** and **Eugénie**, a young former convict. Ostensibly Esther's lady's-maid, she is really Collin's watchdog.

Jacqueline Collin (zhahk-LEEN), sometimes called **Asia**, Collin's aunt, a clever, unprincipled woman who is installed as Esther's cook. She acts for Collin in negotiations with the baron.

Baron Frédéric de Nucingen (fray-day-REEK deh new-sahn-ZHAHN), an elderly banker. No matter how much it costs him, he is determined to possess Esther.

Mademoiselle Clotilde-Fréderique Grandlieu, an unattractive heiress who is desperate to marry Lucien.

Peyrade (pay-RAHD), or **Father Canquoëlle**, an elderly man, formerly a high police official. He loves his illegitimate daughter Lydia dearly.

Corentin (koh-rah[n]-TAHN), a mulatto. Once Peyrade's subordinate, he is now his confederate.

Contenson (koh[n]-teh[n]-ZOH[N]), another spy, a friend of Peyrade and Corentin. He is paid by the baron to discover Esther's identity.

How Much Love May Cost an Old Man, 1844

Jacques Collin, who uses Esther as bait to extort from the baron most of the money that Lucien must have before he can marry. He refuses to be blackmailed by Corentin but instead arranges to have Lydia kidnapped. After Esther's death, he forges a will, by which she leaves her property to Lucien. Both Collin and Lucien are accused of murdering Esther and stealing her money.

Esther Gobseck, who is convinced by Collin that Lucien will go to the gallows if he is exposed. She accepts the baron as her lover. She is unexpectedly left a huge sum of money but kills herself before learning about her inheritance.

Lucien Chardon de Rubempré, who agrees to abandon Esther but loses his chance at marriage when his financial situation is exposed, then is arrested for murder and theft.

Corentin, who, acting as the Grandlieus' agent, discovers the truth about Lucien and tries to blackmail Collin. Corentin is responsible for the arrest of Collin and Lucien.

Peyrade, who learns that Lydia is ill because of her mis-

The End of Bad Roads, 1846

Jacques Collin, who calmly works to clear himself and Lucien.

Lucien Chardon de Rubempré, who ignores Collin's injunction to keep silent and betrays his master, admitting that Don Carlos is in fact Collin. As influential friends are about to have him freed, he panics and hangs himself.

The Last Incarnation of Vautrin, 1847

Jacques Collin, who continues to outmaneuver his enemies. When Europe (Prudence Servien) returns with the missing money and Esther's suicide note, he is cleared of any wrongdoing in her death. Although now known to be Collin, and even by some as the respectable **Vautrin** (voh-TRA[N]), he still has a trump card, Lucien's correspondence, which enables him to save himself, as well as Lucien's predecessor in his

treatment. He dies of apoplexy.

Contenson, who swears revenge on Collin, whom he holds responsible for Peyrade's death. Collin throws him off a roof to his death.

Monsieur Camusot, the timid examining magistrate, who is pressured both by Lucien's friends and by his enemies. He depends on his canny wife for advice.

Bibi-Lupin, the chief of detectives and a former convict. He hates Collin and seeks to have him executed.

affections, Théodore Calvi. He obtains a reward for saving a lady's sanity, claims his inheritance from Lucien, succeeds Bibi-Lupin, and remains chief of detectives for fifteen years.

Corentin, who is forced to offer Collin a pardon and a job.

Bibi-Lipin, who is ordered to leave his old enemy alone, despite all of his crimes, and then loses his job to him.

— *Rosemary M. Canfield Reisman*

THE SPOILERS

Author: Rex Beach (1877-1949)
First published: 1906
Genre: Novel

Locale: The Yukon
Time: During the Alaska gold rush
Plot: Adventure

Roy Glenister, a co-owner of the Midas gold mine. He fights heroically using law and fists to defend himself and his property in the wild Yukon gold country. He falls in love with Helen Chester, until he finds her apparently in league with crooks to cheat the miners of their claims. He is finally convinced of her innocence.

Bill Dextry, a co-owner of the Midas gold mine. He is an old frontiersman who likes living beyond the edge of civilization. When law and order arrive in the gold fields, he announces that he is selling his part of the mine and leaving.

Helen Chester, an American who unwittingly helps a crooked politician in his attempt to steal the miners' claims. With Glenister and Dextry's help, she stows away aboard a ship bound for Alaska. She falls in love with Glenister, finally convinces him of her innocence of wrongdoing, and offers to stay with him in Alaska.

Cherry Malotte, a notorious woman of Nome. She loves

Glenister and tries to help him by telling him of the activities of McNamara, Judge Stillman, and Helen.

Mr. McNamara, a crooked politician. In league with Judge Stillman, he tries to steal the miners' gold claims. He is defeated in his efforts by Glenister, who leads the miners in their fight for justice. He is beaten by Glenister in one of the most famous fistfights in American literature.

Judge Stillman, Helen's uncle and the first federal judge in Alaska. He helps McNamara in the latter's attempts to steal the mining claims.

Mr. Struve, a crooked lawyer who aids McNamara and Judge Stillman in their plots against Glenister and the other miners.

The Broncho Kid, Helen's long-lost brother, a gambler. When Struve attacks Helen because of her knowledge of his dishonest dealings, the Broncho Kid appears and rescues her after shooting Struve.

THE SPOILS OF POYNTON

Author: Henry James (1843-1916)
First published: 1897
Genre: Novel

Locale: England
Time: Late nineteenth century
Plot: Social realism

Mrs. Gereth, the mistress of Poynton. During her husband's lifetime, she and Mr. Gereth had filled Poynton with carefully chosen, exquisite furnishings that had made her beloved house a place of beauty and charm. Apprehensive over the fate of her cherished objects in the hands of Poynton's heir, her insensitive son Owen, she attempts to manipulate his rela-

tionships to guarantee the preservation of the estate and its contents as they are, only to see the house and furnishings finally consumed by fire.

Owen Gereth, Mrs. Gereth's son and the heir to Poynton. Insensitive to the real beauty of Poynton but loving it as his home, he is torn, abetted by his mother's manipulations, between Mona Brigstock, who desires the house for the value of its contents, and Fleda Vetch, who loves it for its beauty. He marries Mona and loses Poynton in a fire.

Mona Brigstock, Owen Gereth's fiancée and later his wife. Although she fails to appreciate Poynton's beauty, she is fully aware of the value of its contents. Finally, triumphant over the

manipulations of Mrs. Gereth, she marries Owen shortly before Poynton and its contents are lost in a fire.

Fleda Vetch, Mrs. Gereth's companion. Loving Poynton for the beauty of the place, she is chosen by Mrs. Gereth as a suitable wife for her son Owen, the heir to Poynton. Fleda falls in love with Owen but loses him to Mona Brigstock.

THE SPOOK WHO SAT BY THE DOOR

Author: Sam Greenlee (1930-   )
First published: 1969
Genre: Novel

Locale: Chicago, Illinois; Washington, D.C.; New York City; and Langley, Virginia
Time: The 1960's
Plot: Social morality

Dan "Turk" Freeman, the protagonist, an idealistic African American who infiltrates the Central Intelligence Agency (CIA) so that he can learn techniques he can develop into guerrilla warfare in the slums of his native Chicago and in other major American cities. He recognizes that he is a "token" of integration. After leaving the CIA, Freeman returns to Chicago as a social worker; organizes the Cobras, a street gang, into a fighting force; and watches them go into action during a civil disturbance.

Pete Dawson, a friend of Freeman's youth, now a Chicago police detective. Freeman hopes to recruit him for the revolution. Instead, when the rioting begins, they become antagonists and eventually fatally wound each other.

Joy, Freeman's college sweetheart, now a buyer for a Chicago department store. Despite sharing Freeman's back-

ground, she is less committed politically and has stronger middle-class aspirations. She decides to marry someone who will provide her with the economic security she thinks she deserves.

The Dahomey Queen, a Washington, D.C., prostitute in whom Freeman tries to instill pride in her African roots. After Freeman leaves the CIA, she becomes the mistress of his former boss.

Pretty Willie Du Bois, the most introspective member of the Cobras. Defensive about the light color of his skin, Pretty Willie is unfocused until Freeman discovers that he writes poetry and short stories and makes him the organization's propagandist.

— *Michael Adams*

SPOON RIVER ANTHOLOGY

Author: Edgar Lee Masters (1868-1950)
First published: 1915
Genre: Poetry

Locale: Spoon River, a Midwestern town
Time: Late nineteenth or early twentieth century
Plot: Social realism

Thomas Rhodes, the president of the bank and the town's most influential citizen. Like the other characters, he is dead and telling his story from a graveyard. A deacon of the town's most prestigious church, he also owned the town store. Under his mismanagement, the bank was ruined, destroying many lives. Although others went to prison, political and social influence allowed Rhodes to plea bargain for an acquittal. When he believed the store manager was stealing blankets to pay his daughter's medical bills, Rhodes hounded him mercilessly. He was a petty, arrogant, self-righteous tyrant who believed that the wealthy deserve rights denied to the poor.

Coolbaugh Whedon, the editor of the *Argus*, Spoon River's conservative newspaper. He served the business interests of the community and admitted to perverting truth for a purpose and accepting money for supporting political candidates. He would publish scandal and crush reputations for business or revenge, or simply to sell more papers. His view of life was negative. From his grave by the river that others find beautiful, he sees only a place where sewage flows, garbage is dumped, and abortions are hidden.

Benjamin Pantier, an attorney, a powerful and strong individual until his wife drove him out of their home. He was then reduced to living in a small room behind his office with his dog, Nig. His wife, who ironically is known only as Mrs.

Benjamin Pantier, loathed him for his drinking and his common nature. The two held opposite views on almost every issue. She was the head of the Social Purity Club, which sought to eliminate drinking, gambling, and horse racing. He enjoyed the saloon and its pleasant camaraderie. Separately, each did good for the community. She campaigned for women's suffrage, and he helped many people in the courtroom. It was only against each other that they unleashed their most destructive forces.

Daisy Frasier, a prostitute who was scorned by the proper citizens. She contributed to the school fund every time she was taken to court. She was more generous and caring than many of the town's more honorable and distinguished citizens. Her house and land were taken away from her because the canning works, run by Ralph Rhodes, son of the bank president, decided it needed her property.

The Reverend Peet, the pastor of the leading church. He often spoke out as the town leaders wished, keeping quiet about many social ills. He was intelligent and well educated, reading Greek as easily as English. After his death, his household goods were auctioned off. The innkeeper bought and burned his sermons.

Indignation Jones, the town carpenter, who was proud of his pure Welsh stock. He was disheveled, with ragged clothes and matted hair. His life had been one disappointment after another. His wife was a slattern. His daughter, Minerva, the town poet, was ridiculed throughout her life for her heavy body and cockeye. After Butch Weldy brutally raped her, she died in an abortion attempt. After this, Indignation Jones simply crept through his life in "impotent revolt."

Doc Meyers, the town doctor, a good-hearted and happy man, content with his life and family. His children were grown and doing well. After Minerva Jones died, he was indicted, and the newspapers pilloried him. He was disgraced, and his wife was unable to forgive him. He was rumored to be the father of Willie Metcalf, the town idiot, who looked a lot like him.

Butch Weldy, a laborer, wild and irresponsible in his youth. When drunk, he not only raped Minerva Jones but also caused an accident that killed Blind Jack, the fiddler. Later, he was blinded in an accident at the canning works. The judge ruled that he would not receive any compensation from the company or Ralph Rhodes, because a fellow worker caused the accident. As jury foreman, Butch helped find Roy Butler guilty of a rape he did not commit.

Mrs. Williams, a milliner, an attractive woman who caught the eye of many of the husbands in Spoon River. She thought it was up to wives to make themselves attractive for their husbands.

Jack McGuire, a friend of Butch Weldy, also wild and irresponsible. One night, while McGuire was walking home drunk, the town marshal, who bitterly opposed drinking, struck him with a club. McGuire killed him and was nearly lynched. He was sentenced to fourteen years in jail instead of life because his lawyer agreed to take pressure off Rhodes in a banking scandal in return for a lighter sentence for his client. He spread the rumors that Willie Metcalf was Doc Meyers' son.

— *Mary E. Mahony*

THE SPORT OF THE GODS

Author: Paul Laurence Dunbar (1872-1906)
First published: 1902; serial form, 1901
Genre: Novel

Locale: A small Southern town and New York City
Time: Late Reconstruction period, c. 1900
Plot: Naturalism

Maurice Oakley, a wealthy Southern businessman and former slaveowner who is kind and generous, especially to his younger half brother, Francis. Maurice becomes a hardened man after making an example of Berry Hamilton, his black butler and trusted servant, who has been accused of stealing a sizable sum of money from Francis. Largely through Oakley's efforts, Berry is sentenced to a long prison term, and his family is evicted from the Oakley estate. Years later, after Francis admits Berry's innocence and his own duplicity, Maurice becomes reclusive and obsessed with hiding this secret. When the truth is exposed by a Northern newspaper, Maurice goes insane.

Berry Hamilton, the trusted butler to Maurice Oakley. Through thrift and industry, Berry has earned a high standing in the community. His fortune changes drastically and immediately when he is falsely convicted of having stolen more than eight hundred dollars from Maurice Oakley's half brother, Francis. Berry spends almost ten years at hard labor, then is pardoned after a New York newspaper exposes the truth. He goes to New York to find his family in shambles and his wife remarried. After reclaiming his wife, Fannie, he returns to the South with her to their old cottage on the Oakley estate, where they live out the rest of their days.

Fannie Hamilton, Berry's proud and illiterate, but thrifty and industrious, wife. She has served as the Oakleys' housekeeper. After Berry's false conviction, she and her children are evicted from the Oakley estate and make their way to New York. There, Fannie helplessly witnesses her family's disintegration. To survive, she marries Tom Gibson, a gambler. After Tom is killed in a fight, Fannie reunites with Berry, and they move back South.

Leslie Oakley, Maurice Oakley's wife. Kindhearted and long-suffering, she nurses her husband in his insanity and makes amends to the Hamiltons by refurnishing their former cottage and inviting them to return to the Oakley estate following Berry's pardon.

Francis (Frank) Oakley, an artist. As the younger half brother of Maurice Oakley, he is pampered and spoiled. He gambles away a large sum of money that his brother provided for him to go to Paris. His fabrication to cover this loss precipitates the charge against Berry Hamilton and Berry's ultimate imprisonment. Years later, when Francis learns of Berry's fate, he confesses his duplicity to his brother, which in turn leads to Maurice's madness.

Joe Hamilton, a barber, Berry and Fannie's son. After Berry is convicted, he loses his job and is unable to find work. When his family is evicted from the Oakley estate, Joe takes his mother and sister to New York. In the city, Joe is defeated by life in the fast lane. He begins drinking heavily and becomes estranged from his mother and sister. Finally, while drunk, he strangles his lover to death and is sent to prison.

Kit Hamilton, a dancer, Berry and Fannie's daughter. She is beautiful, charming, and condescending. After arriving in New York, she begins going out with William Thomas. Unknown to her, he is married. Afterward, she becomes a showgirl in "Martin's Blackbirds," a touring revue.

Hattie Sterling, a dancer. As one of "Martin's Blackbirds," she becomes Joe Hamilton's lover and is instrumental in helping Kit obtain a job in the troupe. Finally tiring of Joe's constant drunkenness, she puts him out. Later that night, he kills her in an act of retaliation.

Mr. Skaggs, a newspaper reporter. As a frequent visitor to Harlem, Skaggs is acquainted with Joe Hamilton. After hearing Joe's account of his father's innocence, Skaggs goes South to the Hamiltons' hometown. There, he forcibly obtains Maurice Oakley's secret about the missing money. His subsequent exposé in the New York *Universe* leads to Berry's pardon and contributes to Maurice's insanity.

Minty Brown, a visitor to New York, originally from the Hamiltons' hometown. Minty calls on the Hamiltons. Having shunned Minty at home, Fannie and Kit Hamilton condescendingly refuse to accept her visit. In retaliation, Minty exposes the Hamiltons' predicament, which results in their eviction from their apartment and being dismissed from their jobs.

Tom Gibson, a gambler on horse races. As a boarder in Fannie Hamilton's flat, he convinces her that Berry's conviction and imprisonment nullified their marriage and convinces her to marry him. After their marriage, Tom frequently beats Fannie. He is killed in a fight at the racetrack.

— *Warren J. Carson*

THE SPORTING CLUB

Author: Thomas McGuane (1939-   )
First published: 1969
Genre: Novel

Locale: Michigan
Time: The 1960's
Plot: Regional

James Quinn, a young Michigan businessman who has recently assumed control of his father's tool and die business. Quinn has retreated to the Centennial Club in the Michigan woods for rest and relaxation. To his dismay, he learns that his old friend and rival, Vernor Stanton, has also arrived. Reluctantly at first, but then with some of his old enthusiasm, Quinn joins Stanton in duels and in his attempts to bring chaos to the Club and its members, eventually participating in the Club's abrupt demise. Throughout the novel, he is in a quandary between fighting Stanton's influence or playing along wholeheartedly and between being the responsible businessman or a fomenter of discord.

Vernor Stanton, a mad, extremely wealthy, and bored man who finds pleasure in disrupting his environment with practical jokes and outright cruelty. Using the Centennial Club as his stage, Stanton enlists the help of Quinn to disrupt and destroy the Club in less than a month. His "jokes" include such acts as dueling with antique pistols loaded with wax bullets in his cellar (a relatively harmless but very painful experience for Quinn), stealing a dignitaries' bus from a bridge dedication ceremony, fomenting the move to fire the Club's manager, and constantly irritating and antagonizing fellow Club members. He eventually goes officially insane, threatening and controlling the assembled Club members with a tripod-mounted machine gun. Some months later, he apparently partially recovers, buys the Club property, returns, and is watched over by Janey and "attendants" who carefully control his activities.

Janey, Stanton's girlfriend, who sticks by him in spite of his cruelty and madness. A physically attractive, concerned, and mild-mannered woman, Janey unintentionally attracts Quinn, who wants to rescue her from Stanton. She is completely loyal to Stanton, however, dismayed by many of his antics but at the same time fascinated by the charm and strength of the man. Her presence forces Quinn to see a side of Stanton that he would rather ignore, and this knowledge forces him to remain concerned and interested in what Stanton does.

Jack Olson, the Club's manager and an accomplished outdoorsman. He is a member of one of the families dispossessed when the Club acquired its extensive acreage, and he has spent a lifetime poaching on and managing Club property. He is so adept at hunting and fishing that he embarrasses the wealthy Club members who associate hunting and fishing with masculinity. He becomes a target for their ire as they plot with Stanton to get rid of him, even though they know that he is irreplaceable as a manager. When he realizes their plans, he hires Earl Olive as his replacement and disappears.

Earl Olive, an uneducated crook and purveyor of live bait. He is hired by Olson as the Club's manager, a move designed by Olson to avenge himself for the treatment he has received. Olive, who has no respect for the Club's "reputation," brings in his crowd of rowdy friends, who party and fornicate openly. Painfully beaten and embarrassed by Stanton in a duel, he dynamites the dam, which drains the lake, and in the resulting chaos he dynamites the main lodge, the lifeguard's platform, and the flagpole. Finally captured by angry Club members, he is freed by Stanton, wielding a machine gun.

Fortescue, an old-time Club member and collector of military miniatures. While the Club is "at war" with Earl Olive and his crowd, Fortescue assumes command as its members attempt to handle Olive without the intervention of the law. He becomes a little despot as he attempts to live out his military fantasies, even to the point of outfitting his "army" at his own expense. As inept as he is enthusiastic, he is ultimately caught and tarred and feathered by Earl Olive and his gang.

Spengler, the Club chronicler. As a means of celebrating the first hundred years of the Club's existence, he has written a history of the Club and the surrounding area, focusing on the illustrious founding fathers and claiming to base all of this on what he calls "solid research." Eventually disillusioned by the antics of the present members, he burns his chronicle before the centennial celebration, which includes the unearthing of the capsule buried by the Club's founders. This capsule contains information that destroys any notion that the founders were illustrious.

Scott, an old-time Club member and obsequious professor. He is basically a non-person, often present and speaking but always ignored.

Charles Murray, an old-time Club member. He is a homosexual, alternately chasing the heavyset daughter of Fortescue, Quinn, and others. He is also basically ignored by the other members, except when they are escaping his advances.

— *David E. Huntley*

THE SPORTSWRITER

Author: Richard Ford (1944-   )
First published: 1986
Genre: Novel

Locale: Haddam, New Jersey
Time: The 1980's
Plot: Character study

Frank Bascombe, a thirty-eight-year-old divorced man who, twelve years earlier, turned his back on a promising literary career to become a sportswriter for a magazine based in New York. Frank took up writing at college in Michigan after a medical discharge from the Navy. In the year following his graduation, he wrote a collection of stories, *Blue Autumn*, that was published to favorable reviews and optioned by a film producer, giving him the financial independence to embark on a writing career in New York. There, he renewed his acquaintance with X, a woman he met at school and whom he marries. Shortly after beginning work on his second novel (his first, written in college, was rejected and lost), he found himself blocked and inexplicably unenthusiastic about his chosen profession. He took the sportswriting job as a respite from fiction writing but knew that he had lost the impetus to complete his novel and would never write fiction again. Frank's growing disaffection with the life he chose was exacerbated several years later by the tragic death of his nine-year-old son, Ralph, from Reye's syndrome. Ralph's death marked the onset of Frank's "dreaminess," a period in which he grew increasingly estranged from X, had affairs with other women, and seemed generally lost. Since emerging from his dreaminess, Frank has come to appreciate the allure that sportswriting has for him. He believes that sports are governed by an orderliness and precision that he cannot find elsewhere in life, and that the best athletes have an admirable one-dimensionality that binds their identities to the games they play. Frank is currently dating Vicki, an earthy younger woman whose directness he finds pleasing, but he remains on good terms with X and his two children, Clarissa and Paul. Although subject to occasional anxieties, he is affable and friendly with everyone he meets and seems relatively content with his current middle-class life. While visiting with Vicki's family for the first time on Easter Sunday, he receives a phone call informing him that Walter Luckett, a member of the informal Divorced Men's Club to which he belongs, has committed suicide. The death catalyzes Vicki's breakup with Frank, just when he thought he would ask her to marry him, and reacquaints him with feelings of grief he has not dealt with since Ralph's death. It also forces him to acknowledge that Walter had been trying for some time to reach out to him for help and that he, in his detachment from others, was oblivious to his friend's needs. The experience leaves him shaken but wiser, and the novel ends with him reassessing his life and wondering where he will go from here.

X, Frank's remarkably patient former wife, whose real first name he never mentions. She is from an affluent family in Michigan, where she spent her school years modeling and training to be a golf professional. She marries Frank shortly after he moves to New York at the start of his literary career, and she gives up her own job to become a housewife when she is pregnant with their first son, Ralph. After Ralph's death, her relationship with Frank turns a corner. In the debris left by robbers who broke into their house, she discovers a secret cache of love letters written to Frank by another woman. Even after the divorce, she shows a fondness for Frank that transcends her interest in keeping what is left of their family together. She is one of the few constants in Frank's life and the only person who understands the full extent of his alienation. Her half-serious talk about remarrying is one of several factors that affect Frank's rapprochement with the world at the novel's end.

Vicki Arcenault, a fun-loving thirty-year-old nurse who projects a matter-of-fact honesty that Frank finds appealing. She started dating Frank shortly after stitching his hand in the emergency room and often travels with him on his assignments. Although she appears to have the sort of one-dimensional personality that Frank envies, she shows surprising perceptiveness when she breaks up with Frank because she realizes that he is using her as an emotional crutch.

Walter Luckett, a pensive and moody businessman who is plunged into self-doubt when his wife runs off with another man. He befriends Frank through the Divorced Men's Club and confides a homosexual encounter he had after the breakup of his marriage. Walter repeatedly tries to get Frank to go out for a drink and probe his life but is always tactfully rebuffed. When he commits suicide, Frank realizes that Walter had lost his emotional bearings and was desperate to communicate with someone whom he thought would understand him.

— *Stefan Dziemianowicz*

SPRING AWAKENING: A Children's Tragedy
(Frühlings Erwachen)

Author: Frank Wedekind (1864-1918)
First published: 1891
Genre: Drama

Locale: Germany
Time: The nineteenth century
Plot: Psychological realism

Melchior Gabor (MEHL-shee-ohr gah-BOHR), a promising high school student. He is beginning to feel the effects of sexual phenomena. In a note, he imparts his knowledge of sex to his friend, Moritz Stiefel. When Moritz commits suicide and the note is found, Melchior is condemned for moral corruption. His mother upholds him until she is confronted with the fact of his classmate Wendla Bergmann's pregnancy, for which he is responsible.

Moritz Stiefel (MOH-rihts STEE-fehl), a friend of Melchior Gabor. Plagued by sexual urges and fear of failure in his studies, he commits suicide.

Wendla Bergmann (VAYN-dlah BEHRG-mahn), a fourteen-year-old who conceives a child by Melchior Gabor. She dies during an attempted abortion.

Mrs. Bergmann, Wendla's mother. She evades the truth in answering her daughter's questions about love and sex.

Mr. Gabor and
Mrs. Gabor, Melchior's parents.

Martha and
Thea, friends of Wendla, with whom she exchanges confidences about love and sex.

Ilse (IHL-seh), a prostitute who attempts to seduce Moritz Stiefel.

Mr. Stiefel, Moritz Stiefel's father, a pensioner.

Dr. Von Brausepulver (BROW-seh-pool-fur) and

Mother Schmidt, abortionists whose concoctions cause Wendla Bergmann's death.

A muffled gentleman, who appears to the ghost of Moritz Stiefel and the living Melchior Gabor as they converse among the graves. He upbraids Moritz for his attempt to lure Melchior into the land of the dead. He and Melchior withdraw together.

SPRING MOON: A Novel of China

Author: Bette Bao Lord (1938-   )
First published: 1981
Genre: Novel

Locale: China
Time: 1892-1972
Plot: Historical realism

Spring Moon, the protagonist and title character. She is the wife of Glad Promise and the niece and mistress of Bold Talent. Under Bold Talent's tutelage, Spring Moon learns to read and write. Though a rebellious youth, she becomes enamored with the idea of marriage and yields unexpectedly and almost enthusiastically to tradition. Only her husband's antipathy for tradition prevents her from becoming a traditional Chinese wife. Throughout her life, Spring Moon adapts to her surroundings, never afraid to change but never eager to abandon the ways of her ancestors. Her pliability represents a sensible mean between the antitraditionalism of Lustrous Jade, her daughter, and the traditionalism of Golden Virtue, Bold Talent's dutiful wife.

Lustrous Jade, the daughter of Spring Moon and Glad Promise. As a child, she is taunted by her peers for having big (or unbound) feet. Her grandmother, Lotus Delight, nicknames her "Worthless Jewel" because she is not a boy. Her grandfather, Fierce Rectitude, refers to her as his "son" on his deathbed, and from that moment on Lustrous Jade is condemned to be her "father's daughter" and her "grandfather's son." Her identity crisis manifests itself as fanaticism, first for Christianity, then for Communism. As an adult, she is a stubborn zealot, disdainful of tradition and often unbending in her convictions.

Bold Talent, the patriarch of the Chang family. In his seventh year at Yale, he receives word of his father's death and must return to China to assume the role of patriarch. Progressive in his ideas, he commits himself to the modernization of China, focusing his efforts mainly on educational and medical reforms. He becomes Spring Moon's tutor and falls in love with her, later taking her as his mistress. Unlike his forebears, he tolerates dissension from the clan women, particularly Lustrous Jade, who argues openly with him and disregards his wishes.

August Winds, a typical capitalist, an orphaned relative of the Chang family. Adopted by Bold Talent, he grows up in the Chang household. When he comes of age, he disappears for several years and returns as a wealthy man. Determined to make Lustrous Jade his wife, he initiates a whirlwind courtship, but Lustrous Jade rejects his proposals, though she ironically accepts his gifts and favors. As an adult, August Winds is confident, shrewd, good natured, and resilient.

Enduring Promise, the illegitimate son of Spring Moon and Bold Talent. In the late 1940's, he immigrates to the West and becomes a professor of Chinese history. Soon after the opening of Communist China in 1972, he returns to Shoochow to find Spring Moon.

Noble Talent, a professional soldier, Spring Moon's unmarried uncle.

Resolute Spirit, Lustrous Jade's husband, the son of a peasant farmer.

— *Edward A. Malone*

THE SPY: A Tale of the Neutral Ground

Author: James Fenimore Cooper (1789-1851)
First published: 1821
Genre: Novel

Locale: New York State
Time: 1780 and 1812
Plot: Historical

Harvey Birch, a peddler, generally believed to be a British spy, in this novel of the American Revolution. He is, however, an American patriot spying against the British.

Mr. Harper, the assumed name of disguised **General George Washington**.

Mr. Wharton, a British sympathizer who extends his hospitality to Mr. Harper during a storm.

Frances Wharton, his daughter, an ideal American woman who is in love with Major Peyton Dunwoodie.

Sarah Wharton, another daughter, whose plans of marriage to Colonel Wellmere are interrupted by news that Wellmere already has a wife who has just crossed from England expecting to join him.

Henry Wharton, the son of Mr. Wharton. A captain in the British army, he is wrongly sentenced to hang as a British spy but escapes through the good offices of Harvey Birch and with the help of Mr. Harper, who thus rewards Mr. Wharton's hospitality.

Major Peyton Dunwoodie, an ideal American officer. He wins the hand of Frances Wharton.

Colonel Wellmere, a British officer who professes to be in love with Sarah Wharton, though he has a wife in England.

Captain Lawton, an American officer finally killed in combat with the British but previously engaged in a gentlemanly pursuit of the supposed British spy Birch.

Isabella Singleton, the sister of an American officer who is recuperating at the Wharton home. Frances believes that Isabella's love for Major Dunwoodie is returned until Isabella, accidentally and fatally wounded, assures her of the contrary.

Miss Jeanette Peyton, the aunt of Sarah and Frances Wharton, also a member of the Wharton household.

Caesar Thompson, the Whartons' black servant.

Captain Wharton Dunwoodie, the son of Major Dunwoodie and Frances. He is an officer in the War of 1812. After a battle, he finds on the body of Harvey Birch a letter that reveals the old man's long years of self-sacrificing patriotism.

A SPY IN THE HOUSE OF LOVE

Author: Anaïs Nin (1903-1977)
First published: 1954
Genre: Novel

Locale: A large city identified with New York and its environs
Time: Late 1940's and early 1950's
Plot: Psychological

Sabina, a thirty-year-old woman who is looking for the ultimate bliss of true love. Extremely attractive and highly sexual but continuously thwarted by guilt, she wastes her energy desperately looking for a satisfying psychosexual relationship. She is married to Alan but has a series of encounters with other men. She assumes a variety of fictive roles, ranging from the prostitute to the spiritual mother, but finds all of them frustrating. She consistently finds herself an onlooker rather than a participant in life and uses her sexual addiction as a means to avoid accepting her inner purity and goodness. She defines herself as a spy in the house of love and, therefore, incapable of sharing in its joys.

The Lie Detector, a mysterious stranger whom Sabina randomly calls on the telephone at the beginning of the novel. They meet from time to time throughout the narrative as he becomes Sabina's confessor and absolver. He delineates for her the variety and levels of guilt and atonement and tells her that they are stratagems by which she avoids uncovering her true nature. Sabina eventually discovers that he is a creation of her own imagination.

Alan, Sabina's thirty-five-year-old, amiable husband. Tall and extremely handsome, with graying sideburns, he protects her from the realities of life. Completely devoted to her, he is the only fixed point in her life and gives her fatherly solicitude. Although sexually desirable, he is passive and does not possess the kind of passionate desire that Sabina finds in other men; he is her guardian angel from whom she wishes absolution because she has been unfaithful to him so often. He is preoccupied by his work and seems oblivious to her affairs.

Philip, a Wagnerian tenor and sometime lover of Sabina. He is a large, powerfully built, broad-shouldered, and handsome man in his thirties. Although he is pursued relentlessly by many women, he finds Sabina an exceptional lover, although his athletic lovemaking fails initially to bring her to climax. After successive tries, he finally breaks through her frigidity and names her "Dona Juana"; that is, he makes her

the feminine counterpart of his own role as an infamous Don Juan.

Donald, a slender, beautiful, and delicate young homosexual who loves Sabina in a passionate but platonic fashion. His seductive voice and passive indolence, combined with his penchant for satirizing everything and everybody, entertain Sabina enormously and relieve her temporarily from her chronic boredom. Sabina becomes for Donald a loving maternal figure. He names her "The Firebird" and makes her feel innocent.

John, a young man in his twenties who has been grounded as a rear gunner from the British Air Corps. Sabina meets him on Long Island, and they are immediately drawn to each other because of their shared incipient madness. He has experienced the hell of war and cannot blot it out. He is an elusive and gentle lover but manages to melt her frigidity. He, too, suffers from sexual guilt, which Sabina wants to help him overcome.

Mambo, a black jazz musician from the Caribbean, in his twenties. He and Sabina become lovers for a while, although he distrusts all white women because he has been their sexual toy for years. He claims that they only want to experience the darkly romantic energy of the tropics but want nothing to do with bearing him black children and living as natives do.

Jay, a painter and former lover of Sabina. They met earlier, in the Montparnasse section of Paris, and experienced an open, sexual relationship. The war forced him back to the United States, however, where he does not seem to be able to produce anything but fragmentary, satiric paintings. He is half bald, has narrow eyes, and resembles Lao Tze.

Djuna, a beautiful, exotic, and highly accomplished dancer in her thirties. Her dancing enables her to distinguish illusion from reality, and she tries to convince Sabina that she is innocent and that it is Sabina's inability to love herself that drives her to fabricate the Lie Detector who, in turn, exacerbates her guilt.

— *Patrick Meanor*

THE SPY WHO CAME IN FROM THE COLD

Author: John le Carré (David John Moore Cornwell, 1931-)
First published: 1963
Genre: Novel

Locale: London, Berlin, and East Germany
Time: Early 1960's
Plot: Spy

Alec Leamas, a British spy, about fifty years old and a loner. Leamas, the former head of a network of undercover agents operating out of Berlin, is directed by British Intelli-

gence to stage a fake defection and bring about the downfall of Hans-Dieter Mundt, a top East German agent. Tough-minded and cynical, Leamas has long avoided the moral and ethical questions raised by his work, adopting the unspoken philosophy of his profession that any action is justified if it achieves the desired results. Divorced and the father of children he rarely sees, Leamas is a case-hardened and emotionally isolated man until he begins a relationship with Liz Gold.

Liz Gold, a woman in her early twenties, naïve, idealistic, and a member of the Communist Party. Liz is working in a London library when she meets Leamas and becomes his lover. Tall, awkward, intelligent, and serious, Liz believes passionately in the future of world communism. She is warm and loving toward Leamas, and she remains ignorant of the true nature of his work until she becomes an unwitting participant in the espionage plot. Her journey to East Germany forces her to confront the realities of life in a communist state and ends with her death at the Berlin Wall.

Control, the head of British Intelligence. Known only by his code name, Control is a mixture of old school manners and ruthless tactics. Detached and enigmatic, he is the master manipulator who pulls the strings that hold the complex espionage operation together, often risking the lives of his agents to achieve the results he wants.

Hans-Dieter Mundt, the deputy director of operations for the East German intelligence community. A onetime Nazi, Mundt is a cruel, ruthless man who has brought about the death of several agents and is disliked and feared even by his own people. He is also, as Leamas at last learns, a highly placed double agent working for the British.

Fiedler, Mundt's second-in-command and a committed Communist. Fiedler, too, is mistrusted by his own people and is infamous among British agents for his savage interrogation techniques. Fiedler, a Jew, has long hated the anti-Semitic Mundt and sees Leamas as the key to his superior's downfall.

Miss Crail, the head librarian at the Bayswater Library for Psychic Research. Spinsterish, sour-tempered, and a stickler for details, Miss Crail takes an immediate dislike to Leamas, who spends a brief period working in the library.

William Ashe, a low-level Eastern bloc agent operating in England. The effete and homosexual Ashe first makes contact with Leamas regarding a possible defection.

Peters, Ashe's superior. Peters is assigned to handle Leamas' defection and to take him to East Berlin.

Karl Riemeck, an East German official who has been acting as a British double agent. Riemeck is the last surviving member of Leamas' Berlin network of spies. He is killed in the book's opening pages as he attempts to cross over to the Western side.

— *Janet Lorenz*

THE SPYGLASS TREE

Author: Albert Murray (1916-   )
First published: 1991
Genre: Novel

Locale: Southern Alabama
Time: The 1910's to the 1930's
Plot: Psychological realism

Scooter, the otherwise unnamed narrator, a young African American boy who grows up in Mobile, Alabama, and later attends Tuskegee Institute in Tuskegee, Alabama. Scooter's childhood consists mainly of baseball and blues music until he begins attending Mobile County Training School, where he falls under the influence of some memorable teachers. They instill in him the belief that nothing can stop him but his own limitations, and they help him to obtain a scholarship to Tuskegee Institute, the famous central Alabama African American college. There Scooter acquires a somewhat eccentric roommate from Chicago and becomes involved with the local jazz performers. He finally puts all of his skills to the test when he helps to end a potential racial conflict by riding shotgun, armed with a .38 automatic.

Little Buddy Marshall, the narrator's best friend while growing up. Little Buddy is in many ways the opposite of the narrator. Instead of excelling at Mobile County Training School, Little Buddy drops out of school and begins to ride the rails.

Luzana Cholly, a blues singer, master of the twelve-string guitar, and mentor to the two boys. Though a rider of the rails himself, he discourages the boys from emulating his life and drifting from town to town.

Lexine Metcalf, one of the teachers at the Mobile County Training School. Her job is to motivate the students to escape the fate of people such as Luzana Cholly and even Little Buddy Marshall. She is the first to recognize Scooter's talent and convinces him to spend extra time at school and at his studies.

B. Franklin Fisher, head of the Mobile County Training School. He helped form the "talented Tenth" of the African American school and required from them more than was expected of other students. He helps to secure Scooter's college scholarship.

T. Jerome Jefferson, Scooter's eccentric college roommate, a native of Chicago. His big-city ways balance Scooter's down-home approach to life.

Giles Cunningham, the owner of a group of jazz and blues clubs and bars in the vicinity of Tuskegee Institute. The climax of the novel is his confrontation with a local white businessman, Dudley Philpot.

Hortense Hightower, a jazz singer at Giles Cunningham's clubs. Hortense initiates Scooter into the world of jazz clubs and into the world of black and white conflict. When Giles Cunningham and Dudley Philpot become enemies, Scooter is asked to ride shotgun as Hortense's bodyguard.

Dudley Philpot, a white businessman and owner of a check-cashing operation. When one of his clients, Will Spradley, has his check cashed by Giles Cunningham, Philpot is deprived of the percentage of the check that he takes as a fee for cashing it. This turf battle leads to the crisis at the end of the novel.

— *Jeff Cupp*

THE STAND

Author: Stephen King (1947-   )
First published: 1978; revised, 1990
Genre: Novel

Locale: The United States
Time: June 16, 1985-Summer, 1986
Plot: Apocalyptic

Stuart Redman, a widowed factory worker. Big and strong, Stu is quiet and competent. As a survivor of the superflu, he serves as a "lab rat" until the death of his captors, who are government employees. He escapes, joins with others, and leads them to Mother Abigail's and on to Colorado, where he becomes a leader, eventually taking a group to the West to take on Flagg. Injured and left on the way, he is the only survivor of the expedition to Las Vegas.

Frannie Goldsmith, a pregnant, unmarried college student. Tall and leggy, with long chestnut hair, Frannie is "prime stuff." The object of Stu Redman's affection as well as Harold Lauder's, she is gentle and understanding, a helpmate and colleague to Stu. Frannie's son is the first child born who contracts and survives the superflu.

Harold Emery Lauder, later called **Hawk**, an exceptionally bright, socially inept teenager. The unwashed, overweight, and unpleasant spoiled child gives way to a hard, determined young man who winds up with the unlikely sobriquet "Hawk." His intelligence guides him, and those who follow, safely to Mother Abigail's and Colorado, but he becomes twisted because he wants Frannie, who loves Stu. He teams with Nadine Cross to destroy the town leaders. After their escape from Boulder, he is injured and abandoned by Nadine Cross. Realizing that he has been and done wrong, he writes an apology (later found by the Las Vegas expedition) and commits suicide.

Larry Underwood, a rock-and-roll singer. Larry is not a nice guy until he confronts himself after his companion's accidental death. After an infatuation with Nadine Cross, he grows to love Lucy Swann, who supports him. First as group leader, then as community leader, he finds the strength to do the right thing in refusing Nadine and later finds the strength again in Las Vegas to not give in to fear or to Randall Flagg, even in the face of death.

Nick Andros, a deaf and mute wanderer. Small, dark, thin, and younger looking than his twenty-two years, Nick is bright, responsible, honest, generous, and compassionate. He looks after victims of the superflu and after Tom Cullen and is an organizer as well as a leader because of his native intelligence. His death at the hands of Harold Lauder and Nadine Cross demoralizes the people of the Free Zone.

Tom Cullen, a mentally deficient man. Near forty but with the mind of a child, Tom is youthful and Nordic looking. Under hypnosis, he becomes God's Tom, cognizant and righteous, and he is sent to spy on Flagg and the evil in Las Vegas. He is the only man of the Free Zone to enter Las Vegas and survive, finding Stu and helping him on his way back to Colorado.

Glendon Pequod Bateman, an aging sociology professor. Gray-haired and sixtyish, Glen is a scholar and adviser. He helps to organize the people of Boulder into a community. He goes to Las Vegas to confront and confound Flagg.

Kojak, a friendly Irish setter. Kojak is Stu Redman's guardian after his injury. He keeps Stu alive until Tom Cullen comes along to help him return to Boulder. The only dog found alive after the superflu, Kojak is a reminder of destruction until a bitch is found, and then they become the hope of a species.

Nadine Cross, a virgin schoolteacher. Pretty, with dark hair turning prematurely white, Nadine is enigmatic. She is destined to bear Flagg's child, dreaming of him and keeping herself for him. A desperate, rebuffed, last-minute bid for Larry convinces her that she is not wanted. She turns wholly to the evil of Flagg, planning the demise of Boulder's leaders, only to discover her grave mistake when she meets Flagg. Her death at his hands is a turning point for evil.

Leo Rockaway, a disturbed boy. First appearing as the feral **Joe** in the care of Nadine Cross, Leo begins to blossom, first as a musical prodigy, then as a clairvoyant. He senses evil about Harold Lauder and refuses to go near him; he knows what is happening elsewhere. Nadine Cross's defection sets him back, and he turns to Larry Underwood for care.

Mother Abigail Freemantle Trotts, an old, religious black woman. Mother Abigail, at the age of 108, is thin, with thinning white hair. She is the spiritual leader of the group in Colorado. Survivors have dreamed of her and sought her out. She is the voice of God and the voice of reason, setting people on the paths chosen for them. She dies after a sojourn in the wilderness.

Randall Flagg, a wicked creature. He is dark, but not identifiable as black or white. People dream of Flagg and see no face, only burning red eyes. Flagg is evil. He draws his followers, keeping them with fear and punishing dissidents with crucifixion. The evil he unleashes goes beyond his control, undermining his power.

Lloyd Henreid, a thief, a murderer, and Flagg's right-hand man. Flagg saves Lloyd from having to resort to cannibalism in his jail cell, and Lloyd becomes his first "convert." Never very bright but easily persuaded, Lloyd is swept along with Flagg until he realizes that he has become smarter. This knowledge comes at about the same time that he notices that things are going wrong.

Donald Merwin "Trashcan Man" Elbert, an imbalanced arsonist. With strange, muddy eyes and one arm a mass of burn scars, Trash is Randall Flagg's secret weapon. He is drawn to instruments of destruction, finally finding the ultimate hardware: a nuclear warhead. He takes it to Flagg in atonement for blowing up his air force. The resultant explosion destroys Las Vegas, Flagg's followers, and some of the surviving members of the expedition from the Free Zone.

— Terry Hays Jackson

STANLEY AND THE WOMEN

Author: Kingsley Amis (1922-1995)
First published: 1984
Genre: Novel

Locale: London, England
Time: Mid-1980's
Plot: Social satire

Stanley Duke, the narrator, the advertising manager of a London newspaper. He is a balding, middle-aged man now in his second marriage. He is intelligent and perceptive; still, he has little understanding of women, at least of the women in his own life. When his son falls ill, he is beleaguered by three women—his former wife, his current wife, and the doctor treating his son—all of whom, he believes, are behaving toward him in a hostile and irrational manner.

Steve Duke, Stanley's nineteen-year-old son, from his first marriage. He is believed to be traveling in Spain with his girlfriend, but he turns up suddenly at Stanley's door. He talks and behaves in a bizarre fashion and eventually is diagnosed as schizophrenic and committed to a hospital for treatment. He is released into his father's care for a time but is recommitted after his stepmother alleges that he attacked and slightly wounded her with a knife.

Nowell Hutchinson, Stanley's first wife, to whom he was married for thirteen years. She is a fading television actress now married to a television producer. She is a selfish woman who has the facility for creating an alternate reality, which always suits her own interests. She attempts to take care of Steve for a day or so but quickly concludes that his illness is his father's fault and that she bears no responsibility.

Susan Duke, Stanley's second wife. She is an assistant literary editor for a London newspaper. A tall brunette, thirty-eight years of age, she is on the surface a perfect wife. She

subtly attempts to force Stanley to choose between his son and her. Finally, she charges that Steve attacked her, but her wound may well have been self-inflicted.

Trish Collings, the psychiatrist in charge of Steve's case. She is a nervous, restless young woman who takes an instant dislike to Stanley. She seems less interested in curing Steve than in proving that Stanley is vaguely responsible for his son's condition.

Bert Hutchinson, Nowell's second husband, the man for whom she left Stanley. He is a television producer. In one scene, he and Stanley get drunk together. They come to share an unspoken camaraderie, based on their common experience of being married to an exceedingly difficult woman.

Lindsey Lucas, a women's page columnist for a London daily. She is a fair, attractive woman with a Northern Ireland accent. She is an exact contemporary of Susan, and Stanley had an affair with her between his marriages. He gets on with her well, probably because he is not married to her.

Lady Daly, Stanley's mother-in-law, the widow of a Conservative member of Parliament. In her middle or late sixties, she is yet another woman with whom Stanley has a tenuous relationship. She is not very bright and is completely lacking in humor. The distant quality of their relationship is characterized by his term of address for her, "lady."

— *Patrick Adcock*

THE STAR OF SEVILLE
(La estrella de Sevilla)

Author: Unknown (but sometimes attributed to Lope de Vega Carpio (1562-1635)
First performed: c. 1617
Genre: Drama

Locale: Seville
Time: The thirteenth century
Plot: Tragedy

Sancho IV (SAHN-choh), called Sancho the Brave, the king of Castile. He falls in love with Estrella Tabera, the betrothed of Don Sancho Ortiz. The king, in disguise, bribes his way into her home but is recognized by her brother, who refuses to acknowledge him as the king, claiming that no ruler would stoop to dishonor. Unable to act in his own person, the king promises Don Sancho any bride he may choose in return for killing an enemy. Don Sancho, finding that he must kill his fiancée's brother, is faithful to his oath of loyalty and kills Don Bustos. Imprisoned, he loyally remains silent, and King Sancho must order his execution. At the plea of Estrella, he gives her the power to decide the fate of Don Sancho. When she frees him, the king is forced to confess his own guilt.

Estrella Tabera (ehs-TREH-yah tah-BEH-rah), the Star of Seville. When her fiancé, Don Sancho, kills her brother at the

king's command, she saves Don Sancho's life but refuses to marry him because of the murder.

Don Bustos Tabera (BEWS-tohs), Estrella's brother, who insults the disguised king and is killed in a duel by his sister's fiancé.

Don Sancho Ortiz (ohr-TEES), Estrella's betrothed. At the king's command, he kills her brother and, unswervingly loyal, refuses to reveal the truth. He is saved from execution by Estrella, but they never marry.

Don Arias (AH-ree-ahs), the king's confidant.

Don Pedro de Guzmán (PEH-droh deh guhs-MAHN) and

Don Farfán de Riviera (fahr-FAHN deh rree-va-rah), alcaldes of Seville.

Matilde (mah-TEEL-deh), a maid who admits the disguised king to Estrella's house. She is hanged by Don Bustos.

Clarindo (klahr-EEN-doh), Don Sancho's servant.

STARING AT THE SUN

Author: Julian Barnes (1946-   )
First published: 1986
Genre: Novel

Locale: Southern England
Time: c. 1930-2020
Plot: Science fiction

Jean Serjeant, the wife of Michael Curtis and mother of Gregory. Jean lives to be ninety-nine years old, and her preoccupation with the wonders of the world and life's disappointments makes her a major voice in the discussion of the significance of human existence in this novel. She is reared as the daughter of a grocer in Bryden and comes to maturity during World War II. As a young woman, Jean is much impressed by the speculations on death, fear, and heroism uttered by the Royal Air Force (RAF) officer who is billeted with her family, but she settles for a marriage to Michael, a police constable. Her life sours as Michael's traditional notions of domestic life and sexuality become increasingly onerous. After almost two decades of married life, Jean leaves her husband when she is thirty-nine years old and seven months pregnant with her first child. She subsequently takes on a number of temporary jobs in pubs and cheap restaurants in an effort to support herself and her son, Gregory. In late middle age, Jean experiences a brief lesbian relationship with Rachel, one of her son's girlfriends, and she becomes preoccupied with foreign travel, particularly with her own list of the seven wonders of the world. In her old age, she turns her attention to the wonders of her life and to the pattern presented by her experiences. At the end of the novel, she joins Gregory in a final airplane ride, which allows them both to confront the brilliant image of the sun.

Sergeant-Pilot Thomas Prosser, a short, slim man with brilliantined black hair and a small mustache. Originally from somewhere near Blackburn in Lancashire, Prosser is a Hurricane IIB fighter pilot in the RAF during World War II. He is grounded temporarily when he is billeted with the Serjeants. Nicknamed "Sun-UP" by his fellow fliers, Prosser is something of a battle ace who has increasingly lost his nerve. In his conversations with Jean, Prosser describes watching the sun rise twice in an early morning flight over the English Channel and the possibility of committing suicide by flying straight into the sun. Prosser later dies by committing suicide in this fashion during a combat mission.

Uncle Leslie, the eccentric brother of Jean's mother. With his well-styled hair and his dark blazer with its regimental badge, Uncle Leslie affects a faded gentility, but he supports himself by gambling, sponging, and various undisclosed employments. Leslie is very fond of Jean, and his sleight-of-hand tricks and ironic gifts introduce her to life's illusions and its disappointments. Before World War II breaks out, he flees to America, but when he returns after the cessation of hostilities, Leslie provides the same introduction to life's absurdities for his nephew Gregory. Leslie dies an old man. Although he alternately rages and trembles at his own mortality, his sense of the absurdity and irony of human existence is well appreciated by Gregory and Jean.

Michael Curtis, a tall man with a fleshy head and a schoolboy's neck. Michael is a police constable and Jean's husband. He first appears to be a charming and unusual figure, much like Uncle Leslie, but he proves to be a stolid and unexceptional husband. He becomes increasingly frustrated with what he describes as his wife's stupidity, and eventually he even strikes her; he is unwilling ever to consider the prospect of his own shortcomings. Curiously, he leaves his house and all of his money to his estranged wife at his death.

Gregory Curtis, the son of Jean and Michael. Gregory begins life as a quiet, passive boy, then grows into a studious, melancholy, and methodical adult. He builds numerous model airplanes while a boy, but his ambition is limited. He never marries. He becomes the unremarkable employee of a life insurance company and lives in the same house as his mother. Like his mother, however, Gregory is much concerned with death and the existence of God. He becomes a fervent interrogator of the state computer information system, and his persistent questions lead him to seek the absolute truth through this system, though without much success.

Rachel, a sometime girlfriend of Gregory and briefly Jean's lesbian lover. After leaving home at the age of sixteen and drifting through several large cities, Rachel has become a militant feminist who works in a neighborhood law center. She is ideologically committed, and her forceful insights are appreciated by Jean, though they often seem discomforting and somewhat distasteful to the older woman.

— *Thomas Carmichael*

STARS IN MY POCKET LIKE GRAINS OF SAND

Author: Samuel R. Delany (1942-   )
First published: 1984
Genre: Novel

Locale: The planets Rhyonon and Velm
Time: The distant future
Plot: Science fiction

Rat Korga, the only survivor of the destruction of the planet Rhyonon. Korga, while a teenager, had chosen to undergo Radical Anxiety Termination (RAT), an operation that destroys those brain cells that produce violent and antisocial behavior, rendering him incapable of anger and destructive emotion. Korga, now called "Rat" because of this surgical procedure, has become a slave of the RAT Institute. After years of slave labor, including an illegal sale to a woman who sexually abuses him, Korga is at work deep below ground when Rhyonon mysteriously experiences a fireball that destroys every living person except him. Discovered by relief members of the Web, an intergalactic organization dedicated to maintaining a communications network among the six thousand inhabited worlds, Korga is healed of his physical wounds and fitted with special rings that reintegrate much of the cranial short-circuiting that Radical Anxiety Termination effected. Now capable of communication and sophisticated social interaction, Korga seeks a new world to replace Rhyonon, the home he never really understood. Korga is taken by the Web to the planet Velm, where he is introduced to Marq Dyeth, whom the Web has identified as his perfect erotic object. Korga and Marq Dyeth begin a homosexual relationship almost immediately; however, when Velm is threatened by the alien race Xlv, the Web chooses to remove Korga from the planet.

Marq Dyeth, an industrial diplomat. A member of the historically powerful Dyeth family, he travels between worlds, easing the difficulty of trade between various cultures and planets. While on a trade mission, he is contacted by the Web and told of the discovery of Korga amid the charred ruins of Rhyonon. The Web intends for them to meet, indicating that

the high level of sexual compatibility between them should make this planned relationship mutually rewarding. Upon his return to his home planet Velm, Marq Dyeth is united with Korga at Dyethshome, the huge ancestral residence of the Dyeth family. While at Dyethshome, Marq Dyeth attempts to introduce Korga to the culture of Velm, providing him with a new world to replace the one he has lost. Together, they discover their erotic compatibility, engage in a traditional Velmian dragon hunt, and take part in a large formal dinner at Dyethshome. Inexplicably, large crowds begin to gather in order to view the survivor of the destroyed planet, all of them drawn by some compulsion to come in contact with Korga. When Korga is spirited away by the Web from the planet, Dyeth is left brokenhearted.

— *Kenneth B. Grant*

STATE FAIR

Author: Phil Stong (1899-1957)
First published: 1932
Genre: Novel

Locale: Iowa
Time: Early 1930's
Plot: Regional

Abel Frake, a prosperous farmer. The story is concerned with his family's preparations for the state fair in Des Moines and with what happens to all of them there. Abel's chief concern is for his fine boar, Blue Boy.

Melissa Frake, his wife. She is anxious over the reception of her jars of pickles; they win three blue ribbons.

Wayne Frake, their son. Before leaving for the fair, he is concerned that his girlfriend seems changed. At the fair, he meets another girl.

Emily, the daughter of a stock-show manager. In her hotel room, she gives Wayne his first taste of liquor and his first sexual experience. She refuses his proposal of marriage because she does not want to settle down on the farm.

Margy Frake, Wayne's sister. At the fair, she meets a newspaper reporter on a roller coaster and falls in love with him. On another night, they ride the roller coaster again and

make love on a grassy spot near the tent grounds.

Pat Gilbert, the reporter Margy meets. He proposes marriage, but Margy refuses because she knows that he would be unhappy as a permanent resident of Des Moines.

Eleanor, Wayne's girlfriend, who is home from her first year in college. She does not want to be committed to promises for the future.

Harry Ware, Margy's suitor at home. Before leaving for the fair, she receives a proposal of marriage from him, but she is not certain of what she wants.

Blue Boy, Abel Frake's boar. He wins.

The storekeeper, a local philosopher who bets Abel five dollars that all will not go well for him at the fair. When Abel returns home, the storekeeper pays the bet but with a sly smile in the direction of Wayne and Margy, as though he senses that he himself has really won the bet.

THE STEPPE: The Story of a Journey
(Step: Istoriya odnoi poezdki)

Author: Anton Chekhov (1860-1904)
First published: 1888
Genre: Novella

Locale: Southern Russia
Time: The 1870's
Plot: Realism

Yegorushka Knyazev (yeh-GOH-rew-shkah KNYA-zehv), called **Georgie**, a boy on the way to his first boarding school. Georgie has been reared by his widowed mother and thus has been, to a degree, sheltered from the world. His unworldliness has been further nurtured by the provincial town in which he has grown up. His journey across the seemingly endless Russian steppe greatly expands his knowledge of both the world and human nature, although he is often frightened or repulsed by his experiences. The boy has a good heart. He sympathizes with the carters, whose difficult lives cause him vicarious pain. On the whole, however, Yegorushka is understandably bored by the lengthy trip and made lonely by the separation from his mother.

Ivan Kuzmichov (kew-ZMIH-chov), Yegorushka's uncle, a provincial merchant. Continually preoccupied with business, reserved, and having the air of a civil servant, Kuzmichov is ambivalent about his nephew. Although he clearly has affection for the boy, the practical businessman has little time for Yegorushka's sensitivity. His chief concern is to settle on a good price for his wool. His secondary errand, escorting the boy to school, is bothersome to him. He grudgingly admits, however, that the boy's education will reflect well on his family.

Father Christopher Siriysky (sih-RIH-skee), a Russian Orthodox priest. Father Christopher, a kindly, gentle man, is Yegorushka's parish priest. His benign, optimistic worldview contrasts favorably with Kuzmichov's hard practicality. Having children himself, Father Christopher understands Yegorushka's homesickness and does his best to lighten the boy's journey. A sincere Christian, he finds authentic delight in the sights of the steppe, making him the only character to do so. His one vanity is his learning, which, with age, he has largely forgotten.

Panteley (pan-teh-LAY), an old carter. His age and his air of wisdom make him the unofficial leader of the wagon train to which Yegorushka becomes attached when his uncle is pressed to hurry. He befriends the boy, taking Yegorushka into his confidence, explaining the histories of the other carters, and pointing out the wonders of the steppe. Panteley is in some ways a mirror image of Father Christopher and acts as his surrogate with Yegorushka: Both men are saintly, calm, and wise in the ways of the world. Short, gaunt men, they even look much alike.

Yemelyan (yeh-MEH-lyan), a carter, formerly a singer. Having lost his once beautiful voice as the result, he claims, of bathing in a cold river, Yemelyan is a melancholy figure. Despite his almost constant *sotto voce* singing, his voice does not improve. As a former professional chorister, however, he still retains his religious devotion.

Dymov (DIH-mov), a young carter. Dymov is rough, gregarious, handsome, and a natural leader. He is also something of a troublemaker. His ennui prompts him to torment Yemelyan and to taunt the other carters. His "rude" behavior, in turn, sparks a confrontation with Yegorushka.

Moses, a peasant innkeeper. Motivated by equal parts of greed and authentic hospitality, Moses alternates between giddiness over the arrival of his guests (Yegorushka, his uncle, and Father Christopher) and despair over the behavior of his brother, Solomon. To an extent, the author's portrait is drawn from nineteenth century stereotypes of Jewish merchants; Moses' dialect, his sycophancy, and his thrift are all caricatured.

Solomon, Moses' brother. Sardonic and embittered, Solomon is considered mad by the other characters. He neither respects his social superiors nor demonstrates affection toward his brother. His role in the story is enigmatic: His half-insane behavior is perhaps a reaction to the rampant anti-Semitism of the period.

Varlamov, a rich peasant. Varlamov is the stereotype of the self-made man. During his brief and almost mythic appearance in the story, the responses of the other characters to him make it abundantly clear that he is a man whom others naturally respect, and possibly fear. Short, powerfully built, and mature, he awes the carters.

Deniska, Kuzmichov's coachman. A simple, good-humored peasant, Deniska shares Yegorushka's boyishness.

Constantine, a newly married man. Constantine appears briefly at the carter's campfire. He has been on a hunting expedition, although his entire attention is centered on his happiness.

— *John Steven Childs*

STEPPENWOLF
(Der Steppenwolf)

Author: Hermann Hesse (1877-1962)
First published: 1927
Genre: Novel

Locale: Germany
Time: The 1920's
Plot: Psychological

Harry Haller, a steppenwolf, part man and part wolf. He has a strange period in his life, when he is fifty years old, in which he haunts taverns and picks up unusual friends, both men and women. Previously a quiet man with suppressed emotions, he finds a new addiction to alcohol, sexual eroticism, and narcotics that helps him to see his many selves for the first time, as exemplified in Pablo's hall of mirrors. There, he encounters Wolfgang Amadeus Mozart, stabs Hermine, and is sentenced by the court to eternal life.

Erica, Harry Haller's wife, a madwoman. Her husband lives away from her and visits her only every few months.

Hermine, a woman Haller meets at a tavern. She helps him so that he will come to love her enough to kill her. She finds Haller a mistress, encourages his love life, and at last brings him to love her.

Maria, a woman introduced to Haller by Hermine. She is an expert in love and becomes Haller's mistress. She has been Hermine's lover as well.

Pablo, a saxophonist who prefers Mozart's music to jazz. He is a fine musician as well as a dope peddler. He becomes Haller's friend and introduces Haller to some strange sides of life. In his hall of mirrors, Pablo becomes Hermine's lover. When the jealous Haller finds them together, he stabs Hermine under the breast.

STEPS

Author: Jerzy Kosinski (1933-1991)
First published: 1968
Genre: Novel

Locale: Indeterminate
Time: Indeterminate
Plot: Existentialism

The narrator, sometimes a voyeur and sometimes a participant in the action. This immigrant to America finds that he does not belong. Because of language barriers and culture shock, he becomes a victim of the city, having to steal to stay alive. He appears to be cold and unemotional, but underneath that exterior is tremendous anger, shown when he fantasizes about destroying the city that gives him so much pain. He is a wanderer searching for his self, but because he practices self-deception, the true self within him remains hidden. He yearns for peace and to be in control of his destiny. As he looks for his identity in the ways he affects others, the roles he creates change him from servant to master, from seducer to seduced, and from victim to victimizer. Everything is negative. An incomplete person molded by a brutal world, he lives at the edge of society. He hates what he is and fears what he might become. When he left a communist country, he expected to find a better life, but he is lost in an uncaring, technological wasteland. He tries in various ways to master his environment. He is cunning and devious as he literally transforms himself into someone else to achieve his goals. A good actor, he successfully fakes deaf mutism for a time. He is a college graduate, but he will do menial labor. He parks cars, works at an archaeology dig, as a photographer, cleans the rust off a ship, and drives a truck. He uses people and fantasizes about killing them. Highly imaginative but spiritually deprived, he plays games with people. His sexual encounters are games, and he tells about shocking games that he has seen others play. Sex verifies life for him, but he shows no desire to please his partner. He wants revenge against those who have hurt him. His greatest desire is to control others. He wants to belong, but he must be the master of every situation. To him, freedom means power and control.

The woman, whom dialogues show to be kind, to admire fairness, and to think the best of everyone. She does not want to make the protagonist feel bad concerning his sexual performance, and she is interested in what he does. She tries to understand him, but she is ignorant about men and about the world. She asks questions to make him feel smart. A Roman Catholic, she goes regularly to confession but is not always honest with the priest. She is unfaithful and can be a liar. She has strong opinions. For example, she tells her lover that circumcision is a mutilation that is cruel to babies. She enjoys sex and will try new things even if she thinks them sinful. Like the narrator, she wants to understand herself, but she, too, practices self-deception. She may be the woman he leaves at the end of the novel, the woman who dives into the ocean. Many readers assume that she is committing suicide, but Kosinski did not intend for her to do that. He explained her action as a celebration of her freedom. The rotted leaf on the surface of the water is her past relationship with the narrator, and all that is left of it is a shadow. When she comes up out of the water, she will leave it behind.

The reader, who becomes a witness to and a participant in the evil portrayed. Forced to confront his own dark side, his first reaction is to recoil from it in horror, but as the emotional bombardment continues, he begins to accept the violence, the sexual manipulation, and the brutality. In a numbness brought on by the constant assault of Kosinski's cold prose, he becomes indifferent to human suffering and suddenly realizes that he is capable of permitting horrors such as the Holocaust by his own inaction or silence. This realization causes him to feel a sour pessimism about the human condition and to be disgusted with himself.

— *Josephine Raburn*

THE STOIC

Author: Theodore Dreiser (1871-1945)
First published: 1947
Genre: Novel

Locale: New York, London, and Paris
Time: Early twentieth century
Plot: Naturalism

Frank A. Cowperwood, a hard-driving, ambitious financier interested in city transportation systems. Failing socially in Chicago, he tries to gain control of the London underground, at the same time endeavoring to please both his wife and his mistress. He hires an artist, Tollifer, to amuse his wife, while he lives with his mistress. Returning to America, he has an affair with a dancer, Lorna Maris. His ambition is to leave his New York house as a museum and to found a hospital. After his death, his fortune evaporates, and his plans come to nothing. His money never brings him happiness.

Aileen Cowperwood, his second wife, whom he neglects. He hires Tollifer to amuse her.

Berenice Fleming, his mistress. After his death, she develops a sense of humanity and founds the hospital he had planned.

Bruce Tollifer, an artist whom Cowperwood hires to amuse his wife.

Lorna Maris, a dancer with whom Cowperwood has an affair.

Lord Stane, an English financier who becomes interested in Berenice.

Philip Henshaw and

Montague Greaves, English engineers who involve Cowperwood in the London underground system.

Dr. Jefferson James, Cowperwood's physician and friend. He becomes head of the hospital that Berenice founds.

THE STONE ANGEL

Author: Margaret Laurence (1926-1987)
First published: 1964
Genre: Novel

Locale: Vancouver, British Columbia, and a town on the Canadian prairie
Time: Mid-1870's to early 1960's
Plot: Psychological realism

Hagar Shipley, née **Currie**, the protagonist, a ninety-year-old woman. She has become too much of a burden to her son and his wife, and even a hazard—bored at the age of eighty, she took up smoking. Daily matters make her aware of her aging body. Her mind is prompted by objects or sounds, such as those in her room or at the doctor's office, to recall episodes of her life filled with her enormous pride and inwardness. As a girl, her shopkeeper father drills her about her Scottish heritage and sends her to an Ontario girls' finishing school. She then works in her father's Manawaka store until she disdains his plan to have her marry well. At the age of twenty-four, she arranges her own wedding without his consent, for she responds to Bram Shipley's dancing and is attracted to his passion. Only once does she nearly express her deep feelings to Bram, whose speech and manners embarrass her. When she can no longer rear her two sons with dignity, she saves money from selling eggs in town and takes the boys to Vancouver. There she keeps house for retired Mr. Oakley, returning only when Bram is dying. Another year, she visits John in Manawaka until his accidental death. With Mr. Oakley's bequest, she buys a house in Vancouver, which she later signs over when Marvin and his wife care for her. Rather than be put in Silverthreads nursing home, she runs away, but she becomes disoriented after alighting from the bus at Shadow Point. As she rests in the abandoned cannery near the beach, she drinks wine with vagrant Murray Lees. After hearing his story, she shares her similar loss of a son. Her collapse comes the next morning. Dying in the hospital, she emerges somewhat from her lifelong inwardness enough to help the girl in the next bed; later, she can even lie to Marvin that he has always been her favorite. Aware that her pride has interfered with her doing more than two independent acts in her life, she expires.

Marvin Shipley, Hagar's eldest son. In consideration of his wife's health, he drives Hagar out to Silverthreads to get her accustomed to the place. Her flashbacks reveal that he knew his parents always liked his younger brother more. He dutifully did farm chores for his father, enlisted in the war, returned to succeed as a salesman, and reliably cared for Hagar, not merely because she had signed over her house and property. Just after Hagar says that he was "a better son than John," realist Marvin tells the nurse, "She's a holy terror."

Doris Shipley, Marvin's wife, who, in her seventies, has difficulty caring for Hagar. She is well-meaning but nosy and talkative. She talks to her, keeps her favorite things near her, takes her to the doctor, and has the minister come.

Bram Shipley, Hagar's husband, a tall, big, and handsome widower with a black beard, fourteen years Hagar's senior. He deteriorated from a sensuous dancer, during courtship, to alcoholism. Although he gives Hagar a crystal and silver decanter as a wedding gift, he provides few amenities on the farm. Although coarse, he continues to evoke a primal response from Hagar, but he embarrasses her. Increasingly repulsive, he drinks heavily with the town half-breed and with his son John, until his liver gives out.

John Shipley, Hagar's younger and favorite son, who learned to lie about Vancouver school friends' social status to please her. He returns to Manawaka to be with his father. Upset by his father's death, John continues his heavy drinking and wildness. He then brings Arlene Telford home often and drinks less, until he becomes enraged that Hagar and Arlene's mother plot to send Arlene to Ontario. John and Arlene die in a dare: He drives his car across the trestle, but a special train comes and hits it.

Murray Ferney Lees, the stranger whom Hagar meets in the abandoned cannery. He willingly shares his bottle of wine and his life story. He had loved the Advocate tabernacle of his grandfather, who was ignored by his mother and father, owners of a shoe store in Blackfly. After marrying Lou, from Bible camp, he continued to sell insurance. He misplaced his faith, though he prayed with her. He blames his drinking and smoking in the basement for their house fire, in which son Donnie died. This prompts Hagar to express her own loss of a son, John, something she previously had been unable to do. After a drafty night and Hagar's collapse, Murray calls Marvin, whose number was in her purse.

— *Greta McCormick Coger*

STONE DESERT
(Desierto de piedra)

Author: Hugo Wast (Gustavo Adolfo Martínez Zuviriá, 1883-1962)
First published: 1925
Genre: Novel

Locale: Northern Argentina
Time: Early twentieth century
Plot: Regional

Don Pedro Pablo Ontiveros (PEH-droh PAHB-loh ohn-tee-VEH-rohs), called **Pepablo** (peh-PAHB-loh), an aged, easygoing Argentine ranch owner. He dies when woodmen start cutting his trees.

Midas Ontiveros (MEE-dahs), Pepablo's heir and a failure at everything.

Marcela (mahr-SEH-lah), Midas' daughter, who wants to restore the rundown ranch but is too proud to follow the practices of the gringos. Finally, she recognizes their good qualities and marries Alfonso.

Aquiles (ah-KEE-lehs) and
Héctor (EHK-tohr), Marcela's brothers.

Doña Claudia (KLOW-dee-ah), Midas' mother-in-law.

Isidro Puentes (ee-SEE-droh PWEHN-tehs), the gringo owner of the adjoining ranch, which once was the property of Carpio.

Alfonso (ahl-FOHN-soh), Isidro's son.

Roque Carpio (RROH-keh KAHR-pee-oh), a former convict who kills his unfaithful wife. While trying to kidnap Marcela, he is stabbed to death with her scissors.

Froilán Palacios (froy-LAHN pah-LAH-see-ohs), the overseer of Pepablo's ranch.

Doña Silvestre (seel-VEHS-treh), his wife.

Difunto (dee-FEWN-toh), another overseer.

Leopolda (leh-oh-POHL-dah), his mannish wife.

Melitón Bazán (meh-lee-TOHN bah-SAHN), a famous hunter.

Don Tertulio (tehr-TEW-lee-oh), who searches Pepablo's ranch house for treasure.

Mónica (MOHN-ee-kah), the daughter of Froilán. She is Carpio's only mourner.

STORM
(Oväder)

Author: August Strindberg (1849-1912)
First published: 1907
Genre: Drama

Locale: Stockholm, Sweden
Time: Early 1900's
Plot: Naturalism

The Gentleman, an aging civil servant living on a pension. Having lost his wife and daughter, he seeks only peace and order in his old age and resists intrusions in his life. He is so inflexible and set in his ways that his desire for peace can be taken as a rationalization based more on a fear of change than on principle. When his young wife and daughter reappear, he remains aloof, even to the point of assuming no responsibility for his child, whom he claims to love. He stresses that he urged his wife to leave him, although the matter remains unclear. He is cynical, somewhat misanthropic, and intolerant.

Karl Fredrik, the Gentleman's brother, a lawyer. He criticizes his brother's isolation and helps Gerda, his brother's former wife, in her flight from her new husband, Fischer. He also defended Gerda during her divorce from the Gentleman. That remains a sore spot in the brothers' relationship. He is a more reasonable and less soured man than his brother.

Gerda, the Gentleman's former wife, his junior by many years. She is emotionally unstable and suffers from her inability to judge men. She marries the sinister Fischer a few years

after divorcing the Gentleman but finally leaves him as well because of his lowly lifestyle.

Louise, the Gentleman's young domestic. Her relationship with the Gentleman verges on romance, although it is carefully controlled by the latter to preclude that possibility. She is loyal and devoted to the Gentleman and spends much of her time playing chess with him.

Fischer, a sinister character, Gerda's new husband. He runs a shady gambling joint in the apartment building where he, Gerda, and the Gentleman live. When Gerda decides to leave him, he abducts her child, Anne-Charlotte, and runs off with a young woman, Agnes, the confectioner's daughter.

Agnes Starck, the confectioner's daughter, an innocent young woman yearning for romance who runs off with Fischer. She soon returns home.

Starck, a confectioner who lives next door to the Gentleman. He is resigned to his life and content in his resignation. He lives for simple pleasures and has few grand illusions.

— *Louis Gallo*

THE STORY OF A BAD BOY

Author: Thomas Bailey Aldrich (1836-1907)
First published: 1869
Genre: Novel

Locale: New Hampshire
Time: The nineteenth century
Plot: Regional

Tom Bailey Aldrich, the narrator, a banker's son, mischievous, high-spirited, and adventurous. After his father's death and Mrs. Aldrich's move to New York, Tom is employed in his uncle's counting house. Tom is a literary forerunner of Tom Sawyer, Huckleberry Finn, and other realistic boys in American fiction.

Captain Nutter, his hale and cheery grandfather.

Miss Abigail, the captain's prim and strict sister who keeps house for him and abhors the odor of tobacco.

Kitty Collins, the Nutter maid, a young Irish woman deserted by her sailor husband, who finally returns to live with her in a seaside cottage.

Bill Conway, Tom's bullying enemy.

Seth Rodgers, another enemy.

Sailor Ben, Tom's friend and Kitty's husband, who shows Tom and his friends how to fire the Trefethen cannon.

Phil Adams, a school friend who teaches Tom how to fight.

Pepper Whitcomb, a friend struck by Tom's misdirected arrow in an amateur production of *William Tell*.

Binny Wallace, Tom's friend who is drowned in the sinking of a drifting boat during a sea storm.

Mr. Grimshaw, the boys' teacher at the Temple Grammar School.

Charley Marden, a schoolboy who almost strangles when a torpedo explodes in school.

Ezra Wingate, a neighbor whose old stagecoach is burned by the boys in a bonfire and who realizes a handsome profit by collecting damages.

Mr. Meeks, the shy druggist whom the Widow Conway is trying to catch for a husband.

Silas Trefethen, an eccentric buyer of cannon for a war with England that never developed.

Nelly Glentworth, Captain Nutter's young visitor, loved by Tom.

THE STORY OF A COUNTRY TOWN

Author: Edgar Watson Howe (1853-1937)
First published: 1883
Genre: Novel

Locale: The Middle West
Time: Mid-nineteenth century
Plot: Social

Abram Nedrow (Ned) Westlock, a Middle Border boy (and man), the narrator of the story. He is a farm helper for his father and later an apprentice in journalism. He becomes a

successful editor of the paper his father leaves him. For years in love with Agnes, he marries her after his mother's death. A close observer of people, he is also a moralist on such matters as temperance and personal industry. As a critic of small-town temperament and mores, he anticipates Sinclair Lewis' Carol Kennicott.

The Reverend John Westlock, his father, a Methodist minister, a strong, capable, independent, and thrifty man. He also is a domestic tyrant, a hard worker, and strongly opinionated. Suffering from a gnawing discontent, he leaves the ministry, becomes the editor of a newspaper, and later deserts his family, informing Ned of a seven-year liaison with Mrs. Tremaine, who accompanies him in his flight.

Mrs. Westlock, the minister's weak, timid, and submissive wife. She dies just before her repentant husband returns.

Jo Erring, her younger brother, in early youth a member of the Westlock household and throughout his life a close friend of Ned. Stout, energetic, and ambitious but rather crude and uneducated, he works hard to prove himself worthy of Mateel. Having learned milling under Damon Barker, he builds a mill of his own and marries Mateel. Doomed from the beginning, the marriage is never happy, and it finally disintegrates. After Mateel divorces him and marries Bragg, Jo murders his successor and later poisons himself in prison.

Mateel Shepherd, Jo Erring's sweetheart. Although she is in love with Bragg, she marries Jo, whom she later divorces to marry Bragg. Driven insane by Bragg's murder, she dies shortly afterward.

Clinton Bragg, Jo's rival for Mateel. He is boastful, sullen, insolent, lazy, an ostentatious drinker, educated, and scornful of others' ignorance. He is murdered by Jo.

Damon Barker (in reality **Captain Deming**), a former ship captain and now a miller, a friend of Ned and Jo. After his wife's death, he reveals his identity to his daughter Agnes, who goes to live with him.

Agnes Deming, his daughter, a young and pretty schoolteacher. Popular in Fairview, she is a kindly friend and adviser to everyone. Although she is older than Ned, she accepts his love. They grow closer when she cares for his ailing mother, and at the end of the story she and Ned have been happily married for several years.

The Reverend Goode Shepherd, the father of Mateel and successor to Mr. Westlock at the Fairview church.

Mrs. Tremaine, the widowed half sister of Damon Barker, for whom she keeps house. She elopes with Mr. Westlock but leaves him when she learns he has left Ned his money and property.

Dad Erring, Jo's father, a shingle-maker. He is nonreligious, eccentric, and reticent, tending to his own business and ignoring that of others.

Mr. Lytle (Little) Biggs, Agnes' uncle, the father of eight children. A small, free-spoken man, he is critical of others' follies and faults as well as his own, such as his penchant for lying.

Big Adam, Mr. Biggs' hired man, a fat, bull-voiced country lout with a habit of drawing imaginary corks and pouring imaginary drinks. He becomes Barker's helper and later the mill operator.

THE STORY OF AN AFRICAN FARM

Author: Olive Schreiner (1855-1920)
First published: 1883
Genre: Novel

Locale: South Africa
Time: The 1880's
Plot: Social realism

Tant' Sannie, a simple, slow, Boer farm woman whom an Englishman marries just before his death so that there will be someone left to care for his daughter and her cousin. She ignores his request to educate the girls because she considers education unnecessary. After the children grow up, she marries a neighboring widower.

Lyndall, Tant' Sannie's stepdaughter, a serious, studious girl. She goes to the city, where her unconventional ideas and conduct lead to her ruin. She lives with a man but, scorning legal ties, will not marry him. Gregory Rose finds her in a hotel room, ill and deserted by her lover. She dies shortly thereafter, and he takes her body back to the farm for burial.

Em, Lyndall's cousin, a more conventional young woman. Betrothed to Gregory Rose, she discovers that she does not love him and breaks off the engagement. After Lyndall's death, Gregory proposes again, and she accepts.

Waldo, the son of the German overseer on the farm. Like Lyndall, he is serious and studious. He leaves the farm and wanders far but returns disillusioned. When he learns that Lyndall, whom he has always loved, is dead, his one desire is to be in the earth with her. One warm sunny day, he dies.

Gregory Rose, a young Englishman who rents part of the farm. He is betrothed to Em until she decides she does not love him. When Lyndall returns home, he is attracted to her and agrees to marry her. She runs off with her lover, however, and he sees no more of her until he finds her deserted by her lover and dying. He takes her body back to the farm. Eventually, he marries Em.

Bonaparte Blenkins, a rascally drifter. Attracted by his glib manner, Tant' Sannie allows him to take over the farm for a time, and he discharges the regular overseer, Waldo's father, who then dies of grief. Jealous and angry when she discovers Bonaparte making love to her niece, Tant' Sannie drives him from the farm.

THE STORY OF BURNT NJAL
(Njáls Saga)

Author: Unknown
First transcribed: The thirteenth century
Genre: Novel

Locale: Iceland
Time: The tenth century
Plot: Adventure

Njal, a man of law. His sons kill his foster son. In the resulting feud, his house is burned. Njal and his wife and sons die.

Bergthora, Njal's wife. When the other women leave the house before it is burned, she stays behind and dies with her husband.

Gunnar Hamondsson, Njal's friend. After Gunnar's first manslaying, Njal predicts truly that Gunnar will be killed if he slays another man in the same family.

Kolskegg Hamondsson, Gunnar's brother.

Hallgerda, Hauskuld Heriolfsson's daughter and a hardhearted woman. Her third marriage is to Gunnar. There is much conflict between her and Bergthora, but the husbands remain friends.

Hauskuld Thrainsson, the foster son of Njal, who gets him a priesthood so that Hildigunna will consent to be his wife. Hauskuld Thrainsson is killed by Njal's sons.

Mord Valgardsson, who sows discord between Hauskuld Thrainsson and Njal's sons.

Hildigunna, the daughter of Flosi and the wife of Hauskuld Thrainsson.

Flosi Thordsson, Hildigunna's father and Njal's enemy. After his son-in-law's death, he attacks Njal's house and burns it.

Helge, Njal's daughter.

Kari Solmundsson, the husband of Helge. He escapes from the fire, but his son is killed. After Flosi has paid atonement for the fire, Kari agrees that the burning is avenged, but not his son Thord's death. After both Kari and Flosi return home from separate pilgrimages, they are fully reconciled.

Hildigunna, the daughter of Flosi's brother. Kari's wife Helge having died, Flosi gives Hildigunna to Kari after the reconciliation.

Thord Karisson, who is killed in the fire.

Skarphedinn Njalsson, who is killed trying to escape from the fire.

Helgi Njalsson, who is killed trying to escape with the women before the fire is set.

Grim Njalsson, who also is killed in the fire.

Thorgeir Craggeir, who becomes briefly involved in the post-fire feud between Kari and Flosi.

Thorgerda, the daughter of Hallgerda.

Thrain Sigfusson, who puts aside his wife to marry Thorgerda. He is killed by Skarphedinn Njalsson.

Kettle of the Mark, Thrain's brother and Njal's son-in-law. He and Njal make atonement for Thrain's death, and Njal takes Hauskuld Thrainsson as his foster son.

Hauskuld Njalsson, a base-born son of Njal. He is killed by Lyting.

Rodny, the mother of Hauskuld Njalsson.

Lyting, Thrain's sister's husband.

Aumund, the blind and base-born son of Hauskuld Njalsson. His eyes are opened just long enough to enable him to kill Lyting.

Otkell Skarfsson, who is killed by Gunnar following a discord beginning with Otkell selling Gunnar a deceitful thrall.

Thorgeir Otkellsson, who is killed by Gunnar when he attempts to ambush Gunnar.

Starkad, an enemy of Gunnar.

Thorgeir Starkadsson, another enemy of Gunnar. He and his father are with Thorgeir in the attempted ambush of Gunnar.

Geir the Priest, who gets up a band to slay Gunnar. The plot succeeds after much slaughter and difficulty.

Hogni Gunnarsson, who, along with Skarphedinn Njalsson, avenges Gunnar's death by slaying Starkad and Thorgeir Starkadsson.

Bork the Waxy-Toothed Blade, the father of Starkad.

Hrut Heriolfsson, who had come to Norway from Iceland to claim an inheritance.

Harold Grayfell, the king of Norway.

Gunnhilda, the mother of the king. Hrut sits in her high seat. Before he returns to Iceland, Gunnhilda puts a spell on him so that he will never have pleasure living with the woman on whom he has set his heart.

Unna, whom Hrut marries after his return to Iceland. The marriage is unhappy, and she leaves him. She enlists Gunnar's aid in getting back her goods from Hrut.

Fiddle Mord, the father of Unna. He asks Hrut to return Unna's goods. When he refuses Hrut's offer to fight him instead, Fiddle Mord gets great shame for his suit.

Hauskuld Heriolfsson, the brother of Hrut and the father of Hallgerda. He makes Hrut return Unna's goods and dowry.

Thorwald Oswifsson, the first husband of Hallgerda.

Glum, the second husband of Hallgerda. He is murdered.

Thiostolf, the foster father of Hallgerda. He kills Thorwald Oswifsson. Hallgerda sends him to tell the news of Glum's death to Hrut, who strikes him dead.

Olof the Hall, the father of Glum.

Olaf Tryggvisson, a later ruler of Norway.

Thangbrand, who is sent by Olaf to preach Christianity in Iceland.

Thorgeir of Lightwater, who challenges any man who speaks against the new Christian law.

Skapti Thorodsson, who, at Lawman Njal's suggestion, brings the Fifth Court into law.

THE STORY OF GÖSTA BERLING
(Gösta Berlings Saga)

Author: Selma Lagerlöf (1858-1940)
First published: 1891
Genre: Novel

Locale: Sweden
Time: Early nineteenth century
Plot: Picaresque

Gösta Berling, a tall, slender, handsome, and poetic but irresponsible priest unfrocked after an investigation of his brandy drinking. He becomes successively a beggar, one of Margareta's Cavalier pensioners, a good Samaritan to Anna, the fiancé of Marianne, the husband of Elizabeth, and at last a good man.

Countess Elizabeth Dohna, a gay, lovely woman married to a stupid husband from whom she escapes to lead a pleasant life. Following the annulment of her marriage, she bears a child and asks Gösta to marry her to give the child a father. They marry, but the child dies a few days later.

Margareta Celsing Samzelius, a once beautiful woman, now the major's aging, influential wife and formerly Altringer's mistress. She is an innocent woman both strengthened and coarsened by her unhappy experiences. Disowned by the major after her admission of adultery and deserted by the Cavaliers she has helped, she becomes a beggar but returns to her estate after her husband's death. She dies shortly afterward.

Marianne Sinclair, a beautiful, witty, and learned young woman in love with Gösta. Scarred by smallpox and rejected by Gösta, she becomes a recluse in her father's home.

Captain Christian Bergh, Gösta's crony and drinking companion. He is a coarse, malicious giant who is stupidly responsible for Gösta's loss of his pulpit. Secretly in love with Margareta for forty years, he sottishly causes her disownment by her husband.

Altringer, Margareta's fiancé and later her lover. He bequeaths his fortune to Major Samzelius so that Margareta may benefit from it.

Sintram, an apelike ironmaster who delights in his own wickedness. He is a demon who blights the lives of others.

Anna Stjärnhök, a wealthy, beautiful young woman who breaks her engagements to two men and elopes with Gösta.

Ferdinand Uggla, Anna's good, gentle, and timid first fiancé with whom she is reunited by Gösta.

Ebba Dohna, a sweetheart of Gösta who sought death because of his deceit.

Count Henrik Dohna, the ugly, wrinkled and stupid but honest brother of Ebba and husband of Elizabeth.

Countess Märta Dohna, the mother of Ebba and Henrik. She dislikes and mistreats Elizabeth.

Major Samzelius, Margareta's ugly, bearlike husband, who dies from the bite of a wounded bear.

Melchior Sinclair, Marianne's wealthy, wife-beating father, who casts her out for loving Gösta.

Dahlberg, a wealthy, little, bald man. He is Anna's second and older fiancé, to whom she becomes engaged because of his money.

Captain Lennart, one of the Cavaliers killed by a drunken brawler.

THE STORYTELLER
(El Hablador)

Author: Mario Vargas Llosa (1936-   )
First published: 1987
Genre: Novel

Locale: Lima, Peru; the Peruvian Amazon; and Florence, Italy
Time: The 1950's to the 1980's
Plot: Philosophical realism

The narrator, a middle-aged Peruvian writer who is similar to and virtually a stand-in for the author. He is a novelist, essayist, and television writer and producer. A consummate intellectual, he is defined by his ideas and his intellectual pursuits; little else of his life is portrayed. The narrator is a man driven by curiosity and his need to clarify mysteries that have hung over his life for decades. His fascination with and affection for his old friend Saúl resulted in a void when Saúl retreated from the narrator's life. The narrator's sense of loss and rejection translate into a nearly obsessive desire for answers, about both Saúl and the Machiguengan people. As a writer, he believes that satisfaction will come through his writing, and he sets for himself the challenge of coming to a logical understanding of what has transpired over the years.

Saúl Zuratas (sah-EWL sur-AH-tahs), a striking, tall man with bright red hair and a consistently disheveled appearance. As a Peruvian Jew, he is somewhat marginalized from the social mainstream. Furthermore, he has an enormous purplish birthmark covering half his face. He has great interest in and sympathy for others who are threatened or marginalized, including endangered peoples and cultures such as the Machiguengas of the Peruvian Amazon. Saúl's nickname, "Mascarita," or "Mask-face," appropriately conveys his detached, distant quality. He is committed to his studies and increasingly to the history of and issues surrounding the indigenous peoples of the Amazon. A fierce debater, Saúl strongly expresses his views to his friend, the novel's narrator, and does not

hesitate to let their intellectual differences come between them. Ultimately, Saúl disappears from the narrator's life and becomes something between a memory and a phantom.

The Storyteller, the narrative voice of the novel's interspersed chapters relating the beliefs and customs of the Machiguengas. The storyteller is a wise and humble man who speaks in a simple, unassertive language that conveys important information without self-consciousness or sophistication. The storyteller has learned all he knows by listening to the Machiguengas. He ultimately takes no responsibility for the stories he tells, following anecdotes and bits of lore with the disclaimer, "That, anyway, is what I have learned." The storyteller relates his fears, emotions, and doubts with candor and a touch of humor. As a storyteller, his life is one of wandering among the jungle from community to community, accompanied by his mascot, a disfigured parrot that sits on his shoulder, regaling his listeners with stories that last for hours on end. He tells of his facial marking and his acceptance into the tribe. It is strongly suggested, but never specifically confirmed, that the storyteller is actually Saúl Zuratas; within the world of the novel, however, they are presented and function as two distinct characters.

Tasurinchi (tah-sewr-EEN-chee), the benevolent Machiguenga creator. The Machiguengas believe that their god is evident in each male, so in referring to one another, and in recounting their stories, they call each man Tasurinchi, differentiating among them with identifiers such as "Tasurinchi, the herb doctor" or "Tasurinchi, the one who used to live by the

Mitaya and now lives in the forest up the Yavero." Tasurinchi is many different characters; the use of the name unifies them into a coherent persona. Tasurinchi is a generally good man who takes lessons from the world around him, lords over his wife, and avoids contact with white people. He has a deathly fear of sneezes, knowing from experience that the white man's common cold means tragedy for the Machiguengas.

The Schneils, a husband-and-wife team of American linguists working with the Machiguengas.

Don Salomón (sah-loh-MOHN), Saúl Zuratas' aging father.

STRAIT IS THE GATE
(La Porte étroite)

Author: André Gide (1869-1951)
First published: 1909
Genre: Novel

Locale: The French province of Normandy
Time: Late nineteenth century
Plot: Psychological realism

Jerome Palissier (zhay-ROHM pah-lees-SYAY), the narrator, a scholar. A sensitive and romantic but passive child (and then young man), he is obsessed with his love for his first cousin Alissa. This love issues from a fascination with virtue and self-abnegation, and from a desire to protect Alissa from life. He is, however, continually frustrated by Alissa's delaying tactics and refusals and by his own inability to overcome his passivity and act. Like Alissa, he fears the physical side of love. After Alissa's death, he remains faithful to her memory.

Alissa Bucolin (ah-LEE-sah bew-koh-LA[N]), Jerome's first cousin, a serious, gentle, and artistic young woman who, repulsed by her mother's sexuality and infidelity, seeks to repress her own love for Jerome by insisting on the necessity of pure spiritual love and self-sacrifice. Her goal becomes nothing less than sainthood, an unmediated relationship with God. To that end, she abandons all nonspiritual concerns (music and literature), devotes herself to an ascetic existence (simple food and dress), and refuses to accept Jerome's timid advances. After her death, her diary reveals the despair that came from her inability to transcend her earthly love for Jerome.

Juliette Bucolin, Alissa's younger sister, an attractive and vivacious girl. Although less religiously oriented than Alissa, she shows an equally strong capacity for self-sacrifice when, despite her love for Jerome, she agrees to marry Édouard Teissières. She does, however, succeed in finding a form of happiness in motherhood and domesticity.

Lucile Bucolin, the adopted daughter of Pastor Vautier, Alissa's mother. She is a strikingly beautiful woman of Creole origin, Her languid, sensual nature makes her feel stifled by the strict Protestant society in which she lives. Toward the start of the novel, she runs off with a lover. Her blatant infidelity to her husband shocks Alissa and Jerome and reinforces their fear of sexuality.

Abel Vautier (ah-BEHL voh-TYAY), the son of Pastor Vautier and friend of Jerome, who falls in love with Juliette. He later writes a novel that Alissa finds shocking.

Félicie Plantier (fay-lee-SEE plahn-TYAY), the cousins' aunt, a good-hearted but slightly scatterbrained woman who tries, with disastrous results, to bring Alissa and Jerome together.

Monsieur Bucolin, Alissa's father and Jerome's maternal uncle. A passive and gentle man, he is crushed by his wife's departure and seeks support and consolation from Alissa, who lives with him until his death.

Madame Palissier, Jerome's mother, a widow who wears only black. She is a strong-willed and conservative woman who regards Lucile Bucolin's nontraditional behavior as both shocking and immoral. She dies while Jerome is still a student.

Robert Bucolin, the younger brother of Alissa and Juliette, a relatively uninteresting boy whom Jerome temporarily takes under his wing in Paris out of a sense of duty.

Pastor Vautier, the father of Abel Vautier and (through adoption) of Lucile Bucolin. The sermon he pronounces after Lucile's desertion of her family contains the biblical verse (Luke 13:24, "Strait is the gate and narrow is the way . . .") from which the novel's title is taken and that so strongly influences Alissa's and Jerome's conduct.

Miss Flora Ashburton, Jerome's mother's former tutor, now her companion.

Édouard Teissières (ay-DWAHR teh-SYEHR), a wine-grower from Nîmes who marries Juliette.

— *Raymond Bach*

THE STRANGE CASE OF DR. JEKYLL AND MR. HYDE

Author: Robert Louis Stevenson (1850-1894)
First published: 1886
Genre: Novella

Locale: London, England
Time: Mid-nineteenth century
Plot: Psychological symbolism

Dr. Henry Jekyll, a well-known London physician who was born into a wealthy family. He is a large man, fifty years old, with a smooth face with something of a sly cast to it. His primary personality characteristic is that although he appears grave and serious in public, he has always felt an inner gaiety that he conceals. Although he does not characterize himself as a hypocrite, he calls himself a double-dealer, insisting that both sides of his dual self are in earnest. Jekyll says that he is no more himself when he labors in the light of day at the furtherance of knowledge and the relief of suffering than he is at night when he lays aside restraint and plunges into what he calls shameful behavior. Realizing that, like himself, all human beings are dual in nature, he seeks a chemical method of separating these dual personalities in order to allow one side to seek pleasure without guilt and the other side to remain steadfast and not be tempted by the pleasure-seeking half. He discovers that once the two personalities are separated, the pleasure-seeking side dominates and the socially responsible side cannot control it. In Freudian psychoanalysis, Dr. Jekyll is the superego, that part of the human personality that represents social order.

Edward Hyde, Dr. Jekyll's evil side. Richard Enfield says there is something wrong with his appearance, something detestable that is hard to explain. Although Hyde gives a strong feeling of deformity, no one can specify the point of deformity. Although characters describing Hyde say that they can see him in their mind's eye, they cannot find the words to account for his appearance. Gabriel John Utterson describes him as pale and dwarfish, with a smile that is a "murderous mixture of timidity and boldness." Utterson says there is something troglodytic about Hyde and that he seems hardly human. Whereas other human beings are commingled out of good and evil, Hyde is the one person in the world who is pure evil. Dr. Jekyll begins to turn into Hyde even without the chemical he has created; moreover, he finds it more difficult to return to being Dr. Jekyll again. In Freudian psychoanalysis, Hyde is the id force, the human drive that knows only "I want."

Gabriel John Utterson, a good friend of Dr. Jekyll, a lawyer with a rugged face that seldom smiles. He is a cold man of little sentiment. Although he is "lean, long, dusty, dreary," he is somehow lovable. His central personality trait is a kind of sardonic tolerance for others; as he says, he is content to "let my brother go to the devil in his own way."

Richard Enfield, a distant kinsman of Utterson and a well-known man about town. The two men often take walks together, but they are so unlike each other that no one can imagine what they have to talk about. Enfield is the first one to witness Hyde's brutal behavior; on one of their walks, he tells Utterson about seeing Hyde knock a child down and trample her.

Sir Danvers Carew, a well-known nobleman and client of Utterson who is killed brutally by Hyde.

Poole, Dr. Jekyll's butler. He helps Utterson break down the door to discover Hyde's body.

Dr. Hastie Lanyon, a well-known and highly respected physician and the oldest friend of Utterson and Dr. Jekyll. Having seen the transformation of Jekyll into Hyde, he is shocked beyond recovery and dies soon after.

Mr. Guest, Utterson's head clerk, who notes the similarity between the handwriting of Dr. Jekyll and Hyde.

— Charles E. May

STRANGE INTERLUDE

Author: Eugene O'Neill (1888-1953)
First published: 1928
Genre: Drama

Locale: New England and New York
Time: The 1920's and 1930's
Plot: Psychological realism

Nina Leeds, a young woman driven to the verge of madness by the wartime death of Gordon Shaw, the man whom she was to marry. After leaving home and going to work as a nurse, Nina gives herself promiscuously to the soldiers in the hospital. To Nina's disturbed mind, this promiscuity is atonement for her failure to give herself to Gordon. Finally, realizing that she needs normal love objects to distract her from her morbid obsession with her own guilt, she marries Sam Evans, only to discover that there is madness in his family. Ridding herself of Sam's unborn child by an operation, Nina takes Dr. Darrell as her lover and becomes pregnant by him. When her child is born, Nina settles down in maternal satisfaction. She is happy until it becomes obvious that her son Gordon cares less for her than for Sam. To add to Nina's misery, Gordon hates his real father, who is still a frequent caller on Nina. When Gordon, at the age of twenty-one, plans to marry, Nina, disturbed and neurotic again, begs Darrell to help her prevent the marriage. He refuses and tells her they already have meddled in too many lives. After Sam dies, Darrell leaves Nina, saying that they are haunted by too many ghosts to be happy. Nina marries faithful Charles Marsden, who offers her peace at last in the autumn of her life.

Edmund "Ned" Darrell, a doctor seven years Nina's senior. Concerned with Nina's condition but unwilling to be distracted from his career by marriage, he persuades Nina to marry Sam Evans. Corrupted and embittered by having to share Nina and his son, he allows his career to be ruined. Having grown rich backing Sam in business, Darrell works sporadically and pays frequent, pathetic visits to Nina and his son. Finally, cured of his love for Nina, he begins a new life as a biologist in the West Indies.

Sam Evans, Nina's boyish, lumbering husband. After Nina has discovered the madness in Sam's background and taken up with Darrell, she can hardly stand to have Sam touch her. Stricken by his wife's rejection, Sam degenerates, drifting from job to job and contemplating suicide. After Nina's baby is born, Sam, swollen with pride of fatherhood, becomes confident and ambitious. Grown rich and masterful, he never suspects the truth about Nina. As a final irony, he leaves Darrell a fortune to carry on his biological work.

Charles Marsden, a writer of popular novels, a bachelor some fifteen years older than Nina. He is vaguely disturbed because she thinks of him as an uncle. At Darrell's urging, he advises Nina to marry Sam. He later discovers that Darrell is Nina's lover and hates him for it. At last, after Sam has died and Darrell has departed, Marsden, who has continued to love Nina without lust, marries her.

Gordon Evans, Nina's son. He becomes, like his namesake, an oarsman and athlete. Handsome and strong but shallow, Gordon, in a rage after his supposed father's death, strikes Darrell. Nina cries that he is hitting his father, but Gordon does not understand. He never learns who his real father is.

Mrs. Amos Evans, Sam's mother. Frail but strong-willed, she tells Nina of the madness in Sam's family and suggests that Nina find a healthy man to father her children.

Professor Henry Leeds, Nina's father, a timid and withdrawn professor of classics at an eastern university. Dependent on Nina and jealous of Gordon Shaw, Leeds had persuaded

Gordon not to marry Nina until after the war. He dies soon after Nina leaves him.

Madeline Arnold, the girl engaged to Gordon Evans. She resembles the young Nina.

Gordon Shaw, the dead man with whom Nina was in love, killed while serving as a flier in World War I. Both Nina and Sam worship his memory.

THE STRANGER
(L'Étranger)

Author: Albert Camus (1913-1960)
First published: 1942
Genre: Novel

Locale: Marengo and Algiers, Algeria
Time: Late 1930's to early 1940's
Plot: Existentialism

Meursault (mur-SOHLT), a young clerk in a business office in Algiers, Algeria. Although not totally disengaged from humanity, Meursault, the narrator and main character, maintains only unemotional and uncommitted relationships with others, even his mother. When called to a home for the aged in Marengo, fifty miles away, for his mother's funeral, he shows no desire to view her body for the last time and shocks the other residents of the home by his seeming indifference. Though physically intimate with his Arab girlfriend, Marie, he regards her desire for marriage as a matter of no consequence. When an acquaintance named Raymond Sintes promises to be Meursault's "pal" for life if he will help him in his own love affair, Meursault replies only that he has "no objection." Meursault is completely but passively amoral. He sees nothing wrong with attending a comic film with Marie immediately after returning from the funeral or in assisting Raymond in the latter's mean-spirited effort to punish his girlfriend for her refusal to submit to his domination. When Meursault and Raymond arm themselves against two Arabs, one of them the brother of the young Arab woman Raymond is attempting to dominate, it occurs to Meursault that whether he shoots or does not shoot the Arabs would amount to the same thing. When he kills one of the Arabs, he acts unconcerned. Another feature of his character, complete resignation to the flow of events, including the consequences of the murder, emerges during his prison experience. If character is created by, and is merely the sum of, a person's decisions, as existentialist philosophy holds, Meursault makes very few true decisions. Even the five shots that he fires into his victim seem to represent something that simply happens to him rather than any conscious choice. Later, in his cell, he contemplates his future calmly, concluding that having lived even one day in the outside world provides a prisoner with enough memories to keep him from ever being bored. He cooperates with his court-appointed lawyer only passively and does nothing to help the latter counter the general impression of callousness toward his mother that the lawyer knows the prosecution will use to sway the jury. Meursault completely lacks faith in God or in the possibility of an afterlife. He rebuffs all soul-saving attempts of the priest who visits him in his cell after his conviction. He possesses only the existentialist certainty of death and feels happy in the awareness that life has emptied him of any hope except the hope that his execution may draw "howls of execration" from a crowd of onlookers.

Marie, Meursault's girlfriend, by contrast a conventional young woman who enjoys the beach and films. She want to settle down with a husband and is willing to marry the indifferent Meursault. By visiting him in prison and attending his trial, she exhibits patient hopefulness in behalf of her hopeless companion.

Raymond Sintes, an aggressive young man who comes closest to being a friend of Meursault. He possesses mostly undesirable traits. Pugnacious and vindictive, he beats his own Arab girlfriend and talks constantly of punishing her and wreaking vengeance on her brother, who appears only to be trying to protect her. It is Raymond's aggressive attitude that draws Meursault into the situation that results in his crime.

The lawyer, unnamed, is a crafty and valiant defense attorney. He is nevertheless unable to elicit from his client the responses that might prevent the imposition of the death penalty.

The priest, also unnamed, is a man of faith, conscientious in his duty. He is knowledgeable about psychology but unsuccessful in his attempts to reclaim Meursault's soul for Christianity. The fact that he is resourceful and persuasive serves to underline the extent of Meursault's resistance to all aspects of conventional faith and hope.

— *Robert P. Ellis*

STRANGER IN A STRANGE LAND

Author: Robert A. Heinlein (1907-1988)
First published: 1961
Genre: Novel

Locale: Bethesda, Maryland; the Poconos; and Las Vegas, Nevada
Time: After World War III, in the near future
Plot: Science fiction

Valentine Michael (Mike) Smith, the protagonist, who was born on Mars of two human scientists but was reared by Martians. "Rescued" and taken to Earth in his mid-twenties, he appears weak and underdeveloped, but his grave eyes reveal his intense curiosity and desire to behave "rightly." Trained by the Martian "Old Ones," he is, at least mentally, more Martian than human and has alien concepts of social and moral relationships. Because water is so scarce on Mars, for example, to share it with another creates an unbreakable bond of trust and mutual responsibility with one's "water brothers." Death, sex, property, lying, guilt, jealousy, and money are all unknown to Martians, whose sole purpose appears to be to "grok" (Martian for "to totally comprehend") everything in the universe. Smith's Martian heritage thus makes him appear extremely innocent to other humans, but, in fact, he has many superhuman powers. These allow him to manipulate, or even separate himself from, his body, to levitate or destroy objects simply through the power of his mind, and to retain and digest immense amounts of information. As the sole survivor of the first, ill-fated expedition to Mars, Smith is both heir to fabulous wealth and the legal "owner" of the entire planet Mars. This makes him a political hot potato for the world government of the Federation, which attempts to keep him incommunicado at the Bethesda hospital complex near Washington, D.C. With the help of newfound human friends, however, he escapes from the clutches of the Federation and begins an odyssey of self-discovery and self-education in the nature of the human condition. He eventually uses his new awareness and Martian powers to develop and propagate a religious philosophy that combines Martian wisdom with sexual ecstasy and openness, as well as a revelation of the universal "Godhood" and individual responsibility of all creatures who "grok" the cosmos.

Ben Caxton, a well-known free-lance investigative reporter. Caxton is streetwise, cynical, persistent, and ruggedly handsome. Extremely hostile to the current political leadership, he attempts to achieve Smith's release from Bethesda but is foiled, drugged, and held captive by the evil police forces of the Federation. Later released, he becomes one of Smith's water brothers and champions but remains skeptical about Smith's new faith. In the end, however, he, like others who become close to Smith, accepts Smith's vision and becomes an important supporter of it.

Gillian (Jill) Boardman, an extremely attractive registered nurse at Bethesda, dedicated both to her profession and to Ben Caxton. Asked by Caxton to spy on Smith, she discovers that the minions of the Federation plan to eliminate him. She dresses Smith as a nurse and escapes with him to the estate of Jubal Harshaw. As Smith's first water brother, as well as his nurse and teacher in the customs of Earth folk, Boardman

accompanies the "Man from Mars" on his voyage of self-discovery and ultimately becomes a high priestess in his universal religion.

Jubal E. Harshaw, a rich and eccentric recluse. The paunchy, curmudgeonly septuagenarian effortlessly churns out an unending series of popular literary works under a variety of pseudonyms. He is also both a brilliant doctor and an incisive lawyer but has refused to involve himself in the affairs of the outside world until Boardman and Smith arrive at his compound as refugees. Intensely interested in Smith's Martian mentality, especially after he learns of the latter's superhuman powers, Harshaw slyly defeats the government's attempts to recapture Smith. He becomes yet another water brother, as well as Smith's spiritual father, and guides the young man's education, expressing a philosophy of skeptical agnosticism and rugged individualism. He then sends Smith and Boardman out into the world to experience it at first hand. Although he is initially distressed by reports that Smith has started a new church, Harshaw ultimately realizes that he himself inspired it and becomes its leader after Smith's sacrificial death.

The Honorable Joseph Edgerton Douglas, the secretary general of the Federation. A middle-aged but handsome politician dominated by his ambitious wife, Douglas stakes his political future on controlling Smith yet does not approve of the violent and underhanded methods used by his subordinates. He is relieved of the need to resolve this conflict by Harshaw, who negotiates to achieve Smith's freedom by giving Douglas general control over both Smith's wealth and future relations with Martians.

The Reverend Doctor Daniel Digby, the supreme bishop of the Fosterite Church of the New Revelation. The leader of a politically powerful religion, Digby is both a cynical con man and a sincere religious leader. The Fosterites combine high-technology showmanship, hard-sell commercialism, and a revivalist theology to convert the masses and dominate politics. Digby attempts to win the "Man from Mars" to the faithful, but Smith senses a great "wrongness" in the Supreme Bishop and sends him directly to the Fosterite heaven. The Fosterites later declare an unsuccessful holy war against Smith and his followers.

— *Thomas C. Schunk*

STRANGERS AND BROTHERS

Author: C. P. Snow (1905-1980)
First published: 1972
Genre: Novels

Locale: England
Time: 1914-1968
Plot: Social

Lewis Eliot, later **Sir Lewis**, the narrator, whose life is traced from youth to old age. His character and experiences partially reflect those of the author. He is the elder son of Bertie and Lena Eliot and the brother of Martin. Eliot rises from humble origins in a small provincial town to be a clerk in a local government office, a barrister, and a Cambridge fellow. He later becomes a consultant to industry and a civil servant. His government service includes involvement with England's wartime development of atomic weapons. Eliot is an ambitious man who prides himself on his judgment and who is

perceived by his friends as a man with great sympathy for others. He is emotional but is highly regarded by some for his ability to control his emotions, a talent that leads others to view him as cold and manipulative. His first marriage, to Sheila Knight, proves disastrous, as he is forced to see the mental deterioration of someone he once loved deeply. His second marriage, to Margaret Davidson, is a far more mutually supportive relationship and one in which Lewis learns to accept that he cannot control the lives of those whom he loves. In the course of the sequence, Eliot comes to better terms with himself and his ambitions, forced to do so by events (including near death while undergoing an eye operation) and by the support of those around him.

Martin Eliot, Lewis' younger brother. There is strong affection between the two but also conflict, because for a long time Lewis has greater hopes and ambition for Martin than Martin himself has. Martin is a physicist and a fellow of the same Cambridge college with which Lewis is affiliated. He is the principal character in *The New Men*, in which he becomes involved in the nation's nuclear weapons research. Lewis believes that his brother is unscrupulous in climbing over friends during an investigation to root out a subversive scientist, but when Martin is offered the post of administrator of the nuclear establishment at Barford, he turns it down and returns to academic life, eventually becoming senior tutor at the Cambridge college. He works closely with Lewis in seeking a reversal of the judgment against Donald Howard in *The Affair*.

Sheila Knight, the daughter of the Reverend Lawrence and Mrs. Knight. She becomes Lewis Eliot's first wife. She is described as very handsome rather than pretty, with magnificent eyes and a dramatic presence. The young Lewis loves her deeply and persuades her to marry him, though she is reluctant because she realizes a personal flaw that makes her incapable of reciprocating that love. She becomes increasingly neurotic, and Lewis must curtail his ambitions so as to pursue a lifestyle that allows him to devote considerable energy to caring for her. The marriage becomes an imprisonment, which ends when Sheila dies of an overdose of drugs.

Margaret Davidson, the younger daughter of art critic Austin Davidson. She becomes Lewis Eliot's second wife. Lewis meets her at a London clinic during the war and romances her, though she is still married to Geoffrey Hollis. After her divorce, she marries Lewis. She is the mother of Maurice Hollis and Charles Eliot.

Bertie Eliot, the father of Lewis and Martin. A mild, self-centered man, he has no great ambitions. He cares more for his position as organist for a church choir than he does for his family and never appreciates the success of his sons.

Lena Eliot, the wife of Bertie and the mother of Lewis and Martin. She is the dominant figure in the Eliot household and invests young Lewis with much of her ambition and drive for betterment.

George Passant, a solicitor's managing clerk in the town of Lewis Eliot's birth and a part-time lecturer at the local technical college. Passant, who is brilliant and unconventional, attracts and inspires a coterie of free-thinking young men and women who are eager to extend themselves and challenge the order of the day. Lewis gives Passant much credit for shaping his early career. Passant's influence on others is less beneficial: He is implicated in a fraud with two members of the group, Jack Cotery and Olive Calvert, and the sexual license that he encourages provides a backdrop for the crimes (including murder) committed by Cora Ross and Kitty Pateman, who were associated with the group after Lewis left town. Lacking discipline and subject to paranoia, Passant fails to achieve the greatness of which Lewis thought him capable.

Roy Calvert, the central figure in *The Light and the Dark*. A brilliant scholar, he is a fellow at the Eliot brothers' Cambridge college and is Lewis' closest friend there. Calvert is a romantic who wants to believe in God but cannot, and who is

also subject to manic-depressive disorder. He can be very caring about others but is reluctant to commit himself in love until he marries Rosalind Wykes. He enlists in the military and serves in bombers during World War II, deliberately choosing that dangerous job. He is killed on a mission over Germany.

Francis Getliffe, later **Sir Francis** and then **Lord Getliffe**, one of Lewis Eliot's oldest friends and a close confidant throughout his career. Getliffe is a brilliant physicist and a fellow of the Cambridge college. He is noted for his strong moralism and personal integrity. He is leftist in his politics. During the war, he is a key figure in England's application of scientific knowledge to develop new weapons and plays a key role in the development of radar. In devoting his energies to the nation, he sacrifices his chance at great scientific discoveries. In the postwar decades, he emerges as a voice against Great Britain's nuclear armament. He is married to Katherine March.

Herbert Getliffe, the half brother of Francis Getliffe. He is a barrister whose chambers Lewis Eliot entered as a young man. Getliffe gives the appearance of being befuddled but is a shrewd, capable man. He is leading counsel for the defense in the trial for fraud of George Passant, Jack Cotery, and Olive Calvert.

Charles March, the son of Leonard March, who is the patriarch of a wealthy Anglo-Jewish family that befriends Lewis Eliot. *The Conscience of the Rich* is the story of Charles March's gradual repudiation of his background as he gives up the law to become a medical general practitioner and then marries outside the Jewish faith. His actions cause his father to disinherit him at great personal cost to both.

Leonard March, the father of Charles March. He is a wealthy Anglo-Jewish banker who has great ambitions for his son and heir, Charles. He is unbending in his opposition to Charles's efforts to carve out his own life, and the clash between them leads to a permanent estrangement.

Ann Simon, an avowed Communist with whom Charles March falls in love and marries. She is a friend of Lewis Eliot, though critical of him for not being as advanced as she would like on various political positions. She is a contributor to the *Note*, a political newsletter.

Donald Howard, the central figure in *The Affair*. He is a fellow of the Cambridge college and is unpopular with many of his colleagues because of his strong communist views. He is dismissed when it is discovered that he incorporated fraudulent data in the scientific publication that earned for him his fellowship. His wife, Laura, forces a reconsideration of the dismissal. Lewis and Martin Eliot, Francis Getliffe, and others defend Howard, whom they dislike, because they believe that an injustice has been done. Lewis is able to persuade the Court of Seniors of the college that Howard's mistake was not fraud but uncritical acceptance of falsified data offered to him by the aged professor under whom he had been working.

Walter Luke, later **Sir Walter** and then **Lord Luke of Salcombe**, a brilliant physicist and fellow of the Cambridge college. He spearheads the drive for nuclear weapons during the war and becomes chief superintendent of the Atomic Energy Establishment and later chief scientist in the Ministry for Defense. Intensely patriotic, he is also brash and impulsive and not well adapted to the compromises of political life.

Roger Quaife, a Conservative member of Parliament who becomes parliamentary secretary in the Ministry for Defense and then is elevated to the post of minister. He is the central figure in *Corridors of Power*. With the support of Lewis Eliot and Francis Getliffe, he tries to turn England away from a policy of nuclear armament, but his career is brought to an end by an extramarital affair with Ellen Smith, the wife of a fellow member of Parliament, whom Quaife eventually marries.

Paul Jago, the senior tutor of the Cambridge college in the years before World War II. He is Lewis Eliot's candidate for master when Vernon Royce dies. His wife, Alice, is socially inept and a political liability. His devotion to her contributes to his defeat in the election and to his eventual withdrawal from college affairs.

Arthur Brown, a junior tutor at the time of the mastership election. He considers Lewis a protégé and has much affection for the younger man. He is an extremely shrewd political tactician whom Lewis respects. He becomes senior tutor after Jago leaves the position. Lewis believes that his role in the Howard affair (supporting the original dismissal) was one of his few political misjudgments.

R. T. A. Crawford, a distinguished scientist who is elected master in preference to Paul Jago. Lewis later acknowledges that Crawford was a good choice because his international scientific reputation contributed to the college's visibility and stature.

Godrey Winslow, another fellow of the college, who served as bursar. He is a man embittered by personal tragedies and a difficult person with whom to get along.

R. E. A. Nightingale, a priggish and contentious fellow to whom Eliot is invariably opposed when he appears in *The Masters*. He succeeds Winslow as bursar after Crawford becomes master and seems to be revitalized, doing much good for the college. At the conclusion of *The Affair*, however, he is found to have destroyed evidence that would have helped Howard, acting to preserve the reputation of the college.

Kitty Pateman and

Cora Ross, residents of the provincial town of Lewis Eliot's youth. They were once affiliated with George Passant's group. They are lesbian lovers who abduct, torture, and kill a young boy in *The Sleep of Reason*.

— *Francis J. Bremer*

STREAMERS

Author: David Rabe (1940-　　　)
First published: 1977
Genre: Drama

Locale: An Army barracks in the United States
Time: The 1960's, during the Vietnam War
Plot: Psychological realism

Richie Douglas, an enlisted man who shares Army quarters with Roger Moore, Billy Wilson, and Martin. Richie is effeminate and open about his homosexuality and his attraction to Billy, though the other men refuse to take him seriously. Deserted by his father at the age of six, Richie is almost paternally protective of the troubled Martin, trying to cover up the suicide attempt and to deal with the problem himself. Richie is immediately suspicious of Carlyle and warns the others that he is dangerous.

Carlyle, a newcomer just out of basic training. An angry black man from the streets, Carlyle is dressed in filthy fatigues and is nervous, fidgety, and suspicious. Drunken and reckless, he takes Roger Moore and Billy to a brothel, then later makes sexual overtures to Richie, who is strangely uncomfortable with these advances. Carlyle starts a fight with Billy, cutting him on the hand and then fatally stabbing him in the stomach. When he is discovered by Sergeant Rooney, Carlyle murders Rooney as well.

Billy Wilson, an enlisted man. White, trim, blond, and in his mid-twenties, Billy is the only one greatly bothered by Richie's jokes about homosexuality. He is also very serious about the Army and the war, though he has a morbid fear of the snakes in Vietnam. A complex, sensitive thinker, Billy has always felt out of place, especially while growing up in Wisconsin, where, at the age of sixteen, he wanted to be a priest so that he could help others. Because Billy refuses to leave Richie and Carlyle alone, Carlyle attacks Billy and kills him.

Roger Moore, an enlisted man and the moral leader of the group. A tall, well-built black man, Roger displays much loyalty to the group and to the Army. He confesses that he cries when he hears the national anthem. Roger is, nevertheless, acutely aware of the oppression of black people by his country.

He is also unsure about the justification for the Army's presence in Vietnam. Having been treated for headaches in the past by a psychiatrist, Roger is consciously trying to be more open and communicative with others. He is a close friend to Billy.

Cokes, a sergeant and old Army buddy of Sergeant Rooney. Cokes is in his fifties and overweight, with short, whitish hair. A bit neater than Rooney, he keeps his jacket tucked in, even when he is drunk. He wears canvas jungle boots, as he has just returned from Vietnam. He wants to return there, but the Army has denied his request because he has been diagnosed with leukemia, an illness that Cokes denies. After the murders of Billy and Rooney, however, Cokes explains to Richie that the fatal disease has made him more tolerant, and he is surprisingly sensitive when he learns of Richie's homosexuality. With Rooney, Cokes teaches the young men the parody of the song "Beautiful Dreamer," called "Beautiful Streamers," legendarily sung by a soldier whose parachute would not open. Cokes sings another version in a mock Korean as the play closes. At one moment, Cokes is drunk and boisterous, bragging about wartime exploits in Korea; the next, he is sad and haunted by the memory of a Korean he killed, an incident that he compares to a Charlie Chaplin film.

Rooney, a sergeant in his fifties, with short, whitish hair and a big belly. Rooney, usually drunk and disheveled, is fond of reliving memories of his airborne missions with Cokes in the Korean War. Rooney discovers Billy's body and is then murdered by Carlyle.

Martin, an enlisted man. Thin, dark, and young, Martin is more openly disturbed than the others by the Army and the prospect of going to Vietnam. After attempting suicide by cutting his wrists, Martin is shipped home.

— *Lou Thompson*

THE STREET

Author: Ann Petry (1908-1997)
First published: 1946
Genre: Novel

Locale: Harlem, New York, and suburban Connecticut
Time: 1944
Plot: Naturalism

Lutie Johnson, a young, divorced African American mother who is characterized by independence of spirit. Lutie is greatly enamored of cultural myths of the self-made American—a figure symbolized for her by the suburban Chandlers, for whom she worked as a maid, and by the larger-than-life image of Benjamin Franklin. After her divorce and a period living briefly with her father, Lutie seeks an apartment for herself and her son, Bub. She soon discovers herself in one of the ill-kept, overcrowded Harlem tenements reserved for African Americans. Moreover, while preoccupied with notions of "pulling oneself up by the bootstraps," Lutie finds herself prey to the desires of those around her—the sexual fantasies of the apartment superintendent, the practiced eye of the resident madame, and the lust of the white slumlord. She survives an attempted rape at the hands of Jones, the superintendent, and by happenstance is presented with the opportunity to escape her environment and realize her dreams by singing. Apparent happenstance is revealed as a plot on the part of Junto, a slumlord and ubiquitous presence, to sacrifice Lutie to his sexual appetite. Faced at the conclusion of the novel with having to solicit money from Junto's middleman, Lutie is consumed with rage at those who manipulate her and at the patent falsehood of American cultural myths in relation to herself and those who share her circumstances. Faced with an imminent rape attempt, Lutie, in her rage, murders Boots, Junto's middleman, and flees Harlem, leaving behind her son—in whose name she had so often fashioned her "American" dreams.

Jones, the superintendent of Lutie's apartment building. Jones has spent his life on board ships and in basements and boiler rooms. He views women almost exclusively as instruments for fulfilling his sexual fantasies. In his life of confinement in the basement of tenements, working for men like Junto, Jones has become an almost subhuman figure. He begins to resemble his alternately cringing and aggressive dog.

Junto, the presiding slumlord who controls the economies of both finance and desire in the environment in which Lutie discovers that she is trapped. In addition to owning the building in which Lutie lives, Junto owns the house of prostitution on the first floor of the apartment building, the bar at the corner where she seeks a momentary respite, and the band and dance hall by means of which it seems Lutie will realize her dreams after all. Much of the latter half of the plot is driven by Junto's desire to possess Lutie.

Boots Smith, the leader of Junto's band, who ultimately is co-opted into attempting to procure Lutie for Junto, despite the fact that he also desires Lutie. Boots is provided with a lifestyle and financial security that he will not risk in defiance of his employer. He has escaped the environment that Lutie wishes to escape, but, ironically, is the very figure that Lutie must kill in order to make her own tattered escape of sorts at the conclusion of the novel.

Mrs. Hedges, an unflappable tenant of Lutie's apartment building who seemingly maintains an omniscient watch over the streets and its people and events. Mrs. Hedges is employed as a madame by Junto, who owns the apartment building, and the two have maintained a long and mutually beneficial business partnership.

Min, the meek, subdued woman who lives with Jones and is thankful foremost for having secured a rent-free situation. She seems to possess little of the mythical American determination and ambition "to better oneself" that is so central a preoccupation for Lutie. She lives meekly in fear of Jones, seeking protection from his brutality from a conjureman. By the end of the novel, she finds the courage to leave Jones.

Bub Johnson, Lutie's young son, who in many ways inherits her uncritical fixation with the American Dream. Once Lutie's downfall occurs, he is abandoned.

The Chandlers, the emotionally troubled and sterile suburban family for whom Lutie worked for a time as a live-in maid. It is from the Chandlers and their constant pursuit of increasing wealth that Lutie learns her most enduring lessons concerning the American Dream. Lutie learns to imitate uncritically their hopes and ambitions, although she also witnesses the shallowness of their lives.

— *Lindon Barrett*

STREET SCENE

Author: Elmer Rice (Elmer Leopold Reizenstein, 1892-1967)
First published: 1929
Genre: Drama

Locale: New York
Time: 1929
Plot: Social realism

Rose Maurrant, the daughter of New York tenement dwellers. She is escorted home by her employer, Harry Easter, who wants to establish her in an apartment and remove her from poverty, an offer that she refuses. Sam Kaplan appears to sympathize with her family problems. Later, Rose tells his sister that she is only slightly attracted to Sam. The next morning, she returns to find that her father has killed her mother and her mother's lover. Rejecting the proffered help of Easter and of Sam, Rose prepares to leave New York, for she feels that no person should belong to another. Perhaps later something will develop for Sam and her.

Frank Maurrant, her father, a stagehand. Although he extols family happiness and propriety, he kills his wife and her lover.

Anna Maurrant, his wife. Her husband kills her and her lover.

Harry Easter, the manager of the office in which Rose works. He tries to establish her in an apartment, but she refuses his offer as well as his proffered help after her mother's murder.

Sam Kaplan, a law student in love with Rose. She will not accept his love, but she holds out a faint hope for the future when they are older and wiser.

Shirley Kaplan, Sam's sister.

Abe Kaplan, Sam's father.

A STREETCAR NAMED DESIRE

Author: Tennessee Williams (Thomas Lanier Williams, 1911-1983)
First published: 1947
Genre: Drama

Locale: The French Quarter, New Orleans, Louisiana
Time: The 1940's
Plot: Tragedy

Blanche DuBois (dew-BWAH), a desperate, neurotic woman who goes to New Orleans to stay with her younger sister Stella after losing her home and job in Mississippi. Blanche is haunted by guilt over the death of her young husband, who committed suicide after she confronted him about his homosexuality. She then became a nymphomaniac, scandalizing her hometown and losing her high school teaching job because of her relationship with a teenage boy. With no money, no home, and fading youth, Blanche clings to romantic illusions to sustain her self-image, even as she depends on Stella for shelter and emotional support. She still sees herself as the beautiful, refined mistress of Belle Reve, the former DuBois family plantation. Unable to accept the changes in her life, she turns to alcohol and romantic fantasy for escape. She hopes to solve her problems by marrying her brother-in-law Stanley's friend Mitch, but he rejects her after discovering the truth about her past. First told to leave and then raped by Stanley, Blanche suffers an emotional collapse, retreating completely into the beautiful but delusional world to which she had tried so desperately to cling in reality.

Stanley Kowalski, Blanche's brother-in-law. Stanley is earthy, unrefined, sensual, and sometimes violent, in every way the opposite of the image of Southern gentility Blanche tries to project. Stanley loves Stella, though he is possessive, dominant, and occasionally abusive toward her. He views Blanche's presence as a threat to his position of power and control in his home. He distrusts her immediately because she cannot adequately explain the loss of Belle Reve, which represents a significant financial setback for him and Stella. He resents Blanche's ill-concealed belief that she is better than him, yet he is sexually attracted to her at the same time. Stanley's sexual frustration resulting from the lack of privacy in the small apartment intensifies his hostility toward Blanche. By informing Mitch of her sordid reputation, telling her to leave his home, and finally raping her, Stanley forces Blanche to acknowledge the truth about herself, but he also destroys her completely in the process, apparently without regret.

Stella Kowalski, Blanche's younger sister and Stanley's wife. Stella is more realistic than her sister, accepting Stanley and his working-class world rather than trying to re-create the life of wealth and privilege that has long since vanished for the DuBois family. Stella also is more shallow and less sensitive than Blanche. Stella loves Blanche and feels sorry for her, but she cannot fully understand the emotional turmoil Blanche is experiencing. After a drunken Stanley hits Stella (who is pregnant), she returns to him partly because the sexual attraction between them is so strong. Stella is furious when Stanley reveals Blanche's past to Mitch and tells her she must leave, but the impending birth of their baby seems to dispel her anger. Even when Blanche is being taken away to a mental hospital, Stella cannot bring herself to acknowledge the truth of what Stanley has done to her sister, refusing to believe Blanche and choosing to stay with Stanley.

Harold Mitchell, called **Mitch**, a friend and coworker of Stanley. Mitch is a simple, kind man, devoted to his dying mother and attracted to Blanche in an old-fashioned, romantic way. He is somewhat shy and socially awkward, but he is the gentlest and most refined of Stanley's friends. He seems to be the only person capable of understanding Blanche's needs and relating to her. Mitch is very traditional, and Stanley's stories of Blanche's sexual escapades embarrass and horrify him. He takes similar offense to her deception, about both her age and her past. Drunk and humiliated, he verbally attacks Blanche, treats her like a prostitute, and brutally rejects her. When Blanche is being led away to the mental hospital, however, Mitch expresses disgust over Stanley's behavior and remorse over his own actions.

Eunice Hubbell, Stanley and Stella's upstairs neighbor. Eunice is a no-nonsense, practical woman who comforts Stella and shelters her after her fight with Stanley. She also encourages Stella not to believe Blanche's story of the rape for the sake of Stella's marriage.

— *Charles Avinger*

STRIFE

Author: John Galsworthy (1867-1933)
First published: 1909
Genre: Drama

Locale: An industrial town near London
Time: Early twentieth century
Plot: Social criticism

John Anthony, the chairman of the board of a sheet metal plant. He is dramatically a fully realized character and also an example of a popular type that figured in early twentieth century industrial disputes. He fights stubbornly for his principles and is uncompromising in his attitude toward petitions from labor factions. Eventually, his resignation is forced by board members eager to compromise with the union.

David Roberts, a zealous leader of the striking workers who is Anthony's counterpart in the ranks of labor. He is typical of the adamant, unyielding element prevalent in labor disputes in the early twentieth century. As Anthony is deserted by the board, so Roberts is abandoned by the union membership, and the strike is compromised.

Annie Roberts, David's wife, who, though not an active character in the play, is an important agent in it. It is her death from the privation caused by the strike that causes the contending forces to think soberly and work out a compromise.

Edgar Anthony, the realistically presented son of John Anthony. He expresses the views that employers of the future might be expected to have where labor is concerned.

Francis and

Enid Underwood, who are sympathetic to labor's cause. Francis, because he is the plant manager, is not as overt in his stand as is Enid. She boldly attempts to reconcile the opposing factions, first by attending Roberts' sick wife and then by pleading personally with Roberts to give up the fight. Significant is the fact that Enid is Anthony's daughter.

Simon Harness, a union officer whose compromise finally is accepted by the contending parties.

STRIKE THE FATHER DEAD

Author: John Wain (1925-1994)
First published: 1962
Genre: Novel

Locale: London, Paris, and an unnamed provincial university town
Time: The 1940's and 1950's
Plot: Bildungsroman

Alfred Coleman, a middle-aged professor of the classics. The son of a minister, Alfred has inherited his father's sense of duty, if not his faith. Except for his wife, Mary, who died after ten years of marriage, Alfred has never permitted himself to become close to anyone. Although he is secretly troubled by the memory of his own wartime weakness, he projects an image of certainty, insisting that everyone accept his values, which are chiefly the suppression of emotion and dedication to learning, particularly to the classics. It is his inflexibility that drives his son, Jeremy Coleman, from home and causes a seventeen-year break in their relationship. Finally, while visiting his son in a hospital, Alfred admits his own vulnerability, enabling father and son to be reconciled.

Jeremy Coleman, the only son of Alfred Coleman and his dead wife. Of average stature, Jeremy is healthy but not athletic. He is bright but not scholarly, tending to drift into daydreams or toward the piano, his chief source of pleasure. Jeremy has always tried to please his father, but at the age of seventeen he realizes that he can find no happiness in Greek books, only in jazz. After running away from school, he eventually becomes a jazz pianist, first in London, then in Paris. After a ten-year period of stagnation, Jeremy once again meets his friend Percy Brett and is inspired to return to his music. Defending Percy in a fight against racist thugs, Jeremy is injured and taken to a hospital. There he and his father are reconciled. At the end of the novel, even though the new popularity of rock and roll means that Jeremy may no longer be able to make a living from jazz, he realizes that even if there is no audience to hear and applaud him, his music makes his life meaningful.

Eleanor Coleman, Alfred Coleman's sister, who acts as his housekeeper. A tenderhearted, gentle, and motherly person, Eleanor loves Jeremy as if he were her own child. Because she is in awe of her older brother Alfred, she rarely disagrees with him, but whenever Jeremy is threatened, she will fight like a tigress. It is at her insistence that Alfred goes to visit Jeremy in the hospital.

Percy Brett, a black musician. Of medium height but massive in stature, he has large, expressive eyes and a melodious voice. When Jeremy meets him in London, he is in the U.S. Air Force, but after World War II, Percy has no desire to return to his native Maryland or to anywhere else in the United States, where he would face racial discrimination. Percy, a brilliant trombonist, introduces Jeremy to real jazz. After Jeremy has been sidetracked by Diana, Percy persuades him to return to his music.

Tim, a friend of Jeremy, an inveterate womanizer, sponger, and scoundrel. Although he is roughly twenty-five years old when he first meets Jeremy, Tim successfully evades wartime service through his facility at lying and scheming and by employing his total lack of shame. Eventually, he sets himself up as Jeremy's public relations man. When Jeremy meets the pathetic wife and young children whom Tim has deserted and who have followed him to Paris, however, Jeremy loses all respect for Tim and breaks off their friendship.

Diana, an English woman. Pretty but discontented, she has a grudge against men because her parents spent all of their money educating her brother so that he could move upward in society. After she has become Jeremy's mistress in Paris, she goes to London, where for eight years she uses him to relieve her sexual frustrations while she seeks a husband. Jeremy blames her physical demands and her psychological attacks for the loss of his musical powers. After she finds a husband and discards Jeremy, he is able to return to his piano.

— *Rosemary M. Canfield Reisman*

STRONG WIND
(Viento fuerte)

Author: Miguel Ángel Asturias (1899-1974)
First published: 1950
Genre: Novel

Locale: An unnamed Latin American country, Chicago, and New York City
Time: Early twentieth century
Plot: Social

Lester Mead, also called **Cosi** and **Lester Stoner**, the green-eyed millionaire organizer of a banana growers' cooperative in an unnamed Latin American country. He left his life as a millionaire for adventure in the tropics. Under the name of Cosi, he is an itinerant salesman of sewing supplies. After his marriage to Leland Foster, he is known as Lester Mead. He buys land and becomes an independent banana grower. When the Tropical Banana Company (Tropbanana) refuses to buy the independent growers' bananas, he organizes them into a cooperative to sell their crop elsewhere. He goes to Tropbanana headquarters to try to convince company executives to stop exploiting the banana growers. When members of his cooperative are jailed for heading an uprising against Tropbanana, he bribes an official to release them. Under his true identity as Lester Stoner, a millionaire and a major stockholder in Tropbanana, he travels to New York to urge other stockholders to pressure the company to treat the growers justly and honestly and thereby ensure for themselves a profitable and stable investment. While in New York, he prepares his will, in which he names his wife as beneficiary and the cooperative as the second beneficiary in the event of her death. When he returns to his banana farm, he is killed by the strong wind conjured up to destroy Tropbanana.

Adelaido Lucero (ah-deh-LAY-doh lew-SEHR-oh), the overseer on a banana plantation. He saves his money to buy land for his sons. They become Mead's partners in the independent banana growers' cooperative. His son Juan is impris-

oned for leading an uprising against Tropbanana. He does not agree with Mead's calls to the cooperative's members to live frugally and save their money as a means to win their struggle for just treatment from Tropbanana.

Leland Foster, the golden-haired wife of Lester Mead. She was divorced from John Pyle so that she could marry Mead. She dies with him in the strong wind. She does not realize that her husband is a millionaire until their trip to New York.

Sarajobalda (sah-rah-hoh-BAHL-dah), an old witch and the godmother of Lino Lucero. Her beating and rape at the hands of representatives of Tropbanana trigger the uprising led by Juan Lucero and Bastiancito Cojubul.

Rito Perraj (REE-toh peh-RRAH), the shaman who conjures up the strong wind to satisfy Hermenegilo Puac's desire for vengeance on Tropbanana for refusing to buy his crop.

Bastiancito Cojubul (bahs-tyahn-SEE-toh koh-hew-BEWL), a highlander who migrated with his wife to the coast to become a banana grower. He is arrested with Juan Lucero for rebellion against Tropbanana.

The Green Pope, the president of Tropical Banana Company, visited by Lester Mead in Chicago. He ordered the company's representatives to stop buying bananas from the growers. He maintains that the stockholders are interested only in dividends and would not be upset if they knew that the company profits came from the merciless, inhuman exploitation of the growers.

— Evelyn Toft

STUDS LONIGAN: A TRILOGY

Author: James T. Farrell (1904-1979)
First published: 1935
Genre: Novel

Locale: Chicago, Illinois
Time: June, 1916-August, 1931
Plot: Naturalism

William "Studs" Lonigan, a young Chicago Irishman who, growing up in the early decades of the twentieth century, is a moral failure. He tries to be tough all his life and succeeds only in leading an empty existence. His thoughts are only of women, drink, and a good time, from his graduation from a parochial grammar school to his sudden death in his thirties.

Patrick Lonigan, Studs's father. He lives in a world that he understands only as he can see it from a narrow point of view. He is a painting contractor who provides for his family in a material way and sees nothing more to do. Only his business failure in the 1930's brings him to believe that he has not done well in this world.

Mrs. Lonigan, Studs's mother. She wants her children to do well. She always thinks the best of her children, even her half-hoodlum son Studs. She is a possessive woman, not wanting to let go of her influence on her children.

Lucy Scanlan, a pretty little neighbor girl whom Studs loves when they are in their early teens.

Catherine Banahan, a young Irishwoman who loves Studs when he is in his thirties. She becomes his mistress. When he dies suddenly, she is left unmarried to bear his child.

Paulie Haggerty, one of Studs's friends. His early death causes Studs to think of his own mortality.

Weary Reilley, a tough contemporary and sometime friend of Studs. Often in and out of scrapes, he eventually is arrested for raping a girl he picks up at a dance.

Frances Lonigan, one of Studs's sisters. She tries to rise out of the intellectual and moral rut of the rest of the family.

Loretta Lonigan, Studs's other sister.

Martin Lonigan, Studs's young brother, who tries to imitate Studs.

Helen Shires, a boyish girl who is Studs's chum when he is a boy.

A STUDY IN SCARLET

Author: Sir Arthur Conan Doyle (1859-1930)
First published: 1887
Genre: Novel

Locale: London, England
Time: The nineteenth century
Plot: Detective and mystery

Sherlock Holmes, a famous detective known for his powers of observation and ability to draw logical conclusions.

Dr. John Watson, Holmes's friend and assistant. He has just returned from the Afghan wars and is a pensioned army doctor newly introduced to Holmes.

Stamford, an old friend of Watson who brings Watson and Holmes together as lodgers at 221B Baker Street.

Tobias Gregson, a detective from Scotland Yard who asks Holmes's help in solving a case.

Enoch J. Drebber, an American found murdered in a deserted house in London. He turns out to be a former Mormon who took Lucy Ferrier as one of his wives against her will. He was murdered by Jefferson Hope, the girl's sweetheart.

Lestrade, a detective from Scotland Yard who works with Gregson.

Stangerson, Drebber's secretary. He is found dead of a stabbing wound in a London hotel. Like Drebber, he has been murdered by Jefferson Hope, who seeks revenge for his sweetheart.

Jefferson Hope, an American. When captured, he is working as the driver of a hansom cab in London. He murdered Drebber and Stangerson because they took Lucy Ferrier from him. He is not punished by the law for his crimes; he dies of a heart attack within a few days of his capture.

Lucy Ferrier, a beautiful young American. Jefferson Hope meets her in Utah and falls in love with her. She is forced by the Mormon elders to marry Drebber even though he already has several wives. She dies within a month of her marriage.

John Ferrier, Lucy's father. He tries to prevent his daughter's having to marry a Mormon, but he is killed by the Mormons. He became a Mormon after he and his child were rescued by a Mormon wagon train while moving West.

THE SUBJECT WAS ROSES

Author: Frank D. Gilroy (1925-   )
First published: 1962
Genre: Drama

Locale: The Bronx, New York
Time: May, 1946
Plot: Realism

John Cleary, a fifty-year-old coffee merchant. John is deeply disappointed with the course his life has taken. He had the opportunity, years ago, to relocate in Brazil, but his wife, Nettie, did not want to make the move. Instead, they settled in the Bronx, near Nettie's mother. The man who took the position in Brazil became rich. Having failed to achieve the American Dream, John now turns his frustration toward others, particularly Nettie and Timmy, his son. John's unhappiness also reveals itself in his rigidity (particularly about morality and religion) and reticence. He is unable to speak about those things that are deeply meaningful to him. He drinks to excess, though he does not approve of his son's drunkenness. John's long-standing estrangement from his wife has intensified during Timmy's absence from home. Now, with Timmy's return, he finds himself both envious of and frustrated by his son. Although he reaches tentative agreement with his son at the end of the play, his deeper problems are unresolved.

Nettie Cleary, John's wife, a bitter, estranged woman. At the age of forty-five, she contrasts her present life with a happier past. She recalls (or imagines) her childhood at home, a world of gentility, culture, and love. She had several suitors and chose John as the most energetic and ambitious of them. He alone, she believed, would be able to give her the life she sought. His failure to do so disappointed her, and her love diminished. To replace her expectations, she has created a life of service to her husband, her mother, her son, and her re-tarded cousin, but it is a life that has left her unfulfilled. The day that she walks out of the house and spends hours wandering around the city is, she says, "the only real freedom I've ever known." Like her husband, Nettie is caught in a self-created worldview, unable to appreciate the different reality of others and unable to communicate with those others. Timmy's return home is yet another failure of reality to meet her expectations.

Timmy Cleary, their son, who left home at the age of eighteen to fight in World War II. Now twenty-one, he returns to his parents' house, precipitating the family crisis for all three characters. Timmy is now better able to perceive his parents' relationship with each other, as well as his relationship with each, though his insight is colored by his own quest for independence. Although he attempts to meet each parent's separate expectations of him, he cannot alter the person he has become. When he tries to reconcile John and Nettie, for example by buying her roses, he fails. Like his father, Timmy drinks excessively, providing a convenient escape from the shattered home he is trying to reenter. His behavior merely makes the situation worse, and although he almost manages some moments of communication, first with Nettie and then with John, his decision to leave home at the end is the only resolution to the family conflict.

— Bruce H. Leland

SUCH IS MY BELOVED

Author: Morley Callaghan (1903-1990)
First published: 1934
Genre: Novel

Locale: Toronto, Canada
Time: The 1930's
Plot: Social

Father Stephen Dowling, a large, handsome young priest, dark-haired and fresh faced, one year out of the seminary. He serves the Roman Catholic cathedral under the pastor, Father Anglin. Father Dowling is interested in social causes, and his fervent sermons frequently disturb the wealthier parishioners. Returning from a deathbed, Father Dowling is accosted by two young prostitutes who do not see the clerical collar under his coat. Initially ignoring them in anger and confusion, he decides to return and speak to them, ashamed of his lack of pity for their wretchedness. Motivated at first by a sense of duty to his parishioners, Father Dowling decides to help the two women, visiting them repeatedly and giving them whatever money he can spare or borrow, even the money he normally sends to help support his mother and brother. Although at rare moments he is tempted physically, his feelings for the women are dominated by a Christian love for the weak and unfortunate. Realizing that one of the women is sick, and that in spite of all that he can give them they continue to work as prostitutes, Father Dowling impulsively appeals to the richest and most powerful of his parishioners, James Robison, to find honest work for them. The meeting with Mr. Robison is a failure: The girls insult him and his wife. Mr. Robison feels compelled to report Father Dowling's involvement with the women to the bishop. Father Dowling continues to visit the women at the hotel where they live and work until, shortly after the meeting with Mr. Robison, the women are arrested and ordered to leave town. Father Dowling is called to see the bishop and told that he has behaved wrongly. He refuses to agree with the bishop that his love for the women is inappropriate, and while he awaits the bishop's discipline, he becomes increasingly withdrawn and depressed. He is unable to reconcile his strong love for the women—and his belief that it is his duty to save them—with the bishop's contention that he loved the women for themselves rather than for the sin from which he might save them. Confined to a sanatorium at the end of the novel, he prays that God will accept his illness as a sacrifice to save the souls of the two women.

Veronica (Ronnie) Olsen, a tall, fair woman who has become a prostitute after losing her job in a shop. She is stubborn and determined not to let life defeat her, eager to travel, and defiant when she feels attacked, as she does by Mrs. Robison. Ronnie cares for Midge, her partner, and especially for Lou, her pimp and occasional lover.

Catherine "Midge" Bourassa, who is smaller than Ronnie and more fragile, both physically and emotionally. She is a dark-haired French Canadian from a typical large Montreal family. She had left home with a man who promised to marry her and has passed from man to man since. Her illness intensifies Father Dowling's desire to help the women by any means possible.

James Robison, the wealthiest and most influential parishioner to remain at the cathedral while other important families have moved to the suburbs. He is sympathetic to Father Dowling in spite of the priest's sermons attacking the bourgeois world for its lack of Christian values. Mr. Robison is generous in charitable giving but demands recognition for his gifts. After Father Dowling brings the prostitutes to his house, however, he feels threatened and, at the urging of his wife, complains to the bishop about Father Dowling, precipitating the arrest of the two women and Father Dowling's breakdown.

Charlie Stewart, a young medical student, Father Dowling's closest friend, the only person with whom Father Dowling feels completely relaxed. He is concerned with social justice and believes in reform through secular means. He and his fiancée, however, ask Father Dowling to marry them in the church. Father Dowling feels uneasy about lying to Charlie and his fiancée about the two women he has befriended. Charlie notices and is frightened by the change in Father Dowling after the women are forced to leave town.

Lou Wilenski, Ronnie's lover and pimp. Lou is a small man who looks and acts tough. He is jealous and suspicious of the girls' involvement with the priest and makes fun of him in his absence, but he is unable to prevent the women from seeing Father Dowling.

Father Jolly, another young priest at the cathedral. He has a room, with bookshelves, that Father Dowling had wanted. When Father Jolly leaves, he offers Father Dowling the room, but Father Dowling is too depressed by his failure with the women to care.

Bishop Foley, a shrewd politician who is more concerned with protecting the church against scandal than with the soul of a young priest or those of two prostitutes. He is presented as a good administrator but not a deeply religious person.

— *Katherine Keller*

SUDDENLY LAST SUMMER

Author: Tennessee Williams (Thomas Lanier Williams, 1911-1983)
First published: 1958
Genre: Drama

Locale: New Orleans, Louisiana
Time: 1936
Plot: Psychological realism

Violet Venable, a wealthy Southern matron of the New Orleans Garden District, mother of the late Sebastian Venable.

She is an aging woman of fading beauty, with light orange or pink hair. She wears a lavender lace dress and has a starfish of diamonds pinned over her "withered bosom." She has devoted her life to her late son, even refusing to return to her critically ill husband so that she could stay with her son and keep him from becoming a Buddhist monk. She and her son traveled every summer, and with her encouragement he wrote one poem each summer. Having suffered a stroke that slightly paralyzed one side of her face, she was rejected as a traveling companion on her son's last and fatal summer voyage and was replaced by her husband's niece, Catharine Holly. Violet is devastated by Sebastian's rejection and death and most of all by Catharine's story of what happened that last summer, a story that is destroying the legend of everything for which Violet has lived. She has proposed to fund young Doctor Cukrowicz's experimental work in exchange for his performing a lobotomy on Catharine to silence her horrible stories. Violet has been accustomed to getting her own way and will use any means at her disposal to get it.

Catharine Holly, the young and beautiful cousin of Sebastian Venable. She wears a suit that was bought for her by her cousin Sebastian, and her hair has been done in a beauty parlor. She is quite nervous, moving about with quick, dance-like movements. She attempts to smoke cigarettes, which her nun attendant does not allow but the doctor permits. She is the niece of Violet's husband and is strongly disliked by Violet. She, her mother, and her brother are dependent on Violet for financial support. Ignored by a weak, indulgent mother and egotistical, self-indulgent brother, Catharine is starved for attention and affection. She is outgoing, aggressive, and unconventional. When her cousin Sebastian shows an interest in her, she accepts his invitation to travel with him. After Sebastian is killed while on their excursion, Catharine tells a story of horror to authorities and is flown home by Violet and committed to a mental hospital. When Catharine continues to repeat her story, despite shock therapy, injections, and other treatments to cure insanity, she is taken to her aunt's home with the intention of having her committed to another sanatorium to undergo a new experimental treatment, a lobotomy, which

Doctor Cukrowicz would perform. In Sebastian's jungle garden, she tells her story of moral degradation and cannibalism to the doctor and her family, including Violet.

Doctor Cukrowicz (kew-KROH-vihts), whose surname means "sugar" in Polish, a young, blond physician. He is extremely handsome and possesses icy charm. He tells Violet that she can call him "Doctor Sugar." He is engaged in experimental brain surgery on mental patients but has a very small budget. He needs money for a separate ward for his patients, for trained assistants, and for a large enough salary to support a wife. He also wants patients in addition to the criminal psychopaths that the state sends to him. He attempts to be fair; he is kind and listens to all sides with an open mind. Violet offers him a subsidy from the Sebastian Venable Memorial Foundation to perform the lobotomy on Catharine Holly, plainly stating that if he refuses to perform the operation, there will be no subsidy.

George Holly, Catharine's brother. A typically handsome man, he is tall, with an elegant figure. He has the best looks in the family. He is ambitious, petulantly spoiled, and concerned about what people will think when they learn that his sister is in a mental hospital. He is also afraid that he will not get his share of Sebastian's money.

Mrs. Holly, the mother of Catharine and George and sister-in-law of Violet Venable. Mrs. Holly is a "fatuous Southern lady who requires no other description." She is upset with her daughter's behavior because she is afraid that Violet will break Sebastian's will, which left money to them. She asks Catharine not to "invent" terrible stories about what happened to Sebastian.

Miss Foxhill, a private nurse for Violet. She moves about nervously in rubber-soled white oxfords and fears displeasing her employer.

Sister Felicity, an attendant nun for Catharine, from the mental hospital. She is dressed in a starched white habit and has difficulty keeping Catharine under her control.

— *Bettye Choate Kash*

SUDER

Author: Percival L. Everett (1956-   )
First published: 1983
Genre: Novel

Locale: Fayetteville, North Carolina; Seattle, Washington; and the Cascade mountain range in Oregon
Time: The second half of the twentieth century
Plot: Picaresque

Craig Suder, the protagonist, a thirty-three-year-old African American who plays third base for the Seattle Mariners. Depressed by career and family problems and haunted by the fear that he may have inherited from his mother a predisposition toward insanity, Suder runs away. On the road, he has a number of improvised adventures that culminate in his attempt to fly under his own power.

Kathy Suder, Craig's mother, whom his father one day pronounces "crazy." Paranoid about her husband's presumed philandering, she wears a full-collared coat in the middle of summer and takes up running to lose weight and thereby regain her husband's affection. Eventually, she establishes the personal goal of running around the city limits of Fayetteville, North Carolina, a distance of twenty-three miles.

Ben Suder, Craig's physician father, a man of infinite patience, understanding, and quiet resignation. He is the point of calm in the Suders' stormy home life. He refuses to consider psychiatric treatment or institutionalization for his wife, calling such responses "white people's foolishness."

Martin Suder, Craig's brother, who shares his distress over their mother's condition and bears most of the brunt of her sexual puritanism. In choosing to become a dentist, he opts for an adult life of method and procedure, as opposed to the often manic improvisation of his mother and Craig.

Bud Powell, a real-life jazz pianist introduced into the fictional narrative. Powell twice stays with the Suders during Craig's youth. It is he who notices Craig's physical resemblance to Charlie "Bird" Parker, a legendary jazz saxophonist.

He also introduces the protagonist to Parker's composition "Ornithology" and reinforces his inherent impulses toward personal freedom.

Lou Tyler, the white manager of the Seattle Mariners, an amateur taxidermist who once offered to stuff Roy Rogers' horse Trigger for free. Tyler's obsession with death and dead things serve as a counterpoint to Craig Suder's instinct for life.

Sid Willis, a retired baseball player and "black Indian" who shelters Suder for a time on his boat. Willis' self-confessed murder of his wife, his dealing in deadly drugs, and his offer to shoot Suder to put him out of his misery clearly align him with the forces inimical to life.

Dr. McCoy, a bigoted, white-haired, white man who runs a "Christian" dental practice, which uses prayer rather than pain killers. He leads a Bible study group that Mrs. Suder hopes to join.

Fat Thomas, a three-hundred-pound, gay, Chinese man who services vending machines. He lives at the Portland boardinghouse where Suder seeks sanctuary for a while. Suder becomes the object of Fat Thomas' affection.

Naomi Watkins, the daughter of the local undertaker, a girl with an inordinate need for affection. She becomes the early focus of Suder's sexual indecision.

Jincy Jessie Jackson, a nine-year-old white girl who is running away from her abusive mother. Suder agrees to make her part of his life, in part because her name "sounds real musical" and in part because her energy matches his.

— *S. Thomas Mack*

THE SUICIDE'S WIFE

Author: David Madden (1933-   )
First published: 1978
Genre: Novel

Locale: San Francisco, West Virginia
Time: 1968
Plot: Tragedy

Ann Harrington, the protagonist, a housewife and mother of three small children. Having grown up in a Polish ghetto in Pittsburgh, Ann attended college only after being urged repeatedly to do so by her high school home economics teacher. At the University of Pittsburgh, she met and later married Wayne Harrington, her English professor. After Wayne commits suicide during a visit to his vacant family home in upstate New York, Ann returns to San Francisco, West Virginia, fearing that Wayne has abandoned her. When the news of his death reaches Ann, she finds herself unable to cope with her new status as the suicide's wife. As she tries to make sense of her life without Wayne, Ann realizes that she was completely dependent on him to fix everything around the house and to make sure that the bills were paid; she cannot even drive Wayne's dilapidated car. Ann starts to grow into an independent woman as she learns to make repairs around the house and as she begins to teach herself how to drive. She soon realizes that she knows very little about Wayne's life. Turning to Max Crane, she learns that Wayne was not admired by his students or his colleagues at the university; in fact, he was regarded as a boring teacher. Ann comes to understand that if Wayne had not committed suicide, she would have continued to live her life in his shadow.

Max Crane, a poet and former colleague of Wayne Harrington. Witty and egotistical, and successful as a poet, Max is popular with his students and faculty coworkers. After Max meets Ann, he tells her much that she never knew about Wayne: that his students found him boring and that the other professors at the university found his work mediocre. While Max relates this information, he also proposes the idea that Wayne may have been killed by Anson Kellor, a radical student who criticized both Wayne and Max. Max wonders if Kellor, a homosexual, may have been attracted to Wayne and may have followed him to New York, killing him because Wayne rejected Kellor's advances. Max even tells Ann that he found himself attracted to Wayne because Wayne's body image contrasted Max's image of his own body and how others perceived him. Eventually, Max invites Ann to a faculty party, but they wind up at his apartment after Ann discovers that she cannot face meeting the people who knew her husband. The two go to bed, but Ann cannot make love to Max. While they lie together, Ann demonstrates how Wayne made her feel sexually violated before he left her to commit suicide. The next day, Max writes a poem titled "The Suicide's Wife," which tries to capture Ann's feelings about her ordeal. The poem, however, leaves Ann angry and confused about her own feelings.

Mark Harrington, Ann's eleven-year-old son, a sensitive boy. Mark writes an imaginative biography about his father. Because Ann cannot answer Mark's questions about Wayne's life, the boy makes up most of the details. When Ann finds the biography, she reads it and discovers that Mark has written nothing about her. Mark becomes openly hostile toward Ann, refusing to complete his chores around the house or to baby-sit his younger brother and sister, Wayne and Annie. Mark eventually fails the sixth grade, which makes Ann realize that while she has worked so hard to make sure everything in her house runs smoothly, she has neglected her children's emotions.

— *Dale Davis*

SULA

Author: Toni Morrison (1931-   )
First published: 1973
Genre: Novel

Locale: Medallion, Ohio
Time: 1919-1965
Plot: Psychological realism

Sula Peace, the protagonist. Sula is different from the other women of the town of Medallion, as willing to feel pain and pleasure as she is to give them. Having lost her best friend, Nel, she looks in vain for friendship in men. After leaving

Medallion to go to college and to travel, she returns as a pariah and is blamed for all the town's misfortunes. She fuels the town's hatred of her by sleeping with married men and with white men. Contrary to the beliefs of the townspeople, who believe that a brighter day will dawn after she dies, her death is followed by a severe ice storm and the catastrophic cave-in of the tunnel.

Nel Wright, Sula's best friend. Reared in an oppressive household, she decides to be her own person, not her mother's daughter. Nel marries the handsome Jude Greene because she wants to be needed. She blames Sula when he leaves her, because Sula seduced Jude. Unlike Sula, she fears change, so much so that she refuses to buy a car. Long after her marriage ends, Nel realizes that she has been mourning for Sula, not for Jude.

Eva Peace, the physically disabled matriarch of the Peace family, Sula's grandmother. She is so preoccupied with her hatred of her womanizing husband and with keeping herself and her family alive that she is unable to show much love to her children. When her husband leaves her, she leaves her children with a neighbor, returns eighteen months later with only one leg, and builds a new home. Her arrogance is apparent in the fancy shoe she wears on her one foot. Strangely, she murders her own son and almost bleeds to death trying to save her daughter.

Shadrack, a shell-shocked veteran of World War I. When he returns to Medallion after the war, he earns the reputation of town character, spending most of his time catching fish to sell, cussing people, acting obscenely, and getting drunk. In 1920, he proclaims January 3 as National Suicide Day, and he commemorates the event every year thereafter by carrying around a hangman's noose and ringing a cowbell. On January 3, 1941, he leads a parade of townspeople to the tunnel, where many of them die in a cave-in.

The Deweys, Eva's three adopted sons, unrelated to one another. Surly and unpredictable, they resist all attempts to distinguish among them. They speak with one voice and think with one mind. After Eva is sent to a nursing home, they live wherever they want. Their bodies are never found after the tunnel collapses.

Hannah Peace, Sula's beautiful and self-indulgent mother. After the death of her husband, Rekus, she takes a series of lovers because of her need to be touched every day. As a result, she is despised by all the women in town. She teaches Sula that sex is pleasurable but otherwise unremarkable. Hannah burns to death while trying to light the yard fire. Eva throws herself out a window trying to save her.

Tar Baby, an alcoholic half-white man who rents a room from Eva. He is arrested for causing a wreck involving the mayor's niece. Tar Baby dies in the cave-in.

Jude Greene, Nel's handsome husband and Sula's lover. Frustrated in his attempt to find work building the New River Road, he marries Nel in his determination to take on a man's role. Even after ten years of marriage, he still feels belittled by white society. Jude leaves Nel shortly after she catches him making love to Sula.

Albert Jacks, called **Ajax**, the one true love in Sula's life, the son of a conjure woman and nine years Sula's senior. Ajax loves women, airplanes, and hot baths. He is the only one of Sula's lovers who actually talks to and listens to her. He senses that she is changing from an unpredictable, spontaneous, and untraditional woman to a more traditional one like those he has previously left. After he is arraigned for arguing with the police, he goes to an air show in Dayton, Ohio, and walks out of Sula's life forever.

Helene Wright, Nel's domineering mother. She moves to Medallion to get as far away as possible from the New Orleans brothel where she was born. In the absence of a Catholic church, she joins the most conservative black church in town and spends her time forcing her daughter to be obedient and polite. Helene saves her own life by refusing to march in the parade to the tunnel.

Plum Peace, Eva's shiftless, spoiled son, to whom she had planned to bequeath everything. He almost dies as a baby because he shoves pebbles up his anus. When he returns to Medallion after serving in World War I, he steals, takes trips to Cincinnati, uses heroin, and sleeps for days in his room with the record player going. Believing that Plum cannot live as a man, Eva sets him afire while he is asleep.

— *Alan Brown*

SUMMER AND SMOKE

Author: Tennessee Williams (Thomas Lanier Williams, 1911-1983)
First published: 1948
Genre: Drama

Locale: Glorious Hill, Mississippi
Time: Early twentieth century
Plot: Psychological

Alma Winemiller, the daughter of a minister in Glorious Hill, a small town in Mississippi. In the prologue, she and John Buchanan are shown as children at a fountain of Eternity in the town in the early years of the twentieth century. The scene shows their pattern as children to foreshadow their pattern as adults: attracted to each other but unable to achieve true communication because she is sensitive and primarily spiritual (as she says, Alma means soul) and he, though capable of a degree of sensitivity, is primarily physical. He is thus representative, in a sense, of the anatomy chart that he shows Alma near the end of the play. As an adult, Alma is given to panic attacks and

frequently goes to John's father for help, even in the middle of the night.

John Buchanan, the son of a physician, frequently at odds with his father. As an adult and a physician himself, he is uncertain that he wants to join his father's practice. The Buchanans and Winemillers are next-door neighbors. In the end, John achieves an understanding of "soul" and will be a successful and empathic physician and husband.

The Reverend Winemiller, Alma's father. Incapable of empathy and lacking genuine faith, he is unsuccessful in all of his roles, as minister, father, and husband.

Mrs. Winemiller, Alma's mother, who is in a permanent psychological state of "perverse childishness." She is primarily interested in eating ice cream.

Dr. Buchanan, John's father. Early in the play, he correctly calls his son a drunkard and a lecher, though it becomes clear that they do feel affection for each other. He treats Alma with great sympathy and does not object to her middle-of-the-night visits.

Rosa Gonzalez, a young Mexican woman whose father owns the gambling casino on Moon Lake and who has a relationship with John.

Nellie Ewell, a younger woman and vocal student of Alma. Her mother goes to trains to attract traveling salesman. As the daughter of a loose woman, Nellie is unaccepted in the community.

Mrs. Bassett, a member of a not-very-successful book club, which has an abortive meeting at Alma's house.

Mr. Gonzalez, Rosa's father. He enters the Buchanan house, seeking Rosa. Dr. Buchanan enters, is insulted at seeing the Gonzalezes in his house, orders them out, and attacks Mr. Gonzalez with a cane. Gonzalez shoots and kills him.

— *Jacob H. Adler*

SUMMER OF THE SEVENTEENTH DOLL

Author: Ray Lawler (1921-   )
First published: 1957
Genre: Drama

Locale: Australia
Time: December, 1952-January, 1953
Plot: Naturalism

Olive Leech, a thirty-seven-year-old barmaid at the same hotel as Pearl. She is cynical but has an "eagerness that properly belongs to extreme youth." She appears to have no frustrations about her dull job and seems to take life as it comes. In adjusting to the unconventional relationship she has with a man who comes to town for only five months out of every year, she has blocked off the other seven months of the year, becoming, as she realizes, "blind to what I want to be." A chance to change the situation with a more conventional arrangement leaves her with a sense of loss and betrayal that borders on the psychotic.

Roo Webber, a sugarcane worker, tall, thirty-seven years old, with light hair starting to gray. He is masculine but has a streak of gentleness, a mixture that invites confidence. He has had a bad working season because of a pretended back injury that he uses as an explanation of his failure to maintain his position as a champion ganger. In his frustration, he fights with his major competitor, Johnny Dowd. He then quits work before the end of the term and returns to the city, eventually getting a job as a painter in a factory, employment he considers degrading. During his annual layoff, he always returns from the fields to live with Olive, to whom he brings, as a symbol of affection, a kewpie doll. This is the seventeenth year for such a present. For him, the relationship with Olive is only a vacation from his real career in the cane fields, where he enjoys a strong sense of community with his fellow workers. He fears making any commitments that will end such bonding but has come to realize that those days are over. He decides to stay in the city and marry Olive, falsely hoping that such stability will redeem his life.

Barney Ibbot, another canecutter, Roo's best friend, a few years older than Roo. He is of medium height and solid build, with the beginning of a pot belly. His manner is assertive and confident. He is a heavy drinker. He has had numerous affairs with women and has fathered three children out of wedlock.

As he gets older, his conquests are more in the telling than in the observance. He cannot admit that the fun is over, however, and lies as a cover-up. His attempt to re-create the past ends in failure.

Pearl Cunningham, a large woman with dyed red hair who contains herself in corsets. She is a widow and mother who earns her living as a barmaid. She feels demeaned by her job and would like to get something more classy. Her friend Olive wants to fix her up with Barney Ibbot, but she is hesitant; she blames her hesitancy on her responsibility in bringing up a teenage daughter. Her suspicious, tentative nature changes to possessiveness when she becomes Barney's lover. Barney does not conform to her idea of respectability. She breaks off the relationship, believing that life should be lived without daydreams.

Emma Leech, Olive's seventy-year-old mother. She owns the house where they live, and Olive pays the bills. Emma is "a wizened, life-battered wisp of a woman . . . with no illusions about humanity." She expects the worst from people and is cynically delighted when her expectations are fulfilled. She is fond of her daughter's friend Roo and offers to lend him money. Wiser than her daughter, she knows the falsity and fragility of a relationship maintained only during a five-month layoff season.

Bubba Ryan, a dark, shy-looking woman of twenty-two, Olive's next-door neighbor. She drops in from time to time, and her visits further plot exposition. She becomes involved with a young canecutter, Johnny Dowd. Life with him, she is convinced, will turn out differently from that lived by Olive and Roo.

Johnny Dowd, another canecutter, a large, boyish, friendly-looking man who is twenty-five years old. In asking Bubba to go with him to the races, he provides evidence that seasonal relationships will survive into a new generation.

— *Wm. Laird Kleine-Ahlbrandt*

THE SUN ALSO RISES

Author: Ernest Hemingway (1899-1961)
First published: 1926
Genre: Novel

Locale: Paris, France, and Pamplona, Spain
Time: The 1920's
Plot: Social realism

Robert Cohn, a Jewish writer living in Paris in the 1920's. He and Jacob Barnes are friends, though Barnes delights in needling him. Cohn seems to mean well, but he has a talent for irritating all of his acquaintances. When Cohn meets Lady Brett Ashley, he immediately brushes off Frances Clyne, his mistress, and spends a few days at San Sebastian with Brett. He now feels that she is his property, though she plans to marry Michael Campbell. Cohn has the temerity to join a group from Paris (including Brett and Michael) going to the fiesta in Pamplona, Spain. Brett is smitten by a young bullfighter and sleeps with him. Cohn, reputedly once a middleweight boxing champion at Princeton, gives the bullfighter a pummeling. Cohn's personality has many contradictions: In general, he is conceited but is unsure of himself as a writer; he seems both obtuse and sensitive; and he evokes pity from his acquaintances, yet they all thoroughly dislike him.

Jacob (Jake) Barnes, the narrator, an American expatriate also living in Paris, where he works as a correspondent for a newspaper. In World War I, he was wounded in the groin and as a result is sexually impotent. This injury negates the love he has for Brett and her love for him. Seeming to work very little, Barnes spends a great deal of time in cafés, drinking and talking. His greatest problems in life are trying to adjust himself to the nature of his injury and trying to work out some sort of personal philosophy; two of his thoughts almost solve the latter problem: "You can't get away from yourself by moving from one place to another" and "Enjoying living was learning to get your money's worth and knowing when you had it." Barnes is a lover of good food and drink, an expert trout fisherman, and an aficionado of the bullfight. Although he drinks as much as the other characters, some of whom are given to passing out, he has the happy faculty of remaining keen and alert.

Lady Brett Ashley, an English woman separated from her husband. Her first lover died of dysentery during the war, and she is getting a divorce from Lord Ashley. She plans to marry Michael Campbell, but she is in love with Barnes, perhaps because she knows he is unattainable, because they can never sexually consummate their love. She is a drunkard and is wildly promiscuous, as is shown by her affairs with Cohn and the young bullfighter, Pedro Romero. She seems as lost in life as Barnes, and she is an appealing woman, one whose successive affairs remind the reader of a little girl trying game after game to keep herself from being bored. In the end, she is determined to settle down with Campbell, even though he is nastily talkative when drunk. In spite of her resolutions, Lady Brett seems destined to work her way through life from bed to bed.

Bill Gorton, a witty American friend of Barnes. With Barnes, he fishes for trout in Spain and attends the fiesta in Pamplona.

Michael Campbell, Lady Brett's fiancé. He is pleasant when sober but very frank and blunt when drunk.

Pedro Romero, a young bullfighter of great promise who has an affair with Brett but who is jilted when he says he wants to marry her and when she realizes she is not good for him.

Count Mippipopolous, a friend of Brett who would like always to drink champagne from magnums. He is kind to Brett and Jake in Paris.

Montoya, the proprietor of the hotel in Pamplona where the established, truly good bullfighters stay; the hotel thus becomes the headquarters of Barnes's wild vacationers.

THE SUNDAY OF LIFE
(Le Dimanche de la vie)

Author: Raymond Queneau (1903-1976)
First published: 1951
Genre: Novel

Locale: Paris, France
Time: Late 1930's and early 1940's
Plot: Domestic

Valentin Brû (vah-lah[n]-TA[N] brew), an army private. Valentin is a very average young man whose real desire in life is to be a street sweeper. He allows himself to be courted by the middle-aged Julia and goes into shopkeeping when he marries her. They move to Paris, where Valentin runs a picture frame shop. He finds success when, disguised as a woman, he becomes a fortune-teller. He is drafted again as World War II approaches. The novel's last image presents him at a train station helping girls and young women into the crowded train and fondling them as he does so. Valentin would like to be a saint, but he is quintessentially a petit bourgeois character who is quite satisfied with the little pleasures of life.

Julia Julie Antoinette Segovie (ahn-twah-NEHT say-goh-VEE), a middle-aged provincial haberdasher. The novel begins with her deciding to marry Valentin, a young soldier whom she has merely seen passing on the street. She succeeds in arranging this marriage, though she cannot take time away from business, so she sends Valentin on a honeymoon trip alone. She inherits a business in Paris from her mother but prefers to become a medium and allows Valentin to run the shop. She becomes ill and allows Valentin to replace her as "Madame Sophie." Julia is a petit bourgeois character incarnating all the comic vices of her class: brashness, vulgarity, avarice, and scheming.

Chantal (shah[n]-TAHL), Julia's sister. She helps her sister in her marriage schemes, even going so far, apparently, as to sleep with Valentin's commanding officer to get Valentin's name. She is an attractive woman, loyal to her family, and her main desire is to see her daughter get her share of the inheritance that Nanette, her mother, leaves to Julia and Valentin.

Paul Bolucra (pohl boh-lew-KRAH), also called **Botucat** (boh-tew-KAH), **Brodago** (broh-dah-GOH), and **Batraga** (bah-trah-GAH), Chantal's husband. The author systematically changes the spelling of the last name of this functionary, an inspector of weights and measures, whose main concerns are whether he is a cuckold, the future of his daughter, and his promotions. He is promoted and is sent from Bordeaux to Paris, where he can consort with Valentin and worry if his wife is doing the same.

Marinette (mah-ree-NEHT), the daughter of Chantal and Paul.

Nanette, Julia and Chantal's mother. She is a lively old woman, which Valentin learns when he meets her, accidentally, on the return trip from Bruges, in Paris, where she is attending her lover's funeral. She leaves her Parisian shop to Valentin and Julia.

Captain Bordeille (bohr-DAY), Valentin's commanding officer. He is a representative of the gallant French soldier and seduces Chantal.

Sergeant Bourrelier (bew-rehl-YAY), another soldier. This friend of Valentin shares frequent drinks with him and comes to visit him in Paris.

Didine (dee-DEEN), a waitress. She gives Valentin advice about marriage and later wants to come to Paris.

Jean-sans-tete (zhahn-sahn-TEHT), or **Jack-Lackwit** in translation, an idiot. This mindless inhabitant of the eleventh arrondissement in Paris carries a broom and is a double for Valentin in his attempt to meditate on nothingness.

— *Allen Thiher*

SUNDOWN

Author: John Joseph Mathews (1895-1979)
First published: 1934
Genre: Novel

Locale: Hills near Kihekah, Oklahoma
Time: c. 1890-1930
Plot: Historical realism

John Windzer, Challenge's father, a representative of the Osages when the government seeks oil rights on Osage land. When Washington reduces its royalties, the Osages blame John and the government brands John a traitor for advocating Osage leases. John turns temporarily to drink. He recovers, however, and continues to work for the Osages, raise horses, and farm—with the help of a tenant—320 acres. John always expresses pride in Challenge. After John's murder, Challenge, now an adult, discovers that John has left $25,000 in the bank for them.

Challenge's mother, who in the beginning dresses in Osage clothing but gives up her blanket, moccasins, and beads when her son goes to the university. She displays Challenge's pictures and books, and she reads all of his college catalog. After John's death, she becomes more verbal. She tells Challenge of John's work for a law to provide care for children and orphans and explains that with money this guardianship will come more easily. She professes that her husband may not have believed that the government would not cheat the Osage and that his death itself shows that civilization has not really come to the Osage Hills.

Challenge, the protagonist. From his birth until his college years, Challenge seems to contemplate each word and action. He proceeds through school and enters the university, where he pledges a fraternity, plays football, and joins the Iron Men cheering squad. Challenge often feels out of step in the outside world. His inner world is a combination of reality and fantasy until he enters the military and begins to fit into "civilization." Challenge becomes a pilot and serves his country. While still an aviator, Challenge learns that his father has been shot and killed. Challenge experiences a conflict in his emotions when he returns to his father's burial and sees the contrast between the old ways and the new ways. Soon he resigns from the military and returns to his hills to drink, ride in fancy cars, try various religions, play pool, and attend dances. He longs to try the tribal dances in public but only dances them in secret. No activity resolves the conflicts that he feels. He loves his mother but is ashamed of her old ways. At last, he realizes that his resentment comes from this Osage woman's being able to see into the heart of a warrior. He decides to attend Harvard law school, then settles back to sleep.

Ellen Windzer, John Windzer's cousin and a teacher in the government school.

Jesus, the one person Challenge thinks much of as a child and who becomes Challenge's friend in fantasy. Challenge finds out about Jesus through Bible cards Ellen Windzer gives him. When Challenge tries to destroy the pictures of the men who are hurting Jesus, Ellen misunderstands, becomes angry with Challenge, and says some things to Challenge that injure his dignity.

Miss Hoover, Challenge's first teacher. A Quaker who wants to teach "little Indian minds," she later leaves her position.

Jep Newberg, the leading merchant and business expert for Kihekah. He dies from a bullet wound to his head.

Charlie Fancher, the trader's son and an early rival of Challenge. Challenge learns from Charlie and the other white boys of the way white people view women and sex: as something interesting and dirty. The Osages view sex merely as a means of procreation.

Jack Fabus, a white boy who persecutes Challenge until Challenge retaliates—according to his father's instructions—with a rock. Challenge receives no punishment because witnesses are honest about what happened.

Sun-on-His-Wings and

Running Elk, Osage friends of Challenge. They are with him as children and even matriculate with him to the university. At the end of the rush and pledge period, however, Sun-on-His-Wings and Running Elk feel violated from the hazing and return to the Osage Hills. Running Elk turns to drink and drugs and dies from a gunshot wound to the head.

Blo Daubency, a popular young white woman at the university who expresses a mild interest in Challenge.

Mr. "Goosie" Granville, a science teacher at the university, an Englishman, Challenge's friend, and the observer of Challenge's first solo acrobatics in an airplane.

Doc Lawes, a profit-maker from the oil wells and victim of a shotgun wound.

Roan Horse, a spokesman for the Osages when the conspiracy to take the land, oil, and money from the Osages reaches trial and when the murders at last go to court when Challenge is a young man.

— *Anita P. Davis*

THE SUNKEN BELL
(Die versunkene Glocke)

Author: Gerhart Hauptmann (1862-1946)
First published: 1896
Genre: Drama

Locale: A mountain, a valley, and the paths between
Time: Indeterminate
Plot: Fantasy

Heinrich (HIN-rihkh), (A Study in Scarlet)a bell-founder who symbolizes the artist against the world. Trying to carry a bell to a mountain church, he is injured by the spirits of wood and water, and his bell is pushed into a lake. He is saved by the mountain sprite Rautendelein, and they fall in love. A rescue party carries him home, but he returns to Rautendelein. His efforts to make a superlative bell are frustrated by the dwarfs. His wife dies, and her dead hand rings the sunken bell. Dying, and renounced by Rautendelein, he tries to reach a flaming cathedral-castle. Wittikin gives him the wines of life and of the questing spirit; Rautendelein, the wine of aspiration. Embraced by Rautendelein, he dies, hearing the chimes of the sun.

Magda (MAHG-dah), his wife.

Rautendelein (row-TEHN-deh-lin), a mountain sprite. She is intended as the bride of the Nickelmann but falls in love with Heinrich. When he is taken home dying, she revives him. Renounced by Heinrich, she marries the Nickelmann but returns to Heinrich as he dies.

Wittikin (VIHT-tih-kihn), a sorceress and the grandmother of Rautendelein.

The Nickelmann, a water spirit whom Rautendelein marries.

The Vicar, representing spirit.

The Schoolteacher, representing mind.

The Barber, representing body.

THE SUNLIGHT DIALOGUES

Author: John Gardner (1933-1982)
First published: 1972
Genre: Novel

Locale: Batavia, New York
Time: August, 1966
Plot: Psychological realism

Taggert Faeley Hodge, a gifted man of forty years, plagued by bad luck, which transforms a gentle idealist into the cynical, fire-scarred **Sunlight Man**. Having failed in all of his efforts to save his wife from insanity and his children from death, he returns to his native Batavia, New York. He is arrested for painting the word "love" on a city street, and he begins using magic tricks to undermine people's faith in law and order and in love. His four "dialogues" with Police Chief Fred Clumly, following the Sunlight Man's escape, are at once seriously learned and blackly humorous, intelligent and insane. Set apart from the rest of humankind as much by his despair and nihilism as by his stench and blasted appearance, he chooses in the end to give himself up, only to be shot dead by a nervous police officer.

Fred Clumly, Batavia's sixty-four-year-old police chief. His beady eyes, large nose, and white, completely hairless body make him a particularly conspicuous figure, especially at the funerals he likes to attend. One year short of retirement, he has become increasingly critical of the modern age. As the crime rate soars, his frustrations, weariness, and paranoia grow, fueled by his noble but decidedly old-fashioned belief in personal responsibility. In a highly irregular maneuver, he agrees to meet secretly with the Sunlight Man following the latter's escape. As a result, he loses his job but acquires a deeper understanding of who and what the Sunlight Man is. This understanding culminates in the speech Clumly delivers at the end of the novel, which enables him to rise above the merely personal and to affirm those "connections" that bind self to community and the individual to the ideal.

Arthur Hodge, Sr., a congressman and patriarch, the builder of Stony Hill, the now-ruined family estate. He was a man of superior mind and virtue blessed by good fortune. His

absolutism, perfection, and idealism come to tyrannize his survivors as they try to live in a less pastoral, more ambiguous age, which the congressman himself foresaw. His wholeness of being and vision lives on in fragmented form, in the specializations of each of his children.

Will Hodge, Sr., the oldest of the congressman's five children. A country lawyer and inveterate toggler committed to shoring up the fragments against last year's ruins, he is a dependable, rueful man, "comfortable in the cage of his limitations" but burdened by guilt and the responsibility he feels for his former wife, his two sons, and his brother Tag, indeed for all humankind.

Millie Jewel Hodge, Will's former wife. Born poor, she tries to win the love of Ben Hodge, drawn by his strength and freedom. Rejected, she takes her revenge by marrying Will (whom she does come to love briefly) and by destroying Stony Hill, and the Hodges with it. Imprisoned by the Sunlight Man, she struggles to maintain her existential autonomy—"I exist, no one else"—but fails. Seeing Tag and hearing the news of her son Luke's death restores this Circe to the world of forgiveness and love.

Luke Hodge, Millie and Will's twenty-two-year-old son. He has an enormous tolerance for the pain caused by his own histamine headaches and his having witnessed his parents' endless bickering. His elephantine ears undermine his romantic tragic-hero pose, just as his will to believe undermines his hard-earned yet nevertheless not-entirely-convincing cynicism. Kept a prisoner in his own house by the Sunlight Man (his uncle), Luke undergoes a significant change. He transforms his adolescent rage into a selfless but suicidal act that will put a stop to the Sunlight Man's madness and Nick Slater's murders. Although Luke dies alone (Tag and Nick having jumped from the truck sometime before Luke drives it off the bridge), it is Luke's death that prompts Tag to give himself up.

Ben Hodge, a large but gentle dairy farmer and lay preacher, fifty years old. Married to Vanessa, a cartoonishly fat but very friendly schoolteacher, he finds his freedom in his visionary sermons and in riding his motorcycle. In his youth, he betrayed Millie Jewel's love, but as an adult he has been both faithful and generous toward others.

Will Hodge, Jr., Luke's older brother, a Buffalo lawyer specializing in legal collection. His earlier idealism—largely destroyed by what he learned when he ran his father's unsuccessful political campaign and by his discovery that the legal system deals with technicalities rather than truth—survives in attenuated form in his commitment to his work and to the Civil Rights movement. He spends much of his time futilely and obsessively tracking down the enigmatic (and, Will believes, dangerous) R. V. Kleppmann.

Esther Clumly, the police chief's blind wife. She met Fred while he was on leave from the Navy and she was a student at the Batavia Blind School, before the onset of the disease that made him "grublike" and before the failure of the operation she underwent to restore her sight. Aging, childless, and emotionally estranged from her husband, she takes refuge in religion, tippling, and self-pity. Her attempt to protect Fred from an imagined conspiracy backfires and contributes to his losing his job. When officials come to the house to collect the tape recordings he has made of the Sunlight Man's dialogues (evidence that will incriminate Fred), Esther comically yet nobly tries to hold them off.

Dominic Sangirgonio, also called **Miller**, a police captain whom Clumly thinks of both as a son and as a rival. A former Marine, he tries as best he can to help Clumly, only to be rebuffed. Eventually (or so the mayor claims), he comes to believe that he can no longer trust the chief.

Stan Kozlowski, who joined the police force to escape his father's farm. Although he may at times be working outside the law (in protecting a prostitute and in accepting free meals), Clumly is nevertheless drawn to Kozlowski, whose ambiguous silence and apparent imperturbability, Clumly says, make a man think. As the story progresses, he becomes more and more Clumly's sole companion and confidant.

John Figlow, Clumly's desk sergeant, who dreams of escaping his unhappy marriage. When the Sunlight Man returns to surrender, it is Figlow who shoots and kills him, understanding only as he fires that the Sunlight Man is not dangerous this time, only once again clowning.

Mickey Salvador, the young, overly trusting police officer who is shot and killed by Nick Slater during the jail break.

Walter Benson, a short, fat, and slightly hunchbacked man who his enormously fat wife, Marguerite, believes is a traveling salesman but who in fact has for the past twenty-two years been the small-time professional thief Walter Boyle. Witness to all that is said and done during his pretrial term in the Batavia jail, he chooses not to become involved, despite the price others must pay for his passivity. He and the Sunlight Man know each other's actual identities (Tag once defended Boyle). Miller, too, discovers Boyle's real identity, but Clumly refuses to use Miller's evidence in court. Returning to Buffalo, Boyle, now Benson, learns that his wife is having an affair

with their boarder. Benson, taking heart from the kitsch poetry he loves to read, decides not to kill the boarder.

Ollie Nuper, Benson's boarder, a man with a silly face, a passion for radical causes, and a distaste for the hypocrisy of others but a self-pitying tolerance for his own. His civil rights activities bring him into contact with Will Hodge, Jr. He is murdered by local neo-Nazis and secretly buried by Benson, who once again chooses not to become involved.

Nick Slater, an eighteen-year-old American Indian who first comes under Luke Hodge's guardianship and then under Ben's. He and his oafish younger brother, Verne, are in jail for their part in a fatal traffic accident. When the Sunlight Man returns to free the prisoners, Nick alone chooses to go, giving up his cell only to become the Sunlight Man's prisoner and slave. He kills a guard during the break and later, more deliberately, murders Will, Sr.'s landlady, Mrs. Palazzo, and Luke's friendly neighbor, Mr. Hardesty.

Kathleen Paxton, the beautiful only daughter of Clive Paxton, whose overprotection made her both gentle and ill-tempered. She became a teacher, married Taggert Hodge against her father's wishes, and gradually lost her mind, coming to prefer the voices she imagined from the past to the harsh reality of her present. Tag and her brothers have spirited her from sanatorium to sanatorium to keep her from again coming under the tyrannical influence of the father who refuses to admit his responsibility for her illness. It apparently was Kathleen who set the fire in which Taggert was badly burned while trying to rescue their two sons.

Clive Paxton, a merciless, self-made businessman and domestic tyrant, feared and hated by most, including his wife, their sons, and the Hodges. He dies at the age of seventy-six on the night before the arrest of the Sunlight Man, who may be implicated in the death.

Elizabeth Paxton, the invalid wife of Clive Paxton, from whose tyranny she took refuge in the love of Professor Combs.

Walt Mullen, Batavia's mayor, an advocate of the time-cost factor in all government affairs, including police work. He is a small man who speaks in clichés and likes to tell off-color jokes. He turns an informal investigation into the formal hearing that ends with Clumly's ouster. He and Phil Uphill (the city fire chief and another of Clumly's critics), however, are the first to congratulate the former police chief for his powerful end-of-the-novel speech.

Sam White, "the oldest judge in the world." He gives Clumly two of Taggert Hodge's essays to read, one on "Police-work and Alienation," the other on Harry Houdini, without, however, divulging that Taggert is the Sunlight Man. Asked by Uphill to help depose Clumly, the judge retreats into silence, acting neither for nor against him.

R. V. Kleppmann, the tall, well-mannered son of Polish Jews whom Will Hodge, Jr., obsessively tries to make live up to his financial responsibilities. His cultivated appearance masks his strong dislike of people, whom he tolerates only insofar as he can use them.

Freeman, a young drifter who appears briefly in Batavia wearing a black coat and an Amish hat, accompanying Will Hodge, Sr., as Hodge trails Clumly. He is "the encourager," but he is also (as Hodge realizes) someone without responsibilities and commitments, who can just pack and leave.

— *Robert A. Morace*

THE SUPPLIANTS
(Hiketides)

Author: Aeschylus (525/524-456/455 B.C.E.)
First performed: 463 B.C.E.?
Genre: Drama

Locale: Argos
Time: The age of myth
Plot: Tragedy

 Danaüs (DAN-ay-uhs), the son of Belus and father of fifty daughters, the Danaïdes. He is a descendant of Io, who was a priestess of Hera and daughter of Inachus, the king of Argos. Io was loved by Zeus, who changed her into a heifer so that she might escape the jealousy of Hera, but Hera sent a gadfly to sting Io and to drive her throughout the world. Having wandered to Egypt, she was touched by Zeus, and from this mystical union was born a son, Epaphus. He, in turn, was the father of Libya, who had two sons, Belus and Agenor. Belus had two sons, Aegyptus and Danaüs. Aegyptus had fifty sons, and Danaüs had fifty daughters. The sons of Aegyptus wished to marry the daughters of Danaüs, but the latter, horrified at the violent lust of their cousins, fled to Argos to seek the protection of their ancestral home. When the play begins, Danaüs, having just landed at Argos, advises his daughters to seek the protection of the local gods. He himself is an old man, unable to protect them from their kinsmen who, as he knows, are sailing in hot pursuit. He asks the aid of Pelasgus, the king of Argos. Having received it and having been given a refuge in the kingdom, he warns his daughters that they must behave in such a fashion as to merit the protection that they have been granted.

 Pelasgus (peh-LAZ-guhs), the king of Argos. He is a vacillating man, torn between his humane desire to grant the protection asked of him and his fear of provoking a war that might well ruin his city. He cannot make up his mind which course to follow until he has obtained the consent of his subjects—an early example of the Greek democratic way of life. Once he

has been backed by the citizens, his better feelings come to the fore, and he not only offers protection to the refugees but also sternly drives off the herald of the sons of Aegyptus and prepares for war.

 The Danaïdes (dah-NAY-ih-deez), or daughters of Danaüs. Although they form the chorus of the drama, they—unlike the usual Greek chorus—act as the chief characters in the play. They are frantic with fear of their pursuing cousins, for they are helpless maidens with only an old and infirm father to protect them. Their barbaric dress arouses the suspicion of the king of Argos, and only through a detailed account of their ancestry do they convince him of their Argive descent. Clinging to the altars of the gods of Argos, they finally threaten to kill themselves if King Pelasgus will not help them. This threat, with its implication of a stain on the kingdom of Argos, helps to persuade the king to offer them protection.

 The herald of Aegyptus (ee-JIHP-tuhs), who speaks for the fifty brothers pursuing the Danaïdes. He lands at Argos just after King Pelasgus has promised his protection to the fugitives. The herald is a heartless ruffian, caring nothing for the gods of Argos, who are not his gods, because he was not born there. He is quite willing to tear the frightened maidens from the altars to which they cling. As suppliants, they are inviolable, but this immemorial, sacred law means nothing to him. He is overawed only by a show of superior force and leaves the stage with a prophecy of war, which was probably fulfilled in the (now lost) subsequent dramas of the trilogy.

THE SUPPLIANTS
(Hiketides)

Author: Euripides (c. 485-406 B.C.E.)
First performed: c. 423 B.C.E.
Genre: Drama

Locale: Eleusis, not far from Athens
Time: Antiquity
Plot: Tragedy

 Theseus (THEE-see-uhs), the young king of Athens, whose aid Adrastus, the king of Argos, seeks in recovering the bodies of the Argive heroes killed in the unsuccessful expedition of the Seven against Thebes. At first he refuses Adrastus' request. He admits that the Thebans should not have withheld the bodies, but he considers the expedition rash and ill-omened, and he is reluctant to identify himself with the bad cause of the Argives. The supplications of the mothers of the fallen heroes, an appeal to pity based on pure sorrow, and of Theseus' mother Aethra, an appeal to pride based on the impiety of the Thebans and the need to uphold the law of Greece, are more successful. Theseus agrees to rescue the dead, by force if necessary. When a herald arrives from the Thebans and asks to speak with the "master" of the city, his innocent remark occasions a largely irrelevant debate between Theseus and the herald on the theme of democracy versus tyranny, in which Theseus is the cham-

pion of democracy as it is practiced in Athens. The herald finally delivers his message, demands that Adrastus be refused sanctuary in Athens, and announces that the bodies shall not be restored to their families, whereupon Theseus summons his warriors. He defeats the Thebans and returns the bodies; however, as an example of the virtue of moderation, he refuses to enter Thebes or sack the conquered city. He oversees the funeral rites of the heroes. Theseus is more successful as a mouthpiece for the glory of Athens than as a man. Although he shows a great love for his mother, he is proud and contentious.

 Adrastus (uh-DRAS-tuhs), the king of Argos, the leader and only survivor among the seven Thebans. He is old, defeated, and disillusioned, and his appeal to Theseus is filled with self-pity; misfortune, he feels, is the common lot of all. Theseus points out Adrastus' own rashness and disregard for the wishes of the gods as the causes of the king's misfortune.

During the play, Adrastus redeems himself, becoming less hysterical and self-pitying. In his funeral oration over the heroes, he speaks out as an advocate of peace.

Aethra (EE-thruh), the mother of Theseus and an example of principled moderation. The mothers of the Seven killed at Thebes come to beg her to intercede with Theseus for recovery of the bodies. Her sympathy for them is genuine and affecting. Although her appeal to Theseus is based on his duty to the gods and Greek law, she realistically plays on his pride.

The Chorus of Argive mothers, who come to plead with Theseus for the recovery of their slain sons. Their odes are the most affecting aspect of the drama.

Evadne (eh-VAD-nee), the widow of Capaneus, who fell in the Theban adventure. Her role is brief but spectacular: She appears, dressed in her wedding finery, on a high rock overlooking the funeral pyre of her husband and, after singing of her sorrow, leaps into the flames. She provides an effective contrast to the moderation of Aethra, and her action horrifies her father and the Chorus.

Iphis (I-fihs), the aged father of Evadne and of Eteocles, one of the Theban adventurers. He comes to bury his son and witnesses the death of his daughter. He departs, completely broken, with words of hatred for old age.

A herald, sent by King Creon from Thebes. He brings news that the bodies will not be restored and insolently engages in a debate with Theseus over democracy versus tyranny. His arguments against democracy are vigorous. He cites its unscrupulous demagogues, the inability of its people to settle policy, and its false equality.

Athena (uh-THEE-nuh), the goddess of wisdom. She appears, *ex machina*, at the close of the play and directs Theseus to extract a pledge from the Argives not to forget what Athens has done for them. She also promises the sons of the Seven future vengeance against Thebes. The play ends with promise of further wars and sorrows.

The sons of the Seven against Thebes, who bring in the ashes of their fathers at the close of the play and look eagerly forward to the time when they will be able to avenge their fathers' deaths.

SURFACING

Author: Margaret Atwood (1939-   )
First published: 1972
Genre: Novel

Locale: A small lake in the Canadian wilderness
Time: Late 1960's
Plot: Psychological symbolism

The narrator, the main protagonist, an unnamed commercial artist and illustrator in her late twenties. She is divorced and the mother of one child. At the beginning of the novel, the narrator is returning to an island on the U.S.-Canadian border, where she will look for her father, a "voluntary recluse" who has disappeared. She spent much of her childhood on this island, except for winters. David and Anna are doing the narrator a favor by driving her and her boyfriend, Joe, to the remote island, which is inaccessible by boat or train. The narrator is disoriented, introverted, and fearful, trying to recover from the shock of an abortion and a broken love affair with a married man. After the four have stayed on the island for a week, the narrator hides from the group and remains on the island when the others leave. She engages in a ritual of grieving for her parents and of shedding the garments and other vestiges of civilization.

Joe, her boyfriend, an avant-garde potter who teaches night school. He seldom speaks. Joe and David are doing a makeshift film, including Anna and the narrator in much of the footage. They plan to put the miscellaneous clips together and call it "Random Samples." After Joe asks the narrator to marry him and she refuses, a series of conflicts unfolds. In the final scene of the novel, Joe returns to the island with Paul to look for her. He calls to her and waits for her response. The novel ends with the narrator on the brink of making this decision.

Anna, the narrator's so-called best friend, though the narrator has known her for only two months. She is somewhat older than the narrator. Insecure in her marriage of nine years to David, Anna dyes her hair, hides behind a coat of makeup, and worries about getting fat and losing David. She suspects him of being unfaithful. To make her week on the island away from the city and civilization tolerable, she reads many detective novels and rations her cigarettes. Although Anna laughs about David's film behind his back and calls it "Random Pimples," she tells on the narrator to David and Joe for throwing their film and camera into the lake at the end of their weeklong stay on the island.

David, Anna's husband, a former radio announcer and Bible salesman, now a teacher of communications at the same night school at which Joe works. He speaks through impersonations and jokes, never saying what he really means. He was studying for the ministry when he met Anna. The oldest member of the group, David fears aging, worries about becoming unattractive, and arranges his hair to conceal his balding. He is the first to suggest that the group stay a full week rather than just the two days that they originally planned. He is angry and distraught when he learns that the narrator has dropped his camera and the film for "Random Samples" into the lake.

Paul, a truck farmer, a neighbor of the narrator's father. Paul writes to the narrator when her father disappears. Although Paul speaks only broken English and the narrator speaks only academic French, they communicate through the ritual of exchanging vegetables. Early in the week, Paul brings Bill Malmstrom to the island and delivers "a huge wad of vegetables from his garden." Later, he comes to the island with Claude to bring word that the narrator's father had been found drowned. Finally, it is Paul who brings Joe to the island in a last search for the narrator.

Madame, Paul's wife, a sturdy woman who has never learned English. She remains nameless and in the background.

Bullhead Evans, "a bulky laconic American" who runs the Blue Moon Cabins. He delivers the group to the island and picks up Joe, Anna, and David a week later.

Bill Malmstrom, a graying executive for "Teenie Town: Togs for Toddlers 'n Tots" in Detroit, Michigan. He identifies himself to the narrator as a "member of the Detroit branch of the Wildlife Protection Association of America." He is looking for a place where the members can meditate, observe, hunt, and fish because their location on Lake Erie is "giving out."

The narrator's former lover, a teacher of lettering who appears only in the narrator's memories. Married, with children, he insists that the narrator have an abortion when she becomes pregnant. The narrator ultimately says of him that he

was "only a normal man, middle-aged, second-rate, selfish and kind in the average proportions."

The narrator's brother, who explores mineral rights in Australia. The family legend of his near drowning as a toddler is important to the narrator. She remembers his "laboratories" in the woods where he kept small animals and insects in jars and often allowed them to die. The narrator has sent him a letter but believes that he has not yet received it.

— *Carol Franks*

THE SURROUNDED

Author: D'Arcy McNickle (1904-1977)
First published: 1936
Genre: Novel

Locale: The Flathead Indian reservation in Montana
Time: Early twentieth century
Plot: Social realism

Archilde Leon (ahr-SHEEL lay-OHN), the mixed-race son of an Indian mother and a European father. He returns home to visit the Flathead Indian reservation in Montana. He expects this to be a brief and final visit before he returns to his life as a musician in Portland, Oregon. A sensitive, intelligent, and careful man, he takes care of his dying father and helps his mother any way that he can. He often seems to be caught up in events and unable to escape the reservation, where he is torn between white and Indian culture.

Catharine LaLoup Leon, the daughter of a Salish chief. She is the mother of Archilde, Louis, and Agnes. One of the tribe's earliest and most enthusiastic converts to Roman Catholicism, Catharine still maintains a rather traditional way of life and eventually renounces her baptism. A strong-willed yet generous and loving old woman, she is very much respected in the Indian community. She is important to Archilde's growing sense of his identity as an Indian, and it is at her death that he feels as if he is a part of the community.

Max Leon, Archilde's father, originally from Spain. His many children have all disappointed him; he had hoped that they would be more manly and less Indian. A wealthy rancher, he drives a flashy blue car and barely speaks to his wife. He is reconciled with Archilde when Archilde helps with the harvest, because he hopes the young man will stay to run the farm after he dies. A gruff man, Max is careful about money. Because of his reluctance to show affection, he lives in isolation from other people.

Mike, Archilde's nephew. A rebellious boy, he is treated harshly at the Indian boarding school and suffers emotional trauma, which is healed by his participation in traditional Indian culture. He and his brother Narcisse reject mainstream culture and try to return to the old ways.

Narcisse (nahr-sees), Mike's brother and constant companion.

Elise, the granddaughter of Modeste. She asserts her interest in Archilde from their first meeting. She is a wild girl, open and expressive, who drinks, smokes, and generally misbehaves. She falls in love with Archilde and kills Dave Quigley in his defense. Elise is not merely rebellious; rather, she is intelligent and strong-willed. Her enthusiastic approach to life charms Archilde.

Modeste, an old Salish chief and a good friend of Catharine. He is often consulted for advice in difficult matters and is the primary source of old stories and native wisdom.

Dave Quigley, the sheriff, disliked and feared by most Indians. A ruthless and cruel man, he hates the Indians and resents his country's protection of them. An excellent tracker, he will stop at nothing to catch and severely punish an Indian.

Louis Leon, Archilde's older brother and a horse thief. Catharine believes that he developed his callous attitude after attending the missionary school. His death brings about her eventual renunciation of Catholicism.

Father Grepilloux, an elderly Franciscan priest who came to the valley with the first group of missionaries. He is writing a history of the mission. He is kindly and affectionate, and he respects the Indians. His attitude is contrasted with that of the more recently arrived priests. He and Max are some of the oldest white settlers in the valley and are good friends.

Agnes Leon, Archilde's widowed sister. She moved into the big house to help take care of her father, Max. Mike and Narcisse are her sons. A quiet woman, she can be very perceptive about human nature.

— *Kelly C. Walter*

SURRY OF EAGLE'S-NEST

Author: John Esten Cooke (1830-1886)
First published: 1866
Genre: Novel

Locale: Virginia
Time: 1861-1863
Plot: Historical

Lieutenant Colonel Surry, an officer of the Confederate Army. He falls in love with May Beverley, who is already engaged. Having been involved in the feud between Mordaunt and Fenwick, and having fought under Jackson, he is able to marry May when her fiancé breaks the engagement.

May Beverley, who marries Surry when her fiancé, Frederick Baskerville, breaks their engagement.

Fenwick, a Yankee spy who has treacherously separated Mordaunt from his wife. Repeatedly escaping Mordaunt's vengeance, he is killed by Achmed.

Colonel Mordaunt, once the rival of Fenwick for the hand of Frances Carleton. Mordaunt had won her, whereupon the rejected Fenwick used forged letters to separate husband and wife. Mordaunt repeatedly seeks revenge, but Fenwick always escapes, until Achmed kills him.

Frances Carleton, Mordaunt's lost wife, who appears as the insane "White Lady." She gives Surry a paper clearing up the mystery of Fenwick's villainy.

Violet Grafton, her cousin and attendant.

Achmed, Mordaunt's Arab companion, who kills Fenwick.

Harry Saltoun, a young Confederate officer who, about to fight a duel with Mordaunt, is revealed as his son.

Mrs. Parkins, Fenwick's confederate.

General Stonewall Jackson,

General J. E. B. Stuart,

General Turner Ashby, and

Major John Pelham, officers of the Confederate Army.

Captain William D. Farley, a Confederate scout.

THE SURVIVOR

Author: Thomas Keneally (1935-   )
First published: 1969
Genre: Novel

Locale: Australia and Antarctica
Time: Mid-1960's
Plot: Tragicomedy

Alexander Ramsey, a former Antarctic explorer, the director of extension studies at a provincial Australian university. A large, homely man of sixty-two, Ramsey is debilitated with guilt at having survived Stephen Leeming, the leader of his Antarctic expedition, and at having slept with Leeming's wife before the journey. Oversensitive to references to Leeming, Ramsey begins the novel by walking out of a Rotary Club meeting because of a casual inquiry. Preoccupied and neglectful of his university work, Ramsey thinks that he is approaching madness when he is informed that Leeming's body has been found and is to be excavated. He flies to the Antarctic to watch the dig. Once it is completed, he achieves a new sense of mental well-being.

Ella Ramsey, Ramsey's wife and a part-time lecturer in the department of history at his university. She is forty-five years old and has an attractive Mediterranean appearance. Her life is dominated by the knowledge of her own infertility; her one pregnancy ended in a stillbirth. From that time, she abandoned her doctoral thesis and has redirected her energies into pottery and sparring with her husband. She has little patience for Ramsey's fixation on Leeming, though she grudgingly supports him otherwise.

The poet, an Australian man of letters, small and intense. The poet is writing an extended poem about the Leeming expedition. He delivers the information of the discovery of Leeming's body to Ramsey, thereby precipitating Ramsey's crisis. Despite some initial distrust, he and Ramsey become friends.

Belle Leeming, the widow of Stephen Leeming. An elderly but still attractive and quick-witted woman, Belle led an unconventional earlier life that included affairs with many men. Her memory of Leeming is practical, whereas Ramsey's is mystical. She goes to the Antarctic to watch the excavation.

Denis Leeming, a doctoral student and the nephew of Belle, in his early thirties. Denis has an impressive academic background, but his thesis cannot be approved. An eccentric, dilettantish man, Denis is excited by the idea of the recovery and reburial of Leeming's body. This plan brings him into conflict with Ramsey. Eventually, Leeming's thesis is accepted for publication as a book.

Stephen Leeming, the leader of the Antarctic expedition. A thin, slight man from a rich family, Leeming was a self-confessed fanatic for polar exploration. Intelligent though ata-

vistic, he led a largely successful exploration but eventually was crippled by a stroke while crossing a glacier.

Morris Pelham, the senior lecturer under Ramsey. A Yorkshire man with a Cambridge education, Pelham is Ramsey's chosen successor to the directorship. Pelham covers up for much of Ramsey's administrative neglect.

Eric Kable, the assistant director of the extension program. An ambitious, unscrupulous man who wants the directorship, Kable plays departmental politics in an attempt to tarnish Ramsey. He supports Denis Leeming.

Valerie Kable, Kable's wife. An attractive woman and amateur actress, she is best known in the university for her promiscuity, which sometimes serves to advance her husband's career.

Arthur Lloyd, a doctor and former Antarctic explorer, now dying. Lloyd accompanied Leeming and Ramsey on the fatal leg of their Antarctic journey. Two weeks before his death, Lloyd tells Ramsey that when they left Leeming, he was not quite dead.

Sir Byron Mews, the vice chancellor of the university, a phlegmatic and political man widely, if secretly, known by his old rugby name, **"Chimpy."** Lord Byron controls the university machinations behind Ramsey, especially with regard to Denis Leeming.

Lady Sadie Mews, Lord Byron's wife, an attractive, girlish, older woman who confides in Ramsey her distrust of her husband.

Brian Sanders, a professor of physics, a handsome man of fifty years. Sanders is a pleasant and honest man but is given to sexual adventuring. As Denis Leeming's supervisor, he tries to prevent him from going to the Antarctic. He almost succeeds in seducing Ella Ramsey, and he makes a student, Sally Bourke, pregnant.

David Hammond, a journalist. A thin, tanned man of thirty-five, Hammond is the Australian journalist assigned to cover the excavation of Leeming. He meets Ramsey in New Zealand on the way to the pole and becomes his confessor, if not friend.

Barbara, Ramsey's secretary, an overweight and pretentious but loyal woman. She runs Ramsey's office for him with motherly efficiency.

— *Paul Budra*

SUTTER'S GOLD
(L'Or: La Merveilleuse Histoire du général Johann August Suter)

Author: Blaise Cendrars (Frédéric Louis Sauser, 1887-1961)
First published: 1925
Genre: Novel

Locale: Switzerland, the United States, and Canada
Time: 1834-1880
Plot: Historical

John Augustus Sutter, a Swiss emigrant to America, a magnificent dreamer and methodical man of action who builds and loses an empire in California. In 1834, he is a penniless Swiss fugitive, vagabond, and swindler named **Johann August Suter**. He deserts his wife and four children and sails for America. His family has no news of him until he becomes famous as General John Augustus Sutter, one of the richest men in the world, the lord of a vast domain in California. Shrewd in maneuvers and a skillful diplomat, he steers a careful course and maintains good relations both with the Mexican authorities who rule California when he arrives and with the forces of American expansion, which will soon claim California as a new state. By the time of statehood, Sutter owns the largest domain in the United States. His vision realized, with his vast farms flourishing with cotton, rice, indigo, livestock, orchards, and vineyards, Sutter longs to settle back into calm and peaceful cultivation of his choice European vine-stocks. At last, he is ready to send for his wife and children, to live out the fulfillment of his grand agrarian dream of New Helvetia in the garden of America. Then gold is discovered on his land. The ensuing chaos, with the inundation of his lands by gold-mad prospectors, settlers, and squatters, shatters his dream and destroys his farms, forts, estates, and villages. The chaos decimates his family and leaves him a ruined, broken man. Aside from the character traits that mark Sutter with a genius for colonization, he possesses a "profound knowledge of the human heart" and a certain "moral ascendancy." When his estates are overrun and the filth of gold hunger seems to have polluted all of California, Sutter wonders whether he is guilty of setting it all in motion, whether it is not somehow his fatal flaw, his overweening ambition, that has caused everything. In this phase of his life, Sutter takes on a certain tragic grandeur. He lives out his final years in Washington, D.C., where he is viewed as something of a joke, as the eccentric old madman seeking an impossible justice. Even General Sutter's death is monumental and symbolic: He dies on the steps of the Capitol and its "gigantic shadow" falls over his corpse. Sutter is one of the most compelling exemplars of the glory and the tragedy of the American Dream. His presence in this novel is so engulfing that he is not merely the only principal character but also, strictly speaking, the only character developed at all.

Anna Sutter, Sutter's wife, abandoned by him and left without word from him for fourteen years. She makes the long, difficult journey to join him, with their children, only to find her husband a ruined man. She dies shortly after her arrival in California.

Judge Thompson, a California magistrate who pronounces Sutter's claims valid. One of the few just and civilized men in the raw territory, Thompson befriends the ruined Sutter. He understands and feels compassion for the general's plight.

Jean Marchais, Sutter's loyal blacksmith, one of the few employees of the general who remains faithful through everything. The Frenchman is finally hanged by the gold-seeking rabble.

Father Gabriel, a missionary and protector of the Indians. Eloquent, just, and firm, he is a friend to Sutter and possesses an intelligent and compassionate understanding of the historical anguish of California and Sutter's role in these events.

Johannes Christitsch, the leader of the Herrenhütter of Lititz, Pennsylvania. A relentless intriguer and self-appointed manager of Sutter's affairs in his last years, he schemes to take advantage of the old general.

— *H. R. Stoneback*

SUTTREE

Author: Cormac McCarthy (1933-   )
First published: 1979
Genre: Novel

Locale: Knoxville, Tennessee, and the surrounding area
Time: 1951-1955
Plot: Impressionistic realism

Cornelius Suttree, called **Buddy** by his family, **Sut** by his friends, and **Youngblood** by Abednego Jones. He is an intelligent and well-educated man of approximately thirty who, for reasons never explicitly divulged, has left his wife and child and gone to live in a houseboat moored to the banks of the Tennessee River. Born with a dead identical twin, Suttree suffers from a sort of double vision: He lives half in this world and half in the next, and he views each from the perspective of the other. He makes a meager living by fishing and spends the rest of his time either taking care of or getting drunk with an assortment of mostly homeless and alcoholic outcasts who are his friends. In the course of his disjointed but thematically coherent adventures, Suttree undergoes a series of encounters with the dead and with death, from the floating corpse that opens the novel to the corpse in his bed that closes it. Not only do many of Suttree's friends die (through violence, neglect, or disaster), but Suttree himself is hospitalized three times in the novel as well, twice as a result of barroom brawls and once for an advanced and untreated case of tuberculosis. Suttree makes three excursions from Knoxville. The first is to attend the funeral of his son; the second is into the Smoky Mountains, where he wanders without food or shelter for more than a month in an effort to lay his demons to rest; and the third is to the French Broads of the Tennessee River, with Reese, in an ill-fated attempt to make money by gathering mussel shells and freshwater pearls. At the end of the novel, most of his friends are dead or gone, and his already tenuous ties to the material world are loosened still further by his lengthy and near-fatal illness. He leaves McAnally Flats one step ahead of the death that hounds him.

Gene Harrogate, also called the **City Mouse**, who meets Suttree in the workhouse, to which he has been sent for the unusual crime of melon-mounting. Harrogate is a misfit even among misfits and serves as Suttree's comic twin; his hare-brained get-rich-quick schemes provide some of the novel's lighter moments.

Abednego (Ab) Jones, a huge black man, one of Suttree's closest friends. With his wife, Doll, Ab runs an unlicensed tavern in his houseboat. Ab tells Suttree that the police "don't like no nigger walkin' around like a man." Because Ab refuses to be intimidated, he is frequently and violently incarcerated. Suttree is involved in Ab's two unsuccessful attempts to get Mother She to destroy his enemies for him and is present during Ab's last epic battle with the police. Ab is finally beaten to death in jail.

Reese, a raft-dwelling ne'er-do-well. He persuades Suttree to undertake his only experiment with earning a living through hard work. The experiment is a miserable failure, and the expedition culminates in death and destruction.

Wanda, Reese's daughter and one of Suttree's lovers. She is killed in a rockfall at the French Broads camp.

Joyce, Suttree's lover after Wanda. Joyce is a prostitute from Chicago who supports Suttree in lavish style until his dependency embitters him, and his bitterness drives her temporarily mad.

Mother She, also called **Miss Mother**, an ancient black witch who takes a particular interest in Suttree. In a hallucinatory episode toward the end of the novel, she gives him "the second sight."

Billy Ray "Red" Callahan, a bully and a petty thief who rescues Harrogate from an assailant in the workhouse, generally wreaks havoc, and is finally shot in the head by a bartender. After the shooting, he lingers in a vegetable state until a hospital orderly pours rubbing alcohol into his wound.

The ragpicker, Suttree's most philosophical friend. Asked whether he believes in God, the ragpicker replies, "I got no reason to think he believes in me."

Michael, an Indian fisherman. He and Suttree become friends when Suttree defends him from a racist attack. He returns to seek help from Suttree during the latter's brief period of prosperity with Joyce, but Suttree ignores his knock.

Daddy Watson, a retired and senile railroad engineer. Until he is committed to an asylum, Daddy lives in an abandoned railroad car near Suttree's houseboat.

Leonard, a male prostitute. Suttree is recruited by Leonard to assist in disposing of the corpse of Leonard's father, which the family has been hiding for months so that they can continue collecting his Social Security payments.

Grace Suttree, Suttree's mother. Grace appears only once in the novel, when she visits Suttree in the workhouse, but she is one of several characters, such as Suttree's dead twin, who are more important than they are visible.

— *John Merritt Unsworth*

SWALLOW BARN: Or, A Sojourn in the Old Dominion

Author: John Pendleton Kennedy (1795-1870)
First published: 1832
Genre: Novel

Locale: Virginia
Time: Early nineteenth century
Plot: Social realism

Mark Littleton, the narrator, a New Yorker visiting his Virginian relations at Swallow Barn. An observant man who enjoys people, he tells his story of the Virginians with relish and with an obvious love of their easygoing way of life. He returns to his New York home after two months in Virginia.

Edward (Ned) Hazard, his New York cousin, high-spirited and given to joking and playing pranks. He is a favorite with children. Although he is the next heir to Swallow Barn, he is glad for Frank to have the responsibility of running the estate. In love with Bel, he encounters difficulties but at last marries her.

Francis (Frank) Meriwether, Ned's middle-aged brother-in-law who operates the Hazard estate. A handsome, portly, and good-humored man, he is unambitious and of a contemplative nature. He is a generous, pleasant host to his many guests and a considerate master to his servants and dependents, who are happy to wait on him. Argumentative about politics, he is little informed about or interested in religion.

Isaac Tracy, an eccentric, elderly gentleman farmer, master of a neighboring estate, The Brakes. A dignified, sober, old-school Virginia gentleman, he occupies much of his time planning and plotting to get one hundred acres of almost worthless marshland lying between The Brakes and the Hazard land.

Bel Tracy, his vivacious younger daughter, pretty, impulsive, flirtatious, and quick-tempered. She is a good horsewoman. Uncertain for a while as to whether Ned is really the man for her, she at last decides he would be a good husband.

Harvey Riggs, a Tracy kinsman, a waggish, warmhearted man of forty who is well liked by everyone.

Scipio, an old freed slave who enjoys recalling older, better times in Virginia.

Lucretia, Frank's wife, a model administrator of domestic affairs at Swallow Barn and a prodigiously fruitful woman.

Mr. Chub, a scholarly, philosophical, plump old gentleman who is a tutor and Presbyterian minister.

Prudence Meriwether, Frank's unmarried sister, who enjoys bewailing the demise of Virginia's golden age.

Carey, an old black man who prides himself on his knowledge of horses.

Barbara Winkle, an old servant who tends to the numerous Meriwether children.

Catharine Tracy, Bel's older sister, well educated and sober-minded.

Ralph Tracy, the younger brother of Catharine and Bel. He is a slovenly, swaggering sportsman.

Singleton Oglethorpe Swansdown, a dandyish bachelor rejected by a bevy of Southern belles. He is Mr. Tracy's arbitrator in the settlement of the boundary line question.

Philpot (Philly) Wart, a popular lawyer and politician who plots with Frank to let Swansdown win in the litigation over the boundary line.

Hafen Blok, a German immigrant popular for his storytelling prowess.

SWAMP ANGEL

Author: Ethel Wilson (1888-1980)
First published: 1954
Genre: Novel

Locale: Vancouver and the interior of British Columbia
Time: Early 1950's
Plot: Regional

Maggie Vardoe, also known as **Maggie Lloyd**, a young widow, married for the second time, to a man whom she detests. Her beauty is not immediately apparent, and she makes no effort to look beautiful, but her eyes are large, gray, and "tranquil," and her body is characterized by "large easy curves." Maggie is self-sufficient, even secretive, and confides very little about her present unhappiness or the pain of losing her first husband and her daughter, even to her closest friends Hilda and Nell Severance. Having decided to leave her second husband, Eddie Vardoe, she ties fishing flies in secret for more than a year to earn money and slips away one night after dinner so unobtrusively that it takes several hours for her husband to notice her absence. Maggie seeks escape and peace away from the city of Vancouver in the mountains of British Columbia, where she tries to re-create the happy setting of her childhood and first marriage at an East Coast fishing lodge. A naturally nurturing and competent woman, Maggie becomes cook and eventually manager of a fishing lodge owned by Haldar and Vera Gunnarsen at Three Loon Lake. Maggie, who had hoped to escape not only her husband but also all emotional involvement with people, finds that she is faced with several crises caused by Vera's envy of Maggie's competence and increasing influence with Haldar and their son, Alan.

Nell Severance, formerly a beautiful circus performer, now in her seventies, her movement limited by obesity. She married into an aristocratic but eccentric English family. Nell has kept the Swamp Angel, a revolver that she used in her juggling act, as a reminder of her lost power. She sends the revolver to Maggie when she realizes that she is no longer independent physically and fears that she is close to death. Nell's powerful personality enables her to control Eddie after Maggie's disappearance. Nell's unconventional life and her love of drama contrast with both her daughter's conventionality and with Maggie's search for tranquillity and disengagement. Despite her nonconformity, Nell provides wisdom and stability to Maggie.

Hilda Severance, later **Hilda Cousins**, an attractive young working woman, the daughter of Nell and Maggie's only friend of her own age. She accepts and respects Maggie's reticence. She cares for her mother, whom she both loves and resents for the irregularity of her childhood, but she is drawn away from her and from Maggie by her marriage to Albert Cousins and the birth of her child.

Edward (Eddie) Vardoe, also called **E. Thompson Vardoe**, a crude, boorish man with "spaniel eyes," a real estate agent with aspirations to own a business. Eddie's uncouth behavior and his petty tyrannizing about money and the running of the household humiliate Maggie and cause her to leave him as quietly as possible, so as not to be subjected to one of his scenes. Having taken Nell's advice to forget Maggie and find someone else, Eddie becomes involved with "a blonde" who manipulates and humiliates him.

Haldar Gunnarsen, the owner of the lodge at Three Loon Lake. He is passionately attached to the land and determined to keep his lodge in spite of a crippling accident that breaks his hip. Haldar is insensitive to his wife's jealousy of the land and her fear of the future. As he depends more and more on Maggie in the running of the lodge, he fails to understand Vera's jealousy of her. His anger at Vera for precipitating Maggie's departure leads to Vera's suicide attempt and the final reconciliation between the Gunnarsens and Maggie.

Vera Gunnarsen, Haldar's wife, a woman reared in the city and unable to understand the reality of running a lodge. She has grandiose dreams of immediate success and wealth. Vera appears to prefer unhappiness to happiness, and she focuses the blame for all of her misery on Maggie. Maggie's patience with her only increases her sense of resentment and jealousy, and finally she forces a confrontation that causes Maggie to leave the lodge temporarily.

— *Katherine Keller*

THE SWAN VILLA
(Das Schwanenhaus)

Author: Martin Walser (1927-)
First published: 1980
Genre: Novel

Locale: Southwestern Germany, near Lake Constance
Time: A summer in the 1970's
Plot: Social realism

Gottlieb Zürn (GOHT-leeb tsewrn), a real estate broker living in the Lake Constance area of southern Germany. He is almost fifty years old and is haunted by a sense of failure and inadequacy in business and family life. He feels harassed by the details of everyday living (such as car insurance) and troubled by inopportune lust. He likes to speculate about the real ages of his acquaintances. People and events in the novel are seen through his eyes, although this is a third-person narrative. His rival real estate agents seem far wealthier and more stylish, enterprising, and successful than he is. He appears less likely than them to obtain the coveted sole agency to sell a magnificent art-nouveau villa on the lake where Gottlieb, who writes poetry, likes to linger in useless melancholy. At parties, he is likely to lose his head in efforts to entertain the company, so that his indiscretions haunt him afterward. On one occasion, he makes extravagant purchases while failing to call on a client through loss of nerve. In family affairs, he believes that he is an inadequate father to his four daughters. He is hot-tempered and impatient in his dealings with them and fails to provide support in their times of need (for example, pregnancy and a wish to "drop out"). He observes that his wife, who bears the brunt of family difficulties, is also more effective than he is at selling real estate. The final discovery that the villa is being demolished at the hands of a rival agent leaves him battered and resigned.

Anna Zürn, Gottlieb's wife, who is burdened with family cares, which include tending a daughter (one of four) who is inexplicably ill. She has a tenacious memory for detail and is perhaps a better agent than her husband. She fends off Gottlieb's amorous advances, often using sobering information for this purpose.

Regina Zürn, their daughter, who is mysteriously ill, often in the hospital. She is a constant worry to her parents.

Rosa Zürn, another daughter, at a university as a student of law. She returns home pregnant by Max, a married man, and decides against an abortion.

Magdalena (Magda) Zürn, another daughter. Approaching her final examinations at school, she is conscientious but not at the top of the class. A vegetarian and a violin player, often listless, she plans, for a time, to drop her studies.

Julia Zürn, another daughter. She plays the piano when her sister plays the violin. She takes the family dog to training classes without success and often seems irritated by her family.

Hortense Leistle (LIST-leh), the wife of a wealthy manufacturer, responsible for the sale of Swan Villa now that her sister has been declared legally incompetent. Gottlieb is eager to get the sole listing, but she refuses to commit herself and ends by allowing the old house to be demolished.

Lissi Reinhold (RIN-hohlt), the wife of a prosperous businessman and a prospective client to Gottlieb, a former tennis partner. She appears everywhere without her husband, accompanied by a bearded young sociologist. She is a formidable woman with a powerful voice. In her presence, Gottlieb is likely to behave foolishly.

Jarl F. Kaltammer (yahrl KAHLT-ahm-mehr), a rival real estate agent. A former student activist with aristocratic pretensions, he finds the local dialect "vulgar." A constructor of shoddy buildings, he prides himself on dealing only in Burgundian chateaus. He outwits all the other agents by arranging for the demolition of Swan Villa.

Paul Schatz (shatz), Gottlieb's principal rival in the real estate business, an autodidact of Hungarian origins. His life, to the envious Gottlieb, seems carefree, and his advertising seems flamboyant. He is prominent in environmental causes and is a painter whose work Mrs. Reinhold admires.

Rudi W. Eitel (I-tehl), another rival to Gottlieb. Rarely in Germany, he cultivates a surrealist appearance and imitates Southern California business methods.

Helmut Maier (MI-ehr), nicknamed **Claims-Maier**, a real estate claims consultant and Gottlieb's drinking companion. He proves to be a competent bidder at the final auction and is good at repartee but is of little assistance to Gottlieb.

Baptist Rauh (row), a composer from the Lake Constance region and a prospective purchaser easily moved to enthusiasm. His wife prefers Hamburg.

Max Stöckl (SHTEH-kehl), a cameraman with ambitions to be a director, Rosa's married boyfriend by whom she is pregnant. He talks incessantly in a Bavarian accent, trying to organize Rosa's life (she should drop law studies, he thinks) and preaching a doctrine of self-assertion. Rosa sends him away.

Eberhard Banzin (BAHN-tsihn), the son of the original owner of Swan Villa and a former schoolmate of Gottlieb. Once a brilliant mathematician, he relapsed into eccentricity and was declared legally incompetent.

— *W. Gordon Cunliffe*

SWEET BIRD OF YOUTH

Author: Tennessee Williams (Thomas Lanier Williams, 1911-1983)
First published: 1959
Genre: Drama

Locale: A fictional Gulf Coast town called St. Cloud
Time: 1959
Plot: Poetic

Chance Wayne, a handsome would-be actor who did not "make it" in Hollywood and is now a gigolo. He has maneuvered his traveling companion, Princess Kosmonopolis, to visit his birthplace, St. Cloud, a small town on the Gulf of Mexico. His plan is to get the princess, who is really a faded film star, Alexandra Del Lago, to help him and Heavenly Finley, the youthful sweetheart he had deserted, begin careers in the motion picture industry. During their short stay, however, he learns that Heavenly has had a hysterectomy, because of his having given her a venereal disease, and that her father, Boss Finley, and her brother, Tom Junior, are waiting to castrate Chance if he ever shows his face in St. Cloud again. As the play ends, Chance recognizes that his youth has passed, that his dreams of stardom and Heavenly will never materialize, and that he must wait for the inevitable with what the

playwright calls "deathbed dignity."

Princess Kosmonopolis, also known as **Alexandra Del Lago**, a film star traveling incognito after fleeing from a preview showing of her "comeback" film. She uses every service and distraction Chance offers, from oxygen, pills, liquor, and hashish to sex. She cannot forget, however, what she believes to be her failed attempt to return to motion pictures as a middle-aged woman. Toward the end of the play, she learns that her film is a success, and she offers to take Chance with her on the return trip to Hollywood, but he declines. She, too, has lost the "sweet bird of youth," but time has allowed her a slight reprieve.

Boss Finley, the father of Heavenly and Tom Junior, a caricature of a "redneck" pre-civil rights politician. His concern for his daughter stems from his fear of what gossip about her will do to his election campaign. He has bullied his son into complete compliance; even his mistress, Miss Lucy, has neither respect nor love for him. As Heavenly reminds him, it was he who drove the young, clean Chance away years ago because he wanted his daughter to marry an older man from whom he hoped to profit. His character becomes clear when he tells his daughter how he had bought her mother a diamond clip as she lay dying—to prove to her that she was going to recover—and then had gotten a refund before the funeral.

Miss Lucy, Boss Finley's mistress for years. She is disloyal to him, secretly encouraging the Heckler, who has interrupted Finley's youth rallies before, by asking questions about Heavenly's operation. She tries unsuccessfully to urge Chance to escape his fated castration by leaving with the princess while he has the opportunity.

Aunt Nonnie, the sister of Heavenly's dead mother, dependent on Boss, who had a part in the original love affair between Chance and Heavenly. Now she reminds Chance that time has passed for Heavenly, too, and that nothing can come of his "plans" for them to win a Youth Search in Hollywood. She warns him to leave St. Cloud while he can.

Heavenly Finley, Chance's sweetheart, who blames her father for much of what has happened to her. She does, however, appear at his side in "virginal white" at his television rally and has agreed to marry Dr. George Scudder, although she threatens going into a convent. She is a very weak person whose only chance for happiness ended when she was not allowed to marry her young lover.

Tom Finley, Jr., Heavenly's brother, a wild young man whose indiscretions have been paid for by his father.

Dr. George Scudder, the chief surgeon at St. Cloud Hospital, which was put up by Boss Finley. He operated on Heavenly and will marry her, but he wants nothing to do with plans for the castration, even though he agrees in principle that it is deserved.

Hatcher, the assistant manager of the Royal Palms Hotel, who tries without success to get the princess to leave St. Cloud.

The Heckler, who has taken a number of beatings but continues to appear whenever Boss Finley holds a rally.

Scotty and

Bud, former friends of Chance. They participate with Tom Junior in the final *coup de grâce* at the end of the play.

Stuff, a bartender in the hotel who remembers Chance from the old days and hates him.

— *Edythe M. McGovern*

THE SWEET DOVE DIED

Author: Barbara Pym (Mary Crampton, 1913-1980)
First published: 1978
Genre: Novel

Locale: London, England
Time: The 1960's
Plot: Sentimental

Leonora Eyre, an aristocratic woman who lives in London, does not work, and is nearing the age of fifty. She is an attractive brunette, especially in the right kinds of light. She dresses well and entertains herself by buying Victorian *objets d'art et de vertu* and by reading. She rather complacently thinks of her life as passion spent and emotion recollected in tranquillity, although she cannot remember just where and when she spent the passion. On a number of occasions, she is faced with the fact that some of her friends think her cold and formidable. She does not accept this judgment, preferring to think her responses to life properly measured and rigorously tasteful.

Humphrey Boyce, the owner of an antique shop in London. Nearing sixty and a widower of many years, Humphrey is tall, slender, and, he thinks, bald in the most distinguished kind of way. He is rather fussy in the shop with Miss Caton, his typist, and with his nephew and employee, James Boyce. He meets Leonora in the book's first chapter at an auction in Bond Street, then later finds himself in a contest for her affections with his nephew.

James Boyce, a twenty-four-year-old graduate of the University of Oxford. Recently orphaned by the death of his mother, he has gone to work for his uncle. He is attractive, well-mannered, and rather passive, falling, as he does, into and out of relationships in a casual and mildly guilt-ridden fashion. Installed by Leonora in a flat above hers, James engages first in a somewhat colorless affair with Phoebe Sharp and, later, in a more spirited liaison with Ned, an American whom he meets in a Spanish post office. Leonora does what she can to end these affairs but is successful only with respect to the former.

Phoebe Sharp, a recent graduate of an unspecified English university. She is brown-eyed, tall, shy, and not overly attractive. Her casual manner of dress is made to look slovenly when she comes up against the immaculate Leonora. She likes James more than he does her but does not have the necessary resources to fight Leonora for his attentions.

Ned, a twenty-nine-year-old, small, neat, fair-haired, and blue-eyed American college English professor. Ned becomes James's lover in Spain and returns to England with him. He is described as having a thin, gnatlike voice. He breaks off the affair with James and prepares to return to his mother in Cambridge, Massachusetts, but not before going to Leonora and announcing his bequeathing of James back to her in a meretricious, cruel, and finally unrewarded play for a show of emotion and of gratitude.

Miss Foxe, a kindly, fragile, white-haired woman of seventy who plays what Leonora considers to be distasteful programs on her radio and whose flat Leonora commandeers to rent to James.

Liz, a neighbor of Leonora whose love of cats has been occasioned by a ruinous marriage.

Meg, a friend of Leonora who is also nearing fifty. She has a homosexual friend named Colin who occasionally leaves her for lovers. She commiserates with Leonora when Ned enters James's life.

Miss Caton, a typist in the employ of Humphrey Boyce. She is admirable, prim, and middle-aged. She takes her tea from a "monstrosity" of a cup and is reproved by Humphrey for so doing.

— *Johnny Wink*

SWEET WHISPERS, BROTHER RUSH

Author: Virginia Hamilton (1936-   )
First published: 1982
Genre: Novel

Locale: A small midwestern town and southwestern Ohio
Time: The 1970's, with flashbacks to the 1960's
Plot: Social realism

Sweet Teresa "Tree" Pratt, a fourteen-year-old black girl responsible for her seventeen-year-old brother, Dab, who is mildly retarded. Because their mother must work away from their home, Tree looks after Dab and herself. Such responsibility has made her very independent, but it also leaves her lonely. When the ghost of Brother Rush suddenly appears and carries her back into the past, Tree learns about her family history and about the sources of the problems that plague the Pratts. By the end, Tree has successfully navigated a set of adolescent rapids, but the trip has not been easy.

Dabney "Dab" Pratt, who is mildly retarded and also suffers from porphyria, a rare genetic disorder. Dab is able to attend school and even bring girls home to his room, but they may be interested only in the drugs he uses to ease his pain.

The porphyria makes him extremely sensitive to light and to touch, and, by the end of the week in which the novel takes places, the disease kills him.

Viola "Muh Vy" Sweet Rush Pratt, Tree and Dab's mother, a live-in nurse who must be away from home most of the time. As a young mother, Vy experienced a double tragedy: Her three brothers all died of porphyria at an early age, and then her husband, Ken, abandoned the family.

Sylvester Wiley D. Smith (Silversmith), Muh Vy's boyfriend, a chauffeur at her present job.

Miss Cenithia Pricherd, a sixty-seven-year-old woman who has been living on the streets. Muh Vy hires her to clean.

— *David Peck*

THE SWISS FAMILY ROBINSON
(Der Schweizerische Robinson)

Authors: Johann David Wyss (1743-1818) and Johann Rudolf
    Wyss (1781-1830)
First published: 1812-1827
Genre: Novel

Locale: An island near New Guinea
Time: Late eighteenth century
Plot: Adventure

Mr. Robinson, an intelligent, resourceful Swiss who, with his family, is shipwrecked on an island near New Guinea. He represents many middle-class virtues and beliefs, including a strong religious sentiment. Because of his good sense, practical knowledge, and understanding of human nature, he and his family succeed in establishing themselves on the island with European-type civilization. When a ship calls at the island, Mr. Robinson decides to remain, hoping that commerce will come and that his little colony will grow and prosper.

Mrs. Robinson, an intelligent, brave, and hardworking woman who is in her way as resourceful as her husband. She improvises a great deal in making her family comfortable and happy. Her tasks are housekeeping and care of the crops and animals. Like her husband, she chooses to remain on the island.

Fritz Robinson, the oldest of the Robinson boys. He grows up on the island to become a gentlemanly, courageous young man. He learns how to accept responsibility and to carry out

difficult tasks requiring initiative and courage. Unlike his father, he wants to return to Europe and does so when the opportunity comes.

Emily Montrose, a young English girl shipwrecked on the island. She is rescued by Fritz, who brings her to his family's settlement. Emily is the daughter of an English army officer and is on her way home from India. She and Fritz fall in love and plan to marry upon their return to Europe.

Ernest Robinson, the second of the Robinson boys. He has a great interest in natural history, and his previous studies help the family very much, for he is able to identify plants and animals for various purposes.

Jack Robinson, the third of the Robinson children. He contributes to the family's welfare by helping his mother tend the animals and crops.

Francis Robinson, the youngest of the Robinson children. He is the pet of the rest of the family and thoroughly enjoys his childhood on the island.

SWORD OF HONOUR

Author: Evelyn Waugh (1903-1966)
First published: 1965
Genre: Novel

Locale: England, Scotland, West Africa, Egypt, Crete, Italy,
    and the Balkans
Time: 1939-1945
Plot: War

Men at Arms, 1952
Guy Crouchback, a thirty-five-year-old Roman Catholic who is reserved and ironic. After his divorce, he lived morosely in a family castle in Italy. When World War II begins, he returns to England, convinced that the Allied cause is just. He

trains in an old-fashioned army unit, the Halberdiers, but gradually becomes disillusioned by the war. He proves his valor in a disastrous expedition ("Skylark") on the West African coast. He generously gives whiskey to a hospitalized friend, who dies as a result. In disgrace, he is sent back to England.

Gervase Crouchback, Guy's saintly father, the book's moral center. Financial problems force him to lease the family home and live in a seaside hotel.

Trimmer, an officer trainee; he is stupid, uncultured, and impudent. He is dismissed from the Halberdiers.

Frank de Sousa, a witty and worldly officer trainee.

Apthorpe, a fellow trainee, then fellow officer, about thirty-five years old. He is burly, mustachioed, occasionally drunken, ambitious, and exceedingly earnest. He tells varying stories about his past, and he has lived in Africa. He often is the target of Guy's ironic remarks. He possesses a large stock of tropical gear, including a portable water closet or "thunderbox." After this object explodes, Apthorpe acts more and more eccentrically. He becomes ill in Africa and dies from drinking too much whiskey.

Virginia Crouchback Blackhouse Troy, a pleasure-loving, witty romantic beauty about thirty years old. She was divorced from Guy to take up with the dashing Tommy Blackhouse, then wedded an American. When Guy tries to seduce her, she is first charmed, then appalled.

Brigadier Ben Ritchie-Hook, the commander of Hazardous Offensive Operations. The one-eyed, irascible, impetuous commander emphasizes attacking ("biffing"). He leads a brigade to West Africa, where a disaster derails his career.

Officers and Gentlemen, 1955

Guy Crouchback, who is now passive and dispirited. He serves first with the Commandos in Scotland and then with Hookforce in Egypt. He finally goes to Crete on an expedition that fails ignominiously. A thoroughly disillusioned Guy is sent back to England. All he has left is his personal sense of honor.

Brigadier Ben Ritchie-Hook, who is now the commander of Hookforce but is still irascible and reckless. He disappears flying over Africa.

Trimmer, a former trainee, revealed as having been a hairdresser named Gustave. He is now a Scottish officer named **McTavish**. For publicity purposes, he leads a foolish military raid that is puffed up by the press. Trimmer becomes the lower-class hero the nation wants.

Virginia Crouchback Blackhouse Troy, who has become increasingly desperate. She sleeps with Trimmer and later, because she needs money, becomes his mistress.

Corporal-Major Ludovic, a man of mystery in his mid-thirties. He writes. He deserts on Crete and is perhaps a murderer. He saves Guy's life.

Unconditional Surrender, 1961

Guy Crouchback, who continues to serve dutifully. Although he wishes to die, he looks for positive acts. He is staying with his uncle Peregrine when Virginia tells him that she is pregnant by Trimmer. He marries her for her unborn child's sake. Although they have a tender month together, he is unmoved by her death. In the Balkans, he meets Mme Kanyi, a leader of some Jewish refugees, and learns how wrong his motives have been. He is further disillusioned when he discovers that his kindness probably led to her death. After the war, he marries Domenica Plessington, and they live on the old Crouchback property and care for their children as well as for Virginia's baby.

Gervase Crouchback, Guy's father, who dies. Many people attend his funeral.

Peregrine Crouchback, Guy's uncle, an innocent man who is a bachelor and a Catholic. He invites Guy to stay with him. He has a memorable dinner with Virginia and is killed by a bomb.

Trimmer, who is increasingly known as a war hero. He inspires the "Sword of Stalingrad." He falls in love with Virginia, who keeps him happy for patriotic appearances. His trip to America for propaganda purposes fails miserably, and he disappears.

Virginia Crouchback Blackhouse Troy, Guy's former wife. When she tells Guy that she is carrying Trimmer's child, Guy agrees to marry her. She effortlessly converts to Catholicism and gives birth to a boy. She is killed by a bomb, but the baby survives.

Frank de Sousa, who is more and more a successful and witty officer but is revealed as a committed communist. In the Balkans, where he is Guy's commanding officer, he makes sure that British forces further communist objectives.

Major-General Ben Ritchie-Hook, who is unhappy because he lacks a real command. Shocked back to his old self by an airplane crash, he recklessly assaults an enemy position and is shot dead.

Major Ludovic, who is still mysterious and possibly insane. When Guy appears at the training unit he commands, he hides and buys a dog. His novel, *The Death Wish*, becomes a bestseller. After the war, he buys the old Crouchback castle in Italy.

Lieutenant Padfield, an American officer who knows everyone and everything. He gathers evidence against Virginia for her divorce. After the war, he becomes Ludovic's assistant.

Mme Kanyi, a leader of displaced Jews. She dies, probably as a result of Guy's kindness.

— *George Soule*

SYBIL: Or, The Two Nations

Author: Benjamin Disraeli (1804-1881)
First published: 1845
Genre: Novel

Locale: London and northern England
Time: 1837-1843
Plot: Political realism

Sybil Gerard, who was brought up at Mowbray Convent. She has been imbued with a deep sense of the deprivations of the Catholic church and of the people by the English aristocracy. She wishes to become a nun and is already engaged in charitable works among the needy inhabitants of Mowbray. She is very close to her father, accompanying him to London for the presentation of the Charter and ministering to him daily during his imprisonment. She has accepted his political idealism, but in her conversations with Egremont and in the failure of Chartism, she comes to realize that some of his beliefs are not based on any real experience. After refusing both Egremont and Morley, she finally accepts the active life and marries Egremont. Benjamin Disraeli portrays her as innately aristocratic, striking, and with a beautiful singing voice and an ability to articulate her ideas forcefully. She delivers several significant speeches. She is capable of considerable physical bravery. She proves herself worthy of reclaiming her rightful title.

Egremont (eh-greh-moh[n]), a younger son. As such, he will not inherit the family estate and needs to find a suitable profession. It is almost by default and certainly by family influence that he becomes a member of Parliament. From his first meeting with the Gerards, a process of political education begins, partly inspired by his growing love for Sybil. Socially, the match would be a disaster: He needs to marry a rich heiress to cover his expenses and maintain his status. Even though he is rejected by Sybil, he speaks in Parliament for receiving the Chartists, though he sees the limitations in Chartism and Morley's radicalism. In the end, he represents the forces of law and order against the disorder of the masses, and it is this that wins Sybil. His brother's death leads to the title: His marriage to Sybil combines his nation with hers. Symbolically, theirs is a marriage of industry and property, of aristocracy and the people, bypassing the capitalism of the middle class.

Walter Gerard, the overseer at Mr. Trafford's factory and, like Trafford, a Catholic. He is a claimant to the Mowbray estates. His energies are of an idealistic nature, channeled into Chartism. He is a popular and respected leader of the workers of Mowbray, a good father to Sybil, and mentor to Egremont. The failure of Chartism saddens but does not break him. His violent death comes as a shock.

Stephen Morley, a radical extremist, editor of a Mowbray newspaper. He rejects tradition, wanting revolution, but goes along with Chartism, partly because of his love for Sybil. At the end, his pacifist views are discredited and he is shot while rifling Mowbray Castle for the Gerard documents.

Lady Deloraine, a typical society aristocrat. Her hobby lies in influencing political decision making. It is her influence that starts Egremont on his political career.

Baptist Hatton, a skilled antiquarian and middleman to titles and estates. He moves discreetly in high society, in contrast to his plebeian brother. Both enjoy the power and prestige they attract.

Devilsdust, who represents the people in their poverty. He is a survivor, able to enjoy life. Given an opportunity, he is capable of doing well and improving himself.

— *David Barratt*

THE SYSTEM OF DANTE'S HELL

Author: Amiri Baraka (Everett LeRoi Jones, 1934-   )
First published: 1965
Genre: Novel

Locale: The Inferno of the Ghetto
Time: Mid-twentieth century
Plot: Autobiographical

The Narrator, the author's persona, also called **Leroi**, **Roi** and **Dante**. He is a black intellectual from lower-middle-class origins, attracted to white culture and Western civilization but guilt-ridden and confused by the resultant denial of his black heritage. The narrator describes himself as in continual flux—"I don't recognize myself 10 seconds later. Who writes this will never read it"—and empty at "the core." He feels trapped in a Dantesque and nightmarish hell, torn between his black identity, which is violent and promiscuous, and his intellectual quest to rise above it. The entrance to his vision of hell, therefore, is inscribed with "You love these demons and will not abandon them." In a disjointed, stream-of-consciousness-like flow of memories, punctuated by black English slang and expletives, he recalls in long and cryptic catalogs the inhabitants of his childhood streets and the ugliness and squalor of their lives; he relives the bewildering seductions of adolescence and the chain of lovers, male and female, who become momentarily tangled in his posing and his longing. People from his past loom up in memory, people doomed to the various circles of hell, and then fade away. The Narrator depicts his youth as a time of excess born of the blues, a time of "violence against others, against one's self, against God, Nature, and Art," a time of hunting and conquest and golden boys, of bisexual use and abuse. He lists the literary greats whose words have lured him toward their value systems (Dylan Thomas, James Joyce, T. S. Eliot, Ezra Pound, and Dante, among others), indicts them as seducers, and cries out in self-disgust: "I am left only with my small words . . . against the day. Against you. Against. My self." He nevertheless expects even those "small words" to be misinterpreted. The Narrator seeks to find some sense in the seemingly meaningless confrontations of his youth: a fight at a party, a homosexual encounter, a rape of an old woman with venereal disease, a "ball" at "The Bottom; where the colored lived," and abuse by whites who define him as a "slick city nigger." In the final circle of hell, he calls himself "an imitation white boy" and "the young wild virgin of the universe" with an Odysseus or a Vergil-like shade pointing the way toward a wilderness "For Madmen Only," a place where he is enslaved by a white prostitute and prostitutes himself for her approval and where he understands himself to be a "nobody." Ultimately, he claims to have a clearer vision of the "inferno" of his frustration and to have found peace in returning to his black self.

46, a nameless representative of "brittle youth" and "dead America," rootless and disillusioned, ignorant and weak, and easily taken. He is a middle-class black person with delusions of hope. The "smooth faced" black youth is sexually seduced by 64.

64, or **Herman Saunders**, a tempting exploiter from Morton Street, an underprivileged black youth who sings the blues. The Narrator calls him "a maelstrom of definitions" and places him in the circle of "Drama" and "False Counsellors." He is both a homosexual seducer and a representative of street knowledge.

Peaches, a fat, white, seventeen-year-old prostitute who tries to rape and then control the Narrator. She has short "baked hair" split at the ends; fat, tiny hands full of rings; perspiring flesh, and a purple dress with wrinkles across the stomach. She laughs at the Narrator and his friend in their military uniforms, and when they try to leave after a few dances, she grabs the Narrator's hat so that he will be technically out of uniform if he tries to return to the base. She then forces the Narrator to spend the evening drinking with her and to come home with her, only to beat him and accuse him of being a homosexual when he cannot perform in bed. Later, when they become lovers, she initially makes him feel as though his past was "all fraud and sickness." Being "Peaches' man," however, eventually helps him to understand how he has prostituted himself to white values and leads him to return to his own people, hellish though their lives may be.

Beverley, one of the women in the Narrator's Newark neighborhood. She is less important for what she is in herself than as an expression of how the opposite sex is perceived.

— Gina Macdonald

TAKE A GIRL LIKE YOU

Author: Kingsley Amis (1922-1995)
First published: 1960
Genre: Novel

Locale: A country town south of London, and London
Time: Late 1950's
Plot: Tragicomedy

Jenny Bunn, a twenty-one-year-old schoolteacher. She is, in most things, an ordinary young woman, pleasant, with average tastes and wants. She is better than average in the domestic virtues, disciplined and orderly in her habits, and accommodating of others. She has a resolute moral compass, and here her problem begins. She is strikingly beautiful, but, with the guidance of her dour, pedestrian, north-of-England morality, she has resolved to remain a virgin until she marries. Being sensible, she has learned to deal with the barrage of sexual attention that comes from almost every quarter, from even the most respectable or homely of men and, occasionally, from women. She has more difficulty with her own divided nature, however, which does and does not want to remain firm. She also surmounts this difficulty. She does want to be married, and here she falters. The men whom she finds who will naturally respect her morality do not interest her. They are the pathetic, homely, and absurd men of the town. The men who do interest her are impatient with her reserve. After Jenny has lived for a time in the company of women for whom virginity is no longer even a wistful memory, and after she has had difficulties with almost every character in the novel (those who have no direct designs on her are offended when Jenny attracts people close to them), she falls prey to the less-than-honorable actions of Patrick Standish, with whom she is in love, and whom she had hoped to marry. She becomes his mistress.

Patrick Standish, a master at a local boys' school. Handsome, intelligent, and cosmopolitan, he is a self-styled rake and playboy and devotes much of his energy to womanizing. He also is a conscientious and concerned teacher, in spite of himself, and he has another nature, less avaricious and more self-content. This other nature, hidden behind the playboy at adolescence, has rarely been seen since. In his adult persona, he has grasped what he thinks he ought to want, at the expense of what he does want. One look at Jenny is enough to bring out the wolf in him, and their first date establishes the pattern that continues through the novel. Patrick behaves badly and then tries to argue her out of her principles. Later, he regrets his boorishness and tries to make amends; Jenny, seeing no ready alternatives, forgives him. Their romance goes thus, up and down through the novel, the down moments being many, and the up moments including a long idyll when it looks as though they will marry, during which Patrick begins to feel something

like his preadolescent contentment. Finally, Patrick gives in to his lesser self. In actions that, if not quite amounting to rape, are certainly more than seduction, he makes Jenny his mistress.

Graham McClintoch, a young chemistry instructor and Patrick's roommate. A would-be Patrick Standish, Graham is the prototype for the homely and pathetic men who would respect Jenny's morality but are quite unfit to be her husband. Although he devotes as much energy as Patrick to sexual misadventures and dotes on Patrick's advice, he has no success. His one date with Jenny falters when he becomes more interested in his own self-pitying fantasies than he is in Jenny. There are good sides to him, and he is not meant to be farcical, except perhaps as a romantic figure. During the crisis at the end of the novel, his natural chivalry proves insufficient to save Jenny from Patrick.

Anna le Page, a French girl who lives in Jenny's boardinghouse. She is a posturing and cosmopolitan woman, the most extreme of the many who appear in the novel. When Jenny makes a sincere try at friendship, Anna gives back only a large dose of polemics on the theme of free love and self-expression and makes a pass at her. By the end of the novel, she has revealed to Jenny that her public persona, by which she was, in her own eyes, a rebel and an outcast, is simple fabrication. Jenny thinks only that in revealing her true self she seems all the more false.

Julian Ormerod, an upper-class friend of the men. He is the master of ceremonies for most of the book's fun and mayhem. He has built up a real charm out of a supercilious manner. He has his own moral compass, and although his north is nowhere near Jenny's, these two are in a way meant for each other. He knows enough not to make an unwelcome proposition, and he knows not to let his desire for a woman run away with his better judgment. He is the prototype of the man who might respect women's virtue, at least in the woman he meant to marry, without being pathetic. As such, he is something of a missing link for the novel, considered a dying breed. At the time of the novel, he is simply not disposed to be married, and he and Jenny quickly establish a solid understanding. He and Jenny may be friends, and she gets some of the benefit of his natural chivalry, but their relations end there.
— *Fritz Monsma*

THE TAKEOVER

Author: Muriel Spark (1918-   )
First published: 1976
Genre: Novel

Locale: Nemi, Italy
Time: 1973-1976
Plot: Satire

Maggie Radcliffe, the **Marchesa Tullio-Friole** (TEW-lee-oh-free-OH-lay), a wealthy American in her forties. Charming and egocentric, Maggie draws to her a dissolute circle who find her great wealth and her prodigality equally attractive. Exhibiting a frivolous, fickle, and careless temperament, she seems to those around her to be easy prey to various criminal schemes. She is, however, relentless in pursuit of those who attempt to bilk her of her fortune and ruthless in meting out what she sees as justice against them. Having been deceived into believing that she is the owner of the sacred wood and sanctuary of Diana of Nemi, she subsequently finds herself dispossessed by a former companion who, having been lent the use of the house, now lays claim to it as a gift. The expulsion of her unwelcome tenant and the pursuit of her unscrupulous business manager, Coco de Renault, who has absconded with her fortune, send her into protracted litigation, and through the financial centers of Europe hunting the elusive confidence man. She plans and has executed a wild kidnapping and ransom scheme to restore all of her money and her rights. Like her ancient predecessor, the goddess of fertility and the hunt, Maggie shows both aspects of Diana in modern society as she seeks to claim what is hers.

Berto, Maggie's devoted and elderly husband. As a descendant of an ancient Italian family, he has vast wealth that encourages a predisposition to security. He, consequently, spends much of his time installing electronic alarms, hiring and maintaining guards, and providing impregnable defenses for his various properties. Although somewhat dismayed by his wife's unpredictability, he nevertheless indulges and supports her unflinchingly.

Hubert Mallindaine, an Englishman and a former companion of Maggie, a tenant of one of her houses. A handsome man of forty-five years, he possesses charisma and personal appearance that draw both men and women to him. He is a charlatan and a thief. He has half-convinced himself, on spurious evidence, that he is the descendant of the goddess Diana and the Roman emperor Caligula, whose ritual marriage took place, according to legend, at Nemi. His imposture as King-of-the-Wood in a quasi-religious cult would deny Maggie, his benefactor, her ownership of the site and make his ownership a claim by divine right. He has been systematically looting her house by replacing her antique furniture and furnishings with fakes.

Pauline Thin, Hubert Mallindaine's secretary. She is attracted to her employer but is brought to a realization that his sexual preference will not admit a more intimate relationship. She assumes a self-appointed prominence in the pagan cult that Hubert has founded. Despite her name, she is plump, with a flair for the dramatic in dress that ill suits her figure and face. She sees herself as chic and fashionable.

Lauro Moretti, a houseboy, first to Hubert Mallindaine and then to Maggie. He later, through polite blackmail, achieves the status of secretary to her. A handsome, graceful opportunist, he deserts a pregnant servant girl, Agata, to marry a middle-class salesclerk in a Roman boutique. Betty, his wife, provides him with a claim to the properties of Nemi and the distinction to which he aspires.

Michael Radcliffe, Maggie's son. Although recently married, he spends much of his time in Rome with a mistress, leaving his wife to her own devices and pleasures.

Mary Radcliffe, Michael's wife, born in California. She is striking, with long blond hair. A certain puritanical sense of orderliness and propriety is evident in her continual keeping of lists. At the top of her list is her duty to succeed in marriage, as did her sister. After a sexual encounter with Lauro, this goal becomes somewhat obscured in her mind.

Dr. Emilio Bernadini (eh-MEE-lyoh behr-nah-DEE-nee), a business lawyer and a tenant of Maggie who introduces her to Coco de Renault. He is sophisticated, fashionably slim, and graceful. His glasses lend a scholarly distinction and seriousness to his pale face.

Letizia Bernadini (leh-TEE-zyah), the eighteen-year-old daughter of Emilio Bernadini. She is full of teenage idealism and good works. She is also a nationalist and a collector of supposed injustices. She enjoys rehabilitating drug addicts and proclaiming Italy for the Italians. Athletic and large of frame, she is also overpowering in her opinions.

Pietro Bernadini (pee-EH-troh), the twenty-year-old son of Emilio Bernadini. He is dark-eyed, with delicate, aristocratic features. His great goal is to become a film star, and he travels with the film set whenever he can.

— *Maureen W. Mills*

THE TAKING OF MISS JANIE

Author: Ed Bullins (1935-   )
First published: 1981
Genre: Drama

Locale: Primarily California
Time: The 1960's
Plot: Social criticism

Monty, a black student in his early twenties attending a West Coast university. He is a poet and the center of a group of campus intellectuals and artists. He is not, however, committed to any system of ideas or movement. Confidence is Monty's most pronounced personality trait and the quality that draws others, particularly women, to him. He is cynical about political strategies and the people who mouth them.

Janie, a white student in her early twenties. Reared by middle-class parents, she has been protected from the harsh realities of American racism and its effects on people and relationships; she is naïve. Janie is attracted to underdogs and believes that all social problems can be solved with goodwill and open dialogue.

Rick, a black man in his early twenties. Rick is in search of a philosophy and a movement in which he can believe. He is passionate in his beliefs, but it is clear that time will present him with other philosophies that he will also embrace.

Len, a roommate of Rick and Monty. He is described by the playwright as intellectual, artistic, and political aware. For Len, race is one of the problems of the 1960's, but it is not the only one.

Sharon, a young white woman who marries Len. She clearly understands the problems in interracialism and is strong enough to fight them.

Peggy, a young black woman who needs and searches for love. She, like the others, has failed in her quest. Her marriage to Monty caused her to drop out of college to put him through school; the failure of that marriage led to a second unsuccessful marriage. Convinced that she cannot find fulfillment in men, she seeks satisfaction in women.

Flossie, a woman who, like Peggy, looked for love but quickly accepted that it was not to be found in black men. Tired of being the third party in a love triangle, she, too, turns to other women.

Lonnie, a white man caught midstream between who he is and who he wants to be. He seeks association with black people and imitates their speech and behavior, but he believes in his own racial superiority.

Mort, a leftover hippie struggling to find a niche. He is an angry man who believes that African Americans and members of other minority groups have failed to acknowledge their debt to him and his kind.

— Donald T. Evans

A TALE OF A TUB

Author: Jonathan Swift (1667-1745)
First published: 1704
Genre: Novel

Locale: England
Time: The seventeenth century
Plot: Satire

Peter, one of three brothers whose father, on his deathbed, wills each of them a new coat that is guaranteed to last a lifetime, given the proper care. The father provides detailed instructions for such care and enjoins his sons Peter, Martin, and Jack to live together peaceably under one roof. Peter goes in search of giants and dragons with his brothers and develops an increasingly enlarged sense of self-importance. When their father's coats no longer reflect the current fashion, the brothers, under Peter's leadership, adjust the coats accordingly. A relentless quest for knowledge, power, and possessions sends Peter in pursuit of experimental science and frenzied finance. He buys a "Large Continent," which he resells numerous times. He discovers a sovereign remedy for worms and engages in other quackery. Dedicated to pride, projects, and knavery, Peter eventually turns into a madman. In his delusions, he calls himself Lord, Emperor, Father, and even God Almighty. His need to make all people subservient soon affects his relationship with his brothers, whom he rules as a despot. They finally rebel and begin their separate existence when Peter, in his rage, turns them out. Allegorically, he represents the pope or the Catholic church.

Jack, Peter's brother. After his break with Peter, he begins to evince the extremist zeal of the dissenter or reformer. He and Martin wish to rediscover and honor their father's will. In trying to rid himself of Peter's influence, Jack tries to remake his father's coat, but his hysterical rage makes him tear it to pieces. Sensing their incompatibility, Jack and Martin separate. Jack's fanatical dissent soon yields to madness, the madness of jealousy, conceit, rebellion, and anarchy. By rejecting Peter, Jack is forced to establish his own tradition of authority. He founds the sect of AEolists, a theology of radical noncon-

formity that holds wind or spirit to be the origin of all things. Filled with this wind of inspiration, Jack is driven to ridiculous excess. A copy of his father's will turns into an object of superstitious veneration. He introduces a new deity known as Babel by some and as Chaos by others. Its shrine is visited by many pilgrims. He covers roguish tricks with shows of devotion. He is strongly averse to music and painting. Jack's nonconformity and dissent are clearly as destructive as Peter's papistry. Both rationalism and emotionalism, as well as both authoritarianism and individualism, turn into religious egotism that perverts and corrupts the simple wishes of the father. Jack allegorically represents John Calvin.

Martin, the third brother, who provides the satiric norm and is as such the least developed and the least interesting of the three. His moderation in all things and sweet reasonableness do not incite the reader's interest, as does the psychopathology of Peter and Jack. Representing Martin Luther and the Church of England, Martin lacks the vitality that animates the radical cause and paranoia of his brothers. The difference is most noticeable in the way he divests his coat of the ornaments that Peter had persuaded his brothers to add. His reformation of the coat proceeds cautiously and discerningly. In contrast, Jack in his impassioned zeal rips not only the decorations but the garment itself, until there is little left of it. When Martin eventually settles in the north, he kindles the wrath of Peter when the people begin to shift their allegiance and financial support from one brother to the other. Bloody battles erupt and the relationship among the three brothers is strained further, until permanent alienation ensues.

— Henry J. Baron

THE TALE OF GENJI
(Genji monogatari)

Author: Murasaki Shikibu (c. 978-c. 1030)
First published: c. 1004
Genre: Novel

Locale: Japan
Time: Early medieval period
Plot: Romance

Prince Genji, the handsome and popular son of the emperor of Japan. This courtly romance of medieval Japan is primarily concerned with Genji's amours.

The emperor of Japan, Genji's father.

Lady Kokiden, the emperor's consort.

Kiritsubo, Genji's mother and the emperor's concubine. Largely as a result of Lady Kokiden's antagonism to her, Kiritsubo dies during Genji's childhood.

Princess Aoi, who is married at the age of sixteen to twelve-year-old Genji. She is unhappy at first as a result of her husband's youth, and later because of his many amours. He does come to appreciate and love her, but her affliction results in her death in childbirth.

Fujitsubo, the emperor's concubine and one of Genji's first paramours. She has a child by Genji, but fortunately for him the resemblance in looks is attributed to fraternity rather than to paternity. After Lady Kokiden's death, Fujitsubo is made official consort.

Utsusemi, a pretty young matron and another of Genji's paramours. Realizing that the affair cannot last, she ends it. While pursuing her again, Genji becomes distracted by another young woman.

Ki no Kami, a young courtier, at whose home Genji meets Utsusemi.

Yūgao, a young noblewoman in love with Genji. They live together in secret within the palace grounds for a time, until Yūgao dies tragically and strangely. Genji's friends act to avert a scandal.

Murasaki, a young orphan girl of good family. Genji secretly rears her and, a year after Princess Aoi's death, when Murasaki is of marriageable age, he makes her his wife.

A TALE OF TWO CITIES

Author: Charles Dickens (1812-1870)
First published: 1859
Genre: Novel

Locale: France and England
Time: During the French Revolution
Plot: Historical

Sydney Carton, the legal assistant to Mr. Stryver, a successful London barrister. A drunkard and a misanthrope, he has no aim or purpose in his life until he meets Lucie Manette and falls secretly in love with her. Because of his remarkable physical resemblance to Charles Darnay, who becomes Lucie's husband, he is able to sacrifice himself on the guillotine in Darnay's place, a deed that finally gives a real meaning to his life in his own eyes.

Charles Darnay, in reality **Charles St. Evrémonde** (shahrl sah[n]-teh-vray-MOHN), an émigré and an antiaristocrat who has renounced his title. In England, where he becomes a teacher of languages, he finds happiness and success as the husband of Lucie Manette. When he returns to France to aid an agent of the St. Evrémonde family who has been captured by the revolutionists, he himself is arrested and condemned to the guillotine. He escapes because Sydney Carton takes his place in prison. Darnay returns to England with his wife and her father.

Lucie Manette (lew-SEE mah-NEHT), a beautiful young French woman, closely connected with political events in France. Her father, a physician, had been a prisoner in the Bastille for many years, sent there because he had acquired knowledge of the hidden crimes of the St. Evrémonde family. Her husband, Charles Darnay, is a member of that family and is condemned to the guillotine during the Revolution. He escapes death through the efforts of his wife, her father, and Sydney Carton. Throughout these trials, Lucie remains level-headed, practical, and devoted.

Dr. Alexander Manette, Lucie's father, a doctor imprisoned for many years in the Bastille in France because he aided a poor servant girl who was forced to become the mistress of the Marquis St. Evrémonde, Charles Darnay's uncle. Dr. Manette loses his mind in the Bastille and becomes obsessed with making shoes. His mind mends after his release, but whenever he is reminded of his prison days, he seeks out his shoe bench and begins work. He tries to free Charles Darnay from the French prison by appealing to the sympathies of the revolutionists, but he is unsuccessful. At Darnay's trial, a document written by the doctor while in prison is presented as evidence to secure the young aristocrat's conviction and sentence of death.

Lucie, her mother's namesake, the small daughter of Charles Darnay and his wife.

Ernest Defarge (deh-FAHRZH), a wineshop keeper in St. Antoine, a suburb of Paris. A former houseservant of Dr. Manette, he cares for his former master after he is released from the Bastille and before he goes to England. He is also one of the most radical of the revolutionists. With his wife, he tries to get Charles Darnay executed by producing the document Dr. Manette had written years before.

Madame Thérèse Defarge (tay-REHZ), the wife of the wineshop keeper, a ruthless, cold woman who hates all aristocrats. Madame Defarge attends every guillotining and knits a stitch for each head that drops. She dies while struggling with Miss Pross, Lucie Darnay's maid.

Mr. Stryver, a self-centered, proud lawyer employed as Charles Darnay's counsel when the young language teacher is accused of carrying treasonous papers between France and England. He is Sydney Carton's patron and employer, a shrewd, determined man who looks years older than his actual age.

Miss Pross, the devoted housekeeper who has looked after Lucie Manette from childhood. She is intelligent and physically strong. Left behind to cover their flight when the Manettes escape from Paris, she struggles with Madame Defarge, who tries to make her confess where the Manettes have gone. Madame Defarge is killed accidentally when her gun goes off. Miss Pross, deafened by the explosion, escapes with Jerry Cruncher and follows her master and mistress to freedom.

Monsieur the Marquis St. Evrémonde, a cruel French aristocrat and Charles Darnay's uncle. He kills a child when his coachman drives his horses too fast. The child's father gains admittance to the chateau and kills the arrogant nobleman. The marquis and his breed are responsible for the peasants' uprising, causing the French Revolution.

Gaspard (gahs-PAHR), the father of the child who was killed by the marquis' fast horses. He succeeds in murdering the marquis by plunging a knife into the sleeping nobleman's heart.

Théophile Gabelle (tay-oh-FEEL zhah-BEHL), a village postmaster and keeper of rents. Arrested by the revolutionists, he appeals to Charles Darnay in England for aid. In response to his plea, Darnay goes on his dangerous errand in France.

Solomon Pross, alias **John Barsad**, Miss Pross's brother. A complete scoundrel, he abandons his sister after obtaining all of her money. Calling himself John Barsad, he becomes a spy for the English. He informs Madame Defarge of Charles Darnay's marriage to Lucie Manette. He is a turnkey at the Conciergerie in Paris while Darnay is imprisoned there. Sydney Carton recognizes him but does not reveal his identity.

Jerry Cruncher, an employee at the London banking house of Tellson and Company by day, a resurrection man (grave robber) by night. Devoted to Lucie and her father, he aids in Charles Darnay's escape from France.

Mrs. Cruncher, his abused wife, whom he calls "Aggerawayter." A pious woman, she thinks her husband's night occupation unspeakably sinful, and she prays for his reformation.

Young Jerry Cruncher, their son. Guessing shrewdly, he has a good idea of the grim trade his father follows at night.

Jarvis Lorry, the confidential clerk of Tellson and Company. He is instrumental in getting Dr. Manette out of France into England, and he goes with the Manettes to Paris during the dark days of the Revolution while Charles Darnay, in prison, awaits his execution.

Jacques One (zhahk),
Jacques Two,
Jacques Three,
Jacques Four, the name taken by Defarge, and
Jacques Five, a group of revolutionists in the suburb of St. Antoine.

The Vengeance, a female revolutionist, Madame Defarge's lieutenant.

Roger Cly, Solomon Pross's partner and Charles Darnay's former servant. He testifies falsely when Darnay is on trial at the Old Bailey. He is supposed to be dead and buried, but Jerry Cruncher knows that his coffin was empty.

THE TALISMAN

Author: Sir Walter Scott (1771-1832)
First published: 1825
Genre: Novel

Locale: The Holy Land
Time: The twelfth century
Plot: Historical

Richard the Lion-Hearted, the English king who leads the Third Crusade to the Holy Land. He is proud and egotistical; the other leaders in the crusade resent him and also his methods. Ill of a fever, he is healed by a Muslim physician sent to him by Saladin, the leader of the Muslims in the Holy War. An attempt is made on Richard's life, but a slave saves him. Richard finally realizes that the crusade is a failure.

Sir Kenneth, Knight of the Couchant Leopard, who is really **David, earl of Huntingdon** and the prince royal of Scotland. He has taken a vow not to reveal his true identity until the Holy City is taken in the crusade. He will not break this oath, even to save his own life. Disguised as a Nubian slave, he is severely wounded by a poisoned knife while saving Richard's life. Richard sucks the poisoned wound and saves him. He is in love with Lady Edith Plantagenet, the king's kinswoman, but they cannot marry because he is a poor Scotsman and she is of royal blood. When Kenneth's true identity becomes known, they do marry.

El Hakim, the physician sent by Saladin to heal Richard. He makes a potion with a talisman he carries, and the potion cures Richard. El Hakim is really **Saladin** in disguise. He gives the talisman to Kenneth and Lady Edith as a wedding present.

Lady Edith Plantagenet (plan-TAJ-eh-neht), Richard's kinswoman, in love with Kenneth. She is lady in waiting to Richard's wife, the queen.

Queen Berengaria (behr-ehn-GAR-ee-uh), the queen of England, who is at a convent because she is making a pilgrimage to pray for the king's recovery. She becomes bored and sends Kenneth a false message saying that Lady Edith wants to see him. He deserts his post of guarding the English royal standard because of this message and thus becomes an outcast from the Christian camp.

Theodorick of Engaddi, a hermit who is a go-between for the Christians and the Muslims.

Conrade, the marquis of Montserrat, a treacherous crusader who plans Richard's death because he wants part of Palestine for himself. Conrade urges the archduke of Austria to place his flag next to that of Richard on the highest place in the camp. He is later responsible for stealing the English flag. He is wounded in a trial by arms and is stabbed by one of his cohorts so that he cannot confess the plot against Richard.

The Grand Master of the Knights Templars, one of the conspirators against Richard. He stabs and kills Conrade while bending over him to hear his confession.

TALLEY AND SON

Author: Lanford Wilson (1937-   )
First published: 1986
Genre: Drama

Locale: The Talley Place, near Lebanon, Missouri
Time: July 4, 1944
Plot: Comic realism

Calvin Stuart Talley, the eighty-year-old patriarch of the Talley family. He is dazed and confused most of the time, but he has flashes of lucidity, during which he asserts his power over Eldon and Lottie, his children, who hate him. As far as Calvin is concerned, the only one of his children who was ever worth anything was Stuart, who has been dead for more than twenty-five years. Calvin is a shrewd and ruthless business-man. He keeps his records locked away and written in code so he will retain control. When a scandal over Eldon's adultery threatens to erupt, Talley manipulates the people involved with no regard for them; his only concern is protecting the family name because of the reflection on the family business. In the end, he loses control to Eldon and slips back into a confused state.

Eldon Talley, Calvin Talley's fifty-two-year-old son. Eldon has always been under his father's thumb at work and has been an irresponsible and adulterous man in his private life. Re-cently, he has been sneaking into his father's office to go through his papers, and he is pleased to see that the family is wealthier than he imagined. He is also excited because his older son, Buddy, is home from the war for a few days, and his younger son, Timmy, is expected soon. He receives a telegram saying that Timmy has been killed, and the local washer-woman demands support for her child by Eldon. As his frus-tration intensifies and he and his father become angrier toward each other, he decides to take control of his life. He outsmarts his father and makes a business deal that will ensure that he gets what he wants, with his father and his ungrateful son Buddy being shut out.

Charlotte (Lottie) Talley, Eldon's younger sister. After graduating from college, Lottie stood up to her father and announced that she was leaving home to work among the poor.

She did some satisfying work teaching poor black children in Chicago and also did a stint at a clock factory in Connecticut. At the age of forty-five, she is back home with her father, dying of cancer she contracted from the radium paint used to paint clock dials. She hates her father and bickers with her brother. Her only happiness comes at the end of the play, when she helps her niece Sally run away without being seen.

Kenneth "Buddy" Talley, Eldon's older son, an army staff sergeant. Buddy, like his father and grandfather, is arrogant and ruthless. He shares his grandfather's interest in the bank-ing business and his father's eye for available women. Not especially clever at business, he nevertheless assumes that he will one day control the bank. He disapproves of his niece's Jewish boyfriend, of Italians, and of his wife wearing pants. Although he has been away from home for some time, he shows no interest in spending time with his wife or his baby daughter. When Eldon trades away his share of the bank, Buddy's plans for his own future evaporate.

Timmy Talley, Eldon's younger son, a Marine. Timmy is the first speaker in the play and reveals that he has been killed in the war. He comments on the action as it unfolds, waiting for his family to get the word of his death. Like his father, he was interested in the garment factory; Eldon assumed that Timmy would take over that business after him. His death forces Eldon to take responsibility for his own life.

Sally Talley, Eldon's daughter. She stays as far as possible from family squabbles. The men's business dealings do not involve her, because she is a daughter, and no one approves of her choice of Matt Friedman, who is Jewish, as a mate. She is seen darting upstairs to avoid the family and sneaking out the door to elope.

— *Cynthia A. Bily*

TALLEY'S FOLLY

Author: Lanford Wilson (1937-   )
First published: 1979
Genre: Drama

Locale: Lebanon, Missouri
Time: July 4, 1944
Plot: Psychological realism

Matt Friedman, a forty-two-year-old Jewish accountant from St. Louis, Missouri. A tall, commanding figure with great warmth and honesty, Matt fell in love with Sally the year before, when he met her during a vacation in her small home-town of Lebanon, Missouri. After having written to her daily for a year and receiving no response, he has returned to her home to face her and ask her to marry him. Matt is not, by his own admission, the romantic type; he is a loner, a European immigrant whose loss of his family in prewar Europe has left him isolated and rootless. He has a strong propensity for mimicry and wit, and he uses these often as defense mecha-nisms to ward off pain, a talent he adopted in having to assuage the painful memories of his childhood. Undaunted by Sally's rejection and demands that he return home, Matt knows that Sally cares for him and refuses to leave until he can

reveal a secret about himself that will affect her marriage decision. With great difficulty, he recounts his life, in the guise of a hypothetical story, detailing the murder of his parents and sister in Europe and his arrival in America. He concludes by revealing the effect that his losses have made on his life: his secret "resolve . . . never to be responsible for bringing into such a world another living soul." He believes that no woman would want a husband who refused to father children, but when Sally finally admits the secret to her life, the secret behind her loneliness and pain, these two displaced and iso-lated people finally make contact and find love and accep-tance.

Sally Talley, a thirty-one-year-old nurse. Born to a wealthy capitalist family, Sally is the outcast, rejected not only because of her socialist beliefs but also because her infertility, brought on by an illness a decade ago, prevented her marriage into another wealthy Lebanon family, a marriage that would have increased her family's fortune during the lean years of the Depression. Sally hates her home life and is eager to move, but because she believes that her only worth as a woman is her ability to procreate, she has decided never to marry and is content to live her life unmarried. For this reason, coupled with her low self-esteem, which has been nurtured by her family's ostracism of her, she has sentenced herself to loneliness and, despite her attraction to Matt, discourages his romantic pursuit of her. Acutely sensitive to her infertility, which she deems antonymous to womanhood, Sally flies into a rage when Matt admits his unwillingness to father children, believing his confession to be a mere fabrication meant to manipulate her into marrying him. Outraged at his seemingly patronizing gesture, she rejects him outright and forcefully for the first time. As Matt pursues the reason for her irrational anger, insisting that his secret resolution is true, Sally eventually believes him and finally, in a most stirring and pathetic moment, lets down her guard and admits her secret: her infertility and the isolation and loneliness it has brought her.

— *B. A. Kachur*

TAMAR

Author: Robinson Jeffers (1887-1962)
First published: 1924
Genre: Poetry

Locale: Carmel Coast Range, California
Time: During World War I
Plot: Psychological

Tamar Cauldwell, a passionate, neurotic, auburn-haired young woman. She tempts her brother Lee to deflower her and continues incest with him until she becomes pregnant. Intending to marry Will Andrews, she seduces him, hoping to hide her incest with Lee. She fails in an attempt to burn the Cauldwell home. In a wild dance on the seashore, she brings on a miscarriage that leaves her ill and embittered at her whole family. She flaunts her body before her father to rouse his enfeebled lust. Taunting her brother with the lie that her lost child was Will's rather than his, she angers Lee until he whips her cruelly. Feigning a desire to reconcile the differences between Lee and Will, she then shows Will the marks of the whip and instigates a bloody fight between him and Lee. Triumphant, she dies by fire, taking her lovers with her. The flames symbolically resemble the fleshly fires that have been consuming the Cauldwells since the old incest of David and Helen.

Lee Cauldwell, her dissolute brother. Nursed to health by Tamar after an accident, he warns Will to stay away from her, then becomes her lover and the father of the child she loses. Tamar prevents Lee from enlisting for World War I but also keeps him from escaping the burning Cauldwell home, and he dies in her locked embrace.

David Cauldwell, her father, a dotard of seventy who in repentance of old sins has turned to his Bible, but too late to save his doomed family.

Jinny Cauldwell, David's mentally disabled sister, a woman of sixty. In youth, she loved her brother, but he was drawn to Helen instead. Jinny, in her madness, innocently causes the fire that brings death to the entire family.

Stella Moreland, the sister of David's dead wife. She acts as nurse to Jinny. Through her as a medium, the voice of Helen reveals much of the sordid past to Tamar. Stella dies with the Cauldwells.

Will Andrews, Tamar's suitor, blond, freckled, and wide-shouldered. He wishes to free Tamar from her family, but she desires only the freedom of death, and Will (already mortally wounded in his fight with Lee) dies in the holocaust that destroys the Cauldwells.

Helen Cauldwell, David's dead sister, with whom he committed incest forty years earlier. After Tamar's orgiastic dance, Helen's spirit voice taunts her, predicts that she will lose her baby, and informs her that her attempt to burn her home will not destroy the corruption of the family.

Ramon Ramirez, the herdsman of the Cauldwell herds.

TAMBURLAINE THE GREAT

Author: Christopher Marlowe (1564-1593)
First published: 1590
Genre: Drama

Locale: Asia
Time: The fourteenth century
Plot: Tragedy

Tamburlaine (TAM-bur-layn), the magniloquent Scythian shepherd who, becoming the ruler of vast lands in Africa and the Middle East, calls himself "the Scourge of God." Absolutely ruthless, he kills the defenseless women and children in conquered cities and stabs his own son when he finds him gambling during an important battle. He is pre-eminently theatrical, delighting in triumphal pageants and in such spectacular effects as changing the color of his tents from white to red to black while he waits outside a city for its surrender or its challenge. This dramatic instinct inspires the imprisonment of Emperor Bajazeth in a cage and the harnessing of four defeated rulers to Tamburlaine's chariot. Invulnerable to injury from men, Tamburlaine wages a strong battle against death and meets it in characteristic theatrical fashion when he has himself carried by his servants and friends to the head of his army.

Zenocrate (zeh-NO-kruh-tee), his wife and the daughter of the soldan of Egypt. Although she is enraged when Tamburlaine captures her, she is quickly enthralled by his grand ambition and proudly wears her crown. She attempts on occasion to assuage her husband's cruelty by pleading for the life of her father and urging tolerance for the weakness of their son, Calyphas.

Bajazeth (BA-ja-zehth), the proud emperor of the Turks.

Defeated by Tamburlaine in spite of his confidence in his own power, he is drawn about in a cage, like a beast, until he submits to his despair and dashes his brains out against the bars of his cage.

Zabina (za-BI-na), the arrogant wife of Bajazeth. She scorns Zenocrate and Tamburlaine even after her capture. She strengthens Bajazeth's resistance as long as possible, but she also recognizes the hopelessness of their state and kills herself as soon as she discovers her husband's body.

Mycetes (mi-SEE-teez), the king of Persia, an incompetent ruler. He resents the insults offered by his brother Cosroe, but he is incapable of defending his realm against him.

Cosroe (kos-ROH-ee), Mycetes' ambitious brother, who criticizes the king's folly and plots the usurpation of his throne to restore the former glory of his nation. He enlists Tamburlaine's help to win Mycetes' crown, but he immediately finds himself deprived of the kingdom by his ally.

Techelles (teh-KEH-leez) and

Usumcasane (ew-suhm-kuh-SA-nee), Asian potentates and Tamburlaine's generals, who are rewarded with large realms.

Theridamas (theh-rih-DA-muhs), a great Persian warrior who becomes one of Tamburlaine's most valued advisers. He falls in love with Olympia, the virtuous widow of one of Tamburlaine's conquered enemies, and asks her to marry him. He does not suspect her motives when she pretends to have a magic ointment that will save her from wounds, and he cuts her throat to test its efficacy.

Olympia (oh-LIHM-pee-uh), the widow of the captain of Balsera. Faithful to her husband's memory, she rejects Theridamas and tricks him into killing her.

Agydas (A-gih-duhs), one of Zenocrate's attendants. He foresees his mistress' love for the Scythian shepherd and the inevitability of his own death as punishment for trying to change her mind, and he forestalls his murderers by committing suicide.

Magnetes (mag-NEE-teez), his companion, another Median lord.

Anippe (a-NIH-pee), Zenocrate's servant, as proud as her master and mistress.

Celebinus (seh-leh-BI-nuhs) and

Amyras (a-MI-ruhs), the bold, self-confident heirs of Tamburlaine and Zenocrate.

Calyphas (KA-lih-fuhs), their brother, a luxury-loving youth, slain by his father, who despises his cowardice.

Callepine (KA-leh-pin), Bajazeth's son, imprisoned by Tamburlaine. He escapes with the help of his jailer and becomes the leader of the forces opposing Tamburlaine.

Orcanes (ohr-KAY-neez),

Gazellus (gah-ZEH-luhs), and

Uribassa (ew-rih-BA-suh), Muslim rulers who attempt to make an alliance with their Christian enemies to halt the power of Tamburlaine.

Sigismund (SIH-gihs-muhnd), the king of Hungary,

Frederick, the lord of Buda, and

Baldwin, the lord of Bohemia, the Christian leaders who break their solemn vows of allegiance to the Muslims, attack them, and lose the battle to those they have betrayed.

The soldan of Egypt, Zenocrate's father, who is enraged at the kidnapping of his daughter.

Meander (mee-AN-dur),

Ortygius (ohr-TIH-jee-uhs),

Ceneus (SEE-nee-uhs), and

Menaphon (MEH-nuh-fon), Persian supporters of Mycetes and Cosroe.

Capolin (KA-poh-lihn), an Egyptian captain.

Philemus (fih-LEE-muhs), the soldan's messenger.

Almeda (al-MEE-duh), Callepine's jailer, who aids him to escape and joins his party.

Perdicas (PUR-dih-kuhs), Calyphas' servant.

THE TAMING OF THE SHREW

Author: William Shakespeare (1564-1616)
First published: 1623
Genre: Drama

Locale: Padua, Italy
Time: The sixteenth century
Plot: Comedy

Katharina (kat-uh-REE-nuh), the "shrew," the spirited elder daughter of Baptista, a well-to-do Paduan gentleman. She storms at her father, her mild young sister, and her tutors until she meets Petruchio, who ignores her protests of rage and marries her while she stands by in stunned amazement. She continues to assert her will, but she finds her husband's even stronger than her own and learns that submission is the surest means to a quiet life. Her transformation is a painful revelation to Lucentio and Hortensio, who must pay Petruchio their wagers and, in addition, live with wives who are less dutiful than they supposed.

Petruchio (peh-TREW-kee-oh), her masterful husband, who comes from Verona to Padua frankly in search of a wealthy wife. He is easily persuaded by his friend Hortensio to court Katharina and pave the way for her younger sister's marriage. Katharina's manners do not daunt him; in truth, his are little better than hers, as his long-suffering servants could testify. He meets insult with insult and storm with storm,

humiliating his bride by appearing at the altar in his oldest garments and keeping her starving and sleepless, all the while pretending the greatest solicitude for her welfare. Using the methods of training hawks, he tames a wife and ensures a happy married life for himself.

Bianca (bee-AHN-kuh), Katharina's pretty, gentle younger sister, for whose hand Lucentio, Hortensio, and Gremio are rivals. Although she is completely charming to her suitors, she is, in her own way, clever and strong-willed, and she chides her bridegroom for being so foolish as to lay wagers on her dutifulness.

Baptista (bap-TEES-tah), her father, a wealthy Paduan. Determined to treat his ill-tempered daughter fairly, he refuses to let Bianca marry before her. Petruchio's courtship is welcome, even though its unorthodoxy disturbs him, and he offers a handsome dowry with Katharina, doubling it when he sees the results of his son-in-law's "taming," which gives him "another daughter." Bianca's marriage without his consent distresses and angers him, but his good nature wins out and he quickly forgives her, watching with delight as Petruchio demonstrates his success with Katharina.

Lucentio (lew-CHEHN-see-oh), the son of a Pisan merchant, who comes to Padua to study. He falls in love with Bianca when he first hears her speak and disguises himself as Cambio, a schoolmaster, to gain access to her, while his servant masquerades as Lucentio. He reveals his identity to his lady and persuades her to wed him secretly, but he finds his happiness somewhat marred when she costs him one hundred crowns by refusing to come at his call.

Hortensio (hohr-TEHN-shee-oh), Petruchio's friend, who presents himself, disguised as a musician, as a teacher for Bianca. Convinced that Katharina is incorrigible, he watches Petruchio's taming of his wife with amusement and skepticism. He weds a rich widow after becoming disillusioned when he sees Bianca embracing the supposed Cambio. Thus he finds himself, like Lucentio, with a wife more willful than he has expected.

Gremio (GREE-mee-oh), an aging Paduan who hires the disguised Lucentio to forward his courtship of Bianca. His hopes are dashed when Tranio, as Lucentio, offers Baptista a large settlement for his daughter, and he is forced to become an observer of others' romances.

Vincentio (veen-CHEHN-see-oh), Lucentio's father. He is first bewildered, then angry, when he arrives in Padua to find an impostor claiming his name, his son missing, and his servant Tranio calling himself Lucentio. Overjoyed to find the real Lucentio alive, he quickly reassures Baptista that an appropriate settlement will be made for Bianca's marriage, saving his anger for the impostors who tried to have him imprisoned.

Tranio (TRAH-nee-oh), Lucentio's servant, who advises his master to follow his inclinations for pleasure, rather than study. He plays his master's part skillfully, courting Bianca to draw her father's attention away from her tutor and even providing himself with a father to approve his courtship. He recognizes trouble in the form of the real Vincentio and attempts to avert it by refusing to recognize his old master and ordering him off to jail. His ruse is unsuccessful, and only nuptial gaiety saves him from the force of Vincentio's wrath.

Grumio (GREW-mee-oh) and

Curtis, Petruchio's long-suffering servants.

Biondello (bee-on-DEHL-oh), Lucentio's servant, who aids in the conspiracy for Bianca's hand.

A pedant, an unsuspecting traveler who is persuaded by Tranio to impersonate Vincentio.

Christopher Sly, a drunken countryman, found unconscious at a tavern by a lord and his huntsmen. They amuse themselves by dressing him in fine clothes and greeting him as a nobleman, newly recovered from insanity. Sly readily accepts their explanations, settles himself in his new luxury, and watches the play of Katharina and Petruchio with waning interest.

A lord, the eloquent nobleman who arranges the jest.

Bartholomew, his page, who pretends to be Sly's noble wife.

TANGO

Author: Sławomir Mrożek (1930-   )
First published: 1964
Genre: Drama

Locale: Unspecified
Time: Mid-twentieth century
Plot: Play of ideas

Arthur, a neat and handsome twenty-five-year-old, dressed until the last act in a freshly pressed suit, white shirt, and tie. He is a counterrevolutionary idealist who rebels against what he considers his family's (and society's) liberalism, ethical relativism, slack permissiveness, disorder, and all-around anarchic individualism. Disgusted by what he regards as his family's immoral refusal to follow firm rules of conduct, he seeks to map out an orderly and respectable way of life, regulated by old-fashioned ceremonies and submission to absolute principles. He persuades his cousin Ala to marry him rather than simply sleep with him and forces his family, by the beginning of act 3, into ill-fitting, outdated, moth-eaten formal clothes for the wedding. He comes to realize that the old order cannot be reestablished at the point of his pistol. When Ala nonchalantly informs him that she had sex with the servant, Eddie, the morning before the marriage vows are to be exchanged, he breaks into tears and becomes easy prey for Eddie, who kills him.

Eddie, the family's muscular, sensual, anti-intellectual servant. He is crude, unshaven, and slovenly, and he sports a small, square mustache. His card playing with Eugene and Eugenia annoys Arthur, but it is his affair with Eleanor that deeply outrages Arthur, who urgently attempts to have his father shoot his mother's lover. When a disillusioned, drunken Arthur raves about the glory of omnipotent power in the final act, Eddie takes him at his word and tries to murder Arthur's uncle Eugene. Ala's declaration of her infidelity causes Arthur to seek Eddie's death. It is the latter, however, who is armed and uses his revolver to stun Arthur, before murdering him with a savage hand blow. Eddie then assumes despotic dominion over the family. The play ends with Eddie dancing all the steps of the tango "La Cumparsita" with old Eugene.

Stomil, Arthur's father, described as "a large, corpulent man with gray hair like a lion's mane." He prefers to wear pajamas that are unbuttoned, thereby angering his son. Stomil is an aesthetic nonconformist who devotes himself to impractical, avant-garde artistic experiments. When Arthur adjures his father to murder Eddie for having made him a cuckold, Stomil repeatedly refuses to make a tragedy out of what he regards as a farce and ends up playing cards with Eddie instead. In act 3, the disillusioned son begs Stomil's forgiveness: "[T]here's no turning back to the old forms. They can't create a reality for us. I was wrong." After Arthur's death, Stomil does forgive him in a generous eulogy.

Eleanor, the middle-aged mother of Arthur and wife of Stomil. She retains a good figure and is casually open about her affair with Eddie. He delights her by lacking complexes, scruples, or any other sort of sophistication, and by what she considers his naturalness and authenticity.

Ala, Arthur's eighteen-year-old cousin. She is pretty, long-haired, flirtatious, and bored by Arthur's long-winded speeches about convention and formal principles. When the dying Arthur tells her that he loved her, she asks him why he had not revealed his heart to her earlier, instead of using her as an audience for his pronouncements.

Eugene, a polite, old former officer, Arthur's great-uncle, who is opportunistic enough to accommodate himself to whatever order, or disorder, governs the family. He is impressed by Arthur's purposefulness and becomes his willing lieutenant when Arthur attempts his return to nineteenth century formalism. When Eddie takes power in the play's final minutes, he orders Eugene to take off his (Eddie's) shoes. Eugene obeys this new regime slavishly.

Eugenia, Arthur's grandmother, lively, irreverent, playful, and indifferent to the philosophic debates that volley in the family. In the opening scene, Arthur insists that she lie on her late husband's catafalque. In the last act, she willingly climbs up on it and dies, thereby upsetting no one but Stomil.

— *Gerhard Brand*

TAPS FOR PRIVATE TUSSIE

Author: Jesse Stuart (1907-1984)
First published: 1943
Genre: Novel

Locale: Kentucky
Time: The twentieth century
Plot: Regional

Grandpa Tussie, the head of the Tussie clan. He lives with his family in a schoolhouse coal shed until the supposed death of a son. After the funeral, the son's wife uses her insurance money to set up the family in a rented mansion, where they and descending relatives live high. Grandpa's relief check is taken away and later, when the last of the insurance money is used to buy a farm in his name, his old-age pension also is taken away.

Grandma Tussie, his wife. When she counts forty-six Tussie relatives living in the mansion, she will stand for no more.

George Tussie, Grandpa's brother, the first relative to move in. A fine fiddle player, he has been married five times. His nephew's "widow" falls in love with his fiddle playing and marries him.

Uncle Mott Tussie, Grandpa's son. He is in love with his brother's wife and therefore hates George. When he finally shoots George's fiddle from his hands, George shoots him through the head.

Aunt Vittie Tussie, the "widow" who has inherited ten thousand dollars in government insurance and spends it lavishly on the family.

Uncle Kim Tussie, the supposedly deceased son. He reappears at the end of the novel; his brother Mott had falsely identified the body in the hope of inheriting his sister-in-law. Family life is resumed as it was before his "death," except for the presence now of Uncle Mott's body.

Sid Seagraves Tussie, a grandson. He is revealed at last by Kim to be Aunt Vittie's son by a rich man who wronged Aunt Vittie and paid Kim to marry her. Now he is to be Kim's and Aunt Vittie's son.

George Rayburn, whose mansion the Tussies rent and almost wreck. He evicts them with difficulty.

Sheriff Whiteapple, who has to serve legal papers before the Tussies will leave the Rayburn mansion. After George Tussie's shooting of Mott, the sheriff comes for George.

Uncle Ben,
Dee,
Young Uncle Ben,
Starkie,
Watt,
Sabie, and
Abe, some of the Tussie relatives who move in. Uncle Mott shoots Young Uncle Ben and Dee for reporting Grandpa to the relief agency.

TAR BABY

Author: Toni Morrison (1931-)
First published: 1981
Genre: Novel

Locale: Isle de Chevaliers in the Caribbean, New York City, and Florida
Time: The 1970's
Plot: Social realism

Jadine Childs, an African American model with a degree in art history from the Sorbonne. Orphaned at the age of twelve, she was taken in by her aunt and uncle, Ondine and Sydney Childs. Their employer, Valerian Street, helped them send Jadine to private schools and to the Sorbonne. Partially because of this upbringing, Jadine experiences conflict between the white society in which she is entrenched and the black culture represented by her uncle and aunt and by Son, her lover. Jadine refuses to conform to the traditional image of womanhood that both Ondine and Son want to impose on her.

At the end of the novel, she returns to her own life in Paris, determined to face her fears alone.

William Green, called **Son**, an African American wanderer from Eloe, Florida. At the beginning of the novel, he escapes from a ship in the Caribbean and slips onto the boat that Jadine and Margaret have borrowed. Son represents everything that Sydney and Ondine have tried to keep from Jadine and everything that she seems to have rejected. To them, he seems to have the qualities of the stereotypical black male—he is shiftless, wild, and unrefined—yet he reveals an honest, direct way of looking at the world. Son, unlike Jadine, seems too nostalgic for the past. Despite initial antagonism, they fall in love.

Valerian Street, a rich, retired white industrialist from Philadelphia. He has retired to the Isle des Chevaliers in the Caribbean. Valerian does not interact well with other people, preferring plants instead. He treats his employees fairly well—better than he treats is wife—but never relinquishes his superior status.

Margaret Street, a beauty queen from Maine who married the much older Valerian and became pregnant soon afterward. She lacks emotional stability and often feels that her husband is closer to Sydney and Ondine than he is to her. She makes Ondine her confidante.

Sydney Childs, an African American who works as a butler for the Streets. Very proud of his "Philadelphia Negro" breeding, he seems to be even tempered, appreciative, and even friendly toward his employer until Son appears. After that, the novel reveals Sydney's resentment of Valerian. At the end, the balance of power between employer and employee shifts. His loving marriage with Ondine is in sharp contrast to the Streets' relationship.

Ondine Childs, Sydney's wife, the Streets' cook. She represents the traditional African American woman. She feels more like the "woman of the house" than does Margaret because of Margaret's inability to nurture her son. Ondine both resents and takes pride in Jadine, praising her accomplishments but wishing that Jadine were more like her; that is, more family-conscious. Like her husband, Ondine is very proud of who she is and patronizes those she considers beneath her, including Son and the local islanders, just as Valerian patronizes her.

Gideon, who is also called **Yardman**,

Thérése, and

Alma Estée, locals who often perform odd chores at the Streets' home. The three black people serve as catalysts for the major action of the novel.

— Lauren Chadwick

TARAS BULBA

Author: Nikolai Gogol (1809-1852)
First published: 1835
Genre: Novel

Locale: Russia
Time: The fifteenth century
Plot: Historical

Taras Bulba (TAH-ruhs BOOL-bah), a sturdy old Cossack warrior and chieftain, restless, fierce, and stubborn. He hates luxury, loves the simple Cossack life, and regards himself as a defender of the Russian Orthodox faith. Elected as leader for the second attack on Dubno, Taras fights bravely; he narrowly avoids capture when the Poles win the battle. Unable to visit the captured Ostap in prison, Taras does witness Ostap's torture and boldly calls out to him before Ostap dies. Disappearing in the crowd watching the torture and execution of the captured Cossacks, Taras escapes from Warsaw and leads many raids of destruction, pillage, and death against the Poles. Finally captured by a superior Polish force, he is burned to death, but not before he has seen the heroic escape of many of his men to whom he has called out defiantly to continue the fight against injustice. Taras is presented as a great folk hero whose epic exploits are reminiscent of those of Homer's warriors.

Ostap (ohs-TAHP), Taras' older son, a former student. At first rebellious against studies, he later ranks high. Loyal to his comrades, he loves war and carousing but is more often a follower than a leader in the academy. As a warrior, however, he shows the cool calculation and tactical ingenuity that seem to predict for him a chieftaincy. In the second battle of Dubno, he is captured and taken to Warsaw, where, after being publicly tortured, he is put to death.

Andrii (ahn-DRIHY), Taras' younger son, also a former student. In the academy, he learned more readily, more willingly, and with less effort than Ostap. He was daring, ingenious, and clever in avoiding punishment, and he early became a lover of women. As a fledgling warrior, he is reckless and intoxicated by battle. Captivated by the memories of a beautiful girl, the daughter of the Polish waiwode of Koven, whose room he once visited, he follows her aged servant secretly into Dubno, taking bread to the starving girl and her relatives during the siege of the town. He deserts to the Polish forces, succumbs to Polish luxury, and leads an assault against the Cossacks. Taras shoots him dead.

Yankel, a Jewish merchant rescued by Taras from Cossack wrath against the Jews. He fails in his attempt to enable Taras—on a promise of a great reward—to visit Ostap in the Warsaw prison. Yankel is a stereotypical Jewish character of the period, by turns greedy, servile, and flattering.

The daughter of the Polish waiwode, or military governor, Andrii's sweetheart. She is beautiful, dark-eyed, and chestnut-haired. Volatile and mischievous when Andrii first sees her, she is more maturely and soberly beautiful when he meets her again in Dubno.

Kirdyaga (kihr-DYAH-guh), the newly elected leader of the Setch (a Cossack encampment) and a close friend of Taras.

Nikolai Pototsky (nih-koh-LI poh-TOHT-skihy), a Polish hetman captured by the Cossacks but freed on a promise to grant religious freedom to all Christian churches and not to exact vengeance against the Cossacks. He later leads the campaign that results in the capture and execution of Taras.

Borodaty (boh-roh-DAH-tihy), a Cossack hetman slain from behind as he despoils a slain Pole. Ostap replaces Borodaty as leader of the Uman company.

Kassian Bovdyug (kah-sih-AHN bohv-DEWG), an old Cossack who nominates Taras as leader of the Cossacks in the second battle at Dubno. Bovdyug dies in the battle.

Mossy Shilo (moh-SIHY SHIH-lo), a powerful Cossack once captured and enslaved by the Turks. Capable of great deeds on occasion, he at other times succumbs to a passion for liquor. He dies bravely in the second battle of Dubno.

TARKA THE OTTER

Author: Henry Williamson (1895-1977)
First published: 1927
Genre: Novel

Locale: The Two Rivers country, somewhere in western England
Time: The 1920's
Plot: Pastoral

Tarka the Otter, whose name means "Little Water Wanderer" or "Wandering as Water." He is presented as both a heroic and a pathetic figure. His short lifetime is filled with threats and enemies, from the owl that almost catches him as a cub, to the trap set for him by the farmer, to the famine winter, to the wild and domestic animals that continually threaten him. His greatest enemies, however, are the otter-hounds and the men and women who hunt him and his family for sport. Tarka's courage in the face of all these adversities is stressed continually, if without open emphasis. He dies like a hero, biting, holding, and drowning the hound who has pursued him all his life and who has worried him to his death. Tarka's second main characteristic is not a traditionally heroic one: his playfulness. He frolics with his sisters, with his mates, and with his children, and he finds a game in every strange object, from empty tins to piers and bridges. The question never asked in the book, but continually implied, is "How can people derive sport from hunting such gallant and charming animals?" Otters are now, in Britain, a protected species.

Deadlock, the pied hound, Tarka's nemesis. He finds Tarka as a cub and might have killed him if the huntsman had not called him off: Hunters allow cubs and pregnant females to live, to give more sport later. Deadlock hunts Tarka through a long day later on and chases him into the sea, where Tarka turns and drags him under in a foreshadowing of the book's final scene. In the end, Deadlock, who gets his name from the remorseless certainty of his pursuits, catches Tarka once more after he seems to have escaped. This time, Tarka gets the "dead lock" on his throat and takes the hound down with him.

Graymuzzle, Tarka's first mate. An old otter with broken teeth, she shows love and forbearance toward the young one and self-sacrificingly stays with him when he is caught in a trap. She gnaws off part of his foot to let him escape, ignoring the bites he gives her in his pain, but is herself caught by the farmer's dog, to be finished off with an iron bar. If Tarka is a defiant hero, Graymuzzle is the book's loving heroine.

Tarka's mother, who is never named. She shows the strongest resistance in the book to anthropomorphism. There is no doubt about her emotions, the human ones of love and fear, but she also shows an animal lack of memory. She grieves for, but soon forgets, the daughter she loses in a trap, the mate caught by hounds, and even Tarka himself when her new mate drives the male cub away.

Marland Jimmy, another old otter, a male who has survived many trials to live a life of solitary amusement. He hides in the funnel of an engine sunk in a pond, sports with the young otters without competing for a mate, and shares a salmon caught in the famine winter. He dies alone, frozen into an icy pond.

White-tip, Tarka's second mate, who also demonstrates the hard life of the hunted animal. Her first litter of cubs is eaten by a passing badger, and her second is drowned by accident in the course of a hunt. She survives and has a happy relationship with Tarka until this too is destroyed by human cruelty.

Bloody Bill Brock, a badger, one of a gallery of named animals who form the background of the otters' life. Just as the otters collectively create an image of the joint character of the species, rather than having developed individual characters of their own, so Brock the badger, Jarrk the seal, Old Nog the heron, and Garbargee the conger eel give a collective picture of natural life. In it, Brock is the ultimate survivor. Too clever to be caught in traps, too thick-skinned to be deterred by otter bite or shotgun pellet, Brock pads through the world unharmed, if unattractive.

— *T. A. Shippey*

TARR

Author: Wyndham Lewis (1882-1957)
First published: 1918
Genre: Novel

Locale: Paris, France
Time: c. 1910
Plot: Psychological realism

Frederick Tarr, an English artist in Paris engaged to Bertha Lunken. Tired of her stupidity, he breaks the engagement and becomes involved with Anastasya Vasek. When Bertha tells him that she is pregnant by Kreisler, he marries her, though he continues to live with Anastasya. Bertha finally divorces him, but he never marries Anastasya.

Bertha Lunken, a sentimental German art student engaged to Tarr. After he breaks the engagement, she turns to Kreisler, who forcibly possesses her. She informs Tarr of her pregnancy and he marries her out of pity, although he continues to live with Anastasya. Bertha eventually divorces Tarr and marries an eye doctor.

Otto Kreisler, a German artist, chronically short of funds. In love with Anastasya, he makes a fool of himself at a party and then gets involved with Bertha. Seeing Anastasya with Soltyk, he challenges the Pole to a duel and kills him. Fleeing to Germany, he is arrested, and he hangs himself in his cell.

Anastasya Vasek, a beautiful Russian beloved by Tarr, Kreisler, and Soltyk. It is over her that Kreisler and Soltyk fight a duel in which Soltyk is killed. She goes to live with Tarr.

Louis Soltyk, a Pole. Because of his attentions to Anastasya, he is challenged and killed by Kreisler.

THE TARTAR STEPPE
(Il deserto dei Tartari)

Author: Dino Buzzati (Dino Buzzati Traverso, 1906-1972)
First published: 1940
Genre: Novel

Locale: A military fort in the mountains and a city
Time: Late nineteenth or early twentieth century
Plot: Metaphysical

Giovanni Drogo (jee-oh-VAHN-nee DROH-goh), a newly commissioned officer posted to Fort Bastiani. Very young when he is first sent to Fort Bastiani, Drogo is sad at leaving the exciting life of the town for the isolated and gloomy fort. Perhaps because of his melancholy and introspective nature, Drogo is self-conscious about every gesture that he makes. As his time at the fort stretches on and on, Drogo loses all contact with the world outside. Like Captain Ortiz, Drogo allows his life to be spent in hope, waiting in vain for the glorious war that seems never to arrive. When it finally does, Drogo is sent away from the fort before the action starts because he is ill. Even though Drogo (now a major) is second in command, he is powerless to prevent his commanding officer, Simeoni, from ignoring his pleas.

Francesco Vescovi (frahn-CHEHS-koh vehs-KOH-vee), a childhood friend of Drogo. Vescovi has chosen the opposite path to Drogo. Drogo has become an officer; Vescovi has stayed in the "easy elegant life" in town, getting fatter as the years go by, in marked contrast to Drogo and the boniness of his frame by the end of the novel. It is Francesco's sister Maria to whom Drogo is unofficially engaged. As the years pass, Drogo drifts apart from both Francesco and Maria.

Captain Ortiz (OHR-teez), a soldier (later a lieutenant colonel) whom Drogo meets on his first trip to the fort. A man of about forty when he first appears in the novel, Ortiz has a "thin, aristocratic face." He stays at Fort Bastiani his entire career, waiting for war and leaving only when he is forced to retire because of his age.

Angustina (AHN-gews-TEE-nah), a lieutenant who is Drogo's friend. Angustina is a pale, sickly man whose pride and arrogance are seen as positive reflections of his strength of character. Although he is described as having a "usual expression of detachment and boredom," Angustina differs from Drogo in that he stays at Fort Bastiani out of pride, rather than because staying is a habit that has become impossible to break. Angustina dies a heroic death, which inspires Drogo when it is his turn to die.

Simeoni (see-meh-OH-nee), another lieutenant at Fort Bastiani. It is Simeoni who first spots the approaching invaders building their road. He relinquishes his telescope and theories easily, however, when they threaten his career. Although he professes to be Drogo's friend, Simeoni sends Drogo away just when it looks as if the long-awaited war will become a reality and justify Drogo's thirty-year wait.

— *T. M. Lipman*

TARTARIN OF TARASCON
(Aventures prodigieuses de Tartarin de Tarascon)

Author: Alphonse Daudet (1840-1897)
First published: 1872
Genre: Novel

Locale: France and North Africa
Time: The nineteenth century
Plot: Satire

Tartarin (tahr-tah-RA[N]), a huntsman of Tarascon who distinguishes himself by growing a garden full of tropical plants in the south of France, keeping a full arsenal of weapons of all nations, using the firearms to shoot holes through the caps of his friends, explaining to citizens the wonders of the mysterious East (though he has never been there), and going on an African lion hunt. In his quest for the beast, he invades Algerian village squares, private gardens, and Muhammadan convent grounds, but he never quite arrives at the lion-infested veldt his numerous noble weapons deserve. He does get his lion, though—a tame, blind, toothless convent pet that comes ambling toward him down the path to a saint's tomb. Tartarin has to sell all of his fine weapons to pay the damages for slaughtering the unfortunate creature.

Prince Grégory (gray-goh-REE), a Montenegrin nobleman and Tartarin's shipmate aboard the *Zouave*. He locates a Moorish maiden who has stolen Tartarin's heart, accompanies him

on a lion hunt, and finally vanishes with his purse.

Baïa (bi-YAH), a twenty-year-old Moorish widow who distracts Tartarin from his hunting mission for a time. They take a house in the native quarter and Baïa entertains her lord, now called Sidi Tart'ri ben Tart'ri, with monotonous songs and the belly dance.

Captain Barbassou (bahr-bah-SEW), the commander of the *Zouave*, the ship that takes Tartarin to Algiers. Wise in the ways of the world, he gives Tartarin some good advice about Montenegrin princes and Moorish widows. Tartarin, unfortunately, does not heed the captain's advice.

Commander Bravida (brah-vee-DAH), a Tarasconese dignitary who, representing community opinion, finally orders Tartarin to leave for Africa and the lion hunt that he has been discussing for months.

Madame Bézuquet (bay-zew-KAY), Tartarin's singing partner at social events.

TARTUFFE
(Tartuffe: Ou, L'Imposteur)

Author: Molière (Jean-Baptiste Poquelin, 1622-1673)
First published: 1669
Genre: Drama

Locale: Paris, France
Time: The seventeenth century
Plot: Comedy

Tartuffe (tahr-TEWF), a religious hypocrite and impostor who uses religious cant and practices to impose on the credulity of a wealthy man who befriends him. To acquire money and cover deceit, he talks of his hair shirt and scourge, prayers, and distributing alms. He also disapproves of immodest dress. Before his first appearance, he is reported by some to be a good man of highest worth and by others to be a glutton, a winebibber, and a hypocrite. Deciding that he wants his patron's daughter as his wife, he uses his seeming piety to convince his host to break his daughter's marriage plans. He then endeavors to seduce his host's wife by holding her hand, patting her knee, fingering her lace collar, and making declarations of love to her. When his conduct is reported to the husband by his wife and their son, the foolish man forgives Tartuffe and gives the hypocrite all his property. Another attempted seduction fails when the husband, hidden, overhears all that happens and orders Tartuffe out of the house. Tartuffe, boasting that the entire property is now his, has an eviction order served on his former patron. When a police officer arrives to carry out the eviction order, the tables are turned. Tartuffe is arrested at the order of the king, who declares him to be a notorious rogue.

Orgon (ohr-GOH[N]), a credulous, wealthy man taken in by Tartuffe, whom he befriends, invites into his home, and proposes as a husband for his daughter, who already is promised to another. Defending Tartuffe against the accusations of his family and servants, he refuses to believe charges that the scoundrel has attempted to seduce his wife. He then disowns his children and signs over all his property to Tartuffe. Only later, when he hides under the table, at the urging of his wife, and overhears Tartuffe's second attempt at seduction, is he convinced that he is harboring a hypocrite and scheming rascal. Orgon is saved from arrest and eviction when Tartuffe is taken away by police officers.

Elmire (ehl-MEER), Orgon's wife. Aware of the wickedness of Tartuffe, she is unable to reveal the hypocrite's true nature to her husband. When she finds herself the object of Tartuffe's wooing, she urges the son not to make the story public, for she believes a discreet and cold denial to be more effective than violent cries of deceit. Finally, by a planned deception of Tartuffe, she convinces her husband of that scoundrel's wickedness.

Dorine (doh-REEN), a maid, a shrewd, outspoken, and witty girl who takes an active part in exposing Tartuffe and assisting the lovers in their plot against him. Much of the humor of the play results from her impertinence. She objects straightforwardly to the forced marriage of Tartuffe to Mariane, and she prevents a misunderstanding between the true lovers.

Mariane (mah-ree-AHN), Orgon's daughter, regarded as a prude by her grandmother. Because she is in love with Valère, she is unhappy over the marriage to Tartuffe proposed by her father. Because of her timidity, her only action at the time is to fall at Orgon's feet and implore him to change his mind.

Damis (dah-MEE), Orgon's son, regarded as a fool by his grandmother. His temper and indiscretion lead him to upset carefully laid plans, as when he suddenly comes out of the closet in which he has listened to Tartuffe's wooing of Elmire and reports the story naïvely to his father. He is outwitted by Tartuffe's calm admission of the charge and his father's belief in Tartuffe's innocence, despite the confession.

Valère (vah-LEHR), Mariane's betrothed. He quarrels with her, after hearing that Orgon intends to marry the young woman to Tartuffe, because she seems not to object to the proposal with sufficient force. In a comedy scene, the maid, running alternately between the lovers, reconciles the pair, and Valère determines that they will be married. He loyally offers to help Orgon flee after the eviction order is served on him by the court.

Madame Pernelle (pehr-NEHL), Orgon's mother, an outspoken old woman. Like her son, she believes in the honesty and piety of Tartuffe, and she hopes that his attitude and teachings may reclaim her grandchildren and brother-in-law from their social frivolity. She defends Tartuffe even after Orgon turns against him. She admits her mistake only after the eviction order is delivered.

Cléante (klay-AH[N]T), Orgon's brother-in-law. He talks in pompous maxims and makes long, tiresome speeches of advice to Orgon and Tartuffe. Both disregard him.

M. Loyal (lwah-YAHL), a tipstaff of the court. He serves the eviction order on Orgon.

A police officer, brought in by Tartuffe to arrest Orgon. Instead, he arrests Tartuffe by order of the king.

Filipote (fee-lee-POHT), Madame Pernelle's servant.

A TASTE OF HONEY

Author: Shelagh Delaney (1939-   )
First published: 1959
Genre: Drama

Locale: Salford, Lancashire
Time: Late 1950's
Plot: Psychological realism

Josephine (Jo), who is about sixteen, in high school but preparing to drop out. She is attractive but without the instinctive sexuality of her mother, with whom she lives in squalor in the tenement slums of Manchester, England. The illegitimate daughter of (according to her mother) a retarded man, Jo is self-contained and more mature than her years, with an acerbic wit that more than matches her mother's hardness, and with some signs of artistic talent. Unable to concentrate on her possibilities because of the transient nature of her upbringing, she tries to avoid succumbing to her mother's lifestyle. She seeks affection in a brief affair with a black sailor, who leaves her pregnant. Fearing that her own father's idiocy will be passed on to the child, she lives through her pregnancy dreading motherhood, cared for only by a homosexual friend.

Helen, Josephine's mother, in her mid- to late thirties but looking younger. She is a "semi-whore"; she enters into relationships with the shared understanding that her needs and wants will be met. She is harsh, independent, and bruised by life's experiences but capable of sustaining herself; she is also a constant and serious drinker. She lives off a series of male friends, moving from place to place to flee more complex relationships, dragging Jo with her from slum to slum. Her motherly instincts are confined to unemotional retreats from real contact, coupled with loud, sarcastic, scourging reprimands laced with indifference and self-indulgence, only occasionally alleviated by real but inarticulate concern. In her mind, there are no moral reservations about her way of life; it is a matter of survival. At her first opportunity, she marries a fairly affluent car salesman, leaving her daughter behind to fend for herself, as she has had to do. Only after he throws her out does she return to help her daughter give birth.

Peter Smith, a successful car salesman, a heavy drinker who is younger than Helen, his lover. When he makes his offer of marriage to her, it is with the understanding that she will desert her daughter, a source of shame to him. He is flippant and disdainful when drunk, wearing a patch over one eye; he becomes vicious and dangerous when approaching sobriety, a state that he never reaches. In his hatred for Jo, which stems partly from repressed sexual attraction to her and partly from jealousy of the mother-daughter bond, he twice forces Helen to choose him over her daughter.

The Boy, "a colored naval rating," Jo's boyfriend, who calls himself "the lascivious Moor." He is young, handsome, romantic, and caring. He has a poetic nature and an unrealistic impression of their chances. On leave at Christmas, he courts Jo by carrying her books from school, offering her a Woolworth engagement ring, kissing her hand, quoting Shakespeare, and reciting nursery rhymes. He gives her the attention her mother never did. He dances with her, sings to her, and leaves her pregnant after the Christmas fair.

Geoffrey Ingram, a young, effeminate boy whom Jo, several months pregnant, picks up and brings home, calling him "a big sister." He is sensitive and loving without making any sexual demands. He is organized and a calming influence on Jo. He moves in and stays with her for the final months of her pregnancy, cooking, cleaning, and preparing to assist in the delivery itself. His attachment to Jo leads him to propose marriage. He leaves reluctantly when Helen returns for the actual birth, not because he is offended by her insults but because Jo, repeating the patterns of her mother, insulates herself against all men and lets him go.

— Thomas J. Taylor

TATTOO THE WICKED CROSS

Author: Floyd Salas (1931-   )
First published: 1967
Genre: Novel

Locale: Golden Gate Institute of Industry and Reform, a prison farm in California
Time: After World War II
Plot: Social realism

Aaron D'Aragon, a Latino adolescent, a pachuco, and a gang leader sent to prison for fighting. He is the protagonist of the novel. Although Aaron is small for his age, he is quite a fighter, like a bantam rooster. Upon entering prison, he is not sure of himself and is intimidated by the director of the prison. He looks forward to seeing an ally while he is in prison, his good friend Barneyway. He hears disturbing rumors that Barneyway is a "queen." Aaron's main tormentor is Buzzer, a cruel and ruthless prison leader. After he is raped by Buzzer and his gang, Aaron vows to Barneyway that they will no longer be victims. Aaron must reconcile his religious beliefs, which say to "turn the other cheek." He decides to take revenge on Buzzer and his gang by poisoning them, but he inadvertently kills Barneyway as well. Because of these acts of murder, he gains the respect and attention of the other inmates, and he begins to serve his time with dignity.

Buzzer, the antagonist of the story. Buzzer represents evil, and Aaron represents good. Buzzer is ruthless and mean, and anyone who crosses his path is dealt with severely. Aaron wants nothing to do with him, but eventually Aaron is brutally sodomized and beaten by Buzzer and his gang. After being hospitalized because of the beating, Aaron feels humiliated, not so much because of the beating but because he has been "gang banged." Buzzer has always had his way and does not think he has anything to fear from Aaron, but he does not reckon with Aaron's fierceness.

Barneyway, Aaron's friend. Barneyway was quite a fighter and tough guy on the streets, but in prison he fell victim to Buzzer's ruthlessness and became a "queen." He learns how to survive in the cruel prison system. Even though he has become a victim of Buzzer and the prison system, Aaron continues to be his friend. Because of Buzzer, their friendship is not the same as it was on the streets.

Rattler, a member of Buzzer's gang. Although he too can be ruthless and cruel, he is only a shadow to Buzzer.

Big Stoop, the brutal giant who runs the institution with a conviction that he is right and the prisoners are wrong. He believes that harsh treatment will strengthen the prisoners' character. He is unaware that the prison system has made him a cruel overseer.

Judith, Aaron's girlfriend. She is the stabilizing element in Aaron's life while in prison. Aaron thinks that she has failed him because she appears for a visit with a tattoo on her cheek. She is no longer a symbol of purity and virtue. There is a close connection between the way Aaron feels toward Judith and the way he feels about his mother's death. He thinks that his mother was taken away by God unfairly and that he has been betrayed by Judith. Aaron believes that he has nothing to hold on to anymore.

The prison chaplain, a Protestant minister who is weak

and effete. Ostensibly he is there to save the souls of the young men, but he is no spiritual leader. In fact, the chaplain is in the service of the state because he acts as an informant. Aaron hates him both because he finds out that he is an informant and because the chaplain has not fulfilled his function as a man of God. His role as an informant makes him a cruel man, exhibiting the opposite of the Christian goodness that he is supposed to represent.

TEA AND SYMPATHY

Author: Robert Anderson (1917-   )
First published: 1953
Genre: Drama

Locale: New England
Time: A few days in early June in the 1950's
Plot: Representational

Laura Reynolds, a young woman in her mid- to late twenties. She has been married for less than a year to Bill Reynolds. Sensitive and compassionate, she is trying to adjust to life at the boys' school where her husband teaches, but she is not one for vigorous outdoor activity or small-minded gossip, both of which seem to be prerequisites for acceptance there. She is also worried by what she perceives as Bill's growing distance from her—physical as well as emotional distance. She is generally cheerful, however, and carries an air of maturity and wisdom about her. When she takes steps to protest an injustice done to Tom Lee, one of the students, she does so thoughtfully and decisively, without histrionics.

Tom Lee, one of the boys living in the house of which Bill Reynolds is housemaster. Almost eighteen years old, midway between boy and man, he is in love with Laura without fully realizing it. Laura, in turn, is touched by Tom's intensity, especially because he reminds her of her first husband, now deceased. The son of divorced parents, reared by a father who does not understand him and scorned by classmates who do not respect him, Tom is very lonely and very sensitive. He spends afternoons listening to his phonograph and playing the guitar. He plans on becoming a folk singer. Although he is the school's tennis champion, that show of athletic prowess fails to help him fit in: He is criticized for winning through technique and control rather than power and strength. Naïve and innocent, Tom has trouble at first understanding why a scandal has erupted over the afternoon he spent sunbathing nude with one of his favorite teachers.

Bill Reynolds, Laura's husband and a teacher at the school. He is about forty years old, large, and strong. He has a tendency to be gruff. It is difficult for him to admit any weaknesses of character, although it was his honesty during an unguarded moment that attracted Laura to him originally. He claims that he was like Tom as a boy, seeking solace for his loneliness in music, but was able to pull himself together to become the outdoorsy man he is today. When Tom is swept up in scandal, Bill worries not about Tom but about how it will reflect on his friendship with Tom's father and his chances of becoming headmaster one day.

Herbert (Herb) Lee, Tom's divorced father, a Boston businessman. He took custody of Tom to ensure that Tom would grow up to become a "regular guy." Extroverted and deeply concerned over appearances, he has no rapport with Tom and is extremely critical of him. Herb confides his concerns to Bill Reynolds, who is an old friend.

Al Thompson, Tom's roommate and captain-elect of the baseball team. A big, brawny athlete and one of the popular guys on campus, Al is everything that Bill and Herb would like Tom to be. Al is also kind and caring, and Tom considers him his closest friend. Al is able to stand up to his peers when they urge him not to room with Tom the next year, but when his father calls with the same advice, Al feels compelled to switch houses.

David Harris, a good-looking young teacher who is kind to Tom. The dean suspects him of homosexual tendencies and informs him that he will not be reappointed for the next year because he was seen sunbathing nude with Tom.

Lilly Sears, a faculty wife in her late thirties. She is flashy and almost gaudy, and she is entertained by the crushes she engenders among the boys. She takes Laura as her confidante.

— *Liz Marshall*

THE TEAHOUSE OF THE AUGUST MOON

Author: John Patrick (John Patrick Goggan, 1905-1995)
First published: 1954
Genre: Drama

Locale: Tobiki, Okinawa, Japan
Time: Late 1940's
Plot: Satire

Sakini, a middle-aged Okinawan interpreter for U.S. occupation forces following World War II. His skillful use of native Okinawan customs, Japanese folk wisdom, parody of Western ways, and naïveté reveal his perceptions of Americans and America. Sakini effectively bridges cross-cultural barriers.

Colonel Purdy, a stout U.S. Army officer assigned to democratize Okinawa following World War II. He is a single-minded individual who follows orders without question. He has rules and signs for the most trivial of situations; when alone, however, Purdy reads *Adventure Magazine* on work time. Outwardly, he guards his reputation, especially because of what his wife might say, but he is not above reversing orders to suit the whims of his superiors.

Captain Fisby, a U.S. Army officer in his late twenties, assigned as aide to Colonel Purdy. He had been an associate professor of humanities and is regarded as a misfit in military matters. Sakini constantly manipulates him into making all sorts of compromises and changes. Gradually, Fisby becomes so acculturated that he disobeys virtually every order that he is given, but in so doing he succeeds in making Tobiki a model village. His role demonstrates that a system is only a framework, within which ideal and reality may differ.

Lotus Blossom, a beautiful, petite Okinawan geisha girl. She has difficulty performing her duties as a geisha because Captain Fisby, to whom she has been given, is ignorant of the true role of the well-trained geisha and assumes her to be a prostitute.

Captain McLean, a psychiatrist in the U.S. Army. He is short and rather fat. His assignment is to make a psychological report on Captain Fisby, whose assimilation of the native ways is interpreted as a sign of mental imbalance. While he is working with Fisby, he is won over by Fisby and his cultural insights.

Sergeant Gregovich, a U.S. Army enlisted man, aide to Colonel Purdy. He goes through the motions of appearing to be efficient.

Old Woman, an Okinawan villager and grandmother of Tobiki's mayor, who rides, over protest, atop a loaded wagon that conveys Captain Fisby to his Tobiki assignment. Not to allow her to ride would make the mayor lose face; thus, she outmaneuvers those in command.

Old Woman's daughter, an Okinawan villager who, along with her three children, rides on the wagon to Tobiki.

Mr. Hokaida, a villager of Tobiki. A stout man in tattered peasant clothes, he presents Captain Fisby with a cricket cage when he arrives in Tobiki.

Mr. Omura, a villager of Tobiki. He welcomes Captain Fisby to Tobiki with chopsticks. He wears a white coat to distinguish himself from the rest of the villagers.

Mr. Sumata, a skilled carpenter in Tobiki. He brings Captain Fisby a geisha girl as a gift, providing a chance to see how cross-cultural misunderstanding can strain relationships.

Mr. Sumata's father, a skilled Tobikian carpenter. He helps to build the five-sided school/teahouse, highlighting the Japanese custom of passing on skills from one generation to the next.

Mr. Seiko, a Tobiki villager. He gives Captain Fisby geta, a kind of wooden sandals, when the officer arrives in Tobiki.

Miss Higa Jiga, an Okinawan villager chosen to be the president of a Ladies' League for Democratic Action. A chunky, flat-faced, unmarried young woman who wears heavy glasses, she makes amusing demands of Fisby in the name of democracy. Thus the Americans see how democracy is perceived by foreigners unaccustomed to the system.

Mr. Keora, an Okinawan villager. He is one of several who are dejected when they cannot sell Okinawan crafts to the U.S. Army personnel because they regard the handcrafted items as inferior to what American technology could produce at lower cost, even though the American goods are of lower quality.

Mr. Oshira, an Okinawan villager. This skilled artisan cannot sell his lacquer cups to soldiers who do not appreciate the time and skill that have gone into making them. He feels that the August moon at the end of summer—the peak between spring, the growing season, and fall, when nature sheds its foliage—symbolizes the maturity and wisdom that the two cultures have attained.

Major McEvoy, a U.S. Army officer. He is to be Captain Fisby's replacement.

Lady Astor, Miss Higa Jiga's goat. If the goat can drink homemade sweet potato brandy without harm, the men will drink it.

— *Victoria Price*

TELL ME THAT YOU LOVE ME, JUNIE MOON

Author: Marjorie Kellogg (1922-   )
First published: 1968
Genre: Novel

Locale: A small U.S. town and a seaside resort
Time: The 1960's
Plot: Social

Junie Moon, a young woman with her face and hands severely disfigured from having acid poured on her by a sexually disturbed assailant. Although her maimed face masks her emotions and her occasional biting words hide her sensitivity, she is the emotional center for the three disabled friends who leave the hospital to set up housekeeping in a run-down shack. Repulsed by the sight of her own face, she nevertheless is sexually attractive to Arthur, with whom she falls in love and has a brief affair before his death, and Mario, with whom she and Warren live after Arthur's death.

Arthur, a young man with an undiagnosed, progressive neurological disease. Walking with a lurching gait and waving his hands wildly around his face, he disguises his feelings by his nervous tics, yet his expressive eyes reveal his deep sensitivity. Deserted by his parents at a state school for the mentally handicapped, he runs away after being humiliated by Ramona, a cook he loves. He works for a time as a Western Union messenger and later is the only one of the three friends to look for a job. Rejected by the fishmonger Mario as a sexual pervert, he disappears to the woods before returning to his friends in a weakened state with a pet dog. On a vacation to the beach, he confesses his love for Junie Moon. He has a brief affair with her, then dies in her arms when they return home.

Warren, a paraplegic who has the idea and makes the arrangements for the three friends to live together. Abandoned by his mother at birth, he lived with Guiles, a young man who was hit by a delivery truck and killed when Warren was seven years old. For the rest of his life, he searches for a man who will love and care for him, thus assuming the role of Guiles. He became a paraplegic at the age of seventeen, when he was shot in the back by Melvin Coffee in a hunting "accident" after confessing his love for his friend.

Mario, the owner of a fish store who befriends Junie Moon, then the two men. Not repulsed by disfigurement because his grandmother had been seriously burned by hot soup, he helps Junie Moon search for the missing Arthur after making the mistake of not hiring him because of the malicious gossip of a neighbor. He provides a truck and money for the three friends to go on vacation when he realizes that Arthur will soon die, and he later shares his home with Warren, Junie Moon, and Arthur's dog.

Minnie, a fifty-two-year-old roommate of Junie Moon whose greatest desire, to be taken from the hospital to live with the three friends, is fulfilled when a sympathetic resident arranges for an ambulance to take her to their home, then picks her up himself later in the afternoon.

Sidney Wyner, a nosy neighbor who spies on the three friends and calls Mario to tell him that Arthur is a sodomist.

Gregory, a wealthy, voyeuristic woman who takes the three friends to her home and tries to convince Warren that he can walk.

Beach Boy, an employee of the resort hotel Patty's Hideaway. He pampers rich people and temporarily takes the place of Guiles in Warren's mind.

Binnie Farber, a sympathetic social worker who helps the three friends obtain welfare money to enable them to live in their own home.

Miss Oxford, a straitlaced head nurse who jealously believes that sex is at the heart of the friends' plan to live together.

— *Donna Maples*

THE TEMPEST

Author: William Shakespeare (1564-1616)
First published: 1623
Genre: Drama

Locale: An island
Time: The fifteenth century
Plot: Fantasy

Prospero (PROS-peh-roh), the former and rightful duke of Milan, now living on an island in the distant seas. Years earlier, he had been deposed by his treacherous younger brother, Antonio, to whom he had given too much power, for Prospero had always been more interested in his books of philosophy and magic than in affairs of state. Antonio had the aid of Alonso, the equally treacherous king of Naples, in his plot against his brother, and the conspirators had set Prospero and his infant daughter, Miranda, adrift in a small boat. They were saved from certain death by the faithful Gonzalo, who provided the boat with food and Prospero's books. Eventually, the craft drifted to an island that formerly had been the domain of the witch Sycorax, whose son, the monster Caliban, still lived there. Through the power of his magic, Prospero subdued Caliban and freed certain good spirits, particularly Ariel, whom Sycorax had imprisoned. Now, in a terrible storm, the ship carrying the treacherous king of Naples, his son Ferdinand, and Antonio is wrecked. They, with their companions, are brought ashore by Ariel. Using Ariel as an instrument, Prospero frustrates the plots of Antonio and Sebastian against the king and of Caliban, Trinculo, and Stephano against himself. He also furthers the romance between Miranda and Ferdinand. Convinced at last that Antonio and Alonso have repented of the wrongs they had done him, Prospero has them brought to his cell, where he reveals his identity and reclaims his dukedom. At the end of the story, he has the satisfaction of releasing Ariel, abandoning his magic, and returning to Milan for the marriage of Miranda and Ferdinand. In the figure of Prospero, some readers have found William Shakespeare's self-portrait; in Prospero's burying of his books on magic, they have found a symbol of Shakespeare's renunciation of the stage.

Miranda (mih-RAN-duh), Prospero's daughter, brought up on the island where her aged father is the only man she has ever seen. She falls instantly in love with Ferdinand. At the end of the play, they are to be married. The character of Miranda often has been taken as the depiction of complete innocence, untouched by the corruption of sophisticated life.

Ferdinand (FUR-dih-nand), the prince of Naples and son of King Alonso. Separated from his father when they reach the island, he is captured by Prospero, who, to test him, puts him at menial tasks. He falls in love with Miranda and she with him. Prospero finally permits their marriage.

Alonso (uh-LON-zoh), the king of Naples and father of Ferdinand. He aided the treacherous Antonio in deposing Prospero. When the castaways reach Prospero's island, Alonso is so grief-stricken by the supposed loss of his son that he repents of his wickedness and is forgiven by Prospero.

Antonio (an-TOH-nee-oh), Prospero's treacherous brother, who has usurped the dukedom of Milan. He is finally forgiven for his crime.

Sebastian (seh-BAS-tyuhn), Alonso's brother. On the island, he plots with Antonio to usurp the throne of Naples. Prospero discovers and frustrates the plot.

Gonzalo (gon-ZAH-loh), a faithful courtier who had saved the lives of Prospero and Miranda.

Ariel (AY-ree-ehl), a spirit imprisoned by Sycorax and released by Prospero, whom he serves faithfully. At the conclusion of the play, having carried out all of Prospero's commands, he is given complete freedom.

Caliban (KAL-ih-ban), the monstrous son of Sycorax, now a servant of Prospero. He represents brute force without intelligence and can be held in check only by Prospero's magic. Some have seen in him Shakespeare's conception of "natural man."

Stephano (STEHF-ah-noh), a drunken butler who plots with Caliban and Trinculo against Prospero and is foiled by Ariel.

Trinculo (TRIHN-kew-loh), a clown, a companion of Stephano and later of Caliban.

THE TEMPLE BEAU

Author: Henry Fielding (1707-1754)
First published: 1730
Genre: Drama

Locale: London, England
Time: The eighteenth century
Plot: Comedy of manners

Sir Harry Wilding, a wealthy Englishman. He is infuriated when he discovers that his son is spending his time as a useless dandy. After being tricked into signing over an annuity to the youth, he is consequently powerless to change his offspring's rakish ways by threats of disinheritance.

Wilding, Sir Harry's son. Supposed to be a law student in London, he is actually a gay young man-about-town. When he falls in love with Bellaria, he employs a ruse to escape potential affairs with Lady Lucy and Lady Gravely. Although he fails to marry Bellaria, he does trick his father into granting him an annuity.

Bellaria, a beautiful young heiress. Although she is loved and wanted by many men, including young Wilding and Valentine, she marries Veromil, who loves her as much as she loves him.

Sir Avarice Pedant, Bellaria's uncle. Although he is supposed to arrange a marriage between his niece and young Wilding, he tries instead to marry her to his own son.

Young Pedant, a young man so interested in his studies that he cannot become interested in women, even beautiful young heiresses.

Lady Lucy, Sir Avarice Pedant's young wife. A coquettish woman, she flirts with young Wilding and with Valentine.

Lady Gravely, Sir Avarice Pedant's sister. She puts on the airs of a prude but discreetly indulges herself in love affairs.

Valentine, a licentious young man who flirts with Lady Lucy. He hopes to marry Bellaria but instead helps his friend Veromil win the woman. He tricks Sir Avarice out of a large sum of money.

Veromil, a fine young man cheated of his inheritance by a dishonest brother. He marries Bellaria after regaining his inheritance.

THE TEMPLE OF THE GOLDEN PAVILION
(Kinkahuji)

Author: Yukio Mishima (Kimitake Hiraoka, 1925-1970)
First published: 1956
Genre: Novel

Locale: Kyoto, Japan
Time: Early 1940's through July 2, 1950
Plot: Psychological realism

Mizoguchi, a young Zen acolyte, from a poverty-stricken background, at the Temple of the Golden Pavilion and a student at Otani University. He is a physically frail only child, and he recognizes early that he is ugly and that his speech impediment (a stutter) locks him away from easy communication with the rest of the world. Alienated and isolated, he lives virtually in an inner world, stubbornly proud that no one understands him. From his youth, he is obsessed with the beauty of the Golden Temple. At the age of twenty-one, to become free of that obsession, he sets fire to the beautiful Zen temple, a revered architectural wonder more than five hundred years old.

Kashiwagi, a clubfooted student at Otani University. Misanthropic and selfish, he uses his disability to take advantage of other people's feelings and to promote his own selfish desires. He is a negative influence who counsels Mizoguchi to be more active in life, but in a selfish, nihilistic manner. By reporting to Father Dosen that Mizoguchi failed to repay a personal loan, Kashiwagi nearly gets Mizoguchi expelled from the temple.

Tsurukawa, a Zen acolyte at the Golden Temple and a student at Otani University. Seemingly cheerful and gentle, he comes from the suburbs of Tokyo, the son of affluent parents. He befriends Mizoguchi, urging him to break out of his quiet isolation. When the two acolytes begin to matriculate at Otani University, their relationship falters. Tsurukawa's death, at first reported as an accident, later is revealed as a probable suicide caused by an unhappy love affair. Letters written by Tsurukawa shortly before his death also call into question his previous seemingly cheerful disposition.

Father Tayama Dosen, a friend of Mizoguchi's father in their seminary days and currently superior of the Temple of the Golden Pavilion. A plump man, he devotes his free time to various satisfactions of the flesh. Although on the surface a fair and impartial superior, Father Dosen shows no feelings for Mizoguchi all the time that he acts as his mentor. He provides the tuition that allows Mizoguchi to attend Otani University, but after Mizoguchi falters in his studies and increasingly becomes more undisciplined at the temple, Father Dosen tells Mizoguchi that he has lost his opportunity to become the superior's successor at the temple.

Uiko, a volunteer nurse at a naval hospital. This proud young woman from a wealthy family attracts the young Mizoguchi. After she tells her parents of Mizoguchi's watching for her as she bicycles to work at dawn, Mizoguchi wishes for her death, thinking that it would end his embarrassment. A few months later, Uiko dies when a Navy deserter, whom she had been secretly aiding, shoots her when she leads the military police to his hiding place. After her death, Mizoguchi continues to be preoccupied with her memory, and he often thinks of her when he comes into contact with other women.

Mizoguchi's father, an impoverished country priest. Knowing that he will soon die from tuberculosis, he takes his adolescent son to see the Temple of the Golden Pavilion, which to the father is a structure of limitless beauty, and to place him under the protection of Father Dosen.

Mizoguchi's mother, a shabby, impoverished wife, then widow. Her ambition is to see her son as the superior of the Golden Temple. She berates Mizoguchi for being undutiful while an acolyte at the temple.

Father Kuwai Zenkai, a Zen priest, the head of Ryoko Temple. Strong and healthy in appearance and character, he serves as a contrast to his two friends from seminary days—Mizoguchi's father and Father Dosen. Father Zenkai is candid when he talks to Mizoguchi a few hours before the temple burns, and Mizoguchi yearns for this priest to understand him.

Mariko, a prostitute a few years older than Mizoguchi. She warns him that he should not frequent the brothel too often.

— *Marion Boyle*

TEMPTATION
(Pokoušení)

Author: Václav Havel (1936-   )
First published: 1986
Genre: Drama

Locale: Soviet Europe
Time: The 1980's
Plot: Social criticism

Dr. Henry Foustka, a scientist employed by the scientific research facility called the Institute. He is secretly exploring the occult, burning candles and reciting incantations alone in his study. Foustka, a Faust figure exploring the possibility that science itself is the worship of the devil, reluctantly employs the services of Fistula, which are essentially the argument by which Foustka realizes his own beliefs. He is damned by Fistula's accusations and disappears in clouds of smoke.

Fistula, an invalid in retirement, sinister and philosophical, who is prone to visiting Foustka unannounced. The Mephistopheles character, he second-guesses Foustka, causing him to make admissions that he does not actually believe, then betrays him to the Director, for whom he has been acting as agent provocateur.

The Director, the head of the Institute, who is in constant need of support staff and yes men. He is strangely attracted to Foustka until his offer of intimate friendship is rebuffed. Both in his position as the head of the Institute and in his duplicity toward Foustka, he is the embodiment of evil, despite his superficial concern for others and his quiet, self-deprecating attitude.

Vilma, a scientist, Foustka's lover, addicted to elaborately staged role-playing scenarios in her love life and accused by Foustka of being responsible for his exposure to the Director. She loses her respect for Foustka when he lies his way out of trouble. Eventually, she acts out what Foustka has always believed to be one of her fantasies, taking up with a dancer who brings her violets every night.

The Deputy Director, an oily and hypocritical man. On the surface, he is the spokesman for the Director, who actually despises him. The Deputy Director acts as facilitator for the Institute. He is always seen with a silent girl, Petruska, who holds his hand at all times, except when she sneaks off to be unfaithful to him with other scientists.

Maggie, a secretary, young and attractive, completely taken in by Foustka's rhetoric. She falls in love with him, believing him to be a clearheaded defender of the world against the devil. She willingly sacrifices herself in his defense when he is condemned by the Director. She goes mad when the Director takes away her job for supporting Foustka.

Lorencova,
Kotrly, and
Neuwirth, the staff scientists for the Institute's work, romantically involved in various combinations. They act as the jury during Foustka's "trial" and attend two parties hosted by the Institute.

Mrs. Houbova, Foustka's elderly landlady. Representing the naïve but unpretentious real world, she is sane and protective of Foustka, with natural instincts of repulsion toward Fistula.

— *Thomas J. Taylor*

THE TEMPTATION OF SAINT ANTHONY
(La Tentation de Saint Antoine)

Author: Gustave Flaubert (1821-1880)
First published: 1874
Genre: Novel

Locale: Egypt
Time: The fourth century
Plot: Historical

Saint Anthony, a hermit for thirty years but now despondent because he feels that his life has been a failure. He is tempted by gluttony, avarice, and lust, but he overcomes them all. His disciple, Hilarion, appears to accuse him of ignorance and to tempt him intellectually by exposing him to all the confusing heresies of the early church and to the false gods of history, each of whom contained some element of truth. He is even carried into space by Satan, to be shown that the universe is limitless and meaningless and to be urged to curse God and acknowledge the Devil. Even this temptation Anthony overcomes, as well as the urgings of Death and Lust that he escape through them the ugliness of the world. When, the next day, Anthony sees the face of Christ in the sun, he knows that he has emerged victorious from his trials.

The Devil, who subjects Anthony to the horror of infinity.

Hilarion, Anthony's former disciple, who exposes him to the sins of the intellect.

The Queen of Sheba, who represents lust.

Tertullian, who drives away the heresiarchs.

Apollonius, who almost conquers Anthony by the offer of the power of having visions and of curing the sick.

Marcellina, a woman who tells Anthony that with the aid of a silver image she can cause Christ to appear.

Montanus, who, according to a strange woman Anthony meets, is the incarnation of the Holy Ghost.

TEN NORTH FREDERICK

Author: John O'Hara (1905-1970)
First published: 1955
Genre: Novel

Locale: Gibbsville, Pennsylvania, and New York City
Time: 1945, with flashbacks
Plot: Realism

Joseph Benjamin (Joe) Chapin, a right-minded snob, born into one of the wealthiest and most socially prominent families of Gibbsville, Pennsylvania. Joe is an only child, dominated by his mother, Charlotte, who has become cold to his father after two miscarriages. Joe has a strong sense of his place in Gibbsville and returns there after attending Yale. With his closest friend, Arthur McHenry, he builds a law practice and establishes a reputation for propriety and discretion. Haunted by the death of Marie Harrison, with whom he had a brief affair while in college and who later died in the abortion of another man's child, he carries on an emotionally intense but sexually restrained courtship of Edith Stokes, whose family has an equal prominence in Gibbsville. Following his marriage to Edith, Joe is particularly fond of their daughter, Ann. He feels diminished, however, when he misses the experience of serving with the military in World War I. He eventually decides to pursue a career in politics, but he is devastated when he learns that he will not get, and never had a real chance at getting, the nomination for lieutenant governor. This revelation, combined with his increasing sense of his wife's selfishness and of their failures with their children, leads him to become an alcoholic, and he eventually dies of cirrhosis.

Edith Stokes Chapin, Joe's wife. Her reserved personality has caused her to be an enigma to almost everyone in Gibbsville. She is actually a very cold person who makes it her purpose in life to "own" her husband emotionally. Jealous of her husband's affection for their daughter and essentially disinterested in their son, she becomes increasingly embittered by the realization that aspects of her husband's life are beyond her control. Physically a very plain woman, she has a Machiavellian attitude toward sex that is apparent in her lesbian affair with Barbara Dantworth, a schoolmate in boarding school, and in her adulterous affair with Lloyd Williams, a brash lawyer who eventually becomes district attorney of Lantenengo County.

Ann Chapin, the beautiful and precocious daughter of Joe and Edith Chapin. She elopes with Charley Bongiorno, a jazz musician, and is permanently scarred when her parents force her to accept an annulment and an abortion. She moves to New York City, works in various offices, and has casual affairs with a number of men until she becomes frightened by her promiscuity. At the time of her father's death, she is living at home, having obtained a separation from her second husband, who is referred to only as Mr. Musgrove.

Joseph (Joby) Chapin, Jr., Edith and Joe's son, a cynic on the verge of becoming an alcoholic. He works with the Office of Strategic Services in Arlington, Virginia. In his adolescence, he compensated for his lack of purpose by playing piano with jazz bands. His knowledge of his mother's affair with Lloyd Williams, of the abortion forced on his sister, and of his mother's willingness to let his father die of alcoholism has permanently disillusioned him.

Mike Slattery, a shrewd politician who has extended his influence far beyond his base as a state senator. Proud of his family and of his Irish ancestry, he views Joe Chapin as a political amateur. Unlike Joe, he is happily married and confides in his wife, trusting her instincts on political matters. He initially encourages Joe's political ambitions, but he is too much the pragmatist to compromise his own influence for the sake of those ambitions.

Arthur McHenry, a man influenced on all sides to be the closest friend and law partner of Joe Chapin. He is levelheaded and unassuming, a loyal confidant. He probably understands Joe better than anyone. His first wife dies of cancer, but, with Joe's insistent encouragement, he rediscovers contentment in marriage to her sister.

— *Martin Kich*

THE TENANT OF WILDFELL HALL

Author: Anne Brontë (1820-1849)
First published: 1848
Genre: Novel

Locale: England
Time: The 1820's
Plot: Social realism

Gilbert Markham, a kindhearted, industrious, and passionate young farmer. In a series of letters written to his brother-in-law, he tells the story of his romance with the mysterious woman who is the new tenant of Wildfell Hall. At first unable to get through her protective shell of coldness and aloofness, Gilbert finally discovers her story, and his sincere sympathy and interest in her work as a landscape painter endear him to her. After several years of separation, faithful Gilbert marries his loved one.

Mrs. Helen Graham, in reality **Mrs. Arthur Huntingdon**, the mysterious tenant of Wildfell Hall. Seemingly a cold and self-contained woman, she jealously guards her son Arthur from any outside interference when she first arrives at Wildfell Hall, where she is content to walk about the countryside and sketch the landscape. The village gossip is that she is carrying on an affair with her landlord, Frederick Lawrence. Eventually, she reveals her story to Gilbert Markham and allows him to read her private journal. He learns that she had been brought up by her rich uncle and aunt and that she had fallen unwisely in love with Arthur Huntingdon, a handsome but wayward young man. Although warned by her aunt not to marry Arthur, Helen did so willfully and thus began a marriage of horror. Faithful and loving, she endured much from her wild and dissipated husband. Finally, when she realized that his profligate ways were affecting their son adversely and that he was carrying on an affair with the wife of one of his friends, Helen left him and fled to Wildfell Hall, to be near the home of her brother. There she meets Gilbert Markham, whose kindness and true affection win her heart.

Arthur Huntingdon, a selfish, reckless young man of profligate habits. Although truly in love with his young wife at the time of their marriage, he cannot give up his former carefree and wicked life, and his character begins to deteriorate. Unable to adapt himself to a domestic situation, he takes more and more journeys to London and then begins to bring his riotous friends home to Grasslands, his country estate. Soon he becomes involved in an affair with Lady Annabella Lowborough, whose husband is one of his friends. When he discovers that his wife Helen is painting pictures to enable her to accumulate enough money to leave him, he has all of her artist's supplies destroyed. He dies a horrible death after drinking wine in defiance of his doctor's orders, and his death leaves Helen free to marry Gilbert Markham. Branwell Brontë served as the model for his sister's portrait of a man wasting his life in dissipation.

Frederick Lawrence, a sheltered, shy, and self-contained man, Helen Graham's brother. No one in the parish knows their relationship, and the gossips believe that he is carrying on an illicit affair with the strange tenant of Wildfell Hall, the family home he had deserted for another residence in a nearby parish. When Gilbert Markham learns the truth after reading Helen's journal, the gossip ceases.

Rose Markham, a tidy, plump young woman with a round face, bright blooming cheeks, glossy clustering curls, and merry brown eyes. Devoted to her brother Gilbert, she hesitates to believe the gossip about Helen Graham. She marries Mr. Halford.

Mrs. Markham, Gilbert's widowed mother. She is a favorite in the parish and often entertains her many friends. Much impressed with Helen Graham, she finds it difficult to believe the gossip about her.

Fergus Markham, Gilbert's younger brother, a good-natured, teasing, and lazy lad who supplies much of the humor in the story.

The Reverend Michael Millward, a tall, ponderous, elderly gentleman of fixed principles, strong prejudices, and regular habits. Because he is intolerant of dissent of any kind and believes that his opinions are always right, he chides Helen Graham for not attending church. He readily believes the stories told about her and attempts to lecture her on her conduct. He is practically turned away from Wildfell Hall for his pains.

Eliza Millward, the vicar's younger daughter, a plump, charming young woman in love with Gilbert Markham. Like a pretty, playful kitten, she is sometimes roguish, sometimes timid and demure. She is responsible for many of the tales told about Helen Graham because she sees in her a rival for Gilbert's hand.

Mary Millward, her sister, several years older, a plain, quiet young woman of warmer disposition than her sister. She has been the family housekeeper and drudge all her life. Gilbert Markham remarks that she is "loved and courted by all the dogs and cats but slighted and neglected by everybody else."

Mrs. Wilson, a narrow-minded, tattling village gossip whose garrulous nature causes her to spread tales about Mrs. Graham.

Robert Wilson, her older son, a rough, countrified bumpkin.

Richard Wilson, her younger son, a retiring and studious young man. With the vicar's assistance, he studies the classics in preparation for college. He plans to enter the church.

Jane Wilson, their sister. She has a boarding school education and elegant manners, but her social ambitions will allow her to take only a gentleman for a husband. She has her eye on Frederick Lawrence, the young squire who formerly occupied Wildfell Hall.

Rachel, Helen Graham's servant and devoted companion. Aware of her mistress' situation at Wildfell Hall, she is cold and suspicious of their neighbors.

Arthur Huntingdon, called **Arthur Graham**, Helen's fun-loving, affectionate small son. Greatly attracted to Gilbert Markham, he serves to introduce that gentleman and his mother.

Mr. Boarham, a fashionable young gentleman and Helen's suitor before her marriage to Arthur Huntingdon. Reflecting his name, Boarham is a boring person, and in spite of her aunt's approval, Helen cannot tolerate him.

Mr. Wilmot, a wealthy old man who pursues Helen. He is greatly surprised by her refusal of his hand.

Annabella, Mr. Wilmot's niece, a dashing young woman who seems too much of a flirt ever to marry. She does marry Lord Lowborough, however, but carries on affairs afterward, including a serious one with Arthur Huntingdon.

Lord Lowborough, Arthur Huntingdon's friend, a sober, tall, and thin gentleman with a sickly, careworn aspect. Through his marriage to Annabella, he hopes to acquire some peace in life, but he fails to do so because of her waywardness.

Millicent Hargrave, Annabella's cousin and Helen's good friend. After Millicent's unfortunate marriage to Mr. Hattersley, she endures the same sort of life that Helen does, having to put up with the drinking bouts and wild conduct of her husband. Her life becomes more comfortable after Mr. Hattersley, observing the fate of Arthur Huntingdon, reforms and becomes a gentle and devoted husband.

Mr. Hattersley, Millicent's wild husband and Arthur Huntingdon's companion on excursions to London. During the early years of their marriage, he browbeats and torments his wife, but eventually he changes for the better.

Walter Hargrave, Millicent's brother. Enamored of Helen, he pursues her with offers of protection and marriage during her unhappy life with Arthur Huntingdon. Although he belongs to the London drinking, gaming, and hunting set, he is less boisterous and more temperate than the others.

Benson, the Huntingdon butler. Devoted to Helen, he helps her to escape from Grasslands.

Miss Myers, a sullen young woman hired by Arthur Huntingdon as a governess for his son when he decides to separate his wife from her child.

Mr. Halford, Gilbert Markham's brother-in-law at a later date, to whom Gilbert writes the letters that tell the story of Helen Graham and his own romance with the tenant of Wildfell Hall.

THE TENANTS OF MOONBLOOM

Author: Edward Lewis Wallant (1926-1962)
First published: 1963
Genre: Novel

Locale: New York City
Time: Early 1960's
Plot: Psychological realism

Norman Moonbloom, a thirty-three-year-old Jew who manages four small, deteriorating tenement buildings owned by his brother. Norman feels like a failure. A kindly, introverted, studious type, he is not cut out to be a businessman but was never comfortable as a student. During fourteen years at the University of Wisconsin, McGill University, the University of Mexico, and Bowdoin College, he tried accounting, art, literature, dentistry, rabbinical studies, and podiatry before becoming his brother's overworked, underpaid agent. Every week, Norman goes around collecting the rents in cash. He and his brother are violating rent control laws by overcharging for scarce accommodations, and they give receipts for less than the tenants pay. Because Norman is exploiting the tenants, he does not want to get friendly with them. Whenever he shows kindness or sympathy, someone takes it for weakness and begins making demands. Norman knows the buildings are falling apart, but his brother allows him only enough to pay for minimal maintenance. The tenants have no respect for Norman; some insult or ridicule him. In spite of himself, he becomes involved with the lives of many tenants. In his eyes, they begin to represent all of suffering humanity. He sees old age, disease, alcoholism, thwarted ambition, grief over the loss of a child, unemployment, marital strife, physical and psychological abuse, and the debilitating fears that haunt most people who live on the edge of poverty. Some were prisoners in World War II Nazi concentration camps and have identification numbers tattooed on their arms. Eventually, Norman experiences a physical and mental breakdown from feeling torn between the conflicting demands of his tenants and those of his greedy brother. When Norman recovers, he is a different person. With the grudging assistance of Gaylord, the maintenance man, Norman begins renovating all four buildings. To economize, he contributes his own labor and even spends $2,000 of his own savings. He begins to have normal human relationships with his tenants. The experience of being useful to others and of being an integral part of humanity makes him feel more content with his role in life than he has ever felt before.

Irwin Moonbloom, Norman's older brother and his employer. He never appears in person but is continually telephoning to complain. Irwin is a typical slumlord interested only in money. He makes the hypersensitive Norman's life miserable by forcing him to squeeze money out of the tenants while refusing to allocate any money for such badly needed services as plumbing repair, elevator maintenance, cockroach and rodent control, painting, lighting, carpeting, and repairs to obsolete heating and cooking appliances. Irwin's character is the exact opposite of his brother's. Irwin, who might be described as a social Darwinist, is blinded by greed and considers his kindly brother to be a useless dreamer doomed to be a hopeless failure.

Gaylord Knight, the African American building superintendent who is responsible for the upkeep of Irwin's properties. He feels doomed to be exploited and confined to menial jobs because of his race. He is understandably determined to do as little as possible for the miserable wages he receives and to try to get as much enjoyment out of life as he can. Irwin regards him as lazy and shiftless without considering that Gaylord has little incentive to work hard and is actually holding down a second part-time job as an elevator operator to make ends meet. Eventually, Gaylord is inspired by Norman's example to find self-fulfillment in helping other people rather than bemoaning his fate.

Basellecci, a cultured old gentleman who makes a bare living teaching his beloved native Italian language. He is dying of cancer of the colon but imagines that his constipation is the result of the terrible condition of his apartment's ancient toilet. His politeness and forbearance make Norman feel especially guilty and help to precipitate the rent collector's dramatic change of character.

Karloff, a powerful Russian-Jewish immigrant who has finally given up the struggle for existence at the age of 104. He speaks garbled English and Yiddish and feigns inability to understand his neighbors' complaints about the roaches and mice he attracts with his atrocious living habits. His abominable apartment is Norman's greatest nightmare and the first unit that Norman and Gaylord attack with detergent, paint, and insecticide.

Sheryl Beeler, a lusty young blonde who seduces Norman in an attempt to get a reduction in her rent. Norman's sexual initiation, although sordid, gives him self-confidence and the ability to love, which inspire him to rebel against Irwin and begin his campaign of building renovation.

— *Bill Delaney*

TENDER IS THE NIGHT

Author: F. Scott Fitzgerald (1896-1940)
First published: 1934
Genre: Novel

Locale: Europe
Time: The 1920's
Plot: Social realism

Dick Diver, a brilliant young psychiatrist who inspires confidence in everyone. As a young man, he met a woman who became a patient and whom he married. He devoted most of his time during the next several years to helping her regain a certain normality. In the process of helping his wife, he loses his own self-respect, alienates most of his friends, and drowns his brilliance in alcohol. His professional position deteriorates to that of a general practitioner in successively smaller towns across the United States.

Nicole Warren Diver, Dick's wife, a fabulously rich American. As a young girl, she had an incestuous relationship with her father and subsequently suffered a mental breakdown. She marries Dick while still a patient and is content to let him guide her in all things for several years. When he begins to drink heavily and make scenes in public, she tries to stop him; in doing so, she begins to gain some moral strength of her own. In a short time, she no longer needs Dick, has a brief affair, and divorces Dick to marry her lover. Apparently aware of her part in Dick's downfall, she continues to be somewhat concerned for him.

Rosemary Hoyt, a beautiful young American film actress. Having fallen in love with Dick, who is several years her senior, on their first meeting, she later has a brief affair with him. When she finally recognizes the decline in him, she is powerless to do anything about it. Although she retains her devotion to both of the Divers, she has never really grown up herself and is incapable of acting positively without direction.

Tommy Barban, a war hero and professional soldier. Typically cold and unfeeling where most people are concerned, he spends much of his time fighting in various wars. He eventually becomes Nicole's lover and then her second husband.

Beth Evan (Baby) Warren, Nicole's older sister. Knowing nothing of the real nature of Nicole's illness, she feels that the family should buy a doctor to marry and care for her. She never fully approves of Dick because her snobbery makes her feel superior to him. After a succession of quiet, well-mannered affairs, she remains without roots or direction in her life.

Mrs. Elsie Speers, Rosemary Hoyt's mother. She devotes her life to making Rosemary a successful actress. She also tries to make her an individual but fails to achieve this goal.

Abe North, an unambitious musician, an early friend of the Divers. He goes consistently downhill and is finally murdered.

Mary North, Abe's wife. She is an ineffectual person while married to Abe; later, she makes a more advantageous marriage and fancies herself one of the queens of the international set.

Collis Clay, a young American friend of Rosemary. Fresh from Yale, he is now studying architecture in Europe and despairs of ever having to go back to Georgia to take over the family business.

Franz Gregorovious, a Swiss psychiatrist who becomes Dick Diver's partner in a clinic they establish with Nicole's money.

Kaethe, his wife, a tactless woman who is envious of Americans and their money.

Gausse, the proprietor of a small hotel on the Riviera where the Divers and their friends often spend their summers.

Mr. and Mrs. McKisco, an American novelist and his wife who, after achieving financial success, lose their sense of inferiority and acquire the superiority and snobbishness typical of the moneyed Americans in the Diver set.

Lady Caroline Sibly-Biers, an English friend of Mary North after her second marriage. She typifies the overbearing attitude of her class.

TENDER MERCIES

Author: Rosellen Brown (1939-   )
First published: 1978
Genre: Novel

Locale: A small town in New Hampshire, with flashbacks in New York City and Boston, Massachusetts
Time: The 1970's
Plot: Domestic realism

Dan Courser, the husband of Laura and primary narrator. He is the father of two children and a graduate of the local vocational college. He is very skilled with his hands and has worked for seven years as a high school shop teacher. He came from a poor home with an abusive and alcoholic father. His mother, who was the best part of that unpleasant home, worked nights in the local paper mill. As an adolescent, he was constantly in trouble for driving while drunk, for vandalizing summer homes, and for suspected paternity. He possessed a "macho" philosophy about women: No girl was too bad for him, and all girls wanted him. His high school English teacher described his style as "braggadocio," a term Dan considered a compliment. Dan thought he could acquire whatever he wanted, like Aladdin with his lamp. His courtship of Laura forced him to "chasten" his impulses, to grow and to change, although he felt he could never catch up with her after his ultimate flamboyant act, which turned Laura into a quadriplegic. Throughout the novel, Dan struggles with his own needs, with the feeling that he must constantly prove himself, and with tremendous guilt for the accident that disabled his wife.

Laura Shurrock Courser, a quadriplegic wife and mother. She has thick reddish hair and a body shaped by dancing, an activity she loved before her accident. Dan describes Laura as not beautiful, but earnest with a no-nonsense nose. She is restrained; she dealt with her anger as a child by holding her breath until she fainted. During her courtship with Dan, she was patient with him and a good listener, unrepulsed by the stories of his father. She came from a well-to-do Boston family and attended Wellesley. She considers herself a "bad girl" and

thinks she married badly because she, like Dan, rejected the conformity of her lifestyle and expected him to change her way of living. After the accident, the degree to which he did change her life strikes her as ironic. Laura attempts to deal with her helplessness with dignity and pride. Through stream-of-consciousness monologues that frequently are accounts of dreams, Laura reveals her reactions to her condition and her longing to escape to a place inside her head that does not hold poisonous memories.

Jonathan Courser, the older of Dan and Laura's two young children. He tries hard not to be embarrassed by his mother and helps as much as he can. He becomes very protective of her when she and his father separate briefly.

Hallie Courser, Dan and Laura's daughter. She has difficulty adjusting to her mother's condition and frequently deals with it by withdrawing. While in New York City during her mother's hospitalization, Hallie disappears overnight and never reveals the circumstances of her absence.

Mr. Shurrock and
Mrs. Shurrock, Laura's parents. They are conservative Bostonians who rush to Laura's aid after the accident, accusing Dan and providing money for Laura's care. They are not strong enough, however, to deal with the practical needs of a person as incapacitated as Laura, and when Dan leaves, they are unable to cope.

Carol Shurrock, Laura's sister. She is the most verbal in her condemnation of Dan, refusing to release him from blame. She also fails in an attempt to assume total care of Laura and retreats into drugs.

John Courser, Dan's older brother. He is more attentive to Laura after the accident than he had ever been before, creating some jealousy in Dan. The relationship between the two brothers has always been physically abusive. The beating John administers in the end seems to absolve Dan and allows him to return to Laura.

— *Karen Ann Pinter*

THE TENNIS PLAYERS
(Tennisspelarna)

Author: Lars Gustafsson (1936-   )
First published: 1977
Genre: Novel

Locale: The University of Texas at Austin
Time: 1974
Plot: Philosophical

Lars Gustafsson (lahrz guhs-TAHF-shuhn), a visiting professor of Scandinavian literature at the University of Texas. Sharing, not coincidentally, both the author's name and profession, the professor reveals that he is glad to have escaped his native Sweden so that he can divide his time between playing tennis in the hot Texas sun and delivering popular lectures at the university. Gustafsson's indolent existence is threatened by the problems presented by two graduate students.

Doobie Smith, the professor's favorite student, an expert on nineteenth century European philosophers. Blonde, blue-eyed, and sensuously plump, Doobie reminds the professor of Friedrich Nietzsche's beloved Lou Salomé. Theoretically a committed Nietzschean, Doobie reverts to her fundamentalist Baptist roots when she discovers that her role as one of the Rhine Maidens in the student production of Richard Wagner's *Das Rheingold* is jeopardized by her refusal to sleep with the conductor. Outraged, Doobie enlists Professor Gustafsson's help in defending her honor.

Bill, a graduate student who has unearthed from the university library a book by Zygmunt I. Pietziewzskoczsky, an obscure Polish writer. Pietziewzskoczsky's book, *Memoires d'un chimiste*, if authenticated, will force a reevaluation of August Strindberg's *Inferno*. Tall, black, and intense, Bill disrupts the professor's graduate seminar when he theorizes that Strindberg's so-called Inferno Crisis is not a product of the author's mad delusions, as Strindberg experts maintain, but stems from a real conspiracy of Polish exiles who were trying to find out the results of Strindberg's chemical experiments.

Chris, a nearsighted computer genius who works part-time at the Strategic Air Command near Fort Worth. Having met Gustafsson on the tennis court, Chris invites the professor to his lodgings to drink beer and to meet the psychiatrist under whose care he has been since his nervous breakdown two years earlier. When Chris learns of Professor Gustafsson's Strindberg problem, he offers to employ the Strategic Air Command's unused memory to collate *Inferno* and *Memoires d'un chimiste* to test whether there is in fact sufficient correlation between the two books to justify an overhaul of Strindberg criticism. Before Chris can complete his task and remove the books from the computer, however, he is arrested during a campus demonstration and fired from his post. As a result, the *Inferno* and the one known copy of *Memoires d'un chimiste* are frozen in the Early Warning System's memory. The professor and other Strindberg authorities are saved from having to go to the trouble of reexamining accepted theories.

Abel, a superb tennis player who has won the Australian open once and reached the finals at Wimbledon twice but who prefers to play pickup matches on public tennis courts. From Abel, the professor learns to improve his serve and to refuse to allow the past to taint the present.

Hugh Frisco, chairman of the board of trustees for the University of Texas. Rich and accustomed to getting his own way, Senator Frisco convenes the board to fire the university's president for defying Frisco's order to replace Wagner's *Das Rheingold* with Giuseppe Verdi's *Aida* as the spring concert.

Geoffrey Gore, an oil magnate and vice chairman of the board of trustees who sides with Frisco in wanting to fire the president.

Professor John R. Perturber, Jr., a former professor of forestry and the current president of the university. The last four university presidents lasted less than one year apiece. The timid Perturber appears to be on his way out when he refuses to give in to the board of trustees on the matter of the spring concert.

Gordon Hugh Smith, a Travis County assistant sheriff who discovers Gore's black Cadillac parked in the middle of the university's baseball field. Smith, sad-faced and rather nondescript, achieves notoriety when he arrests Gore for drunken driving and Frisco for having sex with a waitress, the real scandal being that Frisco chooses for his liaison the batter's box, a spot traditionally reserved for the school's best batter to meet his girlfriend on the night before a big game. As a result of Smith's discovery, Gore and Frisco are fired from the board, President Perturber keeps his job, the spring concert goes on as planned, and Sheriff Smith becomes a local hero.

— *Sandra Hanby Harris*

TENT OF MIRACLES
(Tenda dos milagres)

Author: Jorge Amado (1912-   )
First published: 1969
Genre: Novel

Locale: Salvador, in the state of Bahia, Brazil
Time: 1968-1969 and 1868-1943
Plot: Magical Realism

Pedro Archanjo (PEH-droh ahr-SHAHN-zhoh), a writer and self-taught anthropologist. A brilliant, light-brown, husky mulatto who loves good conversation, riotous celebration, women, and social justice, he earns his living as a runner at Bahia School of Medicine yet writes four insightful anthropological works about the beloved mulatto culture of his native Bahia. One highly controversial work traces the impurities in the aristocratic bloodlines, which infuriates the white supremacists. He is a font of virtue and humanity to the good, a thorn to the proud and hateful. His tremendous powers of observation and language earn for him the folk titles **Ojuobá** (oh-zhew-BAH) and **Eyes of Xangô** (shahng-OH), titles that imply the supernatural and magical. The 1868-1943 frame of the novel follows his fight against white supremacy, especially the promotion of miscegenation. The 1968-1969 frame relates the perverse whitewashing of his image when it becomes profitable to make the neglected writer a national hero.

Fausta Pena (FOWS-tah PEH-nah), a poet, the first-person narrator of the 1968-1969 frame. Fausta, with his beard, long hair, and blue jeans, prides himself on the nickname given him by the female poets—**Wicked Cobra**. When Ana Mercedes betrays him, he experiences severe doubts about his masculinity, literary significance, and political integrity. Fausta accepts a commission from Levenson to research Archanjo's life. This research forms the basis for the 1868-1943 frame. He later realizes that the commission was merely a ruse to clear Levenson's access to Ana Mercedes.

Nilo d'Ávila Argolo de Araújo (NEE-loh DAH-vee-lah AHR-goh-loh deh ah-ROW-zhew), a professor of forensic medicine at the Bahia School of Medicine. He is tall and erect, with a spare, dry, black-clad frame and a forbidding voice and bearing. Argolo uses his considerable force of character to advance racial hatred. He persecutes Archanjo, inciting Archanjo's arrest and the destruction of the Tent of Miracles. His arrogant world falls to pieces when Archanjo's research reveals that Argolo is related to Archanjo.

Lídio Corró (LEE-dee-oh koh-ROH), a miracle painter and printer. She is fortyish, short, and stocky. The shrewd, keen-witted mulatto is Archanjo's best friend and owner of the art and print shop called the Tent of Miracles, where Archanjo and his circle gather to celebrate and converse.

Ana Mercedes, a poet and reporter, Pena's girlfriend. Golden and slender, with slightly fleshy lips, greedy white teeth, and loose black hair, the mulatta Mercedes exudes sexiness and voluptuous insouciance. Mercedes seduces Pena into writing poems over her name, then betrays him for a prestigious affair with Levenson.

James D. Levenson, a scholar, forty-five years old, more than six feet tall, with blond hair and sky-blue eyes. The famous North American Nobel Prize winner disrupts Bahia in 1968 by declaring that he has arrived to study the neglected writer Archanjo. Everyone suddenly clamors to become Archanjo's champion.

Rosa de Oxalá (oh-shah-LAH), Corró's mistress. With languid Yoruba eyes, blue-black skin that exudes a scent of the night, and her body shining with supple power, she laughs lustily while performing the most seductive dances of the celebrations. Archanjo will not consummate their passionate mutual love because of his loyalty to Corró.

Major Damião de Souza (day-MYOW[N] deh SOO-sah), a self-taught lawyer, Archanjo's friend. Always dressed in white, he keeps himself straight and slim as a ramrod with rum and sex. Smoking a cheap cigar, his mouth full of bad teeth, and waving his big, knotty mulatto hands, he rolls out the most exquisite and winning rhetoric in the courtroom, but only in defense of the poor.

Tadeu Canhoto (tah-DEH-ew kahn-OH-toh), a professional engineer, one of Archanjo's illegitimate sons. With a fine-featured, frank copper face, gleaming black hair, and dancing yet bashful eyes, he works brilliantly and diligently to succeed and thus gain the acceptance of the rich white family whose daughter he loves. His marriage to the daughter helps incite a six-year campaign of arrest and destruction by the secret police.

Pedrito Gordo (peh-DREE-toh GOHR-doh), the chief of the secret police. Stoutish, middle-aged, and looking like a dandy, the cane-wielding bully wages brutal war against the mulatto element of Bahia.

Dr. Zèzinho Pinto (zay-ZEE-nyoh PEEN-toh), a newspaper publisher. A stolid, worldly man who thinks of nothing but selling newspapers, he spearheads and profits from the new acclamation of Archanjo and instigates the whitewashing of Archanjo's image.

Kirsi the Swede, one of Archanjo's mistresses. Actually a Finn, very blonde, white, and lovely, she happily returns to Finland to bear Archanjo a son.

Dr. Silva Virajá (vee-rah-ZHAH), a professor. Good-natured and honest, he is Archanjo's friend and mentor within the Bahia School of Medicine.

Professor Azevedo (ah-seh-VEH-doh),

Professor Calazans (kah-lah-SAHNS), and

Professor Ramos (RRAH-mohs), scholars truly interested in science. They resist Pinto's misrepresentation of Archanjo's person and message.

— Timothy C. Davis

THE TENTS OF WICKEDNESS

Author: Peter De Vries (1910-1993)
First published: 1959
Genre: Novel

Locale: Decency, Connecticut
Time: Late 1950's
Plot: Fiction of manners

Charles (Chick) Swallow, a fortyish columnist for the Decency, Connecticut, *Picayune Blade*. His sympathetic pen and ear win him more friends than he wants. His reinvolvement with a girlfriend from adolescence, Sweetie Ap-

pleyard, prompts him to apologize for his excessive conventionality, as opposed to her strained and theatrical feeling that she is special and needs special allowances made for her. He is just silly enough and she just barely reasonable enough that here is some plausibility to each case.

Crystal Swallow, Chick's wife and the mother of his three children. Crystal has a sense that she is trapped in a "chintz prison." She is a pre-women's liberation example of an educated woman who believes that her abilities are not being used well in her role as wife and mother, however urbane the setting.

Elizabeth "Sweetie" Appleyard, a childhood sweetheart of Chick described by her father as an Emily Dickinson without talent. Hers is a case of arrested development—sexual and other—caused, her father thinks, by the traumatic interruption of Chick's early attempted seduction of her. After she has reentered Chick's life as a baby-sitter, her father asks Chick to complete the seduction. Chick fails, and she goes off to the Village to try to live like, if not be, a poet. Damning the bourgeois life, she asks Chick to father a child for her to rear and temporarily fools him into thinking her pregnancy was caused by him. After being found out, she heads for the West Coast, marries a divorced man with two children, and moves to a Los Angeles suburb.

Charles Appleyard, Sweetie's father, a widower who marries during the course of the novel. A failure at almost everything he has attempted, he nevertheless had the good sense to invest inherited money through his French connection—his wife's relatives—and thus is able to present himself as a sort of effete Adlai Stevenson. He probably is the cause of his daughter's holier-than-thou attitude, and he certainly is the cause of her enrichment, because he dies a moment or so before Sweetie's grandmother (both in the same plane crash), thus enabling the fortune to proceed directly to his daughter and not to his newly acquired wife.

Nickie Sherman, Chick's boyhood friend and brother-in-law. Like Chick, Nickie is a failed boulevardier; unlike Chick, however, he has not gone on to find any meaningful work. He cannot come to terms with the ordinariness of life, and his marriage, partly as a result of this failure, is breaking up. After a schizophrenic episode triggered by Chick's well-meaning but ill-conceived intervention, Nickie is shocked back to normality and into responsibility.

Lila Sherman, Chick's intelligent, down-to-earth sister, Nickie's wife. As the mother of two children, she has lost patience with her husband's intellectual philandering and his unwillingness to let his life be "disrupted by routine." When he finally becomes reconciled to reality, however, she accepts him; their lives are normalized, and their marriage is saved.

— *James H. Bowden*

TERMS OF ENDEARMENT

Author: Larry McMurtry (1936-   )
First published: 1975
Genre: Novel

Locale: Houston, Texas; Des Moines, Iowa; and Kearney and Omaha, Nebraska
Time: The 1960's and 1970's
Plot: Domestic realism

Aurora Greenway, a middle-aged, fairly prosperous widow in Houston, Texas. Aurora is incurably selfish but charming. She spends her time encouraging and then terrifying a host of middle-aged beaus. Her principal vanities are her lovely head of auburn hair, her vocabulary, and her authentic Renoir. Her principal disappointment—in addition to the suitors, who always fall short of her expectations—is her daughter, Emma, who is as ordinary as Aurora is eccentric. She bullies Emma and her suitors to make the most of themselves, to be more alive, and to seize the moment; often, though, her encouragements only paralyze them with terror.

Emma Horton, Aurora's only child, who lives in the shadow of her mother. Emma is bright, articulate, and capable of deep emotions, but she is mousy-haired, a little dumpy, and saddled with a bad marriage to a lethargic young English professor, Flap. Emma does not lack a spirit of adventure and has two romantic affairs, but they are without the flair and exuberance of her mother. Her strengths are principally as a mother and surface when she is dying of cancer and must plan for her children's future in the midst of a disintegrating marriage. While Aurora makes trivia into high drama, Emma effaces the great tragedy of her short life into daily domestic detail.

Rosie Dunlop, Aurora's maid, tiny and outspoken, tremendously attached to Emma, and usually at odds with Aurora. Rosie is a counterpoint to the romantic lives of Aurora and Emma. Her perpetual crises with her philandering husband, Royce, are essentially comic because they are forever resolvable. Rosie provides pithy and accurate commentary on the affectations and selfishness of Aurora; like all the others, however, she is under Aurora's spell.

Vernon Dalhart, a Texas oilman, one of Aurora's suitors. He is short and unimposing, and his most memorable feature is that he lives in his Lincoln in a parking garage that he owns in downtown Houston. He never quite succeeds in winning Aurora but is perennially there to solve her problems, help her dependents, and provide absolute adoration.

Hector Scott, a retired general who is Aurora's neighbor and her principal suitor. Hector is tall, gray in both hair and dress, and as rigid and conservative as a proper general should be. Hector is alternately floored and infuriated by Aurora's assumption of command of everyone, including him. His persistence, however, pays off; he is the only beau whom Aurora takes to bed.

Thomas "Flap" Horton, Emma's husband. Flap enters the story as a graduate student, then later is an English professor at small, unremarkable midwestern universities. His only energy is sexual; academically and emotionally, Flap is a wimp. His philandering breaks apart his family before Emma's cancer does. Flap's lethargy pressures Emma as much as her mother's exuberance does. Flap is an intriguing negative balance to Aurora in this novel, and neither values Emma appropriately.

— *Evelyn Romig*

TERRA NOSTRA

Author: Carlos Fuentes (1928-   )
First published: 1975
Genre: Novel

Locale: Rome, Paris, Mexico, and Spain
Time: The first century before Christ to 1999
Plot: Historical

Pollo Phoibee (POH-loh FOY-bee), in Spanish **Polo Febo** (POH-loh FEH-boh), a young man in Paris in 1999 who works as a sidewalk hawker carrying a sandwich board. He is inquisitive, adventurous, and handsome, with shoulder-length blond hair and only one hand. He is proclaimed in the novel as the seeker of ultimate truth and is perhaps the possessor of some mysterious knowledge. He is transformed into one of the three bastard sons of Felipe the Fair and becomes the lover of Joanna Regina, the widow of Felipe. At times, he seems to be one of the narrators of the novel. At the end of the novel, he performs an ecstatic act of love with Celestina, through which the two become one hermaphroditic being who gives birth to the new creature, the New World of the twenty-first century.

Celestina (seh-lehs-TEE-nah), a female pimp, a twentieth century transformation of the female procuress of the same name from the Spanish Renaissance work *Comedia de Calisto y Melibea* (1949; the play of Calisto and Melibea), by Fernando de Rojas. Young and beautiful, she has firm skin like a china teacup, and her lips are tattooed with violet, yellow, and green snakes. Dressed as a male page, she accompanies Pollo Phoibee on his search through history for eternal truth. At times, she seems to be a narrator of the novel as she tells her story, which forms a large part of the narrative. She is also transformed into a bride, raped by Felipe the Fair on her wedding night, who gives birth to one of his three bastard sons, the Pilgrim. She and Pollo Phoibee, in an act of sexual union on the last night of 1999, become transformed into a hermaphroditic creature who produces the new creature, the New World of the twenty-first century.

Felipe (feh-LEE-peh), also called **El Señor**, **Philip II** (1527-1598), the king of Spain from 1556 to 1598. He is portrayed in the novel as the son of Felipe the Fair and the Mad Lady, Joanna Regina, though historically he was their grandson and the son of Charles I, king of Spain from 1516 to 1559, and, as Charles V, was emperor of the Holy Roman Empire from 1519 to 1559. Educated from birth to be a strong monarch, Felipe is a tyrant intent on creating a perfect building, the royal palace and monastery, the Escorial, with the desire to contain, in one place, all time and space and to preserve an ascetic way of life, shutting out all lasciviousness and evil. He marries Elizabeth I of England (though historically Philip II pursued Elizabeth unsuccessfully after the death of his wife, Elizabeth's sister Mary Tudor). When one of the bastard sons of Felipe the Fair returns from an encounter with the Aztecs in the New World, Felipe refuses to admit the possibility of an unknown world beyond the oceans. Felipe orders his scribe, Guzmán, to transcribe his words exactly to create a definitive text of all experience, a document that will encompass all truth and grant Felipe ultimate power over the world.

Isabel (ee-sah-BEHL), also called **La Señora**, **Elizabeth I** (1533-1603), queen of England from 1558 to 1603. She is married to Felipe II (although, historically, she refused his offer of marriage after the death of her sister, Mary Tudor, who was in fact married to Felipe). Frustrated and confused by her husband's attempt to preserve an ascetic way of life within the walls of the royal palace, the Escorial, Isabel remains closeted away in a hidden room of the palace, in which she has created a Moorish pleasure salon furnished with white sand, blue water, and a bed of total sexual abandon. As she cultivates her hedonism, seeking in vain to ward off the devastating effects of the passage of time, she is haunted by a recurring nightmare of a mouse that "knows the truth" and gnaws incessantly at her genitals.

Felipe the Fair, Archduke Philip of Austria (1478-1506), who was **King Philip I** of Spain for several months before his death in 1506. He is the son of Emperor Maximilian (1459-1519) and married to Joanna Regina. He is the father of three bastard sons and of Felipe II (although historically he was the father of Charles V, emperor of the Holy Roman Empire). In the novel, after his death, his embalmed body, preserved against the ravages of time, is transported throughout Spain in a caravan led by his wife, the Mad Lady.

Joanna Regina (1479-1555), in Spanish **Juana la Loca** (HWAH-nah lah LOH-kah), the **Mad Lady**, the daughter of the Catholic monarchs Fernando of Aragon (reigned 1474-1516) and Isabel of Castilla (reigned 1474-1504). She is the widow of Felipe the Fair. Always dressed in mourning and heavily veiled, she travels in a caravan across Spain bearing the embalmed body of her dead husband and finally takes as her lover one of his bastard sons.

Guzmán (gews-MAHN), the secretary of Felipe (El Señor). He is the principal aide to the king, bureaucratic and opportunistic. He is responsible for recording all the king's words to create a compendium of all knowledge so that the king can acquire ultimate power over the world.

Fray Julián (hew-lee-AHN), a court artist commissioned to paint royal portraits. He is also a court confessor and knows the secrets of the palace. He travels to the New World and narrates part of the novel.

Don Juan (hwahn), a handsome and sensuous young man with a birthmark on his back in the shape of a cross. He is one of the three bastard sons of Felipe the Fair, born of Isabel, La Señora. He becomes the lover of first the Mad Lady and then of Isabel, who imprisons him in her bedchamber.

The Pilgrim, a handsome young man with a birthmark on his back in the shape of a cross and with six toes on each foot. He is one of the three bastard sons of Felipe the Fair, born of Celestina. He narrates the second part of the novel as the story of his journey to the New World and his encounter with the Aztecs.

The Idiot Prince, a young man also with a birthmark on his back in the shape of a cross and with six toes on each foot. He is one of the three bastard sons of Felipe the Fair, born of a she-wolf. He is forced by Joanna Regina to be a court jester.

Miguel de Cervantes (mee-GEHL deh sehr-VAHN-tehs), the fictionalized representation of the historical author of *Don Quixote de la Mancha* (1605, 1615). He appears as the chronicler in the novel, narrating a part of the story and transforming it into the story of the knight and his squire, Don Quixote and Sancho Panza.

Ludovico, a flagellant in the Parisian parade. He also appears as a student of theology and finally as the man who plays the role of father of the three mysterious bastard sons of Felipe the Fair.

Tiberius Caesar (ti-BIH-ree-uhs SEE-zur), the emperor of Rome from 14 to 37 C.E., assassinated by the reincarnated Agrippa Postumus, the heir to the throne designated by his father-in-law, Emperor Augustus. Because Tiberius had himself assassinated Agrippa, Tiberius' death is accompanied by a curse, which dictates that Agrippa would be revived in the form of three Caesars, born from the bellies of she-wolves, represented in the novel as the three young men, each with a red birthmark in the shape of a cross on his back and six toes on each foot.

— Gilbert Smith

TESS OF THE D'URBERVILLES: A Pure Woman Faithfully Presented

Author: Thomas Hardy (1840-1928)
First published: 1891
Genre: Novel

Locale: England
Time: Late nineteenth century
Plot: Philosophical realism

Tess Durbeyfield, a naïve country girl. When her father learns that his family is descended from an ancient landed house, the mother, hoping to better her struggling family financially, sends Tess to work for the Stoke-d'Urbervilles, who have recently moved to the locality. In this household, the innocent girl, attractive and mature beyond her years, meets Alec d'Urberville, a dissolute young man. From this time on, she is the rather stoical victim of personal disasters. Seduced by Alec, she gives birth to his child. Later, she works on a dairy farm, where she meets Angel Clare and reluctantly agrees to marry him, even though she is afraid of his reaction if he learns about her past. As she fears, he is disillusioned by her loss of innocence and virtue. Although she is deserted by her husband, she never loses her unselfish love for him. Eventually, pursued by the relentless Alec, she capitulates to his blandishments and goes to live with him at a prosperous resort. When Angel Clare returns to her, she stabs Alec. She spends a few happy days with Clare before she is captured and hanged for her crime.

Angel Clare, Tess's husband. Professing a dislike for effete, worn-out families and outdated traditions, he is determined not to follow family tradition and become a clergyman or a scholar. Instead, he wishes to learn what he can about farming, in the hope of having a farm of his own. When he meets Tess at a dairy farm, he teaches her various philosophical theories that he has gleaned from his reading. He learns that she is descended from the d'Urbervilles and is pleased by the information. After urging reluctant Tess to marry him, at the same time refusing to let her tell him about her past life, he persuades her to accept him; later, he learns to his great mortification about her relations with Alec. Although he himself has confessed to an episode with a woman in London, he is not as forgiving as Tess. After several days, he deserts her and goes to Brazil. Finally, no longer so provincial in his moral views, he remorsefully comes back to Tess, but he returns too late to make amends for his selfish actions toward her.

Alec d'Urberville, Tess's seducer. Lusting after the beautiful girl and making brazen propositions, he boldly pursues her. At first, she resists his advances, but she is unable to stop him from having his way in a lonely wood. For a time, he reforms and assumes the unlikely role of an evangelist. Meeting Tess again, he lusts after her more than ever and hounds her at every turn until she accepts him as her protector. Desperate when Angel Clare returns, she kills her hated lover.

Jack Durbeyfield, a carter of Marlott, Tess's indolent father. After learning of his distinguished forebears, he gives up work almost entirely and spends much of his time drinking beer in the Rolliver Tavern. He thinks that a man who has grand and noble "skillentons" in a family vault at Kingsbere-sub-Greenhill should not have to work.

Joan Durbeyfield, Tess's mother. After her hard labor at her modest home, she likes to sit at Rolliver's Tavern while her husband drinks a few pints and brags about his ancestors. A practical woman in a harsh world, she is probably right when she tells Tess not to reveal her past to Angel Clare.

Sorrow, Tess's child by Alec d'Urberville. The infant lives only a few days. Tess herself performs the rite of baptism before the baby dies.

Eliza-Louisa, called **Liza-Lu**, Tess's younger sister. It is Tess's hope, before her death, that Angel Clare will marry her sister. Liza-Lu waits with Angel during the hour of Tess's execution for the murder of Alec d'Urberville.

Abraham,

Hope, and

Modesty, the son and young daughters of the Durbeyfields.

The Reverend James Clare, Angel Clare's father, a devout man of simple faith but limited vision.

Mrs. Clare, a woman of good works and restricted interests. She shows little understanding of her son Angel.

Felix and

Cuthbert Clare, Angel Clare's conventional, rather snobbish brothers. They are patronizing in their attitude toward him and disapprove of his marriage to Tess Durbeyfield.

Mercy Chant, a young woman interested in church work and charity, whom Angel Clare's parents thought a proper wife for him. Later, she marries his brother Cuthbert.

Mrs. Stoke-d'Urberville, the blind widow of a man who grew rich in trade and added the name of the extinct d'Urberville barony to his own. Her chief interests in life are her wayward son Alec and her poultry.

Car Darch, also called **Dark Car**, a vulgar village woman. Because of her previous relations with Alec d'Urberville, she is jealous of Tess Durbeyfield. Her nickname is the Queen of Spades.

Nancy, her sister, nicknamed the Queen of Diamonds.

Mr. Tringham, the elderly parson and antiquarian who half-jokingly tells Jack Durbeyfield that he is descended from the noble d'Urberville family.

Richard Crick, the owner of Talbothays Farm, where Angel Clare is learning dairy farming. Farmer Crick hires Tess Durbeyfield as a dairymaid after the death of her child. Tess and Angel are married at Talbothays.

Christiana Crick, Farmer Crick's kind and hearty wife.

Marian, a stout, red-faced dairymaid at Talbothays Farm. Later, she takes to drink and becomes a field worker at Flintcomb-Ash Farm. She and Izz Huett write Angel Clare an anonymous letter in which they tell him that his wife is being pursued by Alec d'Urberville.

Izz Huett, a dairymaid at Talbothays Farm who is in love with Angel Clare. She openly declares her feelings after he deserts Tess. He is tempted to take Izz with him to Brazil, but he soon changes his mind. She and Marian write Angel a letter warning him to look after his wife.

Retty Priddle, the youngest of the dairymaids at Talbothays Farm. Also in love with Angel Clare, she tries to drown herself after his marriage.

Farmy Groby, the tightfisted, harsh owner of Flintcomb-Ash Farm, where Tess works in the fields after Angel Clare deserts her.

THADDEUS OF WARSAW

Author: Jane Porter (1776-1850)
First published: 1803
Genre: Novel

Locale: Poland and England
Time: Late eighteenth century
Plot: Historical

Thaddeus Sobieski (tah-DAY-uhsh soh-BEE-skih), actually the illegitimate son of an English aristocrat named Sackville. Reared in Poland by his mother and grandfather, he becomes a Polish patriot, fighting against Russia as long as he can. He finally becomes a refugee in England, taking the name of Mr. Constantine. He is put into debtors' prison because he cannot pay his bills from his small income as a tutor. He is rescued by his friend Pembroke Somerset, who turns out to be his half brother. Somerset recognizes the relationship and gives Thaddeus a portion of the family fortune so that Thaddeus can marry and settle down to a comfortable life as an English gentleman.

Count Sobieski, Thaddeus' grandfather and an enlightened Polish noble. A great Polish patriot and soldier, he is killed while fighting against the Russian oppressors of his country. Proud of his name, he makes Thaddeus promise to use no other.

Pembroke Somerset, a young English adventurer who fights for the Russian czar. He is captured by Thaddeus and becomes his friend. Later, he befriends Thaddeus in England and turns out to be Thaddeus' half brother.

General Kosciusko (kosh-TYEWSH-koh), the famous Polish patriot. He is one of Thaddeus' commanding officers.

General Butzou (BEW-tzuh), a Polish patriot and the friend of Thaddeus' family. Thaddeus befriends him when the two are refugees in London.

Mrs. Robson, Thaddeus' kind landlady in London.

Dr. Vincent, a money-hungry doctor who overcharges Thaddeus in London.

Lady Tinemouth, an Englishwoman rescued by Thaddeus from ruffians in Hyde Park.

Mary Beaufort, a young English woman who befriends Thaddeus, falls in love with him, and marries him. She is Pembroke Somerset's cousin.

Lady Sara Ross, Lady Tinemouth's friend. She tries to involve Thaddeus in an affair.

Dr. Cavendish, a London doctor who is kind to the Polish refugees.

Lady Dundas, an English woman who hires Thaddeus as a tutor for her daughter.

Euphemia Dundas, one of Thaddeus' pupils. She becomes infatuated with him.

Diana Dundas, another of Thaddeus' pupils.

THE THANATOS SYNDROME

Author: Walker Percy (1916-1990)
First published: 1987
Genre: Novel

Locale: Louisiana
Time: The 1980's
Plot: Moral

Thomas More, a psychiatrist, psychiatric outpatient, and bad Catholic in a dissolute and decrepit postmodern Feliciana Parish, Louisiana. Dr. Tom, as he is commonly known, has settled down with his Presbyterian bride, Ellen, into what he believes to be a comfortable, if somewhat unlucrative, private practice. His female patients begin making sexual advances, presenting him with their hindquarters in a gesture that Dr. Tom finds disturbingly simian. He discovers correlating evidence of something awry when a local Catholic priest, Father Smith, holes up in a fire tower and refuses to come down. His fears are confirmed when even his formerly stalwart and conservative wife begins to act strangely and suddenly blossoms into one of the best contract bridge players in the world. All these oddities turn Dr. Tom into a detective. His research eventually leads to his discovery of a physical crisis emblematic of a larger spiritual crisis, a chemically caused worship of death and deviance that has gripped the parish. Dr. Tom reveals the cause of this syndrome, but only after personally facing the temptations offered by the chemical pseudo-cure.

Ellen Oglethorpe More, the former nurse and longtime wife of Dr. Tom. Ellen becomes an inverse of her former self in the first two-thirds of the novel as she is affected by the sodium-based drug that two experimenters, Dr. Bob Comeaux and John Van Dorn, introduce into the water supply of Feliciana Parish. In addition to becoming a wizard at mathematical computations and card playing, Ellen loses her moral grip and has at least one extramarital affair.

Dr. Bob Comeaux, a bureaucrat responsible for the "sodium shunt" that releases a mind-altering drug into the water system. Comeaux, who has a fondness for Mercedes automobiles and Strauss waltzes, is an archetype of the social engineering scientist who prefers order to freedom and the exercise of the individual will. After Dr. Tom proves that the sodium-based drug leads to deviance and perversion, Comeaux skulks away and becomes a free-lance scientist who is said to work as a consultant to authoritarian governments.

John Van Dorn, the despicable counterpart to Comeaux's order-craving scientism. Van Dorn is a pseudoscientist whose health clinic becomes a center for child molestation and perverted sexuality. Poisoned by his own drug, Van Dorn is exposed as a pedophile, leading to the end of the Thanatos experiment.

Father Simon Rinaldo Smith, a Catholic priest who recognizes that the parish is in trouble. Smith's unusual solution is to climb into a fire tower and refuse to come down. Dr. Tom is chosen as ambassador to Smith, and he tries unsuccessfully to convince the priest to leave the tower. Father Smith's Dostoevski-like "confession" to Dr. Tom concerning his temptation by the death-worshiping Nazism of the 1930's forms the dramatic center of the novel. Whether Dr. Tom understands the symbolic importance of Father Smith's fable is uncertain, but he is led to act in a manner that brings to an end the possibility of a similar death cult in the parishes of Louisiana.

Lucy Lipscomb, Dr. Tom's cousin, an epidemiologist who becomes involved in his investigation. Her access to government data banks is a key part of his work.

— *Jeff Cupp*

THAT AWFUL MESS ON VIA MERULANA
(Quer pasticciaccio brutto de via Merulana)

Author: Carlo Emilio Gadda (1893-1973)
First published: 1957
Genre: Novel

Locale: Rome, Italy
Time: February and March, 1927
Plot: Impressionistic realism

Francesco Ingravallo (frahn-CHEHS-koh een-grah-VAHL-loh), also called **Don Ciccio** (CHEE-kee-oh), a Roman police inspector in charge of a robbery and homicide investigation. Don Ciccio is a bachelor but is perhaps a little in love with his good friend, Liliana Balducci, who is murdered. Don Ciccio is a complex figure; his patience, determination, hidden feelings, and skepticism are revealed only through his struggles to find Liliana's murderer. Despite his cynicism, Don Ciccio does not think like most people at his level in society. He always tries to give the poor a chance to defend themselves, rather than assume that they are automatically guilty because of their class.

Liliana Balducci (lee-lee-AH-nah bahl-DEW-chee), an emotionally and physically barren middle-aged woman. She is found in her apartment with her throat cut and her jewels stolen. To Don Ciccio, Liliana symbolized perfect femininity. During the murder investigation, however, a surprising side of Liliana is revealed. Unable to have children, Liliana had poured her affection on some young orphan girls, whom she had employed as housemaids and then helped to make good

marriages. Although she was cheated and disappointed every time by those reprobate young women, Liliana always found the strength to continue in her faith in them, helped by the tacit support of her husband, Remo. It seems probable that Liliana was murdered by one of her former protégées.

Corporal Pestalozzi (pehs-tah-LOHZ-zee), a carabiniere, or member of the national police. A coarse and spiteful man, Corporal Pestalozzi succeeds primarily through use of brute force. It is he (with his men) who brings the case to a head when he locates the jewelry stolen from the apartment building on Via Merulana.

Zamira Pacori (zah-MEE-rah PAH-kohr-ree), a laundress and former prostitute. Zamira is a grotesque old woman whose current occupation is a cover for her activities as a bawd, a sorceress, and a faith healer. She surrounds herself with poor, unfortunate young women just as Liliana did, though for more sinister reasons.

— *Rosaria Pipia*

THAT NIGHT

Author: Alice McDermott (1953-   )
First published: 1987
Genre: Novel

Locale: Long Island, New York
Time: The 1960's to the 1980's
Plot: Social realism

The narrator, never named, who was ten years old at the time of "that night," when the most important episode of the novel occurs. For the narrator, the central love story of a real teenage romance dominates her Barbie doll dreams. As the narrator comes to maturity, she is able to see that the events of "that night," when Rick and his friends were attacked by the men of the neighborhood in defense of Mrs. Sayles, were central not only to her childish dreams but also to the aspirations of all the suburbanites who sought happiness with mates and children in their own single-family houses.

Sheryl Sayles, the fifteen-year-old heartthrob of Rick. Slight of build, with thin nondescript hair and light brown eyes, she wears tight skirts and even tighter sweaters. Her makeup is thick, her eyeliner blotched, and her thin hair teased by a teasing comb she keeps in her purse or back pocket. She wears a "slave chain" on her ankle, along with her young lover's silver I.D. bracelet. Her father died prematurely, leaving her with a void to fill in her young life and a reckless attitude toward living. She is the first female on the block to enter adolescence.

Rick, a seventeen-year-old "hood," complete with hot rod. Rick knows that when Sheryl speaks of death, it is time for him to make love to her. Both of Rick's parents are alive, but his mother is suicidal and his father has given up practicing medicine out of some pride that made it impossible for him to keep accounts of the money his patients owed him or to continue as a professional healer when his wife continued in her attempts to take her own life.

Mrs. Sayles, Sheryl's mother, who is as emptied by her husband's death as Sheryl is. She knows exactly what to do when Sheryl admits her pregnancy to her mother. It is as if the situation already had a script kept in readiness for girls unlucky enough to show material signs of their sexuality. Mrs. Sayles and Sheryl are one family among several—the Evers, the Carpenters, the Rossis, and the narrator's—all of which will come to a time when the poignancy of a first love will be balanced by a long life of everyday reality.

— *Mary Rohrberger*

THAT UNCERTAIN FEELING

Author: Kingsley Amis (1922-1995)
First published: 1955
Genre: Novel

Locale: Aberdarcy, Wales
Time: Mid-1950's
Plot: Ironic

John Lewis, a young assistant librarian in the Welsh community of Aberdarcy. Married five and a half years and the father of two small children, he is restless, bored, and vaguely dissatisfied with his lot, play-acting at life rather than living it. Poorly paid and with only the hypochondriac Mrs. Jenkins as baby-sitter, he and his wife are tied down to their crowded, cluttered flat. Although he loves his wife, he has been faithful more through luck than self-restraint, and he readily becomes involved with local socialite Elizabeth Gruffydd-Williams when she displays an interest in him. Her husband has offered to support Lewis in his application for a more prestigious position at the library. Although he is uncomfortable with the idea of Gruffydd-Williams pulling strings to get him the job, Lewis nevertheless takes up with the local crowd of socialites, simultaneously attracted to and repulsed by this rich, reckless, English-acting, party-going crowd. Enthralled by the prospect of fancy cars, beautiful women, and freedom, he imagines that he fits in with this elite group, but they laugh at him behind his back. Eventually realizing the shallow, even dangerous, nature of these pseudo-English Welshmen, he returns with his family to his hometown, finally comfortable with his Welsh heritage.

Elizabeth Gruffydd-Williams, the beautiful black-haired, fair-skinned wife of a prominent Aberdarcy citizen. Traveling with a fast crowd, she intends to make John Lewis her latest conquest upon their first meeting at the library. A heavy drinker, she has a penchant for stirring up trouble and making romantic conquests. Heedless of the consequences of her actions and of other people's feelings, she exists only to be amused, certain that she will be rescued by her husband if a situation gets out of control.

Jean Lewis, John's wife, a small woman with dark red hair, large eyes, and a thin, full-lipped face. She is visibly tired and drawn from rearing two small, demanding children. Confined to the family's flat day after day, she realizes immediately that her husband is involved with Elizabeth and her crowd. She is deeply hurt and shuts him out of her life until he realizes how foolish he has been.

Vernon Gruffydd-Williams, Elizabeth's husband, a prominent Aberdarcy citizen. A wealthy member of the town council and Library Committee, he is willing to use his authority to get Lewis appointed to the sub-librarian position merely because he wants to irritate a colleague who does not like Lewis. Apparently used to his wife's flings with other men, he is there to bail her out when she gets in over her head.

Ieuan Jenkins, Lewis' coworker at the library. A man in his late forties, Jenkins is desperate to be appointed to the sub-librarian job that Lewis has applied for, knowing that it represents his last chance for relief from his sickly wife's whining.

Mrs. Jenkins, Ieuan Jenkins' wife and occasional baby-sitter for the Lewis children. She constantly complains of her frail health, although doctors have found nothing wrong with her. She insists that her husband must get the sub-librarian job at the Aberdarcy library.

Bill Evans, a member of Elizabeth's crowd. Evans, from all indications, was Elizabeth's most recent fling before her interest in Lewis. Once Lewis enters the picture, Evans is reduced to fetching and carrying for Elizabeth, baby-sitting the Lewis children, and hauling groceries and drinks for parties.

Gareth Probert, a scruffy, poetry-writing office worker who has been taken up by Elizabeth's crowd. He shows some romantic interest in Jean Lewis.

— *Mary Virginia Davis*

THAT VOICE
(Cette Voix)

Author: Robert Pinget (1919-1997)
First published: 1975
Genre: Novel

Locale: The fictional French villages of Fantoine and Agapa
Time: Indeterminate
Plot: Impressionistic realism

Aléxandre Mortin (ah-lehk-SAHNDR mohr-TA[N]), a failed author and would-be historian. At the age of twenty, he published some poems in the *Fantoniard*, the local newspaper, and then earned a scant living as a hack writer. With his small mustache; old, greasy hat; and pince-nez glasses, he was a common sight in the village of Fantoine as he went about collecting all forms of printed matter—newspapers, advertisements, and catalogs—and gossip in an effort to chronicle the history of his family and region. Given to drink and perhaps senile in his later years, he never organizes all the papers he accumulates. His death is mysterious; various accounts claim that he died of a heart attack, committed suicide, was strangled or poisoned, or was stabbed by his maid, by her nephew, or by his own nephew and heir. Aléxandre's failure to make sense of the information he has gathered, like the multiple accounts of his death, reveals the impossibility of knowing, the uncertainty of what passes for truth.

Théodore (tay-oh-DOHR), Aléxandre Mortin's godson and nephew, or great-great-nephew, and heir. As a child, he may have lived with Aléxandre, whom he affectionately called Dieudonne or Dodo, because his own mother was too poor to support him or because Aléxandre bribed her and kept the boy as his homosexual lover. After Aléxandre's death, Théodore attempts to catalog his uncle's papers but fares no better than Mortin. Even wearing his uncle's pince-nez does not help him make sense of the material. His identity fuses with that of his uncle, suggesting again the difficulty of distinguishing fact from fancy, of knowing even oneself.

Alfred Mortin, Aléxandre's older brother, the first historian of the family. His wife ran away with a Spanish juggler. Alfred leaves his house, fortune, and papers to his younger brother, whom he had been supporting. The cause of Alfred's death, like that of his brother (with whom he is sometimes confused), is questionable: He may have died of a heart attack or a stab wound.

Léo (lay-OH), Alfred's favorite nephew. Léo goes to America, where he is presumed to have died, because no one hears from him.

Mademoiselle Moine (mwan), the president of the Dieudonne Foundations. After Théodore's death, she oversees the successful cataloging of Mortin's papers. Because Aléxandre's will prohibits the removal of his papers from his house, Théodore bequeathed the building to the town for its library. Mademoiselle Moine serves as the local librarian and hence as guardian of the material the Mortins accumulated.

Mademoiselle Francine de Bonne-Mesure (frahn-SEEN deh bon-may-ZEWR), a bookbinder who supposedly is rich. She donates her labor and material to bind the catalog that the Dieudonne Foundation has prepared.

Marie, the housekeeper for Alfred and Aléxandre Mortin. She may be given to drink and senility like her master, or she may be a teetotaler who tries to help Théodore organize Aléxandre's papers.

Louis (lwee), Marie's nephew or lover. Perhaps a waiter, he is poor and relies on Marie for money.

— *Joseph Rosenblum*

THE THAW
(Ottepel)

Author: Ilya Ehrenburg (1891-1967)
First published: 1954
Genre: Novel

Locale: A small town in the Soviet Union
Time: Early 1950's
Plot: Social realism

Elena (Lena) Borissovna Zhuravliov (boh-rih-SOHV-nah zhew-rahv-LYOV), a Soviet schoolteacher. Attractive, intelligent, and cultured, she is a thirty-year-old wife and mother who has become dissatisfied with her life. She finds purpose in her career as a teacher but no emotional satisfaction in her relationship with her husband. She unwittingly falls in love with her husband's coworker, Dmitri Koroteyev, who is also cultured and sensitive. When she realizes the seriousness of her affection, she leaves her husband. Mistakenly believing that her love is unrequited, she lives solitarily until a chance encounter brings her and Dmitri together.

Ivan Zhuravliov, a factory manager, several years older than Lena. He has grown stout and sedate with marriage. Committed to increasing production, he puts machines ahead of workers and his job before his family. Soon after Lena leaves him, a storm destroys shoddily built housing that he constructed for employees. Well-meaning but bewildered by private as well as public humiliation, he loses both his family and his career.

Dmitri Koroteyev (DMIH-tree koh-roh-TEH-yehv), an engineer in Zhuravliov's factory. Thirty-five years old and regarded as a model worker, he is quiet and somewhat reclusive. His wife was killed in the Great Patriotic War against the Nazis, and he has since resisted any emotional involvement. His friendship with Lena grows from their mutual love of books and ideas. Unaware of the depth of his passion for her or of her passion for him, he hesitates to act after she leaves Ivan. At the end of a long, bitter winter, he can no longer stifle his need for affection and approaches Lena.

Andrey Pukhov (ahn-DRAY PEW-khov), an old schoolmaster, sixty-four years of age, who acted as Lena's mentor, inspiring her with ideals about learning and living. He supports her separation from Ivan.

Vladimir (Volyoda) Andreyevich Pukhov (vla-DIH-mihr voh-LY-oh-dyah ahn-DREH-yeh-vihch), Andrey's son, an artist. He has grown cynical by painting industrial scenes that sell well to bureaucrats but do not reflect his own aesthetic aspirations. Like Ivan, he has lost the ability to love by concentrating on his social advancement. Although he constantly attracts women, he is unable to find love.

Saburaov (sah-BEW-rov), an artist and friend of Volyoda. He and his wife, Glasha, live miserably on her bookkeeper's salary, but they live contentedly, with passion compensating for poverty.

Sonya, Andrey's daughter, who is studying to be an engineer. Although she loves literature, she is determined to pursue a practical career. At the age of twenty-five, she has just finished school and taken her first job, though it means breaking off a romance with Savchenko, Dmitri's coworker.

Vera Scherer, a physician at the factory. Like Dmitri, she is a veteran of the war whose lover was killed in the fighting. She dedicates herself to work to stifle her own emotions. She is thirteen years older than Lena and serves as Lena's confidant and supporter.

— *Robert M. Otten*

THE THEBAID
(Thebais)

Author: Statius (Publius Papinius Statius, c. 45-c. 96 C.E.)
First transcribed: c. 90 C.E.
Genre: Poetry

Locale: Argos, Nemea, and Thebes
Time: Antiquity
Plot: Epic

Oedipus (EHD-ih-puhs), a king of Thebes. By the time the *Thebaid* opens, he has killed his father and married his mother, has blinded himself, and has been deposed. He does not appear often in the work, but he is important as a motivating force, for it is his curses on his ungrateful sons that set the action of the story in motion. Traditionally, Oedipus has been viewed as a kind of demigod, made more than human by the depths of his fall from glory and by his terrible suffering. The *Thebaid* follows the tradition, surrounding Oedipus with an aura of the more-than-human. Oedipus shows little personality beyond an all-consuming rage.

Jocasta (joh-KAS-tuh), the mother and wife of Oedipus. She plays a small role, but her legendary status makes her larger than life. In book VII, she attempts to arrange a meeting and reconciliation between her two sons, but she fails. Later, she attempts to stab herself over their bodies. If Oedipus is presented almost entirely in terms of rage, Jocasta is the image of grief.

Eteocles (eh-TEE-oh-kleez), one of the two sons of Oedipus. His unwillingness to surrender the throne at the end of his one-year term is the cause of the invasion led by his brother, Polynices. He is presented as the Greek stereotype of the tyrant—greedy, suspicious, cruel, arrogant, and bad-tempered. He is more a type than a person.

Polynices (pol-ih-NI-seez), the exiled son of Oedipus. He leads the Argive invasion of Thebes. Although presented as proud, resentful, and envious, he seems a little less self-assured than his brother. It is only the interference of Tydeus that prevents him from agreeing to a meeting with his brother that might have led to a reconciliation. In general, he is presented as being as proud and egocentric as his brother. If Eteocles is to blame for creating the crisis by not surrendering the throne, Polynices is equally guilty for invading his homeland. Both are also guilty of mistreating their father. Polynices is neither a tragic nor a sympathetic figure.

Tydeus (TI-dews), the prince of Calydon and one of the seven leaders in the war against Thebes. He is small in stature but ferocious in temperament. At their first meeting, he and

Polynices quarrel violently, but they later become allies. Returning from Thebes, he single-handedly kills a large ambushing party. He opposes any move toward peace between the brothers. He also possesses the qualities of honor and loyalty, and he never wavers in his support for Polynices' cause.

Adrastus (uh-DRAS-tuhs), the king of Argos. He is wise and cautious but is drawn into the war by the workings of fate. He is more levelheaded and takes a longer view than do the other characters. In book XI, he attempts to come between the brothers, but he fails to prevent their killing each other. His personality is largely undeveloped.

Hypsipyle (hihp-SIHP-ih-lee), the former queen of Lemnos. After a series of adventures, she becomes a slave of the king and queen of Nemea. Her long account of her misfortunes, which interrupts the action for a full book, is both exotic and pathetic but is not an integral part of the main action. Her character is essentially undeveloped.

Creon (KREE-on), Jocasta's brother, who succeeds Eteocles on the throne of Thebes. His rash refusal to allow the slain Argives to be buried leads to his death and the defeat of Thebes. Although his refusal to allow burial is harsh and impious, it arises from grief over his son's death rather than from a tyrannical nature. He comes to the throne not through his own pride and ambition but because no nearer claimant remains alive.

Tiresias (ti-REE-sih-uhs), a blind seer of Thebes.

Jupiter (Zeus in Greek), the king of the gods, presented as majestic and awe-inspiring, a sort of ideal picture of a Roman emperor. It is his anger at the Greeks that allows the general catastrophe of the war.

Juno (Hera in Greek), the wife of Jupiter. She is generally presented as vile-tempered, jealous, and fiercely protective of those cities dedicated to her. She pleads for peace to protect her city of Argos but is cowed by Jupiter's power.

Venus (Aphrodite in Greek), the goddess of sexual love and beauty. She is not a warrior goddess but is made formidable by her guile and skill at seduction. She is a partisan of Thebes.

— *Jack Hart*

THEIR EYES WERE WATCHING GOD

Author: Zora Neale Hurston (1891-1960)
First published: 1937
Genre: Novel

Locale: Florida
Time: c. 1897-1921
Plot: Bildungsroman

Janie Crawford Killicks Starks Woods, the novel's central character, a beautiful, romantic, and hopeful black woman who, over the course of thirty years and three marriages, grows into an attractive, life-affirming, and independent woman. As an adolescent, Janie imagines life and especially marriage as a blossoming pear tree kissed by singing bees. She has her first experience of sexual ecstacy under the pear tree in her grandmother's backyard. Her first two marriages end in disappoint-

ment, but Tea Cake, her third husband, reminds her of a pear tree blossom in spring. Even after Janie kills Tea Cake in self-defense, he lives in her memory, associated with sunshine and life's plenty.

Nanny Crawford, Janie's grandmother, who rears Janie while keeping house for the white Washburn family. Born into slavery, Nanny flees a Georgia plantation when its white mistress, rightly suspecting Nanny to be her husband's lover, threatens to kill her and sell her daughter Leafy (later Janie's mother). Leafy is raped by her schoolteacher and leaves Janie to be reared by Nanny. Because experience has taught Nanny that "de nigger woman is de mule uh de world," she forces Janie to marry for protection rather than love. Nanny dies a month after Janie's first wedding, unforgiven by Janie.

Logan Killicks, Janie's first husband, an older, responsible, and well-to-do farmer and landowner. Janie, at the age of sixteen, thinks that he looks like "some ole skullhead in de grave yard" and marries him only because Nanny insists. When Logan decides to buy a second mule so that Janie can work in the fields, she runs off with Joe Starks and never sees Logan again.

Joe Starks, Janie's ambitious second husband, whose goal is to become rich and powerful. Janie runs off with him because he promises her comfort and social position and because he reminds her of rich white people. In the black town of Eatonville, Florida, Joe opens a store and is elected mayor. As he gains power, however, he becomes less loving and less loved: He resents Janie's desire for independence, as well as her youthful beauty, and he is resented by the townspeople because he demands their obedience. Mistakenly convinced that Janie is poisoning him, he dies a frightened, solitary, and pathetic man. His death leaves Janie an independently wealthy woman.

Vergible "Tea Cake" Woods, Janie's adored third husband, who is playful, charming, and vital. Although Janie suspects that the much younger Tea Cake might be after her money, she takes a risk, marries him, and never regrets her decision. Tea Cake not only loves Janie but also, unlike Joe, encourages her growth toward independence by teaching her skills and praising her talents. During a hurricane, Tea Cake is bitten by a rabid dog while protecting Janie. When he becomes mad himself, Janie must shoot him to save her own life.

Pheoby Watson, Janie's closest friend, a loyal, intelligent, and affectionate woman. Janie tells the story of her life to Pheoby, with the understanding that Pheoby will share it with others. When Janie finishes, Pheoby says, "Ah done growed ten feet higher from jus' listenin' tuh you."

Mrs. Turner, a prideful, thin-lipped, light-skinned black woman who worships Caucasian traits and cannot stand dark-skinned black people. She tries, but fails, to have her no-account brother win Janie away from Tea Cake.

— *Donald A. Daiker*

THEM

Author: Joyce Carol Oates (1938-   )
First published: 1969
Genre: Novel

Locale: The Midwest
Time: 1937-1967
Plot: Naturalism

Loretta Wendall, née **Botsford**, the mother of Jules and Maureen. A generally passive and not particularly intelligent woman, she has an extravagantly romantic nature that is never satisfied. Her one truly independent gesture, an escape to Detroit from the stifling home of her in-laws, ends in humiliation but does achieve her goal of leaving the country for the city. As she grows older, she becomes more limited in her aspirations and more shrewish in her complaints. She is crudely racist and moralistic but is also a survivor in a brutal and violent environment. She drinks to avoid facing the blankness of much of her life and generally neglects her family. She changes character, dreams, lifestyle, and men, depending on her situation. Her children are baffled and frustrated by her inconsistencies in behavior and in her often irrational and unpredictable actions toward them. The Detroit riots destroy her home, but rather then discouraging or defeating her, this experience actually rekindles some of her old desire for adventure and excitement.

Howard Wendall, Loretta's husband and the father of Jules and Maureen. Stolid and unintelligent, Howard is dominated by his mother. A policeman at the start of the book, he is later forced to work at jobs that he hates. Unable to meet the emotional needs of his wife or of his children, he has become a mere shell by the time of his death.

Jules Wendall, the son of Loretta and Howard. He continues the romantic tendencies of his mother, often to his own destruction. Searching for wealth and adventure, he roams Detroit's streets, stealing and living independently even as a child. When he is older, he runs off with an unstable rich girl, who first abandons and later shoots him. He also becomes involved with a wealthy and bombastic but ineffectual criminal who is murdered. Through each disaster, Jules continues a deep love for his family, none of whom, however, can meet his needs. After a period of severe depression, during which he exists as a pimp, the violence of the Detroit riots serves as a catalyst and reawakens his romantic need for adventure and self-importance.

Maureen Wendall, the daughter of Loretta and Howard. She shares her mother and her brother's romantic nature, but eventually she responds to the brutality of the life around her by abandoning her dreams of being a teacher, repudiating her family, and deliberately entrapping and marrying one of her college professors. She then settles into the highly respectable middle-class life of which her mother had dreamed but never achieved, setting up a barrier between herself and her past. This past includes a brutal and almost fatal beating by one of her mother's husbands, who discovered that she had been prostituting herself to earn money to escape her life at home.

— *Eleanor H. Green*

THEOPHILUS NORTH

Author: Thornton Wilder (1897-1975)
First published: 1973
Genre: Novel

Locale: Newport, Rhode Island
Time: Summer, 1926
Plot: Social realism

Theophilus (Teddy) North, the stiff and stuffy narrator. North has recently quit his teaching job at a prestigious boys' preparatory school in Raritan, New Jersey, and has come back to Newport, Rhode Island, where he was stationed during World War I (1919-1920). He returns older and wiser, having finished college and lived in Europe for a year, to work for the summer as tennis coach, companion, and tutor to the wealthy residents of Newport. Conscious of his own middle-class background, North draws clear lines between himself and his employers (refusing, for example, to be entertained in their homes), but his regular interactions with these rich residents of the seaside resort allow him glimpses into their lives of privilege and leisure. Priggish and pedantic, a real "planner," as one character calls him, North is constantly lecturing his employers about what they should do to change and then setting up elaborate schemes (often involving wild stories or lies) to bring about the necessary transformations. He is both a savior figure and a cupid, either helping people to transform their lives or matching people who should be together. His means and methods are highly manipulative and usually involve some type of deceit. North is, at least in background, a thinly disguised portrait of the author, but his formal manners and didactic relations with others seem closer to the seventy-five-year-old author than to his thirty-year-old character. In contrast to some of the cardboard characters in the various stories, North has a certain three-dimensional, if punctilious, reality.

Diana Bell, the spoiled and headstrong daughter of one of the oldest families of Newport. North is hired by her father to head off her elopement, and he does it in such a way that no one is hurt. Other influential people hear of his exploits.

Miss Norine Wyckoff, the last of a line of Newport aristocrats. Her house supposedly is haunted, but North helps her to dispel that rumor so that servants will again stay there at night and she can as well. This story demonstrates more about how North operates: He digs into the past, finds out much about the residents and their history (here, about how the story of the haunted house got started), sets up an elaborate scheme (as usual involving, often unknowingly, several other characters), and carries it to its successful conclusion.

Flora Deland, a gossip columnist, originally a part of the Newport colony but now an outsider, digging around trying to uncover juicy items for her national gossip columns. She is not a bad person, but her parties are wild "flapper" affairs at which much liquor and indiscretion may flow. She is the object of gossip herself, but North helps her, as he helps so many others, to acquire a better reputation.

Dr. James McHenry Bosworth, a seventy-four-year-old widower and former diplomat who is trapped in his own mansion, Nine Gables, by his family and servants. Dr. Bosworth is interested in philosophy, which he and North read together. As usual, this job soon turns into more, and North helps to free this bright and vibrant man from the prison of his own estate.

Persis Tennyson, Dr. Bosworth's granddaughter, who lives on his estate with her son in a small cottage. North is half in love with Persis himself but works instead to fix her up with Bodo Stams. First, he must clear her name. She is a widow who lost her husband when he shot himself, not out of despon-

dency, but rather, as North proves, because of his own reckless way of living. Persis really loved her husband but lives hidden under the shadow cast by his tragic death until North proves that it was an accident and not suicide.

Baron Bodo von Stams, an Austrian diplomat who summers with friends in Newport. Convivial and loyal, cultured and intelligent, Stams gets as close to North as anyone in Newport does, and he helps North in several of his adventures. In return, North helps Stams to win Persis, with whom he is in love, and the novel closes on the expectation that the two will marry.

Henry Simmons, a British manservant who first befriends North in a pool hall and then introduces him to other people in Newport who become his friends and confidants.

Amelia Cranston, the owner of a servants' boardinghouse, the woman who knows more about what is going on in Newport, and about what has gone on in the past, than perhaps anyone else. Her relations with the chief of police and other officials in the town allow her access to information and assistance when she needs either. She helps North in several of his adventures, and the parlor of her boardinghouse acts as the hub of the wheel for North during this summer.

Edweena Wills, Henry Simmons' fiancée, a woman with whom North spent one night at the end of World War I. Neither of them allows Simmons to learn of this liaison, and the three remain friends. Wills is a ladies' maid who has risen to be respected as the epitome of her profession and now also owns several dress shops and has gained financial independence.

Colonel Nicholas "Rip" Vanwinkle, a World War I flying ace and a classmate of North at Yale. He hires North to help him with his German, for his remaining life's desire is to return to Berlin for a reunion of the flyers on both sides in the air wars of World War I. Vanwinkle is a prime example of what wealth does to a man; in this case, it is his wife's wealth. A true war hero, he is trapped by his wife's wealth, but North helps him to begin to free himself.

Charles Fenwick, a shy and precocious teenager whom North frees from his adolescent hangups about sex. Thanks to North's help, Fenwick is permanently changed and ends his chapter speaking French easily with his tutor and holding sophisticated conversations with his parents.

Myra Granberry, a young woman to whom North reads the classics. She slowly comes to read and enjoy them on her own. What North does in the Granberry household is another one of his miraculous metamorphoses: He gets George Granberry to give up his mistress and recommit himself to his pregnant and insecure wife.

Benjamino "Mino" Matera, a brilliant young man who lost both feet in a childhood accident and is confined to the store/house of his Italian family. He earns money by devising clever puzzles for newspapers. North gets Matera to overcome his self-consciousness about his handicap. By the end of his chapter, he is relating to others much more easily, particularly to women.

Alice, the unhappy wife of a sailor. North meets her in a restaurant one night. She is convinced that her problems will be solved if she has a baby, and North tries to oblige her.

Miss Elspeth Skeel, the young heir of The Deer Park, an extensive estate containing myriad examples of animal life.

She suffers from terrible migraine headaches. North shows that her attacks are the result not of medical problems but rather of the hermetic conditions in which she is kept by her strict Danish father. North "lays hands" on Skeel and cures her, but his success owes less to any shamanistic abilities than to the honest way in which he treats her and the hope that he gives her for her future.

— *David Peck*

THERE ARE CRIMES AND CRIMES
(Brott och Brott)

Author: August Strindberg (1849-1912)
First published: 1899
Genre: Drama

Locale: Paris, France
Time: Late nineteenth century
Plot: Symbolic realism

Maurice, a young Parisian playwright. Assured that his play will be a success, he promises to marry Jeanne, his mistress. She gives him a tie and gloves to wear on the opening night. That afternoon, he meets Henriette, the mistress of his friend Adolphe. Although he is falling in love, he has a presentiment of evil. His play is a triumph, but Maurice, instead of going to the celebration party, meets Henriette, who declares her love and throws Jeanne's gifts into the fire. Planning to flee with Henriette, Maurice visits his daughter Marion. After his visit, the child is found dead, and he and Henriette are arrested for murder. They are released for lack of evidence, but Maurice's career is ruined. He and Henriette, now hating each other, separate. After his exoneration, he regains popularity, and he and Jeanne are reunited.

Jeanne, Maurice's mistress, whom he deserts for Henriette but to whom he returns.
Marion, their young daughter. Maurice is suspected of her murder, but she had died of a rare disease.
Henriette, the mistress of Adolphe and later of Maurice. She has assisted in a fatal abortion and has turned to wantonness through dread of her past. She breaks with Maurice and returns to her home.
Adolphe, a painter and Henriette's lover.
The abbé, who brings Maurice to penitence.
Emile, Jeanne's brother.
Madame Catherine, the proprietor of the crêmerie where Maurice first meets Henriette.

THERE IS A TREE MORE ANCIENT THAN EDEN

Author: Leon Forrest (1937-1997)
First published: 1973
Genre: Novel

Locale: New Orleans, Louisiana; Memphis, Tennessee; and indeterminate locations
Time: Primarily the 1920's through the 1960's
Plot: Stream of consciousness

Nathaniel (Turner) Witherspoon, the boy who recalls most of the events in the book. He is intelligent and has a vivid imagination. His complexion is lighter than those of some of his black friends because his great-grandfather, on his father's side, was a white slave-owner. His father tried to instill in him the cultural myths of both black and white American society; consequently, Nathaniel is torn between the two worlds. He painfully tries to reconstruct his own identity as well as understand his role in a world beset by racial strife. Nathaniel's attempts to resolve his internal conflicts form the basis in the book for questions concerning wider social issues.

Aunt Hattie Breedlove "Breedy" Wordlaw, Nathaniel's aunt, who, aside from his father, is the greatest influence in Nathaniel's life. She is wise and shrewd and tries to counteract the attempts by Nathaniel's father to make his son into a great, heroic "man." She is gentle with Nathaniel but can be tough when necessary. A devout Christian, she believes that only love and self-sacrifice can better the world. Breedy tries to teach Nathaniel love, dignity, pride, and inner strength.

Jamestown Fishbond, Nathaniel's boyhood friend, later an artist and criminal. He is an Afro-Indian described as ebony-black in complexion and six feet, one inch tall. Extremely intelligent, he is a prodigious reader, a very good painter, and a speaker of several languages. He is also a superior chess player and has published articles dealing with jazz. As gifted as Jamestown is, he has also been diagnosed as a manic-depressive and paranoic with a personality dislocation crisis. He struggles with alcoholism and drug addiction, and he serves time in jail on several occasions. Eventually, he becomes involved with violence in Mozambique and is killed. His obvious talents make him the perfect idol for the young Nathaniel, but his hatred of white people and his poor method of dealing with his own identity crisis show Nathaniel how not to be.

Madge Ann Fishbond, Jamestown's older sister. She becomes streetwise at a very young age because she has to survive the terrible poverty that breaks up her family and kills her mother prematurely. Despite the harshness of her surroundings while growing up, she does not become embittered, as Jamestown does. It is through her that the reader learns more about Jamestown and the Fishbond family.

Hilda Mae Fishbond, Jamestown and Madge's mother. She manages to rear her eight children alone after her husband abandons them. The strain becomes too much, and one night she attempts to burn down the tenement where they live. Luckily, everyone escapes. After that, she continues to support her family by working as a cleaning lady for rich, white families. She dies of a heart attack while at her job.

Jericho Witherspoon, Nathaniel's grandfather, a slave and son of a white slave-owner. He was intelligent and deft with his hands. He is described as six feet, five inches tall, with reddish, curly hair and having a reddish brown complexion.

He was taught to read and write by his father. Jericho ran away from his father in 1850 and was considered dangerous. Although he thought of himself as white, he was also said to have hated white society. He worked for the freedom of black people.

Taylor "Warm-Gravy" James, a pianist. He writes scores for musicals and folk operas, eventually becoming quite well known for his work as well as for his political views. He joins the Islamic religion, changing his name to Ebn-Allah, Al-Fatir. He is also a health food addict and does not smoke, use alcohol, or take drugs.

Maxwell "Black-Ball" Saltport, Nathaniel's friend. He has minor scrapes with the law but then seems to become responsible, abruptly, eventually becoming a member of the California state council on prison reforms. He also wins a Medal of Freedom for his drug rehabilitation efforts. Under the influence of his uncle, Grandberry Persons Saltport, he converts to the Nation of Islam, receiving his X in the spring of 1956.

Goodwin "Stale-Bread" Winters, Nathaniel's friend. He is his high school class valedictorian in 1958. Four years later, Stale-Bread dies of a heroin overdose.

— *Ruth Hsu*

THÉRÈSE
(Thérèse Desqueyroux)

Author: François Mauriac (1885-1970)
First published: 1927
Genre: Novel

Locale: France
Time: The twentieth century
Plot: Psychological realism

Thérèse Desqueyroux (tay-REHZ dehs-keh-REW), a charming, introspective woman and the wife of Bernard Desqueyroux. Disgusted by her marriage to a materialistic husband, she is attracted by Jean Azévédo, her sister-in-law's lover. She tries to poison Bernard and is saved from conviction only by his desire to avoid scandal. Bernard allows her to move to Paris, where, years later, she is found by her daughter Marie, who has followed her lover there. Thérèse tries to help Marie, only to find that the lover, Georges Filhot, loves her, not her daughter. She confesses to him her crimes, real and imaginary, and advises him to break with Marie. She then sinks into a paranoiac state, imagining plots against her. Marie takes her back home, where, regaining her sanity, she prepares for death and deliverance from herself.

Bernard Desqueyroux, her husband, a provincial landowner filled with family pride and love of possessions. When Thérèse tries to poison him, he invents an explanation that saves her, thus avoiding scandal.

Marie Desqueyroux, their daughter, in love with Georges Filhot.

Georges Filhot (zhohrzh fee-LOT), a student, Marie's lover; later, he is in love with Thérèse.

Anne de la Trave (ahn deh lah trahv), Bernard's half sister, who is in love with Jean Azévédo.

Jean Azévédo (zhah[n] ah-zay-vay-DOH), a young intellectual, in love with Anne but attracted to Thérèse.

THÉRÈSE RAQUIN
(Un Mariage d'amour)

Author: Émile Zola (1840-1902)
First published: 1867
Genre: Novel

Locale: Paris, France
Time: 1852-1870
Plot: Naturalism

Madame Raquin (rah-KA[N]), a plump, sixty-year-old, doting mother who centers her life on her son, Camille, and gratifies his every whim. When he decides to go to Paris to look for a new position, she leaves her comfortable country retirement at Vernon and uses a portion of her savings to rent a miserable little haberdashery on a wretched Left Bank alley. Camille, his mother, and his wife, Thérèse, live a life of unbroken plainness and regularity until they are enlivened by Camille's vivacious coworker and friend, Laurent. After the seemingly accidental death of Camille, Madame Raquin's sorrow eventually is tempered by her apparently devoted daughter-in-law, Thérèse, and the thoughtful Laurent. She is maneuvered into suggesting their marriage. At first, they guard the secret of their culpability for Camille's death and hide their psychological torment from her. After Madame Raquin suffers a progressively debilitating paralysis, which leaves her unable to move or speak, Laurent, in one of his regular anguished and angry bouts with Thérèse, lets the truth slip out in front of the invalid. Unable to communicate the awful truth to the mem-

bers of the Thursday night gatherings, Madame Raquin festers in her hatred, relishing the destructive behavior of Thérèse and Laurent. She has the ultimate satisfaction of witnessing their double suicide.

Thérèse Raquin (tay-REHZ), the twenty-eight-year-old daughter of Madame Raquin's brother, Captain Degans. He left Thérèse to her aunt's care after the death of the toddler's Algerian mother. Thérèse, a strong and lissome person, has fine features, with dark hair and eyes. Madame Raquin decides that her niece and ward should marry her son, Camille. Although she is deeply repelled by Camille's sickly smell and touch, the passive Thérèse acquiesces. Without protest, she gives up the life in the country, which she loved, for the dismal shop and apartment in Paris. She molders away until her passionate nature is brought to life and unleashed by the advances of Laurent. When their secret but tempestuous affair is threatened by lack of opportunity, it is she who suggests the murder of her husband. After Camille's death, their ardor cools, and in its place grows guilt. They hope that their marriage will bring peace; instead, it brings greater guilt and psychological anguish. They cannot stand to touch each other, and the two engage in protracted bouts of hateful recrimination. Unable to find peace in dissipation, Thérèse, in despair, decides to escape Laurent and her own demons by killing him. Laurent, overwrought by guilt and haunted by the specter of Camille, has decided to poison her at precisely the same time. When they discover their mutual intent, they embrace. Thérèse takes the glass of poisoned water, drinks half, and hands it to Laurent, who consumes the remainder.

Camille Raquin (kah-MEEL), a thirty-year-old clerk. Camille is Madame Raquin's only son, whom she has overprotected because of his frail health. He is a slight, pale, and listless creature with colorless hair and an almost beardless but blotchy face, a mentally dull person devoid of imagination and passion. His only ambition is fulfilled when he obtains a clerical post with the Orleans Railway. He admires the elemental and vivacious Laurent, whom he introduces to his wife and mother. Completely unaware that Laurent has seduced Thérèse, Camille continues to bring him into his household. He does not suspect the fate that is in store for him when he suggests a walk in the country. He allows himself, despite his terror of water, to be shamed into a skiff on the Seine. As Laurent wrestles him out of the boat, Camille takes a deep bite out of his attacker's neck, thus leaving a lasting reminder of the deed.

Laurent (loh-RAH[N]), the tall, square-shouldered, and earthy son of a peasant, who attended school at Vernon with Camille and Thérèse. He went to Paris to study law but concentrated instead on his own ease and enjoyment until his father cut off his subsidies. Attracted by the bohemian lifestyle, he tried his hand at art. His lack of talent forces him to take a job at the office of the Orleans Railway. When he meets Thérèse, he regards her as an easy and insignificant conquest. Her unleashed animality, however, captivates him and awakens in him a latent sensitivity. After drowning Camille, Laurent goes daily to the morgue to look for his body. When the body finally is discovered and displayed, the bloated, decomposing horror of the corpse is deeply etched on Laurent's mind, and the recurring memory consumes him with guilt.

Michaud (mee-SHOH), a retired police superintendent, an old friend of Madame Raquin. He had retired to Paris after having been stationed in Vernon. After a chance meeting with Madame Raquin, the pasty and blotched-faced Michaud becomes a regular guest at her apartment on Thursday evenings, when the Raquins and their guests share tea, conversation, and dominoes. After the murder of Camille, Laurent goes immediately to Michaud, ostensibly for assistance in breaking the news to Madame Raquin. Michaud, whose primary concern is to continue his comfortable Thursday evenings, suspects nothing and gives his support to Laurent's version of the tragedy. He is manipulated into suggesting to Madame Raquin that the apparently pining Thérèse should marry and that the obvious choice is Laurent.

Grivet (gree-VAY), an old employee of the Orleans Railway, Camille's supervisor, and a regular at the Thursday night gatherings. Grivet has narrow features and thin lips but round eyes. The inner turmoil and growing loathing of Thérèse and Laurent for each other remains hidden from him and from the others. His lack of perception and self-centeredness are especially evident when he presumes, always erroneously, to be able to understand the unspoken wishes of Madame Raquin after her paralysis.

Olivier (oh-lee-VYAY), Michaud's son, another habitual participant at the Thursday night gatherings. A thirty-year-old, tall, lean, angular, arrogant, and egotistical chief clerk in the prefecture of police's Department of Public Order and Safety, Olivier unwittingly helps to deflect any possible suspicion from the murderers.

Suzanne, Olivier's small and flabby-faced wife, also a Thursday night regular. An intellectually dull and physically frail person of unattractive appearance, she idolizes Thérèse's vivacity.

— Bernard A. Cook

THESE THOUSAND HILLS

Author: A. B. Guthrie, Jr. (1901-1991)
First published: 1956
Genre: Novel

Locale: Oregon and Montana
Time: The 1880's
Plot: Historical realism

Albert Gallatin (Lat) Evans, a ranch hand and later a rancher. Twenty years old as the story begins, he is an only child, strongly influenced by his strict, upright father and by his good, gentle mother. He is daring, intelligent, and courageous, and he is determined to see life and to make his own way. Although later he passionately desires to be a respectable community leader, he will risk his reputation and even his marriage to save old friends who once helped him.

Tom Ping, Lat's companion, in his late twenties when the novel begins. Tom has dark skin and hair with a forelock that hangs over his forehead, a strong mouth, and even teeth. Having run away from his Texas home when he was ten years old, Tom is more defiant of society and more experienced in life than Lat. Their friendship deepens on the trail and in Indian captivity, but it breaks when Lat disapproves of Tom's marriage to a prostitute. Resentful of Lat's prosperity, Tom insults him in bars, even after Lat has saved him from being caught rustling, but he finally acknowledges publicly how much he admires Lat.

Callie Kash, a young prostitute, sweet-faced, considerate, slim, and pretty, with yellow hair and blue eyes. She goes to her aunt's brothel in Montana after having been seduced by her West Virginia lover. Deeply in love with Lat, she becomes his mistress. It is Callie who loans him her life savings so that he can bet on a horse race and make his fortune. Shielding the black servant who had defended her, Callie is herself accused of murder. Although Lat decides to risk everything to testify for her, Callie and the servant flee and thus protect him.

Joyce Sheridan, Lat's wife. Her coloring is striking: She has very pale skin, black hair, and black eyes. When Lat meets her, she is nineteen or twenty years old and has just finished her schooling. The niece of the storekeeper, she has come west from Indiana to be a schoolteacher. From the first, Joyce admits that she is frightened by the vastness of the new country. Although she admires and loves Lat, Joyce is unable to tolerate the uncouthness and immorality of his friends or to see the nobility often present beneath the rough surface. The revelation of Lat's former relationship with Callie almost destroys her feelings for her husband. Joyce proves to have depths of love that she had not previously sounded, however, and at the end of the novel welcomes him back to her arms.

Mike Carmichael, a trail rider. Short and wiry, he is already middle-aged when young Lat joins the cattle drive. Later, after Mike has been injured and disabled, Lat gives him a job on the ranch. Although Mike understands Tom Ping's continuing rebellion against a new, tamer society, he is willing to settle down with the country. On the hunt for rustlers, Mike keeps quiet about Ping's escape; he points out to Lat that his debt has thus been paid.

Jehu, a wealthy horse fancier. Tall and immaculately dressed, with a gray hat, a pearl-handled revolver, and spotless boots, he wagers that Lat cannot break his horse, Sugar. Lat wins the bet and begins to work for Jehu. Later, when Jehu cheats him out of his pay, Lat outsmarts him. When Sugar later wins a race against an Indian horse, Lat collects enough money to buy his ranch and begin his upward climb.

Brownie Evans, called **Pa**, Lat's father, a poor Oregon rancher. A straitlaced, respected man, he has always been moody and sometimes frighteningly temperamental. Even though the successful Lat avoids visiting his parents, he is strongly influenced by them. His upbringing will not let him marry Callie; instead, he must seek a respectable girl such as Joyce.

— *Rosemary M. Canfield Reisman*

THESMOPHORIAZUSAE
(Thesmophoriazousai)

Author: Aristophanes (c. 450-c. 385 B.C.E.)
First performed: 411 B.C.E.
Genre: Drama

Locale: Athens
Time: The fifth century B.C.E.
Plot: Satire

Euripides (yew-RIH-pih-deez), the tragic poet and a perennial butt of Aristophanes' satire, depicted in the broad strokes appropriate to farce. He is about to be punished by the Thesmophoriazusae, women who are celebrating the Feast of Demeter, because he has presented unflattering portraits of women on the stage and has, in the process, given away too many secrets of the sex. He does not know what fate is in store for him, but he wishes to have a friend at court if possible. He attempts to persuade Agathon to disguise himself as a woman, to mingle with the Thesmophoriazusae, and to speak up for him if need be. When Agathon refuses, Mnesilochus agrees to attempt the deception. In spite of his promise to rescue his friend should the trick not carry, Euripides is obviously much more interested in his own safety than in saving Mnesilochus from discomfiture, but after the disguise is penetrated, he comes to the rescue when Mnesilochus begins to hurl small wooden images from the temple, each inscribed with a plea for help, a parody of a device used by Euripides himself in his *Palamedes*. Once on the scene, Euripides joins Mnesilochus in befuddling the women by reciting wildly burlesqued passages from his own tragedies. When Mnesilochus is arrested and fastened to a post (a situation that permits Euripides to play first Echo and then Perseus to Mnesilochus' Andromeda), Euripides disguises himself as an old bawd and, having promised never to write ill things of women again, releases his friend while the guard is engaged with a dancing girl he has provided.

Mnesilochus (neh-SIH-loh-kuhs), Euripides' madcap friend and father-in-law. After being painfully shaved, depilated, and dressed in a woman's robe, he joins the celebrants in the temple. He presumably would have gone undetected had he been able to keep quiet during the debate on the punishment to be accorded Euripides for his insults to women. In his defense of the poet, however, he insults the women even more. When Clisthenes announces to the enraged women that Euripides has sent a disguised man among them, he is quickly discovered. He attempts to make his escape by snatching a child away from one of the worshipers for a hostage, but the infant turns out to be a wineskin shod with Persian slippers. After being arrested, he is rescued by Euripides. The plot development leads to a series of broadly farcical situations.

Agathon (A-guh-thon), a poet, satirized for his wantonness and voluptuousness. Because of Agathon's effeminacy, Euripides had hoped to send him among the women, but the poet refuses to take the risk.

Clisthenes (KLIS-theh-neez), another effeminate, who warns the women of Euripides' ruse.

A Prytanis (PRIH-tuh-nihs), a member of the council who arrests Mnesilochus for desecrating the Mysteries of Demeter.

A Scythian archer, a barbarian with a thick accent and, apparently, a head to match, left to guard the prisoner. He is easily lured away from his post by a dancing girl.

A Chorus of women, celebrating the Thesmophoria.

THEY SHOOT HORSES, DON'T THEY?

Author: Horace McCoy (1897-1955)
First published: 1935
Genre: Novel

Locale: Hollywood, California
Time: 1935
Plot: Existentialism

Robert Syverten, a young man from Arkansas who has gone to Hollywood in the hope of becoming a film director. Although repeatedly frustrated in his efforts to get work with an established director, he maintains his optimism and holds down a variety of jobs, ranging from soda jerk to film extra, as he continues trying to break into the film business. He has just recovered from a near-fatal case of intestinal flu when he meets Gloria Beatty, an embittered aspiring actress who convinces him to be her partner in a dance marathon being held in a hall on one of the local piers. Robert dreams of winning the contest and using his share of the $1,000 prize money to make a two-reel film that he can use to illustrate his skills to the film studios. He fails in his efforts to cheer up the terminally gloomy Gloria, and as the marathon drags on for thirty-seven days, he becomes infected by her despair. He continues trying to catch an occasional glimpse of sunlight or ocean to remind him of the world outside the dance hall, but his ambitions soon dwindle simply to trying to survive the ordeal of the marathon. When the marathon ends prematurely with no winner, he obliges Gloria's request to shoot her and put her out of her misery, a crime for which he is sentenced to death.

Gloria Beatty, a film extra who has become disillusioned because of her inability to obtain acting work. An orphan who ran away to Dallas from her aunt and uncle's home in Texas, she decided to become an actress while recovering from a suicide attempt brought on by despair over her wretched life. Gloria hitchhiked her way to Hollywood, nurturing the hope of becoming a star overnight, but has since become discouraged with the film industry and with life in general. She repeatedly voices the wish that she were dead. When she asks Robert to be her partner in the dance marathon, it is her final desperate attempt to be noticed by film directors and film stars, who sometimes attend the marathons for their performance value. Cynical and hard-bitten, she picks fights with the dance marathon officials and persistently counsels a pregnant fellow contestant to have an abortion and spare the child a dismal existence. Gloria accepts each new indignity the marathon promoters inflict on the contestants in their effort to turn the contest into a popular spectacle, but she continually hopes out loud that someone will put her out of her misery. Utterly convinced of the futility of life when the marathon is terminated before a winner can be declared, she persuades Robert to "pinch hit for God" and shoot her dead.

Mrs. Layden, an aging woman who frequents dance marathons and laments that she is too old to be in them herself. She subscribes to the romantic fantasy that the promoters build around the contests and is especially drawn to Robert and Gloria, whom she convinces a beer company to sponsor. Secretly, though, she counsels Robert that a relationship with Gloria will only bring him misery. Her death at the dance hall by a stray bullet fired during an altercation at the bar terminates the marathon before a winner can emerge.

Vincent "Socks" Donald, a dance marathon promoter who callously engineers such events as a nightly footrace for the dancers and the marriage of two contestants during the marathon to increase his dance contest's popularity and draw an audience.

— *Stefan Dziemianowicz*

A THIEF OF TIME

Author: Tony Hillerman (1925-   )
First published: 1988
Genre: Novel

Locale: New Mexico
Time: The 1980's
Plot: Detective and mystery

Dr. Eleanor Friedman-Bernal, an anthropologist whose specialty is Anasazi ceramics. Formerly married to an archaeologist who ran off with another woman, Friedman-Bernal is exploring ancient Anasazi burial areas on a New Mexico Navajo reservation in search of potsherds and the occasional intact pot. While exploring the ruins alone one night, she disappears, at about the same time an anonymous caller to the Navajo Tribal Police accuses her of violating the Antiquities Preservation Protection Act.

Joe Leaphorn, a lieutenant with the Navajo Tribal Police who is in the last two weeks of a thirty-day terminal leave prior to retirement. Nevertheless, he becomes involved in what appears to be a series of related events: the disappearance of Friedman-Bernal, the nighttime theft of government vehicles, and a pair of murders. Though a Navajo, he is not afraid of the *chindi*, spirits of the dead, because his career has immunized him against all but one, that of his wife, whose death he continues to mourn.

Jim Chee, also an officer with the Navajo Tribal Police. He has strong ties to tribal traditions and religion, and he is concerned about disturbing the ghosts of the dead. His police responsibilities conflict with his beliefs when he has to search ruins of ancient burial grounds. Chee is *hatathali*, a Navajo singer and medicine man who has been trained to lead curing ceremonies. Having ended a relationship with a non-Navajo woman because of their cultural differences, he is tentatively embarking on a new one, this time with a fellow Navajo, Janet Pete, a lawyer with the tribal legal services office.

Maxie Davis, who is part of a contract archaeology team, with Friedman-Bernal, engaged in dating more than one thousand Anasazi sites, inventorying them, and determining which are significant enough to be preserved. Self-made and class-conscious, Davis remembers having been put down by the upper class over the years, so she instinctively resents someone like Elliot. Davis, who is Friedman-Bernal's friend and neighbor, telephones the sheriff to report her colleague's disappearance.

Randall Elliot, a wealthy former Navy helicopter pilot in Vietnam, now a specialist in cultural anthropology and a coworker of Davis and Friedman-Bernal, particularly of the former. According to Davis, once Elliot and she publish their study of the Anasazi, there will not be anything left for other scholars in the field to write. Elliot, who is very conscious of his upper-class birth and flaunts it, is drawn to Davis despite their different backgrounds. He hopes to impress her with his scholarship and thus overcome her instinctive class-motivated antagonism. To support his theory that genetic flaws could explain the disappearance of the Anasazis, he resorts to illegal digging, and when Friedman-Bernal catches him at it, he tries to kill her. He murders two others to prevent them from talking to the authorities.

Harrison Houk, a wealthy landowner, sometime dealer in Anasazi pots, and survivor. Twenty years earlier, his son Brigham allegedly killed the rest of the family (Brigham's mother, sister, and brother) and then presumably drowned, though his body was not found. Faced with death, Houk hastily scrawls part of a message to Leaphorn, telling him that Friedman-Bernal still is alive. An atypical act for a tough guy and a scoundrel, it is significant to Leaphorn, who believes it is related to Houk's one known soft spot, for his schizophrenic son Brigham. Another discovery Leaphorn makes about Houk is that the arthritic old man took the same downriver kayak journey at night every full moon, a dangerous trip that the detective replicates and that leads him not only to Friedman-Bernal but also to the fugitive Brigham, whose father for two decades had helped him avoid a life sentence in a prison for the criminally insane. These discoveries help Leaphorn solve the case.

Slick Nakai, a fundamentalist Christian evangelist of questionable honesty who tows his revival tent around the reservation, an area larger than that of New England. Although he calls himself simply a preacher, he also deals in ancient pottery, which he willingly takes in lieu of cash contributions and then sells to dealers and collectors such as Harrison Houk. Because of such dealings, Nakai is an early suspect in the disappearance of Friedman-Bernal, particularly after two of his sometime employees are killed.

— *Gerald Strauss*

THE THIN MAN

Author: Dashiell Hammett (1894-1961)
First published: 1934
Genre: Novel

Locale: New York City
Time: The 1930's
Plot: Detective and mystery

Mimi Jorgenson, Clyde Wynant's former wife, a showy blond in whose arms Julia Wolf dies. She is suspected of Julia's murder.

Dorothy Wynant, Mimi's daughter, a small, attractive blond who dislikes her family and who asks Nick to locate Wynant.

Gilbert Wynant, Mimi's son, an odd, extremely inquisitive young man.

Christian Jorgenson, formerly called **Kelterman**, Wynant's former associate who, feeling unfairly treated, breaks with him. Although he already has a wife in Boston, Jorgenson marries Mimi to get his hands on the large divorce settlement Wynant provides for her. Temporarily suspected of Julia's murder, he finally returns to his legal wife in Boston.

Nick Charles, the narrator, a onetime detective, now a lumberman. Humorous, self-possessed, tough, and intelligent, he discovers clues, arranges them, makes deductions, and solves the murders. He then summarizes the whole solution for his admiring wife, Nora.

Nora Charles, his wife, a woman with a well-developed sense of humor who finds Nick fascinating.

Herbert Macaulay, Wynant's thieving attorney, the murderer of Wynant, Julia, and Nunheim. He murders Wynant to rob him, Julia to quiet her, and Nunheim because he was a possible witness to Julia's murder.

Shep Morelli, a gangster and former friend of Julia who thinks Nick knows what happened to her. He shoots Nick and is beaten by the police but is released when Nick does not press charges.

Arthur Nunheim, a former convict who identified Julia's body. He is murdered.

Julia Wolf, a murder victim, Clyde Wynant's secretary and mistress who plotted with Macaulay to get Wynant's money.

Clyde Wynant, a wealthy, eccentric inventor, once a client of Nick. He is a tall, thin man murdered by Macaulay.

Guild, a detective.

THE THIN RED LINE

Author: James Jones (1921-1977)
First published: 1962
Genre: Novel

Locale: Guadalcanal, in the Solomon Islands, and in the western Pacific Ocean
Time: 1942-1943
Plot: Psychological realism

Edward Welsh, the first sergeant in Charlie Company. He enlisted in the Army at the beginning of the Great Depression, believing that he had shrewdly escaped the general economic calamity but convinced that, as a career soldier, he would not escape the next war because of the pattern of America becoming involved in wars at roughly twenty-year intervals. His personality is full of paradoxes. Even though he cynically dismisses all ideals as empty and believes that all wars are struggles over property rights, he is completely uninterested in acquiring property and respects only the most fatalistic acceptance of the insignificance of the individual. Even though he has no combat experience before the Guadalcanal campaign, he instinctively understands and accepts the demands of battle and the likelihood of death. He takes every opportunity to exhibit his contempt for his subordinates and his superiors alike, but he has an underlying pity for their limitations and a desire to compensate for them. He lives up to his nickname of "Mad Welsh," but at bottom he conceals a reflexive compassion to which he will not admit, even to himself. In particular, he singles out Corporal Fife for verbal abuse, recognizing that Fife is too self-reflective and has too strong a sense of self-preservation to be suited to combat. When Fife is finally injured seriously enough to be offered evacuation, it is Welsh's further derision that, ironically, makes him decide to accept the offer. In effect, Welsh has saved Fife by allowing Fife to think that he is spiting him. In another instance, a soldier named Tella is gut-shot and left lying in screaming agony on the open ground cleared by enemy machine-gun fire. When a medic is cut down trying to administer morphine to Tella, Welsh insanely runs across the open ground to the wounded man. Although he cannot rescue Tella, he is able to administer the morphine to relieve his suffering and to quiet the screaming that is unnerving everyone. Afterward, he is so embarrassed at having revealed how much he cares for the men in his company that he loudly threatens Captain Stein for wanting to recommend him for the Silver Star. When the Guadalcanal campaign is almost over, Welsh contracts malaria but refuses to accept evacuation because it will mean being permanently separated from the company.

Storm, the mess sergeant in Charlie Company. In many ways, he is Welsh's opposite. Whereas Welsh is explosively abusive of his men, Storm tries to be consistently self-controlled and reassuring. Whereas Welsh finds his emotional equilibrium in combat, Storm is appalled by the little combat he sees, in particular by his participation in the abuse of some Japanese prisoners after an especially fierce hand-to-hand engagement. When he is wounded, he gladly accepts evacuation, wanting only to prepare one last meal for the company before departing. At bottom, he believes that the levelheaded performance of his duties is all that he owes the men of Charlie Company.

John Bell, a private, later a sergeant, and finally a lieutenant in Charlie Company. A commissioned officer in the regular army in the years before the war, he resigned his commission when given an assignment that would require a prolonged separation from his wife, Marty. When he is drafted as a private into Charlie Company, the other soldiers regard him as something of an enigma because he exhibits no bitterness or presumptuousness about his having been an officer. Initially, Bell goes into combat with an intense underlying fear that he will be killed in battle and that his death will be as essentially meaningless as any other small statistic of battle. He suppresses this fear only by recalling vividly erotic moments with his wife. He begins to volunteer for especially dangerous missions and gradually admits to himself that his wife's vibrant sexuality makes it extremely improbable that she will remain faithful to him. He is, then, not entirely surprised when he receives a Dear John letter from his wife, ironically at about the same time that he receives notification of his reinstatement as an officer. Of all the soldiers in Charlie Company, Bell is the most farsightedly thoughtful in his repeated recognition that giving oneself up to the brutality of combat will leave permanent emotional scars.

Geoffrey Fife, a corporal in Charlie Company. Because his idealistic notions about the nature and purpose of war are essential to his sanity, he is repelled by the continual evidence of the mindless and soulless machinery of war. He cannot accept the notion that his death in battle may be pointless, and he repeatedly confesses his cowardice in the face of such a death, believing that the other men of the company lack the idealism to fear death as he does. In his exaggerated sense of his singular weakness, he begins a homosexual relationship with Private Bead, whom he abuses as a gesture of his self-disgust. When Bead is mortally wounded, he asks Fife to hold his hand. Fife is reluctant, afraid that he will confirm any suspicions about their relationship. When Fife himself receives a minor wound, he is appalled that the wound, which to him seems pointed evidence that he has done his part in the battle, does not make him eligible for evacuation. He transfers out of Charlie Company when Welsh, while Fife is hospitalized for the minor wound, gives his job as company clerk to another soldier. With his new company, Fife participates in the attack on Boola Boola, the last, weakly defended, Japanese stronghold. All of his desperation releases itself in his wild slaughtering of every Japanese soldier he sees. Once the insane exhilaration of the battle has worn off, Fife is haunted by the same anxieties that he has felt since the opening of the campaign.

Don Doll, a private in Charlie Company. In many ways, he is the opposite of Fife. Although he is afraid of dying pointlessly in combat, he recognizes, as Fife does not, that all the soldiers in the company have assumed postures of one sort or another to hide this same fear. Consequently, he assumes a posture of recklessness that the others ironically come to accept as genuine bravery. Aboard the troopship as the landings are under way, he steals a pistol that he hopes will serve as a sort of talisman for his survival, though he knows that it will not be an especially useful weapon in combat. Later, during a night bombardment, he stands in his foxhole, insanely testing his fate with an outward manner of nonchalance. After his first killing of a Japanese soldier, he feels a genuine guilt, but also the strange elation of knowing that his guilt will not result in any corresponding punishment. He begins a strange competition with another private, Charlie Dale, for the most dangerous assignments. Whereas Dale is looking to move up through the ranks as quickly as possible, Doll is motivated more simply by the need to keep up his adrenaline to avoid reflection.

Witt, a private in Charlie Company who transfers to another company because he hates Welsh. A free spirit with inexplicable politics, he deserts his new company to rejoin Charlie Company whenever the fighting becomes especially heavy. The men in Charlie Company are reassured by his presence at critical moments, but they cannot understand the loyalty to them that compels him to endanger himself by rejoining them. Witt himself is unable to articulate the code that drives him.

James "Bugger" Stein, the captain of Charlie Company in the early stages of the Guadalcanal campaign. Nicknamed Bugger by the men in the company, he is a well-meaning but ineffective leader in combat. His training in the Reserve Officers' Training Corps and his six months in the Army Reserve have not given him an understanding of what his men expect from him. He ends up relying on soldierly clichés that, in themselves, cause his men to lose faith in him. He is replaced as the captain of Charlie Company after an especially disastrous battle. Ironically, he allows his superior, Lieutenant Colonel Gordon Tall, to overrule a more effective battle plan that he has devised; Tall then has him transferred.

George "Brass" Band, Captain Stein's replacement in Charlie Company, given his nickname by the men of the company. He devises battle plans without any regard for the casualties entailed. He is eventually replaced when his tactics prove not only costly but also unsuccessful.

Gordon Tall, the battalion commander, a lieutenant colonel with a Machiavellian personality. He views the Guadalcanal campaign as a career opportunity and has little empathy for the circumstances of the ordinary soldiers.

— *Martin Kich*

THINGS FALL APART

Author: Chinua Achebe (1930-   )
First published: 1958
Genre: Novel

Locale: Umuofia, an Ibo society on the lower Nile River
Time: Late nineteenth century
Plot: Tragedy

Okonkwo (oh-KOHN-kwoh), the protagonist, one of the leaders of the Ibo community of Umuofia. He struggles from humble beginnings to achieve high status yet is still haunted by feelings of insecurity associated with his former lack of status. He is now a great warrior and wealthy farmer, with two barns full of yams, three wives, and two titles; he is also a lord in the clan. This string of successes is interrupted when he accidentally kills a man and is forced into exile for seven years. His plans for advancement are of necessity put on hold, and he chafes under this banishment. While he is gone, European missionaries establish themselves in the midst of Umuofia, make converts, and subtly undermine the old order. Under the impact of Westernization and modernization, things begin to fall apart. When Okonkwo returns, he finds Umuofia much changed and its former independence and integrity dangerously threatened by the new ways. He tries to rally his people and save his community. He is the most authentic representative and protector of traditional society. He rejects the new values that are subverting the old order and crosses the point of no return by killing a messenger of the Europeans to force his clansmen to make a choice. When they let the other messengers escape, he realizes that his community will not go to war against the Europeans. He commits suicide, which is a great evil and prevents him from being buried among his people. His tragic end underscores that there can be no compromise between traditional and modern society. Things must of necessity fall apart.

Unoka (ew-NOH-kah), Okonkwo's father. Lazy, shiftless, and always in debt, he is a man without title and unable to provide for his family. He is a good storyteller and a fine musician, the life of any party.

Nwoye (NWOH-yay), Okonkwo's eldest son. Sensitive and deeply troubled by certain Umuofian practices, such as the exposure of twins in the Evil Forest and the sacrifice of his beloved companion, Ikemefuna, he was attracted to the music, hope, and poetry of Christianity, and he converted. His actions remind Okonkwo of the failures of his father and raise the specter that he too might have these flaws.

Chielo (chee-OH-loh), the priestess of Agbala, the Oracle of the Hills and the Caves. Her approval is needed for major decisions, such as going to war. In everyday life, she is an ordinary woman, but as priestess few dare to ignore her divinations.

Ekwefi (ay-KWAY-fee), Okonkwo's second wife. The village beauty, she was captivated by Okonkwo's victory over the Cat in the greatest wrestling match within living memory. She ran away from her husband to live with Okonkwo. She bears ten children but loses nine in infancy. A daughter, Ezinma, survives, and Ekwefi lavishes special care and affection on her.

Ezinma (ay-ZEEN-mah), Okonkwo and Ekwefi's daughter. Intelligent and beautiful, she best understands the complex moods of her father and best interprets the appropriate course of action. Okonkwo wishes she were a male. She is his favorite child, and he plans her marriage as a logical part of his rise to power. Chielo calls her "daughter" and is probably training her to be the new priestess.

Ikemefuna (ee-kay-may-FEW-nah), a fifteen-year-old boy from a neighboring village. Okonkwo treats him like a son, and Nwoye learns under his tutelage and regards him as the older brother he never had. Given to Umuofia in atonement for the murder of a clansman's wife, he is placed under the guardianship of Okonkwo. After about three years, the Oracle of the Hills and the Caves orders his sacrifice. Wishing to show his strength and his loyalty to village traditions, Okonkwo strikes the fatal blow.

Obierika (oh-bee-ay-REE-kah), a friend of Okonkwo. He manages Okonkwo's affairs while Okonkwo is in exile, warns him that the law does not require him to participate in Ikemefuna's sacrifice, and has him buried by outsiders when he commits suicide.

Mr. Brown, the first European missionary in Umuofia. Respectful of Umuofia's traditions, he wisely guides the affairs of the early Christian church, and its membership and power grows.

The Reverend James Smith, a narrow-minded missionary who succeeds Mr. Brown. He brooks no compromises with native traditions and insists on the rights and privileges of the Christian community over those of Umuofia. His fanaticism and nonbending stance set the stage for the imposition of European rule of government and law.

— *Maurice P. Brungardt*

THIRD AND OAK: The Laundromat

Author: Marsha Norman (1947-   )
First published: 1980
Genre: Drama

Locale: Ohio
Time: Late twentieth century
Plot: Naturalism

Alberta "Bertie" Johnson, a retired teacher and Herb's recent widow, a white, middle-aged perfectionist who initially keeps her husband's death secret because she cannot yet deal with letting go of Herb. An isolationist, Alberta is lonely and talks to herself for company. Precise and proper, she is at first taken aback by Deedee's spontaneity and is reluctant to accept help from or be close to Deedee. Bertie also is a caring person and extends herself to help Deedee with issues ranging from getting change for the machines to dealing with her unfaithful husband. Her approach to her world is predominantly logical.

Deedee Johnson, Joe's lonely wife, who addresses envelopes for a secret income and wants to be liked but sees herself as essentially inadequate. In fact, Deedee sabotages her own competence by her impulsive behaviors; she is frequently unprepared for her own actions or for others' reactions to her. Deedee believes that she lacks intelligence. A chocolate lover who belittles herself for responding to her world emotionally, Deedee has tolerated a violent, racist, and unfaithful husband because she needs to be with someone and he has been there for her. Deedee displays both independent thought and independent action in her final exchanges with Alberta in the laundry.

— *Kathleen Mills*

THIRD FACTORY
(Tret'ya fabrika)

Author: Viktor Shklovsky (1893-1984)
First published: 1926
Genre: Novel

Locale: The Soviet Union
Time: c. 1900-1926
Plot: Social realism

Viktor Borisovich Shklovsky (VIHK-tohr boh-RIH-sohvihch SHKLOV-skee), the author, narrator, and subject of this work. Shklovsky sets forth memories and ideas in an autobiographical sketch that was meant also to present his conception of prose fiction and his assessment of other writers who were prominent at the time. Instead of a conventional self-portrait, Shklovsky provides a series of anecdotes that illustrate the development of his own views and feelings, which in their turn are arranged according to his own notions of the Formalist novel. The author's conception of himself is refracted by the technical devices he has chosen to employ, and underlying creative concerns may be found alongside some outwardly offhand notes and observations. According to the author, his existence has been lived in a succession of factories. The first was his home and school; the second was Opoyaz, a literary society of innovative predilections. His employment in the Soviet film industry—the "third factory"—provides a backdrop for his reflections and reminiscences. During passages dealing with the author's early manhood, names and images of writers and theorists flash by along with some blunt and unvarnished recollections of war and revolution. Among many noted figures, Jan Baudouin de Courtenay, a professor of philology and one of Shklovsky's mentors, is mentioned with some respect. Elsewhere, important theorists of the author's own generation, including Roman Osipovich Jakobson, Yury Nikolayevich Tynayanov, and Boris Mikhailovich Eikhenbaum, are the recipients of some reflections on life and language in the guise of open letters. His writing features Tatars and sailors, as well as travel notes and hints of homebound affection for the author's native land. Odd, abrupt changes of subject and wildly humorous interjections occur amid musings on the possibilities and shortcomings of modern literary figures. Through it all, it can hardly be said that the author is prone to taking himself too seriously: He calls attention to his prominently bald, shining head, and, at times, he recoils from a surfeit of his own wit.

— *J. R. Broadus*

THE THIRD LIFE OF GRANGE COPELAND

Author: Alice Walker (1944-   )
First published: 1970
Genre: Novel

Locale: Georgia and New York City
Time: 1920 to the early 1960's
Plot: Family

Grange Copeland, the protagonist, a black sharecropper in Georgia. A tall, gaunt man who has worked hard all of his life, Grange is poor, ignorant, and in debt to the white plantation owner. He abuses his wife and son in response to his own powerlessness and eventually abandons them to try his luck in the North. While living in Harlem, he attacks racism, rather than merely reacting to it as he had done in Georgia. He realizes that he cannot succeed in a one-man attack on racial discrimination and returns to Georgia. On his return, he marries his longtime lover, Josie, but treats her badly and tries in vain to keep his son from making the mistakes that he himself has made. Only his granddaughter, Ruth, receives his love, as he tries to make up for past sins. Grange never loses his hatred of white people, but he comes to realize how his hatred has made him weak. He tries to make a life for himself and for Ruth that will enable them to stay free by never depending on whites for anything.

Margaret Copeland, Grange's first wife and the mother of Brownfield and a bastard son. In the early years of her marriage, Margaret is soft and has sweet breath, and she is as submissive to her husband as a dog. After years of abuse, she becomes hardened and turns to drinking and promiscuity. It is her sexual relationship with the white plantation owner, resulting in the birth of a child, that finally drives Grange away for good. Margaret has never stopped loving Grange, and when he leaves, she kills herself and the baby, leaving fifteen-year-old Brownfield to fend for himself.

Brownfield Copeland, the neglected son of Grange and

Margaret. As a baby, he is unattended, unfed, and unchanged all day because both parents work in the fields. He never attends school and envies his cousins up North. Abandoned by both parents at the age of fifteen, he sets out to find the North but only gets as far as Josie's Dew Drop Inn. After several years of sharing the home and beds of Josie and her daughter, Brownfield falls in love with the beautiful and educated Mem, whom he marries. He comes to resent her accomplishments, however, and to despise her. He begins to repeat his father's life, working long hours as a sharecropper for little reward, beating his wife and children, drinking away his earnings, and spending his nights with Josie. His once-handsome body becomes worn down from hard work and disease. Unlike his father, Brownfield never learns to accept any responsibility for his own failings. He believes that white people have kept him from being a man, and that the only way to assert his manliness is to abuse his family.

Mem Copeland, Brownfield's wife. Cherry brown, plump, quiet, and demure, Mem was educated in Atlanta and speaks a dialect that at first sounds wonderful to Brownfield. She is a schoolteacher for several years and teaches Brownfield to read and write. In the early years of their marriage, she is a happy and devoted wife. Brownfield then begins to beat her, makes her give up teaching to become a domestic, makes her speak the way he speaks, and moves her from one ramshackle cabin to another. Mem is resigned to her own fate but fights back at Brownfield when the children's future is at stake. For a few years, Mem rises to power in the family and there is a surface of domestic harmony, but Brownfield eventually supplants her, and chaos and violence are restored.

Ruth Copeland, the youngest daughter of Brownfield and Mem. Born in a frozen cabin while her drunken father sleeps, Ruth receives her first beating from her father at the age of four, then watches him kill her mother at eight. She moves in with Grange and Josie and becomes the center of Grange's life, squeezing out even Josie. She is spoiled and sassy, and her only friend is Grange. At the age of sixteen, she loves to read and wonders about life outside the farm that Grange has established to protect them from white society. Unlike Grange, she believes that white people could change and that hating them for their ancestors' sins against her ancestors is wrong.

Josie Copeland, a prostitute, Grange's second wife and Brownfield's first lover. She is cantaloupe-colored, fat, and a voracious lover. She and Grange have had a relationship since before his first marriage, and it is to her that he returns after ten years in the North. Josie has spent those years as Brownfield's mistress, and she returns to Brownfield after Ruth steals Grange's heart. Both men abuse her, and she becomes a lonely old woman who realizes that she has never been loved.

— *Cynthia A. Bily*

THE THIRD POLICEMAN

Author: Flann O'Brien (Brian O'Nolan, 1911-1966)
First published: 1967
Genre: Novel

Locale: Rural western Ireland
Time: Late 1930's
Plot: Fantasy

The narrator, who as a child was sent to a fine boarding school after both of his parents died. At the age of sixteen, he becomes obsessed with the thought of a fictional charlatan, de Selby, who believes that most human experiences are illusory. After the narrator leaves school, he loses his left leg in an accident and returns home interested only in continuing his study of de Selby. He joins his dishonest caretaker, John Divney, in a crime to finance the publication of his definitive collation of all the interpretations of de Selby's thought. After Divney murders him, the narrator, not realizing that he is dead, goes to a strange police barracks in search of the lockbox that contains their loot. Amid strange dialogues and disorienting experiences, he is accused by Sergeant Pluck of murder. He narrowly avoids being hanged and escapes on Pluck's animate and gynecomorphic bicycle, toward which he develops amorous feelings. When he reaches his house, the narrator finds Divney and discovers that not three days but sixteen years have passed since he began his search for the box.

John Divney, the man hired to take care of the narrator's farm and tavern while he is at boarding school. Divney is short but well built, with broad shoulders and thick arms. He is brown haired and roughly handsome, with a reassuring face and brooding, brown, and patient eyes. After the narrator returns home, he does not dismiss the lazy and unprincipled Divney, even after he realizes that Divney was stealing from him. Divney convinces the narrator to join him in a plot to rob and murder Mathers, who carries his cash box with him when he walks to the village. After the murder, Divney hides the box and will not tell the narrator where it is. After the narrator shadows him for several years, even to the point of sleeping in the same bed with him, Divney relents. He tells the narrator that he has hidden the strongbox under the floor in Mathers' house, but he has actually planted a bomb there. When the narrator, who is killed by the bomb, comes back to his house, Divney, who alone can see him, is frightened to death. The two, unaware that they are dead, then prepare to repeat the forgotten trials of the narrator.

Phillip Mathers, a wealthy, elderly, retired man who lives alone in a big house three miles from the narrator's house. On a rainy night, the narrator and Divney attack him. After Divney strikes him with a bicycle pump and the narrator finishes him off with a spade, they bury his body in a ditch. He appears to the narrator after the narrator's death. Not aware of his own death, the narrator enters into a conversation with the ghastly and spectral, but apparently alive, Mathers. Mathers directs the narrator to the weird policemen, whom he sought in hope that they could help him locate the missing strongbox.

Joe, the narrator's soul, of whom the narrator becomes aware after his death. Joe is the narrator's companion and adviser, and they carries on dialogues. He is a voice of common sense in the midst of the narrator's disorienting experiences and fantastic theories on the nature of all sorts of things expressed by the policemen.

Martin Finnucane, a robber and murderer whom the narrator encounters on his way to the police barracks. Finnucane also has a wooden left leg and is the leader of a band of one-legged men.

Sergeant Pluck, the head of the constabulary at the strange police station. Pluck is a giant of a man, with a bulging neck and an enormous, fat red face sporting a violent red mustache and topped with abundant and unruly straw-colored hair. Believing that people and bicycles are exchanging identities through too much contact, he continually steals and hides bicycles. To solve a second murder of the dead Mathers, he blames the—this time—innocent narrator. After subjecting the narrator to prolonged interrogations and an escorted tour of an eternity machine, Pluck prepares to hang him but is distracted by the Finnucane gang.

Policeman MacCruiskeen, an inventive policeman who crafts a marvelous but incredible series of Chinese boxes and honed spearpoints, so fine that they are invisible. Dark complexioned, with a hook nose, dark whiskers, and a mass of curly black hair, he is as big and fat as Pluck but has a lean and intelligent face with penetrating eyes. He supervises and adjusts the gauges that control their strange world.

Policeman Fox, the third policeman, a mysterious character whom no one ever sees. The narrator, on his way back home, encounters Fox in his own private station in the walls of Mathers' house. Corpulent and with the face and voice of Mathers, he informs the narrator that the sought-after box contained 4 ounces of omnium, the essence of everything, which could satisfy his every desire.

— Bernard A. Cook

THE THIRTY-NINE STEPS

Author: John Buchan (1875-1940)
First published: 1915
Genre: Novel

Locale: England and Scotland
Time: 1914
Plot: Spy

Richard Hannay, a well-to-do retired mining engineer. Wishing to protect himself from Scudder's murderers and to relay to proper authorities Scudder's secret coded information (in a small black book), Hannay escapes to Scotland to hide but at the same time gives the impression that he killed Scudder. He evades the pursuing Black Stone and the police, as well as decoding Scudder's book; by doing so, he learns of invasion plans against England and informs Sir Walter. Revealing the imposture of the false First Lord of the Admiralty and finally discovering the meaning of the thirty-nine steps, Hannay is able to bring about the capture of the Black Stone.

Franklin Scudder, an American, a private investigator fearful of being murdered because of his knowledge of the

Black Stone's plans. During Hannay's absence, Scudder is stabbed to death in Hannay's flat.

Sir Walter Bullivant, a government official who at first is skeptical of Hannay's information; he is convinced upon learning of Karolides' death. He passes on Hannay's warning to other government officials.

The Black Stone, a group of espionage agents who kill Scudder and Karolides and attempt to prepare for a German invasion of England. They are captured just before escaping from England in a fast yacht.

Constantine Karolides, a Greek diplomat assassinated by the Black Stone.

Sir Harry, a newfound friend of Hannay and godson of Sir Walter.

THIS ABOVE ALL

Author: Eric Knight (1897-1943)
First published: 1941
Genre: Novel

Locale: England
Time: Summer, 1940
Plot: Sentimental

Clive Briggs, a British private. An illegitimate child and a product of the slums, he nevertheless has a good mind and is a deep thinker. After heroic conduct in the rear-guard action at Dunkirk, he is given a furlough and meets Prue Cathaway, the daughter of an upper-middle-class family. They fall in love and go on a ten-day holiday together. Clive is extremely bitter because of the disparity in opportunity among the English classes and decides that he will no longer fight for an England whose citizens are not equal. After his furlough, he fails to return to his military unit and is hunted as a deserter. Slipping into London to meet Prue, who has become pregnant, he is caught in an air raid and suddenly loses his idealistic rebelliousness. As he tries to rescue a woman trapped in the rubble, he is fatally injured by a falling wall.

Prudence (Prue) Cathaway, a member of the W.A.A.F. and the daughter of an upper-middle-class family. When her fiancé proves to be a conscientious objector, her ideals and belief in

English tradition impel her to join the women's army. Educated, refined, and privileged, she is nevertheless strongly attracted to the intense but lower-class Clive. Although she is a virgin, she gives herself to him on their second date. She becomes pregnant during their holiday. After Clive's heroic death, she draws great comfort from the thought of bearing his child.

Monty Montague, Clive's army buddy, also a product of the slums, a wise and reckless private from World War I. He is with Clive in the harrowing rear-guard action at Dunkirk. He joins Prue and Clive for part of their holiday. Although his crude manner is offensive to Prue's sensibilities, she insists that he tell her the details of Clive's heroism, to Clive's disgust. Monty greatly admires Clive's intelligence and courage and delights in giving Prue some insight into her lover's personality.

Dr. Roger Cathaway, Prue's father, a famous brain surgeon. He operates on Clive after the air raid, but even his skill is insufficient to save the doomed man.

Diane Cathaway, Prue's mother, a self-satisfied, nagging woman.

General Hamish Cathaway, Prue's grandfather, a typical upper-middle-class Englishman. He is frustrated because he is too old to fight in World War II.

Willfred Cathaway, the general's second son, an influential politician.

Hamish Cathaway, the general's youngest son, an attorney. He gives up his practice to join the war effort and is happy to get away from his waspish wife.

Iris Saintby Cathaway, Hamish's wife, a cold, vicious woman. She uses her accidentally acquired knowledge of Prue's indiscretions to force Willfred to arrange for her and her children to flee to the safety of the United States.

Prentiss Saintby, Iris' brother, a procurement officer in America. The author uses this character to give a somewhat distorted view of the United States just prior to the attack on Pearl Harbor.

Joe Telson, a drinking acquaintance through whom Clive meets Prue, a blind date.

The Reverend Mr. Polkingthorne, who temporarily shelters Clive and tries to persuade the fugitive to return to his army unit and face the charge of desertion.

THIS CHILD'S GONNA LIVE

Author: Sarah E. Wright (1928-   )
First published: 1969
Genre: Novel

Locale: The eastern shore of Maryland
Time: The late 1920's
Plot: Social realism

Mariah "Rah" Upshur, the protagonist, a young African American woman who is determined to escape from the poverty, ignorance, and religious hypocrisy of her community and save her children, even if it means leaving her husband, Jacob. Earlier, she had been driven from the church because of her pregnancy out of wedlock. Mariah finally is married to Jacob, but she is not reconciled to the church. In the course of the novel, she loses two children, leaves Tangierneck with her family and takes work with them as migrant laborers, and returns to her home.

Jacob Upshur, Mariah's husband, whose commitment to the land being stolen from him by his white relatives leads him to ignore his real circumstances. Though a religious man, he fathers a son, Ned, by his adopted sister, Vyella. He nevertheless condemns Mariah for bearing Dr. Albert Grene's daughter, Bardetta Tometta. He seems unable to break away from his father, who taught him to believe that he is the master of his world. He is well intentioned but ineffectual.

Percy Upshur, Jacob's father, whose sexual relationship with Miss Bannie, a white relative, causes him to lose his land and, ultimately, his life. He rules his family and is responsible for Jacob's weakness.

Bertha Ann Upshur, Percy's wife and a thorn in Mariah's side. To prevent Mariah's marriage to Jacob, she sent him to Baltimore and self-righteously condemned Mariah for her pregnancy.

Horace Upshur, called "Rabbit," Mariah's son. He suffers from a harelip and eventually dies from roundworms and tuberculosis. Bright and creative, he is to be a poet and is Mariah's favorite. In order to save Mariah's life, he takes the fatal blue pills away from her and later uses them himself. Although he is a "real" character, he is also a symbolic one—he is intellect housed in a flawed body, and his death ironically comments on the results of good intentions.

Bardetta Tometta Upshur, Mariah's daughter by Dr. Albert Grene, named for the legendary Bard Tom, Jacob's grandfather, whose rebellion against white society and his subsequent lynching made him a folk hero. The child serves a structural function, in that the novel begins shortly before her birth and ends shortly after her death.

Bannie Upshire Dudley, known as **Miss Bannie**, a white mail carrier, landowner, and lover of Percy Upshur, her relative. She acquires control of the Upshur land, which is passed, after her death, to Mr. Nelson. She is almost drowned by Mariah, who cannot commit murder, and returns her to her home, where she takes the blue pills.

Vyella, Jacob's adopted sister and mother to his child Ned. Mariah's best friend, she is a woman whose "natural" religious feelings lead her to become a preacher and a foil to the religious hypocrites.

Albert Grene, Percy and Miss Bannie's son, a respected physician, and father to Mariah's daughter, Bardetta Tometta.

Haim Crawford, a red-faced, racist patriarch of a family that is the "establishment" in Dormerset County. According to Mariah, he uses African Americans as spittoons.

— *Thomas L. Erskine*

THIS SIDE OF PARADISE

Author: F. Scott Fitzgerald (1896-1940)
First published: 1920
Genre: Novel

Locale: New York City, New Jersey, Philadelphia, Maryland, and Minneapolis
Time: 1896-1919
Plot: Fiction of manners

Amory Blaine, a boy born in the Midwest to a prominent family in the process of losing its fortune. He is a pampered, privileged young boy who embarks on a quest for self-discovery that covers his years at preparatory school, at Princeton University, in the Army, and beginning a life as an adult as he pursues a career in New York. He arrives in the East full of a kind of idealistic innocence, with untested assumptions about courage, honor, duty, and a man's place in the world, but his natural charm, earnestness, amiability, and obvious intelligence enable him to progress toward a firmer understanding of his essential nature. He is almost six feet tall as he enters Princeton, with light hair and penetrating green eyes. He is strikingly but not conventionally handsome, with a kind of slender athleticism to his carriage. Often intoxicated with the splendor of his youth and intensely conscious of his reactions to everything, he is fond of outrageous gestures and desperately concerned about his appearance and status in the eyes of those whom he admires and hopes to equal or emulate. He correctly sees himself as a "romantic egotist," and his attitude toward the world—particularly toward women—has been shaped heavily by his reading, which has tended toward nineteenth century writers with rebellious and ultraromantic philosophies. His inclinations toward social equality and his sensitivity toward the people whom he likes rescue him from his tendencies to be a prototypical snob with a vastly inflated estimate of his own self-worth.

Beatrice O'Hara Blaine, Amory's mother, an extremely theatrical, self-dramatizing woman of exceptional beauty, almost constantly affected in manner, with no sense of monetary value and no real fundamental understanding of life. She lives as she wishes, with few responsibilities and a casually distant relationship to her husband. She is primarily responsible for rearing Amory through his childhood and for almost sealing him in the mold of a precious young prig fascinated with his own glory. She and Amory come to understand each other very well, but he is hardly affected by the news of her death during World War I.

Thayer Darcy, a Catholic monsignor, forty-four years old when Amory meets him, robust, and somewhat stout. He creates an impressive figure in his religious regalia but is much more striking in terms of his warmth, wisdom, and abiding religious faith, which he has won through a test of conscience and experience. He is almost perfect as the surrogate father whom Amory needs: appreciative of Amory's wit, guiding him toward sound moral and aesthetic precepts, and showing him gradually the range and depth of life that Amory has not seen yet. He is encouraging, patient, nonjudgmental, incisive, and philosophic, a constant pleasure to know. He gives Amory a sense of his Irish/Celtic heritage, supports his quest, and accepts his egotism. He is a model on which Amory can pattern himself. His death at the book's end marks the true beginning of Amory's adulthood.

Thomas Parke D'Invilliers, one of Amory's classmates at Princeton, who seems to be eccentrically out of touch with important social customs. He is stoop shouldered and has pale blue eyes. Amory eventually discovers that Thomas is genuinely literary and fundamentally traditional in outlook. He remains one of Amory's best friends and is able to discuss literature with passion and without affectation. He is drawn from the poet John Peale Bishop.

Kerry Holiday and

Burne Holiday, brothers attending Princeton, housemates of Amory during his freshman year. Kerry, good-natured, easygoing, and completely natural, volunteers for and dies in World War I. Burne seems to emerge during his junior year, when he reaches a position of socialism and pacifism and argues his reformist politics with passion, conviction, and an impressive, lucid logic.

Alec Connage, another of Amory's friends at Princeton, basically decent but essentially nondescript. He lacks the special essence of Amory's closest friends.

Rosalind Connage, Alec's sister, the great love of Amory's life, with "glorious yellow hair," an "eternal kissable mouth, small, slightly sensual," and "an unimpeachable skin with two spots of vanishing color." She is physically stunning and mentally overwhelming. She is self-confident and self-possessed, and her offhand, casually witty personality tends to distract people from her perceptive view of the world. She has a gift for romantic banter (possibly based on that of Zelda Sayre), and she and Amory spend five weeks in an all-consuming relationship. Then, ruled by social expectations, she breaks off the affair and marries for money, comfort, and what she refers to as "background." In spite of her appeal, she exhibits tendencies to be vain, lazy, and selfish, tendencies of which Amory is not aware, caught up as he is in blind ardor.

Isabelle Borgé, Amory's first love, a girl from his hometown.

Clara Page, Amory's distant cousin, with whom he falls in love briefly. A beautiful, self-composed, and mature woman, she is both regal in demeanor and democratic in attitude, too advanced for Amory.

Eleanor Savage, an impetuous eighteen-year-old with whom Amory has a brief summer romance shortly after his break with Rosalind. She is a reckless romantic, with a "gorgeous clarity of mind" and a self-destructive streak that recalls some of Edgar Allan Poe's more exotic heroines. Her incipient madness and her atheism attract and frighten Amory.

— *Leon Lewis*

THIS SPORTING LIFE

Author: David Storey (1933-   )
First published: 1960
Genre: Novel

Locale: A North Country industrial town in England
Time: Late 1950's
Plot: Naturalism

Arthur Machin, a professional rugby player for the Primstone Team in northern England. He is in his early thirties, muscular, taciturn, and self-reliant. He also is grimly determined to succeed. Born in the working class, he seeks social respectability through athletic success. Rugby brings him money (and, thus, a car, a television set, and even women) that his full-time job as a machinist could never earn. Money and fame also give him a sense of power over others. In confident moments, he treats friends, parents, and even his lover as opposing players who must be knocked down. On rare occasions, he is a gentle, generous giant.

Valerie Hammond, a widow with two small children, Arthur's landlady. Desperately poor and still grieving for her dead husband, she keeps emotionally and socially distant from Arthur despite his efforts to befriend her. She becomes his mistress when success allows him to treat her and the children to middle-class comforts. She resists Arthur's clumsy efforts at emotional commitment. She breaks off their relationship because of intense neighborhood gossip. Months later, when she suffers an eventually fatal stroke, Arthur is her only visitor.

Johnson, who previously was committee man for the team and is now an aging hanger-on. He gets Arthur a tryout with a team. Although he protests that he wants no reward, he finds that Arthur now treats him contemptibly. As a sop, he is hired as a gardener by one of the team's owners.

Charles Weaver, an industrialist who owns the factory where Arthur works and co-owns the team for which Arthur plays. Annoyed by Arthur's egotism, he constantly votes to dismiss Arthur from the team. Toward the end of the novel, he temporarily succeeds.

Diane Weaver, Charles's wife. Ostensibly dedicated to charitable works, she pursues handsome, young football players. She propositions Arthur, but he resists; later, she spurns his attempt to start a liaison.

Mr. Slomer, a co-owner of the team. An eccentric, reclusive semi-invalid, he is a mysterious figure to the players. He and Charles Weaver battle to control the team by supporting and promoting different players. His death at the end of the novel is regarded by all the characters as a turning point with unpredictable consequences in their lives and in the history of the team.

Frank, a rugby team captain. Like Arthur, he is a taciturn bull of a man. Unlike Arthur, he is content with working in the mines and with a normal domestic life. He also differs in that he puts no emphasis on the pleasures or powers that fame and money buy.

Maurice Braithwaite, Arthur's teammate and an employee at Weaver's factory. He is a thoughtless pleasure seeker and exhibitionist. Reluctantly, he marries Judith, a secretary, when she becomes pregnant by him. Gradually, married life calms his restless instincts.

— *Robert M. Otten*

THIS SUNDAY
(Este domingo)

Author: José Donoso (1924-1996)
First published: 1966
Genre: Novel

Locale: Santiago, Chile
Time: Late 1950's
Plot: Realism

Josefina Rosas de Vives (hoh-seh-FEE-nah RROH-sahs deh VEE-vehs), called **Chepa** (CHEH-pah), the well-to-do daughter of Alejandro Rosas and the wife of the lawyer Alvaro, who likens her to a bitch constantly nursing a vast litter. In her preoccupation with giving aid and sustenance to slum dwellers, she assumes the character of an Artemis of Ephesus and even envisions herself as a many-breasted nurturer who, in giving suck to a multitude, is bitten and consumed. Her ostensible charity is actually an obsession with making others completely dependent on her. In her passion to control others, she develops a strange attachment to a convicted murderer, Maya, whose release from prison she secures and whom she sets up in a leather business. Seeking him in the slums after his desertion of her, she is manhandled by the slum dwellers and loses consciousness. Broken by the experience and by her loss of Maya, she spends the last ten years of her life in silence and sadness and dies at the age of sixty-five.

Alvaro Vives (AHL-vah-roh), a fifty-five-year-old lawyer and husband of Chepa, who is the same age. His cancer, evidenced by a growing mole above his left nipple, will take his life within five months. His youthful sexual affair with Violeta had been followed by dates with many women, eight of whom are named in the novel, and by his marriage to Chepa when both were twenty-two years old. Although he and Chepa have two daughters, his extramarital affairs with Matilde Greene (who later commits suicide), Carmen Méndez, and Picha attest his loveless marriage. Both he and Chepa, each irrefragably self-centered, are incapable of love. They remain married but stop sleeping together after the exposure of Alvaro's affair with Matilde Greene. His grandchildren call the terminally ill Alvaro *La Muñeca* (the Doll) because of his porcelain-like whiteness.

Maya (MI-yah), a convicted murderer. He is tall and ungainly. Like Alvaro, he has a mole, but it is on his upper lip and is not symptomatic of cancer; also like Alvaro, he is compared to a doll, but whereas Alvaro is in metaphor a *muñeca* (female doll), Maya is a *muñeco* (male doll). Maya exploits Chepa's fascination with him by prevailing on her to secure his release from prison. Once released and set up in a leather business, which Chepa provides for him, he resents his subjection to her. She has arranged lodging for him at Violeta's house and keeps close tabs on him until he breaks with her and leaves Violeta's house. He loses all of his money and subsistence by betting on racehorses. His loss of independence frustrates his desire to be his own person. Ultimately, he can assert his individualism only by committing another murder as a means of being returned to prison.

Violeta (vee-oh-LEH-tah), a maid in the household of Don Alvaro and his wife Elena, the parents of Alvaro. She had continued to serve without monetary compensation after a household staff retrenchment and was rewarded after Elena's death with the legacy of a house. She is four years older than Alvaro (the son), although, on the Sunday that she initiates him in sexual union, she is said to be twenty-two years old (instead of twenty) to his sixteen. She remains the young Alvaro's sexual partner for six years, until he marries Chepa. She is abandoned by her lover, Marín, whose child she bears out of wedlock. Each Sunday, she prepares a batch of *empanadas* (meat pastries) for Alvaro, Chepa, and their grandchildren. Eventually, she confesses to Chepa her sexual affair with Alvaro. She is murdered by Maya in his determination to be returned to prison.

Mirella (mee-REH-yah), the illegitimate daughter of Violeta and Marín. She marries an automobile mechanic named Fausto, and they have a daughter named Maruxa Jacqueline.

Meche (MEH-cheh), the daughter of Alvaro and Chepa. She and her husband, Lucho, are the parents of Magdalena, Marta, Luis, and Alberto.

Pina (PEE-nah), the daughter of Alvaro and Chepa. She is married to a doctor.

The grandson of Alvaro and Chepa. The son of Pina and her husband, he narrates the three shorter sections of the novel (the two major parts are in third-person narrative). He is one year younger than Luis and the coeval of Alberto. He is in his mid-fifties as he gives his account of "this Sunday" at the home of his grandparents when they were in their mid-fifties. He and his four cousins played for the last time, on this particular Sunday, their game of Ueks (good people) and Cuecos (villains). The "funeral" of "Mariola Roncafort," the consummate Uek, was played as prelude to her "resurrection," but there was to be no resurrection. The games ended on this Sunday, during which Alvaro learned from his son-in-law, the doctor, about his terminal cancer; Violeta was murdered by Maya; and Chepa, seeking out Maya, was traumatically abused by her slum constituents.

Marujita Bueras (mah-rew-HEE-tah BWEH-rahs), a peddler of shirts, who is married and who both visits Maya in prison and corresponds with him by mail. She proves to be a rival to Chepa for Maya's attentions.

Fanny Rodriguez (rrohd-REE-gehs), a companion of Chepa on her visits to the penitentiary. She suggests that Chepa is in love with Maya and provides Chepa with information on how to use influence to secure Maya's release.

Bartolomé Páez (bahr-toh-loh-MEH PAH-ehs), the warden of the penitentiary. He had been a clerk when Chepa's father was president of the supreme court.

Don Pedro Benitez (PEH-droh beh-NEE-tehs), an official whose aid Chepa solicits in working out the release of Maya.

Gabriel, the manager of the Caja de Crédito Industrial (Industrial Credit Bank), who approves Chepa's request to lend Maya the money for an expensive sewing machine. He has risen from the same poverty that Maya knew. In his success and affluence, he is disappointed that his wife and sister-in-law have gone into a candy-store business because there was no need for them to do so.

Antonia, the maid in the household of Alvaro and Chepa.

— *Roy Arthur Swanson*

A THOUSAND ACRES

Author: Jane Smiley (1949-   )
First published: 1991
Genre: Novel

Locale: Northwestern Iowa
Time: 1979 and 1982
Plot: Domestic realism

Virginia (Ginny) Cook Smith, the narrator and the oldest of Larry Cook's three daughters. Even after marriage to Ty Smith, Ginny is the mainstay of the Cook homestead, tending her widowed father, her ailing sister Rose, and the large farm on which they all live. After repressing the memory, Ginny later accepts the fact that Larry sexually molested his two oldest daughters. Ginny clashes with Larry over management of the farm and with Rose over affection for Jess Clark.

Laurence (Larry) Cook, a proud Iowa farmer. A widower in his sixties, Larry cedes his thousand-acre operation to his daughters. When Caroline, his youngest daughter, proves unenthusiastic, he excludes her. Larry later regrets his premature retirement and, with the help of lawyer Caroline, battles to regain the farm.

Jessie (Jess) Clark, Harold Clark's prodigal son. He deserted from the Army during the Vietnam War. After thirteen years in Vancouver and then Seattle, Jess returns to Iowa as a vegetarian teetotaler who advocates organic farming. After a fling with Ginny, he marries Rose and then vanishes.

Rose Cook Lewis, the second daughter of Larry Cook, whom she resents for abusing her during childhood. She is the mother of Pammy and Linda and the wife of Pete Lewis, after

whose drowning she marries Jess Clark. Rose eventually dies of breast cancer.

Caroline Cook Rasmussen, Larry's youngest daughter, the only one not interested in maintaining the farm. Caroline, a lawyer, moves to Des Moines but returns to help her father press his rights against the two sisters who reared her.

Harold Clark, Jess's father, a farmer who is a neighbor of the Cooks. He tries to mediate the Cooks' dispute. Harold is blinded in a farming accident for which Pete bears responsibility.

Tyler (Ty) Smith, Ginny's husband. A hardworking farmer who respects Larry's devotion to the land, he moves to Texas after the Cook farm fails.

Pete Lewis, Rose's husband. After learning of her relationship with Jess, he goes off in a drunken rage and drives his truck into the quarry, where he drowns.

Loren Clark, Jess's brother. He remains in Zebulon County and works with his father on the Clark family farm.

Pammy Lewis and
Linda Lewis, daughters of Rose and Pete. To safeguard them from Larry's lewd attentions, Rose sends her daughters to boarding school.

— *Steven G. Kellman*

THOUSAND CRANES
(Sembazuru)

Author: Yasunari Kawabata (1899-1972)
First published: 1952; serial form, 1949-1951
Genre: Novel

Locale: Kamakura and Tokyo, Japan
Time: Late 1940's
Plot: Psychological realism

Kikuji Mitani, an orphan and a bachelor in his late twenties. A singularly passive man, he finds himself embroiled in the subtle machinations of his dead father's mistresses without

having any clear sense of what he wants. He is given to much reflection about his father's love life and meditations on the utensils of the tea ceremony connected with Mrs. Ota, but he falls into her arms and later into the arms of her daughter without equal thought. He is attracted to the woman proposed as a bride for him, Yukiko Inamura, but seems unable to wring himself away from the women who were involved with his father.

Chikako Kurimoto, a teacher of the tea ceremony. After a few years as the mistress of Mitani's father, she seems to become sexless and appears to be fated to a lonely life because of a repulsively large black birthmark on her breasts. Unable to let go of the Mitani family after the affair, she becomes a family confidante, spewing her jealous resentment of the last mistress. She insists on being the go-between for Mitani and a young female student of hers. Finding Mitani hesitating between two young women, she tries to punish him by reporting that they are both married.

Yukiko Inamura, Chikako's student and a prospective bride for Mitani. Elegant and pleasing, she carries a pink scarf with a pattern of a thousand cranes, an omen that seems very promising for Mitani's future happiness.

Mrs. Ota, the widow of a fellow tea enthusiast of the elder Mitani. She was his mistress in the last years of his life. In her mid-forties, with a long white neck, small mouth and nose, full shoulders, and a warm, pliant manner, she seems to be attracted to Kikuji as a way of remembering his father. Clinging and affectionate, she is, however, consumed with guilt and commits suicide.

Fumiko Ota, Mrs. Ota's daughter. She has inherited her mother's long neck but has a fuller mouth and very sad eyes. Ashamed of her mother's behavior, she nevertheless is also attracted to Mitani. She disappears mysteriously at the end, and there is a hint that she, too, may have committed suicide.

— *Shakuntala Jayaswal*

THE THREE BLACK PENNYS

Author: Joseph Hergesheimer (1880-1954)
First published: 1917
Genre: Novel

Locale: Pennsylvania
Time: c. 1750-1910
Plot: Historical

Howat Penny, the dark-skinned, somber-eyed, and jut-chinned son of the owner of Myrtle Forge. A free-spirited and strong-willed man, he loves the Pennsylvania wilderness rather than his father's iron works. Once he has fallen in love with Ludowika and possessed her, he has no scruples about taking her from her husband; the theft is unnecessary because Winscombe dies.

Ludowika Winscombe, the young Anglo-Polish wife of an elderly British envoy. She falls in love with Howat Penny and later becomes his wife. Having a background of social life in London, she finds Pennsylvania life interesting but somewhat crude. She submits to Howat's forcefulness, however, and becomes Mrs. Penny.

Jasper Penny, Howat's great-grandson, a widower. He is headstrong, rebellious, and independent like his ancestor, whom he resembles physically. Guilt leads him to rescue Eunice and provide for her. He is unable to persuade Susan to marry him until both have lost their vigor; their son, the second Howat's father, is the weakened product of their diminished selves.

Susan Brundon, Jasper's sweetheart, the mistress of a girls' school and friend of Jasper's cousins, the Jannans. Pale, blue-eyed, and high-cheeked, she is a very proper Victorian and rejects Jasper's marriage proposal because she thinks herself an unsuitable mother for Eunice. After Essie's death, however, she does marry him.

Howat Penny, Jasper's and Susan's grandson, the final issue of a declining family. A delicate aesthete and antiquarian who lives a quiet bachelor life, he is shocked by Mariana's interest in Polder. Howat is a symbol of family decay.

Mariana Jannan, Howat's cousin, a modern young woman whom old-fashioned Howat cannot understand. Howat sees in her something of the first Howat and Jasper combined, a person of vigor and independence in contrast to his own negativity.

James Polder, Mariana's lover, the grandson of Eunice. He is a blunt, self-made man. Deserted by a slatternly wife, he takes Mariana as his mistress until he can get a divorce.

Felix Winscombe, Ludowika's cold, sardonic husband.

Eunice Scofield, Jasper's illegitimate daughter, later legally adopted and named Penny.

Essie Scofield, her repulsive mother, whom Jasper finally pays off permanently.

Gilbert Penny, the first Howat's father.

Stephen Jannan, Jasper's cousin, a lawyer.

Daniel Cusler, Essie's leechlike young lover, who is killed while visiting her.

THE THREE-CORNERED HAT
(El sombrero de tres picos)

Author: Pedro Antonio de Alarcón (1833-1891)
First published: 1874
Genre: Novel

Locale: Spain
Time: Early nineteenth century
Plot: Wit and humor

Lucas, a friendly but ugly miller who, each day, entertains the clergy and the military in the shade of his grape arbor. When Eugenio, the mayor, tries secretly to visit Lucas' wife one evening, Lucas, in Eugenio's cloak and three-cornered hat, goes calling on Eugenio's wife, Doña Mercedes. Each man is quickly rebuffed by the other's faithful wife.

Frasquita (frahs-KEE-tah), Lucas' young and attractive wife, who is completely faithful to him. When the mayor, coming to see her, falls into the millpond, she has Weasel look after him while she goes hunting for Lucas.

Don Eugenio (eh-ew-HEHN-ee-oh), the *corregidor*, or mayor. He has designs on Frasquita. Everybody recognizes his big three-cornered hat.

Doña Mercedes (mehr-SAY-dehs), the wife of Eugenio.

Weasel, the bailiff, who plots to keep Lucas away from the mill overnight so that his master can visit Frasquita.

The bishop, another frequent caller at Lucas' mill.

THE THREE-CORNERED WORLD
(Kusamakura)

Author: Sōseki Natsume (Kinnosuke Natsume, 1867-1916)
First published: 1906
Genre: Novel

Locale: The Japanese resort village of Nakoi
Time: 1905
Plot: Philosophical realism

The narrator, a well-educated connoisseur of both Asian and Western arts, literature, and philosophy. The narrator has fled the capital with its mundane distractions and involvements for a hiking trip to put himself in touch with nature and regain his artistic perspective. As he says, "an artist is a person who lives in the triangle which remains after the angle which we may call common sense has been removed from this four-cornered world." Because the artist lacks common sense, he can approach areas from which the average person shrinks in the worlds of both nature and humanity; there he can find beauty. The narrator spends his time sketching, writing poems, philosophizing about art and life, and soaking up the atmosphere in the Shioda family inn at a small mountain hot spring.

O-Nami Shioda, the beautiful daughter of a wealthy innkeeper. O-Nami was forced to marry the son of a rich man of the local castle town rather than the boy she preferred. When the couple's money evaporated in a business turndown, O-Nami divorced her husband, returned to her father's home, and engaged in increasingly strange behavior. O-Nami entrances the narrator with her bizarre behavior and frank speech. He is awakened by her singing as she strolls through the garden; later, she enters his room while he sleeps and leaves reminders of her presence. She walks the veranda of the inn in her bridal gown and once enters the bathroom naked while the narrator is having a bath, only to run away laughing. O-Nami takes long walks in the mountains alone, writes po-

ems that respond to the narrator's verses, and verbally spars with him as he tries to find out more about her.

The village barber, a rough-speaking village gossip. He provides the village perspective on O-Nami while he gives the narrator a painful shave and shampoo. He relates that a local monk, Taian, fell in love with O-Nami and expressed his affection in a letter. O-Nami responded by disrupting a prayer service and demanding that the monk publicly make love to her in front of the Buddha. He sees her as crazy and warns the narrator against her.

Kyuichi Shioda, a callow young cousin of O-Nami who does amateur paintings in the Western style. Kyuichi is drafted to serve in the army fighting Russians in Manchuria. He is encouraged to die a hero's death on the battlefield by O-Nami, and he has the mark of death already on his countenance as he says good-bye to the Shiodas and the narrator as they see him leave on the same train that takes O-Nami's husband off to Manchuria to begin a new life.

O-Nami's former husband, once a wealthy young man, now a wandering, beaten tramp who meets her in the mountains to beg for money to go to Manchuria. The narrator, who secretly observes them from afar, fears that O-Nami seeks to kill him with the dagger she carries, a present from her father to Kyuichi.

— *Joseph Laker*

THREE LIVES

Author: Gertrude Stein (1874-1946)
First published: 1909
Genre: Novel

Locale: Bridgepoint, in the United States
Time: Late nineteenth and early twentieth centuries
Plot: Psychological realism

Anna Federner, a middle-aged domestic servant, "the good Anna" who provides the title for the first of the three stories in the book. She is a hardworking and clean immigrant German woman who fills her life with service to others. Through caring, she exercises a measure of control over her employers, her dogs, and the young girls who are her assistants in the domestic sphere. Anna is not sophisticated or educated and is used by others because of her desire to be needed. She literally works herself to death being good to others.

Miss Mary Wadsmith, Anna's initial employer in Bridgeport. She is a large, fair, and helpless woman, trying to rear her brother's orphaned children. She lets Anna make all the decisions that pertain to the family. She cannot control her niece, who, as she matures, challenges Anna's control and drives her away.

Miss Mathilda, Anna's second employer. She is a large, careless woman who needs Anna because Anna's willingness to take over the entire domestic sphere frees her to pursue other interests. She listens to Anna's problems and offers the kind of sympathetic understanding proper to a relationship based on class difference. Her interests finally take her to Europe (as the author's own interests did), and Anna is left behind, totally bereaved.

Mrs. Lehntman, Anna's friend and the only love of her life besides her dogs. She is Anna's opposite in her easygoing approach to life and her failure to care about strict codes of behavior. She is a widow and a midwife who acquires an extra child without thinking about financial responsibilities. She borrows money from Anna and others that she cannot repay and appears to be involved in illegal activities with a local doctor. Although she always lands on her feet, she finally alienates Anna.

Melanctha Herbert, who is eighteen years old at the beginning of the second novella, which takes her name. She is somewhat older by the end of her adventures, when she dies, as do all the major female characters of these stories. Melanctha is a mulatto whose mixed race reflects her difficulty in understanding where she belongs. Melanctha is intelligent, adventuresome, and desirous of learning what life means. She lives always in the present in her fearless, apparently undirected way. She naturally accepts the life of feeling and learning as opposed to the life of fixed rules and appearances. As a result, she enters into a number of fluid relationships that bring her disillusionment and disappointment and lead to her death by tuberculosis.

Dr. Jeff Campbell, a hardworking, serious black physician who opposes the fluidity of Melanctha's life and wants to create a life of traditional values for his people. His love affair with Melanctha ends when the conflicts that the two of them represent overwhelm him.

Jane Harden, a hard-drinking, independent, educated mulatto who teaches Melanctha much of what she learns about life. Jane's rebellious understanding takes Melanctha only so far, however, and her influence lessens when Melanctha meets Jeff.

Rose Johnson, a careless, negligent, sullen, childlike, and selfish black woman who allows her child to die as a result of indifference. She is a friend of Melanctha and the opposite of Jane Harden. Rose does not question or seek to learn but accepts things as they are and has her place in the social fabric of the black community. She uses Melanctha until she becomes jealous of Melanctha's friendship with her husband.

Jem Richards, Melanctha's last lover and a gambler, dashing and powerful, honest, and fast in his life. His power attracts Melanctha, but his desire for freedom is greater than hers, and he abandons her. He does not love her but fails to tell her so until she has ended her relationship with Jeff Campbell.

Lena Mainz, the title character of "The Gentle Lena." She is brought to Bridgeport from Germany by her cousin, who is unable to understand that Lena's gentleness is a result of her passivity. So simple is Lena that she seems to have no desires in this world or concern about autonomy of any kind. Manipulated into an unhappy marriage, she bears three children, who bring her no joy. Lena becomes increasingly lifeless in her marriage until she bears a fourth baby, a stillborn child. The birth having taken what life she has, she dies.

Herman Kreder, Lena's husband, a German American tailor who works for his father. He is an unimaginative, spoiled mother's boy who has no will to protect his wife from his mother's interference until he realizes that he will be a father. As Lena becomes more lifeless with each child, Herman becomes more involved in the lives of his children, loving and caring for them because they are his. After Lena's death, he is content not to have a woman always around, for he has his three children.

Mrs. Haydon, Lena's cousin, a hard, ambitious, well-meaning German American woman married to a well-to-do grocer. She exercises power by arranging other people's lives for their own good, and Lena is a victim of her "goodness."

— *Donna Gertsenberger*

THE THREE MARIAS
(As três Marias)

Author: Rachel de Queiroz (1910-   )
First published: 1939
Genre: Novel

Locale: Fortaleza and Rio de Janeiro, Brazil
Time: The 1930's
Plot: Realism

Maria "Guta" Augusta (ow-GEWS-tah), the narrator, a student in a girls' boarding school and later a typist in the city of Fortaleza, Brazil. Awkward and fearful, she is relieved to find friends during her first days at the nuns' school; she, Maria José, and Gloria share one another's hopes, enthusiasms, fantasies, and discouragements. After graduation, Guta tires of the monotony of home life, gets a job in Fortaleza, and soon moves in with Maria José. Guta is intrigued by a middle-aged bohemian painter, Raul; he paints her portrait and almost seduces her. Guta's father sends her money for a trip to Rio because she is depressed after a friend, Aluísio, commits suicide, and in Rio she meets a young Romanian doctor, Isaac, falls in love, and returns to Fortaleza pregnant. After a miscarriage and illness, she returns home to Crato, in the Cariri region, where her father, her dull and virtuous stepmother, and her younger half brothers and half sisters live.

Maria José (hoh-SEH), Guta's closest friend and the first girl to befriend her at the nuns' school. After they have left school and are working, Maria José, who teaches school and is devoutly religious, shares her room in her mother's house with Guta.

Maria da Gloria, called **Gloria**, Guta's other close friend at the convent school and afterward. Orphaned at the age of twelve, Gloria venerated the memory of the poet-father who reared her, and her friends admire her passionate mourning and her talent as a violinist. Soon after they are graduated, she becomes engaged to Afonso, a young college graduate, and she centers her emotional energy on him. Guta and Maria José attend her wedding. The birth of Gloria's son is an important event for her two friends.

Jandira (hahn-DEE-rah), a friend of the three Marias at the school. The illegitimate daughter of a married man and a prostitute, she has been cared for and sent to school by her father's sisters. She marries a seaman during their last year at school, but the marriage is an unhappy one. Their child is almost blind, and Jandira toils as a seamstress to support him. She is left a house and money by her aunt, takes a lover, and is much happier.

Raul (rah-EWL), a middle-aged married painter who fascinates Guta and with whom she imagines herself to be in love for a while. He seems romantic and mysterious to her, and she goes with Maria José and Aluísio to his studio and agrees to model for a portrait. Alternately repelled and attracted, Guta is almost seduced by him but realizes just in time that she does not want to be sexually involved with Raul. Guta is very disillusioned when she sees him as he really is.

Aluísio (ah-lew-EE-see-oh), an emotional young student, a friend of Guta and Maria José who commits suicide and leaves a letter in which he alludes to an unhappy love affair. Everyone assumes that his passion was for Guta. She visits him before he dies and is much distressed, although she knows that his death is not really her fault.

Isaac, a young Romanian Jewish immigrant whom Guta meets at the boardinghouse where she stays when she visits Rio. He is studying to validate his medical diploma and risks being deported if he fails the examination. He talks to Guta about Romania, plays records for her, and encourages her to tell him about her home and memories. She falls in love with him, and they become lovers just before Guta must return to her job in Fortaleza. She never tells him that she is pregnant with his child, and he does not speak to her of plans for a future together, although he writes letters to her.

— *Mary G. Berg*

THREE MEN IN A BOAT (TO SAY NOTHING OF THE DOG)

Author: Jerome K. Jerome (1859-1927)
First published: 1889
Genre: Novel

Locale: The River Thames
Time: Late 1880's
Plot: Wit and humor

J., the narrator and alter ego of the author. He is single and a resident of London. In this wry tale of a holiday on the River Thames, J., of no stated occupation, is representative of the English middle classes. J., who is something of a hypochondriac, commiserates with two friends, George and Harris, about their need for a restful holiday. They decide to embark on a two-week boating trip up the Thames from London to Oxford and back again. Because the adventure is told by J., it is his view of events that prevails, including numerous and amusing digressions from the past such as the time he carried a ripe cheese from Liverpool to London on a crowded railway. Always confident of his own abilities and sure of the rightness of his own motives, J. describes at length the foibles of his companions, with himself the well-meaning, generous, and wise counselor, always above the fray—unless he became a part of it. J. obviously is no better—and no worse—in his abilities and actions than George or Harris.

George, who also is single. He works—or, according to J., sleeps—in a bank in the City of London from ten to four o'clock on weekdays; on Saturdays, he is awakened and expelled at two. It is he who proposes the boating trip. The heavyset and always thirsty George knows every drinking spot in and around London and is thus considered to be a valuable resource for the holiday. Because he has to work part of the day on Saturday, he is unable to join the group until sometime after J. and Harris set out. When he arrives, it is in an unsuitably loud blazer, and he is carrying a banjo that he cannot play.

William Samuel Harris, a man who, according to J., lacks any romance and poetry in his soul. Harris and George are broadly similar types. Like George, Harris organizes his life around eating and drinking. He also has considerable confidence in his musical aptitude, especially singing comic songs, but he can never remember the words. Like George with his banjo, Harris' talent is greatly inferior to his ambition. On one occasion, Harris remains in the boat while George and J. visit a town. When they return, Harris can hardly be roused because of his drunkenness, and all he can talk about is being attacked by differing numbers of swans. At the end of the adventure, heavy rains force them to abandon the wet boat for a dry train back to London, where they will find a theater and a good restaurant. Harris proposes the final toast: "Here's to Three Men well out of a Boat!"

Montmorency, a small fox terrier, the fourth member of the crew. His ambitions in life are to be sworn at by J. and his friends, to be in the way on every occasion possible, and to get into fights with every other dog in whatever neighborhood he finds himself. According to J., the only time Montmorency was stopped in his tracks was when he rushed up to a cat who forced him to retreat with his tail between his legs. Montmorency, as revealed by J., is the voice of realism on the boat. His sardonic attitude is in humorous contrast to the blustering naïveté of the human animals, J., George, and Harris.

— *Eugene Larson*

THE THREE MUSKETEERS
(Les Trois Mousquetaires)

Author: Alexandre Dumas, *père* (1802-1870)
First published: 1844
Genre: Novel

Locale: France
Time: 1626
Plot: Adventure

D'Artagnan (dahr-tahn-YAH[N]), a quick-witted, high-tempered young Gascon who has come to Paris to seek his fortune at the court of King Louis XIII. Having proved his bravery by fighting duels with Athos, Porthos, and Aramis, all members of the King's Musketeers, he becomes friends with each. Through the agency of his landlord's wife, Constance Bonancieux, with whom he has fallen in love, he and his

friends are induced to go to England to reclaim two diamond studs that the queen has imprudently given to her lover, the duke of Buckingham. Athos, Porthos, and Aramis are waylaid by agents of Cardinal Richelieu, but D'Artagnan is successful in completing the mission and saving the honor of the queen. In revenge, Milady, an agent of the cardinal, poisons Madame Bonancieux and tries to poison D'Artagnan. Having failed to prevent the assassination of the duke of Buckingham and having served gallantly at the siege of La Rochelle, D'Artagnan and his friends avenge themselves on Milady by having her beheaded. At the end of the novel, D'Artagnan is made lieutenant of the King's Musketeers.

Athos (ah-TOHS), the name assumed by the Comte de la Fère while serving in the King's Musketeers. When young, he had married a beautiful young woman, only to learn that she had been branded as a thief. She reappears as Milady.

Aramis (ah-rah-MEES), the name taken by the Chevalier d'Herblay when, as the consequence of fighting a duel, he gives up his intention of entering the priesthood and becomes one of the King's Musketeers. At the end of the novel, he is about to return to his religious vocation.

Porthos (pohr-TOHS), the third of the King's Musketeers who welcome D'Artagnan into their fellowship. He is noted for his great strength, vanity, and stupidity.

Milady, known also as **Charlotte Backson**, the **Comtesse de la Fère**, and **Lady de Winter**. She had, when young, first corrupted a priest and then married the Comte de la Fère. Having been revealed as a thief, she married an English nobleman whom she poisoned to secure his estate. In the novel, she is an agent of Cardinal Richelieu, and it is she who steals from the duke of Buckingham the two diamond studs given him by the French queen. D'Artagnan makes love to Milady under a false name. When she discovers the deception, he plans revenge. She is imprisoned in England by her brother-in-law and placed under the guard of John Felton. She corrupts Felton and induces him to stab Buckingham. Fleeing to France after the death of the duke, she revenges herself on D'Artagnan by poisoning his beloved, Constance Bonancieux. Finally, she is captured by the Musketeers and is beheaded.

The Cardinal-Duke de Richelieu (deh reesh-LYEW), the chief minister of King Louis XIII and an enemy of Queen Anne. He tries to ruin her reputation with the king so that she will be sent back to Spain. He orders Milady to steal from the duke of Buckingham the two diamond studs given to him by the queen, a plot intended to uncover the queen's love for the Englishman. The plot is foiled by D'Artagnan and his friends.

Anne of Austria, the unhappy queen of King Louis XIII, in love with the duke of Buckingham. She gives him two of the diamond studs presented to her by the king.

George Villiers (veel-YAY), the duke of Buckingham, the favorite of King Charles I of England and the lover of Anne of Austria, queen of France. He is, through the instigation of Milady, murdered by John Felton.

Lord de Winter, the brother-in-law of Milady, on whose orders she is imprisoned.

John Felton, an officer in the English navy and a Puritan, ordered by Lord de Winter to guard Milady. She seduces him and prevails on him to assassinate the duke of Buckingham.

Constance Bonancieux (boh nah[n]-SYEW), the wife of D'Artagnan's landlord and a confidential servant of the queen. Milady revenges herself on D'Artagnan by poisoning Constance.

The executioner of Lille, the brother of the priest who was Milady's first victim. He beheads her and thus avenges his brother.

De Treville (deh treh-VEEL), the captain of the King's Musketeers and D'Artagnan's patron.

The chevalier de Rochefort (deh rohsh-FOHR), the master of horse to Cardinal de Richelieu and one of his trusted agents.

Planchet (plahn-SHAY), D'Artagnan's servant.

Grimaud (gree-MOH), Athos' taciturn servant.

Musqueton (mews-keh-TOH[N]), Porthos' servant.

THE THREE SISTERS
(Tri sestry)

Author: Anton Chekhov (1860-1904)
First published: 1901; revised, 1904
Genre: Drama

Locale: Russia
Time: The nineteenth century
Plot: Impressionistic realism

Andrey Prozorov (ahn-DRAY proh-ZOH-rof), the son of a high-ranking Russian army officer. He studies to be a professor, but after his marriage he turns to gambling to forget his boorish wife, who takes a lover. He is an ineffective man who accomplishes nothing.

Natasha (nah-TAH-shuh), Andrey's ill-bred, rude, and selfish wife. She takes a local official, Protopopov, as her lover.

Masha (MAH-shuh), one of Andrey's sisters and the wife of Fyodor Kuligin. She once thought her husband clever, but she has been disillusioned. She falls in love with Vershinin, though he cannot leave his wife and children for her.

Fyodor Kuligin (FYOH-dohr KOO-lih-gihn), Masha's husband. He is an ineffective man who teaches in a high school.

Olga Prozorov (OHL-y-guh), one of Andrey's sisters. She wants desperately to return to Moscow. She teaches languages in the town's high school and becomes headmistress, but she is unhappy with her lot.

Irina Prozorov (ihr-IHN-uh), one of Andrey's sisters. Her hopes are dashed when Baron Tusenbach is killed by Captain Solyony in a duel, for she thought she could escape the little garrison town by marrying the baron.

Ivan Tchebutykin (iv-AHN cheh-BOOT-y-kihn), a medical doctor and friend of the Prozorovs. He is an incompetent medical practitioner.

Baron Tusenbach (TOO-sehn-bahch), an army lieutenant in love with Irina Prozorov. He is killed in a duel by Captain Solyony, his rival for Irina's affections.

Captain Vassily Solyony (vah-SIH-lihy soh-ly-ON-y), Baron Tusenbach's rival for Irina Prozorov's love. He kills the baron in a duel over the young woman.

Alexandr Vershinin (ahl-EHKS-andr vehr-SHIH-nihn), an artillery commander. He believes the world and people will get better and better. He falls in love with Masha but cannot leave his family for her.

Protopopov (proh-toh-POH-pof), a local official who becomes Natasha's lover.

THE THREE SISTERS

Author: May Sinclair (1863-1946)
First published: 1914
Genre: Novel

Locale: Garth, a remote village on the northern moors of England
Time: Early 1900's
Plot: Psychological realism

Gwendolyn Cartaret, the defiant and perceptive second daughter of James Cartaret, twenty-five years old when the novel opens. Keenly sensitive to nature, she assumes responsibility for visiting outlying parishioners in the lonely Yorkshire moors and thrives on strenuous hikes in the evenings. Slender, with translucent skin and expressive hands, she is a nervous beauty whose inner strength impresses other characters forcibly. She sees through her father's hypocrisy and maintains an intellectual's reverence for truth yet is susceptible to pointless self-sacrifice. She leaves Steven Rowcliffe, who loves her, in the hope that he will marry Alice. Later, when she returns to Garth to nurse her father after his stroke, she is forced to endure his mistaken choice of Mary.

James Cartaret, the vicar of Garth. His egotism and sensuality oppress his daughters. His fear of public opinion has led him to move to the isolated community of Garth when the novel begins. He is cold, domineering, and unsuited for both his profession and the celibate life that he is forced, by his wife's desertion, to lead. He bullies his daughters endlessly, afraid only of Gwendolyn, who opposes him. His control of his daughters' lives relaxes after a stroke, which renders him a gentle, pathetic old man relying on Gwendolyn for daily care.

Mary Cartaret, the oldest daughter of the vicar, at twenty-seven years of age when the novel opens, responsible for teaching Sunday school. Proud of her own goodness, Mary is a placid, deceptive beauty who encourages Gwendolyn to leave Garth only to woo Steven Rowcliffe herself. After her marriage, her self-deception turns to hypocrisy as she increasingly cultivates acquaintance with "good" society. She becomes a neglectful mother of three children and torments Gwendolyn with evidence of her satisfying marriage to Steven.

Alice Cartaret, the youngest daughter of the vicar, responsible for directing the church choir and playing the organ for church services. At the age of twenty-three, with little outlet for her passionate nature, she is subject to hysteria and responds to her father's bullying by starving herself into serious anemia. Believing that she is in love with the doctor, she blossoms into youthful beauty. Her graceful manner and golden hair and skin attract Jim Greatorex. She forgets the doctor in her quest to reform Jim and matures during the course of their love affair. Her pregnancy by and subsequent marriage to this farmer from a significantly lower social class precipitate the vicar's stroke. Motherhood turns her into a plump, cheerful matron, completely absorbed in her children.

Steven Rowcliffe, the village doctor, who has left a successful practice in Leeds to minister to the needs of country patients. At thirty years of age, he is stimulated by the rough people and countryside and finds that the outdoor demands of his job appeal to his romantic nature. Handsome, somewhat vain, and embracing strenuous activity, he is drawn to Gwendolyn, although he is envious of her capacity to lose herself in the natural beauty of the moors. His egotism is appeased by Mary's attention after Gwendolyn rejects his proposal of marriage and goes to London. Only after Gwendolyn's return does he realize that Mary bores him and has captured him by appealing to his latent laziness. Sensual and passionate, he urges Gwendolyn to have an affair with him; after she refuses, his love for her gradually wanes over the years.

Jim Greatorex, a young farmer who marries Alice after she becomes pregnant with his child. He begins the novel dominated by his physical needs, but his drunkenness and his affairs with village serving girls cease when he falls in love with Alice. Despite his brutishness, he is capable of great gentleness and inarticulate appreciation of natural beauty. Frustrated by a lack of faith, he finds purpose in protecting Alice, and his sensitivity appeals to Gwendolyn, who discovers that he shares her passion for nature.

Essy Gale, a young servant at the vicarage. She is forced to leave her position when the vicar discovers that she is pregnant with Jim Greatorex's child. Despite social ostracism, Essy maintains her dignity by refusing to marry Jim because she knows that he does not love her. She finds solace in the fact that Gwendolyn is genuinely kind to her and later returns to work for the vicar after his stroke has erased the memory of her past mistakes.

— *Gweneth A. Dunleavy*

THREE SOLDIERS

Author: John Dos Passos (1896-1970)
First published: 1921
Genre: Novel

Locale: France
Time: 1917-1919
Plot: Social realism

John Andrews, called **Andy**, a Harvard-trained musician who finds himself in the enlisted ranks during World War I. He is intelligent and sensitive, and he hates the Army for trying to make a machine of him. Returning to his regiment from the hospital after he has suffered a wound in his leg from a bursting shell, he is full of rebellion. He is convinced that humanity should not tolerate war. He goes absent without leave but is caught and sentenced to hard labor. He escapes and hides out at an inn near Paris. There, working on a musical composition, he is again arrested by the military police.

Chrisfield, a violent soldier from Indiana. Chrisfield hates and loves quickly and passionately. He kills a German officer in cold blood and slays a hated American lieutenant named Anderson as the officer, wounded, waits for help in a clearing in a forest. When Chrisfield comes to suspect that the authorities know that he killed Anderson, he goes absent without leave and spends his days as a refugee in France.

Dan Fuselli, a whining, sniveling, and groveling American private from San Francisco whose only ambition is to become a corporal. He spends much of his time in France paying court to noncommissioned officers who might get him promoted.

His French girlfriend, Yvonne, is stolen from him by a sergeant. He becomes a corporal after the Armistice but learns, at about the same time, that his girl back home has married a naval officer.

Geneviève Rod, a young Frenchwoman who admires Andrews' musicianship and his good taste but cannot understand the motive behind his rebellion.

THREE TRAPPED TIGERS
(Tres tristes tigres)

Author: Guillermo Cabrera Infante (1929-   )
First published: 1967
Genre: Novel

Locale: Havana, Cuba
Time: Summer, 1958
Plot: Comic realism

Bustrófedon (bews-TROH-feh-dohn), a character who embodies language and its creative potential. His name, of Greek origin, means "to write alternately from right to left and left to right." He is fascinated with anything reversible: words, numbers, or concepts. He represents an appreciation of the potential of language and of the sheer joy of spontaneous and uninhibited creation. He is a character in the process of discovering and creating himself through language. After his death, he continues to live in the minds of many of the novel's characters.

Silvestre (seel-VEHS-treh), a would-be writer. Estranged from the present, he is obsessed with the past, preferring his memories over experiencing life. He is particularly concerned with ordering the chaos of existence by means of the written word. He is linked to one of the novel's major themes: humanity's attempt to comprehend the implications of formlessness.

Arsenio Cué (kew-EH), a professional actor and television star, and Silvestre's closest friend. His personal and professional lives merge to such an extent that they seem one and the same. He is so often playing a role that it is difficult to know who he is. His humor, his continual role-playing, and his dark sunglasses protect him from the outside world. His playful excursions into the world of fantasy have a serious purpose: He lives in a society that is wasting its energies in useless dissipation, yet he attempts to channel his activities into creative forces. His view is that the universe is dominated by chance rather than by order.

Códac (KOH-dak), a photojournalist. He is first a superficial recorder of the social scene, then later becomes involved

in the more realistic and distasteful journalistic duties of photographing political reality during the last months of the dictatorship of Fulgencio Batista. Although sensitive to visual reality, he is also able to appreciate the beauty beneath superficial appearances, underscoring one of the novel's major themes: the importance of re-creation instead of duplication, creation rather than sterility, and change rather than permanence.

Eribó (eh-ree-BOH), a lonely mulatto bongo player and would-be social climber. He becomes emotionally involved with Vivian Smith Corona, a spoiled and immature member of the upper class, but the relationship leads nowhere. Eribó recognizes the pathos of the situation and views it in ironic terms. His association with Vivian is typical of most of the relationships that exist between men and women in the novel. These relationships, essentially sterile and self-defeating, are also symptomatic of this society.

La Estrella (lah ehs-TREH-yah), a huge mulatta singer of boleros. Although she is obese and generally unattractive, she is an outstanding singer, capable of creating a purity of sound that moves everyone who hears her. La Estrella is a combination of the ugly and the beautiful, a symbol of life itself. Unique uses of language and sound by both her and Bustrófedon represent an attempt to return to origins as a means to capture the freshness of a new beginning. They are, however, an anomaly in a society that is committed to artificiality and illusion.

— *Genevieve Slomski*

THE THREEPENNY OPERA
(Die Dreigroschenoper)

Author: Bertolt Brecht (1898-1956)
First published: 1929
Genre: Drama

Locale: London's Soho district
Time: 1837
Plot: Social satire

Macheath, called **Mac the Knife**, the head of a gang of petty criminals in London. He manages his crooked affairs through "understandings" with Sheriff Brown. An incorrigible philanderer, he is involved with Brown's daughter, Lucy, but also entices Polly, the daughter of "Beggar Boss" Peachum, into matrimony. This act outrages Peachum, who vows to undo Macheath by working a deal with Sheriff Brown. Mac's enemies are convinced that, even when warned that a plot has

been hatched against him, he will not flee far; soon, he is caught while making his habitual turn among the harlots of Turnbridge. Because Mac is an inveterate wheeler and dealer, however, he is able to bribe his way out of the charges and even to obtain recognition for service to the crown.

Jonathan Jeremiah "Beggar Boss" Peachum, the proprietor of Beggar's Friend, Ltd. He organizes London's beggars quarter by quarter, giving them territories and pitiful roles to play. Although Peachum himself is an obvious opportunist, the destitute figures under him provide a channel to convey the social revolutionary theme of the play. Peachum is distracted from organizing an unprecedented parade of beggars at Queen Victoria's coronation by the troublesome scandal of his daughter's marriage to Mac. A mixture of opportunism and pomposity is revealed in Peachum, whose concern over the poor focuses mainly on how to use them to his benefit.

Polly Peachum, the daughter of Jonathan Peachum. Polly marries Macheath in a ceremony that reflects the milieu to which her father, in obvious hypocrisy, objects: The marriage takes place in a "borrowed" stable; all accessories, including furniture, are stolen. Polly is not timid about her association with Mac's gang, prompting her mother's recollection that "even as a child she had a swelled head like the Queen of England." When Mac is pursued by the law, he asks Polly to "manage" the gang's affairs. In her dealings with her parents, as well as in her verbal confrontations with Sheriff Brown's daughter Lucy, who also claims Mac's amorous loyalties, Polly demonstrates an uncanny ability to turn vulnerability into moral superiority.

Jack "Tiger" Brown, the high sheriff of London, Mac's friend since childhood days and a former fellow soldier with him in the colonial army in India. Brown receives a cut from all profits of Mac's gang. He suffers pangs of conscience over his friend's arrest and is only partially embarrassed when Mac escapes. He is soon caught in a quandary, however, when Peachum threatens to compromise the high sheriff by amassing hundreds of beggars at the queen's coronation. Brown learns that, unless Mac hangs, he will have to undergo the unpleasantness of removing the destitute from the shadow of regal splendor by brute force. On the other hand, the sheriff is worried that, if a public execution is carried out, the crowds that would have cheered the queen will throng to the side of the gallows. Brown outdoes himself arranging a deal, gaining not only a reprieve but also the queen's award of an honorary peerage, a pension, and a castle to Mac the Knife. This device satisfies the Peachums.

Lucy Brown, the daughter of High Sheriff Brown. She has been involved amorously with Mac. After her discovery of Mac's marriage and her first confrontation with Polly, her role is that of a frenetic woman propelled by jealousy. As the plot advances, however, and Mac must flee both women to avoid arrest, Lucy's weaknesses show through. Mac succeeds in making her believe that he loves only her, and (perhaps because she is so gullible as to believe Mac) she comes to commiserate with her rival Polly, whom she now calls "Mrs. Macheath." Both women come to the conclusion that men are not worth the frustration that they cause.

— *Byron D. Cannon*

THROUGH THE IVORY GATE

Author: Rita Dove (1952-   )
First published: 1992
Genre: Novel

Locale: Phoenix, Arizona, and Akron and Oberlin, Ohio
Time: Early 1960's to mid-1970's
Plot: Psychological realism

Virginia King, the protagonist, a college-educated puppeteer, musician, and actress. She returns to her hometown of Akron, Ohio, from Phoenix, Arizona, to serve as an artist-in-residence at a public school in Akron. Plagued with unresolved feelings about her family's past, she determines to discover the truth about her family and herself. She has a series of unsatisfactory relationships with men and must decide whether to pursue her career and search for identity or to marry.

Belle King, Virginia's embittered mother, unforgiving of her husband's sexual relationship with his sister and exacting in her demands on her children. She indulges herself in selfish pain. She tries to help her children understand the difficulties of being African American.

Ernest King, Virginia's father, the first African American chemist to work for Goodyear. He is a decent, caring man whose affair with his sister, Carrie, in his youth has driven him to emotional isolation from his wife and a passion for traveling to historical and cultural sites.

Claudia King, Virginia's younger sister, a rebellious teenager experiencing "growing pains."

Ernest King, Jr., Virginia's brother and ally.

Aunt Carrie, Ernest's sister and Virginia's aunt. Unattractive as a child, she was married to an elderly widower who died while she was still a young woman. When Belle discovered Carrie's note about her youthful relationship with Ernest, Ernest moves his family from Akron to Arizona. When Carrie tells her story to Virginia, she purges herself of some of her guilt and provides Virginia with an explanation for her parents' behavior.

Virginia Evans, Virginia's namesake and the matriarch of the family. In her apartment at Saferstein Towers, she sits on "her throne—the *talking seat*"—and not only tells Virginia about her life with her husband but also provides her with counsel about life. Her warning "that you can't hide nothing from nobody in this world" haunts Virginia and applies both to Carrie's story and Virginia's own unresolved feelings about Clayton Everett and Terry Murray.

Clayton Everett, a handsome, tall, talented cellist whom Virginia meets while she is a student at the University of Michigan. Virginia's colleague, tutor, foil, confidant, and friend, Clayton would be the perfect mate for her if he were not a homosexual. Despite his sexual preference, he and she become lovers, but the affair is doomed. Virginia accepts the situation when he invites her to his apartment, where he introduces her to his male lover. At the end of the novel, Virginia believes that she loved Clayton but did not love Terry Murray.

Terry Murray, an educated, handsome, sensitive, available bachelor whose son is one of Virginia's students. The parents of Virginia's students encourage and orchestrate the match, and she is tempted by his sincere declaration that he is "in this for the distance."

Todd Williams, Virginia's handsome high school boyfriend, whom she rejects when she reads his almost illiterate note. Her response and her majorette role reflect her unconscious desire to conform to white society.

Renee Butler, a quiet, musically talented student of Virginia. She is insecure and fixates on Virginia, who encourages her, then ignores her. When Renee jumps and falls, injuring her ankle, her mother chides Virginia for meddling in Renee's life, then ignoring her. Mrs. Butler's admonition applies to the pattern of Virginia's life.

Karen, Virginia's white friend in elementary school. Her racial epithet "nigger" exposes Virginia to racial prejudice.

— *Thomas L. Erskine*

THROUGH THE LOOKING-GLASS: And What Alice Found There

Author: Lewis Carroll (Charles Lutwidge Dodgson, 1832-1898)
First published: 1871
Genre: Novel

Locale: The dreamworld of Alice
Time: The nineteenth century
Plot: Fantasy

Alice, an imaginative English child who has fantastic adventures in Looking-Glass House.

The White Kitten, a good kitten who is not responsible for Alice's adventures.

The Black Kitten, who is told by Alice to pretend that they can go through the mirror to Looking-Glass House.

Dinah, the kittens' mother.

The White Queen, a live chess piece. In Alice's adventures, she becomes a sheep, gives Alice some needles, and tells the little girl to knit. She reappears throughout the story in various guises.

The White King, a live chess piece. He has Alice serve a cake that cuts itself.

Tiger Lily,

Rose, and

Violet, flowers of whom Alice asks the path to take.

Gnat, a pleasant insect as big as a chicken. He melts away.

The Red Queen, a live chess piece. She tells Alice that one has to run to stay in the same place. Later, she turns into the black kitten.

Tweedledum and

Tweedledee, two odd, fat, little men. They speak in ambiguities and recite poems to Alice. They fight over a rattle until frightened away by a crow.

The Red King, a live chess piece. He dreams about Alice, says Tweedledee, and thus gives her reality.

Humpty Dumpty, who has a conversation in riddles with Alice. He explains to her the Jabberwocky poem.

The Lion and

the Unicorn, who fight over the White King's crown.

The Red Knight, a live chess piece who claims Alice as his prisoner.

The White Knight, a live chess piece who also claims Alice as his prisoner. He leads Alice to a brook and tells her to jump into the next square to become a queen herself.

THYESTES

Author: Seneca (4 B.C.E.-65 C.E.)
First performed: c. 40-55 C.E.
Genre: Drama

Locale: Mycenae
Time: Antiquity
Plot: Tragedy

Atreus (AY-tree-uhs), the oldest son of Pelops and the rightful ruler of Mycenae. He is the protagonist in what is arguably the most fiendish revenge play in the history of the theater. He and his brother Thyestes were supposed to alternate in ruling Mycenae, but neither of them respected the other's rights. Having won the latest civil war, Atreus has consolidated his power and is now ready to avenge himself on his brother. Asserting that, as a king, he is not bound by moral law, Atreus formulates his plan. He sends his two sons to Thyestes with a friendly message, inviting him to return to Mycenae and share the throne with Atreus. When Thyestes arrives, Atreus welcomes him warmly; later, however, Atreus kills his nephews, butchers them, cooks the meat, and at a great feast serves it to their unsuspecting father. He concludes by giving Thyestes wine mixed with his children's blood, then reveals the truth by uncovering a platter holding their heads. Gloating over his brother's distress, Atreus claims victory. Now, Atreus says, his marriage bed has been cleansed and he can be sure that his sons are his own. He ends by scoffing at the idea that the gods will punish him.

Thyestes (thi-EHS-teez), Atreus' brother, who seduces his wife and steals the golden ram, the symbol of power in the kingdom. Having been defeated and banished by Atreus, Thyestes accepts with foreboding his brother's invitation to return to Mycenae. When Atreus insists that he accept a crown, Thyestes believes that his brother really has forgiven him, and he relaxes his guard. At the feast in his honor, Thyestes drinks heavily and enjoys his food, although he has a strange premonition of evil. He is fed the bodies of his sons at the banquet. When Atreus reveals the heads of the dead boys and tells their father that he has consumed his own children, Thyestes can only wish for his own death. Although he deserved to suffer, he says, his sons were innocent, and he calls on the gods to avenge them. His greatest regret is his inability to get similar vengeance on Atreus.

Tantalus (TAN-tuh-luhs), a son of Thyestes, his great-grandfather's namesake. He helps convince Thyestes that they should accept Atreus' invitation. He is the first to be slain.

Thyestes' two other sons, murdered by their uncle, who roasts their bodies for their father's banquet.

Agamemnon (a-guh-MEHM-non) and

Menelaus (meh-nuh-LAY-uhs), sons of Atreus.

Megaera (meh-GAY-ruh), one of the Furies. She orders the ghost of Tantalus to goad his descendants into committing evil acts.

The ghost of Tantalus, the former king and the grandfather of Atreus and Thyestes, summoned back from Hades to witness the fury of his descendants and help carry out the gods'

curse on his house. For his sacrifice of his son, Pelops, he was sentenced to eternal torment.

Pelops (PEE-lops), the father of Atreus and Thyestes and the son of Tantalus. He was sacrificed by his father to the gods but restored to life.

— *Rosemary M. Canfield Reisman*

A TICKET TO THE STARS
(Zvezdnyi bilet)

Author: Vassily Aksyonov (1932-   )
First published: 1961
Genre: Novel

Locale: Moscow and the Baltic coast
Time: Summer, 1960
Plot: Social realism

Dimka, a seventeen-year-old who has recently been graduated from high school. He represents the generation of Russian youth born during World War II, who have little firsthand knowledge of the hardships that their parents experienced. Having completed his secondary education, he is faced with the decision of whether to continue his education or to seek a job. Even though he loves his parents and admires his older brother, Victor, a space scientist, Dimka leaves home and Moscow, mainly because he wants to make his own decisions for the first time in his life. This rebelliousness stems from the fact that young people in the Soviet Union are constantly told what to do instead of being allowed to make their own decisions. Even Dimka's successful brother cannot escape the criticism of being too pliant in acquiescing to the system. Dimka is not rebellious solely for the sake of asserting his independence, as shown at the end of the novel, when he returns home after hearing about his brother's fatal accident. Through this act, he confirms his integrity and innate sense of responsibility. This attitude bodes well for the young Soviet generation, showing that its individuals can think and act for themselves after decades of submissiveness.

Yurka, Dimka's classmate, who joins him on the post-graduation journey and becomes a "kilometer eater" instead of meekly accepting the will of his elders. With his feet placed firmly on the ground, Yurka shows promise in the sports field and hopes to become a basketball star. He is willing to forgo the best chance of achieving that goal, which would mean that he would have to stay at home. Like Dimka and others, Yurka is a young man whose behavior is typical for his age, as seen in his desire to have fun and in his falling in love with Galya. He, too, demonstrates a readiness to make his own decisions and to sacrifice the benefits of going along with the system.

Alik, Dimka and Yurka's classmate and trip companion. More withdrawn and art-oriented, Alik hopes to make writing

his career. By asserting his independence and by wasting time in aimless wandering, he risks losing the best chance of learning the writing skills, that of a continuing education. He is willing to take that risk, knowing intuitively that the best way to become a good writer is to get to know the world outside the benevolent but stifling protection of his parents. Like his friends, Alik shows a remarkable maturity for his age and a fiercely independent spirit.

Galya, Dimka's girlfriend and classmate. Galya asserts her will by leaving on the trip with three classmates, against her parents' wishes. She behaves normally for her age when she flirts with Yurka, even though she is Dimka's girlfriend, and when she falls for the tall tales of a middle-aged actor, a chance acquaintance who promises to help her in her acting career. She is a perfect companion for the three boys in showing the same desire for independence. She also demonstrates that this desire is genuine and widespread among the Russian youth.

Victor, Dimka's older brother, a space scientist. A member of a prewar generation, Victor displays a more obedient mentality and a willingness to serve the system. He, too, shows signs of independence when, after discovering new material, he refuses to complete his dissertation only for the sake of getting a degree. He is also more understanding of the young people, as shown in his refusal to interfere with Dimka's decision to leave home, even though he disagrees with it. Victor's lasting legacy is "a ticket to the stars" for the younger generations, which prompts Dimka to abandon his quest for a new life of adventure and uncertainty and to follow in his brother's footsteps. Victor can thus be seen as a middleman between the old and the new generations and a guidepost toward a better future.

— *Vasa D. Mihailovich*

THE TIDINGS BROUGHT TO MARY
(L'Annonce faite à Marie)

Author: Paul Claudel (1868-1955)
First published: 1912
Genre: Drama

Locale: France
Time: Early years of the fifteenth century
Plot: Poetic

Violaine Vercors (vyoh-LEHN vehr-KOHR), the eighteen-year-old daughter of Anne and Elisabeth, and Mara's older sister. She is engaged to marry Jacques Hury, a farmer. In the

prologue, she forgives Pierre de Craon, a mason who had attempted to rape her. He now suffers from leprosy. As he is about to leave their village for Rheims to build a church appropriately named Holy Justice, Violaine gives him her engagement ring as a contribution to the construction costs. She then kisses Pierre as a sign of her forgiveness. She thus becomes infected with leprosy, from which she will die. Although she loves Jacques, her fiancé, she tells him that they can never marry each other. After she leaves their village of Combernon, he marries her younger sister, Mara. When their baby Aubaine dies, Mara implores Violaine to pray to God so that Aubaine may live. Aubaine is miraculously restored to life. As the play ends, Violaine encourages her father, her sister, and her brother-in-law to appreciate God's intense love for humanity.

Pierre de Craon (pyehr deh kra-YOH[N]), a mason who appears only in the prologue. He bitterly regrets his attempted rape of Violaine. He tells her that his leprosy is a divine punishment for his crime. She believes that his repentance is sincere. He is miraculously cured of his leprosy. While in Jerusalem, he meets Violaine's father and gives him her engagement ring.

Anne Vercors, the husband of Elisabeth and father of two grown daughters, Violaine and Mara. After having arranged Violaine's forthcoming marriage to Jacques Hury, he informs his wife and daughters that God needs him to make a pilgrimage to the Holy Land. Anne believes that he must sacrifice his comfortable life in France to serve God. When he returns to his village, he finds Violaine unconscious in the sand. He brings her home and explains to Jacques and Mara that Violaine freely contracted leprosy to serve God through suffering and prayer.

Jacques Hury (zhahk hew-REE), a young and sensible farmer engaged to marry Violaine. When he learns from her that she suffers from leprosy, he agrees with her that they should never marry. He arranges for her to leave Combernon for Chevoche, where she will receive care. Although he does marry Mara, he never stops loving Violaine. As Violaine is dying, Anne tells Jacques that she was inspired by God to sacrifice happiness so that she could dedicate her life to prayer.

Mara Vercors (mah-RAH), Violaine's younger sister, first portrayed as self-centered and manipulative. Mara wanted to marry Jacques; she tells her mother that she will commit suicide if her mother does not prevent Violaine's wedding to Jacques. After Violaine becomes a leper, Mara does marry Jacques. When their baby daughter, Aubaine, dies, Mara implores her sister to intervene with God. While Violaine prays, Mara recites readings from the masses for Christmas Day. Their prayers are answered with Aubaine's miraculous restoration to life. After his return from the Holy Land, Anne helps Mara to understand that altruism can overcome selfishness. Thanks to Anne and Violaine, Mara grows both spiritually and emotionally.

Elisabeth Vercors, the wife of Anne and mother of Violaine and Mara, hurt by her husband's sudden decision to leave for the Holy Land and by Mara's threat to commit suicide. She feels abandoned by her husband, and she cannot understand Mara's extreme selfishness. Elisabeth dies sometime between the wedding of Jacques and Mara and the birth of her granddaughter, Aubaine.

— *Edmund J. Campion*

TIETA, THE GOAT GIRL: Or, The Return of the Prodigal Daughter
(Tiêta do Agreste)

Author: Jorge Amado (1912-   )
First published: 1977
Genre: Novel

Locale: The fictitious town of Sant'Ana do Agreste, Salvador, and São Paulo, Brazil
Time: Mid-1960's
Plot: Melodrama

Antonieta Esteves Cantarelli (ahn-tohn-ee-EH-tah ehs-TEH-vehs kahn-tah-REH-lee), also called **Tieta** (tee-EH-tah), the wealthy owner of the Lord's Retreat, a sophisticated bordello in São Paulo. A middle-aged, curly haired brunette who covers her tall, voluptuous, dark-skinned body in red turbans, blonde wigs, and skin-tight jeans, the sexy Tieta unashamedly lusts for good men, fine food, and unbridled laughter. Her goatlike stubbornness, pragmatism, and flinty hardness sometimes conflict with her genuine loving and kindness but just as often translate her generosity into action. Tieta's arrival in backward Sant'Ana do Agreste to visit her impoverished relatives and birthplace catalyzes changes in the town and crises in many characters. She uses her bordello-related influence to obtain electricity for the town, which attracts the interest of the deadly titanium dioxide industry. Her many acts of goodness earn for her the title of saint, until the town discovers her true profession and her seduction of her nephew.

Ascânio Trindade (ahs-KAYN-yoh treen-DAH-deh), Agreste's county clerk. A good-looking, serious-faced official, twenty-eight years old, Ascânio is frank, friendly, honest, kind, and sometimes excitable in his dreams about a possible bright future for Agreste. He suffers a cruel betrayal by his

betrothed, from which he does not recover until he falls in love with Leonora. In his sincere dreams for progress, the innocent Ascânio becomes the pawn of the titanium dioxide industry as the industry's candidate for mayor. This influence gradually corrupts him. His last vestiges of goodness are shattered when he discovers that Leonora is a prostitute.

Ricardo Batista (rree-KAHR-doh bah-TEES-tah), a seminarian and Perpétua's older son. A tall, dark, muscular, good-looking, husky, and somewhat gangling youth of seventeen with the hint of a mustache, Ricardo exudes innocence and good health in his black cassock. He is tortured by his lust for Tieta, which finally triumphs over his devotion to God. Through a talk with a wise old holy man, however, he finally realizes that he can be both priest and lover. He consequently pursues both paths with such dedication that Tieta throws him naked into the street when she learns of his other lovers. Ricardo matures into a radical champion against the titanium dioxide industry.

Perpétua Esteves Batista (pehr-PEH-tew-ah), Tieta's widowed older sister. A stern-faced, bony-chested, domineering sourpuss with a perpetually constipated face, Perpétua masks her greed and meanness in exaggerated piety. Her covetous wish to have Ricardo become Tieta's heir provides Tieta the chance to seduce him. Perpétua's wrath abates when Tieta compensates her in cash for the seminarian's lost virginity.

Elisa Esteves Simas (eh-LEE-sah ehs-TEH-vehs SEE-mahs), Tieta's younger half sister. Elisa is a slender, graceful, and sensitive brunette whose luxurious hair frames a pretty pale face with full lips and melancholy eyes. She lives in constant sexual frustration because her husband insists on treating her high-haunched, firm-breasted body with delicate respect. Elisa longs to move to exciting São Paulo, even if she must become a prostitute, until Tieta persuades Asterio to make love to Elisa with more force and abandon.

Leonora Cantarelli (leh-oh-NOHR-ah), a prostitute at the Lord's Retreat, a slim, blonde, and youthful sylph who is charming and sweet, with a crystalline laugh. Leonora masquerades as Tieta's stepdaughter. Her impoverished and brutal past has not destroyed a core of innocence and a longing for true love, which she thinks she has found with Ascânio. When she tearfully confesses her true identity, Ascânio rejects her, and she attempts suicide.

Donna Carmosina Sluizer da Consolação (kahr-moh-SEE-nah slo-ZIHR dah kon-soo-lah-SOW), Agreste's postmistress. Light-skinned, with a freckled, broad face, keen eyes, and a keener wit, Carmosina loves life and laughter but grieves that she is still a virgin at the age of fifty. She freely reads everyone's mail and controls local gossip, but she does so with benevolent intentions.

Skipper Dário Queluz (DAH-ree-oh kay-LOOSH), a retired seaman. Athletic but philosophic, Skipper Dário commands love and respect with his integrity and kindly smile. His love for the natural beauty of Agreste makes him sacrifice his reclusive lifestyle to become an antipollution candidate for mayor.

Doctor Mirko Stefano (MEER-koh steh-FAHN-oh), a São Paulo industrialist. With his matinee-idol looks, avant-garde clothes, and prissy, affected voice, the unscrupulous Mirko contrives to establish a deadly titanium dioxide factory in Agreste.

Peto Batista (PEH-toh), Perpétua's youngest son. Peto, a lewd, precocious thirteen-year-old, cannot understand Ricardo's resistance to Tieta's attractions.

Asterio Simas (ahs-TEH-ree-oh), Elisa's husband. Weak-willed and unambitious since giving up the unorthodox sexual practices of his bachelorhood, Asterio finally heeds Tieta's advice to express his deepest desires with his wife.

— *Timothy C. Davis*

TIGER AT THE GATES
(La Guerre de Troie n'aura pas lieu)

Author: Jean Giraudoux (1882-1944)
First published: 1935
Genre: Drama

Locale: Troy
Time: During the Trojan War
Plot: Mythic

Hector, the leader of the Trojan army and son of King Priam, a warrior who understands the costs as well as the attractions of war. Having just returned from the bloody battlefield, he now longs for peace. He is strong, not only physically but also morally, believing in life and responding to all that is natural and good. His overwhelming desire to shut the Gates of War enables him to bend others—Priam, Helen, Paris, and even the Greek Ulysses—to his will. He is determined and confident enough to ignore insults on the way to creating peace. Because of his youth, however, he does not realize that it may be easier to control an army than to control the illogical, emotional behavior of a single individual or to alter fate.

Andromache (an-DRAH-mah-kee), Hector's wife, his match in wisdom, moral strength, and desire for peace. As a woman, she sees only the loss and tragedy of war, and she is unable to understand why poets find glory in death and destruction. She believes in love and honesty, and she laments the fact that hypocrisy, not honor, breeds war. She most regrets that if the war occurs, it will be fought for lovers who do not really love each other.

Helen, the wife of Menelaus, a king of Greece. She represents external beauty and is incapable of any deep feeling. She cares only for things that are vivid or bright enough to catch her attention, and nothing holds her attention long. In many ways, she is the most complicated figure in the play. It is all too easy to characterize her as shallow, as just a pretty face. She is that, but she is more. In her own, admittedly rather self-centered way, she is as much a visionary as Cassandra. A creature of fate, she is also stoic. She readily accepts what must happen. She knows she is hated by the Trojan women, yet she ignores this because there is nothing she can do about it. She does not worry because her beauty will fade and she will grow old. She has no pity for anyone, not even herself.

Demokos, a poet and the leader of the Trojan senate, infatuated with words and images. Those of beauty, blood, courage, honor, glory, and war inspire him. He creates war songs that he hopes will turn men savage. He is an evil man and a bad poet.

Hecuba (HEH-kyuh-buh), Priam's wife, who is caustic and cynical about love, beauty, men, and women. Both clever and realistic, she matches Demokos in a battle of words and insults, proving herself superior. She believes that old men should fight the wars.

Priam (PRI-am), the king of Troy, the father of Hector and Paris, and one of the old men who follow Helen. He leaves the leadership of the army and even the country to Hector, warning him, however, that peace can be dangerous.

Ulysses (yew-LIH-sees), a Greek warrior and diplomat, Hector's counterpart. When the two meet to decide whether war or peace will prevail, he proves more articulate and wiser in both the ways of diplomacy and the ways of the world. He sees the human folly that leads to war, and although he works with Hector to prevent war, he warns Hector that all cunning may be useless in a fight against destiny.

Paris, Hector's younger brother, handsome, shallow, and flighty. He stole Helen after seeing her swimming naked. He is a male counterpart to Helen, moving from one woman to the next because he loves the sensations of romance: first attraction, then consummation, next the tears and tragedy of separation, and finally a search for the next love. Both he and Helen are concerned only with their own feelings; each needs new sensations continually to provide stimulation.

Ajax, a captain in the Greek army, blunt, aggressive, and hard-drinking. Although he initially believes that Hector is a coward, he comes to admire Hector's moral strength and realizes that the two, as warriors, have more in common than citizens who stand by urging a war they will never have to fight.

Cassandra, Hector's sister, a blind prophetess. She insists that her prophecies are not visions but simply predictions based on her knowledge of human nature and of fate. Her warnings follow the movement of events toward their inexorable end: The complacency of Troy will cause the waking of the tiger who has been sleeping at the gates.

— *Mary E. Mahony*

TILL WE HAVE FACES: A Myth Retold

Author: C. S. Lewis (1898-1963)
First published: 1956
Genre: Novel

Locale: Glome, a kingdom in Eastern Europe or Asia Minor
Time: Sometime after the death of Socrates in 399 B.C.
Plot: Mythic

Orual, or **Maia** (MAY-yah), the narrator, the eldest princess of Glome and finally its queen. She is caught between her love of learning as presented in the ideals of Greek philosophy and poetry and her earthy, passionate nature. So ugly as to have no hope of romantic love, Orual attaches herself fiercely to her Greek tutor and her divinely beautiful half sister, Istra/Psyche, while secretly cherishing a love for the soldier who teaches her swordsmanship. Each love is marred by her inability to release its object, a fault most evident with Istra, who is doomed to exile through Orual's possessive jealousy. Orual rules Glome well: She is brave in battle and wise in council. The story is told in her old age, as an accusation against gods and their inscrutable cruelty, and covers Orual's life from childhood. Visions and dreams cause the book to end in understanding and acceptance of the paradox of divinity as Orual dies.

Istra, or **Psyche** (SI-kee), the youngest princess of Glome, the lovely child of the king's second wife. She fills Orual's hungry heart but is too beautiful for a mortal; she is sacrificed to the "Shadow Beast," a manifestation of the son of Glome's patron goddess, Ungit. Ungit is understood as a cultural alternate form of Aphrodite (Venus), and her son is the Glome Eros (Cupid). Thus Istra/Psyche and Ungit's son tie this tale to the Cupid-Psyche myth of antiquity. The princess' sacrifice is also a wedding, and Psyche lives in an invisible palace with a divine husband whom she must never see. When Orual forces a betrayal of the god-bridegroom, Psyche is doomed to lose her love and home and to wander weeping through the world. Before her own death, Orual encounters a shrine where Istra/Psyche is worshiped as a goddess of spring and renewal.

Lysias, the **"Fox,"** a Greek slave bought as a status symbol to teach the children of the king. He stands as an affectionate father to Orual and Istra, teaching them the intellectual ideals of Greek philosophy, yet he is unable to fathom the nature of

divinity manifested in Ungit. He renounces his hope of a return to Greece so that he can stay with Orual as a councillor when she frees him.

Trom, the brutal, selfish king of Glome, who rejects his daughters in the hope of having a son, railing against the gods and fate in his misfortunes of war, famine, and disease. He uses Orual's intellectual gifts but dies in terror of her, realizing in his last illness the growth of her power in his own decline.

Bardia, the captain of the king's guards and councillor to Orual. He teaches her military arts and accompanies her on her first search for the body of the sacrificed Istra. Devoted to martial virtues and common sense, Bardia never sees Orual as a woman or realizes that she loves him. His widow accuses Orual of working her devoted servant to death.

Redival, the middle princess, beautiful in mortal terms, hungry for love, and jealous of Orual's tie to Istra. She is a flirt and a gossip whose indiscretions help lead to Istra's sacrifice. Orual marries her to a neighboring king and adopts her second son as heir to the throne of Glome.

Priest of Ungit, the immensely old and inscrutable representative of the abuses and mystery surrounding the worship of the goddess Ungit. It is he who demands the sacrifice of Princess Istra. He dies, after a long illness, at the same time as does Trom.

Arnom, the successor to the old priest of Ungit. He understands his goddess as a Hellenized and abstract deity, an Aphrodite represented by a Greek statue that displaces Ungit's shapeless, faceless stone. Arnom is a skilled politician, alert to the interests of the temple. His establishment as chief priest is contemporary with Orual's accession to the throne, and they work as allies. He ends the novel with praise of the dead queen.

— *Anne W. Sienkewicz*

THE TILTED CROSS

Author: Hal Porter (1911-1984)
First published: 1961; revised, 1971
Genre: Novel

Locale: Hobart Town, Van Diemen's Land (Hobart, Tasmania)
Time: The 1840's
Plot: Historical realism

Judas Griffin Vaneleigh, an artist and former convict. Once a handsome, dashing figure of consequence in London artistic circles, Vaneleigh has lost his aristocratic air and has turned into a broken man, both in appearance and in spirit, even though he is only in his early forties. Vaneleigh's charac-

ter draws from a historical figure, Thomas Griffiths Wainewright, who, like his fictional counterpart, was convicted of forgery in England and transported to the Australian penal colony, Van Diemen's Land (present-day Tasmania). There Vaneleigh eventually gains release from prison and becomes a "ticket-of-leave man" (parolee), surviving by painting portraits of local socialites. Vaneleigh's assignment at Cindermead, the Knight estate, sets the action in motion. Thereafter, he remains in the background until his death.

Queely Sheill, Vaneleigh's unpaid attendant. In his early twenties, he is strikingly handsome, almost an Adonis-like figure. Although he is a sex object to women and men of all ages, as well as a guardian angel to the downtrodden, Queely appears somewhat stupid and naïve. The son of an itinerant actor, Queely offers his services to Vaneleigh, partly out of pity and partly out of admiration for this rare "gentleman" in a town of convicts and their keepers, ersatz aristocrats, and wretched hangers-on. He accompanies Vaneleigh to Cindermead and there enters into a sexual liaison with a houseguest, the consequences of which determine what little plot the novel possesses. Falsely accused of theft, Queely goes to prison, where he dies, transformed at that point into a Christ figure.

Sir Sydney Knight, the master of Cindermead and a government official. Sir Sydney, approaching middle age, is virile in appearance but in truth is impotent. A caricature of the nineteenth century British colonial civil servant, Sir Sydney is blustering, pompous, petty, ruthless, ambitious, and self-important.

Lady Rose Knight, Sir Sydney's wife. Frustrated by her husband's impotence, Lady Rose takes a series of lovers. In her forties (or perhaps fifties), vicious, stupid, overdressed, and overwrought, she plays the grand lady of Cindermead to the hilt. Her jealousy of Asnetha Sleep's conquest of the handsome Queely leads her to the action that destroys the young man.

Asnetha Sleep, a wealthy English cousin of Sir Sydney and a houseguest at Cindermead. Roughly thirty years old, she is crippled, wears outlandish clothes and jewelry, drinks too much, and behaves in a bizarre manner. Without harm to her reputation, she manages to extricate herself from the affair with Queely and marries a local fortune hunter.

Orfee Maka, called **Teapot**, a West Indian servant to Asnetha Sleep. In his mid-teens, he is inordinately fond of his mistress, who both mistreats him and dotes on him. The exotic, simpleminded Teapot inadvertently becomes involved in Lady Rose's revenge on Asnetha and Queely.

John Death Sheill, an itinerant actor, Queely's father. Monstrously fat, drunken, and womanizing, the elder Sheill serves as the antithesis to his son. Otherwise, his main function is to provide a kind of comic relief, though black in nature, and to heighten the decadence that pervades the novel.

Polidorio Smith, also called **the duchess**, another actor and a housemate of the Sheills. He is of indeterminate age, skinny and angular, drunken, and excessively talkative. He is homosexual and has long been in love with Queely. Like his fellow actor, he serves primarily as a background figure to create a milieu of wretchedness and moral depravity.

— *Robert L. Ross*

TIME AND THE CONWAYS

Author: J. B. Priestley (1894-1984)
First published: 1937
Genre: Drama

Locale: Newlingham, England
Time: 1919 and 1938
Plot: Play of ideas

Mrs. Conway, a widow living in a provincial town. She is in her mid-forties at the start of the play and is well dressed, talkative, and very conscious of her status in local society. She is at her best at parties and other social gatherings; she has little practical knowledge or talent. Her behavior as a mother is a central concern in the play. The promising lives of her children are shown to be wasted, and she herself faces financial ruin at the end of the play.

Alan Conway, the eldest son, a clerk. Rather shy and silent, he is in his early twenties as the play begins. He stammers and dresses shabbily. Initially, he seems a failure in contrast to the other characters. His sense of futility finally extends to the rest of the family. He is truly good-natured and is the person closest to Kay. It is Alan who elaborates for Kay the theory of time at the heart of the play.

Madge Conway, the eldest sister. She is a well-educated and efficient woman, busy with plans for social and political reform. She is the least attractive of the sisters but has a romantic interest in Gerald Thornton early in the play, an interest that might be returned. A possible union with Thornton is thwarted by her mother, who treats her ideas with scorn. Madge ultimately becomes the hostile, defensive headmistress of a girls' school.

Robin Conway, the younger son, his mother's favorite and a loafer with no apparent talent. Robin is returning from World War I as the play begins. He is charming and good-looking and spends much of his time pursuing Joan Helford, to whom he is married and whom he subsequently abandons. He manipulates his mother, who gives him money, but he proves unable to help her when she faces financial difficulties.

Hazel Conway, the most beautiful and popular of the Conway sisters. Fair-haired, elegant, and seemingly self-confident, she is at her best at parties and games. She is pursued by and finally married to Ernest Beevers, a social-climbing young man who represents everything that the Conways scorn. She becomes a weak and terrorized wife.

Kay Conway, an aspiring writer. The play begins at a party celebrating her twenty-first birthday. Not as pretty as Hazel or as serious as Madge, she is sensitive and doubtful of her own talent. Kay's perceptions control the structure of the play; the middle act is her vision of the family's future. Like the other Conways, she fails at what she tries to do: She gives up writing novels for a career as a popular journalist and becomes the mistress of a married man.

Carol Conway, the youngest child. Sixteen years old as the play begins, she is energetic and charming, without the social affectations seen in most of the family. She is also very morbid and is obsessed with thoughts of death, particularly with memories of her father's drowning. She is the only member of the family who welcomes Ernest Beevers into their social circle. Carol dies young, and her death symbolizes the loss of vitality and goodness in the Conways.

Joan Helford, a local woman. Pretty but unexceptional, Joan is a friend of the Conway family. She is in love with Robin, whom she idolizes. This attachment puts her in conflict with Mrs. Conway, who is jealous of Robin's interest in her. Her difficult marriage only promotes her worst qualities, and she becomes a slovenly and irritable middle-aged woman.

Ernest Beevers, a local businessman. He is approximately thirty years old as the play begins. Of a somewhat lower social class than the Conways, he is small and shy but has a growing sense of his own authority. Fascinated by the Conways and in love with Hazel, Beevers is at first awkward and out of place in the Conway home. He comes to dominate Hazel and to sneer at the rest of the family. Ultimately, he will deny them the money needed to make Mrs. Conway financially secure.

Gerald Thornton, the family solicitor. A promising young man of roughly thirty years as the play begins, he is good-looking and well-groomed. He carefully maintains an air of gentility and professionalism. Embarrassed by Mrs. Conway's ridicule of Madge, he proves too weak to pursue his interest in her or in her political ideas, and he lapses into a petty provincial by the end of the play, presiding over the inevitable dismantling of the Conway home.

— *Heidi J. Holder*

THE TIME MACHINE: An Invention

Author: H. G. Wells (1866-1946)
First published: 1895
Genre: Novel

Locale: England
Time: Late nineteenth century
Plot: Science fiction

The Time Traveler, who exhibits his Time Machine one evening after dinner. The next week, his guests arrive for dinner but do not find him home. Informed that they are to proceed without him, they sit down to dinner. Later, their host arrives, dirty and limping. He has traveled to the year 802,701, the time of the sunset of humanity. He tells his guests what he found. The people, weak, rounded creatures about four feet high, are vegetarians called Eloi, living in enormous buildings. Underground live the predatory Morlocks, apelike creatures also descended from humans. They were responsible for the disappearance of the Time Machine, but the Time Traveler says he managed to get it back and take off as the Morlocks sprang at him. Then, after quick and horrifying excursions ahead millions of years to the distant future, when the sun is dying and the earth is enveloped in bitter cold and deathly stillness, he hurried back to the present. The next day, the Time Traveler silences his friends' doubts by departing again on his Time Machine; he does not return, and his friends can only wonder what mishap has made him a lost wanderer in time.

Weena, a girl of the Eloi. The Time Traveler saves her from drowning, and she becomes his friend and guide. After sightseeing, they find that they have walked too far to return that night. They build a fire on a hill to keep away the dark-loving Morlocks, but later the Time Traveler wakes to find the fire out and Weena missing.

THE TIME OF INDIFFERENCE
(Gli indifferenti)

Author: Alberto Moravia (1907-1990)
First published: 1929
Genre: Novel

Locale: Rome, Italy
Time: 1929
Plot: Psychological realism

Mariagrazia Ardengo (mah-ree-ah-GRAH-see-ah ahr-DEHN-goh), a silly, neurotic, middle-aged widow. Mariagrazia's main motivation is to keep her love affair with Leo from expiring. Her jealous scenes, however, drive Leo away, and he begins to focus his interest on Mariagrazia's daughter, Carla. Ultimately, Mariagrazia is willing to share Leo with Carla as long as he does not abandon her altogether.

Leo Merumeci (LEE-oh mehr-EW-meh-see), Mariagrazia's forty-two-year-old lover. Leo is a rough and unscrupulous businessman who is trying to appropriate Mariagrazia's money. His interest in having Carla, even if it means he has to marry her, does not preclude his keeping Mariagrazia as a lover.

Carla Ardengo, Mariagrazia's twenty-four-year-old daughter. Passive and indifferent, Carla is a true victim of the situation who, at times, longs to escape her dreary existence. She witnesses without any sign of rebellion the various events that are used to manipulate her. Carla marries Leo not out of love but out of a desire for change in her life.

Michele Ardengo, Mariagrazia's son, a first-year law student. He has visions of liberation from his indifferent existence, but they are doomed by that very indifference. When he realizes that Leo has seduced Carla, Michele believes that he must do something but cannot find any real emotion for the task. As a result, Michele decides to shoot Leo, but his attempt fails miserably because he forgets to load the gun. From the failure of his action, however, Michele acquires an understanding of the value of love and honesty and the importance of family and society. This new awareness does not help him break out of his passive life. He agrees to see Lisa and start an affair with her, but he does so with no real enthusiasm.

Lisa, Leo's lover before he met Mariagrazia. After losing Leo first to Mariagrazia and then to Carla, Lisa switches her attentions to Michele, whom she seeks to seduce. Lisa also desires change (as does Carla) and passion (as does Michele) in her life. Michele, with his lack of spontaneous emotion, probably will not provide either.

— *Rosaria Pipia*

THE TIME OF MAN

Author: Elizabeth Madox Roberts (1886-1941)
First published: 1926
Genre: Novel

Locale: Kentucky
Time: Early twentieth century
Plot: Regional

Ellen Chesser Kent, a farm girl and woman with an introspective mind and a poetic imagination. Although she is uneducated, she resembles the well-read Diony Hall Jarvis from the author's *The Great Meadow* (1930) in her consciousness of herself as a separate identity. Hate fills her when Jonas deserts her for Sallie Lou, and she hates Hester for the lust she inspires in Jasper.

Henry Chesser, her father, a restless tenant farmer who works for various farmers. He usually is meek and timid but occasionally is roused to anger. He loves to talk.

Nellie Chesser, her mother, a simple farm woman.

Jasper Kent, her husband, a hard worker and a fighter when angered, as when Albert steals his pigs. Accused of barn burning, he is acquitted. Unjustly accused of another burning, he is savagely beaten by masked raiders. He packs up his family to take them far away.

Jonas Prather, Ellen's fiancé, who marries Sallie Lou Brown instead of her.

Hep Bodine,

Mrs. Bodine, and

Emphira Bodine, a family on one farm where the Chessers are tenants.

Tessie, Ellen's friend, a fortune-teller with whom Ellen

wants to travel instead of living on the Bodine farm.

Joe Trent, a college boy and energetic farm worker who likes Ellen but seems to look down on her.

Mr. Al and

Miss Tod Wakefield, owners of the Wakefield farm, on which they raise turkeys.

Scott MacMurtrie, a farmer.

Miss Cassie, his wife, a strong and independent woman who nevertheless hangs herself when Scott and Amanda run away together.

Amanda Cain, a cousin of Miss Cassie.

Dorine Wheatley, a merry, gay friend of Ellen.

Sebe Townley, a kind and gentle friend of Ellen who cannot forget his big ears.

Mrs. Wingate, an old, half-mad woman for whom Jasper sharecrops.

Albert, her son, a heavy-drinking troublemaker who steals Jasper's pigs and sells them. Jasper thrashes him.

Joe Phillips, a farmer who offers Jasper work and a house on his farm and who later becomes interested in Ellen.

Jule Nestor, a prostitute, the memory of whom troubles Jonas' conscience.

Hester Shuck, a wench whom Jasper visits.

THE TIME OF THE HERO
(La ciudad y los perros)

Author: Mario Vargas Llosa (1936-   )
First published: 1962
Genre: Novel

Locale: The military academy Leoncio Prado in Lima, Peru
Time: The 1950's
Plot: Bildungsroman

Porfirio Cava (pohr-FEE-ree-oh KAH-vah), a cadet in the Leoncio Prado Military Academy in Lima, Peru. A highlander with a peasant background, he has chosen to attend the academy because he plans a career in the military. He is one of four members of "the Circle," a group of cadets formed for mutual protection and support. After a losing roll of the dice, he is obligated to steal a chemistry examination for the Circle. During the late-night theft, he accidentally breaks a window. This evidence, coupled with information supplied by the informant Arana, leads to his court-martial and expulsion, ending his chance for a career in the military and the concomitant improvement in economic and social status.

Alberto Fernández Temple (ahl-BEHR-toh fehr-NAHN-dehs TEHM-pleh), **the Poet**, the bourgeois intellectual of the Circle, a cadet whose wit and skill at writing love letters and pornographic stories are admired by the other cadets. His father is a womanizer and his mother a complainer. Like his father, Alberto is preoccupied with women. First he was infatuated with Helena; after she broke off their relationship, his grades suffered and his father sent him to the academy to teach him discipline. Alberto has his first sexual experience with Golden Toes, the prostitute who has serviced half of his class.

At the request of Ricardo, who cannot get a pass, he agrees to meet with Teresa. He takes her to see films, is smitten, and continues to date her. Sustaining a friendship with Ricardo and a relationship with Teresa troubles his conscience. When Ricardo is murdered, Alberto is so overwhelmed with guilt that he denounces the murderer before Lieutenant Gamboa. Academy officials ignore the facts, and nothing is done. As the novel ends, Alberto has finished the academy with high marks, has received a gift from his father as a reward, and will probably go to the United States to study engineering. Influenced by his circle of bourgeois friends outside the academy, he drops Teresa and begins dating Marcela. He probably will repeat his father's philandering ways.

Jaguar (hah-GHWAHR), the leader of the Circle, a violent, fearless cadet who shows his class how to stand up to and beat the system. Before entering the academy, he fell in love with Teresa, but after an argument, they went their separate ways. Poor, his father dead, and his mother old, Jaguar was living with the criminal Skinny Higueras and was leading a life of crime until most of his cohorts were caught during a robbery attempt. After going without food and sleeping in the open, Jaguar finally turned to his godfather, who put him to work in exchange for room and board. With the help of his godfather's wife (whom he had to satisfy sexually), Jaguar has entered the academy, where he has become a natural leader and fighter. He organizes the class and his followers to resist the upperclassmen. He teaches them that there are no moral limits to protecting the group. When Cava is betrayed, Jaguar murders the betrayer, Arana. Jaguar's subsequent ostracism from the group, however, makes him aware of how lonely Arana must have been. Remorseful, Jaguar confesses his crime, but the academy is not interested. In the end, he marries Teresa.

Ricardo Arana (rree-KAHR-doh ah-RAHN-ah), **the Slave**, a timid and shy cadet whom the other cadets ostracize. He has been reared by his mother and his Aunt Adelina in the regional town of Chiclayo; his father was absent during his early upbringing. Suddenly uprooted from this environment and brought to Lima, where his mother moved to live with his father again, Ricardo learned to avoid his father and most social interaction. His father concluded that Ricardo was a mama's boy, ill-adapted to face the world, and saw the military academy as a remedy for these shortcomings in his son. Ricardo has willingly agreed to enroll, but he is not accepted by the other cadets. They make fun of him, abuse him, and exploit his unwillingness to fight back. He finds some solace in his friendship with Alberto and is infatuated with Teresa. Having been confined to the academy, he becomes so desperate for a pass to see his mother that he informs the authorities that Cava stole the examination. In revenge, Ricardo is murdered in an "accident" during a field exercise. The authorities cover up the incident and blame the death on the cadet himself.

Boa, a cadet who sexually molests chickens and his dog Skimpy. He is a member of the Circle and a loyal follower of its leader, Jaguar.

Lieutenant Gamboa (gahm-BOH-ah), a tough, no-nonsense, model officer who believes in a fair and consistent application of the rules and discipline. He reports the murder but finds his career threatened by superiors, who cover up the scandal.

Teresa (teh-REH-sah), a young woman whose interest in Ricardo and Alberto probably results from their higher economic and social background. She finally marries Jaguar.

— *Maurice P. Brungardt*

THE TIME OF YOUR LIFE

Author: William Saroyan (1908-1981)
First published: 1939
Genre: Drama

Locale: San Francisco, California
Time: An afternoon and evening in October, 1939
Plot: Psychological realism

Joe, a young man with money, the initiator of most of the action of the play. He sits at a table in Nick's bar, near the waterfront in San Francisco, observing and commenting on the activities in the bar and trying to help some of the patrons, particularly Kitty Duval and Mary L. He directs his young flunkey, Tom, to run errands for him. When he sees that Tom is falling in love with Kitty, he does everything he can to promote the love affair, including renting a car and taking a romantic drive with the two lovers down the Pacific coast and then installing Kitty in a room at a fancy hotel. Joe gets Tom a job driving a truck and at the end of the play sends the two lovers away to get married. Joe also helps to defend Kitty when Blick, the vice cop, tries to arrest her. Joe states the philosophy that gives the play its title, his belief that one should live so that the time of one's life is not wasted in game-playing, frantic pursuit of money and prestige, or regrets.

Tom, Joe's younger friend, who idolizes Joe and does everything that Joe asks him to do. He is sometimes mystified by his tasks, such as bringing Joe on one occasion a collection of toys and on another a gun. He falls in love with Kitty, and their blossoming romance is the main plot device of the play.

Kitty Duval, a prostitute who wanders into the bar, angry at herself and the world because of her circumstances and occupation. She is revived by Joe, who reminds her that she once had dreams and still is capable of hope.

Nick, the owner of the bar in which most of the action takes place. He is bemused by the actions of most of his patrons but accepts their antics with good nature, although he halfheartedly complains from time to time that he does not understand what is occurring.

Mary L., a woman who comes into the bar and with whom Joe strikes up a slightly drunken conversation when he notices the initials "M. L." on her bag. They realize that they may have fallen in love with each other, but Mary walks out of the bar and does not return.

Harry, a young song and dance man who tries (in vain) to entertain the customers with his comedic monologues.

Wesley, a young black man who plays the piano as entertainment for Nick's customers.

Blick, a vice cop in his mid-forties. He harasses the patrons and provides the conflict in the play when he tries to make Kitty perform the burlesque routine that she did before she drifted into prostitution. Nick throws Blick out of the bar, and he is killed in the street.

McCarthy, a good-natured longshoreman who is on the side of ordinary people in spite of the mess made of the world. He tries to convince Krupp that he is in the wrong line of work.

Krupp, his friend, a slightly dim-witted policeman in his late thirties who is growing tired of his job and is unable to understand why people keep making what is basically a pleasant world worse.

Dudley R. Bostwick, a young man who continually uses the telephone in the bar to contact a girl. Any girl will do, but the one with whom he is in love would be best.

Willie, a young man who plays the pinball machine in the bar, sometimes with spectacular results.

Kit Carson, an old-time cowboy who tells tall tales of his wild adventures fighting Indians. These tales seem to be lies until he shoots and kills Blick offstage near the end of the play.

The Arab, who sits at the bar and mutters the recurring line, "No foundation. All the way down the line."

— *James Baird*

TIMON OF ATHENS

Author: William Shakespeare (1564-1616)
First published: 1623
Genre: Drama

Locale: Athens and the nearby seacoast
Time: The fourth century B.C.E.
Plot: Tragedy

Timon (TI-muhn), a noble Athenian who impoverishes himself through his unceasing generosity to his friends. He lavishes gifts on them, offers help when they find themselves in trouble, and entertains them at extravagant feasts, paying no attention to the warnings of his steward that his fortune is dwindling. Refused at every door when he himself needs assistance, he is so completely disillusioned with human ingratitude that he becomes a misanthrope and flees to the woods to escape humanity. Before his departure, he invites his acquaintances to a final banquet, where he sets before them bowls of water. Bent on avenging his injuries and knowing that wealth breeds discontent and misfortune, he dispenses gold from a newly discovered treasure trove, and he encourages Alcibiades' attack on his native city. He composes his own epitaph as a final defiance of ungrateful humankind: "Pass by, and curse thy fill, but pass and stay not here thy gait."

Alcibiades (al-sih-BI-uh-deez), the great Athenian captain, Timon's friend, and several times the savior of his state. Banished by the senate when he defends one of his soldiers against a death sentence, he later returns with an army to take vengeance on the city and purge it of evil.

Flavius (FLAY-vee-uhs), Timon's loyal steward, who tries to warn his master of impending financial disaster and later attempts to ward off greedy creditors. He, alone, remains virtuous, following his master into exile to offer his money and companionship. Timon can hardly believe that he, too, is not false, but he sends him away with money, advising him to use it to escape the society of men.

Apemantus (ap-eh-MAN-tuhs), a professional misanthrope who wanders through Athens railing at its citizens and commenting cynically on their folly. He greets Timon in the wilderness as a kindred spirit, but he finds himself rejected as one who has no cause for misanthropy; he has never benefited others enough to be able to feel ingratitude.

Lucullus (lew-KUHL-uhs),
Lucius (LEW-shee-uhs), and
Sempronius (sem-PROH-nee-uhs), Athenian lords who ac-

cept Timon's bounteous gifts with pleasure and make weak excuses when they are asked to help him satisfy his creditors.

A Poet,
a painter,
a merchant, and
a jeweler, flattering craftsmen who are also beneficiaries of Timon's generosity. They disappear from view as soon as he loses his money, but the poet and the painter follow him into the forest when they hear rumors of his new treasure. They are beaten and sent away by the misanthrope, who clearly sees their hypocrisy.

Ventidius (vehn-TIHD-ee-uhs), an Athenian nobleman, freed from debtors' prison by Timon. He offers to repay his debt while Timon is still prosperous, but, like all his friends, he refuses his benefactor money when it can obviously bring him nothing in return.

Lucilius (lew-SIHL-ee-uhs),
Flaminius (fluh-MIHN-ee-uhs), and
Servilius (sur-VIHL-ee-uhs), Timon's servants, who try unsuccessfully to persuade rich Athenians to relieve their master's distress.

Hostilius (hos-TIHL-ee-uhs), a foreign visitor who, with two friends, observes the ingratitude that the Athenians show toward Timon and silently condemns them.

Caphis (KAY-fihs),
Titus (TI-tuhs),
Hortensius (horh-TEHN-shee-uhs), and
Philotus (fi-LOH-tuhs), servants of Timon's creditors. They comment cynically on the heartlessness of their respective masters.

Timandra (ti-MAN-druh) and
Phrynia (FRI-nee-uh), courtesans, Alcibiades' companions, whom Timon orders to infect the whole city of Athens, promising them gold.

Cupid (KYEW-pihd), the god of love, who introduces a masque presented by Timon for his friends.

THE TIN DRUM
(Die Blechtrommel)

Author: Günter Grass (1927-   )
First published: 1959
Genre: Novel

Locale: Poland and Germany
Time: 1899-1954
Plot: Social satire

Oscar Matzerath (mat-tseh-RAHT), a deranged dwarf storyteller who willed himself to stop growing at the age of three to protect himself from the insane society of Nazi Germany. Oscar has magical powers imparted to him by a succession of tin drums. He encounters representatives of virtually all segments of German society and beats his drum as these people accommodate themselves to the Nazi regime to a greater or lesser degree.

Agnes Matzerath, Oscar's mother, who carries on a love

affair with her cousin throughout the first part of the novel. Agnes and other female characters suffer the disabilities imparted by the Nazi attitude toward women, which relegates them to a subordinate position in family relationships and the workplace.

Alfred Matzerath, Agnes' husband but probably not Oscar's father. Alfred is a small business owner who willingly embraced the Nazi Party long before Adolf Hitler came to power, as did many other members of his social class. He is myopic and greedy, willing to sacrifice any principle to gain a perceived economic advantage. He dies after the Russian invasion of Danzig by swallowing his Nazi party badge.

Jan Bronski (yahn BRON-skee), Agnes' Polish cousin, her lover, and probably Oscar's father. Jan is good-hearted and generous but either too dense or too indifferent to realize what the Nazi regime truly represents. Jan is devoted to Agnes and becomes close friends with Oscar, but he never takes a stand on political or moral issues.

Mr. Bebra (BEH-brah), a circus midget who befriends Oscar after his mother's death. Bebra is an accomplished artist, talented in many different fields. He is the consummate survivor, showing Oscar how to accommodate himself to virtually any situation. He does not particularly care for the Nazis but is determined to adapt to any situation.

Roswitha Raguna (rohz-VEE-tah rah-GEW-nah), an associate of Bebra who is even shorter than the midget and capable of sleeping anyplace at any time. Although Roswitha displays enough intelligence to realize the evil rampant in Germany, she manages to sleep through most of the Nazi horror.

Herbert Truczinski (trew-TSIHNS-kee), a neighbor of the Matzeraths in Danzig. As was the case with many Germans, he remained convinced that President Paul von Hindenburg ("The Wooden Titan") could control Hitler and the Nazis after 1933. The heavily tattooed Truczinski becomes enamored of the wooden figurehead of a ship and impales himself on it.

Maria Truczinski, Herbert's younger sister, who becomes Oscar's lover in an unlikely relationship. Maria eventually bears Oscar's child and then proceeds to marry his father (despite his Nazi affiliations), who could obviously provide for her and the infant much more readily than could Oscar.

Sister Dorothea Koengetter (doh-roh-TAY-ah KEHN-geht-tehr), a neighbor of Oscar in postwar West Germany and one of the few people in the novel not implicated in any complicity with the Nazi regime. Despite, or perhaps because of, her goodness, Sister Dorothea becomes a murder victim. Oscar is falsely accused of her murder.

Gottfried von Vittlar (GOT-freed fon VIHT-lahr), an acquaintance of both Sister Dorothea and Oscar whose testimony inadvertently results in Oscar's conviction for murder.

— *Paul Madden*

TINKER, TAILOR, SOLDIER, SPY

Author: John le Carré (David John Moore Cornwell, 1931-   )
First published: 1974
Genre: Novel

Locale: England
Time: The 1970's
Plot: Spy

George Smiley, who is released from his work as a spy for British intelligence because he is suspected of compromising secrets, if not actually working for the Russians. Smiley is pressed back into service by his old colleagues, who realize not only that is he not implicated in spying for the other side but also that he is the one man capable of exposing the "mole," the double agent who has infiltrated "the Circus," as British intelligence calls itself. Smiley is well into middle age and weary of Cold War spy games. He is also skeptical of his side's morality, but he has a residual loyalty to his country and to his colleagues as well as a dogged desire to know the truth. His unassuming demeanor often leads people to underestimate him. He is married to a beautiful woman, Ann, who has had several affairs and has left him. To some of his colleagues, Smiley may seem a pathetic character, yet it eventually becomes clear that he has the best mind in the intelligence services.

Karla, the nemesis of British intelligence. He runs the Soviet spy network and is responsible for recruiting and running the mole who has ruined the British spy network in Eastern Europe. Smiley met Karla once and interrogated him, trying unsuccessfully to get his arch adversary to defect. Smiley realizes that Karla cannot be tempted or duped and that he can be defeated only if the mole is found.

Control, the ailing chief of British intelligence and Smiley's mentor. Control realizes that a mole is destroying his organization, but he dies before discovering the double agent.

Percy Alleline, Control's successor, who is responsible for Smiley's dismissal. The ambitious Alleline falls into Karla's trap: Alleline does not realize that the intelligence he is receiv-

ing from the Soviet side actually is being fed to him by Karla's mole.

Bill Haydon, a dashing master of British intelligence. He is worshiped by younger agents such as Peter Guillam. Haydon has had an adventurous career around the world. Quite a man with the ladies, he seduces Ann, Smiley's wife. He is also Smiley's chief competition in the intelligence service, and Smiley realizes that eventually the secret of the mole will lead him to Haydon.

Jim Prideaux, a former intelligence agent now teaching in a private school. He was shot in the back when Alleline's spy network collapsed. Smiley seeks out the uncooperative Prideaux for the details that will help him discover the mole's identity.

Aleksey Polyakov, a Soviet diplomat who, Smiley discovers, actually is a spy. He maintains direct contact with the British mole.

Peter Guillam, one of Bill Haydon's protégés who becomes Smiley's right-hand man. Guillam has idolized Haydon and is devastated by Smiley's discoveries.

Toby Esterhase, one of the more devious agents in British intelligence. One of Percy Alleline's men, he possesses some of the key information that Smiley needs to ferret out the mole.

Ricki Tarr, a low-level British intelligence agent who falls in love with a Soviet spy, Irena, and subsequently provides some of the crucial details that contribute to Smiley's cracking of Karla's conspiracy against British intelligence.

Oliver Lacon, a high-ranking political type in British intelligence. He recruits Smiley back into the service hoping that Smiley can catch the mole.

— *Carl Rollyson*

TINY ALICE

Author: Edward Albee (1928-   )
First published: 1965
Genre: Drama

Locale: The United States
Time: The 1960's
Plot: Absurdist

Julian, a modest, shy, and benevolent Roman Catholic lay brother and personal secretary to the Cardinal. In his benevolence and his desire to serve, he is a victim of the Roman Catholic Church's avarice. After having become disillusioned with other people's images and uses of God, he loses his faith and commits himself to a mental institution for six years. By the beginning of the play, Julian is Brother Julian, the first lay secretary to a cardinal in church history. He is sent by the Cardinal to Miss Alice to work out the details of the $20 billion grant that the church is to receive from Miss Alice. After frequent meetings with Miss Alice, Julian consents to becoming married to her. After the wedding, he is left alone by all the other characters, including his supposed wife. He discovers that he did not really marry Miss Alice but rather Tiny Alice, the occupant of a miniature replica of the castle in which most of the play's action takes place. Julian has to learn that Miss Alice is only the physical representation of Tiny Alice. He refuses to remain in the castle all alone as the trophy that Tiny Alice demanded for her large grant, desiring instead to return to a mental institution. In response, the Lawyer shoots him. Julian, bleeding to death beside the castle replica, becomes a Christlike figure in a crucifixion pose, thinking initially that he has been forsaken by God but then accepting the sacrifice asked of him and addressing Tiny Alice as God.

Miss Alice, a mysterious young woman apparently hired as a representative by Tiny Alice, the occupant of the miniature of Miss Alice's castle. Although at the beginning of the play Miss Alice seems to be the one giving the grant, and although she likes to order others around, her subordinate role becomes increasingly clear. Like the Lawyer and the Butler, she works for Tiny Alice. She may have had love affairs with the Butler and the Lawyer, whom she seems to be giving up for Julian. Miss Alice likes to joke with Julian and does not want to harm him, but she willingly lures him into marriage to make him a sacrifice for Tiny Alice. Although she seems to care for Julian, she does not try to prevent his death but instead follows the orders of the Lawyer, which are implicitly Tiny Alice's orders.

The Lawyer, an aggressive and intimidating man seemingly employed by Miss Alice but ultimately in the service of Tiny Alice. He represents the intelligent and unfeeling leader. He enjoys teasing his former schoolmate, the Cardinal, with whom he starts numerous arguments and whose problematic past he likes to discuss. He plays with the Cardinal's wish to get the $20 billion grant and delights in catching the Cardinal in failures to use the majestic plural. The Butler is another victim of his witty condescension. The Lawyer seems interested in Miss Alice but ultimately does all that he can to serve Tiny Alice, the occupant of the miniature castle. To provide a sacrifice for her, he shoots Julian and refuses to call a doctor for him.

The Butler, a friendly but puzzling servant seemingly working for Miss Alice but ultimately employed by Tiny Alice. He is benevolent and helpful toward Julian and tries to assist him against the Lawyer's intimidations. Although he presents himself as Julian's friend, he refuses to take orders from Julian after the wedding and joins all other characters in avoiding Julian. He also does not try to prevent Julian's murder, reasoning that, because Julian had been chosen as the sacrifice, he might be better off dead than alive.

The Cardinal, the representative of the Roman Catholic Church, who is to receive grant money from Tiny Alice. The Cardinal is used as an illustration of human conduct: The expectation of the grant makes him forget his principles (the use of the majestic plural) and prevents hesitations about sacrificing his secretary, Julian. With the Lawyer, the Cardinal shows his command of the art of argument and insult. He justifies sacrificing Julian by noting the good that this sacrifice would bring to the Roman Catholic Church, but he does not dare to tell Julian what is awaiting him. After Julian is shot, the Cardinal does not attempt to rescue him but asks him to die as a martyr.

— *Josef Raab*

TIRRA LIRRA BY THE RIVER

Author: Jessica Anderson (1916-   )
First published: 1978
Genre: Novel

Locale: Brisbane and Sydney, Australia, and London, England
Time: Early 1900's to 1970
Plot: Psychological realism

Nora Roche Porteous, a retired dressmaker. In her seventies, she returns to her family home in Brisbane, where she recalls her past while recovering from pneumonia. Having lost her father at the age of six, she grew up yearning for escape from the household of her mother and older sister. Marriage to Colin Porteous took her to the comparatively glamorous world of Sydney, but her husband proved unfeeling and ungenerous, installing her in his mother's house and deriding her few contacts with creative friends. Nora turns an early skill at needlework into a profession. Her divorce settlement carries her to London, where she practices her craft for the next thirty-five years. A horrifying illegal abortion and, later, a ruinous face-lift cause greater withdrawal and shyness in a personality always prone to expect loss and disappointment. She concludes, however, that her search for autonomy and self-ratification has been proper and successful.

Grace Roche Chiddy, Nora's older sister. She remained in Brisbane, hoping that submissiveness and moralizing would bolster her faith; in the end, "she had only opinions." Nora's early resentment of Grace is tempered in the narrative present by admiration for her late sister's improvements in the decorating and landscaping of the house.

Olive Partridge, a childhood friend of Nora. She becomes a successful and worldly novelist. She helps Nora to obtain her abortion in London. Nora criticizes Olive's writing for depicting glamorous affairs without advocating sexual responsibility.

Dorothy Irey Rainbow, Nora's childhood model of grace and charm. Marrying at a young age and giving up elegant dreams to remain in Brisbane, she later attacks her husband and children with an ax. The sole surviving child, Dr. Gordon Rainbow, becomes Nora's physician after her return to Australia.

Colin Porteous, a lawyer. Nora marries him more to get away than for his particular qualities: He is egotistical and heavy-handed, demanding that Nora think for herself and then deriding her decisions. Ultimately, he deserts Nora for a more submissive, ornamental partner.

Una Porteous, Colin's mother, the archetypal evil mother-in-law. When Nora and Colin move into her house during the Depression, Una attempts a systematic reduction of Nora's self-confidence. Long after the marriage ends, her name is Nora's catchphrase for hypocrisy and manipulation.

Lewie Johns, an artist in Sydney. Nora builds confidence through her friendship with him, and he takes seriously her search for identity. The narrowness of the role that Colin has assigned to Nora is strongly revealed in his homophobic reaction to her friend. Nora takes comfort in finding "a lesser Lewie" at almost all phases of her later career.

Ida Mayo, a dressmaker in Sydney who encourages Nora to turn her skill at needlework into a career. Her professionalism, like Lewie's friendship, helps Nora to find the confidence to seek personal autonomy.

Liza,

Hilda, and

Fred, Nora's fellow tenants at "number six," a house that they rent together in London. Many of Nora's reminiscences follow recalled patterns of discussion among these friends, so that she can almost hear the questions that they might ask her. The collapse of this supportive household and surrogate family precipitates the aging Nora's lonely return to Australia.

— *John Scheckter*

'TIS PITY SHE'S A WHORE

Author: John Ford (1586-after 1639)
First published: 1633
Genre: Drama

Locale: Parma, Italy
Time: The 1620's
Plot: Tragedy

Florio (FLOH-ree-oh), a gentleman of Parma, the devoted father of Giovanni and Annabella. Concerned about his son's "over-bookish" habits, he places his hope in his beloved daughter and leaves her free to marry for love. He is so shocked by the revelation of his children's incestuous relationship and Annabella's death that he dies almost instantly of a broken heart.

Giovanni (jee-oh-VAHN-nee), his sensitive, intellectual son, who is consumed by his passion for his sister. He maintains steadily the conviction that his love is virtuous and reaffirms his faith in his affection as he kills Annabella and their unborn child to save her honor.

Annabella, his beautiful sister. She rejects the virtuous life her father wants for her and returns Giovanni's love, repenting her actions only when she realizes that Soranzo intends to kill her for her betrayal of him.

Putana (pew-TAH-nah), Annabella's bawdy old servant, who encourages her relationship with Giovanni.

Donado (doh-NAH-doh), the wealthy uncle of one of Annabella's foolish suitors.

Bergetto (behr-GEHT-toh), Donado's tactless, stupid nephew, who courts Annabella with insults, then brags of winning her favor. He is killed by Grimaldi.

Poggio (poh-GEE-oh), Bergetto's servant.

Soranzo (soh-RAHN-zoh), the worldly, well-to-do gentleman whom Annabella marries to save her reputation. He rages and plots her murder when he learns how he has been duped.

Grimaldi (gree-MAHL-dee), a belligerent Roman gentleman, Annabella's admirer. He murders Bergetto by mistake as he attempts to take revenge on his successful rival, Soranzo.

Hippolita, Soranzo's vengeful cast-off mistress.

Richardetto, Hippolita's husband, rumored dead. Disguised as a doctor, he returns to Parma to spy on his wife's infidelities.

Philotis (fee-LOH-tees), Richardetto's niece.

Friar Bonaventura (boh-nah-vehn-TEW-rah), Giovanni's confessor, who tries unsuccessfully to convince him that he is falling deeper and deeper into sin.

Vasques (VAS-kwehz), Soranzo's servant, expert at extracting information and at thwarting conspiracies against his master.

THE TITAN

Author: Theodore Dreiser (1871-1945)
First published: 1914
Genre: Novel

Locale: Chicago, Illinois
Time: The 1890's
Plot: Naturalism

Frank Algernon Cowperwood, a financial genius. Freed from prison in Pennsylvania, where he served a term for embezzlement, he goes to Chicago to make a new fortune. Amoral in business and love, he gains control of many lives and many businesses. He becomes the force behind the Chicago transit system until his greed causes him to lose his

power to obtain franchises through bribery. Defeated, he sells his interests and leaves Chicago.

Aileen Butler Cowperwood, a beautiful young woman, the daughter of an Irish politician in Philadelphia. She becomes Cowperwood's mistress and, later, his wife. In her attempts to enter high society, she is frustrated by her own lack of social poise and by the enmity her husband evokes by his business dealings. Her husband's marital infidelities drive her to take a lover herself. She and Cowperwood are finally divorced to clear the way for a marriage between Cowperwood and Berenice Fleming.

Stephanie Platow, a dark, lush young woman ten years younger than Aileen. She becomes Cowperwood's mistress. She eventually disappoints Cowperwood by taking another lover.

Berenice Fleming, another of Cowperwood's lovers. Although she is the daughter of a procuress, she is educated in a fashionable boarding school, in preparation for a life in high society as Cowperwood's wife.

Peter Laughlin, a Chicago businessman who takes Cowperwood as a business partner, thus giving the Philadelphian his start in the Midwest. Laughlin is left behind, however, as Cowperwood becomes a great force in financial circles.

TITAN: A Romance

Author: Jean Paul (Johann Paul Friedrich Richter, 1763-1825)
First published: 1800-1803
Genre: Novel

Locale: Italy and the mythical principalities of Hohenfliess and Haarhaar in Germany
Time: Probably late eighteenth century
Plot: Epic

Albano (ahl-BAH-noh), the prince of the mythical German principality of Hohenfliess (HOH-ehn-flees). Albano is a young, fiery, and handsome aristocrat. As the novel begins, he is about to meet his assumed father, Gaspar de Cesara, with whom he spent the first three years of his life on the island of Isola Bella. Albano's complicated history is revealed to him in a letter from his mother, Princess Eleonore, toward the end of the novel. Because his real parents, the rulers of Hohenfliess, feared an attempt on his life by their cunning relatives, the rulers of the neighboring principality of Haarhaar, they arranged that their son be reared by the trustworthy burgher Wehrfritz under the supervision of Gaspard. Consequently, Albano is educated in the quiet countryside with the help of several tutors and emerges as a noble and serious young man who does not yet know the world. He admires, respects, and loves unusual and great individuals. His assumed father, a knight of the Golden Fleece, has attained superhuman status for him, primarily by his absence and invisibility. Albano is the central character of this novel, on whom all events and occurrences focus. The purpose of his entry into society, beginning with the return to the island where he spent his infancy, is the formation of Albano as a worthy successor to the throne of Hohenfliess. Eventually, Albano learns who his true parents and siblings are and becomes acquainted with Roquairol von Froulay, the son of the prime minister of Hohenfliess, who had been held up as a model by his teachers. Roquairol proves to be immoral and deceitful, and after the friendship that Albano had sought with him dissolves, Count Cesara sends him on a trip to Rome so that he can learn to appreciate art. Albano, who still does not know that he is next in line to the throne of Hohenfliess, which in the meantime has been claimed by his older and unknown brother Luigi, expresses his republican inclination in his desire to travel to France to assist the revolutionaries. In the course of the novel, Albano succeeds in emancipating himself from his complex family background and from the passivity of the young, disinterested aristocrat. When Luigi dies and Albano is told of his true birth, he gives up the planned trip to France and, along with his bride, Idoine, becomes the enlightened ruler of Hohenfliess.

Julienne, Albano's twin sister, of whose existence he does not know until he is an adult. Along with their older brother Luigi, Julienne was reared at the court of Hohenfliess. The

young princess, whose best friend is Liane von Froulay, shares the sentimentality and tendency toward ecstatic imaginings of her friend. Julienne, who is also Linda's friend, reveals herself to Albano as his sister during his stay in Italy, where she has been visiting with Linda.

Luigi, Albano's older brother, heir to the throne of Hohenfliess. He is a degenerate who wastes his life and suffers from boredom. His face carries an expression of permanent discontent, and his body is bloated from his incontinent eating and drinking habits. When the old prince dies, Luigi, who has married the oldest daughter of the Prince of Haarhaar, becomes ruler of Hohenfliess. He soon dies. Luigi represents the decadent aristocrat who is doomed from birth. Hope lies with Albano, who is not reared at the court.

Liane von Froulay (fon FROW-lay), the daughter of the prime minister of Hohenfliess. Liane is fifteen years old when she first meets Albano, a year and one-half her senior, in the princely gardens of Lilar, where she and her brother are spending some time. Exceptionally beautiful, Liane is also an eager student who excels in music and drawing. Liane and Albano fall in love, but Liane renounces her claim on Albano when she is told his true identity. The young woman, sickly and sentimental, soon becomes fatally ill. On her deathbed, she requests one last visit from Albano. After her death, Albano becomes very ill and recovers only with the appearance of Idoine, his later bride, who resembles Liane.

Roquairol von Froulay (roh-KI-rohl), the son of the prime minister of Hohenfliess. Roquairol is at first Albano's friend but later becomes his enemy. He has a stormy and uneven personality and a temperament given to excess and enthusiasms. In a letter to Albano, he reveals that he has seduced Rabette, believing that Albano will understand his claim that passion has its own rights. Albano's love for his friend turns to hatred after this incident. In the meantime, Roquairol has fallen in love with Linda, who does not return his feelings. He grows to hate Albano and decides to injure his erstwhile friend by deceiving Linda, which he does by imitating Albano's handwriting in a note inviting Linda to a rendezvous. Linda mistakes Roquairol for Albano (she is unable to see well at night) and allows the seduction to take place. Roquairol, who has written a drama titled *Der Trauerspieler* ("the tragedian"), invites everyone to attend its premiere. The script consists of events from Roquairol's life, with the seduction of Linda as the last scene. At the end of the play, and as an action in it, Roquairol fatally shoots himself.

Falterle (FAHL-tehr-leh), Albano's Viennese fencing teacher. He praises Roquairol and his sister Liane and awakens in Albano the desire to meet them. Basically insecure, he hides behind fancy dress and polite manners. He survives life in the country by escaping to the city, Pestitz, three times a week.

Wehmeier (VAY-mi-ehr), one of Albano's tutors. He is approximately fifty years old and is the father of eight children. His knowledge of science and philosophy is limited, but he knows history well.

Dian (dee-AHN), an architect and later a tutor of Albano. Dian is a Greek who was educated in Greece and Rome. He introduces Albano to the works of Homer and Sophocles. Dian's methods of education consist of giving Albano a reading list in which no specific order prevails.

Schoppe (SHOHP-peh), an honorary librarian and a later tutor of Albano. Albano regards Schoppe, who is outspoken and not easily intimidated, to be his special friend. Schoppe is said to have a southern temperament, which is in conflict with northern culture. Schoppe tries to uncover the secret of Albano's origin and, as the result of his activities, is confined to an insane asylum. There he becomes mentally ill. He dies when he sees his friend and double "Siebenkas."

Augusti, a lecturer employed by the prince. Augusti, who is thirty-seven years old but appears to be ten years older because of his experience and mode of dress, becomes Albano's chief tutor. His first meeting with Albano occurs on the island of Isola Bella. Together with Schoppe and Dian, who accompanied Albano to the island, he spends several days with him there. Augusti is a member of the court circle and is therefore important for Albano's later education.

Gaspard de Cesara (gas-PAHRD duh say-ZEH-rah), a knight of the Golden Fleece and Albano's assumed father. The narrator indicates that he himself is not certain whether Gaspard is a Spanish or an Austrian knight of the Golden Fleece. Of advanced age, Gaspard is still extremely vital and active. Gaspard spent his early years traveling from court to court, because one place could not contain his restless energy. As the result of his travels, he became acquainted with important and unimportant individuals and with great and insignificant courts. His attitude toward others is evenhanded and unsentimental; his temperament is composed. When the prince and princess of Hohenfliess searched for a safe haven for Albano, he agreed to become Albano's foster father, provided that Albano would eventually marry his daughter Linda. Gaspard spent only the first three years of Albano's life with him but summons him to return briefly to the island where he spent his infancy when Albano is a young man and ready to enter the world. Gaspard is also responsible for the trip Albano makes to Rome. Such trips were traditional in the aesthetic education of an artist or nobleman. Only after Albano has seen his assumed father is he allowed to visit Pestitz, the major city in Hohenfliess.

Linda de Romeiro, Gaspard's daughter. Albano meets Linda in Italy but does not know that she is his assumed sister because they were reared separately. Linda has the tall and aristocratic bearing of a Spanish noblewoman. Dressed in red silk, she covers her face with a white veil, through which Albano can detect black, serious eyes and a proud, straight nose. Linda and Albano fall in love. In a letter to Albano, Linda describes her travels, which have taken her, like her father, from country to country and court to court. She becomes tired of this mode of life but suffers from the inactivity society forces on women. Linda fears marriage, which she considers to be the end of a woman's freedom and the death of love; she therefore refuses Albano's marriage proposal. When Linda fears that Albano may fall in love with Idoine, who resembles Liane, she decides to marry him after all. After Albano refuses Linda's plea to promise that he never participate in a war, however, Linda leaves. Roquairol, who is also in love with Linda, deceives and seduces her. After Linda, who is now pregnant, discovers her mistake, she leaves, vowing that she hates all men.

Wehrfritz (VEHR-frihts), a landscape architect. Wehrfritz is a good and honest burgher. Albano is reared in his home in Blumenbuhl.

Albine (ahl-BEE-neh), Wehrfritz's wife. She is gentle and concerned about Albano's welfare and loves him like a son.

Rabette (rah-BEHT-teh), Wehrfritz's daughter. Rabette is a healthy and blooming country girl who loves Albano like a brother. She is seduced by Roquairol and spends the rest of her life in mourning and unhappiness.

Idoine (ee-DWAHN), the princess of Haarhaar, the neighboring principality with which Hohenfliess has long been in conflict. Idoine is tall and of noble and majestic appearance. She resembles Liane but has learned self-control and has a well-balanced personality. A friend of Linda and of Julienne, she spent time living in Switzerland, where she improved the economy and life of a village. Ultimately, she marries Albano.

— Helga Stipa Madland

TITUS ANDRONICUS

Author: William Shakespeare (1564-1616)
First published: 1594
Genre: Drama

Locale: Rome and its vicinity
Time: Early in the Christian era
Plot: Tragedy

Titus Andronicus (TI-tuhs an-DRON-ih-kuhs), a noble Roman soldier who has dedicated his life and lost twenty-one of his twenty-five sons in the service of the state. He is not an entirely coherent or consistent character, especially in the first act of the play. In that act, he disdains ambition, offers his support to Saturninus, and mourns the death of the sons whose bodies he brings home from the wars; in the same act, he also sets off a chain of slaughters as he sacrifices the eldest son of the captured Tamora, queen of the Goths, on the tomb of his own sons; slays Mutius, one of his four surviving sons, for daring to cross his father's will; and defends Bassianus' right to Lavinia's hand. After this day, a malignant fate seems to pursue Titus, gradually destroying his sanity. He sees his daughter mutilated and dishonored; his sons falsely condemned for the murder of her husband and eventually executed, in spite of his sacrifice of his hand to save them; and, finally, his one remaining son, Lucius, banished for defending his brothers. His mind turns entirely to the horrors inflicted on him and his daughter. Conceiving a grotesque and dreadful vengeance against his tormenters, Tamora and her sons, he plans a Thyestean banquet for the queen before he kills her and Lavinia.

Aaron (AYR-uhn), the Moor, one of the earliest of the Shakespearean villains who delight in evil for its own sake. He spurs on the efforts of his mistress, Tamora, to avenge the death of her son on the Andronici, and he instigates the rape of Lavinia by Demetrius and Chiron. He reveals a glimmer of human feeling in his defense of his baby son whom Tamora has ordered to be destroyed to conceal her guilt. He exults in his villainy, and, as Lucius sentences him, he repents any good he inadvertently may have done.

Tamora (TAHM-oh-ruh), the barbarian queen brought by Titus to Rome to take part in his triumph. She uses all her influence with her new husband, Emperor Saturninus, to take vengeance on her captor for the killing of her son, Alarbus, at the tomb of the Andronici. As she comes increasingly under the influence of Aaron, she delves more deeply into villainy and joins in the plot to murder Bassianus, mutilate Lavinia, and have Quintus and Martius condemned for these deeds. She masquerades as Revenge to gain access to Titus, but in so doing she causes her own death and that of Demetrius and Chiron. The old man is less mad and more cunning than she realizes, and she must experience the full horror of feasting on her own children before she is stabbed by her enemy.

Saturninus (sat-ur-NIH-nuhs), the luxury-loving, sensuous emperor of Rome who arrogantly accepts Titus' aid in his election and, as a reward, condescends to ask for Lavinia, his brother's betrothed, as his bride. When Titus' sons defend Bassianus' right to their sister, the emperor vows revenge on the Andronici and immediately takes as his wife Tamora, who directs his will and successfully hides from him her affair with Aaron. The assertions of Titus that Quintus and Martius were falsely executed for Bassianus' murder so infuriate him that he is restrained from killing the old man only by his fear of Lucius, who is gathering an army among the Goths. True to his unfaithful wife, he kills Titus to avenge her death.

Lavinia (luh-VIHN-ee-uh), Titus' daughter, the chaste and virtuous wife of Bassianus. She seems to step out of character when she taunts Tamora about her affair with Aaron, for she later pleads for her own honor with an innocence that clashes with the rather vulgar tone of her remarks to the empress. Her emotions for the latter part of the play can be expressed only in tears, because after violating her, Demetrius and Chiron cut out her tongue to protect themselves.

Bassianus (bas-ih-AYN-uhs), Lavinia's husband and the brother of Saturninus, his rival for the emperorship. He seems rather arrogant in his interchanges with Saturninus and Titus, but he stands for virtue and justice against the emperor's vanity and ambition.

Marcus Andronicus (MAHR-kuhs), Titus' brother, a tribune of the people. He attempts to modify his brother's absolute, impulsive actions and comments on each successive family tragedy with wisdom and sorrow.

Lucius (LEW-shee-uhs), Titus' surviving son and heir, who becomes emperor at the end of the play. He defends Bassianus' claim to Lavinia and is banished for attempting to prevent the execution of Quintus and Martius.

Mutius (MEW-shuhs), Lucius' brother, killed by his father as he intercedes to prevent Lavinia's marriage to Saturninus. His is the famous epitaph, "He lives in fame that died in virtue's cause."

Quintus (KWIHN-tuhs) and

Martius (MAHR-shuhs), sons of Titus, trapped and, though innocent, executed for Bassianus' death through the plotting of Aaron and Tamora.

Demetrius (deh-MEE-tree-uhs) and

Chiron (KI-ron), Tamora's bestial sons, who are quarreling over mutual attraction toward Lavinia when Aaron comes upon them and suggests that they kill her husband and take her by force. They are appropriately cast as Rape and Murder in their mother's masquerade. Titus finally kills them and feeds their flesh to their mother at a banquet.

Young Lucius, Titus' grandson, a precocious youth who is deeply upset by his aunt's injuries and vows to help his elders take vengeance on Tamora's sons.

Publius (PUHB-lee-uhs), Marcus' son, who helps capture Demetrius and Chiron.

Aemilius (ee-MIHL-ee-uhs), a Roman messenger.

Alarbus (a-LAHR-buhs), Tamora's son, slain by Titus as a sacrifice for his own sons killed in battle.

TO BE A PILGRIM

Author: Joyce Cary (1888-1957)
First published: 1942
Genre: Novel

Locale: Tolbrook, England
Time: Late 1930's
Plot: Social realism

Tom Wilcher, the dying owner of Tolbrook Manor, the last representative of the old West County liberal and religious tradition. He is concerned about the future of his family, his property, and his convictions. Tom had sacrificed a religious career to handle the family affairs and, although a liberal, he has grown to revere the political and religious values of the past. As he views the unhappy lives of his family, he determines to marry Sara Monday, his ideal of the old, humane, settled life. She also fails him, however, and he returns home and dies.

Ann Wilcher, Tom's niece, a modern, emancipated young doctor. She treats Tom in his last illness.

Robert Brown, Tom's nephew and Ann's husband. A scientific farmer, he represents a return to the soil. He rejects Ann for Molly, but the three are reunited in one household.

Sara Monday, Tom's old housekeeper, jailed by Tom's family for stealing unused articles. She rejects the ideals for which Tom cherishes her.

Edward Wilcher, Tom's brother and Ann's father, a politician.

Lucy Wilcher, Tom's wild sister and Robert's mother.

Puggy Brown, Lucy's adulterous husband, a hypocritical Benjamite preacher.

Julie Eeles, an actress, Edward's mistress and later Tom's mistress.

Bill Wilcher, Tom's settled brother, a military man.

Amy Sprott, Bill's devoted wife.

Loftus Wilcher, their son.

John Wilcher, another son. Disillusioned by World War I, he has lost his concern for religious and family life, and he lives indifferently until killed by an automobile.

Fred, Sara's latest man.

Molly, a young farm girl.

TO HAVE AND HAVE NOT

Author: Ernest Hemingway (1899-1961)
First published: 1937
Genre: Novel

Locale: Florida and the Caribbean
Time: Mid-1930's
Plot: Social realism

Harry Morgan, the owner of a charter fishing boat based in Key West, Florida. He is a big, powerfully built, athletic man in his early forties, ruggedly handsome and scarred by a life of adventure, which has made him even more attractive to women, an attraction enhanced by his indifference to its effect. He knows and loves the sea but has been forced to work as a guide for rich and ignorant tourists. When times are hard, he runs liquor on the Caribbean. Although he is scrupulously honest in his dealings with people, he is worried about his responsibilities to his wife and children. Under the pressures of corrupt and immoral local officials, he moves beyond the law into a series of dangerous and illegal voyages that eventually lead to his death. He tries to be decent and honorable according to his own set of principles, but he is overmatched by evil men and an inclination toward violence that finally goes beyond his control. Even during scenes in the novel in which he is not actively present, his daunting individuality hovers around the other characters as a measure of their courage, wit, and fundamental decency.

Marie Morgan, Harry's wife and the mother of his three daughters, formerly a call girl. She is a big and handsome woman, with bleached blonde hair, still attractive in her mid-forties in a Rubenesque fashion but on the verge of losing her edge and sliding toward excess. She is deeply in love with her husband, strongly attracted to him physically and very dependent on him. Although she has the strength to survive on her own, she has committed her life completely to him and, to a lesser extent, to their children.

Albert Tracy, Morgan's right-hand man and first mate. Tracy is roughly middle-aged, nondescript in appearance, not particularly intelligent, not especially strong, and not at all imaginative. He lives on welfare much of the time and tries to keep his complaining wife moderately satisfied. Morgan likes and trusts him because he is reliable, faithful, loyal, and competent at his job: "dumb but straight and a good man in a boat," Morgan says. He tends to be cautious and has no real driving force in his life, but he shows the kind of courage Morgan values. He dies absurdly, sticking close to Morgan on his last ride.

Eddy, a "rummy" who sometimes works for Morgan. He has lost the courage to act decisively except when fortified by alcohol. Morgan understands him and sympathizes to an extent with his fears, but Morgan is ultimately disgusted with him and regards him as a failure who does not have the character to face death and danger with some degree of grace.

His walk, which is described as "sloppy" with "his joints all slung wrong," typifies his lack of control and his absence of style.

Richard Gordon, a successful novelist, still youthful in the manner of a man who can afford the best clothing and care and the privileged existence of a celebrity. He is not a bad writer, but he has sacrificed a part of his soul to maintain his carefree pattern of living. He and his wife have no children, no permanent residence, and many affairs. Whereas Morgan knows who he is and what he must do to protect his honor, Gordon has no clear conception of himself and is disturbed by his uncertainty about how to act in a crisis. His writing is slick but superficial, contrived to exploit commercial opportunities, and he is no real judge of character, a crucial prerequisite for a real artist. When his wife leaves him for a less flashy but more substantial man, he is thrown into a kind of chaos he cannot resolve.

Helen Gordon, his wife, an extremely attractive woman in her early thirties, with dark hair, clear skin, and a need for something beyond the frivolous existence that they have been leading. She is instinctively aware of some deeper aspects of her character that have been suppressed and is willing to give up the brittle pleasures they share to find something of more enduring value. She and her husband form a kind of parallel to the Morgans, a pair of "haves" in contrast to the Morgans, who are "have nots" in the economic sense. The separation may drive both Helen and her husband into closer contact with the exigencies of life that have shaped Morgan and his wife.

Freddy, a saloon keeper, a friend of Morgan, who appreciates his special character and tries to treat everyone with a degree of honesty and respect. He is one among several minor characters who appear on the streets, wharves, and bars of Key West who are not motivated by selfishness or the pleasures of power and control. He speaks Spanish and English, is worldly and experienced, is basically nonjudgmental, and appears likable in an ordinary way. He is another of the "have nots" who actually has a genuine sense of value and worth.

Wallace Johnston, the owner of a yacht, with a master's degree from Harvard and money from silk mills. At the age of thirty-eight, he is the epitome of the kind of "have" who is essentially harmless but who lacks any kind of insight, knows nothing of life beyond the club, and in his idle ignorance contributes to the economic conditions of the Depression, which have forced men such as Morgan over the line.

— Leon Lewis

TO HAVE AND TO HOLD

Author: Mary Johnston (1870-1936)
First published: 1900
Genre: Novel

Locale: In and near Jamestown, Virginia, and the West Indies
Time: 1621-1622
Plot: Historical

Captain Ralph Percy, a Virginia planter and veteran of the Dutch war for independence. He was among the first settlers at Jamestown. Against his better judgment, he takes the advice of his good friend, John Rolfe, and seeks a wife among the women who arrive in the colony early in 1621. Rescuing her from the rude attentions of some of his fellow colonists, Percy chooses on impulse the haughty but beautiful Jocelyn Leigh. By his marriage, he incurs the wrath of Lord Carnal. He risks imprisonment and death to win the respect and eventually the love of his wife. At the end of this quest, Percy saves Jamestown by warning his fellow settlers of the projected slaughter of all the colonists by the united Indian tribes of eastern Virginia.

Jocelyn Leigh, a ward of the English king, James I. She flees to Virginia under an assumed name to escape being forced into an unwanted marriage with Lord Carnal, a man whom she hates. In desperation, she weds Captain Ralph Percy to gain his protection. Although she confesses her deception to her husband, her pride will not permit her to love the man whose name and devotion she has accepted. When Carnal pursues her to Virginia, Jocelyn realizes that her flight may cost Ralph his life. Slowly she falls in love with the man whose loyalty never falters despite arrest, torture, and almost certain death. Surviving the attack on Jamestown, Jocelyn is reunited with the husband whom she now loves as well as respects.

Lord Carnal, one of the favorites of James I. His personality combines all the loathsome qualities associated with those handsome young men who preyed on the English king's weaknesses. There are no redeeming aspects to Carnal: He follows Jocelyn Leigh to Virginia to force her into an unwanted marriage simply to see her suffer, and he marks Captain Percy for death by thwarting his plan. After an accident robs Carnal of his physical beauty, he escapes from his failures to retain the king's favor and to win Jocelyn Leigh by taking poison.

Jeremy Sparrow, a former actor turned minister. He is a close friend of Captain Ralph Percy and is the clergyman who marries him to Jocelyn Leigh. A giant of a man who possesses both great strength and courage, Sparrow saves Ralph and Jocelyn from certain death and effects their eventual reunion.

A ventriloquist, he uses his talent both to amuse and to serve his friends when they are in danger.

Diccon, who like Percy is a veteran of the Dutch wars. Because of minor criminal offenses, he is indentured to his former commander. Unlike the majority of the novel's characters, Diccon possesses a personality that has real depth. He is both saint and sinner, a surly, brawling man who attempts at one point to murder Ralph Percy, only to sacrifice himself for that same master whom he loves and hates. A man of the lowest social class, he is nevertheless a complex individual, a bundle of contradictions.

John Rolfe, the husband of Pocahontas, the close friend of Captain Ralph Percy and his defender from the attacks of Lord Carnal and the authorities of the Virginia Company. A well-known historical personality, Rolfe was one of the early leaders of England's first successful colony in North America. The tragic early death of his wife left him a widower at the time of the attempted slaughter of the English in Virginia, and he moves through the novel as a sad but ever-noble figure. Endowed with all the virtues associated with persons of gentle birth, he is the obvious opposite of Lord Carnal.

Nicolo, Lord Carnal's physician, the personification of evil. His death by self-administered poison is regretted by no one, including his master. A combination of all the bad qualities attributed by seventeenth century Englishmen to all foreigners, and especially to Italians, Nicolo is woven into the fabric of the story like a dark thread twisted into one of the tapestries favored by the early Virginians.

Nantauquas, the son of Powhatan and the brother-in-law of John Rolfe, the noble savage brought to life. A friend of the English settlers and especially of Captain Ralph Percy, he is haunted by the fear of what may happen to his people and their way of life if the number of colonists increases. Although he reluctantly participates in the massive attack by the Indians on the Virginia colony, he spares the lives of Ralph Percy, Jocelyn Leigh, and Jeremy Sparrow. Sorrow and a certain fatalism cling to Nantauquas like the fur mantle he wears.

— *Clifton W. Potter, Jr.*

TO KILL A MOCKINGBIRD

Author: Harper Lee (1926-   )
First published: 1960
Genre: Novel

Locale: Alabama
Time: 1932-1935
Plot: Bildungsroman

Jean Louise "Scout" Finch, a five-year-old girl when the story begins. She is smart and precocious, having learned to read at an early age by studying her father's law books. A hothead, more willing to fight than to think, she is often in trouble. She serves as a willing accomplice in her older brother's escapades. It is in her clear, honest voice that the story is told.

Jeremy "Jem" Atticus Finch, Scout's brother, nine years old when the novel begins. He is thoughtful, with a slower fuse than Scout, and often acts as interpreter to his sister of the world's confusing contradictions and vagaries. He intends to be a lawyer like his father when he grows up.

Atticus Finch, Scout and Jem's father, a lawyer in Maycomb, Alabama. A widower, almost fifty years old, Atticus responds to the challenge of rearing two small children by treating them as equals, with dignity and honesty. Atticus is a rare man, not only because he is a keen judge of human nature but also because he is able to forgive his fellow citizens their faults. When he defends a black man charged with raping a white woman, he does so knowing full well the wrath he will draw from the community. Standing up to the town's anger and ridicule requires both physical and moral courage, and Atticus shows that he has both.

Calpurnia, the Finch's cook and housekeeper, a self-educated black woman in her fifties. Calpurnia acts as Scout and Jem's substitute mother. It is through Calpurnia that the Finches learn how the black community is responding to the rape charge against Tom Robinson.

Charles "Dill" Baker Harris, a fatherless boy one year older than Scout. Shunted from home to home, Dill comes to Maycomb in the summers to stay with his aunt. A grand storyteller and an inspired actor, he is Scout and Jem's favorite playmate. Dill is based on Truman Capote, Harper Lee's life-long friend from her hometown of Monroeville, Alabama.

Arthur "Boo" Radley, a recluse in his forties who lives with his brother, next door to the Finches. Boo was put under the equivalent of house arrest by his father years ago as punishment for a teenage prank. Few have seen him since, and many of the children's games revolve around trying to make Boo come out.

Tom Robinson, a twenty-five-year-old black laborer, married and the father of three children. Tom is an honest, well-respected man. Although he has a disabled left arm, he is a strong and steady worker. Tom ignores the social dicta that forbid a black man from associating with a white woman, and,

out of pity, helps overworked Mayella Ewell with some of her heavier chores. He is killed trying to escape from prison before Atticus can appeal his conviction for rape.

Helen Robinson, Tom's wife.

Robert (Bob) E. Lee Ewell, a cocky, uneducated widower who spends his relief checks on green whiskey and lets his oldest daughter, Mayella, worry about how to feed herself and the other seven children from what she can forage from the town dump. After Atticus implies in court that Bob, not Tom, beat Mayella, Bob vows revenge. He is found dead with a knife in his ribs after Scout and Jem are attacked.

Mayella Violet Ewell, Bob Ewell's nineteen-year-old daughter. She is a stocky, friendless girl more or less resigned to a difficult life. When her attempt to kiss Tom is discovered, she quickly joins her father in accusing the black man of rape.

Alexandra Finch Hancock, Atticus' married sister. She strongly disapproves of how Atticus is rearing his children, especially Scout. During the trial, she comes to stay with the Finches.

John (Jack) Hale Finch, Atticus' younger brother by ten years, a physician.

Miss Maudie Atkinson, an independent-minded widow who lives near the Finches. Like Atticus, she treats Scout and Jem with respect, and they enjoy her company.

Mrs. Henry Lafayette Dubose, a very old invalid who breaks her addiction to morphine, the painkiller prescribed to her, before she dies.

Miss Stephanie Crawford, the neighborhood busybody.

— Liz Marshall

TO THE LAND OF THE CATTAILS

Author: Aharon Appelfeld (1932-   )
First published: 1986
Genre: Novel

Locale: En route between Austria and Bukovina
Time: 1938-1940
Plot: Allegory

Toni Strauss, née **Rosenfeld**, a Jewish woman who was divorced by her gentile husband when she was only twenty years old; they had been married three years. A dark, beautiful woman, she has had many lovers. A year after an elderly lover dies and leaves her a legacy, Toni decides that she and her son must return to her birthplace. She is short on education and academic knowledge, which leads her son to think that she is a stupid woman, yet people fall in love with her wherever she goes. Toni almost dies of typhus when they are in Buszwyn. Throughout the book, Toni experiences an ever-growing fear. It is an oppression that grows greater as she and Rudi near her parents' village, just as her craving for coffee increases. In the end, she is taken by the Nazis, along with her parents, to the concentration camps.

Rudi Strauss, Toni's son by her gentile husband, August Strauss. Rudi loves his mother but cannot stand the way that her mind seems to be a jumble of thoughts clouded with fear. His connection with animals emphasizes the difference between his mother's hypersensitivity and his insensitivity. After a drunken binge, he recovers to find that his mother has gone

to see her parents without him. He follows, but a day behind, to the railway station. Along the way, he meets Arna and takes her with him.

Rosemarie, the dead owner of a tavern, murdered because she was a Jew. Rosemarie's death is the first real sign of the impending doom that will engulf first Toni and then Rudi.

Tina, a woman at Rosemarie's tavern. At first, Tina is insane with the events that are befalling Jews for no apparent reason. By the end of Toni and Rudi's stay, she seems to have accepted the fate that is approaching them.

Arna, a young Jewish girl. Arna, while at the railroad station with the other Jews awaiting deportation, was sent by her mother to fetch water. When Arna returned, all the people were gone. Arna takes care of Rudi when he falls ill while they are looking for their mothers. Although she is still very young, Arna is wise and helps Rudi to accept himself as a Jew. Arna reassures Rudi that "soon we'll find them all" when he despairs of finding his mother, though finding them all will probably be in death.

— T. M. Lipman

TO THE LIGHTHOUSE

Author: Virginia Woolf (1882-1941)
First published: 1927
Genre: Novel

Locale: The Isle of Skye in the Hebrides
Time: c. 1910-1920
Plot: Stream of consciousness

Mr. Ramsay, a professor of philosophy, a metaphysician of high order, an author, and the father of eight. Not really first-rate, as he realized by the time he was sixty, he knew also that his mind was still agile and his ability to abstract strong. Loved by his wife, he is nevertheless offered sympathy and consolation for the things he is not. Lithe, trim, and the very prototype of the philosopher, he attracts many people to him and uses their feelings to buoy him in his weaknesses. He is not truly a father; his gift for the ironic and sardonic arouses fear and hatred rather than respect among his children. Broken by the deaths of his wife and his oldest son, he continues to endure and to sharpen his mind on the fine whetstone of wit.

Mrs. Ramsay, a beautiful woman even in her aging; she is warm, compassionate, and devoted to the old-fashioned virtues of hearth, husband, and children. With an aura of graciousness and goodness about her, ineffable but pervasive, Mrs. Ramsay gathers about her guests, students, friends, and family at their summer home on the Isle of Skye. Loving and tender to her children, and polite and pleasant to her guests, she impresses on them all the sanctity of life and marriage, the elemental virtues. Her love and reverence of life have its effect on all of her guests, even an atheistic student of her husband and an aloof poet. Mostly she affects women, especially Lily Briscoe, with the need to throw oneself into life, not to limit life but to live it, especially through motherhood.

James, the Ramsays' youngest son and his mother's favorite. He is the child most criticized by the professor because the boy robs him of sympathy that he desperately needs. Sensitive and austere, James at six and sixteen suffers most the loss of his mother, taken from him at first by a calculating father's demands and later by her death. He and his sister Camilla make a pact of war against their father's tyranny of demands and oversights. Finally, on a trip to the lighthouse, the symbol of what had been denied him by his father, Mr. Ramsay praises his son's seamanship.

Prue, who dies in childbirth,

Andrew, who is killed in World War I,

Nancy,

Roger,

Rose,

Jasper, and

Camilla, called Cam, the other children of Mr. and Mrs. Ramsay. All the children resent their father and his dominance. Mrs. Ramsay regrets that they must grow up because of the loss of sensitivity and imagination that will come with adulthood.

Lily Briscoe, an artist and friend of the family who, more than any other, loved the weeks spent with the Ramsays in the Hebrides. Desperately in need of assurance, Lily has withheld love and affection from others until the summer she spends at the Ramsay cottage, where she observes life with its fixed center and raw edges. Completely won over by Mrs. Ramsay, Lily almost gets her chance at life, and had the war not interfered, she might have married. She is not really a great artist, but during a visit to the Ramsay home after the war, she experiences a moment of fulfilled vision, a feeling of devotion to the oldest cause, of a sense of oneness with all time, and of sympathy for the human condition. She is able to express this fleeting moment in a painting she had begun before Mrs. Ramsay's death.

Augustus Carmichael, a minor poet with one major success. He is a hanger-on and is the only one who does not at first love his hostess. He finally discovers her genius years after her death. Laughed at by all the Ramsay children because of his yellow-tinted beard—they imagine the tint is the result of taking opium—he soaks up love and life without himself giving anything. His late fame as a poet is a surprise to all who know him.

Minta Doyle and

Paul Rayley, two handsome guests who become engaged through Mrs. Ramsay's quiet management. Minta is like the young Mrs. Ramsay and sends out an aura of love and passion, whereas Paul, with his good looks and careful dress, is a foil for all affections and strong feelings. The marriage turns out badly. Minta leads her own life, and Paul takes a mistress. No longer lovers, they can afford to be friends.

William Bankes, a botanist, the oldest friend of Mr. Ramsay. An aging widower, he first comes to visit with the Ramsays out of a sense of duty, but he stays on enraptured with life. The object of Lily Briscoe's undisguised affections, he appears to Mrs. Ramsay almost willing to become domesticated in spite of his eccentricities and set ways. Nothing comes of this relationship except a broadening of Lily's views on life.

Charles Tansley, Mr. Ramsay's protégé, a boorish young man who eventually is won over to the warmth and love of Mrs. Ramsay. It is his opinionated conviction that women cannot paint or write. Interested in abstract thought, he makes his career in scholarship.

Mrs. McNab, the old charwoman who acts as caretaker of the Ramsay house in the Hebrides during the ten years it stands empty.

Mrs. Bast, the cottager who helps Mrs. McNab get the house ready for the return of the Ramsay family.

George Bast, her son, who catches the rats and cuts the grass surrounding the Ramsay house.

Macalister, the aged Scottish boatman who takes Mr. Ramsay, Cam, and James on an expedition to the lighthouse. He tells the voyagers tales of winter, storm, and death.

TOBACCO ROAD

Author: Erskine Caldwell (1903-1987)
First published: 1932
Genre: Novel

Locale: Georgia
Time: The 1920's
Plot: Naturalism

Jeeter Lester, a Georgia poor white, the father of seventeen, of whom twelve are surviving and two are still at home. Shiftless but always vaguely hopeful, he makes several half-hearted and futile attempts to feed himself first and his starving family afterward. He burns to death in his shack as a result of a fire he set to burn broomsedge.

Ada Lester, his wife, who shares his fate.

Dude Lester, his sixteen-year-old son, who is persuaded into marriage with a middle-aged widow by her purchase of a Ford, which subsequently runs over and kills a black man and, later, the Lesters' grandmother, both to no one's particular regret.

Bessie Lester, Dude's wife. She uses her authority as a backwoods evangelist to perform her own marriage ceremony.

Pearl Bensey, Jeeter's fifteen-year-old married daughter. After being tied to their bed by her husband, she manages to free herself and run away.

Lov Bensey, Pearl's husband. After Pearl's flight, he is advised by Jeeter to take Ellie May instead.

Ellie May Lester, Jeeter's harelipped daughter, who uses her charms to distract Lov's attention, first from his bag of turnips, then later from his marital loss.

TOBACCO ROAD

Author: Jack Kirkland (1901?-1969)
First published: 1934
Genre: Drama

Locale: Rural Georgia
Time: Early 1930's
Plot: Social realism

Jeeter Lester, a shiftless, starving tobacco farmer living in rural Georgia. He resides in a ramshackle cabin that was once part of a prosperous homestead. The land has since been depleted by generations of tobacco plantings followed by cotton crops. Jeeter has an obsession with the soil, and every spring he promises to plant a cotton crop but somehow never gets around to it. The economic effects of the Depression in the South are too great for him to overcome. He refuses to leave his beloved land to work elsewhere. He says of his plight, "City ways ain't God-given. It wasn't intended for a man with the smell of the land in him to live in a mill in Augusta." Jeeter is a tragic figure who cannot control his own destiny. In the course of the play, Jeeter dramatically demonstrates that he is lazy, selfish, lecherous, and brutally degenerate. Racked by poverty and starvation, and lost in reveries over a spring planting that will never come to pass, Jeeter fights desperately to keep his beloved land. That losing struggle proves to be his one saving grace.

Ada Lester, Jeeter's haggard, pellagra-ridden, and long-suffering wife. Ada, in her mid-fifties, has been married to Jeeter for forty years. She habitually chews on a snuff stick to ease the pangs of hunger. She has given birth to seventeen children, of whom her favorite is the youngest, Pearl, whose biological father was not Jeeter. Throughout the play, Ada expresses one modest wish: that she be buried with a stylish dress. Her selfless love for Pearl leads to the daughter's long-desired freedom, her own accidental death by the new automobile, and Jeeter's loss of the land at the end of the play.

Dude Lester, Jeeter's sixteen-year-old son, as lazy as his father. Dude has no ambition in life except to sit around the yard. Openly contemptuous of his parents and of Ellie May, his sister, he is moved only by the prospect of driving a new car. He accepts Sister Bessie Rice's marriage proposal, despite the fact that she is more than twenty years older than he, when she offers him a new Ford automobile as a wedding present. The ignorant Dude proceeds to destroy the car piece by piece and kills two people with it. One of the victims is Ada, his mother.

Ellie May Lester, Jeeter's silent eighteen-year-old daughter, who is disfigured by a harelip. Ellie May, who is quite self-conscious about her deformity, is secretly in love with her brother-in-law, Lov Bensey, who is married to her much younger and prettier sister, Pearl. She openly flirts with, and attempts to seduce, the love-starved Bensey. Her dearest wish comes true at the tragic conclusion when Jeeter sends her to live with Lov following Pearl's escape and Ada's death.

Pearl Bensey, Ada's pubescent daughter, the youngest of her children. Her mother's favorite, Pearl was fathered by a passing stranger. Sold in marriage by Jeeter to Lov Bensey for seven dollars, Pearl has refused to accept Lov as a husband; ultimately, she escapes from him and her family. Although offstage for most of the play, she is a pivotal figure in the action.

Lov Bensey, Jeeter's disgruntled son-in-law, Pearl's husband. Lov is the only one of the major characters to hold a job and earn a steady income. He is very unhappy with his child-wife because Pearl absolutely refuses to talk to him or share his bed. He tries to bribe, threaten, and beat her into submission, but to no avail. Lov has always been sexually attracted to the older and more voluptuous Ellie May but has been put off by her facial deformity.

Sister Bessie Rice, an itinerant, self-ordained evangelist. Almost forty years old and widowed, Bessie preaches her own version of the gospel without benefit of a church and will do so whenever the spirit moves her. She prays out loud, carrying on a dialogue with God, and He always agrees with her passionate petitions. When, for example, Sister Bessie lusts after the young Dude, she prays for guidance; according to her account, God replies that "Dude Lester is the man I want you to wed." She persuades the reluctant Dude to wed her with the bribe of a new car. Her primary interest is to turn the aimless Dude into a country preacher like herself, with both of them traveling by car and spreading the gospel.

— *Terry Theodore*

THE TOBIAS TRILOGY
(Pilgrimen)

Author: Pär Lagerkvist (1891-1974)
First published: 1966
Genre: Novels

Locale: The Mediterranean and Aegean seas and coastlands
Time: The Middle Ages
Plot: Allegory

The Death of Ahasuerus, 1960

Ahasuerus (ah-hah-sew-AY-ruhs), the legendary Wandering Jew, identified in the narrative only as "the stranger." He meets Tobias and Diana in an inn for pilgrims to the Holy Land and accompanies them until Diana is killed and Tobias subsequently boards a ship falsely represented as bound for the Holy Land. Ahasuerus has been cursed with eternal meaningless life for having refused to let Jesus, bearing his cross to Golgotha, rest against his house. To Ahasuerus, the Holy Land is death, the object of his longing. He finds death, and peace, after realizing that Christ was his brother in suffering, not his savior, and that God is for humans a hindrance to the divine, not the agent of their access to it. Like Sophocles' Oedipus, he acquires his insight after becoming blind; like Saul of Tarsus, he gains his revelation in a burst of bright light.

Pilgrim at Sea, 1962

Tobias, a pilgrim to the Holy Land aboard a pirate ship that is not bound there. When the opportunity to transfer to a veritable pilgrim ship is offered to him, he chooses to remain with the pirates and continue his pilgrimage on the "holy" but meaningless sea (emblematic of existence). Aboard the pirate ship, he listens to the story of Giovanni.

Giovanni, a priest who was defrocked and excommunicated after having been discovered in a love affair with a noblewoman whose confessor he had been. The woman, mar-

The Holy Land, 1964

Tobias, a pilgrim to the Holy Land who has become a member of a pirate crew. He chooses to remain with Giovanni when the pirates maroon the disabled former priest. Living with Giovanni in the ruins of a temple on a bleak coastland, he experiences strange vestiges of the Olympian and Judeo-Christian religions: a nativity attended by herdsmen, an unearthed icon of the temple god, augury, and sacrificial rites. Wearing the empty locket after Giovanni's death, he ascends the hills into Aftonland, a world of perpetual twilight. Resting in an area of diminished darkness, he converses with the blue-clad Virgin Mary, who is transformed into the blue-clad girl whom he had impregnated when he and she were barely pubescent and whose life and death he had obliterated from his memory. With her return to him in Aftonland and her avowal of constant love for him, he realizes that his pilgrimage to the Holy Land has been in

Tobias, a bandit, former soldier, and reluctant pilgrim to the Holy Land. Having chanced upon the day-old corpse of a middle-aged woman, a pilgrim bearing the stigmata (nail-wound scars of the crucified Christ), he vows, perplexedly, to complete her pilgrimage for her. He is followed by her dog, as Tobias in the *Book of Tobit* is followed by a dog. Tobias is a tormented man with repressed memories, an indefinable longing, and a bent for cruelty.

Diana, a huntress living in the wilds who, after being raped by Tobias, attaches herself to him and remains devoted to him despite his despicable treatment of her. She places herself in the path of an arrow aimed directly at Tobias. As she dies, Tobias, at her request, once more calls her Diana, the name he had given her. Tobias and "the stranger" bury her beneath an evergreen oak, the tree sacred to the goddess Diana.

ried, had confessed to him a true love, whose picture she carried in her locket. Giovanni stole the locket and found it empty: Her true love did not exist. He kept the locket and wore it constantly as his most valued possession. Giovanni notes also that the noblewoman had undertaken a pilgrimage of penitence to the Holy Land but failed to reach it. Tobias concludes that true love and the Holy Land exist, but only as illusive human goals.

fact a pilgrimage to the true love that always lay within him. As his true love removes his locket and places it upon herself, he is witness to her bright effulgence and dies in great peace.

Giovanni, the defrocked priest, whose pirate life is ended by old age and blindness. Cared for by Tobias, he remains bitter and cynical until Death, in the form of a lady who carries a venomous snake in a basket, removes his locket and, as Giovanni dies in peace, places it on Tobias' neck. His blindness and death recall the end of Ahasuerus. The removal of the locket defines the end of quests for true love, Giovanni's quest marred by the bitterness of unrequited love, and Tobias' culminating in humanistically salvific love from the Blue Lady.

— *Roy Arthur Swanson*

THE TOILERS OF THE SEA
(Les Travailleurs de la mer)

Author: Victor Hugo (1802-1885)
First published: 1866
Genre: Novel

Locale: The Isle of Guernsey
Time: The 1820's
Plot: Sentimental

Gilliatt (zheel-YAHT), a young recluse living on the Isle of Guernsey and looked on with suspicion by most of his fellow parishioners. He saves his friend's fortune with great difficulty and nobly gives up to another the promised reward of marriage to the girl he loves. Finally, sitting on the very rock from which he once rescued his now successful rival, he lets himself be drowned by the high tide.

Mess Lethierry (leh-tyeh-REE), a shipowner and Gilliatt's friend. His partner having run away with his money, Lethierry attempts to recoup his fortune by buying a steamboat. His treacherous captain sinks it, but Gilliatt succeeds in salvaging the valuable engine.

Deruchette (day-rew-SHEHT), Lethierry's beautiful niece, whom Gilliatt loves.

Ebenezer Caudray (EHB-eh-nee-zur), the new rector. His love for Deruchette is returned. After she is promised to Gilli-

att by Lethierry, Deruchette and Caudray are frustrated in their attempt to marry secretly, but Gilliatt's generosity unites them.

Rantaine (rahn-TEHN), Lethierry's absconding former partner.

Sieur Clubin (syewr klew-BA[N]), the captain of Lethierry's steamboat, a man widely noted for honesty. Clubin takes Lethierry's stolen money from Rantaine at gunpoint. Having arranged to be picked up by smugglers, he sinks Lethierry's steamboat; his scheme is to escape with the money and leave a reputation for heroism as one who "stayed with the ship." He grounds the ship in the wrong place and is, in fact, drowned. Later, his plotting is discovered. Gilliatt, in salvaging the steam engine, also retrieves the money from Clubin's body.

TOLD BY AN IDIOT

Author: Rose Macaulay (1881-1958)
First published: 1923
Genre: Novel

Locale: London, England
Time: 1879 to early 1920's
Plot: Historical

Aubrey Garden, a liberal clergyman. When the story begins, he is fifty years old, distinguished-looking, and melancholy, with bright blue eyes. Earnest and intellectual, he is a spiritual Don Quixote, forever questing after "the truth." His wife and children react with varying degrees of loyalty, sympathy, and ironic tolerance to each spiritual crisis; his switching of faiths usually causes a switching of jobs and living situations. In his intense devotion to various religions, he names his children for their symbols. When he dies in 1914, he has realized that for him, only a combination of all religions equals truth.

Mrs. Garden, his loyal, patient wife. In her mid-forties, she is devoted to her family, adapting serenely to Aubrey's perpetual quest for truth until she finally gets her fill of switching and announces her intention of staying at home while he worships. She secretly grieves over Maurice's unhappy marriage and his perpetual war with society but remains remarkably tolerant of her children's quirks. Even at her death from cancer in 1903, she refuses to burden her children with guilt by bequeathing the care of their bereaved father to them.

Victoria Garden, the eldest daughter, named for her father's temporary victory over unbelief. At the age of twenty-three, she is slim and graceful, with thick chestnut hair and gray eyes. Lively and affectionate, she adores parties, dresses, music, beaux, and aesthetics. She marries Charles Carrington, bears five children, and runs with energy and vivacity a warm if not intellectually stimulating household.

Rome Garden, the second daughter, named (ironically, as she vacillates between agnosticism and atheism) for the Catholic Church. At twenty years of age, she is pale and

slender, with fair hair and intense blue-green eyes. Although she never marries, she falls in love with a married man, Francis Jayne. Contemplating adultery from a "civilized" rather than a moral perspective, she witnesses his murder and never loves again. Even when facing death at sixty-four from cancer (she has told none of her family and is planning suicide to forestall the pain and "uncivilized" messiness), she maintains a detached and ironic view of life, bordering on nihilism. It is from her outlook that the novel takes its title.

Stanley Garden, the third daughter, named for a dean whom her father had admired. Vigorous, stocky, athletic, and independent, she is in her teens when the story begins. An avid reader and worker for social causes, she eventually marries Denman Croft, bears two children (neither of whom shares her political interests), and divorces him for infidelity. She embraces social causes with her father's fervor and fluctuation. As the story ends, she is heading eagerly for Geneva to work for the new League of Nations, optimistic that it can save the world from further war.

Una Garden, the youngest daughter, named for the One Person in whom her father had once believed. Fifteen years old at the outset, she is plump, physically vigorous, cheerful, and attractive, with brown hair and blue eyes. The "least clever and the best balanced of the Gardens," she marries a farmer, settles in the country, bears several healthy children, and remains "attuned to the soil," her contentment a powerful foil for Rome's ironic detachment.

Maurice Garden, the older son, named for a prominent theologian. In his early twenties, Maurice has light, straight hair, a long chin, and thin lips; his glasses make him look scholarly and serious. A rationalist who respects some religions but has no faith, he becomes a radical journalist. He marries the catty Amy Wilbur, fathers two disappointingly shallow children (his son becomes a second-rate novelist whose writing is more esteemed than his intellectual father's erudite prose), and divorces Amy once the children are grown. In late middle age, he finally achieves a truce with life.

Irving Garden, the younger son, named Irving because Aubrey had been an Irvingite, or member of the Catholic Apostolic Church. Handsome, dark, and urbane, Irving is in his middle teens. With his flair for business, he becomes the only financially successful Garden, sharing wealth and opportunities with his siblings. He marries Lady Marjorie Banister

and settles down to rear a family, enjoy life, and make more money. Although he views war and politics only as they affect his finances, he remains genial and affectionate.

Imogen Carrington, Victoria's youngest daughter, one of the "new" generation. Tomboyish and imaginative, she becomes a poet and novelist, never exactly sure what the "proper role" for women should be, and she usually imagines herself as a boy. Like her Aunt Stanley, she is in love with life; like her Aunt Rome, she falls in love with a married man. At the end of the story, she departs with her lover (half in grief, half in joy) to live out her dreams for a year in the South Pacific.

— Sonya H. Cashdan

TOM BROWN'S SCHOOL DAYS: By an Old Boy

Author: Thomas Hughes (1822-1896)
First published: 1857
Genre: Novel

Locale: England
Time: Early nineteenth century
Plot: Social realism

Squire Brown, Tom Brown's father, a man who believes in permitting his children to mingle with all sorts of people, as long as they are honorable.

Dr. Arnold, the fine, gentlemanly, and religious headmaster of Rugby. He is gentle but firm with his charges and understands them thoroughly.

Tom Brown, a good boy who finds himself in a great deal of mischief at Rugby after he gets in with a group of ruffians. Because he is essentially good, he responds to the example of a younger boy who becomes his roommate. Before he finishes his work at Rugby to go to Oxford, Tom becomes a great leader in the school and changes the actions and attitudes of

the boys for the better.

George Arthur, a younger boy at Rugby who, by his moral courage and religious fervor, reforms Tom Brown and Harry East from wild mischief-makers into school leaders. George is the true leader, working through Tom's influence over the other boys.

Harry East, a wild young lad who, under the influence of Tom, George, and Dr. Arnold, becomes a good young man, as he really wants to be. He finds great help in his religion.

Flashman, a bully at Rugby whose power over the younger boys is broken by the stalwart defense of Tom and Harry. Flashman is expelled from Rugby for drunkenness.

TOM BURKE OF "OURS"

Author: Charles James Lever (1806-1872)
First published: 1844
Genre: Novel

Locale: Ireland and France
Time: Early nineteenth century
Plot: Historical

Tom Burke, the younger son of an Irish nobleman. He becomes a soldier of fortune after his father's death. He has many adventures with Irish patriots, the British army, and an evil lawyer. He makes his way to France, attends the École Polytechnique, and becomes an officer under Napoleon, rising to the rank of colonel. He inherits the family estates when his older brother George dies, and he marries Marie de Meudon, a beautiful Frenchwoman and the widow of General d'Auvergne.

Darby M'Keown, an Irish patriot known as **Darby the Blast**. He is Tom's friend.

Charles de Meudon (deh mew-DOH[N]), a young French officer aiding the Irish rebels who becomes Tom's friend and who, just before his death, gives Tom money for passage to France and asks him to look after his sister, Marie de Meudon.

Marie de Meudon, also known as **Mlle de Rochefort** and the **Rose of Provence**. She is Charles Meudon's sister. She marries Tom Burke after she has become a widow and he has inherited the family estates.

Captain Bubbleton, a bombastic, good-hearted English officer who befriends Tom.

Anna Maria Bubbleton, Captain Bubbleton's good-hearted sister, who nurses Tom when he is hurt.

Captain Montague Crofts, a villain who is Tom's enemy and wants, as a distant kinsman, to obtain Tom's estates.

General d'Auvergne (doh-VEHR-nyeh), one of Napoleon's officers, Tom's friend and benefactor. He is the first husband of Marie. He had wanted to adopt Marie, but Napoleon insisted that he marry her instead. He is killed in battle at Chaumière.

The Marquis Henri de Beauvais (ah[n]-REE deh boh-VAY), a royalist who plots against Napoleon. He becomes Tom's friend and clears Tom of charges of treason against Napoleon.

The Abbé d'Ervan (ah-BAY dehr-VAH[N]), a loyalist and a friend of the marquis de Beauvais.

Anthony Basset, an unscrupulous lawyer who cheats Tom as a boy.

The chevalier Duchesne (dew-SHEHZ-neh), a friend of Tom who turns against Napoleon and then tries to incriminate Tom as a traitor.

Napoleon Bonaparte, the French leader, under whom Tom serves against the British. Napoleon notices Tom's excellence as a soldier and grants him preferment and decorations.

Lieutenant Tascher, Madame Bonaparte's nephew and Tom's roommate at the École Polytechnique.

TOM CRINGLE'S LOG

Author: Michael Scott (1789-1835)
First published: 1833; serial form, 1829-1833
Genre: Novel

Locale: The West Indies
Time: The nineteenth century
Plot: Adventure

Tom Cringle, a young man, determined to distinguish himself, who joins the British navy at the age of thirteen. He has many adventures and sees much action on various ships. Eventually, he is promoted to lieutenant and then commander as a reward for his bravery and attention to duty. At the age of twenty-three, he is master of his own ship and a much-trusted officer.

Mary Palma, Cringle's cousin, whom he marries after his promotion to commander.

Obadiah (oh-buh-DI-uh), a pirate responsible for taking Cringle to the lagoon that is the secret lair of the West Indian pirates. When the pirate band is captured, he tries to swim away and is shot.

Captain Transom, the genial commander of the *Firebrand*, an English warship. He has many friends in the islands and takes Cringle to many jolly parties ashore.

Francesco Cangrejo (frahn-SEHS-koh kahn-GREH-hoh), a handsome Spanish pirate. Sentenced to death, he gives Tom a miniature and a crucifix to deliver to his betrothed.

TOM JONES

Author: Henry Fielding (1707-1754)
First published: 1749
Genre: Novel

Locale: England
Time: Early eighteenth century
Plot: Picaresque

Tom Jones, a foundling. Although he is befriended by his foster father, Squire Allworthy, Tom encounters many vicissitudes, some of them of his own making, for he is a somewhat wild and foolish, though good-hearted, young man. His wild ways, exaggerated by enemies, including Master Blifil, cause Tom to be cast off by Squire Allworthy. After Tom's goodness and virtue eventually triumph over disastrous circumstances, the young man is reconciled with the squire and, even more important, with Sophia Western, the beautiful and virtuous woman he loves. He is acknowledged as the squire's nephew when the secret of his real parentage becomes known.

Squire Allworthy, an extremely just and virtuous country gentleman who becomes Tom's foster father after the infant is discovered in the squire's bed. Tom's enemies play upon the squire's gullibility, for Allworthy, like many another honest man, finds it difficult to believe that there is dishonesty in other people. Eventually, he sees Tom's essential goodness, receives him as his nephew, and makes the young man his heir.

Sophia Western, the virtuous daughter of a domineering country squire. She loves Tom, even to facing down her father and aunt when they try to marry her off to Master Blifil and Lord Fellamar. Although she loves Tom, she is disappointed by his escapades, particularly those of an amorous nature, and until she is convinced that he can be a faithful husband, she refuses to accept his suit.

Squire Western, Sophia's domineering, profane father, who loves his hounds, his horses, and his bottle almost as much as his only child. When he insists on forcing her to marry Master Blifil, the husband of his choice, Sophia is forced into running away from home, placing herself and her virtue in the path of adventure and danger. The squire, though uncouth, is a good man at heart. Both he and Squire Allworthy are exceptionally well-drawn characters.

Master Blifil, the villainous son of the squire's sister, Bridget. A great hypocrite, he hides his villainy under a cloak of seeming honesty and virtue. He plays false witness against Tom many times. He becomes Sophia Western's suitor only because he wants her money and hates Tom, the man she loves. His villainy is done in the face of his knowing that Tom is really an older half brother, not a foundling.

Bridget Blifil, Squire Allworthy's seemingly virtuous sister. She bears Tom out of wedlock and lets him become a foundling. Later, she marries and has another son, Master Blifil. On her deathbed, she sends to her brother a letter telling the story of Tom's parentage. The letter is stolen and concealed by her legitimate son.

Captain Blifil, Bridget's husband, who marries her for her money. He dies of apoplexy, however, before he can enjoy any of it.

Mr. Partridge, a schoolteacher and barber-surgeon. Long Tom's loyal, if loquacious, companion, he is for many years suspected of being Tom's father.

Jenny Jones, later **Mrs. Waters**. As a maid in Mr. Partridge's house, she is accused of being Tom's mother, and her surname is given to him. As Mrs. Waters, she has a brief love affair with Tom, much to the horror of some of his acquaintances, who believe that the supposed mother and son have committed incest. Through her testimony, the identity of Tom's real mother becomes known.

Mr. Dowling, a not-so-honest lawyer. Through his testimony, Tom's identity is proved, as he corroborates Jenny Jones's statements. He keeps the secret for many years, thinking that he is following Mr. Allworthy's wishes.

Black George Seagrim, so called because of his extremely black beard, a rustic and poacher. Although he is befriended by Tom, he steals from the young man and plays him ill turns.

Molly Seagrim, a young woman of easy virtue, Black George's daughter. Tom's escapades with her cause him grave trouble until her affairs with other men take some of the blame from him.

The Reverend Roger Thwackum, an Anglican clergyman retained by Mr. Allworthy to tutor Tom and Master Blifil during their boyhood. A self-righteous, bigoted man, he voices his prejudices at all times. He beats Tom often and severely, living up to his name.

Mr. Thomas Square, a deistically inclined philosopher who is a pensioner in Mr. Allworthy's household and is Mr. Thwackum's opponent in endless debates over the efficacy of reason and religious insight. Although he dislikes Tom, he makes a deathbed confession that clears Tom of some of his supposed misdeeds.

Lady Bellaston, a sensual noblewoman of loose morals who takes a fancy to Tom and, when she is spurned, tries to do him much evil.

Mrs. Western, Lady Bellaston's cousin and Sophia's aunt. To satisfy her own social pretensions, she tries to marry off Sophia to Lord Fellamar against the girl's will.

Mrs. Fitzpatrick, Sophia's cousin. They travel to London together.

Mr. Fitzpatrick, her jealous husband. Tom is jailed for wounding him in a duel.

Lord Fellamar, a licentious nobleman who makes love to Sophia and, with Mrs. Western's approval, even attempts to ravish the girl to force her to marry him. Misled by Lady Bellaston's advice, he tries to have Tom impressed into the naval service.

Mrs. Arabella Hunt, a pretty and wealthy widow who offers formally, by letter, to marry Tom. His refusal of this handsome offer helps reestablish Tom with Sophia.

Honour Blackmore, Sophia's loyal, if somewhat selfish, maid, who shares in most of her mistress' adventures.

Mrs. Miller, Tom's landlady in London. Convinced of his virtue by his many good deeds, she pleads on his behalf with Squire Allworthy and is instrumental in helping restore Tom to his foster father's good graces.

Nancy and

Betty Miller, the landlady's daughters.

Mr. Nightingale, Tom's fellow lodger at the Miller house. Tom persuades the elder Nightingale to permit the son to marry Nancy.

Mr. Summer, a handsome young cleric befriended as a student by Mr. Allworthy. It was he who seduced Bridget Allworthy and fathered Tom Jones.

TOM THUMB: A Tragedy

Author: Henry Fielding (1707-1754)
First published: 1730
Genre: Drama

Locale: King Arthur's court
Time: The age of chivalry
Plot: Farce

Tom Thumb, a midget son of peasant parents in King Arthur's time. He accomplishes great deeds, even subduing ten thousand giants. He takes Princess Huncamunca as his bride, but his happiness is short-lived, for after subduing rebels led by Lord Grizzle, he is swallowed at a single gulp by a red cow.

Queen Dollallolla, the wife of King Arthur. She loves drinking, and she loves Tom Thumb. Although she does not fear the king—indeed, he is afraid of her—she does not tell him of her love for the little hero. She is slain by a courtier's mistress in a senseless series of murders.

Queen Glumdalca, a giantess and King Arthur's enemy. She is subdued by Tom Thumb and brought to Arthur's court, where the king falls in love with her. She wants Tom Thumb as her lover, but she settles for the king. She is killed by Lord Grizzle while defending Arthur against the rebels.

King Arthur, the king of England and Tom Thumb's liege lord. He loves Glumdalca and fears his wife. He kills himself after a senseless series of murders leaves him alone.

Princess Huncamunca, the daughter of King Arthur, loved by Tom Thumb. She marries Tom Thumb, whom she has loved for a long time. When she discovers that Lord Grizzle loves her, she wants to have two husbands. She kills her mother's murderer and then is herself slain.

Lord Grizzle, a malcontent. He promises to kill Tom Thumb for Queen Dollallolla. In his rebellion against King Arthur, he is slain by Tom Thumb.

Merlin, the magician at Arthur's court. He grants Tom Thumb a vision in which the little hero foresees that he will be eaten by a red cow.

A TOMB FOR BORIS DAVIDOVICH
(Grobnica za Borisa Davidoviča)

Author: Danilo Kiš (1935-1989)
First published: 1976
Genre: Novel

Locale: Central and Eastern Europe
Time: The 1920's to the 1970's
Plot: Social realism

Boris Davidovich (dah-VIH-doh-vihch), a Jew and a Russian revolutionary. Boris has been imbued with a revolutionary

zeal from his early youth, fighting against the czarist regime and for the Bolsheviks. As a result, a portrait of a classical revolutionary emerges: brave, resolute, bold, cool, resourceful, loyal to the cause, and blind to questioning of his ideology. Although it is not quite clear whether he joins the revolution out of a sense of justice or in quest of action or adventure, he participates in it without any reservations, which leads to a firmness of character that remains throughout his life. When he falls out of grace and is tortured and threatened with death, he refuses to sign a confession that would implicate others; instead, he prefers to be shot as a traitor rather than to be hanged as a common thief. Through his death in a labor camp during an escape attempt, he epitomizes a revolutionary who dies unjustly at the hands of his comrades. He also resembles the numerous revolutionaries throughout the world who, convinced of the rightness of their cause, are nevertheless stymied in their idealistic expectations and sacrificed to the exigencies of the revolution.

A. L. Chelyustnikov (cheh-LYEWST-nih-kov), a Russian revolutionary, another example of a loyal servant of the revolution, yet for entirely different reasons. A boaster and a womanizer, expert at playing cards, he seems to have become a revolutionary out of opportunism or inertia. He is a typical organization man, even to the point of agreeing to be a fall guy to serve the cause. It is not surprising that he survives the ups and downs of the revolutionary struggle, even though he is not without scars or close calls.

Fedukin (feh-DUH-kihn), a secret police investigator. A revolutionary of yet another sort, Fedukin serves the revolution and the state out of a need to do evil and hurt people to satisfy his sadistic impulses. A tall, pockmarked, and unbending interrogator, of modest education but of some literary talent, he derives the greatest pleasure when he investigates and tortures his former comrades, guilty or innocent. His motto is, "Even a stone would talk if you broke its teeth," referring to those victims who have passed through his hands. He believes that it is better to destroy one person's truth than to jeopardize "higher" interests and principles and that to sign a confession for the sake of duty is logical and moral and, therefore, deserving of respect. He simply cannot understand the "sentimental egocentricity of the accused, their pathological need to prove their own innocence, their own little truths." Fedukin thus becomes villainy incarnate, without any alleviating circumstances or rational explanations.

Karl Taube (TAH-uh-beh), a Hungarian revolutionary, representative of a well-meaning European intellectual who joins the revolution as a firm believer in just and idealistic goals. Taube eventually dies during the intraparty intrigues in the Soviet Union. He pays the ultimate price, however, in a bizarre way—he is murdered by common criminals in the prison. He thus becomes a victim of blind fate because, had the leadership not imprisoned him for a flimsy reason, he would not have been killed. Refusing to recognize harsh realities and clinging to his dream of a better life, he perishes for trying to solve problems through reason under circumstances that are governed by passion and blind hatred.

Gould Vershoyle (gewld vur-SHOYL), an Irish revolutionary. His disenchanted search for a better place to live takes him to Spain, where he fights for the Republicans in the civil war, and to Moscow, where he is taken because of his suspicions about the Soviet role in the war. His death in a labor camp in 1945 is another example of a juggernaut crushing everything in its way toward a revolutionary goal.

Miksha, a handyman from Bukovina who works for a Jewish shopkeeper and is a member of the underground. Introduced to the underground by another revolutionary, Aimicke, Miksha sets out to find a traitor in their midst. He suspects a certain girl and kills her, but it was Aimicke who was informing the police. After fleeing to the Soviet Union, Miksha is arrested and forced to confess that he was a Gestapo agent, implicating twelve Russian officials as well; they all get twenty years of hard labor. Miksha thus becomes another example of the revolution devouring its own children.

Eduard Herriot, the leader of the French Radical Socialists. Herriot represents the West European politicians who were unclear about the true nature of the Soviet system. Predictably, he visits the Soviet Union to see whether religion is suppressed there, and he returns convinced that it is not. That is all the more surprising because Herriot is a cautious and sensitive person. Chelyustnikov, who masterminds the official cover-up of the truth during Herriot's visit, signs a guest book in Lyons years later as if thanking Herriot for being so gullible.

Baruch David Neumann, a refugee from Germany and a former Jew. Neumann, who lived in fourteenth century France during the pogroms, suffers the same indignities as those suffered in the twentieth century and, eventually, death for a related reason—human intolerance of different creeds and beliefs. Even though he converts to Christianity to save his life, he later recants, finding it impossible to renounce Judaism. Like Fedukin, Neumann's detractors believe that it is better "to slaughter one mangy sheep than to allow the whole flock to become tainted." This aspect relates Neumann's case to other stories in the novel, proving that intolerance and inhumanity are as old as humankind.

A. A. Darmolatov (dahr-moh-LAH-tov), a Soviet writer. Even though Darmolatov, a minor Soviet poet, is acquainted with Davidovich, a more significant connection is somewhat obscure. It is not quite clear whether his story is included because of his acquaintanceship with Davidovich, because he develops mental problems trying to be a successful writer under oppressive conditions, or because he becomes a medical phenomenon by developing elephantiasis. His is the only story without victims, Jewish or otherwise, and without enforced confessions.

— Vasa D. Mihailovich